IMMIGRATION LAW HANDBOOK

Fifth Edition

MARGARET PHELAN
Barrister
AND
JAMES GILLESPIE
Barrister

UNIVERSITY PRESS

OXFORD
UNIVERSITY PRESS

Great Clarendon Street, Oxford OX2 6DP

Oxford University Press is a department of the University of Oxford.
It furthers the University's objective of excellence in research, scholarship,
and education by publishing worldwide in

Oxford New York

Auckland Cape Town Dar es Salaam Hong Kong Karachi
Kuala Lumpur Madrid Melbourne Mexico City Nairobi
New Delhi Shanghai Taipei Toronto

With offices in

Argentina Austria Brazil Chile Czech Republic France Greece
Guatemala Hungary Italy Japan Poland Portugal Singapore
South Korea Switzerland Thailand Turkey Ukraine Vietnam

Oxford is a registered trade mark of Oxford University Press
in the UK and in certain other countries

Published in the United States
by Oxford University Press Inc., New York

First edition published 2003
Fifth edition published 2007

British Library Cataloguing in Publication Data
Data available

Library of Congress Cataloging-in-Publication Data

Phelan, Margaret, barrister.
Immigration law handbook / Margaret Phelan and James Gillespie.—5th ed.
p. cm.
Includes index.
ISBN–13: 978–0–19–920917–0 (alk. paper)
1. Emigration and immigration law—Great Britain. 2. Aliens—Great Britain.
3. Asylum, Right of—Great Britain. I. Gillespie, James (Michael James) II. Title.
KD4134.A3 2007
342.4108′2—dc22
2006036287

Typeset by RefineCatch Limited, Bungay, Suffolk
Printed in Great Britain
on acid-free paper by
Ashford Colour Press Limited, Gosport, Hampshire

ISBN 978–0–19–920917–0

1 3 5 7 9 10 8 6 4 2

IMMIGRATION LAW HANDBOOK

CONTENTS—SUMMARY

CONTENTS

STATUTES

PROCEDURE RULES

IMMIGRATION RULES

EUROPEAN MATERIALS

INTERNATIONAL MATERIALS

PREFACE

The 5th edition of this handbook is in response to further new legislation, in particular the Immigration, Asylum and Nationality Act 2006, consequential changes to delegated legislation and substantial changes to the immigration rules.

We intend the book to be of practical use to all those working in immigration law.

We are very grateful to UNHCR for their kind permission to reproduce the full text of the UNHCR Handbook on Procedures and Criteria for Determining Refugee Status.

We would also like to thank Mick Chatwin and Matthew Fletcher.

The contents of this edition is up to date as of November 15 2006.

Margaret Phelan
James Gillespie
November 2006

STATUTES

Immigration Act 1971

(1971, c. 77)

Arrangement of Sections

PART I. REGULATION OF ENTRY INTO AND STAY IN UNITED KINGDOM

PART II. APPEALS

. . .

PART III. CRIMINAL PROCEEDINGS

PART IV. SUPPLEMENTARY

SCHEDULES

An Act to amend and replace the present immigration laws, to make certain related changes in the citizenship law and enable help to be given to those wishing to return abroad, and for purposes connected therewith.

[28th October 1971]

Part I

Regulation of Entry Into and Stay In United Kingdom

1. General principles

(1) All those who are in this Act expressed to have the right of abode in the United Kingdom shall be free to live in and to come and go into and from, the United Kingdom without let or hindrance except such as may be required under and in accordance with this Act to enable their right to be established or as may be otherwise lawfully imposed on any person.

(2) Those not having that right may live, work and settle in the United Kingdom by permission and subject to such regulation and control of their entry into, stay in and departure from the United Kingdom as is imposed by this Act; and indefinite leave to enter or remain in the United Kingdom shall, by virtue of this provision, be treated as having been given under this Act to those in the United Kingdom at its coming into force, if they are then settled there (and not exempt under this Act from the provisions relating to leave to enter or remain).

(3) Arrival in and departure from the United Kingdom on a local journey from or to any of the Islands (that is to say, the Channel Islands and Isle of Man) or the Republic of Ireland shall not be subject to control under this Act, nor shall a person require leave to enter the United Kingdom on so arriving, except in so far as any of those places is for any purpose excluded from this subsection under the powers conferred by this Act; and in the Act the United Kingdom and those places, or such of them as are not so excluded, are collectively referred to as 'the common travel area'.

(4) The rules laid down by the Secretary of State as to the practice to be followed in the administration of this Act for regulating the entry into and stay in the United Kingdom of persons not having the right of abode shall include provision for admitting (in such cases and subject to such restrictions as may be provided by the rules, and subject or not to conditions as to length of stay or otherwise) persons coming for the purpose of taking employment, or for purposes of study, or as visitors, or as dependants of persons lawfully in or entering the United Kingdom.

(5) . . .

Note: Section 1(5) repealed by Immigration Act 1988, s 1.

[2. Statement of right of abode in United Kingdom

(1) A person is under this Act to have the right of abode in the United Kingdom if—
  (a) he is a British citizen; or
  (b) he is a Commonwealth citizen who—
    (i) immediately before the commencement of the British Nationality Act 1981 was a Commonwealth citizen having the right of abode in the United Kingdom by virtue of section 2(1)(d) or section 2(2) of this Act as then in force; and
    (ii) has not ceased to be a Commonwealth citizen in the meanwhile.

(2) In relation to Commonwealth citizens who have the right of abode in the United Kingdom by virtue of subsection (1)(b) above, this Act, except this section and [section 5(2)], shall apply as if they were British citizens; and in this Act (except as aforesaid) 'British citizen' shall be construed accordingly.]

Note: Section 2 substituted by British Nationality Act 1981, s 39(2). Words in square brackets in s 2(2) substituted by the Immigration Act 1988, s 3(3).

[2A. Deprivation of right of abode

(1) The Secretary of State may by order remove from a specified person a right of abode in the United Kingdom which he has under section 2(1)(b).

(2) The Secretary of State may make an order under subsection (1) in respect of a person only if the Secretary of State thinks that it would be conducive to the public good for the person to be excluded or removed from the United Kingdom.

(3) An order under subsection (1) may be revoked by order of the Secretary of State.

(4) While an order under subsection (1) has effect in relation to a person—
  (a) section 2(2) shall not apply to him, and
  (b) any certificate of entitlement granted to him shall have no effect.]

Note: Section 2A inserted by Immigration, Asylum and Nationality Act 2006, s 57 from a date to be appointed.

3. General provisions for regulation and control

(1) Except as otherwise provided by or under this Act, where a person is not [a British citizen]—
  (a) he shall not enter the United Kingdom unless given leave to do so in accordance with [the provisions of, or made under,] this Act;
  (b) he may be given leave to enter the United Kingdom (or, when already

there, leave to remain in the United Kingdom) either for a limited or for an indefinite period);

[(c) if he is given limited leave to enter or remain in the United Kingdom, it may be given subject to all or any of the following conditions, namely—

(i) a condition restricting his employment or occupation in the United Kingdom;

(ii) a condition requiring him to maintain and accommodate himself, and any dependants of his, without recourse to public funds; and

(iii) a condition requiring him to register with the police.]

(2) The Secretary of State shall from time to time (and as soon as may be) lay before Parliament statements of the rules, or of any changes in the rules, laid down by him as to the practice to be followed in the administration of this Act for regulating the entry into and stay in the United Kingdom of persons required by this Act to have leave to enter, including any rules as to the period for which leave is to be given and the conditions to be attached in different circumstances; and section 1(4) above shall not be taken to require uniform provision to be made by the rules as regards admission of persons for a purpose or in a capacity specified in section 1(4) (and in particular, for this as well as other purposes of this Act, account may be taken of citizenship or nationality).

If a statement laid before either House of Parliament under this subsection is disapproved by a resolution of that House passed within the period of forty days beginning with the date of laying (and exclusive of any period during which Parliament is dissolved or prorogued or during which both Houses are adjourned for more than four days), then the Secretary of State shall as soon as may be make such changes or further changes in the rules as appear to him to be required in the circumstances, so that the statement of those changes be laid before Parliament at latest by the end of the period of forty days beginning with the date of the resolution (but exclusive as aforesaid).

(3) In the case of a limited leave to enter or remain in the United Kingdom,—

(a) a person's leave may be varied, whether by restricting, enlarging or removing the limit on its duration, or by adding, varying or revoking conditions, but if the limit on its duration is removed, any conditions attached to the leave shall cease to apply; and

(b) the limitation on and any conditions attached to a person's leave [(whether imposed originally or on a variation) shall], if not superseded, apply also to any subsequent leave he may obtain after an absence from the United Kingdom within the period limited for the duration of the earlier leave.

(4) A person's leave to enter or remain in the United Kingdom shall lapse on his going to a country or territory outside the common travel area (whether or not he lands there), unless within the period for which he had leave he returns to the United Kingdom in circumstances in which he is not required to obtain

leave to enter; but, if he does so return, his previous leave (and any limitation on it or conditions attached to it) shall continue to apply.

[(5) A person who is not a British citizen is liable to deportation from the United Kingdom if—

(a) the Secretary of State deems his deportation to be conducive to the public good; or

(b) another person to whose family he belongs is or has been ordered to be deported.]

(6) Without prejudice to the operation of subsection (5) above, a person who is not [a British citizen] shall also be liable to deportation from the United Kingdom if, after he has attained the age of seventeen, he is convicted of an offence for which he is punishable with imprisonment and on his conviction is recommended for deportation by a court empowered by this Act to do so.

(7) Where it appears to Her Majesty proper so to do by reason of restrictions or conditions imposed on [British citizens, British Dependent Territories citizens or British Overseas citizens] when leaving or seeking to leave any country or the territory subject to the government of any country, Her Majesty may be Order in Council make provision for prohibiting persons who are nationals or citizens of that country and are not [British citizens] from embarking in the United Kingdom, or from doing so elsewhere than at a port of exit, or for imposing restrictions or conditions on them when embarking or about to embark in the United Kingdom; and Her Majesty may also make provision by Order in Council to enable those who are not [British citizens] to be, in such cases as may be prescribed by the Order, prohibited in the interests of safety from so embarking on a ship or aircraft specified or indicated in the prohibition.

Any Order in Council under this subsection shall be subject to annulment in pursuance of a resolution of either House of Parliament.

(8) When any question arises under this Act whether or not a person is [a British citizen], or is entitled to any exemption under this Act, it shall lie on the person asserting it to prove that he is.

[(9) A person seeking to enter the United Kingdom and claiming to have the right of abode there shall prove it by means of—

(a) a United Kingdom passport describing him as a British citizen,

(b) a United Kingdom passport describing him as a British subject with the right of abode in the United Kingdom,

(c) an ID card issued under the Identity Cards Act 2006 describing him as a British citizen,

(d) an ID card issued under that Act describing him as a British subject with the right of abode in the United Kingdom, or

(e) a certificate of entitlement.]

Note: Section 3(1)(c) substituted by Asylum and Immigration Act 1996 from 1 November 1996.

Words in square brackets in s 3(6)–(8) and first square brackets in s 3(1) substituted by British Nationality Act 1981. Words in square brackets in s 3(3) and (9) substituted by Immigration Act 1988. Words omitted from s 3(9)(b) by Nationality, Immigration and Asylum Act 2002, s 10 from 1 April 2003 (SI 2003/754). Words in square brackets in s 3(1)(a) inserted by Immigration and Asylum Act 1999 from 14 February 2000. Section 3(5) substituted by Immigration and Asylum Act 1999 from 2 October 2000. Section 3(9) substituted by Immigration, Asylum and Nationality Act 2006 from a date to be appointed.

[3A. Further provision as to leave to enter

(1) The Secretary of State may by order make further provision with respect to the giving, refusing or varying of leave to enter the United Kingdom.

(2) An order under subsection (1) may, in particular, provide for—

(a) leave to be given or refused before the person concerned arrives in the United Kingdom;

(b) the form or manner in which leave may be given, refused or varied;

(c) the imposition of conditions;

(d) a person's leave to enter not to lapse on his leaving the common travel area.

(3) The Secretary of State may be order provide that, in such circumstances as may be prescribed—

(a) an entry visa, or

(b) such other form of entry clearance as may be prescribed, is to have effect as leave to enter the United Kingdom.

(4) An order under subsection (3) may, in particular—

(a) provide for a clearance to have effect as leave to enter—

(i) on a prescribed number of occasions during the period for which the clearance has effect;

(ii) on an unlimited number of occasions during that period;

(iii) subject to prescribed conditions; and

(b) provide for a clearance which has the effect referred to in paragraph (a)(i) or (ii) to be varied by the Secretary of State or an immigration officer so that it ceases to have that effect.

(5) Only conditions of a kind that could be imposed on leave to enter given under section 3 may be prescribed.

(6) In subsections (3), (4) and (5) 'prescribed' means prescribed in an order made under subsection (3).

(7) The Secretary of State may, in such circumstances as may be prescribed in an order made by him, give or refuse leave to enter the United Kingdom.

(8) An order under subsection (7) may provide that, in such circumstances as may be prescribed by the order, paragraphs 2, 4, 6, 7, 8, 9 and 21 of Part I of Schedule 2 to this Act are to be read, in relation to the exercise by the Secretary of State of functions which he has as a result of the order, as if

references to an immigration officer included references to the Secretary of State.

(9) Subsection (8) is not to be read as affecting any power conferred by subsection (10).

(10) An order under this section may—

(a) contain such incidental, supplemental, consequential and transitional provision as the Secretary of State considers appropriate; and

(b) make different provision for different cases.

(11) This Act and any provision made under it has effect subject to any order made under this section.

(12) An order under this section must be made by statutory instrument.

(13) But no such order is to be made unless a draft of the order has been laid before Parliament and approved by a resolution of each House.]

Note: Section 3A inserted by Immigration and Asylum Act 1999 from 14 February 2000.

[3B. Further provision as to leave to remain

(1) The Secretary of State may by order make further provision with respect to the giving, refusing or varying of leave to remain in the United Kingdom.

(2) An order under subsection (1) may, in particular, provide for—

(a) the form or manner in which leave may be given, refused or varied;

(b) the imposition of conditions;

(c) a person's leave to remain in the United Kingdom not to lapse on his leaving the common travel area.

(3) An order under this section may—

(a) contain such incidental, supplemental, consequential and transitional provision as the Secretary of State considers appropriate; and

(b) make different provision for different cases.

(4) This Act and any provision made under it has effect subject to any order made under this section.

(5) An order under this section must be made by statutory instrument.

(6) But no such order is to be made unless a draft of the order has been laid before Parliament and approved by a resolution of each House.]

Note: Section 3B inserted by Immigration and Asylum Act 1999 from 14 February 2000.

[3C. Continuation of leave pending variation decision

(1) This section applies if—

(a) a person who has limited leave to enter or remain in the United Kingdom applies to the Secretary of State for variation of the leave,

(b) the application for variation is made before the leave expires, and
(c) the leave expires without the application for variation having been decided.

(2) The leave is extended by virtue of this section during any period when—
(a) the application for variation is neither decided nor withdrawn,
(b) an appeal under section 82(1) of the Nationality, Asylum and Immigration Act 2002 could be brought [, while the appellant is in the United Kingdom] against the decision on the application for variation (ignoring any possibility of an appeal out of time with permission), or
(c) an appeal under that section against that decision [, brought while the appellant is in the United Kingdom,] is pending (within the meaning of section 104 of that Act).

(3) Leave extended by virtue of this section shall lapse if the applicant leaves the United Kingdom.

(4) A person may not make an application for variation of his leave to enter or remain in the United Kingdom while that leave is extended by virtue of this section.

(5) But subsection (4) does not prevent the variation of the application mentioned in subsection (1)(a).

[(6) The Secretary of State may make regulations determining when an application is decided for the purposes of this section; and the regulations—
(a) may make provision by reference to receipt of a notice,
(b) may provide for a notice to be treated as having been received in specified circumstances,
(c) may make different provision for different purposes or circumstances,
(d) shall be made by statutory instrument, and
(e) shall be subject to annulment in pursuance of a resolution of either House of Parliament.]

Note: Section 3C substituted by Nationality, Immigration and Asylum Act 2002, s 118 from 1 April 2003 (SI 2003/754). Transitional provisions set out in SI 2003/754. Words added to sub-s (2)(b) and (c) and sub-s (6) substituted by Immigration, Nationality and Asylum Act 2006, s 11 from 31 August 2006 (SI 2006/2226), applying to applications made before that date in respect of which no decision has been made, as it applies to applications made on or after that date.

[3D. Continuation of leave following revocation

(1) This section applies if a person's leave to enter or remain in the United Kingdom—
(a) is varied with the result that he has no leave to enter or remain in the United Kingdom, or
(b) is revoked.

(2) The person's leave is extended by virtue of this section during any period when—

(a) an appeal under section 82(1) of the Nationality, Immigration and Asylum Act 2002 could be brought, while the person is in the United Kingdom, against the variation or revocation (ignoring any possibility of an appeal out of time with permission), or

(b) an appeal under that section against the variation or revocation, brought while the appellant is in the United Kingdom, is pending (within the meaning of section 104 of that Act).

(3) A person's leave as extended by virtue of this section shall lapse if he leaves the United Kingdom.

(4) A person may not make an application for variation of his leave to enter or remain in the United Kingdom while that leave is extended by virtue of this section.]

Note: Section 3D inserted by Immigration, Asylum and Nationality Act 2006, s 11 from 31 August 2006 (SI 2006/2226), only in relation to a decision made on or after that date.

4. Administration of control

(1) The power under this Act to give or refuse leave to enter the United Kingdom shall be exercised by immigration officers, and the power to give leave to remain in the United Kingdom, or to vary any leave under section 3(3)(a) (whether as regards duration or conditions), shall be exercised by the Secretary of State; and, unless otherwise [allowed by or under] this Act, those powers shall be exercised by notice in writing given to the person affected, except that the powers under section 3(3)(a) may be exercised generally in respect of any class of persons by order made by statutory instrument.

(2) The provisions of Schedule 2 to this Act shall have effect with respect to—

(a) the appointment and powers of immigration officers and medical inspectors for purposes of this Act;

(b) the examination of persons arriving in or leaving the United Kingdom by ship or aircraft, and the special powers exercisable in the case of those who arrive as, or with a view to becoming, members of the crews of ships and aircraft; and

(c) the exercise by immigration officers of their powers in relation to entry into the United Kingdom, and the removal from the United Kingdom of persons refused leave to enter or entering or remaining unlawfully; and

(d) the detention of persons pending examination or pending removal from the United Kingdom;

and for other purposes supplementary to the foregoing provisions of this Act.

(3) The Secretary of State may by regulations made by statutory instrument, which shall be subject to annulment in pursuance of a resolution of either House of Parliament, make provision as to the effect of a condition under this Act

requiring a person to register with the police; and the regulations may include provision—

(a) as to the officers of police by whom registers are to be maintained, and as to the form and content of the registers;
(b) as to the place and manner in which anyone is to register and as to the documents and information to be furnished by him, whether on registration or on any change of circumstances;
(c) as to the issue of certificates of registration and as to the payment of fees for certificates of registration;

and the regulations may require anyone who is for the time being subject to such a condition to produce a certificate of registration to such persons and in such circumstances as may be prescribed by the regulations.

(4) The Secretary of State may by order made by statutory instrument, which shall be subject to annulment in pursuance of a resolution of either House of Parliament, make such provision as appears to him to be expedient in connection with this Act for records to be made and kept of persons staying at hotels and other premises where lodging or sleeping accommodation is provided, and for persons (whether [British citizens] or not) who stay at any such premises to supply the necessary information.

Note: Words in square brackets in s 4(4) substituted by British Nationality Act 1981, s 39(6). Words in square brackets in s 4(1) substituted by Immigration and Asylum Act 1999 from 14 February 2000.

5. Procedure for, and further provisions as to, deportation

(1) Where a person is under section 3(5) or (6) above liable to deportation, then subject to the following provisions of this Act the Secretary of State may make a deportation order against him, that is to say an order requiring him to leave and prohibiting him from entering the United Kingdom; and a deportation order against a person shall invalidate any leave to enter or remain in the United Kingdom given him before the order is made or while it is in force.

(2) A deportation order against a person may at any time be revoked by a further order of the Secretary of State, and shall cease to have effect if he becomes [a British citizen].

(3) A deportation order shall not be made against a person as belonging to the family of another person if more than eight weeks have elapsed since the other person left the United Kingdom after the making of the deportation order against him; and a deportation order made against a person on that ground shall cease to have effect if he ceases to belong to the family of the other person, or if the deportation order made against the other person ceases to have effect.

(4) For purposes of deportation the following shall be those who are regarded as belonging to another person's family—

(a) where that other person is a man, his wife [or civil partner,] and his or her children under the age of eighteen; and

[(b) where that other person is a woman, her husband [or civil partner,] and her or his children under the age of eighteen;]

and for purposes of this subsection an adopted child, whether legally adopted or not, may be treated as the child of the adopter and, if legally adopted, shall be regarded as the child only of the adopter; an illegitimate child (subject to the foregoing rule as to adoptions) shall be regarded as the child of the mother; and 'wife' includes each of two or more wives.

(5) The provisions of Schedule 3 to this Act shall have effect with respect to the removal from the United Kingdom of persons against whom deportation orders are in force and with respect to the detention or control of persons in connection with deportation.

(6) Where a person is liable to deportation under section [3(5)] or (6) above but, without a deportation order being made against him, leaves the United Kingdom to live permanently abroad, the Secretary of State may make payments of such amounts as he may determine to meet that person's expenses in so leaving the United Kingdom, including travelling expenses for members of his family or household.

Note: Words in square brackets in s 5(2) substituted by British Nationality Act 1981, s 39(6). Figures in square brackets in s 5(6) substituted by Immigration Act 1988, s 10. Section 5(4)(b) substituted by Asylum and Immigration Act 1996 from 1 October 1996. Transitional provisions set out in SI 2003/754. Words in square brackets in sub-s (4) inserted by Sch 27 Civil Partnership Act 2004 from a date to be appointed.

6. Recommendations by court for deportation

(1) Where under section 3(6) above a person convicted of an offence is liable to deportation on the recommendation of a court, he may be recommended for deportation by any court having power to sentence him for the offence unless the court commits him to be sentenced or further dealt with for that offence by another court:

Provided that in Scotland the power to recommend a person for deportation shall be exercisable only by the sheriff or the High Court of Justiciary, and shall not be exercisable by the latter on an appeal unless the appeal is against a conviction on indictment or against a sentence upon such a conviction.

(2) A court shall not recommend a person for deportation unless he has been given not less than seven days notice in writing stating that a person is not liable to deportation if he is [a British citizen] describing the persons who are [British citizens] and stating (so far as material) the effect of section 3(8) above and section 7 below; but the powers of adjournment conferred by [section 10(3) of the Magistrates' Courts Act 1980], [section 179 or 380 of

the Criminal Procedure (Scotland) Act 1975] or any corresponding enactment for the time being in force in Northern Ireland shall include power to adjourn, after convicting an offender, for the purpose of enabling a notice to be given to him under this subsection or, if a notice was so given to him less than seven days previously, for the purpose of enabling the necessary seven days to elapse.

(3) For purposes of section 3(6) above—
   (a) a person shall be deemed to have attained the age of seventeen at the time of his conviction if, on consideration of any available evidence, he appears to have done so to the court making or considering a recommendation for deportation; and
   (b) the question whether an offence is one for which a person is punishable with imprisonment shall be determined without regard to any enactment restricting the imprisonment of young offenders or [persons who have not previously been sentenced to imprisonment];

and for purposes of deportation a person who on being charged with an offence is found to have committed it shall, notwithstanding any enactment to the contrary and notwithstanding that the court does not proceed to conviction, be regarded as a person convicted of the offence, and references to conviction shall be construed accordingly.

(4) Notwithstanding any rule of practice restricting the matters which ought to be taken into account in dealing with an offender who is sentenced to imprisonment, a recommendation for deportation may be made in respect of an offender who is sentenced to imprisonment for life.

(5) Where a court recommends or purports to recommend a person for deportation, the validity of the recommendation shall not be called in question except on an appeal against the recommendation or against the conviction on which it is made; but—
   (a) the recommendation shall be treated as a sentence for the purpose of any enactment providing an appeal against sentence;
   (b) . . .

(6) A deportation order shall not be made on the recommendation of a court so long as an appeal or further appeal is pending against the recommendation or against the conviction on which it was made; and for this purpose an appeal or further appeal shall be treated as pending (where one is competent but has not been brought) until the expiration of the time for bringing that appeal or, in Scotland, until the expiration of twenty-eight days from the date of the recommendation.

(7) For the purpose of giving effect to any of the provisions of this section in its application to Scotland, the High Court of Justiciary shall have power to make rules by act of adjournal.

Note: Words in first and second square brackets in s 6(2) substituted by British Nationality Act 1981, s 39(6). Words in third square brackets in s 6(2) substituted by Magistrates' Courts Act 1980, s 154. Words in fourth square brackets in s 6(2) substituted by Criminal Procedure (Scotland) Act 1975, s 461. Words in square brackets in s 6(3)(b) substituted by Criminal Justice Act 1972, s 64(1). Words omitted from s 6(5) repealed by Criminal Justice (Scotland) Act 1980, s 83(3) and Criminal Justice Act 1982, ss 77, 78.

7. Exemption from deportation for certain existing residents

(1) Notwithstanding anything in section 3(5) or (6) above but subject to the provisions of this section, a Commonwealth citizen or citizen of the Republic of Ireland who was such a citizen at the coming into force of this Act and was then ordinarily resident in the United Kingdom—
  (a) . . .
  [(b) shall not be liable to deportation under section 3(5) if at the time of the Secretary of State's decision he had for the last five years been ordinarily resident in the United Kingdom and Islands;] and
  (c) shall not on conviction of an offence be recommended for deportation under section 3(6) if at the time of the conviction he had for the last five years been ordinarily resident in the United Kingdom and Islands.

(2) A person who has at any time become ordinarily resident in the United Kingdom or in any of the Islands shall not be treated for the purposes of this section as having ceased to be so by reason only of his having remained there in breach of the immigration laws.

(3) The 'last five years' before the material time under subsection (1)(b) or (c) above is to be taken as a period amounting in total to five years exclusive of any time during which the person claiming exemption under this section was undergoing imprisonment or detention by virtue of a sentence passed for an offence on a conviction in the United Kingdom and Islands, and the period for which he was imprisoned or detained by virtue of the sentence amounted to six months or more.

(4) For purposes of subsection (3) above—
  (a) 'sentence' includes any order made on conviction of an offence; and
  (b) two or more sentences for consecutive (or partly consecutive) terms shall be treated as a single sentence; and
  (c) a person shall be deemed to be detained by virtue of a sentence—
    (i) at any time when he is liable to imprisonment or detention by virtue of the sentence, but is unlawfully at large; and
    (ii) (unless the sentence is passed after the material time) during any period of custody by which under any relevant enactment the term to be served under the sentence is reduced.

In paragraph (c)(ii) above 'relevant enactment' means [section 240 of the Criminal Justice Act 2003] (or, before that section operated, section 17(2) of the Criminal

Justice Administration Act 1962) and any similar enactment which is for the time being or has (before or after the passing of this Act) been in force in any part of the United Kingdom and Islands.

(5) Nothing in this section shall be taken to exclude the operation of section 3(8) above in relation to an exemption under this section.

Note: Subsection (1)(a) repealed by Nationality, Immigration and Asylum Act 2002, s 75 from 10 February 2003 (SI 2003/1). Subsection (1)(b) substituted by Nationality, Immigration and Asylum Act 2003, s 75 from 10 February 2003 (SI 2003/1). Words in square brackets in sub-s 4 substituted by Sch 32 Criminal Justice Act 2003 from a date to be appointed.

8. Exceptions for seamen, aircrews and other special cases

(1) Where a person arrives at a place in the United Kingdom as a member of the crew of a ship or aircraft under an engagement requiring him to leave on that ship as a member of the crew, or to leave within seven days on that or another aircraft as a member of its crew, then unless either—
   (a) there is in force a deportation order made against him; or
   (b) he has at any time been refused leave to enter the United Kingdom and has not since then been given leave to enter or remain in the United Kingdom; or
   (c) an immigration officer requires him to submit to examination in accordance with Schedule 2 to this Act;

   he may without leave enter the United Kingdom at that place and remain until the departure of the ship or aircraft on which he is required by his engagement to leave.

(2) The Secretary of State may by order exempt any person or class of persons, either unconditionally or subject to such conditions as may be imposed by or under the order, from all or any of the provisions of this Act relating to those who are not [British citizens].

   An order under this subsection, if made with respect to a class of persons, shall be made by statutory instrument, which shall be subject to annulment in pursuance of a resolution of either House of Parliament.

(3) [Subject to subsection 3A below,] the provisions of this Act relating to those who are not [British citizens] shall not apply to any person so long as he is a member of a mission (within the meaning of the Diplomatic Privileges Act 1964), a person who is a member of the family and forms part of the household of such a member, or a person otherwise entitled to the like immunity from jurisdiction as is conferred by that Act on a diplomatic agent.

([3A) For the purposes of subsection (3), a member of a mission other than diplomatic agent (as defined by the 1964 Act) is not to count as a member of a mission unless—
   (a) he was resident outside the United Kingdom, and was not in the United Kingdom, when he was offered a post as such a member; and

(b) he has not ceased to be such a member after having taken up the post.]

(4) The provisions of this Act relating to those who are not [British citizens], other than the provisions relating to deportation, shall also not apply to any person so long as either—

(a) he is subject, as a member of the home forces, to service law; or

(b) being a member of a Commonwealth force or of a force raised under the law of any associated state, colony, protectorate or protected state, is undergoing or about to undergo training in the United Kingdom with any body, contingent or detachment of the home forces; or

(c) he is serving or posted for service in the United Kingdom as a member of a visiting force or of any force raised as aforesaid or as a member of an international headquarters or defence organisation designated for the time being by an Order in Council under section 1 of the International Headquarters and Defence Organisations Act 1964.

(5) Where a person having a limited leave to enter or remain in the United Kingdom becomes entitled to an exemption under this section, that leave shall continue to apply after he ceases to be entitled to the exemption, unless it has by then expired; and a person is not to be regarded for purposes of this Act as having been [settled in the United Kingdom at any time when he was entitled under the former immigration laws to any exemption corresponding to any of those afforded by subsection (3) or (4)(b) or (c) above or by any order under subsection (2) above].

([5A) An order under subsection (2) above may, as regards any person or class of persons to whom it applies, provide for that person or class to be in specified circumstances regarded (notwithstanding the order) as settled in the United Kingdom for the purposes of section 1(1) of the British Nationality Act 1981.]

(6) In this section 'the home forces' means any of Her Majesty's forces other than a Commonwealth force or a force raised under the law of any associated state, colony, protectorate or protected state; 'Commonwealth force' means a force of any country to which provisions of the Visiting Forces Act 1952 apply without an Order in Council under section 1 of the Act; and 'visiting force' means a body, contingent or detachment of the forces of a country to which any of those provisions apply, being a body, contingent or detachment for the time being present in the United Kingdom on the invitation of Her Majesty's Government in the United Kingdom.

[8A. Persons ceasing to be exempt

(1) A person is exempt for the purposes of this section if he is exempt from provisions of this Act as a result of section 8(2) or (3).

(2) If a person who is exempt—

(a) ceases to be exempt, and
(b) requires leave to enter or remain in the United Kingdom as a result, he is to be treated as if he had been given leave to remain in the United Kingdom for a period of 90 days beginning on the day on which he ceased to be exempt.

(3) If—
(a) a person who is exempt ceases to be exempt, and
(b) there is in force in respect of him leave for him to enter or remain in the United Kingdom which expires before the end of the period mentioned in subsection (2), his leave is to be treated as expiring at the end of that period.]

[8B. Persons excluded from the United Kingdom under international obligations

(1) An excluded person must be refused—
(a) leave to enter the United Kingdom;
(b) leave to remain in the United Kingdom.

(2) A person's leave to enter or remain in the United Kingdom is cancelled on his becoming an excluded person.

(3) A person's exemption from the provisions of this Act as a result of section 8(1), (2) or (3) ceases on his becoming an excluded person.

(4) 'Excluded person' means a person—
(a) named by or under, or
(b) of a description specified in, a designated instrument.

(5) The Secretary of State may by order designate an instrument if it is a resolution of the Security Council of the United Nations or an instrument made by the Council of the European Union and it—
(a) requires that a person is not to be admitted to the United Kingdom (however that requirement is expressed); or
(b) recommends that a person should not be admitted to the United Kingdom (however that recommendation is expressed).

(6) Subsections (1) to (3) are subject to such exceptions (if any) as may specified in the order designating the instrument in question.

(7) An order under this section must be made by statutory instrument.

(8) Such a statutory instrument shall be laid before Parliament without delay.]

Note: First words in square brackets in s 8(3) inserted by Immigration Act 1988. Other words in square brackets in s 8(2), (3), (4) and (5) substituted and s 8(5A) inserted by British Nationality Act 1981. Sections 8(3A), 8A and 8B inserted by Immigration and Asylum Act 1999 from 1 March 2000.

9. Further provisions as to common travel area

(1) Subject to subsection (5) below, the provisions of Schedule 4 to this Act shall have effect for the purpose of taking account in the United Kingdom of the operation in any of the Islands of the immigration laws there.

(2) Persons who lawfully enter the United Kingdom on a local journey from a place in the common travel area after having either—

(a) entered any of the Islands or the Republic of Ireland on coming from a place outside the common travel area; or

(b) left the United Kingdom while having a limited leave to enter or remain which has since expired;

if they are not [British citizens] (and are not to be regarded under Schedule 4 to this Act as having leave to enter the United Kingdom), shall be subject in the United Kingdom to such restrictions on the period for which they may remain, and such conditions restricting their employment or occupation or requiring them to register with the police or both, as may be imposed by an order of the Secretary of State and may be applicable to them.

(3) Any provision of this Act applying to a limited leave or to conditions attached to a limited leave shall, unless otherwise provided, have effect in relation to a person subject to any restriction or condition by virtue of an order under subsection (2) above as if the provisions of the order applicable to him were terms on which he had been given leave under this Act to enter the United Kingdom.

(4) Section 1(3) above shall not be taken to affect the operation of a deportation order; and, subject to Schedule 4 to this Act, a person who is not [a British citizen] may not by virtue of section 1(3) enter the United Kingdom without leave on a local journey from a place in the common travel area if either—

(a) he is on arrival in the United Kingdom given written notice by an immigration officer stating that, the Secretary of State having issued directions for him not to be given entry to the United Kingdom on the ground that his exclusion is conducive to the public good as being in the interests of national security, he is accordingly refused leave to enter the United Kingdom; or

(b) he has at any time been refused leave to enter the United Kingdom and has not since then been given leave to enter or remain in the United Kingdom.

(5) If it appears to the Secretary of State necessary so to do by reason of differences between the immigration laws of the United Kingdom and any of the Islands, he may by order exclude that island from section 1(3) above for such purposes as may be specified in the order, and references in this Act to the Islands shall apply to an island so excluded so far only as may be provided by order of the Secretary of State.

(6) The Secretary of State shall also have power by order to exclude the Republic of Ireland from section 1(3) for such purposes as may be specified in the order.

(7) An order of the Secretary of State under this section shall be made by statutory instrument, which shall be subject to annulment in pursuance of a resolution of either House of Parliament.

Note: Words in square brackets in s 9(2) and (4) substituted by British Nationality Act 1981, s 39(6). Words omitted from s 9(5) repealed by British Nationality Act 1981, s 52(8).

10. Entry otherwise than by sea or air

(1) Her Majesty may by Order in Council direct that any of the provisions of this Act shall have effect in relation to persons entering or seeking to enter the United Kingdom on arrival otherwise than by ship or aircraft as they have effect in the case of a person arriving by ship or aircraft;

[(1A) Her Majesty may by Order in Council direct that paragraph 27B or 27C of Schedule 2 shall have effect in relation to trains or vehicles as it has effect in relation to ships or aircraft.

(1B) Any Order in Council under this section may make—

(a) such adaptations or modifications of the provisions concerned, and

(b) such supplementary provisions,

as appear to Her Majesty to be necessary or expedient for the purposes of the Order.]

(2) The provision made by an Order in Council under [subsection (1)] may include provision for excluding the Republic of Ireland from section 1(3) of this Act either generally or for any specified purposes.

(3) No recommendation shall be made to Her Majesty to make an Order in Council under this section unless a draft of the Order has been laid before Parliament and approved by a resolution of each House of Parliament.

Note: Words omitted from s 10(1), s 10(1A) and words in square brackets in s 10(2) substituted by Immigration and Asylum Act 1999.

11. Construction of references to entry and other phrases relating to travel

(1) A person arriving in the United Kingdom by ship or aircraft shall for purposes of this Act be deemed not to enter the United Kingdom unless and until he disembarks, and on disembarkation at a port shall further be deemed not to enter the United Kingdom so long as he remains in such area (if any) at the port as may be approved for this purpose by an immigration officer; and a person who has not otherwise entered the United Kingdom shall be deemed not to do so as long as he is detained, or temporarily admitted or released while liable to

detention, under the powers conferred by Schedule 2 to this Act [or by Part III of the Immigration and Asylum Act 1999] [or section 62 of the Nationality, Immigration and Asylum Act 2002] [or by section 68 of the Nationality, Immigration and Asylum Act 2002].

(2) In this Act 'disembark' means disembark from a ship or aircraft, and 'embark' means embark in a ship or aircraft; and, except in subsection (1) above,—

(a) references to disembarking in the United Kingdom do not apply to disembarking after a local journey from a place in the United Kingdom or elsewhere in the common travel area; and

(b) references to embarking in the United Kingdom do not apply to embarking for a local journey to a place in the United Kingdom or elsewhere in the common travel area.

(3) Except in so far as the context otherwise requires, references in this Act to arriving in the United Kingdom by ship shall extend to arrival by any floating structure, and 'disembark' shall be construed accordingly; but the provisions of this Act specially relating to members of the crew of a ship shall not by virtue of this provision apply in relation to any floating structure not being a ship.

(4) For purposes of this Act 'common travel area' has the meaning given by section 1(3), and a journey is, in relation to the common travel area, a local journey if but only if it begins and ends in the common travel area and is not made by a ship or aircraft which—

(a) in the case of a journey to a place in the United Kingdom, began its voyage from, or has during its voyage called at, a place not in the common travel area; or

(b) in the case of a journey from a place in the United Kingdom, is due to end its voyage in, or call in the course of its voyage at, a place not in the common travel area.

(5) A person who enters the United Kingdom lawfully by virtue of section 8(1) above, and seeks to remain beyond the time limited by section 8(1), shall be treated for purposes of this Act as seeking to enter the United Kingdom.

Note: Words in first square brackets in sub-s (1) inserted by Immigration and Asylum Act 1999. Words in second square brackets in sub-s (1) inserted by Nationality, Immigration and Asylum Act 2002, s 62 from 10 February 2003 (SI 2003/1). Words in third square brackets inserted by SI 2003/1016 from 4 April 2003.

Part II
Appeals

. . .

Note: Part II repealed by Immigration and Asylum Act 1999 from 2 October 2000 (SI 2000/2444). Transitional provisions set out in SI 2003/754.

Part III

Criminal Proceedings

24. Illegal entry and similar offences

(1) A person who is not [a British citizen] shall be guilty of an offence punishable on summary conviction with a fine of not more than [level 5] on the standard scale or with imprisonment for not more than six months, or with both, in any of the following cases:—

(a) if contrary to this Act he knowingly enters the United Kingdom in breach of a deportation order or without leave;

(aa) . . .

(b) if, having only a limited leave to enter or remain in the United Kingdom, he knowingly either—

(i) remains beyond the time limited by the leave; or

(ii) fails to observe a condition of the leave;

(c) if, having lawfully entered the United Kingdom without leave by virtue of section 8(1) above, he remains without leave beyond the time allowed by section 8(1);

(d) if, without reasonable excuse, he fails to comply with any requirement imposed on him under Schedule 2 to this Act to report to a medical officer of health, or to attend, or submit to a test or examination, as required by such an officer;

(e) if, without reasonable excuse, he fails to observe any restriction imposed on him under Schedule 2 or 3 to this Act as to residence, [as to his employment or occupation] or as to reporting to the police[, to an immigration officer or to the Secretary of State];

(f) if he disembarks in the United Kingdom from a ship or aircraft after being placed on board under Schedule 2 or 3 to this Act with a view to his removal from the United Kingdom;

(g) if he embarks in contravention of a restriction imposed by or under an Order in Council under section 3(7) of this Act.

[(1A) A person commits an offence under subsection (1)(b)(i) above on the day when he first knows that the time limited by his leave has expired and continues to commit it throughout any period during which he is in the United Kingdom thereafter; but a person shall not be prosecuted under that provision more than once in respect of the same limited leave.]

(2) . . .

(3) The extended time limit for prosecutions which is provided for by section 28 below shall apply to offences under [subsection (1)(a) and (c)] above.

(4) In proceedings for an offence against subsection (1)(a) above of entering the United Kingdom without leave,—

(a) any stamp purporting to have been imprinted on a passport or other travel document by an immigration officer on a particular date for the purpose of giving leave shall be presumed to have been duly so imprinted, unless the contrary is proved;

(b) proof that a person had leave to enter the United Kingdom shall lie on the defence if, but only if, he is shown to have entered within six months before the date when the proceedings were commenced.

Note: Words in first square brackets in s 24(1) substituted by British Nationality Act 1981. Words in second square brackets in s 24(1) substituted by Asylum and Immigration Act 1996 from 1 October 1996. Words in first square brackets in s 24(1)(e) added by and words in square brackets in s 24(3) substituted by Immigration Act 1988. Words in second square brackets in sub-s 24(1)(e) substituted by Nationality, Immigration and Asylum Act 2002, s 62, from 10 February 2003 (SI 2003/1). Section 24(1A) added by Immigration Act 1988, s 6, except in relation to persons whose leave had expired before 10 July 1988. Sections 24(1)(aa) and 24(2) omitted by Immigration and Asylum Act 1999 from 14 February 2000.

[24A. Deception

(1) A person who is not a British citizen is guilty of an offence if, by means which include deception by him—

(a) he obtains or seeks to obtain leave to enter or remain in the United Kingdom; or

(b) he secures or seeks to secure the avoidance, postponement or revocation of enforcement action against him.

(2) 'Enforcement action', in relation to a person, means—

(a) the giving of directions for his removal from the United Kingdom ('directions') under Schedule 2 to this Act or section 10 of the Immigration and Asylum Act 1999;

(b) the making of a deportation order against him under section 5 of this Act; or

(c) his removal from the United Kingdom in consequence of directions or a deportation order.

(3) A person guilty of an offence under this section is liable—

(a) on summary conviction, to imprisonment for a term not exceeding six months or to a fine not exceeding the statutory maximum, or to both; or

(b) on conviction on indictment, to imprisonment for a term not exceeding two years or to a fine, or to both.

(4) . . .]

Note: Section 24A inserted by Immigration and Asylum Act 1999 from 14 February 2000. Section 24A(4) repealed by Nationality, Immigration and Asylum Act 2002, s 156 from 10 February 2003 (SI 2003/1).

[25. **Assisting unlawful immigration to member State**

(1) A person commits an offence if he—
(a) does an act which facilitates the commission of a breach of immigration law by an individual who is not a citizen of the European Union,
(b) knows or has reasonable cause for believing that the act facilitates the commission of a breach of immigration law by the individual, and
(c) knows or has reasonable cause for believing that the individual is not a citizen of the European Union.

(2) In subsection (1) 'immigration law' means a law which has effect in a member State and which controls, in respect of some or all persons who are not nationals of the State, entitlement to—
(a) enter the State,
(b) transit across the State, or
(c) be in the State.

(3) A document issued by the government of a member State certifying a matter of law in that State—
(a) shall be admissible in proceedings for an offence under this section, and
(b) shall be conclusive as to the matter certified.

(4) Subsection (1) applies to anything done—
(a) in the United Kingdom,
(b) outside the United Kingdom by an individual to whom subsection (5) applies, or
(c) outside the United Kingdom by a body incorporated under the law of a part of the United Kingdom.

(5) This subsection applies to—
(a) a British citizen,
(b) a British overseas territories citizen,
(c) a British National (Overseas),
(d) a British Overseas citizen,
(e) a person who is a British subject under the British Nationality Act 1981 (c. 61), and
(f) a British protected person within the meaning of that Act.

(6) A person guilty of an offence under this section shall be liable—
(a) on conviction on indictment, to imprisonment for a term not exceeding 14 years, to a fine or to both, or
(b) on summary conviction, to imprisonment for a term not exceeding six months, to a fine not exceeding the statutory maximum or to both.]

[(7) In this section—
(a) a reference to a member State includes a reference to a State on a list prescribed for the purposes of this section by order of the Secretary of

State (to be known as the 'Section 25 List of Schengen Acquis States'), and

(b) a reference to a citizen of the European Union includes a reference to a person who is a national of a State on that list.

(8) An order under subsection (7)(a)—

(a) may be made only if the Secretary of State thinks it necessary for the purpose of complying with the United Kingdom's obligations under the Community Treaties,

(b) may include transitional, consequential or incidental provision,

(c) shall be made by statutory instrument, and

(d) shall be subject to annulment in pursuance of a resolution of either House of Parliament.]

Note: Section 25 substituted by Nationality, Immigration and Asylum Act 2002, s 143, from 10 February 2003 (SI 2003/1). Subsections (7) and (8) inserted by Asylum and Immigration Act 2004, s 1 from 1 October 2004.

[25A. Helping asylum-seeker to enter United Kingdom

(1) A person commits an offence if—

(a) he knowingly and for gain facilitates the arrival in the United Kingdom of an individual, and

(b) he knows or has reasonable cause to believe that the individual is an asylum-seeker.

(2) In this section 'asylum-seeker' means a person who intends to claim that to remove him from or require him to leave the United Kingdom would be contrary to the United Kingdom's obligations under—

(a) the Refugee Convention (within the meaning given by section 167(1) of the Immigration and Asylum Act 1999 (c. 33) (interpretation)), or

(b) the Human Rights Convention (within the meaning given by that section).

(3) Subsection (1) does not apply to anything done by a person acting on behalf of an organisation which—

(a) aims to assist asylum-seekers, and

(b) does not charge for its services.

(4) Subsections (4) to (6) of section 25 apply for the purpose of the offence in subsection (1) of this section as they apply for the purpose of the offence in subsection (1) of that section.]

Note: Section 25A inserted by Nationality, Immigration and Asylum Act 2002, s 143 from 10 February 2003 (SI 2003/1).

[25B. Assisting entry to United Kingdom in breach of deportation or exclusion order

(1) A person commits an offence if he—
 (a) does an act which facilitates a breach of a deportation order in force against an individual who is a citizen of the European Union, and
 (b) knows or has reasonable cause for believing that the act facilitates a breach of the deportation order.

(2) Subsection (3) applies where the Secretary of State personally directs that the exclusion from the United Kingdom of an individual who is a citizen of the European Union is conducive to the public good.

(3) A person commits an offence if he—
 (a) does an act which assists the individual to arrive in, enter or remain in the United Kingdom,
 (b) knows or has reasonable cause for believing that the act assists the individual to arrive in, enter or remain in the United Kingdom, and
 (c) knows or has reasonable cause for believing that the Secretary of State has personally directed that the individual's exclusion from the United Kingdom is conducive to the public good.

(4) Subsections (4) to (6) of section 25 apply for the purpose of an offence under this section as they apply for the purpose of an offence under that section.]

Note: Section 25B inserted by Nationality, Immigration and Asylum Act 2002, s 143 from 10 February 2003 (SI 2003/1).

[25C. Forfeiture of vehicle, ship or aircraft

(1) This section applies where a person is convicted on indictment of an offence under section 25, 25A or 25B.

(2) The court may order the forfeiture of a vehicle used or intended to be used in connection with the offence if the convicted person—
 (a) owned the vehicle at the time the offence was committed,
 (b) was at that time a director, secretary or manager of a company which owned the vehicle,
 (c) was at that time in possession of the vehicle under a hire-purchase agreement,
 (d) was at that time a director, secretary or manager of a company which was in possession of the vehicle under a hire-purchase agreement, or
 (e) was driving the vehicle in the course of the commission of the offence.

(3) The court may order the forfeiture of a ship or aircraft used or intended to be used in connection with the offence if the convicted person—
 (a) owned the ship or aircraft at the time the offence was committed,

(b) was at that time a director, secretary or manager of a company which owned the ship or aircraft,
(c) was at that time in possession of the ship or aircraft under a hire-purchase agreement,
(d) was at that time a director, secretary or manager of a company which was in possession of the ship or aircraft under a hire-purchase agreement,
(e) was at that time a charterer of the ship or aircraft, or
(f) committed the offence while acting as captain of the ship or aircraft.

(4) But in a case to which subsection (3)(a) or (b) does not apply, forfeiture may be ordered only—
(a) in the case of a ship, if subsection (5) or (6) applies;
(b) in the case of an aircraft, if subsection (5) or (7) applies.

(5) This subsection applies where—
(a) in the course of the commission of the offence, the ship or aircraft carried more than 20 illegal entrants, and
(b) a person who, at the time the offence was committed, owned the ship or aircraft or was a director, secretary or manager of a company which owned it, knew or ought to have known of the intention to use it in the course of the commission of an offence under section 25, 25A or 25B.

(6) This subsection applies where a ship's gross tonnage is less than 500 tons.

(7) This subsection applies where the maximum weight at which an aircraft (which is not a hovercraft) may take off in accordance with its certificate of airworthiness is less than 5,700 kilogrammes.

(8) Where a person who claims to have an interest in a vehicle, ship or aircraft applies to a court to make representations on the question of forfeiture, the court may not make an order under this section in respect of the ship, aircraft or vehicle unless the person has been given an opportunity to make representations.

(9) In the case of an offence under section 25, the reference in subsection (5)(a) to an illegal entrant shall be taken to include a reference to—
(a) an individual who seeks to enter a member State in breach of immigration law [(for which purpose 'member State' and 'immigration law' have the meanings given by section 25(2) and (7))] and
(b) an individual who is a passenger for the purpose of section 145 of the Nationality, Immigration and Asylum Act 2002 (traffic in prostitution) [or section 4 of the Asylum and Immigration (Treatment of Claimants, etc.) Act 2004 (trafficking people for exploitation)].

(10) In the case of an offence under section 25A, the reference in subsection (5)(a) to an illegal entrant shall be taken to include a reference to—
(a) an asylum-seeker (within the meaning of that section), and
(b) an individual who is a passenger for the purpose of section 145(1) of the

Nationality, Immigration and Asylum Act 2002 [or section 4 of the Asylum and Immigration (Treatment of Claimants, etc.) Act 2004 (trafficking people for exploitation)].

(11) In the case of an offence under section 25B, the reference in subsection (5)(a) to an illegal entrant shall be taken to include a reference to an individual who is a passenger for the purpose of section 145(1) of the Nationality, Immigration and Asylum Act 2002 [or section 4 of the Asylum and Immigration (Treatment of Claimants, etc.) Act 2004 (trafficking people for exploitation)].

Note: Section 25C inserted by Nationality, Immigration and Asylum Act 2002, s 143 from 10 February 2003 (SI 2003/1). Words in square brackets in sub-s 9(a) substituted by Asylum and Immigration Act 2004, s 1 from 1 October 2004. Other words in square brackets inserted by Asylum and Immigration Act 2004, s 5 from a date to be appointed.

[25D. Detention of ship, aircraft or vehicle

(1) If a person has been arrested for an offence under section 25[, 25A or 25B], a senior officer or a constable may detain a relevant ship, aircraft or vehicle—
   (a) until a decision is taken as to whether or not to charge the arrested person with that offence; or
   (b) if the arrested person has been charged—
      (i) until he is acquitted, the charge against him is dismissed or the proceedings are discontinued; or
      (ii) if he has been convicted, until the court decides whether or not to order forfeiture of the ship, aircraft or vehicle.

(2) A ship, aircraft or vehicle is a relevant ship, aircraft or vehicle, in relation to an arrested person, if it is one which the officer or constable concerned has reasonable grounds for believing could, on conviction of the arrested person for the offence for which he was arrested, be the subject of an order for forfeiture made under [section 25C].

(3) [A person (other than the arrested person) may apply to the court for the release of a ship, aircraft or vehicle on the grounds that—
   (a) he owns the ship, aircraft or vehicle,
   (b) he was, immediately before the detention of the ship, aircraft or vehicle, in possession of it under a hire-purchase agreement, or
   (c) he is a charterer of the ship or aircraft.]

(4) The court to which an application is made under subsection (3) may, on such security or surety being tendered as it considers satisfactory, release the ship, aircraft or vehicle on condition that it is made available to the court if—
   (a) the arrested person is convicted; and
   (b) an order for its forfeiture is made under [section 25C].

(5) In the application to Scotland of subsection (1), for paragraphs (a) and (b) substitute—

'(a) until a decision is taken as to whether or not to institute criminal proceedings against the arrested person for that offence; or

(b) if criminal proceedings have been instituted against the arrested person—

(i) until he is acquitted or, under section 65 or 147 of the Criminal Procedure (Scotland) Act 1995, discharged or liberated or the trial diet is deserted simpliciter;

(ii) if he has been convicted, until the court decides whether or not to order forfeiture of the ship, aircraft or vehicle, and for the purposes of this subsection, criminal proceedings are instituted against a person at whichever is the earliest of his first appearance before the sheriff on petition, or the service on him of an indictment or complaint.'

(6) 'Court' means—

(a) in England and Wales—

[(ia) if the arrested person has not been charged, or he has been charged but proceedings for the offence have not begun to be heard, a magistrates' court;]

(iii) if he has been charged and proceedings for the offence are being heard, the court hearing the proceedings;

(b) in Scotland, the sheriff; and

(c) in Northern Ireland—

(i) if the arrested person has not been charged, the magistrates' court for the county court division in which he was arrested;

(ii) if he has been charged but proceedings for the offence have not begun to be heard, the magistrates' court for the county court division in which he was charged;

(iii) if he has been charged and proceedings for the offence are being heard, the court hearing the proceedings.

(7) . . .

(8) 'Senior officer' means an immigration officer not below the rank of chief immigration officer.]

Note: Section 25D (previously s 25A) renumbered by Nationality, Immigration and Asylum Act 2002 from 10 February 2003 (SI 2003/1) and inserted by Immigration and Asylum Act 1999 from 2 October 2000. Words in square brackets in sub-s (2) substituted by and sub-s (3) inserted by Nationality, Immigration and Asylum Act 2002, s 144 from 10 February 2003 (SI 2003/1). Words in square brackets in sub-s (4)(d) substituted by and sub-s (7) omitted by Nationality, Immigration and Asylum Act 2002, s 144 from 10 February 2003 (SI 2003/1). Words in square brackets in sub-s (6) substituted by Sch 8 Courts Act 2003 from a date to be appointed.

26. General offences in connection with administration of Act

(1) A person shall be guilty of an offence punishable on summary conviction with a fine of not more than [level 5 on the standard scale] or with imprisonment for not more than six months, or with both, in any of the following cases—

(a) if, without reasonable excuse, he refuses or fails to submit to examination under Schedule 2 of this Act;
(b) if, without reasonable excuse, he refuses or fails to furnish or produce any information in his possession, or any documents in his possession or control, which he is on an examination under that Schedule required to furnish or produce;
(c) if on any such examination or otherwise he makes or causes to be made to an immigration officer or other person lawfully acting in the execution of [a relevant enactment] a return, statement or representation which he knows to be false or does not believe to be true;
(d) if, without lawful authority, he alters any [certificate of entitlement], entry clearance, work permit or other document issued or made under or for the purposes of this Act, or uses for the purposes of this Act, or has in his possession for such use, any passport, [certificate of entitlement], entry clearance, work permit or other document which he knows or has reasonable cause to believe to be false;
(e) if, without reasonable excuse, he fails to complete and produce a landing or embarkation card in accordance with any order under Schedule 2 of this Act;
(f) if, without reasonable excuse, he fails to comply with any requirement of regulations under section 4(3) or of an order under section 4(4) above;
(g) if, without reasonable excuse, he obstructs an immigration officer or other person lawfully acting in the execution of this Act.

(2) The extended time limit for prosecutions which is provided for by section 28 below shall apply to offences under subsection (1)(c) and (d) above.

[(3) 'Relevant enactment' means—
(a) this Act;
(b) the Immigration Act 1988;
(c) the Asylum and Immigration Appeals Act 1993 (apart from section 4 or 5); . . .
(d) the Immigration and Asylum Act 1999 (apart from Part VI)]; [or
(e) the Nationality, Immigration and Asylum Act 2002 (apart from Part 5).]

Note: Words in first square brackets in s 26(1) substituted by virtue of Criminal Justice Act 1982, and amended by Asylum and Immigration Act 1996 from 1 October 1996. Words in square brackets in s 26(1)(d) substituted by British Nationality Act 1981, s 39(6). Words in square brackets in s 26(1)(c) and sub-s (3) inserted by Immigration and Asylum Act 1999 from 14 February 2000. Subsection 3(e) inserted by and words in sub-s 3(c) omitted by Nationality, Immigration and Asylum Act 2002, s 151 from 10 February 2003 (SI 2003/1).

[26A. Registration card

(1) In this section 'registration card' means a document which—
(a) carries information about a person (whether or not wholly or partly electronically), and

(b) is issued by the Secretary of State to the person wholly or partly in connection with a claim for asylum (whether or not made by that person).

(2) In subsection (1) 'claim for asylum' has the meaning given by section 18 of the Nationality, Immigration and Asylum Act 2002.

(3) A person commits an offence if he—

(a) makes a false registration card,

(b) alters a registration card with intent to deceive or to enable another to deceive,

(c) has a false or altered registration card in his possession without reasonable excuse,

(d) uses or attempts to use a false registration card for a purpose for which a registration card is issued,

(e) uses or attempts to use an altered registration card with intent to deceive,

(f) makes an article designed to be used in making a false registration card,

(g) makes an article designed to be used in altering a registration card with intent to deceive or to enable another to deceive, or

(h) has an article within paragraph (f or (g) in his possession without reasonable excuse.

(4) In subsection (3) 'false registration card' means a document which is designed to appear to be a registration card.

(5) A person who is guilty of an offence under subsection (3)(a), (b), (d), (e), (f) or (g) shall be liable—

(a) on conviction on indictment, to imprisonment for a term not exceeding ten years, to a fine or to both, or

(b) on summary conviction, to imprisonment for a term not exceeding six months, to a fine not exceeding the statutory maximum or to both.

(6) A person who is guilty of an offence under subsection (3)(c) or (h) shall be liable—

(a) on conviction on indictment, to imprisonment for a term not exceeding two years, to a fine or to both, or

(b) on summary conviction, to imprisonment for a term not exceeding six months, to a fine not exceeding the statutory maximum or to both.

(7) The Secretary of State may by order—

(a) amend the definition of 'registration card' in subsection (1);

(b) make consequential amendment of this section.

(8) An order under subsection (7)—

(a) must be made by statutory instrument, and

(b) may not be made unless a draft has been laid before and approved by resolution of each House of Parliament.]

Note: Section 26A inserted by Nationality, Immigration and Asylum Act 2002, s 148 from 10 February 2003 (SI 2003/1).

[26B. Possession of immigration stamp

(1) A person commits an offence if he has an immigration stamp in his possession without reasonable excuse.

(2) A person commits an offence if he has a replica immigration stamp in his possession without reasonable excuse.

(3) In this section—
   (a) 'immigration stamp' means a device which is designed for the purpose of stamping documents in the exercise of an immigration function,
   (b) 'replica immigration stamp' means a device which is designed for the purpose of stamping a document so that it appears to have been stamped in the exercise of an immigration function, and
   (c) 'immigration function' means a function of an immigration officer or the Secretary of State under the Immigration Acts.

(4) A person who is guilty of an offence under this section shall be liable—
   (a) on conviction on indictment, to imprisonment for a term not exceeding two years, to a fine or to both, or
   (b) on summary conviction, to imprisonment for a term not exceeding six months, to a fine not exceeding the statutory maximum or to both.]

Note: Section 26B inserted by Nationality, Immigration and Asylum Act 2002, s 148 from 10 February 2003 (SI 2003/1).

27. Offences by persons connected with ships or aircraft or with ports

A person shall be guilty of an offence punishable on summary conviction with a fine of not more than [level 5 on the standard scale] or with imprisonment for not more than six months, or with both, in any of the following cases—
   (a) if, being the captain of a ship or aircraft,—
      (i) he knowingly permits a person to disembark in the United Kingdom when required under Schedule 2 or 3 to this Act to prevent it, or fails without reasonable excuse to take any steps he is required by or under Schedule 2 to take in connection with the disembarkation or examination of passengers or for furnishing a passenger list or particulars of members of the crew; or
      (ii) he fails, without reasonable excuse, to comply with any directions given him under Schedule 2 or 3 [or under the Immigration and Asylum Act 1999] with respect to the removal of a person from the United Kingdom;
   (b) if, as owner or agent of a ship or aircraft,—
      (i) he arranges, or is knowingly concerned in any arrangements, for the

ship or aircraft to call at a port other than a port of entry contrary to any provision of Schedule 2 to this Act; or

(ii) he fails, with reasonable excuse, to take any steps required by an order under Schedule 2 for the supply to passengers of landing or embarkation cards; or

(iii) he fails, without reasonable excuse, to make arrangements for [or in connection with] the removal of a person from the United Kingdom when required to do so by directions given under Schedule 2 or 3 to this Act [or under the Immigration and Asylum Act 1999; or

(iv) he fails, without reasonable excuse, to comply with [a requirement imposed by or under Schedule 2]

(c) if, as a person concerned in the management of a port, he fails, without reasonable excuse, to take any steps required by Schedule 2 in relation to the embarkation or disembarkation of passengers where a control area is designated.

Note: Words in first square brackets in s 27 substituted by virtue of Criminal Justice Act 1982, and amended by Asylum and Immigration Act 1996 from 1 October 1996. Words in square brackets in sub-s (b)(iv) substituted and words omitted from sub-s (c) by Immigration, Asylum and Nationality Act 2006, s 31 from a date to be appointed. Other words in square brackets inserted by Immigration and Asylum Act 1999 from 2 October 2000.

28. Proceedings

(1) Where the offence is one to which, under section 24, [. . .] or 26 above, an extended time limit for prosecutions is to apply, then—

(a) an information relating to the offence may in England and Wales be tried by a magistrates' court if it is laid within six months after the commission of the offence, or if it is laid within three years after the commission of the offence and not more than two months after the date certified by [an officer of police above the rank of chief superintendent] to be the date on which evidence sufficient to justify proceedings came to the notice of an officer of [the police force to which he belongs] and;

(b) summary proceedings for the offence may in Scotland be commenced within six months after the commission of the offence, or within three years after the commission of the offence and not more than two months after the date on which evidence sufficient in the opinion of the Lord Advocate to justify proceedings came to his knowledge; and

(c) a complaint charging the commission of the offence may in Northern Ireland be heard and determined by a magistrates' court if it is made within six months after the commission of the offence, or if it is made within three years after the commission of the offence and not more than two months after the date certified by an officer of police not below the rank of assistant chief constable to be the date on which evidence sufficient to justify the proceedings came to the notice of the police in Northern Ireland.

(2) For purposes of subsection (1)(b) above proceedings shall be deemed to be commenced on the date on which a warrant to apprehend or to cite the accused is granted, if such warrant is executed without undue delay; and a certificate of the Lord Advocate as to the date on which such evidence as is mentioned in subsection (1)(b) came to his knowledge shall be conclusive evidence.

(3) For the purposes of the trial of a person for an offence under this Part of this Act, the offence shall be deemed to have been committed either at the place at which it actually was committed or at any place at which he may be.

(4) Any powers exercisable under this Act in the case of any person may be exercised notwithstanding that proceedings for an offence under this Part of this Act have been taken against him.

Note: Words omitted from sub-s (1) by Nationality, Immigration and Asylum Act 2002, s 156 from 10 February 2003 (SI 2003/1). Words in square brackets in s 28(1)(a) substituted by Immigration Act 1988.

[28A. Arrest without warrant

(1) An immigration officer may arrest without warrant a person—
  (a) who has committed or attempted to commit an offence under section 24 or 24A; or
  (b) whom he has reasonable grounds for suspecting has committed or attempted to commit such an offence.

(2) But subsection (1) does not apply in relation to an offence under section 24(1)(d).

(3) An immigration officer may arrest without warrant a person—
  (a) who has committed an offence under section [25, 25A or 25B]; or
  (b) whom he has reasonable grounds for suspecting has committed that offence.

(4) . . .

(5) An immigration officer may arrest without warrant a person ('the suspect') who, or whom he has reasonable grounds for suspecting—
  (a) has committed or attempted to commit an offence under section 26(1)(g); or
  (b) is committing or attempting to commit that offence.

(6) The power conferred by subsection (5) is exercisable only if either the first or the second condition is satisfied.

(7) The first condition is that it appears to the officer that service of a summons (or, in Scotland, a copy complaint) is impracticable or inappropriate because—
  (a) he does not know, and cannot readily discover, the suspect's name;

(b) he has reasonable grounds for doubting whether a name given by the suspect as his name is his real name;
(c) the suspect has failed to give him a satisfactory address for service; or
(d) he has reasonable grounds for doubting whether an address given by the suspect is a satisfactory address for service.

(8) The second condition is that the officer has reasonable grounds for believing that arrest is necessary to prevent the suspect—
(a) causing physical injury to himself or another person;
(b) suffering physical injury; or
(c) causing loss of or damage to property.

(9) For the purposes of subsection (7), an address is a satisfactory address for service if it appears to the officer—
(a) that the suspect will be at that address for a sufficiently long period for it to be possible to serve him with a summons (or copy complaint); or
(b) that some other person specified by the suspect will accept service of a summons (or copy complaint) for the suspect at that address.

[(9A) An immigration officer may arrest without warrant a person—
(a) who has committed an offence under section 26A or 26B; or
(b) who he has reasonable grounds for suspecting has committed an offence under section 26A or 26B.]

(10) In relation to the exercise of the powers conferred by subsections (3)(b) . . . and (5), it is immaterial that no offence has been committed.

(11) In Scotland the powers conferred by subsections (3) . . . and (5) may also be exercised by a constable.]

Note: Section 28A inserted by Immigration and Asylum Act 1999 from 14 February 2000. Words in square brackets in sub-s (3)(a) substituted by and sub-s (4) omitted by Nationality, Immigration and Asylum Act 2002, s 144 from 10 February 2003 (SI 2003/1). Subsection (9A) inserted by Nationality, Immigration and Asylum Act 2002, s 150 from 10 February 2003 (SI 2003/1). Words omitted from sub-ss (10) and (11) by Nationality, Immigration and Asylum Act 2002, s 144 from 10 February 2003 (SI 2003/1). Words in square brackets in sub-ss (1) and (9A) substituted by Serious Organised Crime and Police Act 2005, s 53 from 1 April 2006 (SI 2006/378).

[28AA. Arrest with warrant

(1) This section applies if on an application by an immigration officer a justice of the peace is satisfied that there are reasonable grounds for suspecting that a person has committed an offence under—
(a) section 24(1)(d), or
(b) section 8 of the Asylum and Immigration Act 1996 (c. 49) (employment: offence).

(2) The justice of the peace may grant a warrant authorising any immigration officer to arrest the person.

(3) In the application of this section to Scotland a reference to a justice of the peace shall be treated as a reference to the sheriff or a justice of the peace.]

Note: Section 28AA inserted by Nationality, Immigration and Asylum Act 2002, s 152 from 10 February 2003 (SI 2003/1).

[28B. Search and arrest by warrant

(1) Subsection (2) applies if a justice of the peace is, by written information on oath, satisfied that there are reasonable grounds for suspecting that a person ('the suspect') who is liable to be arrested for a relevant offence is to be found on any premises.

(2) The justice may grant a warrant authorising any immigration officer or constable to enter, if need be by force, the premises named in the warrant for the purpose of searching for and arresting the suspect.

(3) Subsection (4) applies if in Scotland the sheriff or a justice of the peace is by evidence on oath satisfied as mentioned in subsection (1).

(4) The sheriff or justice may grant a warrant authorising any immigration officer or constable to enter, if need be by force, the premises named in the warrant for the purpose of searching for and arresting the suspect.

(5) 'Relevant offence' means an offence under section 24(1)(a), (b), (c), (d), (e) or (f), [24A, 26A or 26B].]

Note: Section 28B inserted by Immigration and Asylum Act 1999 from 14 February 2000. Words in square brackets in sub-s (5) substituted by Nationality, Immigration and Asylum Act 2002, ss 144, 150 from 10 February 2003 (SI 2003/1).

[28C. Search and arrest without warrant

(1) An immigration officer may enter and search any premises for the purpose of arresting a person for an offence under [section 25, 25A or 25B].

(2) The power may be exercised—
   (a) only to the extent that it is reasonably required for that purpose; and
   (b) only if the officer has reasonable grounds for believing that the person whom he is seeking is on the premises.

(3) In relation to premises consisting of two or more separate dwellings, the power is limited to entering and searching—
   (a) any parts of the premises which the occupiers of any dwelling comprised in the premises use in common with the occupiers of any such other dwelling; and
   (b) any such dwelling in which the officer has reasonable grounds for believing that the person whom he is seeking may be.

(4) The power may be exercised only if the officer produces identification showing that he is an immigration officer (whether or not he is asked to do so).]

Note: Section 28C inserted by Immigration and Asylum Act 1999 from 14 February 2000. Words in square brackets in sub-s (1) substituted by Nationality, Immigration and Asylum Act 2002, s 144 from 10 February 2003 (SI 2003/1).

[28CA. Business premises: entry to arrest

(1) A constable or immigration officer may enter and search any business premises for the purpose of arresting a person—
   (a) for an offence under section 24,
   (b) for an offence under section 24A, or
   (c) under paragraph 17 of Schedule 2.

(2) The power under subsection (1) may be exercised only—
   (a) to the extent that it is reasonably required for a purpose specified in subsection (1),
   (b) if the constable or immigration officer has reasonable grounds for believing that the person whom he is seeking is on the premises,
   (c) with the authority of the Secretary of State (in the case of an immigration officer) or a Chief Superintendent (in the case of a constable), and
   (d) if the constable or immigration officer produces identification showing his status.

(3) Authority for the purposes of subsection (2)(c)—
   (a) may be given on behalf of the Secretary of State only by a civil servant of the rank of at least Assistant Director, and
   (b) shall expire at the end of the period of seven days beginning with the day on which it is given.

(4) Subsection (2)(d) applies—
   (a) whether or not a constable or immigration officer is asked to produce identification, but
   (b) only where premises are occupied.

(5) Subsection (6) applies where a constable or immigration officer—
   (a) enters premises in reliance on this section, and
   (b) detains a person on the premises.

(6) A detainee custody officer may enter the premises for the purpose of carrying out a search.

(7) In subsection (6)—
'detainee custody officer' means a person in respect of whom a certificate of authorisation is in force under section 154 of the Immigration and Asylum Act 1999 (c. 33) (detained persons: escort and custody), and

'search' means a search under paragraph 2(1)(a) of Schedule 13 to that Act (escort arrangements: power to search detained person).]

Note: Section 28CA inserted by Nationality, Immigration and Asylum Act 2002 s 153 from 10 February 2003 (SI 2003/1).

[28D. Entry and search of premises

(1) If, on an application made by an immigration officer, a justice of the peace is satisfied that there are reasonable grounds for believing that—
   (a) a relevant offence has been committed,
   (b) there is material on premises specified in the application which is likely to be of substantial value (whether by itself or together with other material) to the investigation of the offence,
   (c) the material is likely to be relevant evidence,
   (d) the material does not consist of or include items subject to legal privilege, excluded material or special procedure material, and
   (e) any of the conditions specified in subsection (2) applies, he may issue a warrant authorising an immigration officer to enter and search the premises.

(2) The conditions are that—
   (a) it is not practicable to communicate with any person entitled to grant entry to the premises;
   (b) it is practicable to communicate with a person entitled to grant entry to the premises but it is not practicable to communicate with any person entitled to grant access to the evidence;
   (c) entry to the premises will not be granted unless a warrant is produced;
   (d) the purpose of a search may be frustrated or seriously prejudiced unless an immigration officer arriving at the premises can secure immediate entry to them.

(3) An immigration officer may seize and retain anything for which a search has been authorised under subsection (1).

(4) 'Relevant offence' means an offence under section 24(1)(a), (b), (c), (d), (e) or (f), [24A, 25, 25A, 25B, 26A or 26B].

(5) In relation to England and Wales, expressions which are given a meaning by the Police and Criminal Evidence Act 1984 have the same meaning when used in this section.

(6) In relation to Northern Ireland, expressions which are given a meaning by the Police and Criminal Evidence (Northern Ireland) Order 1989 have the same meaning when used in this section.

(7) In the application of subsection (1) to Scotland—
   (a) read the reference to a justice of the peace as a reference to the sheriff or a justice of the peace; and

(b) in paragraph (d), omit the reference to excluded material and special procedure material.]

Note: Section 28D inserted by Immigration and Asylum Act 1999 from 14 February 2000. Words in square brackets in sub-s (4) substituted by Nationality, Immigration and Asylum Act 2002, ss 144, 150 from 10 February 2003 (SI 2003/1).

[28E. Entry and search of premises following arrest

(1) This section applies if a person is arrested for an offence under this Part at a place other than a police station.

(2) An immigration officer may enter and search any premises—
  (a) in which the person was when arrested, or
  (b) in which he was immediately before he was arrested, for evidence relating to the offence for which the arrest was made ('relevant evidence').

(3) The power may be exercised—
  (a) only if the officer has reasonable grounds for believing that there is relevant evidence on the premises; and
  (b) only to the extent that it is reasonably required for the purpose of discovering relevant evidence.

(4) In relation to premises consisting of two or more separate dwellings, the power is limited to entering and searching—
  (a) any dwelling in which the arrest took place or in which the arrested person was immediately before his arrest; and
  (b) any parts of the premises which the occupier of any such dwelling uses in common with the occupiers of any other dwellings comprised in the premises.

(5) An officer searching premises under subsection (2) may seize and retain anything he finds which he has reasonable grounds for believing is relevant evidence.

(6) Subsection (5) does not apply to items which the officer has reasonable grounds for believing are items subject to legal privilege.]

Note: Section 28E inserted by Immigration and Asylum Act 1999 from 14 February 2000.

[28F. Entry and search of premises following arrest under section 25, 25A or 25B

(1) An immigration officer may enter and search any premises occupied or controlled by a person arrested for an offence under [section 25, 25A, 25B.]

(2) The power may be exercised—
  (a) only if the officer has reasonable grounds for suspecting that there is relevant evidence on the premises;
  (b) only to the extent that it is reasonably required for the purpose of discovering relevant evidence; and

(c) subject to subsection (3), only if a senior officer has authorised it in writing.

(3) The power may be exercised—

(a) before taking the arrested person to a place where he is to be detained; and

(b) without obtaining an authorisation under subsection (2)(c), if the presence of that person at a place other than one where he is to be detained is necessary for the effective investigation of the offence.

(4) An officer who has relied on subsection (3) must inform a senior officer as soon as is practicable.

(5) The officer authorising a search, or who is informed of one under subsection (4), must make a record in writing of—

(a) the grounds for the search; and

(b) the nature of the evidence that was sought.

(6) An officer searching premises under this section may seize and retain anything he finds which he has reasonable grounds for suspecting is relevant evidence.

(7) 'Relevant evidence' means evidence, other than items subject to legal privilege, that relates to the offence in question.

(8) 'Senior officer' means an immigration officer not below the rank of chief immigration officer.]

Note: Section 28F inserted by Immigration and Asylum Act 1999 from 14 February 2000. Words in square brackets in sub-s (1) substituted by Nationality, Immigration and Asylum Act 2002, s 144 from 10 February 2003 (SI 2003/1).

[28FA. Search for personnel records: warrant unnecessary

(1) This section applies where—

(a) a person has been arrested for an offence under section 24(1) or 24A(1),

(b) a person has been arrested under paragraph 17 of Schedule 2,

(c) a constable or immigration officer reasonably believes that a person is liable to arrest for an offence under section 24(1) or 24A(1), or

(d) a constable or immigration officer reasonably believes that a person is liable to arrest under paragraph 17 of Schedule 2.

(2) A constable or immigration officer may search business premises where the arrest was made or where the person liable to arrest is if the constable or immigration officer reasonably believes—

(a) that a person has committed an immigration employment offence in relation to the person arrested or liable to arrest, and

(b) that employee records, other than items subject to legal privilege, will be found on the premises and will be of substantial value (whether on their own or together with other material) in the investigation of the immigration employment offence.

(3) A constable or officer searching premises under subsection (2) may seize and retain employee records, other than items subject to legal privilege, which he reasonably suspects will be of substantial value (whether on their own or together with other material) in the investigation of—
  (a) an immigration employment offence, or
  (b) an offence under section 105 or 106 of the Immigration and Asylum Act 1999 (c. 33) (support for asylum-seeker: fraud).

(4) The power under subsection (2) may be exercised only—
  (a) to the extent that it is reasonably required for the purpose of discovering employee records other than items subject to legal privilege,
  (b) if the constable or immigration officer produces identification showing his status, and
  (c) if the constable or immigration officer reasonably believes that at least one of the conditions in subsection (5) applies.

(5) Those conditions are—
  (a) that it is not practicable to communicate with a person entitled to grant access to the records,
  (b) that permission to search has been refused,
  (c) that permission to search would be refused if requested, and
  (d) that the purpose of a search may be frustrated or seriously prejudiced if it is not carried out in reliance on subsection (2).

(6) Subsection (4)(b) applies—
  (a) whether or not a constable or immigration officer is asked to produce identification, but
  (b) only where premises are occupied.

(7) In this section 'immigration employment offence' means an offence under section 8 of the Asylum and Immigration Act 1996 (c. 49) (employment).]

Note: Section 28FA inserted by Nationality, Immigration and Asylum Act 2002, s 154 from 10 February 2003 (SI 2003/1).

[28FB. Search for personnel records: with warrant

(1) This section applies where on an application made by an immigration officer in respect of business premises a justice of the peace is satisfied that there are reasonable grounds for believing—
  (a) that an employer has provided inaccurate or incomplete information under section 134 of the Nationality, Immigration and Asylum Act 2002 (compulsory disclosure by employer),
  (b) that employee records, other than items subject to legal privilege, will be found on the premises and will enable deduction of some or all of the information which the employer was required to provide, and

(c) that at least one of the conditions in subsection (2) is satisfied.

(2) Those conditions are—

(a) that it is not practicable to communicate with a person entitled to grant access to the premises,

(b) that it is not practicable to communicate with a person entitled to grant access to the records,

(c) that entry to the premises or access to the records will not be granted unless a warrant is produced, and

(d) that the purpose of a search may be frustrated or seriously prejudiced unless an immigration officer arriving at the premises can secure immediate entry.

(3) The justice of the peace may issue a warrant authorising an immigration officer to enter and search the premises.

(4) Subsection (7)(a) of section 28D shall have effect for the purposes of this section as it has effect for the purposes of that section.

(5) An immigration officer searching premises under a warrant issued under this section may seize and retain employee records, other than items subject to legal privilege, which he reasonably suspects will be of substantial value (whether on their own or together with other material) in the investigation of—

(a) an offence under section 137 of the Nationality, Immigration and Asylum Act 2002 (disclosure of information: offences) in respect of a requirement under section 134 of that Act, or

(b) an offence under section 105 or 106 of the Immigration and Asylum Act 1999 (c. 33) (support for asylum-seeker: fraud).]

Note: Section 28FB inserted by Nationality, Immigration and Asylum Act 2002, s 154 from 10 February 2003 (SI 2003/1).

[28G. Searching arrested persons

(1) This section applies if a person is arrested for an offence under this Part at a place other than a police station.

(2) An immigration officer may search the arrested person if he has reasonable grounds for believing that the arrested person may present a danger to himself or others.

(3) The officer may search the arrested person for—

(a) anything which he might use to assist his escape from lawful custody; or

(b) anything which might be evidence relating to the offence for which he has been arrested.

(4) The power conferred by subsection (3) may be exercised—

(a) only if the officer has reasonable grounds for believing that the arrested person may have concealed on him anything of a kind mentioned in that subsection; and

(b) only to the extent that it is reasonably required for the purpose of discovering any such thing.

(5) A power conferred by this section to search a person is not to be read as authorising an officer to require a person to remove any of his clothing in public other than an outer coat, jacket or glove; but it does authorise the search of a person's mouth.

(6) An officer searching a person under subsection (2) may seize and retain anything he finds, if he has reasonable grounds for believing that that person might use it to cause physical injury to himself or to another person.

(7) An officer searching a person under subsection (3) may seize and retain anything he finds, if he has reasonable grounds for believing—

(a) that that person might use it to assist his escape from lawful custody; or

(b) that it is evidence which relates to the offence in question.

(8) Subsection (7)(b) does not apply to an item subject to legal privilege.]

Note: Section 28G inserted by Immigration and Asylum Act 1999 from 14 February 2000.

[28H. Searching persons in police custody

(1) This section applies if a person—

(a) has been arrested for an offence under this Part; and

(b) is in custody at a police station or in police detention at a place other than a police station.

(2) An immigration officer may at any time, search the arrested person in order to see whether he has with him anything—

(a) which he might use to—

(i) cause physical injury to himself or others;

(ii) damage property;

(iii) interfere with evidence; or

(iv) assist his escape; or

(b) which the officer has reasonable grounds for believing is evidence relating to the offence in question.

(3) The power may be exercised only to the extent that the custody officer concerned considers it to be necessary for the purpose of discovering anything of a kind mentioned in subsection (2).

(4) An officer searching a person under this section may seize anything he finds, if he has reasonable grounds for believing that—

(a) that person might use it for one or more of the purposes mentioned in subsection (2)(a); or

(b) it is evidence relating to the offence in question.

(5) Anything seized under subsection (4)(a) may be.retained by the police.

(6) Anything seized under subsection (4)(b) may be retained by an immigration officer.

(7) The person from whom something is seized must be told the reason for the seizure unless he is—
  (a) violent or appears likely to become violent; or
  (b) incapable of understanding what is said to him.

(8) An intimate search may not be conducted under this section.

(9) The person carrying out a search under this section must be of the same sex as the person searched.

(10) 'Custody officer'—
  (a) in relation to England and Wales, has the same meaning as in the Police and Criminal Evidence Act 1984;
  (b) in relation to Scotland, means the officer in charge of a police station; and
  (c) in relation to Northern Ireland, has the same meaning as in the Police and Criminal Evidence (Northern Ireland) Order 1989.

(11) 'Intimate search'—
  (a) in relation to England and Wales, has the meaning given by section 65 of the Act of 1984;
  (b) in relation to Scotland, means a search which consists of the physical examination of a person's body orifices other than the mouth; and
  (c) in relation to Northern Ireland, has the same meaning as in the 1989 Order.

(12) 'Police detention'—
  (a) in relation to England and Wales, has the meaning given by section 118(2) of the 1984 Act; and
  (b) in relation to Northern Ireland, has the meaning given by Article 2 of the 1989 Order.

(13) In relation to Scotland, a person is in police detention if—
  (a) he has been taken to a police station after being arrested for an-offence; or
  (b) he is arrested at a police station after attending voluntarily at the station, accompanying a constable to it or being detained under section 14 of the Criminal Procedure (Scotland) Act 1995, and is detained there or is detained elsewhere in the charge of a constable, but is not in police detention if he is in court after being charged.]

Note: Section 28H inserted by Immigration and Asylum Act 1999 from 14 February 2000.

[28I. Seized material: access and copying

(1) If a person showing himself—
  (a) to be the occupier of the premises on which seized material was seized, or
  (b) to have had custody or control of the material immediately before it was seized,

asks the immigration officer who seized the material for a record of what he seized, the officer must provide the record to that person within a reasonable time.

(2) If a relevant person asks an immigration officer for permission to be granted access to seized material, the officer must arrange for him to have access to the material under the supervision—
 (a) in the case of seized material within subsection (8)(a), of an immigration officer;
 (b) in the case of seized material within subsection (8)(b), of a constable.

(3) An immigration officer may photograph or copy, or have photographed or copied, seized material.

(4) If a relevant person asks an immigration officer for a photograph or copy of seized material, the officer must arrange for—
 (a) that person to have access to the material for the purpose of photographing or copying it under the supervision—
  (i) in the case of seized material within subsection (8)(a), of an immigration officer;
  (ii) in the case of seized material within subsection (8)(b), of a constable; or
 (b) the material to be photographed or copied.

(5) A photograph or copy made under subsection (4)(b) must be supplied within a reasonable time.

(6) There is no duty under this section to arrange for access to, or the supply of a photograph or copy of, any material if there are reasonable grounds for believing that to do so would prejudice—
 (a) the exercise of any functions in connection with which the material was seized; or
 (b) an investigation which is being conducted under this Act, or any criminal proceedings which may be brought as a result.

(7) 'Relevant person' means—
 (a) a person who had custody or control of seized material immediately before it was seized, or
 (b) someone acting on behalf of such a person.

(8) 'Seized material' means anything—
 (a) seized and retained by an immigration officer, or
 (b) seized by an immigration officer and retained by the police, under this Part.]

Note: Section 28I inserted by Immigration and Asylum Act 1999 from 14 February 2000.

[28J. Search warrants: safeguards

(1) The entry or search of premises under a warrant is unlawful unless it complies with this section and section 28K.

(2) If an immigration officer applies for a warrant, he must—
 (a) state the ground on which he makes the application and the provision of this Act under which the warrant would be issued;
 (b) specify the premises which it is desired to enter and search; and
 (c) identify, so far as is practicable, the persons or articles to be sought.

(3) In Northern Ireland, an application for a warrant is to be supported by a complaint in writing and substantiated on oath.

(4) Otherwise, an application for a warrant is to be made ex parte and supported by an information in writing or, in Scotland, evidence on oath.

(5) The officer must answer on oath any question that the justice of the peace or sheriff hearing the application asks him.

(6) A warrant shall authorise an entry on one occasion only.

(7) A warrant must specify—
 (a) the name of the person applying for it;
 (b) the date on which it is issued;
 (c) the premises to be searched; and
 (d) the provision of this Act under which it is issued.

(8) A warrant must identify, so far as is practicable, the persons or articles to be sought.

(9) Two copies of a warrant must be made.

(10) The copies must be clearly certified as copies.

(11) 'Warrant' means a warrant to enter and search premises issued to an immigration officer under this Part or under paragraph 17(2) of Schedule 2.]

Note: Section 28J inserted by Immigration and Asylum Act 1999 from 14 February 2000.

[28K. Execution of warrants

(1) A warrant may be executed by any immigration officer.

(2) A warrant may authorise persons to accompany the officer executing it.

(3) Entry and search under a warrant must be—
 (a) within one month from the date of its issue; and
 (b) at a reasonable hour, unless it appears to the officer executing it that the purpose of a search might be frustrated.

(4) If the occupier of premises which are to be entered and searched is present at the time when an immigration officer seeks to execute a warrant, the officer must—
 (a) identify himself to the occupier and produce identification showing that he is an immigration officer;
 (b) show the occupier the warrant; and
 (c) supply him with a copy of it.

(5) If—
  (a) the occupier is not present, but
  (b) some other person who appears to the officer to be in charge of the premises is present,

subsection (4) has effect as if each reference to the occupier were a reference to that other person.

(6) If there is no person present who appears to the officer to be in charge of the premises, the officer must leave a copy of the warrant in a prominent place on the premises.

(7) A search under a warrant may only be a search to the extent required for the purpose for which the warrant was issued.

(8) An officer executing a warrant must make an endorsement on it stating—
  (a) whether the persons or articles sought were found; and
  (b) whether any articles, other than articles which were sought, were seized.

(9) A warrant which has been executed, or has not been executed within the time authorised for its execution, must be returned—
  [(a) if issued by a justice of the peace in England and Wales, to the designated officer for the local justice area in which the justice was acting when he issued the warrant;]
  (b) if issued by a justice of the peace in Northern Ireland, to the clerk of petty sessions for the petty sessions district in which the premises are situated;
  (c) if issued by a justice of the peace in Scotland, to the clerk of the district court for the commission area for which the justice of the peace was appointed;
  (d) if issued by the sheriff, to the sheriff clerk.

(10) A warrant returned under subsection (9)(a) must be retained for 12 months by the [designated officer].

(11) A warrant issued under subsection (9)(b) or (c) must be retained for 12 months by the clerk.

(12) A warrant returned under subsection (9)(d) must be retained for 12 months by the sheriff clerk.

(13) If during that 12 month period the occupier of the premises to which it relates asks to inspect it, he must be allowed to do so.

(14) 'Warrant' means a warrant to enter and search premises issued to an immigration officer under this Part or under paragraph 17(2) of Schedule 2.]

Note: Section 28K inserted by Immigration and Asylum Act 1999 from 14 February 2000. Words in square brackets substituted by Sch 3 Courts Act 2003 from a date to be appointed.

[28L. Interpretation of Part III

[(1)] In this Part, 'premises' and 'items subject to legal privilege' have the same meaning—
(a) in relation to England and Wales, as in the Police and Criminal Evidence Act 1984;
(b) in relation to Northern Ireland, as in the Police and Criminal Evidence (Northern Ireland) Order 1989; and
(c) in relation to Scotland, as in section 33 of the Criminal Law (Consolidation) (Scotland) Act 1995.]

[(2) In this Part 'business premises' means premises (or any part of premises) not used as a dwelling.

(3) In this Part 'employee records' means records which show an employee's—
(a) name,
(b) date of birth,
(c) address,
(d) length of service,
(e) rate of pay, or
(f) nationality or citizenship.

(4) The Secretary of State may by order amend section 28CA(3)(a) to reflect a change in nomenclature.

(5) An order under subsection (4)—
(a) must be made by statutory instrument, and
(b) shall be subject to annulment in pursuance of a resolution of either House of Parliament.]

Note: Section 28L inserted by Immigration and Asylum Act 1999 from 14 February 2000. Subsections (2)–(5) inserted by Nationality, Immigration and Asylum Act 2002, s 155 from 10 February 2003 (SI 2003/1).

Part IV

Supplementary

29. . . .

Note: Repealed by Nationality, Immigration and Asylum Act 2002, s 58 and Sch 9 from 1 April 2003 (SI 2003/754).

30. . . .

Note: Repealed by British Nationality Act 1981, s 52(8) and Mental Health (Scotland) Act 1984, s 127(2).

31. Expenses

There shall be defrayed out of moneys provided by Parliament any expenses incurred [by the Lord Chancellor under Schedule 5 to this Act or] by a Secretary of State under or by virtue of this Act—
(a) by way of administrative expenses . . .; or
(b) in connection with the removal of any person from the United Kingdom under Schedule 2 or 3 to this Act or the departure with him of his dependants, or his or their maintenance pending departure; or
(c) . . .
(d) . . .

Note: Words in square brackets in s 31 inserted and s 31(c) repealed by SI 1987/465. Words omitted from s 31(a) repealed by British Nationality Act 1981, s 52(8). Section 31(d) repealed by Nationality, Immigration and Asylum Act 2002, s 58 and Sch 9 from 1 April 2003, (SI 2003/754).

[31A. Procedural requirements as to applications

. . .]

Note: Section 31A repealed by Immigration, Asylum and Nationality Act 2006 from a date to be appointed.

32. General provisions as to Order in Council, etc.

(1) Any power conferred by Part I of this Act to make an Order in Council or order (other than a deportation order) or to give any directions includes power to revoke or vary the Order in Council, order or directions.

(2) Any document purporting to be an order, notice or direction made or given by the Secretary of State for the purposes of [the Immigration Acts] and to be signed by him or on his behalf, and any document purporting to be a certificate of the Secretary of State so given and to be signed by him [or on his behalf] shall be received in evidence, and shall, until the contrary is proved, be deemed to be made or issued by him.

(3) Prima facie evidence of any such order, notice, direction or certificate as afore-said may, in any legal proceedings or [other proceedings under the Immigration Acts], be given by the production of a document bearing a certificate purporting to be signed by or on behalf of the Secretary of State and stating that the document is a true copy of the order, notice, direction or certificate.

(4) Where an order under section 8(2) above applies to persons specified in a schedule to the order, or any directions of the Secretary of State given for the purposes of [the Immigration Acts] apply to persons specified in a schedule to

the directions, prima facie evidence of the provisions of the order or directions other than the schedule and of any entry contained in the schedule may, in any legal proceedings or [other proceedings under the Immigration Acts], be given by the production of a document purporting to be signed by or on behalf of the Secretary of State and stating that the document is a true copy of the said provisions and of the relevant entry.

[(5) . . .]

Note: Words in square brackets in sub-ss (2), (3) and (4) inserted by Immigration and Asylum Act 1999 from 6 December 1999. Subsection (5) substituted by Nationality, Immigration and Asylum Act 2002, s 158 from 10 February 2003 (SI 2003/1). Final words in square brackets substituted by Asylum and Immigration Act 2004, s 44 from 1 October 2004 (SI 2004/2523). Subsection (5) ceases to have effect by Immigration, Asylum and Nationality Act 2006, s 64 and Sch 3 from a date to be appointed.

33. Interpretation

(1) For purposes of this Act, except in so far as the context otherwise requires—

'aircraft' includes hovercraft, 'airport' includes hoverport and 'port' includes airport;

'captain' means master (of a ship) or commander (of an aircraft);

['certificate of entitlement' means a certificate under section 10 of the Nationality, Immigration and Asylum Act 2002 that a person has the right of abode in the United Kingdom];

['Convention adoption' has the same meaning as in the Adoption Act 1976 and the Adoption (Scotland) Act 1978;]

'crew', in relation to a ship or aircraft, means all persons actually employed in the working or service of the ship or aircraft, including the captain, and 'member of the crew' shall be construed accordingly;

['entrant' means a person entering or seeking to enter the United Kingdom and 'illegal entrant' means a person—

(a) unlawfully entering or seeking to enter in breach of a deportation order or of the immigration laws, or

(b) entering or seeking to enter by means which include deception by another person,

and includes also a person who has entered as mentioned in paragraph (a) or (b) above;]

'entry clearance' means a visa, entry certificate or other document which, in accordance with the immigration rules, is to be taken as evidence [or the requisite evidence] of a person's eligibility, though not [a British citizen], for entry into the United Kingdom (but does not include a work permit);

'immigration laws' means this Act and any law for purposes similar to this Act which is for the time being or has (before or after the passing of this Act) been in force in any part of the United Kingdom and Islands;

'immigration rules' means the rules for the time being laid down as mentioned in section 3(2) above;

'the Islands' means the Channel Islands and the Isle of Man, and 'the United Kingdom and Islands' means the United Kingdom and the Islands taken together;

'legally adopted' means adopted in pursuance of an order made by any court in the United Kingdom and Islands [under a Convention adoption] or by any adoption specified as an overseas adoption by order of the Secretary of State under [section 72(2) the Adoption Act 1976];

'limited leave' and 'indefinite leave' mean respectively leave under this Act to enter or remain in the United Kingdom which is, and one which is not, limited as to duration;

'settled' shall be construed in accordance with [subsection (2A) below];

'ship' includes every description of vessel used in navigation;

['United Kingdom passport' means a current passport issued by the Government of the United Kingdom, or by the Lieutenant-Governor of any of the Islands or by the Government of any territory which is for the time being a dependent territory within the meaning of the British Nationality Act 1981;]

'work permit' means a permit indicating, in accordance with the immigration rules, that a person named in it is eligible, though not [a British citizen], for entry into the United Kingdom for the purpose of taking employment.

(1A) A reference to being the owner of a vehicle, ship or aircraft includes a reference to being any of a number of persons who jointly own it.

(2) It is hereby declared that, except as otherwise provided in this Act, a person is not to be treated for the purposes of any provision of this Act as ordinarily resident in the United Kingdom or in any of the Islands at a time when he is there in breach of the immigration laws.

(2A) Subject to section 8(5) above, references to a person being settled in the United Kingdom are references to his being ordinarily resident there without being subject under the immigration laws to any restriction on the period for which he may remain.]

(3) The ports of entry for purposes of this Act, and the ports of exit for purposes of any Order in Council under section 3(7) above, shall be such ports as may from time to time be designated for the purpose by order of the Secretary of State made by statutory instrument.

[(4) For the purposes of this Act, the question of whether an appeal is pending shall be determined {in accordance with section 104 of the Nationality, Immigration and Asylum Act 2002 (pending appeals)}.]

(5) This Act shall not be taken to supersede or impair any power exercisable by Her Majesty in relation to aliens by virtue of Her prerogative.

Note: Definition of certificate of entitlement in s 33(1) substituted by Nationality, Immigration and Asylum Act 2002, s 10, from a date to be appointed. Definition of 'Convention adoption' and amendment to definition of legally adopted inserted by Adoption (Intercountry Aspects) Act 1999, Sch 2 from 1 June 2003 (SI 2003/362). Definition of 'entrant' in s 33(1) substituted by Asylum and Immigration Act 1996 from 1 October 1996. Words in third square brackets in s 33(1) inserted by Immigration Act 1988, s 10. Words in fifth square brackets in s 33(1) substituted by Adoption Act 1976. Other words in square brackets in s 33(1) substituted by British Nationality Act 1981. Subsection (1A) inserted by Nationality, Immigration and Asylum Act 2002, s 144 from 10 February 2003 (SI 2003/1). Subsection (2A) inserted by British Nationality Act 1981. Subsection (4) substituted by Immigration and Asylum Act 1999 from 2 October 2000. Words in curly brackets in sub-s (4) substituted by Sch 7 Nationality, Immigration and Asylum Act 2002 from 1 April 2003 (SI 2003/754).

34. Repeal, transitional and temporary

(1) Subject to the following provisions of this section, the enactments mentioned in Schedule 6 to this Act are hereby repealed, as from the coming into force of this Act, to the extent mentioned in column 3 of the Schedule; and—

(a) this Act, as from its coming into force, shall apply in relation to entrants or others arriving in the United Kingdom at whatever date before or after it comes into force; and

(b) after this Act comes into force anything done under or for the purposes of the former immigration laws shall have effect, in so far as any corresponding action could be taken under or for the purposes of this Act, as if done by way of action so taken, and in relation to anything so done this Act shall apply accordingly.

(2) Without prejudice to the generality of subsection (1)(a) and (b) above, a person refused leave to land by virtue of the Aliens Restriction Act 1914 shall be treated as having been refused leave to enter under this Act, and a person given leave to land by virtue of that Act shall be treated as having been given leave to enter under this Act; and similarly with the Commonwealth Immigrants Acts 1962 and 1968.

(3) A person treated in accordance with subsection (2) above as having leave to enter the United Kingdom—

(a) shall be treated as having an indefinite leave, if he is not at the coming in to force of this Act subject to a condition limiting his stay in the United Kingdom; and

(b) shall be treated, if he is then subject to such a condition, as having a limited leave of such duration, and subject to such conditions (capable of being attached to leave under this Act), as correspond to the conditions to which he is then subject, but not to conditions not capable of being so attached.

This subsection shall have effect in relation to any restriction or requirement imposed by Order in Council under the Aliens Restriction Act 1914 as if it had been imposed by way of a landing condition.

(4) Notwithstanding anything in the foregoing provisions of this Act, the former immigration laws shall continue to apply, and this Act shall not apply,—

(a) in relation to the making of deportation orders and matters connected therewith in any case where a decision to make the order has been notified to the person concerned before the coming into force of this Act;

(b) in relation to removal from the United Kingdom and matters conected therewith (including detention pending removal or pending the giving of directions for removal) in any case where a person is to be removed in pursuance of a decision taken before the coming into force of this Act or in pursuance of a deportation order to the making of which paragraph (a) above applies;

(c) in relation to appeals against any decision taken or other thing done under the former immigration laws, whether taken or done before the coming into force of this Act or by virtue of this subsection.

(5) Subsection (1) above shall not be taken as empowering a court on appeal to recommend for deportation a person whom the court below could not recommend for deportation, or as affecting any right of appeal in respect of a recommendation for deportation made before this Act comes into force, or as enabling a notice given before this Act comes into force and not complying with section 6(2) to take the place of the notice required by section 6(2) to be given before a person is recommended for deportation.

(6) . . .

Note: Section 34(6) repealed by Statute Law (Repeals) Act 1993, s 1.

35. Commencement, and interim provisions

(1) Except as otherwise provided by this Act, Parts I to III of this Act shall come into force on such day as the Secretary of State may appoint by order made by statutory instrument; and references to the coming into force of this Act shall be construed as references to the beginning of the day so appointed.

(2) Section 25 above, except section 25(2), and section 28 in its application to offences under section 25(1) shall come into force at the end of one month beginning with the date this Act is passed.

(3) . . .

(4) . . .

(5) . . .

Note: Section 35(3)–(5) repealed by Statute Law (Repeals) Act 1986.

36. Power to extend to Islands

Her Majesty may by Order in Council direct that any of the provisions of this Act shall extend, with such exceptions, adaptations and modifications, if any, as may be specified in the Order, to any of the Islands; and any Order in Council under this subsection may be varied or revoked by a further Order in Council.

37. Short title and extent

(1) This Act may be cited as the Immigration Act 1971.

(2) It is hereby declared that this Act extends to Northern Ireland, and (without prejudice to any provision of Schedule 1 to this Act as to the extent of that Schedule) where an enactment repealed by this Act extends outside the United Kingdom, the repeal shall be of like extent.

Schedules

Schedule 1

Note: Repealed by British Nationality Act 1981, s 52(8).

Section 4

Schedule 2

Administrative Provisions as to Control on Entry etc.

Part I. General Provisions

Immigration officers and medical inspectors

1.—(1) Immigration officers for the purposes of this Act shall be appointed by the Secretary of State, and he may arrange with the Commissioners of Customs and Excise for the employment of officers of customs and excise as immigration officers under this Act.

(2) Medical inspectors for the purposes of this Act may be appointed by the Secretary of State or, in Northern Ireland, by the Minister of Health and Social Services or other appropriate Minister of the Government of Northern Ireland in pursuance of arrangements made between that Minister and the Secretary of State, and shall be fully qualified medical practitioners.

[(2A) The Secretary of State may direct that his function of appointing medical inspectors under sub-paragraph (2) is also to be exercisable by such persons specified in the direction who exercise functions relating to health in England or Wales.]

(3) In the exercise of their functions under this Act immigration officers shall act in accordance with such instructions (not inconsistent with the immigration rules) as may be given them by the Secretary of State, and medical inspectors shall act in accordance with

such instructions as may be given them by the Secretary of State or, in Northern Ireland, as may be given in pursuance of the arrangements mentioned in sub-paragraph (2) above by the Minister making appointments of medical inspectors in Northern Ireland.

(4) An immigration officer or medical inspector may board any ship [or aircraft] for the purpose of exercising his functions under this Act.

(5) An immigration officer, for the purpose of satisfying himself whether there are persons he may wish to examine under paragraph 2 below, may search any ship [or aircraft] and anything on board it, or any vehicle taken off a ship or aircraft on which it has been brought to the United Kingdom.

Note: Words in square brackets in sub-paras (4) and (5) substituted by SI 1993/1813. Subparagraph (2A) inserted by Health Protection Agency Act 2004, s 12(3) and Sch 3 from 22 September 2004.

Examination by immigration officers, and medical examination

2.—(1) An immigration officer may examine any persons who have arrived in the United Kingdom by ship [or aircraft] (including transit passengers, members of the crew and others not seeking to enter the United Kingdom) for the purpose of determining—

(a) whether any of them is or is not [a British citizen]; and

(b) whether, if he is not, he may or may not enter the United Kingdom without leave; and

[(c) whether, if he may not—

(i) he has been given leave which is still in force,

(ii) he should be given leave and for what period or on what conditions (if any), or

(iii) he should be refused leave.]

(2) Any such person, if he is seeking to enter the United Kingdom, may be examined also by a medical inspector or by any qualified person carrying out a test or examination required by a medical inspector.

(3) A person, on being examined under this paragraph by an immigration officer or medical inspector, may be required in writing by him to submit to further examination; but a requirement under this sub-paragraph shall not prevent a person who arrives as a transit passenger, or as a member of the crew of a ship or aircraft, or for the purpose of joining a ship or aircraft as a member of the crew, from leaving by his intended ship or aircraft.

Note: Words in first square brackets substituted by SI 1993/1813. Words in square brackets in sub-para (1)(a) substituted by British Nationality Act 1981, s 39(6). Subparagraph (1)(c) substituted by Immigration and Asylum Act 1999 from 14 February 2000.

[*Examination of persons who arrive with continuing leave*

2A.—(1) This paragraph applies to a person who has arrived in the United Kingdom with leave to enter which is in force but which was given to him before his arrival.

(2) He may be examined by an immigration officer for the purpose of establishing—

(a) whether there has been such a change in the circumstances of his case, since that leave was given, that it should be cancelled;

(b) whether that leave was obtained as a result of false information given by him or his failure to disclose material facts; or

(c) whether there are medical grounds on which that leave should be cancelled.

[(2A) Where the person's leave to enter derives, by virtue of section 3A(3), from an entry clearance, he may also be examined by an immigration officer for the purpose of establishing whether the leave should be cancelled on the grounds that the person's purpose in arriving in the United Kingdom is different from the purpose specified in the entry clearance.]

(3) He may also be examined by an immigration officer for the purpose of determining whether it would be conducive to the public good for that leave to be cancelled.

(4) He may also be examined by a medical inspector or by any qualified person carrying out a test or examination required by a medical inspector.

(5) A person examined under this paragraph may be required by the officer or inspector to submit to further examination.

(6) A requirement under sub-paragraph (5) does not prevent a person who arrives—

(a) as a transit passenger,

(b) as a member of the crew of a ship or aircraft, or

(c) for the purpose of joining a ship or aircraft as a member of the crew, from leaving by his intended ship or aircraft.

(7) An immigration officer examining a person under this paragraph may by notice suspend his leave to enter until the examination is completed.

(8) An immigration officer may, on the completion of any examination of a person under this paragraph, cancel his leave to enter.

(9) Cancellation of a person's leave under sub-paragraph (8) is to be treated for the purposes of this Act and [Part 5 of the Nationality, Immigration and Asylum Act 2002 (immigration and asylum appeals)] as if he had been refused leave to enter at a time when he had a current entry clearance.

(10) A requirement imposed under sub-paragraph (5) and a notice given under sub-paragraph (7) must be in writing.]

Note: Paragraph 2A inserted by Immigration and Asylum Act 1999 from 14 February 2000. Words in square brackets in para 2A(9) substituted by Sch 7 Nationality, Immigration and Asylum Act 2002 from 1 April 2003 (SI 2003/754). Subsection (2A) inserted by Asylum and Immigration Act 2004, s 18 from 1 October 2004 (SI 2004/2523).

3.—(1) An immigration officer may examine any person who is embarking or seeking to embark in the United Kingdom for the purpose of determining whether he is [a British citizen] and, [if he is not a British citizen, for the purpose of establishing—

(a) his identity;

(b) whether he entered the United Kingdom lawfully;

(c) whether he has complied with any conditions of leave to enter or remain in the United Kingdom;

(d) whether his return to the United Kingdom is prohibited or restricted.

(1A) An immigration officer who examines a person under sub-paragraph (1) may require him, by notice in writing, to submit to further examination for a purpose specified in that sub-paragraph.]

(2) So long as any Order in Council is in force under section 3(7) of this Act, an immigration officer may examine any person who is embarking or seeking to embark in the United Kingdom for the purpose of determining—

(a) whether any of the provisions of the Order apply to him; and
(b) whether, if so, any power conferred by the Order should be exercised in relation to him and in what way.

Note: Words in first square brackets in sub-para (1) substituted by British Nationality Act 1981. Other words in square brackets substituted by Immigration, Asylum and Nationality Act 2006, s 42 from 31 August 2006 (SI 2006/2226).

Information and documents

4.—(1) It shall be the duty of any person examined under paragraph 2 [2A] or 3 above to furnish to the person carrying out the examination all such information in his possession as that person may require for the purpose of his functions under that paragraph.

(2) A person on his examination under paragraph 2, [2A] or 3 above by an immigration officer shall, if so required by the immigration officer—
(a) produce either a valid passport with photograph or some other document satisfactorily establishing his identity and nationality or citizenship; and
(b) declare whether or not he is carrying or conveying [, or has carried or conveyed] documents of any relevant description specified by the immigration officer, and produce any documents of that description which he is carrying or conveying.

In paragraph (b), 'relevant description' means any description appearing to the immigration officer to be relevant for the purposes of the examination.

(3) Where under sub-paragraph (2)(b) above a person has been required to declare whether or not he is carrying or conveying [or has carried or conveyed,] documents of any description.
[(a) he and any baggage or vehicle belonging to him or under his control; and
(b) any ship, aircraft or vehicle in which he arrived in the United Kingdom,]; may be searched with a view to ascertaining whether he is doing, [or, as the case may be, has done], so by the immigration officer or a person acting under the directions of the officer:

Provided that no woman or girl shall be searched except by a woman.

[(4) Where a passport or other document is produced or found in accordance with this paragraph an immigration officer may examine it and detain it—
(a) for the purpose of examining it, for a period not exceeding 7 days;
(b) for any purpose, until the person to whom the document relates is given leave to enter the United Kingdom or is about to depart or be removed following refusal of leave or until it is decided that the person does not require leave to enter;
(c) after a time described in paragraph (b), while the immigration officer thinks that the document may be required in connection with proceedings in respect of an appeal under the Immigration Acts or in respect of an offence.

(5) For the purpose of ascertaining that a passport or other document produced or found in accordance with this paragraph relates to a person examined under paragraph 2, 2A or 3 above, the person carrying out the examination may require the person being examined to provide information (whether or not by submitting to a process by means of which information is obtained or recorded) about his external physical characteristics (which may include, in particular, fingerprints or features of the iris or any other part of the eye).]

Note: Words in square brackets in para 4(1) and (2) inserted by Immigration and Asylum Act 1999 from 14 February 2000. Subparagraph (2A) ceases to have effect and sub-para 4 substituted by Immigration, Asylum and Nationality Act 2006, s 27 from 31 August 2006 (SI 2006/2226). Where, immediately before that date, a passport or other document produced or found in accordance with para 4 is being examined or detained by an immigration officer under para 4(2A) or para 4(4), para 4(4) shall apply to the examination or detention of those documents on or after 31 August 2006 as if it had been in force on the date on which the passport or other document was produced or found, and para 4(2A) shall cease to have effect. Paragraph 4(5) shall apply only where the examination under para 2, 2A or 3 of that Schedule begins on or after 31 August 2006.

5. The Secretary of State may by order made by statutory instrument make provision for requiring passengers disembarking or embarking in the United Kingdom, or any class of such passengers, to produce to an immigration officer, if so required, landing or embarkation cards in such form as the Secretary of State may direct, and for requiring the owners or agents of ships and aircraft to supply such cards to those passengers.

Notice of leave to enter or of refusal of leave

6.—(1) Subject to sub-paragraph (3) below, where a person examined by an immigration officer under paragraph 2 above is to be given a limited leave to enter the United Kingdom or is to be refused leave, the notice giving or refusing leave shall be given not later than [twenty four] hours after the conclusion of his examination (including any further examination) in pursuance of that paragraph; and if notice giving or refusing leave is not given him before the end of those [twenty four] hours, he shall (if not [a British citizen]) be deemed to have been given [leave to enter the United Kingdom for a period of six months subject to a condition prohibiting his taking employment] and the immigration officer shall as soon as may be given him written notice of that leave.

(2) Where on a person's examination under paragraph 2 above he is given notice of leave to enter the United Kingdom, then at any time before the end of [twenty four hours] from the conclusion of the examination he may be given a further notice in writing by an immigration officer cancelling the earlier notice and refusing him leave to enter.

(3) Where in accordance with this paragraph a person is given notice refusing him leave to enter the United Kingdom, that notice may at any time be cancelled by notice in writing given him by an immigration officer; and where a person is given a notice of cancellation under this sub-paragraph, [and the immigration officer does not at the same time give him indefinite or limited leave to enter {or require him to submit to further examination}, he shall be deemed to have been given leave to enter for a period of six months subject to a condition prohibiting his taking employment and the immigration officer shall as soon as may be give him written notice of that leave.]

(4) Where an entrant is a member of a party in charge of a person appearing to the immigration officer to be a responsible person, any notice to be given in relation to that entrant in accordance with this paragraph shall be duly given if delivered to the person in charge of the party.

Note: Words in third square brackets substituted by British Nationality Act 1981, s 39(6); other words in square brackets substituted by Immigration Act 1988, s 10. Words in curly brackets in para 6(3) inserted by Nationality, Immigration and Asylum Act 2002, s 119 from 8 January 2003 (SI 2002/2811).

[Power to require medical examination after entry

7.—(1) This paragraph applies if an immigration officer examining a person under paragraph 2 decides—
(a) that he may be given leave to enter the United Kingdom; but
(b) that a further medical test or examination may be required in the interests of public health.

(2) This paragraph also applies if an immigration officer examining a person under paragraph 2A decides—
(a) that his leave to enter the United Kingdom should not be cancelled; but
(b) that a further medical test or examination may be required in the interests of public health.

(3) The immigration officer may give the person concerned notice in writing requiring him—
(a) to report his arrival to such medical officer of health as may be specified in the notice; and
(b) to attend at such place and time and submit to such test or examination (if any), as that medical officer of health may require.

(4) In reaching a decision under paragraph (b) of sub-paragraph (1) or (2), the immigration officer must act on the advice of—
(a) a medical inspector; or
(b) if no medical inspector is available, a fully qualified medical practitioner.]

Note: Paragraph 7 substituted by Immigration and Asylum Act 1999 from 14 February 2000.

Removal of persons refused leave to enter and illegal entrants

8.—(1) Where a person arriving in the United Kingdom is refused leave to enter, an immigration officer may, subject to sub-paragraph (2) below—
(a) give the captain of the ship or aircraft in which he arrives directions requiring the captain to remove him from the United Kingdom in that ship or aircraft; or
(b) give the owners or agents of that ship or aircraft directions requiring them to remove him from the United Kingdom in any ship or aircraft specified or indicated in the directions, being a ship or aircraft of which they are the owners or agents; or
(c) give those owners or agents directions requiring them to make arrangements for his removal from the United Kingdom in any ship or aircraft specified or indicated in the directions to a country or territory so specified, being either—
(i) a country of which he is a national or citizen; or
(ii) a country or territory in which he has obtained a passport or other document of identity; or
(iii) a country or territory in which he embarked for the United Kingdom; or
(iv) a country or territory to which there is reason to believe that he will be admitted.

(2) No directions shall be given under this paragraph in respect of anyone after the expiration of two months beginning with the date on which he was refused leave to enter the United Kingdom [(ignoring any period during which an appeal by him under the

Immigration Acts is pending)] [except that directions may be given under sub-paragraph (1)(b) or (c) after the end of that period if the immigration officer has within that period given written notice to the owners or agents in question of his intention to give directions to them in respect of that person].

Note: Words in first square brackets in sub-para (2) inserted by Sch 7 Nationality, Immigration and Asylum Act 2002 from 1 April 2003 (SI 2003/754). Words in second square brackets in sub-para (2) added by Immigration Act 1988, s 10. Paragraph 8 modified in relation to certain persons entering or seeking to enter through Republic of Ireland with effect from 17 July 2002: see the Immigration (Entry otherwise than by Sea or Air) Order 2002 (SI 2002/1832).

9.—(1) Where an illegal entrant is not given leave to enter or remain in the United Kingdom, an immigration officer may give any such directions in respect of him as in a case within paragraph 8 above are authorised by paragraph 8(1).

[(2) Any leave to enter the United Kingdom which is obtained by deception shall be disregarded for the purposes of this paragraph.]

Note: Paragraph 9(2) added by Asylum and Immigration Act 1996 from 1 October 1996. Subparagraph (1) modified in relation to certain persons entering or seeking to enter through Republic of Ireland with effect from 17 July 2002: see the Immigration (Entry otherwise than by Sea or Air) Order 2002 (SI 2002/1832).

10.—(1) Where it appears to the Secretary of State either—

(a) that directions might be given in respect of a person under paragraph 8 or 9 above, but that it is not practicable for them to be given or that, if given, they would be ineffective; or

(b) that directions might have been given in respect of a person under paragraph 8 above [but that the requirements of paragraph 8(2) have not been complied with]; then the Secretary of State may give to the owners or agents of any ship or aircraft any such directions in respect of that person as are authorised by paragraph 8(1)(c).

(2) Where the Secretary of State may give directions for a person's removal in accordance with sub-paragraph (1) above, he may instead give directions for his removal in accordance with arrangements to be made by the Secretary of State to any country or territory to which he could be removed under sub-paragraph (1).

(3) The costs of complying with any directions given under this paragraph shall be defrayed by the Secretary of State.

[**10A** Where directions are given in respect of a person under any of paragraphs 8 to 10 above, directions to the same effect may be given under that paragraph in respect of a member of the person's family].

Note: Paragraph 10A inserted by Nationality, Immigration and Asylum Act 2002 from 10 February 2003 (SI 2003/1).

11. A person in respect of whom directions are given under any of paragraphs 8 to 10 above may be placed, under the authority of an immigration officer, on board any ship or aircraft in which he is to be removed in accordance with the directions.

Note: Paragraph 11 modified in relation to certain persons entering or seeking to enter through Republic of Ireland with effect from 17 July 2002: see the Immigration (Entry otherwise than by Sea or Air) Order 2002 (SI 2002/1832).

Seamen and aircrews

12.—(1) If, on a person's examination by an immigration officer under paragraph 2 above, the immigration officer is satisfied that he has come to the United Kingdom for the purpose of joining a ship or aircraft as a member of the crew, then the immigration officer may limit the duration of any leave he gives that person to enter the United Kingdom by requiring him to leave the United Kingdom in a ship or aircraft specified or indicated by the notice giving leave.

(2) Where a person (not being [a British citizen]) arrives in the United Kingdom for the purpose of joining a ship or aircraft as a member of the crew and, having been given leave to enter as mentioned in sub-paragraph (1) above, remains beyond the time limited by that leave, or is reasonably suspected by an immigration officer of intending to do so, an immigration officer may—

(a) give the captain of that ship or aircraft directions requiring the captain to remove him from the United Kingdom in that ship or aircraft; or

(b) give the owners or agents of that ship or aircraft directions requiring them to remove him from the United Kingdom in any ship or aircraft specified or indicated in the directions, being a ship or aircraft of which they are the owners or agents; or

(c) give those owners or agents directions requiring them to make arrangements for his removal from the United Kingdom in any ship or aircraft specified or indicated in the directions to a country or territory so specified, being either—

(i) a country of which he is a national or citizen; or

(ii) a country or territory in which he has obtained a passport or other document of identity; or

(iii) a country or territory in which he embarked for the United Kingdom; or

(iv) a country or territory where he was engaged as a member of the crew of the ship or aircraft which he arrived in the United Kingdom to join; or

(v) a country or territory to which there is reason to believe that he will be admitted.

Note: Words in square brackets substituted by British Nationality Act 1981, s 39(6).

13.—(1) Where a person being a member of the crew of a ship or aircraft is examined by an immigration officer under paragraph 2 above, the immigration officer may limit the duration of any leave he gives that person to enter the United Kingdom—

(a) in the manner authorised by paragraph 12(1) above; or

(b) if that person is to be allowed to enter the United Kingdom in order to receive hospital treatment, by requiring him, on completion of that treatment, to leave the United Kingdom in accordance with arrangements to be made for his repatriation; or

(c) by requiring him to leave the United Kingdom within a specified period in accordance with arrangements to be made for his repatriation.

(2) Where a person (not being [a British citizen]) arrives in the United Kingdom as a member of the crew of a ship or aircraft, and either—

(a) having lawfully entered the United Kingdom without leave by virtue of section 8(1) of this Act, he remains without leave beyond the time allowed by section 8(1), or is reasonably suspected by an immigration officer of intending to do so; or

(b) having been given leave limited as mentioned in sub-paragraph (1) above, he remains beyond the time limited by that leave, or is reasonably suspected by an immigration officer of intending to do so;

an immigration officer may—

(a) give the captain of the ship or aircraft in which he arrived directions requiring the captain to remove him from the United Kingdom in that ship or aircraft; or

(b) give the owners or agents of that ship or aircraft directions requiring them to remove him from the United Kingdom in any ship or aircraft specified or indicated in the directions, being a ship or aircraft of which they are the owners or agents; or

(c) give those owners or agents directions requiring them to make arrangements for his removal from the United Kingdom in any ship or aircraft specified or indicated in the directions to a country or territory so specified, being either—

(i) a country of which he is a national or citizen; or

(ii) a country or territory in which he has obtained a passport or other document of identity; or

(iii) a country in which he embarked for the United Kingdom; or

(iv) a country or territory in which he was engaged as a member of the crew of the ship or aircraft in which he arrived in the United Kingdom; or

(v) a country or territory to which there is reason to believe that he will be admitted.

Note: Words in square brackets substituted by British Nationality Act 1981, s 39(6).

14.—(1) Where it appears to the Secretary of State that directions might be given in respect of a person under paragraph 12 or 13 above, but that it is not practicable for them to be given or that, if given, they would be ineffective, then the Secretary of State may give to the owners or agents of any ship or aircraft any such directions in respect of that person as are authorised by paragraph 12(2)(c) or 13(2)(c).

(2) Where the Secretary of State may give directions for a person's removal in accordance with sub-paragraph (1) above, he may instead give directions for his removal in accordance with arrangements to be made by the Secretary of State to any country or territory to which he could be removed under sub-paragraph (1).

(3) The costs of complying with any directions given under this paragraph shall be defrayed by the Secretary of State.

15. A person in respect of whom directions are given under any of paragraphs 12 to 14 above may be placed, under the authority of an immigration officer, on board any ship or aircraft in which he is to be removed in accordance with the directions.

Detention of persons liable to examination or removal

16.—(1) A person who may be required to submit to examination under paragraph 2 above may be detained under the authority of an immigration officer pending his examination and pending a decision to give or refuse him leave to enter.

[(1A) A person whose leave to enter has been suspended under paragraph 2A may be detained under the authority of an immigration officer pending—

(a) completion of his examination under that paragraph; and

(b) a decision on whether to cancel his leave to enter.]

[(1B) A person who has been required to submit to further examination under paragraph 3(1A) may be detained under the authority of an immigration officer, for a period not exceeding 12 hours, pending the completion of the examination.]

[(2) If there are reasonable grounds for suspecting that a person is someone in respect of whom directions may be given under any of paragraphs [8 to 10A]or 12 to 14, that person may be detained under the authority of an immigration officer pending—

(a) a decision whether or not to give such directions;

(b) his removal in pursuance of such directions.]

(3) A person on board a ship or aircraft may, under the authority of an immigration officer, be removed from the ship or aircraft for detention under this paragraph; but if an immigration officer so requires the captain of a ship or aircraft shall prevent from disembarking in the United Kingdom any person who has arrived in the United Kingdom in the ship or aircraft and been refused leave to enter, and the captain may for that purpose detain him in custody on board the ship or aircraft.

(4) The captain of a ship or aircraft, if so required by an immigration officer, shall prevent from disembarking in the United Kingdom or before the directions for his removal have been fulfilled any person placed on board the ship or aircraft under paragraph 11 or 15 above, and the captain may for that purpose detain him in custody on board the ship or aircraft.

Note: Paragraph 1A inserted by Immigration and Asylum Act 1999 from 14 February 2000, sub-para (2) substituted by Immigration and Asylum Act 1999. Words in square brackets substituted by Nationality, Immigration and Asylum Act 2002 from 10 February 2003 (SI 2003/1). Subparagraph (1B) inserted by Immigration, Asylum and Nationality Act 2006, s 42 from 31 August 2006 (SI 2006/2226).

17.—(1) A person liable to be detained under paragraph 16 above may be arrested without warrant by a constable or by an immigration officer.

(2) If—

(a) a justice of the peace is by written information on oath satisfied that there is reasonable ground for suspecting that a person liable to be arrested under this paragraph is to be found on any premises; or

(b) in Scotland, a sheriff, or a . . . justice of the peace, having jurisdiction in the place where the premises are situated is by evidence on oath so satisfied; he may grant a warrant [authorising any immigration officer or constable to enter], [if need be by reasonable force], the premises named in the warrant for the purpose of searching for and arresting that person.

[(3) Sub-paragraph (4) applies where an immigration officer or constable—

(a) enters premises in reliance on a warrant under sub-paragraph (2), and

(b) detains a person on the premises.

(4) A detainee custody officer may enter the premises, if need be by reasonable force, for the purpose of carrying out a search.

(5) In sub-paragraph (4)—

'detainee custody officer' means a person in respect of whom a certificate of authorisation is in force under section 154 of the Immigration and Asylum Act 1999 (c. 33) (detained persons: escort and custody), and 'search' means a search under paragraph 2(1)(a) of Schedule 13 to that Act (escort arrangements: power to search detained person).]

Note: Words omitted from (2)(b) repealed by Asylum and Immigration Act 1996 from 1 October 1996; other words omitted by Police and Criminal Evidence Act 1984, s 119(2). Words in first square brackets in 2(b) substituted by Immigration and Asylum Act 1999, s 140(2); words in second square brackets substituted by Nationality, Immigration and Asylum Act 2002 from 10 February 2003 (SI 2003/1).

18.—(1) Persons may be detained under paragraph 16 above in such places as the Secretary of State may direct (when not detained in accordance with paragraph 16 on board a ship or aircraft).

(2) Where a person is detained under paragraph 16, any immigration officer, constable or prison officer, or any other person authorised by the Secretary of State, may take all such steps as may be reasonably necessary for photographing, measuring or otherwise identifying him.

[**(2A)** The power conferred by sub-paragraph (2) includes power to take fingerprints.]

(3) Any person detained under paragraph 16 may be taken in the custody of a constable, or of any person acting under the authority of an immigration officer, to and from any place where his attendance is required for the purpose of ascertaining his citizenship or nationality or of making arrangements for his admission to a country or territory other than the United Kingdom, or where he is required to be for any other purpose connected with the operation of this Act.

(4) A person shall be deemed to be in legal custody at any time when he is detained under paragraph 16 or is being removed in pursuance of sub-paragraph (3) above.

Note: Subparagraph 2A inserted by Immigration and Asylum Act 1999 from 11 December 1999 (SI 2000/3099).

19.—(1) Where a person is refused leave to enter the United Kingdom and directions are given in respect of him under paragraph 8 or 10 above, then subject to the provisions of this paragraph the owners or agents of the ship or aircraft in which he arrived shall be liable to pay the Secretary of State on demand any expenses incurred by the latter in respect of the custody, accommodation or maintenance of that person [for any period (not exceeding 14 days)] after his arrival while he was detained or liable to be detained under paragraph 16 above.

(2) Sub-paragraph (1) above shall not apply to expenses in respect of a person who, when he arrived in the United Kingdom, held a [certificate of entitlement] or a current entry clearance or was the person named in a current work permit; and for this purpose a document purporting to be a [certificate of entitlement], entry clearance or work permit is to be regarded as being one unless its falsity is reasonably apparent.

(3) If, before the directions for a person's removal under paragraph 8 or 10 above have been carried out, he is given leave to enter the United Kingdom, or if he is afterwards given that leave in consequence of the determination in his favour of an appeal under this Act (being an appeal against a refusal of leave to enter by virtue of which the directions were given), or it is determined on an appeal under this Act that he does not require leave to enter (being an appeal occasioned by such a refusal), no sum shall be demanded under

sub-paragraph (1) above for expenses incurred in respect of that person and any sum already demanded and paid shall be refunded.

(4) Sub-paragraph (1) above shall not have effect in relation to directions which in consequence of an appeal under this Act, have ceased to have effect or are for the time being of no effect; and the expenses to which that sub-paragraph applies include expenses in conveying the person in question to and from the place where he is detained or accommodated unless the journey is made for the purpose of attending an appeal by him under this Act.

Note: Words in square brackets sub-para (1) substituted by Asylum and Immigration Act 1996 from 1 October 1996. Words in square brackets in sub-para (2) substituted by British Nationality Act 1981, s 39(6).

20.—(1) Subject to the provisions of this paragraph, in either of the following cases, that is to say,—

(a) where directions are given in respect of an illegal entrant under paragraph 9 or 10 above; and

(b) where a person has lawfully entered the United Kingdom without leave by virtue of section 8(1) of this Act, but directions are given in respect of him under paragraph 13(2)(A) above or, in a case within paragraph 13(2)(A), under paragraph 14; the owners or agents of the ship or aircraft in which he arrived in the United Kingdom shall be liable to pay the Secretary of State on demand any expenses incurred by the latter in respect of the custody, accommodation or maintenance of that person [for any period (not exceeding 14 days)] after his arrival while he was detained or liable to be detained under paragraph 16 above.

[(**1A**) Sub-paragraph (1) above shall not apply to expenses in respect of an illegal entrant if he obtained leave to enter by deception and the leave has not been cancelled under paragraph 6(2) above.]

(2) If, before the directions for a person's removal from the United Kingdom have been carried out, he is given leave to remain in the United Kingdom, no sum shall be demanded under sub-paragraph (1) above for expenses incurred in respect of that person and any sum already demanded and paid shall be refunded.

(3) Sub-paragraph (1) above shall not have effect in relation to directions which, in consequence of an appeal under this Act, are for the time being of no effect; and the expenses to which that sub-paragraph applies include expenses in conveying the person in question to and from the place where he is detained or accommodated unless the journey is made for the purpose of attending an appeal by him under this Act.

Note: Words in square brackets substituted and (1A) inserted by Asylum and Immigration Act 1996 from 1 October 1996.

Temporary admission of persons liable to detention

21.—(1) A person liable to detention or detained under paragraph 16 [(1), (1A) or (2)] above may, under the written authority of an immigration officer, be temporarily admitted to the United Kingdom without being detained or be released from detention; but this shall not prejudice a later exercise of the power to detain him.

(2) So long as a person is at large in the United Kingdom by virtue of this paragraph, he

shall be subject to such restrictions as to residence [, as to his employment or occupation] and as to reporting to the police or an immigration officer as may from time to time be notified to him in writing by an immigration officer.

[(2A) The provisions that may be included in restrictions as to residence imposed under sub-paragraph (2) include provisions of such a description as may be prescribed by regulations made by the Secretary of State.

(2B) The regulations may, among other things, provide for the inclusion of provisions—

(a) prohibiting residence in one or more particular areas;

(b) requiring the person concerned to reside in accommodation provided under section 4 of the Immigration and Asylum Act 1999 and prohibiting him from being absent from that accommodation except in accordance with the restrictions imposed on him.

(2C) The regulations may provide that a particular description of provision may be imposed only for prescribed purposes.

(2D) The power to make regulations conferred by this paragraph is exercisable by statutory instrument and includes a power to make different provision for different cases.

(2E) But no regulations under this paragraph are to be made unless a draft of the regulations has been laid before Parliament and approved by a resolution of each House.]

[(3) Sub-paragraph (4) below applies where a person who is at large in the United Kingdom by virtue of this paragraph is subject to a restriction as to reporting to an immigration officer with a view to the conclusion of his examination under paragraph 2 [or 2A] above.

(4) If the person fails at any time to comply with that restriction—

(a) an immigration officer may direct that the person's examination shall be treated as concluded at that time; but

(b) nothing in paragraph 6 above shall require the notice giving or refusing him leave to enter the United Kingdom to be given within twenty-four hours after that time.]

Note: Words in last square brackets in sub-paragraph (1) inserted by Immigration, Asylum and Nationality Act 2006, s 42 from 31 August 2006 (SI 2006/2226). Words in square brackets in sub-para (2) inserted by Immigration Act 1988, s 10; sub-paras (3) and (4) inserted by Asylum and Immigration Act 1996 from 1 October 1996. Paragraphs 2A, 2B, 2C, 2D, and 2E inserted by Immigration and Asylum Act 1999 from 11 November 1999, other words in square brackets inserted and words in sub-para (4)(a) omitted by Immigration and Asylum Act 1999 from 14 February 2000.

Temporary release of persons liable to detention

22.—[(**1**) The following, namely—

(a) a person detained under paragraph 16(1) above pending examination;

[(aa) a person detained under paragraph 16(1A) above pending completion of his examination or a decision on whether to cancel his leave to enter;] and

(b) a person detained under paragraph 16(2) above pending the giving of directions,

may be released on bail in accordance with this paragraph.

(**1A**) An immigration officer not below the rank of chief immigration officer or [the Asylum and Immigration Tribunal] may release a person so detained on his entering into a recognizance or, in Scotland, bail bond conditioned for his appearance before an immigration officer at a time and place named in the recognizance or bail bond or at such other time and place as may in the meantime be notified to him in writing by an immigration officer.

(1B) Sub-paragraph (1)(a) above shall not apply unless seven days have elapsed since the date of the person's arrival in the United Kingdom.]

(2) The conditions of a recognizance or bail bond taken under this paragraph may include conditions appearing to the [immigration officer or [the Asylum and Immigration Tribunal]] to be likely to result in the appearance of the person bailed at the required time and place; and any recognizance shall be with or without sureties as the [officer or [the Asylum and Immigration Tribunal]] may determine.

(3) In any case in which an [immigration officer or [the Asylum and Immigration Tribunal]] has power under this paragraph to release a person on bail, the [officer or [the Asylum and Immigration Tribunal]] may, instead of taking the bail, fix the amount and conditions of the bail (including the amount in which any sureties are to be bound) with a view to its being taken subsequently by any such person as may be specified by the [officer or [the Asylum and Immigration Tribunal]]; and on the recognizance or bail bond being so taken the person to be bailed shall be released.

Note: Subparagraph (1) and words in square brackets in sub-paras (2) and (3) substituted by Asylum and Immigration Act 1996 from 1 October 1996 and amended by Sch 2 Asylum and Immigration Act 1996 from a date to be appointed. Subparagraph (1)(aa) inserted by Immigration and Asylum Act 1999 from 14 February 2000.

23.—(1) Where a recognizance entered into under paragraph 22 above appears to [the Asylum and Immigration Tribunal] to be forfeited, [the Asylum and Immigration Tribunal] may by order declare it to be forfeited and adjudge the persons bound thereby, whether as principal or sureties, or any of them, to pay the sum in which they are respectively bound or such part of it, if any, as [the Asylum and Immigration Tribunal] thinks fit; and an order under this sub-paragraph shall specify a magistrates' court or, in Northern Ireland, court of summary jurisdiction, and—

(a) the recognizance shall be treated for the purposes of collection, enforcement and remission of the sum forfeited as having been forfeited by the court so specified; and

(b) [the Asylum and Immigration Tribunal] shall, as soon as practicable, give particulars of the recognizance to the clerk of that court.

(2) Where a person released on bail under paragraph 22 above as it applies in Scotland fails to comply with the terms of his bail bond, [the Asylum and Immigration Tribunal] may declare the bail to be forefeited, and any bail so forfeited shall be transmitted by [the Asylum and Immigration Tribunal] to the sheriff court having jurisdiction in the area where the proceedings took place, and shall be treated as having been forfeited by that court.

(3) Any sum the payment of which is enforceable by a magistrates' court in England or Wales by virtue of this paragraph shall be treated for the [purposes of section 38 of the Courts Act 2003 (application of receipts of designated officers) as being] due under a recognizance forfeited by such a court . . .

(4) Any sum the payment of which is enforceable by virtue of this paragraph by a court of summary jurisdiction in Northern Ireland shall, for the purposes of section 20(5) of the

Administration of Justice Act (Northern Ireland) 1954, be treated as a forfeited recognizance.

Note: Words in square brackets in sub-para 3 substituted by Justices of the Peace Act 1979; words omitted repealed by Criminal Justice Act 1972. Words in square brackets in sub-s (3) substituted by Sch 8 Courts Act 2003 from a date to be appointed. Other words in square brackets substituted by Sch 2 Asylum and Immigration Act 2004 from a date to be appointed.

24.—(1) An immigration officer or constable may arrest without warrant a person who has been released by virtue of paragraph 22 above—

(a) if he has reasonable grounds for believing that that person is likely to break the condition of his recognizance or bail bond that he will appear at the time and place required or to break any other condition of it, or has reasonable ground to suspect that the person is breaking or has broken any such other condition; or

(b) if, a recognizance with sureties having been taken, he is notified in writing by any surety of the surety's belief that that person is likely to break the first-mentioned condition, and of the surety's wish for that reason to be relieved of his obligations as a surety;

and paragraph 17(2) above shall apply for the arrest of a person under this paragraph as it applies for the arrest of a person under paragraph 17.

(2) A person arrested under this paragraph—

(a) if not required by a condition on which he was released to appear before an immigration officer within twenty-four hours after the time of his arrest, shall as soon as practicable be brought before [the Asylum and Immigration Tribunal] or, if that is not practicable within those twenty-four hours, before a justice of the peace acting for the petty sessions area in which he is arrested or, in Scotland, the sheriff; and

(b) if required by such a condition to appear within those twenty-four hours before an immigration officer, shall be brought before that officer.

(3) [Where a person is brought before the Asylum and Immigration Tribunal, a justice of the peace or the sheriff by virtue of sub-paragraph (2)(a), the Tribunal, justice of the peace or sheriff]—

(a) if of the opinion that that person has broken or is likely to break any condition on which he was released, may either—

(i) direct that he be detained under the authority of the person by whom he was arrested; or

(ii) release him, on his original recognizance or on a new recognizance, with or without sureties, or, in Scotland, on his original bail or on new bail; and

(b) if not of that opinion, shall release him on his original recognizance or bail.

Note: Words in square brackets substituted by Sch 2 Asylum and Immigration Act 2004 from a date to be appointed.

25. The power to make rules of procedure conferred by [section 106 of the Nationality, Immigration and Asylum Act 2002 (appeals)] shall include power to make rules with respect to applications to [the Asylum and Immigration Tribunal] under paragraphs 22 to 24 above and matters arising out of such applications.

Note: Words in first square brackets substituted by Sch 7 Nationality, Immigration and Asylum Act 2002 from 1 April 2003 (SI 2003/754). Other words in square brackets substituted by Sch 2 Asylum and Immigration Act 2004 from a date to be appointed.

[*Entry and search of premises*

25A.—(1) This paragraph applies if—
(a) a person is arrested under this Schedule; or
(b) a person who was arrested by a constable (other than under this Schedule) is detained by an immigration officer under this Schedule.

(2) An immigration officer may enter and search any premises—
(a) occupied or controlled by the arrested person, or
(b) in which that person was when he was arrested, or immediately before he was arrested,

for relevant documents.

(3) The power may be exercised—
(a) only if the officer has reasonable grounds for believing that there are relevant documents on the premises;
(b) only to the extent that it is reasonably required for the purpose of discovering relevant documents; and
(c) subject to sub-paragraph (4), only if a senior officer has authorised its exercise in writing.

(4) An immigration officer may conduct a search under sub-paragraph (2)—
(a) before taking the arrested person to a place where he is to be detained; and
(b) without obtaining an authorisation under sub-paragraph (3)(c), if the presence of that person at a place other than one where he is to be detained is necessary to make an effective search for any relevant documents.

(5) An officer who has conducted a search under sub-paragraph (4) must inform a senior officer as soon as is practicable.

(6) The officer authorising a search, or who is informed of one under subparagraph (5), must make a record in writing of—
(a) the grounds for the search; and
(b) the nature of the documents that were sought.

(7) An officer searching premises under sub-paragraph (2)—
(a) may seize and retain any documents he finds which he has reasonable grounds for believing are relevant documents; but
(b) may not retain any such document for longer than is necessary in view of the purpose for which the person was arrested.

(8) But sub-paragraph (7)(a) does not apply to documents which the officer has reasonable grounds for believing are items subject to legal privilege.

(9) 'Relevant documents' means any documents which might—
(a) establish the arrested person's identity, nationality or citizenship; or
(b) indicate the place from which he has travelled to the United Kingdom or to which he is proposing to go.

(10) 'Senior officer' means an immigration officer not below the rank of chief immigration officer.]

Note: Paragraph 25A inserted by Immigration and Asylum Act 1999 from 14 February 2000.

[*Searching persons arrested by immigration officers*

25B.—(1) This paragraph applies if a person is arrested under this Schedule.

(2) An immigration officer may search the arrested person if he has reasonable grounds for believing that the arrested person may present a danger to himself or others.

(3) The officer may search the arrested person for—
   (a) anything which he might use to assist his escape from lawful custody; or
   (b) any document which might—
      (i) establish his identity, nationality or citizenship; or
      (ii) indicate the place from which he has travelled to the United Kingdom or to which he is proposing to go.

(4) The power conferred by sub-paragraph (3) may be exercised—
   (a) only if the officer has reasonable grounds for believing that the arrested person may have concealed on him anything of a kind mentioned in that sub-paragraph; and
   (b) only to the extent that it is reasonably required for the purpose of discovering any such thing.

(5) A power conferred by this paragraph to search a person is not to be read as authorising an officer to require a person to remove any of his clothing in public other than an outer coat, jacket or glove; but it does authorise the search of a person's mouth.

(6) An officer searching a person under sub-paragraph (2) may seize and retain anything he finds, if he has reasonable grounds for believing that the person searched might use it to cause physical injury to himself or to another person.

(7) An officer searching a person under sub-paragraph (3)(a) may seize and retain anything he finds, if he has reasonable grounds for believing that he might use it to assist his escape from lawful custody.

(8) An officer searching a person under sub-paragraph (3)(b) may seize and retain anything he finds, other than an item subject to legal privilege, if he has reasonable grounds for believing that it might be a document falling within that sub-paragraph.

(9) Nothing seized under sub-paragraph (6) or (7) may be retained when the person from whom it was seized—
   (a) is no longer in custody, or
   (b) is in the custody of a court but has been released on bail.]

Note: Paragraph 25B inserted by Immigration and Asylum Act 1999 from 14 February 2000.

[*Searching persons in police custody*

25C.—(1) This paragraph applies if a person—
   (a) has been arrested under this Schedule; and
   (b) is in custody at a police station.

(2) An immigration officer may, at any time, search the arrested person in order to ascertain whether he has with him—
   (a) anything which he might use to—
      (i) cause physical injury to himself or others;
      (ii) damage property;

(iii) interfere with evidence; or
(iv) assist his escape; or
(b) any document which might—
(i) establish his identity, nationality or citizenship; or
(ii) indicate the place from which he has travelled to the United Kingdom or to which he is proposing to go.

(3) The power may be exercised only to the extent that the officer considers it to be necessary for the purpose of discovering anything of a kind mentioned in sub-paragraph (2).

(4) An officer searching a person under this paragraph may seize and retain anything he finds, if he has reasonable grounds for believing that—
(a) that person might use it for one or more of the purposes mentioned in sub-paragraph (2)(a); or
(b) it might be a document falling within sub-paragraph (2)(b).

(5) But the officer may not retain anything seized under sub-paragraph (2)(a)—
(a) for longer than is necessary in view of the purpose for which the search was carried out; or
(b) when the person from whom it was seized is no longer in custody or is in the custody of a court but has been released on bail.

(6) The person from whom something is seized must be told the reason for the seizure unless he is—
(a) violent or appears likely to become violent; or
(b) incapable of understanding what is said to him.

(7) An intimate search may not be conducted under this paragraph.

(8) The person carrying out a search under this paragraph must be of the same sex as the person searched.

(9) 'Intimate search' has the same meaning as in section 28H(11).]

Note: Paragraph 25C inserted by Immigration and Asylum Act 1999 from 14 February 2000.

[*Access and copying*

25D.—(1) If a person showing himself—
(a) to be the occupier of the premises on which seized material was seized, or
(b) to have had custody or control of the material immediately before it was seized,
asks the immigration officer who seized the material for a record of what he seized, the officer must provide the record to that person within a reasonable time.

(2) If a relevant person asks an immigration officer for permission to be granted access to seized material, the officer must arrange for that person to have access to the material under the supervision of an immigration officer.

(3) An immigration officer may photograph or copy, or have photographed or copied, seized material.

(4) If a relevant person asks an immigration officer for a photograph or copy of seized material, the officer must arrange for—
(a) that person to have access to the material under the supervision of an immigration officer for the purpose of photographing or copying it; or
(b) the material to be photographed or copied.

(5) A photograph or copy made under sub-paragraph (4)(b) must be supplied within a reasonable time.

(6) There is no duty under this paragraph to arrange for access to, or the supply of a photograph or copy of, any material if there are reasonable grounds for believing that to do so would prejudice—

(a) the exercise of any functions in connection with which the material was seized; or

(b) an investigation which is being conducted under this Act, or any criminal proceedings which may be brought as a result.

(7) 'Relevant person' means—

(a) a person who had custody or control of seized material immediately before it was seized, or

(b) someone acting on behalf of such a person.

(8) 'Seized material' means anything which has been seized and retained under this Schedule.]

Note: Paragraph 25D inserted by Immigration and Asylum Act 1999 from 14 February 2000.

[**25E.** Section 28L applies for the purposes of this Schedule as it applies for the purposes of Part III.]

Note: Paragraph 25E inserted by Immigration and Asylum Act 1999 from 14 February 2000.

Supplementary duties of those connected with ships or aircraft or with ports

26.—(1) The owners or agents of a ship or aircraft employed to carry passengers for reward shall not, without the approval of the Secretary of State, arrange for the ship or aircraft to call at a port in the United Kingdom other than a port of entry for the purpose of disembarking passengers, if any of the passengers on board may not enter the United Kingdom without leave, or for the purpose of embarking passengers unless the owners or agents have reasonable cause to believe all of them to be [British citizens].

[(**1A**) Sub-paragraph (1) does not apply in such circumstances, if any, as the Secretary of State may by order prescribe.]

(2) The Secretary of State may from time to time give written notice to the owners or agents of any ships or aircraft designating control areas for the embarkation or disembarkation of passengers in any port in the United Kingdom, and specifying the conditions and restrictions (if any) to be observed in any control area; and where by notice given to any owners or agents a control areas is for the time being designated for the embarkation or disembarkation of passengers at any port, the owners or agents shall take all reasonable steps to secure that, in the case of their ships or aircraft, passengers do not embark or disembark, as the case may be, at the port outside the control area and that any conditions or restrictions notified to them are observed.

(3) The Secretary of State may also from time to time give to any persons concerned with the management of a port in the United Kingdom written notice designating control areas in the port and specifying conditions or restrictions to be observed in any control area; and any such person shall take all reasonable steps to secure that any conditions or restrictions as notified to him are observed.

[(**3A**) The power conferred by sub-paragraph (1A) is exercisable by statutory instrument;

and any such instrument shall be subject to annulment by a resolution of either House of Parliament.]

Note: Words in square brackets substituted by British Nationality Act 1981. Words omitted from para 26(1) and paras 26(1A) and 26(3A) inserted by Immigration and Asylum Act 1999 from 14 February 2000.

27.—(1) The captain of a ship or aircraft arriving in the United Kingdom—

(a) shall take such steps as may be necessary to secure that persons on board do not disembark there unless either they have been examined by an immigration officer, or they disembark in accordance with arrangements approved by an immigration officer, or they are members of the crew who may lawfully enter the United Kingdom without leave by virtue of section 8(1) of this Act; and

(b) where the examination of persons on board is to be carried out on the ship or aircraft, shall take such steps as may be necessary to secure that those to be examined are presented for the purpose in an orderly manner.

[(2) The Secretary of State may by order require, or enable an immigration officer to require, a responsible person in respect of a ship or aircraft to supply—

(a) a passenger list showing the names and nationality or citizenship of passengers arriving or leaving on board the ship or aircraft;

(b) particulars of members of the crew of the ship or aircraft.

(3) An order under sub-paragraph (2) may relate—

(a) to all ships or aircraft arriving or expected to arrive in the United Kingdom;

(b) to all ships or aircraft leaving or expected to leave the United Kingdom;

(c) to ships or aircraft arriving or expected to arrive in the United Kingdom from or by way of a specified country;

(d) to ships or aircraft leaving or expected to leave the United Kingdom to travel to or by way of a specified country;

(e) to specified ships or specified aircraft.

(4) For the purposes of sub-paragraph (2) the following are responsible persons in respect of a ship or aircraft—

(a) the owner or agent, and

(b) the captain.

(5) An order under sub-paragraph (2)—

(a) may specify the time at which or period during which information is to be provided,

(b) may specify the form and manner in which information is to be provided,

(c) shall be made by statutory instrument, and

(d) shall be subject to annulment in pursuance of a resolution of either House of Parliament.]

Note: Subparagraph (2) substituted and sub-paras (3) and (4) inserted by Immigration, Asylum and Nationality Act 2006, s 42 from a date to be appointed.

[*Passenger information*

27B.—(1) This paragraph applies to ships or aircraft—

(a) which have arrived, or are expected to arrive, in the United Kingdom; or

(b) which have left, or are expected to leave, the United Kingdom.

(2) If an immigration officer asks the owner or agent ('the carrier') of a ship or aircraft for passenger information [or service information], the carrier must provide that information to the officer.

(3) The officer may ask for passenger information [or service information] relating to—
  (a) a particular ship or particular aircraft of the carrier;
  (b) particular ships or aircraft (however described) of the carrier; or
  (c) all of the carrier's ships or aircraft.

(4) The officer may ask for—
  (a) all passenger information [or service information] in relation to the ship or aircraft concerned; or
  (b) particular passenger information [or service information] in relation to that ship or aircraft.

[(4A) The officer may ask the carrier to provide a copy of all or part of a document that relates to a passenger and contains passenger information [or service information].]

(5) A request under sub-paragraph (2)—
  (a) must be in writing;
  (b) must state the date on which it ceases to have effect; and
  (c) continues in force until that date, unless withdrawn earlier by written notice by an immigration officer.

(6) The date may not be later than six months after the request is made.

(7) The fact that a request under sub-paragraph (2) has ceased to have effect as a result of sub-paragraph (5) does not prevent the request from being renewed.

(8) The information must be provided—
  (a) in such form and manner as the Secretary of State may direct; and
  (b) at such time as may be stated in the request.

(9) 'Passenger information' [or service information] means such information relating to the passengers carried, or expected to be carried, by the ship or aircraft as may be specified.

[(9A) 'Service information' means such information relating to the voyage or flight undertaken by the ship or aircraft as may be specified.]

(10) 'Specified' means specified in an order made by statutory instrument by the Secretary of State.

(11) Such an instrument shall be subject to annulment in pursuance of a resolution of either House of Parliament.]

Note: Paragraph 27B inserted by Immigration and Asylum Act 1999 from 3 April 2000. Subparagraph 4A inserted by Asylum and Immigration Act 2004, s 16 from a date to be appointed. Words in square brackets and sub-para (9A) inserted by Immigration, Asylum and Nationality Act 2006, s 31 from a date to be appointed.

[*Notification of non-EEA arrivals*

27C.—(1) If a senior officer, or an immigration officer authorised by a senior officer, gives written notice to the owner or agent ('the carrier') of a ship or aircraft, the carrier must inform a relevant officer of the expected arrival in the United Kingdom of any ship or aircraft—

(a) of which he is the owner or agent; and
(b) which he expects to carry a person who is not an EEA national.

(2) The notice may relate to—
(a) a particular ship or particular aircraft of the carrier;
(b) particular ships or aircraft (however described) of the carrier; or
(c) all of the carrier's ships or aircraft.

(3) The notice—
(a) must state the date on which it ceases to have effect; and
(b) continues in force until that date, unless withdrawn earlier by written notice given by a senior officer.

(4) The date may not be later than six months after the notice is given.

(5) The fact that a notice under sub-paragraph (1) has ceased to have effect as a result of sub-paragraph (3) does not prevent the notice from being renewed.

(6) The information must be provided—
(a) in such form and manner as the notice may require; and
(b) before the ship or aircraft concerned departs for the United Kingdom.

(7) If a ship or aircraft travelling to the United Kingdom stops at one or more places before arriving in the United Kingdom, it is to be treated as departing for the United Kingdom when it leaves the last of those places.

(8) 'Senior officer' means an immigration officer not below the rank of chief immigration officer.

(9) 'Relevant officer' means—
(a) the officer who gave the notice under sub-paragraph (1); or
(b) any immigration officer at the port at which the ship or aircraft concerned is expected to arrive.

(10) 'EEA national' means a national of a State which is a Contracting Party to the Agreement on the European Economic Area signed at Oporto on 2nd May 1992 as it has effect for the time being.]

Note: Paragraph 27C inserted by Immigration and Asylum Act 1999 from 3 April 2000.

Part II Effect of Appeals

Stay on directions for removal

28. . . .

Note: Paragraph 28 omitted by Immigration and Asylum Act 1999 from 2 October 2000. Transitional provisions set out in SI 2003/754.

Grant of bail pending appeal

29.—(1) Where a person (in the following provisions of this Schedule referred to as an 'an appellant') has an appeal pending under [Part 5 of the Nationality, Immigration and Asylum Act 2002] and is for the time being detained under Part I of this Schedule, he may be released on bail in accordance with this paragraph.

(2) An immigration officer not below the rank of chief immigration officer or a police officer not below the rank of inspector may release an appellant on his entering into a recognizance or, in Scotland, bail bond conditioned for his appearance before [the Asylum and Immigration Tribunal] at a time and place named in the recognizance or bail bond.

(3) [The Asylum and Immigration Tribunal] may release an appellant on his entering into a recognizance or, in Scotland, bail bond conditioned for his appearance before [the Tribunal] at a time and place named in the recognizance or bail bond; . . .

(4) . . .

(5) The conditions of a recognizance or bail bond taken under this paragraph may include conditions appearing to the person fixing the bail to be likely to result in the appearance of the appellant at the time and place named; and any recognizance shall be with or without sureties as that person may determine.

(6) In any case in which [the Asylum and Immigration Tribunal] has power or is required by this paragraph to release an appellant on bail, [the Tribunal] may, instead of taking the bail, fix the amount and conditions of the bail (including the amount in which any sureties are to be bound) with a view to its being taken subsequently by any such person as may be specified by [the Tribunal]; and on the recognizance or bail bond being so taken the appellant shall be released.

Note: Words in first square brackets substituted by Sch 7 Nationality, Immigration and Asylum Act 2002 from 1 April 2003 (SI 2003/754). Transitional provisions regarding sub-para (1) set out in SI 2003/754. Other words in square brackets substituted by and words omitted by Sch 2 Asylum and Immigration Act 2004 from a date to be appointed.

Restrictions on grant of bail

30.—(1) An appellant shall not be released under paragraph 29 above without the consent of the Secretary of State if directions for the removal of the appellant from the United Kingdom are for the time being in force, or the power to give such directions is for the time being exercisable.

(2) Notwithstanding paragraph 29(3) or (4) above, [the Tribunal] shall not be obliged to release an appellant unless the appellant enters into a proper recognizance, with sufficient and satisfactory sureties if required, or in Scotland sufficient and satisfactory bail is found if so required; and [the Tribunal] shall not be obliged to release an appellant if it appears to [the Tribunal]

(a) that the appellant, having on any previous occasion been released on bail (whether under paragraph 24 or under any other provision), has failed to comply with the conditions of any recognizance or bail bond entered into by him on that occasion;

(b) that the appellant is likely to commit an offence unless he is retained in detention;

(c) that the release of the appellant is likely to cause danger to public health;

(d) that the appellant is suffering from mental disorder and that his continued detention is necessary in his own interests or for the protection of any other person; or

(e) that the appellant is under the age of seventeen, that arrangements ought to be made for his care in the event of his release and that no satisfactory arrangements for that purpose have been made.

Note: Words in square brackets substituted by Sch 2 Asylum and Immigration Act 2004 from 4 April 2005 (SI 2005/565).

Forfeiture of recognizances

31.—(1) Where under paragraph 29 above (as it applies in England and Wales or in Northern Ireland) a recognizance is entered into conditioned for the appearance of an appellant, [before the Tribunal], and it appears to [the Tribunal] to be forfeited, [the Tribunal] may by order declare it to be forfeited and adjudge the persons bound thereby, whether as principal or sureties, or any of them, to pay the sum in which they are respectively bound or such part of it, if any, as [the Tribunal] thinks fit.

(2) An order under this paragraph shall, for the purposes of this sub-paragraph, specify a magistrates' court or, in Northern Ireland, court of summary jurisdiction; and the recognizance shall be treated for the purposes of collection, enforcement and remission of the sum forfeited as having been forfeited by the court so specified.

(3) Where [the Tribunal] makes an order under this paragraph [the Tribunal] shall, as soon as practicable, give particulars of the recognizance to the clerk of the court specified in the order in pursuance of sub-paragraph (2) above.

(4) Any sum the payment of which is enforceable by a magistrates' court in England or Wales by virtue of this paragraph shall be treated for the purposes of the [Justices of the Peace Act 1979 and, in particular, section 61 thereof] as being due under a recognizance forfeited by such a court . . .

(5) Any sum the payment of which is enforceable by virtue of this paragraph by a court of summary jurisdiction in Northern Ireland shall, for the purposes of section 20(5) of the Administration of Justice Act (Northern Ireland) 1954, be treated as a forfeited recognizance.

Note: Words in square brackets in sub-para (4) substituted by Justices of the Peace Act 1979, s 71; words omitted by Criminal Justice Act 1972, s 64a. Other words in square brackets substituted by Sch 2 Asylum and Immigration Act 2004 from 4 April 2005, (SI 2005/565).

32. Where under paragraph 29 above (as it applies in Scotland) a person released on bail fails to comply with the terms of a bail bond conditioned for his appearance [before the Tribunal], [the Tribunal] may declare the bail to be forfeited, and any bail so forfeited shall be transmitted by [the Tribunal] to the sheriff court having jurisdiction in the area where the proceedings took place, and shall be treated as having been forfeited by that court.

Note: Words in square brackets substituted by Sch 2 Asylum and Immigration Act 2004 from 4 April 2005, (SI 2005/565).

Arrest of appellants released on bail

33.—(1) An immigration officer or constable may arrest without warrant a person who has been released by virtue of this Part of this Schedule—

(a) if he has reasonable grounds for believing that that person is likely to break the condition of his recognizance or bail bond that he will appear at the time and place required or to break any other condition of it, or has reasonable ground to suspect that that person is breaking or has broken any such other condition; or

(b) if, a recognizance with sureties having been taken, he is notified in writing by any surety of the surety's belief that that person is likely to break the first-mentioned condition, and of the surety's wish for that reason to be relieved of his obligations as a surety;

and paragraph 17(2) above shall apply for the arrest of a person under this paragraph as it applies for the arrest of a person under paragraph 17.

(2) A person arrested under this paragraph—

(a) if not required by a condition on which he was released to appear [before the Tribunal] within twenty-four hours after the time of his arrest, shall as soon as practicable be brought [before the Tribunal], or, if that is not practicable within those twenty-four hours, before a justice of the peace acting for the petty sessions area in which he is arrested or, in Scotland, the sheriff; and

(b) if required by such a condition to appear within those twenty-four hours [before the Tribunal] shall be brought [before it].

(3) [Where a person is brought before the Asylum and Immigration Tribunal, a justice of the peace or the sheriff by virtue of sub-paragraph (2)(a), the Tribunal, justice of the peace or sheriff—]

(a) if of the opinion that that person has broken or is likely to break any condition on which he was released, may either—

(i) direct that he be detained under the authority of the person by whom he was arrested; or

(ii) release him on his original recognizance or on a new recognizance, with or without sureties, or, in Scotland, on his original bail or on new bail; and

(b) if not of that opinion, shall release him on his original recognizance or bail.

Note: Words in square brackets substituted by Sch 2 Asylum and Immigration Act 2004 from a date to be appointed.

Grant of bail pending removal

[**34.**—(1) Paragraph 22 above shall apply in relation to a person—

(a) directions for whose removal from the United Kingdom are for the time being in force; and

(b) who is for the time being detained under Part I of this Schedule,

as it applies in relation to a person detained under paragraph 16(1) above pending examination [, detained under paragraph 16(1A) above pending completion of his examination or a decision on whether to cancel his leave to enter] or detained under paragraph 16(2) above pending the giving of directions.

(2) Paragraphs 23 to 25 above shall apply as if any reference to paragraph 22 above included a reference to that paragraph as it applies by virtue of this paragraph.]

Note: Paragraph 34 inserted by Asylum and Immigration Act 1996 from 1 October 1996. Words in square brackets inserted by Immigration and Asylum Act 1999 from 2 October 2000.

Section 5

Schedule 3

Supplementary Provisions as to Deportation

Removal of persons liable to deportation

1.—(1) Where a deportation order is in force against any person, the Secretary of State may give directions for his removal to a country or territory specified in the directions being either—

(a) a country of which he is a national or citizen; or

(b) a country or territory to which there is reason to believe that he will be admitted.

(2) The directions under sub-paragraph (1) above may be either—

(a) directions given to the captain of a ship or aircraft about to leave the United Kingdom requiring him to remove the person in question in that ship or aircraft; or

(b) directions given to the owners or agents of any ship or aircraft requiring them to make arrangements for his removal in a ship or aircraft specified or indicated in the directions; or

(c) directions for his removal in accordance with arrangements to be made by the Secretary of State.

(3) In relation to directions given under this paragraph, paragraphs 11 and 16(4) of Schedule 2 to this Act shall apply, with the substitution of references to the Secretary of State for references to an immigration officer, as they apply in relation to directions for removal given under paragraph 8 of that Schedule.

(4) The Secretary of State, if he thinks fit, may apply in or towards payment of the expenses of or incidental to the voyage from the United Kingdom of a person against whom a deportation order is in force, or the maintenance until departure of such a person and his dependants, if any, any money belonging to that person; and except so far as they are paid as aforesaid, those expenses shall be defrayed by the Secretary of State.

Detention or control pending deportation

2.—(1) Where a recommendation for deportation made by a court is in force in respect of any person, [and that person is not detained in pursuance of the sentence or order of any court] he shall, unless the court by which the recommendation is made otherwise directs, [or a direction is given under sub-paragraph (1A) below,] be detained pending the making of a deportation order in pursuance of the recommendation, unless the Secretary of State directs him to be released pending further consideration of his case [or he is released on bail].

[(**1A**) Where—

(a) a recommendation for deportation made by a court on a conviction of a person is in force in respect of him; and

(b) he appeals against his conviction or against that recommendation, the powers that the court determining the appeal may exercise include power to direct him to be released without setting aside the recommendation.]

(2) Where notice has been given to a person in accordance with regulations under [section 105 of the Nationality, Immigration and Asylum Act 2002 (notice of decision)] of a

decision to make a deportation order against him, [and he is not detained in pursuance of the sentence or order of a court], he may be detained under the authority of the Secretary of State pending the making of the deportation order.

(3) Where a deportation order is in force against any person, he may be detained under the authority of the Secretary of State pending his removal or departure from the United Kingdom (and if already detained by virtue of sub-paragraph (1) or (2) above when the order is made, shall continue to be detained unless [he is released on bail or] the Secretary of State directs otherwise).

(4) In relation to detention under sub-paragraph (2) or (3) above, paragraphs 17[,18 and 25A to 25E] of Schedule 2 to this Act shall apply as they apply in relation to detention under paragraph 16 of that Schedule [; and for that purpose the reference in paragraph 17(1) to a person liable to detention includes a reference to a person who would be liable to detention upon receipt of a notice which is ready to be given to him.]

[(4A) Paragraphs 22 to 25 of Schedule 2 to this Act apply in relation to a person detained under sub-paragraph (1), (2) or (3) as they apply in relation to a person detained under paragraph 16 of that Schedule.]

[(5) A person to whom this sub-paragraph applies shall be subject to such restrictions as to residence, [as to his employment or occupation] and as to reporting to the police [or an immigration officer] as may from time to time be notified to him in writing by the Secretary of State.

(6) The persons to whom sub-paragraph (5) above applies are—

(a) a person liable to be detained under sub-paragraph (1) above, while by virtue of a direction of the Secretary of State he is not so detained; and

(b) a person liable to be detained under sub-paragraph (2) or (3) above, while he is not so detained.]

Effect of appeals

[3. So far as they relate to an appeal under section 82(1) of the Nationality, Immigration and Asylum Act 2002 against a decision of the kind referred to in section 82(2)(j) or (k) of that Act (decision to make a deportation order and refusal to revoke deportation order), paragraphs 29 to 33 to this Act shall apply for the purposes of this schedule as if the reference in paragraph 29(1) to Part 1 of that Schedule were a reference to this Schedule.]

[*Powers of courts pending deportation*

4. Where the release of a person recommended for deportation is directed by a court, he shall be subject to such restrictions as to residence [as to his employment or occupation] and as to reporting to the police as the court may direct.

5.—(1) On an application made—

(a) by or on behalf of a person recommended for deportation whose release was so directed; or

(b) by a constable; or

(c) by an Immigration Officer,

the appropriate court shall have the powers specified in sub-paragraph (2) below.

(2) The powers mentioned in sub-paragraph (1) above are—
 (a) if the person to whom the application relates is not subject to any such restrictions imposed by a court as are mentioned in paragraph 4 above, to order that he shall be subject to any such restrictions as the court may direct; and
 (b) if he is subject to restrictions imposed by a court by virtue of that paragraph or this paragraph—
  (i) to direct that any of them shall be varied or shall cease to have effect; or
  (ii) to give further directions as to his residence and reporting.

6.—(1) In this Schedule 'the appropriate court', means except in a case to which sub-paragraph (2) below applies, the court which directed release.

(2) This sub-paragraph applies where the court which directed release was—
 (a) the Crown Court;
 (b) the Court of Appeal;
 (c) the High Court of Justiciary;
 (d) the Crown Court in Northern Ireland; or
 (e) the Court of Appeal in Northern Ireland.

(3) Where the Crown Court or the Crown Court in Northern Ireland directed release, the appropriate court is—
 (a) the court that directed release; or
 (b) a magistrates' court acting for the commission area or county court division where the person to whom the application relates resides.

(4) Where the Court of Appeal or the Court of Appeal in Northern Ireland gave the direction, the appropriate court is the Crown Court or the Crown Court in Northern Ireland, as the case may be.

(5) Where the High Court of Justiciary directed release, the appropriate court is—
 (a) that court; or
 (b) in a case where release was directed by that court on appeal, the court from which the appeal was made.

7.—(1) A constable or Immigration Officer may arrest without warrant any person who is subject to restrictions imposed by a court under this Schedule and who at the time of the arrest is in the relevant part of the United Kingdom—
 (a) if he has reasonable grounds to suspect that that person is contravening or has contravened any of those restrictions; or
 (b) if he has reasonable grounds for believing that that person is likely to contravene any of them.

(2) In sub-paragraph (2) above 'the relevant part of the United Kingdom' means—
 (a) England and Wales, in a case where a court with jurisdiction in England or Wales imposed the restrictions;
 (b) Scotland, in a case where a court with jurisdiction in Scotland imposed them; and
 (c) Northern Ireland, in a case where a court in Northern Ireland imposed them.

8.—(1) A person arrested in England or Wales or Northern Ireland in pursuance of paragraph 7 above shall be brought as soon as practicable and in any event within 24 hours after his arrest before a justice of the peace for the petty sessions area or district in which he was arrested.

(2) In reckoning for the purposes of this paragraph any period of 24 hours, no account shall be taken of Christmas Day, Good Friday or any Sunday.

9.—(1) A person arrested in Scotland in pursuance of paragraph 7 above shall wherever practicable be brought before the appropriate court not later than in the course of the first day after his arrest, such day not being a Saturday, a Sunday or a court holiday prescribed for that court under section 10 of the Bail etc. (Scotland) Act 1980.

(2) Nothing in this paragraph shall prevent a person arrested in Scotland being brought before a court on a Saturday, a Sunday or such a court holiday as is mentioned in sub-paragraph (1) above where the court is, in pursuance of section 10 of the said Act of 1980, sitting on such day for the disposal of criminal business.

10. Any justice of the peace or court before whom a person is brought by virtue of paragraph 8 or 9 above—

(a) if of the opinion that that person is contravening, has contravened or is likely to contravene any restriction imposed on him by a court under this Schedule, may direct—

(i) that he be detained; or

(ii) that he be released subject to such restrictions as to his residence and reporting to the police as the court may direct; and

(b) if not of that opinion, shall release him without altering the restrictions as to his residence and his reporting to the police.]

Note: Paragraph 2: words in second square brackets in para 2(1) and paras 2(1A), 2(5), (6) added by Criminal Justice Act 1982. Words in first square brackets in para 2(2) substituted by Sch 7 Nationality, Immigration and Asylum Act 2002 from 1 April 2003 (SI 2003/754). Other words in square brackets in paras 2(1) and (2) substituted by Sch 2 Asylum and Immigration Act 2004 from a date to be appointed. Other words in square brackets in para 2(2) and para 2(4A) inserted by Immigration and Asylum Act 1999, s 54 from 10 February 2003 (SI 2003/2). Words in first square brackets in para 2(5) added by Immigration Act 1988, s 10, other words in square brackets inserted by Asylum and Immigration Act 1996 from 1 October 1996. Words in last square brackets in para 2(4) inserted by Immigration, Asylum and Nationality Act 2006 from 31 August 2006 (SI 2006/2226). Paragraph 3 substituted by Sch 7 Nationality, Immigration and Asylum Act 2002 from 1 April 2003 (SI 2003/754, which sets out transitional provisions). Paragraphs 4–10: added by Criminal Justice Act 1982. Paragraph 4: words in square brackets added by Immigration Act 1988, s 10.

Section 9

Schedule 4

Integration With United Kingdom Law of Immigration Law of Islands

Leave to enter

1.—(1) Where under the immigration laws of any of the Islands a person is or has been given leave to enter or remain in the island, or is or has been refused leave, this Act shall have effect in relation to him, if he is not [a British citizen], as if the leave were leave (of like duration) given under this Act to enter or remain in the United Kingdom, or, as the case may be, as if he had under this Act been refused leave to enter the United Kingdom.

(2) Where under the immigration laws of any of the Islands a person has a limited leave to

enter or remain in the island subject to any such conditions as are authorised in the United Kingdom by section 3(1) of this Act (being conditions imposed by notice given to him, whether the notice of leave or a subsequent notice), then on his coming to the United Kingdom this Act shall apply, if he is not [a British citizen], as if those conditions related to his stay in the United Kingdom and had been imposed by notice under this Act.

(3) Without prejudice to the generality of sub-paragraphs (1) and (2) above, anything having effect in the United Kingdom by virtue of either of those sub-paragraphs may in relation to the United Kingdom be varied or revoked under this Act in like manner, and subject to the like appeal (if any), as if it had originated under this Act as mentioned in that sub-paragraph.

(4) Where anything having effect in the United Kingdom by virtue of sub-paragraph (1) or (2) above ceases to have effect or is altered in effect as mentioned in sub-paragraph (3) or otherwise by anything done under this Act, sub-paragraph (1) or (2) shall not thereafter apply to it or, as the case may be, shall apply to it as so altered in effect.

(5) Nothing in this paragraph shall be taken as conferring on a person a right of appeal under this Act against any decision or action taken in any of the Islands.

2. Notwithstanding section 3(4) of this Act, leave given to a person under this Act to enter or remain in the United Kingdom shall not continue to apply on his return to the United Kingdom after an absence if he has during that absence entered any of the Islands in circumstances in which he is required under the immigration laws of that island to obtain leave to enter.

Deportation

[3.—(1) This Act has effect in relation to a person who is subject to an Islands deportation order as if the order were a deportation order made against him under this Act.

(2) Sub-paragraph (1) does not apply if the person concerned is—
  (a) a British citizen;
  (b) an EEA national;
  (c) a member of the family of an EEA national; or
  (d) a member of the family of a British citizen who is neither such a citizen nor an EEA national.

(3) The Secretary of State does not, as a result of sub-paragraph (1), have power to revoke an Islands deportation order.

(4) In any particular case, the Secretary of State may direct that paragraph (b), (c) or (d) of sub-paragraph (2) is not to apply in relation to the Islands deportation order.

(5) Nothing in this paragraph makes it unlawful for a person in respect of whom an Islands deportation order is in force in any of the Islands to enter the United Kingdom on his way from that island to a place outside the United Kingdom.

(6) 'Islands deportation order' means an order made under the immigration laws of any of the Islands under which a person is, or has been, ordered to leave the island and forbidden to return.

(7) Subsections (10) and (12) to (14) of section 80 of the Immigration and Asylum Act 1999 apply for the purposes of this section as they apply for the purposes of that section.]

Illegal entrants

4. Notwithstanding anything in section 1(3) of this Act, it shall not be lawful for a person who is not [a British citizen] to enter the United Kingdom from any of the Islands where his presence was unlawful under the immigration laws of that island, unless he is given leave to enter.

Note: Words in square brackets substituted by British Nationality Act 1981, s 39(6). Paragraph 3 substituted by Immigration and Asylum Act 1999 from 2 October 2000.

SCHEDULE 5

Note: Schedule 5 repealed by Immigration and Asylum Act 1999 from 14 February 2000.

Section 34

SCHEDULE 6

...

REPEALS

Race Relations Act 1976
(1976, c. 74)

An Act to make fresh provision with respect to discrimination on racial grounds and relations between people of different racial groups; and to make in the Sex Discrimination Act 1975 amendments for bringing provisions in that Act relating to its administration and enforcement into conformity with the corresponding provisions in this Act. [22 November 1976]

Note: Extracts.

Part I
Discrimination to Which Act Applies

1. Racial discrimination

(**1**) A person discriminates against another in any circumstances relevant for the purposes of any provision of this Act if—
- (a) on racial grounds he treats that other less favourably than he treats or would treat other persons; or
- (b) he applies to that other a requirement or condition which he applies or would apply equally to persons not of the same racial group as that other but—
  - (i) which is such that the proportion of persons of the same racial group as that other who can comply with it is considerably smaller than the proportion of persons not of that racial group who can comply with it; and
  - (ii) which he cannot show to be justifiable irrespective of the colour, race, nationality or ethnic or national origins of the person to whom it is applied; and
  - (iii) which is to the detriment of that other because he cannot comply with it.

[(**1A**) A person also discriminates against another if, in any circumstances relevant for the purposes of any provision referred to in subsection (1B), he applies to that other a provision, criterion or practice which he applies or would apply equally to persons not of the same race or ethnic or national origins as that other, but—
- (a) which puts or would put persons of the same race or ethnic or national origins as that other at a particular disadvantage when compared with other persons,

(b) which puts that other at that disadvantage, and
(c) which he cannot show to be a proportionate means of achieving a legitimate aim.

(1B) The provisions mentioned in subsection (1A) are—
(a) Part II;
(b) sections 17 to 18D;
(c) section 19B, so far as relating to—
(i) any form of social security;
(ii) health care;
(iii) any other form of social protection; and
(iv) any form of social advantage;
which does not fall within section 20;
(d) sections 20 to 24;
(e) sections 26A and 26B;
(f) sections 76 and 76ZA; and
(g) Part IV, in its application to the provisions referred to in paragraphs (a) to (f).

(1C) Where, by virtue of subsection (1A), a person discriminates against another, subsection (1)(b) does not apply to him.]

(2) It is hereby declared that, for the purposes of this Act, segregating a person from other persons on racial grounds is treating him less favourably than they are treated.

Note: Subsections (1A), (1B) and (1C) inserted by SI 2003/1626 from 19 July 2003.

2. Discrimination by way of victimisation

(1) A person ('the discriminator') discriminates against another person ('the person victimised') in any circumstances relevant for the purposes of any provision of this Act if he treats the person victimised less favourably than in those circumstances he treats or would treat other persons, and does so by reason that the person victimised has—
(a) brought proceedings against the discriminator or any other person under this Act; or
(b) given evidence or information in connection with proceedings brought by any person against the discriminator or any other person under this Act; or
(c) otherwise done anything under or by reference to this Act in relation to the discriminator or any other person; or
(d) alleged that the discriminator or any other person has committed an act which (whether or not the allegation so states) would amount to a contravention of this Act,

or by reason that the discriminator knows that the person victimised intends to do any of those things, or suspects that the person victimised has done, or intends to do, any of them.

(2) Subsection (1) does not apply to treatment of a person by reason of any allegation made by him if the allegation was false and not made in good faith.

3. Meaning of 'racial grounds', 'racial group' etc.

(1) In this Act, unless the context otherwise requires—

'racial grounds' means any of the following grounds, namely colour, race, nationality or ethnic or national origins;

'racial group' means a group of persons defined by reference to colour, race, nationality or ethnic or national origins, and references to a person's racial group refer to any racial group into which he falls.

(2) The fact that a racial group comprises two or more distinct racial groups does not prevent it from constituting a particular racial group for the purposes of this Act.

(3) In this Act—

(a) references to discrimination refer to any discrimination falling within section 1 or 2; and

(b) references to racial discrimination refer to any discrimination falling within section 1,

and related expressions shall be construed accordingly.

(4) A comparison of the case of a person of a particular racial group with that of a person not of that group under section 1(1) [or (1A)] must be such that the relevant circumstances in the one case are the same, or not materially different, in the other.

Note: Words in square brackets inserted by SI 2003/1626 from 19 July 2003.

[Harassment

3A.—(1) A person subjects another to harassment in any circumstances relevant for the purposes of any provision referred to in section 1(1B) where, on grounds of race or ethnic or national origins, he engages in unwanted conduct which has the purpose or effect of—

(a) violating that others person's dignity, or

(b) creating an intimidating, hostile, degrading, humiliating or offensive environment for him.

(2) Conduct shall be regarded as having the effect specified in paragraph (a) or (b) of subsection (1) only if, having regard to all the circumstances, including

in particular the perception of that other person, it should reasonably be considered as having that effect.]

Note: Section 3A inserted by SI 2003/1626 from 19 July 2003.

[*Public authorities*

19B. [. . .] public authorities

(1) It is unlawful for a public authority in carrying out any function of the authority to do any act which constitutes discrimination.

(1A) It is unlawful for a public authority to subject a person to harassment in the course of carrying out any functions of the authority which consist of the provision of—
  (a) any form of social security;
  (b) healthcare;
  (c) any other form of social protection; or
  (d) any form of social advantage,
  which does not fall within section 20.

(2) In this section 'public authority'—
  (a) includes any person certain of whose functions are functions of a public nature; but
  (b) does not include any person mentioned in subsection (3).

(3) The persons mentioned in this subsection are—
  (a) either House of Parliament;
  (b) a person exercising functions in connection with proceedings in Parliament;
  (c) the Security Service;
  (d) the Secret Intelligence Service;
  (e) the Government Communications Headquarters; and
  (f) any unit or part of a unit of any of the naval, military or air forces of the Crown which is for the time being required by the Secretary of State to assist the Government Communications Headquarters in carrying out its functions.

(4) In relation to a particular act, a person is not a public authority by virtue only of subsection (2)(a) if the nature of the act is private.

(5) This section is subject to sections 19C to 19F.

(6) Nothing in this section makes unlawful any act of discrimination [or harassment] which—
  (a) is made unlawful by virtue of any other provision of this Act; or
  (b) would be so made but for any provision made by or under this Act.

Note: Section 19B inserted by Race Relations (Amendment) Act 2000 from 2 April 2002,

(SI 2001/566). Words omitted, sub-s (1A) and words in square brackets inserted by SI 2003/1626 from 19 July 2003.

19C. Exceptions or further exceptions from section 19B for judicial and legislative acts etc.

(1) Section 19B does not apply to—

(a) any judicial act (whether done by a court, tribunal or other person); or

(b) any act done on the instructions, or on behalf, of a person acting in a judicial capacity.

(2) Section 19B does not apply to any act of, or relating to, making, confirming or approving any enactment or Order in Council or any instrument made by a Minister of the Crown under an enactment.

(3) Section 19B does not apply to any act of, or relating to, making or 'approving arrangements, or imposing requirements or conditions, of a kind [excepted by] section 41.

(4) Section 19B does not apply to any act of, or relating to, imposing a requirement, or giving an express authorisation, of a kind mentioned in section 19D(3) in relation to the carrying out of [immigration functions].

(5) In this section—

'[immigration functions]' has the meaning given in section 19D; and

'Minister of the Crown' includes the National Assembly for Wales and a member of the Scottish Executive.

Note: Section 19C inserted by Race Relations (Amendment) Act 2000 from 2 April 2002, (SI 2001/566). First words in square brackets inserted by SI 2003/1626 from 19 July 2003. Other words in square brackets substituted by SI 2003/1016 from 4 April 2003.

19D. Exception from section 19B for certain acts in immigration and nationality cases

(1) Section 19B does not make it unlawful for a relevant person to discriminate against another person on grounds of nationality or ethnic or national origins in carrying out [immigration functions].

(2) For the purposes of subsection (1), 'relevant person' means—

(a) a Minister of the Crown acting personally; or

(b) any other person acting in accordance with a relevant authorisation.

(3) In subsection (2), 'relevant authorisation' means a requirement imposed or express authorisation given—

(a) with respect to a particular case or class of case, by a Minister of the Crown acting personally;

(b) with respect to a particular class of case—
(i) by any of the enactments mentioned in subsection (5); or
(ii) by any instrument made under or by virtue of any of those enactments.

[(4) In subsection (1) 'immigration functions' means functions exercisable by virtue of any of the enactments mentioned in subsection (5).

(5) Those enactments are—
(a) the Immigration Acts [(within the meaning of section 44 of the Asylum and Immigration (Treatment of Claimants, etc.) Act 2004)] excluding sections 28A to 28K of the Immigration Act 1971 (c. 77) so far as they relate to offences under Part III of that Act [and excluding section 14 of the Asylum and Immigration (Treatment of Claimants, etc.) Act 2004];
(b) the Special Immigration Appeals Commission Act 1997 (c. 68);
(c) provision made under section 2(2) of the European Communities Act 1972 (c. 68) which relates to immigration or asylum; and
(d) any provision of Community law which relates to immigration or asylum.]

Note: Section 19D inserted by Race Relations (Amendment) Act 2000 from 2 April 2002 (SI 2001/566). Words in square brackets in sub-s (5)(a) substituted by Asylum and Immigration Act 2004, s 14 from 1 December 2004 (SI 2004/2999). Other words in square brackets substituted by Nationality, Immigration and Asylum Act 2002, s 6 from 7 November 2002.

19E. Monitoring of exception in relation to immigration and nationality cases

(1) The Secretary of State shall appoint a person who is not a member of his staff to act as a monitor.

(2) Before appointing any such person, the Secretary of State shall consult the Commission.

(3) The person so appointed shall monitor, in such manner as the Secretary of State may determine—
(a) the likely effect on the operation of the exception in section 19D of any relevant authorisation relating to the carrying out of [immigration functions] which has been given by a Minister of the Crown acting personally; and
(b) the operation of that exception in relation to acts which have been done by a person acting in accordance with such an authorisation.

(4) The monitor shall make an annual report on the discharge of his functions to the Secretary of State.

(5) The Secretary of State shall lay a copy of any report made to him under sub-section (4) before each House of Parliament.

(6) The Secretary of State shall pay to the monitor such fees and allowances (if any) as he may determine.

(7) . . .

Note: Section 19E inserted by Race Relations (Amendment) Act 2000 from 2 April 2002 (SI 2001/566). Words in square brackets substituted and sub-s (7) omitted by Nationality, Immigration and Asylum Act 2002, s 6 from 7 November 2002.

Extent

27. Extent of Part III [etc.]

(1) Sections 17 to 19 do not apply to benefits, facilities or services outside Great Britain except—

(a) travel on a ship registered at a port of registry in Great Britain; and

(b) benefits, facilities or services provided on a ship so registered.

[(**1A**) In its application in relation to granting, entry clearance (within the meaning of the Immigration Act 1971) section 19B applies in relation to acts done outside the United Kingdom, as well as those done within Great Britain.]

Note: Section 27(1A) inserted by Race Relations (Amendment) Act 2000 from 2 April 2001 (SI 2001/566).

57. Claims under Part III [etc.]

(1) A claim by any person ('the claimant') that another person ('the respondent')—

(a) has committed an act [. . .] against the claimant which is unlawful by virtue of Part III [other than, in relation to discrimination on grounds of race or ethnic or national origins, or harassment, section 26A or 26B]; or

(b) is by virtue of section 32 or 33 to be treated as having committed such an act [. . .] against the claimant,

may be made the subject of civil proceedings in like manner as any other claim in tort or (in Scotland) in reparation for breach of statutory duty.

(2) Proceedings under subsection (1)—

(a) shall, in England and Wales, be brought only in a designated county court; and

(b) shall, in Scotland, be brought only in a sheriff court;

but all such remedies shall be obtainable in such proceedings as, apart from this subsection and section 53(1), would be obtainable in the High Court or the Court of Session, as the case may be.

(3) As respects an unlawful act of discrimination falling within section 1 (1)(b) no award of damages shall be made if the respondent proves that the requirement or condition in question was not applied with the intention of treating the claimant unfavourably on racial grounds.

(4) For the avoidance of doubt it is hereby declared that damages in respect of an unlawful act of discrimination may include compensation for injury to feelings whether or not they include compensation under any other head.

[(4A) . . .

(4B) . . .

(4C) . . .

(4D) . . .]

(5) Civil proceedings in respect of a claim by any person that he has been discriminated against in contravention of section 17 or 18 by a body to which section 19(1) applies shall not be instituted unless the claimant has given notice of the claim to the Secretary of State . . .

(6) In Scotland, when any proceedings are brought under this section, in addition to the service on the defender of a copy of the summons or initial writ initiating the action a copy thereof shall be sent as soon as practicable to the Commission in a manner to be prescribed by Act of Sederunt.

Note: Words in square brackets inserted by SI 2003/1626 from 19 July 2003. Subsections (4A)–(4D) refer to Criminal proceedings.

[Burden of Proof: County and Sheriff Courts

57ZA.—(1) This section applies where a claim is brought under section 57 and the claim is that the respondent—

(a) has committed an act of discrimination, on grounds of race or ethnic or national origins, which is unlawful by virtue of any provision referred to in section 1(1B)(b) to (d), or Part IV in its application to those provisions, or

(b) has committed an act of harassment.

(2) Where, on the hearing of the claim, the claimant proves facts from which the court could, apart from this section, conclude in the absence of an adequate explanation that the respondent—

(a) has committed such an act of discrimination or harassment against the claimant, or

(b) is by virtue of section 32 or 33 to be treated as having committed such an act of discrimination or harassment against the claimant,

the court shall uphold the claim unless the respondent proves that he did not commit or, as the case may be, is not to be treated as having committed, that act.]

Note: Section 57ZA inserted by SI 2003/1626 from 19 July 2003.

[57A. Claims under section 19B in immigration cases

(1) No proceedings may be brought by a claimant under section 57(1) in respect of an immigration claim if—

(a) the act to which the claim relates was done in the taking by an immigration authority of a relevant decision and the question whether that act was unlawful by virtue of section 19B has been or could be raised in proceedings on an appeal which is pending, or could be brought, under the 1997 Act or [Part 5 of the 2002 Act]; or

(b) it has been decided in relevant immigration proceedings that that act was not unlawful by virtue of that section.

(2) For the purposes of this section an immigration claim is a claim that a person—

(a) has committed a relevant act of discrimination against the claimant which is unlawful by virtue of section 19B; or

(b) is by virtue of section 32 or 33 to be treated as having committed such an act of discrimination against the claimant.

(3) Where it has been decided in relevant immigration proceedings that an act to which an immigration claim relates was unlawful by virtue of section 19B, any court hearing that claim under section 57 shall treat that act as an act which is unlawful by virtue of section 19B for the purposes of the proceedings before it.

(4) No relevant decision of an immigration authority involving an act to which an immigration claim relates and no relevant decision of an immigration appellate body in relation to such a decision shall be subject to challenge or otherwise affected by virtue of a decision of a court hearing the immigration claim under section 57.

(5) In this section—

['the Immigration Acts' has the meaning given by section 158 of the 2002 Act;]

'immigration appellate body' means [the Asylum and Immigration Tribunal,] the Special Immigration Appeals Commission, the Court of Appeal, the Court of Session or the [Supreme Court];

['immigration authority' means the Secretary of State, an immigration officer or a person responsible for the grant or refusal of entry clearance (within the meaning of section 33(1) of the Immigration Act 1971 (c. 77));]

'immigration claim' has the meaning given by subsection (2) above;

'pending' has the same meaning as in the 1997 Act or, as the case may be, [Part 5 of the 2002 Act];

'relevant act of discrimination' means an act of discrimination done by an immigration authority in taking any relevant decision;

'relevant decision' means—

(a) in relation to an immigration authority, any decision under the Immigration Acts relating to the entitlement of the claimant to enter or remain in the United Kingdom; and

(b) in relation to an immigration appellate body, any decision on an appeal under the 1997 Act or [Part 5 of the 2002 Act] in relation to a decision falling within paragraph (a);

'relevant immigration proceedings' means proceedings on an appeal under the 1997 Act or [Part 5 of the 2002 Act];

'the 1997 Act' means the Special Immigration Appeals Commission Act 1997;

['the 2002 Act' means the Nationality, Immigration and Asylum Act 2002;] and, for the purposes of subsection (1)(a), any power to grant leave to appeal out of time shall be disregarded.]

Note: Section 57A inserted by Race Relations (Amendment) Act 2000 from 2 April 2001 (SI 2001/566). Second words in square brackets in sub-s (5) substituted by Schedule 1 Immigration, Asylum and Nationality Act 2006 from a date to be appointed. Third words in square brackets in sub-s (5) substituted by Sch 9 Constitutional Reform Act 2005 from a date to be appointed. Other words in square brackets substituted by Sch 7 Nationality, Immigration and Asylum Act 2002 from 1 April 2003 (SI 2003/743).

British Nationality Act 1981
(1981, c. 61)

Arrangement of Sections

PART I. BRITISH CITIZENSHIP

Acquisition after commencement

Section

1. Acquisition by birth or adoption.
2. Acquisition by descent.
3. Acquisition by registration: minors.
4. Acquisition by registration: [British overseas territories] citizens etc.

4A. Acquisition by registration: further provision for British overseas territories citizens.

4B. Acquisition by registration: certain persons without other citizenship.

4C. Acquisition by registration: certain persons born between 1961 and 1983.

5. Acquisition by registration: nationals for purposes of the Community Treaties.
6. Acquisition by naturalisation.

Acquisition after commencement: special cases

7. . . .
8. . . .
9. . . .
10. Registration following renunciation of citizenship of UK and Colonies.

Acquisition at commencement

11. Citizens of UK and Colonies who are to become British citizens at commencement.

Renunciation and resumption

12. Renunciation.
13. Resumption.

Supplementary

14. Meaning of British citizen 'by descent'.

An Act to make fresh provision about citizenship and nationality, and to amend the Immigration Act 1971 as regards the right of abode in the United Kingdom. [30th October 1981]

Part I

British Citizenship

Acquisition after commencement

1. Acquisition by birth or adoption

(1) A person born in the United Kingdom after commencement[, or in a qualifying territory on or after the appointed day,] shall be a British citizen if at the time of the birth his father or mother is—
(a) a British citizen; or
(b) settled in the United Kingdom [or that territory].

(2) A new-born infant who, after commencement, is found abandoned in the United Kingdom[, or on or after the appointed day is found abandoned in a qualifying territory,] shall, unless the contrary is shown, be deemed for the purposes of subsection (1)—
(a) to have been born in the United Kingdom after commencement; [or in that territory on or after the appointed day] and
(b) to have been born to a parent who at the time of the birth was a British citizen or settled in the United Kingdom [or that territory].

(3) A person born in the United Kingdom after commencement who is not a British citizen by virtue of subsection (1) or (2) shall be entitled to be registered as a British citizen if, while he is a minor—
(a) his father or mother becomes a British citizen or becomes settled in the United Kingdom; and
(b) an application is made for his registration as a British citizen.

(4) A person born in the United Kingdom after commencement who is not a British citizen by virtue of subsection (1) or (2) shall be entitled, on an application for his registration as a British citizen made at any time after he has attained the age of ten years, to be registered as such a citizen if, as regards each of the first ten years of that person's life, the number of days on which he was absent from the United Kingdom in that year does not exceed 90.

[(5) Where—
(a) any court in the United Kingdom [or, on or after the appointed day, any court in a qualifying territory] makes an order authorising the adoption of a minor who is not a British citizen; or
(b) a minor who is not a British citizen is adopted under a Convention adoption, that minor shall, if the requirements of subsection (5A) are met, be a British citizen as from the date on which the order is made or the Convention adoption is effected, as the case may be.

(5A) Those requirements are that on the date on which the order is made or the Convention adoption is effected (as the case may be)—

(a) the adopter or, in the case of a joint adoption, one of the adopters is a British citizen; and
(b) in a case within subsection (5)(b), the adopter or, in the case of a joint adoption, both of the adopters are habitually resident in the United Kingdom.]

(6) Where an order [or a Convention adoption] in consequence of which any person became a British citizen by virtue of subsection (5) ceases to have effect, whether on annulment or otherwise, the cesser shall not effect the status of that person as a British citizen.

(7) If in the special circumstances of any particular case the Secretary of State thinks fit, he may for the purposes of subsection (4) treat the person to whom the application relates as fulfilling the requirement specified in that subsection although, as regards any one or more of the first ten years of that person's life, the number of days on which he was absent from the United Kingdom in that year or each of the years in question exceeds 90.

(8) In this section and elsewhere in this Act 'settled' has the meaning given by section 50 [and in this section 'Convention adoption' has the same meaning as in the Adoption Act 1976 and the Adoption (Scotland) Act 1978].

Note: Subsection (5) substituted and words in square brackets in sub-ss (6) and (8) inserted by Adoption (Intercountry Aspects) Act 1999, s 7 from 1 June 2003 (SI 2003/362). Other words in square brackets inserted by Sch 1 British Overseas Territories Act 2002, from 21 May 2002 (SI 2002/1252).

2. Acquisition by descent

(1) A person born outside the United Kingdom [and the qualifying territories] after commencement shall be a British citizen if at the time of the birth his father or mother—
(a) is a British citizen otherwise than by descent; or
(b) is a British citizen and is serving outside the United Kingdom[and the qualifying territories] in service to which this paragraph applies, his or her recruitment for that service having taken place in the United Kingdom [or a qualifying territory]; or
(c) is a British citizen and is serving outside the United Kingdom [and the qualifying territories] in service under a Community institution, his or her recruitment for that service having taken place in a country which at the time of the recruitment was a member of the Communities.

(2) Paragraph (b) of subsection (1) applies to—
(a) Crown service under the government of the United Kingdom [or of a qualifying territory]; and
(b) service of any description for the time being designated under subsection (3).

(3) For the purposes of this section the Secretary of State may by order made by statutory instrument designate any description of service which he considers to be closely associated with the activities outside the United Kingdom [and the qualifying territories] of Her Majesty's government in the United Kingdom [or in a qualifying territory].

(4) Any order made under subsection (3) shall be subject to annulment in pursuance of a resolution of either House of Parliament.

Note: Words in square brackets inserted by Sch 1 British Overseas Territories Act 2002 from 21 May 2002 (SI 2002/1252), but without effect to the operation of this section in relation to persons born before that date.

3. Acquisition by registration: minors

(1) If while a person is a minor an application is made for his registration as a British citizen, the Secretary of State may, if he thinks fit, cause him to be registered as such a citizen.

(2) A person born outside the United Kingdom [and the qualifying territories] shall be entitled, on an application for his registration as a British citizen made within the period of twelve months from the date of the birth, to be registered as such a citizen if the requirements specified in subsection (3) or, in the case of a person born stateless, the requirements specified in paragraphs (a) and (b) of that subsection, are fulfilled in the case of either that person's father or his mother ('the parent in question').

(3) The requirements referred to in subsection (2) are—
  (a) that the parent in question was a British citizen by descent at the time of the birth; and
  (b) that the father or mother of the parent in question—
    (i) was a British citizen otherwise than by descent at the time of the birth of the parent in question; or
    (ii) became a British citizen otherwise than by descent at commencement, or would have become such a citizen otherwise than by descent at commencement but for his or her death; and
  (c) that, as regards some period of three years ending with a date not later than the date of the birth—
    (i) the parent in question was in the United Kingdom [or a qualifying territory] at the beginning of that period; and
    (ii) the number of days on which the parent in question was absent from the United Kingdom[and the qualifying territories] in that period does not exceed 270.

(4) If in the special circumstances of any particular case the Secretary of State thinks fit, he may treat subsection (2) as if the reference to twelve months were a reference to six years.

(5) A person born outside the United Kingdom [and the qualifying territories] shall be entitled, on an application for his registration as a British citizen made while he is a minor, to be registered as such a citizen if the following requirements are satisfied, namely—

(a) that at the time of that person's birth his father or mother was a British citizen by descent; and

(b) subject to subsection (6), that that person and his father and mother were in the United Kingdom [or a qualifying territory] at the beginning of the period of three years ending with the date of the application and that, in the case of each of them, the number of days on which the person in question was absent from the United Kingdom [and the qualifying territories] in that period does not exceed 270; and

(c) subject to subsection (6), that the consent of his father and mother to the registration has been signified in the prescribed manner.

(6) In the case of an application under subsection (5) for the registration of a person as a British citizen—

(a) if his father or mother dies, or their marriage [or civil partnership] was terminated, on or before the date of the application, or his father and mother were legally separated on that date, the references to his father and mother in paragraph (b) of that subsection shall be read either as references to his father or as references to his mother; [and]

(b) if his father or mother died on or before that date, the reference to his father and mother in paragraph (c) of that subsection shall be read as a reference to either of them; [. . .]

(c) [. . .]

Note: Last word in square brackets in sub-s (6)(a) inserted and words deleted from sub-ss (6)(b) and (c) by, Nationality, Immigration & Asylum Act 2002, s 9 from 7 November 2002, with effect in relation to children born on or after a date to be appointed. Other words in square brackets inserted by Sch 1 British Overseas Territories Act 2002, from 21 May 2002 (SI 2002/1252) but without effect to the operation of this section in relation to persons born before that date. Words in first square brackets in sub-s (6)(a) inserted by Sch 27 Civil Partnership Act 2004 from a date to be appointed.

4. Acquisition by registration: [British overseas territories] citizens etc.

(1) This section applies to any person who is a [British overseas territories] citizen, [a British National (Overseas)] a British Overseas citizen, a British subject under this Act or a British protected person.

(2) A person to whom this section applies shall be entitled, on an application for his registration as a British citizen, to be registered as such a citizen if the following requirements are satisfied in the case of that person, namely—

(a) subject to subsection (3), that he was in the United Kingdom at the beginning of the period of five years ending with the date of the application and that the number of days on which he was absent from the United Kingdom in that period does not exceed 450; and

(b) that the number of days on which he was absent from the United Kingdom in the period of twelve months so ending does not exceed 90; and

(c) that he was not at any time in the period of twelve months so ending subject under the immigration law to any restriction on the period for which he might remain in the United Kingdom; and

(d) that he was not at any time in the period of five years so ending in the United Kingdom in breach of the immigration laws.

(3) So much of subsection (2)(a) as requires the person in question to have been in the United Kingdom at the beginning of the period there mentioned shall not apply in relation to a person who was settled in the United Kingdom immediately before commencement.

(4) If in the special circumstances of any particular case the Secretary of State thinks fit, he may for the purposes of subsection (2) do all or any of the following things, namely—

(a) treat the person to whom the application relates as fulfilling the requirement specified in subsection (2)(a) or subsection (2)(b), or both, although the number of days on which he was absent from the United Kingdom in the period there mentioned exceeds the number there mentioned;

(b) disregard any such restriction as is mentioned in subsection (2)(c), not being a restriction to which that person was subject on the date of the application;

(c) treat that person as fulfilling the requirement specified in subsection (2)(d) although he was in the United Kingdom in breach of the immigration laws in the period there mentioned.

(5) If, on an application for registration as a British citizen made by a person to whom this section applies, the Secretary of State is satisfied that the applicant has at any time served in service to which this subsection applies, he may, if he thinks fit in the special circumstances of the applicant's case, cause him to be registered as such a citizen.

(6) Subsection (5) applies to—

(a) Crown service under the government of a [British overseas territory]; and

(b) paid or unpaid service (not falling within paragraph (a)) as a member of any body established by law in a [British overseas territory] members of which are appointed by or on behalf of the Crown.

Note: Words in second square brackets in s 4(1) inserted by SI 1986/948. Dependent territories became British overseas territories from 26 February 2002, British Overseas Territories Act 2002, s 1.

[4A. Acquisition by registration: further provision for British overseas territories citizens

(1) If an application is made to register as a British citizen a person who is a British overseas territories citizen, the Secretary of State may if he thinks fit cause the person to be so registered.

(2) Subsection (1) does not apply in the case of a British overseas territories citizen who—
   (a) is such a citizen by virtue only of a connection with the Sovereign Base Areas of Akrotiri and Dhekelia; or
   (b) has ceased to be a British citizen as a result of a declaration of renunciation.]

Note: Section 4A inserted by British Overseas Territories Act, s 4 from 21 May 2002 (SI 2002/1252).

[4B. Acquisition by registration: certain persons without other citizenship

(1) This section applies to a person who has the status of—
   (a) British Overseas citizen,
   (b) British subject under this Act, or
   (c) British protected person.

(2) A person to whom this section applies shall be entitled to be registered as a British citizen if—
   (a) he applies for registration under this section,
   (b) the Secretary of State is satisfied that the person does not have, apart from the status mentioned in subsection (1), any citizenship or nationality, and
   (c) the Secretary of State is satisfied that the person has not after 4th July 2002 renounced, voluntarily relinquished or lost through action or inaction any citizenship or nationality.]

Note: Section 4B inserted by Nationality, Immigration and Asylum Act 2002, s 12 from 30 April 2003 (SI 2003/754).

[4C. Acquisition by registration: certain persons born between 1961 and 1983

(1) A person is entitled to be registered as a British citizen if—
   (a) he applies for registration under this section, and
   (b) he satisfies each of the following conditions.

(2) The first condition is that the applicant was born after 7th February 1961 and before 1st January 1983.

(3) The second condition is that the applicant would at some time before 1st January 1983 have become a citizen of the United Kingdom and Colonies by virtue of section 5 of the British Nationality Act 1948 (c. 56) if that section

had provided for citizenship by descent from a mother in the same terms as it provided for citizenship by descent from a father.

(4) The third condition is that immediately before 1st January 1983 the applicant would have had the right of abode in the United Kingdom by virtue of section 2 of the Immigration Act 1971 (c. 77) had he become a citizen of the United Kingdom and Colonies as described in subsection (3) above.]

Note: Section 4C inserted by Nationality, Immigration and Asylum Act 2002, s 13 from 30 April 2003 (SI 2003/754).

5. Acquisition by registration: nationals for purposes of the Community Treaties

A[British overseas territories] citizen who falls to be treated as a national of the United Kingdom for the purposes of the Community Treaties shall be entitled to be registered as a British citizen if an application is made for his registration as such a citizen.

Note: British dependent territories became British overseas territories from 26 February 2002, British Overseas Territories Act 2002, s 1.

6. Acquisition by naturalisation

(1) If, on an application for naturalisation as a British citizen made by a person of full age and capacity, the Secretary of State is satisfied that the applicant fulfils the requirements of Schedule 1 for naturalisation as such a citizen under this subsection, he may, if he thinks fit, grant to him a certificate of naturalisation as such a citizen.

(2) If, on an application for naturalisation as a British citizen made by a person of full age and capacity who on the date of the application is married to a British citizen [or is the civil partner of a British citizen], the Secretary of State is satisfied that the applicant fulfils the requirements of Schedule 1 for naturalisation as such a citizen under this subsection, he may, if he thinks fit, grant to him a certificate of naturalisation as such a citizen.

Note: Words in square brackets inserted by Sch 27 Civil Partnership Act 2004 from a date to be appointed.

Acquisition after commencement: special cases

7. . . .

Note: Section 7 repealed by Sch 2 of Nationality, Immigration and Asylum Act 2002 from a date to be appointed.

8. . . .

Note: Section 8 repealed by Sch 2 of Nationality, Immigration and Asylum Act 2002 from a date to be appointed.

9. . . .

Note: Section 9 repealed by Sch 2 of Nationality, Immigration and Asylum Act 2002 from a date to be appointed.

10. Registration following renunciation of citizenship of UK and Colonies

(1) Subject to subsection (3), a person shall be entitled, on an application for his registration as a British citizen, to be registered as such a citizen if immediately before commencement he would (had he applied for it) have been entitled under section 1(1) of the British Nationality Act 1964 (resumption of citizenship) to be registered as a citizen of the United Kingdom and Colonies by virtue of having an appropriate qualifying connection with the United Kingdom or, [. . .] by virtue of having been married before commencement to a person who has, or would if living have, such a connection.

(2) On an application for his registration as a British citizen made by a person of full capacity who had before commencement ceased to be a citizen of the United Kingdom and Colonies as a result of a declaration of renunciation, the Secretary of State may, if he thinks fit, cause that person to be registered as a British citizen if that person—

- (a) has an appropriate qualifying connection with the United Kingdom; or
- (b) [. . .] has been married to [, or has been the civil partner of,] a person who has, or would if living have, such a connection.

(3) A person shall not be entitled to registration under subsection (1) on more than one occasion.

(4) For the purposes of this section a person shall be taken to have an appropriate qualifying connection with the United Kingdom if he, his father or his father's father—

- (a) was born in the United Kingdom; or
- (b) is or was a person naturalised in the United Kingdom; or
- (c) was registered as a citizen of the United Kingdom and Colonies in the United Kingdom or in a country which at the time was mentioned in section 1(3) of the 1948 Act.

Note: The words deleted from sub-ss (1) and (2) repealed by Nationality Immigration and Asylum Act 2002, s 5 from a date to be appointed. Words in square brackets in sub-s (2) inserted by Sch 27 Civil Partnership Act 2004 from a date to be appointed.

Acquisition at commencement

11. Citizens of UK and Colonies who are to become British citizens at commencement

(1) Subject to subsection (2), a person who immediately before commencement—
  (a) was a citizen of the United Kingdom and Colonies; and
  (b) had the right of abode in the United Kingdom under the Immigration Act 1971 as then in force,

shall at commencement become a British citizen.

(2) A person who was registered as a citizen of the United Kingdom and Colonies under section 1 of the British Nationality (No. 2) Act 1964 (stateless persons) on the ground mentioned in subsection (1)(a) of that section (namely that his mother was a citizen of the United Kingdom and Colonies at the time when he was born) shall not become a British citizen under subsection (1) unless—
  (a) his mother becomes a British citizen under subsection (1) or would have done so but for her death; or
  (b) immediately before commencement he had the right of abode in the United Kingdom by virtue of section 2(1)(c) of the Immigration Act 1971 as then in force (settlement in United Kingdom, combined with five or more years' ordinary residence there as a citizen of the United Kingdom and Colonies).

(3) A person who—
  (a) immediately before commencement was a citizen of the United Kingdom and Colonies by virtue of having been registered under subsection (6) of section 12 of the 1948 Act (British subjects before commencement of 1948 Act becoming citizens of United Kingdom and Colonies) under arrangements made by virtue of subsection (7) of that section (registration in independent Commonwealth country by United Kingdom High Commissioner); and
  (b) was so registered on an application under the said subsection (6) based on the applicant's descent in the male line from a person ('the relevant person') possessing one of the qualifications specified in subsection (1)(a) and (b) of that section (birth or naturalisation in the United Kingdom and Colonies),

shall at commencement become a British citizen if the relevant person was born or naturalised in the United Kingdom.

Renunciation and resumption

12. Renunciation

(1) If any British citizen of full age and capacity makes in the prescribed manner a declaration of renunciation of British citizenship, then, subject to subsections (3) and (4), the Secretary of State shall cause the declaration to be registered.

(2) On the registration of a declaration made in pursuance of this section the person who made it shall cease to be a British citizen.

(3) A declaration made by a person in pursuance of this section shall not be registered unless the Secretary of State is satisfied that the person who made it will after the registration have or acquire some citizenship or nationality other than British citizenship; and if that person does not have any such citizenship or nationality on the date of registration and does not acquire some such citizenship or nationality within six months from that date, he shall be, and be deemed to have remained, a British citizen notwithstanding the registration.

(4) The Secretary of State may withhold registration of any declaration made in pursuance of this section if it is made during any war in which Her Majesty may be engaged in right of Her Majesty's government in the United Kingdom.

(5) For the purposes of this section any person who has been married [or has formed a civil partnership] shall be deemed to be of full age.

Note: Words in square brackets in sub-s (5) inserted by Sch 27 Civil Partnership Act 2004 from a date to be appointed.

13. Resumption

(1) Subject to subsection (2), a person who has ceased to be a British citizen as a result of a declaration of renunciation shall be entitled, on an application for his registration as a British citizen, to be registered as such a citizen if—
   (a) he is of full capacity; and
   (b) his renunciation of British citizenship was necessary to enable him to retain or acquire some other citizenship or nationality.

(2) A person shall not be entitled to registration under subsection (1) on more than one occasion.

(3) If a person of full capacity who has ceased to be a British citizen as a result of a declaration of renunciation (for whatever reason made) makes an application for his registration as such a citizen, the Secretary of State may, if he thinks fit, cause him to be registered as such a citizen.

Supplementary

14. Meaning of British citizen 'by descent'

(1) For the purposes of this Act a British citizen is a British citizen 'by descent' if and only if—

(a) he is a person born outside the United Kingdom after commencement who is a British citizen by virtue of section 2(1)(a) only or by virtue of registration under section 3(2) or 9; or

(b) subject to subsection (2), he is a person born outside the United Kingdom before commencement who became a British citizen at commencement and immediately before commencement—

(i) was a citizen of the United Kingdom and Colonies by virtue of section 5 of the 1948 Act (citizenship by descent); or

(ii) was a person who, under any provision of the British Nationality Acts 1948 to 1965, was deemed for the purposes of the proviso to section 5(1) of the 1948 Act to be a citizen of the United Kingdom and Colonies by descent only, or would have been so deemed if male; or

(iii) had the right of abode in the United Kingdom by virtue only of paragraph (b) of subsection (1) of section 2 of the Immigration Act 1971 as then in force (connection with United Kingdom through parent or grandparent), or by virtue only of that paragraph and paragraph (c) of that subsection (settlement in United Kingdom with five years' ordinary residence there), or by virtue only of being or having been the wife of a person who immediately before commencement had that right by virtue only of the said paragraph (b) or the said paragraphs (b) and (c); or

(iv) being a woman, was a citizen of the United Kingdom and Colonies as a result of her registration as such a citizen under section 6(2) of the 1948 Act by virtue of having been married to a man who at commencement became a British citizen by descent or would have done so but for his having died or ceased to be a citizen of the United Kingdom and Colonies as a result of a declaration of renunciation; or

(c) he is a British citizen by virtue of registration under section 3(1) and either—

(i) his father or mother was a British citizen at the time of the birth; or

(ii) his father or mother was a citizen of the United Kingdom and Colonies at that time and became a British citizen at commencement, or would have done so but for his or her death; or

(d) he is a British citizen by virtue of registration under [section 4B [4C] or 5]; or

(e) subject to subsection (2), being a woman born outside the United Kingdom before commencement, she is a British citizen as a result of her registration as such a citizen under section 8 by virtue of being or having been married to a man who at commencement became a British citizen by descent or would have done so but for his having died or ceased to be a citizen of the United Kingdom and Colonies as a result of a declaration of renunciation; or

(f) he is a British citizen by virtue of registration under section 10 who, having before commencement ceased to be a citizen of the United Kingdom and Colonies as a result of a declaration of renunciation, would, if he had not so ceased, have at commencement become a British citizen by descent by virtue of paragraph (b); or

(g) he is a British citizen by virtue of registration under section 13 who, immediately before he ceased to be a British citizen as a result of a declaration of renunciation, was such a citizen by descent; or

(h) he is a person born in a [British overseas territory] after commencement who is a British citizen by virtue of paragraph 2 of Schedule 2.

(2) A person born outside the United Kingdom before commencement is not a British citizen 'by descent' by virtue of subsection (1)(b) or (e) if his father was at the time of his birth serving outside the United Kingdom—

(a) in service of a description mentioned in subsection (3), his recruitment for the service in question having taken place in the United Kingdom; or

(b) in service under a Community institution, his recruitment for that service having taken place in a country which at the time of the recruitment was a member of the Communities.

(3) The descriptions of service referred to in subsection (2) are—

(a) Crown service under the government of the United Kingdom; and

(b) service of any description at any time designated under section 2(3).

Note: First words in square brackets in sub-s (1)(d) substituted by Nationality, Immigration and Asylum Act 2002, s 12 from 30 April 2003 (SI 2003/754). Second words in square brackets in sub-s (1)(d) inserted by Nationality, Immigration and Asylum Act 2002, s 13 from 30 April 2003 (SI 2003/754). British dependent territories became British overseas territories from 26 February 2002, British Overseas Territories Act 2002, s 1.

Part II

[British Overseas Territories] Citizenship

Acquisition after commencement

15. Acquisition by birth or adoption

(1) A person born in a [British overseas territory] after commencement shall be a [British overseas territories] citizen if at the time of the birth his father or mother is—

(a) a [British overseas territories] citizen; or
(b) settled in a [British overseas territory].

(2) A new-born infant who, after commencement, is found abandoned in a [British overseas territory] shall, unless the contrary is shown, be deemed for the purposes of subsection (1)—
(a) to have been born in that territory after commencement; and
(b) to have been born to a parent who at the time of the birth was a [British over-seas territories] citizen or settled in a [British overseas territory].

(3) A person born in a [British overseas territory] after commencement who is not a [British overseas territories] citizen by virtue of subsection (1) or (2) shall be entitled to be registered as such a citizen if, while he is a minor—
(a) his father or mother becomes such a citizen or becomes settled in a [British overseas territory]; and
(b) an application is made for his registration as such a citizen.

(4) A person born in a [British overseas territory] after commencement who is not a [British overseas territories] citizen by virtue of subsection (1) or (2) shall be entitled, on an application for his registration as a [British overseas territories] citizen made at any time after he has attained the age of ten years, to be registered as such a citizen if, as regards each of the first ten years of that person's life, the number of days on which he was absent from that territory in that year does not exceed 90.

(5) Where after commencement an order authorising the adoption of a minor who is not a [British overseas territories] citizen is made by a court in any [British overseas territory], he shall be a [British overseas territories] citizen as from the date on which the order is made if the adopter or, in the case of a joint adoption, one of the adopters, is a [British overseas territories] citizen on that date.

(6) Where an order in consequence of which any person became a [British overseas territories] citizen by virtue of subsection (5) ceases to have effect, whether on annulment or otherwise, the cesser shall not affect the status of that person as such a citizen.

(7) If in the special circumstances of any particular case the Secretary of State thinks fit, he may for the purposes of subsection (4) treat the person to whom the application relates as fulfilling the requirements specified in that subsection although, as regards any one or more of the first ten years of that person's life, the number of days on which he was absent from the [British overseas territory] there mentioned in that year or each of the years in question exceeds 90.

Note: British dependent territories became British overseas territories from 26 February 2002, British Overseas Territories Act 2002, s 1.

16. Acquisition by descent

(1) A person born outside the [British overseas territories] after commencement shall be a [British overseas territories] citizen if at the time of the birth his father or mother—
   (a) is such a citizen otherwise than by descent; or
   (b) is such a citizen and is serving outside the [British overseas territories] in service to which this paragraph applies, his or her recruitment for that service having taken place in a [British overseas territory].

(2) Paragraph (b) of subsection (1) applies to—
   (a) Crown service under the government of a [British overseas territory]; and
   (b) service of any description for the time being designated under subsection (3).

(3) For the purposes of this section the Secretary of State may be order made by statutory instrument designate any description of service which he considers to be closely associated with the activities outside the [British overseas territories] of the government of any [British overseas territory].

(4) Any order made under subsection (3) shall be subject to annulment in pursuance of a resolution of either House of Parliament.

Note: British dependent territories became British overseas territories from 26 February 2002, British Overseas Territories Act 2002, s 1.

17. Acquisition by registration: minors

(1) If while a person is a minor an application is made for his registration as a [British overseas territories] citizen the Secretary of State may, if he thinks fit, cause him to be registered as such a citizen.

(2) A person born outside the [British overseas territories] shall be entitled, on an application for his registration as a [British overseas territories] citizen made within the period of twelve months from the date of the birth, to be registered as such a citizen if the requirements specified in subsection (3) or, in the case of a person born stateless, the requirements specified in paragraphs (a) and (b) of that subsection, are fulfilled in the case of either that person's father or his mother ('the parent in question').

(3) The requirements referred to in subsection (2) are—
   (a) that the parent in question was a [British overseas territories] citizen by descent at the time of the birth; and
   (b) that the father or mother of the parent in question—
      (i) was a [British overseas territories] citizen otherwise than by descent at the time of the birth of the parent in question; or
      (ii) became a [British overseas territories] citizen otherwise than by descent

at commencement, or would have become such a citizen otherwise than by descent at commencement but for his or her death; and

(c) that, as regards some period of three years ending with a date not later than the date of the birth—

(i) the parent in question was in a [British overseas territory] at the beginning of that period; and

(ii) the number of days on which the parent in question was absent from that territory in that period does not exceed 270.

(4) If in the special circumstances of any particular case the Secretary of State thinks fit, he may treat subsection (2) as if the reference to twelve months were a reference to six years.

(5) A person born outside the [British overseas territories] shall be entitled, on an application for his registration as a [British overseas territories citizen] made while he is a minor, to be registered as such a citizen if the following requirements are satisfied, namely—

(a) that at the time of that person's birth his father or mother was a [British overseas territories] citizen by descent; and

(b) subject to subsection (6), that that person and his father and mother were in one and the same [British overseas territory] (no matter which) at the beginning of the period of three years ending with the date of the application and that, in the case of each of them, the number of days on which the person in question was absent from the last-mentioned territory in that period does not exceed 270; and

(c) subject to subsection (6), that the consent of his father and mother to the registration has been signified in the prescribed manner.

(6) In the case of an application under subsection (5) for the registration of a person as a [British overseas territories] citizen—

(a) if his father or mother died, or their marriage [or civil partnership] was terminated, on or before the date of the application, or his father and mother were legally separated on that date, the references to his father and mother in paragraph (b) of that subsection shall be read either as references to his father or as references to his mother; [and]

(b) if his father or mother died on or before that date, the reference to his father and mother in paragraph (c) of that subsection shall be read as a reference to either of them; [. . .

(c) . . .]

Note: Last word in square brackets in sub-s (6)(a) inserted, and words deleted from sub-ss (6)(b) and (c) by Nationality, Immigration and Asylum Act 2002, s 9 from 7 November 2002, in relation to children born on or after a date to be appointed. British dependent territories became British overseas territories from 26 February 2002, British Overseas Territories Act 2002, s 1. Words in first square brackets in sub-s (6)(a) inserted by Sch 27 Civil Partnership Act 2004 from a date to be appointed.

18. Acquisition by naturalisation

(1) If, on an application for naturalisation as a [British overseas territories] citizen made by a person of full age and capacity, the Secretary of State is satisfied that the applicant fulfils the requirements of Schedule 1 for naturalisation as such a citizen under this subsection, he may, if he thinks fit, grant to him a certificate of naturalisation as such a citizen.

(2) If, on an application for naturalisation as a [British overseas territories] citizen made by a person of full age and capacity who on the date of the application is married to such a citizen [or is the civil partner of such a citizen] the Secretary of State is satisfied that the applicant fulfils the requirements of Schedule 1 for naturalisation as such a citizen under this subsection, he may, if he thinks fit, grant to him a certificate of naturalisation as such a citizen.

(3) Every application under this section shall specify the [British overseas territory] which is to be treated as the relevant territory for the purposes of that application; and, in relation to any such application, references in Schedule 1 to the relevant territory shall be construed accordingly.

Note: British dependent territories became British overseas territories from 26 February 2002, British Overseas Territories Act 2002, s 1. Words in square brackets in sub-s (2) inserted by Sch 27 Civil Partnership Act 2004 from a date to be appointed.

Acquisition after commencement: special cases

19. . . .

Note: Section 19 repealed by Sch 2 Nationality, Immigration and Asylum Act 2002 from a date to be appointed.

20. . . .

Note: Section 20 repealed by Sch 2 Nationality, Immigration and Asylum Act 2002 from a date to be appointed.

21. . . .

Note: Section 21 repealed by Sch 2 Nationality, Immigration and Asylum Act 2002 from a date to be appointed.

22. Right to registration replacing right to resume citizenship of UK and Colonies

(1) Subject to subsection (3), a person shall be entitled, on an application for his registration as a [British overseas territories] citizen, to be registered as such a

citizen if immediately before commencement he would (had he applied for it) have been entitled under section 1(1) of the British Nationality Act 1964 (resumption of citizenship) to be registered as a citizen of the United Kingdom and Colonies by virtue of having an appropriate qualifying connection with a [British overseas territory] or, [. . .,] by virtue of having been married before commencement to a person who has, or would if living have, such a connection.

(2) On an application for his registration as a [British overseas territories] citizen made by a person of full capacity who had before commencement ceased to be a citizen of the United Kingdom and Colonies as a result of a declaration of renunciation, the Secretary of State may, if he thinks fit, cause that person to be registered as a [British overseas territories] citizen if that person—

(a) has an appropriate qualifying connection with a [British overseas territory]; or

(b) [. . .] has been married to [or has been the civil partner of,] a person who has, or would if living have, such a connection.

(3) A person shall not be entitled to registration under subsection (1) on more than one occasion.

(4) For the purposes of this section a person shall be taken to have an appropriate qualifying connection with a [British overseas territory] if he, his father or his father's father—

(a) was born in that territory; or

(b) is or was a person naturalised in that territory; or

(c) was registered as a citizen of the United Kingdom and Colonies in that territory; or

(d) became a British subject by reason of the annexation of any territory included in that territory.

Note: The words deleted from sub-ss (1) and (2) cease to have effect with regard to applications made after 7 November 2002, or applications not determined before that date: Nationality, Immigration and Asylum Act 2002, s 5. British dependent territories became British overseas territories from 26 February 2002, British Overseas Territories Act 2002, s 1. Words in square brackets in sub-s (2)(b) inserted by Sch 27 Civil Partnership Act 2004 from a date to be appointed.

Acquisition at commencement

23. Citizens of UK and Colonies who are to become [British overseas territories] citizens at commencement

(1) A person shall at commencement become a [British overseas territories] citizen if—

(a) immediately before commencement he was a citizen of the United Kingdom and Colonies who had that citizenship by his birth, naturalisation or registration in a [British overseas territory]; or

(b) he was immediately before commencement a citizen of the United Kingdom and Colonies, and was born to a parent—
   (i) who at the time of the birth ('the material time') was a citizen of the United Kingdom and Colonies; and
   (ii) who either had that citizenship at the material time by his birth, naturalisation or registration in a [British overseas territory] or was himself born to a parent who at the time of that birth so had that citizenship; or

(c) being a woman, she was immediately before commencement a citizen of the United Kingdom and Colonies and either was then, or had at any time been, the wife of a man who under paragraph (a) or (b) becomes a [British overseas territories] citizen at commencement or would have done so but for his death.

(2) A person shall at commencement become a [British overseas territories] citizen if—

(a) immediately before commencement he was a citizen of the United Kingdom and Colonies by virtue of registration under section 7 of the 1948 Act (minor children) or section 1 of the British Nationality (No. 2) Act 1964 (stateless persons); and

(b) he was so registered otherwise than in a [British overseas territory]; and

(c) his father or mother (in the case of a person registered under the said section 7) or his mother (in the case of a person registered under the said section 1)—
   (i) was a citizen of the United Kingdom and Colonies at the time of the registration or would have been such a citizen at that time but for his or her death; and
   (ii) becomes a [British overseas territories] citizen at commencement or would have done so but for his or her death.

(3) A person who—

(a) immediately before commencement was a citizen of the United Kingdom and Colonies by virtue of having been registered under subsection (6) of section 12 of the 1948 Act (British subjects before commencement of 1948 Act becoming citizens of United Kingdom and Colonies) otherwise than in a [British overseas territory]; and

(b) was so registered on an application under that subsection based on the applicant's descent in the male line from a person ('the relevant person') possessing one of the qualifications specified in subsection (1) of that section (birth or naturalisation in the United Kingdom and Colonies, or acquisition of the status of British subject by reason of annexation of territory),

shall at commencement become a [British overseas territories] citizen if the relevant person—

(i) was born or naturalised in a [British overseas territory]; or
(ii) became a British subject by reason of the annexation of any territory included in a [British overseas territory].

(4) A person who—
(a) immediately before commencement was a citizen of the United Kingdom and Colonies by virtue of registration under section 1 of the British Nationality Act 1964 (resumption of citizenship); and
(b) was so registered otherwise than in a [British overseas territory]; and
(c) was so registered by virtue of having an appropriate qualifying connection with a [British overseas territory] or, if a woman, by virtue of having been married to a person who at the time of the registration had or would, if then living, have had such a connection,

shall at commencement become a [British overseas territories] citizen.

(5) For the purposes of subsection (4) a person shall be taken to have an appropriate qualifying connection with a [British overseas territory] if he, his father or his father's father—
(a) was born in a [British overseas territory]; or
(b) is or was a person naturalised in a [British overseas territory]; or
(c) was registered as a citizen of the United Kingdom and Colonies in a [British overseas territory]; or
(d) became a British subject by reason of the annexation of any territory included in a [British overseas territory].

(6) For the purposes of subsection (1)(b) references to citizenship of the United Kingdom and Colonies shall, in relation to a time before the year 1949, be construed as references to British nationality.

Note: British dependent territories became British overseas territories from 26 February 2002, British Overseas Territories Act 2002, s 1.

Renunciation and resumption

24. Renunciation and resumption

The provisions of sections 12 and 13 shall apply in relation to [British overseas territories] citizens and [British Overseas Territories] citizenship as they apply in relation to British citizens and British citizenship.

Note: British dependent territories became British overseas territories from 26 February 2002, British Overseas Territories Act 2002, s 1.

Supplementary

25. Meaning of [British overseas territories] citizen 'by descent'

(1) For the purposes of this Act a [British overseas territories] citizen is such a citizen 'by descent' if and only if—

(a) he is a person born outside the [British overseas territories] after commencement who is a [British overseas territories] citizen by virtue of section 16(1)(a) only or by virtue of registration under section 17(2) or 21; or

(b) subject to subsection (2), he is a person born outside the [British overseas territories] before commencement who became a [British overseas territories] citizen at commencement and immediately before commencement—

(i) was a citizen of the United Kingdom and Colonies by virtue of section 5 of the 1948 Act (citizenship by descent); or

(ii) was a person who, under any provision of the British Nationality Acts 1948 to 1965, was deemed for the purposes of the proviso to section 5(1) of the 1948 Act to be a citizen of the United Kingdom and Colonies by descent only, or would have been so deemed if male; or

(c) he is a [British overseas territories] citizen by virtue of registration under section 17(1) and either—

(i) his father or mother was a [British overseas territories] citizen at the time of the birth; or

(ii) his father or mother was a citizen of the United Kingdom and Colonies at that time and became a [British overseas territories] citizen at commencement, or would have done so but for his or her death; or

(d) subject to subsection (2), he is a person born outside the [British overseas territories] before commencement who became a [British overseas territories] citizen at commencement under section 23(1)(b) only; or

(e) subject to subsection (2), being a woman, she became a [British overseas territories] citizen at commencement under section 23(1)(c) only, and did so only by virtue of having been, immediately before commencement or earlier, the wife of a man who immediately after commencement was, or would but for his death have been, a [British overseas territories] citizen by descent by virtue of paragraph (b) or (d) of this subsection; or

(f) subject to subsection (2), being a woman born outside the [British overseas territories] before commencement, she is a [British overseas territories] citizen as a result of her registration as such a citizen under section 20 by virtue of being or having been married to a man who at commencement became such a citizen by descent or would have done so but for his having died or ceased to be a citizen of the United Kingdom and Colonies as a result of a declaration of renunciation; or

(g) he is a [British overseas territories] citizen by virtue of registration under section 22 who, having before commencement ceased to be a citizen of the

United Kingdom and Colonies as a result of a declaration of renunciation, would, if he had not so ceased, have at commencement become a [British overseas territories] citizen by descent by virtue of paragraph (b), (d) or (e);

(h) he is a [British overseas territories] citizen by virtue of registration under section 13 (as applied by section 24) who, immediately before he ceased to be a [British overseas territories] citizen as a result of a declaration of renunciation, was such a citizen by descent; or

(i) he is a person born in the United Kingdom after commencement who is a [British overseas territories] citizen by virtue of paragraph 1 of Schedule 2.

(2) A person born outside the [British overseas territories] before commencement is not a [British overseas territories] citizen 'by descent' by virtue of subsection (1)(b), (d), (e) or (f) if his father was at the time of his birth serving outside the [British overseas territories] in service of a description mentioned in subsection (3), his recruitment for the service in question having taken place in a [British overseas territory].

(3) The descriptions of service referred to in subsection (2) are—

(a) Crown service under the government of a [British overseas territory]; and

(b) service of any description at any time designated under section 16(3).

Note: British dependent territories became British overseas territories from 26 February 2002, British Overseas Territories Act 2002, s 1.

Part III
British Overseas Citizenship

26. Citizens of UK and Colonies who are to become British Overseas citizens at commencement

Any person who was a citizen of the United Kingdom and Colonies immediately before commencement and who does not at commencement become either a British citizen or a [British overseas territories] citizen shall at commencement become a British Overseas citizen.

Note: British dependent territories became British overseas territories from 26 February 2002, British Overseas Territories Act 2002, s 1.

27. Registration of minors

(1) If while a person is a minor an application is made for his registration as a British Overseas citizen, the Secretary of State may, if he thinks fit, cause him to be registered as such a citizen.

(2) . . .

Note: Section 27(2) repealed by Sch 2 Nationality, Immigration and Asylum Act 2002 from a date to be appointed.

28. . . .

Note: Section 28 repealed by Sch 2 Nationality, Immigration and Asylum Act 2002 from a date to be appointed.

29. Renunciation

The provisions of section 12 shall apply in relation to British Overseas citizens and British Overseas citizenship as they apply in relation to British citizens and British citizenship.

Part IV

British Subjects

30. Continuance as British subjects of existing British subjects of certain descriptions

A person who immediately before commencement was—

(a) a British subject without citizenship by virtue of section 13 or 16 of the 1948 Act; or

(b) a British subject by virtue of section 1 of the British Nationality Act 1965 (registration of alien women who have been married to British subjects of certain descriptions),

shall as from commencement be a British subject by virtue of this section.

31. Continuance as British subjects of certain former citizens of Eire

(1) A person is within this subsection if immediately before 1st January 1949 he was both a citizen of Eire and a British subject.

(2) A person within subsections (1) who immediately before commencement was a British subject by virtue of section 2 of the 1948 Act (continuance of certain citizens of Eire as British subjects) shall as from commencement be a British subject by virtue of this subsection.

(3) If at any time after commencement a citizen of the Republic of Ireland who is within subsection (1) but is not a British subject by virtue of subsection (2) gives notice in writing to the Secretary of State claiming to remain a British subject on either or both of the following grounds, namely—

- (a) that he is or has been in Crown Service under the government of the United Kingdom; and

(b) that he has associations by way of descent, residence or otherwise with the United Kingdom or with any [British overseas territory],

he shall as from that time be a British subject by virtue of this subsection.

(4) A person who is a British subject by virtue of subsection (2) or (3) shall be deemed to have remained a British subject from 1st January 1949 to the time when (whether already a British subject by virtue of the said section 2 or not) he became a British subject by virtue of that subsection.

Note: British dependent territories became British overseas territories from 26 February 2002, British Overseas Territories Act 2002, s 1.

32. Registration of minors

If while a person is a minor an application is made for his registration as a British subject, the Secretary of State may, if he thinks fit, cause him to be registered as a British subject.

33. . . .

Note: Section 33 repealed by Sch 2 Nationality, Immigration and Asylum Act 2002 from a date to be appointed.

34. Renunciation

The provisions of section 12 shall apply in relation to British subjects and the status of a British subject as they apply in relation to British citizens and British citizenship.

35. Circumstances in which British subjects are to lose that status

A person who under this Act is a British subject otherwise than by virtue of section 31 shall cease to be such a subject if, in whatever circumstances and whether under this Act or otherwise, he acquires any other citizenship or nationality whatever.

Part V

Miscellaneous and Supplementary

36. Provisions for reducing statelessness

The provisions of Schedule 2 shall have effect for the purpose of reducing statelessness.

37. Commonwealth citizenship

(1) Every person who—
   (a) under [the British Nationality Acts 1981 and 1983] [or the British Overseas Territories Act 2002] is a British citizen, a [British overseas territories] citizen, [a British National (Overseas)] a British Overseas citizen or a British subject; or
   (b) under any enactment for the time being in force in any country mentioned in Schedule 3 is a citizen of that country,

shall have the status of a Commonwealth citizen.

(2) Her Majesty may by Order in Council amend Schedule 3 by the alteration of any entry, the removal of any entry, or the insertion of any additional entry.

(3) Any Order in Council made under this section shall be subject to annulment in pursuance of a resolution of either House of Parliament.

(4) After commencement no person shall have the status of a Commonwealth citizen or the status of a British subject otherwise than under this Act.

Note: Words in first square brackets in sub-s (1) substituted by British Nationality (Falkland Islands) Act 1983. Words in second square brackets inserted by Sch 1 British Overseas Territories Act 2002 from 21 May 2002 (SI 2002/1252). Words in 4th square brackets in sub-s (1) inserted by SI 1986/948. British dependent territories became British overseas territories from 26 February 2002, British Overseas Territories Act 2002, s 1.

38. British protected persons

(1) Her Majesty may by Order in Council made in relation to any territory which was at any time before commencement—
   (a) a protectorate or protected state for the purposes of the 1948 Act; or
   (b) a United Kingdom trust territory within the meaning of that Act,

declare to be British protected persons for the purposes of this Act any class of persons who are connected with that territory and are not citizens of any country mentioned in Schedule 3 which consists of or includes that territory.

(2) Any Order in Council made under this section shall be subject to annulment in pursuance of a resolution of either House of Parliament.

39. Amendment of Immigration Act 1971

(1) . . .

(2) . . .

(3) . . .

(4) . . .

(5) . . .

(6) . . .

(7) . . .

(8) A certificate of patriality issued under the Immigration Act 1971 and in force immediately before commencement shall have effect after commencement as if it were a certificate of entitlement issued under that Act [as in force after commencement] unless at commencement the holder ceases to have the right of abode in the United Kingdom.

Note: Section 39(1), (2), (4), (6) amend Immigration Act 1971. Section 39(3), (5) repealed, and words in square brackets in sub-s (8) substituted by Immigration Act 1988, s 3. Section 39(7) amended Mental Health Act 1959, Mental Health (Scotland) Act 1960.

[40. Deprivation of citizenship

(1) In this section a reference to a person's 'citizenship status' is a reference to his status as—
  (a) a British citizen,
  (b) a British overseas territories citizen,
  (c) a British Overseas citizen,
  (d) a British National (Overseas),
  (e) a British protected person, or
  (f) a British subject.

[(2) The Secretary of State may by order deprive a person of a citizenship status if the Secretary of State is satisfied that deprivation is conducive to the public good.]

(3) The Secretary of State may by order deprive a person of a citizenship status which results from his registration or naturalisation if the Secretary of State is satisfied that the registration or naturalisation was obtained by means of—
  (a) fraud,
  (b) false representation, or
  (c) concealment of a material fact.

(4) The Secretary of State may not make an order under subsection (2) if he is satisfied that the order would make a person stateless.

(5) Before making an order under this section in respect of a person the Secretary of State must give the person written notice specifying—
  (a) that the Secretary of State has decided to make an order,
  (b) the reasons for the order, and
  (c) the person's right of appeal under section 40A(1) or under section 2B of the Special Immigration Appeals Commission Act 1997 (c. 68).

(6) Where a person acquired a citizenship status by the operation of a law which applied to him because of his registration or naturalisation under an enactment

having effect before commencement, the Secretary of State may by order deprive the person of the citizenship status if the Secretary of State is satisfied that the registration or naturalisation was obtained by means of—

(a) fraud,

(b) false representation, or

(c) concealment of a material fact.

Note: Section 40 substituted by Nationality, Immigration and Asylum Act 2002, s 4 from 1 April 2003 (SI 2003/754). Subsection (2) substituted by Immigration, Asylum and Nationality Act 2006, s 56 from 16 June 2006 (SI 2006/1498).

40A. Deprivation of citizenship: appeal

(1) A person who is given notice under section 40(5) of a decision to make an order in respect of him under section 40 may appeal against the decision to [the Asylum and Immigration Tribunal]

(2) Subsection (1) shall not apply to a decision if the Secretary of State certifies that it was taken wholly or partly in reliance on information which in his opinion should not be made public—

(a) in the interests of national security,

(b) in the interests of the relationship between the United Kingdom and another country, or

(c) otherwise in the public interest.

[(3) The following provisions of the Nationality, Immigration and Asylum Act 2002 (c. 41) shall apply in relation to an appeal under this section as they apply in relation to an appeal under section 82 [,83 or 83A] of that Act—

(a) section 87 (successful appeal: direction) (for which purpose a direction may, in particular, provide for an order under section 40 above to be treated as having had no effect),

(b) sections 103A to 103E (review and appeal),

(c) section 106 (rules),

(d) section 107 (practice directions).] [, and

(e) section 108 (forged document: proceedings in private).]

(6) . . .

(7) . . .

(8) . . .

Note: Section 40A inserted by Nationality, Immigration and Asylum Act 2002, s 4 from 1 April 2003 (SI 2003/754). Words in square brackets substituted by and sub-ss (6)–(8) omitted by Sch 2 Asylum and Immigration Act 2004 from a date to be appointed. Words in square brackets in sub-s (3) and sub-s (3)(e) inserted by Immigration, Asylum and Nationality Act 2006, s 56 from 16 June 2006 (SI 2006/1498).

41. Regulations and Orders in Council

(1) The Secretary of State may by regulations make provision generally for carrying into effect the purposes of this Act, and in particular provision—

(a) for prescribing anything which under this Act is to be prescribed;

(b) for prescribing the manner in which, and the persons to and by whom, applications for registration or naturalisation under any provision of this Act may or must be made;

[(ba) for determining whether a person has sufficient knowledge of a language for the purpose of an application for naturalisation;

(bb) for determining whether a person has sufficient knowledge about life in the United Kingdom for the purpose of an application for naturalisation;]

(c) for the registration of anything required or authorised by or under this Act to be registered;

[(d) for the time within which an obligation to make a citizenship oath and pledge at a citizenship ceremony must be satisfied;

(da) for the time within which an obligation to make a citizenship oath or pledge must be satisfied;

(db) for the content and conduct of a citizenship ceremony;

(dc) for the administration and making of a citizenship oath or pledge;

(dd) for the registration and certification of the making of a citizenship oath or pledge;

(de) for the completion and grant of a certificate of registration or naturalisation;]

(e) for the giving of any notice required or authorised to be given to any person under this Act;

(f) for the cancellation of the registration of, and the cancellation and amendment of certificates of naturalisation relating to, persons deprived of citizenship [or of the status of a British National (overseas)] under this Act, and for requiring such certificates to be delivered up for those purposes;

(g) for the births and deaths of persons of any class or description born or dying in a country mentioned in Schedule 3 to be registered there by the High Commissioner for Her Majesty's government in the United Kingdom or by members of his official staff;

(h) for the births and deaths of persons of any class or description born or dying in a foreign country to be registered there by consular officers or other officers in the service of Her Majesty's government in the United Kingdom;

(i) for enabling the births and deaths of British citizens, [British overseas territories citizens], [British Nationals (Overseas)] British Overseas citizens, British subjects and British protected persons born or dying in any country in which Her Majesty's government in the United Kingdom has for the time being no diplomatic or consular representatives to be registered—

(i) by persons serving in the diplomatic, consular or other foreign service of any country which, by arrangement with Her Majesty's government in the United Kingdom, has undertaken to represent that government's interest in that country, or

(ii) by a person authorised in that behalf by the Secretary of State.

[(j) as to the consequences of failure to comply with provision made under any of paragraphs (a) to (i).]

[(**1A**) Regulations under subsection (1)(ba) or (bb) may, in particular—

(a) make provision by reference to possession of a specified qualification;

(b) make provision by reference to possession of a qualification of a specified kind;

(c) make provision by reference to attendance on a specified course;

(d) make provision by reference to attendance on a course of a specified kind;

(e) make provision by reference to a specified level of achievement;

(f) enable a person designated by the Secretary of State to determine sufficiency of knowledge in specified circumstances;

(g) enable the Secretary of State to accept a qualification of a specified kind as evidence of sufficient knowledge of a language].

(2) . . .

(3) Regulations under subsection (1) . . . may make different provision for different circumstances; and—

(a) regulations under subsection (1) may provide for the extension of any time-limit for the [making of oaths and pledges of citizenship]; and

. . .

[(**3A**) Regulations under subsection (1)(d) to (de) may, in particular—

(a) enable the Secretary of State to designate or authorise a person to exercise a function (which may include a discretion) in connection with a citizenship ceremony or a citizenship oath or pledge;

(b) require, or enable the Secretary of State to require, a local authority to provide specified facilities and to make specified arrangements in connection with citizenship ceremonies;

(c) impose, or enable the Secretary of State to impose, a function (which may include a discretion) on a local authority or on a registrar.

[(**3B**) In subsection (3A)—

'local authority' means—

(a) in relation to England and Wales, a county council, a county borough council, a metropolitan district council, a London Borough Council and the Common Council of the City of London, and

(b) in relation to Scotland, a council constituted under section 2 of the Local Government etc. (Scotland) Act 1994 (c. 39), and

'registrar' means—

(a) in relation to England and Wales, a superintendent registrar of births, deaths and marriages (or, in accordance with section 8 of the Registration Service Act 1953 (c. 37), a deputy superintendent registrar), and

(b) in relation to Scotland, a district registrar within the meaning of section 7(12) of the Registration of Births, Deaths and Marriages (Scotland) Act 1965 (c. 49).]

(4) Her Majesty may by Order in Council provide for any Act or Northern Ireland legislation to which this subsection applies to apply, with such adaptations and modifications as appear to Her necessary, to births and deaths registered—

(a) in accordance with regulations made in pursuance of subsection (1)(g) to (i) of this section or subsection (1)(f) and (g) of section 29 of the 1948 Act; or

(b) at a consulate of Her Majesty in accordance with regulations made under the British Nationality and Status of Aliens Acts 1914 to 1943 or in accordance with instructions of the Secretary of State; or

(c) by a High Commissioner for Her Majesty's government in the United Kingdom or members of his official staff in accordance with instructions of the Secretary of State; and an Order in Council under this subsection may exclude, in relation to births and deaths so registered, any of the provisions of section 45.

(5) Subsection (4) applies to—

(a) the Births and Deaths Registration Act 1953, the Registration Service Act 1953 and the Registration of Births, Deaths and Marriages (Scotland) Act 1965; and

(b) so much of any Northern Ireland legislation for the time being in force (whether passed or made before or after commencement) as relates to the registration of births and deaths.

(6) The power to make regulations under subsection (1) or (2) shall be exercisable by statutory instrument.

(7) Any regulations or Order in Council made under this section shall be subject to annulment in pursuance of a resolution of either House of Parliament.

Note: Words in square brackets in sub-ss (1)(f), (1)(i), (2)(a) and (2)(b) inserted by SI 1986/948. Subsections (1)(ba), (bb) inserted by Nationality, Immigration and Asylum Act 2002, s 1 from 6 July 2004 (SI 2004/1707) and s 1A inserted by s 1 of that Act from 1 November 2005 (SI 2005/2782). Section 41(1)(d) substituted by para 4, Sch 1 Nationality, Immigration and Asylum Act 2002 from 1 January 2004 (SI 2003/3156). Words in square brackets in sub-ss (2)(c) and (3)(a) substituted by para 5, Sch 1 of the Nationality, Immigration and Asylum Act 2002 from 1 January 2004 (SI 2003/3156). Subsections (3A) and (3B) inserted by para 7, Sch 1, Nationality, Immigration and

Asylum Act 2002 from 1 January 2004 (SI 2003/3156). British dependent territories became British overseas territories from 26 February 2002, British Overseas Territories Act 2002, s 1. Subsection (1)(j) inserted and sub-ss (2), (3)(b) and words in (3)(a) omitted by Sch 2 Immigration, Asylum and Nationality Act 2006 from a date to be appointed.

[42. Registration and naturalisation: citizenship ceremony, oath and pledge

(1) A person of full age shall not be registered under this Act as a British citizen unless he has made the relevant citizenship oath and pledge specified in Schedule 5 at a citizenship ceremony.

(2) A certificate of naturalisation as a British citizen shall not be granted under this Act to a person of full age unless he has made the relevant citizenship oath and pledge specified in Schedule 5 at a citizenship ceremony.

(3) A person of full age shall not be registered under this Act as a British overseas territories citizen unless he has made the relevant citizenship oath and pledge specified in Schedule 5.

(4) A certificate of naturalisation as a British overseas territories citizen shall not be granted under this Act to a person of full age unless he has made the relevant citizenship oath and pledge specified in Schedule 5.

(5) A person of full age shall not be registered under this Act as a British Overseas citizen or a British subject unless he has made the relevant citizenship oath specified in Schedule 5.

(6) Where the Secretary of State thinks it appropriate because of the special circumstances of a case he may—
  (a) disapply any of subsections (1) to (5), or
  (b) modify the effect of any of those subsections.

(7) Sections 5 and 6 of the Oaths Act 1978 (c. 19) (affirmation) apply to a citizenship oath; and a reference in this Act to a citizenship oath includes a reference to a citizenship affirmation.]

Note: Section 42 substituted by para 1, Sch 1 Nationality, Immigration and Asylum Act 2002 from a date to be appointed. Section 42A inserted by para 1, Sch 1 Nationality, Immigration and Asylum Act 2002 from a date to be appointed. Ceases to have effect from a date to be appointed, Sch 3 Immigration, Asylum and Nationality Act 2006.

[42B. Registration and naturalisation: timing

(1) A person who is registered under this Act as a citizen of any description or as a British subject shall be treated as having become a citizen or subject—
  (a) immediately on making the required citizenship oath and pledge in accordance with section 42, or
  (b) where the requirement for an oath and pledge is disapplied, immediately on registration.

(2) A person granted a certificate of naturalisation under this Act as a citizen of any description shall be treated as having become a citizen—
   (a) immediately on making the required citizenship oath and pledge in accordance with section 42, or
   (b) where the requirement for an oath and pledge is disapplied, immediately on the grant of the certificate.

(3) In the application of subsection (1) to registration as a British Overseas citizen or as a British subject the reference to the citizenship oath and pledge shall be taken as a reference to the citizenship oath.]

Note: Section 42B inserted by para 1, Sch 1 Nationality, Immigration and Asylum Act 2002 from a date to be appointed.

43. Exercise of functions of Secretary of State by Governors and others

(1) Subject to subsection (3), the Secretary of State may in the case of any of his functions under this Act with respect to any of the matters mentioned in subsection (2), make arrangements for that function to be exercised—
   (a) in any of the Islands, by the Lieutenant-Governor in cases concerning British citizens or British citizenship;
   (b) in any [British overseas territory] [. . .], by the Governor in cases concerning [British overseas territories] citizens or [British overseas territories] citizenship [and in cases concerning British National (Overseas) or the status of a British National (Overseas)];

(2) The said matters are—
   (a) registration and naturalisation; and
   (b) renunciation, resumption and deprivation of British citizenship or [British overseas territories] citizenship.
   [(c) renunciation and deprivation of the status of a British National (Overseas).]

(3) Nothing in this section applies in the case of any power to make regulations or rules conferred on the Secretary of State by this Act.

(4) Arrangements under subsection (1) may provide for any such function as is there mentioned to be exercisable only with the approval of the Secretary of State.

Note: Words in fifth square brackets in sub-s (1)(b) and sub-s (2)(c) added by SI 1986/948. British dependent territories became British overseas territories from 26 February 2002, British Overseas Territories Act 2002, s 1.

44. Decisions involving exercise of discretion

(1) Any discretion vested by or under this Act in the Secretary of State, a Governor or a Lieutenant-Governor shall be exercised without regard to the race, colour or religion of any person who may be affected by its exercise.

(2) . . .

(3) . . .

Note: Subsections (2) and (3) cease to have effect from 7 November 2002, Nationality, Immigration and Asylum Act 2002, s 7.

[44A. Waiver of requirement for full capacity

Where a provision of this Act requires an applicant to be of full capacity, the Secretary of State may waive the requirement in respect of a specified applicant if he thinks it in the applicant's best interests.]

Note: Section 44A inserted by Immigration, Asylum and Nationality Act 2006, s 49 from a date to be appointed.

45. Evidence

(1) Every document purporting to be a notice, certificate, order or declaration, or an entry in a register, or a subscription of an oath of allegiance, given, granted or made under this Act or any of the former nationality Acts shall be received in evidence and shall, unless the contrary is proved, be deemed to have been given, granted or made by or on behalf of the person by whom or on whose behalf it purports to have been given, granted or made.

(2) Prima facie evidence of any such document may be given by the production of a document purporting to be certified as a true copy of it by such person and in such manner as may be prescribed.

(3) Any entry in a register made under this Act or any of the former nationality Acts shall be received as evidence (and in Scotland as sufficient evidence) of the matters stated in the entry.

(4) A certificate given by or on behalf of the Secretary of State that a person was at any time in Crown service under the government of the United Kingdom or that a person's recruitment for such service took place in the United Kingdom shall, for the purposes of this Act, be conclusive evidence of that fact.

46. Offences and proceedings

(1) Any person who for the purpose of procuring anything to be done or not to be done under this Act—
   (a) makes any statement which he knows to be false in a material particular; or
   (b) recklessly makes any statement which is false in a material particular, shall be liable on summary conviction in the United Kingdom to imprisonment for a term not exceeding three months or to a fine not exceeding [level 5 on the standard scale], or both.

(2) Any person who without reasonable excuse fails to comply with any requirement imposed on him by regulations made under this Act with respect to the delivering up of certificates of naturalisation shall be liable on summary conviction in the United Kingdom to a fine not exceeding [level 4 on the standard scale].

(3) In the case of an offence under subsection (1)—

(a) any information relating to the offence may in England and Wales be tried by a magistrates' court if it is laid within six months after the commission of the offence, or if it is laid within three years after the commission of the offence and not more than two months after the date certified by a chief officer of police to be the date on which evidence sufficient to justify proceedings came to the notice of an officer of his police force; and

(b) summary proceedings for the offence may in Scotland be commenced within six months after the commission of the offence, or within three years after the commission of the offence and not more than two months after the date on which evidence sufficient in the opinion of the Lord Advocate to justify proceedings came to his knowledge; and

(c) a complaint charging the commission of the offence may in Northern Ireland be heard and determined by a magistrates' court if it is made within six months after the commission of the offence, or if it is made within three years after the commission of the offence and not more than two months after the date certified by an officer of police not below the rank of assistant chief constable to be the date on which evidence sufficient to justify the proceedings came to the notice of the police in Northern Ireland.

(4) For the purposes of subsection (3)(b) proceedings shall be deemed to be commenced on the date on which a warrant to apprehend or to cite the accused is granted, if such warrant is executed without undue delay; and a certificate of the Lord Advocate as to the date on which such evidence as is mentioned in subsection (3)(b) came to his knowledge shall be conclusive evidence.

(5) For the purposes of the trial of a person for an offence under subsection (1) or (2), the offence shall be deemed to have been committed either at the place at which it actually was committed or at any place at which he may be.

(6) In their application to the Bailiwick of Jersey subsections (1) and (2) shall have effect with the omission of the words 'on summary conviction'.

Note: Words in square brackets in s 46(1), (2), substituted by virtue of Criminal Justice Act 1982, s 46.

47. . . .

Note: Section 47 ceases to have effect in relation to a child born on or after a date to be appointed, from 7 November 2002, Nationality, Immigration and Asylum Act 2002, s 9.

48. Posthumous children

Any reference in this Act to the status of description of the father or mother of a person at the time of that person's birth shall, in relation to a person born after the death of his father or mother, be construed as a reference to the status or description of the parent in question at the time of that parent's death; and where that death occurred before, and the birth occurs after, commencement, the status or description which would have been applicable to the father or mother had he or she died after commencement shall be deemed to be the status or description applicable to him or her at the time of his or her death.

49. Registration and naturalisation under British Nationality Acts 1948 to 1965

. . .

Note: Section 49 repealed by s 52(8) and Sch 9 of this Act.

50. Interpretation

(1) In this Act, unless the context otherwise requires—

'the 1948 Act' means the British Nationality Act 1948;

'alien' means a person who is neither a Commonwealth citizen nor a British protected person nor a citizen of the Republic of Ireland;

['appointed day' means the day appointed by the Secretary of State under section 8 of the British Overseas Territories Act 2002 for the commencement of Schedule 1 to that Act;]

'association' means an unincorporated body of persons;

['British National (Overseas)' means a person who is a British National (Overseas) under the Hong Kong (British Nationality) Order 1986, and 'status of a British National (Overseas)' shall be construed accordingly;

'British Overseas citizen' includes a person who is a British Overseas citizen under the Hong Kong (British Nationality) Order 1986.]

'British protected person' means a person who is a member of any class of persons declared to be British protected persons by an Order in Council for the time being in force under section 38 or is a British protected person by virtue of the Solomon Islands Act 1978;

'commencement', without more, means the commencement of this Act;

'Commonwealth citizen' means a person who has the status of a Commonwealth citizen under this Act;

'company' means a body corporate;

'Crown service' means the service of the Crown, whether within Her Majesty's dominions or elsewhere;

'Crown service under the government of the United Kingdom' means Crown service under Her Majesty's government in the United Kingdom or under Her Majesty's government in Northern Ireland;

[. . .]

'enactment' includes an enactment comprised in Northern Ireland legislation;

'foreign country' means a country other than the United Kingdom, a [British overseas territory], a country mentioned in Schedule 3 and the Republic of Ireland;

'the former nationality Acts' means—

(a) the British Nationality Acts 1948 to 1965;

(b) the British Nationality and Status of Aliens Acts 1914 to 1943; and

(c) any Act repealed by the said Acts of 1914 to 1943 or by the Naturalization Act 1870;

'Governor', in relation to a [British overseas territory], includes the officer for the time being administering the government of that territory;

'High Commissioner' includes an acting High Commissioner;

'immigration laws'—

(a) in relation to the United Kingdom, means the Immigration Act 1971 and any law for purposes similar to that Act which is for the time being or has at any time been in force in any part of the United Kingdom;

(b) in relation to a [British overseas territory], means any law for purposes similar to the Immigration Act 1971 which is for the time being or has at any time been in force in that territory;

'the Islands' means the Channel Islands and the Isle of Man;

'minor' means a person who has not attained the age of eighteen years;

'prescribed' means prescribed by regulations made under section 41;

['qualifying territory' means a British overseas territory other than the Sovereign Base Areas of Akrotiri and Dhekelia;]

'settled' shall be construed in accordance with subsections (2) to (4);

'ship' includes a hovercraft;

'statutory provision' means any enactment or any provision contained in—

(a) subordinate legislation (as defined in section 21(1) of the Interpretation Act 1978); or

(b) any instrument of a legislative character made under any Northern Ireland legislation;

'the United Kingdom' means Great Britain, Northern Ireland and the Islands, taken together;

'United Kingdom consulate' means the office of a consular officer of Her Majesty's government in the United Kingdom where a register of births is kept or, where there is no such office, such office as may be prescribed.

(2) Subject to subsection (3), references in this Act to a person being settled in the United Kingdom or in a [British overseas territory] are references to his being ordinarily resident in the United Kingdom or, as the case may be, in that

territory without being subject under the immigration laws to any restriction on the period for which he may remain.

(3) Subject to subsection (4), a person is not to be regarded for the purposes of this Act—

(a) as having been settled in the United Kingdom at any time when he was entitled to an exception under section 8(3) or (4)(b) or (c) of the Immigration Act 1971 or, unless the order under section 8(2) of that Act conferring the exemption in question provides otherwise, to an exemption under the said section 8(2), or to any corresponding exemption under the former immigration laws; or

(b) as having been settled in a [British overseas territory] at any time when he was under the immigration laws entitled to any exemption corresponding to any such exemption as is mentioned in paragraph (a) (that paragraph being for the purposes of this paragraph read as if the words from 'unless' to 'otherwise' were omitted).

(4) A person to whom a child is born in the United Kingdom after commencement is to be regarded for the purposes of section 1(1) as being settled in the United Kingdom at the time of the birth if—

(a) he would fall to be so regarded but for his being at that time entitled to an exemption under section 8(3) of the Immigration Act 1971; and

(b) immediately before he became entitled to that exemption he was settled in the United Kingdom; and

(c) he was ordinarily resident in the United Kingdom from the time when he became entitled to that exemption to the time of the birth; but this subsection shall not apply if at the time of the birth the child's father or mother is a person on whom any immunity from jurisdiction is conferred by or under the Diplomatic Privileges Act 1964.

(5) It is hereby declared that a person is not to be treated for the purpose of any provision of this Act as ordinarily resident in the United Kingdom or in a [British overseas territory] at a time when he is in the United Kingdom or, as the case may be, in that territory in breach of the immigration laws.

(6) For the purposes of this Act—

(a) a person shall be taken to have been naturalised in the United Kingdom if, but only if, he is—

(i) a person to whom a certificate of naturalisation was granted under any of the former nationality Acts by the Secretary of State or, in any of the Islands, by the Lieutenant-Governor; or

(ii) a person who by virtue of section 27(2) of the British Nationality and Status of Aliens Act 1914 was deemed to be a person to whom a certificate of naturalisation was granted, if the certificate of naturalisation in which his name was included was granted by the Secretary of State; or

(iii) a person who by virtue of section 10(5) of the Naturalization Act 1870 was deemed to be a naturalised British subject by reason of his residence with his father or mother;

(b) a person shall be taken to have been naturalised in a [British overseas territory] if, but only if, he is—

(i) a person to whom a certificate of naturalisation was granted under any of the former nationality Acts by the Governor of that territory or by a person for the time being specified in a direction given in relation to that territory under paragraph 4 of Schedule 3 to the West Indies Act 1967 or for the time being holding an office so specified; or

(ii) a person who by virtue of the said section 27(2) was deemed to be a person to whom a certificate of naturalisation was granted, if the certificate of naturalisation in which his name was included was granted by the Governor of that territory; or

(iii) a person who by the law in force in that territory enjoyed the privileges of naturalisation within that territory only;

and references in this Act to naturalisation in the United Kingdom or in a [British overseas territory] shall be construed accordingly.

(7) For the purposes of this Act a person born outside the United Kingdom aboard a ship or aircraft—

(a) shall be deemed to have been born in the United Kingdom if—

(i) at the time of the birth his father or mother was a British citizen; or

(ii) he would, but for this subsection, have been born stateless,

and (in either case) at the time of the birth the ship or aircraft was registered in the United Kingdom or was an unregistered ship or aircraft of the government of the United Kingdom; but

(b) subject to paragraph (a), is to be regarded as born outside the United Kingdom, whoever was the owner of the ship or aircraft at that time, and irrespective of whether or where it was then registered.

[(7A) For the purposes of this Act a person born outside a qualifying territory aboard a ship or aircraft—

(a) shall be deemed to have been born in that territory if—

(i) at the time of the birth his father or mother was a British citizen or a British overseas territories citizen; or

(ii) he would, but for this subsection, have been born stateless,

and (in either case) at the time of the birth the ship or aircraft was registered in that territory or was an unregistered ship or aircraft of the government of that territory; but

(b) subject to paragraph (a), is to be regarded as born outside that territory, whoever was the owner of the ship or aircraft at the time, and irrespective of whether or where it was then registered.

(**7B**) For the purposes of this Act a person born outside a British overseas territory, other than a qualifying territory, aboard a ship or aircraft—

(a) shall be deemed to have been born in that territory if—

(i) at the time of the birth his father or mother was a British overseas territories citizen; or

(ii) he would, but for this subsection, have been born stateless,

and (in either case) at the time of the birth the ship or aircraft was registered in that territory or was an unregistered ship or aircraft of the government of that territory; but

(b) subject to paragraph (a), is to be regarded as born outside that territory, whoever was the owner of the ship or aircraft at the time, and irrespective of whether or where it was then registered.]

(**8**) For the purposes of this Act an application under any provision thereof shall be taken to have been made at the time of its receipt by a person authorised to receive it on behalf of the person to whom it is made; and references in this Act to the date of such an application are references to the date of its receipt by a person so authorised.

[(**9**) For the purposes of this Act a child's mother is the woman who gives birth to the child.

(**9A**) For the purposes of this Act a child's father is—

(a) the husband, at the time of the child's birth, of the woman who gives birth to the child, or

(b) where a person is treated as the father of the child under section 28 of the Human Fertilisation and Embryology Act 1990 (c. 37) (father), that person, or

(c) where neither paragraph (a) nor paragraph (b) applies, any person who satisfies prescribed requirements as to proof of paternity.

(**9B**) In subsection (9A)(c) 'prescribed' means prescribed by regulations of the Secretary of State; and the regulations—

(a) may confer a function (which may be a discretionary function) on the Secretary of State or another person,

(b) may make provision which applies generally or only in specified circumstances,

(c) may make different provision for different circumstances,

(d) must be made by statutory instrument, and

(e) shall be subject to annulment in pursuance of a resolution of either House of Parliament.

(**9C**) The expressions 'parent', 'child' and 'descended' shall be construed in accordance with subsections (9) and (9A).]

(**10**) For the purposes of this Act—

(a) a period 'from' or 'to' a specified date includes that date; and

(b) any reference to a day on which a person was absent from the United Kingdom or from a [British overseas territory] or from the [British overseas] territories is a reference to a day for the whole of which he was so absent.

(11) For the purposes of this Act—

(a) a person is of full age if he has attained the age of eighteen years, and of full capacity if he is not of unsound mind; and

(b) a person attains any particular age at the beginning of the relevant anniversary of the date of his birth.

(12) References in this Act to any country mentioned in Schedule 3 include references to the dependencies of that country.

(13) Her Majesty may be Order in Council subject to annulment in pursuance of a resolution of either House of Parliament amend Schedule 6 in any of the following circumstances, namely—

(a) where the name of any territory mentioned in it is altered; or

(b) where any territory mentioned in it is divided into two or more territories.

Note: Words in second square brackets in s 50(1) inserted by SI 1986/948. Other words in square brackets inserted in sub-s 1 and sub-ss (7A) and (7B) substituted by Sch 1 British Overseas Territories Act from 21 May 2002 (SI 2002/1252). Subsection (9) substituted by Nationality, Immigration and Asylum Act 2002, s 9, from 7 November 2002, s 9, with effect in relation to children born on or after 1 July 2006 (SI 2006/1498). British dependent territories became British overseas territories from 26 February 2002, British Overseas Territories Act 2002, s 1.

51. Meaning of certain expressions relating to nationality to other Acts and instruments

(1) Without prejudice to subsection (3)(c), in any enactment or instrument whatever passed or made before commencement 'British subject' and 'Commonwealth citizen' have the same meaning, that is—

(a) in relation to any time before commencement—

(i) a person who under the 1948 Act was at that time a citizen of the United Kingdom and Colonies or who, under any enactment then in force in a country mentioned in section 1(3) of that Act as then in force, was at that time a citizen of that country; and

(ii) any other person who had at that time the status of a British subject under that Act or any other enactment then in force;

(b) in relation to any time after commencement, a person who has the status of a Commonwealth citizen under this Act.

(2) In any enactment or instrument whatever passed or made after commencement—

'British subject' means a person who has the status of a British subject under this Act;

'Commonwealth citizen' means a person who has the status of a Commonwealth citizen under this Act.

(3) In any enactment or instrument whatever passed or made before commencement—

(a) 'citizen of the United Kingdom and Colonies'—

(i) in relation to any time before commencement, means a person who under the 1948 Act was at that time a citizen of the United Kingdom and Colonies;

(ii) in relation to any time after commencement, means a person who under [the British Nationality Acts 1981 and 1983] [or the British Overseas Territories Act 2002] is a British citizen, a [British overseas territories] citizen or a British Overseas citizen [or who under the Hong Kong (British Nationality) Order 1986 is a British National (Overseas)];

(b) any reference to ceasing to be a citizen of the United Kingdom and Colonies shall, in relation to any time after commencement, be construed as a reference to becoming a person who is neither a British citizen nor a [British overseas territories] citizen [nor a British National (Overseas)] nor a British Overseas citizen;

(c) any reference to a person who is a British subject (or a British subject without citizenship) by virtue of section 2, 13, or 16 of the 1948 Act or by virtue of, or of section 1 of, the British Nationality Act 1965 shall, in relation to any time after commencement, be construed as a reference to a person who under this Act is a British subject.

(4) In any statutory provision, whether passed or made before or after commencement, and in any other instrument whatever made after commencement 'alien', in relation to any time after commencement, means a person who is neither a Commonwealth citizen nor a British protected person nor a citizen of the Republic of Ireland.

(5) The preceding provisions of this section—

(a) shall not apply in cases where the context otherwise requires; and

(b) shall not apply to this Act or to any instrument made under this Act.

Note: Words in first square brackets in s 51(3) substituted by British Nationality (Falkland Islands) Act 1983. Words in second square brackets inserted by Sch 1 British Overseas Territories Act 2002 from 21 May 2002 (SI 2002/1252). Words in second square brackets in sub-s (3)(b) inserted by SI 1986/948. British dependent territories became British overseas territories from 26 February 2002, British Overseas Territories Act 2002, s 1.

52. Consequential amendments, transitional provisions, repeals and savings

(1) In any enactment or instrument whatever passed or made before commencement, for any reference to section 1(3) of the 1948 Act (list of countries whose

citizens are Commonwealth citizens under that Act) there shall be substituted a reference to Schedule 3 to this Act, unless the context makes that substitution inappropriate.

(2) Subject to subsection (3), Her Majesty may be Order in Council make such consequential modifications of—
(a) any enactment of the Parliament of the United Kingdom passed before commencement;
(b) any provision contained in any Northern Ireland legislation passed or made before commencement; or
(c) any instrument made before commencement under any such enactment or provision,
as appear to Her necessary or expedient for preserving after commencement the substantive effect of that enactment, provision or instrument.

(3) Subsection (2) shall not apply in relation to—
(a) the Immigration Act 1971; or
(b) any provision of this Act not contained in Schedule 7.

(4) Any Order in Council made under subsection (2) shall be subject to annulment in pursuance of a resolution of either House of Parliament.

(5) Any provision made by Order in Council under subsection (2) after commencement may be made with retrospective effect as from commencement or any later date.

(6) The enactments specified in Schedule 7 shall have effect subject to the amendments there specified, being amendments consequential on the provisions of this Act.

(7) This Act shall have effect subject to the transitional provisions contained in Schedule 8.

(8) The enactments mentioned in Schedule 9 are hereby repealed to the extent specified in the third column of that Schedule.

(9) Without prejudice to section 51, nothing in this Act affects the operation, in relation to any time before commencement, of any statutory provision passed or made before commencement.

(10) Nothing in this Act shall be taken as prejudicing the operation of sections 16 and 17 of the Interpretation Act 1978 (which relate to the effect of repeals).

(11) In this section 'modifications' includes additions, omissions and alterations.

53. Citation, commencement and extent

(1) This Act may be cited as the British Nationality Act 1981.

(2) This Act, except the provisions mentioned in subsection (3), shall come into force on such day as the Secretary of State may by order made by statutory

instrument appoint; and references to the commencement of this Act shall be construed as references to the beginning of that day.

(3) Section 49 and this section shall come into force on the passing of this Act.

(4) This Act extends to Northern Ireland.

(5) The provisions of this Act, except those mentioned in subsection (7), extend to the Islands and all [British overseas territories]; and section 36 of the Immigration Act 1971 (power to extend provisions of that Act to Islands) shall apply to the said excepted provisions as if they were provisions of that Act.

(6) For the purposes of section 3(3) of the West Indies Act 1967 it is hereby declared that the provisions of this Act, except those mentioned in subsection (7), extend to all associated states.

(7) The provisions referred to in subsections (5) and (6) are—

(a) section 39 and Schedule 4;

(b) section 52(7) and Schedule 8 so far as they relate to the Immigration Act 1971; and

(c) section 52(8) and Schedule 9 so far as they relate to provisions of the Immigration Act 1971 other than Schedule 1.

Note: British dependent territories became British overseas territories from 26 February 2002, British Overseas Territories Act 2002, s 1.

Schedules

Section 6 and 18

Schedule 1

Requirements For Naturalisation

Naturalisation as a British citizen under section 6(1)

1.—(1) Subject to paragraph 2, the requirements for naturalisation as a British citizen under section 6(1) are, in the case of any person who applies for it—

(a) the requirements specified in sub-paragraph (2) of this paragraph, or the alternative requirement specified in subparagraph (3) of this paragraph; and

(b) that he is of good character; and

(c) that he has a sufficient knowledge of the English, Welsh or Scottish Gaelic language; and

[(ca) that he has sufficient knowledge about life in the United Kingdom; and]

(d) that either—

(i) his intentions are such that, in the event of a certificate of naturalisation as a British citizen being granted to him, his home or (if he has more than one) his principal home will be in the United Kingdom; or

(ii) he intends, in the event of such a certificate being granted to him, to enter into, or continue in, Crown service under the government of the United Kingdom, or service under an international organisation of which the United

Kingdom or Her Majesty's government therein is a member, or service in the employment of a company or association established in the United Kingdom.

(2) The requirement referred to in sub-paragraph (1)(a) of this paragraph are—

(a) that the applicant was in the United Kingdom at the beginning of the period of five years ending with the date of the application, and that the number of days on which he was absent from the United Kingdom in that period does not exceed 450; and

(b) that the number of days on which he was absent from the United Kingdom in the period of twelve months so ending does not exceed 90; and

(c) that he was not at any time in the period of twelve months so ending subject under the immigration laws to any restriction on the period for which he might remain in the United Kingdom; and

(d) that he was not at any time in the period of five years so ending in the United Kingdom in breach of the immigration laws.

(3) The alternative requirement referred to in sub-paragraph (1)(a) of this paragraph is that on the date of the application he is serving outside the United Kingdom in Crown service under the government of the United Kingdom.

2. If in the special circumstances of any particular case the Secretary of State thinks fit, he may for the purposes of paragraph 1 do all or any of the following things, namely—

(a) treat the applicant as fulfilling the requirement specified in paragraph 1(2)(a) or paragraph 1(2)(b), or both, although the number of days on which he was absent from the United Kingdom in the period there mentioned exceeds the number there mentioned;

(b) treat the applicant as having been in the United Kingdom for the whole or any part of any period during which he would otherwise fall to be treated under paragraph 9(1) as having been absent;

(c) disregard any such restriction as is mentioned in paragraph 1(2)(c), not being a restriction to which the applicant was subject on the date of the application;

(d) treat the applicant as fulfilling the requirement specified in paragraph 1(2)(d) although he was in the United Kingdom in breach of the immigration laws in the period there mentioned;

(e) waive the need to fulfil [either or both of the requirements specified in paragraph 1(1)(c) and (ca)] if he considers that because of the applicant's age or physical or mental condition it would be unreasonable to [expect him to fulfil that requirement or those requirements].

Naturalisation as a British citizen under section 6(2)

3. Subject to paragraph 4, the requirements for naturalisation as a British citizen under section 6(2) are, in the case of any person who applies for it—

(a) that he was in the United Kingdom at the beginning of the period of three years ending with the date of the application, and that the number of days on which he was absent from the United Kingdom in that period does not exceed 270; and

(b) that the number of days on which he was absent from the United Kingdom in the period of twelve months so ending does not exceed 90; and

(c) that on the date of the application he was not subject under the immigration laws to any restriction on the period for which he might remain in the United Kingdom; and

(d) that he was not at any time in the period of three years ending with the date of the application in the United Kingdom in breach of the immigration laws; and

(e) the [requirements specified in paragraph 1(1)(b), (c) and (ca)].

4. Paragraph 2 shall apply in relation to paragraph 3 with the following modifications, namely—

(a) the reference to the purposes of paragraph 1 shall be read as a reference to the purposes of paragraph 3;

(b) the references to paragraphs 1(2)(a), 1(2)(b) and 1(2)(d) shall be read as references to paragraphs 3(a), 3(b) and 3(d) respectively;

(c) paragraph 2(c) [. . .] shall be omitted; and

(d) after paragraph (e) there shall be added—

'(f) waive the need to fulfil all or any of the requirements specified in paragraph 3(a) and (b) if on the date of the application the person to whom the applicant is married [, or of whom the applicant is the civil partner,] is serving in service to which section 2(1)(b) applies, that person's recruitment for that service having taken place in the United Kingdom'.

Naturalisation as a [British overseas territories] citizen under section 18(1)

5.—(1) Subject to paragraph 6, the requirements for naturalisation as a [British overseas territories] citizen under section 18(1) are, in the case of any person who applies for it—

(a) the requirements specified in sub-paragraph (2) of this paragraph, or the alternative requirement specified in sub-paragraph (3) of this paragraph; and

(b) that he is of good character; and

(c) that he has a sufficient knowledge of the English language or any other language recognised for official purposes in the relevant territory; and

(d) that either—

(i) his intentions are such that, in the event of a certificate of naturalisation as a [British overseas territories] citizen being granted to him, his home or (if he has more than one) his principal home will be in the relevant territory; or

(ii) he intends, in the event of such a certificate being granted to him, to enter into, or continue in, Crown service under the government of that territory, or service under an international organisation of which that territory or the government of that territory is a member, or service in the employment of a company or association established in that territory.

(2) The requirements referred to in sub-paragraph (1)(a) of this paragraph are—

(a) that he was in the relevant territory at the beginning of the period of five years ending with the date of the application, and that the number of days on which he was absent from that territory in that period does not exceed 450; and

(b) that the number of days on which he was absent from that territory in the period of twelve months so ending does not exceed 90; and

(c) that he was not at any time in the period of twelve months so ending subject under the immigration laws to any restriction on the period for which he might remain in that territory; and

(d) that he was not at any time in the period of five years so ending in that territory in breach of the immigration laws.

(3) The alternative requirement referred to in sub-paragraph (1)(a) of this paragraph is that on the date of the application he is serving outside the relevant territory in Crown service under the government of that territory.

6. If in the special circumstances of any particular case the Secretary of State thinks fit, he may for the purposes of paragraph 5 do all or any of the following things, namely—

(a) treat the applicant as fulfilling the requirement specified in paragraph 5(2)(a) or paragraph 5(2)(b), or both, although the number of days on which he was absent from the relevant territory in the period there mentioned exceeds the number there mentioned;

(b) treat the applicant as having been in the relevant territory for the whole or any part of any period during which he would otherwise fall to be treated under paragraph 9(2) as having been absent;

(c) disregard any such restriction as is mentioned in paragraph 5(2)(c), not being a restriction to which the applicant was subject on the date of the application;

(d) treat the applicant as fulfilling the requirement specified in paragraph 5(2)(d) although he was in the relevant territory in breach of the immigration laws in the period there mentioned;

(e) waive the need to fulfil the requirement specified in paragraph 5(1)(c) if he considers that because of the applicant's age or physical or mental condition it would be unreasonable to expect him to fulfil it.

Naturalisation as a [British overseas territories] citizen under section 18(2)

7. Subject to paragraph 8, the requirements for naturalisation as a [British overseas territories] citizen under section 18(2) are, in the case of any person who applies for it—

(a) that he was in the relevant territory at the beginning of the period of three years ending with the date of the application, and that the number of days on which he was absent from that territory in that period does not exceed 270; and

(b) that the number of days on which he was absent from that territory in the period of twelve months so ending does not exceed 90; and

(c) that on the date of the application he was not subject under the immigration laws to any restriction on the period for which he might remain in that territory; and

(d) that he was not at any time in the period of three years ending with the date of the application in that territory in breach of the immigration laws; and

(e) the [requirements specified in paragraph 5(1)(b) and (c)]

8. Paragraph 6 shall apply in relation to paragraph 7 with the following modifications, namely—

(a) the reference to the purposes of paragraph 5 shall be read as a reference to the purposes of paragraph 7;

(b) the references to paragraphs 5(2)(a), 5(2)(b) and 5(2)(d) shall be read as references to paragraphs 7(a), 7(b) and 7(d) respectively;

(c) paragraph 6(c) [. . .] shall be omitted; and

(d) after paragraph (e) there shall be added—

'(f) waive the need to fulfil all or any of the requirements specified in paragraph 7(a) and (b) if on the date of the application the person to whom the applicant is married [, or of whom the applicant is the civil partner,] is serving in service to which section 16(1)(b) applies, that person's recruitment for that service having taken place in a [British overseas territory]'.

Periods to be treated as periods of absence from UK or a [British overseas territory]

9.—(1) For the purposes of this Schedule a person shall (subject to paragraph 2(b)) be treated as having been absent from the United Kingdom during any of the following periods, that is to say—

(a) any period when he was in the United Kingdom and either was entitled to an exemption under section 8(3) or (4) of the Immigration Act 1971 (exemptions for diplomatic agents etc. and members of the forces) or was a member of the family and formed part of the household of a person so entitled;

(b) any period when he was detained—

(i) in any place of detention in the United Kingdom in pursuance of a sentence passed on him by a court in the United Kingdom or elsewhere for any offence;

(ii) in any hospital in the United Kingdom under a hospital order made under [Part III of the Mental Health Act 1983] or section 175 or 376 of the Criminal Procedure (Scotland) Act 1975 or Part III of the Mental Health [(Northern Ireland) Order 1986], being an order made in connection with his conviction of an offence; or

(iii) under any power of detention conferred by the immigration laws of the United Kingdom;

(c) any period when, being liable to be detained as mentioned in paragraph (b)(i) or (ii) of this sub-paragraph, he was unlawfully at large or absent without leave and for that reason liable to be arrested or taken into custody;

(d) any period when, his actual detention under any such power as is mentioned in paragraph (b)(iii) of this sub-paragraph being required or specifically authorised, he was unlawfully at large and for that reason liable to be arrested.

(2) For the purposes of this Schedule a person shall (subject to paragraph 6(b)) be treated as having been absent from any particular [British overseas territory] during any of the following periods, that is to say—

(a) any period when he was in that territory and either was entitled to an exemption under the immigration laws of that territory corresponding to any such exemption as is mentioned in sub-paragraph (1)(a) or was a member of the family and formed part of the household of a person so entitled;

(b) any period when he was detained—

(i) in any place of detention in the relevant territory in pursuance of a sentence passed on him by a court in that territory or elsewhere for any offence;

(ii) in any hospital in that territory under a direction (however described) made under any law for purposes similar to [Part III of the Mental Health Act 1983] which was for the time being in force in that territory, being a direction made in connection with his conviction of an offence and corresponding to a hospital order under that Part; or

(iii) under any power of detention conferred by the immigration laws of that territory;

(c) any period when, being liable to be detained as mentioned in paragraph (b)(i) or (ii) of this sub-paragraph, he was unlawfully at large or absent without leave and for that reason liable to be arrested or taken into custody;

(d) any period when, his actual detention under any such power as is mentioned in paragraph (b)(iii) of this sub-paragraph being required or specifically authorised, he was unlawfully at large and for that reason liable to be arrested.

Interpretation

10. In this Schedule 'the relevant territory' has the meaning given by section 18(3).

Note: Words in first square brackets in paras 9(1)(b) and 9(2)(b) substituted by Mental Health Act 1983, s 148. Words in second square brackets in para 9(1)(b) substituted by SI 1956/596. Paragraph 1(1)(ca) inserted by and words in square brackets in para 2(e) substituted by Nationality, Immigration and Asylum Act 2002, s 1 and words in square brackets in paras 3(e) and 7(e) substituted by s 2 of that Act from 1 November 2005 (SI 2005/2782). Words in square brackets in paras 4(c) and 8(c) omitted by Nationality, Immigration and Asylum Act 2002, s 2 from 1 November 2005 (SI 20053/2782). British dependent territories became British overseas territories from 26 February 2002, British Overseas Territories Act 2002, s 1. Words in square brackets in sub-paras 4(d) and 8(d) inserted by Sch 27 Civil Partnerships Act 2004 from a date to be appointed.

Section 36

Schedule 2

Provisions For Reducing Statelessness

Persons born in the United Kingdom after commencement

1.—(1) Where a person born in the United Kingdom after commencement would, but for this paragraph, be born stateless, then, subject to sub-paragraph (3)—

(a) if at the time of the birth his father or mother is a citizen or subject of a description mentioned in sub-paragraph (2), he shall be a citizen or subject of that description; and accordingly

(b) [. . .] at the time of the birth each of his parents is a citizen or subject of a different description so mentioned, he shall be a citizen or subject of the same description so mentioned as each of them is respectively at that time.

(2) The descriptions referred to in sub-paragraph (1) are a [British overseas territories] citizen, a British Overseas citizen and a British subject under this Act.

(3) A person shall not be a British subject by virtue of this paragraph if by virtue of it he is a citizen of a description mentioned in sub-paragraph (2).

Persons born in a [British overseas territory] after commencement

2.—(1) Where a person born in a [British overseas territory] after commencement would, but for this paragraph, be born stateless, then, subject to sub-paragraph (3)—

(a) if at the time of the birth his father or mother is a citizen or subject of a description mentioned in sub-paragraph (2), he shall be a citizen or subject of that description; and accordingly

(b) [. . .] at the time of the birth each of his parents is a citizen or subject of a different description so mentioned, he shall be a citizen or subject of the same description so mentioned as each of them is respectively at that time.

(2) The descriptions referred to in sub-paragraph (1) are a British citizen, a British Overseas citizen and a British subject under this Act.

(3) A person shall not be a British subject by virtue of this paragraph if by virtue of it he is a citizen of a description mentioned in sub-paragraph (2).

Persons born in the United Kingdom or a [British overseas territory] after commencement

3.—(1) A person born in the United Kingdom or a [British overseas territory] after commencement shall be entitled, on an application for his registration under this paragraph, to be so registered if the following requirements are satisfied in his case, namely—

(a) that he is and always has been stateless; and

(b) that on the date of the application he [. . .] was under the age of twenty-two; and

(c) that he was in the United Kingdom or a [British overseas territory] (no matter which) at the beginning of the period of five years ending with that date and that (subject to paragraph 6) the number of days on which he was absent from both the United Kingdom and the [British overseas territories] in that period does not exceed 450.

(2) A person entitled to registration under this paragraph—

(a) shall be registered under it as a British citizen if, in the period of five years mentioned in sub-paragraph (1), the number of days wholly or partly spent by him in the United Kingdom exceeds the number of days wholly or partly spent by him in the [British overseas territories];

(b) in any other case, shall be registered under it as a [British overseas territories] citizen.

Persons born outside the United Kingdom and the [British Overseas Territories] after commencement

4.—(1) A person born outside the United Kingdom and the [British overseas territories] after commencement shall be entitled, on an application for his registration under this paragraph, to be so registered if the following requirements are satisfied, namely—

(a) that that person is and always has been stateless; and

(b) that at the time of that person's birth his father or mother was a citizen or subject of a description mentioned in sub-paragraph (4); and

(c) that that person was in the United Kingdom or a [British overseas territory] (no matter which) at the beginning of the period of three years ending with the date of the application and that (subject to paragraph 6) the number of days on which he was absent from both the United Kingdom and the [British overseas territories] in that period does not exceed 270.

(2) A person entitled to registration under this paragraph—

(a) shall be registered under it as a citizen or subject of a description available to him in accordance with sub-paragraph (3); and

(b) if more than one description is so available to him, shall be registered under this paragraph as a citizen of whichever one or more of the descriptions so available to him is or are stated in the application under this paragraph to be wanted.

(3) For the purposes of this paragraph the descriptions of citizen or subject available to a person entitled to registration under this paragraph are—

(a) in the case of a person whose father or mother was at the time of that person's birth a citizen of a description mentioned in sub-paragraph (4), any description of citizen so mentioned which applied to his father or mother at that time;

(b) in any case, a British subject under this Act.

(4) The description referred to in sub-paragraphs (1) to (3) are a British citizen, a [British overseas territories] citizen, a British Overseas citizen and a British subject under this Act.

Persons born stateless before commencement

5.—(1) A person born before commencement shall be entitled, on an application for his registration under this paragraph, to be so registered if the circumstances are such that, if—

(a) this Act had not been passed, and the enactments repealed or amended by this Act had continued in force accordingly; and

(b) an application for the registration of that person under section 1 of the British Nationality (No. 2) Act 1964 (stateless persons) as a citizen of the United Kingdom and Colonies had been made on the date of the application under this paragraph, that person would have been entitled under that section to be registered as such a citizen.

(2) A person entitled to registration under this paragraph shall be registered under it as such a citizen as he would have become at commencement if, immediately before commencement, he had been registered as a citizen of the United Kingdom and Colonies under section 1 of the British Nationality (No. 2) Act 1964 on whichever of the grounds mentioned in subsection (1)(a) to (c) of that section he would have been entitled to be so registered on in the circumstances described in sub-paragraph (1)(a) and (b) of this paragraph.

Supplementary

6. If in the special circumstances of any particular case the Secretary of State thinks fit, he may for the purposes of paragraph 3 or 4 treat the person who is the subject of the application as fulfilling the requirement specified in sub-paragraph (1)(c) of that paragraph although the number of days on which he was absent from both the United Kingdom and the [British overseas territories] in the period there mentioned exceeds the number there mentioned.

Note: British dependent territories became British overseas territories from 26 February 2002, British Overseas Territories Act 2002, s 1. Words deleted from paras 1(1)(b) and 2(1)(b) cease to have effect in relation to children born on or after a date to be appointed from 7 November 2002, Nationality, Immigration and Asylum Act 2002, s 9. Words deleted from para 3(1)(b) cease to have effect in relation to an application made on or after a date to be appointed from 7 November 2002, Nationality, Immigration and Asylum Act 2002, s 8.

Section 37

SCHEDULE 3

COUNTRIES WHOSE CITIZENS ARE COMMONWEALTH CITIZENS

Antigua and Barbuda
Australia
The Bahamas
Bangladesh
Barbados
Belize
Botswana
[Brunei]
[Cameroon]
Canada
Kenya
Kiribati
Lesotho
Malawi
Malaysia
[Maldives]
Malta
Mauritius
[Mozambique]
Nauru
New Zealand
Nigeria
[Pakistan]
Uganda
Vanuatu
Western Samoa
Papua New Guinea
[Saint Christopher and Nevis]
Saint Lucia
Saint Vincent and the Grenadines
Republic of Cyprus
Dominica
Fiji
The Gambia
Ghana
Grenada
Guyana
India
Jamaica
Seychelles
Sierra Leone
Singapore
Solomon Islands
Sri Lanka
Swaziland
Tanzania
Tonga
Trinidad and Tobago
Tuvalu
Zambia
Zimbabwe
[Namibia]

Note: 'Brunei' inserted by SI 1983/1699; 'Maldives' inserted by Brunei and Maldives Act 1985; 'Pakistan' inserted by SI 1989/1331; 'Saint Christopher and Nevis' inserted by SI 1983/882; 'Namibia' inserted by SI 1990/1502. 'Cameroon' and 'Mozambique' inserted by SI 1998/3161 from 25 January 1999. Schedule 4 amends Immigration Act 1971, ss 3–6, 8, 9, 13, 14, 22, 24–26, 29, 33, Schs 2, 4.

Schedule 4

. . .

Section 42(1)

[Schedule 5

Citizenship Oath and Pledge

1. The form of citizenship oath and pledge is as follows for registration of or naturalisation as a British citizen—

OATH

'I, [name], swear by Almighty God that, on becoming a British citizen, I will be faithful and bear true allegiance to Her Majesty Queen Elizabeth the Second, Her Heirs and Successors according to law.'

PLEDGE

'I will give my loyalty to the United Kingdom and respect its rights and freedoms. I will uphold its democratic values. I will observe its laws faithfully and fulfil my duties and obligations as a British citizen.'

2. The form of citizenship oath and pledge is as follows for registration of or naturalisation as a British overseas territories citizen—

OATH

'I, [name], swear by Almighty God that, on becoming a British overseas territories citizen, I will be faithful and bear true allegiance to Her Majesty Queen Elizabeth the Second, Her Heirs and Successors according to law.'

PLEDGE

'I will give my loyalty to [name of territory] and respect its rights and freedoms. I will uphold its democratic values. I will observe its laws faithfully and fulfil my duties and obligations as a British overseas territories citizen.'

3. The form of citizenship oath is as follows for registration of a British Overseas citizen—

'I, [name], swear by Almighty God that, on becoming a British Overseas citizen, I will be faithful and bear true allegiance to Her Majesty Queen Elizabeth the Second, Her Heirs and Successors according to law.'

4. The form of citizenship oath is as follows for registration of a British subject—

'I, [name], swear by Almighty God that, on becoming a British subject, I will be faithful and bear true allegiance to Her Majesty Queen Elizabeth the Second, Her Heirs and Successors according to law.']

Note: Schedule 5 substituted by Nationality, Immigration and Asylum Act 2002, Sch 1, para 2, from a date to be appointed.

Section 50(1)

Schedule 6

[British Overseas Territories]

Anguilla
Bermuda
British Antarctic Territory
British Indian Ocean Territory
Cayman Islands
Falkland Islands [. . .]
Gibraltar
. . .
Montserrat
Pitcarn, Henderson, Ducie and Oeno Islands
. . .
St. Helena and Dependencies
[South Georgia and the South Sandwich Islands]
The Sovereign Base Areas of Akrotiri and Dhekelia (that is to say the areas mentioned in section 2(1) of the Cyprus Act 1960)
Turks and Caicos Islands
Virgin Islands

Note: British dependent territories became British overseas territories from 26 February 2002, British Overseas Territories Act 2002, s 1. First words omitted in Sch 6 repealed by SI 2002/3497. Second words omitted repealed by SI 1986/948. Third words omitted repealed by SI 1983/893. Words in square brackets inserted by SI 2001/3497 from 4 December 2001.

Schedule 7

Consequential Amendments (s. 52(6))

. . .

Schedule 8

Transitional Provisions (s. 52(7))

. . .

Schedule 9

Repeals (s. 52(8))

. . .

Immigration Act 1988
(1988, c. 14)

An Act to make further provision for the regulation of immigration into the United Kingdom; and for connected purposes. [10th May 1988]

1. Termination of saving in respect of Commonwealth citizens settled before 1973

. . .

Note: Section 1 repeals Immigration Act 1971, s 1(5).

2. Restriction on exercise of right of abode in cases of polygamy

(1) this section applies to any woman who—

(a) has the right of abode in the United Kingdom under section 2(1)(b) of the principal Act as, or as having been, the wife of a man ('the husband')—

(i) to whom she is or was polygamously married; and

(ii) who is or was such a citizen of the United Kingdom and Colonies, Commonwealth citizen or British subject as is mentioned in section 2(2)(a) or (b) of that Act as in force immediately before the commencement of the British Nationality Act 1981; and

(b) has not before the coming into force of this section and since her marriage to the husband been in the United Kingdom.

(2) A woman to whom this section applies shall not be entitled to enter the United Kingdom in the exercise of the right of abode mentioned in subsection (1)(a) above or to be granted a certificate of entitlement in respect of that right if there is another woman living (whether or not one to whom this section applies) who is the wife or widow of the husband and who—

(a) is, or at any time since her marriage to the husband has been, in the United Kingdom; or

(b) has been granted a certificate of entitlement in respect of the right of abode mentioned in subsection (1)(a) above or an entry clearance to enter the United Kingdom as the wife of the husband.

(3) So long as a woman is precluded by subsection (2) above from entering the United Kingdom in the exercise of her right of abode or being granted a certificate of entitlement in respect of that right the principal Act shall apply to her as it applies to a person not having a right of abode.

(4) Subsection (2) above shall not preclude a woman from re-entering the United Kingdom if since her marriage to the husband she has at any time previously been in the United Kingdom and there was at that time no such other woman living as is mentioned in that subsection.

(5) Where a woman claims that this section does not apply to her because she had been in the United Kingdom before the coming into force of this section and since her marriage to the husband it shall be for her to prove that fact.

(6) For the purposes of this section a marriage may by polygamous although at its inception neither party has any spouse additional to the other.

(7) For the purposes of subsection (1)(b), (2)(a), (4) and (5) above there shall be disregarded presence in the United Kingdom as a visitor or an illegal entrant and presence in circumstances in which a person is deemed by section 11(1) of the principal Act not to have entered the United Kingdom.

(8) In subsection (2)(b) above the reference to a certificate of entitlement includes a reference to a certificate treated as such a certificate by virtue of section 39(8) of the British Nationality Act 1981.

(9) No application by a woman for a certificate of entitlement in respect of such a right of abode as is mentioned in subsection (1)(a) above or for an entry clearance shall be granted if another application for such a certificate or clearance is pending and that application is made by a woman as the wife or widow of the same husband.

(10) For the purposes of subsection (9) above an application shall be regarded as pending so long as it and any appeal proceedings relating to it have not been finally determined.

3. Proof of right of abode

. . .

Note: Amends Immigration Act 1971, ss 3(9), 13(3), 2(2); British Nationality Act 1981, s 39.

4. Members of diplomatic missions

. . .

Note: Amends Immigration Act 1971, s 8.

5. . . .

Note: Section 5 repealed by Immigration and Asylum Act 1999 from 2 October 2000, transitional provisions set out in SI 2003/754.

6. Knowingly overstaying limited leave

(1) . . .

(2) . . .

(3) These amendments do not apply in relation to a person whose leave has expired before the coming into force of this section.

Note: Section 6(1) and (2) amend Immigration Act 1971, s 24.

7. Persons exercising Community rights and nationals of Member States

(1) A person shall not under the principal Act require leave to enter or remain in the United Kingdom in any case in which he is entitled to do so by virtue of an enforceable Community right or of any provision made under section 2(2) of the European Communities Act 1972.

(2) The Secretary of State may be order made by statutory instrument give leave to enter the United Kingdom for a limited period to any class of persons who are nationals of member States but who are not entitled to enter the United Kingdom as mentioned in subsection (1) above; and any such order may give leave subject to such conditions as may be imposed by the order.

(3) References in the principal Act to limited leave shall include references to leave given by an order under subsection (2) above and a person having leave by virtue of such an order shall be treated as having been given that leave by a notice given to him by an immigration officer within the period specified in paragraph 6(1) of Schedule 2 to that Act.

8. . . .

Note: Section 8 repealed by Immigration and Asylum Act 1999.

9. . . .

Note: Section 9 repealed by Immigration and Asylum Act 1999.

10. Miscellaneous minor amendments

The principal Act shall have effect with the amendments specified in the Schedule to this Act.

11. Expenses and receipts

(1) There shall be paid out of money provided by Parliament any expenses incurred by the Secretary of State in consequences of this Act.

(2) Any sums received by the Secretary of State by virtue of this Act shall be paid into the Consolidated Fund.

12. Short title, interpretation, commencement and extent

(1) This Act may be cited as the Immigration Act 1988.

(2) In this Act 'the principal Act' means the Immigration Act 1971 and any expression which is also used in that Act has the same meaning as in that Act.

(3) Except as provided in subsection (4) below this Act shall come into force at the end of the period of two months beginning with the day on which it is passed.

(4) Sections 1, 2, 3, 4, 5 and 7(1) and paragraph 1 of the Schedule shall come into force on such day as may be appointed by the Secretary of State by an order made by statutory instrument; and such an order may appoint different days for different provisions and contain such transitional provisions and savings as the Secretary of State thinks necessary or expedient in connection with any provision brought into force.

(5) This Act extends to Northern Ireland and section 36 of the principal Act (power to extend any of its provisions to the Channel Islands or the Isle of Man) shall apply also to the provisions of this Act.

Section 10 **SCHEDULE**

MINOR AMENDMENTS

. . .

Asylum and Immigration Appeals Act 1993
(1993, c. 23)

An Act to make provision about persons who claim asylum in the United Kingdom and their dependants; to amend the law with respect to certain rights of appeal under the Immigration Act 1971; and to extend the provisions of the Immigration (Carriers' Liability) Act 1987 to transit passengers. [1st July 1993]

Introductory

1. Interpretation

In this Act—

'the 1971 Act' means the Immigration Act 1971;

'claim for asylum' means a claim made by a person (whether before or after the coming into force of this section) that it would be contrary to the United Kingdom's obligations under the Convention for him to be removed from, or required to leave, the United Kingdom; and

'the Convention' means the Convention relating to the Status of Refugees done at Geneva on 28th July 1951 and the Protocol to that Convention.

2. Primacy of Convention

Nothing in the immigration rules (within the meaning of the 1971 Act) shall lay down any practice which would be contrary to the Convention.

Treatment of persons who claim asylum

3. . . .

Note: Section 3 repealed by Immigration and Asylum Act 1999 from 11 December 2000.

4. . . .

Note: Section 4 repealed by Immigration and Asylum Act 1999 from 3 April 2000.

5. . . .

Note: Section 5 repealed by Immigration and Asylum Act 1999 from 3 April 2000.

6. . . .

Note: Section 6 repealed by Immigration and Asylum Act 1999 from 11 November 1999, with effect from 26 July 1993.

7. . . .

Note: Section 7 repealed by Immigration and Asylum Act 1999 from 2 October 2000.

8. . . .

Note: Section 8 repealed by Immigration and Asylum Act 1999 from 2 October 2000, transitional provisions set out in SI 2003/754.

9. . . .

Note: Section 9 repealed by Immigration and Asylum Act 1999 from 2 October 2000.

[9A. . . .

Note: Section 9A repealed by Sch 2 Asylum and Immigration Act 2004 from 4 April 2005 (SI 2005/565).

10. Visitors, short-term and and prospective students and their dependants

. . .

Note: Section 10 repealed by Immigration and Asylum Act 1999 from 2 October 2000.

11. Refusals which are mandatory under immigration rules

. . .

Note: Section 11 repealed by Immigration and Asylum Act 1999 from 2 October 2000.

12. . . .

Note: Section 12 repealed by Immigration and Asylum Act 1999.

Supplementary

13. Financial provision

(1) There shall be paid out of money provided by Parliament—
   (a) any expenditure incurred by the Secretary of State under this Act; and
   (b) any increase attributable to this Act in the sums payable out of such money under any other enactment.

(2) Any sums received by the Secretary of State by virtue of this Act shall be paid into the Consolidated Fund.

14. Commencement

(1) Sections 4 to 11 above (and section 1 above so far as it relates to those sections) shall not come into force until such day as the Secretary of State may by order appoint, and different days may be appointed for provisions or for different purposes.

(2) An order under subsection (1) above—
  (a) shall be made by statutory instrument; and
  (b) may contain such transitional and supplemental provisions as the Secretary of State thinks necessary or expedient.

(3) Without prejudice to the generality of subsections (1) and (2) above, with respect to any provision of section 4 above an order under subsection (1) above may appoint different days in relation to different descriptions of asylum-seekers and dependants of asylum-seekers; and any such descriptions may be framed by reference to nationality, citizenship, origin or other connection with any particular country or territory, but not by reference to race, colour or religion.

15. Extent

(1) Her Majesty may by Order in Council direct that any of the provisions of this Act shall extend, with such modifications as appear to Her Majesty to be appropriate, to any of the Channel Islands or the Isle of Man.

(2) This Act extends to Northern Ireland.

16. Short title

This Act may be cited as the Asylum and Immigration Appeals Act 1993.

Schedules

Schedule 1

. . .

Note: Schedule 1 repealed by Immigration and Asylum Act 1999 from 3 April 2000.

Section 8(6)

Schedule 2

Note: Schedule 2 repealed by Immigration and Asylum Act 1999 from 2 October 2000.

Special Immigration Appeals Commission Act 1997
(1997, c. 68)

An Act to establish the Special Immigration Appeals Commission; to make provision with respect to its jurisdiction; and for connected purposes.

[17 December 1997]

1. Establishment of the commission

(1) There shall be a commission, known as the Special Immigration Appeals Commission, for the purpose of exercising the jurisdiction conferred by this Act.

(2) Schedule 1 to this Act shall have effect in relation to the Commission.

[(3) The Commission shall be a superior court of record.

(4) A decision of the Commission shall be questioned in legal proceedings only in accordance with—

(a) section 7, or

(b) . . .

Note: Words in square brackets inserted by Anti-terrorism, Crime and Security Act 2001, s 35 from 13 December 2001. Subsection 4(b) repealed by Prevention of Terrorism Act 2005, s 16 from 14 March 2005.

[2. Jurisdiction: appeals

(1) A person may appeal to the Special Immigration Appeals Commission against a decision if—

(a) he would be able to appeal against the decision under section 82(1) [83(2) or 83A(2)] of the Nationality, Immigration and Asylum Act 2002 but for a certificate of the Secretary of State under section 97 of that Act (national security &c.), or

(b) an appeal against the decision under section 82(1) [83(2) or 83A(2)] of that Act lapsed under section 99 of that Act by virtue of a certificate of the Secretary of State under section 97 of that Act.

(2) The following provisions shall apply, with any necessary modifications, in relation to an appeal against an immigration decision under this section as they apply in relation to an appeal under section 82(1) of the Nationality, Immigration and Asylum Act 2002—

(a) section 3C [or 3D] of the Immigration Act 1971 (c. 77) [continuation of leave],

(b) section 78 of the Nationality, Immigration and Asylum Act 2002 (no removal while appeal pending),
(c) section 79 of that Act (deportation order: appeal),
(d) section 82(3) of that Act (variation or revocation of leave to enter or remain: appeal),
(e) section 84 of that Act (grounds of appeal),
(f) section 85 of that Act (matters to be considered),
(g) section 86 of that Act (determination of appeal),
(h) section 87 of that Act (successful appeal: direction),
(i) section 96 of that Act (earlier right of appeal),
(j) section 104 of that Act (pending appeal),
(k) section 105 of that Act (notice of immigration decision), and
(l) section 110 of that Act (grants).

(3) The following provisions shall apply, with any necessary modifications, in relation to [an appeal against a decision other than an immigration decision] under this section as they apply in relation to an appeal under section 83(2) [or 83A(2)] of the Nationality, Immigration and Asylum Act 2002—
(a) section 85(4) of that Act (matters to be considered),
(b) section 86 of that Act (determination of appeal),
(c) section 87 of that Act (successful appeal direction), and
(d) section 110 of that Act (grants).

(4) An appeal against the rejection of a claim for asylum under this section shall be treated as abandoned if the appellant leaves the United Kingdom.

(5) A person may bring or continue an appeal against an immigration decision under this section while he is in the United Kingdom only if he would be able to bring or continue the appeal while he was in the United Kingdom if it were an appeal under section 82(1) of that Act.

(6) In this section 'immigration decision' has the meaning given by section 82(2) of the Nationality, Immigration and Asylum Act 2002.]

[**2A.** . . .

[**2B.** A person may appeal to the Special Immigration Appeals Commission against a decision to make an order under section 40 of the British Nationality Act 1981 (c. 61) (deprivation of citizenship) if he is not entitled to appeal under section 40A(1) of that Act because of a certificate under section 40A(2)] [and section 40A(3)(a) shall have effect in relation to appeals under this section.]

Note: Section 2 substituted and s 2A cease to have effect by Sch 7 Nationality, Immigration and Asylum Act 2002 from 1 April 2003 (SI 2003/754). Words in square brackets in s 2 inserted or substituted by Sch 1 Immigration, Asylum and Nationality Act 2006 from a date to be appointed. Section 2B inserted by Nationality, Immigration and Asylum Act 2002, s 4 from 1 April 2003 (SI 2003/754). Transitional provisions set out in SI 2003/754. Words in second square brackets in s 2B inserted by Sch 2 Asylum and Immigration Act 2004 from a date to be appointed.

3. Jurisdiction: bail

(1) In the case of a person to whom subsection (2) below applies, the provisions of Schedule 2 to the Immigration Act 1971 specified in Schedule 3 to this Act shall have effect with the modifications set out there.

(2) This subsection applies to a person who is detained under the Immigration Act 1971 [or the Nationality, Immigration and Asylum Act 2002] if—
   (a) the Secretary of State certifies that his detention is necessary in the interests of national security,
   (b) he is detained following a decision to refuse him leave to enter the United Kingdom on the ground that his exclusion is in the interests of national security, or
   (c) he is detained following a decision to make a deportation order against him on the ground that his deportation is in the interests of national security.

Note: Words in square brackets inserted from 4 April 2003 (SI 2003/1016).

4. . . .

Note: Section 4 ceases to have effect from 1 April 2003 (SI 2003/754), Sch 7 Nationality, Immigration and Asylum Act 2002. Transitional provisions set out in SI 2003/754.

5. Procedure in relation to jurisdiction under sections 2 and 3

(1) The Lord Chancellor may make rules—
   (a) for regulating the exercise of the rights of appeal conferred by section 2 [or 2B] . . . above,
   (b) for prescribing the practice and procedure to be followed on or in connection with appeals under [section 2 [or 2B] . . .] above, including the mode and burden of proof and admissibility of evidence on such appeals, and
   (c) for other matters preliminary or incidental to or arising out of such appeals, including proof of the decisions of the Special Immigration Appeals Commission.

(2) Rules under this section shall provide that an appellant has the right to be legally represented in any proceedings before the Commission on an appeal under section 2 [or 2B] [. . .] above, subject to any power conferred on the Commission by such rules.

[(2A) Rules under this section may, in particular, do anything which may be done by rules under section 106 of the Nationality, Immigration and Asylum Act 2002 (appeals:rules).]

(3) Rules under this section may, in particular—

(a) make provision enabling proceedings before the Commission to take place without the appellant being given full particulars of the reasons for the decision which is the subject of the appeal,

(b) make provision enabling the Commission to hold proceedings in the absence of any person, including the appellant and any legal representative appointed by him,

(c) make provision about the functions in proceedings before the Commission of persons appointed under section 6 below, and

(d) make provision enabling the Commission to give the appellant a summary of any evidence taken in his absence.

(4) Rules under this section may also include provision—

(a) enabling any functions of the Commission which relate to matters preliminary or incidental to an appeal, or which are conferred by Part II of Schedule 2 to the Immigration Act 1971, to be performed by a single member of the Commission, or

(b) conferring on the Commission such ancillary powers as the Lord Chancellor thinks necessary for the purposes of the exercise of its functions.

(5) The power to make rules under this section shall include power to make rules with respect to applications to the Commission under paragraphs 22 to 24 of Schedule 2 to the Immigration Act 1971 and matters arising out of such applications.

(6) In making rules under this section, the Lord Chancellor shall have regard, in particular, to—

(a) the need to secure that decisions which are the subject of appeals are properly reviewed, and

(b) the need to secure that information is not disclosed contrary to the public interest.

(7) Section 9(1) of the Interception of Communications Act 1985 (exclusion of evidence) shall not apply to proceedings before the Commission.

(8) The power to make rules under this section shall be exercisable by statutory instrument.

(9) No rules shall be made under this section unless a draft of them has been laid before and approved by resolution of each House of Parliament.

Note: Words deleted from and words in square brackets in sub-ss 5(1) and 5(2), and sub-s 5(2A) inserted by Sch 7 Nationality, Immigration and Asylum Act 2002 from 1 April 2003 (SI 2003/754, which sets out transitional provisions).

6. Appointment of person to represent the appellant's interests

(1) The relevant law officer may appoint a person to represent the interests of an appellant in any proceedings before the Special Immigration Appeals

Commission from which the appellant and any legal representative of his are excluded.

(2) For the purposes of subsection (1) above, the relevant law officer is—
  (a) in relation to proceedings before the Commission in England and Wales, the Attorney General,
  (b) in relation to proceedings before the Commission in Scotland, the Lord Advocate, and
  (c) in relation to proceedings before the Commission in Northern Ireland, the Attorney General for Northern Ireland.

(3) A person appointed under subsection (1) above—
  (a) if appointed for the purposes of proceedings in England and Wales, shall have a general qualification for the purposes of section 71 of the Courts and Legal Services Act 1990,
  (b) if appointed for the purposes of proceedings in Scotland, shall be—
    (i) an advocate, or
    (ii) a solicitor who has by virtue of section 25A of the Solicitors (Scotland) Act 1980 rights of audience in the Court of Session and the High Court of Justiciary, and
  (c) if appointed for the purposes of proceedings in Northern Ireland, shall be a member of the Bar of Northern Ireland.

(4) A person appointed under subsection (1) above shall not be responsible to the person whose interests he is appointed to represent.

7. Appeals from the Commission

(1) Where the Special Immigration Appeals Commission has made a final determination of an appeal, any party to the appeal may bring a further appeal to the appropriate appeal court on any question of law material to that determination.

(2) An appeal under this section may be brought only with the leave of the Commission or, if such leave is refused, with the leave of the appropriate appeal court.

(3) In this section 'the appropriate appeal court' means—
  (a) in relation to a determination made by the Commission in England and Wales, the Court of Appeal,
  (b) in relation to a determination made by the Commission in Scotland, the Court of Session, and
  (c) in relation to a determination made by the Commission in Northern Ireland, the Court of Appeal in Northern Ireland.

(4) . . .

Note: Section 7(4) omitted and 7A inserted by Immigration and Asylum Act 1999 from 2 October 2000. Section 7A ceases to have effect from 1 April 2003 (SI 2003/754), Sch 7 Nationality, Immigration and Asylum Act 2002. SI 2003/754 sets out transitional provisions.

8. Procedure on applications to the Commission for leave to appeal

(1) The Lord Chancellor may make rules regulating, and prescribing the procedure to be followed on, applications to the Special Immigration Appeals Commission for leave to appeal under section 7 above.

(2) Rules under this section may include provision enabling an application for leave to appeal to be heard by a single member of the Commission.

(3) The power to make rules under this section shall be exercisable by statutory instrument.

(4) No rules shall be made under this section unless a draft of them has been laid before and approved by resolution of each House of Parliament.

9. Short title, commencement and extent

(1) This Act may be cited as the Special Immigration Appeals Commission Act 1997.

(2) This Act, except for this section, shall come into force on such day as the Secretary of State may by order made by statutory instrument appoint; and different days may be so appointed for different purposes.

(3) Her Majesty may by Order in Council direct that any of the provisions of this Act shall extend, with such modifications as appear to Her Majesty to be appropriate, to any of the Channel Islands or the Isle of Man.

(4) This Act extends to Northern Ireland.

Note: Commencement: s 9 on 17 December 1997, ss 5 and 8 on 11 June 1998, remainder of Act on 3 August 1998.

Schedules

Section 1

Schedule 1

The Commission

Members

1.—(1) The Special Immigration Appeals Commission shall consist of such number of members appointed by the Lord Chancellor as he may determine.

(2) A member of the Commission shall hold and vacate office in accordance with the terms of his appointment and shall, on ceasing to hold office, be eligible for reappointment.

(3) A member of the Commission may resign his office at any time by notice in writing to the Lord Chancellor.

Chairman

2. The Lord Chancellor shall appoint one of the members of the Commission to be its chairman.

Payments to members

3.—(1) The Lord Chancellor may pay to the members of the Commission such remuneration and allowances as he may determine.

(2) The Lord Chancellor may, if he thinks fit in the case of any member of the Commission pay such pension, allowance or gratuity to or in respect of the member, or such sums towards the provision of such pension, allowance or gratuity, as he may determine.

(3) If a person ceases to be a member of the Commission and it appears to the Lord Chancellor that there are special circumstances which make it right that the person should receive compensation, he may pay to that person a sum of such amount as he may determine.

Proceedings

4. The Commission shall sit at such times and in such places as the Lord Chancellor may direct and may sit in two or more divisions.

5. The Commission shall be deemed to be duly constituted if it consists of three members of whom—

(a) at least one holds or has held high judicial office (within the meaning of the Appellate Jurisdiction Act 1876), and

[(b) at least one is or has been a legally qualified member of the Asylum and Immigration Tribunal.]

Note: Paragraph 5(b) substituted by Sch 2 Asylum and Immigration Act 2004 from 4 April 2005, (SI 2005/565).

6. The chairman or, in his absence, such other member of the Commission as he may nominate, shall preside at sittings of the Commission and report its decisions.

Staff

7. The Lord Chancellor may appoint such officers and servants for the Commission as he thinks fit.

Expenses

8. The Lord Chancellor shall defray the remuneration of persons appointed under paragraph 7 above and such expenses of the Commission as he thinks fit.

Section 2

Schedule 2

Appeals: Supplementary

. . .

Note: Schedule 2 ceases to have effect from 1 April 2003 (SI 2003/754), Sch 7 Nationality, Immigration and Asylum Act 2002. SI 2003/754 sets out transitional provisions.

Section 3 SCHEDULE 3

BAIL: MODIFICATIONS OF SCHEDULE 2 TO THE IMMIGRATION ACT 1971

1.—(1) Paragraph 22 shall be amended as follows.

(2) In sub-paragraph (1A), for the words from the beginning to ['Tribunal'] there shall be substituted 'The Special Immigration Appeals Commission'.

(3) In sub-paragraph (2)—

(a) for the words 'immigration officer or ["The Asylum and Immigration Tribunal"]' there shall be substituted 'Special Immigration Appeals Commission', and

(b) for the words 'officer or ["The Asylum and Immigration Tribunal"]' there shall be substituted 'Commission'.

(4) In sub-paragraph (3)—

(a) for 'an immigration officer or ["The Asylum and Immigration Tribunal"]' there shall be substituted 'the Special Immigration Appeals Commission', and

(b) for 'officer or ["The Asylum and Immigration Tribunal"]', in both places, there shall be substituted 'Commission'.

2.—(1) Paragraph 23 shall be amended as follows.

(2) In sub-paragraph (1)—

(a) for ['The Asylum and Immigration Tribunal'] there shall be substituted 'the Special Immigration Appeals Commission', and

(b) for ['The Asylum and Immigration Tribunal'], in each place, there shall be substituted 'the Commission'.

(3) In sub-paragraph (2)—

(a) for ['The Asylum and Immigration Tribunal'] there shall be substituted 'the Special Immigration Appeals Commission', and

(b) for ['The Asylum and Immigration Tribunal'] there shall be substituted 'the Commission'.

3.—(1) Paragraph 24 shall be amended as follows.

(2) For sub-paragraph (2), there shall be substituted—

'(2) A person arrested under this paragraph shall be brought before the Special Immigration Appeals Commission within twenty-four hours.'

(3) In sub-paragraph (3), for the words from the beginning to 'above' there shall be substituted 'Where a person is brought before the Special Immigration Appeals Commission by virtue of sub-paragraph (2) above, the Commission—'.

4.—(1) Paragraph 29 shall be amended as follows.

(2) For sub-paragraphs (2) to (4) there shall be substituted—

'(2) The Special Immigration Appeals Commission may release an appellant on his entering into a recognizance or, in Scotland, bail bond conditioned for his appearance before the Commission at a time and place named in the recognizance or bail bond.'

(3) For sub-paragraph (6) there shall be substituted—

'(6) In any case in which the Special Immigration Appeals Commission has power to release an appellant on bail, the Commission may, instead of taking the bail, fix the amount and conditions of the bail (including the amount in which any sureties are to be bound) with a view to its being taken subsequently by any such person as may be specified by the Commission; and on the recognizance or bail bond being so taken the appellant shall be released.'

5. Paragraph 30(2) shall be omitted.

6.—(1) Paragraph 31 shall be amended as follows.

(2) In sub-paragraph (1)—

(a) for ['the Tribunal'] there shall be substituted 'the Special Immigration Appeals Commission',

(b) for ['the Tribunal'] there shall be substituted 'the Commission', and

(c) for ['the Tribunal'], in both places, there shall be substituted 'the Commission'.

(3) In sub-paragraph (3)—

(a) for ['the Tribunal'] there shall be substituted 'the Special Immigration Appeals Commission,' and

(b) for ['the Tribunal'] there shall be substituted 'it'.

7. Paragraph 32 shall be amended as follows—

(a) for ['the Tribunal'] there shall be substituted 'the Special Immigration Appeals Commission',

(b) for ['the Tribunal'] there shall be substituted 'the Commission', and

(c) for ['the Tribunal'] there shall be substituted 'the Commission'.

8.—(1) Paragraph 33 shall be amended as follows.

(2) For sub-paragraph (2), there shall be substituted—

'(2) A person arrested under this paragraph shall be brought before the Special Immigration Appeals Commission within twenty-four hours.'

(3) In sub-paragraph (3), for the words from the beginning to 'above' there shall be substituted 'Where a person is brought before the Special Immigration Appeals Commission by virtue of sub-paragraph (2) above, the Commission—'.

Note: Extends jurisdiction of Tribunal to Special Immigration Appeals Commission in paras 22–24, 29, 31–33. Words in square brackets substituted by Sch 2 Asylum and Immigration Act 2004 from 4 April 2005 (SI 2005/565).

Human Rights Act 1998
(1998, c. 42)

Arrangement of Sections

Introduction

An Act to give further effect to rights and freedoms guaranteed under the European Convention on Human Rights; to make provision with respect to holders of certain judicial offices who become judges of the European Court of Human Rights; and for connected purposes. [9 November 1998]

Introduction

1. The Convention Rights

(1) In this Act 'the Convention rights' means the rights and fundamental freedoms set out in—
  (a) Articles 2 to 12 and 14 of the Convention,
  (b) Articles 1 to 3 of the First Protocol, and
  (c) [Article 1 of the Thirteenth Protocol]
  as read with Articles 16 to 18 of the Convention.

(2) Those Articles are to have effect for the purposes of this Act subject to any designated derogation or reservation (as to which see sections 14 and 15).

(3) The Articles are set out in Schedule 1.

(4) The Secretary of State may by order make such amendments to this Act as he considers appropriate to reflect the effect, in relation to the United Kingdom, of a protocol.

(5) In subsection (4) 'protocol' means a protocol to the Convention—
   (a) which the United Kingdom has ratified; or
   (b) which the United Kingdom has signed with a view to ratification.

(6) No amendment may be made by an order under subsection (4) so as to come into force before the protocol concerned is in force in relation to the United Kingdom.

Note: Commencement 2 October 2000. Words in square brackets in sub-s (1)(c) substituted from 22 June 2004 (SI 2004/1574).

2. Interpretation of Convention rights

(1) A court or tribunal determining a question which has arisen in connection with a Convention right must take into account any—
   (a) judgment, decision, declaration or advisory opinion of the European Court of Human Rights,
   (b) opinion of the Commission given in a report adopted under Article 31 of the Convention,
   (c) decision of the Commission in connection with Article 26 or 27(2) of the Convention, or
   (d) decision of the Committee of Ministers taken under Article 46 of the Convention,

whenever made or given, so far as, in the opinion of the court or tribunal, it is relevant to the proceedings in which that question has arisen.

(2) Evidence of any judgment, decision, declaration or opinion of which account may have to be taken under this section is to be given in proceedings before any court or tribunal in such manner as may be provided by rules.

(3) In this section 'rules' means rules of court or, in the case of proceedings before a tribunal, rules made for the purposes of this section—
   (a) by the Lord Chancellor or the Secretary of State, in relation to any proceedings outside Scotland;
   (b) by the Secretary of State, in relation to proceedings in Scotland; or
   (c) by a Northern Ireland department, in relation to proceedings before a tribunal in Northern Ireland—
      (i) which deals with transferred matters; and
      (ii) for which no rules made under paragraph (a) are in force.

Note: Commencement 2 October 2000.

Legislation

3. Interpretation of legislation

(1) So far as it is possible to do so, primary legislation and subordinate legislation

must be read and given effect in a way which is compatible with the Convention rights.

(2) This section—
  (a) applies to primary legislation and subordinate legislation whenever enacted;
  (b) does not affect the validity, continuing operation or enforcement of any incompatible primary legislation; and
  (c) does not affect the validity, continuing operation or enforcement of any incompatible subordinate legislation if (disregarding any possibility of revocation) primary legislation prevents removal of the incompatibility.

Note: Commencement 2 October 2000.

4. Declaration of incompatibility

(1) Subsection (2) applies in any proceedings in which a court determines whether a provision of primary legislation is compatible with a Convention right.

(2) If the court is satisfied that the provision is incompatible with a Convention right, it may make a declaration of that incompatibility.

(3) Subsection (4) applies in any proceedings in which a court determines whether a provision of subordinate legislation, made in the exercise of a power conferred by primary legislation, is compatible with a Convention right.

(4) If the court is satisfied—
  (a) that the provision is incompatible with a Convention right, and
  (b) that (disregarding any possibility of revocation) the primary legislation concerned prevents removal of the incompatibility,

it may make a declaration of that incompatibility.

(5) In this section 'court' means—
  (a) the House of Lords;
  (b) the Judicial Committee of the Privy Council;
  (c) the Courts-Martial Appeal Court;
  (d) in Scotland, the High Court of Justiciary sitting otherwise than as a trial court or the Court of Session;
  (e) in England and Wales or Northern Ireland, the High Court or the Court of Appeal.

(6) A declaration under this section ('a declaration of incompatibility')—
  (a) does not affect the validity, continuing operation or enforcement of the provision in respect of which it is given; and
  (b) is not binding on the parties to the proceedings in which it is made.

Note: Commencement 2 October 2000.

5. Right of Crown to intervene

(1) Where a court is considering whether to make a declaration of incompatibility, the Crown is entitled to notice in accordance with rules of court.

(2) In any case to which subsection (1) applies—
  (a) a Minister of the Crown (or a person nominated by him),
  (b) a member of the Scottish Executive,
  (c) a Northern Ireland Minister,
  (d) a Northern Ireland department, is entitled, on giving notice in accordance with rules of court, to be joined as a party to the proceedings.

(3) Notice under subsection (2) may be given at any time during the proceedings.

(4) A person who has been made a party to criminal proceedings (other than in Scotland) as the result of a notice under subsection (2) may, with leave, appeal to the House of Lords against any declaration of incompatibility made in the proceedings.

(5) In subsection (4)—
'criminal proceedings' includes all proceedings before the Courts-Martial Appeal Court; and
'leave' means leave granted by the court making the declaration of incompatibility or by the House of Lords.

Public authorities

6. Acts of public authorities

(1) It is unlawful for a public authority to act in a way which is incompatible with a Convention right.

(2) Subsection (1) does not apply to an act if—
  (a) as the result of one or more provisions of primary legislation, the authority could not have acted differently; or
  (b) in the case of one or more provisions of, or made under, primary legislation which cannot be read or given effect in a way which is compatible with the Convention rights, the authority was acting so as to give effect to or enforce those provisions.

(3) In this section 'public authority' includes—
  (a) a court or tribunal, and
  (b) any person certain of whose functions are functions of a public nature,
but does not include either House of Parliament or a person exercising functions in connection with proceedings in Parliament.

(4) In subsection (3) 'Parliament' does not include the House of Lords in its judicial capacity.

(5) In relation to a particular act, a person is not a public authority by virtue only of subsection (3)(b) if the nature of the act is private.

(6) 'An act' includes a failure to act but does not include a failure to—
 (a) introduce in, or lay before, Parliament a proposal for legislation; or
 (b) make any primary legislation or remedial order.

Note: Commencement 2 October 2000.

7. Proceedings

(1) A person who claims that a public authority has acted (or proposes to act) in a way which is made unlawful by section 6(1) may—
 (a) bring proceedings against the authority under this Act in the appropriate court or tribunal, or
 (b) rely on the Convention right or rights concerned in any legal proceedings,
 but only if he is (or would be) a victim of the unlawful act.

(2) In subsection (1)(a) 'appropriate court or tribunal' means such court or tribunal as may be determined in accordance with rules; and proceedings against an authority include a counterclaim or similar proceeding.

(3) If the proceedings are brought on an application for judicial review, the applicant is to be taken to have a sufficient interest in relation to the unlawful act only if he is, or would be, a victim of that act.

(4) If the proceedings are made by way of a petition for judicial review in Scotland, the applicant shall be taken to have title and interest to sue in relation to the unlawful act only if he is, or would be, a victim of that act.

(5) Proceedings under subsection (1)(a) must be brought before the end of—
 (a) the period of one year beginning with the date on which the act complained of took place; or
 (b) such longer period as the court or tribunal considers equitable having regard to all the circumstances,

but that is subject to any rule imposing a stricter time limit in relation to the procedure in question.

(6) In subsection (1)(b) 'legal proceedings' includes—
 (a) proceedings brought by or at the instigation of a public authority; and
 (b) an appeal against the decision of a court or tribunal.

(7) For the purposes of this section, a person is a victim of an unlawful act only if he would be a victim for the purposes of Article 34 of the Convention if proceedings were brought in the European Court of Human Rights in respect of that act.

(8) Nothing in this Act creates a criminal offence.

(9) In this section 'rules' means—
 (a) in relation to proceedings before a court or tribunal outside Scotland, rules

made by the Lord Chancellor or the Secretary of State for the purposes of this section or rules of court,

(b) in relation to proceedings before a court or tribunal in Scotland, rules made by the Secretary of State for those purposes,

(c) in relation to proceedings before a tribunal in Northern Ireland—

(i) which deals with transferred matters; and

(ii) for which no rules made under paragraph (a) are in force,

rules made by a Northern Ireland department for those purposes, and includes provision made by order under section 1 of the Courts and Legal Services Act 1990.

(10) In making rules, regard must be had to section 9.

(11) The Minister who has power to make rules in relation to a particular tribunal may, to the extent he considers it necessary to ensure that the tribunal can provide an appropriate remedy in relation to an act (or proposed act) of a public authority which is (or would be) unlawful as a result of section 6(1), by order add to—

(a) the relief or remedies which the tribunal may grant; or

(b) the grounds on which it may grant any of them.

(12) An order made under subsection (11) may contain such incidental, supplemental, consequential or transitional provision as the Minister making it considers appropriate.

(13) 'The Minister' includes the Northern Ireland department concerned.

Note: Commencement 2 October 2000.

8. Judicial remedies

(1) In relation to any act (or proposed act) of a public authority which the court finds is (or would be) unlawful, it may grant such relief or remedy, or make such order, within its powers as it considers just and appropriate.

(2) But damages may be awarded only by a court which has power to award damages, or to order the payment of compensation, in civil proceedings.

(3) No award of damages is to be made unless, taking account of all the circumstances of the case, including—

(a) any other relief or remedy granted, or order made, in relation to the act in question (by that or any other court), and

(b) the consequences of any decision (of that or any other court) in respect of that act,

the court is satisfied that the award is necessary to afford just satisfaction to the person in whose favour it is made.

(4) In determining—

(a) whether to award damages, or

(b) the amount of an award,

the court must take into account the principles applied by the European Court of Human Rights in relation to the award of compensation under Article 41 of the Convention.

(5) A public authority against which damages are awarded is to be treated—

(a) in Scotland, for the purposes of section 3 of the Law Reform (Miscellaneous Provisions) (Scotland) Act 1940 as if the award were made in an action of damages in which the authority has been found liable in respect of loss or damage to the person to whom the award is made;

(b) for the purposes of the Civil Liability (Contribution) Act 1978 as liable in respect of damage suffered by the person to whom the award is made.

(6) In this section—

'court' includes a tribunal;

'damages' means damages for an unlawful act of a public authority; and

'unlawful' means unlawful under section 6(1).

Note: Commencement 2 October 2000.

9. Judicial acts

(1) Proceedings under section 7(1)(a) in respect of a judicial act may be brought only—

(a) by exercising a right of appeal;

(b) on an application (in Scotland a petition) for judicial review; or

(c) in such other forum as may be prescribed by rules.

(2) That does not affect any rule of law which prevents a court from being the subject of judicial review.

(3) In proceedings under this Act in respect of a judicial act done in good faith, damages may not be awarded otherwise than to compensate a person to the extent required by Article 5(5) of the Convention.

(4) An award of damages permitted by subsection (3) is to be made against the Crown; but no award may be made unless the appropriate person, if not a party to the proceedings, is joined.

(5) In this section—

'appropriate person' means the Minister responsible for the court concerned, or a person or government department nominated by him;

'court' includes a tribunal;

'judge' includes a member of a tribunal, a justice of the peace and a clerk or other officer entitled to exercise the jurisdiction of a court;

'judicial act' means a judicial act of a court and includes an act done on the instructions, or on behalf, of a judge; and

'rules' has the same meaning as in section 7(9).

Note: Commencement 2 October 2000.

Remedial action

10. Power to take remedial action

(1) This section applies if—
  (a) a provision of legislation has been declared under section 4 to be incompatible with a Convention right and, if an appeal lies—
    (i) all persons who may appeal have stated in writing that they do not intend to do so;
    (ii) the time for bringing an appeal has expired and no appeal has been brought within that time; or
    (iii) an appeal brought within that time has been determined or abandoned; or
  (b) it appears to a Minister of the Crown or Her Majesty in Council that, having regard to a finding of the European Court of Human Rights made after the coming into force of this section in proceedings against the United Kingdom, a provision of legislation is incompatible with an obligation of the United Kingdom arising from the Convention.

(2) If a Minister of the Crown considers that there are compelling reasons for proceeding under this section, he may by order make such amendments to the legislation as he considers necessary to remove the incompatibility.

(3) If, in the case of subordinate legislation, a Minister of the Crown considers—
  (a) that it is necessary to amend the primary legislation under which the subordinate legislation in question was made, in order to enable the incompatibility to be removed, and
  (b) that there are compelling reasons for proceeding under this section, he may by order make such amendments to the primary legislation as he considers necessary.

(4) This section also applies where the provision in question is in subordinate legislation and has been quashed, or declared invalid, by reason of incompatibility with a Convention right and the Minister proposes to proceed under paragraph 2(b) of Schedule 2.

(5) If the legislation is an Order in Council, the power conferred by subsection (2) or (3) is exercisable by Her Majesty in Council.

(6) In this section 'legislation' does not include a Measure of the Church Assembly or of the General Synod of the Church of England.

(7) Schedule 2 makes further provision about remedial orders.

Note: Commencement 2 October 2000.

Other rights and proceedings

11. Safeguard for existing human rights

A person's reliance on a Convention right does not restrict—

(a) any other right or freedom conferred on him by or under any law having effect in any part of the United Kingdom; or

(b) his right to make any claim or bring any proceedings which he could make or bring apart from sections 7 to 9.

Note: Commencement 2 October 2000.

12. Freedom of expression

(1) This section applies if a court is considering whether to grant any relief which, if granted, might affect the exercise of the Convention right to freedom of expression.

(2) If the person against whom the application for relief is made ('the respondent') is neither present nor represented, no such relief is to be granted unless the court is satisfied—

(a) that the applicant has taken all practicable steps to notify the respondent; or

(b) that there are compelling reasons why the respondent should not be notified.

(3) No such relief is to be granted so as to restrain publication before trial unless the court is satisfied that the applicant is likely to establish that publication should not be allowed.

(4) The court must have particular regard to the importance of the Convention right to freedom of expression and, where the proceedings relate to material which the respondent claims, or which appears to the court, to be journalistic, literary or artistic material (or to conduct connected with such material), to—

(a) the extent to which—

(i) the material has, or is about to, become available to the public; or

(ii) it is, or would be, in the public interest for the material to be published;

(b) any relevant privacy code.

(5) In this section—

'court' includes a tribunal; and

'relief' includes any remedy or order (other than in criminal proceedings).

Note: Commencement 2 October 2000.

13. Freedom of thought, conscience and religion

(1) If a court's determination of any question arising under this Act might affect the exercise by a religious organisation (itself or its members collectively) of the Convention right to freedom of thought, conscience and religion, it must have particular regard to the importance of that right.

(2) In this section 'court' includes a tribunal.

Note: Commencement 2 October 2000.

Derogations and reservations

14. Derogations

(1) In this Act 'designated derogation' means[. . .] any derogation by the United Kingdom from an Article of the Convention, or of any protocol to the Convention, which is designated for the purposes of this Act in an order made by the Secretary of State.

(2) . . .

(3) If a designated derogation is amended or replaced it ceases to be a designated derogation.

(4) But subsection (3) does not prevent the Secretary of State from exercising his power under subsection (1)[. . .] to make a fresh designation order in respect of the Article concerned.

(5) The Secretary of State must by order make such amendments to Schedule 3 as he considers appropriate to reflect—
- (a) any designation order; or
- (b) the effect of subsection (3).

(6) A designation order may be made in anticipation of the making by the United Kingdom of a proposed derogation.

Note: Commencement 2 October 2000. Words omitted from 1 April 2001 (SI 2001/1216).

15. Reservations

(1) In this Act 'designated reservation' means—
- (a) the United Kingdom's reservation to Article 2 of the First Protocol to the Convention; and
- (b) any other reservation by the United Kingdom to an Article of the Convention, or of any protocol to the Convention, which is designated for the purposes of this Act in an order made by the Secretary of State.

(2) The text of the reservation referred to in subsection (1)(a) is set out in Part II of Schedule 3.

(3) If a designated reservation is withdrawn wholly or in part it ceases to be a designated reservation.

(4) But subsection (3) does not prevent the Secretary of State from exercising his power under subsection (1)(b) to make a fresh designation order in respect of the Article concerned.

(5) The Secretary of State must by order make such amendments to this Act as he considers appropriate to reflect—

(a) any designation order; or

(b) the effect of subsection (3).

Note: Commencement 2 October 2000.

16. Period for which designated derogations have effect

(1) If it has not already been withdrawn by the United Kingdom, a designated derogation ceases to have effect for the purposes of this Act—

[. . .] at the end of the period of five years beginning with the date on which the order designation it was made.

(2) At any time before the period—

(a) fixed by subsection (1) [. . .], or

(b) extended by an order under this subsection,

comes to an end, the Secretary of State may by order extend it by a further period of five years.

(3) An order under section 14(1)[. . .] ceases to have effect at the end of the period for consideration, unless a resolution has been passed by each House approving the order.

(4) Subsection (3) does not affect—

(a) anything done in reliance on the order; or

(b) the power to make a fresh order under section 14(1)[. . .].

(5) In subsection (3) 'period for consideration' means the period of forty days beginning with the day on which the order was made.

(6) In calculating the period for consideration, no account is to be taken of any time during which—

(a) Parliament is dissolved or prorogued; or

(b) both Houses are adjourned for more than four days.

(7) If a designated derogation is withdrawn by the United Kingdom, the Secretary of State must by order make such amendments to this Act as he considers are required to reflect that withdrawal.

Note: Commencement 2 October 2000. Words omitted from 1 April 2001 (SI 2001/1216).

17. Periodic review of designated reservations

(1) The appropriate Minister must review the designated reservation referred to in section 15(1)(a)—
   (a) before the end of the period of five years beginning with the date on which section 1(2) came into force; and
   (b) if that designation is still in force, before the end of the period of five years beginning with the date on which the last report relating to it was laid under subsection (3).

(2) The appropriate Minister must review each of the other designated reservations (if any)—
   (a) before the end of the period of five years beginning with the date on which the order designating the reservation first came into force; and
   (b) if the designation is still in force, before the end of the period of five years beginning with the date on which the last report relating to it was laid under subsection (3).

(3) The Minister conducting a review under this section must prepare a report on the result of the review and lay a copy of it before each House of Parliament.

Note: Commencement 2 October 2000.

Judges of the European Court of Human Rights

18. Appointment to European Court of Human Rights

(1) In this section 'judicial office' means the office of—
   (a) Lord Justice of Appeal, Justice of the High Court or Circuit judge, in England and Wales;
   (b) judge of the Court of Session or sheriff, in Scotland;
   (c) Lord Justice of Appeal, judge of the High Court or county court judge, in Northern Ireland.

(2) The holder of a judicial office may become a judge of the European Court of Human Rights ('the Court') without being required to relinquish his office.

(3) But he is not required to perform the duties of his judicial office while he is a judge of the Court.

(4) In respect of any period during which he is a judge of the Court—
   (a) a Lord Justice of Appeal or Justice of the High Court is not to count as a judge of the relevant court for the purposes of section 2(1) or 4(1) of the Supreme Court Act 1981 (maximum number of judges) nor as a judge of the Supreme Court for the purposes of section 12(1) to (6) of that Act (salaries etc.);
   (b) a judge of the Court of Session is not to count as a judge of that court for

the purposes of section 1(1) of the Court of Session Act 1988 (maximum number of judges) or of section 9(1)(c) of the Administration of Justice Act 1973 ('the 1973 Act') (salaries etc.);

(c) a Lord Justice of Appeal or judge of the High Court in Northern Ireland is not to count as a judge of the relevant court for the purposes of section 2(1) or 3(1) of the Judicature (Northern Ireland) Act 1978 (maximum number of judges) nor as a judge of the Supreme Court of Northern Ireland for the purposes of section 9(1)(d) of the 1973 Act (salaries etc.);

(d) a Circuit judge is not to count as such for the purposes of section 18 of the Court Act 1971 (salaries etc.);

(e) a sheriff is not to count as such for the purposes of section 14 of the Sheriff Courts (Scotland) Act 1907 (salaries etc.);

(f) a county court judge of Northern Ireland is not to count as such for the purposes of section 106 of the County Courts Act (Northern Ireland) 1959 (salaries etc.).

(5) If a sheriff principal is appointed a judge of the Court, section 11(1) of the Sheriff Courts (Scotland) Act 1971 (temporary appointment of sheriff principal) applies, while he holds that appointment, as if his office is vacant.

(6) Schedule 4 makes provision about judicial pensions in relation to the holder of a judicial office who serves as a judge of the Court.

(7) The Lord Chancellor or the Secretary of State may by order make such transitional provision (including, in particular, provision for a temporary increase in the maximum number of judges) as he considers appropriate in relation to any holder of a judicial office who has completed his service as a judge of the Court.

Note: Commencement 9 November 1998.

Parliamentary procedure

19. Statements of compatibility

(1) A Minister of the Crown in charge of a Bill in either House of Parliament must, before Second Reading of the Bill—

(a) make a statement to the effect that in his view the provisions of the Bill are compatible with the Convention rights ('a statement of compatibility'); or

(b) make a statement to the effect that although he is unable to make a statement of compatibility the government nevertheless wishes the House to proceed with the Bill.

(2) The statement must be in writing and be published in such manner as the Minister making it considers appropriate.

Note: Commencement 24 November 1998.

Supplemental

20. Orders etc. under this Act

(1) Any power of a Minister of the Crown to make an order under this Act is exercisable by statutory instrument.

(2) The power of the Lord Chancellor or the Secretary of State to make rules (other than rules of court) under section 2(3) or 7(9) is exercisable by statutory instrument.

(3) Any statutory instrument made under section 14, 15 or 16(7) must be laid before Parliament.

(4) No order may be made by the Lord Chancellor or the Secretary of State under section 1(4), 7(11) or 16(2) unless a draft of the order has been laid before, and approved by, each House of Parliament.

(5) Any statutory instrument made under section 18(7) or Schedule 4, or to which subsection (2) applies, shall be subject to annulment in pursuance of a resolution of either House of Parliament.

(6) The power of a Northern Ireland department to make—
(a) rules under section 2(3)(c) or 7(9)(c), or
(b) an order under section 7(11),
is exercisable by statutory rule for the purposes of the Statutory Rules (Northern Ireland) Order 1979.

(7) Any rules made under section 2(3)(c) or 7(9)(c) shall be subject to negative resolution; and section 41(6) of the Interpretation Act (Northern Ireland) 1954 (meaning of 'subject to negative resolution') shall apply as if the power to make the rules were conferred by an Act of the Northern Ireland Assembly.

(8) No order may be made by a Northern Ireland department under section 7(11) unless a draft of the order has been laid before, and approved by, the Northern Ireland Assembly.

Note: Commencement 9 November 1998.

21. Interpretation, etc

(1) In this Act—
'amend' includes repeal and apply (with or without modifications);
'the appropriate Minister' means the Minister of the Crown having charge of the appropriate authorised government department (within the meaning of the Crown Proceedings Act 1947);
'the Commission' means the European Commission of Human Rights;
'the Convention' means the Convention for the Protection of Human Rights and Fundamental Freedoms, agreed by the Council of Europe at Rome on

4th November 1950 as it has effect for the time being in relation to the United Kingdom;

'declaration of incompatibility' means a declaration under section 4;

'Minister of the Crown' has the same meaning as in the Ministers of the Crown Act 1975;

'Northern Ireland Minister' includes the First Minister and the deputy First Minister in Northern Ireland;

'primary legislation' means any—

(a) public general Act;
(b) local and personal Act;
(c) private Act;
(d) Measure of the Church Assembly;
(e) Measure of the General Synod of the Church of England;
(f) Order in Council—
  (i) made in exercise of Her Majesty's Royal Prerogative;
  (ii) made under section 38(1)(a) of the Northern Ireland Constitution Act 1973 or the corresponding provision of the Northern Ireland Act 1998; or
  (iii) amending an Act of a kind mentioned in paragraph (a), (b) or (c); and includes an order or other instrument made under primary legislation (otherwise than by the National Assembly for Wales, a member of the Scottish Executive, a Northern Ireland Minister or a Northern Ireland department) to the extent to which it operates to bring one or more provisions of that legislation into force or amends any primary legislation;

'the First Protocol' means the protocol to the Convention agreed at Paris on 20th March 1952;

. . .

'the Eleventh Protocol' means the protocol to the Convention (restructuring the control machinery established by the Convention) agreed at Strasbourg on 11th May 1994;

['the Thirteenth Protocol' means the protocol to the Convention (concerning the abolition of the death penalty in all circumstances) agreed at Vilnius on 3rd May 2002;]

'remedial order' means an order under section 10;

'subordinate legislation' means any—

(a) Order in Council other than one—
  (i) made in exercise of Her Majesty's Royal Prerogative;
  (ii) made under section 38(1)(a) of the Northern Ireland Constitution Act 1973 or the corresponding provision of the Northern Ireland Act 1998; or
  (iii) amending an Act of a kind mentioned in the definition of primary legislation;

(b) Act of the Scottish Parliament;
(c) Act of the Parliament of Northern Ireland;
(d) Measure of the Assembly established under section 1 of the Northern Ireland Assembly Act 1973;
(e) Act of the Northern Ireland Assembly;
(f) order, rules, regulations, scheme, warrant, byelaw or other instrument made under primary legislation (except to the extent to which it operates to bring one or more provisions of that legislation into force or amends any primary legislation);
(g) order, rules, regulations, scheme, warrant, byelaw or other instrument made under legislation mentioned in paragraph (b), (c), (d) or (e) or made under an Order in Council applying only to Northern Ireland;
(h) order, rules, regulations, scheme, warrant, byelaw or other instrument made by a member of the Scottish Executive, a Northern Ireland Minister or a Northern Ireland department in exercise of prerogative or other executive functions of Her Majesty which are exercisable by such a person on behalf of Her Majesty;

'transferred matters' has the same meaning as in the Northern Ireland Act 1998; and

'tribunal' means any tribunal in which legal proceedings may be brought.

(2) The references in paragraphs (b) and (c) of section 2(1) to Articles are to Articles of the Convention as they had effect immediately before the coming into force of the Eleventh Protocol.

(3) The reference in paragraph (d) of section 2(1) to Article 46 includes a reference to Articles 32 and 54 of the Convention as they had effect immediately before the coming into force of the Eleventh Protocol.

(4) The references in section 2(1) to a report or decision of the Commission or a decision of the Committee of Ministers include references to a report or decision made as provided by paragraphs 3, 4 and 6 of Article 5 of the Eleventh Protocol (transitional provisions).

(5) Any liability under the Army Act 1955, the Air Force Act 1955 or the Naval Discipline Act 1957 to suffer death for an offence is replaced by a liability to imprisonment for life or any less punishment authorised by those Acts; and those Acts shall accordingly have effect with the necessary modifications.

Note: Commencement of s 21(5) on 9 November 1998, remainder of s 21 on 2 October 2000. Words in sub-s (1) omitted and substituted by SI 2004/1574 from 22 June 2004.

22. Short title, commencement, application and extent

(1) This Act may be cited as the Human Rights Act 1998.

(2) Sections 18, 20 and 21(5) and this section come into force on the passing of this Act.

(3) The other provisions of this Act come into force on such day as the Secretary of State may by order appoint; and different days may be appointed for different purposes.

(4) Paragraph (b) of subsection (1) of section 7 applies to proceedings brought by or at the instigation of a public authority whenever the act in question took place; but otherwise that subsection does not apply to an act taking place before the coming into force of that section.

(5) This Act binds the Crown.

(6) This Act extends to Northern Ireland.

(7) Section 21(5), so far as it relates to any provision contained in the Army Act 1955, the Air Force Act 1955 or the Naval Discipline Act 1957, extends to any place to which that provision extends.

Note: Commencement 9 November 1998.

Schedules

Section 1(3)

Schedule 1

The Articles

Part I

The Convention Rights and Freedoms

Article 2 *Right to life*

1. Everyone's right to life shall be protected by law. No one shall be deprived of his life intentionally save in the execution of a sentence of a court following his conviction of a crime for which this penalty is provided by law.
2. Deprivation of life shall not be regarded as inflicted in contravention of this Article when it results from the use of force which is no more than absolutely necessary:
   (a) in defence of any person from unlawful violence;
   (b) in order to effect a lawful arrest or to prevent the escape of a person lawfully detained;
   (c) in action lawfully taken for the purpose of quelling a riot or insurrection.

Article 3 *Prohibition of torture*

No one shall be subjected to torture or to inhuman or degrading treatment or punishment.

Article 4 *Prohibition of slavery and forced labour*

1. No one shall be held in slavery or servitude.
2. No one shall be required to perform forced or compulsory labour.

3. For the purpose of this Article the term 'forced or compulsory labour' shall not include:
   (a) any work required to be done in the ordinary course of detention imposed according to the provisions of Article 5 of this Convention or during conditional release from such detention;
   (b) any service of a military character or, in case of conscientious objectors in countries where they are recognised, service exacted instead of compulsory military service;
   (c) any service exacted in case of an emergency or calamity threatening the life or well-being of the community;
   (d) any work or service which forms part of normal civic obligations.

Article 5 *Right to liberty and security*

1. Everyone has the right to liberty and security of person. No one shall be deprived of his liberty save in the following cases and in accordance with a procedure prescribed by law:
   (a) the lawful detention of a person after conviction by a competent court;
   (b) the lawful arrest or detention of a person for non-compliance with the lawful order of a court or in order to secure the fulfilment of any obligation prescribed by law;
   (c) the lawful arrest or detention of a person effected for the purpose of bringing him before the competent legal authority on reasonable suspicion of having committed an offence or when it is reasonably considered necessary to prevent his committing an offence or fleeing after having done so;
   (d) the detention of a minor by lawful order for the purpose of educational supervision or his lawful detention for the purpose of bringing him before the competent legal authority;
   (e) the lawful detention of persons for the prevention of the spreading of infectious diseases, of persons of unsound mind, alcoholics or drug addicts or vagrants;
   (f) the lawful arrest or detention of a person to prevent his effecting an unauthorised entry into the country or of a person against whom action is being taken with a view to deportation or extradition.
2. Everyone who is arrested shall be informed promptly, in a language which he understands, of the reasons for his arrest and of any charge against him.
3. Everyone arrested or detained in accordance with the provisions of paragraph 1(c) of this Article shall be brought promptly before a judge or other officer authorised by law to exercise judicial power and shall be entitled to trial within a reasonable time or to release pending trial. Release may be conditioned by guarantees to appear for trial.
4. Everyone who is deprived of his liberty by arrest or detention shall be entitled to take proceedings by which the lawfulness of his detention shall be decided speedily by a court and his release ordered if the detention is not lawful.
5. Everyone who has been the victim of arrest or detention in contravention of the provisions of this Article shall have an enforceable right to compensation.

Article 6 *Right to a fair trial*

1. In the determination of his civil rights and obligations or of any criminal charge against him, everyone is entitled to a fair and public hearing within a reasonable time by an

independent and impartial tribunal established by law. Judgment shall be pronounced publicly but the press and public may be excluded from all or part of the trial in the interest of morals, public order or national security in a democratic society, where the interests of juveniles or the protection of the private life of the parties so require, or to the extent strictly necessary in the opinion of the court in special circumstances where publicity would prejudice the interests of justice.

2. Everyone charged with a criminal offence shall be presumed innocent until proved guilty according to law.
3. Everyone charged with a criminal offence has the following minimum rights:
   (a) to be informed promptly, in a language which he understands and in detail, of the nature and cause of the accusation against him;
   (b) to have adequate time and facilities for the preparation of his defence;
   (c) to defend himself in person or through legal assistance of his own choosing or, if he has not sufficient means to pay for legal assistance, to be given it free when the interests of justice so require;
   (d) to examine or have examined witnesses against him and to obtain the attendance and examination of witnesses on his behalf under the same conditions as witnesses against him;
   (e) to have the free assistance of an interpreter if he cannot understand or speak the language used in court.

Article 7 *No punishment without law*

1. No one shall be held guilty of any criminal offence on account of any act or omission which did not constitute a criminal offence under national or international law at the time when it was committed. Nor shall a heavier penalty be imposed than the one that was applicable at the time the criminal offence was committed.
2. This Article shall not prejudice the trial and punishment of any person for any act or omission which, at the time when it was committed, was criminal according to the general principles of law recognised by civilised nations.

Article 8 *Right to respect for private and family life*

1. Everyone has the right to respect for his private and family life, his home and his correspondence.
2. There shall be no interference by a public authority with the exercise of this right except such as is in accordance with the law and is necessary in a democratic society in the interests of national security, public safety or the economic well being of the country, for the prevention of disorder or crime, for the protection of health or morals, or for the protection of the rights and freedoms of others.

Article 9 *Freedom of thought, conscience and religion*

1. Everyone has the right to freedom of thought, conscience and religion; this right includes freedom to change his religion or belief and freedom, either alone or in community with others and in public or private, to manifest his religion or belief, in worship, teaching, practice and observance.

2. Freedom to manifest one's religion or beliefs shall be subject only to such limitations as are prescribed by law and are necessary in a democratic society in the interests of public safety, for the protection of public order, health or morals, or for the protection of the rights and freedoms of others.

Article 10 *Freedom of expression*

1. Everyone has the right to freedom of expression. This right shall include freedom to hold opinions and to receive and impart information and ideas without interference by public authority and regardless of frontiers. This Article shall not prevent States from requiring the licensing of broadcasting, television or cinema enterprises.
2. The exercise of these freedoms, since it carries with it duties and responsibilities, may be subject to such formalities, conditions, restrictions or penalties as are prescribed by law and are necessary in a democratic society, in the interests of national security, territorial integrity or public safety, for the prevention of disorder or crime, for the protection of health or morals, for the protection of the reputation or rights of others, for preventing the disclosure of information received in confidence, or for maintaining the authority and impartiality of the judiciary.

Article 11 *Freedom of assembly and association*

1. Everyone has the right to freedom of peaceful assembly and to freedom of association with others, including the right to form and to join trade unions for the protection of his interests.
2. No restrictions shall be placed on the exercise of these rights other than such as are prescribed by law and are necessary in a democratic society in the interests of national security or public safety, for the prevention of disorder or crime, for the protection of health or morals or for the protection of the rights and freedoms of others. This Article shall not prevent the imposition of lawful restrictions on the exercise of these rights by members of the armed forces, of the police or of the administration of the State.

Article 12 *Right to marry*

Men and women of marriageable age have the right to marry and to found a family, according to the national laws governing the exercise of this right.

Article 14 *Prohibition of discrimination*

The enjoyment of the rights and freedoms set forth in this Convention shall be secured without discrimination on any ground such as sex, race, colour, language, religion, political or other opinion, national or social origin, association with a national minority, property, birth or other status.

Article 16 *Restrictions on political activity of aliens*

Nothing in Articles 10, 11 and 14 shall be regarded as preventing the High Contracting Parties from imposing restrictions on the political activity of aliens.

Article 17 *Prohibition of abuse of rights*

Nothing in this Convention may be interpreted as implying for any State, group or person any right to engage in any activity or perform any act aimed at the destruction of any of the rights and freedoms set forth herein or at their limitation to a greater extent than is provided for in the Convention.

Article 18 *Limitation on use of restrictions on rights*

The restrictions permitted under this Convention to the said rights and freedoms shall not be applied for any purpose other than those for which they have been prescribed.

Part II

The First Protocol

Article 1 *Protection of property*

Every natural or legal person is entitled to the peaceful enjoyment of his possessions. No one shall be deprived of his possessions except in the public interest and subject to the conditions provided for by law and by the general principles of international law.

The preceding provisions shall not, however, in any way impair the right of a State to enforce such laws as it deems necessary to control the use of property in accordance with the general interest or to secure the payment of taxes or other contributions or penalties.

Article 2 *Right to education*

No person shall be denied the right to education. In the exercise of any functions which it assumes in relation to education and to teaching, the State shall respect the right of parents to ensure such education and teaching in conformity with their own religious and philosophical convictions.

Article 3 *Right to free elections*

The High Contracting Parties undertake to hold free elections at reasonable intervals by secret ballot, under conditions which will ensure the free expression of the opinion of the people in the choice of the legislature.

[Part III

Article 1 of the Thirteenth Protocol

Abolition of the death penalty

The death penalty shall be abolished. No one shall be condemned to such penalty or executed.]

Note: Part 3 substituted from 22 June 2004 (SI 2004/1574).

Section 10

Schedule 2

Remedial Orders

Orders

1.—(1) A remedial order may—

(a) contain such incidental, supplemental, consequential or transitional provision as the person making it considers appropriate;

(b) be made so as to have effect from a date earlier than that on which it is made;

(c) make provision for the delegation of specific functions;

(d) make different provision for different cases.

(2) The power conferred by sub-paragraph (1)(a) includes—

(a) power to amend primary legislation (including primary legislation other than that which contains the incompatible provision); and

(b) power to amend or revoke subordinate legislation (including subordinate legislation other than that which contains the incompatible provision).

(3) A remedial order may be made so as to have the same extent as the legislation which it affects.

(4) No person is to be guilty of an offence solely as a result of the retrospective effect of a remedial order.

Procedure

2. No remedial order may be made unless—

(a) a draft of the order has been approved by a resolution of each House of Parliament made after the end of the period of 60 days beginning with the day on which the draft was laid; or

(b) it is declared in the order that it appears to the person making it that, because of the urgency of the matter, it is necessary to make the order without a draft being so approved.

Orders laid in draft

3.—(1) No draft may be laid under paragraph 2(a) unless—

(a) the person proposing to make the order has laid before Parliament a document which contains a draft of the proposed order and the required information; and

(b) the period of 60 days, beginning with the day on which the document required by this sub-paragraph was laid, has ended.

(2) If representations have been made during that period, the draft laid under paragraph 2(a) must be accompanied by a statement containing—

(a) a summary of the representations; and

(b) if, as a result of the representations, the proposed order has been changed, details of the changes.

Urgent cases

4.—(1) If a remedial order ('the original order') is made without being approved in draft, the person making it must lay it before Parliament, accompanied by the required information, after it is made.

(2) If representations have been made during the period of 60 days beginning with the day on which the original order was made, the person making it must (after the end of that period) lay before Parliament a statement containing—

(a) a summary of the representations; and

(b) if, as a result of the representations, he considers it appropriate to make changes to the original order, details of the changes.

(3) If sub-paragraph (2)(b) applies, the person making the statement must—

(a) make a further remedial order replacing the original order; and

(b) lay the replacement order before Parliament.

(4) If, at the end of the period of 120 days beginning with the day on which the original order was made, a resolution has not been passed by each House approving the original or replacement order, the order ceases to have effect (but without that affecting anything previously done under either order or the power to make a fresh remedial order).

Definitions

5. In this Schedule—

'representations' means representations about a remedial order (or proposed remedial order) made to the person making (or proposing to make) it and includes any relevant Parliamentary report or resolution; and

'required information' means—

(a) an explanation of the incompatibility which the order (or proposed order) seeks to remove, including particulars of the relevant declaration, finding or order; and

(b) a statement of the reasons for proceeding under section 10 and for making an order in those terms.

Calculating periods

6. In calculating any period for the purposes of this Schedule, no account is to be taken of any time during which—

(a) Parliament is dissolved or prorogued; or

(b) both Houses are adjourned for more than four days.

Section 14 and 15

Schedule 3

Derogation and Reservation

Note: Part 1 repealed from 8 April 2005, (SI 2005/1071).

Part II
Reservation

At the time of signing the present (First) Protocol, I declare that, in view of certain provisions of the Education Acts in the United Kingdom, the principle affirmed in the second sentence of Article 2 is accepted by the United Kingdom only so far as it is compatible with the provision of efficient instruction and training, and the avoidance of unreasonable public expenditure.

Dated 20 march 1952. Made by the United Kingdom Permanent Representative to the Council of Europe.

Note: Part 1 repealed from 1 April 2001 (SI 2001/1216), current Part 1 inserted from 20 December 2001 (SI 2001/4032).

Section 18(6)

Schedule 4
Judicial Pensions

. . .

Immigration and Asylum Act 1999
(1999, c. 33)

Arrangement of Sections

Monitoring entry clearance

23. Monitoring refusals of entry clearance.

Reporting suspicious marriages

24. Duty to report suspicious marriages.
24A. Duty to report suspicious civil partnerships.

Immigration control: facilities and charges

25. Provision of facilities for immigration control at ports.
26. Charges: immigration control.

Charges: travel documents

27. . . .

Offences

28. . . .
29. . . .
30. . . .
31. Defences based on Article 31(1) of the Refugee Convention.

PART II. CARRIERS' LIABILITY

Clandestine entrants

32. Penalty for carrying clandestine entrants.
32A. Level of penalty: code of practice.
33. Prevention of clandestine entrants: code of practice.
34. Defences to claim that penalty is due under section 32.
35. Procedure.
35A. Appeal
36. Power to detain vehicles etc. in connection with penalties under section 32.
36A. Detention in default of payment.
37. Effect of detention.
38. . . .
39. . . .

Passengers without proper documents

40. Charges in respect of passengers without proper documents.
40A. Notification and objection.
40B. Appeal.

41. Visas for transit passengers.
42. . . .

Interpretation

43. Interpretation of Part II.

Part III. Bail

Routine bail hearings

44.–52. . . .

Bail hearings under other enactments

53. Applications for bail in immigration cases.
54. Extension of right to apply for bail in deportation cases.

Grants

55. . . .

Part IV. Appeals

. . .

Part V. Immigration Advisers and Immigration Service Providers

Interpretation

82. Interpretation of Part V.

The immigration services commissioner

83. The Commissioner.

The general prohibition

84. Provision of immigration services.
85. Registration and exemption by the Commissioner.
86. Designated professional bodies.

The immigration services tribunal

87. The Tribunal.
88. Appeal upheld by the Tribunal.
89. Disciplinary charge upheld by the Tribunal.
90. Orders by disciplinary bodies.

Enforcement

91. Offences.

An Act to make provision about immigration and asylum; provision about procedures in connection with marriage on superintendant registrar's certificate; and for connected purposes. [11 November 1999]

Part I

Immigration: General

Leave to enter, or remain in, the United Kingdom

1. . . .

Note: Amends Immigration Act 1971, s 3A.

2. . . .

Note: Amends Immigration Act 1971, s 3B.

3. . . .

Note: Amends Immigration Act 1971, s 3C.

4. Accommodation

(1) The Secretary of State may provide, or arrange for the provision of, facilities for the accommodation of persons—
   (a) temporarily admitted to the United Kingdom under paragraph 21 of Schedule 2 to the 1971 Act;
   (b) released from detention under that paragraph; or
   (c) released on bail from detention under any provision of the Immigration Acts.

[(2) The Secretary of State may provide, or arrange for the provision of, facilities for the accommodation of a person if—
   (a) he was (but is no longer) an asylum-seeker, and
   (b) his claim for asylum was rejected.

(3) The Secretary of State may provide, or arrange for the provision of, facilities for the accommodation of a dependant of a person for whom facilities may be provided under subsection (2).

(4) The following expressions have the same meaning in this section as in Part VI of this Act (as defined in section 94)—
   (a) asylum-seeker,
   (b) claim for asylum, and
   (c) dependant.]

[(5) The Secretary of State may make regulations specifying criteria to be used in determining—
   (a) whether or not to provide accommodation, or arrange for the provision of accommodation, for a person under this section;
   (b) whether or not to continue to provide accommodation, or arrange for the provision of accommodation, for a person under this section.

(6) The regulations may, in particular—
   (a) provide for the continuation of the provision of accommodation for a person to be conditional upon his performance of or participation in community activities in accordance with arrangements made by the Secretary of State;
   (b) provide for the continuation of the provision of accommodation to be subject to other conditions;
   (c) provide for the provision of accommodation (or the continuation of the provision of accommodation) to be a matter for the Secretary of State's discretion to a specified extent or in a specified class of case.

(7) For the purposes of subsection (6)(a)—
   (a) 'community activities' means activities that appear to the Secretary of State to be beneficial to the public or a section of the public, and
   (b) the Secretary of State may, in particular—
      (i) appoint one person to supervise or manage the performance of or participation in activities by another person;
      (ii) enter into a contract (with a local authority or any other person) for the provision of services by way of making arrangements for community activities in accordance with this section;
      (iii) pay, or arrange for the payment of, allowances to a person performing or participating in community activities in accordance with arrangements under this section.

(8) Regulations by virtue of subsection (6)(a) may, in particular, provide for a condition requiring the performance of or participation in community activities to apply to a person only if the Secretary of State has made arrangements for community activities in an area that includes the place where accommodation is provided for the person.

(9) A local authority or other person may undertake to manage or participate in arrangements for community activities in accordance with this section.]

[(**10**) The Secretary of State may make regulations permitting a person who is provided with accommodation under this section to be supplied also with services or facilities of a specified kind.

(**11**) Regulations under subsection (10)—

(a) may, in particular, permit a person to be supplied with a voucher which may be exchanged for goods or services,

(b) may not permit a person to be supplied with money,

(c) may restrict the extent or value of services or facilities to be provided, and

(d) may confer a discretion.]

Note: Commencement 11 November 1999. Heading substituted and sub-s (2) inserted by Nationality, Immigration and Asylum Act 2002, s 49 from 7 November 2002. Subsections (5)–(9) inserted by Asylum and Immigration Act 2004, s 10 from 1 December 2004 (SI 2004/2999). Subsections (10)–(11) inserted by Immigration, Asylum and Nationality Act 2006, s 43 from 16 June 2006 (SI 2006/1497).

5. . . .

Note: Ceases to have effect from a date to be appointed, Sch 2 Immigration, Asylum and Nationality Act 2006 (SI 2006/1497).

Exemption from immigration control

6. . . .

Note: Amends Immigration Act 1971, s 8.

7. . . .

Note: Amends Immigration Act 1971, s 8.

8. . . .

Note: Amends Immigration Act 1971, s 8.

Removal from the United Kingdom

9. Treatment of certain overstayers

(1) During the regularisation period overstayers may apply, in the prescribed manner, for leave to remain in the United Kingdom.

(2) The regularisation period begins on the day prescribed for the purposes of this subsection and is not to be less than three months.

(3) The regularisation period ends—

(a) on the day prescribed for the purposes of this subsection; or

(b) if later, on the day before that on which section 65 comes into force.

(4) Section 10 and paragraph 12 of Schedule 15 come into force on the day after that on which the regularisation period ends.

(5) The Secretary of State must publicise the effect of this section in the way appearing to him to be best calculated to bring it to the attention of those affected.

(6) 'Overstayer' means a person who, having only limited leave to enter or remain in the United Kingdom, remains beyond the time limited by the leave.

Note: Commencement 11 November 1999, s 170.

10. Removal of certain persons unlawfully in the United Kingdom

(1) A person who is not a British citizen may be removed from the United Kingdom, in accordance with directions given by an immigration officer, if—

(a) having only a limited leave to enter or remain, he does not observe a condition attached to the leave or remains beyond the time limited by the leave;

[(b) he uses deception in seeking (whether successfully or not) leave to remain;

(ba) his indefinite leave to enter or remain has been revoked under section 76(3) of the Nationality, Immigration and Asylum Act 2002 (person ceasing to be refugee);] or

(c) directions [. . .] have been given for the removal, under this section, of a person [. . .] to whose family he belongs.

(2) Directions may not be given under subsection (1)(a) if the person concerned has made an application for leave to remain in accordance with regulations made under section 9.

[(3) Directions for the removal of a person may not be given under subsection (1)(c) unless the Secretary of State has given the person written notice of the intention to remove him.

(4) A notice under subsection (3) may not be given if—

(a) the person whose removal under subsection (1)(a) or (b) is the cause of the proposed directions under subsection (1)(c) has left the United Kingdom, and

(b) more than eight weeks have elapsed since that person's departure.

(5) If a notice under subsection (3) is sent by first class post to a person's last known address, that subsection shall be taken to be satisfied at the end of the second day after the day of posting.

(5A) Directions for the removal of a person under subsection (1)(c) cease to have effect if he ceases to belong to the family of the person whose removal under subsection (1)(a) or (b) is the cause of the directions under subsection (1)(c).]

(6) Directions under this section—
   (a) may be given only to persons falling within a prescribed class;
   (b) may impose any requirements of a prescribed kind.

(7) In relation to any such directions, paragraphs 10, 11, 16 to 18, 21 and 22 to 24 of Schedule 2 to the 1971 Act (administrative provisions as to control of entry), apply as they apply in relation to directions given under paragraph 8 of that Schedule.

[(8) When a person is notified that a decision has been made to remove him in accordance with this section, the notification invalidates any leave to enter or remain in the United Kingdom previously given to him.]

(9) The costs of complying with a direction given under this section (so far as reasonably incurred) must be met by the Secretary of State.

[(10) A person shall not be liable to removal from the United Kingdom under this section at a time when section 7(1)(b) of the Immigration Act 1971 (Commonwealth and Irish citizens ordinarily resident in United Kingdom) would prevent a decision to deport him.]

Note: Section 10(6) commenced 22 May 2000, SI 2000/282, remainder of s 10 on 2 October 2000, SI 2000/244. Subsection (1)(b) substituted by and sub-s (1)(ba) inserted by Nationality, Immigration and Asylum Act 2002, ss 74 and 76 from 10 February 2003 (SI 2003/1). Subsections (3)–(5A) substituted by Nationality, Immigration and Asylum Act 2002 from 10 February 2003 (SI 2003/1). Subsection (10) inserted by Nationality, Immigration and Asylum Act 2002, s 75 from 10 February 2003 (SI 2003/1). Transitional provisions set out in SI 2003/754. Subsection (8) substituted by Immigration, Asylum and Nationality Act 2006, s 48 from 16 June 2006 (SI 2006/1497).

11. . . .

Note: Section 11 ceased to have effect from 1 October 2004, Asylum and Immigration Act 2004, s 33 (SI 2004/2523).

12. . . .

Note: Section 12 ceased to have effect from 1 October 2004, Asylum and Immigration Act 2004, s 33 (SI 2004/2523).

13. Proof of identity of persons to be removed or deported

(1) This section applies if a person—
   (a) is to be removed from the United Kingdom to a country of which he is a national or citizen; but
   (b) does not have a valid passport or other document establishing his identity and nationality or citizenship and permitting him to travel.

(2) If the country to which the person is to be removed indicates that he will not be admitted to it unless identification data relating to him are provided by the Secretary of State, he may provide them with such data.

(3) In providing identification data, the Secretary of State must not disclose whether the person concerned has made a claim for asylum.

(4) For the purposes of paragraph 4(1) of Schedule 4 to the Data Protection Act 1998, the provision under this section of identification data is a transfer of personal data which is necessary for reasons of substantial public interest.

(5) 'Identification data' means—
   (a) fingerprints taken under section 141; or
   (b) data collected in accordance with regulations made under section 144.

(6) 'Removed' means removed as a result of directions given under section 10 or under Schedule 2 or 3 to the 1971 Act.

Note: Commenced 11 December 2000, SI 2000/3099.

14. Escorts for persons removed from the United Kingdom under directions

(1) Directions for, or requiring arrangements to be made for, the removal of a person from the United Kingdom may include or be amended to include provision for the person who is to be removed to be accompanied by an escort consisting of one or more persons specified in the directions.

(2) The Secretary of State may by regulations make further provision supplementing subsection (1).

(3) The regulations may, in particular, include provision—
   (a) requiring the person to whom the directions are given to provide for the return of the escort to the United Kingdom;
   (b) requiring him to bear such costs in connection with the escort (including, in particular, remuneration) as may be prescribed;
   (c) as to the cases in which the Secretary of State is to bear those costs;
   (d) prescribing the kinds of expenditure which are to count in calculating the costs incurred in connection with escorts.

Note: Commencement 1 March 2000 (SI 2000/168).

15. . . .

Note: Section 15 repealed by Nationality, Immigration and Asylum Act 2002, s 77 from 1 April 2003 (SI 2003/754).

Provision of financial security

16. Security on grant of entry clearance

(1) In such circumstances as may be specified, the Secretary of State may require security to be given, with respect to a person applying for entry clearance, before clearance is given.

(2) In such circumstances as may be specified—
(a) the Secretary of State may accept security with respect to a person who is applying for entry clearance but for whom security is not required; and
(b) in determining whether to give clearance, account may be taken of any security so provided.

(3) 'Security' means—
(a) the deposit of a sum of money by the applicant, his agent or any other person, or
(b) the provision by the applicant, his agent or any other person of a financial guarantee of a specified kind,

with a view to securing that the applicant will, if given leave to enter the United Kingdom for a limited period, leave the United Kingdom at the end of that period.

(4) Immigration rules must make provision as to the circumstances in which a security provided under this section—
(a) is to be repaid, released or otherwise cancelled; or
(b) is to be forfeited or otherwise realised by the Secretary of State.

(5) No security provided under this section may be forfeited or otherwise realised unless the person providing it has been given an opportunity, in accordance with immigration rules, to make representations to the Secretary of State.

(6) Immigration rules may, in particular—
(a) fix the maximum amount that may be required, or accepted, by way of security provided under this section;
(b) specify the form and manner in which such a security is to be given or may be accepted;
(c) make provision, where such a security has been forfeited or otherwise realised, for the person providing it to be reimbursed in such circumstances as may be specified;
(d) make different provision for different cases or descriptions of case.

(7) 'Specified' means specified by immigration rules.

(8) Any security forfeited or otherwise realised by the Secretary of State under this section must be paid into the Consolidated Fund.

Note: Commencement on a date to be appointed.

17. Provision of further security on extension of leave

(1) This section applies if security has been provided under section 16(1) or (2) with respect to a person who, having entered the United Kingdom (with leave to do so), applies—
(a) to extend his leave to enter the United Kingdom; or
(b) for leave to remain in the United Kingdom for a limited period.

(2) The Secretary of State may refuse the application if security of such kind as the Secretary of State considers appropriate is not provided, or continued, with respect to the applicant.

(3) Immigration rules must make provision as to the circumstances in which a security provided under this section—
   (a) is to be repaid, released or otherwise cancelled; or
   (b) is to be forfeited or otherwise realised by the Secretary of State.

(4) No security provided under this section may be forfeited or otherwise realised unless the person providing it has been given an opportunity, in accordance with immigration rules, to make representations to the Secretary of State.

(5) Subsection (7) of section 16 applies in relation to this section as it applies in relation to that section.

(6) Any security forfeited or otherwise realised by the Secretary of State under this section must be paid into the Consolidated Fund.

Note: Commencement on a date to be appointed.

Information

18. . . .

Note: Amends para 27B, Sch 2 Immigration Act 1971.

19. . . .

Note: Amends para 27C, Sch 2 Immigration Act 1971.

20. Supply of information to Secretary of State

(1) This section applies to information held by—
   (a) a chief officer of police;
   (b) the Director General of the National Criminal Intelligence Service;
   (c) the Director General of the National Crime Squad;
   (d) the Commissioners of Customs and Excise, or a person providing services to them in connection with the provision of those services;
   (e) a person with whom the Secretary of State has made a contract or other arrangements under section 95 or 98 or a sub-contractor of such a person; or
   (f) any specified person, for purposes specified in relation to that person.

[(1A) This section also applies to a document or article which—
   (a) comes into the possession of a person listed in subsection (1) or someone acting on his behalf, or

(b) is discovered by a person listed in subsection (1) or someone acting on his behalf.]

(2) The information[, document or article] may be supplied to the Secretary of State for use for immigration purposes.

[(2A) The Secretary of State may—

(a) retain for immigration purposes a document or article supplied to him under subsection (2), and

(b) dispose of a document or article supplied to him under subsection (2) in such manner as he thinks appropriate (and the reference to use in subsection (2) includes a reference to disposal).]

(3) 'Immigration purposes' means any of the following—

(a) the administration of immigration control under the Immigration Acts;

(b) the prevention, detection, investigation or prosecution of criminal offences under those Acts;

(c) the imposition of penalties or charges under Part II;

(d) the provision of support for asylum-seekers and their dependants under Part VI;

(e) such other purposes as may be specified.

(4) 'Chief officer of police' means—

(a) the chief officer of police for a police area in England and Wales;

(b) the chief constable of a police force maintained under the Police (Scotland) Act 1967;

(c) the Chief Constable of the Royal Ulster Constabulary.

(5) 'Specified' means specified in an order made by the Secretary of State.

(6) This section does not limit the circumstances in which information[, documents or articles] may be supplied apart from this section.

Note: Commencement 1 January 2000 (SI 1999/3190). Subsection (1A) and sub-s (2A) inserted by Nationality, Immigration and Asylum Act 2002, s 132 from 10 February 2003 (SI 2003/1). Words in square brackets in sub-ss (2) and (6) inserted by Nationality, Immigration and Asylum Act 2002, s 132 from 10 February 2003 (SI 2003/1).

21. Supply of information by Secretary of State

(1) This section applies to information held by the Secretary of State in connection with the exercise of functions under any of the Immigration Acts.

(2) The information may be supplied to—

(a) a chief officer of police, for use for police purposes;

(b) the Director General of the National Criminal Intelligence Service, for use for NCIS purposes;

(c) the Director General of the National Crime Squad, for use for NCS purposes;

(d) the Commissioners of Customs and Excise, or a person providing services to them, for use for customs purposes; or
(e) any specified person, for use for purposes specified in relation to that person.

(3) 'Police purposes' means any of the following—
(a) the prevention, detection, investigation or prosecution of criminal offences;
(b) safeguarding national security;
(c) such other purposes as may be specified.

(4) 'NCIS purposes' means any of the functions of the National Criminal Intelligence Service mentioned in section 2 of the Police Act 1997.

(5) 'NCS purposes' means any of the functions of the National Crime Squad mentioned in section 48 of that Act.

(6) 'Customs purposes' means any of the Commissioners' functions in relation to—
(a) the prevention, detection, investigation or prosecution of criminal offences;
(b) the prevention, detection or investigation of conduct in respect of which penalties which are not criminal penalties are provided for by or under any enactment;
(c) the assessment or determination of penalties which are not criminal penalties;
(d) checking the accuracy of information relating to, or provided for purposes connected with, any matter under the care and management of the Commissioners or any assigned matter (as defined by section 1(1) of the Customs and Excise Management Act 1979);
(e) amending or supplementing any such information (where appropriate);
(f) legal or other proceedings relating to anything mentioned in paragraphs (a) to (e);
(g) safeguarding national security; and
(h) such other purposes as may be specified.

(7) 'Chief officer of police' and 'specified' have the same meaning as in section 20.

(8) This section does not limit the circumstances in which information may be supplied apart from this section.

Note: Commencement 1 January 2000 (SI 1999/3190).

22. . . .

Note: Amends Asylum and Immigration Act 1996, s 8A.

Monitoring entry clearance

23. Monitoring refusals of entry clearance

(1) The Secretary of State must appoint a person to monitor, in such a manner as the Secretary of State may determine, refusals of entry clearance in cases where there is, as a result of [section 90 or 91 of the Nationality, Immigration and Asylum Act 2002], no right of appeal.

(2) But the Secretary of State may not appoint a member of his staff.

(3) The monitor must make an annual report on the discharge of his functions to the Secretary of State.

(4) The Secretary of State must lay a copy of any report made to him under subsection (3) before each House of Parliament.

(5) The Secretary of State may pay to the monitor such fees and allowances as he may determine.

Note: Commencement 2 October 2000 (SI 2000/2444). Words in square brackets in sub-s (1) substituted by Sch 7 Nationality, Immigration and Asylum Act 2002 from 1 April 2003 (SI 2003/754).

Reporting suspicious marriages

24. Duty to report suspicious marriages

(1) Subsection (3) applies if—

(a) a superintendent registrar to whom a notice of marriage has been given under section 27 of the Marriage Act 1949,

(b) any other person who, under section 28(2) of that Act, has attested a declaration accompanying such a notice,

(c) a district registrar to whom a marriage notice or an approved certificate has been submitted under section 3 of the Marriage (Scotland) Act 1977, or

(d) a registrar or deputy registrar to whom notice has been given under section 13 of the Marriages (Ireland) Act 1844 or section 4 of the Marriage Law (Ireland) Amendment Act 1863,

has reasonable grounds for suspecting that the marriage will be a sham marriage.

(2) Subsection (3) also applies if—

(a) a marriage is solemnized in the presence of a registrar of marriages or, in relation to Scotland, an authorised registrar (within the meaning of the Act of 1977); and

(b) before, during or immediately after solemnization of the marriage, the registrar has reasonable grounds for suspecting that the marriage will be, or is, a sham marriage.

(3) The person concerned must report his suspicion to the Secretary of State without delay and in such form and manner as may be prescribed by regulations.

(4) The regulations are to be made—
  (a) in relation to England and Wales, by the Registrar General for England and Wales with the approval of the Chancellor of the Exchequer;
  (b) in relation to Scotland, by the Secretary of State after consulting the Registrar General of Births, Deaths and Marriages for Scotland;
  (c) in relation to Northern Ireland, by the Secretary of State after consulting the Registrar General in Northern Ireland.

(5) 'Sham marriage' means a marriage (whether or not void)—
  (a) entered into between a person ('A') who is neither a British citizen nor a national of an EEA State other than the United Kingdom and another person (whether or not such a citizen or such a national); and
  (b) entered into by A for the purpose of avoiding the effect of one or more provisions of United Kingdom immigration law or the immigration rules.

Note: Commencement 1 January 2001 (SI 2000/2698).

[24A. Duty to report suspicious civil partnerships

(1) Subsection (3) applies if—
  (a) a registration authority to whom a notice of proposed civil partnership has been given under section 8 of the Civil Partnership Act 2004,
  (b) any person who, under section 8 of the 2004 Act, has attested a declaration accompanying such a notice,
  (c) a district registrar to whom a notice of proposed civil partnership has been given under section 88 of the 2004 Act, or
  (d) a registrar to whom a civil partnership notice has been given under section 139 of the 2004 Act,

has reasonable grounds for suspecting that the civil partnership will be a sham civil partnership.

(2) Subsection (3) also applies if—
  (a) two people register as civil partners of each other under Part 2, 3 or 4 of the 2004 Act in the presence of the registrar, and
  (b) before, during or immediately after they do so, the registrar has reasonable grounds for suspecting that the civil partnership will be, or is, a sham civil partnership.

(3) The person concerned must report his suspicion to the Secretary of State without delay and in such form and manner as may be prescribed by regulations.

(4) The regulations are to be made—
  (a) in relation to England and Wales, by the Registrar General for England and Wales with the approval of the Chancellor of the Exchequer;

(b) in relation to Scotland, by the Secretary of State after consulting the Registrar General of Births, Deaths and Marriages for Scotland;

(c) in relation to Northern Ireland, by the Secretary of State after consulting the Registrar General in Northern Ireland.

(5) 'Sham civil partnership' means a civil partnership (whether or not void)—

(a) formed between a person ('A') who is neither a British citizen nor a national of an EEA State other than the United Kingdom and another person (whether or not such a citizen or such a national), and

(b) formed by A for the purpose of avoiding the effect of one or more provisions of United Kingdom immigration law or the immigration rules.

(6) 'The registrar' means—

(a) in relation to England and Wales, the civil partnership registrar acting under Part 2 of the 2004 Act;

(b) in relation to Scotland, the authorised registrar acting under Part 3 of the 2004 Act;

(c) in relation to Northern Ireland, the registrar acting under Part 4 of the 2004 Act.]

Note: Section 24A inserted by Sch 27 Civil Partnership Act 2004 from a date to be appointed.

Immigration control: facilities and charges

25. Provision of facilities for immigration control at ports

(1) The person responsible for the management of a control port ('the manager') must provide the Secretary of State free of charge with such facilities at the port as the Secretary of State may direct as being reasonably necessary for, or in connection with, the operation of immigration control there.

(2) Before giving such a direction, the Secretary of State must consult such persons likely to be affected by it as he considers appropriate.

(3) If the Secretary of State gives such a direction, he must send a copy of it to the person appearing to him to be the manager.

(4) If the manager persistently fails to comply with the direction (or part of it), the Secretary of State may—

(a) in the case of a control port which is not a port of entry, revoke any approval in relation to the port given under paragraph 26(1) of Schedule 2 to the 1971 Act;

(b) in the case of a control port which is a port of entry, by order revoke its designation as a port of entry.

(5) A direction under this section is enforceable, on the application of the Secretary of State—

(a) by injunction granted by a county court; or

(b) in Scotland, by an order under section 45 of the Court of Session Act 1988.

(6) 'Control port' means a port in which a control area is designated under paragraph 26(3) of Schedule 2 to the 1971 Act.

(7) 'Facilities' means accommodation, facilities, equipment and services of a class or description specified in an order made by the Secretary of State.

Note: Commenced on 17 February 2003 for the purpose of enabling the Secretary of State to exercise power to make subordinate legislation; otherwise commences on 1 April 2003 (SI 2003/2).

26. Charges: immigration control

(1) The Secretary of State may, at the request of any person and in consideration of such charges as he may determine, make arrangements—
   (a) for the provision at any control port of immigration officers or facilities in addition to those (if any) needed to provide a basic service at the port;
   (b) for the provision of immigration officers or facilities for dealing with passengers of a particular description or in particular circumstances.

(2) 'Control port' has the same meaning as in section 25.

(3) 'Facilities' includes equipment.

(4) 'Basic service' has such meaning as may be prescribed.

Note: Commenced on 5 June 2003 for purpose of enabling Secretary of State to make subordinate legislation; remainder commenced on 30 June 2003 (SI 2003/1469).

Charges: travel documents

27. . . .

Note: Commencement 11 November 1999, s 170. Ceases to have effect from a date to be appointed, Sch 2 Immigration, Asylum and Nationality Act 2006.

Offences

28. . . .

Note: Amends Immigration Act 1971, s 24A.

29. . . .

Note: Repealed by Nationality, Immigration and Asylum Act 2002 from a date to be appointed.

30. . . .

Note: Amends Immigration Act 1971, s 26.

31. Defences based on Article 31(1) of the Refugee Convention

(1) It is a defence for a refugee charged with an offence to which this section applies to show that, having come to the United Kingdom directly from a country where his life or freedom was threatened (within the meaning of the Refugee Convention), he—

(a) presented himself to the authorities in the United Kingdom without delay;
(b) showed good cause for his illegal entry or presence; and
(c) made a claim for asylum as soon as was reasonably practicable after his arrival in the United Kingdom.

(2) If, in coming from the country where his life or freedom was threatened, the refugee stopped in another country outside the United Kingdom, subsection (1) applies only if he shows that he could not reasonably have expected to be given protection under the Refugee Convention in that other country.

(3) In England and Wales and Northern Ireland the offences to which this section applies are any offence, and any attempt to commit an offence, under—

(a) Part I of the Forgery and Counterfeiting Act 1981 (forgery and connected offences);
[(aa) section 25(1) or (5) of the Identity Cards Act 2006;]
(b) section 24A of the 1971 Act (deception); or
(c) section 26(1)(d) of the 1971 Act (falsification of documents).

(4) In Scotland, the offences to which this section applies are those—

(a) of fraud,
(b) of uttering a forged document,
[(ba) under section 25(1) or (5) of the Identity Cards Act 2006;]
(c) under section 24A of the 1971 Act (deception), or
(d) under section 26(1)(d) of the 1971 Act (falsification of documents),

and any attempt to commit any of those offences.

(5) A refugee who has made a claim for asylum is not entitled to the defence provided by subsection (1) in relation to any offence committed by him after making that claim.

(6) 'Refugee' has the same meaning as it has for the purposes of the Refugee Convention.

(7) If the Secretary of State has refused to grant a claim for asylum made by a person who claims that he has a defence under subsection (1), that person is to be taken not to be a refugee unless he shows that he is.

(8) A person who—

(a) was convicted in England and Wales or Northern Ireland of an offence to which this section applies before the commencement of this section, but

(b) at no time during the proceedings for that offence argued that he had a defence based on Article 31(1), may apply to the Criminal Cases Review Commission with a view to his case being referred to the Court of Appeal by the Commission on the ground that he would have had a defence under this section had it been in force at the material time.

(9) A person who—

(a) was convicted in Scotland of an offence to which this section applies before the commencement of this section, but

(b) at no time during the proceedings for that offence argued that he had a defence based on Article 31(1),

may apply to the Scottish Criminal Cases Review Commission with a view to his case being referred to the High Court of Justiciary by the Commission on the ground that he would have had a defence under this section had it been in force at the material time.

(10) The Secretary of State may by order amend—

(a) subsection (3), or

(b) subsection (4),

by adding offences to those for the time being listed there.

(11) Before making an order under subsection (10)(b), the Secretary of State must consult the Scottish Ministers.

Note: Commencement 11 November 1999, s 170. Subsections (3)(aa) and (4)(ba) inserted by Identity Cards Act 2006, s 30 from 7 June 2006 (SI 2006/1439).

Part II

Carriers' Liability

Clandestine entrants

32. Penalty for carrying clandestine entrants

(1) A person is a clandestine entrant if—

(a) he arrives in the United Kingdom concealed in a vehicle, ship or aircraft,

[(aa) he arrives in the United Kingdom concealed in a rail freight wagon,]

(b) he passes, or attempts to pass, through immigration control concealed in a vehicle, or

(c) he arrives in the United Kingdom on a ship or aircraft, having embarked—

(i) concealed in a vehicle; and

(ii) at a time when the ship or aircraft was outside the United Kingdom,

and claims, or indicates that he intends to seek, asylum in the United Kingdom or evades, or attempts to evade, immigration control.

[(2) The Secretary of State may require a person who is responsible for a clandestine entrant to pay—

(a) a penalty in respect of the clandestine entrant;
(b) a penalty in respect of any person who was concealed with the clandestine entrant in the same transporter.]

[(2A) In imposing a penalty under subsection (2) the Secretary of State—
(a) must specify an amount which does not exceed the maximum prescribed for the purpose of this paragraph,
(b) may, in respect of a clandestine entrant or a concealed person, impose separate penalties on more than one of the persons responsible for the clandestine entrant, and
(c) may not impose penalties in respect of a clandestine entrant or a concealed person which amount in aggregate to more than the maximum prescribed for the purpose of this paragraph.]

(3) A penalty imposed under this section must be paid to the Secretary of State before the end of the prescribed period.

[(4) Where a penalty is imposed under subsection (2) on the driver of a vehicle who is an employee of the vehicle's owner or hirer—
(a) the employee and the employer shall be jointly and severally liable for the penalty imposed on the driver (irrespective of whether a penalty is also imposed on the employer), and
(b) a provision of this Part about notification, objection or appeal shall have effect as if the penalty imposed on the driver were also imposed on the employer (irrespective of whether a penalty is also imposed on the employer in his capacity as the owner or hirer of the vehicle).]

[(4A) In the case of a detached trailer, subsection (4) shall have effect as if a reference to the driver were a reference to the operator.]

(5) In the case of a clandestine entrant to whom subsection (1)(a) applies, each of the following is a responsible person—
(a) if the transporter is a ship or aircraft, the owner [and] captain;
(b) if it is a vehicle (but not a detached trailer), the owner, hirer [and] driver of the vehicle;
(c) if it is a detached trailer, the owner, hirer [and] operator of the trailer.

[(5A) In the case of a clandestine entrant to whom subsection (1)(aa) applies, the responsible person is—
(a) where the entrant arrived concealed in a freight train, the train operator who, at the train's last scheduled stop before arrival in the United Kingdom, was responsible for certifying it as fit to travel to the United Kingdom, or
(b) where the entrant arrived concealed in a freight shuttle wagon, the operator of the shuttle-train of which the wagon formed part.]

(6) In the case of a clandestine entrant to whom subsection (1)(b) or (c) applies, each of the following is a responsible person—

(a) if the transporter is a detached trailer, the owner, hirer [and] operator of the trailer;
(b) if it is not, the owner, hirer [and] driver of the vehicle.

[(6A) Where a person falls within the definition of responsible person in more than one capacity, a separate penalty may be imposed on him under subsection (2) in respect of each capacity.]

(7) Subject to any defence provided by section 34, it is immaterial whether a responsible person knew or suspected—
(a) that the clandestine entrant was concealed in the transporter; or
(b) that there were one or more other persons concealed with the clandestine entrant in the same transporter.

(8) Subsection (9) applies if a transporter ('the carried transporter') is itself being carried in or on another transporter.

(9) If a person is concealed in the carried transporter, the question whether any other person is concealed with that person in the same transporter is to be determined by reference to the carried transporter and not by reference to the transporter in or on which it is carried.

(10) 'Immigration control' means United Kingdom immigration control and includes any United Kingdom immigration control operated in a prescribed control zone outside the United Kingdom.

Note: Sections 32(2)(a), 32(3) and 32(10) commenced 6 December 1999 (SI 1999/3190), remainder on 3 April 2000 (SI 2000/464). Subsections (1)(aa), (2A), (4A), (5A) and (6A) inserted by Sch 8 Nationality, Immigration and Asylum Act 2002 from 14 November 2002 (SI 2002/2811). Subsections (2) and (4) substituted by and words in square brackets in sub-ss (5) and (6) inserted by Sch 8 Nationality, Immigration and Asylum Act 2002 from 14 November 2002 (SI 2002/2811).

[32A. Level of penalty: code of practice

(1) The Secretary of State shall issue a code of practice specifying matters to be considered in determining the amount of a penalty under section 32.

(2) The Secretary of State shall have regard to the code (in addition to any other matters he thinks relevant)—
(a) when imposing a penalty under section 32, and
(b) when considering a notice of objection under section 35(4).

(3) Before issuing the code the Secretary of State shall lay a draft before Parliament.

(4) After laying the draft code before Parliament the Secretary of State may bring the code into operation by order.

(5) The Secretary of State may from time to time revise the whole or any part of the code and issue the code as revised.

(6) Subsections (3) and (4) also apply to a revision or proposed revision of the code.]

Note: Section 32A inserted by Sch 8 Nationality, Immigration and Asylum Act 2002 from 14 November 2002 for the purpose of enabling the Secretary of State to exercise the power under s 32A(1), (3) and (4); otherwise takes effect from 8 December 2002 (SI 2002/2811).

33. [Prevention of clandestine entrants: code of practice]

(1) The Secretary of State must issue a code of practice to be followed by any person operating a system for preventing the carriage of clandestine entrants.

(2) Before issuing the code, the Secretary of State must—
   (a) consult such persons as he considers appropriate; and
   (b) lay a draft before . . . Parliament.

(3) The requirement of subsection (2)(a) may be satisfied by consultation before the passing of this Act.

(4) After laying the draft code before Parliament, the Secretary of State may bring the code into operation by an order.

(5) The Secretary of State may from time to time revise the whole or any part of the code and issue the code as revised.

(6) Subsections (2) and (4) also apply to any revision, or proposed revision, of the code.

Note: Commenced 6 December 1999 (SI 1999/3190). Heading substituted and words omitted from sub-s (2)(b) by Sch 8 Nationality, Immigration and Asylum Act 2002 from 8 December 2002 (SI 2002/2811).

34. Defences to claim that penalty is due under section 32

[(1) A person ('the carrier') shall not be liable to the imposition of a penalty under section 32(2) if he has a defence under this section.]

(2) It is a defence for the carrier to show that he, or an employee of his who was directly responsible for allowing the clandestine entrant to be concealed, was acting under duress.

(3) It is also a defence for the carrier to show that—
   (a) he did not know, and had no reasonable grounds for suspecting, that a clandestine entrant was, or might be, concealed in the transporter;
   (b) an effective system for preventing the carriage of clandestine entrants was in operation in relation to the transporter; and
   (c) . . . on the occasion in question the person or persons responsible for operating that system did so properly.

[(3A) It is also a defence for the carrier to show that—
   (a) he knew or suspected that a clandestine entrant was or might be concealed in a rail freight wagon, having boarded after the wagon began its journey to the United Kingdom;

(b) he could not stop the train or shuttle-train of which the wagon formed part without endangering safety;
(c) an effective system for preventing the carriage of clandestine entrants was in operation in relation to the train or shuttle-train; and
(d) on the occasion in question the person or persons responsible for operating the system did so properly.]

(4) In determining, for the purposes of this section, whether a particular system is effective, regard is to be had to the code of practice issued by the Secretary of State under section 33.

(5) . . .

[(6) Where a person has a defence under subsection (2) in respect of a clandestine entrant, every other responsible person in respect of the clandestine entrant is also entitled to the benefit of the defence.]

Note: Commencement 3 April 2000 (SI 2000/464). Subsections (1) and (6) substituted by and sub-s (3A) inserted by and words in sub-s (3)(c) omitted by and sub-s (5) omitted by Sch 8 Nationality, Immigration and Asylum Act 2002 from 8 December 2002 (SI 2002/2811).

35. Procedure

(1) If the Secretary of State decides that a person ('P') is liable to one or more penalties under section 32, he must notify P of his decision.

(2) A notice under subsection (1) (a 'penalty notice') must—
(a) state the Secretary of State's reasons for deciding that P is liable to the penalty (or penalties);
(b) state the amount of the penalty (or penalties) to which P is liable;
(c) specify the date before which, and the manner in which, the penalty (or penalties) must be paid; and
(d) include an explanation of the steps—
(i) that P [may] take if he objects to the penalty;
(ii) that the Secretary of State may take under this Part to recover any unpaid penalty.

[(3) Subsection (4) applies where a person to whom a penalty notice is issued objects on the ground that—
(a) he is not liable to the imposition of a penalty, or
(b) the amount of the penalty is too high.

(4) The person may give a notice of objection to the Secretary of State.

(5) A notice of objection must—
(a) be in writing,
(b) give the objector's reasons, and
(c) be given before the end of such period as may be prescribed.

(6) Where the Secretary of State receives a notice of objection to a penalty in accordance with this section he shall consider it and—
(a) cancel the penalty,
(b) reduce the penalty,
(c) increase the penalty, or
(d) determine to take no action under paragraphs (a) to (c).

(7) Where the Secretary of State considers a notice of objection under subsection (6) he shall—
(a) inform the objector of his decision before the end of such period as may be prescribed or such longer period as he may agree with the objector,
(b) if he increases the penalty, issue a new penalty notice under subsection (1), and
(c) if he reduces the penalty, notify the objector of the reduced amount.]

(8) . . .

(9) The Secretary of State may be regulations provide, in relation to detached trailers, for a penalty notice which is [issued] in such manner as may be prescribed to have effect as a penalty notice properly [issued to] the responsible person or persons concerned under this section.

(10) Any sum payable to the Secretary of State as a penalty under section 32 may be recovered by the Secretary of State as a debt due to him.

[(11) In proceedings for enforcement of a penalty under subsection (10) no question may be raised as to—
(a) liability to the imposition of the penalty, or
(b) its amount.

(12) A document which is to be issued to or served on a person outside the United Kingdom for the purpose of subsection (1) or (7) or in the course of proceedings under subsection (10) may be issued or served—
(a) in person,
(b) by post,
(c) by facsimile transmission, or
(d) in another prescribed manner.

(13) The Secretary of State may by regulations provide that a document issued or served in a manner listed in subsection (12) in accordance with the regulations is to be taken to have been received at a time specified by or determined in accordance with the regulations.]

Note: Section 35(7)–(9) commenced 6 December 1999 (SI 1999/3190), remainder 3 April 2000 (SI 2000/464). Subsections (3)–(7) substituted by and sub-s (8) omitted by and sub-ss (11)–(13) inserted by and words in square brackets in sub-s (2) and (9) substituted by Sch 8 Nationality, Immigration and Asylum Act 2002 from 8 December 2002 (SI 2002/2811).

[35A. Appeal

(1) A person may appeal to the court against a penalty imposed on him under section 32 on the ground that—
   (a) he is not liable to the imposition of a penalty, or
   (b) the amount of the penalty is too high.

(2) On an appeal under this section the court may—
   (a) allow the appeal and cancel the penalty,
   (b) allow the appeal and reduce the penalty, or
   (c) dismiss the appeal.

(3) An appeal under this section shall be a re-hearing of the Secretary of State's decision to impose a penalty and shall be determined having regard to—
   (a) any code of practice under section 32A which has effect at the time of the appeal,
   (b) the code of practice under section 33 which had effect at the time of the events to which the penalty relates, and
   (c) any other matters which the court thinks relevant (which may include matters of which the Secretary of State was unaware).

(4) Subsection (3) has effect despite any provision of Civil Procedure Rules.

(5) An appeal may be brought by a person under this section against a penalty whether or not—
   (a) he has given notice of objection under section 35(4);
   (b) the penalty has been increased or reduced under section 35(6).]

Note: Section 35A inserted by Sch 8 Nationality, Immigration and Asylum Act 2002 from 8 December 2002 (SI 2002/2811).

36. Power to detain vehicles etc. in connection with penalties under section 32

(1) If a penalty notice has been [issued] under section 35, a senior officer may detain any relevant—
   (a) vehicle,
   (b) small ship, . . .
   (c) small aircraft, . . . [or
   (d) rail freight wagon,]

   until all penalties to which the notice relates, and any expenses reasonably incurred by the Secretary of State in connection with the detention, have been paid.

(2) That power—
   (a) may be exercised only if, in the opinion of the senior officer concerned, there is a significant risk that the penalty (or one or more of the penalties)

will not be paid before the end of the prescribed period if the transporter is not detained; and

(b) may not be exercised if alternative security which the Secretary of State considers is satisfactory, has been given.

[(2A) A vehicle may be detained under subsection (1) only if—

(a) the driver of the vehicle is an employee of its owner or hirer,

(b) the driver of the vehicle is its owner or hirer, or

(c) a penalty notice is issued to the owner or hirer of the vehicle.

(2B) A senior officer may detain a relevant vehicle, small ship, small aircraft or rail freight wagon pending—

(a) a decision whether to issue a penalty notice,

(b) the issue of a penalty notice, or

(c) a decision whether to detain under subsection (1).

(2C) That power may not be exercised in any case—

(a) for longer than is necessary in the circumstances of the case, or

(b) after the expiry of the period of 24 hours beginning with the conclusion of the first search of the vehicle, ship, aircraft or wagon by an immigration officer after it arrived in the United Kingdom.]

(3) If a transporter is detained under this section, the owner, consignor or any other person who has an interest in any freight or other thing carried in or on the transporter may remove it, or arrange for it to be removed, at such time and in such way as is reasonable.

(4) The detention of a transporter under this section is lawful even though it is subsequently established that the penalty notice on which the detention was based was ill-founded in respect of all or any of the penalties to which it related.

(5) But subsection (4) does not apply if the Secretary of State was acting unreasonably in issuing the penalty notice.

Note: Section 36(2)(a) commenced 6 December 1999 (SI 1999/3190), remainder 3 April 2000 (SI 2000/464). Subsections (2A), (2B) and (2C) inserted by and words in square brackets in sub-s (1) substituted by Sch 8 Nationality Immigration and Asylum Act 2002 from 8 December 2002 (SI 2002/2811).

[36A. Detention in default of payment

(1) This section applies where a person to whom a penalty notice has been issued under section 35 fails to pay the penalty before the date specified in accordance with section 35(2)(c).

(2) The Secretary of State may make arrangements for the detention of any vehicle, small ship, small aircraft or rail freight wagon which the person to whom the penalty notice was issued uses in the course of a business.

(3) A vehicle, ship, aircraft or wagon may be detained under subsection (2) whether or not the person to whom the penalty notice was issued owns it.

(4) But a vehicle may be detained under subsection (2) only if the person to whom the penalty notice was issued—
   (a) is the owner or hirer of the vehicle, or
   (b) was an employee of the owner or hirer of the vehicle when the penalty notice was issued.

(5) The power under subsection (2) may not be exercised while an appeal against the penalty under section 35A is pending or could be brought (ignoring the possibility of an appeal out of time with permission).

(6) The Secretary of State shall arrange for the release of a vehicle, ship, aircraft or wagon detained under this section if the person to whom the penalty notice was issued pays—
   (a) the penalty, and
   (b) expenses reasonably incurred in connection with the detention.]

Note: Section 36A inserted by Sch 8 Nationality, Immigration and Asylum Act 2002 from 8 December 2002 (SI 2002/2811).

37. Effect of detention

(1) This section applies if a transporter is detained under [section 36(1)].

(2) The person to whom the penalty notice was addressed, or the owner or any other person [whose interests may be affected by detention of the transporter], may apply to the court for the transporter to be released.

(3) The court may release the transporter if it considers that—
   (a) satisfactory security has been tendered in place of the transporter for the payment of the penalty alleged to be due and connected expenses;
   (b) there is no significant risk that the penalty (or one or more of the penalties) and any connected expenses will not be paid; or
   (c) there is a significant doubt as to whether the penalty is payable. . . .

[(**3A**) The court may also release the transporter on the application of the owner of the transporter under subsection (2) if—
   (a) a penalty notice was not issued to the owner or an employee of his, and
   (b) the court considers it right to release the transporter.

(**3B**) In determining whether to release a transporter under subsection (3A) the court shall consider—
   (a) the extent of any hardship caused by detention,
   (b) the extent (if any) to which the owner is responsible for the matters in respect of which the penalty notice was issued, and
   (c) any other matter which appears to the court to be relevant (whether specific to the circumstances of the case or of a general nature).]

(4) If the court has not ordered the release of the transporter, the Secretary of State may sell it if the penalty in question and connected expenses are not paid before the end of the period of 84 days beginning with the date on which the detention began.

(5) 'Connected expenses' means expenses reasonably incurred by the secretary of State in connection with the detention.

[(5A) The power of sale under subsection (4) may be exercised only when no appeal against the imposition of the penalty is pending or can be brought (ignoring the possibility of an appeal out of time with permission).

(5B) The power of sale under subsection (4) shall lapse if not exercised within a prescribed period.]

(6) Schedule 1 applies to the sale of transporters under this section.

[(7) This section applies to a transporter detained under section 36A as it applies to a transporter detained under section 36(1); but for that purpose—

(a) the court may release the transporter only if the court considers that the detention was unlawful or under subsection (3A) (and subsection (3) shall not apply), and

(b) the reference in subsection (4) to the period of 84 days shall be taken as a reference to a period prescribed for the purpose of this paragraph.]

Note: Section 37(6) commenced 6 December 1999 (SI 1999/3190), remainder 3 April 2000 (SI 2000/464). Subsections (3A)–(3B), (5A)–(5B) and (7) inserted by Sch 8 Nationality, Immigration and Asylum Act 2002 from 8 December 2002 (SI 2002/2811). Words in square brackets in sub-ss (1) and (2) and words in sub-s (3)(c) omitted by Sch 8 Nationality, Immigration and Asylum Act 2002 from 8 December 2002 (SI 2002/2811).

38. Assisting illegal entry and harbouring

. . .

Note: Amends Immigration Act 1971, s 25 from 3 April 2000. Subsections (1) and (3) repealed by Nationality, Immigration and Asylum Act 2002 from a date to be appointed.

39. . . .

Note: Section 39 repealed by Sch 8 Nationality, Immigration and Asylum Act 2002 from 8 December 2002 (SI 2002/2811).

Passengers without proper documents

[40. Charge in respect of passenger without proper documents

(1) This section applies if an individual requiring leave to enter the United Kingdom arrives in the United Kingdom by ship or aircraft and, on being required to do so by an immigration officer, fails to produce—

(a) an immigration document which is in force and which satisfactorily establishes his identity and his nationality or citizenship, and
(b) if the individual requires a visa, a visa of the required kind.

(2) The Secretary of State may charge the owner of the ship or aircraft; in respect of the individual, the sum of £2,000.

(3) The charge shall be payable to the Secretary of State on demand.

(4) No charge shall be payable in respect of any individual who is shown by the owner to have produced the required document or documents to the owner or his employee or agent when embarking on the ship or aircraft for the voyage or flight to the United Kingdom.

(5) For the purpose of subsection (4) an owner shall be entitled to regard a document as—
(a) being what it purports to be unless its falsity is reasonably apparent, and
(b) relating to the individual producing it unless it is reasonably apparent that it does not relate to him.

(6) For the purposes of this section an individual requires a visa if—
(a) under the immigration rules he requires a visa for entry into the United Kingdom, or
(b) as a result of section 41 he requires a visa for passing through the United Kingdom.

(7) The Secretary of State may by order amend this section for the purpose of applying it in relation to an individual who—
(a) requires leave to enter the United Kingdom, and
(b) arrives in the United Kingdom by train.

(8) An order under subsection (7) may provide for the application of this section—
(a) except in cases of a specified kind;
(b) subject to a specified defence.

(9) In this section 'immigration document' means—
(a) a passport, and
(b) a document which relates to a national of a country other than the United Kingdom and which is designed to serve the same purpose as a passport.

(10) The Secretary of State may by order substitute a sum for the sum in subsection (2).]

Note: Section 40 substituted by Sch 8 Nationality, Immigration and Asylum Act 2002 from 8 December 2002 (SI 2003/2811).

40A. Notification and objection

(1) If the Secretary of State decides to charge a person under section 40, the Secretary of State must notify the person of his decision.

(2) A notice under subsection (1) (a 'charge notice') must—
 (a) state the Secretary of State's reasons for deciding to charge the person,
 (b) state the amount of the charge,
 (c) specify the date before which, and the manner in which, the charge must be paid,
 (d) include an explanation of the steps that the person may take if he objects to the charge, and
 (e) include an explanation of the steps that the Secretary of State may take under this Part to recover any unpaid charge.

(3) Where a person on whom a charge notice is served objects to the imposition of the charge on him, he may give a notice of objection to the Secretary of State.

(4) A notice of objection must—
 (a) be in writing,
 (b) give the objector's reasons, and
 (c) be given before the end of such period as may be prescribed.

(5) Where the Secretary of State receives a notice of objection to a charge in accordance with this section, he shall—
 (a) consider it, and
 (b) determine whether or not to cancel the charge.

(6) Where the Secretary of State considers a notice of objection, he shall inform the objector of his decision before the end of—
 (a) such period as may be prescribed, or
 (b) such longer period as he may agree with the objector.

(7) Any sum payable to the Secretary of State as a charge under section 40 may be recovered by the Secretary of State as a debt due to him.

(8) In proceedings for enforcement of a charge under subsection (7) no question may be raised as to the validity of the charge.

(9) Subsections (12) and (13) of section 35 shall have effect for the purpose of this section as they have effect for the purpose of section 35(1), (7) and (10).]

Note: Section 40A inserted by Sch 8 Nationality, Immigration and Asylum Act 2002 from 8 December 2002 (SI 2002/2811).

40B. Appeal

(1) A person may appeal to the court against a decision to charge him under section 40.

(2) On an appeal under this section the court may—
 (a) allow the appeal and cancel the charge, or
 (b) dismiss the appeal.

(3) An appeal under this section—

(a) shall be a re-hearing of the Secretary of State's decision to impose a charge, and
(b) may be determined having regard to matters of which the Secretary of State was unaware.

(4) Subsection (3)(a) has effect despite any provision of Civil Procedure Rules.

(5) An appeal may be brought by a person under this section against a decision to charge him whether or not he has given notice of objection under section 40A(3).

Note: Section 40B inserted by Sch 8 Nationality, Immigration and Asylum Act 2002 from 8 December 2002 (SI 2002/2811).

41. Visas for transit passengers

(1) The Secretary of State may by order require transit passengers to hold a transit visa.

(2) 'Transit passengers' means persons of any description specified in the order who on arrival in the United Kingdom pass through to another country without entering the United Kingdom; and 'transit visa' means a visa for that purpose.

(3) The order—
(a) may specify a description of persons by reference to nationality, citizenship, origin or other connection with any particular country but not by reference to race, colour or religion;
(b) may not provide for the requirement imposed by the order to apply to any person who under the 1971 Act has the right of abode in the United Kingdom;
(c) may provide for any category of persons of a description specified in the order to be exempt from the requirement imposed by the order;
(d) may make provision about the method of application for visas required by the order.

Note: Commenced 8 December 2002 (SI 2002/2815).

42. . . .

Note: Section 42 repealed by Sch 8 Nationality, Immigration and Asylum Act from 8 December 2002 (SI 2002/2811).

Interpretation

43. Interpretation of Part II

(1) In this Part—
'aircraft' includes hovercraft;
'captain' means the master of a ship or commander of an aircraft;

'concealed' includes being concealed in any freight, stores or other thing carried in or on the vehicle, ship [,aircraft or rail freight wagon] concerned;

. . .

'detached trailer' means a trailer, semi-trailer, caravan or any other thing which is designed or adapted for towing by a vehicle but which has been detached for transport—
- (a) in or on the vehicle concerned; or
- (b) in the ship or aircraft concerned (whether separately or in or on a vehicle);

'equipment', in relation to an aircraft, includes—
- (a) any certificate of registration, maintenance or airworthiness of the aircraft;
- (b) any log book relating to the use of the aircraft; and
- (c) any similar document;

['freight shuttle wagon' means a wagon which—
- (a) forms part of a shuttle-train, and
- (b) is designed to carry commercial goods vehicles;

'freight train' means any train other than—
- (a) a train engaged on a service for the carriage of passengers, or
- (b) a shuttle-train;]

'hirer', in relation to a vehicle, means any person who has hired the vehicle from another person;

'operating weight', in relation to an aircraft, means the maximum total weight of the aircraft and its contents at which the aircraft may take off anywhere in the world, in the most favourable circumstances, in accordance with the certificate of airworthiness in force in respect of the aircraft;

'owner' includes—
- (a) in relation to a ship or aircraft, the agent or operator of the ship or aircraft;

. . .
- (b) . . .

and in relation to a transporter which is the subject of a hire-purchase agreement, includes the person in possession of it under that agreement;

'penalty notice' has the meaning given in section 35(2);

['rail freight wagon' means—
- (a) any rolling stock, other than a locomotive, which forms part of a freight train, or
- (b) a freight shuttle wagon,

and for the purpose of this definition, 'rolling stock' and 'locomotive' have the meanings given by section 83 of the Railways Act 1993 (c.43);]

'senior officer' means an immigration officer not below the rank of chief immigration officer;

'ship' includes every description of vessel used in navigation;

['shuttle-train' has the meaning given by section 1(9) of the Channel Tunnel Act 1987 (c. 53);]

'small aircraft' means an aircraft which has an operating weight of less than 5,700 kilogrammes;

'small ship' means a ship which has a gross tonnage of less than 500 tonnes;

'train' means a train which—

(a) is engaged on an international service as defined by section 13(6) of the Channel Tunnel Act 1987; but

(b) is not a shuttle train as defined by section 1(9) of that Act;

'train operator', in relation to a person arriving in the United Kingdom on a train, means the operator of trains who embarked that person on that train for the journey to the United Kingdom;

'transporter' means a vehicle, ship, [aircraft or rail freight wagon] together with—

(a) its equipment; and

(b) any stores for use in connection with its operation;

'vehicle' includes a trailer, semi-trailer, caravan or other thing which is designed or adapted to be towed by another vehicle.

[(2) A reference in this Part to 'the court' is a reference—

(a) in England and Wales, to a country court,

(b) in Scotland, to the sheriff, and

(c) in Northern Ireland, to a country court.

(3) But—

(a) a county court may transfer proceedings under this Part to the High Court, and

(b) the sheriff may transfer proceedings under this Part to the Court of Session.]

Note: Commenced 6 December 1999 (SI 1999/3190). Subsection (2) and words in square brackets in sub-s (1) inserted by and words in sub-s (1) omitted by Sch 8 Nationality, Immigration and Asylum Act from 8 December 2002 (SI 2002/2811)

Part III
Bail

Routine bail hearings

. . .

44–52. . . .

Note: Sections 44 to 52 repealed by the Nationality, Immigration and Asylum Act 2002, s 68 from 10 February 2003 (SI 2003/1).

Bail hearings under other enactments

53. Applications for bail in immigration cases

(1) The Secretary of State may by regulations make new provision in relation to applications for bail by persons detained under the 1971 Act [or under section 62 of the Nationality, Immigration and Asylum Act 2002].

(2) The regulations may confer a right to be released on bail in prescribed circumstances.

(3) The regulations may, in particular, make provision—
   (a) creating or transferring jurisdiction to hear an application for bail by a person detained under the 1971 Act [or under section 62 of the Nationality, Immigration and Asylum Act 2002];
   (b) as to the places in which such an application may be held;
   (c) as to the procedure to be followed on, or in connection with, such an application;
   (d) as to circumstances in which, and conditions (including financial conditions) on which, an applicant may be released on bail;
   (e) amending or repealing any enactment so far as it relates to such an application.

(4) The regulations must include provision for securing that an application for bail made by a person who has brought an appeal under any provision of [the Nationality, Immigration and Asylum Act 2002] or the Special Immigration Appeals Commission Act 1997 is heard by the appellate authority hearing that appeal.

(5) . . .

(6) Regulations under this section require the approval of the Lord Chancellor.

[(6A) In so far as regulations under this section relate to England and Wales, the Lord Chancellor must consult the Lord Chief Justice of England and Wales before giving his approval.

(6B) In so far as regulations under this section relate to Northern Ireland, the Lord Chancellor must consult the Lord Chief Justice of Northern Ireland before giving his approval.]

(7) In so far as regulations under this section relate to the sheriff or the Court of Session, the Lord Chancellor must obtain the consent of the Scottish Ministers before giving his approval.

[(8) The Lord Chief Justice of England and Wales may nominate a judicial office holder (as defined in section 109(4) of the Constitutional Reform Act 2005) to exercise his functions under this section.

(9) The Lord Chief Justice of Northern Ireland may nominate any of the following to exercise his functions under this section—

(a) the holder of one of the offices listed in Schedule 1 to the Justice (Northern Ireland) Act 2002;

(b) a Lord Justice of Appeal (as defined in section 88 of that Act).]

Note: Section 53 commenced 10 February 2003 (SI 2003/2). Words in square brackets in sub-ss (1) and (3) inserted by and sub-s (5) omitted by Nationality, Immigration and Asylum Act 2002, ss 62, 68 from 10 February 2003 (SI 2003/1). Words in square brackets in sub-s (4) substituted by Sch 7 Nationality, Immigration and Asylum Act 2002 from 1 April 2003 (SI 2003/754). Subsections (6A), (8)–(9) inserted by Sch 4 Constitutional Reform Act 2005 from 3 April 2006 (SI 2006/1014). Any function of the Lord Chancellor under sub-s (6) to become a protected function from a date to be appointed, Sch 7 Constitutional Reform Act 2005.

54. Extension of right to apply for bail in deportation cases

Note: Amends para 2, Sch 3 Immigration Act 1971.

Grants

55. . . .

Note: Section 55 ceases to have effect from 10 February 2003, Nationality, Immigration and Asylum Act 2002, s 68.

Part IV

Appeals

. . .

Note: Part IV repealed by the Nationality, Immigration and Asylum Act 2002, s 114 and Sch 9 from 1 April 2003 (SI 2003/754, which sets out transitional provisions).

Part V

Immigration Advisers and Immigration Service Providers

Interpretation

82. Interpretation of Part V

(1) In this Part—

'claim for asylum' means a claim that it would be contrary to the United Kingdom's obligations under—

(a) the Refugee Convention, or

(b) Article 3 of the Human Rights Convention,

for the claimant to be removed from, or required to leave, the United Kingdom;

'the Commissioner' means the Immigration Services Commissioner,

'the complaints scheme' means the scheme established under paragraph 5(1) of Schedule 5;

'designated judge' has the same meaning as in section 119(1) of the Courts and Legal Services Act 1990;

'designated professional body' has the meaning given by section 86;

'immigration advice' means advice which—

(a) relates to a particular individual;

(b) is given in connection with one or more relevant matters;

(c) is given by a person who knows that he is giving it in relation to a particular individual and in connection with one or more relevant matters; and

(d) is not given in connection with representing an individual before a court in criminal proceedings or matters ancillary to criminal proceedings;

'immigration services' means the making of representations on behalf of a particular individual—

(a) in civil proceedings before a court, tribunal or adjudicator in the United Kingdom, or

(b) in correspondence with a Minister of the Crown or government department,

in connection with one or more relevant matters;

'Minister of the Crown' has the same meaning as in the Ministers of the Crown Act 1975;

'qualified person' means a person who is qualified for the purposes of section 84;

'registered person' means a person who is registered with the Commissioner under section 85;

'relevant matters' means any of the following—

(a) a claim for asylum;

(b) an application for, or for the variation of, entry clearance or leave to enter or remain in the United Kingdom;
[(ba) an application for an immigration employment document;]
(c) unlawful entry into the United Kingdom;
(d) nationality and citizenship under the law of the United Kingdom;
(e) citizenship of the European Union;
(f) admission to Member States under Community law;
(g) residence in a Member State in accordance with rights conferred by or under Community law;
(h) removal or deportation from the United Kingdom;
(i) an application for bail under the Immigration Acts or under the Special Immigration Appeals Commission Act 1997;
(j) an appeal against, or an application for judicial review in relation to, any decision taken in connection with a matter referred to in paragraphs (a) to (i); and

'the Tribunal' means the Immigration Services Tribunal.

(2) In this Part, references to the provision of immigration advice or immigration services are to the provision of such advice or services by a person—
(a) in the United Kingdom (regardless of whether the persons to whom they are provided are in the United Kingdom or elsewhere); and
(b) in the course of a business carried on (whether or not for profit) by him or by another person.

[(3) In the definition of 'relevant matters' in subsection (1) 'immigration employment document' means—
(a) a work permit (within the meaning of section 33(1) of the Immigration Act 1971 (interpretation)), and
(b) any other document which relates to employment and is issued for a purpose of immigration rules or in connection with leave to enter or remain in the United Kingdom.]

Note: Commenced 22 May 2000 (SI 2000/1282). Words in square brackets in sub-s (1) and sub-s (3) inserted by Nationality, Immigration and Asylum Act 2002, s 123 from 1 April 2004 (SI 2003/2993).

The Immigration Services Commissioner

83. The Commissioner

(1) There is to be an Immigration Services Commissioner (referred to in this Part as 'the Commissioner').

(2) The Commissioner is to be appointed by the Secretary of State after consulting the Lord Chancellor and the Scottish Ministers.

(3) It is to be the general duty of the Commissioner to promote good practice by those who provide immigration advice or immigration services.

(4) In addition to any other functions conferred on him by this Part, the Commissioner is to have the regulatory functions set out in Part I of Schedule 5.

(5) The Commissioner must exercise his functions so as to secure, so far as is reasonably practicable, that those who provide immigration advice or immigration services—
  (a) are fit and competent to do so;
  (b) act in the best interests of their clients;
  (c) do not knowingly mislead any court, tribunal or adjudicator in the United Kingdom;
  (d) do not seek to abuse any procedure operating in the United Kingdom in connection with immigration or asylum (including any appellate or other judicial procedure);
  (e) do not advise any person to do something which would amount to such an abuse.

(6) The Commissioner—
  (a) must arrange for the publication, in such form and manner and to such extent as he considers appropriate, of information about his functions and about matters falling within the scope of his functions; and
  (b) may give advice about his functions and about such matters.

(7) Part II of Schedule 5 makes further provision with respect to the Commissioner.

Note: Section 83(4) and (5) commenced 22 May 2000 for the purposes of Sch 5, and 30 October 2000 (SI 2000/1985).

The General prohibition

84. Provision of immigration services

(1) No person may provide immigration advice or immigration services unless he is a qualified person.

[(2) A person is a qualified person if he is—
  (a) a registered person,
  (b) authorised by a designated professional body to practise as a member of the profession whose members the body regulates,
  (c) the equivalent in an EEA State of—
    (i) a registered person, or
    (ii) a person within paragraph (b),
  (d) a person permitted, by virtue of exemption from a prohibition, to provide in an EEA State advice or services equivalent to immigration advice or services, or
  (e) acting on behalf of, and under the supervision of, a person within any of paragraphs (a) to (d) (whether or not under a contract of employment).

(3) Subsection (2)(a) and (e) are subject to any limitation on the effect of a person's registration imposed under paragraph 2(2) of Schedule 6.]

(4) Subsection (1) does not apply to a person who—
 (a) is certified by the Commissioner as exempt ('an exempt person');
 (b) is employed by an exempt person;
 (c) works under the supervision of an exempt person or an employee of an exempt person; or
 (d) who falls within a category of person specified in an order made by the Secretary of State for the purposes of this subsection.

(5) A certificate under subsection (4)(a) may relate only to a specified description of immigration advice or immigration services.

(6) Subsection (1) does not apply to a person—
 (a) holding an office under the Crown, when acting in that capacity;
 (b) employed by, or for the purposes of, a government department, when acting in that capacity;
 (c) acting under the control of a government department; or
 (d) otherwise exercising functions on behalf of the Crown.

(7) An exemption given under subsection (4) may be withdrawn by the Commissioner.

Note: Subsections (4)(a) and (d), (5) and (7) commenced 30 October 2000 (SI 2000/1985), remainder on 30 April 2001 (SI 2001/1394). Subsections (2) and (3) substituted by Asylum and Immigration Act 2004, s 37 from 1 October 2004 (SI 2004/2523).

85. Registration and exemption by the Commissioner

(1) The Commissioner must prepare and maintain a register for the purposes of section 84(2)(a) . . .

(2) The Commissioner must keep a record of the persons to whom he has issued a certificate of exemption under section 84(4)(a).

(3) Schedule 6 makes further provision with respect to registration.

Note: Subsection (3) commenced 1 August 2000, remainder 30 October 2000 (SI 2000/1985). Words omitted from sub-s (1) by Asylum and Immigration Act 2004, s 37 from 1 October 2004 (SI 2004/2523).

86. Designated professional bodies

(1) 'Designated professional body' means—
 (a) The Law Society;
 (b) The Law Society of Scotland;
 (c) The Law Society of Northern Ireland;
 (d) The Institute of Legal Executives;
 (e) The General Council of the Bar;

(f) The Faculty of Advocates; or
(g) The General Council of the Bar of Northern Ireland.

[(2) The Secretary of State may by order remove a body from the list in subsection (1) if he considers that the body—
(a) has failed to provide effective regulation of its members in their provision of immigration advice or immigration services, or
(b) has failed to comply with a request of the Commissioner for the provision of information (whether general or in relation to a particular case or matter).]

(3) If a designated professional body asks the Secretary of State to amend subsection (1) so as to remove its name, the Secretary of State may by order do so.

(4) If the Secretary of State is proposing to act under subsection (2) he must, before doing so—
(a) consult the Commissioner;
(b) consult the Legal Services Ombudsman, if the proposed order would affect a designated professional body in England and Wales;
(c) consult the Scottish Legal Services Ombudsman, if the proposed order would affect a designated professional body in Scotland;
(d) consult the lay observers appointed under Article 42 of the Solicitors (Northern Ireland) Order 1976, if the proposed order would affect a designated professional body in Northern Ireland;
(e) notify the body concerned of his proposal and give it a reasonable period within which to make representations; and
(f) consider any representations so made.

(5) An order under subsection (2) requires the approval of—
(a) the Lord Chancellor, if it affects a designated professional body in England and Wales or Northern Ireland;
(b) the Scottish Ministers, if it affects a designated professional body in Scotland.

(6) Before deciding whether or not to give his approval under subsection (5)(a), the Lord Chancellor must consult—
(a) the designated judges, if the order affects a designated professional body in England and Wales;
(b) the Lord Chief Justice of Northern Ireland, if it affects a designated professional body in Northern Ireland.

(7) Before deciding whether or not to give their approval under subsection (5)(b), the Scottish Ministers must consult the Lord President of the Court of Session.

(8) If the Secretary of State considers that a body which—
(a) is concerned (whether wholly or in part) with regulating the legal profession, or a branch of it, in an EEA State,
(b) is not a designated professional body, and

(c) is capable of providing effective regulation of its members in their provision of immigration advice or immigration services, ought to be designated, he may by order amend subsection (1) to include the name of that body.

(9) The Commissioner must—

(a) keep under review the list of designated professional bodies set out in subsection (1); and

[(b) report to the Secretary of State if the Commissioner considers that a designated professional body—

(i) is failing to provide effective regulation of its members in their provision of immigration advice or immigration services, or

(ii) has failed to comply with a request of the Commissioner for the provision of information (whether general or in relation to a particular case or matter).]

[**(9A)** A designated professional body shall comply with a request of the Commissioner for the provision of information (whether general or in relation to a specified case or matter).]

(10) For the purpose of meeting the costs incurred by the Commissioner in discharging his functions under this Part, each designated professional body must pay to the Commissioner, in each year and on such date as may be specified, such fee as may be specified.

(11) Any unpaid fee for which a designated professional body is liable under subsection (10) may be recovered from that body as a debt due to the Commissioner.

(12) 'Specified' means specified by an order made by the Secretary of State.

Note: Subsections (1)–(9) commenced 22 May 2000 (SI 2000/1282), remainder 30 October 2000 (SI 2000/1985). Words in square brackets substituted by Asylum and Immigration Act 2004, s 41 from 1 October 2004 (SI 2004/2523).

The Immigration Services Tribunal

87. The Tribunal

(1) There is to be a tribunal known as the Immigration Services Tribunal (referred to in this Part as 'the Tribunal').

(2) Any person aggrieved by a relevant decision of the Commissioner may appeal to the Tribunal against the decision.

(3) 'Relevant decision' means a decision—

(a) to refuse an application for registration made under paragraph 1 of Schedule 6;

(b) to withdraw an exemption given under section 84(4)(a);

(c) under paragraph 2(2) of that Schedule to register with limited effect;

(d) to refuse an application for continued registration made under paragraph 3 of that Schedule;

(e) to vary a registration on an application under paragraph 3 of that Schedule;

[(ea) to vary a registration under paragraph 3A of that Schedule;] or

(f) . . .

(4) The Tribunal is also to have the function of hearing disciplinary charges laid by the Commissioner under paragraph 9(1)(e) of Schedule 5.

(5) Schedule 7 makes further provision with respect to the Tribunal and its constitution and functions.

Note: Subsection (5) commenced 1 August 2000, remainder 30 October 2000 (SI 2000/1985). Words in square brackets inserted by Nationality, Immigration and Asylum Act 2002, s 140 from 8 January 2003 (SI 2003/1). Words omitted by Asylum and Immigration Act 2004, s 40 from 1 October 2004 (SI 2004/2523).

88. Appeal upheld by the Tribunal

(1) This section applies if the Tribunal allows an appeal under section 87.

(2) If the Tribunal considers it appropriate, it may direct the Commissioner—

(a) to register the applicant or to continue the applicant's registration;

(b) to make or vary the applicant's registration so as to have limited effect in any of the ways mentioned in paragraph 2(2) of Schedule 6;

(c) to restore an exemption granted under section 84(4)(a); or

(d) to quash a decision recorded under paragraph 9(1)(a) of Schedule 5 and the record of that decision.

Note: Commenced 30 October 2000 (SI 2000/1985).

89. Disciplinary charge upheld by the Tribunal

(1) This section applies if the Tribunal upholds a disciplinary charge laid by the Commissioner under paragraph 9(1)(e) of Schedule 5 against a person ('the person charged').

[(2) If the person charged is a registered person or acts on behalf of a registered person, the Tribunal may—

(a) direct the Commissioner to record the charge and the Tribunal's decision for consideration in connection with the registered person's next application for continued registration;

(b) direct the registered person to apply for continued registration as soon as is reasonably practicable.]

(4) If the person charged is certified by the Commissioner as exempt under section 84(4)(a), the Tribunal may direct the Commissioner to consider whether to withdraw his exemption.

(5) If the person charged is found to have charged unreasonable fees for

immigration advice or immigration services, the Tribunal may direct him to repay to the clients concerned such portion of those fees as it may determine.

(6) The Tribunal may direct the person charged to pay a penalty to the Commissioner of such sum as it considers appropriate.

(7) A direction given by the Tribunal under subsection (5) (or under subsection (6)) may be enforced by the clients concerned (or by the Commissioner)—
  (a) as if it were an order of a county court; or
  (b) in Scotland, as if it were an extract registered decree arbitral bearing a warrant for execution issued by the sheriff court of any sheriffdom in Scotland.

(8) The Tribunal may direct that the person charged or any person [acting on his behalf or] under his supervision is to be—
  (a) subject to such restrictions on the provision of immigration advice or immigration services as the Tribunal considers appropriate;
  (b) suspended from providing immigration advice or immigration services for such period as the Tribunal may determine; or
  (c) prohibited from providing immigration advice or immigration services indefinitely.

(9) The Commissioner must keep a record of the persons against whom there is in force a direction given by the Tribunal under subsection (8).

Note: Commenced 30 October 2000 (SI 2000/1985). Words in square brackets substituted by Asylum and Immigration Act 2004, s 37 from 1 October 2004 (SI 2004/2523).

90. Orders by disciplinary bodies

(1) A disciplinary body may make an order directing that a person subject to its jurisdiction is to be—
  (a) subject to such restrictions on the provision of immigration advice or immigration services as the body considers appropriate;
  (b) suspended from providing immigration advice or immigration services for such period as the body may determine; or
  (c) prohibited from providing immigration advice or immigration services indefinitely.

(2) 'Disciplinary body' means any body—
  (a) appearing to the Secretary of State to be established for the purpose of hearing disciplinary charges against members of a designated professional body; and
  (b) specified in an order made by the Secretary of State.

(3) The Secretary of State must consult the designated professional body concerned before making an order under subsection (2)(b).

(4) For the purposes of this section, a person is subject to the jurisdiction of a

disciplinary body if he is an authorised person or [acting on his behalf or] an authorised person.

(5) 'Authorised person' means a person who is authorised by the designated professional body concerned to practise as a member of the profession whose members are regulated by that body.

Note: Commenced 1 August 2000 (SI 2000/1985). Words in square brackets substituted by Asylum and Immigration Act 2004, s 37 from 1 October 2004 (SI 2004/2523).

Enforcement

91. Offences

(1) A person who provides immigration advice or immigration services in contravention of section 84 or of a restraining order is guilty of an offence and liable—
   (a) on summary conviction, to imprisonment for a term not exceeding six months or to a fine not exceeding the statutory maximum, or to both; or
   (b) on conviction on indictment, to imprisonment for a term not exceeding two years or to a fine, or to both.

(2) 'Restraining order' means—
   (a) a direction given by the Tribunal under section 89(8) or paragraph 9(3) of Schedule 5; or
   (b) an order made by a disciplinary body under section 90(1).

(3) If an offence under this section committed by a body corporate is proved—
   (a) to have been committed with the consent or connivance of an officer, or
   (b) to be attributable to neglect on his part, the officer as well as the body corporate is guilty of the offence and liable to be proceeded against and punished accordingly.

(4) 'Officer', in relation to a body corporate, means a director, manager, secretary or other similar officer of the body, or a person purporting to act in such a capacity.

(5) If the affairs of a body corporate are managed by its members, subsection (3) applies in relation to the acts and defaults of a member in connection with his functions of management as if he were a director of the body corporate.

(6) If an offence under this section committed by a partnership in Scotland is proved—
   (a) to have been committed with the consent or connivance of a partner, or
   (b) to be attributable to neglect on his part,

   the partner as well as the partnership is guilty of the offence and liable to be proceeded against and punished accordingly.

(7) 'Partner' includes a person purporting to act as a partner.

Note: Commenced 30 April 2001 (SI 2001/1394).

92. Enforcement

(1) If it appears to the Commissioner that a person—
   (a) is providing immigration advice or immigration services in contravention of section 84 or of a restraining order, and
   (b) is likely to continue to do so unless restrained,

   the Commissioner may apply to a county court for an injunction, or to the sheriff for an interdict, restraining him from doing so.

(2) If the court is satisfied that the application is well-founded, it may grant the injunction or interdict in the terms applied for or in more limited terms.

(3) 'Restraining order' has the meaning given by section 91.

Note: Commenced 30 April 2001 (SI 2001/1394).

[92A. Investigation of offence: power of entry

(1) On an application made by the Commissioner a justice of the peace may issue a warrant authorising the Commissioner to enter and search premises.

(2) A justice of the peace may issue a warrant in respect of premises only if satisfied that there are reasonable grounds for believing that—
   (a) an offence under section 91 has been committed,
   (b) there is material on the premises which is likely to be of substantial value (whether by itself or together with other material) to the investigation of the offence, and
   (c) any of the conditions specified in subsection (3) is satisfied.

(3) Those conditions are—
   (a) that it is not practicable to communicate with a person entitled to grant entry to the premises,
   (b) that it is not practicable to communicate with a person entitled to grant access to the evidence,
   (c) that entry to the premises will be prevented unless a warrant is produced, and
   (d) that the purpose of a search may be frustrated or seriously prejudiced unless the Commissioner can secure immediate entry on arrival at the premises.

(4) The Commissioner may seize and retain anything for which a search is authorised under this section.

(5) A person commits an offence if without reasonable excuse he obstructs the Commissioner in the exercise of a power by virtue of this section.

(6) A person guilty of an offence under subsection (5) shall be liable on summary conviction to—
   (a) imprisonment for a term not exceeding six months,

(b) a fine not exceeding level 5 on the standard scale, or
(c) both.

(7) In this section—
(a) a reference to the Commissioner includes a reference to a member of his staff authorised in writing by him,
(b) a reference to premises includes a reference to premises used wholly or partly as a dwelling, and
(c) a reference to material—
(i) includes material subject to legal privilege within the meaning of the Police and Criminal Evidence Act 1984 (c. 60),
(ii) does not include excluded material or special procedure material,
(iii) includes material whether or not it would be admissible in evidence at a trial.

(8) In the application of this section to Scotland—
(a) a reference to a justice of the peace shall be taken as a reference to the sheriff,
(b) for sub-paragraph (i) of subsection (7)(c) there is substituted—
'(i) includes material comprising items subject to legal privilege (as defined by section 412 of the Proceeds of Crime Act 2002 (c. 29)),' and
(c) sub-paragraph (ii) of subsection (7)(c) shall be ignored.

(9) In the application of this section to Northern Ireland the reference to the Police and Criminal Evidence Act 1984 shall be taken as a reference to the Police and Criminal Evidence (Northern Ireland) Order 1989 (S.I. 1989/1341 (N.I. 12)).]

Note: Section 92A inserted by Asylum and Immigration Act 2004, s 38 from 1 October 2004 (SI 2004/2523).

[92B. Advertising

(1) A person commits an offence if—
(a) he offers to provide immigration advice or immigration services, and
(b) provision by him of the advice or services would constitute an offence under section 91.

(2) For the purpose of subsection (1) a person offers to provide advice or services if he—
(a) makes an offer to a particular person or class of person,
(b) makes arrangements for an advertisement in which he offers to provide advice or services, or
(c) makes arrangements for an advertisement in which he is described or presented as competent to provide advice or services.

(3) A person guilty of an offence under this section shall be liable on summary conviction to a fine not exceeding level 4 on the standard scale.

(4) Subsections (3) to (7) of section 91 shall have effect for the purposes of this section as they have effect for the purposes of that section.

(5) An information relating to an offence under this section may in England and Wales be tried by a magistrates' court if—
  (a) it is laid within the period of six months beginning with the date (or first date) on which the offence is alleged to have been committed, or
  (b) it is laid—
    (i) within the period of two years beginning with that date, and
    (ii) within the period of six months beginning with a date certified by the Immigration Services Commissioner as the date on which the commission of the offence came to his notice.

(6) In Scotland, proceedings for an offence under this section may be commenced—
  (a) at any time within the period of six months beginning with the date (or first date) on which the offence is alleged to have been committed, or
  (b) at any time within both—
    (i) the period of two years beginning with that date, and
    (ii) the period of six months beginning with a date specified, in a certificate signed by or on behalf of the procurator fiscal, as the date on which evidence sufficient in his opinion to warrant such proceedings came to his knowledge,

  and any such certificate purporting to be so signed shall be deemed so signed unless the contrary is proved and be conclusive as to the facts stated in it.

(7) Subsection (3) of section 136 of the Criminal Procedure (Scotland) Act 1995 (c. 46) (date on which proceedings are deemed commenced) has effect to the purposes of subsection (6) as it has effect for the purposes of that section.

(8) A complaint charging the commission of an offence under this section may in Northern Ireland be heard and determined by a magistrates' court if—
  (a) it is made within the period of six months beginning with the date (or first date) on which the offence is alleged to have been committed, or
  (b) it is made—
    (i) within the period of two years beginning with that date, and
    (iii) within the period of six months beginning with a date certified by the Immigration Services Commissioner as the date on which the commission of the offence came to his notice.]

Note: Section 92B inserted by Asylum and Immigration Act 2004, s 39 from 1 October 2004 (SI 2004/2523).

Miscellaneous

93. Information

(1) No enactment or rule of law prohibiting or restricting the disclosure of information prevents a person from—
   (a) giving the Commissioner information which is necessary for the discharge of his functions; or
   (b) giving the Tribunal information which is necessary for the discharge of its functions.

(2) No relevant person may at any time disclose information which—
   (a) has been obtained by, or given to, the Commissioner under or for purposes of this Act,
   (b) relates to an identified or identifiable individual or business, and
   (c) is not at that time, and has not previously been, available to the public from other sources,

unless the disclosure is made with lawful authority.

(3) For the purposes of subsection (2), a disclosure is made with lawful authority only if, and to the extent that—
   (a) it is made with the consent of the individual or of the person for the time being carrying on the business;
   (b) it is made for the purposes of, and is necessary for, the discharge of any of the Commissioner's functions under this Act or any Community obligation of the Commissioner;
   (c) it is made for the purposes of any civil or criminal proceedings arising under or by virtue of this Part, or otherwise; or
   (d) having regard to the rights and freedoms or legitimate interests of any person, the disclosure is necessary in the public interest.

(4) A person who knowingly or recklessly discloses information in contravention of subsection (2) is guilty of an offence and liable—
   (a) on summary conviction, to a fine not exceeding the statutory maximum; or
   (b) on conviction on indictment, to a fine.

(5) 'Relevant person' means a person who is or has been—
   (a) the Commissioner;
   (b) a member of the Commissioner's staff; or
   (c) an agent of the Commissioner.

Note: Commenced 22 May 2000 (SI 2000/1282).

Part VI

Support For Asylum-Seekers

Interpretation

94. Interpretation of Part VI

(1) In this Part—

'adjudicator' has the meaning given in section 102(2);

['asylum-seeker' means a person—

(a) who is at least 18 years old,

(b) who is in the United Kingdom.

(c) who has made a claim for asylum at a place designated by the Secretary of State,

(d) whose claim has been recorded by the Secretary of State, and

(e) whose claim has not been determined;]

'claim for asylum' means a claim that it would be contrary to the United Kingdom's obligations under the Refugee Convention, or under Article 3 of the Human Rights Convention, for the claimant to be removed from, or required to leave, the United Kingdom;

'the Department' means the Department of Health and Social Services for Northern Ireland;

['dependant' in relation to an asylum-seeker or a supported person means a person who—

(a) is in the United Kingdom, and

(b) is within a prescribed class;]

'the Executive' means the Northern Ireland Housing Executive;

'housing accommodation' includes flats, lodging houses and hostels;

'local authority' means—

(a) in England and Wales, a country council, a county borough council, a district council, a London borough council, the Common Council of the City of London or the Council of the Isles of Scilly;

(b) in Scotland, a council constituted under section 2 of the Local Government etc. (Scotland) Act 1994;

['Northern Ireland authority' has the meaning given by section 110(9).]

'supported person' means—

(a) an asylum-seeker, or

(b) a dependant of an asylum-seeker,

who has applied for support and for whom support is provided under section 95.

(2) References in this Part to support provided under section 95 include references to support which is provided under arrangements made by the Secretary of State under that section.

[(3) A claim for asylum shall be treated as determined for the purposes of subsection (1) at the end of such period as may be prescribed beginning with—
   (a) the date on which the Secretary of State notifies the claimant of his decision on the claim, or
   (b) if the claimant appeals against the Secretary of State's decision, the date on which the appeal is disposed of.

(3A) A person shall continue to be treated as an asylum-seeker despite paragraph (e) of the definition of 'asylum-seeker' in subsection (1) while—
   (a) his household includes a dependant child who is under 18, and
   (b) he does not have leave to enter or remain in the United Kingdom.]

(4) An appeal is disposed of when it is no longer pending for the purposes of the Immigration Acts or the Special Immigration Appeals Commission Act 1997.

(5) . . .

(6) . . .

(7) For the purposes of this Part, the Secretary of State may inquire into, and decide, the age of any person.

(8) A notice under subsection (3) must be given in writing.

(9) If such a notice is sent by the Secretary of State by first class post, addressed—
   (a) to the asylum-seeker's representative, or
   (b) to the asylum-seeker's last known address,

   it is to be taken to have been received by the asylum-seeker on the second day after the day on which it was posted.

Note: Commenced 11 November 1999, s 170. Words in first and second square brackets in sub-s (1) substituted by Nationality, Immigration and Asylum Act 2002, s 44 from a date to be appointed and words in third square brackets in sub-s (1) inserted by the same Act, s 60 from 10 February 2003 (SI 2003/1). Subsection (3) substituted by and sub-s (3A) inserted by and sub-ss (5) and (6) omitted by Nationality, Immigration and Asylum Act 2002, s 44 from a date to be appointed. Definition of 'asylum-seeker' modified in relation to ss 110 and 111 from 11 November 2002 so as not to exclude persons under 18 (Nationality, Immigration and Asylum Act 2002, s 48).

Provision of support

95. Persons for whom support may be provided

(1) The Secretary of State may provide, or arrange for the provision of, support for—
   (a) asylum-seekers, or
   (b) dependants of asylum-seekers,

   who appear to the Secretary of State to be destitute or to be likely to become destitute within such period as may be prescribed.

[(2) Where a person has dependants, he had his dependants are destitute for the purpose of this section if they do not have and cannot obtain both—

(a) adequate accommodation, and
(b) food and other essential items.

(3) Where a person does not have dependants, he is destitute for the purpose of this section if he does not have and cannot obtain both—
(a) adequate accommodation, and
(b) food and other essential items.

(4) In determining whether accommodation is adequate for the purposes of subsection (2) or (3) the Secretary of State must have regard to any matter prescribed for the purposes of this subsection.

(5) In determining whether accommodation is adequate for the purposes of subsection (2) or (3) the Secretary of State may not have regard to—
(a) whether a person has an enforceable right to occupy accommodation,
(b) whether a person shares all or part of accommodation,
(c) whether accommodation is temporary or permanent,
(d) the location of accommodation, or
(e) any other matter prescribed for the purposes of this subsection.

(6) The Secretary of State may by regulations specify items which are or are not to be treated as essential items for the purposes of subsections (2) and (3).

(7) The Secretary of State may by regulations—
(a) provide that a person is not to be treated as destitute for the purposes of this Part in specified circumstances;
(b) enable or require the Secretary of State in deciding whether a person is destitute to have regard to income which he or a dependant of his might reasonably be expected to have;
(c) enable or require the Secretary of State in deciding whether a person is destitute to have regard to support which is or might reasonably be expected to be available to the person or a dependant of his;
(d) enable or require the Secretary of State in deciding whether a person is destitute to have regard to assets of a prescribed kind which he or a dependant of his has or might reasonably be expected to have;
(e) make provision as to the valuation of assets.]

(9) Support may be provided subject to conditions.

[(9A) A condition imposed under subsection (9) may, in particular, relate to—
(a) any matter relating to the use of the support provided, or
(b) compliance with a restriction imposed under paragraph 21 of Schedule 2 to the 1971 Act (temporary admission or release from detention) or paragraph 2 or 5 of Schedule 3 to that Act (restriction pending deportation).]

(10) The conditions must be set out in writing.

(11) A copy of the conditions must be given to the supported person.

(12) Schedule 8 gives the Secretary of State power to make regulations supplementing this section.

(13) Schedule 9 makes temporary provision for support in the period before the coming into force of this section.

Note: Commenced in part 11 November 1999 and 6 December 1999, remainder 1 January 2000 (SI 1999/3190). Subsections (2)–(8) substituted by Nationality, Immigration and Asylum Act 2002, s 44 from a date to be appointed and sub-s 9A inserted by Nationality, Immigration and Asylum Act 2002, s 50 from 7 November 2002.

96. Ways in which support may be provided

(1) Support may be provided under section 95—

(a) by providing accommodation appearing to the Secretary of State to be adequate for the needs of the supported person and his dependants (if any);

[(b) by providing the supported person and his dependants (if any) with food or other essential items;]

(c) to enable the supported person (if he is the asylum-seeker) to meet what appear to the Secretary of State to be expenses (other than legal expenses or other expenses of a prescribed description) incurred in connection with his claim for asylum;

(d) to enable the asylum-seeker and his dependants to attend bail proceedings in connection with his detention under any provision of the Immigration Acts; or

(e) to enable the asylum-seeker and his dependants to attend bail proceedings in connection with the detention of a dependant of his under any such provision.

(2) If the Secretary of State considers that the circumstances of a particular case are exceptional, he may provide support under section 95 in such other ways as he considers necessary to enable the supported person and his dependants (if any) to be supported.

(3) Unless the circumstances of a particular case are exceptional, support provided by the Secretary of State under subsection (1)(a) or (b) or (2) must not be wholly or mainly by way of payments made (by whatever means) to the supported person or to his dependants (if any).

(4) . . .

(5) . . .

(6) . . .

Note: Commenced 3 April 2000 (SI 2000/464). Subsection 1(b) substituted by Nationality, Immigration and Asylum Act 2002, s 45 from a date to be appointed. Subsections (4)–(6) repealed by the same Act, s 61 from 7 November 2002.

97. Supplemental

(1) When exercising his power under section 95 to provide accommodation, the Secretary of State must have regard to—

(a) the fact that the accommodation is to be temporary pending determination of the asylum-seeker's claim;
(b) the desirability, in general, of providing accommodation in areas in which there is a ready supply of accommodation; and
(c) such other matters (if any) as may be prescribed.

(2) But he may not have regard to—
(a) any preference that the supported person or his dependants (if any) may have as to the locality in which the accommodation is to be provided; or
(b) such other matters (if any) as may be prescribed.

(3) The Secretary of State may by order repeal all or any of the following—
(a) subsection (1)(a);
(b) subsection (1)(b);
(c) subsection (2)(a).

(4) When exercising his power under section 95 to provide [food and other essential items], the Secretary of State—
(a) must have regard to such matters as may be prescribed for the purposes of this paragraph; but
(b) may not have regard to such other matters as may be prescribed for the purposes of this paragraph.

(5) In addition, when exercising his power under section 95 to provide [food and other essential items], the Secretary of State may limit the overall amount of the expenditure which he incurs in connection with a particular supported person—
(a) to such portion of the income support applicable amount provided under section 124 of the Social Security Contributions and Benefits Act 1992, or
(b) to such portion of any components of that amount,

as he considers appropriate having regard to the temporary nature of the support that he is providing.

(6) For the purposes of subsection (5), any support of a kind falling within section 96(1)(c) is to be treated as if it were the provision of essential [items].

(7) In determining how to provide, or arrange for the provision of, support under section 95, the Secretary of State may disregard any preference which the supported person or his dependants (if any) may have as to the way in which the support is to be given.

Note: Commenced for the purposes of enabling subordinate legislation 1 January 2000 (SI 1999/3190), remainder 3 April 2000 (SI 2000/464). Words in square brackets substituted by Nationality, Immigration and Asylum Act 2002, s 45 from a date to be appointed.

98. Temporary support

(1) The Secretary of State may provide, or arrange for the provision of, support for—
   (a) asylum-seekers, or
   (b) dependants of asylum-seekers,
   who it appears to the Secretary of State may be destitute.

(2) Support may be provided under this section only until the Secretary of State is able to determine whether support may be provided under section 95.

(3) Subsections (2) to (11) of section 95 apply for the purposes of this section as they apply for the purposes of that section.

Note: Subsection (3) commenced for the purposes of enabling subordinate legislation 1 March 2000, remainder 3 April 2000 (SI 2000/464).

Support and assistance by local authorities etc.

99. Provision of support by local authorities

(1) A local authority [or Northern Ireland authority] may provide support for [persons] in accordance with arrangements made by the Secretary of State under section [4,] 95 [or 98].

(2) Support may be provided by an authority in accordance with arrangements made with the authority or with another person.

(3) Support may be provided by an authority in accordance with arrangements made under section 95 only in one or more of the ways mentioned in section 96(1) and (2).

(4) [An authority] may incur reasonable expenditure in connection with the preparation of proposals for entering into arrangements under section [4,] 95 [or 98].

(5) The powers conferred on [an authority] by this section include power to—
   (a) provide services outside their area;
   (b) provide services jointly with one or more[other bodies];
   (c) form a company for the purpose of providing services;
   (d) tender for contracts (whether alone or with any other person).

Note: Subsections (1)–(3) commenced 3 April 2000 (SI 2000/464). Subsections (4) and (5) commenced 11 November 1999, s 170. Words in second and third square brackets in sub-s (1) and second square brackets in sub-s (4) substituted by Immigration, Nationality and Asylum Act 2006, s 43 from 16 June 2006 (SI 2006/1497). Subsections (2) and (3) substituted by and other words in square brackets substituted by Nationality, Immigration and Asylum Act 2002, s 56 from 7 November 2002.

100. Local authority and other assistance for Secretary of State

(1) This section applies if the Secretary of State asks—
(a) a local authority,
(b) a registered social landlord,
(c) a registered housing association in Scotland or Northern Ireland, or
(d) the Executive,
to assist him to exercise his power under section 95 to provide accommodation.

(2) The person to whom the request is made must co-operate in giving the Secretary of State such assistance in the exercise of that power as is reasonable in the circumstances.

(3) Subsection (2) does not require a registered social landlord to act beyond its powers.

(4) A local authority must supply to the Secretary of State such information about their housing accommodation (whether or not occupied) as he may from time to time request.

(5) The information must be provided in such form and manner as the Secretary of State may direct.

(6) 'Registered social landlord' has the same meaning as in Part I of the Housing Act 1996.

(7) 'Registered housing association' has the same meaning—
(a) in relation to Scotland, as in the Housing Associations Act 1985; and
(b) in relation to Northern Ireland, as in Part II of the Housing (Northern Ireland) Order 1992.

Note: Commenced 3 April 2000 (SI 2000/464).

101. Reception zones

(1) The Secretary of State may by order designate as reception zones—
(a) areas in England and Wales consisting of the areas of one or more local authorities;
(b) areas in Scotland consisting of the areas of one or more local authorities;
(c) Northern Ireland.

(2) Subsection (3) applies if the Secretary of State considers that—
(a) a local authority whose area is within a reception zone has suitable housing accommodation within that zone; or
(b) the Executive has suitable housing accommodation.

(3) The Secretary of State may direct the local authority or the Executive to make available such of the accommodation as may be specified in the direction for a period so specified—
(a) to him for the purpose of providing support under section 95; or

(b) to a person with whom the Secretary of State has made arrangements under section 95.

(4) A period specified in a direction under subsection (3)—
(a) begins on a date so specified; and
(b) must not exceed five years.

(5) A direction under subsection (3) is enforceable, on an application made on behalf of the Secretary of State, by injunction or in Scotland an order under section 45(b) of the Court of Session Act 1988.

(6) The Secretary of State's power to give a direction under subsection (3) in respect of a particular reception zone must be exercised by reference to criteria specified for the purposes of this subsection in the order designating that zone.

(7) The Secretary of State may not give a direction under subsection (3) in respect of a local authority in Scotland unless the Scottish Ministers have confirmed to him that the criteria specified in the designation order concerned are in their opinion met in relation to that authority.

(8) Housing accommodation is suitable for the purposes of subsection (2) if it—
(a) is unoccupied;
(b) would be likely to remain unoccupied for the foreseeable future if not made available; and
(c) is appropriate for the accommodation of persons supported under this Part or capable of being made so with minor work.

(9) If housing accommodation for which a direction under this section is, for the time being, in force—
(a) is not appropriate for the accommodation of persons supported under this Part, but
(b) is capable of being made so with minor work, the direction may require the body to whom it is given to secure that that work is done without delay.

(10) The Secretary of State must make regulations with respect to the general management of any housing accommodation for which a direction under subsection (3) is, for the time being, in force.

(11) Regulations under subsection (10) must include provision—
(a) as to the method to be used in determining the amount of rent or other charges to be payable in relation to the accommodation;
(b) as to the times at which payments of rent or other charges are to be made;
(c) as to the responsibility for maintenance of, and repairs to, the accommodation;
(d) enabling the accommodation to be inspected, in such circumstances as may be prescribed, by the body to which the direction was given;
(e) with respect to the condition in which the accommodation is to be returned when the direction ceases to have effect.

(12) Regulations under subsection (10) may, in particular, include provision—
  (a) for the cost, or part of the cost, of minor work required by a direction under this section to be met by the Secretary of State in prescribed circumstances;
  (b) as to the maximum amount of expenditure which a body may be required to incur as a result of a direction under this section.

(13) The Secretary of State must by regulations make provision ('the dispute resolution procedure') for resolving disputes arising in connection with the operation of any regulations made under subsection (10).

(14) Regulations under subsection (13) must include provision—
  (a) requiring a dispute to be resolved in accordance with the dispute resolution procedure;
  (b) requiring the parties to a dispute to comply with obligations imposed on them by the procedure; and
  (c) for the decision of the person resolving a dispute in accordance with the procedure to be final and binding on the parties.

(15) Before—
  (a) designating a reception zone in Great Britain,
  (b) determining the criteria to be included in the order designating the zone, or
  (c) making regulations under subsection (13),

the Secretary of State must consult such local authorities, local authority associations and other persons as he thinks appropriate.

(16) Before—
  (a) designating Northern Ireland as a reception zone, or
  (b) determining the criteria to be included in the order designating Northern Ireland,

the Secretary of State must consult the Executive and such other persons as he thinks appropriate.

(17) Before making regulations under subsection (10) which extend only to Northern Ireland, the Secretary of State must consult the Executive and such other persons as he thinks appropriate.

(18) Before making any other regulations under subsection (10), the Secretary of State must consult—
  (a) such local authorities, local authority associations and other persons as he thinks appropriate; and
  (b) if the regulations extend to Northern Ireland, the Executive.

Note: Commenced 3 April 2000 (SI 2000/464).

Appeals

102. Asylum Support Adjudicators

(1) There are to be adjudicators to hear appeals under this Part.

(2) A person appointed as an adjudicator under this Part is to be known as an Asylum Support Adjudicator (but is referred to in this Part as 'an adjudicator').

(3) Schedule 10 makes further provision with respect to adjudicators.

Note: Commenced 3 April 2000 (SI 2000/464).

[103. Appeals: general

[(1) This section applies where a person has applied for support under all or any of the following provisions—
  (a) section 4,
  (b) section 95, and
  (c) section 17 of the Nationality, Immigration and Asylum Act 2002]

(2) The person may appeal to an adjudicator against a decision that the person is not qualified to receive the support for which he has applied.

(3) The person may also appeal to an adjudicator against a decision to stop providing support under a provision mentioned in subsection (1).

(4) But subsection (3) does not apply—
  (a) to a decision to stop providing support under one of the provisions mentioned in subsection (1) if it is to be replaced immediately by support under [another of those provisions], or
  (b) to a decision taken on the ground that the person is no longer an asylum-seeker or the dependant of an asylum-seeker.

(5) On an appeal under this section an adjudicator may—
  (a) require the Secretary of State to reconsider a matter;
  (b) substitute his decision for the decision against which the appeal is brought;
  (c) dismiss the appeal.

(6) An adjudicator must give his reasons in writing.

(7) If an appeal under this section is dismissed the Secretary of State shall not consider any further application by the appellant for support under a provision mentioned in [subsection (1)] unless the Secretary of State thinks there has been a material change in circumstances.

(8) An appeal under this section may not be brought or continued by a person who is outside the United Kingdom.]

Note: Section 103 substituted by Nationality, Immigration and Asylum Act 2002, s 53 from a date to be appointed. Words in square brackets inserted by Asylum and Immigration Act 2004, s 10 from 31 March 2005 (SI 2005/372).

[103A. Appeals: location of support under [section 4 or 95]

(1) The Secretary of State may by regulations provide for a decision as to where support provided under [section 4 or 95] is to be provided to be appealable to an adjudicator under this Part.

(2) Regulations under this section may provide for a provision of section 103 to have effect in relation to an appeal under the regulations with specified modifications.

Note: Section 103A inserted by Nationality, Immigration and Asylum Act 2002, s 53 from a date to be appointed. Words in square brackets inserted by Asylum and Immigration Act 2004, s 10 from 31 March 2005 (SI 2005/372).

103B. Appeals: travelling expenses

The Secretary of State may pay reasonable travelling expenses incurred by an appellant in connection with attendance for the purposes of an appeal under or by virtue of section 103 or 103A.]

Note: Section 103B inserted by Nationality, Immigration and Asylum Act 2002, s 53 from a date to be appointed.

104. Secretary of State's rules

(1) The Secretary of State may make rules regulating—
- (a) the bringing of appeals under this Part; and
- (b) the practice and procedure of the adjudicators.

(2) The rules may, in particular, make provision—
- (a) for the period within which an appeal must be brought;
- (b) as to the burden of proof on an appeal;
- (c) as to the giving and admissibility of evidence;
- (d) for summoning witnesses;
- (e) for an appeal to be heard in the absence of the appellant;
- (f) for determining an appeal without a hearing;
- (g) requiring reports of decisions of adjudicators to be published;
- (h) conferring such ancillary powers on adjudicators as the Secretary of State considers necessary for the proper discharge of their functions.

(3) In making the rules, the Secretary of State must have regard to the desirability of securing, so far as is reasonably practicable, that appeals are brought and disposed of with the minimum of delay.

Note: Commenced 1 January 2000 (SI 1999/3190).

Offences

105. False representations

(1) A person is guilty of an offence if, with a view to obtaining support for himself or any other person under any provision made by or under this Part, he—
  (a) makes a statement or representation which he knows is false in a material particular;
  (b) produces or gives to a person exercising functions under this Part, or knowingly causes or allows to be produced or given to such a person, any document or information which he knows is false in a material particular;
  (c) fails, without reasonable excuse, to notify a change of circumstances when required to do so in accordance with any provision made by or under this Part; or
  (d) without reasonable excuse, knowingly causes another person to fail to notify a change of circumstances which that other person was required to notify in accordance with any provision made by or under this Part.

(2) A person guilty of an offence under this section is liable on summary conviction to imprisonment for a term not exceeding three months or to a fine not exceeding level 5 on the standard scale, or to both.

Note: Commenced 11 November 1999, s 170.

106. Dishonest representations

(1) A person is guilty of an offence if, with a view to obtaining any benefit or other payment or advantage under this Part for himself or any other person, he dishonestly—
  (a) makes a statement or representation which is false in a material particular;
  (b) produces or gives to a person exercising functions under this Part, or causes or allows to be produced or given to such a person, any document or information which is false in a material particular;
  (c) fails to notify a change of circumstances when required to do so in accordance with any provision made by or under this Part; or
  (d) causes another person to fail to notify a change of circumstances which that other person was required to notify in accordance with any provision made by or under this Part.

(2) A person guilty of an offence under this section is liable—
  (a) on summary conviction, to imprisonment for a term not exceeding six months or to a fine not exceeding the statutory maximum, or to both; or
  (b) on conviction on indictment, to imprisonment for a term not exceeding seven years or to a fine, or to both.

(3) In the application of this section to Scotland, in subsection (1) for 'dishonestly' substitute 'knowingly'.

Note: Commenced 11 November 1999, s 170.

107. Delay or obstruction

(1) A person is guilty of an offence if, without reasonable excuse, he—
 (a) intentionally delays or obstructs a person exercising functions conferred by or under this Part; or
 (b) refuses or neglects to answer a question, give any information or produce a document when required to do so in accordance with any provision made by or under this Part.

(2) A person guilty of an offence under subsection (1) is liable on summary conviction to a fine not exceeding level 3 on the standard scale.

Note: Commenced 11 November 1999, s 170.

108. Failure of sponsor to maintain

(1) A person is guilty of an offence if, during any period in respect of which he has given a written undertaking in pursuance of the immigration rules to be responsible for the maintenance and accommodation of another person—
 (a) he persistently refuses or neglects, without reasonable excuse, to maintain that person in accordance with the undertaking; and
 (b) in consequence of his refusal or neglect, support under any provision made by or under this Part is provided for or in respect of that person.

(2) A person guilty of an offence under this section is liable on summary conviction to imprisonment for a term not exceeding 3 months or to a fine not exceeding level 4 on the standard scale, or to both.

(3) For the purposes of this section, a person is not to be taken to have refused or neglected to maintain another person by reason only of anything done or omitted in furtherance of a trade dispute.

Note: Commenced 11 November 1999, s 170.

109. Supplemental

(1) If an offence under section 105, 106, 107 or 108 committed by a body corporate is proved—
 (a) to have been committed with the consent or connivance of an officer, or
 (b) to be attributable to neglect on his part,

 the officer as well as the body corporate is guilty of the offence and liable to be proceeded against and punished accordingly.

(2) 'Officer', in relation to a body corporate, means a director, manager, secretary or other similar officer of the body, or a person purporting to act in such a capacity.

(3) If the affairs of a body corporate are managed by its members, subsection (1)

applies in relation to the acts and defaults of a member in connection with his functions of management as if he were a director of the body corporate.

(4) If an offence under section 105, 106, 107 or 108 committed by a partnership in Scotland is proved—
(a) to have been committed with the consent or connivance of a partner, or
(b) to be attributable to neglect on his part,
the partner as well as the partnership is guilty of the offence and liable to be proceeded against and punished accordingly.

(5) 'Partner' includes a person purporting to act as a partner.

Note: Commenced 11 November 1999, s 170.

Expenditure

110. Payments to local authorities

(1) The Secretary of State may from time to time pay to any local authority or Northern Ireland authority such sums as he considers appropriate in respect of expenditure incurred, or to be incurred, by the authority in connection with—
(a) persons who are, or have been, asylum-seekers; and
(b) their dependants.

(2) The Secretary of State may from time to time pay to any—
(a) local authority,
(b) local authority association, or
(c) Northern Ireland authority,
such sums as he considers appropriate in respect of services provided by the authority or association in connection with the discharge of functions under this Part.

(3) The Secretary of State may make payments to any local authority towards the discharge of any liability of supported persons or their dependants in respect of council tax payable to that authority.

(4) The Secretary of State must pay to a body to which a direction under section 101(3) is given such sums as he considers represent the reasonable costs to that body of complying with the direction.

(5) The Secretary of State must pay to a directed body sums determined to be payable in relation to accommodation made available by that body under section 101(3)(a).

(6) The Secretary of State may pay to a directed body sums determined to be payable in relation to accommodation made available by that body under section 101(3)(b).

(7) in subsections (5) and (6)—

'determined' means determined in accordance with regulations made by virtue of subsection (11)(a) of section 101, and
'directed body' means a body to which a direction under subsection (3) of section 101 is given.

(8) Payments under subsection (1), (2) or (3) may be made on such terms, and subject to such conditions, as the Secretary of State may determine.

(9) 'Northern Ireland authority' means—
(a) the Executive; or
(b) a Health and Social Services Board established under Article 16 of the Health and Personal Social Services (Northern Ireland) Order 1972 [; or
(c) a Health and Social Services trust established under the Health and Personal Social Services (Northern Ireland) Order 1991 (S.I. 1991/194 (N.I. 1).]

Note: Subsections (1), (2) and (8) commenced 11 November 1999, s 170, sub-s (9) 6 December 1999 (SI 1999/3190), remainder 3 April 2000 (SI 2000/464). Subsection (9)(1(c) inserted by Nationality, Immigration and Asylum Act 2002, s 60 from 7 November 2002.

111. Grants to voluntary organisations

(1) The Secretary of State may make grants of such amounts as he thinks appropriate to voluntary organisations in connection with—
(a) the provision by them of support (of whatever nature) to persons who are, or have been, asylum-seekers and to their dependants; and
(b) connected matters.

(2) Grants may be made on such terms, and subject to such conditions, as the Secretary of State may determine.

Note: Commenced 11 November 1999, s 170.

112. Recovery of expenditure on support: misrepresentation etc.

(1) This section applies if, on an application made by the Secretary of State, the court determines that—
(a) a person ('A') has misrepresented or failed to disclose a material fact (whether fraudulently or otherwise); and
(b) as a consequence of the misrepresentation or failure, support has been provided under section 95 or 98 (whether or not to A).

(2) If the support was provided by the Secretary of State, the court may order A to pay to the Secretary of State an amount representing the monetary value of the support which would not have been provided but for A's misrepresentation or failure.

(3) If the support was provided by another person ('B') in accordance with arrangements made with the Secretary of State under section 95 or 98, the court may order A to pay to the Secretary of State an amount representing the

payment to B which would not have been made but for A's misrepresentation or failure.

(4) 'Court' means a county court or, in Scotland, the sheriff.

Note: Commenced 3 April 2000 (SI 2000/464).

113. Recovery of expenditure on support from sponsor

(1) This section applies if—

(a) a person ('the sponsor') has given a written undertaking in pursuance of the immigration rules to be responsible for the maintenance and accommodation of another person; and

(b) during any period in relation to which the undertaking applies, support under section 95 is provided to or in respect of that other person.

(2) The Secretary of State may make a complaint against the sponsor to a magistrates' court for an order under this section.

(3) The court—

(a) must have regard to all the circumstances (and in particular to the sponsor's income); and

(b) may order him to pay to the Secretary of State such sum (weekly or otherwise) as it considers appropriate.

(4) But such a sum is not to include any amount attributable otherwise than to support provided under section 95.

(5) In determining—

(a) whether to order any payments to be made in respect of support provided under section 95 for any period before the complaint was made, or

(b) the amount of any such payments,

the court must disregard any amount by which the sponsor's current income exceeds his income during that period.

(6) An order under this section is enforceable as a magistrates' court maintenance order within the meaning of section 150(1) of the Magistrates' Courts Act 1980.

(7) In the application of this section to Scotland—

(a) omit subsection (6);

(b) for references to a complaint substitute references to an application; and

(c) for references to a magistrates' court substitute references to the sheriff.

(8) In the application of this section to Northern Ireland, for references to a magistrates' court substitute references to a court of summary jurisdiction and for subsection (6) substitute—

'(6) An order under this section is an order to which Article 98(11) of the Magistrates' Courts (Northern Ireland) Order 1981 applies.'

Note: Commenced 3 April 2000 (SI 2000/464).

114. Overpayments

(1) Subsection (2) applies if, as a result of an error on the part of the Secretary of State, support has been provided to a person under section 95 or 98.

(2) The Secretary of State may recover from a person who is, or has been, a supported person an amount representing the monetary value of support provided to him as a result of the error.

(3) An amount recoverable under subsection (2) may be recovered as if it were a debt due to the Secretary of State.

(4) The Secretary of State may by regulations make provision for other methods of recovery, including deductions from support provided under section 95.

Note: Commenced 1 January 2000 for the purposes of enabling subordinate legislation (SI 1999/3190).

Exclusions

115. Exclusion from benefits

(1) No person is entitled to income-based jobseeker's allowance under the Jobseekers Act 1995 or to—
   (a) attendance allowance,
   (b) severe disablement allowance,
   (c) invalid care allowance,
   (d) disability living allowance,
   (e) income support,
   (f) working families' tax credit,
   (g) disabled person's tax credit,
   (h) a social fund payment,
   (i) child benefit,
   (j) housing benefit, or
   (k) council tax benefit,

   under the Social Security Contributions and Benefits Act 1992 while he is a person to whom this section applies.

(2) No person in Northern Ireland is entitled to—
   (a) income-based jobseeker's allowance under the Jobseekers (Northern Ireland) Order 1995, or
   (b) any of the benefits mentioned in paragraphs (a) to (j) of subsection (1), under the Social Security Contributions and Benefits (Northern Ireland) Act 1992 while he is a person to whom this section applies.

(3) This section applies to a person subject to immigration control unless he falls within such category or description, or satisfies such conditions, as may be prescribed.

(4) Regulations under subsection (3) may provide for a person to be treated for prescribed purposes only as not being a person to whom this section applies.

(5) In relation to the benefits mentioned in subsection (1)(f) or (g), 'prescribed' means prescribed by regulations made by the Treasury.

(6) In relation to the matters mentioned in subsection (2) (except so far as it relates to the benefits mentioned in subsection (1)(f) or (g)), 'prescribed' means prescribed by regulations made by the Department.

(7) Section 175(3) to (5) of the Social Security Contributions and Benefits Act 1992 (supplemental powers in relation to regulations) applies to regulations made by the Secretary of State or the Treasury under subsection (3) as it applies to regulations made under that Act.

(8) Sections 133(2), 171(2) and 172(4) of the Social Security Contributions and Benefits (Northern Ireland) Act 1992 apply to regulations made by the Department under subsection (3) as they apply to regulations made by the Department under that Act.

(9) 'A person subject to immigration control' means a person who is not a national of an EEA State and who—

(a) requires leave to enter or remain in the United Kingdom but does not have it;

(b) has leave to enter or remain in the United Kingdom which is subject to a condition that he does not have recourse to public funds;

(c) has leave to enter or remain in the United Kingdom given as a result of a maintenance undertaking; or

(d) has leave to enter or remain in the United Kingdom only as a result of paragraph 17 of Schedule 4.

(10) 'Maintenance undertaking', in relation to any person, means a written undertaking given by another person in pursuance of the immigration rules to be responsible for that person's maintenance and accommodation.

Note: Commenced for the purposes of enabling subordinate legislation 1 January 2000 (SI 1999/3190), remainder 3 April 2000 (SI 2000/464).

116. . . .

Note: Amends National Assistance Act 1948, s 21.

117. . . .

Note: Amends Health Services and Public Health Act 1968, s 4; Sch 8 National Health Service Act 1977; and Housing Act 1996, ss 161, 185–187.

118. Housing authority accommodation

(1) Each housing authority must secure that, so far as practicable, a tenancy of, or licence to occupy, housing accommodation provided under the

accommodation provisions is not granted to a person subject to immigration control unless—

(a) he is of a class specified in an order made by the Secretary of State; or

(b) the tenancy of, or licence to occupy, such accommodation is granted in accordance with arrangements made under section [4, 95 or 98].

(2) 'Housing authority' means—

(a) in relation to England and Wales, a local housing authority within the meaning of the Housing Act 1985;

(b) in relation to Scotland, a local authority within the meaning of the Housing (Scotland) Act 1987; and

(c) in relation to Northern Ireland, the Executive.

(3) 'Accommodation provisions' means—

(a) in relation to England and Wales, Part II of the Housing Act 1985;

(b) in relation to Scotland, Part I of the Housing (Scotland) Act 1987;

(c) in relation to Northern Ireland, Part II of the Housing (Northern Ireland) Order 1981.

(4) 'Licence to occupy', in relation to Scotland, means a permission or right to occupy.

(5) 'Tenancy', in relation to England and Wales, has the same meaning as in the Housing Act 1985.

(6) 'Person subject to immigration control' means a person who under the 1971 Act requires leave to enter or remain in the United Kingdom (whether or not such leave has been given).

(7) This section does not apply in relation to any allocation of housing to which Part VI of the Housing Act 1996 (allocation of housing accommodation) applies.

Note: Commenced 1 January 2000 for purposes of enabling subordinate legislation (SI 1999/3190), remainder 1 March 2000 (SI 2000/464). Words in square brackets in sub-s (1)(b) substituted by Immigration, Nationality and Asylum Act 2006, s 43 from 16 June 2006 (SI 2006/1497).

119. Homelessness: Scotland and Northern Ireland

(1) A person subject to immigration control—

(a) is not eligible for accommodation or assistance under the homelessness provisions, and

(b) is to be disregarded in determining for the purposes of those provisions, whether another person—

(i) is homeless or is threatened with homelessness, or

(ii) has a priority need for accommodation,

unless he is of a class specified in an order made by the Secretary of State.

(2) An order under subsection (1) may not be made so as to include in a specified class any person to whom section 115 applies.

(3) 'The homelessness provisions' means—
  (a) in relation to Scotland, Part II of the Housing (Scotland) Act 1987; and
  (b) in relation to Northern Ireland, Part II of the Housing (Northern Ireland) Order 1988.

(4) 'Person subject to immigration control' has the same meaning as in section 118.

Note: Commenced 1 January 2000 for purposes of enabling subordinate legislation, remainder 1 March 2000 (SI 2000/464).

120. . . .

Note: Amends Social Work (Scotland) Act 1968, ss 2 and 13, Mental Health (Scotland) Act 1984, ss 7–8 and Asylum and Immigration Appeals Act 1993, ss 4–5 and Sch 1.

121. . . .

Note: Amends Health and Personal Social Services (Northern Ireland) Order 1972.

[122. Family with children

(1) This section applies where a person ('the asylum-seeker') applies for support under section 95 of this Act or section 17 of the Nationality, Immigration and Asylum Act 2002 (accommodation centres) if—
  (a) the Secretary of State thinks that the asylum-seeker is eligible for support under either or both of those sections, and
  (b) the asylum-seeker's household includes a dependant child who is under 18.

(2) The Secretary of State must offer the provision of support for the child, as part of the asylum-seeker's household, under one of the sections mentioned in subsection (1).

(3) A local authority (or, in Northern Ireland, an authority) may not provide assistance for a child if—
  (a) the Secretary of State is providing support for the child in accordance with an offer under subsection (2),
  (b) an offer by the Secretary of State under subsection (2) remains open in respect of the child, or
  (c) the Secretary of State has agreed that he would make an offer in respect of the child under subsection (2) if an application were made as described in subsection (1).

(4) In subsection (3) 'assistance' means assistance under—
  (a) section 17 of the Children Act 1989 (c. 41) (local authority support),
  (b) section 22 of the Children (Scotland) Act 1995 (c. 36) (similar provision for Scotland), or

(c) Article 18 of the Children (Northern Ireland) Order 1995 (S.I. 1995/775 (N.I. 2)) (similar provision for Northern Ireland).

(5) The Secretary of State may by order disapply subsection (3) in specified circumstances.

(6) Where subsection (3) ceases to apply to a child because the Secretary of State stops providing support, no local authority may provide assistance for the child except the authority for the area within which the support was provided.]

Note: Section 122 substituted by Nationality, Immigration and Asylum Act 2002, s 47 from a date to be appointed.

123. Back-dating of benefits where person recorded as refugee

. . .

Note: Section 123 ceases to have effect from a date to be appointed, Asylum and Immigration Act 2004, s 12.

Miscellaneous

124. Secretary of State to be corporation sole for purposes of Part VI

(1) For the purpose of exercising his functions under this Part, the Secretary of State is a corporation sole.

(2) Any instrument in connection with the acquisition, management or disposal of property, real or personal, heritable or moveable, by the Secretary of State under this Part may be executed on his behalf by a person authorised by him for that purpose.

(3) Any instrument purporting to have been so executed on behalf of the Secretary of State is to be treated, until the contrary is proved, to have been so executed on his behalf.

Note: Commenced 11 November 1999, s 170.

125. Entry of premises

(1) This section applies in relation to premises in which accommodation has been provided under section 95 or 98 for a supported person.

(2) If, on an application made by a person authorised in writing by the Secretary of State, a justice of the peace is satisfied that there is reason to believe that—

(a) the supported person or any dependants of his for whom the accommodation is provided is not resident in it,

(b) the accommodation is being used for any purpose other than the accommodation of the asylum-seeker or any dependant of his, or

(c) any person other than the supported person and his dependants (if any) is residing in the accommodation,

he may grant a warrant to enter the premises to the person making the application.

(3) A warrant granted under subsection (2) may be executed—

(a) at any reasonable time;

(b) using reasonable force.

(4) In the application of subsection (2) to Scotland, read the reference to a justice of the peace as a reference to the sheriff or a justice of the peace.

Note: Commenced 3 April 2000 (SI 2000/464).

126. Information from property owners

(1) The power conferred by this section is to be exercised with a view to obtaining information about premises in which accommodation is or has been provided for supported persons.

(2) The Secretary of State may require any person appearing to him—

(a) to have any interest in, or

(b) to be involved in any way in the management or control of, such premises, or any building which includes such premises,

to provide him with such information with respect to the premises and the persons occupying them as he may specify.

(3) A person who is required to provide information under this section must do so in accordance with such requirements as may be prescribed.

(4) Information provided to the Secretary of State under this section may be used by him only in the exercise of his functions under this Part.

Note: Commenced 3 April 2000 (SI 2000/464).

127. Requirement to supply information about redirection of post

(1) The Secretary of State may require any person conveying postal packets to supply redirection information to the Secretary of State—

(a) for use in the prevention, detection, investigation or prosecution of criminal offences under this Part;

(b) for use in checking the accuracy of information relating to support provided under this Part; or

(c) for any other purpose relating to the provision of support to asylum-seekers.

(2) The information must be supplied in such manner and form, and in accordance with such requirements, as may be prescribed.

(3) The Secretary of State must make payments of such amount as he considers reasonable in respect of the supply of information under this section.

(4) 'Postal packet' has the same meaning as in the Post Office Act 1953.

(5) 'Redirection information' means information relating to arrangements made with any person conveying postal packets for the delivery of postal packets to addresses other than those indicated by senders on the packets.

Note: Commenced 3 April 2000 (SI 2000/464).

Part VII

Power to Arrest, Search and Fingerprint

Power to arrest

128. . . .

Note: Amends Immigration Act 1971, s 28.

Power to search and arrest

129. . . .

Note: Amends Immigration Act 1971, s 28.

130. . . .

Note: Amends Immigration Act 1971, s 28.

Power to enter and search premises

131. . . .

Note: Amends Immigration Act 1971, s 28.

132. . . .

Note: Amends Immigration Act 1971, s 28 and Sch 2, para 25.

133. . . .

Note: Amends Immigration Act 1971, s 28.

Power to search persons

134. . . .

Note: Amends Immigration Act 1971, s 28 and Sch 2, para 25.

135. . . .

Note: Amends Immigration Act 1971, s 28 and Sch 2, para 25.

Seized material: access and copying

136. . . .

Note: Amends Immigration Act 1971, s 28 and Sch 2, para 25.

Search warrants

137. . . .

Note: Amends Immigration Act 1971, s 28.

138. . . .

Note: Amends Immigration Act 1971, s 28.

139. . . .

Note: Amends Immigration Act 1971, s 28 and Sch 2, para 25.

Detention

140. . . .

Note: Amends Immigration Act 1971, Sch 2, paras 16–17.

Fingerprinting

141. Fingerprinting

(1) Fingerprints may be taken by an authorised person from a person to whom this section applies.

(2) Fingerprints may be taken under this section only during the relevant period.

(3) Fingerprints may not be taken under this section from a person under the age of sixteen ('the child') except in the presence of a person of full age who is—
   (a) the child's parent or guardian; or
   (b) a person who for the time being takes responsibility for the child.

(4) The person mentioned in subsection (3)(b) may not be—
   (a) an officer of the Secretary of State who is not an authorised person;
   (b) an authorised person.

(5) 'Authorised person' means—
(a) a constable;
(b) an immigration officer;
(c) a prison officer;
(d) an officer of the Secretary of State authorised for the purpose; or
(e) a person who is employed by a contractor in connection with the discharge of the contractor's duties under a [removal centre] contract.

(6) In subsection (5)(e) 'contractor' and '[removal centre] contract' have the same meaning as in Part VIII.

(7) This section applies to—
(a) any person ('A') who, on being required to do so by an immigration officer on his arrival in the United Kingdom, fails to produce a valid passport with photograph or some other document satisfactorily establishing his identity and nationality or citizenship;
(b) any person ('B') who has been refused leave to enter the United Kingdom but has been temporarily admitted under paragraph 21 of Schedule 2 to the 1971 Act if an immigration officer reasonably suspects that B might break any condition imposed on him relating to residence or as to reporting to the police or an immigration officer;
[(c) any person ('C') in respect of whom a relevant immigration decision has been made;]
(d) any person ('D') who has been [detained under paragraph 16 of Schedule 2 to the 1971 Act or arrested under paragraph 17 of that Schedule;]
(e) any person ('E') who has made a claim for asylum;
(f) any person ('F') who is a dependant of any of those persons.

(8) 'The relevant period' begins—
(a) for A, on his failure to produce the passport or other document;
(b) for B, on the decision to admit him temporarily;
[(c) for C, on the service on him of notice of the relevant immigration decision by virtue of section 105 of the Nationality, Immigration and Asylum Act 2002 (c. 41);]
(d) for D, on his [detention or arrest;]
(e) for E, on the making of his claim for asylum; and
(f) for F, at the same time as for the person whose dependant he is.

(9) 'The relevant period' ends on the earliest of the following—
(a) the grant of leave to enter or remain in the United Kingdom;
(b) for A, B, C or D, his removal or deportation from the United Kingdom;
[(c) for C—
(i) the time when the relevant immigration decision ceases to have effect, whether as a result of an appeal or otherwise, or
(ii) if a deportation order has been made against him, its revocation or its otherwise ceasing to have effect;]

(d) for D, his release if he is no longer liable to be detained under paragraph 16 of Schedule 2 to the 1971 Act;
(e) for E, the final determination or abandonment of his claim for asylum; and
(f) for F, at the same time as for the person whose dependant he is.

(10) No fingerprints may be taken from A if the immigration officer considers that A has a reasonable excuse for the failure concerned.

(11) No fingerprints may be taken from B unless the decision to take them has been confirmed by a chief immigration officer.

(12) An authorised person may not take fingerprints from a person under the age of sixteen unless his decision to take them has been confirmed—
(a) if he is a constable, by a person designated for the purpose by the chief constable of his police force;
(b) if he is a person mentioned in subsection (5)(b) or (e), by a chief immigration officer;
(c) if he is a person officer, by a person designated for the purpose by the governor of the prison;
(d) if he is an officer of the Secretary of State, by a person designated for the purpose by the Secretary of State.

(13) Neither subsection (3) nor subsection (12) prevents an authorised person from taking fingerprints if he reasonably believes that the person from whom they are to be taken is aged sixteen or over.

(14) For the purposes of subsection (7)(f), a person is a dependant of another person if—
(a) he is that person's spouse or child under the age of eighteen; and
(b) he does not have a right of abode in the United Kingdom or indefinite leave to enter or remain in the United Kingdom.

(15) 'Claim for asylum' has the same meaning as in Part VI.

[(16) 'Relevant immigration decision' means a decision of the kind mentioned in section 82(2)(g), (h), (i), (j) or (k) of the Nationality, Immigration and Asylum Act 2002 (c. 41).]

[(17) Section 157(1) applies to this section (in so far as it relates to removal centres by virtue of subsection (5)(e)) as it applies to Part VIII.]

Note: Commenced 11 December 2000 (SI 2000/3099). Words in first and second square brackets substituted by Nationality, Immigration and Asylum Act 2002, s 66 from 10 February 2003 (SI 2003/1). Words in square brackets in sub-ss (7)(c), (8)(c) and (9)(c) substituted and sub-s (16) added by Asylum and Immigration Act 2004, s 15 from 1 October 2004 (SI 2004/2523). Words in square brackets in sub-ss (7)(d) and (8)(d) substituted and sub-s (17) added by Immigration, Asylum and Nationality Act 2006, s 28 from 31 August 2006 (SI 2006/2226).

142. Attendance for fingerprinting

(1) The Secretary of State may, by notice in writing, require a person to whom section 141 applies to attend at a specified place for fingerprinting.

[(2) In the case of a notice given to a person of a kind specified in section 141(7)(a) to (d) or (f) (in so far as it applies to a dependant of a person of a kind specified in section 141(7)(a) to (d)), the notice—

(a) must require him to attend during a specified period of at least seven days beginning with a day not less than seven days after the date given in the notice as its date of issue, and

(b) may require him to attend at a specified time of day or during specified hours.

(2A) In the case of a notice given to a person of a kind specified in section 141(7)(e) or (f) (in so far as it applies to a dependant of a person of a kind specified in section 141(7)(e)), the notice—

(a) may require him to attend during a specified period beginning with a day not less than three days after the date given in the notice as its date of issue,

(b) may require him to attend on a specified day not less than three days after the date given in the notice as its date of issue, and

(c) may require him to attend at a specified time of day or during specified hours.]

(3) A constable or immigration officer may arrest without warrant a person who has failed to comply with a requirement imposed on him under this section (unless the requirement has ceased to have effect).

(4) Before a person arrested under subsection (3) is released—

(a) he may be removed to a place where his fingerprints may conveniently be taken; and

(b) his fingerprints may be taken (whether or not he is so removed).

(5) A requirement imposed under subsection (1) ceases to have effect at the end of the relevant period (as defined by section 141).

Note: Commenced 11 December 2000 (SI 2000/3099). Subsection (2) substituted and sub-s 2A inserted by Immigration, Asylum and Nationality Act 2006, s 29 from 31 August 2006 (SI 2006/2226).

143. Destruction of fingerprints

(1) If they have not already been destroyed, fingerprints must be destroyed before the end of the specified period beginning with the day on which they were taken.

(2) If a person from whom fingerprints were taken proves that he is—

(a) a British citizen, or

(b) a Commonwealth citizen who has a right of abode in the United Kingdom as a result of section 2(1)(b) of the 1971 Act,

the fingerprints must be destroyed as soon as reasonably practicable.

(3) . . .

(4) . . .

(5) . . .

(6) . . .

(7) . . .

(8) . . .

(9) Fingerprints taken from F [within the meaning of section 141(7)] must be destroyed when fingerprints taken from the person whose dependant he is have to be destroyed.

(10) The obligation to destroy fingerprints under this section applies also to copies of fingerprints.

(11) The Secretary of State must take all reasonably practicable steps to secure—

(a) that data which are held in electronic form and which relate to fingerprints which have to be destroyed as a result of this section are destroyed or erased; or

(b) that access to such data is blocked.

(12) The person to whom the data relate is entitled, on request, to a certificate issued by the Secretary of State to the effect that he has taken the steps required by subsection (11).

(13) A certificate under subsection (12) must be issued within three months of the date of the request for it.

(14) . . .

(15) 'Specified period' means—

(a) such period as the Secretary of State may specify by order;

(b) if no period is so specified, ten years.

Note: Commenced 11 December 2000 (SI 2000/3099). Subsections (3)–(8) and (14) cease to have effect and words in square brackets in sub-s (9) inserted by Anti-terrorism, Crime and Security Act 2001, s 36 14 December 2001 with effect to fingerprints whether taken before or after 14 December 2001. Those fingerprints which were required by s 143 to be destroyed before 14 December 2001 shall be treated as though these amendments had effect before the requirement arose.

144. Other methods of collecting data about physical characteristics

[(1)] The Secretary of State may make regulations containing provisions equivalent to sections 141, 142 and 143 in relation to such other methods of collecting data about external physical characteristics as may be prescribed.

[(2) In subsection (1) 'external physical characteristics' includes, in particular, features of the iris or any other part of the eye.]

Note: Commenced 11 December 2000 (SI 2000/3099). Subsection (2) inserted by Nationality, Immigration and Asylum Act 2002, s 128 from 10 February 2003 (SI 2003/1).

Codes of practice

145. Codes of practice

(1) An immigration officer exercising any specified power to—
   (a) arrest, question, search or take fingerprints from a person,
   (b) enter and search premises, or
   (c) seize property found on persons or premises,
   must have regard to such provisions of a code as may be specified.

(2) Subsection (1) also applies to an authorised person exercising the power to take fingerprints conferred by section 141.

[(2A) A person exercising a power under regulations made by virtue of section 144 must have regard to such provisions of a code as may be specified.]

(3) Any specified provision of a code may have effect for the purposes of this section subject to such modifications as may be specified.

(4) 'Specified' means specified in a direction given by the Secretary of State.

(5) 'Authorised person' has the same meaning as in section 141.

(6) 'Code' means—
   (a) in relation to England and Wales, any code of practice for the time being in force under the Police and Criminal Evidence Act 1984;
   (b) in relation to Northern Ireland, any code of practice for the time being in force under the Police and Criminal Evidence (Northern Ireland) Order 1989.

(7) This section does not apply to any person exercising powers in Scotland.

Note: Commenced 11 November 1999, s 170. Subsection (2A) inserted by Nationality, Immigration and Asylum Act 2002, s 128 from 10 February 2003 (SI 2003/1).

Use of force

146. Use of force

(1) An immigration officer exercising any power conferred on him by the 1971 Act or this Act may, if necessary, use reasonable force.

[(2) A person exercising a power under any of the following may if necessary use reasonable force—

(a) section 28CA, 28FA or 28FB of the 1971 Act (business premises: entry to arrest or search),
(b) section 141 or 142 of this Act, and
(c) regulations under section 144 of this Act.]

Note: Subsection (2) substituted by Nationality, Immigration and Asylum Act 2002, s 153 from 8 January 2003 (SI 2003/1).

Part VIII

Detention Centres and Detained Persons

Interpretation

147. Interpretation of Part VIII

In this Part—

'certificate of authorisation' means a certificate issued by the Secretary of State under section 154;

'certified prisoner custody officer' means a prisoner custody officer certified under section 89 of the Criminal Justice Act 1991, or section 114 of the Criminal Justice and Public Order Act 1994, to perform custodial duties;

'contract monitor' means a person appointed by the Secretary of State under section 149(4);

'contracted out [removal centre]' means a [removal centre] in relation to which a [removal centre] contract is in force;

'contractor', in relation to a [removal centre] which is being run in accordance with a [removal centre] contract, means the person who has contracted to run it;

'custodial functions' means custodial functions at a [removal centre];

'detained persons' means persons detained or required to be detained under the 1971 Act [or under section 62 of the Nationality, Immigration and Asylum Act 2002 (detention by Secretary of State);]

'detainee custody officer' means a person in respect of whom a certificate of authorisation is in force;

. . .

'[removal centre] contract' means a contract entered into by the Secretary of State under section 149;

'[removal] centre rules' means rules made by the Secretary of State under section 153;

'directly managed [removal centre]' means a [removal centre] which is not a contracted out [removal centre];

'escort arrangements' means arrangements made by the Secretary of State under section 156;

'escort functions' means functions under escort arrangements;

'escort monitor' means a person appointed under paragraph 1 of Schedule 13;

'prisoner custody officer'—

(a) in relation to England and Wales, has the same meaning as in the Criminal Justice Act 1991;

(b) in relation to Scotland, has the meaning given in section 114(1) of the Criminal Justice and Public Order Act 1994;

(c) in relation to Northern Ireland, has the meaning given in section 122(1) of that Act of 1994;

['removal centre' means a place which is used solely for the detention of detained persons but which is not a short-term holding facility, a prison or part of a prison;]

'short-term holding facility' means a place used solely for the detention of detained persons for a period of not more than seven days or for such other period as may be prescribed.

Note: Commenced 1 August 2000 (SI 2000/1985). Definition of removal centre inserted by Nationality, Immigration and Asylum Act 2002, s 66 from 10 February 2003 (SI 2003/1). Definition of detained persons amended by Nationality, Immigration and Asylum Act 2002, s 62 from 10 February 2003 (SI 2003/1). Other words in square brackets inserted by Nationality, Immigration and Asylum Act 2002, s 66 from 10 February 2003 (SI 2003/1).

Removal centres

148. Management of [removal centres]

(1) A manager must be appointed for every [removal centre].

(2) In the case of a contracted out [removal centre], the person appointed as manager must be a detainee custody officer whose appointment is approved by the Secretary of State.

(3) The manager of a [removal centre] is to have such functions as are conferred on him by [removal centre] rules.

(4) The manager of a contracted out [removal centre] may not—

(a) enquire into a disciplinary charge laid against a detained person;

(b) conduct the hearing of such a charge; or

(c) make, remit or mitigate an award in respect of such a charge.

(5) The manager of a contracted out [removal centre] may not, except in cases of urgency, order—

(a) the removal of a detained person from association with other detained persons;

(b) the temporary confinement of a detained person in special accommodation; or

(c) the application to a detained person of any other special control or restraint (other than handcuffs).

Note: Subsection (3) commenced 1 August 2000 (SI 2000/1985). Remainder commenced 2 April 2001 (SI 2001/239). Words in square brackets substituted by Nationality, Immigration and Asylum Act 2002, s 66 from 10 February 2003 (SI 2003/1).

149. Contracting out of certain [removal centres]

(1) The Secretary of State may enter into a contract with another person for the provision or running (or the provision and running) by him, or (if the contract so provides) for the running by sub-contractors of his, of any [removal centre] or part of a [removal centre].

(2) While a [removal centre] contract for the running of a [removal centre] or part of a [removal centre] is in force—
- (a) the [removal centre] or part is to be run subject to and in accordance with the provisions of or made under this Part; and
- (b) in the case of a part, that part and the remaining part are to be treated for the purposes of those provisions as if they were separate [removal centres].

(3) If the Secretary of State grants a lease or tenancy of land for the purposes of a detention centre contract, none of the following enactments applies to the lease or tenancy—
- (a) Part II of the Landlord and Tenant Act 1954 (security of tenure);
- (b) section 146 of the Law of Property Act 1925 (restrictions on and relief against forfeiture);
- (c) section 19(1), (2) and (3) of the Landlord and Tenant Act 1927 and the Landlord and Tenant Act 1988 (covenants not to assign etc.);
- (d) the Agricultural Holdings Act 1986;
- (e) sections 4 to 7 of the Law Reform (Miscellaneous Provisions) (Scotland) Act 1985 (irritancy clauses);
- (f) the Agricultural Holdings (Scotland) Act 1991;
- (g) section 14 of the Conveyancing Act 1881;
- (h) the Conveyancing and Law of Property Act 1892;
- (i) the Business Tenancies (Northern Ireland) Order 1996.

(4) The Secretary of State must appoint a contract monitor for every contracted out [removal centre].

(5) A person may be appointed as the contract monitor for more than one [removal centre].

(6) The contract monitor is to have—
- (a) such functions as may be conferred on him by [removal centre] rules;
- (b) the status of a Crown servant.

(7) The contract monitor must—
- (a) keep under review, and report to the Secretary of State on, the running of a [removal centre] for which he is appointed; and
- (b) investigate, and report to the Secretary of State on, any allegations made against any person performing custodial functions at that centre.

(8) The contractor, and any sub-contractor of his, must do all that he reasonably can (whether by giving directions to the officers of the [removal centre] or otherwise) to facilitate the exercise by the contract monitor of his functions.

(9) 'Lease or tenancy' includes an underlease, sublease or sub-tenancy.

(10) In relation to a [removal centre] contract entered into by the Secretary of State before the commencement of this section, this section is to be treated as having been in force at that time.

Note: Subsections (1), (3), (6)(a) and (9) commenced 1 August 2000 (SI 2000/1985). Remainder commenced 2 April 2001, s 66 (SI 2001/239). Words in square brackets substituted by Nationality, Immigration and Asylum Act 2002, s 66 from 10 February 2003 (SI 2003/1).

150. Contracted out functions at directly managed [removal centres]

(1) The Secretary of State may enter into a contract with another person—
   (a) for functions at, or connected with, a directly managed [removal centre] to be performed by detainee custody officers provided by that person; or
   (b) for such functions to be performed by certified prisoner custody officers who are provided by that person.

(2) For the purposes of this section '[removal centre]' includes a short-term holding facility.

Note: Commenced 2 April 2001 (SI 2001/239). Words in square brackets substituted by Nationality, Immigration and Asylum Act 2002, s 66 from 10 February 2003 (SI 2003/1).

151. Intervention by Secretary of State

(1) The Secretary of State may exercise the powers conferred by this section if it appears to him that—
   (a) the manager of a contracted out [removal centre] has lost, or is likely to lose, effective control of the centre or of any part of it; or
   (b) it is necessary to do so in the interests of preserving the safety of any person, or of preventing serious damage to any property.

(2) The Secretary of State may appoint a person (to be known as the Controller) to act as manager of the [removal centre] for the period—
   (a) beginning with the time specified in the appointment; and
   (b) ending with the time specified in the notice of termination under subsection (5).

(3) During that period—
   (a) all the functions which would otherwise be exercisable by the manager or the contract monitor are to be exercisable by the Controller;
   (b) the contractor and any sub-contractor of his must do all that he reasonably can to facilitate the exercise by the Controller of his functions; and
   (c) the staff of the detention centre must comply with any directions given by the Controller in the exercise of his functions.

(4) The Controller is to have the status of a Crown servant.

(5) If the Secretary of State is satisfied that a Controller is no longer needed for a particular detention centre, he must (by giving notice to the Controller) terminate his appointment at a time specified in the notice.

(6) As soon as practicable after making an appointment under this section, the Secretary of State must give notice of the appointment to those entitled to notice.

(7) As soon as practicable after terminating an appointment under this section, the Secretary of State must give a copy of the notice of termination to those entitled to notice.

(8) Those entitled to notice are the contractor, the manager, the contract monitor and the Controller.

Note: Commenced 2 April 2001 (SI 2001/239). Words in square brackets substituted by Nationality, Immigration and Asylum Act 2002, s 66 from 10 February 2003 (SI 2003/1).

152. Visiting Committees and inspections

(1) The Secretary of State must appoint a committee (to be known as the Visiting Committee) for each detention centre.

(2) The functions of the Visiting Committee for a [removal centre] are to be such as may be prescribed by the [removal centre] rules.

(3) Those rules must include provision—

(a) as to the making of visits to the centre by members of the Visiting Committee;

(b) for the hearing of complaints made by persons detained in the centre;

(c) requiring the making of reports by the Visiting Committee to the Secretary of State.

(4) Every member of the Visiting Committee for a [removal centre] may at any time enter the centre and have free access to every part of it and to every person detained there.

(5) . . .

Note: Subsections (2) and (3) commenced for the purposes of enabling subordinate legislation 1 August 2000 (SI 2000/1985). Otherwise commenced 2 April 2001 (SI 2001/239). Subsection (5) amends the Prison Act, 1952, s 5A. Words in square brackets substituted by Nationality, Immigration and Asylum Act 2002, s 66 from 10 February 2003 (SI 2003/1).

153. [Removal centre] rules

(1) The Secretary of State must make rules for the regulation and management of [removal centres].

(2) [Removal centre] rules may, among other things, make provision with respect to the safety, care, activities, discipline and control of detained persons.

Note: Commenced for the purposes of enabling subordinate legislation 1 August 2000 (SI 2000/1985). Otherwise commenced 2 April 2001 (SI 2001/239). Words in square brackets substituted by Nationality, Immigration and Asylum Act 2002, s 66 from 10 February 2003 (SI 2003/1).

[153A. Detained persons: national minimum wage

A detained person does not qualify for the national minimum wage in respect of work which he does in pursuance of removal centre rules.]

Note: Inserted by Immigration, Asylum and Nationality Act 2006, s 59 from a date to be appointed.

Custody and movement of detained persons

154. Detainee custody officers

(1) On an application made to him under this section, the Secretary of State may certify that the applicant—
   (a) is authorised to perform escort functions; or
   (b) is authorised to perform both escort functions and custodial functions.

(2) The Secretary of State may not issue a certificate of authorisation unless he is satisfied that the applicant—
   (a) is a fit and proper person to perform the functions to be authorised; and
   (b) has received training to such standard as the Secretary of State considers appropriate for the performance of those functions.

(3) A certificate of authorisation continues in force until such date, or the occurrence of such event, as may be specified in the certificate but may be suspended or revoked under paragraph 7 of Schedule 11.

(4) A certificate which authorises the performance of both escort functions and custodial functions may specify one date or event for one of those functions and a different date or event for the other.

[(5) The Secretary of State may confer functions of detainee custody officers on prison officers or prisoner custody officers.]

(6) A prison officer acting under arrangements made under subsection (5) has all the powers, authority, protection and privileges of a constable.

(7) Schedule 11 makes further provision about detainee custody officers.

Note: Commenced 2 April 2001 (SI 2001/239). Subsection (5) substituted by Nationality, Immigration and Asylum Act 2002, s 65 from 10 February 2003 (SI 2003/1).

155. Custodial functions and discipline etc. at [removal centres]

(1) Custodial functions may be discharged at a [removal centre] only by—
   (a) a detainee custody officer authorised, in accordance with section 154(1), to perform such functions; or

(b) a prison officer, or a certified prisoner custody officer, exercising functions in relation to the [removal centre]—
   (i) in accordance with arrangements made under section 154(5); or
   (ii) as a result of a contract entered into under section 150(1)(b).

(2) Schedule 12 makes provision with respect to discipline and other matters at [removal centres] and short-term holding facilities.

Note: Subsection (2) commenced 1 August 2000 (SI 2000/1985). Remainder commenced 2 April 2001 (SI 2001/239). Words in square brackets substituted by Nationality, Immigration and Asylum Act 2002, s 66 from 10 February 2003 (SI 2003/1).

156. Arrangements for the provision of escorts and custody

(1) The Secretary of State may make arrangements for—
   (a) the delivery of detained persons to premises in which they may lawfully be detained;
   (b) the delivery of persons from any such premises for the purposes of their removal from the United Kingdom in accordance with directions given under the 1971 Act or this Act;
   (c) the custody of detained persons who are temporarily outside such premises;
   (d) the custody of detained persons held on the premises of any court.

(2) Escort arrangements may provide for functions under the arrangements to be performed, in such cases as may be determined by or under the arrangements, by detainee custody officers.

(3) 'Court' includes—
   [(a) the Asylum and Immigration Tribunal;]
   (c) the Commission.

(4) Escort arrangements may include entering into contracts with other persons for the provision by them of—
   (a) detainee custody officers; or
   (b) prisoner custody officers who are certified under section 89 of the Criminal Justice Act 1991, or section 114 or 122 of the Criminal Justice and Public Order Act 1994, to perform escort functions.

(5) Schedule 13 makes further provision about escort arrangements.

(6) A person responsible for performing a function of a kind mentioned in subsection (1), in accordance with a transfer direction, complies with the direction if he does all that he reasonably can to secure that the function is performed by a person acting in accordance with escort arrangements.

(7) 'Transfer direction' means a transfer direction given under—
   (a) section 48 of the Mental Health Act 1983 or section 71 of the Mental Health (Scotland) Act 1984 (removal to hospital of, among others, persons detained under the 1971 Act); or

(b) in Northern Ireland, article 54 of the Mental Health (Northern Ireland) Order 1986 (provision corresponding to section 48 of the 1983 Act).

Note: Subsection (5) commenced 1 August 2000 (SI 2000/1985). Remainder commenced 2 April 2001 (SI 2001/239). Words in square brackets substituted by Sch 2 Asylum and Immigration Act 2004 from 4 April 2005 (SI 2005/565).

157. Short-term holding facilities

(1) The Secretary of State may be regulations extend any provision made by or under this Part in relation to [removal centres] (other than one mentioned in subsection (2)) to short-term holding facilities.

(2) Subsection (1) does not apply to section 150.

(3) The Secretary of State may make rules for the regulation and management of short-term holding facilities.

Note: Commenced for the purposes of enabling subordinate legislation 1 August 2000 (SI 2000/1985). Otherwise commenced 2 April 2001 (SI 2001/239). Words in square brackets substituted by Nationality, Immigration and Asylum Act 2002, s 66 from 10 February 2003 (SI 2003/1).

Miscellaneous

158. Wrongful disclosure of information

(1) A person who is or has been employed (whether as a detainee custody officer, prisoner custody officer or otherwise)—
   (a) in accordance with escort arrangements,
   (b) at a contracted out [removal centre], or
   (c) to perform contracted out functions at a directly managed detention centre,
is guilty of an offence if he discloses, otherwise than in the course of his duty or as authorised by the Secretary of State, any information which he acquired in the course of his employment and which relates to a particular detained person.

(2) A person guilty of such an offence is liable—
   (a) on conviction on indictment, to imprisonment for a term not exceeding two years or to a fine or to both;
   (b) on summary conviction, to imprisonment for a term not exceeding six months or to a fine not exceeding the statutory maximum or to both.

(3) 'Contracted out functions' means functions which, as the result of a contract entered into under section 150, fall to be performed by detainee custody officers or certified prisoner custody officers.

Note: Commenced 2 April 2001 (SI 2001/239). Words in square brackets substituted by Nationality, Immigration and Asylum Act 2002, s 66 from 10 February 2003 (SI 2003/1).

159. Power of constable to act outside his jurisdiction

(1) For the purpose of taking a person to or from a [removal centre] under the order of any authority competent to give the order, a constable may act outside the area of his jurisdiction.

(2) When acting under this section, the constable concerned retains all the powers, authority, protection and privileges of his office.

Note: Commenced 2 April 2001 (SI 2001/239). Words in square brackets substituted by Nationality, Immigration and Asylum Act 2002, s 66 from 10 February 2003 (SI 2003/1).

Part IX

Registrar's Certificates: Procedure

160. . . .

Note: Amends Marriage Act 1949, ss 26–7, 31.

161. . . .

Note: Amends the Marriage Act 1949, ss 26–7 and the Marriage Law (Ireland) Amendment Act 1863, s 2.

162. . . .

Note: Amends the Marriage Act 1949, s 28 and the Marriage Law (Ireland) Amendment Act 1863 s 3.

163. . . .

Note: Amends the Marriage Act 1949, s 31 and the Marriages (Ireland) Act 1844, s 16.

Part X

Miscellaneous and Supplemental

164. . . .

Note: Amends the Prosecution of Offences Act 1985, s 3.

165. . . .

Note: Amends Immigration Act 1971, s 31.

166. Regulations and orders

(1) Any power to make rules, regulations or orders conferred by this Act is exercisable by statutory instrument.

(2) But subsection (1) does not apply in relation to [orders made under section 90(1),] rules made under paragraph 1 of Schedule 5 or immigration rules.

(3) Any statutory instrument made as a result of subsection (1) may—
   (a) contain such incidental, supplemental, consequential and transitional provision as the person making it considers appropriate;
   (b) make different provision for different cases or descriptions of case; and
   (c) make different provision for different areas.

(4) No order is to be made under—
   (a) section 20,
   (b) section 21,
   (c) section 31(10),
   (d) section 86(2),
   (e) . . .
   (f) section 97(3),
   (g) section 143(15), or
   (h) paragraph 4 of Schedule 5,
   unless a draft of the order has been laid before Parliament and approved by a resolution of each House.

(5) No regulations are to be made under—
   [(za) section 4(5),]
   (a) section 9,
   (b) section 46(8);
   (c) section 53, or
   (d) section 144,
   unless a draft of the regulations has been laid before Parliament and approved by a resolution of each House.

(6) Any statutory instrument made under this Act, apart from one made—
   (a) under any of the provisions mentioned in subsection (4) or (5), or
   (b) under section 24(3) [,24A(3)] or 170(4) or (7),
   shall be subject to annulment by a resolution of either House of Parliament.

Note: Commencement 11 November 1999, s 170. Subsection (4)(e) omitted by Nationality, Immigration and Asylum Act 2002, s 61 from 7 November 2002. Words in square brackets in sub-s (2) inserted by Asylum and Immigration Act 2004, s 41 from 1 October 2004 (SI 2004/2523), sub-s 5(za) inserted by Asylum and Immigration Act 2004, s 10 from 1 December 2004 (SI 2004/2999). Words in Square brackets in sub-s 6(b) inserted by Civil Partnership Act 2004 from a date to be appointed.

167. Interpretation

(1) In this Act—

'the 1971 Act' means the Immigration Act 1971;

'adjudicator' (except in Part VI) means an adjudicators appointed under section 57;

'Chief Adjudicator' means the person appointed as Chief Adjudicator under section 57(2);

'claim for asylum' (except in Parts V and VI and section 141) means a claim that it would be contrary to the United Kingdom's obligations under the Refugee Convention for the claimant to be removed from, or required to leave, the United Kingdom;

'the Commission' means the Special Immigration Appeals Commission;

'country' includes any territory;

'EEA State' means a State which is a Contracting Party to the Agreement on the European Economic Area signed at Oporto on 2nd May 1992 as it has effect for the time being;

'the Human Rights Convention' means the Convention for the Protection of Human Rights and Fundamental Freedoms, agreed by the Council of Europe at Rome on 4th November 1950 as it has effect for the time being in relation to the United Kingdom;

'prescribed' means prescribed by regulations made by the Secretary of State;

'the Refugee Convention' means the Convention relating to the Status of Refugees done at Geneva on 28 July 1951 and the Protocol to the Convention;

'voluntary organisations' means bodies (other than public or local authorities) whose activities are not carried on for profit.

(2) The following expressions have the same meaning as in the 1971 Act—

'certificate of entitlement';

'entry clearance';

'illegal entrant';

'immigration officer';

'immigration rules';

'port';

'United Kingdom passport';

'work permit'.

Note: Commencement 11 November 1999, s 170. Words in square brackets substituted by Nationality, Immigration and Asylum Act 2002, s 158 from 10 February 2003 (SI 2003/1) , and cease to have effect from a date to be appointed, Immigration, Asylum and Nationality Act 2006, s. 64.

168. Expenditure and receipts

(1) There is to be paid out of money provided by Parliament—

(a) any expenditure incurred by the Secretary of State or the Lord Chancellor in consequence of this Act; and
(b) any increase attributable to this Act in the sums so payable by virtue of any other Act.

(2) Sums received by the Secretary of State under section 5, 32, 40, 112 or 113 or by the Lord Chancellor under section 48(4) or 49(4) must be paid into the Consolidated Fund.

Note: Commencement 11 November 1999, s 170.

169. Minor and consequential amendments, transitional provisions and repeals

(1) Schedule 14 makes minor and consequential amendments.

(2) Schedule 15 contains transitional provisions and savings.

(3) The enactments set out in Schedule 16 are repealed.

170. Short title, commencement and extent

(1) This Act may be cited as the Immigration and Asylum Act 1999.

(2) Subsections (1) and (2) of section 115 come into force on the day on which the first regulations made under Schedule 8 come into force.

(3) The following provisions come into force on the passing of this Act—
(a) section 4;
(b) section 9;
(c) section 15;
(d) section 27;
(e) section 31;
(f) section 94;
(g) section 95(13);
(h) section 99(4) and (5);
(i) sections 105 to 109;
(j) section 110(1), (2) and (8) (so far as relating to subsections (1) and (2));
(k) section 111;
(l) section 124;
(m) section 140;
(n) section 145;
(o) section 146(1);
(p) sections 166 to 168;
(q) this section;
(r) Schedule 9;
(s) paragraphs 62(2), 73, 78, 79, 81, 82, 87, 88 and 102 of Schedule 14;
(t) paragraph 2 and 13 of Schedule 15.

(4) The other provisions of this Act, except section 10 and paragraph 12 of Schedule

15 (which come into force in accordance with section 9), come into force on such day as the Secretary of State may by order appoint.

(5) Different days may be appointed for different purposes.

(6) This Act extends to Northern Ireland.

(7) Her Majesty may by Order in Council direct that any of the provisions of this Act are to extend, with such modifications (if any) as appear to Her Majesty to be appropriate, to any of the Channel Islands or the Isle of Man.

Note: Commenced 11 November 1999.

Schedules

Sections 37(6) and 42(8)

Schedule 1

Sale of Transporters

. . .

Section 56(2)

Schedule 2

The Immigration Appeal Tribunal

. . .

Note: Schedule 2 repealed by Sch 9 Nationality, Immigration and Asylum Act 2002 from 1 April 2003 (SI 2003/754, which sets out transitional provisions).

Schedule 3

Adjudicators

. . .

Note: Schedule 3 repealed by Sch 9 Nationality, Immigration and Asylum Act 2002 from 1 April 2003 (SI 2003/754, which sets out transitional provisions).

Schedule 4

Appeals

. . .

Note: Schedule 4 repealed by Sch 9 Nationality, Immigration and Asylum Act 2002 from 1 April 2003 (SI 2003/754, which sets out transitional provisions).

Section 83

SCHEDULE 5

THE IMMIGRATION SERVICES COMMISSIONER

PART I

REGULATORY FUNCTIONS

The Commissioner's rules

1.—(1) The Commissioner may make rules regulating any aspect of the professional practice, conduct or discipline of—
(a) registered persons, and
[(b) those acting on behalf of registered persons.]

(2) Before making or altering any rules, the Commissioner must consult such persons appearing to him to represent the views of persons engaged in the provision of immigration advice or immigration services as he considers appropriate.

(3) In determining whether a registered person is competent or otherwise fit to provide immigration advice or immigration services, the Commissioner may take into account any breach of the rules by—
(a) that person; and
[(b) any person acting on behalf of that person.]

(4) The rules may, among other things, make provision requiring the keeping of accounts or the obtaining of indemnity insurance.

2.—(1) The Commissioner's rules must be made or altered by an instrument in writing.

(2) Such an instrument must specify that it is made under this Schedule.

(3) Immediately after such an instrument is made, it must be printed and made available to the public.

(4) The Commissioner may charge a reasonable fee for providing a person with a copy of the instrument.

(5) A person is not to be taken to have contravened a rule made by the Commissioner if he shows that at the time of the alleged contravention the instrument containing the rule had not been made available in accordance with this paragraph.

(6) The production of a printed copy of an instrument purporting to be made by the Commissioner on which is endorsed a certificate signed by an officer of the Commissioner authorised by him for that purpose and stating—
(a) that the instrument was made by the Commissioner,
(b) that the copy is a true copy of the instrument, and
(c) that on a specified date the instrument was made available to the public in accordance with this paragraph, is evidence (or in Scotland sufficient evidence) of the facts stated in the certificate.

(7) A certificate purporting to be signed as mentioned in sub-paragraph (6) is to be treated as having been properly signed unless the contrary is shown.

(8) A person who wishes in any legal proceedings to rely on an instrument containing the

Commissioner's rules may require him to endorse a copy of the instrument with a certificate of the kind mentioned in sub-paragraph (6).

Code of Standards

3.—(1) The Commissioner must prepare and issue a code setting standards of conduct which those to whom the code applies are expected to meet.

(2) The code is to be known as the Code of Standards but is referred to in this Schedule as 'the Code'.

(3) The Code is to apply to any person providing immigration advice or immigration services other than—

(a) a person who is authorised by a designated professional body to practise as a member of the profession whose members are regulated by that body;

[(b) a person who is acting on behalf of a person who is within paragraph (a);]

(4) It is the duty of any person to whom the Code applies to comply with its provisions in providing immigration advice or immigration services.

(5) If the Commissioner alters the Code, he must re-issue it.

(6) Before issuing the Code or altering it, the Commissioner must consult—

(a) each of the designated professional bodies;
(b) the designated judges;
(c) the Lord President of the Court of Session;
(d) the Lord Chief Justice of Northern Ireland; and
(e) such other persons appearing to him to represent the views of persons engaged in the provision of immigration advice or immigration services as he considers appropriate.

(7) The Commissioner must publish the Code in such form and manner as the Secretary of State may direct.

Extension of scope of the Code

4.—(1) The Secretary of State may by order provide for the provisions of the Code, or such provisions of the Code as may be specified by the order, to apply to—

(a) persons authorised by any designated professional body to practise as a member of the profession whose members are regulated by that body; and

[(b) persons acting on behalf of persons who are within paragraph (a).]

(2) If the Secretary of State is proposing to act under sub-paragraph (1) he must, before doing so, consult—

(a) the Commissioner;
(b) the Legal Services Ombudsman, if the proposed order would affect a designated professional body in England and Wales;
(c) the Scottish Legal Services Ombudsman, if the proposed order would affect a designated professional body in Scotland;
(d) the lay observers appointed under Article 42 of the Solicitors (Northern Ireland)

Order 1976, if the proposed order would affect a designated professional body in Northern Ireland.

(3) An order under sub-paragraph (1) requires the approval of—

(a) the Lord Chancellor, if it affects a designated professional body in England and Wales or Northern Ireland;

(b) the Scottish Ministers, if it affects a designated professional body in Scotland.

(4) Before deciding whether or not to give his approval under sub-paragraph (3)(a), the Lord Chancellor must consult—

(a) the designated judges, if the order affects a designated professional body in England and Wales;

(b) the Lord Chief Justice of Northern Ireland, if it affects a designated professional body in Northern Ireland.

(5) Before deciding whether or not to give their approval under subparagraph (3)(b), the Scottish Ministers must consult the Lord President of the Court of Session.

Investigation of complaints

5.—(1) The Commissioner must establish a scheme ('the complaints scheme') for the investigation by him of relevant complaints made to him in accordance with the provisions of the scheme.

(2) Before establishing the scheme or altering it, the Commissioner must consult—

(a) each of the designated professional bodies; and

(b) such other persons appearing to him to represent the views of persons engaged in the provision of immigration advice or immigration services as he considers appropriate.

(3) A complaint is a relevant complaint if it relates to—

(a) the competence or fitness of a person to provide immigration advice or immigration services,

(b) the competence or fitness of a person [acting on behalf of] a person providing immigration advice or immigration services,

(c) an alleged breach of the Code,

(d) an alleged breach of one or more of the Commissioner's rules by a person to whom they apply, or

[(e) an alleged breach of a rule of a relevant regulatory body.]

(4) The Commissioner may, on his own initiative, investigate any matter which he would have power to investigate on a complaint made under the complaints scheme.

(5) In investigating any such matter on his own initiative, the Commissioner must proceed as if his investigation were being conducted in response to a complaint made under the scheme.

6.—(1) The complaints scheme must provide for a person who is the subject of an investigation under the scheme to be given a reasonable opportunity to make representations to the Commissioner.

(2) Any person who is the subject of an investigation under the scheme must—
  (a) take such steps as are reasonably required to assist the Commissioner in his investigation; and
  (b) comply with any reasonable requirement imposed on him by the Commissioner.

(3) If a person fails to comply with sub-paragraph (2)(a) or with a requirement imposed under sub-paragraph (2)(b) the Commissioner may—
  (a) in the ease of a registered person, cancel his registration;
  (b) in the case of a person certified by the Commissioner as exempt under section 84(4)(a), withdraw his exemption; or
  [(c) in any other case, refer the matter to any relevant regulatory body.]

Power to enter premises

7.—(1) This paragraph applies if—
  (a) the Commissioner is investigating a complaint under the complaints scheme;
  (b) the complaint falls within paragraph 5(3)(a), (b) [(c)] or (d); and
  (c) there are reasonable grounds for believing that particular premises are being used in connection with the provision of immigration advice or immigration services by a [registered or exempt person.]

[(1A) This paragraph also applies if the Commissioner is investigating a matter under paragraph 5(5) and—
  (a) the matter is of a kind described in paragraph 5(3)(a), (b) [(c)] or (d) (for which purpose a reference to an allegation shall be treated as a reference to a suspicion of the Commissioner), and
  (b) there are reasonable grounds for believing that particular premises are being used in connection with the provision of immigration advice or immigration services by a [registered or exempt person.]

(2) The Commissioner, or a member of his staff authorised in writing by him, may enter the premises at reasonable hours.

(3) Sub-paragraph (2) does not apply to premises to the extent to which they constitute a private residence.

(4) A person exercising the power given by sub-paragraph (2) ('the investigating officer') may—
  (a) take with him such equipment as appears to him to be necessary;
  (b) require any person on the premises—
    (i) to produce any document which he considers relates to any matter relevant to the investigation; and
    (ii) if the document is produced, to provide an explanation of it;
  (c) require any person to state, to the best of his knowledge and belief, where any such document is to be found;
  (d) take copies of, or extracts from, any document which is produced;
  (e) require any information which is held in a computer and is accessible from the premises and which the investigating officer considers relates to any matter relevant to the investigation, to be produced in a form—

(i) in which it can be taken away; and
(ii) in which it is visible and legible.

(5) Instead of exercising the power under sub-paragraph (2), the Commissioner may require such person as he may determine ('his agent') to make a report on the provision of immigration advice or immigration services from the premises.

(6) If the Commissioner so determines, his agent may exercise the power conferred by sub-paragraph (2) as if he were a member of the Commissioner's staff appropriately authorised.

(7) If a registered person fails without reasonable excuse to allow access under sub-paragraph (2) or (6) to any premises under his occupation or control, the Commissioner may cancel his registration.

(8) The Commissioner may also cancel the registration of a registered person who—
(a) without reasonable excuse fails to comply with a requirement imposed on him under sub-paragraph (4);
(b) intentionally delays or obstructs any person exercising functions under this paragraph; or
(c) fails to take reasonable steps to prevent an employee of his from obstructing any person exercising such functions.

[(9) Sub-paragraphs (7) and (8) shall apply to an exempt person as they apply to a registered person, but with a reference to cancellation of registration being treated as a reference to withdrawal of exemption.

(10) In this paragraph 'exempt person' means a person certified by the Commissioner as exempt under section 84(4)(a).]

Determination of complaints

8.—(1) On determining a complaint under the complaints scheme, the Commissioner must give his decision in a written statement.

(2) The statement must include the Commissioner's reasons for his decision.

(3) A copy of the statement must be given by the Commissioner to—
(a) the person who made the complaint; and
(b) the person who is the subject of the complaint.

9.—(1) On determining a complaint under the complaints scheme, the Commissioner may—
(a) if the person to whom the complaint relates is a registered person [or is acting on behalf of] a registered person, record the complaint and the decision on it for consideration when that registered person next applies for his registration to be continued;
(b) if the person to whom the complaint relates is a registered person [or is acting on behalf of] a registered person and the Commissioner considers the matter sufficiently serious to require immediate action, require that registered person to apply for continued registration without delay;
[(c) refer the complaint and his decision on it to a relevant regulatory body;]

(d) if the person to whom the complaint relates is certified by the Commissioner as exempt under section 84(4)(a) or is employed by, or working under the supervision of, such a person, consider whether to withdraw that person's exemption;

(e) lay before the Tribunal a disciplinary charge against a relevant person.

(2) Sub-paragraph (3) applies if—

(a) the Tribunal is considering a disciplinary charge against a relevant person; and

(b) the Commissioner asks it to exercise its powers under that subparagraph.

(3) The Tribunal may give directions (which are to have effect while it is dealing with the charge)—

[(a) imposing restrictions on the provision of immigration advice or immigration services by the relevant person or by a person acting on his behalf or under his supervision;

(b) prohibiting the provision of immigration advice or immigration services by the relevant person or a person acting on his behalf or under his supervision.]

(4) 'Relevant person' means a person providing immigration advice or immigration services who is—

(a) a registered person;

[(b) a person acting on behalf of a registered person;]

(e) a person certified by the Commissioner as exempt under section 84(4)(a);

(f) a person to whom section 84(4)(d) applies; or

(g) a person employed by, or working under the supervision of, a person to whom paragraph (e) or (f) applies.

Complaints referred to designated professional bodies

10.—(1) This paragraph applies if the Commissioner refers a complaint to a designated professional body under paragraph 9(1)(c).

(2) The Commissioner may give directions setting a timetable to be followed by the designated professional body—

(a) in considering the complaint; and

(b) if appropriate, in taking disciplinary proceedings in connection with the complaint.

(3) In making his annual report to the Secretary of State under paragraph 21, the Commissioner must take into account any failure of a designated professional body to comply (whether wholly or in part) with directions given to it under this paragraph.

(4) Sub-paragraph (5) applies if the Commissioner or the Secretary of State considers that a designated professional body has persistently failed to comply with directions given to it under this paragraph.

(5) The Commissioner must take the failure into account in determining whether to make a report under section 86(9)(b) and the Secretary of State must take it into account in determining whether to make an order under section 86(2).

Note: Paragraph 7(1A) inserted by Nationality, Immigration and Asylum Act 2002, s 140 from 8 January 2003 (SI 2003/1). Other words in square brackets substituted or inserted by Asylum and Immigration Act 2004, ss 37 and 38 from 1 October 2004 (SI 2004/2523).

Part II

Commissioner's Status, Remuneration and Staff etc

. . .

Section 85(3)

Schedule 6

Registration

Applications for registration

1.—(1) An application for registration under section 84(2)(a) . . . must—

(a) be made to the Commissioner in such form and manner, and

(b) be accompanied by such information and supporting evidence,

as the Commissioner may from time to time determine.

(2) When considering an application for registration, the Commissioner may require the applicant to provide him with such further information or supporting evidence as the Commissioner may reasonably require.

Registration

2.—(1) If the Commissioner considers that an applicant for registration is competent and otherwise fit to provide immigration advice and immigration services, he must register the applicant.

(2) Registration may be made so as to have effect—

(a) only in relation to a specified field of advice or services;

(b) only in relation to the provision of advice or services to a specified category of person;

(c) only in relation to the provision of advice or services to a member of a specified category of person; or

(d) only in specified circumstances.

Review of qualifications

3.—(1) At such intervals as the Commissioner may determine, each registered person must submit an application for his registration to be continued.

(2) Different intervals may be fixed by the Commissioner in relation to different registered persons or descriptions of registered person.

(3) An application for continued registration must—

(a) be made to the Commissioner in such form and manner, and

(b) be accompanied by such information and supporting evidence, as the Commissioner may from time to time determine.

(4) When considering an application for continued registration, the Commissioner may require the applicant to provide him with such further information or supporting evidence as the Commissioner may reasonably require.

(5) If the Commissioner considers that an applicant for continued registration is no longer competent or is otherwise unfit to provide immigration advice or immigration services, he must cancel the applicant's registration.

(6) Otherwise, the Commissioner must continue the applicant's registration but may, in doing so, vary the registration—
   (a) so as to make it have limited effect in any of the ways mentioned in paragraph 2(2); or
   (b) so as to make it have full effect.

(7) If a registered person fails, without reasonable excuse—
   (a) to make an application for continued registration as required by subparagraph (1) or by a direction given by the Tribunal under [section 89(2)(b)], or
   (b) to provide further information or evidence under sub-paragraph (4),

the Commissioner may cancel the person's registration as from such date as he may determine.

[*Variation of registration*

3A. The Commissioner may vary a person's registration—
   (a) so as to make it have limited effect in any of the ways mentioned in paragraph 2(2); or
   (b) so as to make it have full effect.]

Disqualification of certain persons

4. A person convicted of an offence under section 25 or 26(1)(d) or (g) of the 1971 Act is disqualified for registration under paragraph 2 or for continued registration under paragraph 3.

Fees

5.—(1) The Secretary of State may by order specify fees for the registration or continued registration of persons on the register.

(2) No application under paragraph 1 or 3 is to be entertained by the Commissioner unless it is accompanied by the specified fee.

Open registers

6.—(1) The register must be made available for inspection by members of the public in a legible form at reasonable hours.

(2) A copy of the register or of any entry in the register must be provided—
   (a) on payment of a reasonable fee;
   (b) in written or electronic form; and
   (c) in a legible form.

(3) Sub-paragraphs (1) and (2) also apply to—
   (a) the record kept by the Commissioner of the persons to whom he has issued a certificate of exemption under section 84(4)(a); and

(b) the record kept by the Commissioner of the persons against whom there is in force a direction given by the Tribunal under section 89(8).

Note: Paragraph 3A inserted by Nationality, Immigration and Asylum Act 2002, s 140 from 8 January 2003 (SI 2003/1).

Section 87(5)

SCHEDULE 7

THE IMMIGRATION SERVICES TRIBUNAL

Members

1.—(1) The Tribunal is to consist of such number of members as the Lord Chancellor may determine.

(2) The members are to be appointed by the Lord Chancellor.

(3) A person may be appointed as a member only if—

(a) he is legally qualified; or

(b) he appears to the Lord Chancellor to have had substantial experience in immigration services or in the law and procedure relating to immigration.

The President

2. The Tribunal is to have a President appointed by the Lord Chancellor from among those of its members who are legally qualified.

Terms and conditions of appointment

3.—(1) Each member is to hold and vacate office in accordance with the terms of his appointment.

(2) A member is eligible for re-appointment when his term of office ends.

(3) A member may resign at any time by notice in writing given to the Lord Chancellor.

(4) The Lord Chancellor may dismiss a member on the ground of incapacity or misconduct.

[(5) The Lord Chancellor may dismiss a person under sub-paragraph (4) only with the concurrence of the appropriate senior judge.

(6) The appropriate senior judge is the Lord Chief Justice of England and Wales, unless—

(a) the person to be dismissed exercises functions wholly or mainly in Scotland, in which case it is the Lord President of the Court of Session, or

(b) that person exercises functions wholly or mainly in Northern Ireland, in which case it is the Lord Chief Justice of Northern Ireland.]

Note: Subsections (5) and (6) inserted by Sch 4 Constitutional Reform Act 2005 from 3 April 2006 (SI 2006/1014).

Remuneration and expenses

4. The Lord Chancellor may pay to any member such remuneration and expenses as he may determine.

Proceedings

5. The Tribunal is to sit at such times and in such places as the Lord Chancellor may direct.

6.—(1) The Commissioner is entitled to be represented before the Tribunal, in relation to the hearing of appeals or disciplinary charges, by such persons as he may authorise.

(2) The Commissioner may authorise a person to represent him before the Tribunal in relation to—
   (a) specified proceedings; or
   (b) all or specified categories of proceedings.

(3) 'Specified' means specified by the Commissioner.

Rules of procedure

7.—(1) The Lord Chancellor may make rules as to the procedure and practice to be followed in relation to the exercise of the Tribunal's functions.

(2) Before making or altering any such rules, the Lord Chancellor must consult the Scottish Ministers.

(3) Subject to the provisions of this Schedule and the rules, the Tribunal may determine its own procedure.

(4) The rules must make provision for any person appealing to the Tribunal or otherwise subject to its jurisdiction to be entitled to be legally represented.

(5) The rules may, in particular, make provision—
   (a) as to the mode and burden of proof and the giving and admissibility of evidence;
   (b) for proceedings before the Tribunal to be capable of being determined in the absence of any party to the proceedings if that party has failed, without reasonable excuse, to appear before the Tribunal or has failed to comply with any reasonable directions given by the Tribunal as to the conduct of the proceedings;
   (c) with respect to other matters preliminary or incidental to, or arising out of, any matter with respect to which the Tribunal is or may be exercising functions;
   (d) as to the period within which an appeal against a decision of the Commissioner can be brought;
   (e) authorising such functions of the Tribunal as may be specified in the rules to be exercised by a single member.

Suspending the effect of a relevant decision

8.—(1) A relevant decision of the Commissioner is not to have effect while the period within which an appeal may be brought against the decision is running.

(2) If the appellant applies to the Tribunal under this paragraph, the Tribunal may direct that while the appeal is being dealt with—
   (a) no effect is to be given to the decision appealed against; or
   (b) only such limited effect is to be given to it as may be specified in the direction.

(3) Rules under paragraph 7 must include provision requiring the Tribunal to consider applications by the Commissioner for the cancellation or variation of directions given under this paragraph.

Staff

9.—(1) The Lord Chancellor may appoint such staff for the Tribunal as he considers appropriate.

(2) The Lord Chancellor may pay, or provide for the payment of, such pensions, allowances or gratuities (including by way of compensation for loss of office or employment) to or in respect of the Tribunal's staff as he considers appropriate.

Expenditure

10. The Lord Chancellor may pay such other expenses of the Tribunal as he considers appropriate.

Meaning of 'legally qualified'

11. A person is legally qualified for the purposes of this Schedule if—

(a) he has a 7 year general qualification, within the meaning of section 71 of the Courts and Legal Services Act 1990;

(b) he is an advocate or solicitor in Scotland of at least 7 years' standing; or

(c) he is a member of the Bar of Northern Ireland or solicitor of the Supreme Court of Northern Ireland of at least 7 years' standing.

Disqualification for House of Commons

12. . . .

Note: Amends House of Commons Disqualification Act 1975.

Disqualification for Northern Ireland Assembly

13. . . .

Note: Amends Northern Ireland Assembly Disqualification Act 1975.

Section 95(12)

Schedule 8

Provision of Support: Regulations

. . .

Section 95(13)

Schedule 9

Asylum Support: Interim Provisions

. . .

Section 102(3)

Schedule 10

Asylum Support Adjudicators

. . .

Section 154(7)

Schedule 11

Detainee Custody Officers

. . .

Section 155(2)

Schedule 12

Discipline etc at [Removal Centres]

. . .

Section 156(5)

Schedule 13

Escort Arrangements

. . .

Section 169(1)

Schedule 14

Consequential Amendments

. . .

Section 169(2)

Schedule 15

Transitional Provisions and Savings

Leave to enter or remain

1.—(1) An order made under section 3A of the 1971 Act may make provision with respect to leave given before the commencement of section 1.

(2) An order made under section 3B of the 1971 Act may make provision with respect to leave given before the commencement of section 2.

Section 2 of the Asylum and Immigration Act 1996

2.—(1) This paragraph applies in relation to any time before the commencement of the repeal by this Act of section 2 of the Asylum and Immigration Act 1996.

(2) That section has effect, and is to be deemed always to have had effect, as if the

reference to section 6 of the Asylum and Immigration Appeals Act 1993 were a reference to section 15, and any certificate issued under that section is to be read accordingly.

Adjudicators and the Tribunal

3.—(1) Each existing member of the Tribunal is to continue as a member of the Tribunal as if he had been duly appointed by the Lord Chancellor under Schedule 2.

(2) Each existing adjudicator is to continue as an adjudicator as if he had been duly appointed by the Lord Chancellor under Schedule 3.

(3) The terms and conditions for a person to whom sub-paragraph (1) or (2) applies remain those on which he held office immediately before the appropriate date.

(4) The provisions of Schedule 7 to the Judicial Pensions and Retirement Act 1993 (transitional provisions for retirement dates), so far as applicable in relation to an existing member or adjudicator immediately before the appropriate date, continue to have effect.

(5) The repeal by this Act of Schedule 5 to the 1971 Act (provisions with respect to adjudicators and the Tribunal) does not affect any entitlement which an existing member or adjudicator had immediately before the appropriate date as a result of a determination made under paragraph 3(1)(b) or 9(1)(b) of that Schedule

(6) 'The appropriate date' means—

(a) in relation to existing members of the Tribunal, the date on which section 56 comes into force; and

(b) in relation to existing adjudicators, the date on which section 57 comes into force.

(7) 'Existing member' means a person who is a member of the Tribunal immediately before the appropriate date.

(8) 'Existing adjudicator' means a person who is an adjudicator immediately before the appropriate date.

References to justices' chief executive

4. . . .

Duties under national Assistance Act 1948

5. . . .

Duties under Health Services and Public Health Act 1968

6. . . .

Duties under Social Work (Scotland) Act 1968

7. . . .

Duties under Health and Personal Social Services (Northern Ireland) Order 1972

8. . . .

Duties under National Health Service Act 1977

9. . . .

Duties under Mental Health (Scotland) Act 1984

10. . . .

Appeals relating to deportation orders

11. Section 15 of the 1971 Act, section 5 of the Immigration Act 1988 and the Immigration (Restricted Right of Appeal against Deportation) (Exemption) Order 1993 are to continue to have effect in relation to any person on whom the Secretary of State has, before the commencement of the repeal of those sections, served a notice of his decision to make a deportation order.

12.—(1) Sub-paragraph (2) applies if, on the coming into force of section 10, sections 15 of the 1971 Act and 5 of the Immigration Act 1988 have been repealed by this Act.

(2) Those sections are to continue to have effect in relation to any person—

(a) who applied during the regularisation period fixed by section 9, in accordance with the regulations made under that section, for leave to remain in the United Kingdom, and

(b) on whom the Secretary of State has since served a notice of his decision to make a deportation order.

Assistance under Part VII of the Housing Act 1996

13. . . .

Provision of support

14. . . .

Section 169(3)

SCHEDULE 16

REPEALS

. . .

British Overseas Territories Act 2002
(2002, c. 14)

An Act to make provision about the name 'British overseas territories' and British citizenship so far as relating to the British overseas territories.

[26th February 2002]

Change of names

1. British overseas territories

(1) As the territories mentioned in Schedule 6 to the British Nationality Act 1981 (c. 61) are now known as 'British overseas territories'—
  (a) . . .
  (b) . . .
  (c) . . .

(2) In any other enactment passed or made before the commencement of this section (including an enactment comprised in subordinate legislation), any reference to a dependent territory within the meaning of the British Nationality Act 1981 shall be read as a reference to a British overseas territory.

(3) . . .

Note: Subsection (1)(a)–(c) amends British Nationality Act 1981, sub-s (3) amends Sch 1 Interpretation Act 1978. Commenced 26 February 2002.

2. British overseas territories citizenship

(1) Pursuant to section 1, British Dependent Territories citizenship is renamed 'British overseas territories citizenship'; and a person having that citizenship is a 'British overseas territories citizen'.

(2) . . .

(3) In any other enactment passed or made before the commencement of this section (including an enactment comprised in subordinate legislation), any reference to British Dependent Territories citizenship, or a British Dependent Territories citizen, shall be read as a reference to British overseas territories citizenship, or a British overseas territories citizen.

Note: Subsection (2) amends British Nationality Act 1981. Commenced 26 February 2002.

British citizenship

3. Conferral on British overseas territories citizens

(1) Any person who, immediately before the commencement of this section, is a British overseas territories citizen shall, on the commencement of this section, become a British citizen.

(2) Subsection (1) does not apply to a person who is a British overseas territories citizen by virtue only of a connection with the Sovereign Base Areas of Akrotiri and Dhekelia.

(3) A person who is a British citizen by virtue of this section is a British citizen by descent for the purposes of the British Nationality Act 1981 if, and only if—
   (a) he was a British overseas territories citizen by descent immediately before the commencement of this section, and
   (b) if at that time he was a British citizen as well as a British overseas territories citizen, he was a British citizen by descent.

Note: Commenced 21 May 2002 (SI 2002/1252).

4. Acquisition by British overseas territories citizens by registration

. . .

Note: Amends British Nationality Act1981, s 4.

5. Acquisition by reference to the British overseas territories

Schedule 1 (which makes provision about the acquisition of British citizenship by reference to the British overseas territories) has effect.

Note: Commenced 21 May 2002 (SI 2002/1252).

Supplementary

6. The Ilois: citizenship

(1) A person shall become a British citizen on the commencement of this section if—
   (a) he was born on or after 26 April 1969 and before 1 January 1983,
   (b) he was born to a woman who at the time was a citizen of the United Kingdom and Colonies by virtue of her birth in the British Indian Ocean Territory, and
   (c) immediately before the commencement of this section he was neither a British citizen nor a British overseas territories citizen.

(2) A person who is a British citizen by virtue of subsection (1) is a British citizen by descent for the purposes of the British Nationality Act 1981 (c. 61).

(3) A person shall become a British overseas territories citizen on the commencement of this section if—
   (a) subsection (1)(a) and (b) apply in relation to him, and
   (b) immediately before the commencement of this section he was not a British overseas territories citizen.

(4) A person who is a British overseas territories citizen by virtue of subsection (3) is such a citizen by descent for the purposes of the British Nationality Act 1981.

Note: Commenced 21 May 2002 (SI 2002/1252).

7. Repeals

The enactments mentioned in Schedule 2 (which include some which are spent or effectively superseded) are repealed to the extent specified there.

Note: Commenced 26 February 2002, save in relation to the British Nationality (Falkland Islands) Act 1983, where commencement is 21 May 2002 (SI 2002/1252).

8. Short title, commencement and extent

(1) This Act may be cited as the British Overseas Territories Act 2002.

(2) The following provisions of this Act are to come into force on such day as the Secretary of State may by order made by statutory instrument appoint—
   (a) sections 3 to 5 and Schedule 1,
   (b) section 6, and
   (c) section 7 and Schedule 2, so far as relating to the British Nationality (Falkland Islands) Act 1983 (c. 6).

(3) An order under subsection (2) may—
   (a) appoint different days for different purposes, and
   (b) include such transitional provision as the Secretary of State considers expedient.

(4) This Act extends to—
   (a) the United Kingdom,
   (b) the Channel Islands and the Isle of Man, and
   (c) the British overseas territories.

Schedule 1

British Citizenship and The British Overseas Territories

Birth or adoption

1. . . .

Descent

2. . . .

Registration of minors

3. . . .

Commonwealth citizens

4. . . .

Interpretation

5. . . .
6. . . .

Note: Amends British Nationality Act 1981, ss 1, 2, 3, 37(1)(a), 50, 51(3)(a) from 21 May 2002 (SI 2002/1252).

Schedule 2

Repeals

. . .

Note: Commencement 26 February 2002.

Nationality, Immigration and Asylum Act 2002
(2002, c. 41)

Arrangement of Sections

PART I. NATIONALITY

Operation of centres

27. Resident of centre
28. Manager of centre
29. Facilities
30. Conditions of residence
31. Financial contribution by resident
32. Tenure
33. Advisory Groups

General

34. The Monitor of Accommodation Centres
35. Ancillary provisions
36. Education: general
37. Education: special cases
38. Local authority
39. 'Prescribed': orders and regulations
40. Scotland
41. Northern Ireland
42. Wales

PART III. OTHER SUPPORT AND ASSISTANCE

43. Asylum-seeker: form of support
44. . . .
45. . . .
46. . . .
47. . . .
48. Young asylum-seeker
49. . . .
50. . . .
51. Choice of form of support
52. . . .
53. . . .
54. Withholding and withdrawal of support
55. Late claim for asylum: refusal of support
56. . . .
57. . . .
58. Voluntary departure from United Kingdom
59. International projects
60. . . .
61. . . .

PART IV. DETENTION AND REMOVAL

PART V. IMMIGRATION AND ASYLUM APPEALS

Part VI. Immigration Procedure

Applications

118. . . .
119. . . .
120. Requirement to state additional grounds for application
121. . . .

Work permit

122. . . .
123. . . .

Authority-to-carry scheme

124. Authority to carry

Evasion of procedure

125. Carriers' liability

Provision of information by traveller

126. Physical data: compulsory provision
127. Physical data: voluntary provision
128. . . .

Disclosure of information by public authority

129. Local authority
130. Inland Revenue
131. Police, &c.
132. . . .
133. Medical inspectors

Disclosure of information by private person

134. Employer
135. Financial institution
136. Notice
137. Disclosure of information: offences
138. Offence by body
139. Privilege against self-incrimination

Immigration services

140. . . .

Immigration control

141. EEA ports: juxtaposed controls

An Act to make provision about nationality, immigration and asylum; to create offences in connection with international traffic in prostitution; to make provision about international projects connected with migration; and for connected purposes. [7th November 2002]

Part I
Nationality

1. Naturalisation: knowledge of language and society

. . .

Note: Amends British Nationality Act 1981, s 41 and Sch 1.

2. Naturalisation: spouse of citizen

. . .

Note: Amends Sch 1 British Nationality Act 1981.

3. Citizenship ceremony, oath and pledge

Schedule 1 (which makes provision about citizenship ceremonies, oaths and pledges) shall have effect.

Note: Commencement 1 January 2004 (SI 2003/3516).

4. Deprivation of citizenship

(1) . . .

Note: Amends British Nationality Act 1981, s 40.

(2) . . .

Note: Amends Special Immigration Appeals Commission Act 1997, s 2.

(3) . . .

Note: Amends Special Immigration Appeals Commission Act 1997, s 5.

(4) In exercising a power under section 40 of the British Nationality Act 1981 after the commencement of subsection (1) above the Secretary of State may have regard to anything which—
- (a) occurred before commencement, and
- (b) he could have relied on (whether on its own or with other matters) in making an order under section 40 before commencement.

Note: Commencement from 1 April 2003 (SI 2003/754).

5. Resumption of citizenship

. . .

Note: Amends British Nationality Act 1981, ss 10, 22.

6. Nationality decision: discrimination

. . .

Note: Amends Race Relations Act 1976, ss 19 and 71.

7. Nationality decision: reasons and review

(1) . . .

Note: Amends British Nationality Act 1981, s 44.

(2) . . .

Note: Amends British Nationality (Hong Kong) Act 1990, s 1.

8. Citizenship: registration

. . .

Note: Amends para 3, Sch 2 British Nationality Act 1981.

9. Legitimacy of child

(1) . . .

Note: Amends British Nationality Act 1981, s 50(9).

(2) . . .

Note: Amends British Nationality Act 1981, s 3(6).

(3) . . .

Note: Amends British Nationality Act 1981, s 17(6).

(4) . . .

Note: Amends British Nationality Act 1981, s 47.

(5) . . .

Note: Amends paras 1, 2, Sch 2 British Nationality Act 1981.

10. Right of abode: certificate of entitlement

(1) The Secretary of State may by regulations make provision for the issue to a person of a certificate that he has the right of abode in the United Kingdom.

(2) The regulations may, in particular—
(a) specify to whom an application must be made;
(b) specify the place (which may be outside the United Kingdom) to which an application must be sent;
(c) provide that an application must be [accompanied by specified information;]
(d) provide that an application must be accompanied by specified documents;
(e) . . .
(f) specify the consequences of failure to comply with a requirement under any of paragraphs [(a) to (d)] above;
(g) provide for a certificate to cease to have effect after a period of time specified in or determined in accordance with the regulations;
(h) make provision about the revocation of a certificate.

(3) The regulations may—
(a) make provision which applies generally or only in specified cases or circumstances;
(b) make different provision for different purposes;
(c) include consequential, incidental or transitional provision.

(4) The regulations—
(a) must be made by statutory instrument, and
(b) shall be subject to annulment in pursuance of a resolution of either House of Parliament.

(5) . . .

(6) Regulations under this section may, in particular, include provision saving, with or without modification, the effect of a certificate which—
(a) is issued before the regulations come into force, and
(b) is a certificate of entitlement for the purposes of sections 3(9) and 33(1) of the Immigration Act 1971 as those sections have effect before the commencement of subsection (5) above.

Note: Subsection (5) amends Immigration Act 1971, ss 3, 33. Subsections (1)–(4) and (6) commenced on 7 November 2002, s 162, remainder at a date to be appointed. Subsection (2)(e) ceases to have effect and words in square brackets in sub-s (2) substituted by Immigration, Asylum and Nationality Act 2006, s 50 and Sch 2 from a date to be appointed.

11. Unlawful presence in United Kingdom

(1) This section applies for the construction of a reference to being in the United Kingdom 'in breach of the immigration laws' in section 4(2) or (4) or 50(5) of, or Schedule 1 to, the British Nationality Act 1981 (c. 61).

(2) A person is in the United Kingdom in breach of the immigration laws if (and only if) he—
(a) is in the United Kingdom,

(b) does not have the right of abode in the United Kingdom within the meaning of section 2 of the Immigration Act 1971,
(c) does not have leave to enter or remain in the United Kingdom (whether or not he previously had leave),
(d) is not a qualified person within the meaning of the Immigration (European Economic Area) Regulations 2000 (S.I. 2000/2326) (person entitled to reside in United Kingdom without leave) (whether or not he was previously a qualified person),
(e) is not a family member of a qualified person within the meaning of those regulations (whether or not he was previously a family member of a qualified person),
(f) is not entitled to enter and remain in the United Kingdom by virtue of section 8(1) of the Immigration Act 1971 (crew) (whether or not he was previously entitled), and
(g) does not have the benefit of an exemption under section 8(2) to (4) of that Act (diplomats, soldiers and other special cases) (whether or not he previously had the benefit of an exemption).

(3) Section 11(1) of the Immigration Act 1971 (person deemed not to be in United Kingdom before disembarkation, while in controlled area or while under immigration control) shall apply for the purposes of this section as it applies for the purposes of that Act.

(4) This section shall be treated as always having had effect except in relation to a person who on the commencement of this section is, or has been at any time since he last entered the United Kingdom—
(a) a qualified person within the meaning of the regulations referred to in subsection (2)(d), or
(b) a family member of a qualified person within the meaning of those regulations.

(5) This section is without prejudice to the generality of—
(a) a reference to being in a place outside the United Kingdom in breach of immigration laws, and
(b) a reference in a provision other than one specified in subsection (1) to being in the United Kingdom in breach of immigration laws.

Note: Commenced 7 November 2002, s 162.

12. British citizenship: registration of certain persons without other citizenship

. . .

Note: Amends British Nationality Act 1981, ss 4, 14.

13. British citizenship: registration of certain persons born between 1961 and 1983

. . .

Note: Amends British Nationality Act 1981, ss 4, 14.

14. Hong Kong

A person may not be registered as a British overseas territories citizen under a provision of the British Nationality Act 1981 (c. 61) by virtue of a connection with Hong Kong.

Note: Commencement from 1 January 2004 (SI 2003/3156).

15. Repeal of spent provisions

Schedule 2 (which repeals spent provisions) shall have effect.

Note: Commencement 7 November 2002, s 162.

Part II

Accommodation Centres

Establishment

16. Establishment of centres

(1) The Secretary of State may arrange for the provision of premises for the accommodation of persons in accordance with this Part.

(2) A set of premises provided under this section is referred to in this Act as an 'accommodation centre'.

(3) The Secretary of State may arrange for—

(a) the provision of facilities at or near an accommodation centre for sittings of adjudicators appointed for the purpose of Part 5 in accordance with a determination . . . under paragraph 2 of Schedule 4;

(b) the provision of facilities at an accommodation centre for the taking of steps in connection with the determination of claims for asylum (within the meaning of section 18(3)).

Note: Commencement 7 November 2002, s 162. Words deleted by Sch 18 Constitutional Reform Act 2004 from 3 April 2006.

Use of centres

17. Support for destitute asylum-seeker

(1) The Secretary of State may arrange for the provision of accommodation for a person in an accommodation centre if—
  (a) the person is an asylum-seeker or the dependant of an asylum-seeker, and
  (b) the Secretary of State thinks that the person is destitute or is likely to become destitute within a prescribed period.

(2) The Secretary of State may make regulations about procedure to be followed in respect of the provision of accommodation under this section.

(3) The regulations may, in particular, make provision—
  (a) specifying procedure to be followed in applying for accommodation in an accommodation centre;
  (b) providing for an application to be combined with an application under or in respect of another enactment;
  (c) requiring an applicant to provide information;
  (d) specifying circumstances in which an application may not be considered (which provision may, in particular, provide for an application not to be considered where the Secretary of State is not satisfied that the information provided is complete or accurate or that the applicant is co-operating with enquiries under paragraph (e));
  (e) about the making of enquiries by the Secretary of State;
  (f) requiring a person to notify the Secretary of State of a change in circumstances.

(4) Sections 18 to 20 define the following expressions for the purpose of this Part—
  (a) asylum-seeker,
  (b) dependant, and
  (c) destitute.

Note: Commencement from a date to be appointed.

18. Asylum-seeker: definition

(1) For the purposes of this Part a person is an 'asylum-seeker' if—
  (a) he is at least 18 years old,
  (b) he is in the United Kingdom,
  (c) a claim for asylum has been made by him at a place designated by the Secretary of State,
  (d) the Secretary of State has recorded the claim, and
  (e) the claim has not been determined.

(2) A person shall continue to be treated as an asylum-seeker despite subsection (1)(e) while—

(a) his household includes a dependent child who is under 18, and
(b) he does not have leave to enter or remain in the United Kingdom.

(3) A claim for asylum is a claim by a person that to remove him from or require him to leave the United Kingdom would be contrary to the United Kingdom's obligations under—
(a) the Convention relating to the Status of Refugees done at Geneva on 28th July 1951 and its Protocol, or
(b) Article 3 of the Convention for the Protection of Human Rights and Fundamental Freedoms agreed by the Council of Europe at Rome on 4th November 1950.

Note: Commenced for the purposes of ss 55(9), 70(3) and para 17(1)(b) of Sch 3 on 8 January 2003 (SI 2003/1). For the purposes of Immigration Act 1971, s 26A(2) and this Act, s 71(5), 10 February 2003 (SI 2003/01).

19. Destitution: definition

(1) Where a person has dependants, he and his dependants are destitute for the purpose of this Part if they do not have and cannot obtain both—
(a) adequate accommodation, and
(b) food and other essential items.

(2) Where a person does not have dependants, he is destitute for the purpose of this Part if he does not have and cannot obtain both—
(a) adequate accommodation, and
(b) food and other essential items.

(3) In determining whether accommodation is adequate for the purposes of subsection (1) or (2) the Secretary of State must have regard to any matter prescribed for the purposes of this subsection.

(4) In determining whether accommodation is adequate for the purposes of subsection (1) or (2) the Secretary of State may not have regard to—
(a) whether a person has an enforceable right to occupy accommodation,
(b) whether a person shares all or part of accommodation,
(c) whether accommodation is temporary or permanent,
(d) the location of accommodation, or
(e) any other matter prescribed for the purposes of this subsection.

(5) The Secretary of State may by regulations specify items which are or are not to be treated as essential items for the purposes of subsections (1) and (2).

(6) The Secretary of State may by regulations—
(a) provide that a person is not to be treated as destitute for the purposes of this Part in specified circumstances;
(b) enable or require the Secretary of State in deciding whether a person is destitute to have regard to income which he or a dependant of his might reasonably be expected to have;

(c) enable or require the Secretary of State in deciding whether a person is destitute to have regard to support which is or might reasonably be expected to be available to the person or a dependant of his;
(d) enable or require the Secretary of State in deciding whether a person is destitute to have regard to assets of a prescribed kind which he or a dependant of his has or might reasonably be expected to have;
(e) make provision as to the valuation of assets.

Note: Commencement at a date to be appointed.

20. Dependant: definition

For the purposes of this Part a person is a 'dependant' of an asylum-seeker if (and only if) that person—
(a) is in the United Kingdom, and
(b) is within a prescribed class.

Note: Commencement at a date to be appointed.

21. Sections 17 to 20: supplementary

(1) This section applies for the purposes of sections 17 to 20.

(2) The Secretary of State may inquire into and decide a person's age.

(3) A claim for asylum shall be treated as determined at the end of such period as may be prescribed beginning with—
(a) the date on which the Secretary of State notifies the claimant of his decision on the claim, or
(b) if the claimant appeals against the Secretary of State's decision, the date on which the appeal is disposed of.

(4) A notice under subsection (3)(a)—
(a) must be in writing, and
(b) if sent by first class post to the claimant's last known address or to the claimant's representative, shall be treated as being received by the claimant on the second day after the day of posting.

(5) An appeal is disposed of when it is no longer pending for the purpose of—
(a) Part 5 of this Act, or
(b) the Special Immigration Appeals Commission Act 1997 (c. 68).

Note: Commencement at a date to be appointed.

22. Immigration and Asylum Act 1999, s. 95

The Secretary of State may provide support under section 95 of the Immigration and Asylum Act 1999 (c. 33) (destitute asylum-seeker) by arranging for the provision of accommodation in an accommodation centre.

Note: Commencement at a date to be appointed.

23. Person subject to United Kingdom entrance control

(1) A residence restriction may include a requirement to reside at an accommodation centre.

(2) In subsection (1) 'residence restriction' means a restriction imposed under—

(a) paragraph 21 of Schedule 2 to the Immigration Act 1971 (c. 77) (temporary admission or release from detention), or

(b) paragraph 2(5) of Schedule 3 to that Act (control pending deportation).

(3) Where a person is required to reside in an accommodation centre by virtue of subsection (1) the Secretary of State must arrange for the provision of accommodation for the person in an accommodation centre.

(4) But if the person is required to leave an accommodation centre by virtue of section 26 or 30 he shall be treated as having broken the residence restriction referred to in subsection (1).

(5) The Secretary of State may provide support under section 4 of the Immigration and Asylum Act 1999 (persons subject to entrance control) (including that section as amended by section 49 of this Act) by arranging for the provision of accommodation in an accommodation centre.

Note: Commencement at a date to be appointed.

24. Provisional assistance

(1) If the Secretary of State thinks that a person may be eligible for the provision of accommodation in an accommodation centre under section 17, he may arrange for the provision for the person, pending a decision about eligibility, of—

(a) accommodation in an accommodation centre, or

(b) other support or assistance (of any kind).

(2) Section 99 of the Immigration and Asylum Act 1999 (c. 33) (provision of support by local authority) shall have effect in relation to the provision of support for persons under subsection (1) above as it has effect in relation to the provision of support for asylum-seekers under sections 95 and 98 of that Act.

Note: Commencement at a date to be appointed.

25. Length of stay

(1) The Secretary of State may not arrange for the provision of accommodation for a person in an accommodation centre if he has been a resident of an accommodation centre for a continuous period of six months.

(2) But—

(a) subsection (1) may be disapplied in respect of a person, generally or to a specified extent, by agreement between the Secretary of State and the person, and
(b) if the Secretary of State thinks it appropriate in relation to a person because of the circumstances of his case, the Secretary of State may direct that subsection (1) shall have effect in relation to the person as if the period specified in that subsection were the period of nine months.

(3) Section 51 is subject to this section.

(4) The Secretary of State may by order amend subsection (1) or (2)(b) so as to substitute a shorter period for a period specified.

Note: Commencement at a date to be appointed.

26. Withdrawal of support

(1) The Secretary of State may stop providing support for a person under section 17 or 24 if—
(a) the Secretary of State suspects that the person or a dependant of his has committed an offence by virtue of section 35, or
(b) the person or a dependant of his has failed to comply with directions of the Secretary of State as to the time or manner of travel to accommodation provided under section 17 or 24.

(2) The Secretary of State may be regulations specify other circumstances in which he may stop providing support for a person under section 17 or 24.

(3) In determining whether or not to provide a person with support or assistance under section 17 or 24 of this Act or section 4, 95 or 98 of the Immigration and Asylum Act 1999 (asylum-seeker) the Secretary of State may take into account the fact that—
(a) he has withdrawn support from the person by virtue of this section or section 30(4) or (5), or
(b) circumstances exist which would have enabled the Secretary of State to withdraw support from the person by virtue of this section had he been receiving support.

(4) This section is without prejudice to section 103 of the Immigration and Asylum Act 1999 (c. 33) (appeal against refusal to support).

Note: Commencement at a date to be appointed.

Operation of centres

27. Resident of centre

A reference in this Part to a resident of an accommodation centre is a reference to a person for whom accommodation in the centre is provided—

(a) under section 17,
(b) by virtue of section 22,
(c) by virtue of section 23, or
(d) under section 24.

Note: Commencement at a date to be appointed.

28. Manager of centre

A reference in this Part to the manager of an accommodation centre is a reference to a person who agrees with the Secretary of State to be wholly or partly responsible for the management of the centre.

Note: Commencement at a date to be appointed.

29. Facilities

(1) The Secretary of State may arrange for the following to be provided to a resident of an accommodation centre—
  (a) food and other essential items;
  (b) money;
  (c) assistance with transport for the purpose of proceedings under the Immigration Acts or in connection with a claim for asylum;
  (d) transport to and from the centre;
  (e) assistance with expenses incurred in connection with carrying out voluntary work or other activities;
  (f) education and training;
  (g) facilities relating to health;
  (h) facilities for religious observance;
  (i) anything which the Secretary of State thinks ought to be provided for the purpose of providing a resident with proper occupation and for the purpose of maintaining good order;
  (j) anything which the Secretary of State thinks ought to be provided for a person because of his exceptional circumstances.

(2) The Secretary of State may make regulations specifying the amount or maximum amount of money to be provided under subsection (1)(b).

(3) The Secretary of State may arrange for the provision of facilities in an accommodation centre for the use of a person in providing legal advice to a resident of the centre.

(4) The Secretary of State shall take reasonable steps to ensure that a resident of an accommodation centre has an opportunity to obtain legal advice before any appointment made by an immigration officer or an official of the Secretary of

State for the purpose of obtaining information from the resident to be used in determining his claim for asylum.

(5) The Secretary of State may by order amend subsection (1) so as to add a reference to facilities which may be provided.

Note: Commencement at a date to be appointed.

30. Conditions of residence

(1) The Secretary of State may make regulations about conditions to be observed by residents of an accommodation centre.

(2) Regulations under subsection (1) may, in particular, enable a condition to be imposed in accordance with the regulations by—

   (a) the Secretary of State, or

   (b) the manager of an accommodation centre.

(3) A condition imposed by virtue of this section may, in particular—

   (a) require a person not to be absent from the centre during specified hours without the permission of the Secretary of State or the manager;

   (b) require a person to report to an immigration officer or the Secretary of State.

(4) If a resident of an accommodation centre breaches a condition imposed by virtue of this section, the Secretary of State may—

   (a) require the resident and any dependant of his to leave the centre;

   (b) authorise the manager of the centre to require the resident and any dependant of his to leave the centre.

(5) If a dependant of a resident of an accommodation centre breaches a condition imposed by virtue of this section, the Secretary of State may—

   (a) require the resident and any dependant of his to leave the centre;

   (b) authorise the manager of the centre to require the resident and any dependant of his to leave the centre.

(6) Regulations under this section must include provision for ensuring that a person subject to a condition is notified of the condition in writing.

(7) A condition imposed by virtue of this section is in addition to any restriction imposed under paragraph 21 of Schedule 2 to the Immigration Act 1971 (c. 77) (control of entry to United Kingdom) or under paragraph 2(5) of Schedule 3 to that Act (control pending deportation).

(8) A reference in this Part to a condition of residence is a reference to a condition imposed by virtue of this section.

Note: Commencement at a date to be appointed.

31. Financial contribution by resident

(1) A condition of residence may, in particular, require a resident of an accommodation centre to make payments to—
  (a) the Secretary of State, or
  (b) the manager of the centre.

(2) The Secretary of State may make regulations enabling him to recover sums representing the whole or part of the value of accommodation and other facilities provided to a resident of an accommodation centre if—
  (a) accommodation is provided for the resident in response to an application by him for support,
  (b) when the application was made the applicant had assets which were not capable of being realised, and
  (c) the assets have become realisable.

(3) In subsection (2) 'assets' includes assets outside the United Kingdom.

(4) An amount recoverable by virtue of regulations made under subsection (2) may be recovered—
  (a) as a debt due to the Secretary of State;
  (b) by another prescribed method (which may include the imposition or variation of a residence condition).

Note: Commencement at a date to be appointed.

32. Tenure

(1) A resident of an accommodation centre shall not be treated as acquiring a tenancy of or other interest in any part of the centre (whether by virtue of an agreement between the resident and another person or otherwise).

(2) Subsection (3) applies where—
  (a) the Secretary of State decides to stop arranging for the provision of accommodation in an accommodation centre for a resident of the centre, or
  (b) a resident of an accommodation centre is required to leave the centre in accordance with section 30.

(3) Where this subsection applies—
  (a) the Secretary of State or the manager of the centre may recover possession of the premises occupied by the resident, and
  (b) the right under paragraph (a) shall be enforceable in accordance with procedure prescribed by regulations made by the Secretary of State.

(4) Any licence which a resident of an accommodation centre has to occupy premises in the centre shall be an excluded licence for the purposes of the Protection from Eviction Act 1977 (c. 43).

(5) . . .

(6) . . .

(7) In this section a reference to an accommodation centre includes a reference to premises in which accommodation is provided under section 24(1)(b).

Note: Subsection (5) amends Protection from Eviction Act 1977, s 3A(7A), sub-s (6) amends Rent (Scotland) Act 1984, s 23A(5A) . Commencement at a date to be appointed.

33. Advisory Groups

(1) The Secretary of State shall appoint a group (to be known as an Accommodation Centre Advisory Group) for each accommodation centre.

(2) The Secretary of State may be regulations—
- (a) confer functions on Advisory Groups;
- (b) make provision about the constitution and proceedings of Advisory Groups.

(3) Regulations under subsection (2)(a) must, in particular, provide for members of an accommodation centre's Advisory Group—
- (a) to visit the centre;
- (b) to hear complaints made by residents of the centre;
- (c) to report to the Secretary of State.

(4) The manager of an accommodation centre must permit a member of the centre's Advisory Group on request—
- (a) to visit the centre at any time;
- (b) to visit any resident of the centre at any time, provided that the resident consents.

(5) A member of an Advisory Group shall hold and vacate office in accordance with the terms of his appointment (which may include provision about retirement, resignation or dismissal).

(6) The Secretary of State may—
- (a) defray expenses of members of an Advisory Group;
- (b) make facilities available to members of an Advisory Group.

Note: Commencement at a date to be appointed.

General

34. The Monitor of Accommodation Centres

(1) The Secretary of State shall appoint a person as Monitor of Accommodation Centres.

(2) The Monitor shall monitor the operation of this Part of this Act and shall, in particular, consider—

(a) the quality and effectiveness of accommodation and other facilities provided in accommodation centres,
(b) the nature and enforcement of conditions of residence,
(c) the treatment of residents, and
(d) whether, in the case of any accommodation centre, its location prevents a need of its residents from being met.

(3) In exercising his functions the Monitor shall consult—
(a) the Secretary of State, and
(b) such other persons as he considers appropriate.

(4) The Monitor shall report to the Secretary of State about the matters considered by the Monitor in the course of the exercise of his functions—
(a) at least once in each calendar year, and
(b) on such occasions as the Secretary of State may request.

(5) Where the Secretary of State receives a report under subsection (4)(a) he shall lay a copy before Parliament as soon as is reasonably practicable.

(6) The Monitor shall hold and vacate office in accordance with the terms of his appointment (which may include provision about retirement, resignation or dismissal).

(7) The Secretary of State may—
(a) pay fees and allowances to the Monitor;
(b) defray expenses of the Monitor;
(c) make staff and other facilities available to the Monitor.

(8) The Secretary of State may appoint more than one person to act jointly as Monitor (in which case they shall divide or share functions in accordance with the terms of their appointment and, subject to that, by agreement between them).

(9) A person who is employed within a government department may not be appointed as Monitor of Accommodation Centres.

Note: Commencement at a date to be appointed.

35. Ancillary provisions

(1) The following provisions of the Immigration and Asylum Act 1999 (c. 33) shall apply for the purposes of this Part as they apply for the purposes of Part VI of that Act (support for asylum-seeker)—
(a) section 105 (false representation),
(b) section 106 (dishonest representation),
(c) section 107 (delay or obstruction),
(d) section 108 (failure of sponsor to maintain),
(e) section 109 (offence committed by body),
(f) section 112 (recovery of expenditure),

(g) section 113 (recovery of expenditure from sponsor),
(h) section 124 (corporation sole), and
(i) section 127 (redirection of post).

(2) In the application of section 112 a reference to something done under section 95 or 98 of that Act shall be treated as a reference to something done under section 17 or 24 of this Act.

(3) In the application of section 113 a reference to section 95 of that Act shall be treated as a reference to section 17 of this Act.

Note: Subsection (1)(h) commenced on 7 November 2002, s 162. Remainder to commence on a date to be appointed.

36. Education: general

(1) For the purposes of section 13 of the Education Act 1996 (c. 56) (general responsibility of local education authority) a resident of an accommodation centre shall not be treated as part of the population of a local education authority's area.

(2) A child who is a resident of an accommodation centre may not be admitted to a maintained school or a maintained nursery (subject to section 37).

(3) But subsection (2) does not prevent a child's admission to a school which is—
(a) a community special school or a foundation special school, and
(b) named in a statement in respect of the child under section 324 of the Education Act 1996 (c. 56) (special educational needs).

(4) In subsections (2) and (3)—
(a) 'maintained school' means a maintained school within the meaning of section 20(7) of the School Standards and Framework Act 1998 (c. 31) (definition), and
(b) 'maintained nursery' means a facility for nursery education, within the meaning of section 117 of that Act, provided by a local education authority.

(5) The following shall not apply in relation to a child who is a resident of an accommodation centre (subject to section 37)—
(a) section 86(1) and (2) of the School Standards and Framework Act 1998 (parental preference),
(b) section 94 of that Act (appeal),
(c) section 19 of the Education Act 1996 (education out of school),
(d) section 316(2) and (3) of that Act (child with special educational needs to be educated in mainstream school), and
(e) paragraphs 3 and 8 of Schedule 27 to that Act (special education needs: making of statement: parental preference).

(6) The power of the Special Educational Needs Tribunal under section 326(3) of the Education Act 1996 (appeal against content of statement) is subject to subsection (2) above.

(7) A person exercising a function under this Act or the Education Act 1996 shall (subject to section 37) secure that a child who is a resident of an accommodation centre and who has special educational needs shall be educated by way of facilities provided under section 29(1)(f) of this Act unless that is incompatible with—

(a) his receiving the special educational provision which his learning difficulty calls for,

(b) the provision of efficient education for other children who are residents of the centre, or

(c) the efficient use of resources.

(8) A person may rely on subsection (7)(b) only where there is no action—

(a) which could reasonably be taken by that person or by another person who exercises functions, or could exercise functions, in respect of the accommodation centre concerned, and

(b) as a result of which subsection (7)(b) would not apply.

(9) An accommodation centre is not a school within the meaning of section 4 of the Education Act 1996 (definition); but—

(a) [Part 1 of the Education Act 2005 (school inspections)] shall apply to educational facilities provided at an accommodation centre as if the centre were a school (for which purpose a reference to the appropriate authority shall be taken as a reference to the person (or persons) responsible for the provision of education at the accommodation centre),

(b) section 329A of the Education Act 1996 (review or assessment of educational needs at request of responsible body) shall have effect as if—

(i) an accommodation centre were a relevant school for the purposes of that section,

(ii) a child for whom education is provided at an accommodation centre under section 29(1)(f) were a registered pupil at the centre, and

(iii) a reference in section 329A to the responsible body in relation to an accommodation centre were a reference to any person providing education at the centre under section 29(1)(f), and

(c) section 140 of the Learning and Skills Act 2000 (c. 21) (learning difficulties: assessment of post-16 needs) shall have effect as if an accommodation centre were a school.

(10) Subsections (1), (2) and (5) shall not apply in relation to an accommodation centre if education is not provided for children who are residents of the centre under section 29(1)(f).

(11) An expression used in this section and in the Education Act 1996 (c. 56) shall have the same meaning in this section as in that Act.

Note: Commencement at a date to be appointed. Words in square brackets in sub-s (9) substituted by Education Act 2005, s 61 and Sch 9 from a date to be appointed.

37. Education: special cases

(1) This section applies to a child if a person who provides education to residents of an accommodation centre recommends in writing to the local education authority for the area in which the centre is that this section should apply to the child on the grounds that his special circumstances call for provision that can only or best be arranged by the authority.

(2) A local education authority may—
  (a) arrange for the provision of education for a child to whom this section applies;
  (b) disapply a provision of section 36 in respect of a child to whom this section applies.

(3) In determining whether to exercise a power under subsection (2) in respect of a child a local education authority shall have regard to any relevant guidance issued by the Secretary of State.

(4) The governing body of a maintained school shall comply with a requirement of the local education authority to admit to the school a child to whom this section applies.

(5) Subsection (4) shall not apply where compliance with a requirement would prejudice measures taken for the purpose of complying with a duty arising under section 1(6) of the School Standards and Framework Act 1998 (c. 31) (limit on infant class size).

(6) A local education authority may not impose a requirement under subsection (4) in respect of a school unless the authority has consulted the school in accordance with regulations made by the Secretary of State.

(7) In the case of a maintained school for which the local education authority are the admission authority, the authority may not arrange for the admission of a child to whom this section applies unless the authority has notified the school in accordance with regulations made by the Secretary of State.

(8) In this section—
  (a) 'maintained school' means a maintained school within the meaning of section 20(7) of the School Standards and Framework Act 1998 (definition), and
  (b) an expression which is also used in the Education Act 1996 (c. 56) shall have the same meaning as it has in that Act.

Note: Commencement at a date to be appointed.

38. Local authority

(1) A local authority may in accordance with arrangements made by the Secretary of State—
  (a) assist in arranging for the provision of an accommodation centre;
  (b) make premises available for an accommodation centre;
  (c) provide services in connection with an accommodation centre.

(2) In particular, a local authority may—
  (a) incur reasonable expenditure;
  (b) provide services outside its area;
  (c) provide services jointly with another body;
  (d) form a company;
  (e) tender for or enter into a contract;
  (f) do anything (including anything listed in paragraphs (a) to (e)) for a preparatory purpose.

(3) In this section 'local authority' means—
  (a) a local authority within the meaning of section 94 of the Immigration and Asylum Act 1999 (c. 33), and
  (b) a Northern Ireland authority within the meaning of section 110 of that Act and an Education and Library Board established under Article 3 of the Education and Libraries (Northern Ireland) Order 1986 (S.I. 1986/594 (N.I. 3)).

Note: Commenced 7 November 2002, s 162.

39. 'Prescribed': orders and regulations

(1) In this Part 'prescribed' means prescribed by the Secretary of State by order or regulations.

(2) An order or regulations under this Part may—
  (a) make provision which applies generally or only in specified cases or circumstances (which may be determined wholly or partly by reference to location);
  (b) make different provision for different cases or circumstances;
  (c) include consequential, transitional or incidental provision.

(3) An order or regulations under this Part must be made by statutory instrument.

(4) An order or regulations under any of the following provisions of this Part shall be subject to annulment in pursuance of a resolution of either House of Parliament—
  (a) section 17,
  (b) section 19,
  (c) section 20,

(d) section 21,
(e) section 26,
(f) section 29,
(g) section 31,
(h) section 32,
(i) section 33,
(j) section 37,
(k) section 40, and
(l) section 41.

(5) An order under section 25 or regulations under section 30 may not be made unless a draft has been laid before and approved by resolution of each House of Parliament.

Note: Commencement at a date to be appointed.

40. Scotland

(1) The Secretary of State may not make arrangements under section 16 for the provision of premises in Scotland unless he has consulted the Scottish Ministers.

(2) The Secretary of State may by order make provision in relation to the education of residents of accommodation centres in Scotland.

(3) An order under subsection (2) may, in particular—
(a) apply, disapply or modify the effect of an enactment (which may include a provision made by or under an Act of the Scottish Parliament);
(b) make provision having an effect similar to the effect of a provision of section 36 or 37.

Note: Subsection (1) commenced on 7 November 2002, s 162. Remainder at a date to be appointed.

41. Northern Ireland

(1) The Secretary of State may not make arrangements under section 16 for the provision of premises in Northern Ireland unless he has consulted the First Minister and the deputy First Minister.

(2) The Secretary of State may by order make provision in relation to the education of residents of accommodation centres in Northern Ireland.

(3) An order under subsection (2) may, in particular—
(a) apply, disapply or modify the effect of an enactment (which may include a provision made by or under Northern Ireland legislation);
(b) make provision having an effect similar to the effect of a provision of section 36 or 37.

Note: Subsection (1) commenced on 7 November 2002, s 162. Remainder at a date to be appointed.

42. Wales

The Secretary of State may not make arrangements under section 16 for the provision of premises in Wales unless he has consulted the National Assembly for Wales.

Note: Commenced 7 November 2002, s 162.

Part III

Other Support and Assistance

43. Asylum-seeker: form of support

(1) The Secretary of State may make an order restricting the application of section 96(1)(b) of the Immigration and Asylum Act 1999 (c. 33) (support for asylum-seeker: essential living needs)—
   (a) in all circumstances, to cases in which support is being provided under section 96(1)(a) (accommodation), or
   (b) in specified circumstances only, to cases in which support is being provided under section 96(1)(a).

(2) An order under subsection (1)(b) may, in particular, make provision by reference to—
   (a) location;
   (b) the date of an application.

(3) An order under subsection (1) may include transitional provision.

(4) An order under subsection (1)—
   (a) must be made by statutory instrument, and
   (b) may not be made unless a draft has been laid before and approved by resolution of each House of Parliament.

Note: Commenced 7 November 2002, s 162.

44. Destitute asylum-seeker

. . .

Note: Amends Immigration and Asylum Act 1999, ss 94, 95 (c. 33).

45. Section 44: supplemental

(1) . . .

Note: Amends Immigration and Asylum Act 1999, s 96.

(2) . . .

Note: Amends Immigration and Asylum Act 1999, s 97.

(3) . . .

Note: Amends Immigration and Asylum Act 1999, Sch 8, paras 2, 6.

(4) . . .

Note: Amends para 3, Sch 9 Immigration and Asylum Act 1999.

(5) . . .

Note: Amends National Assistance Act 1948, s 21 (1B) (c. 29).

(6) . . .

Note: Amends Health Services and Public Health Act 1968, s 45(4B).

(7) . . .

Note: Amends para 2(2B), Sch 8 National Health Service Act 1977.

46. Section 44: supplemental: Scotland and Northern Ireland

(1–3) . . .

Note: Amends the Social Work (Scotland) Act 1968.

(4–5) . . .

Note: Amends the Mental Health (Scotland) Act 1984.

(6–7) . . .

Note: Amends the Health and Personal Social Services (Northern Ireland) Order 1972 (SI 1972/1265 (NI 14)).

47. Asylum-seeker: family with children

. . .

Note: Amends Immigration and Asylum Act 1999, s 122.

48. Young asylum-seeker

The following provisions of the Immigration and Asylum Act 1999 (c. 33) shall have effect as if the definition of asylum-seeker in section 94(1) of that Act did not exclude persons who are under 18—
(a) section 110 (local authority expenditure on asylum-seekers), and
(b) section 111 (grants to voluntary organisations).

Note: Commenced on 7 November 2002, s 162.

49. Failed asylum-seeker

. . .

Note: Amends Immigration and Asylum Act 1999, s 4.

50. Conditions of support

. . .

Note: Amends Immigration and Asylum Act 1999, s 95 and Sch 9.

51. Choice of form of support

(1) The Secretary of State may refuse to provide support for a person under a provision specified in subsection (2) on the grounds that an offer has been made to the person of support under another provision specified in that subsection.

(2) The provisions are—
 (a) sections 17 and 24 of this Act,
 (b) section 4 of the Immigration and Asylum Act 1999 (accommodation for person temporarily admitted or released from detention), and
 (c) sections 95 and 98 of that Act (support for destitute asylum-seeker).

(3) In deciding under which of the provisions listed in subsection (2) to offer support to a person the Secretary of State may—
 (a) have regard to administrative or other matters which do not concern the person's personal circumstances;
 (b) regard one of those matters as conclusive;
 (c) apply different criteria to different persons for administrative reasons (which may include the importance of testing the operation of a particular provision).

Note: Commencement at a date to be appointed.

52. Back-dating of benefit for refugee

. . .

Note: Amends Immigration and Asylum Act 1999, s 123.

53. Asylum-seeker: appeal against refusal to support

. . .

Note: Amends Immigration and Asylum Act 1999, s 103.

54. Withholding and withdrawal of support

Schedule 3 (which makes provision for support to be withheld or withdrawn in certain circumstances) shall have effect.

Note: Commenced for the purpose of making subordinate legislation 8 December 2002. Remainder commenced 8 January 2003 (SI 2002/2811).

55. Late claim for asylum: refusal of support

(1) The Secretary of State may not provide or arrange for the provision of support to a person under a provision mentioned in subsection (2) if—
  (a) the person makes a claim for asylum which is recorded by the Secretary of State, and
  (b) the Secretary of State is not satisfied that the claim was made as soon as reasonably practicable after the person's arrival in the United Kingdom.

(2) The provisions are—
  (a) sections 4, 95 and 98 of the Immigration and Asylum Act 1999 (c. 33) (support for asylum-seeker, &c.), and
  (b) sections 17 and 24 of this Act (accommodation centre).

(3) An authority may not provide or arrange for the provision of support to a person under a provision mentioned in subsection (4) if—
  (a) the person has made a claim for asylum, and
  (b) the Secretary of State is not satisfied that the claim was made as soon as reasonably practicable after the person's arrival in the United Kingdom.

(4) The provisions are—
  (a) section 29(1)(b) of the Housing (Scotland) Act 1987 (c. 26) (accommodation pending review),
  (b) section 188(3) or 204(4) of the Housing Act 1996 (c. 52) (accommodation pending review or appeal), and
  (c) section 2 of the Local Government Act 2000 (c. 22) (promotion of well-being).

(5) This section shall not prevent—
  (a) the exercise of a power by the Secretary of State to the extent necessary for the purpose of avoiding a breach of a person's Convention rights (within the meaning of the Human Rights Act 1998 (c. 42)),
  (b) the provision of support under section 95 of the Immigration and Asylum Act 1999 (c. 33) or section 17 of this Act in accordance with section 122 of that Act (children), or
  (c) the provision of support under section 98 of the Immigration and Asylum Act 1999 or section 24 of this Act (provisional support) to a person under the age of 18 and the household of which he forms part.

(6) An authority which proposes to provide or arrange for the provision of support to a person under a provision mentioned in subsection (4)—
  (a) must inform the Secretary of State if the authority believes that the person has made a claim for asylum,
  (b) must act in accordance with any guidance issued by the Secretary of State to determine whether subsection (3) applies, and
  (c) shall not be prohibited from providing or arranging for the provision of support if the authority has complied with paragraph (a) and (b) and concluded that subsection (3) does not apply.

(7) The Secretary of State may by order—
  (a) add, remove or amend an entry in the list in subsection (4);
  (b) provide for subsection (3) not to have effect in specified cases or circumstances.

(8) An order under subsection (7)—
  (a) may include transitional, consequential or incidental provision,
  (b) must be made by statutory instrument, and
  (c) may not be made unless a draft has been laid before and approved by resolution of each House of Parliament.

(9) For the purposes of this section 'claim for asylum' has the same meaning as in section 18.

(10) A decision of the Secretary of State that this section prevents him from providing or arranging for the provision of support to a person is not a decision that the person does not qualify for support for the purpose of section 103 of the Immigration and Asylum Act 1999 (appeals).

(11) This section does not prevent a person's compliance with a residence restriction imposed in reliance on section 70 (induction).

Note: Commenced 8 January 2003 (SI 2002/2811).

56. Provision of support by local authority

. . .

Note: Amends Immigration and Asylum Act 1999, s 99.

57. Application for support: false or incomplete information

. . .

Note: Amends para 12, Sch 8 Immigration and Asylum Act 1999.

58. Voluntary departure from United Kingdom

(1) A person is a 'voluntary leaver' for the purposes of this section if—
   (a) he is not a British citizen or an EEA national,
   (b) he leaves the United Kingdom for a place where he hopes to take up permanent residence (his 'new place of residence'), and
   (c) the Secretary of State thinks that it is in the person's interest to leave the United Kingdom and that the person wishes to leave.

(2) The Secretary of State may make arrangements to—
   (a) assist voluntary leavers;
   (b) assist individuals to decide whether to become voluntary leavers.

(3) The Secretary of State may, in particular, make payments (whether to voluntary leavers or to organisations providing services for them) which relate to—
   (a) travelling and other expenses incurred by or on behalf of a voluntary leaver, or a member of his family or household, in leaving the United Kingdom;
   (b) expenses incurred by or on behalf of a voluntary leaver, or a member of his family or household, on or shortly after arrival in his new place of residence;
   (c) the provision of services designed to assist a voluntary leaver, or a member of his family or household, to settle in his new place of residence;
   (d) expenses in connection with a journey undertaken by a person (with or without his family or household) to prepare for, or to assess the possibility of, his becoming a voluntary leaver.

(4) In subsection (1)(a) 'EEA national' means a national of a State which is a contracting party to the Agreement on the European Economic Area signed at Oporto on 2nd May 1992 (as it has effect from time to time).

(5) . . .

Note: Subsection (5) repeals Immigration Act 1971, ss 29 and 31(d). Commenced 7 November 2002, s 162.

59. International projects

(1) The Secretary of State may participate in a project which is designed to—
   (a) reduce migration,
   (b) assist or ensure the return of migrants,
   (c) facilitate co-operation between States in matters relating to migration,
   (d) conduct or consider research about migration, or
   (e) arrange or assist the settlement of migrants (whether in the United Kingdom or elsewhere).

(2) In particular, the Secretary of State may—
   (a) provide financial support to an international organisation which arranges or participates in a project of a kind described in subsection (1);

(b) provide financial support to an organisation in the United Kingdom or another country which arranges or participates in a project of that kind;
(c) provide or arrange for the provision of financial or other assistance to a migrant who participates in a project of that kind;
(d) participate in financial or other arrangements which are agreed between Her Majesty's Government and the government of one or more other countries and which are or form part of a project of that kind.

(3) In this section—
(a) 'migrant' means a person who leaves the country where he lives hoping to settle in another country (whether or not he is a refugee within the meaning of any international Convention), and
(b) 'migration' shall be construed accordingly.

(4) Subsection (1) does not—
(a) confer a power to remove a person from the United Kingdom, or
(b) affect a person's right to enter or remain in the United Kingdom.

Note: Commenced 7 November 2002, s 162.

60. Northern Ireland authorities

. . .

Note: Amends Immigration and Asylum Act 1999, ss 94 and 110.

61. Repeal of spent provisions

. . .

Note: Repeals Immigration and Asylum Act 1999, ss 96(4)–(6), 166(4)(e).

Part IV

Detention and Removal

Detention

62. Detention by Secretary of State

(1) A person may be detained under the authority of the Secretary of State pending—
(a) a decision by the Secretary of State whether to give directions in respect of the person under paragraph 10, 10A or 14 of Schedule 2 to the Immigration Act 1971 (c. 77) (control of entry: removal), or
(b) removal of the person from the United Kingdom in pursuance of directions given by the Secretary of State under any of those paragraphs.

(2) Where the Secretary of State is empowered under section 3A of that Act (powers of Secretary of State) to examine a person or to give or refuse a person

leave to enter the United Kingdom, the person may be detained under the authority of the Secretary of State pending—

(a) the person's examination by the Secretary of State,

(b) the Secretary of State's decision to give or refuse the person leave to enter,

(c) a decision by the Secretary of State whether to give directions in respect of the person under paragraph 8 or 9 of Schedule 2 to that Act (removal), or

(d) removal of the person in pursuance of directions given by the Secretary of State under either of those paragraphs.

(3) A provision of Schedule 2 to that Act about a person who is detained or liable to detention under that Schedule shall apply to a person who is detained or liable to detention under this section: and for that purpose—

(a) a reference to paragraph 16 of that Schedule shall be taken to include a reference to this section,

(b) a reference in paragraph 21 of that Schedule to an immigration officer shall be taken to include a reference to the Secretary of State, and

(c) a reference to detention under that Schedule or under a provision or Part of that Schedule shall be taken to include a reference to detention under this section.

(4) In the case of a restriction imposed under paragraph 21 of that Schedule by virtue of this section—

(a) a restriction imposed by an immigration officer may be varied by the Secretary of State, and

(b) a restriction imposed by the Secretary of State may be varied by an immigration officer.

(5) In subsection (1) the reference to paragraph 10 of that Schedule includes a reference to that paragraph as applied by virtue of section 10 of the Immigration and Asylum Act 1999 (c. 33) (persons unlawfully in United Kingdom: removal).

(6) Subsection (5) is without prejudice to the generality of section 159.

(7) A power under this section which is exercisable pending a decision of a particular kind by the Secretary of State is exercisable where the Secretary of State has reasonable grounds to suspect that he may make a decision of that kind.

(8–16) . . .

Note: Subsections 8–16 amend Immigration Act 1971, ss 11, 24; Mental Health Act 1983, ss 48, 53, Mental Health (Scotland) Act 1984, ss 71, 74; Mental Health (Northern Ireland) Order 1986, Arts 54, 59; Immigration and Asylum Act 1999, ss 53, 147; Anti-terrorism, Crime and Security Act 2001, ss 23, 24. Commencement 10 February 2003 (SI 2003/1).

63. Control of entry to United Kingdom, &c.: use of force

. . .

Note: Amends para 17(2), Sch 2 Immigration Act 1971.

64. Escorts

. . .

Note: Amends para 17, Sch 2 Immigration Act 1971.

65. Detention centres: custodial functions

. . .

Note: Amends Immigration and Asylum Act 1999, s 154 and Sch 11.

66. Detention centres: change of name

(1)–(3) . . .

(4) A reference in an enactment or instrument to a detention centre within the meaning of Part VIII of the Immigration and Asylum Act 1999 (c. 33) shall be construed as a reference to a removal centre within the meaning of that Part.

Note: Subsections (1)–(3) amend Immigration and Asylum Act 1999, ss 141, 147–53, 155, 157–9 and Schs 11–13; Prison Act 1952, s 5A; Sch 4A Water Industry Act 1991.

67. Construction of reference to person liable to detention

(1) This section applies to the construction of a provision which—
   (a) does not confer power to detain a person, but
   (b) refers (in any terms) to a person who is liable to detention under a provision of the Immigration Acts.

(2) The reference shall be taken to include a person if the only reason why he cannot not be detained under the provision is that—
   (a) he cannot presently be removed from the United Kingdom, because of a legal impediment connected with the United Kingdom's obligations under an international agreement,
   (b) practical difficulties are impeding or delaying the making of arrangements for his removal from the United Kingdom, or
   (c) practical difficulties, or demands on administrative resources, are impeding or delaying the taking of a decision in respect of him.

(3) This section shall be treated as always having had effect.

Note: Commenced 7 November 2002, s 162.

Temporary release

68. Bail

(1) This section applies in a case where an immigration officer not below the rank of chief immigration officer has sole or shared power to release a person on bail in accordance with—

(a) a provision of Schedule 2 to the Immigration Act 1971 (c. 77) (control of entry) (including a provision of that Schedule applied by a provision of that Act or by another enactment), or

(b) section 9A of the Asylum and Immigration Appeals Act 1993 (c. 23) (pending appeal from Immigration Appeal Tribunal).

(2) In respect of an application for release on bail which is instituted after the expiry of the period of eight days beginning with the day on which detention commences, the power to release on bail—

(a) shall be exercisable by the Secretary of State (as well as by any person with whom the immigration officer's power is shared under the provision referred to in subsection (1)), and

(b) shall not be exercisable by an immigration officer (except where he acts on behalf of the Secretary of State).

(3) In relation to the exercise by the Secretary of State of a power to release a person on bail by virtue of subsection (2), a reference to an immigration officer shall be construed as a reference to the Secretary of State.

(4) The Secretary of State may by order amend or replace subsection (2) so as to make different provision for the circumstances in which the power to release on bail may be exercised by the Secretary of State and not by an immigration officer.

(5) An order under subsection (4)—

(a) may include consequential or transitional provision,

(b) must be made by statutory instrument, and

(c) may not be made unless a draft has been laid before and approved by resolution of each House of Parliament.

(6) . . .

Note: Subsection (6) repeals Immigration and Asylum Act 1999, ss 44–52, 53(5) and 55, from 10 February 2003 (SI 2003/1). Remainder of s 68 commenced 1 April 2003 (SI 2003/754).

69. Reporting restriction: travel expenses

(1) The Secretary of State may make a payment to a person in respect of travelling expenses which the person has incurred or will incur for the purpose of complying with a reporting restriction.

(2) In subsection (1) 'reporting restriction' means a restriction which—
  (a) requires a person to report to the police, an immigration officer or the Secretary of State, and
  (b) is imposed under a provision listed in subsection (3).

(3) Those provisions are—
  (a) paragraph 21 of Schedule 2 to the Immigration Act 1971 (c. 77) (temporary admission or release from detention),
  (b) paragraph 29 of that Schedule (bail), and
  (c) paragraph 2 or 5 of Schedule 3 to that Act (pending deportation).

Note: Commenced 7 November 2002, s 162.

70. Induction

(1) A residence restriction may be imposed on an asylum-seeker or a dependant of an asylum-seeker without regard to his personal circumstances if—
  (a) it requires him to reside at a specified location for a period not exceeding 14 days, and
  (b) the person imposing the residence restriction believes that a programme of induction will be made available to the asylum-seeker at or near the specified location.

(2) In subsection (1) 'residence restriction' means a restriction imposed under—
  (a) paragraph 21 of Schedule 2 to the Immigration Act 1971 (temporary admission or release from detention), or
  (b) paragraph 2(5) of Schedule 3 to that Act (control pending deportation).

(3) In this section—

'asylum-seeker' has the meaning given by section 18 of this Act but disregarding section 18(1)(a),

'dependent of an asylum-seeker' means a person who appears to the Secretary of State to be making a claim or application in respect of residence in the United Kingdom by virtue of being a dependant of an asylum-seeker, and

'programme of induction' means education about the nature of the asylum process.

(4) Regulations under subsection (3)—
  (a) may make different provision for different circumstances,
  (b) must be made by statutory instrument, and
  (c) shall be subject to annulment in pursuance of a resolution of either House of Parliament.

(5) Subsection (6) applies where the Secretary of State arranges for the provision of a programme of induction (whether or not he also provides other facilities to persons attending the programme and whether or not all the persons attending the programme are subject to residence restrictions).

(6) A local authority may arrange for or participate in the provision of the programme or other facilities.

(7) In particular, a local authority may—
- (a) incur reasonable expenditure;
- (b) provide services outside its area;
- (c) provide services jointly with another body;
- (d) form a company;
- (e) tender for or enter into a contract;
- (f) do anything (including anything listed in paragraphs (a) to (e)) for a preparatory purpose.

(8) In this section 'local authority' means—
- (a) a local authority within the meaning of section 94 of the Immigration and Asylum Act 1999 (c. 33), and
- (b) a Northern Ireland authority within the meaning of section 110 of that Act.

Note: Commenced 7 November 2002, s 162.

71. Asylum-seeker: residence, &c. restriction

(1) This section applies to—
- (a) a person who makes a claim for asylum at a time when he has leave to enter or remain in the United Kingdom, and
- (b) a dependant of a person within paragraph (a).

(2) The Secretary of State or an immigration officer may impose on a person to whom this section applies any restriction which may be imposed under paragraph 21 of Schedule 2 to the Immigration Act 1971 (c. 77) (control of entry: residence, reporting and occupation restrictions) on a person liable to detention under paragraph 16 of that Schedule.

(3) Where a restriction is imposed on a person under subsection (2)—
- (a) the restriction shall be treated for all purposes as a restriction imposed under paragraph 21 of that Schedule, and
- (b) if the person fails to comply with the restriction he shall be liable to detention under paragraph 16 of that Schedule.

(4) A restriction imposed on a person under this section shall cease to have effect if he ceases to be an asylum-seeker or the dependant of an asylum-seeker.

(5) In this section—

'asylum-seeker' has the same meaning as in section 70,

'claim for asylum' has the same meaning as in section 18, and

'dependant' means a person who appears to the Secretary of State to be making a claim or application in respect of residence in the United Kingdom by virtue of being a dependant of another person.

(6) Regulations under subsection (5)—
  (a) may make different provision for different circumstances,
  (b) must be made by statutory instrument, and
  (c) shall be subject to annulment in pursuance of a resolution of either House of Parliament.

Note: Commenced 10 February 2003 (SI 2003/1).

Removal

72. Serious criminal

(1) This section applies for the purpose of the construction and application of Article 33(2) of the Refugee Convention (exclusion from protection).

(2) A person shall be presumed to have been convicted by a final judgment of a particularly serious crime and to constitute a danger to the community of the United Kingdom if he is—
  (a) convicted in the United Kingdom of an offence, and
  (b) sentenced to a period of imprisonment of at least two years.

(3) A person shall be presumed to have been convicted by a final judgment of a particularly serious crime and to constitute a danger to the community of the United Kingdom if—
  (a) he is convicted outside the United Kingdom of an offence,
  (b) he is sentenced to a period of imprisonment of at least two years, and
  (c) he could have been sentenced to a period of imprisonment of at least two years had his conviction been a conviction in the United Kingdom of a similar offence.

(4) A person shall be presumed to have been convicted by a final judgment of a particularly serious crime and to constitute a danger to the community of the United Kingdom if—
  (a) he is convicted of an offence specified by order of the Secretary of State, or
  (b) he is convicted outside the United Kingdom of an offence and the Secretary of State certifies that in his opinion the offence is similar to an offence specified by order under paragraph (a).

(5) An order under subsection (4)—
  (a) must be made by statutory instrument, and
  (b) shall be subject to annulment in pursuance of a resolution of either House of Parliament.

(6) A presumption under subsection (2), (3) or (4) that a person constitutes a danger to the community is rebuttable by that person.

(7) A presumption under subsection (2), (3) or (4) does not apply while an appeal against conviction or sentence—

(a) is pending, or
(b) could be brought (disregarding the possibility of appeal out of time with leave).

(8) Section 34(1) of the Anti-terrorism, Crime and Security Act 2001 (c. 24) (no need to consider gravity of fear or threat of persecution) applies for the purpose of considering whether a presumption mentioned in subsection (6) has been rebutted as it applies for the purpose of considering whether Article 33(2) of the Refugee Convention applies.

(9) Subsection (10) applies where—
(a) a person appeals under section 82, 83 [, 83A] or 101 of this Act or under section 2 of the Special Immigration Appeals Commission Act 1997 (c. 68) wholly or partly on the ground that to remove him from or to require him to leave the United Kingdom would breach the United Kingdom's obligations under the Refugee Convention, and
(b) the Secretary of State issues a certificate that presumptions under subsection (2), (3) or (4) apply to the person (subject to rebuttal).

(10) The [. . .] Tribunal or Commission hearing the appeal—
(a) must begin substantive deliberation on the appeal by considering the certificate, and
(b) if in agreement that presumptions under subsection (2), (3) or (4) apply (having given the appellant an opportunity for rebuttal) must dismiss the appeal in so far as it relies on the ground specified in subsection (9)(a).

(11) For the purposes of this section—
(a) 'the Refugee Convention' means the Convention relating to the Status of Refugees done at Geneva on 28th July 1951 and its Protocol, and
(b) a reference to a person who is sentenced to a period of imprisonment of at least two years—
(i) does not include a reference to a person who receives a suspended sentence (unless at least two years of the sentence are not suspended),
(ii) includes a reference to a person who is sentenced to detention, or ordered or directed to be detained, in an institution other than a prison (including, in particular, a hospital or an institution for young offenders), and
(iii) includes a reference to a person who is sentenced to imprisonment or detention, or ordered or directed to be detained, for an indeterminate period (provided that it may last for two years).

Note: Subsections (1)–(8) and (11) commenced 10 February 2003 (SI 2003/1), remainder on 1 April 2003 (SI 2003/754). Word omitted by Sch 2 Asylum and Immigration Act 2004 from 4 April 2005 (SI 2005/565). Serious offences for the purposes of sub-s (4)(a) set out in SI 2004/1910. Words in square brackets in sub-s (9) inserted by Sch 1 Immigration, Asylum and Nationality Act 2006 from a date to be appointed.

73. Family

. . .

Note: Amends Sch 2 Immigration Act 1971 (c. 77); Immigration and Asylum Act 1999, s 10.

74. Deception

. . .

Note: Amends Immigration and Asylum Act 1999, s 10(1).

75. Exemption from deportation

. . .

Note: Amends Immigration Act 1971, s 7; Immigration and Asylum Act 1999, s 10.

76. Revocation of leave to enter or remain

(1) The Secretary of State may revoke a person's indefinite leave to enter or remain in the United Kingdom if the person—
 (a) is liable to deportation, but
 (b) cannot be deported for legal reasons.

(2) The Secretary of State may revoke a person's indefinite leave to enter or remain in the United Kingdom if—
 (a) the leave was obtained by deception,
 (b) the person would be liable to removal because of the deception, but
 (c) the person cannot be removed for legal or practical reasons.

(3) The Secretary of State may revoke a person's indefinite leave to enter or remain in the United Kingdom if the person, or someone of whom he is a dependant, ceases to be a refugee as a result of—
 (a) voluntarily availing himself of the protection of his country of nationality,
 (b) voluntarily re-acquiring a lost nationality,
 (c) acquiring the nationality of a country other than the United Kingdom and availing himself of its protection, or
 (d) voluntarily establishing himself in a country in respect of which he was a refugee.

(4) In this section—
 'indefinite leave' has the meaning given by section 33(1) of the Immigration Act 1971 (c. 77) (interpretation),
 'liable to deportation' has the meaning given by section 3(5) and (6) of that Act (deportation),
 'refugee' has the meaning given by the Convention relating to the Status of Refugees done at Geneva on 28th July 1951 and its Protocol, and
 'removed' means removed from the United Kingdom under—

(a) paragraph 9 or 10 of Schedule 2 to the Immigration Act 1971 (control of entry: directions for removal), or

(b) section 10(1)(b) of the Immigration and Asylum Act 1999 (c. 33) (removal of persons unlawfully in United Kingdom: deception).

(5) A power under subsection (1) or (2) to revoke leave may be exercised—

(a) in respect of leave granted before this section comes into force;

(b) in reliance on anything done before this section comes into force.

(6) A power under subsection (3) to revoke leave may be exercised—

(a) in respect of leave granted before this section comes into force, but

(b) only in reliance on action taken after this section comes into force.

(7) . . .

Note: Subsection (7) amends Immigration and Asylum Act 1999, s 10(1). Commencement 10 February 2003 (SI 2003/1).

77. No removal while claim for asylum pending

(1) While a person's claim for asylum is pending he may not be—

(a) removed from the United Kingdom in accordance with a provision of the Immigration Acts, or

(b) required to leave the United Kingdom in accordance with a provision of the Immigration Acts.

(2) In this section—

(a) 'claim for asylum' means a claim by a person that it would be contrary to the United Kingdom's obligations under the Refugee Convention to remove him from or require him to leave the United Kingdom, and

(b) a person's claim is pending until he is given notice of the Secretary of State's decision on it.

(3) In subsection (2) 'the Refugee Convention' means the Convention relating to the Status of Refugees done at Geneva on 28th July 1951 and its Protocol.

(4) Nothing in this section shall prevent any of the following while a claim for asylum is pending—

(a) the giving of a direction for the claimant's removal from the United Kingdom,

(b) the making of a deportation order in respect of the claimant, or

(c) the taking of any other interim or preparatory action.

(5) . . .

Note: Subsection (5) repeals Immigration and Asylum Act 1999, s 15. Commencement 1 April 2003 (SI 2003/754). Has effect in relation to a claim for asylum pending on 31 March 2003 as it has effect in relation to claims pending under the 2002 Act (SI 2003/754).

78. No removal while appeal pending

(1) While a person's appeal under section 82(1) is pending he may not be—
   (a) removed from the United Kingdom in accordance with a provision of the Immigration Acts, or
   (b) required to leave the United Kingdom in accordance with a provision of the Immigration Acts.

(2) In this section 'pending' has the meaning given by section 104.

(3) Nothing in this section shall prevent any of the following while an appeal is pending—
   (a) the giving of a direction for the appellant's removal from the United Kingdom,
   (b) the making of a deportation order in respect of the appellant (subject to section 79), or
   (c) the taking of any other interim or preparatory action.

(4) This section applies only to an appeal brought while the appellant is in the United Kingdom in accordance with section 92.

Note: Commencement 1 April 2003 (SI 2003/754). Has effect in relation to appeals pending under the old appeal provisions as it has effect in relation to an appeal pending under s 82(1) of the 2002 Act.

79. Deportation order: appeal

(1) A deportation order may not be made in respect of a person while an appeal under section 82(1) against the decision to make the order—
   (a) could be brought (ignoring any possibility of an appeal out of time with permission), or
   (b) is pending.

(2) In this section 'pending' has the meaning given by section 104.

Note: Commencement 1 April 2003 (SI 2003/754). Has effect in relation to an appeal pending under the old appeals provisions as it has effect in relation to an appeal pending under s 82(1) of the 2002 Act.

80. Removal of asylum-seeker to third country

. . .

Note: Amends Immigration and Asylum Act 1999, s 11.

Part V

Immigration and Asylum Appeals

[*Appeal to Tribunal*

81. The Asylum and Immigration Tribunal

(1) There shall be a tribunal to be known as the Asylum and Immigration Tribunal.

(2) Schedule 4 (which makes provision about the Tribunal) shall have effect.

(3) A reference in this Part to the Tribunal is a reference to the Asylum and Immigration Tribunal.]

Note: Section 81 substituted by Asylum and Immigration Act 2004, s 26 from 4 April 2005 (SI 2005/565)

82. Right of appeal: general

(1) Where an immigration decision is made in respect of a person he may appeal [to the Tribunal].

(2) In this Part 'immigration decision' means—
- (a) refusal of leave to enter the United Kingdom,
- (b) refusal of entry clearance,
- (c) refusal of a certificate of entitlement under section 10 of this Act,
- (d) refusal to vary a person's leave to enter or remain in the United Kingdom if the result of the refusal is that the person has no leave to enter or remain,
- (e) variation of a person's leave to enter or remain in the United Kingdom if when the variation takes effect the person has no leave to enter or remain,
- (f) revocation under section 76 of this Act of indefinite leave to enter or remain in the United Kingdom,
- (g) a decision that a person is to be removed from the United Kingdom by way of directions under [section 10(1)(a), (b), (ba) or (c)] of the Immigration and Asylum Act 1999 (c. 33) (removal of person unlawfully in United Kingdom),
- (h) a decision that an illegal entrant is to be removed from the United Kingdom by way of directions under paragraphs 8 to 10 of Schedule 2 to the Immigration Act 1971 (c. 77) (control of entry: removal),
- [(ha) a decision that a person is to be removed from the United Kingdom by way of directions under section 47 of the Immigration, Asylum and Nationality Act 2006 (removal: persons with statutorily extended leave),]
- (i) a decision that a person is to be removed from the United Kingdom by way of directions given by virtue of paragraph 10A of that Schedule (family),

[(ia) a decision that a person is to be removed from the United Kingdom by way of directions under paragraph 12(2) of Schedule 2 to the Immigration Act 1971 (c. 77) (seamen and aircrews),]

[(ib) a decision to make an order under section 2A of that Act (deprivation of right of abode),]

(j) a decision to make a deportation order under section 5(1) of that Act, and

(k) refusal to revoke a deportation order under section 5(2) of that Act.

(3) . . .

(4) The right of appeal under subsection (1) is subject to the exceptions and limitations specified in this Part.

Note: Commencement from 1 April 2003 (SI 2003/754, which sets out transitional provisions). Words in square brackets in sub-s (1) substituted by Asylum and Immigration Act 2004, s 26 from 4 April 2005 (SI 2005/565). Subsection (2)(ia) inserted by Asylum and Immigration Act 2004, s 26 from 4 April 2005 (SI 2005/565). Words in square brackets in sub-s (2)(g) substituted by Immigration Asylum and Nationality Act 2006, s 2 from 31 August 2006 (SI 2006/2226) in respect of decisions made on or after that date. Subsection (2)(ha) inserted by s 47 of that Act from a date to be appointed. Subsection (2)(ib) inserted by Immigration, Asylum and Nationality Act 2006, s 57 from 16 June 2006 (SI 2006/1497). Subsection (3) ceases to have effect from 31 August 2006 (SI 2006/2226), Immigration, Asylum and Nationality Act 2006, s 11, but continues to have effect in relation to decisions made before that date.

83. Appeal: asylum claim

(1) This section applies where a person has made an asylum claim and—

(a) his claim has been rejected by the Secretary of State, but

(b) he has been granted leave to enter or remain in the United Kingdom for a period exceeding one year (or for periods exceeding one year in aggregate).

(2) The person may appeal [to the Tribunal] against the rejection of his asylum claim.

Note: Commencement from 1 April 2003 (SI 2003/754, which sets out transitional provisions). Words in square brackets in sub-s (2) substituted by Asylum and Immigration Act 2004, s 26 from 4 April 2005 (SI 2005/565).

[83A. Appeal: variation of limited leave

(1) This section applies where—

(a) a person has made an asylum claim,

(b) he was granted limited leave to enter or remain in the United Kingdom as a refugee within the meaning of the Refugee Convention,

(c) a decision is made that he is not a refugee, and

(d) following the decision specified in paragraph (c) he has limited leave to enter or remain in the United Kingdom otherwise than as a refugee.

(2) The person may appeal to the Tribunal against the decision to curtail or to refuse to extend his limited leave.]

Note: Section 83A inserted by Immigration, Asylum and Nationality Act 2006, s 1 from 31 August 2006 (SI 2006/2226) in respect of decisions made on or after that date.

84. Grounds of appeal

(1) An appeal under section 82(1) against an immigration decision must be brought on one or more of the following grounds—
   (a) that the decision is not in accordance with immigration rules;
   (b) that the decision is unlawful by virtue of section 19B of the Race Relations Act 1976 (c. 74) (discrimination by public authorities);
   (c) that the decision is unlawful under section 6 of the Human Rights Act 1998 (c. 42) (public authority not to act contrary to Human Rights Convention) as being incompatible with the appellant's Convention rights;
   (d) that the appellant is an EEA national or a member of the family of an EEA national and the decision breaches the appellant's rights under the Community Treaties in respect of entry to or residence in the United Kingdom;
   (e) that the decision is otherwise not in accordance with the law;
   (f) that the person taking the decision should have exercised differently a discretion conferred by immigration rules;
   (g) that removal of the appellant from the United Kingdom in consequence of the immigration decision would breach the United Kingdom's obligations under the Refugee Convention or would be unlawful under section 6 of the Human Rights Act 1998 as being incompatible with the appellant's Convention rights.

(2) In subsection (1)(d) 'EEA national' means a national of a State which is a contracting party to the Agreement on the European Economic Area signed at Oporto on 2nd May 1992 (as it has effect from time to time).

(3) An appeal under section 83 must be brought on the grounds that removal of the appellant from the United Kingdom would breach the United Kingdom's obligations under the Refugee Convention.

[(4) An appeal under section 83A must be brought on the grounds that removal of the appellant from the United Kingdom would breach the United Kingdom's obligations under the Refugee Convention.]

Note: Commencement from 1 April 2003 (SI 2003/754, which sets out transitional provisions). Subsection (4) inserted by Immigration, Asylum and Nationality Act 2006, s 3 from 31 August 2006 (SI 2006/2226) in respect of decisions made on or after that date.

85. Matters to be considered

(1) An appeal under section 82(1) against a decision shall be treated by [the Tribunal] as including an appeal against any decision in respect of which the appellant has a right of appeal under section 82(1).

(2) If an appellant under section 82(1) makes a statement under section 120, [the

Tribunal] shall consider any matter raised in the statement which constitutes a ground of appeal of a kind listed in section 84(1) against the decision appealed against.

(3) Subsection (2) applies to a statement made under section 120 whether the statement was made before or after the appeal was commenced.

(4) On an appeal under section 82(1) [, 83(2) or 83A(2)] against a decision [the Tribunal] may consider evidence about any matter which [it] thinks relevant to the substance of the decision, including evidence which concerns a matter arising after the date of the decision.

(5) But in relation to an appeal under section 82(1) against refusal of entry clearance or refusal of a certificate of entitlement under section 10—
 (a) subsection (4) shall not apply, and
 (b) [the Tribunal] may consider only the circumstances appertaining at the time of the decision to refuse.

Note: Commencement from 1 April 2003 (SI 2003/754, which sets out transitional provisions). First words in square brackets in sub-s (4) substituted by Sch 1 Immigration, Asylum and Nationality Act 2006 from a date to be appointed. Other words in square brackets substituted by Sch 2 Asylum and Immigration Act 2004 from 4 April 2005 (SI 2005/565).

86. Determination of appeal

(1) This section applies on an appeal under section 82(1) [, 83 or 83A.]

(2) [the Tribunal] must determine—
 (a) any matter raised as a ground of appeal (whether or not by virtue of section 85(1)), and
 (b) any matter which section 85 requires [it] to consider.

(3) [the Tribunal] must allow the appeal in so far as [it] thinks that—
 (a) a decision against which the appeal is brought or is treated as being brought was not in accordance with the law (including immigration rules), or
 (b) a discretion exercised in making a decision against which the appeal is brought or is treated as being brought should have been exercised differently.

(4) For the purposes of subsection (3) a decision that a person should be removed from the United Kingdom under a provision shall not be regarded as unlawful if it could have been lawfully made by reference to removal under another provision.

(5) In so far as subsection (3) does not apply, [the Tribunal] shall dismiss the appeal.

(6) Refusal to depart from or to authorise departure from immigration rules is not the exercise of a discretion for the purposes of subsection (3)(b).

Note: Commencement from 1 April 2003 (SI 2003/754, which sets out transitional provisions). Words in square brackets in sub-s (1) substituted by Sch 1 Immigration, Asylum and Nationality Act 2006 from a date to be appointed. Other words in square brackets substituted by Sch 2 Asylum and Immigration Act 2004 from 4 April 2005 (SI 2005/565).

87. Successful appeal: direction

(1) If [the Tribunal] allows an appeal under section 82 [, 83 or 83A] [it] may give a direction for the purpose of giving effect to [its] decision.

(2) A person responsible for making an immigration decision shall act in accordance with any relevant direction under subsection (1).

[(3) But a direction under this section shall not have effect while—

(a) an application under section 103A(1) (other than an application out of time with permission) could be made or is awaiting determination,

(b) reconsideration of an appeal has been ordered under section 103A(1) and has not been completed,

(c) an appeal has been remitted to the Tribunal and is awaiting determination,

(d) an application under section 103B or 103E for permission to appeal (other than an application out of time with permission) could be made or is awaiting determination,

(e) an appeal under section 103B or 103E is awaiting determination, or

(f) a reference under section 103C is awaiting determination.]

(4) A direction under subsection (1) shall be treated [as part of the Tribunal's decision on the appeal for the purposes of section 103A]

Note: Commencement from 1 April 2003 (SI 2003/754, which sets out transitional provisions). Second words in square brackets in sub-s (1) substituted by Sch 1 Immigration, Asylum and Nationality Act 2006 from a date to be appointed. Other words in square brackets substituted by Sch 2 Asylum and Immigration Act 2004 from 4 April 2005 (SI 2005/565).

Exceptions and limitations

88. Ineligibility

(1) This section applies to an immigration decision of a kind referred to in section 82(2)(a), (b), (d) or (e).

(2) A person may not appeal under section 82(1) against an immigration decision which is taken on the grounds that he or a person of whom he is a dependant—

(a) does not satisfy a requirement as to age, nationality or citizenship specified in immigration rules,

(b) does not have an immigration document of a particular kind (or any immigration document),

[(ba) has failed to supply a medical report or a medical certificate in accordance with a requirement of immigration rules,]

(c) is seeking to be in the United Kingdom for a period greater than that permitted in his case by immigration rules, or
(d) is seeking to enter or remain in the United Kingdom for a purpose other than one for which entry or remaining is permitted in accordance with immigration rules.

(3) In subsection (2)(b) 'immigration document' means—
(a) entry clearance,
(b) a passport,
(c) a work permit or other immigration employment document within the meaning of section 122, and
(d) a document which relates to a national of a country other than the United Kingdom and which is designed to serve the same purpose as a passport.

(4) Subsection (2) does not prevent the bringing of an appeal on any or all of the grounds referred to in section 84(1)(b), (c) and (g).

Note: Commencement from 1 April 2003 (SI 2003/754, which sets out transitional provisions). Subsection (2)(ba) inserted by Immigration, Asylum and Nationality Act 2006, s 5 from 31 August 2006 (SI 2006/2226) in respect of decisions made on or after that date.

[88A. Entry clearance

(1) A person may not appeal under section 82(1) against refusal of an application for entry clearance unless the application was made for the purpose of—
(a) visiting a person of a class or description prescribed by regulations for the purpose of this subsection, or
(b) entering as the dependant of a person in circumstances prescribed by regulations for the purpose of this subsection.

(2) Regulations under subsection (1) may, in particular—
(a) make provision by reference to whether the applicant is a member of the family (within such meaning as the regulations may assign) of the person he seeks to visit;
(b) provide for the determination of whether one person is dependent on another;
(c) make provision by reference to the circumstances of the applicant, of the person whom the applicant seeks to visit or on whom he depends, or of both (and the regulations may, in particular, include provision by reference to—
(i) whether or not a person is lawfully settled in the United Kingdom within such meaning as the regulations may assign;
(ii) the duration of two individuals' residence together);
(d) make provision by reference to an applicant's purpose in entering as a dependant;
(e) make provision by reference to immigration rules;
(f) confer a discretion.

(3) Subsection (1)—
   (a) does not prevent the bringing of an appeal on either or both of the grounds referred to in section 84(1)(b) and (c), and
   (b) is without prejudice to the effect of section 88 in relation to an appeal under section 82(1) against refusal of entry clearance.]

Note: Section 88A substituted for ss 88A, 90 and 91 by Immigration, Asylum and Nationality Act 2006, s 4 from a date to be appointed.

[89. Refusal of leave to enter

(1) A person may not appeal under section 82(1) against refusal of leave to enter the United Kingdom unless—
   (a) on his arrival in the United Kingdom he had entry clearance, and
   (b) the purpose of entry specified in the entry clearance is the same as that specified in his application for leave to enter.

(2) Subsection (1) does not prevent the bringing of an appeal on any or all of the grounds referred to in section 84(1)(b), (c) and (g).]

Note: Section 89 substituted by Immigration, Asylum and Nationality Act 2006, s 6 from 31 August 2006 (SI 2006/2226), without effect in relation to decisions made before that date.

90. . . .

Note: See note to s. 88A above.

91. . . .

Note: See note to s. 88A above.

92. Appeal from within United Kingdom: general

(1) A person may not appeal under section 82(1) while he is in the United Kingdom unless his appeal is of a kind to which this section applies.

(2) This section applies to an appeal against an immigration decision of a kind specified in section 82(2)(c), (d), (e), (f) [, (ha)] and (j).

[(3) This section also applies to an appeal against refusal of leave to enter the United Kingdom if—
   (a) at the time of the refusal the appellant is in the United Kingdom, and
   (b) on his arrival in the United Kingdom the appellant had entry clearance.

(3A) But this section does not apply by virtue of subsection (3) if subsection (3B) or (3C) applies to the refusal of leave to enter.

(3B) This subsection applies to a refusal of leave to enter which is a deemed refusal under paragraph 2A(9) of Schedule 2 to the Immigration Act 1971 (c. 77) resulting from cancellation of leave to enter by an immigration officer—
   (a) under paragraph 2A(8) of that Schedule, and
   (b) on the grounds specified in paragraph 2A(2A) of that Schedule.

(3C) This subsection applies to a refusal of leave to enter which specifies that the grounds for refusal are that the leave is sought for a purpose other than that specified in the entry clearance.

(3D) This section also applies to an appeal against refusal of leave to enter the United Kingdom if at the time of the refusal the appellant—
- (a) is in the United Kingdom,
- (b) has a work permit, and
- (c) is any of the following (within the meaning of the British Nationality Act 1981 (c. 61))—
  - (i) a British overseas territories citizen,
  - (ii) a British Overseas citizen,
  - (iii) a British National (Overseas),
  - (iv) a British protected person, or
  - (v) a British subject.]

(4) This section also applies to an appeal against an immigration decision if the appellant—
- (a) has made an asylum claim, or a human rights claim, while in the United Kingdom, or
- (b) is an EEA national or a member of the family of an EEA national and makes a claim to the Secretary of State that the decision breaches the appellant's rights under the Community Treaties in respect of entry to or residence in the United Kingdom.

Note: Commencement from 1 April 2003 (SI 2003/754, which sets out transitional provisions). Subsection (3) substituted by Asylum and Immigration Act 2004, s 28 from 1 October 2004 (SI 2004/2523). Words in square brackets in sub-s (2) substituted by Immigration, Asylum and Nationality Act 2006, s 47 from a date to be appointed.

93. Appeal from within United Kingdom: 'third country' removal

. . .

Note: Section 93 ceased to have effect from 1 October 2004, Asylum and Immigration Act 2004, s 33 (SI 2004/2523).

94. Appeal from within United Kingdom: unfounded human rights or asylum claim

(1) This section applies to an appeal under section 82(1) where the appellant has made an asylum claim or a human rights claim (or both).

[(1A) A person may not bring an appeal against an immigration decision of a kind specified in section 82(2)(c), (d) [(e) or (ha)] in reliance on section 92(2) if the Secretary of State certifies that the claim or claims mentioned in subsection (1) above is or are clearly unfounded.]

(2) A person may not bring an appeal to which this section applies [in reliance on

section 92(4)(a)] if the Secretary of State certifies that the claim or claims mentioned in subsection (1) is or are clearly unfounded.

(3) If the Secretary of State is satisfied that an asylum claimant or human rights claimant is entitled to reside in a State listed in subsection (4) he shall certify the claim under subsection (2) unless satisfied that it is not clearly unfounded.

(4) Those States are—

(a)–(j) . . .
[(k) the Republic of Albania,
(l) Bulgaria,
(m) Serbia and Montenegro,
(n) Jamaica,
(o) Macedonia,
(p) the Republic of Moldova, and
(q) Romania.]
[(r) . . .
(s) Bolivia,
(t) Brazil,
(u) Ecuador,
(v) Sri Lanka,
(w) South Africa, and
(x) Ukraine.]
[(z) Mongolia,
(aa) Ghana (in respect of men),
(bb) Nigeria (in respect of men).]

(5) The Secretary of State may by order add a State, or part of a State, to the list in subsection (4) if satisfied that—

(a) there is in general in that State or part no serious risk of persecution of persons entitled to reside in that State or part, and
(b) removal to that State or part of persons entitled to reside there will not in general contravene the United Kingdom's obligations under the Human Rights Convention.

[(5A) If the Secretary of State is satisfied that the statements in subsection (5) (a) and (b) are true of a State or part of a State in relation to a description of person, an order under subsection (5) may add the State or part to the list in subsection (4) in respect of that description of person.

(5B) Where a State or part of a State is added to the list in subsection (4) in respect of a description of person, subsection (3) shall have effect in relation to a claimant only if the Secretary of State is satisfied that he is within that description (as well as being satisfied that he is entitled to reside in the State or part).

(5C) A description for the purposes of subsection (5A) may refer to—

(a) gender,
(b) language,
(c) race,
(d) religion,
(e) nationality,
(f) membership of a social or other group,
(g) political opinion, or
(h) any other attribute or circumstance that the Secretary of State thinks appropriate.]

[(**6**) The Secretary of State may by order amend the list in subsection (4) so as to omit a State or part added under subsection (5); and the omission may be—
- (a) general, or
- (b) effected so that the State or part remains listed in respect of a description of person.]

[(**6A**) Subsection (3) shall not apply in relation to an asylum claimant or human rights claimant who—
- (a) is the subject of a certificate under section 2 or 70 of the Extradition Act 2003 (c. 41),
- (b) is in custody pursuant to arrest under section 5 of that Act,
- (c) is the subject of a provisional warrant under section 73 of that Act,
- (d) is the subject of an authority to proceed under section 7 of the Extradition Act 1989 (c. 33) or an order under paragraph 4(2) of Schedule 1 to that Act, or
- (e) is the subject of a provisional warrant under section 8 of that Act or of a warrant under paragraph 5(1)(b) of Schedule 1 to that Act.]

[(**6B**) A certificate under subsection (1A) or (2) may not be issued (and subsection (3) shall not apply) in relation to an appeal under section 82(2)(d) or (e) against a decision relating to leave to enter or remain in the United Kingdom, where the leave was given in circumstances specified for the purposes of this subsection by order of the Secretary of State.]

(**7**) A person may not bring an appeal to which this section applies in reliance on section 92(4) if the Secretary of State certifies that—
- (a) it is proposed to remove the person to a country of which he is not a national or citizen, and
- (b) there is no reason to believe that the person's rights under the Human Rights Convention will be breached in that country.

(**8**) In determining whether a person in relation to whom a certificate has been issued under subsection (7) may be removed from the United Kingdom, the country specified in the certificate is to be regarded as—
- (a) a place where a person's life and liberty is not threatened by reason of his race, religion, nationality, membership of a particular social group, or political opinion, and
- (b) a place from which a person will not be sent to another country otherwise than in accordance with the Refugee Convention.

(**9**) Where a person in relation to whom a certificate is issued under this section subsequently brings an appeal under section 82(1) while outside the United Kingdom, the appeal shall be considered as if he had not been removed from the United Kingdom.

Note: Subsection (5) commenced 10 February 2003 for the purposes of enabling subordinate legislation, SI 2003/249. Remainder from 1 April 2003 (SI 2003/754, which sets out transitional provisions). Words in square brackets in sub-s (1A) substituted by Immigration, Asylum and

Nationality Act 2006, s 47 from a date to be appointed. Subsection (6B) inserted by Immigration, Asylum and Nationality Act 2006, s 13 from a date to be appointed. Subsection 4: words in first square brackets added by SI 2003/970 from 1 April 2003, words in 2nd square brackets added by SI 2003/1919 from 23 July 2003, Bangladesh omitted and last words in square brackets inserted from December 2005 (SI 2005/3306). First words omitted and other words in square brackets substituted or added by Asylum and Immigration Act 2004, s 27 from 1 October 2004 (SI 2004/2523). Other word omitted from 22 April 2005 (SI 2005/1016).

95. Appeal from outside United Kingdom: removal

A person who is outside the United Kingdom may not appeal under section 82(1) on the ground specified in section 84(1)(g) (except in a case to which section 94(9) applies).

Note: Commencement from 1 April 2003 (SI 2003/754, which sets out transitional provisions).

96. Earlier right of appeal

[(1) An appeal under section 82(1) against an immigration decision ('the new decision') in respect of a person may not be brought if the Secretary of State or an immigration officer certifies—

(a) that the person was notified of a right of appeal under that section against another immigration decision ('the old decision') (whether or not an appeal was brought and whether or not any appeal brought has been determined),

(b) that the claim or application to which the new decision relates relies on a matter that could have been raised in an appeal against the old decision, and

(c) that, in the opinion of the Secretary of State or the immigration officer, there is no satisfactory reason for that matter not having been raised in an appeal against the old decision.

(2) An appeal under section 82(1) against an immigration decision ('the new decision') in respect of a person may not be brought if the Secretary of State or an immigration officer certifies—

(a) that the person received a notice under section 120 by virtue of an application other than that to which the new decision relates or by virtue of a decision other than the new decision,

(b) that the new decision relates to an application or claim which relies on a matter that should have been, but has not been, raised in a statement made in response to that notice, and

(c) that, in the opinion of the Secretary of State or the immigration officer, there is no satisfactory reason for that matter not having been raised in a statement made in response to that notice.]

(4) In subsection (1) 'notified' means notified in accordance with regulations under section 105.

(5) [Subsections (1) and (2) apply to prevent] a person's right of appeal whether or

not he has been outside the United Kingdom since an earlier right of appeal arose or since a requirement under section 120 was imposed.

(6) In this section a reference to an appeal under section 82(1) includes a reference to an appeal under section 2 of the Special Immigration Appeals Commission Act 1997 (c. 68) which is or could be brought by reference to an appeal under section 82(1).

[(7) A certificate under subsection (1) or (2) shall have no effect in relation to an appeal instituted before the certificate is issued.]

Note: Commencement from 1 April 2003 (SI 2003/754, which sets out transitional provisions). Words in square brackets substituted and sub-s (7) added by Asylum and Immigration Act 2004, s 30 from 1 October 2004 (SI 2004/2523).

97. National security, &c.

(1) An appeal under section 82(1) [, 83(2) or 83A(2)] against a decision in respect of a person may not be brought or continued if the Secretary of State certifies that the decision is or was taken—

(a) by the Secretary of State wholly or partly on a ground listed in subsection (2), or

(b) in accordance with a direction of the Secretary of State which identifies the person to whom the decision relates and which is given wholly or partly on a ground listed in subsection (2).

(2) The grounds mentioned in subsection (1) are that the person's exclusion or removal from the United Kingdom is—

(a) in the interests of national security, or

(b) in the interests of the relationship between the United Kingdom and another country.

(3) An appeal under section 82(1) [, 83(2) or 83A(2)] against a decision may not be brought or continued if the Secretary of State certifies that the decision is or was taken wholly or partly in reliance on information which in his opinion should not be made public—

(a) in the interests of national security,

(b) in the interests of the relationship between the United Kingdom and another country, or

(c) otherwise in the public interest.

(4) In subsections (1)(a) and (b) and (3) a reference to the Secretary of State is to the Secretary of State acting in person.

Note: Commencement from 1 April 2003 (SI 2003/754, which sets out transitional provisions). Words in square brackets in sub-ss (1) and (3) substituted by Sch 1 Immigration, Asylum and Nationality Act 2006 from a date to be appointed.

[97A. National security: deportation

(1) This section applies where the Secretary of State certifies that the decision to

make a deportation order in respect of a person was taken on the grounds that his removal from the United Kingdom would be in the interests of national security.

(2) Where this section applies—
  (a) section 79 shall not apply,
  (b) the Secretary of State shall be taken to have certified the decision to make the deportation order under section 97, and
  (c) for the purposes of section 2(5) of the Special Immigration Appeals Commission Act 1997 (c. 68) (appeals from within United Kingdom) it shall be assumed that section 92 of this Act—
    (i) would not apply to an appeal against the decision to make the deportation order by virtue of section 92(2) to (3D),
    (ii) would not apply to an appeal against that decision by virtue of section 92(4)(a) in respect of an asylum claim, and
    (iii) would be capable of applying to an appeal against that decision by virtue of section 92(4)(a) in respect of a human rights claim unless the Secretary of State certifies that the removal of the person from the United Kingdom would not breach the United Kingdom's obligations under the Human Rights Convention.

(3) A person in respect of whom a certificate is issued under subsection (2)(c)(iii) may appeal to the Special Immigration Appeals Commission against the issue of the certificate; and for that purpose the Special Immigration Appeals Commission Act 1997 shall apply as to an appeal against an immigration decision to which section 92 of this Act applies.

(4) The Secretary of State may repeal this section by order.]

Note: Section 97A inserted by Immigration, Asylum and Nationality Act 2006, s 7 from 31 August 2006 (SI 2006/2226).

98. Other grounds of public good

(1) This section applies to an immigration decision of a kind referred to in section 82(2)(a) or (b).

(2) An appeal under section 82(1) against an immigration decision may not be brought or continued if the Secretary of State certifies that the decision is or was taken—
  (a) by the Secretary of State wholly or partly on the ground that the exclusion or removal from the United Kingdom of the person to whom the decision relates is conducive to the public good, or
  (b) in accordance with a direction of the Secretary of State which identifies the person to whom the decision relates and which is given wholly or partly on that ground.

(3) In subsection (2)(a) and (b) a reference to the Secretary of State is to the Secretary of State acting in person.

(4) Subsection (2) does not prevent the bringing of an appeal on either or both of the grounds referred to in section 84(1)(b) and (c).

(5) Subsection (2) does not prevent the bringing of an appeal against an immigration decision of the kind referred to in section 82(2)(a) on the grounds referred to in section 84(1)(g).

Note: Commencement from 1 April 2003 (SI 2003/754, which sets out transitional provisions).

99. Sections 96 to 98: appeal in progress

(1) This section applies where a certificate is issued under section 96(1) or (2), 97 or 98 in respect of a pending appeal.

(2) The appeal shall lapse.

Note: Commencement from 1 April 2003 (SI 2003/754, which sets out transitional provisions).

Appeal from adjudicator

100. Immigration Appeal Tribunal

. . .

Note: Section 100 ceases to have effect, Asylum and Immigration Act 2004, s 26 from 4 April 2005 (SI 2005/565).

101. Appeal to Tribunal

. . .

Note: Section 101 ceases to have effect, Asylum and Immigration Act 2004, s 26 from 4 April 2005 (SI 2005/565).

102. Decision

. . .

Note: Section 102 ceases to have effect from 4 April 2005 (SI 2005/565), Asylum and Immigration Act 2004, s 26.

103. Appeal from Tribunal

. . .

Note: Section 103 ceases to have effect from 4 April 2005 (SI 2005/565), Asylum and Immigration Act 2004, s 26.

[103A. Review of Tribunal's decision

(1) A party to an appeal under section 82 [, 83 or 83A] may apply to the appropriate court, on the grounds that the Tribunal made an error of law, for an order requiring the Tribunal to reconsider its decision on the appeal.

(2) The appropriate court may make an order under subsection (1)—
   (a) only if it thinks that the Tribunal may have made an error of law, and
   (b) only once in relation to an appeal.

(3) An application under subsection (1) must be made—
(a) in the case of an application by the appellant made while he is in the United Kingdom, within the period of 5 days beginning with the date on which he is treated, in accordance with rules under section 106, as receiving notice of the Tribunal's decision,
(b) in the case of an application by the appellant made while he is outside the United Kingdom, within the period of 28 days beginning with the date on which he is treated, in accordance with rules under section 106, as receiving notice of the Tribunal's decision, and
(c) in the case of an application brought by a party to the appeal other than the appellant, within the period of 5 days beginning with the date on which he is treated, in accordance with rules under section 106, as receiving notice of the Tribunal's decision.

(4) But—
(a) rules of court may specify days to be disregarded in applying subsection (3)(a), (b) or (c), and
(b) the appropriate court may permit an application under subsection (1) to be made outside the period specified in subsection (3) where it thinks that the application could not reasonably practicably have been made within that period.

(5) An application under subsection (1) shall be determined by reference only to—
(a) written submissions of the applicant, and
(b) where rules of court permit, other written submissions.

(6) A decision of the appropriate court on an application under subsection (1) shall be final.

(7) In this section a reference to the Tribunal's decision on an appeal does not include a reference to—
(a) a procedural, ancillary or preliminary decision, or
(b) a decision following remittal under section 103B, 103C or 103E.

(8) This section does not apply to a decision of the Tribunal where its jurisdiction is exercised by three or more legally qualified members.

(9) In this section 'the appropriate court' means—
(a) in relation to an appeal decided in England or Wales, the High Court,
(b) in relation to an appeal decided in Scotland, the Court of Session, and
(c) in relation to an appeal decided in Northern Ireland, the High Court in Northern Ireland.

(10) An application under subsection (1) to the Court of Session shall be to the Outer House.

103B. Appeal from Tribunal following reconsideration

(1) Where an appeal to the Tribunal has been reconsidered, a party to the appeal may bring a further appeal on a point of law to the appropriate appellate court.

(2) In subsection (1) the reference to reconsideration is to reconsideration pursuant to—
  (a) an order under section 103A(1), or
  (b) remittal to the Tribunal under this section or under section 103C or 103E.

(3) An appeal under subsection (1) may be brought only with the permission of—
  (a) the Tribunal, or
  (b) if the Tribunal refuses permission, the appropriate appellate court.

(4) On an appeal under subsection (1) the appropriate appellate court may—
  (a) affirm the Tribunal's decision;
  (b) make any decision which the Tribunal could have made;
  (c) remit the case to the Tribunal;
  (d) affirm a direction under section 87;
  (e) vary a direction under section 87;
  (f) give a direction which the Tribunal could have given under section 87.

(5) In this section 'the appropriate appellate court' means—
  (a) in relation to an appeal decided in England or Wales, the Court of Appeal,
  (b) in relation to an appeal decided in Scotland, the Court of Session, and
  (c) in relation to an appeal decided in Northern Ireland, the Court of Appeal in Northern Ireland.

(6) An appeal under subsection (1) to the Court of Session shall be to the Inner House.

103C. Appeal from Tribunal instead of reconsideration

(1) On an application under section 103A in respect of an appeal the appropriate court, if it thinks the appeal raises a question of law of such importance that it should be decided by the appropriate appellate court, may refer the appeal to that court.

(2) On a reference under subsection (1) the appropriate appellate court may—
  (a) affirm the Tribunal's decision;
  (b) make any decision which the Tribunal could have made;
  (c) remit the case to the Tribunal;
  (d) affirm a direction under section 87;
  (e) vary a direction under section 87;
  (f) give a direction which the Tribunal could have given under section 87;
  (g) restore the application under section 103A to the appropriate court.

(3) In this section—

'the appropriate court' has the same meaning as in section 103A, and
'the appropriate appellate court' has the same meaning as in section 103B.

(4) A reference under subsection (1) to the Court of Session shall be to the Inner House.

103D. Reconsideration: legal aid

(1) On the application of an appellant under section 103A, the appropriate court may order that the appellant's costs in respect of the application under section 103A shall be paid out of the Community Legal Service Fund established under section 5 of the Access to Justice Act 1999 (c. 22).

(2) Subsection (3) applies [where an order for reconsideration is made]—
  (a) under section 103A(1), and
  (b) on the application of the appellant.

[(3) The Tribunal may order payment out of that Fund of the appellant's costs—
  (a) in respect of the application for reconsideration;
  (b) in respect of preparation for reconsideration;
  (c) in respect of the reconsideration.]

(4) The Secretary of State may make regulations about the exercise of the powers in subsections (1) and (3).

(5) Regulations under subsection (4) may, in particular, make provision—
  (a) specifying or providing for the determination of the amount of payments;
  (b) about the persons to whom the payments are to be made;
  (c) restricting the exercise of the power (whether by reference to the prospects of success in respect of the appeal at the time when the application for reconsideration was made, the fact that a reference has been made under section 103C(1), the circumstances of the appellant, the nature of the appellant's legal representatives, or otherwise).

(6) Regulations under subsection (4) may make provision—
  (a) conferring a function on the Legal Services Commission;
  (b) modifying a duty or power of the Legal Services Commission in respect of compliance with orders under subsection (3);
  (c) applying (with or without modifications), modifying or disapplying a provision of, or of anything done under, an enactment relating to the funding of legal services.

(7) Before making regulations under subsection (4) the Secretary of State shall consult such persons as he thinks appropriate.

(8) This section has effect only in relation to an appeal decided in—
  (a) England,
  (b) Wales, or
  (c) Northern Ireland.

(9) In relation to an appeal decided in Northern Ireland this section shall have effect—
   (a) as if a reference to the Community Legal Service Fund were to the fund established under paragraph 4(2)(a) of Schedule 3 to the Access to Justice (Northern Ireland) Order 2003 (S.I. 2003/ 435 (N.I. 10)), and
   (b) with any other necessary modifications.

103E. Appeal from Tribunal sitting as panel

(1) This section applies to a decision of the Tribunal on an appeal under section 82 [, 83 or 83A] where its jurisdiction is exercised by three or more legally qualified members.

(2) A party to the appeal may bring a further appeal on a point of law to the appropriate appellate court.

(3) An appeal under subsection (2) may be brought only with the permission of—
   (a) the Tribunal, or
   (b) if the Tribunal refuses permission, the appropriate appellate court.

(4) On an appeal under subsection (2) the appropriate appellate court may—
   (a) affirm the Tribunal's decision;
   (b) make any decision which the Tribunal could have made;
   (c) remit the case to the Tribunal;
   (d) affirm a direction under section 87;
   (e) vary a direction under section 87;
   (f) give a direction which the Tribunal could have given under section 87.

(5) In this section 'the appropriate appellate court' means—
   (a) in relation to an appeal decided in England or Wales, the Court of Appeal,
   (b) in relation to an appeal decided in Scotland, the Court of Session, and
   (c) in relation to an appeal decided in Northern Ireland, the Court of Appeal in Northern Ireland.

(6) A further appeal under subsection (2) to the Court of Session shall be to the Inner House.

(7) In this section a reference to the Tribunal's decision on an appeal does not include a reference to—
   (a) a procedural, ancillary or preliminary decision, or
   (b) a decision following remittal under section 103B or 103C.]

Note: Sections 103A–E inserted by Asylum and Immigration Act 2004, s 26 from 4 April 2005 (SI 2005/565). Words in square brackets in sub-ss 103A(1) and 103E(1) substituted by Sch 1 Immigration, Asylum and Nationality Act 2006 from a date to be appointed. Words in square brackets in sub-s 103D substituted by Immigration, Asylum and Nationality Act 2006, s 8 from a date to be appointed.

Procedure

104. Pending appeal

(1) An appeal under section 82(1) is pending during the period—
   (a) beginning when it is instituted, and
   (b) ending when it is finally determined, withdrawn or abandoned (or when it lapses under section 99).

[(2) An appeal under section 82(1) is not finally determined for the purposes of subsection (1)(b) while—
   (a) an application under section 103A(1) (other than an application out of time with permission) could be made or is awaiting determination,
   (b) reconsideration of an appeal has been ordered under section 103A(1) and has not been completed,
   (c) an appeal has been remitted to the Tribunal and is awaiting determination,
   (d) an application under section 103B or 103E for permission to appeal (other than an application out of time with permission) could be made or is awaiting determination,
   (e) an appeal under section 103B or 103E is awaiting determination, or
   (f) a reference under section 103C is awaiting determination.]

(3) . . .

[(4) An appeal under section 82(1) brought by a person while he is in the United Kingdom shall be treated as abandoned if the appellant leaves the United Kingdom.

(4A) An appeal under section 82(1) brought by a person while he is in the United Kingdom shall be treated as abandoned if the appellant is granted leave to enter or remain in the United Kingdom (subject to subsections (4B) and (4C)).

(4B) Subsection (4A) shall not apply to an appeal in so far as it is brought on the ground relating to the Refugee Convention specified in section 84(1)(g) where the appellant—
   (a) is granted leave to enter or remain in the United Kingdom for a period exceeding 12 months, and
   (b) gives notice, in accordance with any relevant procedural rules (which may include provision about timing), that he wishes to pursue the appeal in so far as it is brought on that ground.

(4C) Subsection (4A) shall not apply to an appeal in so far as it is brought on the ground specified in section 84(1)(b) where the appellant gives notice, in accordance with any relevant procedural rules (which may include provision about timing), that he wishes to pursue the appeal in so far as it is brought on that ground.]

(5) An appeal under section 82(2)(a), (c), (d), (e) or (f) shall be treated as finally determined if a deportation order is made against the appellant.

Note: Commencement from 1 April 2003 (SI 2003/754). Subsection (2) substituted and sub-s (3) omitted by Sch 2 Asylum and Immigration Act 2004 from 4 April 2005 (SI 2005/565). Subsection (4) substituted and sub-ss (4A)–(4C) inserted by Immigration, Asylum and Nationality Act 2006, s 9 from 13 November 2006 (SI 2006/2838).

105. Notice of immigration decision

(1) The Secretary of State may make regulations requiring a person to be given written notice where an immigration decision is taken in respect of him.

(2) The regulations may, in particular, provide that a notice under subsection (1) of a decision against which the person is entitled to appeal under section 82(1) must state—

(a) that there is a right of appeal under that section, and

(b) how and when that right may be exercised.

(3) The regulations may make provision (which may include presumptions) about service.

Note: Commencement from 1 April 2003 (SI 2003/754).

106. Rules

(1) The Lord Chancellor may make rules—

(a) regulating the exercise of the right of appeal under section 82, [[, 83 or 83A] or by virtue of section 109]

(b) prescribing procedure to be followed in connection with proceedings under section 82, [[, 83 or 83A] or by virtue of section 109]

[(1A) In making rules under subsection (1) the Lord Chancellor shall aim to ensure—

(a) that the rules are designed to ensure that proceedings before the Tribunal are handled as fairly, quickly and efficiently as possible, and

(b) that the rules where appropriate confer on members of the Tribunal responsibility for ensuring that proceedings before the Tribunal are handled as fairly, quickly and efficiently as possible.]

(2) In particular, rules under subsection (1)—

(a) must entitle an appellant to be legally represented at any hearing of his appeal;

(b) may enable or require an appeal to be determined without a hearing;

(c) may enable or require an appeal to be dismissed without substantive consideration where practice or procedure has not been complied with;

(d) may enable or require [the Tribunal] to treat an appeal as abandoned in specified circumstances;

(e) may enable or require . . . the Tribunal to determine an appeal in the absence of parties in specified circumstances;
(f) may enable or require . . . the Tribunal to determine an appeal by reference only to written submissions in specified circumstances;
(g) may make provision about the adjournment of an appeal by [the Tribunal] (which may include provision prohibiting [the Tribunal] from adjourning except in specified circumstances);
(h) may make provision about the treatment of adjourned appeals by [the Tribunal] (which may include provision requiring [the Tribunal] to determine an appeal within a specified period);
(i) may make provision about the use of electronic communication in the course of or in connection with a hearing;
(j) . . .
(k) . . .
(l) may enable the Tribunal to set aside a decision of the Tribunal;
(m) must make provision about the consolidation of appeals . . .
(n) may make provision (which may include presumptions) about service;
(o) may confer ancillary powers on . . . the Tribunal;
(p) may confer a discretion on . . . the Tribunal;
(q) may require . . . the Tribunal to give notice of a determination to a specified person;
(r) may require or enable notice of a determination to be given on behalf of . . . the Tribunal;
(s) may make provision about the grant of bail by an adjudicator or the Tribunal (which may, in particular, include provision which applies or is similar to any enactment).
[(t) may make provision about the number of members exercising the Tribunal's jurisdiction;
(u) may make provision about the allocation of proceedings among members of the Tribunal (which may include provision for transfer);
(v) may make provision about reconsideration of a decision pursuant to an order under section 103A(1) (which may, in particular, include provision about the action that may be taken on reconsideration and about the matters and evidence to which the Tribunal may have regard);
(w) shall provide that a party to an appeal is to be treated as having received notice of the Tribunal's decision, unless the contrary is shown, at such time as may be specified in, or determined in accordance with, the rules;
(x) may make provision about proceedings under paragraph 30 of Schedule 2 to the Asylum and Immigration (Treatment of Claimants, etc.) Act 2004 (transitional filter of applications for reconsideration from High Court to Tribunal) (and may, in particular, make provision of a kind that may be made by rules of court under section 103A(5)(b));

(y) may make provision about the form and content of decisions of the Tribunal.]

(3) Rules under subsection (1)—
(a) may enable . . . the Tribunal to make an award of costs or expenses,
(b) may make provision (which may include provision conferring discretion on a court) for the taxation or assessment of costs or expenses,
(c) may make provision about interest on an award of costs or expenses (which may include provision conferring a discretion or providing for interest to be calculated in accordance with provision made by the rules),
(d) may enable . . . the Tribunal to disallow all or part of a representative's costs or expenses,
(e) may enable . . . the Tribunal to require a representative to pay specified costs or expenses, and
[(f) may enable the Tribunal to certify that an appeal had no merit (and shall make provision for the consequences of the issue of a certificate).]

(4) A person commits an offence if without reasonable excuse he fails to comply with a requirement imposed in accordance with rules under subsection (1) to attend before . . . the Tribunal—
(a) to give evidence, or
(b) to produce a document.

(5) A person who is guilty of an offence under subsection (4) shall be liable on summary conviction to a fine not exceeding level 3 on the standard scale.

Note: Commencement from 1 April 2003 (SI 2003/754). Amended by Sch 2 Asylum and immigration Act 2004, from 4 April 2005 (SI 2005/565). Words in first square brackets in sub-ss (1)(a) and (b) substituted by Sch 1 Immigration, Asylum and Nationality Act 2006 from a date to be appointed.

107. Practice directions

(1) The President of [the Tribunal] may give directions as to the practice to be followed by the Tribunal.

(2) . . .

[(3) A practice direction may, in particular, require the Tribunal to treat a specified decision of the Tribunal as authoritative in respect of a particular matter.]

Note: Commencement from 1 April 2003 (SI 2003/754). Amended by Sch 2 Asylum and immigration Act 2004, from 4 April 2005 (SI 2005/565).

108. Forged document: proceedings in private

(1) This section applies where it is alleged—
(a) that a document relied on by a party to an appeal under section 82, [, 83 or 83A] is a forgery, and

(b) that disclosure to that party of a matter relating to the detection of the forgery would be contrary to the public interest.

(2) [The Tribunal]

(a) must investigate the allegation in private, and

(b) may proceed in private so far as necessary to prevent disclosure of the matter referred to in subsection (1)(b).

Note: Commencement from 1 April 2003 (SI 2003/754). Amended by Sch 2 Asylum and immigration Act 2004, from 4 April 2005 (SI 2005/565). Words in square brackets in sub-s (1)(a) substituted by Sch 1 Immigration, Asylum and Nationality Act 2006 from a date to be appointed.

General

109. European Union and European economic area

(1) Regulations may provide for, or make provision about, an appeal against an immigration decision taken in respect of a person who has or claims to have a right under any of the Community Treaties.

(2) The regulations may—

(a) apply a provision of this Act or the Special Immigration Appeals Commission Act 1997 (c. 68) with or without modification;

(b) make provision similar to a provision made by or under this Act or that Act;

(c) disapply or modify the effect of a provision of this Act or that Act.

(3) In subsection (1) 'immigration decision' means a decision about—

(a) a person's entitlement to enter or remain in the United Kingdom, or

(b) removal of a person from the United Kingdom.

Note: Commencement from 1 April 2003 (SI 2003/754).

110. Grants

. . .

Note: Commencement from 1 April 2003 (SI 2003/754). Ceased to have effect from 16 June 2006, Immigration, Asylum and Nationality Act 2006, s 10 (SI 2006/1497).

111. Monitor of certification of claims as unfounded

(1) The Secretary of State shall appoint a person to monitor the use of the powers under sections 94(2) and 115(1).

(2) The person appointed under this section shall make a report to the Secretary of State—

(a) once in each calendar year, and

(b) on such occasions as the Secretary of State may request.

(3) Where the Secretary of State receives a report under subsection (2)(a) he shall lay a copy before Parliament as soon as is reasonably practicable.

(4) The person appointed under this section shall hold and vacate office in accordance with the terms of his appointment (which may include provision about retirement, resignation or dismissal).

(5) The Secretary of State may—
 (a) pay fees and allowances to the person appointed under this section;
 (b) defray expenses of the person appointed under this section.

(6) A person who is employed within a government department may not be appointed under this section.

Note: Commencement from 1 April 2003 (SI 2003/754).

112. Regulations, &c.

(1) Regulations under this Part shall be made by the Secretary of State.

(2) Regulations and rules under this Part [other than regulations under section 103D(4)]—
 (a) must be made by statutory instrument, and
 (b) shall be subject to annulment in pursuance of a resolution of either House of Parliament.

(3) Regulations and rules under this Part—
 (a) may make provision which applies generally or only in a specified case or in specified circumstances,
 (b) may make different provision for different cases or circumstances,
 (c) may include consequential, transitional or incidental provision, and
 (d) may include savings.

[(3A) An order under section 88A—
 (a) must be made by statutory instrument,
 (b) may not be made unless a draft has been laid before and approved by resolution of each House of Parliament, and
 (c) may include transitional provision.]

(4) An order under section 94(5) or 115(8)—
 (a) must be made by statutory instrument,
 (b) may not be made unless a draft has been laid before and approved by resolution of each House of Parliament, and
 (c) may include transitional provision.

(5) An order under section [94(6) or (6B)] or 115(9)—
 (a) must be made by statutory instrument,
 (b) shall be subject to annulment in pursuance of a resolution of either House of Parliament, and
 (c) may include transitional provision.

[(**5A**) If an instrument makes provision under section 94(5) and 94(6)—
- (a) subsection (4)(b) above shall apply, and
- (b) subsection (5)(b) above shall not apply.]

[(**5B**) An order under section 97A(4)—
- (a) must be made by statutory instrument,
- (b) shall be subject to annulment in pursuance of a resolution of either House of Parliament, and
- (c) may include transitional provision.]

[(**6**) Regulations under section 103D(4)—
- (a) must be made by statutory instrument, and
- (b) shall not be made unless a draft has been laid before and approved by resolution of each House of Parliament.

(7) An order under paragraph 4 of Schedule 4—
- (a) may include consequential or incidental provision (which may include provision amending, or providing for the construction of, a reference in an enactment, instrument or other document to a member of the Asylum and Immigration Tribunal),
- (b) must be made by statutory instrument, and
- (c) shall be subject to annulment in pursuance of a resolution of either House of Parliament.]

Note: Commenced 10 February 2003 (SI 2003/249). Words in square brackets in sub-s (2) inserted and sub-s (6) substituted by Sch 2 Asylum and Immigration Act 2004 from 4 April 2005 (SI 2005/565). Subsection (3A) and (5A) inserted by Asylum and Immigration Act 2004, ss 29 and 27 respectively from 1 October 2004 (SI 2004/2523). Words in square brackets in sub-s (5) substituted by Sch 1 from a date to be appointed and sub-s (5B) inserted by Immigration, Asylum and Nationality Act 2006, s 7 from 31 August 2006 (SI 2006/2226).

113. Interpretation

(**1**) In this Part, unless a contrary intention appears—

['asylum claim'—
- (a) means a claim made by a person that to remove him from or require him to leave the United Kingdom would breach the United Kingdom's obligations under the Refugee Convention, but
- (b) does not include a claim which, having regard to a former claim, falls to be disregarded for the purposes of this Part in accordance with immigration rules,]

'entry clearance' has the meaning given by section 33(1) of the Immigration Act 1971 (c. 77) (interpretation),

['human rights claim'—
- (a) means a claim made by a person that to remove him from or require him to leave the United Kingdom would be unlawful under section 6 of the Human Rights Act 1998 (c. 42) (public authority not to act

contrary to Convention) as being incompatible with his Convention rights, but

(b) does not include a claim which, having regard to a former claim, falls to be disregarded for the purposes of this Part in accordance with immigration rules,]

'the Human Rights Convention' has the same meaning as 'the Convention' in the Human Rights Act 1998 and 'Convention rights' shall be construed in accordance with section 1 of that Act,

'illegal entrant' has the meaning given by section 33(1) of the Immigration Act 1971,

'immigration rules' means rules under section 1(4) of that Act (general immigration rules),

'prescribed' means prescribed by regulations,

'the Refugee Convention' means the Convention relating to the Status of Refugees done at Geneva on 28th July 1951 and its Protocol,

'visitor' means a visitor in accordance with immigration rules, and

'work permit' has the meaning given by section 33(1) of the Immigration Act 1971 (c. 77) (interpretation).

(2) A reference to varying leave to enter or remain in the United Kingdom does not include a reference to adding, varying or revoking a condition of leave.

Note: Commenced 10 February 2003 (SI 2003/249). Definitions of asylum claim and human rights claim substituted by Immigration, Asylum and Nationality Act 2006, s 12 from a date to be appointed.

114. Repeal

(1) . . .

(2) Schedule 6 (which makes transitional provision in connection with the repeal of Part IV of that Act and its replacement by this Part) shall have effect.

(3) Schedule 7 (consequential amendments) shall have effect.

Note: Subsection (1) repeals Part IV of the Immigration and Asylum Act 1999. Subsection (3) Commenced 10 February 2003 (SI 2003/1). Remainder from 1 April 2003 (SI 2003/754).

115. Appeal from within United Kingdom: unfounded human rights or asylum claim: transitional provision

(1) A person may not bring an appeal under section 65 or 69 of the Immigration and Asylum Act 1999 (human rights and asylum) while in the United Kingdom if—

(a) the Secretary of State certifies that the appeal relates to a human rights claim or an asylum claim which is clearly unfounded, and

(b) the person does not have another right of appeal while in the United Kingdom under Part IV of that Act.

(2) A person while in the United Kingdom may not bring an appeal under section 69 of that Act, or raise a question which relates to the Human Rights Convention under section 77 of that Act, if the Secretary of State certifies that—

(a) it is proposed to remove the person to a country of which he is not a national or citizen, and

(b) there is no reason to believe that the person's rights under the Human Rights Convention will be breached in that country.

(3) A person while in the United Kingdom may not bring an appeal under section 65 of that Act (human rights) if the Secretary of State certifies that—

(a) it is proposed to remove the person to a country of which he is not a national or citizen, and

(b) there is no reason to believe that the person's rights under the Human Rights Convention will be breached in that country.

(4) In determining whether a person in relation to whom a certificate has been issued under subsection (2) or (3) may be removed from the United Kingdom, the country specified in the certificate is to be regarded as—

(a) a place where a person's life and liberty is not threatened by reason of his race, religion, nationality, membership of a particular social group, or political opinion, and

(b) a place from which a person will not be sent to another country otherwise than in accordance with the Refugee Convention.

(5) Where a person in relation to whom a certificate is issued under this section subsequently brings an appeal or raises a question under section 65, 69 or 77 of that Act while outside the United Kingdom, the appeal or question shall be considered as if he had not been removed from the United Kingdom.

(6) If the Secretary of State is satisfied that a person who makes a human rights claim or an asylum claim is entitled to reside in a State listed in subsection (7), he shall issue a certificate under subsection (1) unless satisfied that the claim is not clearly unfounded.

(7) Those States are—

(a) the Republic of Cyprus,
(b) the Czech Republic,
(c) the Republic of Estonia,
(d) the Republic of Hungary,
(e) the Republic of Latvia,
(f) the Republic of Lithuania,
(g) the Republic of Malta,
(h) the Republic of Poland,
(i) the Slovak Republic, and
(j) the Republic of Slovenia.
[(k) the Republic of Albania,
(l) Bulgaria,
(m) Serbia and Montenegro,
(n) Jamaica,
(o) Macedonia,
(p) the Republic of Moldova, and
(q) Romania.]

(8) The Secretary of State may be order add a State, or part of a State, to the list in subsection (7) if satisfied that—
   (a) there is in general in that State or part no serious risk of persecution of persons entitled to reside in that State or part, and
   (b) removal to that State or part of persons entitled to reside there will not in general contravene the United Kingdom's obligations under the Human Rights Convention.

(9) The Secretary of State may by order remove from the list in subsection (7) a State or part added under subsection (8).

(10) In this section 'asylum claim' and 'human rights claim' have the meanings given by section 113 but—
   (a) a reference to a claim in that section shall be treated as including a reference to an allegation, and
   (b) a reference in that section to making a claim at a place designated by the Secretary of State shall be ignored.

Note: Commenced 7 November 2002, s 162. Continues to have effect in relation to any person who made an asylum or human rights claim (as defined in sub-s (10)) on or after 1 April 2003. Words in square brackets added by SI 2003/970 from 1 April 2003.

116. Special Immigration Appeals Commission: Community Legal Service

. . .

Note: Amends para 2(1), Sch 2 Access to Justice Act 1999.

117. Northern Ireland appeals: legal aid

. . .

Note: Amends Part 1, Sch 1 Legal Aid, Advice and Assistance (Northern Ireland) Order 1981.

Part VI

Immigration Procedure

Applications

118. Leave pending decision on variation application

. . .

Note: Amends Immigration Act 1971, s 3C.

119. Deemed leave on cancellation of notice

. . .

Note: Amends para 6(3), Sch 2 Immigration Act 1971.

120. Requirement to state additional grounds for application

(1) This section applies to a person if—
  (a) he has made an application to enter or remain in the United Kingdom, or
  (b) an immigration decision within the meaning of section 82 has been taken or may be taken in respect of him.

(2) The Secretary of State or an immigration officer may be notice in writing require the person to state—
  (a) his reasons for wishing to enter or remain in the United Kingdom,
  (b) any grounds on which he should be permitted to enter or remain in the United Kingdom, and
  (c) any grounds on which he should not be removed from or required to leave the United Kingdom.

(3) A statement under subsection (2) need not repeat reasons or grounds set out in—
  (a) the application mentioned in subsection (1)(a), or
  (b) an application to which the immigration decision mentioned in subsection (1)(b) relates.

Note: Commencement from 1 April 2003 (SI 2003/754).

121. Compliance with procedure

. . .

Note: Amends Immigration Act 1971, s 31A.

Work permit

122. . . .

Note: Commenced 10 February 2003 (SI 2003/1). Ceases to have effect by Sch 2 Immigration, Asylum and Nationality Act 2006 from a date to be appointed.

123. Advice about work permit, &c.

. . .

Note: Amends Immigration and Asylum Act 1999, s 82.

Authority-to-carry scheme

124. Authority to carry

(1) Regulations made by the Secretary of State may authorise him to require a person (a 'carrier') to pay a penalty if the carrier brings a passenger to the United Kingdom and—

(a) the carrier was required by an authority-to-carry scheme to seek authority under the scheme to carry the passenger, and
(b) the carrier did not seek authority before the journey to the United Kingdom commenced or was refused authority under the scheme.

(2) An 'authority-to-carry scheme' is a scheme operated by the Secretary of State which requires carriers to seek authority to bring passengers to the United Kingdom.

(3) An authority-to-carry scheme must specify—
(a) the class of carrier to which it applies (which may be defined by reference to a method of transport or otherwise), and
(b) the class of passenger to which it applies (which may be defined by reference to nationality, the possession of specified documents or otherwise).

(4) The Secretary of State may operate different authority-to-carry schemes for different purposes.

(5) Where the Secretary of State makes regulations under subsection (1) he must—
(a) identify in the regulations the authority-to-carry scheme to which they refer, and
(b) lay the authority-to-carry scheme before Parliament.

(6) Regulations under subsection (1) may, in particular—
(a) apply or make provision similar to a provision of sections 40 to 43 of and Schedule 1 to the Immigration and Asylum Act 1999 (c. 33) (charge for passenger without document);
(b) do anything which may be done under a provision of any of those sections;
(c) amend any of those sections.

(7) Regulations by virtue of subsection (6)(a) may, in particular—
(a) apply a provision with modification;
(b) apply a provision which confers power to make legislation.

(8) The grant or refusal of authority under an authority-to-carry scheme shall not be taken to determine whether a person is entitled or permitted to enter the United Kingdom.

(9) Regulations under this section—
(a) must be made by statutory instrument, and
(b) may not be made unless a draft has been laid before and approved by resolution of each House of Parliament.

Note: Commencement at a date to be appointed.

Evasion of procedure

125. Carriers' liability

Schedule 8 (which amends Part II of the Immigration and Asylum Act 1999 (carriers' liability)) shall have effect.

Note: Commencement 14 November 2002 for the purpose of enabling subordinate legislation; 8 December 2002 for the purposes of clandestine entrants and carrier's liability (SI 2002/2811).

Provision of information by traveller

126. Physical data: compulsory provision

(1) The Secretary of State may by regulations—
  (a) require an immigration application to be accompanied by specified information about external physical characteristics of the applicant;
  (b) enable an authorised person to require an individual who makes an immigration application to provide information about his external physical characteristics;
  (c) enable an authorised person to require an entrant to provide information about his external physical characteristics.

(2) In subsection (1) 'immigration application' means an application for—
  (a) entry clearance,
  (b) leave to enter or remain in the United Kingdom, or
  (c) variation of leave to enter or remain in the United Kingdom.

(3) Regulations under subsection (1) may not—
  (a) impose a requirement in respect of a person to whom section 141 of the Immigration and Asylum Act 1999 (c. 33) (fingerprinting) applies, during the relevant period within the meaning of that section, or
  (b) enable a requirement to be imposed in respect of a person to whom that section applies, during the relevant period within the meaning of that section.

(4) Regulations under subsection (1) may, in particular—
  (a) require, or enable an authorised person to require, the provision of information in a specified form;
  (b) require an individual to submit, or enable an authorised person to require an individual to submit, to a specified process by means of which information is obtained or recorded;
  (c) make provision about the effect of failure to provide information or to submit to a process (which may, in particular, include provision for an application to be disregarded or dismissed if a requirement is not satisfied);

(d) confer a function (which may include the exercise of a discretion) on an authorised person;
(e) require an authorised person to have regard to a code (with or without modification);
(f) require an authorised person to have regard to such provisions of a code (with or without modification) as may be specified by direction of the Secretary of State;
(g) make provision about the use and retention of information provided (which may include provision permitting the use of information for specified purposes which do not relate to immigration);
(h) make provision which applies generally or only in specified cases or circumstances;
(i) make different provision for different cases or circumstances.

(5) Regulations under subsection (1) must—
(a) include provision about the destruction of information obtained or recorded by virtue of the regulations,
(b) require the destruction of information at the end of the period of ten years beginning with the day on which it is obtained or recorded in a case for which destruction at the end of another period is not required by or in accordance with the regulations, and
(c) include provision similar to section 143(2) and (10) to (13) of the Immigration and Asylum Act 1999 (c. 33) (fingerprints: destruction of copies and electronic data).

(6) In so far as regulations under subsection (1) require an individual under the age of 16 to submit to a process, the regulations must make provision similar to section 141(3) to (5) and (13) of the Immigration and Asylum Act 1999 (fingerprints: children).

(7) In so far as regulations under subsection (1) enable an authorised person to require an individual under the age of 16 to submit to a process, the regulations must make provision similar to section 141(3) to (5), (12) and (13) of that Act (fingerprints: children).

(8) Regulations under subsection (1)—
(a) must be made by statutory instrument, and
(b) shall not be made unless a draft of the regulations has been laid before and approved by resolution of each House of Parliament:

(9) In this section—
'authorised person' has the meaning given by section 141(5) of the Immigration and Asylum Act 1999 (authority to take fingerprints),
'code' has the meaning given by section 145(6) of that Act (code of practice),
'entrant' has the meaning given by section 33(1) of the Immigration Act 1971 (c. 77) (interpretation),

'entry clearance' has the meaning given by section 33(1) of that Act, and
'external physical characteristics' includes, in particular, features of the iris or any other part of the eye.

Note: Commencement from 1 April 2003 (SI 2003/754).

127. Physical data: voluntary provision

(1) The Secretary of State may operate a scheme under which an individual may supply, or submit to the obtaining or recording of, information about his external physical characteristics to be used (wholly or partly) in connection with entry to the United Kingdom.

(2) In particular, the Secretary of State may—
   (a) require an authorised person to use information supplied under a scheme;
   (b) make provision about the collection, use and retention of information supplied under a scheme (which may include provision requiring an authorised person to have regard to a code);
   (c) charge for participation in a scheme.

(3) In this section the following expressions have the same meaning as in section 126—
   (a) 'authorised person',
   (b) 'code', and
   (c) 'external physical characteristics'.

Note: Commencement from 10 December 2004 (SI 2004/2998).

128. Data collection under Immigration and Asylum Act 1999

. . .

Note: Amends Immigration and Asylum Act 1999, ss 144, 145.

Disclosure of information by public authority

129. Local authority

(1) The Secretary of State may require a local authority to supply information for the purpose of establishing where a person is if the Secretary of State reasonably suspects that—
   (a) the person has committed an offence under section 24(1)(a), (b), (c), (e) or (f), 24A(1) or 26(1)(c) or (d) of the Immigration Act 1971 (c. 77) (illegal entry, deception, &c.), and
   (b) the person is or has been resident in the local authority's area.

(2) A local authority shall comply with a requirement under this section.

(3) In the application of this section to England and Wales 'local authority' means—
(a) a county council,
(b) a county borough council,
(c) a district council,
(d) a London borough council,
(e) the Common Council of the City of London, and
(f) the Council of the Isles of Scilly.

(4) In the application of this section to Scotland 'local authority' means a council constituted under section 2 of the Local Government etc. (Scotland) Act 1994 (c. 39).

(5) In the application of this section to Northern Ireland—
(a) a reference to a local authority shall be taken as a reference to the Northern Ireland Housing Executive, and
(b) the reference to a local authority's area shall be taken as a reference to Northern Ireland.

Note: Commencement from 30 July 2003 (SI 2003/1747).

130. Inland Revenue

(1) The Commissioners of Inland Revenue may supply the Secretary of State with information for the purpose of establishing where a person is if the Secretary of State reasonably suspects—
(a) that the person does not have leave to enter or remain in the United Kingdom, and
(b) that the person does not have permission to work in accordance with section 1(2) of the Immigration Act 1971 (c. 77) (general principles).

(2) The Commissioners of Inland Revenue may supply the Secretary of State with information for the purpose of establishing where a person is if the Secretary of State reasonably suspects that the person has undertaken employment in the United Kingdom in breach of—
(a) a condition attached to leave to enter or remain in the United Kingdom,
(b) a restriction imposed under paragraph 21 of Schedule 2 to the Immigration Act 1971 (control of entry), or
(c) a restriction imposed under paragraph 2 of Schedule 3 to that Act (deportation).

(3) The Commissioners of Inland Revenue may supply the Secretary of State with information for the purpose of determining whether an applicant for naturalisation under the British Nationality Act 1981 (c. 61) is of good character.

(4) The Commissioners of Inland Revenue may supply the Secretary of State with information for the purpose of applying, in the case of an applicant for entry

clearance within the meaning of section 33 of the Immigration Act 1971, a provision of rules under section 3 of that Act relating to maintenance or accommodation.

(5) Information supplied to the Secretary of State under any of subsections (1) to (4) may be supplied by him to another person only—
   (a) for a purpose specified in any of those subsections,
   (b) for the purpose of legal proceedings, or
   (c) with consent (which may be general or specific) of the Commissioners of Inland Revenue, for a purpose for which the Commissioners could supply the information.

(6) A power of the Commissioners of Inland Revenue under this section—
   (a) may be exercised on their behalf only by a person authorised (generally or specifically) for the purpose, and
   (b) may be exercised despite any statutory or other requirement of confidentiality.

Note: Commencement from 1 April 2003 (SI 2003/754).

131. Police, &c.

Information may be supplied under section 20 of the Immigration and Asylum Act 1999 (c. 33) (supply of information to Secretary of State) for use for the purpose of determining whether an applicant for naturalisation under the British Nationality Act 1981 is of good character.

Note: Commencement 10 February 2003 (SI 2001/1).

132. Supply of document, &c. to Secretary of State

. . .

Note: Amends Immigration and Asylum Act 1999, s 20.

133. Medical inspectors

(1) This section applies to a person if an immigration officer acting under Schedule 2 to the Immigration Act 1971 (c. 77) (control on entry, &c.) has brought the person to the attention of—
   (a) a medical inspector appointed under paragraph 1(2) of that Schedule, or
   (b) a person working under the direction of a medical inspector appointed under that paragraph.

(2) A medical inspector may disclose to a health service body—
   (a) the name of a person to whom this section applies,
   (b) his place of residence in the United Kingdom,

(c) his age,
(d) the language which he speaks,
(e) the nature of any disease with which the inspector thinks the person may be infected,
(f) relevant details of the person's medical history,
(g) the grounds for an opinion mentioned in paragraph (e) (including the result of any test or examination which has been carried out), and
(h) the inspector's opinion about action which the health service body should take.

(3) A disclosure may be made under subsection (2) only if the medical inspector thinks it necessary for the purpose of—
(a) preventative medicine,
(b) medical diagnosis,
(c) the provision of care or treatment, or
(d) the management of health care services.

(4) For the purposes of this section 'health service body' in relation to a person means a body which carries out functions in an area which includes his place of residence and which is—
(a) in relation to England—
(i) a Primary Care Trust established under section 16A of the National Health Service Act 1977 (c. 49),
(ii) a National Health Service Trust established under section 5 of the National Health Service and Community Care Act 1990 (c. 19),
(iii) a Strategic Health Authority established under section 8 of the National Health Service Act 1977,
(iv) a Special Health Authority established under section 11 of that Act, or
(v) the Public Health Laboratory Service Board,
[or
(vi) the Health Protection Agency.]
(b) in relation to Wales—
(i) a Health Authority or Local Health Board established under section 8 or 16BA of that Act,
(ii) a National Health Service Trust established under section 5 of the National Health Service and Community Care Act 1990, or
(iii) the Public Health Laboratory Service Board,
[or
(iv) the Health Protection Agency.]
(c) in relation to Scotland—
(i) a Health Board, Special Health Board or National Health Service Trust established under section 2 or 12A of the National Health Service (Scotland) Act 1978 (c. 29),. . .

(ii) the Common Services Agency for the Scottish Health Service established under section 10 of that Act, or

[(iii) the Health Protection Agency, or]

(d) in relation to Northern Ireland—

(i) a Health and Social Services Board established under the Health and Personal Social Services (Northern Ireland) Order 1972 (S.I. 1972/1265 (N.I. 14)),

(ii) a Health and Social Services trust established under the Health and Personal Social Services (Northern Ireland) Order 1991 (S.I. 1991/194 (N.I. 1)), . . .

(iii) the Department of Health, Social Services and Public Safety.

[or

(iv) the Health Protection Agency.]

Note: Commencement 10 February 2003 (SI 2003/1). Words in square brackets inserted and words omitted by Sch 3 Health Protection Agency Act from a date to be appointed.

Disclosure of information by private person

134. Employer

(1) The Secretary of State may require an employer to supply information about an employee whom the Secretary of State reasonably suspects of having committed an offence under—

(a) section 24(1)(a), (b), (c), (e) or (f), 24A(1) or 26(1)(c) or (d) of the Immigration Act 1971 (c. 77) (illegal entry, deception, &c.),

(b) section 105(1)(a), (b) or (c) of the Immigration and Asylum Act 1999 (c. 33) (support for asylum-seeker: fraud), or

(c) section 106(1)(a), (b) or (c) of that Act (support for asylum-seeker: fraud).

(2) The power under subsection (1) may be exercised to require information about an employee only if the information—

(a) is required for the purpose of establishing where the employee is, or

(b) relates to the employee's earnings or to the history of his employment.

(3) In this section a reference to an employer or employee—

(a) includes a reference to a former employer or employee, and

(b) shall be construed in accordance with section 8(8) of the Asylum and Immigration Act 1996 (c. 49) (restrictions on employment).

(4) Where—

(a) a business (the 'employment agency') arranges for one person (the 'worker') to provide services to another (the 'client'), and

(b) the worker is not employed by the employment agency or the client, this section shall apply as if the employment agency were the worker's employer while he provides services to the client.

Note: Commencement from 30 July 2003 (SI 2003/1747).

135. Financial institution

(1) The Secretary of State may require a financial institution to supply information about a person if the Secretary of State reasonably suspects that—
  (a) the person has committed an offence under section 105(1)(a), (b) or (c) or 106(1)(a), (b) or (c) of the Immigration and Asylum Act 1999 (c. 33) (support for asylum-seeker: fraud),
  (b) the information is relevant to the offence, and
  (c) the institution has the information.

(2) In this section 'financial institution' means—
  (a) a person who has permission under Part 4 of the Financial Services and Markets Act 2000 (c. 8) to accept deposits, and
  (b) a building society (within the meaning given by the Building Societies Act 1986 (c. 53)).

Note: Commencement from 30 July 2003 (SI 2003/1747).

136. Notice

(1) A requirement to provide information under section 134 or 135 must be imposed by notice in writing specifying—
  (a) the information,
  (b) the manner in which it is to be provided, and
  (c) the period of time within which it is to be provided.

(2) A period of time specified in a notice under subsection (1)(c)—
  (a) must begin with the date of receipt of the notice, and
  (b) must not be less than ten working days.

(3) A person on whom a notice is served under subsection (1) must provide the Secretary of State with the information specified in the notice.

(4) Information provided under subsection (3) must be provided—
  (a) in the manner specified under subsection (1)(b), and
  (b) within the time specified under subsection (1)(c).

(5) In this section 'working day' means a day which is not—
  (a) Saturday,
  (b) Sunday,
  (c) Christmas Day,
  (d) Good Friday, or
  (e) a day which is a bank holiday under the Banking and Financial Dealings Act 1971 (c. 80) in any part of the United Kingdom.

Note: Commencement from 30 July 2003 (SI 2003/1747).

137. Disclosure of information: offences

(1) A person commits an offence if without reasonable excuse he fails to comply with section 136(3).

(2) A person who is guilty of an offence under subsection (1) shall be liable on summary conviction to—
   (a) imprisonment for a term not exceeding three months,
   (b) a fine not exceeding level 5 on the standard scale, or
   (c) both.

Note: Commencement from 30 July 2003 (SI 2003/1747).

138. Offence by body

(1) Subsection (2) applies where an offence under section 137 is committed by a body corporate and it is proved that the offence—
   (a) was committed with the consent or connivance of an officer of the body, or
   (b) was attributable to neglect on the part of an officer of the body.

(2) The officer, as well as the body, shall be guilty of the offence.

(3) In this section a reference to an officer of a body corporate includes a reference to—
   (a) a director, manager or secretary,
   (b) a person purporting to act as a director, manager or secretary, and
   (c) if the affairs of the body are managed by its members, a member.

(4) Where an offence under section 137 is committed by a partnership (other than a limited partnership), each partner shall be guilty of the offence.

(5) Subsection (1) shall have effect in relation to a limited partnership as if—
   (a) a reference to a body corporate were a reference to a limited partnership, and
   (b) a reference to an officer of the body were a reference to a partner.

Note: Commencement from 30 July 2003 (SI 2003/1747).

139. Privilege against self-incrimination

(1) Information provided by a person pursuant to a requirement under section 134 or 135 shall not be admissible in evidence in criminal proceedings against that person.

(2) This section shall not apply to proceedings for an offence under section 137.

Note: Commencement from 30 July 2003 (SI 2003/1747).

Immigration services

140. Immigration Services Commissioner

. . .

Note: Amends, Immigration and Asylum Act 1999 s 87(3), Sch 5, para 7 and Sch 6, para 3.

Immigration control

141. EEA ports: juxtaposed controls

(1) The Secretary of State may by order make provision for the purpose of giving effect to an international agreement which concerns immigration control at an EEA port (whether or not it also concerns other aspects of frontier control at the port).

(2) An order under this section may make any provision which appears to the Secretary of State—
   (a) likely to facilitate implementation of the international agreement (including those aspects of the agreement which relate to frontier control other than immigration control), or
   (b) appropriate as a consequence of provision made for the purpose of facilitating implementation of the agreement.

(3) In particular, an order under this section may—
   (a) provide for a law of England and Wales to have effect, with or without modification, in relation to a person in a specified area or anything done in a specified area;
   (b) provide for a law of England and Wales not to have effect in relation to a person in a specified area or anything done in a specified area;
   (c) provide for a law of England and Wales to be modified in its effect in relation to a person in a specified area or anything done in a specified area;
   (d) disapply or modify an enactment in relation to a person who has undergone a process in a specified area;
   (e) disapply or modify an enactment otherwise than under paragraph (b), (c) or (d);
   (f) make provision conferring a function (which may include—
      (i) provision conferring a discretionary function;
      (ii) provision conferring a function on a servant or agent of the government of a State other than the United Kingdom);
   (g) create or extend the application of an offence;
   (h) impose or permit the imposition of a penalty;
   (i) require the payment of, or enable a person to require the payment of, a charge or fee;

(j) make provision about enforcement (which may include—
   (i) provision conferring a power of arrest, detention or removal from or to any place;
   (ii) provision for the purpose of enforcing the law of a State other than the United Kingdom);
(k) confer jurisdiction on a court or tribunal;
(l) confer immunity or provide for indemnity;
(m) make provision about compensation;
(n) impose a requirement, or enable a requirement to be imposed, for a person to co-operate with or to provide facilities for the use of another person who is performing a function under the order or under the international agreement (which may include a requirement to provide facilities without charge);
(o) make provision about the disclosure of information.

(4) An order under this section may—
(a) make provision which applies generally or only in specified circumstances;
(b) make different provision for different circumstances;
(c) amend an enactment.

(5) An order under this section—
(a) must be made by statutory instrument,
(b) may not be made unless the Secretary of State has consulted with such persons as appear to him to be appropriate, and
(c) may not be made unless a draft has been laid before and approved by resolution of each House of Parliament.

(6) In this section—
'EEA port' means a port in an EEA State from which passengers are commonly carried by sea to or from the United Kingdom,
'EEA State' means a State which is a contracting party to the Agreement on the European Economic Area signed at Oporto on 2nd May 1992 (as it has effect from time to time),
'frontier control' means the enforcement of law which relates to, or in so far as it relates to, the movement of persons or goods into or out of the United Kingdom or another State,
'immigration control' means arrangements made in connection with the movement of persons into or out of the United Kingdom or another State,
'international agreement' means an agreement made between Her Majesty's Government and the government of another State, and
'specified area' means an area (whether of the United Kingdom or of another State) specified in an international agreement.

Note: Commenced 8 January 2003 (SI 2002/2811).

Country information

142. Advisory Panel on Country Information

(1) The Secretary of State shall appoint a group of not fewer than ten nor more than 20 individuals (to be known as the Advisory Panel on Country Information).

(2) The Secretary of State shall appoint one member of the Advisory Panel as its Chairman.

(3) The function of the Advisory Panel shall be to consider and make recommendations to the Secretary of State about the content of country information.

(4) In this section 'country information' means information about conditions in countries outside the United Kingdom which the Secretary of State compiles and makes available, for purposes connected with immigration, to—
   (a) immigration officers, and
   (b) other officers of the Secretary of State.

(5) The function of the Advisory Panel shall be shared among its members in accordance with arrangements made by the Chairman.

(6) A member of the Advisory Panel shall hold and vacate office in accordance with the terms of his appointment (which may include provision about retirement, resignation or dismissal).

(7) The Secretary of State may—
   (a) pay fees and allowances to members of the Advisory Panel;
   (b) defray expenses of members of the Advisory Panel;
   (c) make staff and other facilities available to the Advisory Panel.

Note: Commencement from 1 April 2003 (SI 2003/754).

Part VII
Offences

Substance

143. Assisting unlawful immigration, &c.

. . .

Note: Amends Immigration Act 1971, s 25.

144. Section 143: consequential amendments

. . .

Note: Amends Immigration Act 1971, ss 25A, 28A, 28B, 28C, 28D, 28F and 33.

145. Traffic in prostitution

(1) A person commits an offence if he arranges or facilitates the arrival in the United Kingdom of an individual (the 'passenger') and—
  (a) he intends to exercise control over prostitution by the passenger in the United Kingdom or elsewhere, or
  (b) he believes that another person is likely to exercise control over prostitution by the passenger in the United Kingdom or elsewhere.

(2) A person commits an offence if he arranges or facilitates travel within the United Kingdom by an individual (the 'passenger') in respect of whom he believes that an offence under subsection (1) may have been committed and—
  (a) he intends to exercise control over prostitution by the passenger in the United Kingdom or elsewhere, or
  (b) he believes that another person is likely to exercise control over prostitution by the passenger in the United Kingdom or elsewhere.

(3) A person commits an offence if he arranges or facilitates the departure from the United Kingdom of an individual (the 'passenger') and—
  (a) he intends to exercise control over prostitution by the passenger outside the United Kingdom, or
  (b) he believes that another person is likely to exercise control over prostitution by the passenger outside the United Kingdom.

(4) For the purposes of subsections (1) to (3) a person exercises control over prostitution by another if for purposes of gain he exercises control, direction or influence over the prostitute's movements in a way which shows that he is aiding, abetting or compelling the prostitution.

(5) A person guilty of an offence under this section shall be liable—
  (a) on conviction on indictment, to imprisonment for a term not exceeding 14 years, to a fine or to both, or
  (b) on summary conviction, to imprisonment for a term not exceeding six months, to a fine not exceeding the statutory maximum or to both.

Note: Commenced 10 February 2003 (SI 2003/1).

146. Section 145: supplementary

(1) Subsections (1) to (3) of section 145 apply to anything done—
  (a) in the United Kingdom,
  (b) outside the United Kingdom by an individual to whom subsection (2) applies, or
  (c) outside the United Kingdom by a body incorporated under the law of a part of the United Kingdom.

(2) This subsection applies to—
(a) a British citizen,
(b) a British overseas territories citizen,
(c) a British National (Overseas),
(d) a British Overseas citizen,
(e) a person who is a British subject under the British Nationality Act 1981 (c. 61), and
(f) a British protected person within the meaning of that Act.

(3) Sections 25C and 25D of the Immigration Act 1971 (c. 77) (forfeiture or detention of vehicle, &c.) shall apply in relation to an offence under section 145 of this Act as they apply in relation to an offence under section 25 of that Act.

(4) . . .

Note: Subsection (4) amends para 2, Sch 4 Criminal Justice and Court Services Act 2000. Commenced 10 February 2003 (SI 2003/1).

147. Employment

. . .

Note: Amends Asylum and Immigration Act 1996, s 8.

148. Registration card

. . .

Note: Amends Immigration Act 1971, s 26.

149. Immigration stamp

. . .

Note: Inserts s 26B into the Immigration Act 1971.

150. Sections 148 and 149: consequential amendments

. . .

Note: Amends Immigration Act 1971, ss 28A, 28B and 28D.

151. False information

. . .

Note: Amends Immigration Act 1971, s 26(3).

Procedure

152. Arrest by immigration officer

. . .

Note: Inserts s 28AA into the Immigration Act 1971.

153. Power of entry

. . .

Note: Inserts s 28CA into the Immigration Act 1971; amends Immigration and Asylum Act 1999, s 146.

154. Power to search for evidence

. . .

Note: Inserts ss 28FA, 28FB into the Immigration Act 1971.

155. Sections 153 and 154: supplemental

. . .

Note: Amends Immigration Act 1971, s 28L.

156. Time limit on prosecution

. . .

Note: Amends Immigration Act 1971, ss 24A, 28(1).

Part VIII

General

157. Consequential and incidental provision

(1) The Secretary of State may be order make consequential or incidental provision in connection with a provision of this Act.

(2) An order under this section may, in particular—
   (a) amend an enactment;
   (b) modify the effect of an enactment.

(3) An order under this section must be made by statutory instrument.

(4) An order under this section which amends an enactment shall not be made

unless a draft has been laid before and approved by resolution of each House of Parliament.

(5) Any other order under this section shall be subject to annulment pursuant to a resolution of either House of Parliament.

Note: Commenced 7 November 2002, s 162 and 8 January 2003 (SI 2002/2811).

158. Interpretation: 'the Immigration Acts'

. . .

Note: Ceases to have effect from a date to be appointed, Immigration, Asylum and Nationality Act 2006, s 64.

159. Applied provision

(1) Subsection (2) applies where this Act amends or refers to a provision which is applied by, under or for purposes of—
   (a) another provision of the Act which contains the provision, or
   (b) another Act.

(2) The amendment or reference shall have effect in relation to the provision as applied.

(3) Where this Act applies a provision of another Act, a reference to that provision in any enactment includes a reference to the provision as applied by this Act.

Note: Commenced 10 February 2003 (SI 2003/1).

160. Money

(1) Expenditure of the Secretary of State or the Lord Chancellor in connection with a provision of this Act shall be paid out of money provided by Parliament.

(2) An increase attributable to this Act in the amount payable out of money provided by Parliament under another enactment shall be paid out of money provided by Parliament.

(3) A sum received by the Secretary of State or the Lord Chancellor in connection with a provision of this Act shall be paid into the Consolidated Fund.

Note: Commenced 7 November 2002, s 162.

161. Repeals

The provisions listed in Schedule 9 are hereby repealed to the extent specified.

Note: Commenced 8 December 2002 (SI 2002/2811) and 10 February 2003 (SI 2003/1).

162. Commencement

(1) Subject to subsections (2) to (5), the preceding provisions of this Act shall come into force in accordance with provision made by the Secretary of State by order.

(2) The following provisions shall come into force on the passing of this Act—

(a) section 6,
(b) section 7,
(c) section 10(1) to (4) and (6),
(d) section 11,
(e) section 15 (and Schedule 2),
(f) section 16,
(g) section 35(1)(h),
(h) section 38,
(i) section 40(1),
(j) section 41(1),
(k) section 42,
(l) section 43,
(m) section 48,
(n) section 49,
(o) section 50,
(p) section 56,
(q) section 58,
(r) section 59,
(s) section 61,
(t) section 67,
(u) section 69,
(v) section 70,
(w) section 115 and paragraph 29 of Schedule 7 (and the relevant entry in Schedule 9)
(x) section 157, and
(y) section 160.

(3) Section 5 shall have effect in relation to—

(a) an application made after the passing of this Act, and
(b) an application made, but not determined, before the passing of this Act.

(4) Section 8 shall have effect in relation to—

(a) an application made on or after a date appointed by the Secretary of State by order, and
(b) an application made, but not determined, before that date.

(5) Section 9 shall have effect in relation to a child born on or after a date appointed by the Secretary of State by order.

(6) An order under subsection (1) may—

(a) make provision generally or for a specified purpose only (which may include the purpose of the application of a provision to or in relation to a particular place or area);
(b) make different provision for different purposes;
(c) include transitional provision;
(d) include savings;
(e) include consequential provision;
(f) include incidental provision.

(7) An order under this section must be made by statutory instrument.

Note: The date appointed for the purpose of sub-s (5) is 1 July 2006 (SI 2006/1498).

163. Extent

(1) A provision of this Act which amends or repeals a provision of another Act or inserts a provision into another Act has the same extent as the provision amended or repealed or as the Act into which the insertion is made (ignoring, in any case, extent by virtue of an Order in Council).

(2) Sections 145 and 146 extend only to—
(a) England and Wales, and
(b) Northern Ireland.

(3) A provision of this Act to which neither subsection (1) nor subsection (2) applies extends to—
(a) England and Wales,
(b) Scotland, and
(c) Northern Ireland.

(4) Her Majesty may by Order in Council direct that a provision of this Act is to extend, with or without modification or adaptation, to—
(a) any of the Channel Islands;
(b) the Isle of Man.

(5) Subsection (4) does not apply in relation to the extension to a place of a provision which extends there by virtue of subsection (1).

164. Short title

This Act may be cited as the Nationality, Immigration and Asylum Act 2002.

SCHEDULES

Section 3

SCHEDULE 1

CITIZENSHIP CEREMONY, OATH AND PLEDGE

1.—7. . . .

8. The Secretary of State may make a payment to a local authority in respect of anything done by the authority in accordance with regulations made by virtue of section 41(3A) of the British Nationality Act 1981 (c. 61).

9.—(1) A local authority must—
(a) comply with a requirement imposed on it by regulations made by virtue of that section, and
(b) carry out a function imposed on it by regulations made by virtue of that section.

(2) A local authority on which a requirement or function is imposed by regulations made by virtue of that section—

(a) may provide facilities or make arrangements in addition to those which it is required to provide or make, and
(b) may make a charge for the provision of facilities or the making of arrangements under paragraph (a) which does not exceed the cost of providing the facilities or making the arrangements.

Note: Paragraphs 1–7 amend the British Nationality Act 1981. Commencement at a date to be appointed.

Section 15

SCHEDULE 2

NATIONALITY: REPEAL OF SPENT PROVISIONS

1. . . .

2 Nothing in this Schedule has any effect in relation to a registration made under a provision before its repeal.

Note: Paragraph 1 repeals parts of British Nationality Act 1981. Commencement from 1 January 2004 (SI 2003/3156).

Section 54

SCHEDULE 3

WITHHOLDING AND WITHDRAWAL OF SUPPORT

Ineligibility for support

1.—(1) A person to whom this paragraph applies shall not be eligible for support or assistance under—

(a) section 21 or 29 of the National Assistance Act 1948 (c. 29) (local authority: accommodation and welfare),
(b) section 45 of the Health Services and Public Health Act 1968 (c. 46) (local authority: welfare of elderly),
(c) section 12 or 13A of the Social Work (Scotland) Act 1968 (c. 49) (social welfare services),
(d) Article 7 or 15 of the Health and Personal Social Services (Northern Ireland) Order 1972 (S.I. 1972/1265 (N.I. 14)) (prevention of illness, social welfare, &c.),
(e) section 21 of and Schedule 8 to the National Health Service Act 1977 (c. 49) (social services),
(f) section 29(1)(b) of the Housing (Scotland) Act 1987 (c. 26) (interim duty to accommodate in case of apparent priority need where review of a local authority decision has been requested),
(g) section 17, 23C, 24A or 24B of the Children Act 1989 (c. 41) (welfare and other powers which can be exercised in relation to adults),
(h) Article 18, 35 or 36 of the Children (Northern Ireland) Order 1995 (S.I. 1995/ 755 (N.I. 2)) (welfare and other powers which can be exercised in relation to adults),
(i) sections 22, 29 and 30 of the Children (Scotland) Act 1995 (c. 36) (provisions analogous to those mentioned in paragraph (g)),

(j) section 188(3) or 204(4) of the Housing Act 1996 (c. 52) (accommodation pending review or appeal),
(k) section 2 of the Local Government Act 2000 (c. 22) (promotion of well-being),
(l) a provision of the Immigration and Asylum Act 1999 (c. 33), or
(m) a provision of this Act.

(2) A power or duty under a provision referred to in sub-paragraph (1) may not be exercised or performed in respect of a person to whom this paragraph applies (whether or not the person has previously been in receipt of support or assistance under the provision).

(3) An approval or directions given under or in relation to a provision referred to in sub-paragraph (1) shall be taken to be subject to sub-paragraph (2).

Exceptions

2.—(1) Paragraph 1 does not prevent the provision of support or assistance—
(a) to a British citizen, or
(b) to a child, or
(c) under or by virtue of regulations made under paragraph 8, 9 or 10 below, or
(d) in a case in respect of which, and to the extent to which, regulations made by the Secretary of State disapply paragraph 1, or
(e) in circumstances in respect of which, and to the extent to which, regulations made by the Secretary of State disapply paragraph 1.

(2) Regulations under sub-paragraph (1)(d) may confer a discretion on the Secretary of State.

(3) Regulations under sub-paragraph (1)(e) may, in particular, disapply paragraph 1 to the provision of support or assistance by a local authority to a person where the authority—
(a) has taken steps in accordance with guidance issued by the Secretary of State to determine whether paragraph 1 would (but for the regulations) apply to the person, and
(b) has concluded on the basis of those steps that there is no reason to believe that paragraph 1 would apply.

(4) Regulations under sub-paragraph (1)(d) or (e) may confer a discretion on an authority.

(5) A local authority which is considering whether to give support or assistance to a person under a provision listed in paragraph 1(1) shall act in accordance with any relevant guidance issued by the Secretary of State under sub-paragraph (3)(a).

(6) A reference in this Schedule to a person to whom paragraph 1 applies includes a reference to a person in respect of whom that paragraph is disapplied to a limited extent by regulations under sub-paragraph (1)(d) or (e), except in a case for which the regulations provide otherwise.

3. Paragraph 1 does not prevent the exercise of a power or the performance of a duty if, and to the extent that, its exercise or performance is necessary for the purpose of avoiding a breach of—
(a) a person's Convention rights, or
(b) a person's rights under the Community Treaties.

First class of ineligible person: refugee status abroad

4.—(1) Paragraph 1 applies to a person if he—
(a) has refugee status abroad, or
(b) is the dependant of a person who is in the United Kingdom and who has refugee status abroad.

(2) For the purposes of this paragraph a person has refugee status abroad if—
(a) he does not have the nationality of an EEA State, and
(b) the government of an EEA State other than the United Kingdom has determined that he is entitled to protection as a refugee under the Refugee Convention.

Second class of ineligible person: citizen of other EEA State

5. Paragraph 1 applies to a person if he—
(a) has the nationality of an EEA State other than the United Kingdom, or
(b) is the dependant of a person who has the nationality of an EEA State other than the United Kingdom.

Third class of ineligible person: failed asylum-seeker

6.—(1) Paragraph 1 applies to a person if—
(a) he was (but is no longer) an asylum-seeker, and
(b) he fails to cooperate with removal directions issued in respect of him.

(2) Paragraph 1 also applies to a dependant of a person to whom that paragraph applies by virtue of sub-paragraph (1).

Fourth class of ineligible person: person unlawfully in United Kingdom

7. Paragraph 1 applies to a person if—
(a) he is in the United Kingdom in breach of the immigration laws within the meaning of section 11, and
(b) he is not an asylum-seeker.

[7A *Fifth class of ineligible person: failed asylum-seeker with family*

(1) Paragraph 1 applies to a person if—
(a) he—
(i) is treated as an asylum-seeker for the purposes of Part VI of the Immigration and Asylum Act 1999 (c. 33) (support) by virtue only of section 94(3A) (failed asylum-seeker with dependent child), or
(ii) is treated as an asylum-seeker for the purposes of Part 2 of this Act by virtue only of section 18(2),
(b) the Secretary of State has certified that in his opinion the person has failed without reasonable excuse to take reasonable steps—
(i) to leave the United Kingdom voluntarily, or
(ii) to place himself in a position in which he is able to leave the United Kingdom voluntarily,
(c) the person has received a copy of the Secretary of State's certificate, and

(d) the period of 14 days, beginning with the date on which the person receives the copy of the certificate, has elapsed.

(2) Paragraph 1 also applies to a dependant of a person to whom that paragraph applies by virtue of sub-paragraph (1).

(3) For the purpose of sub-paragraph (1)(d) if the Secretary of State sends a copy of a certificate by first class post to a person's last known address, the person shall be treated as receiving the copy on the second day after the day on which it was posted.

(4) The Secretary of State may be regulations vary the period specified in sub-paragraph (1)(d).]

Travel assistance

8. The Secretary of State may make regulations providing for arrangements to be made enabling a person to whom paragraph 1 applies by virtue of paragraph 4 or 5 to leave the United Kingdom.

Temporary accommodation

9.—(1) The Secretary of State may make regulations providing for arrangements to be made for the accommodation of a person to whom paragraph 1 applies pending the implementation of arrangements made by virtue of paragraph 8.

(2) Arrangements for a person by virtue of this paragraph—
(a) may be made only if the person has with him a dependent child, and
(b) may include arrangements for a dependent child.

10.—(1) The Secretary of State may make regulations providing for arrangements to be made for the accommodation of a person if—
(a) paragraph 1 applies to him by virtue of paragraph 7, and
(b) he has not failed to cooperate with removal directions issued in respect of him.

(2) Arrangements for a person by virtue of this paragraph—
(a) may be made only if the person has with him a dependent child, and
(b) may include arrangements for a dependent child.

Assistance and accommodation: general

11. Regulations under paragraph 8, 9 or 10 may—
(a) provide for the making of arrangements under a provision referred to in paragraph 1(1) or otherwise;
(b) confer a function (which may include the exercise of a discretion) on the Secretary of State, a local authority or another person;
(c) provide that arrangements must be made in a specified manner or in accordance with specified principles;
(d) provide that arrangements may not be made in a specified manner;
(e) require a local authority or another person to have regard to guidance issued by the Secretary of State in making arrangements;
(f) require a local authority or another person to comply with a direction of the Secretary of State in making arrangements.

12.—(1) Regulations may, in particular, provide that if a person refuses an offer of arrangements under paragraph 8 or fails to implement or cooperate with arrangements made for him under that paragraph—

(a) new arrangements may not be made for him under paragraph 8, but

(b) new arrangements may not be made for him under paragraph 9.

(2) Regulations by virtue of this paragraph may include exceptions in the case of a person who—

(a) has a reason of a kind specified in the regulations for failing to implement or cooperate with arrangements made under paragraph 8, and

(b) satisfies any requirements of the regulations for proof of the reason.

Offences

13.—(1) A person who leaves the United Kingdom in accordance with arrangements made under paragraph 8 commits an offence if he—

(a) returns to the United Kingdom, and

(b) requests that arrangements be made for him by virtue of paragraph 8, 9 or 10.

(2) A person commits an offence if he—

(a) requests that arrangements be made for him by virtue of paragraph 8, 9 or 10, and

(b) fails to mention a previous request by him for the making of arrangements under any of those paragraphs.

(3) A person who is guilty of an offence under this paragraph shall be liable on summary conviction to imprisonment for a term not exceeding six months.

Information

14.—(1) If it appears to a local authority that paragraph 1 applies or may apply to a person in the authority's area by virtue of [paragraph 6, 7 or 7A], the authority must inform the Secretary of State.

(2) A local authority shall act in accordance with any relevant guidance issued by the Secretary of State for the purpose of determining whether paragraph 1 applies or may apply to a person in the authority's area by virtue of [paragraph 6, 7 or 7A].

Power to amend Schedule

15. The Secretary of State may be order amend this Schedule so as—

(a) to provide for paragraph 1 to apply or not to apply to a class of person;

(b) to add or remove a provision to or from the list in paragraph 1(1);

(c) to add, amend or remove a limitation of or exception to paragraph 1.

Orders and regulations

16.—(1) An order or regulations under this Schedule must be made by statutory instrument.

(2) An order or regulations under this Schedule may—

(a) make provision which applies generally or only in specified cases or circumstances or only for specified purposes;

(b) make different provision for different cases, circumstances or purposes;

(c) make transitional provision;

(d) make consequential provision (which may include provision amending a provision made by or under this or another Act).

(3) An order under this Schedule, regulations under paragraph 2(1)(d) or (e) or other regulations which include consequential provision amending an enactment shall not be made unless a draft has been laid before and approved by resolution of each House of Parliament.

(4) Regulations under this Schedule to which sub-paragraph (3) does not apply shall be subject to annulment in pursuance of a resolution of either House of Parliament.

Interpretation

17.—(1) In this Schedule—

'asylum-seeker' means a person—

(a) who is at least 18 years old,

(b) who has made a claim for asylum (within the meaning of section 18(3)), and

(c) whose claim has been recorded by the Secretary of State but not determined,

'Convention rights' has the same meaning as in the Human Rights Act 1998 (c. 42),

'child' means a person under the age of eighteen,

'dependant' and 'dependent' shall have such meanings as may be prescribed by regulations made by the Secretary of State,

'EEA State' means a State which is a contracting party to the Agreement on the European Economic Area signed at Oporto on 2nd May 1992 (as it has effect from time to time),

'local authority'—

(a) in relation to England and Wales, has the same meaning as in section 129(3),

(b) in relation to Scotland, has the same meaning as in section 129(4), and

(c) in relation to Northern Ireland, means a health service body within the meaning of section 133(4)(d) and the Northern Ireland Housing Executive (for which purpose a reference to the authority's area shall be taken as a reference to Northern Ireland),

'the Refugee Convention' means the Convention relating to the status of Refugees done at Geneva on 28th July 1951 and its Protocol, and

'removal directions' means directions under Schedule 2 to the Immigration Act 1971 (c. 77) (control of entry, &c.), under Schedule 3 to that Act (deportation) or under section 10 of the Immigration and Asylum Act 1999 (c. 33) (removal of person unlawfully in United Kingdom).

(2) For the purpose of the definition of 'asylum-seeker' in sub-paragraph (1) a claim is determined if—

(a) the Secretary of State has notified the claimant of his decision,

(b) no appeal against the decision can be brought (disregarding the possibility of an appeal out of time with permission), and

(c) any appeal which has already been brought has been disposed of.

(3) For the purpose of sub-paragraph (2)(c) an appeal is disposed f when it is no longer pending for the purpose of—

(a) Part 5 of this Act, or
(b) the Special Immigration Appeals Commission Act 1997 (c. 68).

(4) The giving of directions in respect of a person under a provision of the Immigration Acts is not the provision of assistance to him for the purposes of this Schedule.

Note: Paragraphs 2, 8, 9, 10, 11, 12, 15 and 16 commenced on 8 December 2002, for the purpose of enabling subordinate legislation. Remainder of Schedule commenced 8 January 2003 (SI 2002/2811). Paragraph (7A) inserted and words in square brackets in para 14 substituted by Asylum and Immigration Act 2004, s 9 from 1 December 2004 (SI 2004/2999).

Section 81

[SCHEDULE 4

THE ASYLUM AND IMMIGRATION TRIBUNAL

Membership

1. The Lord Chancellor shall appoint the members of the Asylum and Immigration Tribunal.

2.—(1) A person is eligible for appointment as a member of the Tribunal only if he—
(a) has a seven year general qualification within the meaning of section 71 of the Courts and Legal Services Act 1990 (c. 41),
(b) is an advocate or solicitor in Scotland of at least seven years' standing,
(c) is a member of the Bar of Northern Ireland, or a solicitor of the Supreme Court of Northern Ireland, of at least seven years' standing,
(d) in the Lord Chancellor's opinion, has legal experience which makes him as suitable for appointment as if he satisfied paragraph (a), (b) or (c), or
(e) in the Lord Chancellor's opinion, has non-legal experience which makes him suitable for appointment.

(2) A person appointed under sub-paragraph (1)(a) to (d) shall be known as a legally qualified member of the Tribunal.

3.—(1) A member—
(a) may resign by notice in writing to the Lord Chancellor,
(b) shall cease to be a member on reaching the age of 70, and
(c) otherwise, shall hold and vacate office in accordance with the terms of his appointment (which may include provision—
(i) about the training, appraisal and mentoring of members of the Tribunal by other members, and
(ii) for removal).

(2) Sub-paragraph (1)(b) is subject to section 26(4) to (6) of the Judicial Pensions and Retirement Act 1993 (c. 8) (extension to age 75).

4. The Lord Chancellor may by order make provision for the title of members of the Tribunal.

Presidency

5.—(1) The Lord Chancellor shall appoint—

(a) a member of the Tribunal, who holds or has held high judicial office within the meaning of [Part 3 of Constitutional Reform Act 2005 or who is or has been a member of the Judicial Committee of the Privy Council], as President of the Tribunal, and

(b) one or more members of the Tribunal as Deputy President.

(2) A Deputy President—

(a) may act for the President if the President is unable to act or unavailable, and

(b) shall perform such functions as the President may delegate or assign to him.

Proceedings

6. The Tribunal shall sit at times and places determined by the Lord Chancellor.

7.—(1) The jurisdiction of the Tribunal shall be exercised by such number of its members as the President, having regard to the complexity and other circumstances of particular cases or classes of case, may direct.

(2) A direction under this paragraph—

(a) may relate to the whole or part of specified proceedings or to the whole or part of proceedings of a specified kind,

(b) may enable jurisdiction to be exercised by a single member,

(c) may require or permit the transfer of the whole or part of proceedings—

(i) from one member to another,

(ii) from one group of members to another,

(iii) from one member to a group of members, or

(iv) from a group of members to one member,

(d) may be varied or revoked by a further direction, and

(e) is subject to rules under section 106.

8.—(1) The President may make arrangements for the allocation of proceedings to members of the Tribunal.

(2) Arrangements under this paragraph—

(a) may permit allocation by the President or another member of the Tribunal,

(b) may permit the allocation of a case to a specified member or to a specified class of member,

(c) may include provision for transfer, and

(d) are subject to rules under section 106.

Staff

9. The Lord Chancellor may appoint staff for the Tribunal.

Money

10. The Lord Chancellor—

(a) may pay remuneration and allowances to members of the Tribunal,

(b) may pay remuneration and allowances to staff of the Tribunal, and

(c) may defray expenses of the Tribunal.

11. The Lord Chancellor may pay compensation to a person who ceases to be a member of the Tribunal if the Lord Chancellor thinks it appropriate because of special circumstances.]

Note: Schedule 4 substituted by Asylum and Immigration Act 2004, s 26 from 4 April 2005 (SI 2005/565). Words in square brackets in para 5(1) substituted by Sch 17 Constitutional Reform Act 2005 from a date to be appointed.

Section 100

Schedule 5

The Immigration Appeal Tribunal

...

Note: Schedule 5 ceases to have effect from 4 April 2005 (SI 2005/565), Asylum and Immigration Act 2004, s 26.

Section 114

Schedule 6

Immigration and Asylum Appeals: Transitional Provision

'Commencement'

1. In this Schedule 'commencement' means the coming into force of Part 5 of this Act.

Adjudicator

2. Where a person is an adjudicator under section 57 of the Immigration and Asylum Act 1999 (c. 33) immediately before commencement his appointment shall have effect after commencement as if made under section 81 of this Act.

Tribunal

3.—(1) Where a person is a member of the Immigration Appeal Tribunal immediately before commencement his appointment shall have effect after commencement as if made under Schedule 5.

(2) Where a person is a member of staff of the Immigration Appeal Tribunal immediately before commencement his appointment shall have effect after commencement as if made under Schedule 5.

Earlier appeal

4. In the application of section 96—
   (a) a reference to an appeal or right of appeal under a provision of this Act includes a reference to an appeal or right of appeal under the Immigration and Asylum Act 1999,
   (b) a reference to a requirement imposed under this Act includes a reference to a requirement of a similar nature imposed under that Act,
   (c) a reference to a statement made in pursuance of a requirement imposed under

a provision of this Act includes a reference to anything done in compliance with a requirement of a similar nature under that Act, and

(d) a reference to notification by virtue of this Act includes a reference to notification by virtue of any other enactment.

Saving

5.—(1) This Schedule is without prejudice to the power to include transitional provision in an order under section 162.

(2) An order under that section may, in particular, provide for a reference to a provision of Part 5 of this Act to be treated as being or including a reference (with or without modification) to a provision of the Immigration and Asylum Act 1999 (c. 33).

Note: Commencement from 1 April 2003 (SI 2003/754)

Section 114

SCHEDULE 7

IMMIGRATION AND ASYLUM APPEALS: CONSEQUENTIAL AMENDMENTS

. . .

Section 125

SCHEDULE 8

CARRIERS' LIABILITY

. . .

Note: Amends the Immigration and Asylum Act 1999.

Section 161

SCHEDULE 9

REPEALS

. . .

Asylum and Immigration (Treatment of Claimants, etc.) Act 2004
(2004, c. 19)

Arrangement of Sections

Offences

Treatment of claimants

Enforcement powers

Procedure for marriage

An Act to make provision about asylum and immigration. [22nd July 2004]

Offences

1. Assisting unlawful immigration

. . .

Note: Amends Immigration Act 1971, ss 25 and 25C.

2. Entering United Kingdom without passport, &c.

(1) A person commits an offence if at a leave or asylum interview he does not have with him an immigration document which—
   (a) is in force, and
   (b) satisfactorily establishes his identity and nationality or citizenship.

(2) A person commits an offence if at a leave or asylum interview he does not have with him, in respect of any dependent child with whom he claims to be travelling or living, an immigration document which—
   (a) is in force, and
   (b) satisfactorily establishes the child's identity and nationality or citizenship.

(3) But a person does not commit an offence under subsection (1) or (2) if—
   (a) the interview referred to in that subsection takes place after the person has entered the United Kingdom, and
   (b) within the period of three days beginning with the date of the interview the person provides to an immigration officer or to the Secretary of State a document of the kind referred to in that subsection.

(4) It is a defence for a person charged with an offence under subsection (1)—
   (a) to prove that he is an EEA national,
   (b) to prove that he is a member of the family of an EEA national and that he is exercising a right under the Community Treaties in respect of entry to or residence in the United Kingdom,
   (c) to prove that he has a reasonable excuse for not being in possession of a document of the kind specified in subsection (1),
   (d) to produce a false immigration document and to prove that he used that document as an immigration document for all purposes in connection with his journey to the United Kingdom, or
   (e) to prove that he travelled to the United Kingdom without, at any stage since he set out on the journey, having possession of an immigration document.

(5) It is a defence for a person charged with an offence under subsection (2) in respect of a child—
   (a) to prove that the child is an EEA national,

(b) to prove that the child is a member of the family of an EEA national and that the child is exercising a right under the Community Treaties in respect of entry to or residence in the United Kingdom,
(c) to prove that the person has a reasonable excuse for not being in possession of a document of the kind specified in subsection (2),
(d) to produce a false immigration document and to prove that it was used as an immigration document for all purposes in connection with the child's journey to the United Kingdom, or
(e) to prove that he travelled to the United Kingdom with the child without, at any stage since he set out on the journey, having possession of an immigration document in respect of the child.

(6) Where the charge for an offence under subsection (1) or (2) relates to an interview which takes place after the defendant has entered the United Kingdom—
(a) subsections (4)(c) and (5)(c) shall not apply, but
(b) it is a defence for the defendant to prove that he has a reasonable excuse for not providing a document in accordance with subsection (3).

(7) For the purposes of subsections (4) to (6)—
(a) the fact that a document was deliberately destroyed or disposed of is not a reasonable excuse for not being in possession of it or for not providing it in accordance with subsection (3), unless it is shown that the destruction or disposal was—
(i) for a reasonable cause, or
(ii) beyond the control of the person charged with the offence, and
(b) in paragraph (a)(i) 'reasonable cause' does not include the purpose of—
(i) delaying the handling or resolution of a claim or application or the taking of a decision,
(ii) increasing the chances of success of a claim or application, or
(iii) complying with instructions or advice given by a person who offers advice about, or facilitates, immigration into the United Kingdom, unless in the circumstances of the case it is unreasonable to expect non-compliance with the instructions or advice.

(8) A person shall be presumed for the purposes of this section not to have a document with him if he fails to produce it to an immigration officer or official of the Secretary of State on request.

(9) A person guilty of an offence under this section shall be liable—
(a) on conviction on indictment, to imprisonment for a term not exceeding two years, to a fine or to both, or
(b) on summary conviction, to imprisonment for a term not exceeding twelve months, to a fine not exceeding the statutory maximum or to both.

(10) If a constable or immigration officer reasonably suspects that a person has committed an offence under this section he may arrest the person without warrant.

(11) An offence under this section shall be treated as—
(a) a relevant offence for the purposes of sections 28B and 28D of the Immigration Act 1971 (c. 77) (search, entry and arrest), and
(b) an offence under Part III of that Act (criminal proceedings) for the purposes of sections 28(4), 28E, 28G and 28H (search after arrest, &c.) of that Act.

(12) In this section—
'EEA national' means a national of a State which is a contracting party to the Agreement on the European Economic Area signed at Oporto on 2nd May 1992 (as it has effect from time to time),
'immigration document' means—
(a) a passport, and
(b) a document which relates to a national of a State other than the United Kingdom and which is designed to serve the same purpose as a passport, and
'leave or asylum interview' means an interview with an immigration officer or an official of the Secretary of State at which a person—
(a) seeks leave to enter or remain in the United Kingdom, or
(b) claims that to remove him from or require him to leave the United Kingdom would breach the United Kingdom's obligations under the Refugee Convention or would be unlawful under section 6 of the Human Rights Act 1998 (c. 42) as being incompatible with his Convention rights.

(13) For the purposes of this section—
(a) a document which purports to be, or is designed to look like, an immigration document, is a false immigration document, and
(b) an immigration document is a false immigration document if and in so far as it is used—
(i) outside the period for which it is expressed to be valid,
(ii) contrary to provision for its used made by the person issuing it, or
(iii) by or in respect of a person other than the person to or for whom it was issued.

(14) Section 11 of the Immigration Act 1971 (c. 77) shall have effect for the purpose of the construction of a reference in this section to entering the United Kingdom.

(15) In so far as this section extends to England and Wales, subsection (9)(b) shall, until the commencement of section 154 of the Criminal Justice Act 2003 (c. 44) (increased limit on magistrates' power of imprisonment), have effect as if the reference to twelve months were a reference to six months.

(16) In so far as this section extends to Scotland, subsection (9)(b) shall have effect as if the reference to twelve months were a reference to six months.

(17) In so far as this section extends to Northern Ireland, subsection (9)(b) shall have effect as if the reference to twelve months were a reference to six months.

Note: Commenced 22 September 2004, s 48.

3. Immigration documents: forgery

. . .

Note: Section 3 repealed from 7 June 2006, Identity Cards Act 2006, s 44 and Sch 2.

4. Trafficking people for exploitation

(1) A person commits an offence if he arranges or facilitates the arrival in the United Kingdom of an individual (the 'passenger') and—
- (a) he intends to exploit the passenger in the United Kingdom or elsewhere, or
- (b) he believes that another person is likely to exploit the passenger in the United Kingdom or elsewhere.

(2) A person commits an offence if he arranges or facilitates travel within the United Kingdom by an individual (the 'passenger') in respect of whom he believes that an offence under subsection (1) may have been committed and—
- (a) he intends to exploit the passenger in the United Kingdom or elsewhere, or
- (b) he believes that another person is likely to exploit the passenger in the United Kingdom or elsewhere.

(3) A person commits an offence if he arranges or facilitates the departure from the United Kingdom of an individual (the 'passenger') and—
- (a) he intends to exploit the passenger outside the United Kingdom, or
- (b) he believes that another person is likely to exploit the passenger outside the United Kingdom.

(4) For the purposes of this section a person is exploited if (and only if)—
- (a) he is the victim of behaviour that contravenes Article 4 of the Human Rights Convention (slavery and forced labour),
- (b) he is encouraged, required or expected to do anything as a result of which he or another person would commit an offence under the Human Organ Transplants Act 1989 (c. 31) or the Human Organ Transplants (Northern Ireland) Order 1989 (S.I. 1989/2408 (N.I. 21)),
- (c) he is subjected to force, threats or deception designed to induce him—
  - (i) to provide services of any kind,
  - (ii) to provide another person with benefits of any kind, or
  - (iii) to enable another person to acquire benefits of any kind, or
- (d) he is requested or induced to undertake any activity, having been chosen as the subject of the request or inducement on the grounds that—

(i) he is mentally or physically ill or disabled, he is young or he has a family relationship with a person, and
(ii) a person without the illness, disability, youth or family relationship would be likely to refuse the request or resist the inducement.

(5) A person guilty of an offence under this section shall be liable—
(a) on conviction on indictment, to imprisonment for a term not exceeding 14 years, to a fine or to both, or
(b) on summary conviction, to imprisonment for a term not exceeding twelve months, to a fine not exceeding the statutory maximum or to both.

Note: Commencement at 1 December 2004 (SI 2004/2999).

5. Section 4: supplemental

(1) Subsections (1) to (3) of section 4 apply to anything done—
(a) in the United Kingdom,
(b) outside the United Kingdom by an individual to whom subsection (2) below applies, or
(c) outside the United Kingdom by a body incorporated under the law of a part of the United Kingdom.

(2) This subsection applies to—
(a) a British citizen,
(b) a British overseas territories citizen,
(c) a British National (Overseas),
(d) a British Overseas citizen,
(e) a person who is a British subject under the British Nationality Act 1981 (c. 61), and
(f) a British protected person within the meaning of that Act.

(3) In section 4(4)(a) 'the Human Rights Convention' means the Convention for the Protection of Human Rights and Fundamental Freedoms agreed by the Council of Europe at Rome on 4th November 1950.

(4) Section 25C and 25D of the Immigration Act 1971 (c. 77) (forfeiture or detention of vehicle, &c.) shall apply in relation to an offence under section 4 of this Act as they apply in relation to an offence under section 25 of that Act.

(5) . . .

Note: Amends Immigration Act 1971, s 25C(9)(b), (10)(b) and (11).

(6) . . .

Note: Amends para 2, Sch 4 Criminal Justice and Court Services Act 2000.

(7) . . .

Note: Amends para 4, Sch 2 Proceeds of Crime Act 2002.

(8) . . .

Note: Amends para 4, Sch 4 Proceeds of Crime Act 2002.

(9) . . .

Note: Amends para 4, Sch 5 Proceeds of Crime Act 2002.

(10) . . .

Note: Amends para 2(1), Sch Protection of Children and Vulnerable Adults (Northern Ireland) Order 2003.

(11) In so far as section 4 extends to England and Wales, subsection (5)(b) shall, until the commencement of section 154 of the Criminal Justice Act 2003 (c. 44) (increased limit on magistrates' power of imprisonment), have effect as if the reference to twelve months were a reference to six months.

(12) In so far as section 4 extends to Scotland, subsection (5)(b) shall have effect as if the reference to twelve months were a reference to six months.

(13) In so far as section 4 extends to Northern Ireland, subsection (5)(b) shall have effect as if the reference to twelve months were a reference to six months.

Note: Commenced 1 December 2004 (SI 2004/2999).

6. Employment

. . .

Note: Amends Asylum and Immigration Act 1996, s 8.

7. Advice of Director of Public Prosecutions

. . .

Note: Amends Prosecution of Offences Act 1985, s 3(2).

Treatment of claimants

8. Claimant's credibility

(1) In determining whether to believe a statement made by or on behalf of a person who makes an asylum claim or a human rights claim, a deciding authority shall take account, as damaging the claimant's credibility, of any behaviour to which this section applies.

(2) This section applies to any behaviour by the claimant that the deciding authority thinks—

(a) is designed or likely to conceal information,

(b) is designed or likely to mislead, or

(c) is designed or likely to obstruct or delay the handling or resolution of the claim or the taking of a decision in relation to the claimant.

(3) Without prejudice to the generality of subsection (2) the following kinds of behaviour shall be treated as designed or likely to conceal information or to mislead—

(a) failure without reasonable explanation to produce a passport on request to an immigration officer or to the Secretary of State,

(b) the production of a document which is not a valid passport as if it were,

(c) the destruction, alteration or disposal, in each case without reasonable explanation, of a passport,

(d) the destruction, alteration or disposal, in each case without reasonable explanation, of a ticket or other document connected with travel, and

(e) failure without reasonable explanation to answer a question asked by a deciding authority.

(4) This section also applies to failure by the claimant to take advantage of a reasonable opportunity to make an asylum claim or human rights claim while in a safe country.

(5) This section also applies to failure by the claimant to make an asylum claim or human rights claim before being notified of an immigration decision, unless the claim relies wholly on matters arising after the notification.

(6) This section also applies to failure by the claimant to make an asylum claim or human rights claim before being arrested under an immigration provision, unless—

(a) he had no reasonable opportunity to make the claim before the arrest, or

(b) the claim relies wholly on matters arising after the arrest.

(7) In this section—

'asylum claim' has the meaning given by section 113(1) of the Nationality, Immigration and Asylum Act 2002 (c. 41) (subject to subsection (9) below),

'deciding authority' means—

(a) an immigration officer,

(b) the Secretary of State,

(c) the Asylum and Immigration Tribunal, or

(d) the Special Immigration Appeals Commission,

'human rights claim' has the meaning given by section 113(1) of the Nationality, Immigration and Asylum Act 2002 (subject to subsection (9) below),

'immigration decision' means—

(a) refusal of leave to enter the United Kingdom,

(b) refusal to vary a person's leave to enter or remain in the United Kingdom,

(c) grant of leave to enter or remain in the United Kingdom,

(d) a decision that a person is to be removed from the United Kingdom by way of directions under section 10(1)(a), (b), (ba) or (c) of the Immigration and Asylum Act 1999 (c. 33) (removal of persons unlawfully in United Kingdom),

(e) a decision that a person is to be removed from the United Kingdom by way of directions under paragraphs 8 to 12 of Schedule 2 to the Immigration Act 1971 (c. 77) (control of entry: removal),

(f) a decision to make a deportation order under section 5(1) of that Act, and

(g) a decision to take action in relation to a person in connection with extradition from the United Kingdom,

'immigration provision' means—

(a) sections 28A, 28AA, 28B, 28C and 28CA of the Immigration Act 1971 (immigration offences: enforcement),

(b) paragraph 17 of Schedule 2 to that Act (control of entry),

(c) section 14 of this Act, and

(d) a provision of the Extradition Act 1989 (c. 33) or 2003 (c. 41),

'notified' means notified in such manner as may be specified by regulations made by the Secretary of State,

'passport' includes a document which relates to a national of a country other than the United Kingdom and which is designed to serve the same purpose as a passport, and

'safe country' means a country to which Part 2 of Schedule 3 applies.

(8) A passport produced by or on behalf of a person is valid for the purposes of subsection (3)(b) if it—

(a) relates to the person by whom or on whose behalf it is produced,

(b) has not been altered otherwise than by or with the permission of the authority who issued it, and

(c) was not obtained by deception.

(9) In subsection (4) a reference to an asylum claim or human rights claim shall be treated as including a reference to a claim of entitlement to remain in a country other than the United Kingdom made by reference to the rights that a person invokes in making an asylum claim or a human rights claim in the United Kingdom.

(10) Regulations under subsection (7) specifying a manner of notification may, in particular—

(a) apply or refer to regulations under section 105 of the Nationality, Immigration and Asylum Act 2002 (c. 41) (notice of immigration decisions);

(b) make provision similar to provision that is or could be made by regulations under that section;

(c) modify a provision of regulations under that section in its effect for the purpose of regulations under this section;

(d) provide for notice to be treated as received at a specified time if sent to a specified class of place in a specified manner.

(11) Regulations under subsection (7) specifying a manner of notification—

(a) may make incidental, consequential or transitional provision,

(b) shall be made by statutory instrument, and

(c) shall be subject to annulment in pursuance of a resolution of either House of Parliament.

(12) This section shall not prevent a deciding authority from determining not to believe a statement on the grounds of behaviour to which this section does not apply.

(13) Before the coming into force of section 26 a reference in this section to the Asylum and Immigration Tribunal shall be treated as a reference to—

(a) an adjudicator appointed, or treated as if appointed; under section 81 of the Nationality, Immigration and Asylum Act 2002 (c. 41) (appeals), and

(b) the Immigration Appeal Tribunal.

Note: Commencement 1 January 2005 (SI 2004/3398).

9. Failed asylum seekers: withdrawal of support

(1) . . .

Note: Amends Sch 3 Nationality, Immigration and Asylum Act 2002.

(2) . . .

Note: Amends Sch 3 Nationality, Immigration and Asylum Act 2002.

(3) No appeal may be brought under section 103 of the Immigration and Asylum Act 1999 (asylum support appeal) against a decision—

(a) that by virtue of a provision of Schedule 3 to the Nationality, Immigration and Asylum Act 2002 (c. 41) other than paragraph 7A a person is not qualified to receive support, or

(b) on the grounds of the application of a provision of that Schedule other than paragraph 7A, to stop providing support to a person.

(4) On an appeal under section 103 of the Immigration and Asylum Act 1999 (c. 33) against a decision made by virtue of paragraph 7A of Schedule 3 to the Nationality, Immigration and Asylum Act 2002 the adjudicator may, in particular—

(a) annul a certificate of the Secretary of State issued for the purposes of that paragraph;

(b) require the Secretary of State to reconsider the matters certified.

(5) An order under section 48 providing for this section to come into force may, in particular, provide for this section to have effect with specified modifications

before the coming into force of a provision of the Nationality, Immigration and Asylum Act 2002.

Note: Commencement 1 December 2004 (SI 2004/2999).

10. Failed asylum seekers: accommodation

(1) . . .

Note: Amends Immigration and Asylum Act 1999, s 4.

(2) . . .

Note: Amends Immigration and Asylum Act 1999, s 166(5).

(3) . . .

Note: Amends Immigration and Asylum Act 1999, s 103.

(4) . . .

Note: Amends Immigration and Asylum Act 1999, s 103.

(5) . . .

Note: Amends Immigration and Asylum Act 1999, s 103A.

(6) In an amendment made by this section a reference to providing accommodation includes a reference to arranging for the provision of accommodation.

(7) Regulations under section 4(5)(b) of the Immigration and Asylum Act 1999 (c. 33) (as inserted by subsection (1) above) may apply to persons receiving support under section 4 when the regulations come into force.

Note: Subsections (1), (2), (6) and (7) commenced 1 December 2004 (SI 2004/2999).

11. Accommodation for asylum seekers: local connection

(1) . . .

Note: Amends Housing Act 1996, s 199.

(2) Subsection (3) applies where—
- (a) a local housing authority would (but for subsection (3)) be obliged to secure that accommodation is available for occupation by a person under section 193 of the Housing Act 1996 (homeless persons),
- (b) the person was (at any time) provided with accommodation in a place in Scotland under section 95 of the Immigration and Asylum Act 1999 (support for asylum seekers),
- (c) the accommodation was not provided in an accommodation centre by virtue of section 22 of the Nationality, Immigration and Asylum Act 2002 (use of accommodation centres for section 95 support), and

(d) the person has neither—
(i) a local connection with the district of a local housing authority (in England or Wales) within the meaning of section 199 of the Housing Act 1996 as amended by subsection (1) above, nor
(ii) a local connection with a district (in Scotland) within the meaning of section 27 of the Housing (Scotland) Act 1987 (c. 26).

(3) Where this subsection applies—
(a) the duty of the local housing authority under section 193 of the Housing Act 1996 in relation to the person shall not apply, but
(b) the local housing authority—
(i) may secure that accommodation is available for occupation by the person for a period giving him a reasonable opportunity of securing accommodation for his occupation, and
(ii) may provide the person (or secure that he is provided with) advice and assistance in any attempts he may make to secure that accommodation becomes available for his occupation.

Note: Commenced 4 January 2005 (SI 2004/2999).

12. Refugee: back-dating of benefits

(1) . . .

Note: Repeals Immigration and Asylum Act 1999, s 123.

(2) . . .

Note: Amends SI 1987/1967, SR 1987/459, SI 1987/1968, SR 1987/465, SI 1987/1971, SR 1987/461, SI 1992/1814.

(3) . . .

Note: Amends SI 2000/636.

(4) . . .

Note: Amends SR 2000/71.

(5) An order under section 48 bringing this section into force may, in particular, provide for this section to have effect in relation to persons recorded as refugees after a specified date (irrespective of when the process resulting in the record was begun).

Note: Commencement at a date to be appointed.

13. Integration loan for refugees

(1) The Secretary of State may make regulations enabling him to make loans [—

(a) to refugees, and
(b) to such other classes of person, or to persons other than refugees in such circumstances, as the regulations may prescribe.]

(2) A person is a refugee for the purpose of subsection (1) if the Secretary of State has—
(a) recorded him as a refugee within the meaning of the Convention relating to the Status of Refugees done at Geneva on 28 July 1951, and
(b) granted him indefinite leave to enter or remain in the United Kingdom (within the meaning of section 33(1) of the Immigration Act 1971 (c. 77)).

(3) Regulations under subsection (1)—
(a) shall specify matters which the Secretary of State shall, in addition to other matters appearing to him to be relevant, take into account in determining whether or not to make a loan (and those matters may, in particular, relate to—
(i) a person's income or assets,
(ii) a person's likely ability to repay a loan, or
(iii) the length of time since a person was recorded as a refugee),
(b) shall enable the Secretary of State to specify (and vary from time to time) a minimum and a maximum amount of a loan,
(c) shall prevent a person from receiving a loan if—
(i) he is under the age of 18,
(ii) he is insolvent, within a meaning given by the regulations, or
(iii) he has received a loan under the regulations,
(d) shall make provision about repayment of a loan (and may, in particular, make provision—
(i) about interest;
(ii) for repayment by deduction from a social security benefit or similar payment due to the person to whom the loan is made),
(e) shall enable the Secretary of State to attach conditions to a loan (which may include conditions about the use of the loan),
(f) shall make provision about—
(i) the making of an application for a loan, and
(ii) the information, which may include information about the intended use of a loan, to be provided in or with an application,
(g) may make provision about steps to be taken by the Secretary of State in establishing an applicant's likely ability to repay a loan,
(h) may make provision for a loan to be made jointly to more than one refugee, and
(i) may confer a discretion on the Secretary of State.

(4) Regulations under this section—
(a) shall be made by statutory instrument, and

(b) may not be made unless a draft has been laid before and approved by resolution of each House of Parliament.

Note: Commencement 29 June 2006 (SI 2006/1517). Words in square brackets in sub-s (1) substituted from 30 June 2006, Immigration, Nationality and Asylum Act 2006, s 45(1).

Enforcement powers

14. Immigration officer: power of arrest

(1) Where an immigration officer in the course of exercising a function under the Immigration Acts forms a reasonable suspicion that a person has committed or attempted to commit an offence listed in subsection (2), he may arrest the person without warrant.

(2) Those offences are—

(a) the offence of conspiracy at common law (in relation to conspiracy to defraud),

(b) at common law in Scotland, any of the following offences—

(i) fraud,

(ii) conspiracy to defraud,

(iii) uttering and fraud,

(iv) bigamy,

(v) theft, and

(vi) reset,

(c) an offence under section 57 of the Offences against the Person Act 1861 (c. 100) (bigamy),

(d) an offence under section 3 or 4 of the Perjury Act 1911 (c. 6) (false statements),

(e) an offence under section 7 of that Act (aiding, abetting &c.) if it relates to an offence under section 3 or 4 of that Act,

(f) an offence under section 53 of the Registration of Births, Deaths and Marriages (Scotland) Act 1965 (c. 49) (knowingly giving false information to district registrar, &c.),

(g) an offence under any of the following provisions of the Theft Act 1968 (c. 60)—

(i) section 1 (theft),

(ii) section 15 (obtaining property by deception),

(iii) section 16 (obtaining pecuniary advantage by deception),

(iv) section 17 (false accounting), and

(v) section 22 (handling stolen goods),

(h) an offence under section 1, 15, 16, 17 or 21 of the Theft Act (Northern Ireland) 1969 (c. 16) (N.I.),

(i) an offence under section 1 or 2 of the Theft Act 1978 (c. 31) (obtaining services, or evading liability, by deception),

(j) an offence under Article 3 or 4 of the Theft (Northern Ireland) Order 1978 (S.I. 1978/1407 (N.I. 23)),
(k) an offence under Article 8 or 9 of the Perjury (Northern Ireland) Order 1979 (S.I. 1979/1714 (N.I. 19)),
(l) an offence under Article 12 of that Order if it relates to an offence under Article 8 or 9 of that Order,
(m) an offence under any of the following provisions of the Forgery and Counterfeiting Act 1981 (c. 45)—
  (i) section 1 (forgery),
  (ii) section 2 (copying false instrument),
  (iii) section 3 (using false instrument),
  (iv) section 4 (using copy of false instrument), and
  (v) section 5(1) and (3) (false documents),
(n) an offence under any of sections 57 to 59 of the Sexual Offences Act 2003 (c. 42) (trafficking for sexual exploitation),
(o) an offence under section 22 of the Criminal Justice (Scotland) Act 2003 (asp 7) (trafficking in prostitution), . . .
(p) an offence under section 4 of this Act.
[(q) an offence under section 25 of the Identity Cards Act 2006]

(3) The following provisions of the Immigration Act 1971 (c. 77) shall have effect for the purpose of making, or in connection with, an arrest under this section as they have effect for the purpose of making, or in connection with, arrests for offences under that Act—
(a) section 28C (entry and search before arrest),
(b) sections 28E and 28F (entry and search after arrest),
(c) sections 28G and 28H (search of arrested person), and
(d) section 28I (seized material).

(4) . . .

Note: Subsection (4) amends Race Relations Act 1976, s 19D. Commencement 1 December 2004 (SI 2004/2999). Words in sub-s 14(2)(o) omitted and words in sub-s 14(2)(q) inserted from 7 June 2006, Identity Cards Act 2006, s 30 and Sch 2.

15. Fingerprinting

. . .

Note: Amends Immigration and Asylum Act 1999, s 141.

16. Information about passengers

. . .

Note: Amends para 27B, Sch 2 Immigration Act 1971.

17. Retention of documents

Where a document comes into the possession of the Secretary of State or an immigration officer in the course of the exercise of an immigration function, the Secretary of State or an immigration officer may retain the document while he suspects that—

(a) a person to whom the document relates may be liable to removal from the United Kingdom in accordance with a provision of the Immigration Acts, and

(b) retention of the document may facilitate the removal.

Note: Commencement at 1 December 2004 (SI 2004/2999).

18. Control of entry

. . .

Note: Amends para 2A, Sch 2 Immigration Act 1971.

Procedure for marriage

19. England and Wales

(1) This section applies to a marriage—

(a) which is to be solemnised on the authority of certificates issued by a superintendent registrar under Part III of the Marriage Act 1949 (c. 76), and

(b) a party to which is subject to immigration control.

(2) In relation to a marriage to which this section applies, the notices under section 27 of the Marriage Act 1949—

(a) shall be given to the superintendent registrar of a registration district specified for the purpose of this paragraph by regulations made by the Secretary of State,

(b) shall be delivered to the superintendent registrar in person by the two parties to the marriage,

(c) may be given only if each party to the marriage has been resident in a registration district for the period of seven days immediately before the giving of his or her notice (but the district need not be that in which the notice is given and the parties need not have resided in the same district), and

(d) shall state, in relation to each party, the registration district by reference to which paragraph (c) is satisfied.

(3) The superintendent registrar shall not enter in the marriage notice book notice of a marriage to which this section applies unless satisfied, by the provision of specified evidence, that the party subject to immigration control—

(a) has an entry clearance granted expressly for the purpose of enabling him to marry in the United Kingdom,
(b) has the written permission of the Secretary of State to marry in the United Kingdom, or
(c) falls within a class specified for the purpose of this paragraph by regulations made by the Secretary of State.

(4) For the purposes of this section—
(a) a person is subject to immigration control if—
(i) he is not an EEA national, and
(ii) under the Immigration Act 1971 (c. 77) he requires leave to enter or remain in the United Kingdom (whether or not leave has been given),
(b) 'EEA national' means a national of a State which is a contracting party to the Agreement on the European Economic Area signed at Oporto on 2nd May 1992 (as it has effect from time to time),
(c) 'entry clearance' has the meaning given by section 33(1) of the Immigration Act 1971, and
(d) 'specified evidence' means such evidence as may be specified in guidance issued by the Registrar General.

Note: Commencement 1 February 2005 (SI 2004/3398).

20. England and Wales: supplemental

(1) The Marriage Act 1949 (c. 76) shall have effect in relation to a marriage to which section 19 applies—
(a) subject to that section, and
(b) with any necessary consequential modification.

(2) In particular—
(a) section 28(1)(b) of that Act (declaration: residence) shall have effect as if it required a declaration that—
(i) the notice of marriage is given in compliance with section 19(2) above, and
(ii) the party subject to immigration control satisfies section 19(3)(a), (b) or (c), and
(b) section 48 of that Act (proof of certain matters not essential to validity of marriage) shall have effect as if the list of matters in section 48(1)(a) to (e) included compliance with section 19 above.

(3) Regulations of the Secretary of State under section 19(2)(a) or (3)(c)—
(a) may make transitional provision,
(b) shall be made by statutory instrument, and
(c) shall be subject to annulment in pursuance of a resolution of either House of Parliament.

(4) Before making regulations under section 19(2)(a) the Secretary of State shall consult the Registrar General.

(5) An expression used in section 19 or this section and in Part III of the Marriage Act 1949 (c. 76) has the same meaning in section 19 or this section as in that Part.

(6) An order under the Regulatory Reform Act 2001 (c. 6) may include provision—
   (a) amending section 19, this section or section 25 in consequence of other provision of the order, or
   (b) repealing section 19, this section and section 25 and re-enacting them with modifications consequential upon other provision of the order.

Note: Commenced 1 February 2005 (SI 2004/3398).

21. Scotland

(1) This section applies to a marriage—
   (a) which is intended to be solemnised in Scotland, and
   (b) a party to which is subject to immigration control.

(2) In relation to a marriage to which this section applies, notice under section 3 of the Marriage (Scotland) Act 1977 (c. 15)—
   (a) may be submitted to the district registrar of a registration district prescribed for the purposes of this section, and
   (b) may not be submitted to the district registrar of any other registration district.

(3) Where the district registrar to whom notice is submitted by virtue of subsection (2) is the district registrar for the registration district in which the marriage is to be solemnised, he shall not make an entry under section 4, or complete a Marriage Schedule under section 6, of the Marriage (Scotland) Act 1977 in respect of the marriage unless satisfied, by the provision of specified evidence, that the party subject to immigration control—
   (a) has an entry clearance granted expressly for the purpose of enabling him to marry in the United Kingdom,
   (b) has the written permission of the Secretary of State to marry in the United Kingdom, or
   (c) falls within a class specified for the purpose of this paragraph by regulations made by the Secretary of State.

(4) Where the district registrar to whom notice is submitted by virtue of subsection (2) (here the 'notified registrar') is not the district registrar for the registration district in which the marriage is to be solemnised (here the 'second registrar')—
   (a) the notified registrar shall, if satisfied as is mentioned in subsection (3), send the notices and any fee, certificate or declaration which accompanied them, to the second registrar, and

(b) the second registrar shall be treated as having received the notices from the parties to the marriage on the dates on which the notified registrar received them.

(5) Subsection (4) of section 19 applies for the purposes of this section as it applies for the purposes of that section except that for the purposes of this section the reference in paragraph (d) of that subsection to guidance issued by the Registrar General shall be construed as a reference to guidance issued by the Secretary of State after consultation with the Registrar General for Scotland.

Note: Commenced 1 February 2005 (SI 2004/3398).

22. Scotland: supplemental

(1) The Marriage (Scotland) Act 1977 shall have effect in relation to a marriage to which section 21 applies—
   (a) subject to that section, and
   (b) with any necessary consequential modification.

(2) In subsection (2)(a) of that section 'prescribed' means prescribed by regulations made by the Secretary of State after consultation with the Registrar General for Scotland; and other expressions used in subsections (1) to (4) of that section and in the Marriage (Scotland) Act 1977 have the same meaning in those subsections as in that Act.

(3) Regulations made by of the Secretary of State under subsection (2)(a) or (3)(c) of that section—
   (a) may make transitional provision,
   (b) shall be made by statutory instrument, and
   (c) shall be subject to annulment in pursuance of a resolution of either House of Parliament.

Note: Commenced 1 February 2005 (SI 2004/3398).

23. Northern Ireland

(1) This section applies to a marriage—
   (a) which is intended to be solemnised in Northern Ireland, and
   (b) a party to which is subject to immigration control.

(2) In relation to a marriage to which this section applies, the marriage notices—
   (a) shall be given only to a prescribed registrar, and
   (b) shall, in prescribed cases, be given by both parties together in person at a prescribed register office.

(3) The prescribed registrar shall not act under Article 4 or 7 of the Marriage (Northern Ireland) Order 2003 (S.I. 2003/413 (N.I.3)) (marriage notice book, list of intended marriages and marriage schedule) unless he is satisfied,

by the provision of specified evidence, that the party subject to immigration control—

(a) has an entry clearance granted expressly for the purpose of enabling him to marry in the United Kingdom,

(b) has the written permission of the Secretary of State to marry in the United Kingdom, or

(c) falls within a class specified for the purpose of this paragraph by regulations made by the Secretary of State.

(4) Subject to subsection (5), if the prescribed registrar is not the registrar for the purposes of Article 4 of that Order, the prescribed registrar shall send him the marriage notices and he shall be treated as having received them from the parties to the marriage on the dates on which the prescribed registrar received them.

(5) The prescribed registrar shall not act under subsection (4) unless he is satisfied as mentioned in subsection (3).

(6) For the purposes of this section—

(a) a person is subject to immigration control if—

(i) he is not an EEA national, and

(ii) under the Immigration Act 1971 (c. 77) he requires leave to enter or remain in the United Kingdom (whether or not leave has been given),

(b) 'EEA national' means a national of a State which is a contracting party to the Agreement on the European Economic Area signed at Oporto on 2nd May 1992 (as it has effect from time to time),

(c) 'entry clearance' has the meaning given by section 33(1) of the Immigration Act 1971, and

(d) 'specified evidence' means such evidence as may be specified in guidance issued by the Secretary of State after consulting the Registrar General for Northern Ireland.

Note: Commenced 1 February 2005 (SI 2004/3398).

24. Northern Ireland: supplemental

(1) The Marriage (Northern Ireland) Order 2003 (S.I. 2003/413 (N.I.3)) shall have effect in relation to a marriage to which section 23 applies—

(a) subject to section 23, and

(b) with any necessary consequential modification.

(2) In section 23 'prescribed' means prescribed for the purposes of that section by regulations made by the Secretary of State after consulting the Registrar General for Northern Ireland and other expressions used in that section or this section and the Marriage (Northern Ireland) Order 2003 have the same meaning in section 23 or this section as in that Order.

(3) Section 18(3) of the Interpretation Act (Northern Ireland) 1954 (c.33 (N.I.)) (provisions as to holders of offices) shall apply to section 23 as if that section were an enactment within the meaning of that Act.

(4) Regulations of the Secretary of State under section 23—
   (a) may make transitional provision,
   (b) shall be made by statutory instrument, and
   (c) shall be subject to annulment in pursuance of a resolution of either House of Parliament.

Note: Commenced 1 February 2005 (SI 2004/3398).

25. Application for permission under section 19(3)(b), 21(3)(b) or 23(3)(b)

(1) The Secretary of State may make regulations requiring a person seeking permission under section 19(3)(b), 21(3)(b) or 23(3)(b)—
   (a) to make an application in writing, and
   (b) to pay a fee.

(2) The regulations shall, in particular, specify—
   (a) the information to be contained in or provided with the application,
   (b) the amount of the fee, and
   (c) how and to whom the fee is to be paid.

(3) The regulations may, in particular, make provision—
   (a) excepting a specified class of persons from the requirement to pay a fee;
   (b) permitting a specified class of persons to pay a reduced fee;
   (c) for the refund of all or part of a fee in specified circumstances.

(4) Regulations under this section—
   (a) shall be made by statutory instrument, and
   (b) shall be subject to annulment in pursuance of a resolution of either House of Parliament.

Note: Commenced 1 December 2004 (SI 2004/2999).

Appeals

26. Unification of appeal system

(1) . . .

Note: Amends Nationality, Immigration and Asylum Act 2002, s 81.

(2) . . .

Note: Amends Nationality, Immigration and Asylum Act 2002, s 82(1).

(3) . . .

Note: Amends Nationality, Immigration and Asylum Act 2002, s 83(2).

(4) . . .

Note: Amends Sch 4 Nationality, Immigration and Asylum Act 2002.

(5) . . .

Note: Amends Nationality, Immigration and Asylum Act 2002, ss 100–103 and Sch 5.

(6) . . .

Note: Amends Nationality, Immigration and Asylum Act 2002, s 104.

(7) Schedule 2 (which makes amendments consequential on this section, and transitional provision) shall have effect.

(8) The Lord Chancellor may by order vary a period specified in—
(a) section 103A(3)(a), (b) or (c) of the Nationality, Immigration and Asylum Act 2002 (c. 41) (review of Tribunal's decision) (as inserted by subsection (6) above), or
(b) paragraph 30(5)(b) of Schedule 2 to this Act.

(9) An order under subsection (8)—
(a) may make provision generally or only for specified cases or circumstances,
(b) may make different provision for different cases or circumstances,
(c) shall be made by statutory instrument, and
(d) shall be subject to annulment in pursuance of a resolution of either House of Parliament.

(10) Before making an order under subsection (8) the Lord Chancellor shall consult—
(a) the Lord Chief Justice, if the order affects proceedings in England and Wales,
(b) the Lord President of the Court of Session, if the order affects proceedings in Scotland, and
(c) the Lord Chief Justice of Northern Ireland, if the order affects proceedings in Northern Ireland.

Note: Commencement from 1 December 2004 (SI 2004/2999).

27. Unfounded human rights or asylum claim

. . .

Note: Amends Nationality, Immigration and Asylum Act 2002, ss 94 and 112 from 1 October 2004 (SI 2004/2523).

28. Appeal from within United Kingdom

. . .

Note: Amends Nationality, Immigration and Asylum Act 2002, s 92(3) from 1 October 2004 (SI 2004/2523).

29. Entry clearance

. . .

Note: Amends Nationality, Immigration and Asylum Act 2002, ss 88 and 112 from 1 October 2004 (SI 2004/2523).

30. Earlier right of appeal

. . .

Note: Amends Nationality, Immigration and Asylum Act 2002, s 96 from 1 October 2004 (SI 2004/2523).

31. Seamen and aircrews: right of appeal

. . .

Note: Amends Nationality, Immigration and Asylum Act 2002, s 82 from 1 October 2004 (SI 2004/2523).

32. Suspected international terrorist: bail

. . .

Note: Section 32 repealed from 14 March 2005, Prevention of Terrorism Act 2005, s 16(2).

Removal and detention

33. Removing asylum seeker to safe country

(1) Schedule 3 (which concerns the removal of persons claiming asylum to countries known to protect refugees and to respect human rights) shall have effect.

(2) . . .

Note: Repeals Immigration and Asylum Act 1999, ss 11 and 12.

(3) . . .

Note: Repeals Nationality, Immigration and Asylum Act 2002, ss 80 and 93. Commencement 1 October 2004 (SI 2004/2523).

34. Detention pending deportation

. . .

Note: Amends para 2, Sch 3 Immigration Act 1971 from 1 October 2004 (SI 2004/2523).

35. Deportation or removal: cooperation

(1) The Secretary of State may require a person to take specified action if the Secretary of State thinks that—
   (a) the action will or may enable a travel document to be obtained by or for the person, and
   (b) possession of the travel document will facilitate the person's deportation or removal from the United Kingdom.

(2) In particular, the Secretary of State may require a person to—
   (a) provide information or documents to the Secretary of State or to any other person;
   (b) obtain information or documents;
   (c) provide fingerprints, submit to the taking of a photograph or provide information, or submit to a process for the recording of information, about external physical characteristics (including, in particular, features of the iris or any other part of the eye);
   (d) make, or consent to or cooperate with the making of, an application to a person acting for the government of a State other than the United Kingdom;
   (e) cooperate with a process designed to enable determination of an application;
   (f) complete a form accurately and completely;
   (g) attend an interview and answer questions accurately and completely;
   (h) make an appointment.

(3) A person commits an offence if he fails without reasonable excuse to comply with a requirement of the Secretary of State under subsection (1).

(4) A person guilty of an offence under subsection (3) shall be liable—
   (a) on conviction on indictment, to imprisonment for a term not exceeding two years, to a fine or to both, or
   (b) on summary conviction, to imprisonment for a term not exceeding twelve months, to a fine not exceeding the statutory maximum or to both.

(5) If a constable or immigration officer reasonably suspects that a person has committed an offence under subsection (3) he may arrest the person without warrant.

(6) An offence under subsection (3) shall be treated as—
   (a) a relevant offence for the purposes of sections 28B and 28D of the Immigration Act 1971 (c. 77) (search, entry and arrest), and
   (b) an offence under Part III of that Act (criminal proceedings) for the purposes of sections 28(4), 28E, 28G and 28H (search after arrest, &c.) of that Act.

(7) In subsection (1)—

'travel document' means a passport or other document which is issued by or for Her Majesty's Government or the government of another State and which enables or facilitates travel from the United Kingdom to another State, and

'removal from the United Kingdom' means removal under—

(a) Schedule 2 to the Immigration Act 1971 (control on entry) (including a provision of that Schedule as applied by another provision of the Immigration Acts),
(b) section 10 of the Immigration and Asylum Act 1999 (c. 33) (removal of person unlawfully in United Kingdom), or
(c) Schedule 3 to this Act.

(8) While sections 11 and 12 of the Immigration and Asylum Act 1999 continue to have effect, the reference in subsection (7)(c) above to Schedule 3 to this Act shall be treated as including a reference to those sections.

(9) In so far as subsection (3) extends to England and Wales, subsection (4)(b) shall, until the commencement of section 154 of the Criminal Justice Act 2003 (c. 44) (increased limit on magistrates' power of imprisonment), have effect as if the reference to twelve months were a reference to six months.

(10) In so far as subsection (3) extends to Scotland, subsection (4)(b) shall have effect as if the reference to twelve months were a reference to six months.

(11) In so far as subsection (3) extends to Northern Ireland, subsection (4)(b) shall have effect as if the reference to twelve months were a reference to six months.

Note: Commencement 1 October 2004 (s 48).

36. Electronic monitoring

(1) In this section—

(a) 'residence restriction' means a restriction as to residence imposed under—
    (i) paragraph 21 of Schedule 2 to the Immigration Act 1971 (c. 77) (control on entry) (including that paragraph as applied by another provision of the Immigration Acts), or
    (ii) Schedule 3 to that Act (deportation),
(b) 'reporting restriction' means a requirement to report to a specified person imposed under any of those provisions,
(c) 'employment restriction' means a restriction as to employment or occupation imposed under any of those provisions, and
(d) 'immigration bail' means—
    (i) release under a provision of the Immigration Acts on entry into a recognizance or bail bond,
    (ii) bail granted in accordance with a provision of the Immigration Acts by a court, a justice of the peace, the sheriff, the Asylum and Immigration

Tribunal, the Secretary of State or an immigration officer (but not by a police officer), and

(iii) bail granted by the Special Immigration Appeals Commission.

(2) Where a residence restriction is imposed on an adult—

(a) he may be required to cooperate with electronic monitoring, and

(b) failure to comply with a requirement under paragraph (a) shall be treated for all purposes of the Immigration Acts as failure to observe the residence restriction.

(3) Where a reporting restriction could be imposed on an adult—

(a) he may instead be required to cooperate with electronic monitoring, and

(b) the requirement shall be treated for all purposes of the Immigration Acts as a reporting restriction.

(4) Immigration bail may be granted to an adult subject to a requirement that he cooperate with electronic monitoring; and the requirement may (but need not) be imposed as a condition of a recognizance or bail bond.

(5) In this section a reference to requiring an adult to cooperate with electronic monitoring is a reference to requiring him to cooperate with such arrangements as the person imposing the requirement may specify for detecting and recording by electronic means the location of the adult, or his presence in or absence from a location—

(a) at specified times,

(b) during specified periods of time, or

(c) throughout the currency of the arrangements.

(6) In particular, arrangements for the electronic monitoring of an adult—

(a) may require him to wear a device;

(b) may require him to make specified use of a device;

(c) may prohibit him from causing or permitting damage of or interference with a device;

(d) may prohibit him from taking or permitting action that would or might prevent the effective operation of a device;

(e) may require him to communicate in a specified manner and at specified times or during specified periods of time;

(f) may involve the performance of functions by persons other than the person imposing the requirement to cooperate with electronic monitoring (and those functions may relate to any aspect or condition of a residence restriction, of a reporting restriction, of an employment restriction, of a requirement under this section or of immigration bail).

(7) In this section 'adult' means an individual who is at least 18 years old.

(8) The Secretary of State—

(a) may make rules about arrangements for electronic monitoring for the purposes of this section, and

(b) when he thinks that satisfactory arrangements for electronic monitoring are available in respect of an area, shall notify persons likely to be in a position to exercise power under this section in respect of the area.

(9) Rules under subsection (8)(a) may, in particular, require that arrangements for electronic monitoring impose on a person of a specified description responsibility for specified aspects of the operation of the arrangements.

(10) A requirement to cooperate with electronic monitoring—

(a) shall comply with rules under subsection (8)(a), and

(b) may not be imposed in respect of an adult who is or is expected to be in an area unless the person imposing the requirement has received a notification from the Secretary of State under subsection (8)(b) in respect of that area.

(11) Rules under subsection (8)(a)—

(a) may include incidental, consequential or transitional provision,

(b) may make provision generally or only in relation to specified cases, circumstances or areas,

(c) shall be made by statutory instrument, and

(d) shall be subject to annulment in pursuance of a resolution of either House of Parliament.

(12) Before the commencement of section 26 a reference in this section to the Asylum and Immigration Tribunal shall be treated as a reference to—

(a) a person appointed, or treated as if appointed, as an adjudicator under section 81 of the Nationality, Immigration and Asylum Act 2002 (c. 41) (appeals), and

(b) the Immigration Appeal Tribunal.

Note: Commencement 1 October 2004 (SI 2004/2523).

Immigration services

37. Provision of immigration services

Note: Amends Immigration and Asylum Act 1999, ss 84, 85, 89, 90 and Sch 5 and 6.

38. Immigration Services Commissioner: power of entry

. . .

Note: Amends Immigration and Asylum Act 1999, s 92 and Sch 5, para 7.

39. Offence of advertising services

. . .

Note: Amends Immigration and Asylum Act 1999, s 92.

40. Appeal to Immigration Services Tribunal

. . .

Note: Repeals Immigration and Asylum Act 1999, s 87(3)(f).

41. Professional bodies

. . .

Note: Amends Immigration and Asylum Act 1999, ss 86, 166 and Sch 5, para 21.

Fees

42. Amount of fees

(1) [In prescribing a fee under section 51 of the Immigration, Asylum and Nationality Act 2006 (fees) in connection with a matter specified in subsection (2)] the Secretary of State may, . . . prescribe an amount which is intended to—
   (a) exceed the administrative costs of determining the application or undertaking the process, and
   (b) reflect benefits that the Secretary of State thinks are likely to accrue to the person who makes the application, to whom the application relates or by or for whom the process is undertaken, if the application is successful or the process is completed.

[(2) Those matters are—
   (a) anything done under, by virtue of or in connection with a provision of the British Nationality Act 1981 (c. 61) or of the former nationality Acts (within the meaning given by section 50(1) of that Act),
   (b) an application for leave to remain in the United Kingdom,
   (c) an application for the variation of leave to enter, or remain in, the United Kingdom,
   (d) section 10 of the Nationality, Immigration and Asylum Act 2002 (c. 41) (right of abode: certificate of entitlement),
   (e) a work permit, and
   (f) any other document which relates to employment and is issued for a purpose of immigration rules or in connection with leave to enter or remain in the United Kingdom.]

(3) An Order in Council under section 1 of the Consular Fees Act 1980 (c. 23) (fees) which prescribes a fee in relation to an application for the issue of a certificate under section 10 of the Nationality, Immigration and Asylum Act 2002 (right of abode: certificate of entitlement) may prescribe an amount which is intended to—

(a) exceed the administrative costs of determining the application, and
(b) reflect benefits that in the opinion of Her Majesty in Council are likely to accrue to the applicant if the application is successful.

(4) Where an instrument prescribes a fee in reliance on this section it may include provision for the refund, where an application is unsuccessful or a process is not completed, of that part of the fee which is intended to reflect the matters specified in subsection (1)(b) or (3)(b).

(5) Provision included by virtue of subsection (4)—
(a) may determine, or provide for the determination of, the amount to be refunded;
(b) may confer a discretion on the Secretary of State or another person (whether in relation to determining the amount of a refund or in relation to determining whether a refund should be made).

(6) An instrument may not be made in reliance on this section unless the Secretary of State has consulted with such persons as appear to him to be appropriate.

(7) An instrument may not be made in reliance on this section unless a draft has been laid before and approved by resolution of each House of Parliament (and any provision making the instrument subject to annulment in pursuance of a resolution of either House of Parliament shall not apply).

(8) This section is without prejudice to the power to make an order under section 102 of the Finance (No. 2) Act 1987 (c. 51) (government fees and charges) in relation to a power under a provision specified in this section.

Note: Commencement 1 October 2004 (SI 2004/2523). Words omitted from and words in square brackets in sub-s (1) substituted by para 6, Sch 2 Asylum, Immigration and Nationality Act 2006 from a date to be appointed.

43. Transfer of leave stamps

. . .

Note: Amends Immigration and Asylum Act 1999, s 5.

General

44. Interpretation: 'the Immigration Acts'

(1) A reference to 'the Immigration Acts' is to—
(a) the Immigration Act 1971 (c. 77),
(b) the Immigration Act 1988 (c. 14),
(c) the Asylum and Immigration Appeals Act 1993 (c. 23),
(d) the Asylum and Immigration Act 1996 (c. 49),

(e) the Immigration and Asylum Act 1999,

(f) the Nationality, Immigration and Asylum Act 2002 (c. 41), and

(g) this Act.

(2) This section has effect in relation to a reference in this Act or any other enactment (including an enactment passed or made before this Act).

(3) . . .

(4) . . .

Note: Subsection (3) amends Nationality, Immigration and Asylum Act 2002, s 58. Subsection (4) amends Immigration Act 1971, s 32 and Immigration and Asylum Act 1999, s 167. Commencement 1 October 2004 (SI 2004/2523). Section 44 repealed by Immigration, Asylum and Nationality Act 2006, s 64(3) from a date to be appointed.

45. Interpretation: immigration officer

In this Act 'immigration officer' means a person appointed by the Secretary of State as an immigration officer under paragraph 1 of Schedule 2 to the Immigration Act 1971.

Note: Commencement 1 October 2004 (SI 2004/2523).

46. Money

There shall be paid out of money provided by Parliament—

(a) any expenditure incurred by a Minister of the Crown in connection with this Act, and

(b) any increase attributable to this Act in the sums payable under any other enactment out of money provided by Parliament.

Note: Commencement 1 October 2004 (SI 2004/2523).

47. Repeals

. . .

48. Commencement

(1) Sections 2, 32(2) and 35 shall come into force at the end of the period of two months beginning with the date on which this Act is passed.

(2) Section 32(1) shall have effect in relation to determinations of the Special Immigration Appeals Commission made after the end of the period of two months beginning with the date on which this Act is passed.

(3) The other preceding provisions of this Act shall come into force in accordance with provision made—

(a) in the case of section 26 or Schedule 1 or 2, by order of the Lord Chancellor,
(b) in the case of sections 4 and 5 in so far as they extend to Scotland, by order of the Scottish Ministers, and
(c) in any other case, by order of the Secretary of State.

(4) An order under subsection (3)—
(a) may make transitional or incidental provision,
(b) may make different provision for different purposes, and
(c) shall be made by statutory instrument.

(5) Transitional provision under subsection (4)(a) in relation to the commencement of section 26 may, in particular, make provision in relation to proceedings which, immediately before commencement—
(a) are awaiting determination by an adjudicator appointed, or treated as if appointed, under section 81 of the Nationality, Immigration and Asylum Act 2002 (c. 41),
(b) are awaiting determination by the Immigration Appeal Tribunal,
(c) having been determined by an adjudicator could be brought before the Immigration Appeal Tribunal,
(d) are awaiting the determination of a further appeal brought in accordance with section 103 of that Act,
(e) having been determined by the Immigration Appeal Tribunal could be brought before another court by way of further appeal under that section,
(f) are or could be made the subject of an application under section 101 of that Act (review of decision on permission to appeal to Tribunal), or
(g) are or could be made the subject of another kind of application to the High Court or the Court of Session.

(6) Provision made under subsection (5) may, in particular—
(a) provide for the institution or continuance of an appeal of a kind not generally available after the commencement of section 26,
(b) provide for the termination of proceedings, or
(c) make any other provision that the Lord Chancellor thinks appropriate.

49. Extent

(1) This Act extends (subject to subsection (2)) to—
(a) England and Wales,
(b) Scotland, and
(c) Northern Ireland.

(2) An amendment effected by this Act has the same extent as the enactment, or as the relevant part of the enactment, amended (ignoring extent by virtue of an Order in Council).

(3) Her Majesty may by Order in Council direct that a provision of this Act is to extend, with or without modification or adaptation, to—

(a) any of the Channel Islands;
(b) the Isle of Man.

50. Short title

This Act may be cited as the Asylum and Immigration (Treatment of Claimants, etc.) Act 2004.

Schedules

Schedule 1

Section 26

New Schedule 4 to the Nationality, Immigration and Asylum Act 2002

...

Schedule 2

Section 26

Asylum and Immigration Tribunal: Consequential Amendments and Transitional Provision

Part 1

Consequential Amendments

...

Part 2

Transitional Provision

26. In this Part 'commencement' means the coming into force of section 26.

27. A person who immediately before commencement is, or is to be treated as, an adjudicator appointed under section 81 of the Nationality, Immigration and Asylum Act 2002 (c. 41) (appeals) (as it has effect before commencement) shall be treated as having been appointed as a member of the Asylum and Immigration Tribunal under paragraph 1 of Schedule 4 to that Act (as it has effect after commencement) immediately after commencement.

28. Where immediately before commencement a person is a member of the Immigration Appeal Tribunal—
   (a) he shall be treated as having been appointed as a member of the Asylum and Immigration Tribunal under paragraph 1 of Schedule 4 to that Act immediately after commencement, and
   (b) if he was a legally qualified member of the Immigration Appeal Tribunal (within

the meaning of Schedule 5 to that Act) he shall be treated as having been appointed as a legally qualified member of the Asylum and Immigration Tribunal.

29. A person who immediately before commencement is a member of staff of adjudicators appointed or treated as appointed under section 81 of the Nationality, Immigration and Asylum Act 2002 (c. 41) or of the Immigration Appeal Tribunal shall be treated as having been appointed as a member of the staff of the Asylum and Immigration Tribunal under paragraph 9 of Schedule 4 to the Nationality, Immigration and Asylum Act 2002 immediately after commencement.

30.—(1) This paragraph shall have effect in relation to applications under section 103A(1) or for permission under section 103A(4)(b) made—

(a) during the period beginning with commencement and ending with such date as may be appointed by order of the Lord Chancellor, and

(b) during any such later period as may be appointed by order of the Lord Chancellor.

(2) An application in relation to which this paragraph has effect shall be considered by a member of the Asylum and Immigration Tribunal (in accordance with arrangements under paragraph 8(1) of Schedule 4 to the Nationality, Immigration and Asylum Act 2002 (inserted by Schedule 1 above)).

(3) For the purposes of sub-paragraph (2)—

(a) references in section 103A to the appropriate court shall be taken as references to the member of the Tribunal who is considering the application or who is to consider the application,

(b) rules of court made for the purpose of section 103A(4)(a) in relation to the court to which an application is made shall have effect in relation to the application despite the fact that it is considered outside the appropriate court, and

(c) section 103A(6) shall be subject to sub-paragraph (5) below.

(4) Where a member of the Tribunal considers an application under section 103A(1) or 103A(4)(b) by virtue of this paragraph—

(a) he may make an order under section 103A(1) or grant permission under section 103A(4)(b), and

(b) if he does not propose to make an order or grant permission, he shall notify the appropriate court and the applicant.

(5) Where notice is given under sub-paragraph (4)(b)—

(a) the applicant may notify the appropriate court that he wishes the court to consider his application under section 103A(1) or 103A(4)(b),

(b) the notification must be given within the period of 5 days beginning with the date on which the applicant is treated, in accordance with rules under section 106 of the Nationality, Immigration and Asylum Act 2002, as receiving the notice under sub-paragraph (4)(b) above, and

(c) the appropriate court shall consider the application under section 103A(1) or 103A(4)(b) if—

(i) the applicant has given notice in accordance with paragraphs (a) and (b) above, or

(ii) the applicant has given notice under paragraph (a) above outside the period specified in paragraph (b) above, but the appropriate court concludes that the application should be considered on the grounds that the notice could not reasonably practicably have been given within that period.

(6) Rules of court may specify days to be disregarded in applying sub-paragraph (5)(b).

(7) A member of the Tribunal considering an application under section 103A(1) by virtue of this paragraph may not make a reference under section 103C.

(8) An order under sub-paragraph (1)(a) or (b)—

(a) shall be made by statutory instrument,

(b) shall not be made unless the Lord Chancellor has consulted such persons as he thinks appropriate, and

(c) shall not be made unless a draft has been laid before and approved by resolution of each House of Parliament.

Note: Commencement at a date to be appointed.

SCHEDULE 3

Section 33 REMOVAL OF ASYLUM SEEKER TO SAFE COUNTRY

PART 1

INTRODUCTORY

1.—(1) In this Schedule—

'asylum claim' means a claim by a person that to remove him from or require him to leave the United Kingdom would breach the United Kingdom's obligations under the Refugee Convention,

'Convention rights' means the rights identified as Convention rights by section 1 of the Human Rights Act 1998 (c. 42) (whether or not in relation to a State that is a party to the Convention),

'human rights claim' means a claim by a person that to remove him from or require him to leave the United Kingdom would be unlawful under section 6 of the Human Rights Act 1998 (public authority not to act contrary to Convention) as being incompatible with his Convention rights,

'immigration appeal' means an appeal under section 82(1) of the Nationality, Immigration and Asylum Act 2002 (c. 41) (appeal against immigration decision), and

'the Refugee Convention' means the Convention relating to the Status of Refugees done at Geneva on 28th July 1951 and its Protocol.

(2) In this Schedule a reference to anything being done in accordance with the Refugee Convention is a reference to the thing being done in accordance with the principles of the Convention, whether or not by a signatory to it.

PART 2

FIRST LIST OF SAFE COUNTRIES (REFUGEE CONVENTION AND HUMAN RIGHTS (1))

2. This Part applies to—

(a) Austria,

(b) Belgium,

(c) Republic of Cyprus,

(d) Czech Republic,

(e) Denmark,
(f) Estonia,
(g) Finland,
(h) France,
(i) Germany,
(j) Greece,
(k) Hungary,
(l) Iceland,
(m) Ireland,
(n) Italy,
(o) Latvia,
(p) Lithuania,
(q) Luxembourg,
(r) Malta,
(s) Netherlands,
(t) Norway,
(u) Poland,
(v) Portugal,
(w) Slovak Republic,
(x) Slovenia,
(y) Spain, and
(z) Sweden.

3.—(1) This paragraph applies for the purposes of the determination by any person, tribunal or court whether a person who has made an asylum claim or a human rights claim may be removed—

(a) from the United Kingdom, and
(b) to a State of which he is not a national or citizen.

(2) A State to which this Part applies shall be treated, in so far as relevant to the question mentioned in sub-paragraph (1), as a place—

(a) where a person's life and liberty are not threatened by reason of his race, religion, nationality, membership of a particular social group or political opinion,
(b) from which a person will not be sent to another State in contravention of his Convention rights, and
(c) from which a person will not be sent to another State otherwise than in accordance with the Refugee Convention.

4. Section 77 of the Nationality, Immigration and Asylum Act 2002 (c. 41) (no removal while claim for asylum pending) shall not prevent a person who has made a claim for asylum from being removed—

(a) from the United Kingdom, and
(b) to a State to which this Part applies;

provided that the Secretary of State certifies that in his opinion the person is not a national or citizen of the State.

5.—(1) This paragraph applies where the Secretary of State certifies that—

(a) it is proposed to remove a person to a State to which this Part applies, and
(b) in the Secretary of State's opinion the person is not a national or citizen of the State.

(2) The person may not bring an immigration appeal by virtue of section 92(2) or (3) of that Act (appeal from within United Kingdom: general).

(3) The person may not bring an immigration appeal by virtue of section 92(4)(a) of that Act (appeal from within United Kingdom: asylum or human rights) in reliance on—

(a) an asylum claim which asserts that to remove the person to a specified State to which this Part applies would breach the United Kingdom's obligations under the Refugee Convention, or
(b) a human rights claim in so far as it asserts that to remove the person to a specified State to which this Part applies would be unlawful under section 6 of the Human

Rights Act 1998 because of the possibility of removal from that State to another State.

(4) The person may not bring an immigration appeal by virtue of section 92(4)(a) of that Act in reliance on a human rights claim to which this sub-paragraph applies if the Secretary of State certifies that the claim is clearly unfounded; and the Secretary of State shall certify a human rights claim to which this sub-paragraph applies unless satisfied that the claim is not clearly unfounded.

(5) Sub-paragraph (4) applies to a human rights claim if, or in so far as, it asserts a matter other than that specified in sub-paragraph (3)(b).

6. A person who is outside the United Kingdom may not bring an immigration appeal on any ground that is inconsistent with treating a State to which this Part applies as a place—

(a) where a person's life and liberty are not threatened by reason of his race, religion, nationality, membership of a particular social group or political opinion,

(b) from which a person will not be sent to another State in contravention of his Convention rights, and

(c) from which a person will not be sent to another State otherwise than in accordance with the Refugee Convention.

Part 3

Second List of Safe Countries (Refugee Convention and Human Rights (2))

7.—(1) This Part applies to such States as the Secretary of State may by order specify.

(2) An order under this paragraph—

(a) shall be made by statutory instrument, and

(b) shall not be made unless a draft has been laid before and approved by resolution of each House of Parliament.

8.—(1) This paragraph applies for the purposes of the determination by any person, tribunal or court whether a person who has made an asylum claim may be removed—

(a) from the United Kingdom, and

(b) to a State of which he is not a national or citizen.

(2) A State to which this Part applies shall be treated, in so far as relevant to the question mentioned in sub-paragraph (1), as a place—

(a) where a person's life and liberty are not threatened by reason of his race, religion, nationality, membership of a particular social group or political opinion, and

(b) from which a person will not be sent to another State otherwise than in accordance with the Refugee Convention.

9. Section 77 of the Nationality, Immigration and Asylum Act 2002 (c. 41) (no removal while claim for asylum pending) shall not prevent a person who has made a claim for asylum from being removed—

(a) from the United Kingdom, and

(b) to a State to which this Part applies;

provided that the Secretary of State certifies that in his opinion the person is not a national or citizen of the State.

10.—(1) This paragraph applies where the Secretary of State certifies that—

(a) it is proposed to remove a person to a State to which this Part applies, and

(b) in the Secretary of State's opinion the person is not a national or citizen of the State.

(2) The person may not bring an immigration appeal by virtue of section 92(2) or (3) of that Act (appeal from within United Kingdom: general).

(3) The person may not bring an immigration appeal by virtue of section 92(4)(a) of that Act (appeal from within United Kingdom: asylum or human rights) in reliance on an asylum claim which asserts that to remove the person to a specified State to which this Part applies would breach the United Kingdom's obligations under the Refugee Convention.

(4) The person may not bring an immigration appeal by virtue of section 92(4)(a) of that Act in reliance on a human rights claim if the Secretary of State certifies that the claim is clearly unfounded; and the Secretary of State shall certify a human rights claim where this paragraph applies unless satisfied that the claim is not clearly unfounded.

11. A person who is outside the United Kingdom may not bring an immigration appeal on any ground that is inconsistent with treating a State to which this Part applies as a place—

(a) where a person's life and liberty are not threatened by reason of his race, religion, nationality, membership of a particular social group or political opinion, and

(b) from which a person will not be sent to another State otherwise than in accordance with the Refugee Convention.

Part 4

Third List of Safe Countries (Refugee Convention Only)

12.—(1) This Part applies to such States as the Secretary of State may by order specify.

(2) An order under this paragraph—

(a) shall be made by statutory instrument, and

(b) shall not be made unless a draft has been laid before and approved by resolution of each House of Parliament.

13.—(1) This paragraph applies for the purposes of the determination by any person, tribunal or court whether a person who has made an asylum claim may be removed—

(a) from the United Kingdom, and

(b) to a State of which he is not a national or citizen.

(2) A State to which this Part applies shall be treated, in so far as relevant to the question mentioned in sub-paragraph (1), as a place—

(a) where a person's life and liberty are not threatened by reason of his race, religion, nationality, membership of a particular social group or political opinion, and

(b) from which a person will not be sent to another State otherwise than in accordance with the Refugee Convention.

14. Section 77 of the Nationality, Immigration and Asylum Act 2002 (c. 41) (no removal while claim for asylum pending) shall not prevent a person who has made a claim for asylum from being removed—

(a) from the United Kingdom, and
(b) to a State to which this Part applies;

provided that the Secretary of State certifies that in his opinion the person is not a national or citizen of the State.

15.—(1) This paragraph applies where the Secretary of State certifies that—

(a) it is proposed to remove a person to a State to which this Part applies, and
(b) in the Secretary of State's opinion the person is not a national or citizen of the State.

(2) The person may not bring an immigration appeal by virtue of section 92(2) or (3) of that Act (appeal from within United Kingdom: general).

(3) The person may not bring an immigration appeal by virtue of section 92(4)(a) of that Act (appeal from within United Kingdom: asylum or human rights) in reliance on an asylum claim which asserts that to remove the person to a specified State to which this Part applies would breach the United Kingdom's obligations under the Refugee Convention.

(4) The person may not bring an immigration appeal by virtue of section 92(4)(a) of that Act in reliance on a human rights claim if the Secretary of State certifies that the claim is clearly unfounded.

16. A person who is outside the United Kingdom may not bring an immigration appeal on any ground that is inconsistent with treating a State to which this Part applies as a place—

(a) where a person's life and liberty are not threatened by reason of his race, religion, nationality, membership of a particular social group or political opinion, and
(b) from which a person will not be sent to another State otherwise than in accordance with the Refugee Convention.

Part 5

Countries Certified as Safe for Individuals

17. This Part applies to a person who has made an asylum claim if the Secretary of State certifies that—

(a) it is proposed to remove the person to a specified State,
(b) in the Secretary of State's opinion the person is not a national or citizen of the specified State, and
(c) in the Secretary of State's opinion the specified State is a place—
    (i) where the person's life and liberty will not be threatened by reason of his race, religion, nationality, membership of a particular social group or political opinion, and
    (ii) from which the person will not be sent to another State otherwise than in accordance with the Refugee Convention.

18. Where this Part applies to a person section 77 of the Nationality, Immigration and Asylum Act 2002 (c. 41) (no removal while claim for asylum pending) shall not prevent his removal to the State specified under paragraph 17.

19. Where this Part applies to a person—

(a) he may not bring an immigration appeal by virtue of section 92(2) or (3) of that Act (appeal from within United Kingdom: general),
(b) he may not bring an immigration appeal by virtue of section 92(4)(a) of that Act (appeal from within United Kingdom: asylum or human rights) in reliance on an asylum claim which asserts that to remove the person to the State specified under paragraph 17 would breach the United Kingdom's obligations under the Refugee Convention,
(c) he may not bring an immigration appeal by virtue of section 92(4)(a) of that Act in reliance on a human rights claim if the Secretary of State certifies that the claim is clearly unfounded, and
(d) he may not while outside the United Kingdom bring an immigration appeal on any ground that is inconsistent with the opinion certified under paragraph 17(c).

Part 6

Amendment of Lists

20.—(1) The Secretary of State may by order add a State to the list specified in paragraph 2.

(2) The Secretary of State may by order—
(a) add a State to a list specified under paragraph 7 or 12, or
(b) remove a State from a list specified under paragraph 7 or 12.

21.—(1) An order under paragraph 20(1) or (2)(a)—
(a) shall be made by statutory instrument,
(b) shall not be made unless a draft has been laid before and approved by resolution of each House of Parliament, and
(c) may include transitional provision.

(2) An order under paragraph 20(2)(b)—
(a) shall be made by statutory instrument,
(b) shall be subject to annulment in pursuance of a resolution of either House of Parliament, and
(c) may include transitional provision.

Note: Commencement at a date to be appointed.

Schedule 4

Section 47

Repeals

. . .

Immigration, Asylum and Nationality Act 2006
(2006, c. 13)

CONTENTS

Appeals

Schedules

An Act to make provision about immigration, asylum and nationality; and for connected purposes. [30th March 2006]

Appeals

1. Variation of leave to enter or remain

...

Note: Amends Nationality, Immigration and Asylum Act 2002, s 83.

2. Removal

...

Note: Amends Nationality, Immigration and Asylum Act 2002, s 82(2).

3. Grounds of appeal

...

Note: Amends Nationality, Immigration and Asylum Act 2002, s 84(3).

4. Entry clearance

(1) ...

(2) ...

(3) Within the period of three years beginning with the commencement (for any purpose) of subsection (1), the Secretary of State shall lay before Parliament a report about the effect of that subsection; and the report—

- (a) must specify the number of applications for entry clearance made during that period,
- (b) must specify the number of those applications refused,
- (c) must specify the number of those applications granted, after an initial indication to the applicant of intention to refuse the application, as a result of further consideration in accordance with arrangements established by the Secretary of State,
- (d) must describe those arrangements,

(e) must describe the effect of regulations made under section 88A(1)(a) or (b) as substituted by subsection (1) above,
(f) may include other information about the process and criteria used to determine applications for entry clearance, and
(g) may record opinions.

Note: Subsection(1) amends Nationality, Immigration and Asylum Act 2002, s 88A, sub-s (2) amends Immigration and Asylum Act 1999, s 23. Commencement at a date to be appointed.

5. Failure to provide documents

. . .

Note: Amends Nationality, Immigration and Asylum Act 2002, s 88(2).

6. Refusal of leave to enter

. . .

Note: Amends Nationality, Immigration and Asylum Act 2002, s 89.

7. Deportation

. . .

Note: Amends Nationality, Immigration and Asylum Act 2002, ss 97, 112.

8. Legal aid

. . .

Note: Amends Nationality, Immigration and Asylum Act 2002, s 103D.

9. Abandonment of appeal

. . .

Note: Amends Nationality, Immigration and Asylum Act 2002, s 104(4).

10. Grants

. . ..

Note: Amends Nationality, Immigration and Asylum Act 2002, s 110.

11. Continuation of leave

. . .

Note: Amends Immigration Act 1971, s 3C and Nationality, Immigration and Asylum Act 2002, s 82(3).

12. Asylum and human rights claims: definition

. . .

Note: Amends Nationality, Immigration and Asylum Act 2002, s 113.

13. Appeal from within United Kingdom: certification of unfounded claim

. . .

Note: Amends Nationality, Immigration and Asylum Act 2002, s 94.

14. Consequential amendments

Schedule 1 (which makes amendments consequential on the preceding provisions of this Act) shall have effect.

Note: Commencement at a date to be appointed.

Employment

15. Penalty

(1) It is contrary to this section to employ an adult subject to immigration control if—
  (a) he has not been granted leave to enter or remain in the United Kingdom, or
  (b) his leave to enter or remain in the United Kingdom—
    (i) is invalid,
    (ii) has ceased to have effect (whether by reason of curtailment, revocation, cancellation, passage of time or otherwise), or
    (iii) is subject to a condition preventing him from accepting the employment.

(2) The Secretary of State may give an employer who acts contrary to this section a notice requiring him to pay a penalty of a specified amount not exceeding the prescribed maximum.

(3) An employer is excused from paying a penalty if he shows that he complied with any prescribed requirements in relation to the employment.

(4) But the excuse in subsection (3) shall not apply to an employer who knew, at any time during the period of the employment, that it was contrary to this section.

(5) The Secretary of State may give a penalty notice without having established whether subsection (3) applies.

(6) A penalty notice must—
  (a) state why the Secretary of State thinks the employer is liable to the penalty,
  (b) state the amount of the penalty,
  (c) specify a date, at least 28 days after the date specified in the notice as the date on which it is given, before which the penalty must be paid,
  (d) specify how the penalty must be paid,
  (e) explain how the employer may object to the penalty, and
  (f) explain how the Secretary of State may enforce the penalty.

(7) An order prescribing requirements for the purposes of subsection (3) may, in particular—
  (a) require the production to an employer of a document of a specified description;
  (b) require the production to an employer of one document of each of a number of specified descriptions;
  (c) require an employer to take specified steps to verify, retain, copy or record the content of a document produced to him in accordance with the order;
  (d) require action to be taken before employment begins;
  (e) require action to be taken at specified intervals or on specified occasions during the course of employment.

Note: Commencement at a date to be appointed.

16. Objection

(1) This section applies where an employer to whom a penalty notice is given objects on the ground that—
  (a) he is not liable to the imposition of a penalty,
  (b) he is excused payment by virtue of section 15(3), or
  (c) the amount of the penalty is too high.

(2) The employer may give a notice of objection to the Secretary of State.

(3) A notice of objection must—
  (a) be in writing,
  (b) give the objector's reasons,
  (c) be given in the prescribed manner, and
  (d) be given before the end of the prescribed period.

(4) Where the Secretary of State receives a notice of objection to a penalty he shall consider it and—
  (a) cancel the penalty,
  (b) reduce the penalty,
  (c) increase the penalty, or
  (d) determine to take no action.

(5) Where the Secretary of State considers a notice of objection he shall—

(a) have regard to the code of practice under section 19 (in so far as the objection relates to the amount of the penalty),
(b) inform the objector of his decision before the end of the prescribed period or such longer period as he may agree with the objector,
(c) if he increases the penalty, issue a new penalty notice under section 15, and
(d) if he reduces the penalty, notify the objector of the reduced amount.

Note: Commencement at a date to be appointed.

17. Appeal

(1) An employer to whom a penalty notice is given may appeal to the court on the ground that—
(a) he is not liable to the imposition of a penalty,
(b) he is excused payment by virtue of section 15(3), or
(c) the amount of the penalty is too high.

(2) The court may—
(a) allow the appeal and cancel the penalty,
(b) allow the appeal and reduce the penalty, or
(c) dismiss the appeal.

(3) An appeal shall be a re-hearing of the Secretary of State's decision to impose a penalty and shall be determined having regard to—
(a) the code of practice under section 19 that has effect at the time of the appeal (in so far as the appeal relates to the amount of the penalty),
and
(b) any other matters which the court thinks relevant (which may include matters of which the Secretary of State was unaware);
and this subsection has effect despite any provision of rules of court.

(4) An appeal must be brought within the period of 28 days beginning with—
(a) the date specified in the penalty notice as the date upon which it is given, or
(b) if the employer gives a notice of objection and the Secretary of State reduces the penalty, the date specified in the notice of reduction as the date upon which it is given, or
(c) if the employer gives a notice of objection and the Secretary of State determines to take no action, the date specified in the notice of that determination as the date upon which it is given.

(5) An appeal may be brought by an employer whether or not—
(a) he has given a notice of objection under section 16;
(b) the penalty has been increased or reduced under that section.

(6) In this section 'the court' means—
(a) where the employer has his principal place of business in England and Wales, a county court,

(b) where the employer has his principal place of business in Scotland, the sheriff, and
(c) where the employer has his principal place of business in Northern Ireland, a county court.

Note: Commencement at a date to be appointed.

18. Enforcement

(1) A sum payable to the Secretary of State as a penalty under section 15 may be recovered by the Secretary of State as a debt due to him.
(2) In proceedings for the enforcement of a penalty no question may be raised as to—
(a) liability to the imposition of the penalty,
(b) the application of the excuse in section 15(3), or
(c) the amount of the penalty.
(3) Money paid to the Secretary of State by way of penalty shall be paid into the Consolidated Fund.

Note: Commencement at a date to be appointed.

19. Code of practice

(1) The Secretary of State shall issue a code of practice specifying factors to be considered by him in determining the amount of a penalty imposed under section 15.
(2) The code—
(a) shall not be issued unless a draft has been laid before Parliament, and
(b) shall come into force in accordance with provision made by order of the Secretary of State.
(3) The Secretary of State shall from time to time review the code and may revise and re-issue it following a review; and a reference in this section to the code includes a reference to the code as revised.

Note: Commencement 31 August 2006 (SI 2006/2226).

20. Orders

(1) An order of the Secretary of State under section 15, 16 or 19—
(a) may make provision which applies generally or only in specified circumstances,
(b) may make different provision for different circumstances,
(c) may include transitional or incidental provision, and
(d) shall be made by statutory instrument.

(2) An order under section 15(2) may not be made unless a draft has been laid before and approved by resolution of each House of Parliament.

(3) Any other order shall be subject to annulment in pursuance of a resolution of either House of Parliament.

Note: Commencement at a date to be appointed.

21. Offence

(1) A person commits an offence if he employs another ('the employee') knowing that the employee is an adult subject to immigration control and that—
  (a) he has not been granted leave to enter or remain in the United Kingdom, or
  (b) his leave to enter or remain in the United Kingdom—
    (i) is invalid,
    (ii) has ceased to have effect (whether by reason of curtailment, revocation, cancellation, passage of time or otherwise), or
    (iii) is subject to a condition preventing him from accepting the employment.

(2) A person guilty of an offence under this section shall be liable—
  (a) on conviction on indictment—
    (i) to imprisonment for a term not exceeding two years,
    (ii) to a fine, or
    (iii) to both, or
  (b) on summary conviction—
    (i) to imprisonment for a term not exceeding 12 months in England and Wales or 6 months in Scotland or Northern Ireland,
    (ii) to a fine not exceeding the statutory maximum, or
    (iii) to both.

(3) An offence under this section shall be treated as—
  (a) a relevant offence for the purpose of sections 28B and 28D of the Immigration Act 1971 (c. 77) (search, entry and arrest), and
  (b) an offence under Part III of that Act (criminal proceedings) for the purposes of sections 28E, 28G and 28H (search after arrest).

(4) In relation to a conviction occurring before the commencement of section 154(1) of the Criminal Justice Act 2003 (c. 44) (general limit on magistrates' powers to imprison) the reference to 12 months in subsection (2)(b)(i) shall be taken as a reference to 6 months.

Note: Commencement at a date to be appointed.

22. Offence: bodies corporate, &c.

(1) For the purposes of section 21(1) a body (whether corporate or not) shall be treated as knowing a fact about an employee if a person who has responsibility within the body for an aspect of the employment knows the fact.

(2) If an offence under section 21(1) is committed by a body corporate with the consent or connivance of an officer of the body, the officer, as well as the body, shall be treated as having committed the offence.

(3) In subsection (2) a reference to an officer of a body includes a reference to—
   (a) a director, manager or secretary,
   (b) a person purporting to act as a director, manager or secretary, and
   (c) if the affairs of the body are managed by its members, a member.

(4) Where an offence under section 21(1) is committed by a partnership (whether or not a limited partnership) subsection (2) above shall have effect, but as if a reference to an officer of the body were a reference to—
   (a) a partner, and
   (b) a person purporting to act as a partner.

Note: Commencement at a date to be appointed.

23. Discrimination: code of practice

(1) The Secretary of State shall issue a code of practice specifying what an employer should or should not do in order to ensure that, while avoiding liability to a penalty under section 15 and while avoiding the commission of an offence under section 21, he also avoids contravening—
   (a) the Race Relations Act 1976 (c. 74), or
   (b) the Race Relations (Northern Ireland) Order 1997 (S.I. 869 (N.I. 6)).

(2) Before issuing the code the Secretary of State shall—
   (a) consult—
      (i) the Commission for Equality and Human Rights,
      (ii) the Equality Commission for Northern Ireland,
      (iii) such bodies representing employers as he thinks appropriate, and
      (iv) such bodies representing workers as he thinks appropriate,
   (b) publish a draft code (after that consultation),
   (c) consider any representations made about the published draft, and
   (d) lay a draft code before Parliament (after considering representations under paragraph (c) and with or without modifications to reflect the representations).

(3) The code shall come into force in accordance with provision made by order of the Secretary of State; and an order—
   (a) may include transitional provision,

(b) shall be made by statutory instrument, and
(c) shall be subject to annulment in pursuance of a resolution of either House of Parliament.

(4) A breach of the code—
(a) shall not make a person liable to civil or criminal proceedings, but
(b) may be taken into account by a court or tribunal.

(5) The Secretary of State shall from time to time review the code and may revise and re-issue it following a review; and a reference in this section to the code includes a reference to the code as revised.

(6) Until the dissolution of the Commission for Racial Equality, the reference in subsection (2)(a)(i) to the Commission for Equality and Human Rights shall be treated as a reference to the Commission for Racial Equality.

Note: Commencement 31 August 2006 (SI 2006/2226).

24. Temporary admission, &c.

Where a person is at large in the United Kingdom by virtue of paragraph 21(1) of Schedule 2 to the Immigration Act 1971 (c. 77) (temporary admission or release from detention)—
(a) he shall be treated for the purposes of sections 15(1) and 21(1) as if he had been granted leave to enter the United Kingdom, and
(b) any restriction as to employment imposed under paragraph 21(2) shall be treated for those purposes as a condition of leave.

Note: Commencement at a date to be appointed.

25. Interpretation

In sections 15 to 24—
(a) 'adult' means a person who has attained the age of 16,
(b) a reference to employment is to employment under a contract of service or apprenticeship, whether express or implied and whether oral or written,
(c) a person is subject to immigration control if under the Immigration Act 1971 he requires leave to enter or remain in the United Kingdom, and
(d) 'prescribed' means prescribed by order of the Secretary of State.

Note: Commencement at a date to be appointed.

26. Repeal

. . .

Note: Repeals Asylum and Immigration Act 1996, ss 8 and 8A

Information

27. Documents produced or found

. . .

Note: Amends para 4, Sch 2 Immigration Act 1971.

28. Fingerprinting

. . .

Note: Amends Immigration and Asylum Act 1999, s 141

29. Attendance for fingerprinting

. . .

Note: Amends Immigration and Asylum Act 1999, s 142(2)

30. Proof of right of abode

. . .

Note: Amends Immigration Act 1971, s 3(9)

31. Provision of information to immigration officers

. . .

Note: Subsections (1)–(3) amend para 27, Sch 2 Immigration Act 1971, sub-s (4) amends s 27 of that Act.

32. Passenger and crew information: police powers

(1) This section applies to ships and aircraft which are—

(a) arriving, or expected to arrive, in the United Kingdom, or

(b) leaving, or expected to leave, the United Kingdom.

(2) The owner or agent of a ship or aircraft shall comply with any requirement imposed by a constable of the rank of superintendent or above to provide passenger or service information.

(3) A passenger or member of crew shall provide to the owner or agent of a ship or aircraft any information that he requires for the purpose of complying with a requirement imposed by virtue of subsection (2).

(4) A constable may impose a requirement under subsection (2) only if he thinks it necessary—

(a) in the case of a constable in England, Wales or Northern Ireland, for police purposes, or
(b) in the case of a constable in Scotland, for police purposes which are or relate to reserved matters.

(5) In this section—
(a) 'passenger or service information' means information which is of a kind specified by order of the Secretary of State and which relates to—
(i) passengers,
(ii) members of crew, or
(iii) a voyage or flight,
(b) 'police purposes' has the meaning given by section 21(3) of the Immigration and Asylum Act 1999 (c. 33) (disclosure by Secretary of State), and
(c) 'reserved matters' has the same meaning as in the Scotland Act 1998 (c. 46).

(6) A requirement imposed under subsection (2)—
(a) must be in writing,
(b) may apply generally or only to one or more specified ships or aircraft,
(c) must specify a period, not exceeding six months and beginning with the date on which it is imposed, during which it has effect,
(d) must state—
(i) the information required, and
(ii) the date or time by which it is to be provided.

(7) The Secretary of State may make an order specifying a kind of information under subsection (5)(a) only if satisfied that the nature of the information is such that there are likely to be circumstances in which it can be required under subsection (2) without breaching Convention rights (within the meaning of the Human Rights Act 1998 (c. 42)).

(8) An order under subsection (5)(a)—
(a) may apply generally or only to specified cases or circumstances,
(b) may make different provision for different cases or circumstances,
(c) may specify the form and manner in which information is to be provided,
(d) shall be made by statutory instrument, and
(e) shall be subject to annulment in pursuance of a resolution of either House of Parliament.

Note: Commencement at a date to be appointed.

33. Freight information: police powers

(1) This section applies to ships, aircraft and vehicles which are—
(a) arriving, or expected to arrive, in the United Kingdom, or
(b) leaving, or expected to leave, the United Kingdom.

(2) If a constable of the rank of superintendent or above requires a person specified in subsection (3) to provide freight information he shall comply with the requirement.

(3) The persons referred to in subsection (2) are—
(a) in the case of a ship or aircraft, the owner or agent,
(b) in the case of a vehicle, the owner or hirer, and
(c) in any case, persons responsible for the import or export of the freight into or from the United Kingdom.

(4) A constable may impose a requirement under subsection (2) only if he thinks it necessary—
(a) in the case of a constable in England, Wales or Northern Ireland, for police purposes, or
(b) in the case of a constable in Scotland, for police purposes which are or relate to reserved matters.

(5) In this section—
(a) 'freight information' means information which is of a kind specified by order of the Secretary of State and which relates to freight carried,
(b) 'police purposes' has the meaning given by section 21(3) of the Immigration and Asylum Act 1999 (c. 33) (disclosure by Secretary of State), and
(c) 'reserved matters' has the same meaning as in the Scotland Act 1998 (c. 46).

(6) A requirement imposed under subsection (2)—
(a) must be in writing,
(b) may apply generally or only to one or more specified ships, aircraft or vehicles,
(c) must specify a period, not exceeding six months and beginning with the date on which it is imposed, during which it has effect, and
(d) must state—
(i) the information required, and
(ii) the date or time by which it is to be provided.

(7) The Secretary of State may make an order specifying a kind of information under subsection (5)(a) only if satisfied that the nature of the information is such that there are likely to be circumstances in which it can be required under subsection (2) without breaching Convention rights (within the meaning of the Human Rights Act 1998 (c. 42)).

(8) An order under subsection (5)(a)—
(a) may apply generally or only to specified cases or circumstances,
(b) may make different provision for different cases or circumstances,
(c) may specify the form and manner in which the information is to be provided,
(d) shall be made by statutory instrument, and

(e) shall be subject to annulment in pursuance of a resolution of either House of Parliament.

Note: Commencement at a date to be appointed.

34. Offence

(1) A person commits an offence if without reasonable excuse he fails to comply with a requirement imposed under section 32(2) or (3) or 33(2).

(2) But—

(a) a person who fails without reasonable excuse to comply with a requirement imposed under section 32(2) or 33(2) by a constable in England and Wales or Northern Ireland otherwise than in relation to a reserved matter (within the meaning of the Scotland Act 1998 (c. 46)) shall not be treated as having committed the offence in Scotland (but has committed the offence in England and Wales or Northern Ireland), and

(b) a person who fails without reasonable excuse to comply with a requirement which is imposed under section 32(3) for the purpose of complying with a requirement to which paragraph (a) applies—

(i) shall not be treated as having committed the offence in Scotland, but

(ii) shall be treated as having committed the offence in England and Wales or Northern Ireland.

(3) A person who is guilty of an offence under subsection (1) shall be liable on summary conviction to—

(a) imprisonment for a term not exceeding 51 weeks in England and Wales or 6 months in Scotland or Northern Ireland,

(b) a fine not exceeding level 4 on the standard scale, or

(c) both.

(4) In relation to a conviction occurring before the commencement of section 281(5) of the Criminal Justice Act 2003 (c. 44) (51 week maximum term of sentences) the reference to 51 weeks in subsection (2)(a) shall be taken as a reference to three months.

Note: Commencement at a date to be appointed.

35. Power of Revenue and Customs to obtain information

. . .

Note: Amends Customs and Excise Management Act 1979, s 35

36. Duty to share information

(1) This section applies to—

(a) the Secretary of State in so far as he has functions under the Immigration Acts,
(b) a chief officer of police, and
(c) Her Majesty's Revenue and Customs.

(2) The persons specified in subsection (1) shall share information to which subsection (4) applies and which is obtained or held by them in the course of their functions to the extent that the information is likely to be of use for—
(a) immigration purposes,
(b) police purposes, or
(c) Revenue and Customs purposes.

(3) But a chief officer of police in Scotland shall share information under subsection (2) only to the extent that it is likely to be of use for—
(a) immigration purposes,
(b) police purposes, in so far as they are or relate to reserved matters within the meaning of the Scotland Act 1998, or
(c) Revenue and Customs purposes other than the prosecution of crime.

(4) This subsection applies to information which—
(a) is obtained or held in the exercise of a power specified by the Secretary of State and the Treasury jointly by order and relates to—
(i) passengers on a ship or aircraft,
(ii) crew of a ship or aircraft,
(iii) freight on a ship or aircraft, or
(iv) flights or voyages, or
(b) relates to such other matters in respect of travel or freight as the Secretary of State and the Treasury may jointly specify by order.

(5) The Secretary of State and the Treasury may make an order under subsection (4) which has the effect of requiring information to be shared only if satisfied that—
(a) the sharing is likely to be of use for—
(i) immigration purposes,
(ii) police purposes, or
(iii) Revenue and Customs purposes, and
(b) the nature of the information is such that there are likely to be circumstances in which it can be shared under subsection (2) without breaching Convention rights (within the meaning of the Human Rights Act 1998 (c. 42)).

(6) Information shared in accordance with subsection (2)—
(a) shall be made available to each of the persons specified in subsection (1), and
(b) may be used for immigration purposes, police purposes or Revenue and Customs purposes (regardless of its source).

(7) An order under subsection (4) may not specify—
(a) a power of Her Majesty's Revenue and Customs if or in so far as it relates to a matter to which section 7 of the Commissioners for Revenue and Customs Act 2005 (c. 11) (former Inland Revenue matters) applies, or
(b) a matter to which that section applies.

(8) An order under subsection (4)—
(a) shall be made by statutory instrument, and
(b) may not be made unless a draft has been laid before and approved by resolution of each House of Parliament.

(9) In this section—

'chief officer of police' means—
(a) in England and Wales, the chief officer of police for a police area specified in section 1 of the Police Act 1996 (c. 16),
(b) in Scotland, the chief constable of a police force maintained under the Police (Scotland) Act 1967 (c. 77), and
(c) in Northern Ireland, the chief constable of the Police Service of Northern Ireland,

'immigration purposes' has the meaning given by section 20(3) of the Immigration and Asylum Act 1999 (c. 33) (disclosure to Secretary of State),

'police purposes' has the meaning given by section 21(3) of that Act (disclosure by Secretary of State), and

'Revenue and Customs purposes' means those functions of Her Majesty's Revenue and Customs specified in section 21(6) of that Act.

(10) This section has effect despite any restriction on the purposes for which information may be disclosed or used.

Note: Commencement at a date to be appointed.

37. Information sharing: code of practice

(1) The Secretary of State and the Treasury shall jointly issue one or more codes of practice about—
(a) the use of information shared in accordance with section 36(2), and
(b) the extent to which, or form or manner in which, shared information is to be made available in accordance with section 36(6).

(2) A code—
(a) shall not be issued unless a draft has been laid before Parliament, and
(b) shall come into force in accordance with provision made by order of the Secretary of State and the Treasury jointly.

(3) The Secretary of State and the Treasury shall jointly from time to time review a code and may revise and re-issue it following a review; and subsection (2) shall apply to a revised code.

(4) An order under subsection (2)—
   (a) shall be made by statutory instrument, and
   (b) shall be subject to annulment in pursuance of a resolution of either House of Parliament.

Note: Commencement at a date to be appointed.

38. Disclosure of information for security purposes

(1) A person specified in subsection (2) may disclose information obtained or held in the course of his functions to a person specified in subsection (3) if he thinks that the information is likely to be of use for a purpose specified in—
   (a) section 1 of the Security Service Act 1989 (c. 5), or
   (b) section 1 or 3 of the Intelligence Services Act 1994 (c. 13).

(2) The persons who may disclose information in accordance with subsection (1) are—
   (a) the Secretary of State in so far as he has functions under the Immigration Acts,
   (b) a chief officer of police, and
   (c) Her Majesty's Revenue and Customs.

(3) The persons to whom information may be disclosed in accordance with subsection (1) are—
   (a) the Director-General of the Security Service,
   (b) the Chief of the Secret Intelligence Service, and
   (c) the Director of the Government Communications Headquarters.

(4) The information referred to in subsection (1) is information—
   (a) which is obtained or held in the exercise of a power specified by the Secretary of State and the Treasury jointly by order and relates to—
      (i) passengers on a ship or aircraft,
      (ii) crew of a ship or aircraft,
      (iii) freight on a ship or aircraft, or
      (iv) flights or voyages, or
   (b) which relates to such other matters in respect of travel or freight as the Secretary of State and the Treasury may jointly specify by order.

(5) In subsection (2) 'chief officer of police' means—
   (a) in England and Wales, the chief officer of police for a police area specified in section 1 of the Police Act 1996 (c. 16),
   (b) in Scotland, the chief constable of a police force maintained under the Police (Scotland) Act 1967 (c. 77), and
   (c) in Northern Ireland, the chief constable of the Police Service of Northern Ireland.

(6) An order under subsection (4) may not specify—

(a) a power of Her Majesty's Revenue and Customs if or in so far as it relates to a matter to which section 7 of the Commissioners for Revenue and Customs Act 2005 (c. 11) (former Inland Revenue matters) applies, or

(b) a matter to which that section applies.

(7) An order under this section—

(a) shall be made by statutory instrument, and

(b) may not be made unless a draft has been laid before and approved by resolution of each House of Parliament.

(8) This section has effect despite any restriction on the purposes for which information may be disclosed or used.

Note: Commencement at a date to be appointed.

39. Disclosure to law enforcement agencies

(1) A chief officer of police may disclose information obtained in accordance with section 32 or 33 to—

(a) the States of Jersey police force;

(b) the salaried police force of the Island of Guernsey;

(c) the Isle of Man constabulary;

(d) any other foreign law enforcement agency.

(2) In subsection (1) 'foreign law enforcement agency' means a person outside the United Kingdom with functions similar to functions of—

(a) a police force in the United Kingdom, or

(b) the Serious Organised Crime Agency.

(3) In subsection (1) 'chief officer of police' means—

(a) in England and Wales, the chief officer of police for a police area specified in section 1 of the Police Act 1996,

(b) in Scotland, the chief constable of a police force maintained under the Police (Scotland) Act 1967, and

(c) in Northern Ireland, the chief constable of the Police Service of Northern Ireland.

Note: Commencement at a date to be appointed.

40. Searches: contracting out

(1) An authorised person may, in accordance with arrangements made under this section, search a searchable ship, aircraft, vehicle or other thing for the purpose of satisfying himself whether there are individuals whom an immigration officer might wish to examine under paragraph 2 of Schedule 2 to the Immigration Act 1971 (c. 77) (control of entry: administrative provisions).

(2) For the purposes of subsection (1)—

(a) 'authorised' means authorised for the purpose of this section by the Secretary of State, and
(b) a ship, aircraft, vehicle or other thing is 'searchable' if an immigration officer could search it under paragraph 1(5) of that Schedule.

(3) The Secretary of State may authorise a specified class of constable for the purpose of this section.

(4) The Secretary of State may, with the consent of the Commissioners for Her Majesty's Revenue and Customs, authorise a specified class of officers of Revenue and Customs for the purpose of this section.

(5) The Secretary of State may authorise a person other than a constable or officer of Revenue and Customs for the purpose of this section only if—
(a) the person applies to be authorised, and
(b) the Secretary of State thinks that the person is—
(i) fit and proper for the purpose, and
(ii) suitably trained.

(6) The Secretary of State—
(a) may make arrangements for the exercise by authorised constables of the powers under subsection (1),
(b) may make arrangements with the Commissioners for Her Majesty's Revenue and Customs for the exercise by authorised officers of Revenue and Customs of the powers under subsection (1), and
(c) may make arrangements with one or more persons for the exercise by authorised persons other than constables and officers of Revenue and Customs of the power under subsection (1).

(7) Where in the course of a search under this section an authorised person discovers an individual whom he thinks an immigration officer might wish to examine under paragraph 2 of that Schedule, the authorised person may—
(a) search the individual for the purpose of discovering whether he has with him anything of a kind that might be used—
(i) by him to cause physical harm to himself or another,
(ii) by him to assist his escape from detention, or
(iii) to establish information about his identity, nationality or citizenship or about his journey;
(b) retain, and as soon as is reasonably practicable deliver to an immigration officer, anything of a kind described in paragraph (a) found on a search under that paragraph;
(c) detain the individual, for a period which is as short as is reasonably necessary and which does not exceed three hours, pending the arrival of an immigration officer to whom the individual is to be delivered;
(d) take the individual, as speedily as is reasonably practicable, to a place for the purpose of delivering him to an immigration officer there;

(e) use reasonable force for the purpose of doing anything under paragraphs (a) to (d).

(8) Despite the generality of subsection (7)—

(a) an individual searched under that subsection may not be required to remove clothing other than an outer coat, a jacket or a glove (but he may be required to open his mouth), and

(b) an item may not be retained under subsection (7)(b) if it is subject to legal privilege—

(i) in relation to a search carried out in England and Wales, within the meaning of the Police and Criminal Evidence Act 1984 (c. 60),

(ii) in relation to a search carried out in Scotland, within the meaning of section 412 of the Proceeds of Crime Act 2002 (c. 29), and

(iii) in relation to a search carried out in Northern Ireland, within the meaning of the Police and Criminal Evidence (Northern Ireland) Order 1989 (S.I. 1989/1341 (N.I. 12)).

Note: Commencement 31 August 2006 (SI 2006/2226).

41. Section 40: supplemental

(1) Arrangements under section 40(6)(c) must include provision for the appointment of a Crown servant to—

(a) monitor the exercise of powers under that section by authorised persons (other than constables or officers of Revenue and Customs),

(b) inspect from time to time the way in which the powers are being exercised by authorised persons (other than constables or officers of Revenue and Customs), and

(c) investigate and report to the Secretary of State about any allegation made against an authorised person (other than a constable or officer of Revenue and Customs) in respect of anything done or not done in the purported exercise of a power under that section.

(2) The authorisation for the purpose of section 40 of a constable or officer of Revenue and Customs or of a class of constable or officer of Revenue and Customs—

(a) may be revoked, and

(b) shall have effect, unless revoked, for such period as shall be specified (whether by reference to dates or otherwise) in the authorisation.

(3) The authorisation of a person other than a constable or officer of Revenue and Customs for the purpose of section 40—

(a) may be subject to conditions,

(b) may be suspended or revoked by the Secretary of State by notice in writing to the authorised person, and

(c) shall have effect, unless suspended or revoked, for such period as shall be specified (whether by reference to dates or otherwise) in the authorisation.

(4) A class may be specified for the purposes of section 40(3) or (4) by reference to—

(a) named individuals,

(b) the functions being exercised by a person,

(c) the location or circumstances in which a person is exercising functions,

or

(d) any other matter.

(5) An individual or article delivered to an immigration officer under section 40 shall be treated as if discovered by the immigration officer on a search under Schedule 2 to the Immigration Act 1971 (c. 77).

(6) A person commits an offence if he—

(a) absconds from detention under section 40(7)(c),

(b) absconds while being taken to a place under section 40(7)(d) or having been taken to a place in accordance with that paragraph but before being delivered to an immigration officer,

(c) obstructs an authorised person in the exercise of a power under section 40, or

(d) assaults an authorised person who is exercising a power under section 40.

(7) But a person does not commit an offence under subsection (6) by doing or failing to do anything in respect of an authorised person who is not readily identifiable—

(a) as a constable or officer of Revenue and Customs, or

(b) as an authorised person (whether by means of a uniform or badge or otherwise).

(8) A person guilty of an offence under subsection (6) shall be liable on summary conviction to—

(a) imprisonment for a term not exceeding 51 weeks, in the case of a conviction in England and Wales, or six months, in the case of a conviction in Scotland or Northern Ireland,

(b) a fine not exceeding level 5 on the standard scale, or

(c) both.

(9) In relation to a conviction occurring before the commencement of section 281(5) of the Criminal Justice Act 2003 (c. 44) (51 week maximum term of sentences) the reference in subsection (8)(a) to 51 weeks shall be treated as a reference to six months.

Note: Commencement at a date to be appointed.

42. Information: embarking passengers

. . .

Note: Amends Sch 2 Immigration Act 1971 (c. 77).

Claimants and applicants

43. Accommodation

(1) . . .

(2) . . .

(3) . . .

(4) . . .

(5) A tenancy is not a Scottish secure tenancy (within the meaning of the Housing (Scotland) Act 2001 (asp 10)) if it is granted in order to provide accommodation under section 4 of the Immigration and Asylum Act 1999 (accommodation).

(6) A tenancy which would be a Scottish secure tenancy but for subsection (4) becomes a Scottish secure tenancy if the landlord notifies the tenant that it is to be regarded as such.

(7) . . .

Note: Subsections (1) and (2) amend Immigration and Asylum Act 1999, s 99. Subsection (3) amends s 118 and sub-s 7 amends s 4 of that Act. Subsection (4) amends Protection from Eviction Act 1977, s 3A; para 3A, Sch 2 Housing (Northern Ireland Order 1983 (SI 1983/1118, NI 15); Rent (Scotland) Act 1984, s 23A; para 4A, Sch 1 Housing Act 1985; para 1B, Sch 4 Housing (Scotland) Act 1988; para 12A, Sch 1 Housing Act 1988. Commenced 16 June 2006 (SI 2006/1497).

44. Failed asylum-seekers: withdrawal of support

(1) The Secretary of State may by order provide for paragraph 7A of Schedule 3 to the Nationality, Immigration and Asylum Act 2002 (c. 41) (failed asylum seeker with family: withdrawal of support) to cease to have effect.

(2) An order under subsection (1) shall also provide for the following to cease to have effect—

(a) section 9(1), (2) and (4) of the Asylum and Immigration (Treatment of Claimants, etc.) Act 2004 (c. 19) (which insert paragraph 7A of Schedule 3 and make consequential provision), and

(b) in section 9(3)(a) and (b) of that Act, the words 'other than paragraph 7A.'

(3) An order under subsection (1)—

(a) may include transitional provision,

(b) shall be made by statutory instrument, and

(c) shall be subject to annulment in pursuance of a resolution of either House of Parliament.

Note: Commencement at a date to be appointed.

45. Integration loans

. . .

Note: Amends Asylum and Immigration (Treatment of Claimants, etc.) Act 2004, s 13.

46. Inspection of detention facilities

. . .

Note: Amends Prison Act 1952, ss 5 and 5A.

47. Removal: persons with statutorily extended leave

(1) Where a person's leave to enter or remain in the United Kingdom is extended by section 3C(2)(b) or 3D(2)(a) of the Immigration Act 1971 (c. 77) (extension pending appeal), the Secretary of State may decide that the person is to be removed from the United Kingdom, in accordance with directions to be given by an immigration officer if and when the leave ends.

(2) Directions under this section may impose any requirements of a kind prescribed for the purpose of section 10 of the Immigration and Asylum Act 1999 (c. 33) (removal of persons unlawfully in United Kingdom).

(3) In relation to directions under this section, paragraphs 10, 11, 16 to 18, 21 and 22 to 24 of Schedule 2 to the Immigration Act 1971 (administrative provisions as to control of entry) apply as they apply in relation to directions under paragraph 8 of that Schedule.

(4) The costs of complying with a direction given under this section (so far as reasonably incurred) must be met by the Secretary of State.

(5) A person shall not be liable to removal from the United Kingdom under this section at a time when section 7(1)(b) of the Immigration Act 1971 (Commonwealth and Irish citizens ordinarily resident in United Kingdom) would prevent a decision to deport him.

(6). . .

(7). . .

(8). . .

Note: Subsection (6) amends Nationality, Immigration and Asylum Act 2002, s 82, sub-s (7) amends s 92 and sub-s (8) amends s 94(1A) of that Act. Commenced 16 June 2006 (SI 2006/1497).

48. Removal: cancellation of leave

...

Note: Amends Immigration and Asylum Act 1999, s 10(8).

49. Capacity to make nationality application

...

Note: Amends British Nationality Act 1981, s 44.

50. Procedure

(1) Rules under section 3 of the Immigration Act 1971 (c. 77)—

(a) may require a specified procedure to be followed in making or pursuing an application or claim (whether or not under those rules or any other enactment),

(b) may, in particular, require the use of a specified form and the submission of specified information or documents,

(c) may make provision about the manner in which a fee is to be paid, and

(d) may make provision for the consequences of failure to comply with a requirement under paragraph (a), (b) or (c).

(2) In respect of any application or claim in connection with immigration (whether or not under the rules referred to in subsection (1) or any other enactment) the Secretary of State—

(a) may require the use of a specified form,

(b) may require the submission of specified information or documents, and

(c) may direct the manner in which a fee is to be paid; and the rules referred to in subsection (1) may provide for the consequences of failure to comply with a requirement under paragraph (a), (b) or (c).

(3) ...

(4) ...

(5) ...

(6) ...

Note: Subsection (3) repeals Immigration Act 1971, s 31A and Asylum and Immigration (Treatment of Claimants etc) Act 2004, s 25 Subsection (4) amends British Nationality Act 1981, s 41. Subsection (5) amends Nationality, Immigration and Asylum Act 2002, s 10. Subsection (6) repeals para 2(3), Sch 23 Civil Partnership Act 2004. Commencement at a date to be appointed.

51. Fees

(1) The Secretary of State may by order require an application or claim in connection with immigration or nationality (whether or not under an enactment) to be accompanied by a specified fee.

(2) The Secretary of State may by order provide for a fee to be charged by him, by an immigration officer or by another specified person in respect of—
  (a) the provision on request of a service (whether or not under an enactment) in connection with immigration or nationality,
  (b) a process (whether or not under an enactment) in connection with immigration or nationality,
  (c) the provision on request of advice in connection with immigration or nationality, or
  (d) the provision on request of information in connection with immigration or nationality.

(3) Where an order under this section provides for a fee to be charged, regulations made by the Secretary of State—
  (a) shall specify the amount of the fee,
  (b) may provide for exceptions,
  (c) may confer a discretion to reduce, waive or refund all or part of a fee,
  (d) may make provision about the consequences of failure to pay a fee,
  (e) may make provision about enforcement, and
  (f) may make provision about the time or period of time at or during which a fee may or must be paid.

(4) Fees paid by virtue of this section shall—
  (a) be paid into the Consolidated Fund, or
  (b) be applied in such other way as the relevant order may specify.

Note: Commencement at a date to be appointed.

52. Fees: supplemental

(1) A fee imposed under section 51 may relate to a thing whether or not it is done wholly or partly outside the United Kingdom; but that section is without prejudice to—
  (a) section 1 of the Consular Fees Act 1980 (c. 23), and
  (b) any other power to charge a fee.

(2) Section 51 is without prejudice to the application of section 102 of the Finance (No. 2) Act 1987 (c. 51) (government fees and charges); and an order made under that section in respect of a power repealed by Schedule 2 to this Act shall have effect as if it related to the powers under section 51 above in so far as they relate to the same matters as the repealed power.

(3) An order or regulations under section 51—
  (a) may make provision generally or only in respect of specified cases or circumstances,
  (b) may make different provision for different cases or circumstances,
  (c) may include incidental, consequential or transitional provision, and
  (d) shall be made by statutory instrument.

(4) An order under section 51—
  (a) may be made only with the consent of the Treasury, and
  (b) may be made only if a draft has been laid before and approved by resolution of each House of Parliament.

(5) Regulations under section 51—
  (a) may be made only with the consent of the Treasury, and
  (b) shall be subject to annulment in pursuance of a resolution of either House of Parliament.

(6) A reference in section 51 to anything in connection with immigration or nationality includes a reference to anything in connection with an enactment (including an enactment of a jurisdiction outside the United Kingdom) that relates wholly or partly to immigration or nationality.

(7) Schedule 2 (consequential amendments) shall have effect.

Note: Commencement at a date to be appointed.

Miscellaneous

53. Arrest pending deportation

. . .

Note: Amends para 2(4), Sche 3 Immigration Act 1971.

54. Refugee Convention: construction

(1) In the construction and application of Article 1(F)(c) of the Refugee Convention the reference to acts contrary to the purposes and principles of the United Nations shall be taken as including, in particular—
  (a) acts of committing, preparing or instigating terrorism (whether or not the acts amount to an actual or inchoate offence), and
  (b) acts of encouraging or inducing others to commit, prepare or instigate terrorism (whether or not the acts amount to an actual or inchoate offence).

(2) In this section—

'the Refugee Convention' means the Convention relating to the Status of Refugees done at Geneva on 28th July 1951, and 'terrorism' has the meaning given by section 1 of the Terrorism Act 2000 (c. 11).

Note: Commencement at a date to be appointed.

55. Refugee Convention: certification

(1) This section applies to an asylum appeal where the Secretary of State issues a certificate that the appellant is not entitled to the protection of Article 33(1) of the Refugee Convention because—
   (a) Article 1(F) applies to him (whether or not he would otherwise be entitled to protection), or
   (b) Article 33(2) applies to him on grounds of national security (whether or not he would otherwise be entitled to protection).

(2) In this section—
   (a) 'asylum appeal' means an appeal—
      (i) which is brought under section 82, 83 or 101 of the Nationality, Immigration and Asylum Act 2002 (c. 41) or section 2 of the Special Immigration Appeals Commission Act 1997 (c. 68), and
      (ii) in which the appellant claims that to remove him from or require him to leave the United Kingdom would be contrary to the United Kingdom's obligations under the Refugee Convention, and
   (b) 'the Refugee Convention' means the Convention relating to the Status of Refugees done at Geneva on 28th July 1951.

(3) The Asylum and Immigration Tribunal or the Special Immigration Appeals Commission must begin substantive deliberations on the asylum appeal by considering the statements in the Secretary of State's certificate.

(4) If the Tribunal or Commission agrees with those statements it must dismiss such part of the asylum appeal as amounts to an asylum claim (before considering any other aspect of the case).

(5) Section 72(10)(a) of the Nationality, Immigration and Asylum Act 2002 (serious criminal: Tribunal or Commission to begin by considering certificate) shall have effect subject to subsection (3) above.

(6)...

Note: Subsection (6) repeals Anti-terrorism, Crime and Security Act 2001, s 33. Commencement 31 August 2006 (SI 2006/2226).

56. Deprivation of citizenship

(1)...

(2)...

Note: Subsection (1) amends of the British Nationality Act 1981, s 42(2) sub-s (2) amends s 40A of that Act.

57. Deprivation of right of abode

(1). . .

(2). . .

Note: Subsection (1) amends Immigration Act 1971, s 2 sub-s (2) amends Nationality, Immigration and Asylum Act 2002. s 82.

58. Acquisition of British nationality, &c.

(1) The Secretary of State shall not grant an application for registration of an adult or young person as a citizen of any description or as a British subject under a provision listed in subsection (2) unless satisfied that the adult or young person is of good character.

(2) Those provisions are—

(a) sections 1(3) and (4), 3(1) and (5), 4(2) and (5), 4A, 4C, 5, 10(1) and (2), 13(1) and (3) of the British Nationality Act 1981 (c. 61) (registration as British citizen),

(b) sections 15(3) and (4), 17(1) and (5), 22(1) and (2), 24, 27(1) and 32 of that Act (registration as British overseas territories citizen, &c.),

(c) section 1 of the Hong Kong (War Wives and Widows) Act 1996 (c. 41) (registration as British citizen), and

(d) section 1 of the British Nationality (Hong Kong) Act 1997 (c. 20) (registration as British citizen).

(3) In subsection (1) 'adult or young person' means a person who has attained the age of 10 at the time when the application is made.

(4) Where the Secretary of State makes arrangements under section 43 of the British Nationality Act 1981 for a function to be exercised by some other person, subsection (1) above shall have effect in relation to that function as if the reference to the Secretary of State were a reference to that other person.

Note: Commencement from 4 December 2006, but without effect in relation to any application under the provisions listed in subsection (2) which was made before that date, SI 2006/2838. Section 50(8) of the British Nationality Act 1981 applies for the purpose of this section.

59. Detained persons: national minimum wage

(1). . .

(2). . .

Note: Subsection (1) amends Immigration and Asylum Act 1999, s 153, sub-s (2) amends National Minimum Wage Act 1998, s 45A.

General

60. Money

There shall be paid out of money provided by Parliament—
(a) any expenditure of the Secretary of State in connection with this Act, and
(b) any increase attributable to this Act in sums payable under another enactment out of money provided by Parliament.

Note: Commenced 16 June 2006 (SI 2006/1497).

61. Repeals

Schedule 3 (repeals) shall have effect.

Note: Commenced with regard to British Nationality Act 1981, s 40A(3) 16 June 2006 (SI 2006/1497). Remainder from 31 August 2006 (SI 2006/2226).

62. Commencement

(1) The preceding provisions of this Act shall come into force in accordance with provision made by order of the Secretary of State.

(2) An order under subsection (1)—
(a) may make provision generally or only for specified purposes,
(b) may make different provision for different purposes,
(c) may include transitional or incidental provision or savings, and
(d) shall be made by statutory instrument.

63. Extent

(1) This Act extends to—
(a) England and Wales,
(b) Scotland, and
(c) Northern Ireland.

(2) But—
(a) an amendment by this Act of another Act has the same extent as that Act or as the relevant part of that Act (ignoring extent by virtue of an Order in Council), and
(b) a provision of this Act shall, so far as it relates to nationality, have the same extent as the British Nationality Act 1981 (c. 61) (disregarding excepted provisions under section 53(7) of that Act).

(3) Her Majesty may by Order in Council direct that a provision of this Act is to extend, with or without modification or adaptation, to—
(a) any of the Channel Islands;
(b) the Isle of Man.

(4) Subsection (3) does not apply in relation to the extension to a place of a provision which extends there by virtue of subsection (2)(b).

Note: Commencement at a date to be appointed.

64. Citation

(1) This Act may be cited as the Immigration, Asylum and Nationality Act 2006.

(2) A reference (in any enactment, including one passed or made before this Act) to 'the Immigration Acts' is to—
- (a) the Immigration Act 1971 (c. 77),
- (b) the Immigration Act 1988 (c. 14),
- (c) the Asylum and Immigration Appeals Act 1993 (c. 23),
- (d) the Asylum and Immigration Act 1996 (c. 49),
- (e) the Immigration and Asylum Act 1999 (c. 33),
- (f) the Nationality, Immigration and Asylum Act 2002 (c. 41),
- (g) the Asylum and Immigration (Treatment of Claimants, etc.) Act 2004 (c. 19), and
- (h) this Act.

(3). . .

(4). . .

Note: Subsection (3) repeals the definition of the Immigration Acts in Immigration Act 1971, s 32(5) Immigration and Asylum Act 1999, s 167(1) Nationality, Immigration and Asylum Act 2002, s 158 and Asylum and Immigration (Treatment of Claimants, etc) Act 2004, s 44. Subsection (4) amends Sch 1 Interpretation Act 1978. Commencement at a date to be appointed.

SCHEDULES

Section 14

SCHEDULE 1

IMMIGRATION AND ASYLUM APPEALS: CONSEQUENTIAL AMENDMENTS

. . .

Section 52

SCHEDULE 2

FEES: CONSEQUENTIAL AMENDMENTS

. . .

Section 61

SCHEDULE 3

REPEALS

. . .

PROCEDURE RULES

The Asylum and Immigration Tribunal (Procedure) Rules 2005
(SI 2005, No. 230)

Arrangement of Rules

PART 1

Introduction

PART 2

Appeals to the Tribunal

Part 5

General Provisions

Part 6

Revocation and Transitional Provisions

Schedule

Part 1

Introduction

Citation and commencement

1. These Rules may be cited as the Asylum and Immigration Tribunal (Procedure) Rules 2005 and shall come into force on 4th April 2005.

Interpretation

2. In these Rules—

'the 2002 Act' means the Nationality, Immigration and Asylum Act 2002;

'the 2004 Act' means the Asylum and Immigration (Treatment of Claimants, etc.) Act 2004;

'appellant' means a person who has given a notice of appeal to the Tribunal against a relevant decision in accordance with these Rules;

'appropriate appellate court' has the meaning given in sections 103B(5) and 103E(5) of the 2002 Act;

'apropriate court' has the meaning given in section 103A(9) of the 2002 Act;

'appropriate prescribed form' means the appropriate form in the Schedule to these Rules, or that form with any variations that the circumstances may require;

'asylum claim' has the meaning given in section 113(1) of the 2002 Act;

'business day' means any day other than a Saturday or Sunday, a bank holiday, 25th to 31st December or Good Friday;

'determination', in relation to an appeal, means a decision by the Tribunal in writing to allow or dismiss the appeal, and does not include a procedural, ancillary or preliminary decision;

'the Immigration Acts' means the Acts referred to in section 44(1) of the 2004 Act;

'immigration decision' means a decision of a kind listed in section 82(2) of the 2002 Act;

'immigration rules' means the rules referred to in section 1(4) of the Immigration Act 1971;

'order for reconsideration' means an order under section 103A(1) or any other statutory provision requiring the Tribunal to reconsider its decision on an appeal;

'President' means the President of the Tribunal;

'relevant decision' means a decision against which there is an exercisable right of appeal to the Tribunal;

'respondent' means the decision maker specified in the notice of decision against which a notice of appeal has been given;

'section 103A' means section 103A of the 2002 Act (Review of Tribunal's decision) and 'section 103A application' means an application under section 103A;

'Tribunal' means the Asylum and Immigration Tribunal;

'United Kingdom Representative' means the United Kingdom Representative of the United Nations High Commissioner for Refugees.

Scope of these Rules

3.—(1) These Rules apply to the following proceedings—

(a) appeals to the Tribunal;

(b) section 103A applications which are considered by a member of the Tribunal in accordance with paragraph 30 of Schedule 2 to the 2004 Act;
(c) reconsideration of appeals by the Tribunal;
(d) applications to the Tribunal for permission to appeal to the Court of Appeal, the Court of Session, or the Court of Appeal in Northern Ireland;
(e) applications to the Tribunal for bail [; and
(f) proceedings incidental to any of the above proceedings, including in particular applications relating to the Tribunal's exercise of its powers under section 103D of the 2002 Act (Reconsideration: legal aid).]

(2) These Rules apply subject to any other Rules made under section 106 of the 2002 Act which apply to specific classes of proceedings.

Note: Subparagraph (f) inserted from 4 April 2005 (SI 2005/569).

Overriding objective

4. The overriding objective of these Rules is to secure that proceedings before the Tribunal are handled as fairly, quickly and efficiently as possible; and, where appropriate, that members of the Tribunal have responsibility for ensuring this, in the interests of the parties to the proceedings and in the wider public interest.

PART 2

Appeals to the Tribunal

Scope of this Part

5. This Part applies to appeals to the Tribunal.

Giving notice of appeal

6.—(1) An appeal to the Tribunal may only be instituted by giving notice of appeal against a relevant decision in accordance with these Rules.

(2) Subject to paragraphs (3) and (4), notice of appeal must be given by filing it with the Tribunal in accordance with rule 55(1).

(3) A person who is in detention under the Immigration Acts may give notice of appeal either—
(a) in accordance with paragraph (2); or
(b) by serving it on the person having custody of him.

(4) A person who is outside the United Kingdom and wishes to appeal against a decision of an entry clearance officer may give notice of appeal either—
(a) in accordance with paragraph (2); or
(b) by serving it on the entry clearance officer.

(5) Where a notice of appeal is served on a custodian under paragraph (3)(b), that person must—
(a) endorse on the notice the date that it is served on him; and
(b) forward it to the Tribunal within 2 days.

(6) Where a notice of appeal is served on an entry clearance officer under paragraph (4)(b), the officer must—
(a) endorse on the notice the date that it is served on him;
(b) forward it to the Tribunal as soon as reasonably practicable, and in any event within 10 days; and
(c) if it is practicable to do so within the time limit in sub-paragraph (b), send to the Tribunal with the notice of appeal a copy of the documents listed in rule 13(1).

Time limit for appeal

7.—(1) A notice of appeal by a person who is in the United Kingdom must be given—
(a) if the person is in detention under the Immigration Acts when he is served with notice of the decision against which he is appealing, not later than 5 days after he is served with that notice; and
(b) in any other case, not later than 10 days after he is served with notice of the decision.

(2) A notice of appeal by a person who is outside the United Kingdom must be given—
(a) if the person—
(i) was in the United Kingdom when the decision against which he is appealing was made; and
(ii) may not appeal while he is the United Kingdom by reason of a provision of the 2002 Act,

not later than 28 days after his departure from the United Kingdom; or
(b) in any other case, not later than 28 days after he is served with notice of the decision.

(3) Where a person—
(a) is served with notice of a decision to reject an asylum claim; and
(b) on the date of being served with that notice does not satisfy the condition in section 83(1)(b) of the 2002 Act, but later satisfies that condition,

paragraphs (1) and (2)(b) apply with the modification that the time for giving notice of appeal under section 83(2) runs from the date on which the person is served with notice of the decision to grant him leave to enter or remain in the United Kingdom by which he satisfies the condition in section 83(1)(b).

Form and contents of notice of appeal

8.—(1) The notice of appeal must be in the appropriate prescribed form and must—
(a) state the name and address of the appellant; and

(b) state whether the appellant has authorised a representative to act for him in the appeal and, if so, give the representative's name and address;
(c) set out the grounds for the appeal;
(d) give reasons in support of those grounds; and
(e) so far as reasonably practicable, list any documents which the appellant intends to rely upon as evidence in support of the appeal.

(2) The notice of appeal must if reasonably practicable be accompanied by the notice of decision against which the appellant is appealing, or a copy of it.

(3) The notice of appeal must be signed by the appellant or his representative, and dated.

(4) If a notice of appeal is signed by the appellant's representative, the representative must certify in the notice of appeal that he has completed it in accordance with the appellant's instructions.

Rejection of invalid notice of appeal

9.—(1) Where—
(a) a person has given a notice of appeal to the Tribunal; and
(b) there is no relevant decision,
the Tribunal shall not accept the notice of appeal.

(2) Where the Tribunal does not accept a notice of appeal, it must—
(a) notify the person giving the notice of appeal and the respondent; and
(b) take no further action.

Late notice of appeal

10.—(1) If a notice of appeal is given outside the applicable time limit, it must include an application for an extension of time for appealing, which must—
(a) include a statement of the reasons for failing to give the notice within that period; and
(b) be accompanied by any written evidence relied upon in support of those reasons.

(2) If a notice of appeal appears to the Tribunal to have been given outside the applicable time limit but does not include an application for an extension of time, unless the Tribunal extends the time for appealing of its own initiative, it must notify the person giving notice of appeal in writing that it proposes to treat the notice of appeal as being out of time.

(3) Where the Tribunal gives notification under paragraph (2), if the person giving notice of appeal contends that—
(a) the notice of appeal was given in time, or

(b) there were special circumstances for failing to give the notice of appeal in time which could not reasonably have been stated in the notice of appeal,

he may file with the Tribunal written evidence in support of that contention.

(4) Written evidence under paragraph (3) must be filed—

(a) if the person giving notice of appeal is in the United Kingdom, not later than 3 days; or

(b) if the person giving notice of appeal is outside the United Kingdom, not later than 10 days,

after notification is given under paragraph (2).

(5) Where the notice of appeal was given out of time, the Tribunal may extend the time for appealing if satisfied that by reason of special circumstances it would be unjust not to do so.

(6) The Tribunal must decide any issue as to whether a notice of appeal was given in time, or whether to extend the time for appealing, as a preliminary decision without a hearing, and in doing so may only take account of—

(a) the matters stated in the notice of appeal;

(b) any evidence filed by the person giving notice of appeal in accordance with paragraph (1) or (3); and

(c) any other relevant matters of fact within the knowledge of the Tribunal.

(7) Subject to paragraphs (8) and (9), the Tribunal must serve written notice of any decision under this rule on the parties.

(8) Where—

(a) a notice of appeal under section 82 of the 2002 Act which relates in whole or in part to an asylum claim was given out of time;

(b) the person giving notice of appeal is in the United Kingdom; and

(c) the Tribunal refuses to extend the time for appealing,

the Tribunal must serve written notice of its decision on the respondent, which must—

(i) serve the notice of decision on the person giving notice of appeal not later than 28 days after receiving it from the Tribunal; and

(ii) as soon as practicable after serving the notice of decision, notify the Tribunal on what date and by what means it was served.

(9) Where paragraph (8) applies, if the respondent does not give the Tribunal notification under sub-paragraph (ii) within 29 days after the Tribunal serves the notice of decision on it, the Tribunal must serve the notice of decision on the person giving notice of appeal as soon as reasonably practicable thereafter.

Special provisions for imminent removal cases

11.—(1) This rule applies in any case in which the respondent notifies the Tribunal that removal directions have been issued against a person who has given notice of appeal, pursuant to which it is proposed to remove him from the United Kingdom within 5 calendar days of the date on which the notice of appeal was given.

(2) The Tribunal must, if reasonably practicable, make any preliminary decision under rule 10 before the date and time proposed for his removal.

(3) Rule 10 shall apply subject to the modifications that the Tribunal may—
   (a) give notification under rule 10(2) orally, which may include giving it by telephone;
   (b) shorten the time for giving evidence under rule 10(3); and
   (c) direct that any evidence under rule 10(3) is to be given orally, which may include requiring the evidence to be given by telephone, and hold a hearing or telephone hearing for the purpose of receiving such evidence.

Service of notice of appeal on respondent

12.—(1) Subject to paragraph (2), when the Tribunal receives a notice of appeal it shall serve a copy upon the respondent as soon as reasonably practicable.

(2) Paragraph (1) does not apply where the notice of appeal was served on an entry clearance officer under rule 6(4)(b).

Filing of documents by respondent

13.—(1) When the respondent is served with a copy of a notice of appeal, it must (unless it has already done so) file with the Tribunal a copy of—
   (a) the notice of the decision to which the notice of appeal relates, and any other document served on the appellant giving reasons for that decision;
   (b) any—
      (i) statement of evidence form completed by the appellant; and
      (ii) record of an interview with the appellant,
   in relation to the decision being appealed;
   (c) any other unpublished document which is referred to in a document mentioned in sub-paragraph (a) or relied upon by the respondent; and
   (d) the notice of any other immigration decision made in relation to the appellant in respect of which he has a right of appeal under section 82 of the 2002 Act.

(2) Subject to paragraph (3), the respondent must file the documents listed in paragraph (1)—
   (a) in accordance with any directions given by the Tribunal; and
   (b) if no such directions are given, as soon as reasonably practicable and in any event not later than 2.00 p.m. on the business day before the earliest date appointed for any hearing of or in relation to the appeal.

(3) If the Tribunal considers the timeliness of a notice of appeal as a preliminary issue under rule 10, the respondent must file the documents listed in paragraph (1) as soon as reasonably practicable after being served with a decision of the Tribunal allowing the appeal to proceed, and in any event not later than 2.00 p.m. on the business day before the earliest date appointed for any hearing of or in relation to the appeal following that decision.

(4) The respondent must, at the same time as filing them, serve on the appellant a copy of all the documents listed in paragraph (1), except for documents which the respondent has already sent to the appellant.

Variation of grounds of appeal

14. Subject to section 85(2) of the 2002 Act, the appellant may vary his grounds of appeal only with the permission of the Tribunal.

Method of determining appeal

15.—(1) Every appeal must be considered by the Tribunal at a hearing, except where—

(a) the appeal—

(i) lapses pursuant to section 99 of the 2002 Act;

(ii) is treated as abandoned pursuant to section 104(4) of the 2002 Act;

(iii) is treated as finally determined pursuant to section 104(5) of the 2002 Act; or

(iv) is withdrawn by the appellant or treated as withdrawn in accordance with rule 17;

(b) paragraph (2) of this rule applies; or

(c) any other provision of these Rules or of any other enactment permits or requires the Tribunal to dispose of an appeal without a hearing.

(2) The Tribunal may determine an appeal without a hearing if—

(a) all the parties to the appeal consent;

(b) the appellant is outside the United Kingdom or it is impracticable to give him notice of a hearing and, in either case, he is unrepresented;

(c) a party has failed to comply with a provision of these Rules or a direction of the Tribunal, and the Tribunal is satisfied that in all the circumstances, including the extent of the failure and any reasons for it, it is appropriate to determine the appeal without a hearing; or

(d) subject to paragraph (3), the Tribunal is satisfied, having regard to the material before it and the nature of the issues raised, that the appeal can be justly determined without a hearing.

(3) Where paragraph (2)(d) applies, the Tribunal must not determine the appeal without a hearing without first giving the parties notice of its intention to do

so, and an opportunity to make written representations as to whether there should be a hearing.

Certification of pending appeal

16.—(1) If the Secretary of State or an immigration officer issues a certificate under section 97 or 98 of the 2002 Act which relates to a pending appeal, he must file notice of the certification with the Tribunal.

(2) Where a notice of certification is filed under paragraph (1), the Tribunal must—
- (a) notify the parties; and
- (b) take no further action in relation to the appeal.

Withdrawal of appeal

17.—(1) An appellant may withdraw an appeal—
- (a) orally, at a hearing; or
- (b) at any time, by filing written notice with the Tribunal.

(2) An appeal shall be treated as withdrawn if the respondent notifies the Tribunal that the decision (or, where the appeal relates to more than one decision, all of the decisions) to which the appeal relates has been withdrawn.

(3) If an appeal is withdrawn or treated as withdrawn, the Tribunal must serve on the parties a notice that the appeal has been recorded as having been withdrawn.

Abandonment of appeal

18.—(1) Any party to a pending appeal must notify the Tribunal if they are aware that an event specified in—
- (a) section 104(4) or (5) of the 2002 Act; or
- (b) regulation 33(1A) of the Immigration (European Economic Area) Regulations 2000 ('the 2000 Regulations'), [or, on or after 30th April 2006, paragraph 4(2) of Schedule 2 to the Immigration (European Economic Area) Regulations 2006 ('the 2006 Regulations')],

has taken place.

(2) Where an appeal is treated as abandoned pursuant to section 104(4) of the 2002 Act or regulation 33(1A) of the 2000 Regulations, [or paragraph 4(2) of Schedule 2 to the 2006 Regulations], or finally determined pursuant to section 104(5) of the 2002 Act, the Tribunal must—
- (a) serve on the parties a notice informing them that the appeal is being treated as abandoned or finally determined; and
- (b) take no further action in relation to the appeal.

Note: Words in square brackets inserted from 30 April 2006 (SI 2006/1003).

Hearing appeal in absence of a party

19.—(1) The Tribunal must hear an appeal in the absence of a party or his representative, if satisfied that the party or his representative—

(a) has been given notice of the date, time and place of the hearing, and

(b) has given no satisfactory explanation for his absence.

(2) Where paragraph (1) does not apply, the Tribunal may hear an appeal in the absence of a party if satisfied that—

(a) a representative of the party is present at the hearing;

(b) the party is outside the United Kingdom;

(c) the party is suffering from a communicable disease or there is a risk of him behaving in a violent or disorderly manner;

(d) the party is unable to attend the hearing because of illness, accident or some other good reason;

(e) the party is unrepresented and it is impracticable to give him notice of the hearing; or

(f) the party has notified the Tribunal that he does not wish to attend the hearing.

Hearing two or more appeals together

20. Where two or more appeals are pending at the same time, the Tribunal may direct them to be heard together if it appears that—

(a) some common question of law or fact arises in each of them;

(b) they relate to decisions or action taken in respect of persons who are members of the same family; or

(c) for some other reason it is desirable for the appeals to be heard together.

Adjournment of appeals

21.—(1) Where a party applies for an adjournment of a hearing of an appeal, he must—

(a) if practicable, notify all other parties of the application;

(b) show good reason why an adjournment is necessary; and

(c) produce evidence of any fact or matter relied upon in support of the application.

(2) The Tribunal must not adjourn a hearing of an appeal on the application of a party, unless satisfied that the appeal cannot otherwise be justly determined.

(3) The Tribunal must not, in particular, adjourn a hearing on the application of a party in order to allow the party more time to produce evidence, unless satisfied that—

(a) the evidence relates to a matter in dispute in the appeal;

(b) it would be unjust to determine the appeal without permitting the party a further opportunity to produce the evidence; and
(c) where the party has failed to comply with directions for the production of the evidence, he has provided a satisfactory explanation for that failure.

(4) Where the hearing of an appeal is adjourned, the Tribunal will fix a new hearing date which—
(a) shall be not more than 28 days after the original hearing date, unless the Tribunal is satisfied that because of exceptional circumstances the appeal cannot justly be heard within that time; and
(b) shall in any event be not later than is strictly required by the circumstances necessitating the adjournment.

Giving of determination

22.—(1) Except in cases to which rule 23 applies, where the Tribunal determines an appeal it must serve on every party a written determination containing its decision and the reasons for it.

(2) The Tribunal must send its determination—
(a) if the appeal is considered at a hearing, not later than 10 days after the hearing finishes; or
(b) if the appeal is determined without a hearing, not later than 10 days after it is determined.

Special procedures and time limits in asylum appeals

23.—(1) This rule applies to appeals under section 82 of the 2002 Act where—
(a) the appellant is in the United Kingdom; and
(b) the appeal relates, in whole or in part, to an asylum claim.

(2) Subject to paragraph (3)—
(a) where an appeal is to be considered by the Tribunal at a hearing, the hearing must be fixed for a date not more than 28 days after the later of—
(i) the date on which the Tribunal receives the notice of appeal; or
(ii) if the Tribunal makes a preliminary decision under rule 10 (late notice of appeal), the date on which notice of that decision is served on the appellant; and
(b) where an appeal is to be determined without a hearing, the Tribunal must determine it not more than 28 days after the later of those dates.

(3) If the respondent does not file the documents specified in rule 13(1) within the time specified in rule 13 or directions given under that rule—
(a) paragraph (2) does not apply; and
(b) the Tribunal may vary any hearing date that it has already fixed in accordance with paragraph (2)(a), if it is satisfied that it would be unfair to the appellant to proceed with the hearing on the date fixed.

(4) The Tribunal must serve its determination on the respondent—
   (a) if the appeal is considered at a hearing, by sending it not later than 10 days after the hearing finishes; or
   (b) if the appeal is determined without a hearing, by sending it not later than 10 days after it is determined.

(5) The respondent must—
   (a) serve the determination on the appellant—
      (i) if the respondent makes a section 103A application or applies for permission to appeal under section 103B or 103E of the 2002 Act, by sending, delivering or personally serving the determination not later than the date on which it makes that application; and
      (ii) otherwise, not later than 28 days after receiving the determination from the Tribunal; and
   (b) as soon as practicable after serving the determination, notify the Tribunal on what date and by what means it was served.

(6) If the respondent does not give the Tribunal notification under paragraph (5)(b) within 29 days after the Tribunal serves the determination on it, the Tribunal must serve the determination on the appellant as soon as reasonably practicable thereafter.

(7) In paragraph (2) of this rule, references to a hearing do not include a case management review hearing or other preliminary hearing.

PART 3

Reconsideration of Appeals etc.

Scope of this Part

24.—(1) Section 1 of this Part applies to section 103A applications made during any period in which paragraph 30 of Schedule 2 to the 2004 Act has effect, which are considered by an immigration judge in accordance with that paragraph.

(2) Section 2 of this Part applies to reconsideration of appeals by the Tribunal pursuant to—
   (a) an order under section 103A(1) made by—
      (i) the appropriate court; or
      (ii) an immigration judge in accordance with paragraph 30 of Schedule 2 to the 2004 Act; and
   (b) remittal by the appropriate appellate court under section 103B(4)(c), 103C(2)(c) or 103E(4)(c) of the 2002 Act.

(3) Section 3 of this Part applies to applications for permission to appeal to the appropriate appellate court.

Section 1

Section 103A applications considered by members of the Tribunal

Procedure for applying for review

25. Where paragraph 30 of Schedule 2 to the 2004 Act has effect in relation to a section 103A application, the application must be made in accordance with relevant rules of court (including any practice directions supplementing those rules).

Deciding applications for review

26.—(1) A section 103A application shall be decided by an immigration judge authorised by the President to deal with such applications.

(2) The immigration judge shall decide the application without a hearing, and by reference only to the applicant's written submissions and the documents filed with the application notice.

(3) The immigration judge is not required to consider any grounds for ordering the Tribunal to reconsider its decision other than those set out in the application notice.

(4) The application must be decided not later than 10 days after the Tribunal receives the application notice.

(5) In deciding a section 103A application, the immigration judge may—

- (a) in relation to an application for permission under section 103A(4)(b), either—
  - (i) permit the application to be made outside the period specified in section 103A(3); or
  - (ii) record that he does not propose to grant permission; and
- (b) in relation to an application for an order under section 103A(1), either—
  - (i) make an order for reconsideration; or
  - (ii) record that he does not propose to make such an order.

(6) The immigration judge may make an order for reconsideration only if he thinks that—

- (a) the Tribunal may have made an error of law; and
- (b) there is a real possibility that the Tribunal would decide the appeal differently on reconsideration.

Form and service of decision

27.—(1) Where an immigration judge decides a section 103A application, he must give written notice of his decision, including his reasons which may be in summary form.

(2) Where an immigration judge makes an order for reconsideration—
   (a) his notice of decision must state the grounds on which the Tribunal is ordered to reconsider its decision on the appeal; and
   (b) he may give directions for the reconsideration of the decision on the appeal which may—
      (i) provide for any of the matters set out in rule 45(4) which he considers appropriate to such reconsideration; and
      (ii) specify the number or class of members of the Tribunal to whom the reconsideration shall be allocated.

(3) The Tribunal must, except in cases to which paragraph (5) applies—
   (a) serve a copy of the notice of decision and any directions on every party to the appeal to the Tribunal; and
   (b) where the immigration judge makes an order for reconsideration, serve on the party to the appeal other than the party who made the section 103A application a copy of the application notice and any documents which were attached to it.

(4) Paragraph (5) applies to reviews of appeals under section 82 of the 2002 Act where—
   (a) the appellant is in the United Kingdom; and
   (b) the appeal relates, in whole or in part, to an asylum claim.

(5) In cases to which this paragraph applies—
   (a) the Tribunal must send to the respondent to the appeal—
      (i) the notice of decision,
      (ii) any directions, and
      (iii) the application notice and any documents which were attached to it (unless the respondent to the appeal made the application for reconsideration);
   (b) the respondent must serve on the appellant—
      (i) the notice of decision and any directions; and
      (ii) the application notice and any documents which were attached to it (unless the appellant made the application for reconsideration),

   not later than 28 days after receiving them from the Tribunal;
   (c) the respondent must, as soon as practicable after serving the documents mentioned in sub-paragraph (b), notify the Tribunal on what date and by what means they were served; and
   (d) if the respondent does not give the Tribunal notification under sub-paragraph (c) within 29 days after the Tribunal serves the notice of decision on it, the Tribunal must serve the documents mentioned in sub-paragraph (b) on the appellant as soon as reasonably practicable thereafter.

Sending notice of decision to the appropriate court

28. The Tribunal must send to the appropriate court copies of—

(a) the notice of decision; and

(b) the application notice and any documents which were attached to it, upon being requested to do so by the appropriate court.

[Orders for funding on section 103A applications

28A.—(1) This rule applies where a section 103A application has been made by an appellant in relation to an appeal decided in England, Wales or Northern Ireland.

(2) If an immigration judge, when he considers a section 103A application, makes an order under section 103D(1) of the 2002 Act, the Tribunal must send a copy of that order to—

(a) the appellant's representative; and

(b) the relevant funding body.

(3) If, pursuant to regulations under section 103D of the 2002 Act, the appellant's representative applies for an order under section 103D(1) of the 2002 Act where an immigration judge has made an order for reconsideration of an appeal but the reconsideration does not proceed—

(a) the immigration judge may decide that application without a hearing; and

(b) the Tribunal must send notice of his decision to—

(i) the appellant's representative; and

(ii) if he makes an order under section 103D(1), the relevant funding body.

(4) In a case to which rule 27(5) applies, the Tribunal must not send an order or decision under this rule to the appellant's representative until either—

(a) the respondent has notified the Tribunal under rule 27(5)(c) that it has served the documents mentioned in rule 27(5)(b) on the appellant; or

(b) the Tribunal has served those documents on the appellant under rule 27(5)(d).

(5) In this rule, 'relevant funding body' has the same meaning as in rule 33.]

Note: Rule 28A inserted from 4 April 2005 (SI 2005/569).

Section 2

Reconsideration of appeals

Rules applicable on reconsideration of appeal

29. Rules 15 to 23, except for rule 23(2) and (3), and Part 5 of these Rules apply to the reconsideration of an appeal as they do to the initial determination of an appeal, and references in those rules to an appeal shall be interpreted as including proceedings for the reconsideration of an appeal.

Reply

30.—(1) When the other party to the appeal is served with an order for reconsideration, he must, if he contends that the Tribunal should uphold the initial determination for reasons different from or additional to those given in the determination, file with the Tribunal and serve on the applicant a reply setting out his case.

(2) The other party to the appeal must file and serve any reply not later than 5 days before the earliest date appointed for any hearing of or in relation to the reconsideration of the appeal.

(3) In this rule, 'other party to the appeal' means the party other than the party on whose application the order for reconsideration was made.

Procedure for reconsideration of appeal

31.—(1) Where an order for reconsideration has been made, the Tribunal must reconsider an appeal as soon as reasonably practicable after that order has been served on both parties to the appeal.

(2) Where the reconsideration is pursuant to an order under section 103A—

(a) the Tribunal carrying out the reconsideration must first decide whether the original Tribunal made a material error of law; and

(b) if it decides that the original Tribunal did not make a material error of law, the Tribunal must order that the original determination of the appeal shall stand.

(3) Subject to paragraph (2), the Tribunal must substitute a fresh decision to allow or dismiss the appeal.

(4) In carrying out the reconsideration, the Tribunal—

(a) may limit submissions or evidence to one or more specified issues; and

(b) must have regard to any directions given by the immigration judge or court which ordered the reconsideration.

(5) In this rule, a 'material error of law' means an error of law which affected the Tribunal's decision upon the appeal.

Evidence on reconsideration of appeal

32.—(1) The Tribunal may consider as evidence any note or record made by the Tribunal of any previous hearing at which the appeal was considered.

(2) If a party wishes to ask the Tribunal to consider evidence which was not submitted on any previous occasion when the appeal was considered, he must file with the Tribunal and serve on the other party written notice to that effect, which must—

(a) indicate the nature of the evidence; and
(b) explain why it was not submitted on any previous occasion.

(3) A notice under paragraph (2) must be filed and served as soon as practicable after the parties have been served with the order for reconsideration.

(4) If the Tribunal decides to admit additional evidence, it may give directions as to—
(a) the manner in which; and
(b) the time by which,

the evidence is to be given or filed.

Orders for funding on reconsideration

33.—(1) This rule applies where—
(a) the Tribunal has reconsidered an appeal following a section 103A application made by the appellant in relation to an appeal decided in England, Wales or Northern Ireland; and
(b) the appellant's representative has specified that he seeks an order under section 103D of the 2002 Act for his costs to be paid out of the relevant fund.

(2) The Tribunal must make a separate determination ('the funding determination') stating whether it orders that the appellant's costs—
(a) in respect of the application for reconsideration; and
(b) in respect of the reconsideration,
are to be paid out of the relevant fund.

(3) The Tribunal must send the funding determination to—
(a) the appellant's representative; and
(b) if the Tribunal has made an order under section 103D, the relevant funding body.

(4) Where the determination of the reconsidered appeal ('the principal determination') is served in accordance with rule 23, the Tribunal must not send the funding determination to the appellant's representative until—
(a) the respondent has notified the Tribunal under rule 23(5)(b) that it has served the principal determination on the appellant; or
(b) the Tribunal has served the principal determination on the appellant under rule 23(6).

[(4A) Where, in accordance with regulations under section 103D of the 2002 Act, a senior immigration judge reviews a decision by the Tribunal not to make an order under section 103D(3), the Tribunal must send notice of the decision upon that review to—
(a) the appellant's representative; and
(b) if the senior immigration judge makes an order under section 103D(3), the relevant funding body.]

(5) In this Rule—
  (a) 'relevant fund' means—
    (i) in relation to an appeal decided in England or Wales, the Community Legal Service Fund established under section 5 of the Access to Justice Act 1999;
    (ii) in relation to an appeal decided in Northern Ireland, the fund established under paragraph 4(2)(a) of Schedule 3 to the Access to Justice (Northern Ireland) Order 2003; and
  (b) 'relevant funding body' means—
    (i) in relation to an appeal decided in England or Wales, the Legal Services Commission;
    (ii) in relation to an appeal decided in Northern Ireland, the Northern Ireland Legal Services Commission.

Note: Paragraph 4A inserted from 4 April 2005 (SI 2005/569).

Section 3

Applications for permission to appeal to the appropriate appellate court

Applying for permission to appeal

34.—(1) An application to the Tribunal under this Section must be made by filing with the Tribunal an application notice for permission to appeal.

(2) The application notice for permission to appeal must—
  (a) be in the appropriate prescribed form;
  (b) state the grounds of appeal; and
  (c) be signed by the applicant or his representative, and dated.

(3) If the application notice is signed by the applicant's representative, the representative must certify in the application notice that he has completed the application notice in accordance with the applicant's instructions.

(4) As soon as practicable after an application notice for permission to appeal is filed, the Tribunal must notify the other party to the appeal to the Tribunal that it has been filed.

Time limit for application

35.—(1) In application notice for permission to appeal must be filed in accordance with rule 34—
  (a) if the applicant is in detention under the Immigration Acts when he is served with the Tribunal's determination, not later than 5 days after he is served with that determination;

(b) in any other case, not later than 10 days after he is served with the Tribunal's determination.

(2) The Tribunal may not extend the time limits in paragraph (1).

Determining the application

36.—(1) An application for permission to appeal must be determined by a senior immigration judge without a hearing.

(2) The Tribunal may either grant or refuse permission to appeal.

(3) Where the Tribunal intends to grant permission to appeal it may, if it thinks that the Tribunal has made an administrative error in relation to the proceedings, instead set aside the Tribunal's determination and direct that the proceedings be reheard by the Tribunal.

(4) The Tribunal must serve on every party written notice of its decision, including its reasons, which may be in summary form.

Part 4

Bail

Scope of this Part and interpretation

37.—(1) This Part applies to applications under the Immigration Acts to the Tribunal, by persons detained under those Acts, to be released on bail.

(2) In this Part, 'applicant' means a person applying to the Tribunal to be released on bail.

(3) The parties to a bail application are the applicant and the Secretary of State.

Applications for bail

38.—(1) An application to be released on bail must be made by filing with the Tribunal an application notice in the appropriate prescribed form.

(2) The application notice must contain the following details—
   (a) the applicant's—
      (i) full name;
      (ii) date of birth; and
      (iii) date of arrival in the United Kingdom;
   (b) the address of the place where the applicant is detained;
   (c) whether an appeal by the applicant to the Tribunal is pending;
   (d) the address where the applicant will reside if his application for bail is granted, or, if he is unable to give such an address, the reason why an address is not given;

(e) where the applicant is aged 18 or over, whether he will, if required, agree as a condition of bail to co-operate with electronic monitoring under section 36 of the 2004 Act;
(f) the amount of the recognizance in which he will agree to be bound;
(g) the full names, addresses, occupations and dates of birth of any persons who have agreed to act as sureties for the applicant if bail is granted, and the amounts of the recognizances in which they will agree to be bound;
(h) the grounds on which the application is made and, where a previous application has been refused, full details of any change in circumstances which has occurred since the refusal; and
(i) whether an interpreter will be required at the hearing, and in respect of what language or dialect.

(3) The application must be signed by the applicant or his representative or, in the case of an applicant who is a child or is for any other reason incapable of acting, by a person acting on his behalf.

Bail hearing

39.—(1) Where an application for bail is filed, the Tribunal must—
(a) as soon as reasonably practicable, serve a copy of the application on the Secretary of State; and
(b) fix a hearing.

(2) If the Secretary of State wishes to contest the application, he must file with the Tribunal and serve on the applicant a written statement of his reasons for doing so—
(a) not later than 2.00 p.m. on the business day before the hearing; or
(b) if he was served with notice of the hearing less than 24 hours before that time, as soon as reasonably practicable.

(3) The Tribunal must serve written notice of its decision on—
(a) the parties; and
(b) the person having custody of the applicant.

(4) Where bail is granted, the notice must include—
(a) the conditions of bail; and
(b) the amount in which the applicant and any sureties are to be bound.

(5) Where bail is refused, the notice must include reasons for the refusal.

Recognizances

40.—(1) The recognizance of an applicant or a surety must be in writing and must state—
(a) the amount in which he agrees to be bound; and
(b) that he has read and understood the bail decision and that he agrees to pay

that amount of money if the applicant fails to comply with the conditions set out in the bail decision.

(2) The recognizance must be—
 (a) signed by the applicant or surety; and
 (b) filed with the Tribunal.

Release of applicant

41. The person having custody of the applicant must release him upon—
 (a) being served with a copy of the decision to grant bail; and
 (b) being satisfied that any recognizances required as a condition of that decision have been entered into.

Application of this Part to Scotland

42. This Part applies to Scotland with the following modifications—
 (a) in rule 38, for paragraph (2)(f) and (g) substitute—
  '(f) the amount, if any, to be deposited if bail is granted;
  (g) the full names, addresses and occupations of any persons offering to act as cautioners if the application for bail is granted;';
 (b) in rule 39, for paragraph (4)(b) substitute—
  '(b) the amount (if any) to be deposited by the applicant and any cautioners.';
 (c) rule 40 does not apply; and
 (d) in rule 41, for sub-paragraph (b) substitute—
  '(b) being satisfied that the amount to be deposited, if any, has been deposited.'

Part 5

General Provisions

Conduct of appeals and applications

43.—(1) The Tribunal may, subject to these Rules, decide the procedure to be followed in relation to any appeal or application.

(2) Anything of a formal or administrative nature which is required or permitted to be done by the Tribunal under these Rules may be done by a member of the Tribunal's staff.

Constitution of the Tribunal

44.—(1) The Tribunal shall be under no duty to consider any representations by a party about the number or class of members of the Tribunal which should exercise the jurisdiction of the Tribunal.

(2) Where the President directs that the Tribunal's jurisdiction shall be exercised by more than one member, unless the President's direction specifies otherwise a single immigration judge may—
   (a) conduct a case management review hearing;
   (b) give directions to the parties; and
   (c) deal with any other matter preliminary or incidental to the hearing of an appeal or application.

Directions

45.—(1) The Tribunal may give directions to the parties relating to the conduct of any appeal or application.

(2) The power to give directions is to be exercised subject to any specific provision of these Rules.

(3) Directions must be given orally or in writing to every party.

(4) Directions of the Tribunal may, in particular—
   (a) relate to any matter concerning the preparation for a hearing;
   (b) specify the length of time allowed for anything to be done;
   (c) vary any time limit in these Rules or in directions previously given by the Tribunal for anything to be done by a party;
   (d) provide for—
      (i) a particular matter to be dealt with as a preliminary issue;
      (ii) a case management review hearing to be held;
      (iii) a party to provide further details of his case, or any other information which appears to be necessary for the determination of the appeal;
      (iv) the witnesses, if any, to be heard;
      (v) the manner in which any evidence is to be given (for example, by directing that witness statements are to stand as evidence in chief);
   (e) require any party to file and serve—
      (i) statements of the evidence which will be called at the hearing;
      (ii) a paginated and indexed bundle of all the documents which will be relied on at the hearing;
      (iii) a skeleton argument which summarises succinctly the submissions which will be made at the hearing and cites all the authorities which will be relied on, identifying any particular passages to be relied on;
      (iv) a time estimate for the hearing;
      (v) a list of witnesses whom any party wishes to call to give evidence;
      (vi) a chronology of events; and
      (vii) details of whether an interpreter will be required at the hearing, and in respect of what language and dialect;
   (f) limit—

(i) the number or length of documents upon which a party may rely at a hearing;
(ii) the length of oral submissions;
(iii) the time allowed for the examination and cross-examination of witnesses; and
(iv) the issues which are to be addressed at a hearing; and

(g) require the parties to take any steps to enable two or more appeals to be heard together under rule 20.
(h) provide for a hearing to be conducted or evidence given or representations made by video link or by other electronic means; and
(i) make provision to secure the anonymity of a party or a witness.

(5) The Tribunal must not direct an unrepresented party to do something unless it is satisfied that he is able to comply with the direction.

(6) The President may direct that, in individual cases or in such classes of case as he shall specify, any time period in these Rules for the Tribunal to do anything shall be extended by such period as he shall specify.

Notification of hearings

46.—(1) When the Tribunal fixes a hearing it must serve notice of the date, time and place of the hearing on every party.

(2) The Tribunal may vary the date of a hearing, but must serve notice of the new date, time and place of the hearing on every party.

Adjournment

47. Subject to any provision of these Rules, the Tribunal may adjourn any hearing.

Representation

48.—(1) An appellant or applicant for bail may act in person or be represented by any person not prohibited from representing him by section 84 of the Immigration and Asylum Act 1999.

(2) A respondent to an appeal, the Secretary of State or the United Kingdom Representative may be represented by any person authorised to act on his behalf.

(3) If a party to whom paragraph (1) applies is represented by a person not permitted by that paragraph to represent him, any determination given or other step taken by the Tribunal in the proceedings shall nevertheless be valid.

(4) Where a representative begins to act for a party, he must immediately notify the Tribunal and the other party of that fact.

(5) Where a representative is acting for a party, he may on behalf of that party do anything that these Rules require or permit that party to do.

(6) Where a representative is acting for an appellant, the appellant is under a duty—

(a) to maintain contact with his representative until the appeal is finally determined; and

(b) to notify the representative of any change of address.

(7) Where a representative ceases to act for a party, the representative and the party must immediately notify the Tribunal and the other party of that fact, and of the name and address of any new representative (if known).

(8) Notification under paragraph (4) or (7)—

(a) may be given orally at a hearing to the Tribunal and to any other party present at that hearing; but

(b) must otherwise be given in writing.

(9) Until the Tribunal is notified that a representative has ceased to act for a party, any document served on that representative shall be deemed to be properly served on the party he was representing.

United Kingdom Representative

49.—(1) The United Kingdom Representative may give notice to the Tribunal that he wishes to participate in any proceedings where the appellant has made an asylum claim.

(2) Where the United Kingdom Representative has given notice under paragraph (1)—

(a) rules 54(6) and 55(7) shall apply; and

(b) the Tribunal must permit him to make representations in the proceedings if he wishes to do so, and may give directions for that purpose.

Summoning of witnesses

50.—(1) The Tribunal may, by issuing a summons ('a witness summons'), require any person in the United Kingdom—

(a) to attend as a witness at the hearing of an appeal; and

(b) subject to rule 51(2), at the hearing to answer any questions or produce any documents in his custody or under his control which relate to any matter in issue in the appeal.

(2) A person is not required to attend a hearing in obedience to a witness summons unless—

(a) the summons is served on him; and

(b) the necessary expenses of his attendance are paid or tendered to him.

(3) If a witness summons is issued at the request of a party, that party must pay or tender the expenses referred to in paragraph (2)(b).

Evidence

51.—(1) The Tribunal may allow oral, documentary or other evidence to be given of any fact which appears to be relevant to an appeal or an application for bail, even if that evidence would be inadmissible in a court of law.

(2) The Tribunal may not compel a party or witness to give any evidence or produce any document which he could not be compelled to give or produce at the trial of a civil claim in the part of the United Kingdom in which the hearing is taking place.

(3) The Tribunal may require the oral evidence of a witness to be given on oath or affirmation.

(4) Where the Tribunal has given directions setting time limits for the filing and serving of written evidence, it must not consider any written evidence which is not filed or served in accordance with those directions unless satisfied that there are good reasons to do so.

(5) Where a party seeks to rely upon a copy of a document as evidence, the Tribunal may require the original document to be produced.

(6) In an appeal to which section 85(5) of the 2002 Act applies, the Tribunal must only consider evidence relating to matters which it is not prevented by that section from considering.

(7) Subject to section 108 of the 2002 Act, the Tribunal must not take account of any evidence that has not been made available to all the parties.

Language of documents

52.—(1) Subject to paragraph (2)—

(a) any notice of appeal or application notice filed with the Tribunal must be completed in English; and

(b) any other document filed with the Tribunal must be in English, or accompanied by a translation into English signed by the translator to certify that the translation is accurate.

(2) In proceedings in or having a connection with Wales, a document may be filed with the Tribunal in Welsh.

(3) The Tribunal shall be under no duty to consider a document which is not in English (or, where paragraph (2) applies, in Welsh), or accompanied by a certified translation.

Burden of proof

53.—(1) If an appellant asserts that a relevant decision ought not to have been taken against him on the ground that the statutory provision under which that decision was taken does not apply to him, it is for that party to prove that the provision does not apply to him.

(2) If—

(a) an appellant asserts any fact; and

(b) by virtue of an Act, statutory instrument or immigration rules, if he had made such an assertion to the Secretary of State, an immigration officer or an entry clearance officer, it would have been for him to satisfy the Secretary of State or officer that the assertion was true,

it is for the appellant to prove that the fact asserted is true.

Admission of public to hearings

54.—(1) Subject to the following provisions of this rule, every hearing before the Tribunal must be held in public.

(2) Where the Tribunal is considering an allegation referred to in section 108 of the 2002 Act—

(a) all members of the public must be excluded from the hearing, and

(b) any party or representative of a party may be excluded from the hearing.

(3) The Tribunal may exclude any or all members of the public from any hearing or part of a hearing if it is necessary—

(a) in the interests of public order or national security; or

(b) to protect the private life of a party or the interests of a minor.

(4) The Tribunal may also, in exceptional circumstances, exclude any or all members of the public from any hearing or part of a hearing to ensure that publicity does not prejudice the interests of justice, but only if and to the extent that it is strictly necessary to do so.

(5) A member of the Council on Tribunals or of its Scottish Committee acting in that capacity is entitled to attend any hearing and may not be excluded pursuant to paragraph (2), (3) or (4) of this rule.

(6) The United Kingdom Representative, where he has given notice to the Tribunal under rule 49, is entitled to attend any hearing except where paragraph (2) applies, and may not be excluded pursuant to paragraph (3) or (4) of this rule.

Filing and service of documents

55.—(1) Any document which is required or permitted by these Rules or by a direction of the Tribunal to be filed with the Tribunal, or served on any person may be—

(a) delivered, or sent by post, to an address;

(b) sent via a document exchange to a document exchange number or address;
(c) sent by fax to a fax number; or
(d) sent by e-mail to an e-mail address,

specified for that purpose by the Tribunal or person to whom the document is directed.

(2) A document to be served on an individual may be served personally by leaving it with that individual.

(3) Where a person has notified the Tribunal that he is acting as the representative of an appellant and has given an address for service, if a document is served on the appellant, a copy must also at the same time be sent to the appellant's representative.

(4) If any document is served on a person who has notified the Tribunal that he is acting as the representative of a party, it shall be deemed to have been served on that party.

(5) Subject to paragraph (6), any document that is served on a person in accordance with this rule shall, unless the contrary is proved, be deemed to be served—

(a) where the document is sent by post or document exchange from and to a place within the United Kingdom, on the second day after it was sent;
(b) where the document is sent by post or document exchange from or to a place outside the United Kingdom, on the twenty-eighth day after it was sent; and
(c) in any other case, on the day on which the document was sent or delivered to, or left with, that person.

(6) Any notice of appeal which is served on a person under rule 6(3)(b) or 6(4)(b) shall be treated as being served on the day on which it is received by that person.

(7) Where the United Kingdom Representative has given notice to the Tribunal under rule 49 in relation to any proceedings, any document which is required by these Rules or by a direction of the Tribunal to be served on a party in those proceedings must also be served on the United Kingdom Representative.

Address for service

56.—(1) Every party, and any person representing a party, must notify the Tribunal in writing of a postal address at which documents may be served on him and of any changes to that address.

(2) Until a party or representative notifies the Tribunal of a change of address, any document served on him at the most recent address which he has notified to the Tribunal shall be deemed to have been properly served on him.

Calculation of time

57.—(1) Where a period of time for doing any act is specified by these Rules or by a direction of the Tribunal, that period is to be calculated—

(a) excluding the day on which the period begins; and
(b) where the period is 10 days or less, excluding any day which is not a business day (unless the period is expressed as a period of calendar days).

(2) Where the time specified by these Rules or by a direction of the Tribunal for doing any act ends on a day which is not a business day, that act is done in time if it is done on the next business day.

Signature of documents

58. Any requirement in these Rules for a document to be signed by a party or his representative shall be satisfied, in the case of a document which is filed or served electronically in accordance with these rules, by the person who is required to sign the document typing his name or producing it by computer or other mechanical means.

Errors of procedure

59.—(1) Where, before the Tribunal has determined an appeal or application, there has been an error of procedure such as a failure to comply with a rule—
(a) subject to these Rules, the error does not invalidate any step taken in the proceedings, unless the Tribunal so orders; and
(b) the Tribunal may make any order, or take any other step, that it considers appropriate to remedy the error.

(2) In particular, any determination made in an appeal or application under these Rules shall be valid notwithstanding that—
(a) a hearing did not take place; or
(b) the determination was not made or served,

within a time period specified in these Rules.

Correction of orders and determinations

60.—(1) The Tribunal may at any time amend an order, notice of decision or determination to correct a clerical error or other accidental slip or omission.

(2) Where an order, notice of decision or determination is amended under this rule—
(a) the Tribunal must serve an amended version on the party or parties on whom it served the original; and
(b) if rule 10(8) and (9), rule 23(5) and (6) or rule 27(5)(b)-(d) applied in relation to the service of the original, it shall also apply in relation to the service of the amended version.

(3) The time within which a party may apply for permission to appeal against, or for a review of, an amended determination runs from the date on which the party is served with the amended determination.

Part 6

Revocation and Transitional Provisions

Revocation

61. The Immigration and Asylum Appeals (Procedure) Rules 2003 are revoked.

Transitional provisions

62.—(1) Subject to the following paragraphs of this rule, these Rules apply to any appeal or application to an adjudicator or the Immigration Appeal Tribunal which was pending immediately before 4th April 2005, and which continues on or after that date as if it had been made to the Tribunal by virtue of a transitional provisions order.

(2) Where a notice of a relevant decision has been served before 4th April 2005 and the recipient gives notice of appeal against the decision on or after 4th April 2005—

(a) rules 6–8, 12 and 13 of these Rules shall not apply; and

(b) rules 6–9 of the 2003 Rules shall continue to apply as if those Rules had not been revoked, but subject to the modifications in paragraph (4).

(3) Where a notice of appeal to an adjudicator has been given before 4th April 2005, but the respondent has not filed the notice of appeal with the appellate authority in accordance with rule 9 of the 2003 Rules—

(a) rules 12 and 13 of these Rules shall not apply; and

(b) rule 9 of the 2003 Rules shall continue to apply as if it had not been revoked, but subject to the modifications in paragraph (4).

(4) The modifications referred to in paragraphs (2)(b) and (3)(b) are that—

(a) references to an adjudicator or the appellate authority shall be treated as referring to the Tribunal;

(b) in rule 9(1) of the 2003 Rules—

(i) the words 'Subject to rule 10' shall be omitted; and

(ii) for 'together with' there shall be substituted 'and must also when directed by the Asylum and Immigration Tribunal file'; and

(c) for rule 9(2) of the 2003 Rules there shall be substituted—

'(2) The respondent must, as soon as practicable after filing the notice of appeal, serve on the appellant—

(a) a copy of all the documents listed in paragraph (1), except for documents which the respondent has already sent to the appellant; and

(b) notice of the date on which the notice of appeal was filed.'.

(5) Where, pursuant to a transitional provisions order, the Tribunal considers a section 103A application for a review of an adjudicator's determination of an

appeal, Section 1 of Part 3 of these Rules shall apply subject to the modifications that—

(a) in rules 26(3) and 27(2), the references to 'its decision' shall be interpreted as referring to the adjudicator's decision; and

(b) in rules 26(6)(a) and 27(3)(a), the references to 'the Tribunal' shall be interpreted as referring to the adjudicator.

(6) Where, pursuant to a transitional provisions order, the Tribunal reconsiders an appeal which was originally determined by an adjudicator, Section 2 of Part 3 shall apply to the reconsideration, subject to paragraph (7).

(7) Where—

(a) a party has been granted permission to appeal to the Immigration Appeal Tribunal against an adjudicator's determination before 4th April 2005, but the appeal has not been determined by that date; and

(b) by virtue of a transitional provisions order the grant of permission to appeal is treated as an order for the Tribunal to reconsider the adjudicator's determination,

the reconsideration shall be limited to the grounds upon which the Immigration Appeal Tribunal granted permission to appeal.

(8) Any time limit in these Rules for the Tribunal to do anything shall not apply in relation to proceedings to which these Rules apply by virtue of paragraph (1) of this rule.

(9) In relation to proceedings which were pending immediately before 4th April 2005—

(a) unless the Tribunal directs otherwise—

(i) anything done or any directions given before 4th April 2005 under the 2003 Rules (including anything which, pursuant to rule 61(3) of those Rules, was treated as if done or given under those Rules) shall continue to have effect on and after that date;

(ii) anything done or any directions given by the appellate authority shall be treated as if done or given by the Tribunal; and

(iii) any document served on the appellate authority shall be treated as if served on the Tribunal;

(b) unless the context requires otherwise, any reference in a document to an adjudicator, the Immigration Appeal Tribunal or the appellate authority shall, insofar as it relates to an event on or after 4th April 2005, be treated as a reference to the Tribunal.

(10) In this rule—

(a) 'the 2003 Rules' means the Immigration and Asylum Appeals (Procedure) Rules 2003;

(b) 'adjudicator' and 'appellate authority' have the same meaning as in the 2003 Rules; and

(c) 'a transitional provisions order' means an order under section 48(3)(a) of the 2004 Act containing transitional provisions.

Schedule
Forms

ASYLUM AND IMMIGRATION
(TREATMENT OF CLAIMANTS, ETC.)
ACT 2004

Notice of appeal to the Asylum and Immigration Tribunal (United Kingdom)

Form AIT-1

In country

Complete this form if you want to appeal from **inside** the United Kingdom and you have the right to do so.

If you want to appeal from **outside** the United Kingdom, you must use:

appeal form AIT-2 if you are appealing against an Entry Clearance Officer's decision

or appeal form AIT-3 if your right of appeal can only be exercised after having left the United Kingdom or you have chosen to leave the United Kingdom before exercising your right of appeal.

- ❑ To complete this appeal form, **please refer to the information leaflet** that was sent to you with your notice of decision and this form. You can also find the leaflet on www.ait.gov.uk.
- ❑ Please complete this form in English. It is in your interest to complete this form as thoroughly as possible, and state all of your grounds in order for your appeal to be dealt with efficiently.
- ❑ Please complete Section 1 of this form by referring to the notice of decision that was sent to you by the Home Office.
- ❑ Where there is a check box ☐, put a check (**X**) in it to show your answer.
- ❑ You should send your notice of decision with this form. If you do not send the notice of decision with your appeal form, you must give your reasons in Section 8.

Section 1 — Your decision

A	Home Office reference number	
B	Case Outcome ID	
C	Type of Decision	Non-asylum ☐ Asylum ☐
D	Date original application made	/ /
E	Date of Service	/ /
F	Deadline to appeal	/ /
G	Method of Service	Post ☐ Fax or Personal Service ☐

Section 2 — Late appeal and application for extension of time

The deadline to appeal is:

- ❑ **5 business days** from the date you were served with the decision, if you are detained under the Immigration Acts.
- ❑ **10 business days** from the date you were served with the decision, if you are not detained under the Immigration Acts.

Your appeal must be received by the Tribunal by the end of this period.

If you know your appeal is late, **or** if you are not sure your appeal will be received by the deadline date, **you must apply for an extension of time, and give your reasons for failing to submit your appeal in time, in the box →**

- ❑ Attach any evidence to the form.
- ❑ Use additional sheets of paper if you need to.

AIT-1(5.05) Rule 6, Asylum and Immigration Tribunal (Procedure) Rules 2005. Version 1.2 [12 May 2005] **1** of 9

Section 3 — Personal information

A Your Surname or family name
Please use CAPITAL LETTERS

B Your other names

C Address where you can be contacted
Notice:
If you change your address, you **must** notify the Asylum and Immigration Tribunal immediately, in writing. The address of the Tribunal is at the end of this form.

Number/Street

Town

Post Code

D Telephone number
Give a number where the Tribunal may contact you during the day

E Your date of birth
Please give as Day/Month/Year

/ /

F Are you male or female?

Male ☐ Female ☐

G Nationality (or nationalities) or citizenship

H Do you have a representative?

No ☐ Yes ☐ ▶ Your representative should complete Section 6 on page 8.

I Have **you** appealed against any other immigration decision made in the United Kingdom?

No ☐ Yes ☐ ▶ What type of decision did you appeal against?
Asylum ☐ Non-asylum ☐

Date of the appeal / /

What is the appeal number, if you know it?

J **1** To the best of your knowledge, does any member of **your family** have an appeal pending in the United Kingdom?

No ☐ Yes ☐ ▼

Name(s)	Relationship	Appeal number, if you know it

J **2** To the best of your knowledge, is any member of **your family** intending to appeal against an immigration decision?

No ☐ Yes ☐

Name(s)	Relationship	Home Office reference number, if you know it

K Do you wish to have your appeal decided at an **oral hearing**?

No ☐ Please go directly to Section 4 on page 4.

Yes ☐

L If you want an oral hearing, who will be present?

Yourself ☐

Your representative ☐

Witness/es ☐

If you want a witness to attend your hearing, please give their name and Home Office reference number, if applicable.

M If you, your representative or a witness are attending the hearing, will you or they need **an interpreter**?

No ☐ Yes ☐

Which language will be needed?
Language:

Dialect (if applicable):

N If you, your representative or a witness has a disability, please explain any special arrangements needed for the hearing.

Section 4

Grounds of your appeal

In this section you must set out the **grounds for your appeal** and give **the reasons** in support of these grounds – that is, why you disagree with the decision. You must do this **now** because you may not be allowed to mention any further grounds at a later date.

- ❑ If your appeal relates in whole or in part to an **asylum** decision, complete all of boxes **A** to **E** that apply to you.
- ❑ If you are not sure which boxes apply to you or there are other points of the refusal letter that you disagree with, write your grounds in box **F**.
- ❑ If your appeal relates to a **non-asylum** decision, go to box **G** and complete it.

Please refer to the paragraphs of the refusal letter when possible.

You should include in this section any parts of your claim that you think have not been addressed in the refusal letter. You must say if you have raised these issues before.

Asylum decision

Give as much detail as possible: use additional sheets of paper if you need to.

A If you disagree with the Home Office's interpretation of **the situation in your country**, please explain why in this box, and give reasons to support your point of view.

B If the Home Office has suggested that you could **live safely in another part of your country of origin**, and you disagree, please explain why in this box.

C If the Home Office has stated that your claim is **not credible**, and you disagree, please explain why in this box.

D If the Home Office has stated that you do not qualify as a refugee on grounds of race, religion, nationality, membership of a particular social group, or political opinion (**under the criteria of the 1951 Geneva Convention**), and you disagree, please explain why in this box.

E If the Home Office has stated that specific articles of the **European Convention on Human Rights** (ECHR) do not apply to your case, and you disagree, please explain why in this box.

F If there is **anything else** that you disagree with in the Home Office letter, please explain why in this box.

- **Please now go to section 5, 'Statement of additional grounds', on page 7.**

Non-asylum decision

G If your appeal relates to a non-asylum decision with which you disagree, you must give your reasons below and refer to the paragraphs of the refusal letter.

Section 5 — Statement of additional grounds

If your notice of decision requires you to make a **Statement of additional grounds**, you should make the statement in this box.
This section refers to any **other reasons** why you think:

- ❑ you should be allowed to stay in the United Kingdom, including any reasons relating to the European Convention on Human Rights
- ❑ you should not be removed or required to leave.

Do not repeat here any grounds and reasons that you have already given in Section 4.

You must give all these additional grounds and reasons **now** because you may not be able to make any other applications to appeal if this current application is refused. You should explain why you did not give these reasons before.

Section 6 Representation

If you have a representative, he or she must complete this section.

A **Declaration by the Representative**

I, the representative, am giving this notice of appeal in accordance with the appellant's instructions, and the appellant believes that the facts stated in this notice of appeal are true.

Representative's signature and date   /   /

B Name of the representative
Please use CAPITAL LETTERS

C Name of the representative's organisation

D Postal address of organisation

Number / Street

Town

Post Code

E Reference for correspondence

F Telephone number

G Mobile number

H Fax number

I Email address

J Are you an organisation regulated by the Office of the Immigration Services Commissioner (OISC)?

No ☐ Yes ☐ ▶ Please provide the OISC reference:

K Has the appellant been granted publicly funded legal representation?

No ☐ Yes ☐ ▶ Please provide the LSC reference number, if applicable:

Notice to representatives

You must also notify the Asylum and Immigration Tribunal, and other parties, if you cease to represent the appellant. If the appellant changes representative, details of the new representative should be sent to the same address to which you are sending this form. Please give the **appellant's full name, address,** and **Home Office reference number.**

Section 7 — Declaration by appellant

If you are the appellant and you are completing this form yourself, you must complete the declaration.

A **Declaration by the Appellant**

I, the appellant, believe that the facts stated in this notice of appeal are true.

Appellant's signature and date

/ /

B Name of appellant
Please use CAPITAL LETTERS

Section 8 — When you have completed the form

What to do next

Keep a copy of this form for your own use. Then **either**:

- ❑ **send** the original form to: **Asylum and Immigration Tribunal**
  PO Box 7866
  Loughborough
  LE11 2XZ
- ❑ **or fax** the form to: **01509 221699**

Send the notice of decision with this form.

To make sure that you are sending your notice of decision with this form, please tick this box. ☐

If you do not send the notice of decision with the appeal form, you must state the reason here.

Documents to support you application

If you are sending any other documents with this form to support your appeal, please list them here.

If you are intending to send other documents that are not yet available to you, please list them here.

If you need to contact the Tribunal

If you need to contact the Asylum and Immigration Tribunal, use your Home Office reference number and your Case Outcome ID in your correspondence.

Changes to your personal information

You must notify the Tribunal if you change your address, and/or if you appoint a new representative.

Data Protection Statement

Information, including personal details, that you have provided in this form will not be used by the Asylum and Immigration Tribunal for any purpose other than the determination of your application. The information may be disclosed to other government departments and public authorities only, for related immigration or asylum purposes.

AIT-1(5.05) Rule 6, Asylum and Immigration Tribunal (Procedure) Rules 2005. Version 1.2 [12 May 2005] **9** of 9

ASYLUM AND IMMIGRATION
(TREATMENT OF CLAIMANTS, ETC.)
ACT 2004

Notice of appeal to the Asylum and Immigration Tribunal (United Kingdom)

Form AIT-2
Overseas-Entry Clearance

Complete this form if you are appealing against a decision of an Entry Clearance Officer.

If you are appealing from **outside the United Kingdom** against any other decision, you must use appeal form AIT-3.

- ❑ To complete this appeal form, **please refer to the information leaflet** that was sent to you with your notice of refusal and this form. You can also find the leaflet on www.ait.gov.uk.
- ❑ Please complete this form in English. It is in your interest to complete this form as thoroughly as possible, and state all of your grounds in order for your appeal to be dealt with efficiently.
- ❑ Please complete Section 1 of this form by referring to the notice of refusal that was sent to you by the Entry Clearance Officer.
- ❑ Where there is a check box ☐, put a check (**X**) in it to show your answer.
- ❑ You should send your notice of refusal with this form. If you do not send the notice of refusal with your appeal form, you must give your reasons in Section 7.

Section 1 — Your decision

A Post reference number	
B Type of Decision	Settlement ☐ Non-Settlement ☐ Family Visit Visa ☐
C Name of British Mission Overseas	
D Date of Service	/ /
E Deadline to appeal	/ /
F Method of Service	Post ☐ Fax or Personal Service ☐

Section 2 — Late appeal and application for extension of time

The deadline to appeal is **28 calendar days** from the date you were served with the decision. Your appeal must be received by the Visa Section or the Tribunal by the end of this period. **In accordance with the Asylum and Immigration Tribunal (Procedure) Rules 2005, you must not send your appeal to both locations.**

If you know your appeal is late, **or** if you are not sure your appeal will be received by the deadline date, **you must apply for an extension of time, and give your reasons for failing to submit your appeal in time, in the box →**

- ❑ Attach any evidence to the form.
- ❑ Use additional sheets of paper if you need to.

Section 3 — Personal information

A Your Surname or family name
Please use CAPITAL LETTERS

B Your other names

C Address where you can be contacted
Notice:
If you change your address, you **must** notify the Asylum and Immigration Tribunal immediately, in writing. The address of the Tribunal is at the end of this form.

Number/Street

Town / Post Code

Country

D Telephone number
Give a number where the Tribunal may contact you during the day

E Your date of birth
Please give as Day/Month/Year

/ /

F Are you male or female?

Male ☐ Female ☐

G Nationality (or nationalities) or citizenship

H Do you have a representative?

No ☐ Yes ☐ ▶ Your representative should complete Section 5 on page 5.

I Have **you** appealed against any other immigration decision made **either** in the United Kingdom or overseas?

No ☐ Yes ☐ ▶ What type of decision did you appeal against?
Asylum ☐ Non-asylum ☐

Date of the appeal / /

What is the appeal number, if you know it?

J **1** To the best of your knowledge, does any member of **your family** have an appeal pending in the United Kingdom?

No ☐ Yes ☐ ▼

Name(s)	Relationship	Appeal number, if you know it

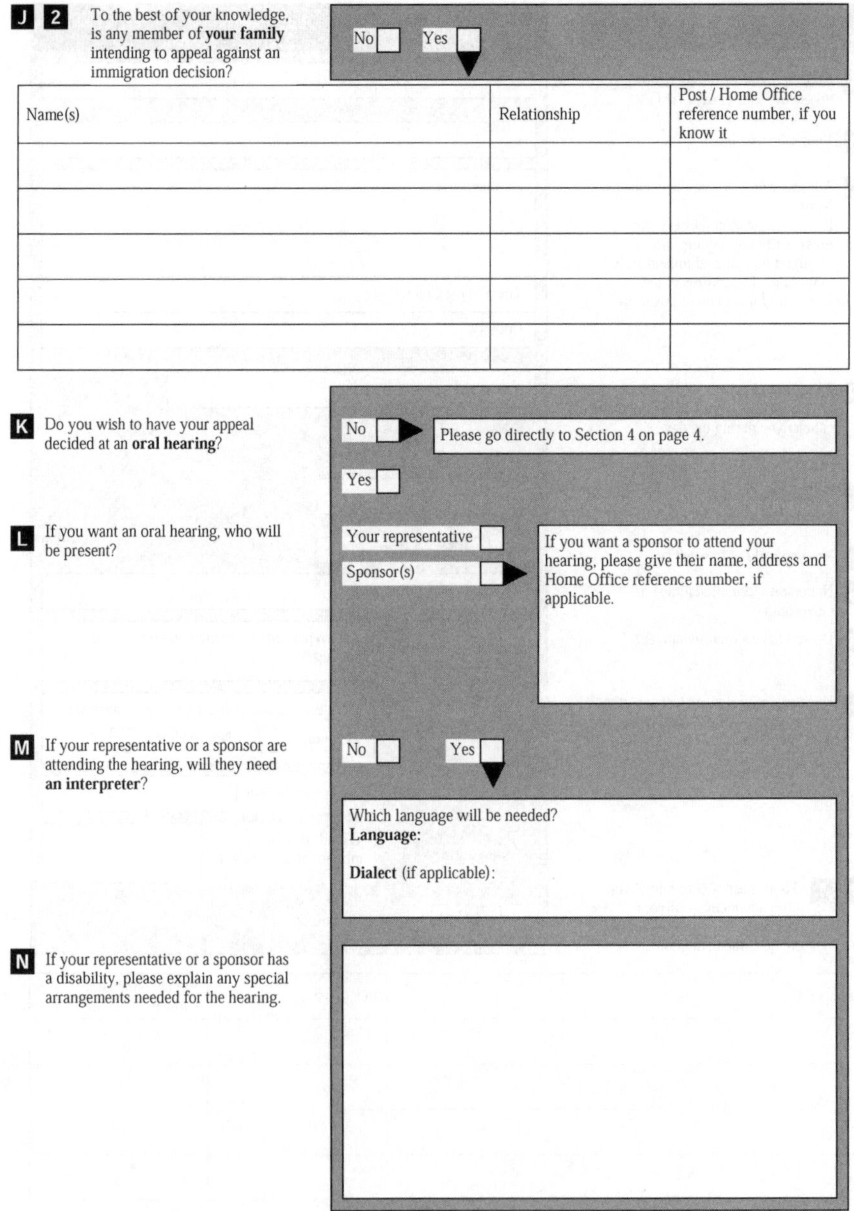

J 2 To the best of your knowledge, is any member of **your family** intending to appeal against an immigration decision?

No ☐ Yes ☐

Name(s)	Relationship	Post / Home Office reference number, if you know it

K Do you wish to have your appeal decided at an **oral hearing**?

No ☐ ▶ Please go directly to Section 4 on page 4.

Yes ☐

L If you want an oral hearing, who will be present?

Your representative ☐

Sponsor(s) ☐ ▶ If you want a sponsor to attend your hearing, please give their name, address and Home Office reference number, if applicable.

M If your representative or a sponsor are attending the hearing, will they need **an interpreter**?

No ☐ Yes ☐

Which language will be needed?
Language:

Dialect (if applicable):

N If your representative or a sponsor has a disability, please explain any special arrangements needed for the hearing.

Section 4

Grounds of your appeal

- In this section you must set out the **grounds for your appeal** and give **the reasons** in support of these grounds – that is, why you disagree with the decision. You must do this **now** because you may not be allowed to mention any further grounds at a later date.
- Please set out your grounds, and reasons in support of those grounds, in the box below.
- Please refer to the paragraphs of the refusal letter when possible.
- You should include in this section any parts of your claim that you think have not been addressed in the refusal letter. You must say if you have raised these issues before.
- Give as much detail as possible: use additional sheets of paper if you need to.

Section 5 Representation

If you have a representative, he or she must complete this section.

A **Declaration by the Representative**

I, the representative, am giving this notice of appeal in accordance with the appellant's instructions, and the appellant believes that the facts stated in this notice of appeal are true.

Representative's signature and date   / /

B Name of the representative
Please use CAPITAL LETTERS

C Name of the representative's organisation

D Postal address of organisation

Number / Street

Town

Post Code

E Reference for correspondence

F Telephone number

G Mobile number

H Fax number

I Email address

J Are you an organisation regulated by the Office of the Immigration Services Commissioner (OISC)?

No ☐ Yes ☐ Please provide the OISC reference:

K Has the appellant been granted publicly funded legal representation?

No ☐ Yes ☐ Please provide the LSC reference number, if applicable:

Notice to representatives

You must notify the Asylum and Immigration Tribunal, the Visa Section in the country where you applied, and other parties, if you cease to represent the appellant. If the appellant changes representative, details of the new representative should be sent to the same address to which you are sending this form. Please give the **appellant's full name, address,** and **Post reference number.**

Section 6

Declaration by appellant

If you are the appellant and you are completing this form yourself, you must complete the declaration.

A Declaration by the Appellant

I, the appellant, believe that the facts stated in this notice of appeal are true.

Appellant's signature and date

/ /

B Name of appellant
Please use CAPITAL LETTERS

Section 7

When you have completed the form

What to do next

Keep a copy of this form for your own use. Then send the original form to either **1** or **2** below, but **not** to both:

1 The Visa Section in the country where you applied; **or**

2 The Asylum and Immigration Tribunal. You may send the form to the Tribunal, either by sending it to: **Asylum and Immigration Tribunal**
PO Box 7866
Loughborough, United Kingdom
LE11 2XZ

Or by faxing it to: **+44 (0)15 09 221 699**

Please tick **one** of boxes **1** or **2** below to show where you will send the form

1 Visa Section ☐ **2** Tribunal ☐

Send the notice of refusal with this form.

To make sure that you are sending your notice of refusal with this form, please tick this box. ☐

If you do not send the notice of decision with the appeal form, you must state the reason here.

Documents to support your application

If you are sending any other documents with this form to support your appeal, please list them here:

If you are intending to send other documents that are not yet available to you, please list them here:

If you need to contact the Tribunal

If you need to contact the Asylum and Immigration Tribunal, use your Post reference number in your correspondence.

Changes to your personal information

You must notify the Tribunal if you change your address, and/or if you appoint a new representative.

Data Protection Statement

Information, including personal details, that you have provided in this form will not be used by the Visa Section, or Asylum and Immigration Tribunal, for any purpose other than the determination of your application. The information may be disclosed to other government departments and public authorities only, for related immigration or asylum purposes.

AIT-2 (5.05) Rule 6, Asylum and Immigration Tribunal (Procedure) Rules 2005. Version 1.2 [12 May 2005] **6** of 6

ASYLUM AND IMMIGRATION (TREATMENT OF CLAIMANTS, ETC.) ACT 2004

Notice of appeal to the Asylum and Immigration Tribunal (United Kingdom)

Form AIT-3
Overseas – Non-Entry Clearance

Complete this form if:
your right of appeal can only be exercised after having left the United Kingdom
or you have chosen to leave the United Kingdom before exercising your right of appeal.

If you are appealing from outside the United Kingdom against a decision of an Entry Clearance Officer, you must use appeal form AIT-2.

- To complete this appeal form, **please refer to the information leaflet** that was sent to you with your notice of decision and this form. You can also find the leaflet on www.ait.gov.uk.
- Please complete this form in English. It is in your interest to complete this form as thoroughly as possible, and state all of your grounds in order for your appeal to be dealt with efficiently.
- Please complete Section 1 of this form by referring to the notice of decision that was sent to you by the Home Office.
- Where there is a check box ☐, put a check (**X**) in it to show your answer.
- You should send your notice of decision with this form. If you do not send the notice of decision with your appeal form, you must give your reasons in Section 7.

Section 1 — Your decision

A	Home Office reference number	
B	Case Outcome ID	
C	Type of Decision	Non-asylum ☐ Asylum ☐
D	Date of Service	/ /
E	Deadline to appeal	/ /
F	Method of Service	Post ☐ Fax or Personal Service ☐

Section 2 — Late appeal and application for extension of time

The deadline to appeal is:

- **28 calendar days** from the date of your departure from the United Kingdom when your right of appeal can only be exercised after you have left the United Kingdom.
- **28 calendar days** from the date when you received your decision in all other cases.

Your appeal must be received by the Tribunal by the end of this period.

If you know your appeal is late, **or** if you are not sure your appeal will be received by the deadline date, **you must apply for an extension of time, and give your reasons for failing to submit your appeal in time, in the box →**

- Attach any evidence to the form.
- Use additional sheets of paper if you need to.

Section 3 — Personal information

A Your Surname or family name
Please use CAPITAL LETTERS

B Your other names

C Address where you can be contacted
Notice:
If you change your address, you **must** notify the Asylum and Immigration Tribunal immediately, in writing. The address of the Tribunal is at the end of this form.

Number/Street

Town / Post Code

Country

D Telephone number
Give a number where the Tribunal may contact you during the day

E Your date of birth
Please give as Day/Month/Year

/ /

F Are you male or female?

Male ☐ Female ☐

G Nationality (or nationalities) or citizenship

H Do you have a representative?

No ☐ Yes ☐ ▶ Your representative should complete Section 5 on page 7.

I Have **you** appealed against any other immigration decision made in the United Kingdom?

No ☐ Yes ☐ ▶ What type of decision did you appeal against?
Asylum ☐ Non-asylum ☐

Date of the appeal / /

What is the appeal number, if you know it?

J **1** To the best of your knowledge, does any member of **your family** have an appeal pending in the United Kingdom?

No ☐ Yes ☐ ▼

Name(s)	Relationship	Appeal number, if you know it

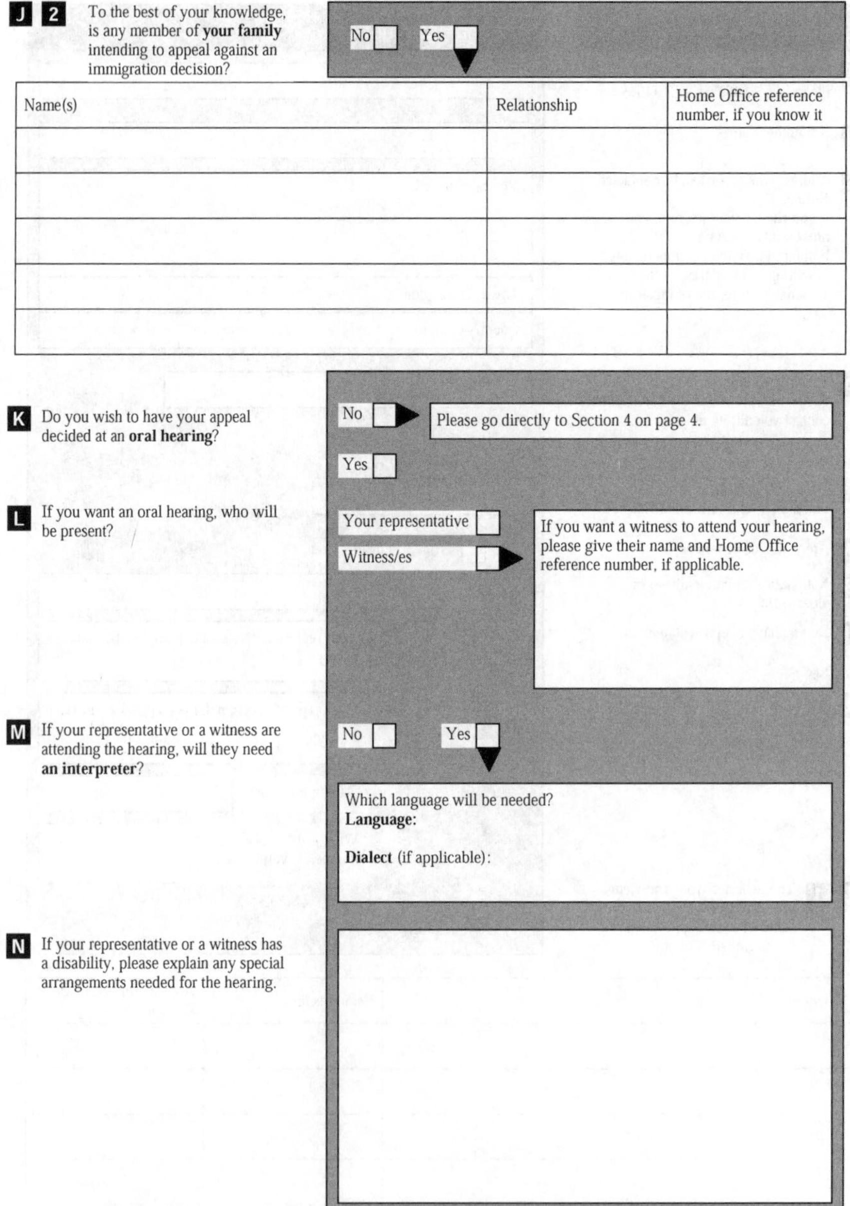

J 2 To the best of your knowledge, is any member of **your family** intending to appeal against an immigration decision?

No ☐ Yes ☐

Name(s)	Relationship	Home Office reference number, if you know it

K Do you wish to have your appeal decided at an **oral hearing**?

No ☐ → Please go directly to Section 4 on page 4.

Yes ☐

L If you want an oral hearing, who will be present?

Your representative ☐

Witness/es ☐ → If you want a witness to attend your hearing, please give their name and Home Office reference number, if applicable.

M If your representative or a witness are attending the hearing, will they need **an interpreter**?

No ☐ Yes ☐

Which language will be needed?
Language:

Dialect (if applicable):

N If your representative or a witness has a disability, please explain any special arrangements needed for the hearing.

AIT-3(5.05) Rule 6, Asylum and Immigration Tribunal (Procedure) Rules 2005. Version 1.2 [12 May 2005] **3** of 8

Section 4

Grounds of your appeal

In this section you must set out the **grounds for your appeal** and give **the reasons** in support of these grounds – that is, why you disagree with the decision. You must do this **now** because you may not be allowed to mention any further grounds at a later date.

- If your appeal relates in whole or in part to an **asylum** decision, complete all of boxes **A** to **E** that apply to you.
- If you are not sure which boxes apply to you or there are other points of the refusal letter that you disagree with, write your grounds in box **F**.
- If your appeal relates to a **non-asylum** claim, go to box **G** and complete it.

Please refer to the paragraphs of the refusal letter when possible.

You should include in this section any parts of your claim that you think have not been addressed in the refusal letter. You must say if you have raised these issues before.

Give as much detail as possible: use additional sheets of paper if you need to.

Asylum decision

A If you disagree with the Home Office's interpretation of **the situation in your country**, please explain why in this box, and give reasons to support your point of view.

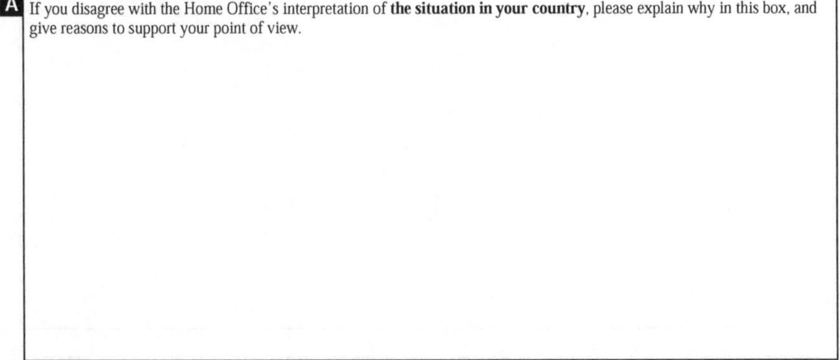

B If the Home Office has suggested that you could **live safely in another part of your country of origin**, and you disagree, please explain why in this box.

C If the Home Office has stated that your claim is **not credible**, and you disagree, please explain why in this box.

D If the Home Office has stated that you do not qualify as a refugee on grounds of race, religion, nationality, membership of a particular social group, or political opinion (**under the criteria of the 1951 Geneva Convention**), and you disagree, please explain why in this box.

E If the Home Office has stated that specific articles of the **European Convention on Human Rights** (ECHR) do not apply to your case, and you disagree, please explain why in this box.

F If there is **anything else** that you disagree with in the Home Office letter, please explain why in this box.

Non-asylum decision

G If your appeal relates to a non-asylum decision with which you disagree, you must give your reasons below and refer to the paragraphs of the refusal letter.

Section 5 — Representation

If you have a representative, he or she must complete this section.

A Declaration by the Representative

I, the representative, am giving this notice of appeal in accordance with the appellant's instructions, and the appellant believes that the facts stated in this notice of appeal are true.

Representative's signature and date / /

B Name of the representative
Please use CAPITAL LETTERS

C Name of the representative's organisation

D Postal address of organisation

Number / Street

Town

Post Code

E Reference for correspondence

F Telephone number

G Mobile number

H Fax number

I Email address

J Are you an organisation regulated by the Office of the Immigration Services Commissioner (OISC)?

No ☐ Yes ☐ ▶ Please provide the OISC reference:

K Has the appellant been granted publicly funded legal representation?

No ☐ Yes ☐ ▶ Please provide the LSC reference number, if applicable:

Notice to representatives

You must notify the Asylum and Immigration Tribunal, and other parties, if you cease to represent the appellant. If the appellant changes representative, details of the new representative should be sent to the same address to which you are sending this form. Please give the **appellant's full name, address,** and **Home Office reference number.**

Section 6 — Declaration by appellant

If you are the appellant and you are completing this form yourself, you must complete the declaration.

A Declaration by the Appellant

I, the Appellant, believe that the facts stated in this notice of appeal are true.

Appellant's signature and date

/ /

B Name of appellant
Please use CAPITAL LETTERS

Section 7 — When you have completed the form

What to do next

Keep a copy of this form for your own use. Then **either**:

- **Send** the original form to:
  Asylum and Immigration Tribunal
  PO Box 7866
  Loughborough, United Kingdom
  LE11 2XZ

- **or fax** the form to: **+44 (0)15 09 221 699**

Send the notice of decision.

To make sure that you are sending your notice of decision with this form, please tick this box ☐

If you do not send the notice of decision with the appeal form, you must state the reason here.

Documents to support you application

If you are sending any other documents with this form to support your appeal, please list them here.

If you are intending to send other documents that are not yet available to you, please list them here.

If you need to contact the Tribunal

If you need to contact the Asylum and Immigration Tribunal, use you Home Office reference number and your Case Outcome ID in your correspondence.

Changes to your personal information

You must notify the Tribunal if you change your address and/or if you appoint a new representative.

Data Protection Statement

Information, including personal details, that you have provided in this form will not be used by the Asylum and Immigration Tribunal for any purpose other than the determination of your application. The information may be disclosed to other government departments and public authorities only, for related immigration or asylum purposes.

AIT-3(5.05) Rule 6, Asylum and Immigration Tribunal (Procedure) Rules 2005. Version 1.2 [12 May 2005] **8** of 8

ASYLUM AND IMMIGRATION
(TREATMENT OF CLAIMANTS, ETC.)
ACT 2004

Application to the Asylum and Immigration Tribunal for permission to appeal to the Court of Appeal or Court of Session

Form AIT-4

Complete this form if you want to challenge the Asylum and Immigration Tribunal determination **on a point of law** by appealing to the Court of Appeal, or the Court of Session when the decision of the Tribunal was made in Scotland

- Please complete this form in English. It is in your interest to complete this form as thoroughly as possible, and state all your grounds in order for your application to be dealt with efficiently.
- Please complete Section 1 of this form by referring to the determination that the Tribunal sent you.
- Where there is a check box ☐, put a check **(X)** in it to show your answer.
- You should send your determination with this form.

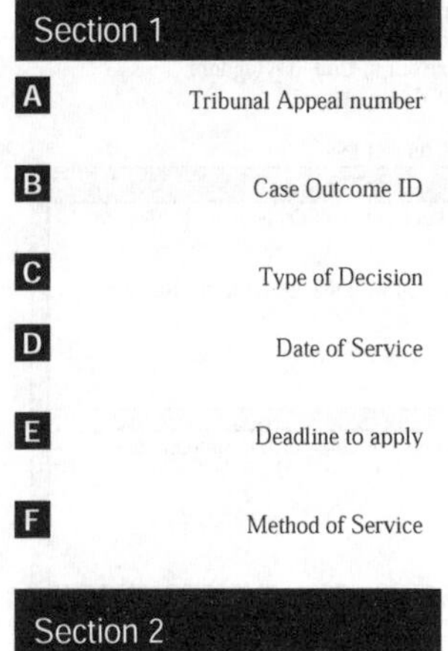

Section 1

A Tribunal Appeal number

B Case Outcome ID

C Type of Decision

D Date of Service

E Deadline to apply

F Method of Service

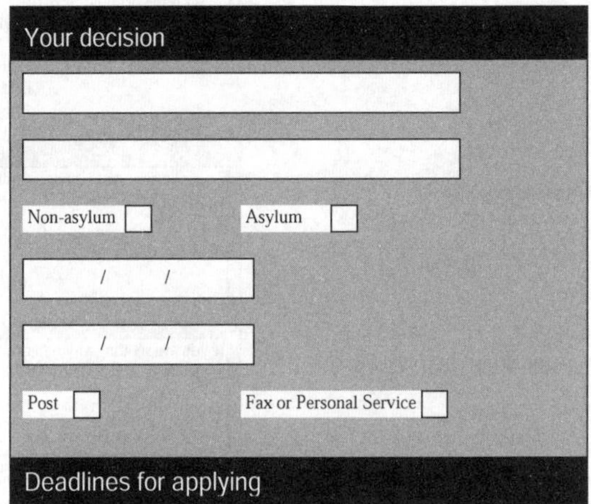

Your decision

Non-asylum ☐ Asylum ☐

/ /

/ /

Post ☐ Fax or Personal Service ☐

Section 2

Deadlines for applying

The deadline to apply is:

- **5 business days** from the date you were served with the decision, if you are detained under the Immigration Acts.
- **10 business days** from the date you were served with the decision, if you are not detained under the Immigration Acts.

Your application must be received by the Tribunal by the end of this period.

Section 3

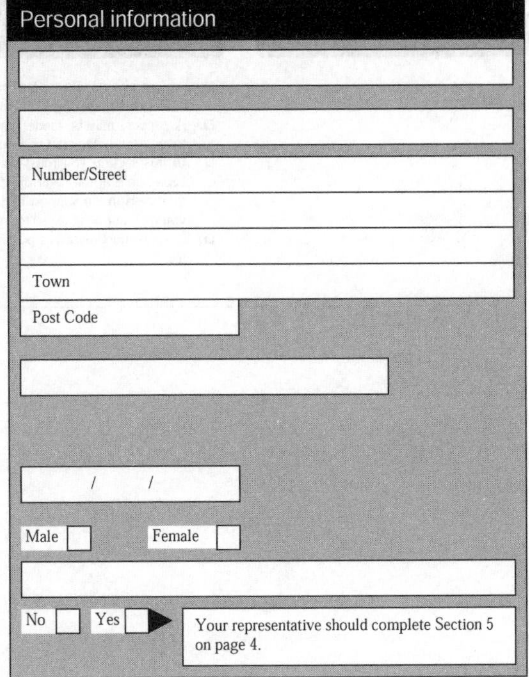

Personal information

A Your Surname or family name Please use CAPITAL LETTERS	
B Your other names	
C Address where you can be contacted **Notice:** If you change your address, you **must** notify the Asylum and Immigration Tribunal immediately, in writing. The address of the Tribunal is at the end of this form.	Number/Street Town Post Code
D Telephone number Give a number where the Tribunal may contact you during the day	
E Your date of birth Please give as Day/Month/Year	/ /
F Are you male or female?	Male ☐ Female ☐
G Nationality (or nationalities) or citizenship	
H Do you have a representative?	No ☐ Yes ☐ ▶ Your representative should complete Section 5 on page 4.

Please turn to section 4 on page 3 →

Section 4

Grounds of your appeal to the Court of Appeal or Court of Session

- An appeal to the Court of Appeal or Court of Session against a determination by the Tribunal is permissible only on a **point of law.**
- An appeal may be made against a point of law in a determination relating to an asylum decision or a non-asylum decision.
- In this section you must set out the **errors of law** that you believe have been made in the determination that you would like to appeal against and give **reasons** in support of these beliefs. You must do this **now** because you may not be allowed to mention any further points of law at a later date.
- Give as much detail as possible: use additional sheets of paper if you need to.

Section 5 | Representation

If you have a representative, he or she must complete this section.

A Declaration by the Representative

I, the representative, am making this application in accordance with the appellant's instructions, and the appellant believes that the facts stated in this application are true.

Representative's signature and date   / /

B Name of the representative
Please use CAPITAL LETTERS

C Name of the representative's organisation

D Postal address of organisation

Number / Street

Town

Post Code

E Reference for correspondence

F Telephone number

G Mobile number

H Fax number

I Email address

J Are you an organisation regulated by the Office of the Immigration Services Commissioner (OISC)?

No ☐ Yes ☐ Please provide the OISC reference:

K Has the appellant been granted publicly funded legal representation?

No ☐ Yes ☐ Please provide the LSC reference number, if applicable:

Notice to representatives

You must notify the Asylum and Immigration Tribunal, and other parties, if you cease to represent the appellant. If the appellant changes representative, details of the new representative should be sent to the same address to which you are sending this form. Please give the **appellant's full name, address,** and **Tribunal appeal number.**

Section 6 — Declaration by appellant

If you are the appellant and you are completing this form yourself, you must complete the declaration.

A Declaration by the Appellant

I, the appellant, believe that the facts stated in this application are true.

Appellant's signature and date

/ /

B Name of appellant
Please use CAPITAL LETTERS

Section 7 — When you have completed the form

What to do next

Keep a copy of this form for your own use. Then **either**:

- **send** the original form to:

  Asylum and Immigration Tribunal
  PO Box 6987
  Leicester
  LE1 6ZX

- **or fax** the form to: **0116 249 4214**

Send your determination with this form

To make sure that you are sending your determination with this form, please tick this box ☐

Documents to support you application

If you are sending any other documents with this form to support your application and appeal, please list them here.

If you need to contact the Tribunal

If you need to contact the Asylum and Immigration Tribunal, use the Tribunal appeal number and your Case Outcome ID in your correspondence.

Changes to your personal information

You must notify the Tribunal if you change your address, and/or if you appoint a new representative.

Data Protection Statement

Information, including personal details, that you have provided in this form will not be used by the Asylum and Immigration Tribunal for any purpose other than the determination of your application. The information may be disclosed to other government departments and public authorities only, for related immigration or asylum purposes.

ASYLUM AND IMMIGRATION (TREATMENT OF CLAIMANTS, ETC.) ACT 2004

Application to be released on bail

Form B1

Section 1 Personal information

A Home Office reference number

B Your surname or family name
Please use CAPITAL LETTERS

C Your other names

D Address where you are detained

Post Code

E Your date of birth
Please give as Day / Month / Year

/ /

F Are you male or female?

Male ☐ Female ☐

G Nationality (or nationalities) or citizenship

H Date of arrival in the United Kingdom

/ /

I Do you have a representative?

No ☐ Yes ☐ ▶ Your representative should complete Section 7 on page 4.

Section 2 About your application

A Do you have an appeal pending?

No ☐ Yes ☐ ▶ What is the appeal number, if you know it?

B Have you lodged a bail application before?

No ☐ Yes ☐ ▶ What is the bail reference number, if you know it?

C The address where you plan to live, if your application for bail is granted

Number/Street

Town

Post Code

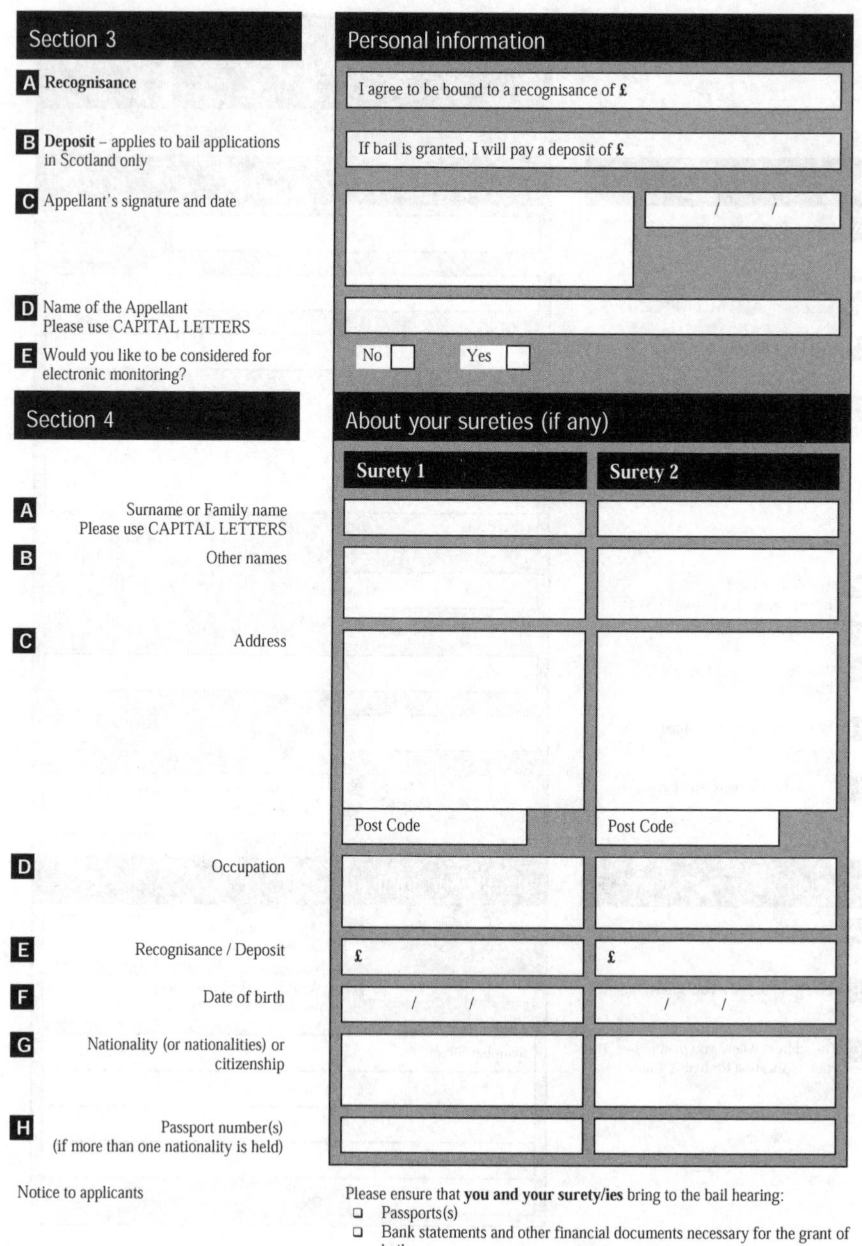

Section 3	Personal information	
A **Recognisance**	I agree to be bound to a recognisance of **£**	
B **Deposit** – applies to bail applications in Scotland only	If bail is granted, I will pay a deposit of **£**	
C Appellant's signature and date		/ /
D Name of the Appellant Please use CAPITAL LETTERS		
E Would you like to be considered for electronic monitoring?	No ☐	Yes ☐

Section 4	About your sureties (if any)	
	Surety 1	**Surety 2**
A Surname or Family name Please use CAPITAL LETTERS		
B Other names		
C Address	Post Code	Post Code
D Occupation		
E Recognisance / Deposit	£	£
F Date of birth	/ /	/ /
G Nationality (or nationalities) or citizenship		
H Passport number(s) (if more than one nationality is held)		

Notice to applicants

Please ensure that **you and your surety/ies** bring to the bail hearing:

- ☐ Passports(s)
- ☐ Bank statements and other financial documents necessary for the grant of bail

Section 5

The grounds on which you are applying for bail

- In this section you must set out all the reasons why you think you should be released.
- If you have had a previous application for bail refused, give full details of any change in circumstances since then.
- Give as much detail as possible: use additional sheets of paper if you need to, and attach them to this form.

In this box, give all the reason(s) why you think you should be released.

Section 6

At the hearing of your application

A Will you or your surety need an interpreter?

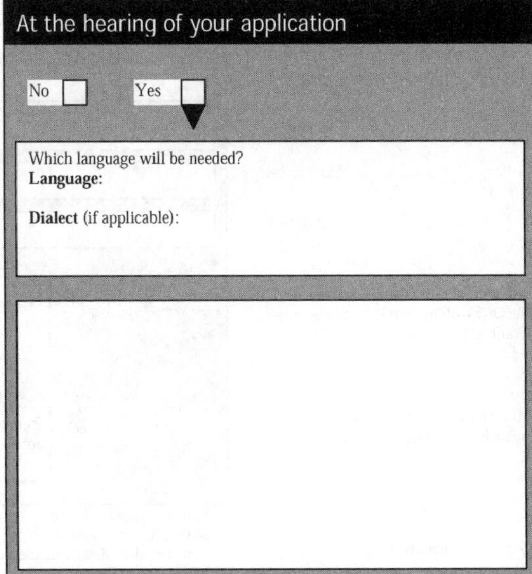
No ☐ Yes ☐

Which language will be needed?
Language:

Dialect (if applicable):

B If you or your legal representative has a disability, please explain any special arrangements needed for the hearing.

Section 7 Representation

If you have a representative, he or she must complete this section

A Declaration by the Representative

I, the representative, am making this application in accordance with the appellant's instructions, and the appellant believes that the facts stated in this application are true.

Representative's signature and date   / /

B Name of the representative
Please use CAPITAL LETTERS

C Name of the representative's organisation

D Postal address of organisation

Number / Street

Town

Post Code

E Reference for correspondence

F Telephone number

G Mobile number

H Fax number

I Email address

J Are you an organisation regulated by the Office of the Immigration Services Commissioner (OISC)?

No ☐ Yes ☐ ▶ Please provide the OISC reference:

K Has the appellant been granted publicly funded legal representation?

No ☐ Yes ☐ ▶ Please provide the LSC reference number, if applicable:

Notice to representatives

You must notify the court in which the bail application is made, and other parties, if you cease to represent the appellant. If the appellant changes representative, details of the new representative should be sent to the same address to which you are sending this form. Please give the **appellant's full name, address,** and **Home Office reference number.**

Section 8 — Declaration by appellant

If you are the appellant and you are completing this form yourself, you must complete the declaration.

A Declaration by the Appellant

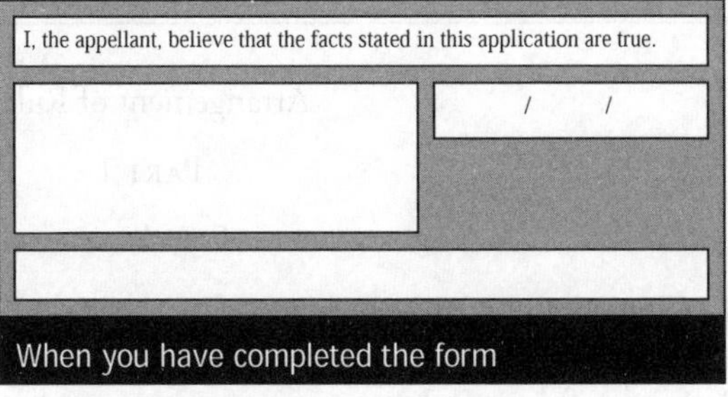
I, the appellant, believe that the facts stated in this application are true.

Appellant's signature and date

/ /

B Name of appellant
Please use CAPITAL LETTERS

Section 9 — When you have completed the form

What to do next

Keep a copy of this form for your own use. Send or deliver the original form to the court to which you intend to make your application for bail.

Data Protection Statement

Information, including personal details, that you have provided in this form will not be used by the Asylum and Immigration Tribunal for any purpose other than the determination of your application. The information may be disclosed to other government departments and public authorities only, for related immigration or asylum purposes.

The Asylum and Immigration Tribunal (Fast Track Procedure) Rules 2005
(SI 2005, No. 560 [L.12])

Arrangement of Rules

Part 1

Introduction

Citation and commencement

1. These Rules may be cited as the Asylum and Immigration Tribunal (Fast Track Procedure) Rules 2005 and shall come into force on 4th April 2005.

Interpretation

2.—(1) In these Rules, 'the Principal Rules' means the Asylum and Immigration Tribunal (Procedure) Rules 2005.

(2) Subject to paragraph (3), words and expressions used in these Rules which are defined in rule 2 of the Principal Rules have the same meaning in these Rules as in the Principal Rules.

(3) In these Rules, and in any provision of the Principal Rules which applies by virtue of these Rules, 'business day' means any day other than a Saturday or Sunday, a bank holiday, 24th to 31st December, Maundy Thursday, Good Friday or the Tuesday after the last Monday in May.

(4) In a provision of the Principal Rules which applies by virtue of these Rules, a reference to an 'appropriate prescribed form' means, in relation to a notice of appeal or an application notice for permission to appeal to the appropriate appellate court, the appropriate form in Schedule 1 to these Rules, or that form with any variations that the circumstances may require.

(5) Where a provision of the Principal Rules applies by virtue of these Rules—
   (a) any reference in that provision to the Principal Rules is to be interpreted as including a reference to these Rules; and
   (b) any reference in that provision to a specific Part or rule in the Principal Rules is to be interpreted as including a reference to any equivalent Part or rule in these Rules.

Scope of these Rules

3.—(1) Part 2 of these Rules applies to appeals to the Tribunal in the circumstances specified in rule 5.

(2) Part 3 applies to proceedings before the Tribunal of the types described in rule 24 of the Principal Rules in the circumstances specified in rule 15.

(3) Part 4 applies to proceedings before the Tribunal to which Part 2 or 3 applies.

(4) Part 5 applies to proceedings before the Tribunal to which Part 2 or 3 applies or has applied.

(5) For the purpose of rules 5 and 15, a party does not cease to satisfy a condition that he must have been continuously in detention under the Immigration Acts at a place or places specified in Schedule 2 to these Rules by reason only of—
   (a) being transported from one place of detention specified in that Schedule to another place which is so specified; or
   (b) leaving and returning to such a place of detention for any purpose between the hours of 6 a.m. and 10 p.m.

Application of the Principal Rules

4.—(1) Rule 4 of the Principal Rules (Overriding objective) applies to these Rules.

(2) Where Part 2 or 3 of these Rules applies to proceedings before the Tribunal, the Principal Rules also apply to the extent specified in rules 6, 16, 20, 24 and 27 of these Rules.

Part 2

Appeals to the Tribunal

Scope of this Part

5.—(1) This Part applies to an appeal to the Tribunal where the person giving notice of appeal—
   (a) was in detention under the Immigration Acts at a place specified in Schedule 2 when he was served with notice of the immigration decision against which he is appealing; and
   (b) has been continuously in detention under the Immigration Acts at a place or places specified in Schedule 2 since that notice was served on him.

(2) This Part shall cease to apply if the Tribunal makes an order under rule 30(1).

Application of Part 2 of the Principal Rules

6. Where this Part applies to an appeal, the following provisions of Part 2 of the Principal Rules apply—
   (a) rule 6(1) to (3), omitting the reference to rule 6(4) in rule 6(2);
   (b) rule 8;
   (c) rule 10(1);
   (d) rule 13(1) and (4);
   (e) rule 14; and
   (f) rules 17 to 19.

Giving notice of appeal

7. Where a notice of appeal is served on a custodian under rule 6(3)(b) of the Principal Rules, the custodian must—
   (a) endorse on the notice the date that it is served on him; and
   (b) forward it to the Tribunal immediately.

Time limit

8.—(1) A person who wishes to appeal must give a notice of appeal not later than 2 days after the day on which he is served with notice of the immigration decision against which he is appealing.

(2) Where a notice of appeal is given outside the time limit in paragraph (1), the Tribunal must not extend the time for appealing unless it is satisfied that, because of circumstances outside the control of the person giving notice of appeal or his representative, it was not practicable for the notice of appeal to be given within that time limit.

Service of notice of appeal on respondent

9. When the Tribunal receives a notice of appeal it shall immediately serve a copy upon the respondent.

Filing of documents by respondent

10. The respondent must file the documents listed in rule 13(1) of the Principal Rules not later than 2 days after the day on which the Tribunal serves the respondent with the notice of appeal.

Listing

11.—(1) The Tribunal shall fix a hearing date which is—
   (a) not later than 2 days after the day on which the respondent files the documents under rule 10; or
   (b) if the Tribunal is unable to arrange a hearing within that time, as soon as practicable thereafter.

(2) The Tribunal must serve notice of the date, time and place of the hearing on every party as soon as practicable, and in any event not later than noon on the business day before the hearing.

Deciding timeliness issues

12.—(1) The Tribunal shall consider any issue as to—

(a) whether a notice of appeal was given outside the applicable time limit; and

(b) whether to extend the time for appealing where the notice of appeal was given outside that time limit,

as a preliminary issue at the hearing fixed under rule 11, subject to paragraph (2) of this rule.

(2) Rule 13 applies to the consideration and decision of such an issue as it applies to the consideration and determination of an appeal.

(3) Where the notice of appeal was given outside the applicable time limit and the Tribunal does not grant an extension of time, the Tribunal must take no further action in relation to the notice of appeal, except that it must serve written notice of its decision under this rule on the parties not later than 1 day after the day on which that decision is made.

Method of determining appeal

13. The Tribunal must consider the appeal at the hearing fixed under rule 11 except where—

(a) the appeal—

(i) lapses pursuant to section 99 of the 2002 Act;

(ii) is treated as abandoned pursuant to section 104(4) of the 2002 Act;

(iii) is treated as finally determined pursuant to section 104(5) of the 2002 Act; or

(iv) is withdrawn by the appellant or treated as withdrawn in accordance with rule 17 of the Principal Rules;

(b) the Tribunal adjourns the hearing under rule 28 or 30(2)(a) of these Rules; or

(c) all of the parties to the appeal consent to the Tribunal determining the appeal without a hearing.

Giving of determination

14.—(1) Where the Tribunal determines an appeal, it must give a written determination containing its decision and the reasons for it.

(2) The Tribunal must serve its determination on every party to the appeal—

(a) if the appeal is considered at a hearing, not later than 2 days after the day on which the hearing of the appeal finishes; or

(b) if the appeal is determined without a hearing, not later than 2 days after the day on which it is determined.

PART 3

Reconsideration of Appeals, etc.

Scope of this Part

15.—(1) This Part applies to proceedings before the Tribunal of a type specified in rule 24 of the Principal Rules, where—

(a) Part 2 of these Rules applied at all times to the appeal to the Tribunal;

(b) Part 3 of these Rules applied at all times to any other proceedings before the Tribunal of a type specified in rule 24 of the Principal Rules which related to that appeal; and

(c) the appellant has been continuously in detention under the Immigration Acts at a place or places specified in Schedule 2 to these Rules since being served with notice of the immigration decision against which he is appealing.

(2) This Part shall cease to apply if the Tribunal makes an order under rule 30(1).

SECTION 1

Section 103A applications considered by members of the Tribunal

Application of Section 1 of Part 3 of the Principal Rules

16. Where this Part applies to a section 103A application, the following provisions of Section 1 of Part 3 of the Principal Rules apply—

(a) rule 25;

(b) rule 26, omitting paragraphs (2) and (4) of that rule;

(c) rule 27(1) and (2); and

(d) rule 28.

Service of application and response

17. Where a section 103A application to which this Part applies is filed with the Tribunal—

(a) the Tribunal must serve copies of the application notice and any documents which were attached to it on the party to the appeal other than the party who made the section 103A application as soon as practicable; and

(b) the party to the appeal other than the party who made the section 103A application may file submissions in response to the application not later than 1 day after the day on which it is served with the application.

Method of deciding applications for review

18. The immigration judge shall decide the application without a hearing, and by reference only to—

(a) the applicant's written submissions and the documents filed with the application notice; and

(b) any submissions filed in response to the application under rule 17(b).

Service of decision

19. The Tribunal must serve a copy of the notice of decision and any directions given under rule 27(2)(b) of the Principal Rules on every party to the appeal—

(a) if submissions were filed in response to the application under rule 17(b), not later than 1 day after they were filed; or

(b) if no submissions were filed within the period specified in rule 17(b), not later than 1 day after the end of that period.

Section 2

Reconsideration of appeals

Application of the Principal Rules

20.—(1) Where this Part applies to the reconsideration of an appeal, the following provisions of Section 2 of Part 3 of the Principal Rules apply—

(a) rule 31(2) to (5); and

(b) rule 32(1).

(2) Rules 17 to 19 and Part 5 of the Principal Rules apply, with any necessary modifications, to the reconsideration of an appeal under this Part to the extent that they would apply to the initial determination of an appeal under Part 2 of these Rules.

Procedure for reconsideration of appeal

21.—(1) Where an order for reconsideration has been made, the Tribunal must fix a hearing date for the reconsideration of its decision on the appeal which is—

(a) not later than 2 days after the day on which that order has been served on both parties to the appeal; or

(b) if the Tribunal is unable to arrange a hearing within that time, as soon as practicable thereafter.

(2) The Tribunal must serve notice of the date, time and place of the reconsideration hearing on every party not later than noon on the business day before the hearing.

Fresh evidence on reconsideration of appeal

22.—(1) If a party wishes to ask the Tribunal to consider evidence which was not submitted on any previous occasion when it considered the appeal, he must notify the Tribunal and the other party of—
(a) the nature of the evidence; and
(b) the reasons why it was not submitted on any previous occasion.

(2) Wherever practicable, notification under paragraph (1) must be given before the date fixed for the reconsideration hearing under rule 21.

Determination on reconsideration

23.—(1) The Tribunal must reconsider its decision on the appeal at the hearing fixed under rule 21 except where—
(a) any of the circumstances set out in rule 13 applies;
(b) a party has failed to comply with a provision of these Rules or a direction of the Tribunal, and the Tribunal is satisfied that in all the circumstances, including the extent of the failure and any reasons for it, it is appropriate to reconsider its decision on the appeal without a hearing; or
(c) the Tribunal is satisfied, having regard to the material before it and the nature of the issues raised, that its decision on the appeal can be justly reconsidered without a hearing.

(2) Rule 14 applies to the reconsideration of an appeal as it applies to the initial determination of an appeal.

Section 3

Applications for permission to appeal to the appropriate appellate court

Application of Section 3 of Part 3 of the Principal Rules

24. Where this Part applies to an application for permission to appeal to the appropriate appellate court, the following provisions of Section 3 of Part 3 of the Principal Rules apply—
(a) rule 34(1) to (3); and
(b) rule 36.

Time limits for filing and serving application

25.—(1) An application notice for permission to appeal must be filed not later than 2 days after the day on which the appellant is served with the Tribunal's determination.

(2) The Tribunal may not extend the time limit in paragraph (1).

(3) Immediately upon an application notice for permission to appeal being filed, the Tribunal must notify the other party to the appeal to the Tribunal that it has been filed.

Time limit for determining the application

26. The Tribunal must determine the application for permission to appeal, and serve its determination on every party, not later than 1 day after the day on which the Tribunal receives the application notice.

Part 4

General Provisions

Application of Part 5 of the Principal Rules

27. Where this Part applies, Part 5 of the Principal Rules applies, except that—
   (a) rule 47 applies subject to rule 28 of these Rules; and
   (b) rule 60(2) does not apply.

Adjournment

28. The Tribunal may only adjourn a hearing where—
   (a) it is necessary to do so because there is insufficient time to hear the appeal or application which is before the Tribunal;
   (b) a party has not been served with notice of the hearing in accordance with these Rules;
   (c) the Tribunal is satisfied by evidence filed or given by or on behalf of a party that—
      (i) the appeal or application cannot be justly determined on the date on which it is listed for hearing; and
      (ii) there is an identifiable future date, not more than 10 days after the date on which the appeal or application is listed for hearing, by which it can be justly determined; or
   (d) the Tribunal makes an order under rule 30.

Correction of orders and determinations

29. Where an order, notice of decision or determination is amended under rule 60(1) of the Principal Rules, the Tribunal must, not later than 1 day after making the amendment, serve an amended version on every party on whom it served the original.

Part 5

Removal of Pending Proceedings from Fast Track

Transfer out of fast track procedure

30.—(1) Where Part 2 or 3 of these Rules applies to an appeal or application, the Tribunal must order that that Part shall cease to apply—

(a) if all the parties consent;

(b) if it is satisfied by evidence filed or given by or on behalf of a party that there are exceptional circumstances which mean that the appeal or application cannot otherwise be justly determined; or

(c) if—

(i) the respondent to the appeal has failed to comply with a provision of these Rules, or the Principal Rules as applied by these Rules, or a direction of the Tribunal; and

(ii) the Tribunal is satisfied that the appellant would be prejudiced by that failure if the appeal or application were determined in accordance with these Rules.

(2) When making an order under paragraph (1), the Tribunal may—

(a) adjourn any hearing of the appeal or application; and

(b) give directions relating to the further conduct of the appeal or application.

(3) Where the Tribunal adjourns a hearing under paragraph (2)(a)—

(a) it must fix a new date, time and place for the hearing; and

(b) in the case of an adjournment of an appeal, rule 21(4) of the Principal Rules shall apply.

Application of the Principal Rules on transfer out of fast track

31.—(1) This rule applies where Part 2 or 3 of these Rules ceases to apply to an appeal or application because—

(a) the conditions in rule 5 or 15 cease to apply; or

(b) the Tribunal makes an order under rule 30(1).

(2) Subject to paragraph (3), the Principal Rules shall apply to the appeal or application from the date on which these Rules cease to apply.

(3) Where—

(a) a period of time for doing something has started to run under a provision of these Rules; and

(b) that provision ceases to apply,

if the Principal Rules contain a time limit for doing the same thing, the time limit in the Principal Rules shall apply, and the relevant period of time shall be treated as running from the date on which the period of time under these Rules started to run.

Part 6

Revocation and Transitional Provisions

Revocation

32. The Immigration and Asylum Appeals (Fast Track Procedure) Rules 2003 are revoked.

Transitional provisions

33.—(1) Subject to the following paragraphs of this rule, these Rules apply to any pending appeal or application to an adjudicator or the Immigration Appeal Tribunal which was subject to the 2003 Fast Track Rules immediately before 4th April 2005, and which continues on or after that date as if it had been made to the Tribunal by virtue of a transitional provisions order.

(2) Where a notice of a relevant decision has been served before 4th April 2005 and the recipient gives notice of appeal against the decision on or after 4th April 2005—

(a) rules 7 to 10 of these Rules, and rules 6(1) to (3), 8 and 13(1) and (4) of the Principal Rules, shall not apply; and

(b) rule 6 of the 2003 Fast Track Rules and rules 6 and 8 of the 2003 Principal Rules shall continue to apply as if those rules had not been revoked, with the modification that references to an adjudicator or the appellate authority shall be treated as referring to the Tribunal.

(3) Where a notice of appeal to an adjudicator has been given before 4th April 2005, but the respondent has not filed the notice of appeal with the appellate authority in accordance with rule 6(3)(a) of the 2003 Fast Track Rules—

(a) rules 9 and 10 of these Rules, and rule 13(1) and (4) of the Principal Rules, shall not apply; and

(b) rule 6(3) of the 2003 Fast Track Rules shall continue to apply as if it had not been revoked, with the modification that the reference to the appellate authority shall be treated as referring to the Tribunal.

(4) Where, pursuant to a transitional provisions order, the Tribunal reconsiders an appeal which was originally determined by an adjudicator, Section 2 of Part 3 shall apply to the reconsideration, subject to paragraph (5).

(5) Where—

(a) a party has been granted permission to appeal to the Immigration Appeal Tribunal against an adjudicator's determination before 4th April 2005, but the appeal has not been determined by that date; and

(b) by virtue of a transitional provisions order the grant of permission to appeal is treated as an order for the Tribunal to reconsider the adjudicator's determination,

the reconsideration shall be limited to the grounds upon which the Immigration Appeal Tribunal granted permission to appeal.

(6) In relation to proceedings which were pending immediately before 4th April 2005—

(a) unless the Tribunal directs otherwise—

(i) anything done or any directions given before 4th April 2005 under the 2003 Fast Track Rules shall continue to have effect on and after that date;

(ii) anything done or any directions given by the appellate authority shall be treated as if done or given by the Tribunal; and

(iii) any document served on the appellate authority shall be treated as if served on the Tribunal;

(b) unless the context requires otherwise, any reference in a document to an adjudicator, the Immigration Appeal Tribunal or the appellate authority shall, insofar as it relates to an event on or after 4th April 2005, be treated as a reference to the Tribunal.

(7) In this rule—

(a) 'the 2003 Fast Track Rules' means the Immigration and Asylum Appeals (Fast Track Procedure) Rules 2003;

(b) 'the 2003 Principal Rules' means the Immigration and Asylum Appeals (Procedure) Rules 2003[6];

(c) 'adjudicator' and 'appellate authority' have the same meaning as in the 2003 Fast Track Rules and 2003 Principal Rules; and

(d) 'a transitional provisions order' means an order under section 48(3)(a) of the 2004 Act containing transitional provisions.

Schedule 1

Rule 2(4)

Forms

ASYLUM AND IMMIGRATION
(TREATMENT OF CLAIMANTS, ETC.)
ACT 2004

Notice of appeal to the Asylum and Immigration Tribunal (United Kingdom)

Form
AIT-1-FT

Fast Track

- To complete this appeal form, **please refer to the information leaflet** that was sent to you with your notice of decision and this form. You can also find the leaflet on www.ait.gov.uk.
- Please complete this form in English. It is in your interest to complete this form as thoroughly as possible, and state all of your grounds in order for your appeal to be dealt with efficiently.
- Please complete Section 1 of this form by referring to the notice of decision that was sent to you by the Home Office.
- Where there is a check box ☐, put a check (**X**) in it to show your answer.
- You should send your notice of decision with this form. If you do not send the notice of decision with your appeal form, you must give your reasons in Section 8.

Section 1 — Your decision

A Home Office reference number

B Case Outcome ID

C Type of Decision — Non-asylum ☐ Asylum ☐

D Date of Service / /

E Deadline to appeal / /

F Removal Centre Address

Post Code

G Removal Centre Telephone Number

Section 2 — Personal information

A Your Surname or family name
Please use CAPITAL LETTERS

B Your other names

C Your date of birth
Please give as Day/Month/Year / /

D Are you male or female? Male ☐ Female ☐

E Nationality (or nationalities) or citizenship

F Do you have a representative? No ☐ Yes ☐ ▶ Your representative should complete Section 6 on page 8.

G Have **you** appealed against any other immigration decision made in the United Kingdom? No ☐ Yes ☐ ▶ What type of decision did you appeal against? Asylum ☐ Non-asylum ☐

Date of the appeal / /

What is the appeal number, if you know it?

H **1** To the best of your knowledge, does any member of **your family** have an appeal pending in the United Kingdom? No ☐ Yes ☐ ▼

Name(s)	Relationship	Appeal number, if you know it

H 2 To the best of your knowledge, is any member of **your family** intending to appeal against an immigration decision?

No ☐ Yes ☐

Name(s)	Relationship	Home Office reference number, if you know it

I Do you wish to have your appeal decided at an **oral hearing**?

No ☐ Please go directly to Section 3 on page 4.

Yes ☐

J If you want an oral hearing, who will be present?

Yourself ☐

Your representative ☐

Witness/es ☐

If you want a witness to attend your hearing, please give their name and Home Office reference number, if applicable.

K If you, your representative or a witness are attending the hearing, will you or they need **an interpreter**?

No ☐ Yes ☐

Which language will be needed?
Language:

Dialect (if applicable):

L If you, your representative or a witness has a disability, please explain any special arrangements needed for the hearing.

Section 3

Grounds of your appeal

In this section you must set out the **grounds for your appeal** and give **the reasons** in support of these grounds – that is, why you disagree with the decision. You must do this **now** because you may not be allowed to mention any further grounds at a later date.

Please refer to the paragraphs of the refusal letter when possible.

You should include in this section any parts of your claim that you think have not been addressed in the refusal letter. You must say if you have raised these issues before.

Give as much detail as possible: use additional sheets of paper if you need to.

Section 4

Statement of additional grounds

If your notice of decision requires you to make a **Statement of additional grounds**, you should make that statement in this box.
This section refers to any **other reasons** why you think:

- ❑ you should be allowed to stay in the United Kingdom, including any reasons relating to the European Convention on Human Rights
- ❑ you should not be removed or required to leave

Do not repeat here any grounds and reasons that you have already given in Section 3.

You must give all these additional grounds and reasons **now** because you may not be able to make any other applications to appeal if this current application is refused. You should explain why you did not give these reasons before.

Section 5

Late appeal and application for extension of time

The deadline to appeal is **2 business days** from the date you received the decision. Your appeal must be received by the Tribunal or by the person having custody of you by the end of this period.

If you know your appeal is late, **or** if you are not sure your appeal will be received by the deadline date, **you must apply for an extension of time, and give your reasons for failing to submit your appeal in time.**

Section 6 — Representation

If you have a representative, he or she must complete this section.

A Declaration by the Representative

I, the representative, am giving this notice of appeal in accordance with the appellant's instructions, and the appellant believes that the facts stated in this notice of appeal are true.

Representative's signature and date / /

B Name of the representative
Please use CAPITAL LETTERS

C Name of the representative's organisation

D Fax number of organisation
Note: It is important that you provide a fax number to ensure that you receive documents from the Tribunal as quickly as possible

E Postal address of organisation

Number / Street

Town

Post Code

F Reference for correspondence

G Telephone number

H Mobile number

I Email address

J Are you an organisation regulated by the Office of the Immigration Services Commissioner (OISC)?

No ☐ Yes ☐ ► Please provide the OISC reference:

K Is the appellant receiving publicly funded legal representation?

No ☐ Yes ☐

Notice to representatives

You must also immediately notify the Asylum and Immigration Tribunal, and other parties, if you cease to represent the appellant or if your address and/or fax number changes. If the appellant changes representative, details of the new representative should be sent to the same address to which you are sending this form. Please give the **appellant's full name, address,** and **Home Office reference number.**

Section 7

Declaration by appellant

If you are the appellant and you are completing this form yourself, you must complete the declaration.

A Declaration by the Appellant

I, the appellant, believe that the facts stated in this notice of appeal are true.

Appellant's signature and date

/ /

B Name of appellant
Please use CAPITAL LETTERS

Section 8

When you have completed the form

What to do next

Keep a copy of this form for your own use. Then send the original form to:

Harmondsworth AIT Hearing Centre,
Colnbrook By Pass,
Harmondsworth
Middlesex, UB7 OHD

or fax the form to: **0208 750 7771**

or hand the form to the person having custody of you

Send the notice of decision with this form.

To make sure that you are sending your notice of decision with this form, please tick this box. ☐

If you do not send the notice of decision with the appeal form, you must state the reason here.

Documents to support you application

If you are sending any other documents with this form to support your appeal, please list them here.

If you are intending to send other documents that are not yet available to you, please list them here.

If you need to contact the Tribunal

If you need to contact the Asylum and Immigration Tribunal, use your Home Office reference number and your Case Outcome ID in your correspondence.

Changes to your personal information

You must notify the Tribunal if you change your address, or if you appoint a new representative, or both.

Data Protection Statement

Information, including personal details, that you have provided in this form will not be used by the Asylum and Immigration Tribunal for any purpose other than the determination of your application. The information may be disclosed to other government departments and public authorities only, for related immigration or asylum purposes.

AIT-1-FT (5.05) Rule 6, Asylum and Immigration Tribunal (Procedure) Rules 2005. Version 1.2 [12 May 2005] **7** of 7

ASYLUM AND IMMIGRATION
(TREATMENT OF CLAIMANTS, ETC.)
ACT 2004

Application to the Asylum and Immigration Tribunal for permission to appeal to the Court of Appeal

Form AIT-4-FT

Fast Track

Complete this form if you want to challenge the Asylum and Immigration Tribunal determination **on a point of law** by appealing to the Court of Appeal.

- Please complete this form in English. It is in your interest to complete this form as thoroughly as possible, and state all your grounds in order for your application to be dealt with efficiently.
- Please complete Section 1 of this form by referring to the determination that the Tribunal sent you.
- Where there is a check box ☐, put a check (**X**) in it to show your answer.
- You should send your determination with this form.
- The deadline to appeal is **2 business days** from the date you were served with the decision. Your appeal must be received by the Tribunal by the end of this period.

Section 1 — Your decision

A Tribunal Appeal number

B Case Outcome ID

C Type of Decision — Non-asylum ☐ Asylum ☐

D Date of Service — / /

E Deadline to appeal — / /

F Removal Centre Address

Post Code

G Removal Centre Telephone Number

Section 2 — Personal information

A Your Surname or family name
Please use CAPITAL LETTERS

B Your other names

C Your date of birth
Please give as Day/Month/Year — / /

D Are you male or female? — Male ☐ Female ☐

E Nationality (or nationalities) or citizenship

F Do you have a representative? — No ☐ Yes ☐ ▶ Your representative should complete Section 4 on page 3.

Section 3

Grounds of your appeal to the Court of Appeal

- An appeal to the Court of Appeal against a determination by the Tribunal is permissible only on a **point of law.**
- An appeal may be made against a point of law in a determination relating to an asylum decision or a non-asylum decision.
- In this section you must set out the **errors of law** that you believe have been made in the determination that you would like to appeal against and give **reasons** in support of these beliefs. You must do this **now** because you may not be allowed to mention any further points of law at a later date.
- Give as much detail as possible: use additional sheets of paper if you need to.

Section 4 — Representation

If you have a representative, he or she must complete this section.

A Declaration by the Representative

I, the representative, am making this application in accordance with the appellant's instructions, and the appellant believes that the facts stated in this application are true.

Representative's signature and date ______ / /

B Name of the representative
Please use CAPITAL LETTERS ______

C Name of the representative's organisation ______

D Fax number of organisation ______
Note: It is important that you provide a fax number to ensure that you receive documents from the Tribunal as quickly as possible

E Postal address of organisation

Number / Street ______

Town ______

Post Code ______

F Reference for correspondence ______

G Telephone number ______

H Mobile number ______

I Email address ______

J Are you an organisation regulated by the Office of the Immigration Services Commissioner (OISC)?

No ☐ Yes ☐ ► Please provide the OISC reference:

K Is the appellant receiving publicly funded legal representation?

No ☐ Yes ☐

Notice to representatives

You must immediately notify the Asylum and Immigration Tribunal, and other parties, if you cease to represent the appellant or if your address and/or fax number changes. If the appellant changes representative, details of the new representative should be sent to the same address to which you are sending this form. Please give the **appellant's full name, address,** and **Tribunal appeal number.**

Section 5

Declaration by appellant

If you are the appellant and you are completing this form yourself, you must complete the declaration.

A Declaration by the Appellant

I, the appellant, believe that the facts stated in this application are true.

Appellant's signature and date

/ /

B Name of appellant
Please use CAPITAL LETTERS

Section 6

When you have completed the form

What to do next

Keep a copy of this form for your own use. Then **send** the original form to:

Harmondsworth AIT Hearing Centre,
Colnbrook By Pass,
Harmondsworth
Middlesex, UB7 OHD

or fax the form to: **0208 750 7771**
or hand the form to the person having custody of you

Send your determination with this form

To make sure that you are sending your determination with this form, please tick this box ☐

Documents to support you application

If you are sending any other documents with this form to support your application and appeal, please list them here.

If you need to contact the Tribunal

If you need to contact the Asylum and Immigration Tribunal, use the Tribunal appeal number and your Case Outcome ID in your correspondence.

Changes to your personal information

You must notify the Tribunal if you change your address, and/or if you appoint a new representative.

Data Protection Statement

Information, including personal details, that you have provided in this form will not be used by the Asylum and Immigration Tribunal for any purpose other than the determination of your application. The information may be disclosed to other government departments and public authorities only, for related immigration or asylum purposes.

AIT-4 (4.05) Rule 34, Asylum and Immigration Tribunal Procedure Rules 2005 **4** of 4

Schedule 2

Rules 5 and 15

Specified Places of Detention

Harmondsworth Immigration Removal Centre, Harmondsworth, Middlesex
Campsfield House Immigration Removal Centre, Kidlington, Oxfordshire
Colnbrook House Immigration Removal Centre, Harmondsworth, Middlesex
Yarls Wood Immigration Removal Centre, Clapham, Bedfordshire

Civil Procedure Rules Part 54
Judicial Review and Statutory Review

I. Judicial Review

...

II. Statutory Review under the Nationality, Immigration and Asylum Act 2002

...

III. Applications for Statutory Review under Section 103A of the Nationality, Immigration and Asylum Act 2002

54.28. Scope and interpretation

(1) This Section of this Part contains rules about applications to the High Court under section 103A of the Nationality, Immigration and Asylum Act 2002 for an order requiring the Asylum and Immigration Tribunal to reconsider its decision on an appeal.

(2) In this Section—

(a) 'the 2002 Act' means the Nationality, Immigration and Asylum Act 2002;

(b) 'the 2004 Act' means the Asylum and Immigration (Treatment of Claimants, etc.) Act 2004;

(c) 'appellant' means the appellant in the proceedings before the Tribunal;

(d) 'applicant' means a person applying to the High Court under section 103A;

(e) 'asylum claim' has the meaning given in section 113(1) of the 2002 Act;

(ea) 'fast track case' means any case in relation to which an order made under section 26(8) of the 2004 Act provides that the time period for making an application under section 103A(1) of the 2002 Act or giving notification under paragraph 30(5) of Schedule 2 to the 2004 Act is less than 5 days;

(f) 'filter provision' means paragraph 30 of Schedule 2 to the 2004 Act;

(g) 'order for reconsideration' means an order under section 103A(1) requiring the Tribunal to reconsider its decision on an appeal;

(h) 'section 103A' means section 103A of the 2002 Act;

(i) 'Tribunal' means the Asylum and Immigration Tribunal.

(3) Any reference in this Section to a period of time specified in—

(a) section 103A(3) for making an application for an order under section 103A(1); or
(b) paragraph 30(5)(b) of Schedule 2 to the 2004 Act for giving notice under that paragraph,

includes a reference to that period as varied by any order under section 26(8) of the 2004 Act.

(4) Rule 2.8 applies to the calculation of the periods of time specified in—
(a) section 103A(3); and
(b) paragraph 30(5)(b) of Schedule 2 to the 2004 Act.

(5) Save as provided otherwise, the provisions of this Section apply to an application under section 103A regardless of whether the filter provision has effect in relation to that application.

54.28A. Representation of applicants while filter provision has effect

(1) This rule applies during any period in which the filter provision has effect.

(2) An applicant may, for the purpose of taking any step under rule 54.29 or 54.30, be represented by any person permitted to provide him with immigration advice or immigration services under section 84 of the Immigration and Asylum Act 1999.

(3) A representative acting for an applicant under paragraph (2) shall be regarded as the applicant's legal representative for the purpose of rule 22.1 (Documents to be verified by a statement of truth) regardless of whether he would otherwise be so regarded.

54.28B. Service of documents on appellants within the jurisdiction

(1) In proceedings under this Section, rules 6.4(2) and 6.5(5) do not apply to the service of documents on an appellant who is within the jurisdiction.

(2) Where a representative is acting for an appellant who is within the jurisdiction, a document must be served on the appellant by—
(a) serving it on his representative; or
(b) serving it on the appellant personally or sending it to his address by first class post,

but if the document is served on the appellant under sub-paragraph (b), a copy must also at the same time be sent to his representative.

54.29. Application for review

(1) Subject to paragraph (5), an application for an order for reconsideration must be made by filing an application notice—

(a) during a period in which the filter provision has effect, with the Tribunal at the address specified in the relevant practice direction; and
(b) at any other time, at the Administrative Court Office.

(2) During any period in which the filter provision does not have effect, the applicant must file with the application notice—
(a) the notice of the immigration, asylum or nationality decision to which the appeal related;
(b) any other document which was served on the appellant giving reasons for that decision;
(c) the grounds of appeal to the Tribunal;
(d) the Tribunal's determination on the appeal; and
(e) any other documents material to the application which were before the Tribunal.

(2A) During any period in which the filter provision has effect, the applicant must file with the application notice a list of the documents referred to in paragraph (2)(a) to (e).

(3) The applicant must also file with the application notice written submissions setting out—
(a) the grounds upon which it is contended that the Tribunal made an error of law which may have affected its decision; and
(b) reasons in support of those grounds.

(4) Where the applicant—
(a) was the respondent to the appeal; and
(b) was required to serve the Tribunal's determination on the appellant,
the application notice must contain a statement of the date on which, and the means by which, the determination was served.

(5) Where the applicant is in detention under the Immigration Acts, the application may be made either—
(a) in accordance with paragraphs (1) to (3); or
(b) by serving the documents specified in paragraphs (1) to (3) on the person having custody of him.

(6) Where an application is made in accordance with paragraph (5)(b), the person on whom the application notice is served must—
(a) endorse on the notice the date that it is served on him;
(b) give the applicant an acknowledgment in writing of receipt of the notice; and
(c) forward the notice and documents within 2 days
(i) during a period in which the filter provision has effect, to the Tribunal; and
(ii) at any other time, to the Administrative Court Office.

54.30. Application to extend time limit

An application to extend the time limit for making an application under section 103A(1) must—

(a) be made in the application notice;

(b) set out the grounds on which it is contended that the application notice could not reasonably practicably have been filed within the time limit; and

(c) be supported by written evidence verified by a statement of truth.

54.31. Procedure while filter provision has effect

(1) This rule applies during any period in which the filter provision has effect.

(2) Where the applicant receives notice from the Tribunal that it—

(a) does not propose to make an order for reconsideration; or

(b) does not propose to grant permission for the application to be made outside the relevant time limit,

and the applicant wishes the court to consider the application, the applicant must file a notice in writing at the Administrative Court Office in accordance with paragraph 30(5)(b) of Schedule 2 to the 2004 Act.

(3) Where the applicant—

(a) was the respondent to the appeal; and

(b) was required to serve the notice from the Tribunal mentioned in paragraph (2) on the appellant,

the notice filed in accordance with paragraph 30(5)(b) of Schedule 2 to the 2004 Act must contain a statement of the date on which, and the means by which, the notice from the Tribunal was served.

(4) A notice which is filed outside the period specified in paragraph 30(5)(b) must—

(a) set out the grounds on which it is contended that the notice could not reasonably practicably have been filed within that period; and

(b) be supported by written evidence verified by a statement of truth.

(5) If the applicant wishes to respond to the reasons given by the Tribunal for its decision that it –

(a) does not propose to make an order for reconsideration; or

(b) does not propose to grant permission for the application to be made outside the relevant time limit,

the notice filed in accordance with paragraph 30(5)(b) of Schedule 2 to the 2004 Act must be accompanied by written submissions setting out the grounds upon which the applicant disputes any of the reasons given by the Tribunal and giving reasons in support of those grounds.

54.32. Procedure in fast track cases while filter provision does not have effect

(1) This rule applies only during a period in which the filter provision does not have effect.

(2) Where a party applies for an order for reconsideration in a fast track case—
   (a) the court will serve copies of the application notice and written submissions on the other party to the appeal; and
   (b) the other party to the appeal may file submissions in response to the application not later than 2 days after being served with the application.

54.33. Determination of the application by the Administrative Court

(1) This rule, and rules 54.34 and 54.35, apply to applications under section 103A which are determined by the Administrative Court.

(2) The application will be considered by a single judge without a hearing.

(3) Unless it orders otherwise, the court will not receive evidence which was not submitted to the Tribunal.

(4) Subject to paragraph (5), where the court determines an application for an order for reconsideration, it may—
   (a) dismiss the application;
   (b) make an order requiring the Tribunal to reconsider its decision on the appeal under section 103A(1) of the 2002 Act; or
   (c) refer the appeal to the Court of Appeal under section 103C of the 2002 Act.

(5) The court will only make an order requiring the Tribunal to reconsider its decision on an appeal if it thinks that—
   (a) the Tribunal may have made an error of law; and
   (b) there is a real possibility that the Tribunal would make a different decision on reconsidering the appeal (which may include making a different direction under section 87 of the 2002 Act).

(6) Where the Court of Appeal has restored the application to the court under section 103C(2)(g) of the 2002 Act, the court may not refer the appeal to the Court of Appeal.

(7) The court's decision shall be final and there shall be no appeal from that decision or renewal of the application.

54.34. Service of order

(1) The court will send copies of its order to—
   (a) the applicant and the other party to the appeal, except where paragraph (2) applies; and
   (b) the Tribunal.

(2) Where the appellant is within the jurisdiction and the application relates, in whole or in part, to an asylum claim, the court will send a copy of its order to the Secretary of State.

(2A) Paragraph (2) does not apply in a fast track case.

(3) Where the court sends an order to the Secretary of State under paragraph (2), the Secretary of State must –
  (a) serve the order on the appellant; and
  (b) immediately after serving the order, notify –
    (i) the court; and
    (ii) where the order requires the Tribunal to reconsider its decision on the appeal, the Tribunal,

  on what date and by what method the order was served.

(4) The Secretary of State must provide the notification required by paragraph (3)(b) no later than 28 days after the date on which the court sends him a copy of its order.

(5) If, 28 days after the date on which the court sends a copy of its order to the Secretary of State in accordance with paragraph (2), the Secretary of State has not provided the notification required by paragraph (3)(b)(i), the court may serve the order on the appellant.

(5A) Where the court serves an order for reconsideration under paragraph (5), it will notify the Tribunal of the date on which the order was served.

(6) If the court makes an order under section 103D(1) of the 2002 Act, it will send copies of that order to –
  (a) the appellant's legal representative; and
  (b) the Legal Services Commission.

(7) Where paragraph (2) applies, the court will not serve copies of an order under section 103D(1) of the 2002 Act until either—
  (a) the Secretary of State has provided the notification required by paragraph (3)(b); or
  (b) 28 days after the date on which the court sent a copy of its order to the Secretary of State,

  whichever is the earlier.

54.35. Costs

The court shall make no order as to the costs of an application under this Section except, where appropriate, an order under section 103D(1) of the 2002 Act.

IMMIGRATION RULES

Immigration Rules
(HC 395)

Laid before Parliament on 23 May 1994 under section 3(2) of the Immigration Act 1971

Arrangement of Rules

Part 2. Persons Seeking to Enter or Remain in the United Kingdom for Visits

Part 3. Persons Seeking to Enter or Remain in the United Kingdom for Studies

Part 4. Persons Seeking to Enter or Remain in the United Kingdom in an 'Au Pair' Placement, as a Working Holidaymaker or for Training or Work Experience

Part 7. Other Categories

Part 8. Family Members

Part 9. General Grounds for the Refusal of Entry Clearance, Leave to Enter or Variation of Leave to Enter or Remain in the United Kingdom

Introduction

1. The Home Secretary has made changes in the Rules laid down by him as to the practice to be followed in the administration of the Immigration Acts for regulating entry into and the stay of persons in the United Kingdom and contained in the statement laid before Parliament on 23 March 1990 (HC 251) (as amended). This statement contains the Rules as changed and replaces the provisions of HC 251 (as amended).

2. Immigration Officers, Entry Clearance Officers and all staff of the Home Office Immigration and Nationality [Directorate] will carry out their duties without regard to the race, colour or religion of persons seeking to enter or remain in the United Kingdom [and in compliance with the provisions of the Human Rights Act 1998].

Note: Words in square brackets inserted from 2 October 2000 (Cm 4851).

3. In these Rules words importing the masculine gender include the feminine unless the contrary intention appears.

Implementation and transitional provisions

4. These Rules come into effect on 1 October 1994 and will apply to all decisions taken on or after that date save that any application made before 1 October 1994 for entry clearance, leave to enter or remain or variation of leave to enter or remain [other than an application for leave by a person seeking asylum,] shall be decided under the provisions of HC 251, as amended, as if these Rules had not been made.

Note: Inserted from 1 September 1996 (Cm 3365).

Application

[**5.** Save where expressly indicated, these Rules do not apply to those persons who are entitled to enter or remain in the United Kingdom by virtue of the provisions of {the 2006 EEA Regulations}. But any person who is not entitled to rely on the provisions of those Regulations is covered by these Rules.]

Note: Substituted from 2 October 2000 (Cm 4851). Words in curly brackets substituted from 30 April 2006 (HC 1053).

Interpretation

6. In these Rules the following interpretations apply:

'the Immigration Acts' mean the Immigration Act 1971 and the Immigration Act 1988.

'the 1993 Act' is the Asylum and Immigration Appeals Act 1993.

['the 1996 Act' is the Asylum and Immigration Act 1996.]

['the 2006 EEA Regulations' means the Immigration (European Economic Area) Regulations 2006.]

['adoption' unless the contrary intention appears, includes a de facto adoption in accordance with the requirements of paragraph 309A of these Rules, and 'adopted' and 'adoptive parent' should be construed accordingly;]

['Approved Destination Status Agreement with China' means the Memorandum of Understanding on visa and related issues concerning tourist groups from the People's Republic of China to the United Kingdom as a approved destination, signed on 21 January 2005.]

['civil partner' means a civil partnership which exists under or by virtue of the Civil Partnership Act 2004 (and any reference to a civil partner is to be read accordingly);]

['degree level study' means a course which leads to a recognised United Kingdom degree at bachelor's level or above, or an equivalent qualification at level 6 or above of the revised National Qualifications Framework, or level 9 or above of the Scottish Credit and Qualifications Framework;]

['EEA national' has the meaning given in regulation 2(1) of the 2006 Regulations.]

'United Kingdom passport' bears the meaning it has in the Immigration Act 1971.

['a UK Bachelors degree' means–

- (a) A programme of study or research which leads to the award, by or on behalf of a university, college or other body which is authorised by Royal Charter or by or under an Act of Parliament to grant degrees, of a qualification designated by the awarding institution to be of Bachelors degree level; or
- (a) A programme of study or research, which leads to a recognised award for the purposes of section 214(2)(c) of the Education Reform Act 1988, of a qualification designated by the awarding institution to be of Bachelors degree level.]

'Immigration Officer' includes a Customs Officer acting as an Immigration Officer.

['public funds' means—

- (a) housing under Part VI or VII of the Housing Act 1996 and under Part II of the Housing Act 1985, Part I or II of the Housing (Scotland) Act 1987, Part II of the Housing (Northern Ireland) Order 1981 or Part II of the Housing (Northern Ireland) Order 1988;

(b) attendance allowance, severe disablement allowance, {carer's allowance} and disability living allowance under Part III of the Social Security Contribution and Benefits Act 1992; income support, . . . council tax benefit, . . . and housing benefit under Part VII of that Act; a social fund payment under Part VIII of that Act; child benefit under Part IX of that Act; income based jobseeker's allowance under the Jobseekers Act 1995; {state pension credit under the State Pensions Credit Act 2002; or child tax credit and working tax credit under Part 1 of the Tax Credits Act 2002.}

(c) attendance allowance, severe disablement allowance, {carer's allowance} and disability living allowance under Part III of the Social Security Contribution and Benefits (Northern Ireland) Act 1992; income support, . . . council tax benefit, . . . housing benefit under Part VII of that Act; a social fund payment under Part VIII of that Act; child benefit under Part IX of that Act; or income based jobseeker's allowance under the Jobseekers (Northern Ireland) Order 1995.

(d) . . .]

'settled in the United Kingdom' means that the person concerned:

(a) is free from any restriction on the period for which he may remain save that a person entitled to an exemption under Section 8 of the Immigration Act 1971) otherwise than as a member of the home forces) is not to be regarded as settled in the United Kingdom except in so far as Section 8(5A) so provides; and

(b) is either:

(i) ordinarily resident in the United Kingdom without having entered or remained in breach of the immigration laws; or

(ii) despite having entered or remained in breach of the immigration laws, has subsequently entered lawfully or has been granted leave to remain and is ordinarily resident.

'a parent' includes

(a) the stepfather of a child whose father is dead [(and the reference to a stepfather includes a relationship arising through civil partnership)];

(b) the stepmother of a child whose mother is dead; [(and the reference to a stepmother includes a relationship arising through civil partnership)];

(c) the father as well as the mother of an illegitimate child where he is proved to be the father;

(d) an adoptive parent, where a child was adopted in accordance with a decision taken by the competent administrative authority or court in a country whose adoption orders are recognised by the United Kingdom or where a child is the subject of a de facto adoption in accordance with the requirements of paragraph 309A of these Rules (except that an adopted child or child who is the subject of a de facto adoption may not make an application for leave to enter or remain in order to accompany, join or remain with an adoptive parent under paragraphs 297 to 303);

(e) in the case of a child born in the United Kingdom who is not a British citizen, a person to whom there has been a genuine transfer of parental responsibility on the ground of the original parent(s)' inability to care for the child.

['visa nationals' are the persons specified in Appendix 1 to these Rules who need a visa for the United Kingdom.] ['Non-visa nationals' are persons who are not specified in Appendix 1 to the Rules.]

. . .

['intention to live permanently with the other' means an intention to live together, evidenced by a clear commitment from both parties that they will live together permanently in the United Kingdom immediately following the outcome of the application in question or as soon as circumstances permit thereafter, and 'intends to live permanently with the other' shall be construed accordingly;]

['present and settled' means that the person concerned is settled in the United Kingdom, and, at the time that an application under these Rules is made, is physically present here or is coming here with or to join the applicant and intends to make the United Kingdom their home with the applicant if the application is successful;]

['sponsor' means the person in relation to whom an applicant is seeking leave to enter or remain as their {spouse, fiancé, civil partner, proposed civil partner, unmarried partner, same-sex partner} or dependent relative, as the case may be, under paragraphs 277 to 2950 or 317 to 319;]

'employment', unless the contrary intention appears, includes paid and unpaid employment, self-employment and engaging in business or any professional activity.

['the Human Rights Convention' means the Convention for the Protection of Human Rights and Fundamental Freedoms, agreed by the Council of Europe at Rome on 4th November 1950 as it has effect for the time being in relation to the United Kingdom.]

['Immigration employment document' means a work permit or any other document which relates to employment and is issued for the purpose of these Rules or in connection with leave to enter or remain in the United Kingdom.]

Note: Definition of 'the 2000 EEA Regulations' and 'the Human Rights Convention' inserted from 2 October 2000 (Cm 4851). Definition of 'the 1996 Act' inserted from 1 September 1996 (HC 31). Definition of 'visa nationals' substituted from 11 November 1998 (Cm 3953). Definitions of 'EEA national' and 'public funds' substituted from and definition of 'immigration employment document' inserted from 18 September 2002 (Cm 5597). Definition of 'adoption' substituted from 1 April 2003 (HC 538). Definition of 'parent' amended from 1 April 2003 (HC 538). Definitions of 'intention to live permanently with the other', 'present and settled' inserted from 1 April 2003 (HC

538). Definition of 'specified national' inserted from 13 November 2003 (HC 1224). Definition of 'degree level study' inserted from 1 October 2004 (Cm 6339). Definition of 'sponsor' subsituted from 1 October 2004 (Cm 6339). Definition of 'Accession State National' inserted from 1 May 2004 (HC 523). Paragraphs 6(b) and 6(c) amended and para 6(d) deleted from 15 March 2005 (HC 346). Definition of 'Approved Destination Status Agreement with China' inserted from 5 April 2005 (HC 486). Definition of 'civil partner' inserted and definition of 'parent' and 'sponsor' amended from 14 November 2005 (HC 582). Definition of 'non-visa national' inserted from 3 April 2006 (HC 1016). Definition of 'the 2006 EEA Regulations' inserted and definition of 'EEA national' substituted from 30 April 2006 (HC 1053).

[**6A.** For the purpose of these Rules, a person is not to be regarded as having (or potentially having) recourse to public funds merely because he is (or will be) reliant in whole or in part on public funds provided to his sponsor, unless, as a result of his presence in the United Kingdom, the sponsor is (or would be) entitled to increased or additional public funds.]

Note: Paragraph 6A inserted from 2 October 2000 (Cm 4851).

[**6B.** A person shall not be regarded as having recourse to public funds if he is a person who is not excluded from specified benefits under section 115 of the Immigration and Asylum Act 1999 by virtue of regulations made under sub-sections (3) and (4) of that section or section 42 of the Tax Credits Act 2002.]

Note: Paragraph 6B inserted from 15 March 2005 (HC 346).

Part 1

General Provisions Regarding Leave to Enter or Remain in the United Kingdom

7. [A person who is neither a British citizen nor a Commonwealth citizen with the right of abode nor a person who is entitled to enter or remain in the United Kingdom by virtue of the provisions of {the 2006 EEA Regulations} requires leave to enter the United Kingdom.]

Note: Substituted from 2 October 2000 (Cm 4851). Words in curly brackets substituted from 30 April 2006 (HC 1053).

[**8.** Under Sections 3 and 4 of the Immigration Act 1971 an Immigration Officer when admitting to the United Kingdom a person subject to immigration control under that Act may give leave to enter for a limited period and, if he does, may impose all or any of the following conditions:

(i) a condition restricting employment or occupation in the United Kingdom;

(ii) a condition requiring the person to maintain and accommodate himself, and any dependants of his, without recourse to public funds; and

(iii) a condition requiring the person to register with the police.

He may also require him to report to the appropriate Medical Officer of Environmental Health. Under Section 24 of the 1971 Act it is an offence knowingly to remain beyond the time limit or fail to comply with such a condition or requirement.]

Note: Paragraph 8 substituted from 1 November 1996 (Cm 3365).

[9. The time limit and any conditions attached will normally be made known to the person concerned either:

(i) by written notice given to him or endorsed by the immigration officer in his passport or travel document; or

(ii) in any other manner permitted by the Immigration (Leave to Enter and Remain) Order 2000.]

Note: Substituted from 30 July 2000 (HC 704).

[Exercise of the power to refuse leave to enter the United Kingdom or to cancel leave to enter or remain which is in force]

10. The power to refuse leave to enter the United Kingdom [or to cancel leave to enter or remain which is already in force] is not to be exercised by an Immigration Officer acting on his own. The authority of a Chief Immigration Officer or of an Immigration Inspector must always be obtained.

Note: Words in square brackets inserted from 30 July 2000 (HC 704).

[Suspension of leave to enter or remain in the United Kingdom

10A. Where a person has arrived in the United Kingdom with leave to enter or remain which is in force but which was given to him before his arrival he may be examined by an Immigration Officer under paragraph 2A of Schedule 2 to the Immigration Act 1971. An Immigration Officer examining a person under paragraph 2A may suspend that person's leave to enter or remain in the United Kingdom until the examination is completed.

Cancellation of leave to enter or remain in the United Kingdom

10B. Where a person arrives in the United Kingdom with leave to enter or remain in the United Kingdom which is already in force, an Immigration Officer may cancel that leave.]

Note: Paragraphs 10A and 10B inserted from 30 July 2000 (HC 704).

Requirement for persons arriving in the United Kingdom or seeking entry through the Channel Tunnel to produce evidence of identity and nationality

11. A person must, on arrival in the United Kingdom or when seeking entry through the Channel Tunnel, produce on request by the Immigration Officer:

(i) a valid national passport or other document satisfactorily establishing his identity and nationality; and

(ii) such information as may be required to establish whether he requires leave to enter the United Kingdom and, if so, whether and on what terms leave to enter should be given.

Requirement for a person not requiring leave to enter the United Kingdom to prove that he has the right of abode

12. A person claiming to be a British citizen must prove that he has the right of abode in the United Kingdom by producing either:

(i) a United Kingdom passport describing him as a British citizen or as a citizen of the United Kingdom and Colonies having the right of abode in the United Kingdom; or

(ii) a certificate of entitlement duly issued by or on behalf of the Government of the United Kingdom certifying that he has the right of abode.

13. A person claiming to be a Commonwealth citizen with the right of abode in the United Kingdom must prove that he has the right of abode by producing a certificate of entitlement duly issued to him by or on behalf of the Government of the United Kingdom certifying that he has the right of abode.

14. A Commonwealth citizen who has been given limited leave to enter the United Kingdom may later claim to have the right of abode. The time limit on his stay may be removed if he is able to establish a claim to the right of abode, for example by showing that:

(i) immediately before the commencement of the British Nationality Act 1981 he was a Commonwealth citizen born to or legally adopted by a parent who at the time of the birth had citizenship of the United Kingdom and Colonies by his birth in the United Kingdom or any of the Islands; and

(ii) he has not ceased to be a Commonwealth citizen in the meanwhile.

Common travel area

15. The United Kingdom, the Channel Islands, the Isle of Man and the Republic of Ireland collectively form a common travel area. A person who has been examined for the purpose of immigration control at the point at which he entered the area does not normally require leave to enter any other part of it. However certain persons subject to the Immigration (Control of Entry through the Republic of Ireland) Order 1972 (as amended) who enter the United Kingdom through the Republic of Ireland do require leave to enter. This includes:

(i) those who merely passed through the Republic of Ireland;

(ii) persons requiring visas;

(iii) persons who entered the Republic of Ireland unlawfully;

(iv) persons who are subject to directions given by the Secretary of State for their exclusion from the United Kingdom on the ground that their exclusion is conducive to the public good;

(v) persons who entered the Republic of Ireland from the United Kingdom and Islands after entering there unlawfully or overstaying their leave.

Admission of certain British passport holders

16. A person in any of the following categories may be admitted freely to the United Kingdom on production of a United Kingdom passport issued in the United Kingdom and Islands or the Republic of Ireland prior to 1 January 1973, unless his passport has been endorsed to show that he was subject to immigration control:

(i) a British Dependent Territories citizen;
(ii) a British National (Overseas);
(iii) a British Overseas citizen;
(iv) a British protected person;
(v) a British subject by virtue of Section 30(a) of the British Nationality Act 1981, (who, immediately before the commencement of the 1981 Act, would have been a British subject not possessing citizenship of the United Kingdom and Colonies or the citizenship of any other Commonwealth country or territory).

17. British Overseas citizens who hold United Kingdom passports wherever issued and who satisfy the Immigration Officer that they have, since 1 March 1968, been given indefinite leave to enter or remain in the United Kingdom may be given indefinite leave to enter.

[Persons outside the United Kingdom

17A. Where a person is outside the United Kingdom but wishes to travel to the United Kingdom an Immigration Officer may give or refuse him leave to enter. An Immigration Officer may exercise these powers whether or not he is, himself, in the United Kingdom. However, an Immigration Officer is not obliged to consider an application for leave to enter from a person outside the United Kingdom.

17B. Where a person, having left the common travel area, has leave to enter the United Kingdom which remains in force under article 13 of the Immigration (Leave to Enter and Remain) Order 2000, an Immigration Officer may cancel that leave. An Immigration Officer may exercise these powers whether or not he is, himself, in the United Kingdom. If a person outside the United Kingdom has leave to remain in the United Kingdom which is in force in this way, the Secretary of State may cancel that leave.].

Note: Paragraphs 17A and 17B inserted from 30 July 2000 (HC 704).

Returning residents

18. A person seeking leave to enter the United Kingdom as a returning resident may be admitted for settlement provided the Immigration Officer is satisfied that the person concerned:

(i) had indefinite leave to enter or remain in the United Kingdom when he last left; and

(ii) has not been away from the United Kingdom for more than 2 years; and
(iii) did not receive assistance from public funds towards the cost of leaving the United Kingdom; and
(iv) now seeks admission for the purpose of settlement.

19. A person who does not benefit from the preceding paragraph by reason only of having been away from the United Kingdom too long may nevertheless be admitted as a returning resident if, for example, he has lived here for most of his life.

[**19A.** Where a person who has indefinite leave to enter or remain in the United Kingdom accompanies, on a tour of duty abroad, a {spouse, civil partner, unmarried partner or same-sex partner} who is a member of HM Forces serving overseas, or a permanent member of HM Diplomatic Service, or a comparable United Kingdom-based staff member of the British Council, or a staff member of the Department for International Development who is a British Citizen or is settled in the United Kingdom, sub-paragraphs (ii) and (iii) of paragraph 18 shall not apply.]

Note: Paragraph 19A substituted from 18 September 2002 (Cm 5597). Words in curly brackets substituted from 5 December 2005 (HC 582).

20. The leave of a person whose stay in the United Kingdom is subject to a time limit lapses on his going to a country or territory outside the common travel area [if the leave was given for a period of six months or less or conferred by a visit visa. In other cases, leave lapses on the holder remaining outside the United Kingdom for a continuous period of more than two years]. [A person whose leave has lapsed and] who returns after a temporary absence abroad within the period of this earlier leave has no claim to admission as a returning resident. His application to re-enter the United Kingdom should be considered in the light of all the relevant circumstances. The same time limit and any conditions attached will normally be reimposed if he meets the requirements of these Rules, unless he is seeking admission in a different capacity from the one in which he was last given leave to enter or remain.

Note: Amended from 30 July 2000 (HC 704).

[Non-lapsing leave

20A. Leave to enter or remain in the United Kingdom will usually lapse on the holder going to a country or territory outside the common travel area. However, under article 13 of the Immigration (Leave to Enter and Remain) Order 2000 such leave will not lapse where it was conferred by means of an entry clearance (other than a visit visa).]

Note: Inserted from 30 July 2000 (HC704).

Holders of restricted travel documents and passports

21. The leave to enter or remain in the United Kingdom of the holder of a passport or travel document whose permission to enter another country has to be exercised before a given date may be restricted so as to terminate at least 2 months before that date.

22. If his passport or travel document is endorsed with a restriction on the period for which he may remain outside his country of normal residence, his leave to enter or remain in the United Kingdom may be limited so as not to extend beyond the period of authorised absence.

23. The holder of a travel document issued by the Home Office should not be given leave to enter or remain for a period extending beyond the validity of that document. This paragraph and paragraphs 21–22 do not apply to a person who is eligible for admission for settlement or to a spouse [or civil partner] who is eligible for admission under paragraph 282 or to a person who qualifies for the removal of the time limit on his stay.

Note: Words in square brackets inserted from 5 December 2005 (HC 582).

[Leave to enter granted on arrival in the United Kingdom

[**23A.** A person who is not a visa national and who is seeking leave to enter on arrival in the United Kingdom for a period not exceeding 6 months for a purpose for which prior entry clearance is not required under these Rules may be granted such leave, for a period not exceeding 6 months.

This paragraph does not apply where the person is a British National (Overseas), a British overseas territories citizen, a British Overseas citizen, a British protected person, or a person who under the British Nationality Act 1981 is a British subject.]

Note: Paragraph 23A substituted from 13 November 2005 (HC 645).

[**23B.** A person who is a British National (Overseas), a British overseas territories citizen, a British Overseas citizen, a British protected person, or a person who under the British Nationality Act 1981 is a British subject, and who is seeking leave to enter on arrival in the United Kingdom for a purpose for which prior entry clearance is not required under these Rules may be granted such leave, irrespective of the period of time for which he seeks entry, for a period not exceeding 6 months.]

Note: Paragraph 23B inserted from 13 November 2005 (HC 645).

Entry clearance

[**24.** The following must produce to the Immigration Officer a valid Passport or other identity document endorsed with a United Kingdom entry clearance issued to him for the purpose for which he seeks entry:

(i) a visa national;

(ii) any other person (other than British Nationals (Overseas), a British overseas territories citizen, a British Overseas citizen, a British protected person or a person who under the British Nationality Act 1981 is a British subject) who is seeking entry for a period exceeding six months or is seeking entry for a purpose for which prior entry clearance is required under these Rules.

Such a person will be refused leave to enter if he has no such current entry clearance. Any other person who wishes to ascertain in advance whether he is eligible for admission to the United Kingdom may apply for the issue of an entry clearance.]

Note: Paragraph 24 substituted from 13 November 2005 (HC 645).

25. Entry clearance takes the form of a visa (for visa nationals) or an entry certificate (for non-visa nationals). These documents are to be taken as evidence of the holder's eligibility for entry into the United Kingdom, and accordingly accepted as 'entry clearances' within the meaning of the Immigration Act 1971.

25A. An entry clearance which satisfies the requirements set out in article 3 of the Immigration (Leave to Enter and Remain) Order 2000 will have effect as leave to enter the United Kingdom. The requirements are that the entry clearance must specify the purpose for which the holder wishes to enter the United Kingdom and should be endorsed with the conditions to which it is subject or with a statement that it has effect as indefinite leave to enter the United Kingdom. The holder of such an entry clearance will not require leave to enter on arrival in the United Kingdom and, for the purposes of these Rules, will be treated as a person who has arrived in the United Kingdom with leave to enter the United Kingdom which is in force but which was given to him before his arrival.]

Note: Paragraph 25A inserted from 30 July 2000 (HC 704).

26. An application for entry clearance will be considered in accordance with the provisions in these Rules governing the grant or refusal of leave to enter. Where appropriate, the term 'Entry Clearance Officer' should be substituted for 'Immigration Officer'.

27. An application for entry clearance is to be decided in the light of the circumstances existing at the time of the decision, except that an applicant will not be refused an entry clearance where entry is sought in one of the categories contained in paragraphs 296–316 solely on account of his attaining the age of 18 years between receipt of his application and the date of the decision on it.

28. An applicant for an entry clearance must be outside the United Kingdom and Islands at the time of the application. An applicant for an entry clearance who is seeking entry as a visitor must apply to a post designated by the Secretary of State to accept applications for entry clearance for that purpose and from that category of applicant. Any other application must be made to the post in the country or territory where the applicant is living which has been designated by the Secretary of State to accept applications for entry clearance for that purpose and from that category of applicant. Where there is no such post the applicant must apply to the appropriate designated post outside the country or territory where he is living.

29. For the purposes of paragraph 28 'post' means a British Diplomatic Mission, British Consular post or the office of any person outside the United Kingdom and Islands who has been authorised by the Secretary of State to accept applications for entry clearance. A list of designated posts is published by the Foreign and Commonwealth Office.

30. An application for an entry clearance is not made until any fee required to be paid under the Consular Fees Act 1980 (including any Regulations or Orders made under that Act) has been paid.

[**30A.** An entry clearance may be revoked if the Entry Clearance Officer is satisfied that:

(i) whether or not to the holder's knowledge, false representations were employed or material facts were not disclosed, either in writing, or orally for the purpose of obtaining the entry clearance; or

(ii) a change of circumstances since the entry clearance was issued has removed the basis of the holder's claim to be admitted to the United Kingdom, except where the change of circumstances amounts solely to his exceeding the age for entry in one of the categories contained in paragraphs 296–316 of these Rules since the issue of the entry clearance; or

(iii) the holder's exclusion from the United Kingdom would be conducive to the public good.]

Note: Paragraph 30A inserted from 1 November 1996 (HC 31).

[**30B.** An entry clearance shall cease to have effect where the entry clearance has effect as leave to enter and an Immigration Officer cancels that leave in accordance with paragraph 2A(8) of Schedule 2 to the Immigration Act 1971.

30C. An Immigration Officer may cancel an entry clearance which is capable of having effect as leave to enter if the holder arrives in the United Kingdom before the day on which the entry clearance becomes effective or if the holder seeks to enter the United Kingdom for a purpose other than the purpose specified in the entry clearance.]

Note: Paragraph 30B and 30C inserted from 30 July 2000 (HC 704).

Variation of leave to enter or remain in the United Kingdom

31. Under Section 3(3) of the 1971 Act a limited leave to enter or remain in the United Kingdom may well be varied by extending or restricting its duration, by adding, varying or revoking conditions or by removing the time limit (whereupon any condition attached to the leave ceases to apply). When leave to enter or remain is varied an entry is to be made in the applicant's passport or travel document (and his registration certificate where appropriate) or the decision may be made known in writing in some other appropriate way.

[**31A.** Where a person has arrived in the United Kingdom with leave to enter or remain in the United Kingdom which is in force but was given to him before his arrival, he may apply, on arrival at a port of entry in the United Kingdom, for variation of that leave. An Immigration Officer acting on behalf of the Secretary of State may vary the leave at the port of entry but is not obliged to consider an application for variation made at the port of entry. If an Immigration Officer acting on behalf of the Secretary of State has declined to consider an application for variation of leave at a port of entry but the leave has not been cancelled under paragraph 2A(8) of Schedule 2 to the Immigration Act 1971, the person seeking variation should apply to the Home Office under paragraph 32.]

Note: Paragraph 31A inserted from 30 July 2000 (HC 704).

32. After admission to the United Kingdom any application for an extension of the time limit on or variation of conditions attached to a person's stay in the United Kingdom must be made to the Home Office before the applicant's current leave to enter or remain expires.
[With the exception of applications made under [paragraph 31A (applications at the port of entry)] and paragraph 33 (work permits), [33A (applications made outside the United Kingdom)], paragraphs 255 to 257 (EEA nationals) and Part 11 (asylum), all applications for variation of leave to enter or remain must be made using the form prescribed for the purpose by the Secretary of State, which must be completed in the manner required by the form and to be accompanied by the documents and photographs specified in the form. An application for such a variation made in any other way is not valid.]

Note: Second para inserted by HC 395 from 25 November 1996. Other words in square brackets inserted from 30 July 2000 (HC 704).

33. Where the application is in respect of employment for which a work permit or a permit for training or work experience is required or is in respect of the spouse [or civil partner] or child of a person who is making such an application, the application should be made direct to the Department of Employment Overseas Labour Service.

Note: Words in square brackets inserted from 5 December 2005 (HC 852).

[**33A.** Where a person, having left the common travel area, has leave to enter or remain in the United Kingdom which remains in force under article 13 of the Immigration (Leave to Enter and Remain) Order 2000, his leave may be varied (including any conditions to which it is subject) in such form and manner as permitted for the giving of leave to enter. However, the Secretary of State is not obliged to consider an application for variation of leave to enter or remain from a person outside the United Kingdom.]

Note: Inserted from 30 July 2000 (HC 704).

Withdrawn applications for variation of leave to enter or remain in the United Kingdom

34. Where a person whose application for variation of leave to enter or remain is being considered requests the return of his passport for the purpose of travel outside the common travel area, the application for variation of leave shall, provided it has not already been determined, be treated as withdrawn as soon as the passport is returned in response to that request. . . .

Note: Words omitted from 2 October 2000 (Cm 4851).

Undertakings

35. A sponsor of a person seeking leave to enter or variation of leave to enter or remain in the United Kingdom may be asked to give an undertaking in writing to be responsible for that person's maintenance and accommodation for the period of any leave granted, including any further variation. Under the Social Security Administration Act 1992 and the Social Security Administration (Northern Ireland) Act 1992, the Department of Social Security or, as the case may be, the Department of Health and Social Services in Northern Ireland may seek to recover from the person giving such an undertaking any income support paid to meet the needs of the person in respect of whom the undertaking has been given.
[Under the Immigration and Asylum Act 1999 the Home Office may seek to recover from the person giving such an undertaking amounts attributable to any support provided under section 95 of the Immigration and Asylum Act 1999 (support for asylum seekers) to, or in respect of, the person in respect of whom the undertaking has been given. Failure by the sponsor to maintain that person in accordance with the undertaking, may also be an offence under section 105 of the Social Security Administration Act 1992 and/or under section 108 of the Immigration and Asylum Act 1999 if, as a consequence, asylum support and/or income support is provided to, or in respect of, that person.]

Note: Words in square brackets inserted from 2 October 2000 (Cm 4851).

Medical

36. A person who intends to remain in the United Kingdom for more than 6 months should normally be referred to the Medical Inspector for examination. If he produces a medical certificate he should be advised to hand it to the Medical Inspector. Any person seeking entry who mentions health or medical treatment as a reason for his visit, or who appears not to be in good mental or physical health, should also be referred to the Medical Inspector; and the Immigration Officer has discretion, which should be exercised sparingly, to refer for examination in any other case.

37. Where the Medical Inspector advises that a person seeking entry is suffering from a specified disease or condition which may interfere with his ability to support himself or his dependants, the Immigration Officer should take account of this, in conjunction with other factors, in deciding whether to admit that person. The Immigration Officer should also take account of the Medical Inspector's assessment of the likely course of treatment in deciding whether a person seeking entry for private medical treatment has sufficient means at his disposal.

38. A returning resident should not be refused leave to enter [or have existing leave to enter or remain cancelled] on medical grounds. But where a person would be refused leave to enter [or have existing leave to enter or remain cancelled] on medical grounds if he were not a returning resident, or in any case where it is decided on compassionate grounds not to exercise the power to refuse leave to enter [or to cancel have existing leave to enter or remain], or in any other case where the Medical Inspector so recommends, the Immigration Officer should give the person concerned a notice requiring him to report to the Medical Officer of Environmental Health designated by the Medical Inspector with a view to further examination and any necessary treatment.

Note: Words in square brackets inserted from 30 July 2000 (HC 704).

39. The Entry Clearance Officer has the same discretion as an Immigration Officer to refer applicants for entry clearance for medical examination and the same principles will apply to the decision whether or not to issue an entry clearance.

[Students

39A. An application for a variation of leave to enter or remain made by a student who is sponsored by a government or international sponsorship agency may be refused if the sponsor has not given written consent to the proposed variation.]

Note: Paragraph 39A inserted from 4 April 1996 (HC 329).

Part 2

Persons Seeking to Enter or Remain in the United Kingdom for Visits

Visitors

Requirements for leave to enter as a visitor

40. For the purpose of paragraphs 41–46 a visitor includes a person living and working outside the United Kingdom who comes to the United Kingdom to transact business (such as attending meetings and briefings, fact finding, negotiating or making contracts with United Kingdom businesses to buy or sell goods or services). A visitor seeking leave to enter or remain for private medical treatment must meet the requirements of paragraphs 51 or 54. [A visitor seeking leave to enter for the purposes of marriage must meet the requirements of paragraph 56D.]

Note: Words in square brackets inserted from 15 March 2005 (HC 346).

41. The requirements to be met by a person seeking leave to enter the United Kingdom as a visitor are that he:

- (i) is genuinely seeking entry as a visitor for a limited period as started by him, not exceeding 6 months; and
- (ii) intends to leave the United Kingdom at the end of the period of the visit as stated by him; and
- (iii) does not intend to take employment in the United Kingdom; and
- (iv) does not intend to produce goods or provide services within the United Kingdom, including the selling of goods or services direct to members of the public; and
- (v) does not intend to study at a maintained school; and
- (vi) will maintain and accommodate himself and any dependants adequately out of resources available to him without recourse to public funds or taking employment; or will, with any dependants, be maintained and accommodated adequately by relatives or friends; and
- (vii) can meet the cost of the return or onward journey; [and
- (viii) is not a child under the age of 18.]

Note: Subparagraph (viii) inserted from 12 February 2006 (HC 819).

Leave to enter as a visitor

42. A person seeking leave to enter the United Kingdom as a visitor may be admitted for a period not exceeding 6 months, subject to a condition prohibiting employment, provided the Immigration Officer is satisfied that each of the requirements of paragraph 41 is met.

Refusal of leave to enter as a visitor

43. Leave to enter as a visitor is to be refused if the Immigration Officer is not satisfied that each of the requirements of paragraph 41 is met.

Requirements for an extension of stay as a visitor

44. Six months is the maximum permitted leave which may be granted to a visitor. The requirements for an extension of stay as a visitor are that the applicant:

- (i) meets the requirements of paragraph 41 (ii)–(vii); and
- (ii) has not already spent, or would not as a result of an extension of stay spend, more than 6 months in total in the United Kingdom as a visitor[; and
- (iii) was not last admitted to the United Kingdom under the Approved Destination Status Agreement with China.]

Any period spent as a seasonal agricultural worker is to be counted as a period spent as a visitor.

Note: Paragraph 44(iii) inserted from 5 April 2005 (HC 486).

Extension of stay as a visitor

45. An extension of stay as a visitor may be granted, subject to a condition prohibiting employment, provided the Secretary of State is satisfied that each of the requirements of paragraph 44 is met.

Refusal of extension of stay as a visitor

46. An extension of stay as a visitor is to be refused if the Secretary of State is not satisfied that each of the requirements of paragraph 44 is met.

Child visitors

Requirements for leave to enter as a child visitor

[**46A.** The requirements to be met by a person seeking leave to enter the United Kingdom as a child visitor are that he:

(i) meets the requirements of paragraph 41 (i)–(vii); and
(ii) is under the age of 18; and
(iii) can demonstrate that suitable arrangements have been made for his travel to, and reception and care in the United Kingdom; and
(iv) has a parent or guardian in his home country or country of habitual residence who is responsible for his care; and
(v) if a visa national:
 (a) holds a valid United Kingdom entry clearance for entry as an accompanied child visitor and is travelling in the company of the adult identified on his entry clearance, who is on the same occasion being admitted to the United Kingdom; or
 (b) holds a valid United Kingdom entry clearance for entry as an unaccompanied child visitor.]

Note: Paragraph 46A inserted from 12 February 2006 (HC 819).

Leave to enter as a child visitor

[**46B.** A person seeking leave to enter the United Kingdom as a child visitor may be admitted for a period not exceeding 6 months, subject to a condition prohibiting employment, providing that the Immigration Officer is satisfied that each of the requirements of paragraph 46A is met.]

Note: Paragraph 46B inserted from 12 February 2006 (HC 819).

Refusal of leave to enter as a child visitor

[**46C.** Leave to enter as a child visitor is to be refused if the Immigration Officer is not satisfied that each of the requirements of paragraph 46A is met.]

Note: Paragraph 46C inserted from 12 February 2006 (HC 819).

Requirements for an extension of stay as a child visitor

[**46D.** Six months is the maximum permitted leave which may be granted to a child visitor. The requirements for an extension of stay as a child visitor are that the applicant:

- (i) meets the requirements of paragraph 41 (ii) to (vii); and
- (ii) is under the age of 18; and
- (iii) can demonstrate that there are suitable arrangements for his care in the United Kingdom; and
- (iv) has a parent or guardian in his home country or country of habitual residence who is responsible for his care; and
- (v) has not already spent, or would not as a result of an extension of stay spend, more than 6 months in total in the United Kingdom as a child visitor.]

Note: Paragraph 46D inserted from 12 February 2006 (HC 819).

Extension of stay as a child visitor

[**46E.** An extension of stay as a child visitor may be granted, subject to a condition prohibiting employment, provided the Secretary of State is satisfied that each of the requirements of paragraph 46D is met.]

Note: Paragraph 46E inserted from 12 February 2006 (HC 819).

Refusal of extension of stay as a child visitor

[**46F.** An extension of stay as a child visitor is to be refused if the Secretary of State is not satisfied that each of the requirements of paragraph 46D is met.]

Note: Paragraph 46F inserted from 12 February 2006 (HC 819).

Visitors in transit

Requirements for admission as a visitor in transit to another country

47. The requirements to be met by a person (not being a member of the crew of a ship, aircraft, hovercraft, hydrofoil or train) seeking leave to enter the United Kingdom as a visitor in transit to another country are that he:

(i) is in transit to a country outside the common travel area; and
(ii) has both the means and the intention of proceeding at once to another country; and
(iii) is assured of entry there; and
(iv) intends and is able to leave the United Kingdom within 48 hours.

Leave to enter as a visitor in transit

48. A person seeking leave to enter the United Kingdom as a visitor in transit may be admitted for a period not exceeding 48 hours with a prohibition on employment provided the Immigration Officer is satisfied that each of the requirements of paragraph 47 is met.

Refusal of leave to enter as a visitor in transit

49. Leave to enter as a visitor in transit is to be refused if the Immigration Officer is not satisfied that each of the requirements of paragraph 47 is met.

Extension of stay as a visitor in transit

50. The maximum permitted leave which may be granted to a visitor in transit is 48 hours. An application for an extension of stay beyond 48 hours from a person admitted in this category is to be refused.

Visitors seeking to enter or remain for private medical treatment

Requirements for leave to enter as a visitor for private medical treatment

51. The requirements to be met by a person seeking leave to enter the United Kingdom as a visitor for private medical treatment are that he:
(i) meets the requirements set out in paragraph 41 (iii)–(vii) for entry as a visitor; and
(ii) in the case of a person suffering from a communicable disease, has satisfied the Medical Inspector that there is no danger to public health; and
(iii) can show, if required to do so, that any proposed course of treatment is of finite duration; and
(iv) intends to leave the United Kingdom at the end of his treatment; and
(v) can produce satisfactory evidence, if required to do so, of:
(a) the medical condition requiring consultation or treatment; and
(b) satisfactory arrangements for the necessary consultation or treatment at his own expense; and
(c) the estimated costs of such consultation or treatment; and
(d) the likely duration of his visit; and
(e) sufficient funds available to him in the United Kingdom to meet the estimated costs and his undertaking to do so.

Leave to enter as a visitor for private medical treatment

52. A person seeking leave to enter the United Kingdom as a visitor for private medical treatment may be admitted for a period not exceeding 6 months, subject to a condition prohibiting employment, provided the Immigration Officer is satisfied that each of the requirements of paragraph 51 is met.

Refusal of leave to enter as a visitor for private medical treatment

53. Leave to enter as a visitor for private medical treatment is to be refused if the Immigration Officer is not satisfied that each of the requirements of paragraph 51 is met.

Requirements for an extension of stay as a visitor for private medical treatment

54. The requirements for an extension of stay as a visitor to undergo or continue private medical treatment are that the applicant:

(i) meets the requirements set out in paragraph 41 (iii)–(vii) and paragraph 51 (ii)–(v); and

[(ii) has produced evidence from a registered medical practitioner who holds an NHS consultant post or who appears in the Specialist Register of the General Medical Council of satisfactory arrangements for private medical consultation or treatment and its likely duration; and, where treatment has already begun, evidence as to its progress; and]

(iii) can show that he has met, out of the resources available to him, any costs and expenses incurred in relation to his treatment in the United Kingdom; and

(iv) has sufficient funds available to him in the United Kingdom to meet the likely costs of his treatment and intends to meet those costs[; and

(v) was not last admitted to the United Kingdom under the Approved Destination Status Agreement with China.]

Note: Paragraph 54(ii) substituted from 2 October 2000 (Cm 4851). Paragraph 54(v) inserted from 5 April 2005 (HC 486).

Extension of a stay as a visitor for private medical treatment

55. An extension of stay to undergo or continue private medical treatment may be granted, with a prohibition on employment, provided the Secretary of State is satisfied that each of the requirements of paragraph 54 is met.

Refusal of extension of stay as a visitor for private medical treatment

56. An extension of stay as a visitor to undergo or continue private medical treatment is to be refused if the Secretary of State is not satisfied that each of the requirements of paragraph 54 is met.

[Parent of a Child at School

Requirements for leave to enter or remain as the parent of a child at school

56A. The requirements to be met by a person seeking leave to enter or remain in the United Kingdom as the parent of a child at school are that:

(i) the parent meets the requirements set out in paragraph 41 (ii)–(vii); and
(ii) the child is attending an independent fee paying day school and meets the requirements set out in paragraph 57 (i)–(vi); and
(iii) the child is under 12 years of age; and
(iv) the parent can provide satisfactory evidence of adequate and reliable funds for maintaining a second home in the United Kingdom; and
(v) the parent is not seeking to make the United Kingdom his main home[; and
(vi) the parent was not last admitted to the United Kingdom under the Approved Destination Status Agreement with China.]

Leave to enter or remain as the parent of a child at school

56B. A person seeking leave to enter or remain in the United Kingdom as the parent of a child at school may be admitted or allowed to remain for a period not exceeding 12 months, subject to a condition prohibiting employment, provided the Immigration Officer or, in the case of an application for limited leave to remain, the Secretary of State is satisfied that each of the requirements of paragraph 56A is met.

Refusal of leave to enter or remain as the parent of a child at school

56C. Leave to enter or remain in the United Kingdom as the parent of a child at school is to be refused if the Immigration Officer or, in the case of an application for limited leave to remain, the Secretary of State is not satisfied that each of the requirements of paragraph 56A is met.]

Note: Paragraphs 56A–C inserted from 2 October 2000 (CM 4851). Paragraph 56A (vi) inserted from 5 April 2005 (HC 486).

Visitors seeking to enter for the purposes of marriage [or civil partnership]

Requirements for leave to enter as a visitor for marriage [or civil partnership]

[**56D.** The requirements to be met by a person seeking leave to enter the United Kingdom as a visitor for marriage [or civil partnership] are that he:

(i) meets the requirements set out in paragraph 41 for entry as a visitor; and
(ii) can show that he intends to give notice of marriage [or civil partnership], or marry [or form a civil partnership], in the United Kingdom within the period for which entry is sought; and

(iii) can produce satisfactory evidence, if required to do so, of the arrangements for giving notice of marriage [or civil partnership], or for his wedding [or civil partnership] ceremony to take place, in the United Kingdom during the period for which entry is sought; and
(iv) holds a valid United Kingdom entry clearance for entry in this capacity.]

Note: Paragraph 56D inserted from 15 March 2005 (HC 346). References to civil partnership inserted from 14 November 2005 (HC 582).

Leave to enter as a visitor for marriage [or civil partnership]

[**56E.** A person seeking leave to enter the United Kingdom as a visitor for marriage [or civil partnership] may be admitted for a period not exceeding 6 months, subject to a condition prohibiting employment, provided the Immigration Officer is satisfied that each of the requirements of paragraph 56D is met.]

Note: Paragraph 56E inserted from 15 March 2005 (HC 346). References to civil partnership inserted from 14 November 2005 (HC 582).

Refusal of leave to enter as a visitor for marriage [or civil partnership]

[**56F.** Leave to enter as a visitor for marriage [or civil partnership] is to be refused if the Immigration Officer is not satisfied that each of the requirements of paragraph 56D is met.]

Note: Paragraph 56F inserted from 15 March 2005 (HC 346). References to civil partnership inserted from 14 November 2005 (HC 582).

[Visitors Seeking Leave to Enter Under the Approved Destination Status (ADS) Agreement with China

Requirements for leave to enter as a visitor under the Approved Destination Status Agreement with China ('ADS Agreement')

56G. The requirements to be met by a person seeking leave to enter the United Kingdom as a visitor under the ADS Agreement with China are that he:

(i) meets the requirements set out in paragraph 41 (ii)–(vii); and
(ii) is a national of the People's Republic of China; and
(iii) is genuinely seeking entry as a visitor for a limited period as stated by him, not exceeding 30 days; and
(iv) intends to enter, leave and travel within the territory of the United Kingdom as a member of a tourist group under the ADS Agreement; and
(v) holds a valid ADS Agreement visit visa.

Leave to enter as a visitor under the ADS Agreement with China

56H. A person seeking leave to enter the United Kingdom as a visitor under the ADS Agreement may be admitted for a period not exceeding 30 days, subject to a condition prohibiting employment, provided they hold an ADS Agreement visit visa.

Refusal of leave to enter as a visitor under the ADS Agreement with China

56I. Leave to enter as a visitor under the ADS Agreement with China is to be refused if the person does not hold an ADS Agreement visit visa.

Extension of stay as a visitor under the ADS Agreement with China

56J. Any application for an extension of stay as a visitor under the ADS Agreement with China is to be refused.]

Note: Paragraphs 56G–56J inserted from 5 April 2005 (HC 486).

Part 3

Persons Seeking to Enter or Remain in the United Kingdom for Studies

Students

Requirements for leave to enter as a student

57. The requirements to be met by a person seeking leave to enter the United Kingdom as a student are that he:
[(i) has been accepted for a course of study which is to be provided by an organisation which is included on the Department for Education and Skills' Register of Education and Training Providers, and is at either;
(a) a publicly funded institution of further or higher education; or
(b) a bona fide private education institution which maintains satisfactory records of enrolment and attendance; or
(c) an independent fee paying school outside the maintained sector; and]
(ii) is able and intends to follow either:
(a) a recognised full-time degree course at a publicly funded institution of further or higher education; or
(b) a weekday full-time course involving attendance at a single institution for a minimum of 15 hours organised daytime study per week of a single subject or directly related subjects; or
(c) a full-time course of study at an independent fee paying school; and
(iii) if under the age of 16 years is enrolled at an independent fee paying

school on a full-time course of studies which meets the requirements of the Education Act 1944; and

(iv) intends to leave the United Kingdom at the end of his studies; and

(v) does not intend to engage in business or to take employment, except part-time or vacation work undertaken with the consent of the Secretary of State for Employment; and

(vi) is able to meet the costs of his course and accommodation and the maintenance of himself and any dependants without taking employment or engaging in business or having recourse to public funds.

Note: Paragraph 57(i) substituted from 1 January 2005 (HC 164).

Leave to enter as a student

58. A person seeking leave to enter the United Kingdom as a student may be admitted for an appropriate period depending on the length of his course of study and his means, and with a condition restricting his freedom to take employment, provided the Immigration Officer is satisfied that each of the requirements of paragraph 57 is met.

Refusal of leave to enter as a student

59. Leave to enter as a student is to be refused if the Immigration Officer is not satisfied that each of the requirements of paragraph 57 is met.

Requirements for an extension of stay as a student

60. The requirements for an extension of stay as a student are that the applicant:

[(i) was last admitted to the UK in possession of a valid entry clearance in accordance with paragraphs 57–75M or 82–87F of these Rules, unless the applicant:

(a) was originally admitted to the UK with entry clearance in accordance with paragraphs 57–75M or 82–87F of these rules which has since expired, but has subsequently been granted leave to remain in accordance with paragraphs 57–75M or 82–87F of these Rules; or

(b) is a non-visa national who has been accepted for a course of study at degree level or above, and who entered the UK with leave as a visitor in accordance with paragraphs 40–46F of these Rules on or before 1 July 2006; or

(c) is a non-visa national who has been accepted for a course of study at degree level or above, and who entered the UK with leave in accordance with the provisions of any category of these Rules, other than paragraphs 40–56J, 82–87, 104–121, and 135I–135N; or

(d) is a non-visa national who has been accepted for a course of study below degree level, and has valid leave in accordance with paragraphs 63–69, 69M–81, Part 2 (other than paragraphs 47–56J), or Parts 4–8 (other than paragraphs 104–121 and 135I–135N) of these Rules, which was granted on or before 22 July 2004; or

(e) is a non-visa national who has been accepted for a course of study below degree level, and has valid leave as a student to study below degree level in accordance with paragraphs 57–62 of these Rules, or has valid leave in accordance with paragraphs 69A–69L or 82–87F of these Rules, which was granted on or before 30 September 2004; and]

(ii) meets the requirements for admission as a student set out in paragraph 57(i)–(vi); and

(iii) has produced evidence of his enrolment on a course which meets the requirements of paragraph 57; and

(iv) can produce satisfactory evidence of regular attendance during any course which he has already begun; or any other course for which he has been enrolled in the past; and

(v) can show evidence of satisfactory progress in his course of study including the taking and passing of any relevant examinations; and

(vi) would not, as a result of an extension of stay, spend more than [2] years on short courses [below degree level] (ie courses of less than [1] years duration, or longer courses broken off before completion); and

(vii) has not come to the end of a period of government or international scholarship agency sponsorship, or has the written consent of his [official] sponsor for a further period of study in the United Kingdom and satisfactory evidence that sufficient sponsorship funding is available.

Note: Paragraph 60(i) substituted from 3 April 2006 (HC 1016). Word in square brackets in para 60(vii) substituted from 2 October 2000 (Cm 4851). Words in square brackets in sub-para (vi) inserted or substituted from 1 October 2004 (Cm 6339).

Extension of stay as a student

61. An extension of stay as a student may be granted, subject to a restriction on his freedom to take employment, provided the Secretary of State is satisfied that the applicant meets each of the requirements of paragraph 60.

Refusal of extension of stay as a student

62. An extension of stay as a student is to be refused if the Secretary of State is not satisfied that each of the requirements of paragraph 60 is met.

Student nurses

Definition of student nurse

63. For the purposes of these Rules the term student nurse means a person accepted for training as a student nurse or midwife leading to a registered nursing qualification. [. . .]

Note: Words deleted from 30 November 2005 (HC 645).

Requirements for leave to enter as a student nurse

64. The requirements to be met by a person seeking leave to enter the United Kingdom as a student nurse are that the person:

(i) comes within the definition set out in paragraph 63 above; and

(ii) has been accepted for a course of study in a recognised nursing educational establishment offering nursing training which meets the requirements of the [Nursing and Midwifery Council]; and

[(iii) did not obtain acceptance on the course of study referred to in (ii) above by misrepresentation;] and

(iv) is able and intends to follow the course; and

(v) does not intend to engage in business or take employment except in connection with the training course; and

(vi) intends to leave the United Kingdom at the end of the course; and

(vii) has sufficient funds available for accommodation and maintenance for himself and any dependants without engaging in business or taking employment (except in connection with the training course) or having recourse to public funds. The possession of a Department of Health bursary may be taken into account in assessing whether the student meets the maintenance requirement.

Note: Subparagraph (iii) substituted from 30 November 2005 (HC 645). Words in square brackets in sub-para (ii) substituted from 30 November 2005 (HC 645).

Leave to enter the United Kingdom as a student nurse

65. A person seeking leave to enter the United Kingdom as a student nurse may be admitted for the duration of the [. . .] course, with a restriction on his freedom to take employment, provided the Immigration Officer is satisfied that each of the requirements of paragraph 64 is met.

Note: Word deleted from 30 November 2005 (HC 645).

Refusal of leave to enter as a student nurse

66. Leave to enter as a student nurse is to be refused if the Immigration Officer is not satisfied that each of the requirements of paragraph 64 is met.

Requirements for an extension of stay as a student nurse

67. The requirements for an extension of stay as a student nurse are that the applicant:

[(i) was last admitted to the United Kingdom in possession of a valid student entry clearance, or valid prospective student entry clearance in accordance with paragraphs 82 to 87 of these Rules, if he is a person specified in Appendix 1 to these Rules; and]
(ii) meets the requirements set out in paragraph 64(i)–(vii); and
(iii) has produced evidence of enrolment at a recognised nursing educational establishment; and
(iv) can provide satisfactory evidence of regular attendance during any course which he has already begun; or any other course for which he has been enrolled in the past; and
(v) would not, as a result of an extension of stay, spend more than 4 years in obtaining the relevant qualification; and
(vi) has not come to the end of a period of government or international scholarship agency sponsorship, or has the written consent of his [official] sponsor for a further period of study in the United Kingdom and evidence that sufficient sponsorship funding is available.

Note: Paragraph 67(i) substituted from 18 September 2002 (Cm 5597).

Extension of stay as a student nurse

68. An extension of stay as a student nurse may be granted, subject to a restriction that the applicant on his freedom to take employment, provided the Secretary of State is satisfied that the applicant meets each of the requirements of paragraph 67.

Refusal of extension of stay as a student nurse

69. An extension of stay as a student nurse is to be refused if the Secretary of State is not satisfied that each of the requirements of paragraph 67 is met.

[*Re-sits of examinations*

Requirements for leave to enter to re-sit an examination

69A. The requirements to be met by a person seeking leave to enter the United Kingdom in order to re-sit an examination are that the applicant:

- (i) (a) meets the requirements for admission as a student set out in paragraph 57 (i)–(vi); or
  - (b) met the requirements for admission as a student set out in paragraph 57 (i)–(iii) in the previous academic year and continues to meet the requirements of paragraph 57 (iv)–(vi); and
- (ii) has produced written confirmation from the education institution or independent fee paying school which he attends or attended in the previous academic year that he is required to re-sit an examination; and
- (iii) can provide satisfactory evidence of regular attendance during any course which he has already begun; or any other course for which he has been enrolled in the past; and
- (iv) has not come to the end of a period of government or international scholarship agency sponsorship, or has the written consent of his official sponsor for a further period of study in the United Kingdom and satisfactory evidence that sufficient sponsorship funding is available; and
- (v) has not previously been granted leave to re-sit the examination.

Leave to enter to re-sit an examination

69B. A person seeking leave to enter the United Kingdom in order to re-sit an examination may be admitted for a period sufficient to enable him to re-sit the examination at the first available opportunity with a condition restricting his freedom to take employment, provided the Immigration Officer is satisfied that each of the requirements of paragraph 69A is met.

Refusal of leave to enter to re-sit an examination

69C. Leave to enter to re-sit an examination is to be refused if the Immigration Officer is not satisfied that each of the requirements of paragraph 69A is met.

Requirements for an extension of stay to re-sit an examination

69D. The requirements for an extension of stay to re-sit an examination are that the applicant:

- (i) was admitted to the United Kingdom with a valid student entry clearance if he was then a visa national; and
- (ii) meets the requirements set out in paragraph 69A (i)–(v).

Extension of stay to re-sit an examination

69E. An extension of stay to re-sit an examination may be granted for a period sufficient to enable the applicant to re-sit the examination at the first available opportunity, subject to a restriction on his freedom to take employment, provided the Secretary of State is satisfied that the applicant meets each of the requirements of paragraph 69D.

Refusal of extension of stay to re-sit an examination

69F. An extension of stay to re-sit an examination is to be refused if the Secretary of State is not satisfied that each of the requirements of paragraph 69D is met.

Writing up a thesis

Requirements for leave to enter to write up a thesis

69G. The requirements to be met by a person seeking leave to enter the United Kingdom in order to write up a thesis are that the applicant:

(i) (a) meets the requirements for admission as a student set out in paragraph 57 (i)–(vi); or
(b) met the requirements for admission as a student set out in paragraph 57 (i)–(iii) in the previous academic year and continues to meet the requirements of paragraph 57 (iv)–(vi); and

(ii) can provide satisfactory evidence that he is a postgraduate student enrolled at an education institution as either a full time, part time or writing up student; and

(iii) can demonstrate that his application is supported by the education institution; and

(iv) has not come to the end of a period of government or international scholarship agency sponsorship, or has the written consent of his official sponsor for a further period of study in the United Kingdom and satisfactory evidence that sufficient sponsorship funding is available; and

(v) has not previously been granted 12 months leave to write up the same thesis.

Leave to enter to write up a thesis

69H. A person seeking leave to enter the United Kingdom in order to write up a thesis may be admitted for 12 months with a condition restricting his freedom to take employment, provided the Immigration Officer is satisfied that each of the requirements of paragraph 69G is met.

Refusal of leave to enter to write up a thesis

69I. Leave to enter to write up a thesis is to be refused if the Immigration Officer is not satisfied that each of the requirements of paragraph 69G is met.

Requirements for an extension of stay to write up a thesis

69J. The requirements for an extension of stay to write up a thesis are that the applicant:

(i) was admitted to the United Kingdom with a valid student entry clearance if he was then a visa national; and
(ii) meets the requirements set out in paragraph 69G (i)–(v).

Extension of stay to write up a thesis

69K. An extension of stay to write up a thesis may be granted for 12 months subject to a restriction on his freedom to take employment, provided the Secretary of State is satisfied that the applicant meets each of the requirements of paragraph 69J.

Refusal of extension of stay to write up a thesis

69L. An extension of stay to write up a thesis is to be refused if the Secretary of State is not satisfied that each of the requirements of paragraph 69J is met.].

Note: Paragraphs 69A–L inserted from 2 October 2000 (Cm 4851).

Requirements for leave to enter as an overseas qualified nurse or Midwife

[**69M.** The requirements to be met by a person seeking leave to enter as an overseas qualified nurse or midwife are that the applicant:
(i) has obtained confirmation from the Nursing and Midwifery Council that he is eligible:
(a) for admission to the Overseas Nurses Programme; or
(b) to undertake a period of supervised practice; or
(c) to undertake an adaptation programme leading to registration as a midwife; and
(ii) has been offered:
(a) a supervised practice placement through an education provider that is recognised by the Nursing and Midwifery Council; or
(b) a supervised practice placement in a setting approved by the Nursing and Midwifery Council; or
(c) a midwifery adaptation programme placement in a setting approved by the Nursing and Midwifery Council; and
(iii) did not obtain acceptance of the offer referred to in paragraph 69 (ii) by misrepresentation; and
(iv) is able and intends to undertake the supervised practice placement or midwife adaptation programme; and
(v) does not intend to engage in business or take employment, except:
(a) in connection with the supervised practice placement or midwife adaptation programme; or
(b) part-time work of a similar nature to the work undertaken on the supervised practice placement or midwife adaptation programme; and

(vi) is able to maintain and accommodate himself and any dependants without recourse to public funds.]

Note: Paragraph 69M inserted from 30 November 2005 (HC 645).

Leave to enter the United Kingdom as an overseas qualified nurse or midwife

[**69N.** Leave to enter the United Kingdom as an overseas qualified nurse or midwife may be granted for a period not exceeding 18 months, provided the Immigration Officer is satisfied that each of the requirements of paragraph 69M is met.]

Note: Paragraph 69N inserted from 30 November 2005 (HC 645).

Refusal of leave to enter as an overseas qualified nurse or midwife

[**69O.** Leave to enter the United Kingdom as an overseas qualified nurse or midwife is to be refused if the Immigration Officer is not satisfied that each of the requirements of paragraph 69M is met.]

Note: Paragraph 69O inserted from 30 November 2005 (HC 645).

Requirements for an extension of stay as an overseas qualified nurse or midwife

[**69P.** The requirements to be met by a person seeking an extension of stay as an overseas qualified nurse or midwife are that the applicant:

(i) has leave to enter or remain in the United Kingdom as a prospective student in accordance with paragraphs 82–87 of these Rules; or

(ii) has leave to enter or remain in the United Kingdom as a student in accordance with paragraphs 57 to 69L of these Rules; or

(iii) has leave to enter or remain in the United Kingdom as a working holiday-maker in accordance with paragraphs 95 to 97 of these Rules and has spent more than 12 months in total in the UK in this capacity; or

{(iii) (a) has leave to enter or remain in the United Kingdom as a work permit holder in accordance with paragraphs 128 to135 of these Rules; or}

(iv) has leave to enter or remain as an overseas qualified nurse or midwife in accordance with paragraphs 69M–69R of these Rules; and

(v) meets the requirements set out in paragraph 69M (i)–(vi); and

(vi) can provide satisfactory evidence of regular attendance during any previous period of supervised practice or midwife adaptation course; and

(vii) if he has previously been granted leave:

(a) as an overseas qualified nurse or midwife under paragraphs 69M–69R of these Rules, or

(b) to undertake an adaptation course as a student nurse under paragraphs 63–69 of these Rules; is not seeking an extension of stay in this category which, when amalgamated with those previous periods of leave, would total more than 18 months; and

(viii) if his previous studies, supervised practice placement or midwife adaptation programme placement were sponsored by a government or international scholarship agency, he has the written consent of his official sponsor to remain in the United Kingdom as an overseas qualified nurse or midwife.]

Note: Paragraph 69P inserted from 30 November 2005 (HC 645). Subparagraph (iii)(a) inserted from 3 April 2006 (HC 1016).

Extension of stay as an overseas qualified nurse or midwife

[**69Q.** An extension of stay as an overseas qualified nurse or midwife may be granted for a period not exceeding 18 months, provided that the Secretary of State is satisfied that each of the requirements of para 69P is met.]

Note: Paragraph 69Q inserted from 30 November 2005 (HC 645).

Refusal of extension of stay as an overseas qualified nurse or midwife

[**69R.** An extension of stay as an overseas qualified nurse or midwife is to be refused if the Secretary of State is not satisfied that each of the requirements of paragraph 69P is met.]

Note: Paragraph 69R inserted from 30 November 2005 (HC 645).

[Requirements for leave to enter the United Kingdom as a postgraduate doctor or dentist]

[**70.** The requirements to be met by a person seeking leave to enter the UK as a postgraduate doctor or dentist are that the applicant:

(i) has successfully completed and obtained a recognised UK degree in medicine or dentistry from either:
  (a) a UK publicly funded institution of further or higher education; or
  (b) a UK bona fide private education institution which maintains satisfactory records of enrolment and attendance; and

(ii) has previously been granted leave:
  (a) in accordance with paragraphs 57 to 69L of these Rules for the final academic year of the studies referred to in (i) above; and
  (b) as a student under paragraphs 57 to 62 of these Rules for at least one other academic year (aside from the final year) of the studies referred to in (i) above; and

(iii) holds a letter from the Postgraduate Dean confirming he has a full-time place on a recognised Foundation Programme; and

(iv) intends to train full time in his post on the Foundation Programme; and

(v) is able to maintain and accommodate himself and any dependants without recourse to public funds; and

(vi) intends to leave the United Kingdom if, on expiry of his leave under this paragraph, he has not been granted leave to remain in the United Kingdom as:

(a) a doctor or dentist undertaking a period of clinical attachment or a dental observer post in accordance with paragraphs 75G to 75M of these Rules; or

(b) a work permit holder in accordance with paragraphs 128 to 135 of these Rules; or

(c) a highly skilled migrant in accordance with paragraphs 135A to 135H of these Rules; or

(d) a person intending to establish themselves in business in accordance with paragraphs 200 to 210 of these Rules; or

(e) an innovator in accordance with paragraphs 210A to 210H of these Rules; and

(vii) if his study at medical school or dental school, or any subsequent studies he has undertaken, were sponsored by a government or international scholarship agency, he has the written consent of his sponsor to enter or remain in the United Kingdom as a postgraduate doctor or dentist; and

(viii) if he has not previously been granted leave in this category, has completed his medical or dental degree in the 12 months preceding this application; and

(ix) if he has previously been granted leave as a postgraduate doctor or dentist, is not seeking leave to enter to a date beyond 3 years from the date on which he was first granted leave to enter or remain in this category; and

(x) holds a valid entry clearance for entry in this capacity except where he is a British National (Overseas), a British overseas territories citizen, a British Overseas citizen, a British protected person or a person who under the British Nationality Act 1981 is a British subject.]

Note: Paragraph 70 substituted from 3 April 2006 (HC 1016).

Leave to enter as a postgraduate doctor or dentist

[71. Leave to enter the United Kingdom as a postgraduate doctor or dentist may be granted for the duration of the Foundation Programme, for a period not exceeding 26 months, provided the Immigration Officer is satisfied that each of the requirements of paragraph 70 is met.]

Note: Paragraph 71 substituted from 3 April 2006 (HC 1016).

Refusal of leave to enter as a postgraduate doctor or dentist

[72. Leave to enter as a postgraduate doctor or dentist is to be refused if the Immigration Officer is not satisfied that each of the requirements of paragraph 70 is met.]

Note: Paragraph 72 substituted from 3 April 2006 (HC 1016).

Requirements for an extension of stay as a postgraduate doctor or dentist

[73. The requirements to be met by a person seeking an extension of stay as a postgraduate doctor or dentist are that the applicant:

- (i) meets the requirements of paragraph 70 (i) to (vii); and
- (ii) has leave to enter or remain in the United Kingdom as either:
  - (a) a student in accordance with paragraphs 57 to 69L of these Rules; or
  - (b) a postgraduate doctor or dentist in accordance with paragraphs 70 to 75 of these Rules; or
  - (c) a doctor or dentist undertaking a period of clinical attachment or a dental observer post in accordance with paragraphs 75G to 75M of these Rules.
- (iii) if he has not previously been granted leave in this category, has completed his medical or dental degree in the last 12 months;
- (iv) would not, as a result of an extension of stay, remain in the United Kingdom as a postgraduate doctor or dentist to a date beyond 3 years from the date on which he was first given leave to enter or remain in this capacity.]

Note: Paragraph 73 substituted from 3 April 2006 (HC 1016).

Extension of stay as a postgraduate doctor or dentist

[74. An extension of stay as a postgraduate doctor or dentist may be granted for the duration of the Foundation Programme, for a period not exceeding 3 years, provided the Secretary of State is satisfied that each of the requirements of paragraph 73 is met.]

Note: Paragraph 74 substituted from 3 April 2006 (HC 1016).

Refusal of an extension of stay as a postgraduate doctor or dentist

[75. An extension of stay as a postgraduate doctor or dentist is to be refused if the Secretary of State is not satisfied that each of the requirements of paragraph 73 is met.]

Note: Paragraph 75 substituted from 3 April 2006 (HC 1016).

Requirements for leave to enter the United Kingdom to take the PLAB Test

[75A. The requirements to be met by a person seeking leave to enter in order to take the PLAB Test are that the applicant:

(i) is a graduate from a medical school and intends to take the PLAB Test in the United Kingdom; and

(ii) can provide documentary evidence of a confirmed test date or of his eligibility to take the PLAB Test; and

(iii) meets the requirements of paragraph 41 (iii)–(vii) for entry as a visitor; and

(iv) intends to leave the United Kingdom at the end of his leave granted under this paragraph unless he is successful in the PLAB Test and granted leave to remain:

(a) as a postgraduate doctor or trainee general practitioner in accordance with paragraphs 70 to 75; or

(b) to undertake a clinical attachment in accordance with paragraphs 75G to 75M of these Rules; or

(c) as a work permit holder for employment in the United Kingdom as a doctor in accordance with paragraphs 128 to 135; or

(d) as a doctor under the highly skilled migrant programme in accordance with paragraphs 135A to 135H.]

Note: Paragraph 75A inserted from 15 March 2005 (HC 364).

Leave to enter to take the PLAB Test

[75B. A person seeking leave to enter the United Kingdom to take the PLAB Test may be admitted for a period not exceeding 6 months, provided the Immigration Officer is satisfied that each of the requirements of paragraph 75A is met.]

Note: Paragraph 75B inserted from 15 March 2005 (HC 364).

Refusal of leave to enter to take the PLAB Test

[75C. Leave to enter the United Kingdom to take the PLAB Test is to be refused if the Immigration Officer is not satisfied that each of the requirements of paragraph 75A is met.]

Note: Paragraph 75C inserted from 15 March 2005 (HC 364).

Requirements for an extension of stay in order to take the PLAB Test

[75D. The requirements for an extension of stay in the United Kingdom in order to take the PLAB Test are that the applicant:

(i) was given leave to enter the United Kingdom for the purposes of taking the PLAB Test in accordance with paragraph 75B of these Rules; and

(ii) intends to take the PLAB Test and can provide documentary evidence of a confirmed test date; and

(iii) meets the requirements set out in paragraph 41 (iii)–(vii); and

(iv) intends to leave the United Kingdom at the end of his leave granted under this paragraph unless he is successful in the PLAB Test and granted leave to remain:

(a) as a postgraduate doctor or trainee general practitioner in accordance with paragraphs 70 to 75; or

(b) to undertake a clinical attachment in accordance with paragraphs 75G to 75M of these Rules; or

(c) as a work permit holder for employment in the United Kingdom as a doctor in accordance with paragraphs 128 to 135; or

(d) as a doctor under the highly skilled migrant programme in accordance with paragraphs 135A to 135H; and

(v) would not as a result of an extension of stay spend more than 18 months in the United Kingdom for the purpose of taking the PLAB Test.]

Note: Paragraph 75D inserted from 15 March 2005 (HC 364).

Extension of stay to take the PLAB Test

[75E. A person seeking leave to remain in the United Kingdom to take the PLAB Test may be granted an extension of stay for a period not exceeding 6 months, provided the Secretary of State is satisfied that each of the requirements of paragraph 75D is met.]

Note: Paragraph 75E inserted from 15 March 2005 (HC 364).

Refusal of extension of stay to take the PLAB Test

[75F. Leave to remain in the United Kingdom to take the PLAB Test is to be refused if the Secretary of State is not satisfied that each of the requirements of paragraph 75D is met.]

Note: Paragraph 75F inserted from 15 March 2005 (HC 364).

Requirements for leave to enter to undertake a clinical attachment or dental observer post

[75G. The requirements to be met by a person seeking leave to enter to undertake a clinical attachment or dental observer post are that the applicant:

(i) is a graduate from a medical or dental school and intends to undertake a clinical attachment or dental observer post in the United Kingdom; and

(ii) can provide documentary evidence of the clinical attachment or dental observer post which will:

(a) be unpaid; and
(b) only involve observation, not treatment, of patients; and

(iii) meets the requirements of paragraph 41 (iii)–(vii) of these Rules; and

(iv) intends to leave the United Kingdom at the end of his leave granted under this paragraph unless he is granted leave to remain:
(a) as a postgraduate doctor, dentist or trainee general practitioner in accordance with paragraphs 70 to 75;
(b) as a work permit holder for employment in the United Kingdom as a doctor or dentist in accordance with paragraphs 128 to 135; or
(c) as a General Practitioner under the highly skilled migrant programme in accordance with paragraphs 135A to 135H; {and

(v) if he has previously been granted leave in this category, is not seeking leave to enter which, when amalgamated with those previous periods of leave, would total more than 6 months.}]

Note: Paragraph 75G inserted from 15 March 2005 (HC 364). Subparagraph (v) inserted from 3 April 2006 (HC 1016).

Leave to enter to undertake a clinical attachment or dental observer post

[75H. A person seeking leave to enter the United Kingdom to undertake a clinical attachment or dental observer post may be admitted for the period of the clinical attachment or dental observer post {up to a maximum of 6 weeks at a time or 6 months in total in this capacity}, provided the Immigration Officer is satisfied that each of the requirements of paragraph 75G is met.]

Note: Paragraph 75H inserted from 15 March 2005 (HC 364). Words in curly brackets substituted from 3 April 2006 (HC 1016).

Refusal of leave to enter to undertake a clinical attachment or dental observer post

[75J. Leave to enter the United Kingdom to undertake a clinical attachment or dental observer post is to be refused if the Immigration Officer is not satisfied that each of the requirements of paragraph 75G is met.]

Note: Paragraph 75J inserted from 15 March 2005 (HC 364).

Requirements for an extension of stay in order to undertake a clinical attachment or dental observer post

[75K. The requirements to be met by a person seeking an extension of stay to undertake a clinical attachment or dental observer post are that the applicant:

(i) was given leave to enter or remain in the United Kingdom to undertake a clinical attachment or dental observer post or:
(a) for the purposes of taking the PLAB Test in accordance with paragraphs 75A to 75F and has passed both parts of the PLAB Test;

(b) as a postgraduate doctor, dentist or trainee general practitioner in accordance with paragraphs 70 to 75; or

(c) as a work permit holder for employment in the UK as a doctor or dentist in accordance with paragraphs 128 to 135; and

(ii) is a graduate from a medical or dental school and intends to undertake a clinical attachment or dental observer post in the United Kingdom; and

(iii) can provide documentary evidence of the clinical attachment or dental observer post which will:

(a) be unpaid; and

(b) only involve observation, not treatment, of patients; and

(iv) intends to leave the United Kingdom at the end of his period of leave granted under this paragraph unless he is granted leave to remain:

(a) as a postgraduate doctor, dentist or trainee general practitioner in accordance with paragraphs 70 to 75; or

(b) as a work permit holder for employment in the United Kingdom as a doctor or dentist in accordance with paragraphs 128 to 135; or

(c) as a General Practitioner under the highly skilled migrant programme in accordance with paragraphs 135A to 135H.; and

(v) meets the requirements of paragraph 41 (iii)–(vii) of these Rules;] {and

(vi) if he has previously been granted leave in this category, is not seeking an extension of stay which, when amalgamated with those previous periods of leave, would total more than 6 months.}]

Note: Paragraph 75K inserted from 15 March 2005 (HC 364). Words in curly brackets inserted from 3 April 2006 (HC 1016).

Extension of stay to undertake a clinical attachment or dental observer post

[**75L.** A person seeking leave to remain in the United Kingdom to undertake a clinical attachment or dental observer post may be granted an extension of stay for the period of their clinical attachment or dental observer post {up to a maximum of 6 weeks at a time or 6 months in total in this category}, provided that the Secretary of State is satisfied that each of the requirements of paragraph 75K is met.]

Note: Paragraph 75L inserted from 15 March 2005 (HC 364). Words in curly brackets inserted from 3 April 2006 (HC 1016).

Refusal of extension of stay to undertake a clinical attachment or dental observer post

[**75M.** Leave to remain in the United Kingdom to undertake a clinical attachment or dental observer post is to be refused if the Secretary of State is not satisfied that each of the requirements of paragraph 75K is met.]

Note: Paragraph 75M inserted from 15 March 2005 (HC 364).

Spouses [or civil partners] of students

Requirements for leave to enter or remain as the spouse [or civil partner] of a student [or prospective student]

76. The requirements to be met by a person seeking leave to enter or remain in the United Kingdom as the spouse [or civil partner] of a student are that:

(i) the applicant is married to [or the civil partner of] a person admitted to or allowed to remain in the United Kingdom under paragraphs 57–75 [or 82–87]; and

(ii) each of the parties intends to live with the other as his or her spouse [or civil partner] during the applicant's stay and the marriage [or civil partnership] is subsisting; and

(iii) there will be adequate accommodation for the parties and any dependants without recourse to public funds; and

(iv) the parties will be able to maintain themselves and any dependants adequately without recourse to public funds; and

(v) the applicant does not intend to take employment except as permitted under paragraph 77 below; and

(vi) the applicant intends to leave the United Kingdom at the end of any period of leave granted to him.

Note: Words in square brackets inserted from 1 November 1996 (HC 31). References to civil partnership inserted from 5 December 2005 (HC 582).

Leave to enter or remain as the spouse [or civil partner] of a student [or prospective student]

[**77.** A person seeking leave to enter or remain in the United Kingdom as the spouse [or civil partner] of a student may be admitted or allowed to remain for a period not in excess of that granted to the student provided the Immigration Officer or, in the case of an application for limited leave to remain, the Secretary of State is satisfied that each of the requirements of paragraph 76 is met. Employment may be permitted where the period of leave granted to the student is, or was, 12 months or more.]

Note: Words in square brackets inserted from 1 November 1996 (HC 31). Paragraph 77 substituted from 2 October 2000 (Cm 4851). References to civil partnership inserted from 5 December 2005 (HC 582).

Refusal of leave to enter or remain as the spouse [or civil partner] of a student [or prospective student]

78. Leave to enter or remain as the spouse [or civil partner] of a student is to be refused if the Immigration Officer or, in the case of an application for a limited leave to remain, the Secretary of State is not satisfied that each of the requirements of paragraph 76 is met.

Note: Words in square brackets inserted from 1 November 1996 (HC 31). References to civil partnership inserted from 5 December 2005 (HC 582).

Children of students

Requirements for leave to enter or remain as the child of a student [or prospective student]

79. The requirements to be met by a person seeking leave to enter or remain in the United Kingdom as the child of a student are that he:

(i) is the child of a parent admitted to or allowed to remain in the United Kingdom as a student under paragraphs 57–75 [or 82–87]; and
(ii) is under the age of 18 or has current leave to enter or remain in this capacity; and
(iii) is unmarried, has not formed an independent family unit and is not leading an independent life; and
(iv) can, and will, be maintained and accommodated adequately without recourse to public funds; and
(v) will not stay in the United Kingdom beyond any period of leave granted to his parent.

Note: Words in square brackets inserted from 1 November 1996 (HC 31).

Leave to enter or remain as the child of a student

[**80.** A person seeking leave to enter or remain in the United Kingdom as the child of a student may be admitted to remain for a period not in excess of that granted to the student provided the Immigration Officer or, in the case of an application for limited leave to remain, the Secretary of State is satisfied that each of the requirements of paragraph 79 is met. Employment may be permitted where the period of leave granted to the student is, or was 12 months or more.]

Note: Substituted from 2 October 2000 (Cm 4851).

Refusal of leave to enter or remain as the child of a student

81. Leave to enter or remain in the United Kingdom as the child of a student is to be refused if the Immigration Officer or, in the case of an application for limited leave to remain, the Secretary of State is not satisfied that each of the requirements of paragraph 79 is met.

Prospective students

Requirements for leave to enter as a prospective student

82. The requirements to be met by a person seeking leave to enter the United Kingdom as a prospective student are that he:

[(i) can demonstrate a genuine and realistic intention of undertaking, within 6 months of his date of entry:
    (a) a course of study which would meet the requirements for an extension of stay as a student under paragraphs 60 to 67 of these Rules; or
    (b) a supervised practice placement or midwife adaptation course which would meet the requirements for an extension of stay as an overseas qualified nurse or midwife under paragraphs 69P to 69R of these Rules; and]

[(ii) intends to leave the United Kingdom on completion of his studies or on the expiry of his leave to enter if he is not able to meet the requirements for an extension of stay:
    (a) as a student in accordance with paragraph 60 or 67 of these Rules; or
    (b) as an overseas qualified nurse or midwife in accordance with paragraph 69P of these Rules; and]

(iii) is able without working or recourse to public funds to meet the costs of his intended course and accommodation and the maintenance of himself and any dependants while making arrangements to study and during the course of his studies.

Note: Sub paragraphs (i) and (ii) substituted from 30 November 2005 (HC 645).

Leave to enter as a prospective student

83. A person seeking leave to enter the United Kingdom as a prospective student may be admitted for a period not exceeding 6 months with a condition prohibiting employment, provided the Immigration Officer is satisfied that each of the requirements of paragraph 82 is met.

Refusal of leave to enter as a prospective student

84. Leave to enter as a prospective student is to be refused if the Immigration Officer is not satisfied that each of the requirements of paragraph 82 is met.

Requirements for extension of stay as a prospective student

85. Six months is the maximum permitted leave which may be granted to a prospective student. The requirements for an extension of stay as a prospective student are that the applicant:

(i) was admitted to the United Kingdom with a valid prospective student entry clearance if he is a person specified in [Appendix 1] to these Rules; and
(ii) meets the requirements of paragraph 82; and
(iii) would not, as a result of an extension of stay, spend more than 6 months in the United Kingdom.

Note: Words in square brackets substituted from 11 May 1998 (Cm 3953).

Extension of stay as a prospective student

86. An extension of stay as a prospective student may be granted, with a prohibition on employment, provided the Secretary of State is satisfied that each of the requirements of paragraph 85 is met.

Refusal of extension of stay as a prospective student

87. An extension of stay as a prospective student is to be refused if the Secretary of State is not satisfied that each of the requirements of paragraph 85 is met.

[*Students' unions sabbatical officers*

Requirements for leave to enter as a sabbatical officer

87A. The requirements to be met by a person seeking leave to enter the United Kingdom as a sabbatical officer are that the person:
(i) has been elected to a full-time salaried post as a sabbatical officer at an educational establishment at which he is registered as a student;
(ii) meets the requirements set out in paragraph 57 (i)–(ii) or met the requirements set out in paragraph 57 (i)–(ii) in the academic year prior to the one in which he took up or intends to take up sabbatical office; and
(iii) does not intend to engage in business or take employment except in connection with his sabbatical post; and
(iv) is able to maintain and accommodate himself and any dependants adequately without recourse to public funds; and
(v) at the end of the sabbatical post he intends to:
  (a) complete a course of study which he has already begun; or
  (b) take up a further course of study which has been deferred to enable the applicant to take up the sabbatical post; or
  (c) leave the United Kingdom; and
(vi) has not come to the end of a period of government or international scholarship agency sponsorship, or has the written consent of his official sponsor to take up a sabbatical post in the United Kingdom; and
(vii) has not already completed 2 years as a sabbatical officer.

Leave to enter the United Kingdom as a sabbatical officer

87B. A person seeking leave to enter the United Kingdom as a sabbatical officer may be admitted for a period not exceeding 12 months on conditions specifying his employment provided the Immigration Officer is satisfied that each of the requirements of paragraph 87A is met.

Refusal of leave to enter the United Kingdom as a sabbatical officer

87C. Leave to enter as a sabbatical officer is to be refused if the Immigration Officer is not satisfied that each of the requirements of paragraph 87A is met.

Requirements for an extension of stay as a sabbatical officer

87D. The requirements for an extension of stay as a sabbatical officer are that the applicant:

(i) was admitted to the United Kingdom with a valid student entry clearance if he was then a visa national; and

(ii) meets the requirements set out in paragraph 87A (i)–(vi); and

(iii) would not, as a result of an extension of stay, remain in the United Kingdom as a sabbatical officer to a date beyond 2 years from the date on which he was first given leave to enter the United Kingdom in this capacity.

Extension of stay as a sabbatical officer

87E. An extension of stay as a sabbatical officer may be granted for a period not exceeding 12 months on conditions specifying his employment provided the Secretary of State is satisfied that the applicant meets each of the requirements of paragraph 87D.

Refusal of extension of stay as a sabbatical officer

87F. An extension of stay as a sabbatical officer is to be refused if the Secretary of State is not satisfied that each of the requirements of paragraph 87D is met.

Note: Paragraphs 87A–F inserted from 2 October 2000 (Cm 4851).

Part 4

Persons Seeking to Enter or Remain in the United Kingdom in an 'au pair' Placement, as a Working Holidaymaker, or for Training or Work Experience

'Au pair' placements

Definition of an 'au pair' placement

88. For the purposes of these Rules an 'au pair' placement is an arrangement whereby a young person:

(a) comes to the United Kingdom for the purpose of learning the English language; and

(b) lives for a time as a member of an English speaking family with appropriate opportunities for study; and

(c) helps in the home for a maximum of 5 hours per day in return for a reasonable allowance and with two free days per week.

Requirements for leave to enter as an 'au pair'

89. The requirements to be met by a person seeking leave to enter the United Kingdom as an 'au pair' are that he:

(i) is seeking entry for the purpose of taking up an arranged placement which can be shown to fall within the definition set out in paragraph 88; and

(ii) is aged between 17–27 inclusive or was so aged when first given leave to enter in this capacity; and

(iii) is unmarried [and is not a civil partner]; and

(iv) is without dependants; and

(v) [is a national of one of the following countries: Andorra, Bosnia-Herzegovina, Republic of Bulgaria, Croatia, The Faroes, Greenland, Macedonia, Monaco, Romania, San Marino, or Turkey; and]

(vi) does not intend to stay in the United Kingdom for more than 2 years as an 'au pair'; and

(vii) intends to leave the United Kingdom on completion of his stay as an 'au pair'; and

(viii) if he has previously spent time in the United Kingdom as an 'au pair', is not seeking leave to enter to a date beyond 2 years from the date on which he was first given leave to enter the United Kingdom in this capacity [; and

(ix) is able to maintain and accommodate himself without recourse to public funds.]

Note: Paragraph (ix) inserted from 1 November 1996 (HC 31). Paragraph 89 (v) substituted from 1 May 2004 (HC 523). Words in square brackets in para 89(iii) inserted from 5 December 2005 (HC 582).

Leave to enter as an 'au pair'

90. A person seeking leave to enter the United Kingdom as an 'au pair' may be admitted for a period not exceeding 2 years with a prohibition on employment except as an 'au pair', provided the Immigration Officer is satisfied that each of the requirements of paragraph 89 is met. (A non-visa national who wishes to ascertain in advance whether a proposed 'au pair' placement is likely to meet the requirements of paragraph 89 is advised to obtain an entry clearance before travelling to the United Kingdom).

Refusal of leave to enter as an 'au pair'

91. An application for leave to enter as an 'au pair' is to be refused if the Immigration Officer is not satisfied that each of the requirements of paragraph 89 is met.

Requirements for an extension of stay as an 'au pair'

92. The requirements for an extension of stay as an 'au pair' are that the applicant:

- (i) was given leave to enter the United Kingdom as an 'au pair' under paragraph 90; and
- (ii) is undertaking an arranged 'au pair' placement which can be shown to fall within the definition set out in paragraph 88; and
- (iii) meets the requirements of paragraph [89 (ii)–(ix)]; and
- (iv) would not, as a result of an extension of stay, remain in the United Kingdom as an 'au pair' to a date beyond 2 years from the date on which he was first given leave to enter the United Kingdom in this capacity.

Note: Words in square brackets substituted from 1 November 1996 (HC 31).

Extension of stay as an 'au pair'

93. An extension of stay as an 'au pair' may be granted with a prohibition on employment except as an 'au pair', provided the Secretary of State is satisfied that each of the requirements of paragraph 92 is met.

Refusal of extension of stay as an 'au pair'

94. An extension of stay as an 'au pair' is to be refused if the Secretary of State is not satisfied that each of the requirements of paragraph 92 is met.

Working holidaymakers

Requirements for leave to enter as a working holidaymaker

[95. The requirements to be met by a person seeking leave to enter the United Kingdom as a working holidaymaker are that he:

(i) is a national or citizen of a country listed in Appendix 3 of these Rules, or a British Overseas Citizen; a British Overseas Territories Citizen; or a British National (Overseas); and

(ii) is aged between 17 and 30 inclusive or was so aged at the date of his application for leave to enter; and

(iii) (a) is unmarried and is not a civil partner, or

(b) is married to, or the civil partner of, a person who meets the requirements of this paragraph and the parties to the marriage or civil partnership intend to take a working holiday together; and]

(iv) has the means to pay for his return or onward journey; and

(v) is able and intends to maintain and accommodate himself without recourse to public funds; and

(vi) is intending only to take employment incidental to a holiday, and not to engage in business, or to provide services as a professional sportsperson, and in any event not to work for more than 12 months during his stay; and

(vii) does not have dependent children any of whom are 5 years of age or over or who will reach 5 years of age before the applicant completes his working holiday; and

(viii) intends to leave the UK at the end of his working holiday: and

(ix) has not spent time in the United Kingdom on a previous working holidaymaker entry clearance; and

(x) holds a valid United Kingdom entry clearance, granted for a limited period not exceeding 2 years, for entry in this capacity.]]

Note: Paragraph 95 substituted from 8 February 2005 (HC 302). Subparagraph (iii) substituted from 5 December 2005 (HC 582) and sub-para (x) substituted from 6 July 2005 (HC 104).

Leave to enter as a working holidaymaker

[**96.** A person seeking to enter the United Kingdom as a working holidaymaker may be admitted provided he is able to produce on arrival a valid United Kingdom entry clearance granted for a period not exceeding 2 years for entry in this capacity.]

Note: Paragraph 96 substituted from 6 July 2005 (HC 104).

Refusal of leave to enter as a working holidaymaker

97. Leave to enter as a working holidaymaker is to be refused if a valid United

Kingdom entry clearance for entry in this capacity is not produced to the Immigration Officer on arrival.

98.–100.

Note: Paragraphs 98–100 deleted from 8 February 2005 (HC 302).

Children of working holidaymakers

Requirements for leave to enter or remain as the child of a working holidaymaker

[**101.** The requirements to be met by a person seeking leave to enter or remain in the United Kingdom as the child of a working holidaymaker are that:

(i) he is the child of a parent admitted to, and currently present in, the United Kingdom as a working holidaymaker; and

(ii) he is under the age of 5 and will leave the United Kingdom before reaching that age; and

(iii) he can and will be maintained and accommodated adequately without recourse to public funds or without his parent(s) engaging in employment except as provided by paragraph 95 above; and

(iv) both parents are being or have been admitted to the United Kingdom, save where:

(a) the parent he is accompanying or joining is his sole surviving parent; or

(b) the parent he is accompanying or joining has had sole responsibility for his upbringing; or

(c) there are serious and compelling family or other considerations which make exclusion from the United Kingdom undesirable and suitable arrangements have been made for his care; and

(v) he holds a valid United Kingdom entry clearance for entry in this capacity or, if seeking leave to remain, was admitted with a valid United Kingdom entry clearance for entry in this capacity, and is seeking leave to a date not beyond the date to which his parent(s) have leave to enter in the working holidaymaker category.]

Note: Paragraph 101 substituted from 8 February 2005 (HC 302).

Leave to enter [or remain] as the child of a working holidaymaker

[**102.** A person seeking to enter the United Kingdom as the child of working holidaymaker/s must be able to produce on arrival a valid United Kingdom entry clearance for entry in this capacity.]

Note: Paragraph 102 substituted from 8 February 2005 (HC 302).

Refusal of leave to enter or remain as the child of a working holidaymaker

103. Leave to enter or remain in the United Kingdom as the child of a working holidaymaker is to be refused if, in relation to an application for leave to enter, a valid United Kingdom entry clearance for entry in this capacity is not produced to the Immigration Officer on arrival or, in the case of an application for leave to remain, the applicant was not admitted with a valid United Kingdom entry clearance for entry in this capacity or is unable to satisfy the Secretary of State that each of the requirements of paragraph 101(i)–(iv) is met.

Seasonal workers at agricultural camps

Requirements for leave to enter as a seasonal [agricultural] worker [. . .]

104. The requirements to be met by a person seeking leave to enter the United Kingdom as a seasonal [agricultural] worker [. . .] are that he:

(i) is a student in full-time education aged [18 or over] and

(ii) holds [an immigration employment document in the form of] a valid Home Office work card issued by the operator of a scheme approved by the Secretary of State; and

(iii) intends to leave the United Kingdom at the end of his period of leave as a seasonal worker; and

(iv) does not intend to take employment except [as permitted by his work card and within the terms of this paragraph] [; and

[(v) is not seeking leave to enter on a date less than 3 months from the date on which an earlier period of leave to enter or remain granted to him in this capacity expired; and]

(vi) is able to maintain and accommodate himself [. . .] without recourse to public funds.]

Note: Subparagraph (v) substituted from 13 November 2003 (HC 1224). Words deleted from 1 April 2003 (HC 538). Word 'agricultural' inserted from 13 November 2003 (HC 1224).

Leave to enter as a seasonal [agricultural] worker [. . .]

[**105.** A person seeking leave to enter the United Kingdom as a seasonal agricultural worker may be admitted with a condition restricting his freedom to take employment for a period not exceeding 6 months, provided the Immigration Officer is satisfied that each of the requirements of paragraph 104 is met.]

Note: Paragraph 105 substituted and words in heading inserted from 13 November 2003 (HC 1224).

Refusal of leave to enter as a seasonal [agricultural] worker [. . .]

106. Leave to enter the United Kingdom as a seasonal [agricultural] worker [. . .] is to be refused if the Immigration Officer is not satisfied that each of the requirements of paragraph 104 is met.

Note: Words deleted from 1 April 2003 (HC 538). Word 'agricultural' inserted from 13 November 2003 (HC 1224).

Requirements for extension of stay as a seasonal [agricultural] worker [. . .]

[**107.** The requirements for an extension of stay as a seasonal agricultural worker are that the applicant:

- (i) entered the United Kingdom as a seasonal agricultural worker under paragraph 105; and
- (ii) has an immigration employment document in the form of a Home Office work card issued by an operator approved by the Home Office that is valid for the duration of the period of the requested extension of stay; and
- (iii) meets the requirements of paragraph 104(iii)–(vi); and
- (iv) would not, as a result of the extension of stay sought, remain in the United Kingdom as a seasonal agricultural worker beyond 6 months from the date on which he was given leave to enter the United Kingdom on this occasion in this capacity.]

Note: Paragraph 107 substituted and word in heading inserted from 13 November 2003 (HC 1224).

Extension of stay as a seasonal [agricultural] worker [. . .]

[**108.** An extension of stay as a seasonal agricultural worker may be granted with a condition restricting his freedom to take employment for a period which does not extend beyond 6 months from the date on which he was given leave to enter the United Kingdom on this occasion in this capacity, provided the Secretary of State is satisfied that the applicant meets each of the requirements of paragraph 107.]

Note: Paragraph 108 substituted and words in heading inserted from 13 November 2003 (HC 1224).

Refusal of extension of stay as a seasonal [agricultural] worker [. . .]

109. An extension of stay as a seasonal [agricultural] worker [. . .] is to be refused if the Secretary of State is not satisfied that each of the requirements of paragraph 107 is met.

Note: Words deleted from 1 April 2003 (HC 538). Word 'agricultural' inserted from 13 November 2003 (HC 1224).

Teachers and language assistants coming to the United Kingdom under approved exchange schemes

Requirements for leave to enter as a teacher or language assistant under an approved exchange scheme

110. The requirements to be met by a person seeking leave to enter the United Kingdom as a teacher or language assistant on an approved exchange scheme are that he:

[(i) is coming to an educational establishment in the United Kingdom under an exchange scheme approved by the Department for Education and Skills, the Scottish or Welsh Office of Education or the Department of Education, Northern Ireland, or administered by the British Council's Education and Training Group or the League for the Exchange of Commonwealth Teachers; and]

(ii) intends to leave the United Kingdom at the end of his exchange period; and

(iii) does not intend to take employment except in the terms of this paragraph; and

(iv) is able to maintain and accommodate himself and any dependants without recourse to public funds; and

(v) holds a valid United Kingdom entry clearance for entry in this capacity.

Note: Subparagraph (i) substituted from 1 October 2004 (Cm 6339).

Leave to enter as a teacher or language assistant under an exchange scheme

111. A person seeking leave to enter the United Kingdom as a teacher or language assistant under an approved exchange scheme may be given leave to enter for a period not exceeding 12 months provided he is able to produce to the Immigration Officer, on arrival, a valid United Kingdom entry clearance for entry in this capacity.

Refusal of leave to enter as a teacher or language assistant under an approved exchange scheme

112. Leave to enter the United Kingdom as a teacher or language assistant under an approved exchange scheme is to be refused if a valid United Kingdom entry clearance for entry in this capacity is not produced to the Immigration Officer on arrival.

Requirements for extension of stay as a teacher or language assistant under an approved exchange scheme

113. The requirements for an extension of stay as a teacher or language assistant under an approved exchange scheme are that the applicant:

(i) entered the United Kingdom with a valid United Kingdom entry clearance as a teacher or language assistant; and
(ii) is still engaged in the employment for which his entry clearance was granted; and
(iii) is still required for the employment in question, as certified by the employer; and
(iv) meets the requirements of paragraph 110(ii)–(iv); and
(v) would not, as a result of an extension of stay, remain in the United Kingdom as an exchange teacher or language assistant for more than 2 years from the date on which he was first given leave to enter the United Kingdom in this capacity.

Extension of stay as a teacher or language assistant under an approved exchange scheme

114. An extension of stay as a teacher or language assistant under an approved exchange scheme may be granted for a further period not exceeding 12 months provided the Secretary of State is satisfied that each of the requirements of paragraph 113 is met.

Refusal of extension of stay as a teacher or language assistant under an approved exchange scheme

115. An extension of stay as a teacher or language assistant under an approved exchange scheme is to be refused if the Secretary of State is not satisfied that each of the requirements of paragraph 113 is met.

[Home Office] approved training or work experience

Requirements for leave to enter for [Home Office] approved training or work experience

116. The requirements to be met by a person seeking leave to enter the United Kingdom for [Home Office] approved training or work experience are that he:
(i) holds a valid work permit from the [Home Office] issued under the Training and Work Experience Scheme; and
(ii) . . .
(iii) is capable of undertaking the training or work experience as specified in his work permit; and
(iv) intends to leave the United Kingdom on the completion of his training or work experience; and
(v) does not intend to take employment except as specified in his work permit; and
(vi) is able to maintain and accommodate himself and any dependants adequately without recourse to public funds; [and]

[(vii) holds a valid United Kingdom entry clearance for entry in this capacity except where he holds a work permit valid for 6 months or less . . . {or he is a British National (Overseas), a British protected person or a person who under the British Nationality Act 1981 is a British subject.}]

Note: Subparagraph (ii) deleted from 1 April 2003 (HC 538). Subparagraph (vii) inserted from 13 November 2003 (HC 1224). Words deleted from sub-para (vii) from 1 May 2004 (HC 523). Words in curly brackets in sub-para (vii) inserted from 13 January 2003 (HC 176). Words 'Home Office' substituted from 27 August 2001 (Cmnd 5253).

Leave to enter for [Home Office] approved training or work experience

[**117.** A person seeking leave to enter the United Kingdom for the purpose of approved training or approved work experience under the Training and Work Experience Scheme may be admitted to the United Kingdom for a period not exceeding the period of training or work experience approved by the Home Office for this purpose (as specified in his work permit) subject to a condition restricting him to that approved employment, provided he is able to produce to the Immigration Officer, on arrival, a valid United Kingdom entry clearance for entry in this capacity or, where entry clearance is not required, provided the Immigration Officer is satisfied that each of the requirements of paragraph 116(i)–(v) is met.]

Note: Paragraph 117 substituted from 13 November 2003 (HC 1224). Words 'Home Office' substituted from 27 August 2001 (Cmnd 5253).

Refusal of leave to enter for [Home Office] approved training or work experience

[**118.** Leave to enter the United Kingdom for Home Office approved training or work experience under the Training and Work Experience scheme is to be refused if a valid United Kingdom entry clearance for entry in this capacity is not produced to the Immigration Officer on arrival or, where entry clearance is not required, if the Immigration officer is not satisfied that each of the requirements of paragraph 116(i)–(vi) is met.]

Note: Paragraph 118 substituted from 13 November 2003 (HC 1224). Words 'Home Office' substituted from 27 August 2001 (Cmnd 5253).

Requirements for extension of stay for [Home Office] approved training or work experience

119. The requirements for an extension of stay for Department of Employment approved training or work experience are that the applicant:

(i) entered the United Kingdom with a valid work permit under paragraph 117 or was admitted or allowed to remain in the United Kingdom as a student; and

(ii) has written approval from the [Home Office] for an extension of stay in this category; and
(iii) meets the requirements of paragraph 116(ii)–(vi); and
(iv) . . .

Note: Paragraph 119(iv) deleted from 18 September 2002 (Cm 5597). Words 'Home Office' substituted from 27 August 2001 (Cmnd 5253).

Extension of stay for [Home Office] approved training or work experience

[**120.** An extension of stay for approved training or approved work experience under the Training and Work Experience scheme may be granted for a further period not exceeding the extended period of training or work experience approved by the Home Office for this purpose (as specified in the work permit), provided that in each case the Secretary of State is satisfied that the requirements of paragraph 119 are met. An extension of stay is to be subject to a condition permitting the applicant to take or change employment only with the permission of the Home Office.]

Note: Paragraph 120 substituted from 13 November 2003 (HC 1224). Words 'Home Office' substituted from 27 August 2001 (Cmnd 5253).

Refusal of extension of stay for [Home Office] approved training or work experience

[**121.** An extension of stay for approved training or approved work experience under the Training and Work Experience scheme is to be refused if the Secretary of State is not satisfied that each of the requirements of paragraph 119 is met.]

Note: Paragraph 121 substituted from 13 November 2003 (HC 1224). Words 'Home Office' substituted from 27 August 2001 (Cmnd 5253).

Spouses [or civil partners] of persons with limited leave to enter or remain under paragraphs 110–121

Requirements for leave to enter or remain as the spouse [or civil partner] of a person with limited leave to enter or remain in the United Kingdom under paragraphs 110–121

122. The requirements to be met by a person seeking leave to enter or remain in the United Kingdom as the spouse [or civil partner] of a person with limited leave to enter or remain in the United Kingdom under paragraphs 110–121 are that:

(i) the applicant is married to [or the civil partner of] a person with limited leave to enter or remain in the United Kingdom under paragraphs 110–121; and

(ii) each of the parties intends to live with the other as his or her spouse [or civil partner] during the applicant's stay and the marriage [or civil partnership] is subsisting; and
(iii) there will be adequate accommodation for the parties and any dependants without recourse to public funds in accommodation which they own or occupy exclusively; and
(iv) the parties will be able to maintain themselves and any dependants adequately without recourse to public funds; and
(v) the applicant does not intend to stay in the United Kingdom beyond any period of leave granted to his spouse [or civil partner]; and
(vi) if seeking leave to enter, the applicant holds a valid United Kingdom entry clearance for entry in this capacity or, if seeking leave to remain, was admitted with a valid United Kingdom entry clearance for entry in this capacity.

Note: References to civil partnership inserted from 5 December 2005 (HC 582).

Leave to enter or remain as the spouse [or civil partner] of a person with limited leave to enter or remain in the United Kingdom under paragraphs 110–121

123. A person seeking leave to enter or remain in the United Kingdom as the spouse [or civil partner] of a person with limited leave to enter or remain in the United Kingdom under paragraphs 110–121 may be given leave to enter or remain in the United Kingdom for a period of leave not in excess of that granted to the person with limited leave to enter or remain under paragraphs 110–121 provided that, in relation to an application for leave to enter, he is able, on arrival, to produce to the Immigration Officer a valid United Kingdom entry clearance for entry in this capacity or, in the case of an application for limited leave to remain, was admitted with a valid United Kingdom entry clearance for entry in this capacity and is able to satisfy the Secretary of State that each of the requirements of paragraph 122(i)–(v) is met.

Note: References to civil partnership inserted from 5 December 2005 (HC 582).

Refusal of leave to enter or remain as the spouse [or civil partner] of a person with limited leave to enter or remain in the United Kingdom under paragraphs 110–121

124. Leave to enter or remain in the United Kingdom as the spouse [or civil partner] of a person with limited leave to enter or remain in the United Kingdom under paragraphs 110–121 is to be refused if, in relation to an application for leave to enter, a valid United Kingdom entry clearance for entry in this capacity is not produced to the Immigration Officer on arrival or, in the case of an application for limited leave to remain, if the applicant was not admitted with a valid United

Kingdom entry clearance for entry in this capacity or is unable to satisfy the Secretary of State that each of the requirements of paragraph 112(i)–(v) is met.

Note: References to civil partnership inserted from 5 December 2005 (HC 582).

Children of persons admitted or allowed to remain under paragraphs 110–121

Requirements for leave to enter or remain as the child of a person with limited leave to enter or remain in the United Kingdom under paragraphs 110–121

125. The requirements to be met by a person seeking leave to enter or remain in the United Kingdom as the child of a person with limited leave to enter or remain in the United Kingdom under paragraphs 110–121 are that:

(i) he is the child of a parent who has limited leave to enter or remain in the United Kingdom under paragraphs 110–121; and

(ii) he is under the age of 18 or has current leave to enter or remain in this capacity; and

(iii) he is unmarried [and is not a civil partner], has not formed an independent family unit and is not leaving an independent life; and

(iv) he can, and will, be maintained and accommodated adequately without recourse to public funds in accommodation which his parent(s) own or occupy exclusively; and

(v) he will not stay in the United Kingdom beyond any period of leave granted to his parent(s); and

(vi) both parents are being or have been admitted to or allowed to remain in the United Kingdom save where:

  (a) the parent he is accompanying or joining is his sole surviving parent: or

  (b) the parent he is accompanying or joining has had sole responsibility for his upbringing; or

  (c) there are serious and compelling family or other considerations which make exclusion from the United Kingdom undesirable and suitable arrangements have been made for his care; and

(vii) if seeking leave to enter, he holds a valid United Kingdom entry clearance for entry in this capacity or, if seeking leave to remain, was admitted with a valid United Kingdom entry clearance for entry in this capacity.

Note: Words in square brackets in sub-para (iii) inserted from 5 December 2005 (HC 582).

Leave to enter or remain as the child of a person with limited leave to enter or remain in the United Kingdom under paragraphs 110–121

126. A person seeking leave to enter or remain in the United Kingdom as the child of a person with limited leave to enter or remain in the United Kingdom under paragraphs 110–121 may be given leave to enter or remain in the United Kingdom for a period of leave not in excess of that granted to the person with limited leave to enter or remain under paragraphs 110–121 provided that, in relation to an application for leave to enter, he is able, on arrival, to produce to the Immigration Officer a valid United Kingdom entry clearance for entry in this capacity or, in the case of an application for limited leave to remain, he was admitted with a valid United Kingdom entry clearance for entry in this capacity and is able to satisfy the Secretary of State that each of the requirements of paragraph 125(i)–(vi) is met.

Refusal of leave to enter or remain as the child of a person with limited leave to enter or remain in the United Kingdom under paragraphs 110–121

127. Leave to enter or remain in the United Kingdom as the child of a person with limited leave to enter or remain in the United Kingdom under paragraphs 110–121 is to be refused if, in relation to an application for leave to enter, a valid United Kingdom entry clearance for entry in this capacity is not produced to the Immigration Officer on arrival or, in the case of an application for limited leave to remain, if the applicant was not admitted with a valid United Kingdom entry clearance for entry in this capacity or is unable to satisfy the Secretary of State that each of the requirements of paragraph 125(i)–(vi) is met.

Part 5

Persons Seeking to Enter or Remain in the United Kingdom for Employment

Work permit employment

Requirements for leave to enter the United Kingdom for work permit employment

128. The requirements to be met by a person coming to the United Kingdom to seek or take employment (unless he is otherwise eligible for admission for employment under these Rules or is eligible for admission as a seaman under contract to join a ship due to leave British waters) are that he:

- (i) holds a valid [Home Office] work permit; and
- (ii) is not of an age which puts him outside the limits for employment; and
- (iii) is capable of undertaking the employment specified in the work permit; and
- (iv) does not intend to take employment except as specified in his work permit; and
- (v) is able to maintain and accommodate himself and any dependants adequately without recourse to public funds; and
- (vi) in the case of a person in possession of a work permit which is valid for a period of 12 months or less, intends to leave the United Kingdom at the end of his approved employment; [and

(vii) holds a valid United Kingdom entry clearance for entry in this capacity except where he holds a work permit valid for 6 months or less . . . {or he is a British National (Overseas), a British protected person or a person who under the British Nationality Act 1981 is a British subject.}]

Note: Subparagraph (vii) inserted from 13 November 2003 (HC 1224). Words deleted from sub-para (vii) from 1 May 2004 (HC 523). Words in curly brackets in sub-para (vii) inserted from 13 January 2003 (HC 176). Word 'Home Office' substituted from 27 August 2001 (Cmnd 5253).

Leave to enter for work permit employment

[**129.** A person seeking leave to enter the United Kingdom for the purpose of work permit employment may be admitted for a period not exceeding the period of employment approved by the Home Office (as specified in his work permit), subject to a condition restricting him to that employment, provided he is able to produce to the Immigration Officer, on arrival, a valid United Kingdom entry clearance for entry in this capacity, or, where entry clearance is not required, provided that the Immigration Officer is satisfied that each of the requirements of paragraph 128(i)–(vi) is met.]

Note: Paragraph 129 substituted from 13 November 2003 (HC 1224).

Refusal of leave to enter for employment

[**130.** Leave to enter for the purposes of work permit employment is to be refused if a valid United Kingdom entry clearance for entry in this capacity is not produced to the Immigration Officer on arrival, or, where entry clearance is not required, if the Immigration Officer is not satisfied that each of the requirements of paragraph 128(i)–(vi) is met.]

Note: Paragraph 130 substituted from 13 November 2003 (HC 1224).

Requirements for an extension of stay for work permit employment

131. The requirements for an extension of stay to seek or take employment (unless the applicant is otherwise eligible for an extension or stay for employment under these Rules) are that the applicant:

(i) entered the United Kingdom with a valid work permit under paragraph 129 . . .; and

(ii) has written approval from the [Home Office] for the continuation of his employment; and

(iii) meets the requirements of paragraph 128(ii)–(v).

Note: Words in para 131(i) deleted from 30 May 2003 (Cm 5829). Word 'Home Office' substituted from 27 August 2001 (Cmnd 5253).

[**131A.** The requirements for an extension of stay to take employment (unless the applicant is otherwise eligible for an extension of stay for employment under these Rules) for a student are that the applicant:

(i) entered the United Kingdom or was given leave to remain as a student in accordance with paragraphs 57 to 62 of these Rules; and

(ii) has obtained a degree qualification on a recognised degree course at either a United Kingdom publicly funded further or higher education institution or a bona fide United Kingdom private education institution which maintains satisfactory records of enrolment and attendance; and

(iii) holds a valid Home Office immigration employment document for employment; and

(iv) has the written consent of his official sponsor to such employment if he is a member of a government or international scholarship agency sponsorship and that sponsorship is either ongoing or has recently come to an end at the time of the requested extension; and

(v) meets each of the requirements of paragraph 128 (ii) to (vi).]

Note: Paragraph 131A inserted from 18 September 2002 (Cm 5597).

[**131B.** The requirements for an extension of stay to take employment (unless the applicant is otherwise eligible for an extension of stay for employment under these Rules) for a student nurse, postgraduate doctor or postgraduate dentist are that the applicant:

(i) entered the United Kingdom or was given leave to remain as a student nurse [overseas qualified nurse or midwife,] in accordance with paragraphs 63 to 69 of these Rules; or

[(ia) entered the United Kingdom or was given leave to remain as an overseas qualified nurse or midwife in accordance with paragraphs 69M to 69R of these Rules; and]

(ii) entered the United Kingdom or was given leave to remain as a postgraduate doctor or a postgraduate dentist in accordance with paragraph 70 to 75 of these Rules; and

(iii) holds a valid Home Office immigration employment document for employment as a nurse, doctor or dentist; and

(iv) has the written consent of his official sponsor to such employment if he is a member of a government or international scholarship agency sponsorship and that sponsorship is either ongoing or has recently come to an end at the time of the requested extension; and

(v) meets each of the requirements of paragraph 128 (ii) to (vi).]

Note: Paragraph 131B inserted from 18 September 2002 (Cm 5597). Words in square brackets in sub-para (i) inserted from 30 November 2005 (HC 645). Subparagraph (ia) inserted from 30 November 2005 (HC 645).

[**131C.** The requirements for an extension of stay to take employment for a Science and Engineering Graduate Scheme participant are that the applicant:

(i) entered the United Kingdom or was given leave to remain as a Science and Engineering Graduate Scheme participant in accordance with paragraphs 135O to 135T of these Rules; and
(ii) holds a valid Home Office immigration employment document for employment; and
(iii) meets each of the requirements of paragraph 128 (ii) to (vi).]

Note: Paragraph 131C substituted from 1 October 2004 (Cm 6339).

[**131D.** The requirements for an extension of stay to take employment (unless the applicant is otherwise eligible for an extension of stay for employment under these Rules) for a working holidaymaker are that the applicant:
(i) entered the United Kingdom as a working holidaymaker in accordance with paragraphs 95 to 96 of these Rules; and
(ii) he has spent more than 12 months in total in the UK in this capacity; and
(iii) holds a valid Home Office immigration employment document for employment in an occupation listed on the Work Permits (UK) shortage occupations list; and
(iv) meets each of the requirements of paragraph 128 (ii) to (vi).]

Note: Paragraph 131D substituted from 8 February 2005 (HC 302).

[**131E.** The requirements for an extension of stay to take employment for a highly skilled migrant are that the applicant:
(i) entered the United Kingdom or was given leave to remain as a highly skilled migrant in accordance with paragraphs 135A to 135E of these Rules; and
(ii) holds a valid work permit; and
(iii) meets each of the requirements of paragraph 128(ii) to (vi).]

Note: Paragraph 131E inserted from 1 October 2004 (Cm 6339).

[**131F.** The requirements for an extension of stay to take employment (unless the applicant is otherwise eligible for an extension of stay for employment under these Rules) for an Innovator are that the applicant:
(i) entered the United Kingdom or was given leave to remain as an Innovator in accordance with paragraphs 210A to 210E of these Rules; and
(ii) holds a valid Home Office immigration employment document for employment; and
(iii) meets each of the requirements of paragraph 128(ii) to (vi).]

Note: Paragraph 131E inserted from 1 October 2004 (Cm 6339).

[**131G.** The requirements for an extension of stay to take employment (unless the applicant is otherwise eligible for an extension of stay for employment under these Rules) for an individual who has leave to enter or leave to remain in the United

Kingdom to take the PLAB Test or to undertake a clinical attachment or dental observer post are that the applicant:

(i) entered the United Kingdom or was given leave to remain for the purposes of taking the PLAB Test in accordance with paragraphs 75A to 75F of these Rules; or

(ii) entered the United Kingdom or was given leave to remain to undertake a clinical attachment or dental observer post in accordance with paragraphs 75G to 75M of these Rules; and

(iii) holds a valid Home Office immigration employment document for employment as a doctor or dentist; and

(iv) meets each of the requirements of paragraph 128 (ii) to (vi).]

Note: Paragraph 131G inserted from 15 March 2005 (HC 346).

[**131H.** The requirements for an extension of stay to take employment (unless the applicant is otherwise eligible for an extension of stay for employment under these Rules) in the case of a person who has leave to enter or remain as a Fresh Talent: Working in Scotland scheme participant are that the applicant:

(i) entered the United Kingdom or was given leave to remain as a Fresh Talent: Working in Scotland scheme participant in accordance with paragraphs 143A to 143F of these Rules; and

(ii) holds a valid Home Office immigration employment document for employment in Scotland; and

(iii) has the written consent of his official sponsor to such employment if the studies which led to him being granted leave under the Fresh Talent: Working in Scotland scheme in accordance with paragraphs 143A to 143F of these Rules, or any studies he has subsequently undertaken, were sponsored by a government or international scholarship agency; and

(iv) meets each of the requirements of paragraph 128 (ii) to (vi).]

Note: Paragraph 131H inserted from 22 June 2005 (HC 104).

Extension of stay for work permit employment

[**132.** An extension of stay for work permit employment may be granted for a period not exceeding the period of approved employment recommended by the Home Office provided the Secretary of State is satisfied that each of the requirements of paragraphs 131, 131A, 131B, 131C, 131D, 131E, 131F, 131G or 131H is met. An extension of stay is to be subject to a condition restricting the applicant to employment approved by the Home Office.]

Note: Paragraph 132 substituted from 22 June 2005 (HC 104).

[**133.** An extension of stay for employment is to be refused if the Secretary of State is not satisfied that each of the requirements of paragraphs 131, 131A, 131B, 131C,

131D, 131E, 131F, 131G or 131H is met (unless the applicant is otherwise eligible for an extension of stay for employment under these Rules).]

Note: Paragraph 133 substituted from 22 June 2005 (HC 104).

Indefinite leave to remain for a work permit holder

134. Indefinite leave to remain may be granted, on application, to a person admitted as a work permit holder provided:

(i) he has spent a continuous period [5] years in the United Kingdom in this capacity; and

[(ii) he has met the requirements of paragraph 128(i) to (v) throughout the 5 year period; and]

(iii) he is still required for the employment in question, as certified by his employer.

Note: Words in square brackets in sub-para (i) and (ii) substituted from 3 April 2006 (HC 1016).

Refusal of indefinite leave to remain for a work permit holder

135. Indefinite leave to remain in the United Kingdom for a work permit holder is to be refused if the Secretary of State is not satisfied that each of the requirements of paragraph 134 is met.

Highly skilled migrants

[Requirements for leave to enter the United Kingdom as a highly skilled migrant

135A. The requirements to be met by a person seeking leave to enter as a highly skilled migrant are that the applicant:

(i) must produce a valid document issued by the Home Office confirming that he meets, at the time of the issue of that document, the criteria specified by the Secretary of State for entry to the United Kingdom under the Highly Skilled Migrant Programme; and

(ii) intends to make the United Kingdom his main home; and

(iii) is able to maintain and accommodate himself and any dependants adequately without recourse to public funds; and

(iv) holds a valid United Kingdom entry clearance for entry in this capacity.]

Note: Paragraph 135A inserted from 1 April 2003 (HC 538).

[Leave to enter as a highly skilled migrant

135B. A person seeking leave to enter the United Kingdom as a highly skilled migrant may be admitted for a period not exceeding {2 years}, provided the

Immigration Officer is satisfied that each of the requirements of paragraph 135A is met.]

Note: Paragraph 135B inserted from 1 April 2003 (HC 538). Words in curly brackets substituted from 3 April 2006 (HC 1016).

[Refusal of leave to enter as a highly skilled migrant

135C. Leave to enter as a highly skilled migrant is to be refused if the Immigration Officer is not satisfied that each of the requirements of paragraph 135A is met.]

Note: Paragraph 135C inserted from 1 April 2003 (HC 538).

135D–135F

Note: Paragraphs 135D-135F deleted from 8 November 2006 and substituted in part by the following paragraphs from 5 December 2006 (HC 1702).

Requirements for an extension of stay as a highly skilled migrant

[**135D.** The requirements for an extension of stay as a highly skilled migrant for a person who has previously been granted entry clearance or leave in this capacity, are that the applicant:

(i) entered the United Kingdom with a valid United Kingdom entry clearance as a highly skilled migrant, or has previously been granted leave in accordance with paragraphs 135DA-135DH of these Rules; and

(ii) has achieved at least 75 points in accordance with the criteria specified in Appendix 4 of these Rules, having provided all the documents which are set out in Appendix 5 (Part I) of these Rules which correspond to the points which he is claiming; and

(iii) (a) has produced an International English Language Testing System certificate issued to him to certify that he has achieved at least band 6 competence in English; or

(b) has demonstrated that he holds a qualification which was taught in English and which is of an equivalent level to a UK Bachelors degree by providing both documents which are set out in Appendix 5 (Part II) of these Rules; and

(iv) meets the requirements of paragraph 135A(ii)–(iii).]

Note: Paragraph 135D inserted from 5 December 2006 (HC 1702).

[**135DA.** The requirements for an extension of stay as a highly skilled migrant for a work permit holder are that the applicant:

(i) entered the United Kingdom or was given leave to remain as a work permit holder in accordance with paragraphs 128 to 132 of these Rules; and

(ii) meets the requirements of paragraph 135A (i)–(iii).]

Note: Paragraph 135DA inserted from 5 December 2006 (HC 1702).

[**135DB.** The requirements for an extension of stay as a highly skilled migrant for a student are that the applicant:

(i) entered the United Kingdom or was given leave to remain as a student in accordance with paragraphs 57 to 62 of these Rules; and

(ii) has obtained a degree qualification on a recognised degree course at either a United Kingdom publicly funded further or higher education institution or a bona fide United Kingdom private education institution which maintains satisfactory records of enrolment and attendance; and

(iii) has the written consent of his official sponsor to remain as a highly skilled migrant if he is a member of a government or international scholarship agency sponsorship and that sponsorship is either ongoing or has recently come to an end at the time of the requested extension; and

(iv) meets the requirements of paragraph 135A(i)–(iii).]

Note: Paragraph 135DB inserted from 5 December 2006 (HC 1702).

[**135DC.** The requirements for an extension of stay as a highly skilled migrant for a postgraduate doctor or postgraduate dentist are that the applicant:

(i) entered the United Kingdom or was given leave to remain as a postgraduate doctor or a postgraduate dentist in accordance with paragraphs 70 to 75 of these Rules; and

(ii) has the written consent of his official sponsor to such employment if he is a member of a government or international scholarship agency sponsorship and that sponsorship is either ongoing or has recently come to an end at the time of the requested extension; and

(iii) meets the requirements of paragraph 135A(i)–(iii).]

Note: Paragraph 135DC inserted from 5 December 2006 (HC 1702).

[**135DD.** The requirements for an extension of stay as a highly skilled migrant for a working holidaymaker are that the applicant:

(i) entered the United Kingdom as a working holidaymaker in accordance with paragraphs 95 to 96 of these Rules; and

(ii) meets the requirements of paragraph 135A(i)–(iii).]

Note: Paragraph 135DD inserted from 5 December 2006 (HC 1702).

[**135DE.** The requirements for an extension of stay as a highly skilled migrant for a participant in the Science and Engineering Graduates Scheme are that the applicant:

(i) entered the United Kingdom or was given leave to remain as a participant in the Science and Engineering Graduates Scheme in accordance with paragraphs 135O to 135T of these Rules; and

(ii) meets the requirements of paragraph 135A(i)–(iii).]

Note: Paragraph 135DE inserted from 5 December 2006 (HC 1702).

[**135DF.** The requirements for an extension of stay as a highly skilled migrant for an innovator are that the applicant:

(i) entered the United Kingdom or was given leave to remain as an innovator in accordance with paragraphs 210A to 210E of these Rules; and

(ii) meets the requirements of paragraph 135A(i)–(iii).]

Note: Paragraph 135DF inserted from 5 December 2006 (HC 1702).

[**135DG.**

Note: Paragraph 135DG deleted from 8 November 2006 (HC 1702).

[**135DH.** The requirements for an extension of stay as a highly skilled migrant for a participant in the Fresh Talent: Working in Scotland scheme are that the applicant:

(i) entered the United Kingdom or was given leave to remain as a Fresh Talent: Working in Scotland scheme participant in accordance with paragraphs 143A to 143F of these Rules; and

(ii) has the written consent of his official sponsor to such employment if the studies which led to him being granted leave under the Fresh Talent: Working in Scotland scheme in accordance with paragraphs 143A to 143F of these Rules, or any studies he has subsequently undertaken, were sponsored by a government or international scholarship agency; and

(iii) meets the requirements of paragraph 135A(i)–(iii).]

Note: Paragraph 135DH inserted from 5 December 2006 (HC 1702).

Extension of stay as a highly skilled migrant

[**135E.** An extension of stay as a highly skilled migrant may be granted for a period not exceeding 3 years, provided that the Secretary of State is satisfied that each of the requirements of paragraph 135D, 135DA, 135DB, 135DC, 135DD, 135DE, 135DF or 135DH is met and that the application does not fall for refusal under paragraph 135HA.]

Note: Paragraph 135E inserted from 5 December 2006 (HC 1702).

Refusal of extension of stay as a highly skilled migrant

[**135F.** An extension of stay as a highly skilled migrant is to be refused if the Secretary of State is not satisfied that each of the requirements of paragraph 135D, 135DA, 135DB, 135DC, 135DD, 135DE, 135DF or 135DH is met or if the application falls for refusal under paragraph 135HA.]

Note: Paragraph 135F inserted from 5 December 2006 (HC 1702).

Requirements for indefinite leave to remain as a highly skilled migrant

[**135G.** The requirements for indefinite leave to remain for a person who has been granted leave as a highly skilled migrant are that the applicant:

(i) has spent a continuous period of 5 years lawfully in the United Kingdom, of which the most recent period must have been spent with leave as a highly skilled migrant (in accordance with paragraphs 135A to 135F of these Rules), and the remainder must be made up of leave as a highly skilled migrant, leave as a work permit holder (under paragraphs 128 to 133 of these Rules), or leave as an Innovator (under paragraphs 210A to 210F of these Rules); and

(ii) throughout the five years spent in the United Kingdom has been able to maintain and accommodate himself and any dependants adequately without recourse to public funds; and

(iii) is lawfully economically active in the United Kingdom in employment, self-employment or a combination of both.]

Note: Paragraph 135G substituted from 5 December 2006 (HC 1702).

Indefinite leave to remain as a highly skilled migrant

[**135GA.** Indefinite leave to remain may be granted provided that the Secretary of State is satisfied that each of the requirements of paragraph 135G is met and that the application does not fall for refusal under paragraph 135HA.]

Note: Paragraph 135GA substituted from 5 December 2006 (HC 1702).

Refusal of indefinite leave to remain as a highly skilled migrant

[**135H.** Indefinite leave to remain in the United Kingdom is to be refused if the Secretary of State is not satisfied that each of the requirements of paragraph 135G is met or if the application falls for refusal under paragraph 135HA.]

Note: Paragraph 135H substituted from 5 December 2006 (HC 1702).

Additional grounds for refusal for highly skilled migrants

[**135HA.** An application under paragraphs 135A-135H of these Rules is to be refused, even if the applicant meets all the requirements of those paragraphs, if:

(i) the applicant submits any document which, whether or not it is material to his application, is forged or not genuine, unless the Immigration Officer or Secretary of State is satisfied that the applicant is unaware that the document is forged or not genuine; or

(ii) the Immigration Officer or Secretary of State has cause to doubt the genuineness of any document submitted by the applicant and, having taken reasonable steps to verify the document, has been unable to verify that it is genuine.]

Note: Paragraph 135HA inserted from 5 December 2006 (HC 1702).

Sectors-Based Scheme

Requirements for leave to enter the United Kingdom for the purpose of employment under the Sectors-Based Scheme

[**135I.** The requirements to be met by a person seeking leave to enter the United Kingdom for the purpose of employment under the Sectors-Based Scheme are that he:

(i) holds a valid Home Office immigration employment document issued under the Sectors-Based Scheme; and

[(ii) is aged between 18 and 30 inclusive or was so aged at the date of his application for leave to enter; and]

(iii) is capable of undertaking the employment specified in the immigration employment document; and

(iv) does not intend to take employment except as specified in his immigration employment document; and

(v) is able to maintain and accomodate himself adequately without recourse to public funds; and

(vi) intends to leave the United Kingdom at the end of his approved employment; and

{(vii) holds a valid United Kingdom entry clearance for entry in this capacity.}]

Note: Paragraph 135I inserted from 30 May 2003 (Cm 5829). Subparagraph (vii) substituted from 1 May 2004 (HC 523). Subparagraph (ii) substituted from 30 November 2005 (HC 645).

Leave to enter for the purpose of employment under the Sectors-Based Scheme

135J. A person seeking leave to enter the United Kingdom for the purpose of employment under the Sectors-Based Scheme may be admitted for a period not exceeding 12 months (normally as specified in his work permit), subject to a condition restricting him to employment approved by the Home Office, provided the Immigration Officer is satisfied that each of the requirements of paragraph 135I is met.

Note: Inserted from 30 May 2003 (Cm 5829).

Refusal of leave to enter for the purpose of employment under the Sectors-Based Scheme

135K. Leave to enter the united Kingdom for the purpose of employment under the Sectors-Based Scheme is to be refused if the Immigration Officer is not satisfied that each of the requirements of paragraph 135I is met.

Note: Inserted from 30 May 2003 (Cm 5829).

Requirements for an extension of stay for Sector-Based employment

[**135L.** The requirements for an extension of stay for Sector-Based employment are that the applicant:

(i) entered the United Kingdom with a valid Home Office immigration employment document issued under the Sectors-Based Scheme and;

(ii) has written approval from the Home Office for the continuation of his employment under the Sectors-Based Scheme; and

(iii) meets the requirements of paragraph 135I (ii) to (vi); and

(iv) would not, as a result of the extension of stay sought, remain in the United Kingdom for Sector-Based Scheme employment to a date beyond 12 months from the date on which he was given leave to enter the United Kingdom on this occasion in this capacity.]

Note: Paragraph 135L inserted from 1 April 2004 (HC 464).

Extension of stay for Sectors-Based Scheme employment

[**135M.** An extension of stay for Sectors-Based Scheme employment may be granted for a period not exceeding the period of approved employment recommended by the Home Office provided the Secretary of State is satisfied that each of the requirements of paragraph 135L are met. An extension of stay is to be subject to a condition restricting the applicant to employment approved by the Home Office.]

Note: Paragraph 135M inserted from 1 April 2004 (HC 464).

Refusal of extension of stay for Sectors-Based Scheme employment

[**135N.** An extension of stay for Sectors-Based Scheme employment is to be refused if the Secretary of State is not satisfied that each of the requirements of paragraph 135L is met.]

Note: Paragraph 135N inserted from 1 April 2004 (HC 464).

Science and Engineering Graduates Scheme

Requirements for leave to enter as a participant in the Science and Engineering Graduates Scheme

[**135O.** The requirements to be met by a person seeking leave to enter as a participant in the Science and Engineering Graduates Scheme are that he:

(i) has successfully completed and obtained either:
 (a) a UK recognised degree (with second class honours or above), Master's degree or PhD in a subject approved by the Department for Education and Skills for the purposes of this scheme at either:
  (i) a publicly funded institution of further or higher education; or
  (ii) a bona fide private education institution which maintains satisfactory records of enrolment and attendance; or
 (b) a UK recognised Master's degree or PhD in any subject, where study for this qualification commenced on or after 1 May 2006, at an institution which is on the Department for Education and Skills' Register of Education and Training Providers, and is either:
  (i) a publicly funded institution of further or higher education; or
  (ii) a bona fide private education institution which maintains satisfactory records of enrolment and attendance; and}

(ii) intends to seek and take work during the period for which leave is granted in this capacity;

(iii) can maintain and accommodate himself and any dependants without recourse to public funds;

(iv) completed his degree, masters or PhD in the approved subject in the last 12 months;

(v) if he has previously spent time in the UK as a participant in the Science and Engineering Graduates Scheme, is not seeking leave to enter to a date beyond 12 months from the date he was first given leave to enter or remain in this capacity;

(vi) intends to leave the United Kingdom if, on expiry of his leave under this scheme, he has not been granted leave to remain in the United Kingdom in accordance with paragraphs 128–135H or 200–210H of these Rules;

(vii) has the written consent of his official sponsor to enter or remain in the United Kingdom under the Science and Engineering Graduate Scheme if his approved studies, or any studies he has subsequently undertaken, were sponsored by a government or international scholarship agency; and

(viii) holds a valid entry clearance for entry in this capacity except where he is a British National (Overseas), a British Overseas Territories citizen, a British Overseas citizen, a British protected person or a person who under the British Nationality Act 1981 is a British subject.]

Note: Paragraph 135O inserted from 25 October 2004 (Cm 6339). Subparagraph (i) substituted from 3 April 2006 (HC 1016).

Leave to enter as a participant in the Science and Engineering Graduates Scheme

[**135P.** A person seeking leave to enter the United Kingdom as a participant in the Science and Engineering Graduates Scheme may be admitted for a period not exceeding 12 months provided he is able to produce to the Immigration Officer, on arrival, a valid United Kingdom entry clearance for entry in this capacity.]

Note: Paragraph 135P inserted from 25 October 2004 (Cm 6339).

Refusal of leave to enter as a participant in the Science and Engineering Graduates Scheme

[**135Q.** Leave to enter as a participant in the Science and Engineering Graduates Scheme is to be refused if the Immigration Officer is not satisfied that each of the requirements of paragraph 135O is met.]

Note: Paragraph 135Q inserted from 25 October 2004 (Cm 6339).

Requirements for leave to remain as a participant in the Science and Engineering Graduates Scheme

[**135R.** The requirements to be met by a person seeking leave to remain as a participant in the Science and Engineering Graduates Scheme are that he:

(i) meets the requirements of paragraph 135O(i) to (vii); and

(ii) has leave to enter or remain as a student or as a participant in the Science and Engineering Graduates Scheme in accordance with paragraphs 57–69L or 135O–135T of these Rules;

(iii) would not, as a result of an extension of stay, remain in the United Kingdom as a participant in the Science and Engineering Graduates Scheme to a date beyond 12 months from the date on which he was first given leave to enter or remain in this capacity.]

Note: Paragraph 135R inserted from 25 October 2004 (Cm 6339).

Leave to remain as a participant in the Science and Engineering Graduates Scheme

[**135S.** Leave to remain as a participant in the Science and Engineering Graduates Scheme may be granted if the Secretary of State is satisfied that the applicant meets each of the requirements of paragraph 135R.]

Note: Paragraph 135S inserted from 25 October 2004 (Cm 6339).

Refusal of leave to remain as a participant in the Science and Engineering Graduates Scheme

[**135T.** Leave to remain as a participant in the Science and Engineering Graduates Scheme is to be refused if the Secretary of State is not satisfied that each of the requirements of paragraph 135R is met]

Note: Paragraph 135T inserted from 25 October 2004 (Cm 6339).

Representatives of overseas newspapers, news agencies and broadcasting organisations

Requirements for leave to enter as a representative of an overseas newspaper, news agency or broadcasting organisation

136. The requirements to be met by a person seeking leave to enter the United Kingdom as a representative of an overseas newspaper, news agency or broadcasting organisation are that he:

(i) has been engaged by that organisation outside the United Kingdom and is being posted to the United Kingdom on a long-term assignment as a representative; and
(ii) intends to work full-time as a representative of that overseas newspaper, news agency or broadcasting organisation; and
(iii) does not intend to take employment except within the terms of this paragraph; and
(iv) can maintain and accommodate himself and any dependants adequately without recourse to public funds; and
(v) holds a valid United Kingdom entry clearance for entry in this capacity.

Leave to enter as a representative of an overseas newspaper, news agency or broadcasting organisation

137. A person seeking leave to enter the United Kingdom as a representative of an overseas newspaper, news agency or broadcasting organisation may be admitted for a period not exceeding [2 years] provided he is able to produce to the Immigration Officer, on arrival, a valid United Kingdom entry clearance for entry in this capacity.

Note: Words in square brackets substituted from 3 April 2006 (HC 1016).

Refusal of leave to enter as a representative of an overseas newspaper, news agency or broadcasting organisation

138. Leave to enter as a representative of an overseas newspaper, news agency or broadcasting organisation is to be refused if a valid United Kingdom entry clearance for entry in this capacity is not produced to the Immigration Officer on arrival.

Requirements for an extension of stay as a representative of an overseas newspaper, news agency or broadcasting organisation

139. The requirements for an extension of stay as a representative of an overseas newspaper, news agency or broadcasting organisation are that the applicant:

(i) entered the United Kingdom with a valid United Kingdom entry clearance as a representative of an overseas newspaper, news agency or broadcasting organisation; and

(ii) is still engaged in the employment for which his entry clearance was granted; and
(iii) is still required for the employment in question, as certified by his employer; and
(iv) meets the requirements of paragraph 136(ii)–(iv).

Extension of stay as a representative of an overseas newspaper, news agency or broadcasting organisation

140. An extension of stay as a representative of an overseas newspaper, news agency or broadcasting organisation may be granted for a period not exceeding 3 years provided the Secretary of State is satisfied that each of the requirements of paragraph 139 is met.

Refusal of extension of stay as a representative of an overseas newspaper, news agency or broadcasting organisation

141. An extension of stay as a representative of an overseas newspaper, news agency or broadcasting organisation is to be refused if the Secretary of State is not satisfied that each of the requirements of paragraph 139 is met.

Indefinite leave to remain for a representative of an overseas newspaper, news agency or broadcasting organisation

142. Indefinite leave to remain may be granted, on application, to a representative of an overseas newspaper, news agency or broadcasting organisation provided:
(i) he has spent a continuous period of [5 years] in the United Kingdom in this capacity; and
(ii) he has met the requirements of paragraph 139 throughout the [5 year] period; and
(iii) he is still required for the employment in question, as certified by his employer.

Note: Words in square brackets substituted from 3 April 2006 (HC 1016).

Refusal of indefinite leave to remain for a representative of an overseas newspaper, news agency or broadcasting organisation

143. Indefinite leave to remain in the United Kingdom for a representative of an overseas newspaper, news agency or broadcasting organisation is to be refused if the Secretary of State is not satisfied that each of the requirements of paragraph 142 is met.

Requirements for leave to enter the United Kingdom as a Fresh Talent: Working in Scotland scheme participant

[**143A.** The requirements to be met by a person seeking leave to enter as a Fresh Talent: Working in Scotland scheme participant are that the applicant:

(i) has been awarded an HND, or a UK recognised undergraduate degree, Master's degree or PhD by either:
  (a) a Scottish publicly funded institution of further or higher education; or
  (b) a Scottish bona fide private education institution which maintains satisfactory records of enrolment and attendance; and

(ii) has lived in Scotland for an appropriate period of time whilst studying for the HND, undergraduate degree, Master's degree or PhD referred to in (i) above; and

(iii) intends to seek and take employment in Scotland during the period of leave granted under this paragraph; and

(iv) is able to maintain and accommodate himself and any dependants adequately without recourse to public funds; and

(v) has completed the HND, undergraduate degree, Master's degree or PhD referred to in (i) above in the last 12 months; and

(vi) intends to leave the United Kingdom if, on expiry of his leave under this paragraph, he has not been granted leave to remain in the United Kingdom as:
  (a) a work permit holder in accordance with paragraphs 128–135 of these Rules; or
  (b) under the highly skilled migrant programme in accordance with paragraphs 135A–135H of these Rules; or
  (c) a person intending to establish themselves in business in accordance with paragraphs 200–210 of these Rules; or
  (d) an innovator in accordance with paragraphs 210A–210H of these Rules; and

(vii) has the written consent of his official sponsor to enter or remain in the United Kingdom as a Fresh Talent: Working in Scotland scheme participant, if the studies which led to his qualification under (i) above (or any studies he has subsequently undertaken) were sponsored by a government or international scholarship agency; and

(viii) if he has previously been granted leave as either:
  (a) a Fresh Talent: Working in Scotland scheme participant in accordance with this paragraph; and/or
  (b) a participant in the Science and Engineering Graduates Scheme in accordance with paragraphs 135O–135T of these Rules

  is not seeking leave to enter under this paragraph which, when amalgamated with any previous periods of leave granted in either of these two categories, would total more than 24 months; and

(ix) holds a valid entry clearance for entry in this capacity except where he is a British National (Overseas), a British overseas territories citizen, a British Overseas citizen, a British protected person or a person who under the British Nationality Act 1981 is a British subject.]

Note: Paragraph 143A inserted from 22 June 2005 (HC 104).

Leave to enter as a Fresh Talent: Working in Scotland scheme participant

[**143B.** A person seeking leave to enter the United Kingdom as a Fresh Talent: Working in Scotland scheme participant may be admitted for a period not exceeding 24 months provided the Immigration Officer is satisfied that each of the requirements of paragraph 143A is met.]

Note: Paragraph 143B inserted from 22 June 2005 (HC 104).

Refusal of leave to enter as a Fresh Talent: Working in Scotland scheme participant

[**143C.** Leave to enter as a Fresh Talent: Working in Scotland scheme participant is to be refused if the Immigration Officer is not satisfied that each of the requirements of paragraph 143A is met.]

Note: Paragraph 143C inserted from 22 June 2005 (HC 104).

Requirements for an extension of stay as a Fresh Talent: Working in Scotland scheme participant

[**143D.** The requirements to be met by a person seeking an extension of stay as a Fresh Talent: Working in Scotland scheme participant are that the applicant:

- (i) meets the requirements of paragraph 143A (i) to (vii); and
- (ii) has leave to enter or remain in the United Kingdom as either:
  - (a) a student in accordance with paragraphs 57–69L of these Rules; or
  - (b) a participant in the Science and Engineering Graduates Scheme in accordance with paragraphs 135O–135T of these Rules; or
  - (c) a Fresh Talent: Working in Scotland scheme participant in accordance with paragraphs 143A–143F of these Rules; and
- (iii) if he has previously been granted leave as either:
  - (a) a Fresh Talent: Working in Scotland scheme participant in accordance with paragraphs 143A–143F of these Rules; and/or
  - (b) a Science and Engineering Graduates Scheme participant in accordance with paragraphs 135O–135T of these Rules is not seeking leave to remain under this paragraph which, when amalgamated with any previous periods of leave granted in either of these two categories, would total more than 24 months.]

Note: Paragraph 143D inserted from 22 June 2005 (HC 104).

Extension of stay as a Fresh Talent: Working in Scotland scheme participant

[**143E.** An extension of stay as a Fresh Talent: Working in Scotland scheme participant may be granted for a period not exceeding 24 months if the Secretary of State is satisfied that each of the requirements of paragraph 143D is met.]

Note: Paragraph 143E inserted from 22 June 2005 (HC 104).

Refusal of an extension of stay as a Fresh Talent: Working in Scotland scheme participant

[**143F.** An extension of stay as a Fresh Talent: Working in Scotland scheme participant is to be refused if the Secretary of State is not satisfied that each of the requirements of paragraph 143D is met.]

Note: Paragraph 143F inserted from 22 June 2005 (HC 104).

Representatives of overseas firms which have no branch, subsidiary or other representative in the United Kingdom (sole representatives)

Requirements for leave to enter as a sole representative

144. The requirements to be met by a person seeking leave to enter the United Kingdom as a sole representative are that he:

- (i) has been recruited and taken on as an employee outside the United Kingdom as a representative of a firm which has its headquarters and principal place of business outside the United Kingdom and which has no branch, subsidiary or other representative in the United Kingdom; and
- (ii) seeks entry to the United Kingdom as a senior employee with full authority to take operational decisions on behalf of the overseas firm for the purpose of representing it in the United Kingdom by establishing and operating a registered branch or wholly-owned subsidiary of that overseas firm; and
- (iii) intends to be employed full-time as a representative of that overseas firm; and
- (iv) is not a majority shareholder in that overseas firm; and
- (v) does not intend to take employment except within the terms of this paragraph; and
- (vi) can maintain and accommodate himself and any dependants adequately without recourse to public funds; and
- (vii) holds a valid United Kingdom entry clearance for entry in this capacity.

Leave to enter as a sole representative

145. A person seeking leave to enter the United Kingdom as a sole representative may be admitted for a period not exceeding [2 years] provided he is able to produce to the Immigration Officer, on arrival, a valid United Kingdom entry clearance for entry in this capacity.

Note: Words in square brackets substituted from 3 April 2006 (HC 1016).

Refusal of leave to enter as a sole representative

146. Leave to enter as a sole representative is to be refused if a valid United Kingdom entry clearance for entry in this capacity is not produced to the Immigration Officer on arrival.

Requirements for an extension of stay as a sole representative

147. The requirements for an extension of stay as a sole representative are that the applicant:

- (i) entered the United Kingdom with a valid United Kingdom entry clearance as a sole representative of an overseas firm: and
- (ii) can show that the overseas firm still has its headquarters and principal place of business outside the United Kingdom; and
- (iii) is employed full-time as a representative of that overseas firm and has established and is in charge of its registered branch or wholly-owned subsidiary; and
- (iv) is still required for the employment in question, as certified by his employer; and
- (v) meets the requirements of paragraph 144(iii)–(vi).

Extension of stay as a sole representative

148. An extension of stay not exceeding 3 years as a sole representative may be granted provided the Secretary of State is satisfied that each of the requirements of paragraph 147 is met.

Refusal of extension of stay as a sole representative

149. An extension of stay as a sole representative is to be refused if the Secretary of State is not satisfied that each of the requirements of paragraph 147 is met.

Indefinite leave to remain for a sole representative

150. Indefinite leave to remain may be granted, on application, to a sole representative provided:

- (i) he has spent a continuous period of [5 years] in the United Kingdom in this capacity; and
- (ii) he has met the requirements of paragraph 147 throughout the [5 year] period; and

(iii) he is still required for the employment in question, as certified by his employer.

Note: Words in square brackets substituted from 3 April 2006 (HC 1016).

Refusal of indefinite leave to remain for a sole representative

151. Indefinite leave to remain in the United Kingdom for a sole representative is to be refused if the Secretary of State is not satisfied that each of the requirements of paragraph 150 is met.

Private servants in diplomatic households

Requirements for leave to enter as a private servant in a diplomatic household

152. The requirements to be met by a person seeking leave to enter the United Kingdom as a private servant in a diplomatic household are that he:

(i) is aged 18 or over; and
(ii) is employed as a private servant in the household of a member of staff of a diplomatic or consular mission who enjoys diplomatic privileges and immunity within the meaning of the Vienna Convention on Diplomatic and Consular Relations or a member of the family forming part of the household of such a person; and
(iii) intends to work full-time as a private servant within the terms of this paragraph; and
(iv) does not intend to take employment except within the terms of this paragraph; and
(v) can maintain and accommodate himself and any dependants adequately without recourse to public funds; and
(vi) holds a valid United Kingdom entry clearance for entry in this capacity.

Leave to enter as a private servant in a diplomatic household

153. A person seeking leave to enter the United Kingdom as a private servant in a diplomatic household may be given leave to enter for a period not exceeding 12 months provided he is able to produce to the Immigration Officer, on arrival, a valid United Kingdom entry clearance for entry in this capacity.

Refusal of leave to enter as a private servant in a diplomatic household

154. Leave to enter as a private servant in a diplomatic household is to be refused if a valid United Kingdom entry clearance for entry in this capacity is not produced to the Immigration Officer on arrival.

Requirements for an extension of stay as a private servant in a diplomatic household

155. The requirements for an extension of stay as a private servant in a diplomatic household are that the applicant:

(i) entered the United Kingdom with a valid United Kingdom entry clearance as a private servant in a diplomatic household; and

(ii) is still engaged in the employment for which his entry clearance was granted; and

(iii) is still required for the employment in question, as certified by the employer; and

(iv) meets the requirements of paragraph 152(iii)–(v).

Extension of stay as a private servant in a diplomatic household

156. An extension of stay as a private servant in a diplomatic household may be granted for a period not exceeding 12 months [at a time] provided the Secretary of State is satisfied that each of the requirements of paragraph 155 is met.

Note: Words in square brackets inserted from 3 April 2006 (HC 1016).

Refusal of extension of stay as a private servant in a diplomatic household

157. An extension of stay as a private servant in a diplomatic household is to be refused if the Secretary of State is not satisfied that each of the requirements of paragraph 155 is met.

Indefinite leave to remain for a servant in a diplomatic household

158. Indefinite leave to remain may be granted, on application, to a private servant in a diplomatic household provided:

(i) he has spent a continuous period of [5 years] in the United Kingdom in this capacity; and

(ii) he has met the requirements of paragraph 155 throughout the [5 year] period; and

(iii) he is still required for the employment in question, as certified by his employer.

Note: Words in square brackets inserted from 3 April 2006 (HC 1016).

Refusal of indefinite leave to remain for a servant in a diplomatic household

159. Indefinite leave to remain in the United Kingdom for a private servant in a diplomatic household is to be refused if the Secretary of State is not satisfied that each of the requirements of paragraph 158 is met.

Domestic Workers in Private Households

Requirements for leave to enter as a domestic worker in a private household

[**159A.** The requirements to be met by a person seeking leave to enter the United Kingdom as a domestic worker in a private household are that he:

(i) is aged 18–65 inclusive;

(ii) has been employed as a domestic worker for one year or more immediately prior to application for entry clearance under the same roof as his employer or in a household that the employer uses for himself on a regular basis and where there is evidence that there is a connection between employer and employee;

(iii) that he intends to travel to the United Kingdom in the company of his employer, his employer's spouse [or civil partner] or his employer's minor child;

(iv) intends to work full time as a domestic worker under the same roof as his employer or in a household that the employer uses for himself on a regular basis and where there is evidence that there is a connection between employer and employee;

(v) does not intend to take employment except within the terms of this paragraph; and

(vi) can maintain and accommodate himself adequately without recourse to public funds; and

(vii) holds a valid United Kingdom entry clearance for entry in this capacity.

Note: Paragraph 159A inserted from 18 September 2002 (Cm 5597). Words in square brackets in sub-para (iii) inserted from 5 December 2005 (HC 582).

Leave to enter as a domestic worker in a private household

[**159B.** A person seeking leave to enter the United Kingdom as a domestic worker in a private household may be given leave to enter for that purpose for a period not exceeding 12 months [at a time] provided he is able to produce to the Immigration Officer, on arrival, a valid United Kingdom entry clearance for entry in this capacity.]

Note: Paragraph 159B inserted from 18 September 2002 (Cm 5597).

Refusal of leave to enter as a domestic worker in a private household

[**159C.** Leave to enter as a domestic worker in a private household is to be refused if a valid United Kingdom entry clearance for entry in this capacity is not produced to the Immigration Officer on arrival.]

Note: Paragraph 159C inserted from 18 September 2002 (Cm 5597).

Requirements for extension of stay as a domestic worker in a private household

[**159D.** The requirements for an extension of stay as a domestic worker in a private household are that the applicant:

(i) entered the United Kingdom with a valid United Kingdom entry clearance as a domestic worker in a private household; and

(ii) has continued to be employed for the duration of his leave as a domestic worker in a private household; and

(iii) continues to be required for employment for the period of the extension sought as a domestic worker in a private household within the terms of paragraph 159A as certified by his current employer; and

(iv) meets each of the requirements of paragraph 159A(i) to (vi).]

Note: Paragraph 159D inserted from 18 September 2002 (Cm 5597).

Extension of stay as a domestic worker in a private household

[**159E.** An extension of stay as a domestic worker in a private household may be granted for a period not exceeding 12 months {at a time} provided the Secretary of State is satisfied that each of the requirements of paragraph 159D is met.]

Note: Paragraph 159E inserted from 18 September 2002 (Cm 5597). Words in curly brackets inserted from 3 April 2006 (HC 1016).

Refusal of extension of stay as a domestic worker in a private household

[**159F.** An extension of stay as a domestic worker may be refused if the Secretary of State is not satisfied that each of the requirements of paragraph 159D is met.]

Note: Paragraph 159F inserted from 18 September 2002 (Cm 5597).

Indefinite leave to remain for a domestic worker in a private household

[**159G.** Indefinite leave to remain may be granted, on application, to a domestic worker in a private household provided that:

(i) he has spent a continuous period of [5 years] in the United Kingdom employed in this capacity; and

(ii) he has met the requirements of paragraph 159A throughout the [5 year] period; and

(iii) he is still required for employment as a domestic worker in a private household, as certified by the current employer.]

Note: Paragraph 159G inserted from 18 September 2002 (Cm 5597). Words in square brackets in sub-paras (i) and (ii) substituted from 3 April 2006 (HC 1016).

Refusal of indefinite leave to remain for a domestic worker in a private household

[**159H.** Indefinite leave to remain in the United Kingdom for a domestic worker in a private household is to be refused if the Secretary of State is not satisfied that each of the requirements of paragraph 159G is met.]

Note: Paragraph 159H inserted from 18 September 2002 (Cm 5597).

Overseas government employees

Requirements for leave to enter as an overseas government employee

160. For the purposes of these Rules an overseas government employee means a person coming for employment by an overseas government or employed by the United Nations Organisation or other international organisation of which the United Kingdom is a member.

161. The requirements to be met by a person seeking leave to enter the United Kingdom as an overseas government employee are that he:

- (i) is able to produce either a valid United Kingdom entry clearance for entry in this capacity or satisfactory documentary evidence of his status as an overseas government employee; and
- (ii) intends to work full time for the government or organisation concerned; and
- (iii) does not intend to take employment except within the terms of this paragraph; and
- (iv) can maintain and accommodate himself and any dependants adequately without recourse to public funds.

Leave to enter as an overseas government employee

162. A person seeking leave to enter the United Kingdom as an overseas government employee may be given leave to enter for a period not exceeding [2 years], provided he is able, on arrival, to produce to the Immigration Officer a valid United Kingdom entry clearance for entry in this capacity or satisfy the Immigration Officer that each of the requirements of paragraph 161 is met.

Note: Words in square brackets substituted from 3 April 2006 (HC 1016).

Refusal of leave to enter as an overseas government employee

163. Leave to enter as an overseas government employee is to be refused if a valid United Kingdom entry clearance for entry in this capacity is not produced to the Immigration Officer on arrival or if the Immigration Officer is not satisfied that each of the requirements of paragraph 161 is met.

Requirements for an extension of stay as an overseas government employee

164. The requirements to be met by a person seeking an extension of stay as an overseas government employee are that the applicant:

(i) was given leave to enter the United Kingdom under paragraph 162 as an overseas government employee; and

(ii) is still engaged in the employment in question; and

(iii) is still required for the employment in question, as certified by the employer; and

(iv) meets the requirements of paragraph 161(ii)–(iv).

Extension of stay as an overseas government employee

165. An extension of stay as an overseas government employee may be granted for a period not exceeding 3 years provided the Secretary of State is satisfied that each of the requirements of paragraph 164 is met.

Refusal of extension of stay as an overseas government employee

166. An extension of stay as an overseas government employee is to be refused if the Secretary of State is not satisfied that each of the requirements of paragraph 164 is met.

Indefinite leave to remain for an overseas government employee

167. Indefinite leave to remain may be granted, on application, to an overseas government employee provided:

(i) he has spent a continuous period of [5 years] in the United Kingdom in this capacity; and

(ii) he has met the requirements of paragraph 164 throughout the [5 year] period; and

(iii) he is still required for the employment in question, as certified by his employer.

Note: Words in square brackets substituted from 3 April 2006 (HC 1016).

Refusal of indefinite leave to remain for an overseas government employee

168. Indefinite leave to remain in the United Kingdom for an overseas government employee is to be refused if the Secretary of State is not satisfied that each of the requirements of paragraph 167 is met.

Ministers of religion, missionaries and members of religious orders

169. For the purposes of these Rules:

(i) a minister of religion means a religious functionary whose main regular duties comprise the leading of a congregation in performing the rites and rituals of the faith and in preaching the essentials of the creed;
(ii) a missionary means a person who is directly engaged in spreading a religious doctrine and whose work is not in essence administrative or clerical;
(iii) a member of a religious order means a person who is coming to live in a community run by that order.

Requirements for leave to enter as a minister of religion, missionary or member of a religious order

170. The requirements to be met by a person seeking leave to enter the United Kingdom as a minister of religion, missionary or member of a religious order are that he:

(i) (a) if seeking leave to enter as a minister of religion has either been working for at least one year as a minister of religion [in any of the 5 years immediately prior to the date on which the application is made] or, where ordination is prescribed by a religious faith as the sole means of entering the ministry, has been ordained as a minister or religion following at least one year's full-time or two years' part-time training for the ministry; or
(b) if seeking leave to enter as a missionary has been trained as a missionary or has worked as a missionary and is being sent to the United Kingdom by an overseas organisation; or
(c) if seeking leave to enter as a member of a religious order is coming to live in a community maintained by the religious order of which he is a member and, if intending to teach, does not intend to do so save at an establishment maintained by his order; and
(ii) intends to work full-time as a minister of religion, missionary or for the religious order of which he is a member; and
(iii) does not intend to take employment except within the terms of this paragraph; and
(iv) can maintain and accommodate himself and any dependants adequately without recourse to public funds; and
[(iva) if seeking entry as a minister of religion, can produce an International English Language Testing System Certificate issued to him to certify that he has achieved level 4 competence in spoken English and that is dated not more than two years prior to the date on which the application is made.]
(v) holds a valid United Kingdom entry clearance for entry in this capacity.

Note: Words in square brackets in sub-para (i)(a) and sub-para (iva), inserted from 23 August 2004 (Cm 6297).

Leave to enter as a minister of religion, missionary or member of a religious order

171. A person seeking leave to enter the United Kingdom as a minister of religion, missionary or member of a religious order may be admitted for a period not exceeding [2 years] provided he is able to produce to the Immigration Officer, on arrival, a valid United Kingdom entry clearance for entry in this capacity.

Note: Words in square brackets substituted from 3 April 2006 (HC 1016).

Refusal of leave to enter as a minister of religion, missionary or member of a religious order

172. Leave to enter as a minister or religion, missionary or member of a religious order is to be refused if a valid United Kingdom entry clearance for entry in this capacity is not produced to the Immigration Officer on arrival.

[Requirements for an extension of stay as a minister of religion where entry to the United Kingdom was granted in that capacity]

173. The requirements for an extension of stay as a minister of religion [where entry to the United Kingdom was granted in that capacity,] missionary or member of a religion order are that the applicant:

(i) entered the United Kingdom with a valid United Kingdom entry clearance as a minister of religion, missionary or member of a religious order; and

(ii) is still engaged in the employment for which his entry clearance was granted; and

(iii) is still required for the employment in question as certified by the leadership of his congregation, his employer or the head of his religious order; and

[(iv) (a) if he entered the United Kingdom as a minister of religion in accordance with sub-paragraph (i) prior to 23 August 2004 or as a missionary or member of a religious order meets the requirements of paragraph 170(ii)–(iv);

(b) if he entered the United Kingdom as a minister of religion in accordance with sub-paragraph (i) after 23 August 2004, or was granted entry clearance in accordance with paragraph 174B after that date, meets the requirements of paragraph 170(ii)–(iva); or[*sic*]]

Note: Heading and para (iv) substituted, and words inserted, from 23 August 2004 (Cm 6297).

Extension of stay as a minister of religion, missionary or member of a religious order

174. An extension of stay as a minister of religion, missionary or member of a religious order may be granted for a period not exceeding 3 years provided the

Secretary of State is satisfied that each of the requirements of paragraph 173 is met.

[Requirements for an extension of stay as a minister of religion where entry to the United Kingdom was not granted in that capacity]

[**174A.** The requirements for an extension of stay as a minister of religion for an applicant who did not enter the United Kingdom in that capacity are that he:

(i) entered the United Kingdom, or was given an extension of stay, in accordance with these Rules, except as a minister of religion or as a visitor under paragraphs 40–56 of these Rules, and has spent a continuous period of at least 12 months here pursuant to that leave immediately prior to the application being made; and

(ii) has either been working for at least one year as a minister of religion in any of the 5 years immediately prior to the date on which the application is made (provided that, when doing so, he was not in breach of a condition of any subsisting leave to enter or remain) or, where ordination is prescribed by a religious faith as the sole means of entering the ministry, has been ordained as a minister of religion following at least one year's full-time or two years' part-time training for the ministry; and

(iii) is imminently to be appointed, or has been appointed, to a position as a minister of religion in the United Kingdom and is suitable for such a position, as certified by the leadership of his prospective congregation; and

(iv) meets the requirements of paragraph 170(ii)–(iva).]

Note: Paragraph 174A inserted from 23 August 2004 (Cm 6297).

[Extension of stay as a minister of religion where leave to enter was not granted in that capacity]

[**174B.** An extension of stay as a minister of religion may be granted for a period not exceeding {3 years at a time} provided the Secretary of State is satisfied that each of the requirements of paragraph 174A is met.]

Note: Paragraph 174B inserted from 23 August 2004 (Cm 6297). Words in curly brackets inserted from 3 April 2006 (HC 1016).

Refusal of extension of stay as a minister of religion, missionary or member of a religious order

175. An extension of stay as a minister of religion, missionary or member of a religious order is to be refused if the Secretary of State is not satisfied that each of the requirements of paragraph 173 [or 174A] is met.

Note: Words in square brackets inserted from 23 August 2004 (Cm 6297).

Indefinite leave to remain for a minister of religion, missionary or member of a religious order

176. Indefinite leave to remain may be granted, on application, to a person admitted as a minister of religion, missionary or member of a religious order provided:

(i) he has spent a continuous period of {5 years} in the United Kingdom in this capacity; and

(ii) he has met the requirements of paragraph 173 [or 174A] throughout the {5 year} period; and

(iii) he is still required for the employment in question as certified by the leadership of his congregation, his employer or the head of the religious order to which he belongs.

Note: Words in square brackets inserted from 23 August 2004 (Cm 6297). Words in curly brackets in sub-para (i) substituted from 3 April (HC 1016).

Refusal of indefinite leave to remain for a minister of religion, missionary or member of a religious order

177. Indefinite leave to remain in the United Kingdom for a minister of religion, missionary or member of a religious order is to be refused if the Secretary of State is not satisfied that each of the requirements of paragraph 176 is met.

[**177A.** For the purposes of these Rules:

(i) a visiting religious worker means a person coming to the UK for a short period to perform religious duties at one or more locations in the UK;

(ii) a religious worker in a non-pastoral role means a person employed in the UK by the faith he is coming here to work for, whose duties include performing religious rites within the religious community, but not preaching to a congregation.]

Note: Paragraph 177A inserted from 9 January 2006 (HC 769).

Requirements for leave to enter the United Kingdom as a visiting religious worker or a religious worker in a non-pastoral role

[**177B.** The requirements to be met by a person seeking leave to enter as a visiting religious worker or a religious worker in a non-pastoral role are that the applicant:

(i) (a) if seeking leave to enter as a visiting religious worker:

(i) is an established religious worker based overseas; and

(ii) submits a letter(s) from a senior member or senior representative of one or more local religious communities in the UK confirming that he is invited to perform religious duties as a visiting religious worker at one or more locations in the UK and confirming the expected duration of that employment; and

(iii) if he has been granted leave as a visiting religious worker in the last 12 months, is not seeking leave to enter which, when amalgamated with his previous periods of leave in this category in the last 12 months, would total more than 6 months; or

(b) if seeking leave to enter as a religious worker in a non-pastoral role:

(i) has at least one year of full time training or work experience, or a period of part time training or work experience equivalent to one year full time training or work experience, accrued in the five years preceding the application in the faith with which he has employment in the UK; and

(ii) can show that, at the time of his application, at least one full-time member of staff of the local religious community which the applicant is applying to join in the UK has a sufficient knowledge of English; and

(iii) submits a letter from a senior member or senior representative of the local religious community which has invited him to the UK, confirming that he has been offered employment as religious worker in a non-pastoral role in that religious community, and confirming the duration of that employment; and

(ii) does not intend to take employment except as a visiting religious worker or religious worker in a non-pastoral role, whichever is the basis of his application; and

(iii) does not intend to undertake employment as a Minister of Religion, Missionary or Member of a Religious Order, as described in paragraphs 169-177 of these Rules; and

(iv) is able to maintain and accommodate himself and any dependants without recourse to public funds, or will, with any dependants, be maintained and accommodated adequately by the religious community employing him; and

(v) intends to leave the UK at the end of his leave in this category; and

(vi) holds a valid entry clearance for entry in this capacity except where he is a British National (Overseas), a British overseas territories citizen, a British Overseas citizen, a British protected person or a person who under the British Nationality Act 1981 is a British subject.]

Note: Paragraph 177B inserted from 9 January 2006 (HC 769).

Leave to enter as a visiting religious worker or a religious worker in a non-pastoral role

[177C. Leave to enter the United Kingdom as a visiting religious worker or a religious worker in a non-pastoral role may be granted:

(a) as a visiting religious worker, for a period not exceeding 6 months; or
(b) as a religious worker in a non-pastoral role, for a period not exceeding 12 months; provided the Immigration Officer is satisfied that each of the requirements of paragraph 177B is met.]

Note: Paragraph 177C inserted from 9 January 2006 (HC 769).

Refusal of leave to enter as a visiting religious worker or a religious worker in a non-pastoral role

[**177D.** Leave to enter as a visiting religious worker or a religious worker in a non-pastoral role is to be refused if the Immigration Officer is not satisfied that each of the requirements of paragraph 177B is met.]

Note: Paragraph 177D inserted from 9 January 2006 (HC 769).

Requirements for an extension of stay as a visiting religious worker or a religious worker in a non-pastoral role

[**177E.** The requirements to be met by a person seeking an extension of stay as a visiting religious worker or a religious worker in a non-pastoral role are that the applicant:

(i) entered the United Kingdom with a valid entry clearance in this capacity or was given leave to enter as a visiting religious worker or a religious worker in a non-pastoral role; and
(ii) intends to continue employment as a visiting religious worker or a religious worker in a non-pastoral role; and
(iii) if seeking an extension of stay as a visiting religious worker:
  (a) meets the requirement of paragraph 177B(i)(a)(i) above; and
  (b) submits a letter from a senior member or senior representative of one or more local religious communities in the UK confirming that he is still wanted to perform religious duties as a visiting religious worker at one or more locations in the UK and confirming the expected duration of that employment; and
  (c) would not, as the result of an extension of stay, be granted leave as a visiting religious worker which, when amalgamated with his previous periods of leave in this category in the last 12 months, would total more than 6 months; or
(iv) if seeking an extension of stay as a religious worker in a non-pastoral role:
  (a) meets the requirements of paragraph 177B(i)(b)(i) and (ii); and
  (b) submits a letter from a senior member or senior representative of the local religious community for which he works in the UK confirming that his employment as a religious worker in a non-pastoral role in that

religious community will continue, and confirming the duration of that employment; and

(c) would not, as the result of an extension of stay, remain in the UK for a period of more than 24 months as a religious worker in a non-pastoral role; and

(v) meets the requirements of paragraph 177B (ii) to (v); and [*sic*]]

Note: Paragraph 177E inserted from 9 January 2006 (HC 769).

Extension of stay as a visiting religious worker or a religious worker in a non-pastoral role

[177F. An extension of stay as a visiting religious worker or a religious worker in a non-pastoral role may be granted:

(a) as a visiting religious worker, for a period not exceeding 6 months; or

(b) as a religious worker in a non-pastoral role, for a period not exceeding 24 months;

if the Secretary of State is satisfied that each of the requirements of paragraph 177E is met.]

Note: Paragraph 177F inserted from 9 January 2006 (HC 769).

Refusal of an extension of stay as a visiting religious worker or a religious worker in a non-pastoral role

[**177G.** An extension of stay as a visiting religious worker or a religious worker in a non-pastoral role is to be refused if the Secretary of State is not satisfied that each of the requirements of paragraph 177E is met.]

Note: Paragraph 177G inserted from 9 January 2006 (HC 769).

Airport-based operational ground staff of overseas-owned airlines

Requirements for leave to enter the United Kingdom as a member of the operational ground staff of an overseas-owned airline

178. The requirements to be met by a person seeking leave to enter the United Kingdom as a member of the operational ground staff of an overseas-owned airline are that he:

(i) has been transferred to the United Kingdom by an overseas-owned airline operating services to and from the United Kingdom to take up duty at an international airport as station manager, security manager or technical manager; and

(ii) intends to work full-time for the airline concerned; and

(iii) does not intend to take employment except within the terms of this paragraph; and
(iv) can maintain and accommodate himself and any dependants without recourse to public funds; and
(v) holds a valid United Kingdom entry clearance for entry in this capacity.

Leave to enter as a member of the operational ground staff of an overseas-owned airline

179. A person seeking leave to enter the United Kingdom as a member of the operational ground staff of an overseas-owned airline may be given leave to enter for a period not exceeding [2 years], provided he is able to produce to the Immigration Officer, on arrival, a valid United Kingdom entry clearance for entry in this capacity.

Note: Words in square brackets substituted from 3 April 2006 (HC 1016).

Refusal of leave to enter as a member of the operational ground staff of an overseas-owned airline

180. Leave to enter as a member of the operational ground staff of an overseas-owned airline is to be refused if a valid United Kingdom entry clearance for entry in this capacity is not produced to the Immigration Officer on arrival.

Requirements for an extension of stay as a member of the operational ground staff of an overseas-owned airline

181. The requirements to be met by a person seeking an extension of stay as a member of the operational ground staff of an overseas-owned airline are that the applicant:
(i) entered the United Kingdom with a valid United Kingdom entry clearance as a member of the operational ground staff of an overseas-owned airline; and
(ii) is still engaged in the employment for which entry was granted; and
(iii) is still required for the employment in question, as certified by the employer; and
(iv) meets the requirements of paragraph 178(ii)–(iv).

Extension of stay as a member of the operational ground staff of an overseas-owned airline

182. An extension of stay as a member of the operational ground staff of an overseas-owned airline may be granted for a period not exceeding 3 years, provided the Secretary of State is satisfied that each of the requirements of paragraph 181 is met.

Refusal of extension of stay as a member of the operational ground staff of an overseas-owned airline

183. An extension of stay as a member of the operational ground staff of an overseas-owned airline is to be refused if the Secretary of State is not satisfied that each of the requirements of paragraph 181 is met.

Indefinite leave to remain for a member of the operational ground staff of an overseas-owned airline

184. Indefinite leave to remain may be granted, on application, to a member of the operational ground staff of an overseas-owned airline provided:

(i) he has spent a continuous period of [5 years] in the United Kingdom in this capacity; and

(ii) he has met the requirements of paragraph 181 throughout the [5 year] period; and

(iii) he is still required for the employment in question, as certified by the employer.

Note: Words in square brackets substituted from 3 April 2006 (HC 1016).

Refusal of indefinite leave to remain for a member of the operational ground staff of an overseas-owned airline

185. Indefinite leave to remain in the United Kingdom for a member of the operational ground staff of an overseas-owned airline is to be refused if the Secretary of State is not satisfied that each of the requirements of paragraph 184 is met.

Persons with United Kingdom ancestry

Requirements for leave to enter on the grounds of United Kingdom ancestry

186. The requirements to be met by a person seeking leave to enter the United Kingdom on the grounds of his United Kingdom ancestry are that he:

(i) is a Commonwealth citizen; and

(ii) is aged 17 or over; and

(iii) is able to provide proof that one of his grandparents was born in the United Kingdom and Islands [and that any such grandparent is the applicant's blood grandparent or grandparent by reason of an adoption recognised by the laws of the United Kingdom relating to adoption]; and

(iv) is able to work and intends to take or seek employment in the United Kingdom; and

(v) will be able to maintain and accommodate himself and any dependants adequately without recourse to public funds; and

(vi) holds a valid United Kingdom entry clearance for entry in this capacity.

Note: Words in square brackets in para 186(iii) inserted from 25 August 2003 (Cm 5949).

Leave to enter the United Kingdom on the grounds of United Kingdom ancestry

187. A person seeking leave to enter the United Kingdom on the grounds of his United Kingdom ancestry may be given leave to enter for a period not exceeding [5 years] provided he is able to produce to the Immigration Officer, on arrival, a valid United Kingdom entry clearance for entry in this capacity.

Note: Words in square brackets substituted from 3 April 2006 (HC 1016).

Refusal of leave to enter on the grounds of United Kingdom ancestry

188. Leave to enter the United Kingdom on the grounds of United Kingdom ancestry is to be refused if a valid United Kingdom entry clearance for entry in this capacity is not produced to the Immigration Officer on arrival.

Requirements for an extension of stay on the grounds of United Kingdom ancestry

[**189.** The requirements to be met by a person seeking an extension of stay on the grounds of United Kingdom ancestry are that:

(i) he is able to meet each of the requirements of paragraph 186 (i)–(v); and

(ii) he was admitted to the United Kingdom on the grounds of United Kingdom ancestry in accordance with paragraphs 186 to 188 or has been granted an extension of stay in this capacity.]

Note: Paragraph 189 substituted from 25 October 2004 (Cm 1112).

Extension of stay on the grounds of United Kingdom ancestry

190. An extension of stay on the grounds of United Kingdom ancestry may be granted for a period not exceeding {5 years} provided the Secretary of State is satisfied that each of the requirements of paragraph [189] is met.

Note: Words in square brackets substituted from 25 October 2004 (Cm 1112). Words in curly brackets substituted from 3 April 2006 (HC 1016).

Refusal of extension of stay on the grounds of United Kingdom ancestry

191. An extension of stay on the grounds of United Kingdom ancestry is to be refused if the Secretary of State is not satisfied that each of the requirements of paragraph [189] is met.

Note: Words in square brackets substituted from 25 October 2004 (Cm 1112).

Indefinite leave to remain on the grounds of United Kingdom ancestry

192. Indefinite leave to remain may be granted, on application, to a Commonwealth citizen with a United Kingdom born grandparent provided:

(i) he meets the requirements of paragraph 186(i)–(v); and

(ii) he has spent a continuous period of [5 years] in the United Kingdom in this capacity.

Note: Words in square brackets substituted from 3 April 2006 (HC 1016).

Refusal of indefinite leave to remain on the grounds of United Kingdom ancestry

193. Indefinite leave to remain in the United Kingdom on the grounds of a United Kingdom born grandparent is to be refused if the Secretary of State is not satisfied that each of the requirements of paragraph 192 is met.

Spouses [or civil partners] of persons with limited leave to enter or remain under paragraph 128–193

Requirements for leave to enter or remain as the spouse [or civil partner] of a person with limited leave to enter or remain in the United Kingdom under paragraphs 128–193

194. The requirements to be met by a person seeking leave to enter or remain in the United Kingdom as the spouse [or civil partner] of a person with limited leave to enter or remain in the United Kingdom under paragraphs 128–193 [but not paragraphs 135I–135K] are that:

(i) the applicant is married to [or the civil partner of] a person with limited leave to enter or remain in the United Kingdom under paragraphs 128–193 [but not paragraphs 135I–135K]; and

(ii) each of the parties intends to live with the other as his or her spouse [or civil partner] during the applicant's stay and the marriage [or civil partnership] is subsisting; and

(iii) there will be adequate accommodation for the parties and any dependants without recourse to public funds in accommodation which they own or occupy exclusively; and

(iv) the parties will be able to maintain themselves and any dependants adequately without recourse to public funds; and

(v) the applicant does not intend to stay in the United Kingdom beyond any period of leave granted to his spouse [or civil partner]; and

(vi) if seeking leave to enter, the applicant holds a valid United Kingdom entry clearance for entry in this capacity or, if seeking leave to remain, was admitted with a valid United Kingdom entry clearance for entry in this capacity.

Note: Words in square brackets inserted from 30 May 2003 (Cm 5829). References to civil partnership inserted from 5 December 2005 (HC 582).

Leave to enter or remain as the spouse [or civil partner] of a person with limited leave to enter or remain in the United Kingdom under paragraphs 128–193

195. A person seeking leave to enter or remain in the United Kingdom as the spouse [or civil partner] of a person with limited leave to enter or remain in the United Kingdom under paragraphs 128–193 [but not paragraphs 135I–135K] may be given leave to enter or remain in the United Kingdom for a period of leave not in excess of that granted to the person with limited leave to enter or remain under paragraphs 128–193 [but not paragraphs 135I–135K] provided that, in relation to an application for leave to enter, he is able, on arrival, to produce to the Immigration Officer a valid United Kingdom entry clearance for entry in this capacity or, in the case of an application for limited leave to remain, he was admitted with a valid United Kingdom entry clearance for entry in this capacity and is able to satisfy the Secretary of State that each of the requirements of paragraph 194(i)–(v) is met. An application for indefinite leave to remain in this category may be granted provided the applicant was admitted with a valid United Kingdom entry clearance for entry in this capacity and is able to satisfy the Secretary of State that each of the requirements of paragraph 194(i)–(v) is met and provided indefinite leave to remain is, at the same time, being granted to the person with limited leave to enter or remain under paragraphs 128–193 [but not paragraphs 135I–135K].

Note: Words in square brackets inserted from 30 May 2003 (Cm 5829). References to civil partnership inserted from 5 December 2005 (HC 582).

Refusal of leave to enter or remain as the spouse [or civil partner] of a person with limited leave to enter or remain in the United Kingdom under paragraphs 128–193

196. Leave to enter or remain in the United Kingdom as the spouse [or civil partner] of a person with limited leave to enter or remain in the United Kingdom under paragraphs 128–193 [but not paragraphs 135I–135K] is to be refused if, in relation to an application for leave to enter, a valid United Kingdom entry clearance for entry in this capacity is not produced to the Immigration Officer on arrival or, in the case of an application for limited leave to remain, if the applicant was not admitted with a valid United Kingdom entry clearance for entry in this capacity or is unable to satisfy the Secretary of State that each of the requirements of paragraph 194(i)–(v) is met. An application for indefinite leave to remain in this category is to be refused if the applicant was not admitted with a valid United Kingdom entry clearance for entry in this capacity or is unable to satisfy the

Secretary of State that each of the requirements of paragraph 194(i)–(v) is met or if indefinite leave to remain is not, at the same time, being granted to the person with limited leave to enter or remain under paragraphs 128–193 [but not paragraphs 135I–135K].

Note: Words in square brackets inserted from 30 May 2003 (Cm 5829). References to civil partnership inserted from 5 December 2005 (HC 582).

Children of persons with limited leave to enter or remain in the United Kingdom under paragraphs 128–193

Requirements for leave to enter or remain as the child of a person with limited leave to enter or remain in the United Kingdom under paragraphs 128–193

197. The requirements to be met by a person seeking leave to enter or remain in the United Kingdom as a child of a person with limited leave to enter or remain in the United Kingdom under paragraphs 128–193 [but not paragraphs 135I–135K] are that:

(i) he is the child of a parent with limited leave to enter or remain in the United Kingdom under paragraphs 128–193 [but not paragraphs 135I–135K]; and

(ii) he is under the age of 18 or has current leave to enter or remain in this capacity; and

(iii) he is unmarried [and is not a civil partner], has not formed an independent family unit and is not leading an independent life; and

(iv) he can and will be maintained and accommodated adequately without recourse to public funds in accommodation which his parent(s) own or occupy exclusively; and

(v) he will not stay in the United Kingdom beyond any period of leave granted to his parent(s); and

(vi) both parents are being or have been admitted to or allowed to remain in the United Kingdom save where:

(a) the parent he is accompanying or joining is his sole surviving parent; or

(b) the parent he is accompanying or joining has had sole responsibility for his upbringing; or

(c) there are serious and compelling family or other considerations which make exclusion from the United Kingdom undesirable and suitable arrangements have been made for his care; and

(vii) if seeking leave to enter, he holds a valid United Kingdom entry clearance for entry in this capacity or, if seeking leave to remain, was admitted with a valid United Kingdom entry clearance for entry in this capacity.

Note: Words in square brackets inserted from 30 May 2003 (Cm 5829). Words in square brackets in sub-para (iii) inserted from 5 December 2006 (HC 582).

Leave to enter or remain as the child of a person with limited leave to enter or remain in the United Kingdom under paragraphs 128–193

198. A person seeking leave to enter or remain in the United Kingdom as the child of a person with limited leave to enter or remain in the United Kingdom under paragraphs 128–193 [but not paragraphs 135I–135K] may be given leave to enter or remain in the United Kingdom for a period of leave not in excess of that granted to the person with limited leave to enter or remain under paragraphs 128–193 [but not paragraphs 135I–135K] provided that, in relation to an application for leave to enter, he is able to produce to the Immigration Officer, on arrival, a valid United Kingdom entry clearance for entry in this capacity or, in the case of an application for limited leave to remain, he was admitted with a valid United Kingdom entry clearance for entry in this capacity and is able to satisfy the Secretary of State that each of the requirements of paragraph 197(i)–(vi) is met. An application for indefinite leave to remain in this category may be granted provided the applicant was admitted with a valid United Kingdom entry clearance for entry in this capacity and is able to satisfy the Secretary of State that each of the requirements of paragraph 197(i)–(vi) is met and provided indefinite leave to remain is, at the same time, being granted to the person with limited leave to enter or remain under paragraphs 128–193 [but not paragraphs 135I–135K].

Note: Words in square brackets inserted from 30 May 2003 (Cm 5829).

Refusal of leave to enter or remain as the child of a person with limited leave to enter or remain in the United Kingdom under paragraphs 128–193.

199. Leave to enter or remain in the United Kingdom as the child of a person with limited leave to enter or remain in the United Kingdom under paragraphs 128–193 [but not paragraphs 135I–135K] is to be refused if, in relation to an application for leave to enter, a valid United Kingdom entry clearance for entry in this capacity is not produced to the Immigration Officer on arrival or, in the case of an application for limited leave to remain, if the applicant was not admitted with a valid United Kingdom entry clearance for entry in this capacity or is unable to satisfy the Secretary of State that each of the requirements of paragraph 197(i)–(vi) is met. An application for indefinite leave to remain in this category is to be refused if the applicant was not admitted with a valid United Kingdom entry clearance for entry in this capacity or is unable to satisfy the Secretary of State that each of the requirements of paragraph 197(i)–(vi) is met or if indefinite leave to remain is not, at the same time, being granted to the person with limited leave to enter or remain under paragraphs 128–193 [but not paragraphs 135I–135K].

Note: Words in square brackets inserted from 30 May 2003 (Cm 5829).

Multiple entry work permit employment

Requirements for leave to enter for Multiple Entry work permit employment

[**199A.** The requirements to be met by a person coming to the United Kingdom to seek or take Multiple Entry work permit employment are that he:

(i) holds a valid work permit;
(ii) is not of an age which puts him outside the limits for employment;
(iii) is capable of undertaking the employment specified in the work permit;
(iv) does not intend to take employment except as specified in his work permit;
(v) is able to maintain and accommodate himself adequately without recourse to public funds; and
(vi) intends to leave the United Kingdom at the end of the employment covered by the Multiple Entry work permit.]
[(vii) holds a valid United Kingdom entry clearance for entry into this capacity except where he holds a work permit valid for 6 months or less . . . or he is a British National (Overseas), a British protected person or a person who under the British Nationality Act 1981 is a British subject.]

Note: Paragraph 199A inserted from 18 September 2002 (Cm 5597). Subparagraph (vii) inserted from 13 January 2004 (HC 176). Words deleted from sub-para (vii) from 1 May 2004 (HC 523).

Leave to enter for Multiple Entry work permit employment

[**199B.** A person seeking leave to enter the United Kingdom for the purpose of Multiple Entry work permit employment may be admitted for a period not exceeding 2 years provided that the immigration Officer is satisfied that each of the requirements of paragraph 199A are met.]

Note: Paragraph 199B inserted from 18 September 2002 (Cm 5597).

Refusal of leave to enter for Multiple Entry work permit employment

[**199C.** Leave to enter for the purpose of Multiple Entry work permit employment is to be refused if the Immigration Officer is not satisfied that each of the requirements of paragraph 199A is met.]

Note: Paragraph 199C inserted from 18 September 2002 (Cm 5597).

Part 6

Persons Seeking to Enter or Remain in the United Kingdom as a Businessman, Self-Employed Person, Investor, Writer, Composer or Artist

Persons intending to establish themselves in business

Requirements for leave to enter the United Kingdom as a person intending to establish himself in business

200. For the purpose of paragraphs 201–210 a business means an enterprise as:
- a sole trader; or
- a partnership; or
- a company registered in the United Kingdom.

201. The requirements to be met by a person seeking leave to enter the United Kingdom to establish himself in business are:

(i) that he satisfies the requirements of either paragraph 202 or paragraph 203; and

(ii) that he has not less than £200,000 of his own money under his control and disposable in the United Kingdom which is held in his own name and not by a trust or other investment vehicle and which he will be investing in the business in the United Kingdom; and

(iii) that until his business provides him with an income he will have sufficient additional funds to maintain and accommodate himself and any dependants without recourse to employment (other than his work for the business) or to public funds; and

(iv) that he will be actively involved full-time in trading or providing services on his own account or in partnership, or in the promotion and management of the company as a director; and

(v) that his level of financial investment will be proportional to his interest in the business; and

(vi) that he will have either a controlling or equal interest in the business and that any partnership or directorship does not amount to disguised employment; and

(vii) that he will be able to bear his share of liabilities; and

(viii) that there is a genuine need for his investment and services in the United Kingdom; and

(ix) that his share of the profits of the business will be sufficient to maintain and accommodate himself and any dependants without recourse to employment (other than his work for the business) or to public funds; and

(x) that he does not intend to supplement his business activities by taking or seeking employment in the United Kingdom other than his work for the business; and

(xi) that he holds a valid United Kingdom entry clearance for entry in this capacity.

202. Where a person intends to take over or join as a partner or director an existing business in the United Kingdom he will need, in addition to meeting the requirements at paragraph 201, to produce:

(i) a written statement of the terms on which he is to take over or join the business; and

(ii) audited accounts for the business for previous years; and

(iii) evidence that his services and investment will result in a net increase in the employment provided by the business to persons settled here to the extent of creating at least 2 new full-time jobs.

203. Where a person intends to establish a new business in the United Kingdom he will need, in addition to meeting the requirements at paragraph 201 above, to produce evidence:

(i) that he will be bringing into the country sufficient funds of his own to establish a business; and

(ii) that the business will create full-time paid employment for at least 2 persons already settled in the United Kingdom.

Leave to enter the United Kingdom as a person seeking to establish himself in business

204. A person seeking leave to enter the United Kingdom to establish himself in business may be admitted for a period not exceeding [2 years] with a condition restricting his freedom to take employment provided he is able to produce to the Immigration Officer, on arrival, a valid United Kingdom entry clearance for entry in this capacity.

Note: Words in square brackets substituted from 3 April 2006 (HC 1016).

Refusal of leave to enter the United Kingdom as a person seeking to establish himself in business

205. Leave to enter the United Kingdom as a person seeking to establish himself in business is to be refused if a valid United Kingdom entry clearance for entry in this capacity is not produced to the Immigration Officer on arrival.

Requirements for an extension of stay in order to remain in business

206. The requirements for an extension of stay in order to remain in business in the United Kingdom are that the applicant can show:

(i) that he entered the United Kingdom with a valid United Kingdom entry clearance as a businessman; and

(ii) audited accounts which show the precise financial position of the business and which confirm that he has invested not less than £200,000 of his own money directly into the business in the United Kingdom; and

(iii) that he is actively involved on a full-time basis in trading or providing services on his own account or in partnership or in the promotion and management of the company as a director; and

(iv) that his level of financial investment is proportional to his interest in the business; and

(v) that he has either a controlling or equal interest in the business and that any partnership or directorship does not amount to disguised employment; and

(vi) that he is able to bear his share of any liability the business may incur; and

(vii) that there is a genuine need for his investment and services in the United Kingdom; and

(viii) (a) that where he has established a new business, new full-time paid employment has been created in the business for at least 2 persons settled in the United Kingdom; or

(b) that where he has taken over or joined an existing business, his services and investment have resulted in a net increase in the employment provided by the business to persons settled here to the extent of creating at least 2 new full-time jobs; and

(ix) that his share of the profits of the business is sufficient to maintain and accommodate him and any dependants without recourse to employment (other than his work for the business) or to public funds; and

(x) that he does not and will not have to supplement his business activities by taking or seeking employment in the United Kingdom other than his work for the business.

[**206A.** The requirements for an extension of stay as a person intending to establish himself in business in the United Kingdom for a person who has leave to enter or remain for work permit employment are that the applicant:

(i) entered the United Kingdom or was given leave to remain as a work permit holder in accordance with paragraphs 128 to 133 of these Rules; and

(ii) meets each of the requirements of paragraph 201 (i)–(x).]

Note: Paragraph 206A inserted from 15 March 2005 (HC 346).

[**206B.** The requirements for an extension of stay as a person intending to establish himself in business in the United Kingdom for a highly skilled migrant are that the applicant:

(i) entered the United Kingdom or was given leave to remain as a highly skilled migrant in accordance with paragraphs 135A to 135F of these Rules; and

(ii) meets each of the requirements of paragraph 201 (i)–(x).]

Note: Paragraph 206B inserted from 15 March 2005 (HC 346).

[**206C.** The requirements for an extension of stay as a person intending to establish himself in business in the United Kingdom for a participant in the Science and Engineering Graduates Scheme are that the applicant:

- (i) entered the United Kingdom or was given leave to remain as a participant in the Science and Engineering Graduates Scheme in accordance with paragraphs 135O to 135T of these Rules; and
- (ii) meets each of the requirements of paragraph 201 (i)–(x).]

Note: Paragraph 206B inserted from 15 March 2005 (HC 346).

[**206D.** The requirements for an extension of stay as a person intending to establish himself in business in the United Kingdom for an innovator are that the applicant:

- (i) entered the United Kingdom or was given leave to remain as an innovator in accordance with paragraphs 210A to 210F of these Rules; and
- (ii) meets each of the requirements of paragraph 201 (i)–(x).]

Note: Paragraph 206D inserted from 15 March 2005 (HC 346).

[**206E.** The requirements for an extension of stay as a person intending to establish himself in business in the United Kingdom for a student are that the applicant:

- (i) entered the United Kingdom or was given leave to remain as a student in accordance with paragraphs 57 to 62 of these Rules; and
- (ii) has obtained a degree qualification on a recognised degree course at either a United Kingdom publicly funded further or higher education institution or a bona fide United Kingdom private education institution which maintains satisfactory records of enrolment and attendance; and
- (iii) has the written consent of his official sponsor to such self employment if he is a member of a government or international scholarship agency sponsorship and that sponsorship is either ongoing or has recently come to an end at the time of the requested extension; and
- (iv) meets each of the requirements of paragraph 201 (i)–(x).]

Note: Paragraph 206E inserted from 15 March 2005 (HC 346).

[**206F.** The requirements for an extension of stay as a person intending to establish himself in business in the United Kingdom for a working holidaymaker are that the applicant:

- (i) entered the United Kingdom or was given leave to remain as a working holidaymaker in accordance with paragraphs 95 to 100 of these Rules; and
- (ii) has spent more than 12 months in total in the UK in this capacity; and
- (iii) meets each of the requirements of paragraph 201 (i)–(x).]

Note: Paragraph 206F inserted from 15 March 2005 (HC 346).

[**206G.** The requirements for an extension of stay as a person intending to establish himself in business in the United Kingdom in the case of a person who has leave to enter or remain as a Fresh Talent: Working in Scotland scheme participant are that the applicant:

(i) entered the United Kingdom or was given leave to remain as a Fresh Talent: Working in Scotland scheme participant in accordance with paragraphs 143A to 143F of these Rules; and

(ii) has the written consent of his official sponsor to such employment if the studies which led to him being granted leave under the Fresh Talent: Working in Scotland scheme in accordance with paragraphs 143A to 143F of these Rules, or any studies he has subsequently undertaken, were sponsored by a government or international scholarship agency; and

(iii) meets each of the requirements of paragraph 201(i)–(x).]

Note: Paragraph 206G inserted from 22 June 2005 (HC 104).

[**206H.** The requirements for an extension of stay as a person intending to establish himself in business in the United Kingdom for a Postgraduate Doctor or Dentist are that the applicant:

(i) entered the United Kingdom or was given leave to remain as a Postgraduate Doctor or Dentist in accordance with paragraphs 70 to 75 of these Rules; and

(ii) has the written consent of his official sponsor to such self-employment if he is a member of a government or international scholarship agency sponsorship and that sponsorship is either ongoing or has recently come to an end at the time of the requested extension; and

(iii) meets each of the requirements of paragraph 201(i)–(x).]

Note: Paragraph 206H inserted from 3 April 2006 (HC 1016).

Extension of stay in order to remain in business

[**207.** An extension of stay in order to remain in business with a condition restricting his freedom to take employment may be granted for a period not exceeding 3 years {at a time} provided the Secretary of State is satisfied that each of the requirements of paragraph 206, 206A, 206B, 206C, 206D, 206E, 206F or 206G is met.]

Note: Paragraph 207 substituted from 22 June 2005 (HC 104). Words in curly brackets inserted from 3 April 2006 (HC 1016).

Refusal of extension of stay in order to remain in business

[**208.** An extension of stay in order to remain in business is to be refused if the Secretary of State is not satisfied that each of the requirements of paragraph 206, 206A, 206B, 206C, 206D, 206E, 206F, {206G or 206H} is met.]

Note: Paragraph 208 substituted from 22 June 2005 (HC 104). Words in curly brackets substituted from 3 April 2006 (HC 1016).

Indefinite leave to remain for a person established in business

209. Indefinite leave to remain may be granted, on application, to a person established in business provided he:

(i) has spent a continuous period of [5 years] in the United Kingdom in this capacity and is still engaged in the business in question; and

(ii) has met the requirements of paragraph 206 throughout the [5 year] period; and

[(iii) submits audited accounts for the first 4 years of trading and management accounts for the 5th year.]

Note: Words in square brackets substituted from 3 April 2006 (HC 1016).

Refusal of indefinite leave to remain for a person established in business

210. Indefinite leave to remain in the United Kingdom for a person established in business is to be refused if the Secretary of State is not satisfied that each of the requirements of paragraph 209 is met.

Innovators

[Requirements for leave to enter the United Kingdom as an innovator

210A. The requirements to be met by a person seeking leave to enter as an innovator are that the applicant:

(i) is approved by the Home Office as a person who meets the criteria specified by the Secretary of State for entry under the innovator scheme at the time that approval is sought under that scheme;

(ii) intends to set up a business that will create full-time paid employment for at least 2 persons already settled in the UK; and

(iii) intends to maintain a minimum five per cent shareholding of the equity capital in that business, once it has been set up, throughout the period of his stay as an innovator; and

(iv) will be able to maintain and accommodate himself and any dependants adequately without recourse to public funds or to other employment; and

(v) holds a valid United Kingdom entry clearance for entry in this capacity.]

Note: Paragraph 210A inserted from 1 April 2003 (HC 538).

[Leave to enter as an innovator

210B. A person seeking leave to enter the United Kingdom as an innovator may be admitted for a period not exceeding {2 years}, provided the Immigration Officer is satisfied that each of the requirements of paragraph 21OA is met.]

Note: Paragraph 210B inserted from 1 April 2003 (HC 538). Words in curly brackets substituted from 3 April 2006 (HC 1016).

[Refusal of leave to enter as an innovator

210C. Leave to enter as an innovator is to be refused if the Immigration Officer is not satisfied that each of the requirements of paragraph 210A are met.]

Note: Paragraph 210C inserted from 1 April 2003 (HC 538).

[Requirements for an extension of stay as an innovator

[**210D.** The requirements for an extension of stay in the United Kingdom as an innovator, in the case of a person who was granted leave to enter under paragraph 210A, are that the applicant:

(i) has established a viable trading business, by reference to the audited accounts and trading records of that business; and

(ii) continues to meet the requirements of paragraph 210A (i) and (iv); and has set up a business that will create full-time paid employment for at least 2 persons already settled in the UK; and

(iii) has maintained a minimum five per cent shareholding of the equity capital in that business, once it has been set up, throughout the period of his stay.]

Note: Paragraph 210D substituted from 1 October 2004 (Cm 6339).

[**210DA.** The requirements for an extension of stay in the United Kingdom as an innovator, in the case of a person who has leave for the purpose of work permit employment are that the applicant:

(i) entered the United Kingdom or was given leave to remain as a work permit holder in accordance with paragraphs 128 to 132 of these Rules; and

(ii) meets the requirements of paragraph 210A (i)–(iv).]

Note: Paragraph 210DA inserted from 1 October 2004 (Cm 6339).

[**210DB.** The requirements for an extension of stay in the United Kingdom as an innovator in the case of a person who has leave as a student are that the applicant:

(i) entered the United Kingdom or was given leave to remain as a student in accordance with paragraphs 57 to 62 of these Rules; and

(ii) has obtained a degree qualification on a recognised degree course at either a United Kingdom publicly funded further or higher education institution or a bona fide United Kingdom private education institution which maintains satisfactory records of enrolment and attendance; and

(iii) has the written consent of his official sponsor to remain under the Innovator category if he is a member of a government or international scholarship agency sponsorship and that sponsorship is either ongoing or has recently come to an end at the time of the requested extension; and

(iv) meets the requirements of paragraph 210(i)–(iv).]

Note: Paragraph 210DB inserted from 1 October 2004 (Cm 6339).

[**210DC.** The requirements to be met for an extension of stay as an innovator, for a person who has leave as a working holidaymaker are that the applicant:

(i) entered the United Kingdom as a working holidaymaker in accordance with paragraphs 95 to 96 of these Rules; and

(ii) meets the requirements of paragraph 210A(i)–(iv).]

Note: Paragraph 210DC inserted from 1 October 2004 (Cm 6339).

[**210DD.** The requirements to be met for an extension of stay as an innovator, for a postgraduate doctor, postgraduate dentist or trainee general practitioner are that the applicant:

(i) entered the United Kingdom or was given leave to remain as a postgraduate doctor, postgraduate dentist or trainee general practitioner in accordance with paragraphs 70 to 75 of these Rules; and

(ii) has the written consent of his official sponsor to remain under the innovator category if he is a member of a government or international scholarship agency sponsorship and that sponsorship is either ongoing or has recently come to an end at the time of the requested extension; and

(iii) meets the requirements of paragraph 210(i)–(iv).]

Note: Paragraph 210DD inserted from 25 October 2004 (Cm 1112).

[**210DE.** The requirements to be met for an extension of stay as an innovator, for a participant in the Science and Engineering Graduate Scheme are that the applicant:

(i) entered the United Kingdom or was given leave to remain as a participant in the Science and Engineering Graduate Scheme in accordance with paragraphs 135O to 135T of these Rules; and

(ii) meets the requirements of paragraph 210A(i)–(iv).]

Note: Paragraph 210DE inserted from 25 October 2004 (Cm 1112).

[**210DF.** The requirements to be met for an extension of stay as an innovator, for a highly skilled migrant are that the applicant:

(i) entered the United Kingdom or was given leave to remain as a highly skilled migrant in accordance with paragraphs 135A to 135E of these Rules; and

(ii) meets the requirements of paragraph 210A(i)–(iv).]

Note: Paragraph 210DF inserted from 25 October 2004 (Cm 1112).

[**210DG.** The requirements to be met for an extension of stay as an innovator, for a person in the United Kingdom to establish themselves or remain in business are that the applicant:

(i) entered the United Kingdom or was granted leave to remain as a person intending to establish themselves or remain in business in accordance with paragraphs 201–208 of these Rules; and
(ii) meets the requirements of paragraph 210 (i)–(iv).]

Note: Paragraph 210DG inserted from 15 March 2005 (HC 346).

[**210DH.** The requirements to be met for an extension of stay as an innovator, in the case of a person who has leave to enter or remain as a Fresh Talent: Working in Scotland scheme participant are that the applicant:
(i) entered the United Kingdom or was given leave to remain as a Fresh Talent: Working in Scotland scheme participant in accordance with paragraphs 143A to 143F of these Rules; and
(ii) has the written consent of his official sponsor to such employment if the studies which led to him being granted leave under the Fresh Talent: Working in Scotland scheme in accordance with paragraphs 143A to 143F of these Rules, or any studies he has subsequently undertaken, were sponsored by a government or international scholarship agency; and
(iii) meets each of the requirements of paragraph 210(i)–(iv).]

Note: Paragraph 210DH inserted from 22 June 2005 (HC 104).

Extension of stay as an innovator

[**210E.** An extension of stay as an innovator may be granted for a period not exceeding {3 years at a time} provided the Secretary of State is satisfied that each of the requirements of paragraph 210D, 210DA, 210DB, 210DC, 210DD, 210DE, 210DF, 210DG or 210DH is met.]

Note: Paragraph 210E substituted from 22 June 2005 (HC 104). Words in curly brackets substituted from 3 April 2006 (HC 1016).

Refusal of extension of stay as an innovator

[**210F.** An extension of stay as an innovator is to be refused if the Secretary of State is not satisfied that each of the requirements of paragraph 210D, 210DA, 210DB, 210DC, 210DD, 210DE, 210DF, 210DG or 210DH is met.]

Note: Paragraph 210F substituted from 22 June 2005 (HC 104).

[Indefinite leave to remain for an innovator

210G. Indefinite leave to remain may be granted, on application, to a person currently with leave as an innovator provided that he:
(i) has spent a continuous period of at least {5 years} leave in the United Kingdom in this capacity; and

(ii) has met the requirements of paragraph 210D throughout the {5 year} period.]

Note: Paragraph 210G inserted from 1 April 2003 (HC 538). Words in curly brackets substituted from 3 April 2006 (HC 1016).

[Refusal of indefinite leave to remain as an innovator

210H. Indefinite leave to remain in the United Kingdom as a person currently with leave as a innovator is to be refused if the Secretary of State is not satisfied that each of the requirements of paragraph 210G is met.]

Note: Paragraph 210H inserted from 1 April 2003 (HC 538).

Persons intending to establish themselves in business under provisions of EC Association Agreements

Requirements for leave to enter the United Kingdom as a person intending to establish himself in business under the provisions of an EC Association Agreement

211. For the purpose of paragraphs 212–223 a business means an enterprise as:
- a sole trader; or
- a partnership; or
- a company registered in the United Kingdom.

212. The requirements to be met by a person seeking leave to enter the United Kingdom to establish himself in business are that:

(i) he satisfies the requirements of either paragraph 213 or paragraph 214; and

(ii) the money he is putting into the business is under his control and sufficient to establish himself in business in the United Kingdom; and

(iii) until his business provides him with an income he will have sufficient additional funds to maintain and accommodate himself and any dependants without recourse to employment (other than his work for the business) or to public funds; and

(iv) his share of the profits of the business will be sufficient to maintain and accommodate himself and any dependants without recourse to employment (other than his work for the business) or to public funds; and

(v) he does not intend to supplement his business activities by taking or seeking employment in the United Kingdom other than his work for the business; and

(vi) he holds a valid United Kingdom entry clearance for entry in this capacity.

213. Where a person intends to establish himself in a company in the United Kingdom which he effectively controls he will need, in addition to meeting the requirements at paragraph 212, to show:

[(i) that he is a national of Bulgaria or Romania; and]
(ii) that he will have a controlling interest in the company; and
(iii) that he will be actively involved in the promotion and management of the company; and
(iv) that the company will be registered in the United Kingdom and be trading or providing services in the United Kingdom; and
(v) that the company will be the owner of the assets of the business; and
(vi) where he is taking over an existing company, a written statement of the terms on which he is to take over the business and audited accounts for the business for previous years.

Note: Subparagraph (i) substituted from 1 May 2004 (HC 523).

214. Where a person intends to establish himself in self-employment or in partnership in the United Kingdom he will need, in addition to meeting the requirements at 212 above, to show:

[(i) that he is a national of Bulgaria or Romania; and]
(ii) that he will be actively involved in trading or providing services on his own account or in partnership in the United Kingdom; and
(iii) that he, or he together with his partners, will be the owner of the assets of the business; and
(iv) in the case of a partnership, that his part in the business will not amount to disguised employment; and
(v) where he is taking over or joining an existing business a written statement of the terms on which he is to take over or join the business and audited accounts for the business for previous years.

Note: Subparagraph (i) substituted from 1 May 2004 (HC 523).

Leave to enter the United Kingdom as a person seeking to establish himself in business under the provisions of an EC Association Agreement

215. A person seeking leave to enter the United Kingdom to establish himself in business may be admitted for a period not exceeding [2 years] with a condition restricting his freedom to take employment provided he is able to produce to the Immigration Officer, on arrival, a valid United Kingdom entry clearance for entry in this capacity.

Note: Words in square brackets substituted from 3 April 2006 (HC 1016).

Refusal of leave to enter the United Kingdom as a person seeking to establish himself in business under the provisions of an EC Association Agreement

216. Leave to enter the United Kingdom as a person seeking to establish himself in business is to be refused if a valid United Kingdom entry clearance for entry in this capacity is not produced to the Immigration Officer on arrival.

Requirements for an extension of stay in order to remain in business under the provisions of an EC Association Agreement

217. The requirement for an extension of stay in order to remain in business in the United Kingdom are that the applicant can show that:

[(i) he entered the United Kingdom with a valid United Kingdom entry clearance as a person intending to establish himself in business under the provisions of an EC Association Agreement; and

(ia) he has established himself in business in the United Kingdom; and]

(ii) his share of the profits of the business is sufficient to maintain and accommodate himself and any dependants without recourse to employment (other than his work for the business) or to public funds; and

(iii) he does not and will not supplement his business activities by taking or seeking employment in the United Kingdom other than his work for the business; and

(iv) in addition he satisfies the requirements of either paragraph 218 or paragraph 219.

Note: Subparagraphs (i) and (ia) substituted from 9 August 2004 (Cm 6297).

218. Where a person has established himself in a company in the United Kingdom which he effectively controls he will need, in addition to meeting the requirements at paragraph 217 above, to show:

[(i) that he is a national of Bulgaria or Romania; and]

(ii) that he is actively involved in the promotion and management of the company; and

(iii) that he has a controlling interest in the company; and

(iv) that the company is registered in the United Kingdom and trading or providing services in the United Kingdom; and

(v) that the company is the owner of the assets of the business; and

(vi) the current financial position in the form of audited accounts for the company.

Note: Subparagraph (i) substituted from 1 May 2004 (HC 523).

219. Where a person has established himself as a sole trader or in partnership in the United Kingdom he will need, in addition to meeting the requirements at 217 above, to show:

[(i) that he is a national of Bulgaria or Romania; and]

(ii) that he is actively involved in trading or providing services on his own account or in partnership in the United Kingdom; and

(iii) that he, or he together with his partners, is the owner of the assets of the business; and

(iv) in the case of a partnership, that his part in the business does not amount to disguised employment; and

(v) the current financial position in the form of audited accounts for the business.

Note: Subparagraph (i) substituted from 1 May 2004 (HC 523).

Extension of stay in order to remain in business under the provisions of an EC Association Agreement

220. An extension of stay in order to remain in business with a condition restricting his freedom to take employment may be granted for a period not exceeding 3 years provided the Secretary of State is satisfied that each of the requirements of paragraphs 217 and 218 or 219 is met.

Refusal of extension of stay in order to remain in business under the provisions of an EC Association Agreement

221. An extension of stay in order to remain in business is to be refused if the Secretary of State is not satisfied that each of the requirements of paragraphs 217 and 218 or 219 is met.

Indefinite leave to remain for a person established in business under the provisions of an EC Association Agreement

222. Indefinite leave to remain may be granted, on application, to a person established in business provided he:

(i) has spent a continuous period of [5 years] in the United Kingdom in this capacity and is still so engaged; and
(ii) has met the requirements of paragraphs 217 and 218 or 219 throughout the [5 years]; and
[(iii) submits audited accounts for the first 4 years of trading and management accounts for the 5th year.]

Note: Words in square brackets substituted from 3 April 2006 (HC 1016).

Refusal of indefinite leave to remain for a person established in business under the provision of an EC Association Agreement

223. Indefinite leave to remain in the United Kingdom for a person established in business is to be refused if the Secretary of State is not satisfied that each of the requirements of paragraph 222 is met.

Investors

Requirements for leave to enter the United Kingdom as an investor

224. The requirements to be met by a person seeking leave to enter the United Kingdom as an investor are that he:

[(i) (a) has money of his own under his control in the United Kingdom amounting to no less than £1 million; or

(b)(i) owns personal assets which, taking into account any liabilities to which he is subject, have value exceeding £2 million; and

(ii) has money under his control in the United Kingdom amounting to no less than £1 million, which may include money loaned to him provided that it was loaned by a financial institution regulated by the Financial Services Authority; and]

(ii) intends to invest not less than £750,000 of his capital in the United Kingdom by way of United Kingdom Government bonds, share capital or loan capital in active and trading United Kingdom registered companies (other than those principally engaged in property investment and excluding investment by the applicant by way of deposits with a bank, building society or other enterprise whose normal course of business includes the acceptance of deposits); and

(iii) intends to make the United Kingdom his main home; and

(iv) is able to maintain and accommodate himself and any dependants without taking employment (other than self-employment or business) or recourse to public funds; and

(v) holds a valid United Kingdom entry clearance for entry in this capacity.

Note: Subparagraph (i) substituted from 13 January 2004 (HC 176).

Leave to enter as an investor

225. A person seeking to enter the United Kingdom as an investor may be admitted for a period not exceeding [2 years] with a restriction on his right to take employment, provided he is able to produce to the Immigration Officer, on arrival, a valid United Kingdom entry clearance for entry in this capacity.

Note: Words in square brackets substituted from 3 April 2006 (HC 1016).

Refusal of leave to enter as an investor

226. Leave to enter as an investor is to be refused if a valid United Kingdom entry clearance for entry in this capacity is not produced to the Immigration Officer on arrival.

Requirements for an extension of stay as an investor

227. The requirements for an extension of stay as an investor are that the applicant:

(i) entered the United Kingdom with a valid United Kingdom entry clearance as an investor; and

[(ii)(a) has money of his own under his control in the United Kingdom amounting to no less than £1 million; or (b)(i) owns personal assets which, taking into account any liabilities to which he is subject, have value exceeding £2 million; and

(ii) has money under his control in the United Kingdom amounting to no less than £1 million, which may include money loaned to him provided that it was loaned by a financial institution regulated by the Financial Services Authority; and]

(iii) has invested not less than £750,000 of his capital in the United Kingdom on the terms set out in paragraph 224(ii) above and intends to maintain that investment on the terms set out in paragraph 224(ii); and

(iv) has made the United Kingdom his main home; and

(v) is able to maintain and accommodate himself and any dependants without taking employment (other than his self-employment or business) or recourse to public funds.

Note: Subparagraph (ii) substituted from 13 January 2004 (HC 176).

[**227A.** The requirements to be met for an extension of stay as an investor, for a person who has leave to enter or remain in the United Kingdom as a work permit holder are that the applicant:

(i) entered the United Kingdom or was granted leave to remain as a work permit holder in accordance with paragraphs 128 to 133 of these Rules; and

(ii) meets the requirements of paragraph 224 (i)–(iv).]

Note: Paragraph 227A inserted from 15 March 2005 (HC 346).

[**227B.** The requirements to be met for an extension of stay as an investor, for a person in the United Kingdom as a highly skilled migrant are that the applicant:

(i) entered the United Kingdom or was granted leave to remain as a highly skilled migrant in accordance with paragraphs 135A to 135F of these Rules; and

(ii) meets the requirements of paragraph 224 (i)–(iv).]

Note: Paragraph 227B inserted from 15 March 2005 (HC 346).

[**227C.** The requirements to be met for an extension of stay as an investor, for a person in the United Kingdom to establish themselves or remain in business are that the applicant:

(i) entered the United Kingdom or was granted leave to remain as a person intending to establish themselves or remain in business in accordance with paragraphs 201 to 208 of these Rules; and

(ii) meets the requirements of paragraph 224 (i)–(iv).]

Note: Paragraph 227C inserted from 15 March 2005 (HC 346).

[**227D.** The requirements to be met for an extension of stay as an investor, for a person in the United Kingdom as an innovator are that the applicant:

(i) entered the United Kingdom or was granted leave to remain as an innovator in accordance with paragraphs 210A to 210F of these Rules; and
(ii) meets the requirements of paragraph 224 (i)–(iv).]

Note: Paragraph 227D inserted from 15 March 2005 (HC 346).

Extension of stay as an investor

[**228.** An extension of stay as an investor, with a restriction on the taking of employment, may be granted for a . . . period {not exceeding 3 years at a time}, provided the Secretary of State is satisfied that each of the requirements of paragraph 227, 227A, 227B, 227C or 227D is met.]

Note: Paragraph 228 substituted from 15 March 2005 (HC 346). Words deleted and words in square brackets substituted from 3 April 2006 (HC 1016).

Refusal of extension of stay as an investor

[**229.** An extension of stay as an investor is to be refused if the Secretary of State is not satisfied that each of the requirements of paragraph 227, 227A, 227B, 227C or 227D is met.]

Note: Paragraph 229 substituted from 15 March 2005 (HC 346).

Indefinite leave to remain for an investor

230. Indefinite leave to remain may be granted, on application, to a person admitted as an investor provided he:
(i) has spent a continuous period of [5 years] in the United Kingdom in this capacity; and
(ii) has met the requirements of paragraph 227 throughout the [5 year] period including the requirement as to the investment of £750,000 and continues to do so.

Note: Words in square brackets substituted from 3 April 2006 (HC 1016).

Refusal of indefinite leave to remain for an investor

231. Indefinite leave to remain in the United Kingdom for an investor is to be refused if the Secretary of State is not satisfied that each of the requirements of paragraph 230 is met.

Writers, composers and artists

Requirements for leave to enter the United Kingdom as a writer, composer or artist

232. The requirements to be met by a person seeking leave to enter the United Kingdom as a writer, composer or artist are that he:

(i) has established himself outside the United Kingdom as a writer, composer or artist primarily engaged in producing original work which has been published (other than exclusively in newspapers or magazines), performed or exhibited for its literary, musical or artistic merit; and

(ii) does not intend to work except as related to his self-employment as a writer, composer or artist; and

(iii) has for the preceding year been able to maintain and accommodate himself and any dependants from his own resources without working except as a writer, composer or artist; and

(iv) will be able to maintain and accommodate himself and any dependants from his own resources without working except as a writer, composer or artist and without recourse to public funds; and

(v) holds a valid United Kingdom entry clearance for entry in this capacity.

Leave to enter as a writer, composer or artist

233. A person seeking leave to enter the United Kingdom as a writer, composer or artist may be admitted for a period not exceeding [2 years] subject to a condition restricting his freedom to take employment, provided he is able to produce to the Immigration Officer, on arrival, a valid United Kingdom entry clearance for entry in this capacity.

Note: Words in square brackets substituted from 3 April 2006 (HC 1016).

Refusal of leave to enter as a writer, composer or artist

234. Leave to enter as a writer, composer or artist is to be refused if a valid United Kingdom entry clearance for entry in this capacity is not produced to the Immigration Officer on arrival.

Requirements for an extension of stay as a writer, composer or artist

235. The requirements for an extension of stay as a writer, composer or artist are that the applicant:

(i) entered the United Kingdom with a valid United Kingdom entry clearance as a writer, composer or artist; and

(ii) meets the requirements of paragraph 232(ii)–(iv).

Extension of stay as a writer, composer or artist

236. An extension of stay as a writer, composer or artist may be granted for a period not exceeding 3 years with a restriction on his freedom to take employment, provided the Secretary of State is satisfied that each of the requirements of paragraph 235 is met.

Refusal of extension of stay as a writer, composer or artist

237. An extension of stay as a writer, composer or artist is to be refused if the Secretary of State is not satisfied that each of the requirements of paragraph 235 is met.

Indefinite leave to remain for a writer, composer or artist

238. Indefinite leave to remain may be granted, on application, to a person admitted as a writer, composer or artist provided he:

(i) has spent a continuous period of [5 years] in the United Kingdom in this capacity; and

(ii) has met the requirements of paragraph 235 throughout the [5 year] period.

Note: Words in square brackets substituted from 3 April 2006 (HC 1016).

Refusal of indefinite leave to remain for a writer, composer or artist

239. Indefinite leave to remain for a writer, composer or artist is to be refused if the Secretary of State is not satisfied that each of the requirements of paragraph 238 is met.

Spouses [or civil partners] of persons with limited leave to enter or remain under paragraphs 200–239

Requirements for leave to enter or remain as the spouse [or civil partner] of a person with limited leave to enter or remain under paragraphs 200–239

240. The requirements to be met by a person seeking leave to enter or remain in the United Kingdom as the spouse [or civil partner] of a person with limited leave to enter or remain in the United Kingdom under paragraphs 200–239 are that:

(i) the applicant is married to [or the civil partner of] a person with limited leave to enter or remain in the United Kingdom under paragraphs 200–239; and

(ii) each of the parties intends to live with the other as his or her spouse during the applicant's stay and the marriage [or civil partnership] is subsisting; and

(iii) there will be adequate accommodation for the parties and any dependants without recourse to public funds in accommodation which they own or occupy exclusively; and

(iv) the parties will be able to maintain themselves and any dependants adequately without recourse to public funds; and
(v) the applicant does not intend to stay in the United Kingdom beyond any period of leave granted to his spouse [or civil partner]; and
(vi) if seeking leave to enter, the applicant holds a valid United Kingdom entry clearance for entry in this capacity or, if seeking leave to remain, was admitted with a valid United Kingdom entry clearance for entry in this capacity.

Note: References to civil partnership inserted from 5 December 2005 (HC 582).

Leave to enter or remain as the spouse [or civil partner] of a person with limited leave to enter or remain in the United Kingdom under paragraphs 200–239

241. A person seeking leave to enter or remain in the United Kingdom as the spouse [or civil partner] of a person with limited leave to enter or remain in the United Kingdom under paragraphs 200–239 may be given leave to enter or remain in the United Kingdom for a period of leave not in excess of that granted to the person with limited leave to enter or remain under paragraphs 200–239 provided that, in relation to an application for leave to enter, he is able, on arrival, to produce to the Immigration Officer a valid United Kingdom entry clearance for entry in this capacity or, in the case of an application for limited leave to remain, he was admitted with a valid United Kingdom entry clearance for entry in this capacity and is able to satisfy the Secretary of State that each of the requirements of paragraph 240(i)–(v) is met. An application for indefinite leave to remain in this category may be granted provided the applicant was admitted with a valid United Kingdom entry clearance for entry in this capacity and is able to satisfy the Secretary of State that each of the requirements of paragraph 240(i)–(v) is met and provided indefinite leave to remain is, at the same time, being granted to the person with limited leave to remain under paragraphs 200–239.

Note: References to civil partnership inserted from 5 December 2005 (HC 582).

Refusal of leave to enter or remain as the spouse [or civil partner] of a person with limited leave to enter or remain in the United Kingdom under paragraphs 200–239

242. Leave to enter or remain in the United Kingdom as the spouse [or civil partner] of a person with limited leave to enter or remain in the United Kingdom under paragraphs 200–239 is to be refused if, in relation to an application for leave to enter, a valid United Kingdom entry clearance for entry in this capacity is not produced to the Immigration Officer on arrival or, in the case of an application for limited leave to remain, if the applicant was not admitted with a valid United Kingdom entry clearance for entry in this capacity or is unable to satisfy the

Secretary of State that each of the requirements of paragraph 240(i)–(v) is met. An application for indefinite leave to remain in this category is to be refused if the applicant was not admitted with a valid United Kingdom entry clearance for entry in this capacity or is unable to satisfy the Secretary of State that each of the requirements of paragraph 240(i)–(v) is met or if indefinite leave to remain is not, at the same time, being granted to the person with limited leave to remain under paragraphs 200–239.

Note: References to civil partnership inserted from 5 December 2005 (HC 582).

Children of persons with limited leave to enter or remain under paragraphs 200–239

Requirements for leave to enter or remain as the child of a person with limited leave to enter or remain in the United Kingdom under paragraphs 200–239

243. The requirements to be met by a person seeking leave to enter or remain in the United Kingdom as a child of a person with limited leave to enter or remain in the United Kingdom under paragraphs 200–239 are that:

(i) he is the child of a parent who has leave to enter or remain in the United Kingdom under paragraphs 200–239; and

(ii) he is under the age of 18 or has current leave to enter or remain in this capacity; and

(iii) he is unmarried [and is not a civil partner], has not formed an independent family unit and is not leading an independent life; and

(iv) he can and will be maintained and accommodated adequately without recourse to public funds in accommodation which his parent(s) own of occupy exclusively; and

(v) he will not stay in the United Kingdom beyond any period of leave granted to his parent(s); and

(vi) both parents are being or have been admitted to or allowed to remain in the United Kingdom save where:

  (a) the parent he is accompanying or joining is his sole surviving parent; or

  (b) the parent he is accompanying or joining has had sole responsibility for his upbringing; or

  (c) there are serious and compelling family or other considerations which make exclusion from the United Kingdom undesirable and suitable arrangements have been made for his care; and

(vii) if seeking leave to enter, he holds a valid United Kingdom entry clearance for entry in this capacity or, if seeking leave to remain, was admitted with a valid United Kingdom entry clearance for entry in this capacity.

Note: Words in square brackets in sub-para (iii) inserted from 5 December 2005 (HC 582).

Leave to enter or remain as the child of a person with limited leave to enter or remain in the United Kingdom under paragraphs 200–239

244. A person seeking leave to enter or remain in the United Kingdom as the child of a person with limited leave to enter or remain in the United Kingdom under paragraphs 200–239 may be admitted to or allowed to remain in the United Kingdom for the same period of leave as that granted to the person given limited leave to enter or remain under paragraphs 200–239 provided that, in relation to an application for leave to enter, he is able to produce to the Immigration Officer, on arrival, a valid United Kingdom entry clearance for entry in this capacity or, in the case of an application for limited leave to remain, he was admitted with a valid United Kingdom entry clearance for entry in this capacity and is able to satisfy the Secretary of State that each of the requirements of paragraph 243(i)–(vi) is met. An application for indefinite leave to remain in this category may be granted provided the applicant was admitted with a valid United Kingdom entry clearance for entry in this capacity and is able to satisfy the Secretary of State that each of the requirements of paragraph 243(i)–(vi) is met and provided indefinite leave to remain is, at the same time, being granted to the person with limited leave to remain under paragraphs 200–239.

Refusal of leave to enter or remain as the child of a person with limited leave to enter or remain in the United Kingdom under paragraphs 200–239

245. Leave to enter or remain in the United Kingdom as the child of a person with limited leave to enter or remain in the United Kingdom under paragraphs 200–239 is to be refused if, in relation to an application for leave to enter, a valid United Kingdom entry clearance for entry in this capacity is not produced to the Immigration Officer on arrival or, in the case of an application for limited leave to remain, if the applicant was not admitted with a valid United Kingdom entry clearance for entry in this capacity or is unable to satisfy the Secretary of State that each of the requirements of paragraph 243(i)–(vi) is met. An application for indefinite leave to remain in this capacity is to be refused if the applicant was not admitted with a valid United Kingdom entry clearance for entry in this capacity or is unable to satisfy the Secretary of State that each of the requirements of paragraph 243(i)–(vi) is met or if indefinite leave to remain is not, at the same time, being granted to the person with limited leave to remain under paragraphs 200–239.

Part 7
Other Categories

[Requirements for leave to enter the United Kingdom as a person exercising rights of access to a child resident in the United Kingdom

246. The requirements to be met by a person seeking leave to enter the United

Kingdom to exercise access rights to a child resident in the United Kingdom are that:

(i) the applicant is the parent of a child who is resident in the United Kingdom; and

(ii) the parent or carer with whom the child permanently resides is resident in the United Kingdom; and

(iii) the applicant produces evidence that he has access rights to the child in the form of:

(a) a Residence Order or a Contact Order granted by a Court in the United Kingdom; or

(b) a certificate issued by a district judge confirming the applicant's intention to maintain contact with the child; and

(iv) the applicant intends to continue to take an active role in the child's upbringing; and

(v) the child is under the age of 18; and

(vi) there will be adequate accommodation for the applicant and any dependants without recourse to public funds in accommodation which the applicant owns or occupies exclusively; and

(vii) the applicant will be able to maintain himself and any dependants adequately without recourse to public funds; and

(viii) the applicant holds a valid United Kingdom entry clearance for entry in this capacity.]

Note: Substituted from 2 October 2000 (Cm 4851).

[Leave to enter the United Kingdom as a person exercising rights of access to a child resident in the United Kingdom

247. Leave to enter as a person exercising access rights to a child resident in the United Kingdom may be granted for 12 months in the first instance, provided that a valid United Kingdom entry clearance for entry in this capacity is produced to the Immigration Officer on arrival.]

Note: Substituted from 2 October 2000 (Cm 4851).

[Refusal of leave to enter the United Kingdom as a person exercising rights of access to a child resident in the United Kingdom

248. Leave to enter as a person exercising rights of access to a child resident in the United Kingdom is to be refused if a valid United Kingdom entry clearance for entry in this capacity is not produced to the Immigration Officer on arrival.]

Note: Substituted from 2 October 2000 (Cm 4851).

[Requirements for leave to remain in the United Kingdom as a person exercising rights of access to a child resident in the United Kingdom

248A. The requirements to be met by a person seeking leave to remain in the United Kingdom to exercise access rights to a child resident in the United Kingdom are that:

(i) the applicant is the parent of a child who is resident in the United Kingdom; and

(ii) the parent or carer with whom the child permanently resides is resident in the United Kingdom; and

(iii) the applicant produces evidence that he has access rights to the child in the form of:

(a) a Residence Order or a Contact Order granted by a Court in the United Kingdom; or

(b) a certificate issued by a district judge confirming the applicant's intention to maintain contact with the child; or

(c) a statement from the child's other parent (or, if contact is supervised, from the supervisor) that the applicant is maintaining contact with the child; and

(iv) the applicant takes and intends to continue to take an active role in the child's upbringing; and

(v) the child visits or stays with the applicant on a frequent and regular basis and the applicant intends this to continue; and

(vi) the child is under the age of 18; and

(vii) the applicant has limited leave to remain in the United Kingdom as the [spouse, civil partner, unmarried partner or same-sex partner] of a person present and settled in the United Kingdom who is the other parent of the child; and

(viii) the applicant has not remained in breach of the immigration laws; and

(ix) there will be adequate accommodation for the applicant and any dependants without recourse to public funds in accommodation which the applicant owns or occupies exclusively; and

(x) the applicant will be able to maintain himself and any dependants adequately without recourse to public funds.

Note: Words in square brackets substituted from 5 December 2005 (HC 582).

Leave to remain in the United Kingdom as a person exercising rights of access to a child resident in the United Kingdom

248B. Leave to remain as a person exercising access rights to a child resident in the United Kingdom may be granted for 12 months in the first instance, provided the Secretary of State is satisfied that each of the requirements of paragraph 248A is met.

Refusal of leave to remain in the United Kingdom as a person exercising rights of access to a child resident in the United Kingdom

248C. Leave to remain as a person exercising rights of access to a child resident in the United Kingdom is to be refused if the Secretary of State is not satisfied that each of the requirements of paragraph 248A is met.

Indefinite leave to remain in the United Kingdom as a person exercising rights of access to a child resident in the United Kingdom

248D. The requirements for indefinite leave to remain in the United Kingdom as a person exercising rights of access to a child resident in the United Kingdom are that:

(i) the applicant was admitted to the United Kingdom or granted leave to remain in the United Kingdom for a period of 12 months as a person exercising rights of access to a child and has completed a period of 12 months as a person exercising rights of access to a child; and

(ii) the applicant takes and intends to continue to take an active role in the child's upbringing; and

(iii) the child visits or stays with the applicant on a frequent and regular basis and the applicant intends this to continue; and

(iv) there will be adequate accommodation for the applicant and any dependants without recourse to public funds in accommodation which the applicant owns or occupies exclusively; and

(v) the applicant will be able to maintain himself and any dependants adequately without recourse to public funds; and

(vi) the child is under 18 years of age.

Indefinite leave to remain as a person exercising rights of access to a child resident in the United Kingdom

248E. Indefinite leave to remain as a person exercising rights of access to a child may be granted provided the Secretary of State is satisfied that each of the requirements of paragraph 248D is met.

Refusal of indefinite leave to remain in the United Kingdom as a person exercising rights of access to a child resident in the United Kingdom

248F. Indefinite leave to remain as a person exercising rights of access to a child is to be refused if the Secretary of State is not satisfied that each of the requirements of paragraph 248D is met.]

Note: Paragraphs 248A–F inserted from 2 October 2000 (Cm 4851).

Holders of special vouchers

Note: Paragraphs 249–54 deleted from 18 September 2002 (Cm 5597).

EEA nationals and their families

255.–255B. . . .

Note: Paragraphs 255–255B deleted from 30 April 2006, subject to transitional provisions (HC 1053).

256. . . .

Note: Deleted from 2 October 2000 (Cm 4851).

257.–257B. . . .

Note: Paragraphs 257, 257A and 257B deleted from 30 April 2006, subject to transitional provisions (HC 1053).

Requirements for leave to enter or remain as the primary carer or relative of an EEA national self-sufficient child

[**257C.** The requirements to be met by a person seeking leave to enter or remain as the primary carer or relative of an EEA national self-sufficient child are that the applicant:

(i) is:

(a) the primary carer; or

(b) the parent; or

(c) the sibling,

of an EEA national under the age of 18 who has a right of residence in the United Kingdom under [the 2006 EEA Regulations] as a self-sufficient person; and

(ii) is living with the EEA national or is seeking entry to the United Kingdom in order to live with the EEA national; and

(iii) in the case of a sibling of the EEA national:

(a) is under the age of 18 or has current leave to enter or remain in this capacity; and

(b) is unmarried [and is not a civil partner], has not formed an independent family unit and is not leading an independent life; and

(iv) can, and will, be maintained and accommodated without taking employment or having recourse to public funds; and

(v) if seeking leave to enter, holds a valid United Kingdom entry clearance for entry in this capacity.

In this paragraph, 'sibling', includes a half-brother or half-sister and a stepbrother or stepsister.]

Note: Paragraph 257C inserted from 1 January 2005 (HC 164). Words in square brackets in sub-para (i)(c) substituted from 30 April 2006 (HC 1053). Words in square brackets in sub-para (iii) inserted from 5 December 2005 (HC 582).

Leave to enter or remain as the primary carer or relative of an EEA national self-sufficient child

[**257D.** Leave to enter or remain in the United Kingdom as the primary carer or relative of an EEA national self-sufficient child may be granted for a period not exceeding five years or the remaining period of validity of any residence permit held by the EEA national under the 2000 EEA Regulations, whichever is the shorter, provided that, in the case of an application for leave to enter, the applicant is able to produce to the Immigration Officer, on arrival a valid entry clearance for entry in this capacity or, in the case of an application for leave to remain, the applicant is able to satisfy the Secretary of State that each of the requirements of paragraph 257C(i) to (iv) is met. Leave to enter or remain is to be subject to a condition prohibiting employment and recourse to public funds.]

Note: Paragraph 257D inserted from 1 January 2005 (HC 164).

Refusal of leave to enter or remain as the primary carer or relative of an EEA national self-sufficient child

[**257E.** Leave to enter or remain in the United Kingdom as the primary carer or relative of an EEA national self-sufficient child is to be refused if, in the case of an application for leave to enter, the applicant is unable to produce to the Immigration Officer on arrival a valid United Kingdom entry clearance for entry in this capacity or, in the case of an application for leave to remain, if the applicant is unable to satisfy the Secretary of State that each of the requirements of paragraph 257C(i) to (iv) is met.]

Note: Paragraph 257C inserted from 1 January 2005 (HC 164).

258–261. . . .

Note: Paragraphs 258–261 deleted from 2 October 2000 (Cm 4851).

Registration with the police for family members of EEA nationals

262. . . .

Note: Deleted from 11 May 1998 (Cm 3953).

Retired persons of independent means

Requirements for leave to enter the United Kingdom as a retired person of independent means

263. The requirements to be met by a person seeking leave to enter the United Kingdom as a retired person of independent means are that he:

(i) is at least 60 years old; and
(ii) has under his control and disposable in the United Kingdom an income of his own of not less than £25,000 per annum; and
(iii) is able and willing to maintain and accommodate himself and any dependants indefinitely in the United Kingdom from his own resources with no assistance from any other person and without taking employment or having recourse to public funds; and
(iv) can demonstrate a close connection with the United Kingdom; and
(v) intends to make the United Kingdom his main home; and
(vi) holds a valid United Kingdom entry clearance for entry in this capacity.

Leave to enter as a retired person of independent means

264. A person seeking leave to enter the United Kingdom as a retired person of independent means may be admitted subject to a condition prohibiting employment for a period not exceeding [5 years], provided he is able to produce to the Immigration Officer, on arrival, a valid United Kingdom entry clearance for entry in this capacity.

Note: Words in square brackets substituted from 3 April 2006 (HC 1016).

Refusal of leave to enter as a retired person of independent means

265. Leave to enter as a retired person of independent means is to be refused if a valid United Kingdom entry clearance for entry in this capacity is not produced to the Immigration Officer on arrival.

Requirements for an extension of stay as a retired person of independent means

266. The requirements for an extension of stay as a retired person of independent means are that the applicant:
(i) entered the United Kingdom with a valid United Kingdom entry clearance as a retired person of independent means; and
(ii) meets the requirements of paragraph 263(ii)–(iv); and
(iii) has made the United Kingdom his main home.

[266A. The requirements for an extension of stay as a retired person of independent means for a person in the United Kingdom as a work permit holder are that the applicant:
(i) entered the United Kingdom or was granted leave to remain as a work permit holder in accordance with paragraphs 128 to 133 of these Rules; and
(ii) meets the requirements of paragraph 263 (i)–(v).]

Note: Paragraph 266A inserted from 15 March 2005 (HC 346).

[**266B.** The requirements for an extension of stay as a retired person of independent means for a person in the United Kingdom as a highly skilled migrant are that the applicant:
- (i) entered the United Kingdom or was granted leave to remain as a highly skilled migrant in accordance with paragraphs 135A to 135F of these Rules; and
- (ii) meets the requirements of paragraph 263 (i)–(v).]

Note: Paragraph 266B inserted from 15 March 2005 (HC 346).

[**266C.** The requirements for an extension of stay as a retired person of independent means for a person in the United Kingdom to establish themselves or remain in business are that the applicant:
- (i) entered the United Kingdom or was granted leave to remain as a person intending to establish themselves or remain in business in accordance with paragraphs 201 to 208 of these Rules; and
- (ii) meets the requirements of paragraph 263 (i)–(v).]

Note: Paragraph 266C inserted from 15 March 2005 (HC 346).

[**266D.** The requirements for an extension of stay as a retired person of independent means for a person in the United Kingdom as an innovator are that the applicant:
- (i) entered the United Kingdom or was granted leave to remain as an innovator in accordance with paragraphs 210A to 210F of these Rules; and
- (ii) meets the requirements of paragraph 263 (i)–(v).]

Note: Paragraph 266D inserted from 15 March 2005 (HC 346).

Extension of stay as a retired person of independent means

[**267.** An extension of stay as a retired person of independent means, with a prohibition on the taking of employment, may be granted so as to bring the person's stay in this category up to a maximum of {5 years} in aggregate, provided the Secretary of State is satisfied that each of the requirements of paragraph 266 is met. An extension of stay as a retired person of independent means, with a prohibition on the taking of employment, may be granted for a maximum period of {5 years}, provided the Secretary of State is satisfied that each of the requirements of paragraph 266A, 266B, 266C or 266D is met.]

Note: Paragraph 267 substituted from 15 March 2005 (HC 346). Words in curly brackets substituted from 3 April 2006 (HC 1016).

Refusal of extension of stay as a retired person of independent means

[**268.** An extension of stay as a retired person of independent means is to be refused if the Secretary of State is not satisfied that each of the requirements of paragraph 266, 266A, 266B, 266C or 266D is met.]

Note: Paragraph 268 substituted from 15 March 2005 (HC 346).

Indefinite leave to remain for a retired person of independent means

269. Indefinite leave to remain may be granted, on application, to a person admitted as a retired person of independent means provided he:

(i) has spent a continuous period of [5 years] in the United Kingdom in this capacity; and
(ii) has met the requirements of paragraph 266 throughout the [5 year] period and continues to do so.

Note: Words in square brackets substituted from 3 April 2006 (HC 1016).

Refusal of indefinite leave to remain for a retired person of independent means

270. Indefinite leave to remain in the United Kingdom for a retired person of independent means is to be refused if the Secretary of State is not satisfied that each of the requirements of paragraph [269] is met.

Note: Number in square brackets substituted from 1 September 1996 (Cm 3365).

Spouses [or civil partners] of persons with limited leave to enter or remain in the United Kingdom as retired persons of independent means

Requirements for leave to enter or remain as the spouse [or civil partner] of a person with limited leave to enter or remain in the United Kingdom as a retired person of independent means

271. The requirements to be met by a person seeking leave to enter or remain in the United Kingdom as the spouse [or civil partner] of a person with limited leave to enter or remain in the United Kingdom as a retired person of independent means are that:

(i) the applicant is married [or the civil partner of] to a person with limited leave to enter or remain in the United Kingdom as a retired person of independent means; and
(ii) each of the parties intends to live with the other as his or her spouse [or civil partner] during the applicant's stay and the marriage [or civil partnership] is subsisting; and
(iii) there will be adequate accommodation for the parties and any dependants without recourse to public funds in accommodation which they own or occupy exclusively; and
(iv) the parties will be able to maintain themselves and any dependants adequately without recourse to public funds; and

(v) the applicant does not intend to stay in the United Kingdom beyond any period of leave granted to his spouse [or civil partner]; and

(vi) if seeking leave to enter, the applicant holds a valid United Kingdom entry clearance for entry in this capacity or, if seeking leave to remain, was admitted with a valid United Kingdom entry clearance for entry in this capacity.

Note: References to civil partnership inserted from 5 December 2005 (HC 582).

Leave to enter or remain as the spouse [or civil partner] of a person with limited leave to enter or remain in the United Kingdom as a retired person of independent means

272. A person seeking leave to enter or remain in the United Kingdom as the spouse [or civil partner] of a person with limited leave to enter or remain in the United Kingdom as a retired person of independent means may be given leave to enter or remain in the United Kingdom for a period not in excess of that granted to the person given limited leave to enter or remain as a retired person of independent means provided that, in relation to an application for leave to enter, he is able to produce to the Immigration Officer, on arrival, a valid United Kingdom entry clearance for entry in this capacity, or, in the case of an application for limited leave to remain, he was admitted with a valid United Kingdom entry clearance for entry in this capacity and is able to satisfy the Secretary of State that each of the requirements of paragraph 271(i)–(v) is met. An application for indefinite leave to remain in this category may be granted provided the applicant was admitted with a valid United Kingdom entry clearance for entry in this capacity and is able to satisfy the Secretary of State that each of the requirements of paragraph 271(i)–(v) is met and provided indefinite leave to remain is, at the same time, being granted to the person with limited leave to enter or remain as a retired person of independent means. Leave to enter or remain is to be subject to a condition prohibiting employment except in relation to the grant of indefinite leave to remain.

Note: References to civil partnership inserted from 5 December 2005 (HC 582).

Refusal of leave to enter or remain as the spouse [or civil partner] of a person with limited leave to enter or remain in the United Kingdom as a retired person of independent means

273. Leave to enter or remain in the United Kingdom as the spouse [or civil partner] of a person with limited leave to enter or remain in the United Kingdom as a retired person of independent means is to be refused if, in relation to an application for leave to enter, a valid United Kingdom entry clearance for entry in this capacity is not produced to the Immigration Officer on arrival or, in the case of an application for limited leave to remain, if the applicant was not admitted with a valid United Kingdom entry clearance for entry in this capacity or is unable to satisfy the Secretary of State that each of the requirements of paragraph 271(i)–(v) is met. An application for indefinite leave to remain in this category is to be refused if the applicant was not admitted with a valid United Kingdom entry clearance for entry in this capacity or is unable to satisfy the Secretary of State that each of the requirements of paragraph 271(i)–(v) is met or if indefinite leave to remain is not, at the same time, being granted to the person with limited leave to enter or remain as a retired person of independent means.

Note: References to civil partnership inserted from 5 December 2005 (HC 582).

Children of persons with limited leave to enter or remain in the United Kingdom as retired persons of independent means

Requirements for leave to enter or remain as the child of a person with limited leave to enter or remain in the United Kingdom as a retired person of independent means

274. The requirements to be met by a person seeking leave to enter or remain in the United Kingdom as the child of a person with limited leave to enter or remain in the United Kingdom as a retired person of independent means are that:

(i) he is the child of a parent who has been admitted to or allowed to remain in the United Kingdom as a retired person of independent means; and

(ii) he is under the age of 18 or has current leave to enter or remain in this capacity; and

(iii) he is unmarried [and is not a civil partner], has not formed an independent family unit and is not leading an independent life; and

(iv) he can, and will, be maintained and accommodated adequately without recourse to public funds in accommodation which his parent(s) own or occupy exclusively; and

(v) he will not stay in the United Kingdom beyond any period of leave granted to his parent(s); and

(vi) both parents are being or have been admitted to or allowed to remain in the United Kingdom save where:

(a) the parent he is accompanying or joining is his sole surviving parent; or

(b) the parent he is accompanying or joining has had sole responsibility for his upbringing; or

(c) there are serious and compelling family or other considerations which make exclusion from the United Kingdom undesirable and suitable arrangements have been made for his care; and

(vii) if seeking leave to enter, he holds a valid United Kingdom entry clearance for entry in this capacity or, if seeking leave to remain, was admitted with a valid United Kingdom entry clearance for entry in this capacity.

Note: Words in square brackets in sub-para (iii) inserted from 5 December 2005 (HC 582).

Leave to enter or remain as the child of a person with limited leave to enter or remain in the United Kingdom as a retired person of independent means

275. A person seeking leave to enter or remain in the United Kingdom as the child of a person with limited leave to enter or remain in the United Kingdom as a retired person of independent means may be given leave to enter or remain in the United Kingdom for a period of leave not in excess of that granted to the person with limited leave to enter or remain as a retired person of independent means provided that, in relation to an application for leave to enter, he is able to produce to the Immigration Officer, on arrival, a valid United Kingdom entry clearance for entry in this capacity or, in the case of an application for limited leave to remain, he was admitted with a valid United Kingdom entry clearance for entry in this capacity and is able to satisfy the Secretary of State that each of the requirements of paragraph 274(i)–(vi) is met. An application for indefinite leave to remain in this category may be granted provided the applicant was admitted to the United Kingdom with a valid United Kingdom entry clearance for entry in this capacity and is able to satisfy the Secretary of State that each of the requirements of paragraph 274(i)–(vi) is met and provided indefinite leave to remain is, at the same time, being granted to the person with limited leave to enter or remain as a retired person of independent means. Leave to enter or remain is to be subject to a condition prohibiting employment except in relation to the grant of indefinite leave to remain.

Refusal of leave to enter or remain as the child of a person with limited leave to enter or remain in the United Kingdom as a retired person of independent means

276. Leave to enter or remain in the United Kingdom as the child of a person with limited leave to enter or remain in the United Kingdom as a retired person of independent means is to be refused if, in relation to an application for leave to enter, a valid United Kingdom entry clearance for entry in this capacity is not produced to the Immigration Officer on arrival, or in the case of an application for limited leave to remain, if the applicant was not admitted with a valid United Kingdom entry clearance for entry in this capacity or is unable to satisfy the Secretary of State that each of the requirements of paragraph 274(i)–(vi) is met. An application for indefinite leave to remain in this category is to be refused if the applicant was not admitted with a valid United Kingdom entry clearance for entry in this capacity or is unable to satisfy the Secretary of State that each of the requirements of paragraph 274(i)–(vi) is met or if indefinite leave to remain is not, at the same time, being granted to the person with limited leave to enter or remain as a retired person of independent means.

Long residence

[Long residence in the United Kingdom

276A. For the purposes of paragraphs 276B to 276D:

(a) 'continuous residence' means residence in the United Kingdom for an unbroken period, and for these purposes a period shall not be considered to have been broken where an applicant is absent from the United Kingdom for a period of 6 months or less at any one time, provided that the applicant in question has existing limited leave to enter or remain upon their departure and return, but shall be considered to have been broken if the applicant:

(i) has been removed under Schedule 2 of the 1971 Act, section 10 of the 1999 Act, has been deported or has left the United Kingdom having been refused leave to enter or remain here; or

(ii) has left the United Kingdom and, on doing so, evidenced a clear intention not to return; or

(iii) left the United Kingdom in circumstances in which he could have had no reasonable expectation at the time of leaving that he would lawfully be able to return; or

(iv) has been convicted of an offence and was sentenced to a period of imprisonment or was directed to be detained in an institution other than a prison (including, in particular, a hospital or an institution for young offenders), provided that the sentence in question was not a suspended sentence; or

(v) has spent a total of more than 18 months absent from the United Kingdom during the period in question.

(b) 'lawful residence' means residence which is continuous residence pursuant to:

(i) existing leave to enter or remain; or

(ii) temporary admission within section 11 of the 1971 Act where leave to enter or remain is subsequently granted; or

(iii) an exemption from immigration control, including where an exemption ceases to apply if it is immediately followed by a grant of leave to enter or remain.]

Note: Paragraph 276A inserted from 1 April 2003 (HC 538).

[Requirements for indefinite leave to remain on the ground of long residence in the United Kingdom

276B. The requirements to be met by an applicant for indefinite leave to remain on the ground of long residence in the United Kingdom are that:

(i) (a) he has had at least 10 years continuous lawful residence in the United Kingdom; or [(b) he has had at least 14 years continuous residence in the United Kingdom, excluding any period spent in the United Kingdom following service of notice of liability to removal or notice of a decision to remove by way of directions under paragraphs 8 to 10A, or 12 to 14, of Schedule 2 to the Immigration Act 1971 or section 10 of the Immigration and Asylum Act 1999, or of a notice of intention to deport him from the United Kingdom; and]

(ii) having regard to the public interest there are no reasons why it would be undesirable for him to be given indefinite leave to remain on the ground of long residence, taking into account his:
(a) age; and
(b) strength of connections in the United Kingdom; and
(c) personal history, including character, conduct, associations and employment record; and
(d) domestic circumstances; and
(e) previous criminal record and the nature of any offence of which the person has been convicted; and
(f) compassionate circumstances; and
(g) any representations received on the person's behalf.]

Note: Paragraph 276B inserted from 1 April 2003 (HC 538). Subparagraph (i)(b) substituted from 1 October 2004 (Cm 6339).

[Indefinite leave to remain on the ground of long residence in the United Kingdom

276C. Indefinite leave to remain on the ground of long residence in the United Kingdom may be granted provided that the Secretary of State is satisfied that each of the requirements of paragraph 276B is met.]

Note: Paragraph 276C inserted from 1 April 2003 (HC 538).

[Refusal of indefinite leave to remain on the ground of long residence in the United Kingdom

276D. Indefinite leave to remain on the ground of long residence in the United Kingdom is to be refused if the Secretary of State is not satisfied that each of the requirements of paragraph 276B is met.]

Note: Paragraph 276D inserted from 1 April 2003 (HC 538).

HM Forces

Definition of Gurkha

[**276E.** For the purposes of these Rules the term 'Gurkha' means a citizen or national of Nepal who has served in the Brigade of Gurkhas of the British Army under the Brigade of Gurkhas' terms and conditions of service.]

Note: Paragraph 276E inserted from 25 October 2004 (Cm 1112).

Leave to enter or remain in the United Kingdom as a Gurkha discharged from the British Army

Requirements for indefinite leave to enter the United Kingdom as a Gurkha discharged from the British Army

[276F. The requirements for indefinite leave to enter the United Kingdom as a Gurkha discharged from the British Army are that:

(i) the applicant has completed at least four years' service as a Gurkha with the British Army; and

(ii) was discharged from the British Army in Nepal on completion of engagement on or after 1 July 1997; and

(iii) was not discharged from the British Army more than 2 years prior to the date on which the application is made; and

(iv) holds a valid United Kingdom entry clearance for entry in this capacity.]

Note: Paragraph 276F inserted from 25 October 2004 (Cm 1112).

Indefinite leave to enter the United Kingdom as a Gurkha discharged from the British Army

[**276G.** A person seeking indefinite leave to enter the United Kingdom as a Gurkha discharged from the British Army may be granted indefinite leave to enter provided a valid United Kingdom entry clearance for entry in this capacity is produced to the Immigration Officer on arrival.]

Note: Paragraph 276G inserted from 25 October 2004 (Cm 1112).

Refusal of indefinite leave to enter the United Kingdom as a Gurkha discharged from the British Army

276H. Indefinite leave to enter the United Kingdom as a Gurkha discharged from the British Army is to be refused if a valid United Kingdom entry clearance for entry in this capacity is not produced to the Immigration Officer on arrival.

Note: Paragraph 276H inserted from 25 October 2004 (Cm 1112).

Requirements for indefinite leave to remain in the United Kingdom as a Gurkha discharged from the British Army

[**276I.** The requirements for indefinite leave to remain in the United Kingdom as a Gurkha discharged from the British Army are that:

(i) the applicant has completed at least four years' service as a Gurkha with the British Army; and
(ii) was discharged from the British Army in Nepal on completion of engagement on or after 1 July 1997; and
(iii) was not discharged from the British Army more than 2 years prior to the date on which the application is made; and
(iv) on the date of application has leave to enter or remain in the United Kingdom.]

Note: Paragraph 276I inserted from 25 October 2004 (Cm 1112).

Indefinite leave to remain in the United Kingdom as a Gurkha discharged from the British Army

[**276J.** A person seeking indefinite leave to remain in the United Kingdom as a Gurkha discharged from the British Army may be granted indefinite leave to remain provided the Secretary of State is satisfied that each of the requirements of paragraph 276I is met.]

Note: Paragraph 276J inserted from 25 October 2004 (Cm 1112).

Refusal of indefinite leave to remain in the United Kingdom as a Gurkha discharged from the British Army

[**276K.** Indefinite leave to remain in the United Kingdom as a Gurkha discharged from the British Army is to be refused if the Secretary of State is not satisfied that each of the requirements of paragraph 276I is met.]

Note: Paragraph 276K inserted from 25 October 2004 (Cm 1112).

Leave to enter or remain in the United Kingdom as a foreign or Commonwealth citizen discharged from HM forces

Requirements for indefinite leave to enter the United Kingdom as a foreign or Commonwealth citizen discharged from HM Forces

[**276L.** The requirements for indefinite leave to enter the United Kingdom as a foreign or Commonwealth citizen discharged from HM Forces are that:
(i) the applicant has completed at least four years' service with HM Forces; and
(ii) was discharged from HM Forces on completion of engagement; and
(iii) was not discharged from HM Forces more than 2 years prior to the date on which the application is made; and
(iv) holds a valid United Kingdom entry clearance for entry in this capacity.]

Note: Paragraph 276L inserted from 25 October 2004 (Cm 1112).

Indefinite leave to enter the United Kingdom as a foreign or Commonwealth citizen discharged from HM Forces

[**276M.** A person seeking indefinite leave to enter the United Kingdom as a foreign or Commonwealth citizen discharged from HM Forces may be granted indefinite leave to enter provided a valid United Kingdom entry clearance for entry in this capacity is produced to the Immigration Officer on arrival.]

Note: Paragraph 276M inserted from 25 October 2004 (Cm 1112).

Refusal of indefinite leave to enter the United Kingdom as a foreign or Commonwealth citizen discharged from HM Forces

[**276N.** Indefinite leave to enter the United Kingdom as a foreign or Commonwealth citizen discharged from HM Forces is to be refused if a valid United Kingdom entry clearance for entry in this capacity is not produced to the Immigration Officer on arrival.]

Note: Paragraph 276N inserted from 25 October 2004 (Cm 1112).

Requirements for indefinite leave to remain in the United Kingdom as a foreign or Commonwealth citizen discharged from HM Forces

[**276O.** The requirements for indefinite leave to remain in the United Kingdom as a foreign or Commonwealth citizen discharged from HM Forces are that:

(i) the applicant has completed at least four years' service with HM Forces; and

(ii) was discharged from HM Forces on completion of engagement; and

(iii) was not discharged from HM Forces more than 2 years prior to the date on which the application is made; and

(iv) on the date of application has leave to enter or remain in the United Kingdom.]

Note: Paragraph 276O inserted from 25 October 2004 (Cm 1112).

Indefinite leave to remain in the United Kingdom as a foreign or Commonwealth citizen discharged from HM Forces

[**276P.** A person seeking indefinite leave to remain in the United Kingdom as a foreign or Commonwealth citizen discharged from HM Forces may be granted indefinite leave to remain provided the Secretary of State is satisfied that each of the requirements of paragraph 276O is met.]

Note: Paragraph 276P inserted from 25 October 2004 (Cm 1112).

Refusal of indefinite leave to remain in the United Kingdom as a foreign or Commonwealth citizen discharged from HM Forces

[276Q. Indefinite leave to remain in the United Kingdom as a foreign or Commonwealth citizen discharged from HM Forces is to be refused if the Secretary of State is not satisfied that each of the requirements of paragraph 276O is met.]

Note: Paragraph 276Q inserted from 25 October 2004 (Cm 1112).

Spouses [or civil partners] of persons settled or seeking settlement in the United Kingdom in accordance with paragraphs 276E to 276Q (HM Forces rules)

Leave to enter or remain in the UK as the spouse of a person present and settled in the United Kingdom or being granted settlement on the same occasion in accordance with paragraphs 276E to 276Q

Requirements for indefinite leave to enter the United Kingdom as the spouse [or civil partner] of a person present and settled in the United Kingdom or being admitted on the same occasion for settlement under paragraphs 276E to 276Q

[276R. The requirements to be met by a person seeking indefinite leave to enter the United Kingdom as the spouse [or civil partner] of a person present and settled in the United Kingdom or being admitted on the same occasion for settlement in accordance with paragraphs 276E to 276Q are that:

(i) the applicant is married to [, or the civil partner of] a person present and settled in the United Kingdom or who is being admitted on the same occasion for settlement in accordance with paragraphs 276E to 276Q; and
(ii) the parties to the marriage [or civil partnership] have met; and
(iii) the parties were married [or formed a civil partnership] at least 2 years ago; and
(iv) each of the parties intends to live permanently with the other as his or her spouse [or civil partner], and
(v) the marriage [or civil partnership] is subsisting; and
(vi) the applicant holds a valid United Kingdom entry clearance for entry in this capacity.]

Note: Paragraph 276R inserted from 1 January 2005 (HC 164). References to civil partnership inserted from 5 December 2005 (HC 582).

Indefinite leave to enter the United Kingdom as the spouse [or civil partner] of a person present and settled in the United Kingdom or being admitted on the same occasion for settlement in accordance with paragraphs 276E to 276Q

[276S. A person seeking leave to enter the United Kingdom as the spouse [or civil partner] of a person present and settled in the United Kingdom or being admitted on the same occasion for settlement in accordance with paragraphs 276E to 276Q may be granted indefinite leave to enter provided a valid United Kingdom entry clearance for entry in this capacity is produced to the Immigration Officer on arrival.]

Note: Paragraph 276S inserted from 1 January 2005 (HC 164). References to civil partnership inserted from 5 December 2005 (HC 582).

Refusal of indefinite leave to enter the United Kingdom as the spouse [or civil partner] of a person present and settled in the UK or being admitted on the same occasion for settlement in accordance with paragraphs 276E to 276Q

[276T. Leave to enter the United Kingdom as the spouse [or civil partner] of a person present and settled in the United Kingdom or being admitted on the same occasion for settlement in accordance with paragraphs 276E to 276Q is to be refused if a valid United Kingdom entry clearance for entry in this capacity is not produced to the Immigration Officer on arrival.]

Note: Paragraph 276T inserted from 1 January 2005 (HC 164). References to civil partnership inserted from 5 December 2005 (HC 582).

Requirements for indefinite leave to remain in the United Kingdom as the spouse [or civil partner] of a person present and settled in the United Kingdom or being granted settlement on the same occasion in accordance with paragraphs 276E to 276Q

[276U. The requirements to be met by a person seeking indefinite leave to remain in the United Kingdom as the spouse [or civil partner] of a person present and settled in the United Kingdom or being granted settlement on the same occasion in accordance with paragraphs 276E to 276Q are that:

(i) the applicant is married to [, or the civil partner of] a person present and settled in the United Kingdom or being granted settlement on the same occasion in accordance with paragraphs 276E to 276Q; and
(ii) the parties to the marriage [or civil partnership] have met; and
(iii) the parties were married [or formed a civil partnership] at least 2 years ago; and
(iv) each of the parties intends to live permanently with the other as his or her spouse [or civil partner]; and
(v) the marriage [or civil partnership] is subsisting; and
(vi) has leave to enter or remain in the United Kingdom.]

Note: Paragraph 276U inserted from 1 January 2005 (HC 164). References to civil partnership inserted from 5 December 2005 (HC 582).

Indefinite leave to remain in the United Kingdom as the spouse [or civil partner] of a person present and settled in the United Kingdom or being granted settlement on the same occasion in accordance with paragraphs 276E to 276Q

[276V. Indefinite leave to remain in the United Kingdom as the spouse [or civil partner] of a person present and settled in the United Kingdom or being granted settlement on the same occasion in accordance with paragraphs 276E to 276Q may be granted provided the Secretary of State is satisfied that each of the requirements of paragraph 276U is met.]

Note: Paragraph 276V inserted from 1 January 2005 (HC 164). References to civil partnership inserted from 5 December 2005 (HC 582).

Refusal of indefinite leave to remain in the United Kingdom as the spouse [or civil partner] of a person present and settled in the United Kingdom or being granted settlement on the same occasion in accordance with paragraphs 276E to 276Q

[276W. Indefinite leave to remain in the United Kingdom as the spouse [or civil partner] of a person present and settled in the United Kingdom or being granted settlement on the same occasion in accordance with paragraphs 276E to 276Q is to be refused if the Secretary of State is not satisfied that each of the requirements of paragraph 276U is met.]

Note: Paragraph 276W inserted from 1 January 2005 (HC 164). References to civil partnership inserted from 5 December 2005 (HC 582).

Children of a parent, parents or a relative settled or seeking settlement in the United Kingdom under paragraphs 276E to 276Q (HM Forces rules)

Leave to enter or remain in the United Kingdom as the child of a parent, parents or a relative present and settled in the United Kingdom or being granted settlement on the same occasion in accordance with paragraphs 276E to 276Q

Requirements for indefinite leave to enter the United Kingdom as the child of a parent, parents or a relative present and settled in the United Kingdom or being admitted for settlement on the same occasion in accordance with paragraphs 276E to 276Q

[276X. The requirements to be met by a person seeking indefinite leave to enter the United Kingdom as the child of a parent, parents or a relative present and settled in the United Kingdom or being admitted for settlement on the same occasion in accordance with paragraphs 276E to 276Q are that:

(i) the applicant is seeking indefinite leave to enter to accompany or join a parent, parents or a relative in one of the following circumstances:

(a) both parents are present and settled in the United Kingdom; or
(b) both parents are being admitted on the same occasion for settlement; or
(c) one parent is present and settled in the United Kingdom and the other is being admitted on the same occasion for settlement; or
(d) one parent is present and settled in the United Kingdom or being admitted on the same occasion for settlement and the other parent is dead; or
(e) one parent is present and settled in the United Kingdom or being admitted on the same occasion for settlement and has had sole responsibility for the child's upbringing; or
(f) one parent or a relative is present and settled in the United Kingdom or being admitted on the same occasion for settlement and there are serious and compelling family or other considerations which make exclusion of the child undesirable and suitable arrangements have been made for the child's care; and

(ii) is under the age of 18; and
(iii) is not leading an independent life, is unmarried [and is not a civil partner], and has not formed an independent family unit; and
(iv) holds a valid United Kingdom entry clearance for entry in this capacity.]

Note: Paragraph 276X inserted from 1 January 2005 (HC 164). References to civil partner inserted from 5 December 2005 (HC 582).

Indefinite leave to enter the United Kingdom as the child of a parent, parents or a relative present and settled in the United Kingdom or being admitted for settlement on the same occasion in accordance with paragraphs 276E to 276Q

[**276Y.** Indefinite leave to enter the United Kingdom as the child of a parent, parents or a relative present and settled in the United Kingdom or being admitted for settlement on the same occasion in accordance with paragraphs 276E to 276Q may be granted provided a valid United Kingdom entry clearance for entry in this capacity is produced to the Immigration Officer on arrival.]

Note: Paragraph 276Y inserted from 1 January 2005 (HC 164).

Refusal of indefinite leave to enter the United Kingdom as the child of a parent, parents or a relative present and settled in the United Kingdom or being admitted for settlement on the same occasion in accordance with paragraphs 276E to 276Q

[**276Z.** Indefinite leave to enter the United Kingdom as the child of a parent, parents, or a relative present and settled in the United Kingdom or being admitted for settlement on the same occasion in accordance with paragraphs 276E to 276Q is to be refused if a valid United Kingdom entry clearance for entry in this capacity is not produced to the Immigration Officer on arrival.]

Note: Paragraph 276Z inserted from 1 January 2005 (HC 164).

Requirements for indefinite leave to remain in the United Kingdom as the child of a parent, parents or a relative present and settled in the United Kingdom or being granted settlement on the same occasion in accordance with paragraphs 276E to 276Q

[**276AA.** The requirements to be met by a person seeking indefinite leave to remain in the United Kingdom as the child of a parent, parents or a relative present and settled in the United Kingdom or being granted settlement on the same occasion in accordance with paragraphs 276E to 276Q are that:

(i) the applicant is seeking indefinite leave to remain with a parent, parents or a relative in one of the following circumstances:
  - (a) both parents are present and settled in the United Kingdom or being granted settlement on the same occasion; or
  - (b) one parent is present and settled in the United Kingdom or being granted settlement on the same occasion and the other parent is dead; or
  - (c) one parent is present and settled in the United Kingdom or being granted settlement on the same occasion and has had sole responsibility for the child's upbringing; or
  - (d) one parent or a relative is present and settled in the United Kingdom or being granted settlement on the same occasion and there are serious and compelling family or other considerations which make exclusion of the child undesirable and suitable arrangements have been made for the child's care; and

(ii) is under the age of 18; and

(iii) is not leading an independent life, is unmarried [and is not a civil partner], and has not formed an independent family unit; and

(iv) has leave to enter or remain in the United Kingdom.]

Note: Paragraph 276AA inserted from 1 January 2005 (HC 164). Reference to civil partner inserted from 5 December 2005 (HC 582).

Indefinite leave to remain in the United Kingdom as the child of a parent, parents or a relative present and settled in the United Kingdom or being granted settlement on the same occasion in accordance with paragraphs 276E to 276Q

[**276AB.** Indefinite leave to remain in the United Kingdom as the child of a parent, parents or a relative present and settled in the United Kingdom or being granted settlement on the same occasion in accordance with paragraphs 276E to 276Q may be granted if the Secretary of State is satisfied that each of the requirements of paragraph 276AA is met.]

Note: Paragraph 276AB inserted from 1 January 2005 (HC 164).

Refusal of indefinite leave to remain in the United Kingdom as the child of a parent, parents or a relative present and settled in the United Kingdom or being granted settlement on the same occasion in accordance with paragraphs 276E to 276Q

[**276AC.** Indefinite leave to remain in the United Kingdom as the child of a parent, parents or a relative present and settled in the United Kingdom or being granted settlement on the same occasion in accordance with paragraphs 276E to 276Q is to be refused if the Secretary of State is not satisfied that each of the requirements of paragraph 276AA is met.]

Note: Paragraph 276AC inserted from 1 January 2005 (HC 164).

Spouses [or civil partners] of Armed Forces members who are exempt from immigration control under Section 8(4) of the Immigration Act 1971

Requirements for leave to enter or remain as the spouse [or civil partner] of an armed forces member who is exempt from immigration control under section 8(4) of the Immigration Act 1971

[**276AD.** The requirements to be met by a person seeking leave to enter or remain in the United Kingdom as the spouse [or civil partner] of an armed forces member who is exempt from immigration control under section 8(4) of the Immigration Act 1971 are that:

(i) the applicant is married [, or the civil partner of] to an armed forces member who is exempt from immigration control under section 8(4) of the Immigration Act 1971; and
(ii) each of the parties intends to live with the other as his or her spouse [or civil partner] during the applicant's stay and the marriage [or civil partnership] is subsisting; and
(iii) there will be adequate accommodation for the parties and any dependants without recourse to public funds in accommodation which they own or occupy exclusively; and
(iv) the parties will be able to maintain themselves and any dependants adequately without recourse to public funds; and
(v) the applicant does not intend to stay in the United Kingdom beyond his or her spouse's [or civil partner's] enlistment in the home forces, or period of posting or training in the United Kingdom.]

Note: Paragraph 276AD inserted from 15 March 2005 (HC 346). References to civil partnership inserted from 5 December 2005 (HC 582).

Leave to enter or remain as the spouse [or civil partner] of an armed forces member who is exempt from immigration control under section 8(4) of the Immigration Act 1971

[**276AE.** A person seeking leave to enter or remain in the United Kingdom as the spouse [or civil partner] of an armed forces member who is exempt from immigration control under section 8(4) of the Immigration Act 1971 may be given leave to enter or remain in the United Kingdom for a period not exceeding 4 years or the duration of the enlistment, posting or training of his or her spouse [or civil partner], whichever is shorter, provided that the Immigration Officer, or in the case of an application for leave to remain, the Secretary of State, is satisfied that each of the requirements of paragraph 276AD (i)–(v) is met.]

Note: Paragraph 276AE inserted from 15 March 2005 (HC 346). References to civil partner inserted from 5 December 2005 (HC 582).

Refusal of leave to enter or remain as the spouse [or civil partner] of an armed forces member who is exempt from immigration control under section 8(4) of the Immigration Act 1971

[**276AF.** Leave to enter or remain in the United Kingdom as the spouse [or civil partner] of an armed forces member who is exempt from immigration control under section 8(4) of the Immigration Act 1971 is to be refused if the Immigration Officer, or in the case of an application for leave to remain, the Secretary of State, is not satisfied that each of the requirements of paragraph 276AD (i)–(v) is met.]

Note: Paragraph 276AF inserted from 15 March 2005 (HC 346). References to civil partner inserted from 5 December 2005 (HC 852).

Children of Armed Forces members who are exempt from immigration control under section 8(4) of the Immigration Act 1971

Requirements for leave to enter or remain as the child of an armed forces member exempt from immigration control under section 8(4) of the Immigration Act 1971

[**276AG.** The requirements to be met by a person seeking leave to enter or remain in the United Kingdom as the child of an armed forces member exempt from immigration control under section 8(4) of the Immigration Act 1971 are that:

(i) he is the child of a parent who is an armed forces member exempt from immigration control under section 8(4) of the Immigration Act 1971; and

(ii) he is under the age of 18 or has current leave to enter or remain in this capacity; and

(iii) he is unmarried [and is not a civil partner] has not formed an independent family unit and is not leading an independent life; and
(iv) he can and will be maintained and accommodated adequately without recourse to public funds in accommodation which his parent(s) own or occupy exclusively; and
(v) he will not stay in the United Kingdom beyond the period of his parent's enlistment in the home forces, or posting or training in the United Kingdom; and
(vi) his other parent is being or has been admitted to or allowed to remain in the United Kingdom save where:
  (a) the parent he is accompanying or joining is his sole surviving parent; or
  (b) the parent he is accompanying or joining has had sole responsibility for his upbringing; or
  (c) there are serious and compelling family or other considerations which make exclusion from the United Kingdom undesirable and suitable arrangements have been made for his care.]

Note: Paragraph 276AG inserted from 15 March 2005 (HC 346). Reference to civil partner inserted from 5 December 2005 (HC 582).

Leave to enter or remain as the child of an armed forces member exempt from immigration control under section 8(4) of the Immigration Act 1971

[**276AH.** A person seeking leave to enter or remain in the United Kingdom as the child of an armed forces member exempt from immigration control under section 8(4) of the Immigration Act 1971 may be given leave to enter or remain in the United Kingdom for a period not exceeding 4 years or the duration of the enlistment, posting or training of his parent, whichever is the shorter, provided that the Immigration Officer, or in the case of an application for leave to remain, the Secretary of State, is satisfied that each of the requirements of 276AG (i)–(vi) is met.]

Note: Paragraph 276AH inserted from 15 March 2005 (HC 346).

Refusal of leave to enter or remain as the child of an armed forces member exempt from immigration control under section 8(4) of the Immigration Act 1971

[**276AI.** Leave to enter or remain in the United Kingdom as the child of an armed forces member exempt from immigration control under section 8(4) of the Immigration Act 1971 is to be refused if the Immigration Officer, or in the case of an application for leave to remain, the Secretary of State, is not satisfied that each of the requirements of paragraph 276AG (i)–(vi) is met.]

Note: Paragraph 276AI inserted from 15 March 2005 (HC 346).

Part 8

Family Members

Spouses [and civil partners]

277. Nothing in these Rules shall be construed as permitting a person to be granted entry clearance, leave to enter, leave to remain or variation of leave as a spouse [or civil partner] of another if [either the applicant] [or the sponsor will be aged under 18] on the date of arrival in the United Kingdom or (as the case may be) on the date on which the leave to remain or variation of leave would be granted.

Note: Words in first square brackets substituted from 21 December 2004 (HC 164) and words in second square brackets inserted from 1 April 2003 (HC 538). References to civil partners inserted from 5 December 2005 (HC 582).

[**278.** Nothing in these Rules shall be construed as allowing a person to be granted entry clearance, leave to enter, leave to remain or variation of leave as the spouse of a man or woman (the sponsor) if:

(i) his or her marriage to the sponsor is polygamous; and

(ii) there is another person living who is the husband or wife of the sponsor and who:

(a) is, or at any time since his or her marriage to the sponsor has been, in the United Kingdom; or

(b) has been granted a certificate of entitlement in respect of the right of abode mentioned in Section 2(1)(a) of the Immigration Act 1988 or an entry clearance to enter the United Kingdom as the husband or wife of the sponsor.

For the purpose of this paragraph a marriage may be polygamous although at its inception neither party had any other spouse.]

Note: Substituted from 2 October 2000 (Cm 4851).

[**279.** Paragraph 278 does not apply to any person who seeks entry clearance, leave to enter, leave to remain or variation of leave where:

(i) he or she has been in the United Kingdom before 1 August 1988 having been admitted for the purpose of settlement as the husband or wife of the sponsor; or

(ii) he or she has, since their marriage to the sponsor, been in the United Kingdom at any time when there was no such other spouse living as is mentioned in paragraph 278(ii).

But where a person claims that paragraph 278 does not apply to them because they have been in the United Kingdom in circumstances which cause them to fall within sub-paragraphs (i) or (ii) of that paragraph, it shall be for them to prove that fact.]

Note: Substituted from 2 October 2000 (Cm 4851).

[**280.** For the purposes of paragraphs 278 and 279 the presence of any wife or husband in the United Kingdom in any of the following circumstances shall be disregarded:

(i) as a visitor; or

(ii) as an illegal entrant; or

(iii) in circumstances whereby a person is deemed by virtue of Section 11(1) of the Immigration Act 1971 not to have entered the United Kingdom.]

Note: Substituted from 2 October 2000 (Cm 4851).

Spouses [or civil partners] of persons present and settled in the United Kingdom or being admitted on the same occasion for settlement

Requirements for leave to enter the United Kingdom with a view to settlement as the spouse [or civil partner] of a person present and settled in the United Kingdom or being admitted on the same occasion for settlement

[**281.** The requirements to be met by a person seeking leave to enter the United Kingdom with a view to settlement as the spouse [or civil partner] of a person present and settled in the United Kingdom or who is on the same occasion being admitted for settlement are that:

{(i) (a) the applicant is married to [, or the civil partner of] a person present and settled in the United Kingdom or who is on the same occasion being admitted for settlement; or

(b) the applicant is married to [, or the civil partner of] a person who has a right of abode in the United Kingdom or indefinite leave to enter or remain in the United Kingdom and is on the same occasion seeking admission to the United Kingdom for the purposes of settlement and the parties were married [or formed a civil partnership] at least 4 years ago, since which time they have been living together outside the United Kingdom; and}

(ii) the parties to the marriage have met; and

(iii) each of the parties intends to live permanently with the other as his or her spouse [or civil partner] and the marriage [or civil partnership] is subsisting; and

(iv) there will be adequate accommodation for the parties and any dependants without recourse to public funds in accommodation which they own or occupy exclusively; and

(v) the parties will be able to maintain themselves and any dependants adequately without recourse to public funds; and

(vi) the applicant holds a valid United Kingdom entry clearance for entry in this capacity.]

[For the purposes of this paragraph and paragraphs 282–289 a member of HM Forces serving overseas, or a permanent member of HM Diplomatic Service or a comparable UK-based staff member of the British Council on a tour of duty abroad, or a staff member of the Department for International Development who is a British citizen or is settled in the United Kingdom, is to be regarded as present and settled in the United Kingdom.]

Note: Paragraph 281 substituted from 5 June 1997 (HC 26). Words following sub-para (vi) substituted from 18 September 2002 (Cm 5597). Words in curly brackets substituted from 1 April 2003 (HC 358). References to civil partnership inserted from 5 December 2005 (HC 582).

Leave to enter as the spouse {or civil partner} of a person present and settled in the United Kingdom or being admitted for settlement on the same occasion

282. A person seeking leave to enter the United Kingdom as the spouse {or civil partner} of a person present and settled in the United Kingdom or who is on the same occasion being admitted for settlement may[, in the case of a person within paragraph 281(i)(a),] be admitted for an initial period not exceeding [2 years or, in the case of a person within paragraph 281(i)(b), indefinite leave to enter may be granted] provided a valid United Kingdom entry clearance for entry [in the appropriate] capacity is produced to the Immigration Officer on arrival.

Note: Words in first square brackets inserted and words in other square brackets substituted from 1 April 2003 (HC 538). Reference to civil partners inserted from 5 December 2005 (HC 582).

Refusal of leave to enter as the spouse [or civil partner] of a person present and settled in the United Kingdom or being admitted on the same occasion for settlement

283. Leave to enter the United Kingdom as the spouse [or civil partner] of a person present and settled in the United Kingdom or who is on the same occasion being admitted for settlement is to be refused if a valid United Kingdom entry clearance for entry in this capacity is not produced to the Immigration Officer on arrival.

Requirements for an extension of stay as the spouse [or civil partner] of a person present and settled in the United Kingdom

[**284.** The requirements for an extension of stay as the spouse [or civil partner] of a person present and settled in the United Kingdom are that:

[(i) the applicant has limited leave to enter or remain in the United Kingdom {which was given in accordance with any of the provisions of these Rules} other than where as a result of that leave he would not have been in the United Kingdom beyond 6 months from the date on which he was admitted to the United Kingdom on this occasion in accordance with these Rules, unless the leave in question is limited leave to enter as a fiancé {or proposed civil partner}; and]

(ii) is married to [, or the civil partner of] a person present and settled in the United Kingdom; and
(iii) the parties to the marriage [or civil partnership] have met; and
(iv) the applicant has not remained in breach of the immigration laws; and
(v) the marriage has not taken place after a decision has been made to deport the applicant or he has been recommended for deportation or been given notice under Section 6(2) of the Immigration Act 1971; and
(vi) each of the parties intends to live permanently with the other as his or her spouse [or civil partner] and the marriage [or civil partnership] is subsisting; and
(vii) there will be adequate accommodation for the parties and any dependants without recourse to public funds in accommodation which they own or occupy exclusively; and
(viii) the parties will be able to maintain themselves and any dependants adequately without recourse to public funds.]

Note: Substituted from 5 June 1997 (HC 26). Subparagraph (i) substituted from 25 August 2003 (Cm 5949). Words in first curly brackets in sub-paragraph (i) inserted from 1 October 2004 (Cm 6339). Words in second curly brackets in sub-para (i) inserted from 3 April 2006 (HC 1016). Other references to civil partnership inserted from 5 December 2005 (HC 582).

Extension of stay as the spouse {or civil partner} of a person present and settled in the United Kingdom

285. An extension of stay as the spouse {or civil partner} of a person present and settled in the United Kingdom may be granted for a period of [2 years] in the first instance, provided the Secretary of State is satisfied that each of the requirements of paragraph 284 is met.

Note: Words in square brackets substituted from 1 April 2003 (HC 538). References to civil partners inserted from 5 December 2005 (HC 582).

Refusal of extension of stay as the spouse [or civil partner] of a person present and settled in the United Kingdom

286. An extension of stay as the spouse [or civil partner] of a person present and settled in the United Kingdom is to be refused if the Secretary of State is not satisfied that each of the requirements of paragraph 284 is met.

Requirements for indefinite leave to remain for the spouse {or civil partner} of a person present and settled in the United Kingdom

[**287.**—(a) The requirements for indefinite leave to remain for the spouse {or civil partner} of a person present and settled in the United Kingdom are that:

[(i) (a) the applicant was admitted to the United Kingdom or given an extension of stay for a period of 2 years in accordance with paragraphs 281 to 286 of these Rules and has completed a period of 2 years as the spouse {or civil partner} of a person present and settled in the United Kingdom; or

(b) the applicant was admitted to the United Kingdom or given an extension of stay for a period of 2 years in accordance with paragraphs 295AA to 295F of these Rules and during that 2 year period married {or formed a civil partnership with} the person whom he or she was admitted or granted an extension of stay to join and has completed a period of 2 years as the unmarried {or same-sex} partner and then the spouse {or civil partner} of a person present and settled in the United Kingdom; and]

(ii) the applicant is still the spouse {or civil partner} of the person he or she was admitted or granted an extension of stay to join and the marriage {or civil partnership} is subsisting; and

(iii) each of the parties intends to live permanently with the other as his or her spouse {or civil partner}; and

(iv) there will be adequate accommodation for the parties and any dependants without recourse to public funds in accommodation which they own or occupy exclusively; and

(v) the parties will be able to maintain themselves and any dependants adequately without recourse to public funds.

(b) The requirements for indefinite leave to remain for the bereaved spouse {or civil partner} of a person who was present and settled in the United Kingdom are that:

[(i) (a) the applicant was admitted to the United Kingdom or given an extension of stay for a period of 2 years as the spouse {or civil partner} of a person present and settled in the United Kingdom in accordance with paragraphs 281 to 286 of these Rules; or

(b) the applicant was admitted to the United Kingdom or given an extension of stay for a period of 2 years as the unmarried {or same-sex} partner of a person present and settled in the United Kingdom in accordance with paragraphs 295AA to 295F of these Rules and during that 2 year period married {or formed a civil partnership with} the person whom he or she was admitted or granted an extension of stay to join; and]

(ii) the person whom the applicant was admitted or granted an extension of stay to join died during that [2 years] period; and

(iii) the applicant was still the spouse {or civil partner} of the person he or she was admitted or granted an extension of stay to join at the time of the death; and

(iv) each of the parties intended to live permanently with the other as his or her spouse {or civil partner} and the marriage [or civil partnership] was subsisting at the time of the death.]

Note: Substituted from 2 October 2000 (Cm 4851). Words in square brackets in sub-para (b)(ii) substituted from 1 April 2003 (HC 538). Sub-paragraphs (a)(i) and (b)(i) substituted from 1 October 2004 (Cm 6339). References to civil partnership inserted from 5 December 2005 (HC 582).

Indefinite leave to remain for the spouse [or civil partner] of a person present and settled in the United Kingdom

288. Indefinite leave to remain for the spouse [or civil partner] of a person present and settled in the United Kingdom may be granted provided the Secretary of State is satisfied that each of the requirements of paragraph 287 is met.

Refusal of indefinite leave to remain for the spouse [or civil partner] of a person present and settled in the United Kingdom

289. Indefinite leave to remain for the spouse [or civil partner] of a person present and settled in the United Kingdom is to be refused if the Secretary of State is not satisfied that each of the requirements of paragraph 287 is met.

Note: References to civil partners inserted from 5 December 2005 (HC 582).

[Requirements for indefinite leave to remain in the United Kingdom as the victim of domestic violence

289A. The requirements to be met by a person who is the victim of domestic violence and who is seeking indefinite leave to remain in the United Kingdom are that the applicant:

(i) was admitted to the United Kingdom or given an extension of stay for a period of {2 years} as the spouse [or civil partner] of a person present and settled here; or

(ii) was admitted to the United Kingdom or given an extension of stay for a period of 2 years as the unmarried [or same-sex] partner of a person present and settled here; or

(iii) the relationship with their [spouse, civil partner, unmarried partner or same-sex partner], as appropriate, was subsisting at the beginning of the relevant period of leave or extension of stay referred to in (i) or (ii) above; and

(iv) is able to produce such evidence as may be required by the Secretary of State to establish that the relationship was caused to permanently break down before the end of that period as a result of domestic violence.]

Note: Paragraph 289A inserted from 18 December 2002 (HC 104). Words in curly brackets in sub-para (i) substituted from 1 April 2003 (HC 538). Words in square brackets in sub-paras (i), (ii) and (iii) inserted from 5 December 2005 (HC 582).

[Indefinite leave to remain as the victim of domestic violence

289B. Indefinite leave to remain as the victim of domestic violence may be granted provided the Secretary of State is satisfied that each of the requirements of paragraph 289A is met.]

Note: Paragraph 289B inserted from 1 April 2003 (HC 538).

[Refusal of indefinite leave to remain as the victim of domestic violence

289C. Indefinite leave to remain as the victim of domestic violence is to be refused if the Secretary of State is not satisfied that each of the requirements of paragraph 289A is met.]

Note: Paragraph 289C inserted from 1 April 2003 (HC 538).

Fiancé(e)s [and proposed civil partners]

[**289AA.** Nothing is these Rules shall be construed as permitting a person to be granted entry clearance, leave to enter or variation of leave as a fiancé(e) [or proposed civil partner] if {either the applicant} or the sponsor will be aged under 18 on the date of arrival of the applicant in the United Kingdom or (as the case may be) on the date on which the leave to enter or variation of leave would be granted.]

Note: Paragraph 289AA inserted from 1 April 2003 (HC 538). Words in curly brackets inserted from 21 December 2004 (HC 164). References to civil partnership inserted from 5 December 2005 (HC 582).

Requirements for leave to enter the United Kingdom as a fiancé(e) [or proposed civil partner] (ie with a view to marriage and permanent settlement in the United Kingdom)

[**290.** The requirements to be met by a person seeking leave to enter the United Kingdom as a fiancé(e) [or proposed civil partner] are that:

(i) the applicant is seeking leave to enter the United Kingdom for marriage [or civil partnership] to a person present and settled in the United Kingdom or who is on the same occasion being admitted for settlement; and

(ii) the parties to the proposed marriage [or civil partnership] have met; and

(iii) each of the parties intends to live permanently with the other as his or her spouse [or civil partner] after the marriage [or civil partnership]; and

(iv) adequate maintenance and accommodation without recourse to public funds will be available for the applicant until the date of the marriage [or civil partnership]; and

(v) there will, after the marriage [or civil partnership], be adequate accommodation for the parties and any dependants without recourse to public funds in accommodation which they own or occupy exclusively; and
(vi) the parties will be able after the marriage [or civil partnership] to maintain themselves and any dependants adequately without recourse to public funds; and
(vii) the applicant holds a valid United Kingdom entry clearance for entry in this capacity.]

Note: Substituted from 5 June 1997 (HC 26). References to civil partnership inserted from 5 December 2005 (HC 582).

[**290A.** For the purposes of paragraph 290 and paragraphs 291–295, an EEA national who holds a registration certificate or a document certifying permanent residence issued under the 2006 EEA Regulations (including an EEA national who holds a residence permit issued under the Immigration (European Economic Area) Regulations 2000 which is treated as if it were such a certificate or document by virtue of Schedule 4 to the 2006 EEA Regulations) is to be regarded as present and settled in the United Kingdom.]

Note: Paragraph 290A substituted from 30 April 2006 (HC 1053).

Leave to enter as a fiancé(e) [or proposed civil partner]

291. A person seeking leave to enter the United Kingdom as a fiancé(e) [or proposed civil partner] may be admitted, with a prohibition on employment, for a period not exceeding 6 months to enable the marriage [or civil partnership] to take place provided a valid United Kingdom entry clearance for entry in this capacity is produced to the Immigration Officer on arrival.

Note: References to civil partnership inserted from 5 December 2005 (HC 582).

Refusal of leave to enter as a fiancé(e) [or proposed civil partner]

292. Leave to enter the United Kingdom as a fiancé(e) [or proposed civil partner] is to be refused if a valid United Kingdom entry clearance for entry in this capacity is not produced to the Immigration Officer on arrival.

Note: References to civil partnership inserted from 5 December 2005 (HC 582).

Requirements for an extension of stay as a fiancé(e) [or proposed civil partner]

293. The requirements for an extension of stay as a fiancé(e) [or proposed civil partner] are that:
(i) the applicant was admitted to the United Kingdom with a valid United Kingdom entry clearance as a fiancé(e) [or proposed civil partner]; and

(ii) good cause is shown why the marriage [or civil partnership] did not take place within the initial period of leave granted under paragraph 291; and
(iii) there is satisfactory evidence that the marriage [or civil partnership] will take place at an early date; and
[(iv) the requirements of paragraph 290(ii)–(vi) are met.]

Note: Subparagraph (iv) substituted from 5 June 1997 (HC 26).

Extension of stay as a fiancé(e) [or proposed civil partner]

294. An extension of stay as a fiancé(e) [or proposed civil partner] may be granted for an appropriate period with a prohibition on employment to enable the marriage [or civil partnership] to take place provided the Secretary of State is satisfied that each of the requirements of paragraph 293 is met.

Note: References to civil partnership inserted from 5 December 2005 (HC 582).

Refusal of extension of stay as a fiancé(e) [or proposed civil partner]

295. An extension of stay is to be refused if the Secretary of State is not satisfied that each of the requirements of paragraph 293 is met.

[Leave to enter as the unmarried [or same-sex] partner of a person present and settled in the United Kingdom or being admitted on the same occasion for settlement

[**295AA.** Nothing in these Rules shall be construed as permitting a person to be granted entry clearance, leave to enter or variation of leave as an unmarried [or same-sex] partner if {either the applicant} or the sponsor will be aged under 18 on the date of arrival of the applicant in the United Kingdom or (as the case may be) on the date on which the leave to enter or variation of leave would be granted.]

Note: Paragraph 295AA inserted from 1 April 2003 (HC 538). Words in curly brackets inserted from 21 December 2004 (HC 164). References to same-sex partners inserted from 5 December 2005 (HC 582).

[Requirements for leave to enter the United Kingdom with a view to settlement as the unmarried [or same-sex] partner of a person present and settled in the United Kingdom or being admitted on the same occasion for settlement

295A. The requirements to be met by a person seeking leave to enter the United Kingdom with a view to settlement as the unmarried [or same-sex] partner of a person present and settled in the United Kingdom or being admitted on the same occasion for settlement, are that:

[(i) (a) the applicant is the unmarried [or same-sex] partner of a person present and settled in the United Kingdom or who is on the same occasion being admitted for settlement and the parties have been living together in a relationship akin to marriage which has subsisted for two years or more; or

(b) the applicant is the unmarried [or same-sex] partner of a person who has a right of abode in the United Kingdom or indefinite leave to enter or remain in the United Kingdom and is on the same occasion seeking admission to the United Kingdom for the purposes of settlement and the parties have been living together outside the United Kingdom in a relationship akin to marriage which has subsisted for 4 years or more; and]

(ii) any previous marriage (or similar relationship) by either partner has permanently broken down; and

[(iii) the parties are not involved in a consanguineous relationship with one another; and]

(iv) . . .

(v) there will be adequate accommodation for the parties and any dependants without recourse to public funds in accommodation which they own or occupy exclusively; and

(vi) the parties will be able to maintain themselves and any dependants adequately without recourse to public funds; and

(vii) the parties intend to live together permanently: and

(viii) the applicant holds a valid United Kingdom entry clearance for entry in this capacity.

[For the purpose of this paragraph and paragraphs 295B–295I, a member of HM Forces serving overseas, or a permanent member of HM Diplomatic Service or a comparable UK-based staff member of the British Council on a tour of duty abroad, or a staff member of the Department for International Development who is a British citizen or is settled in the United Kingdom, is to be regarded as present and settled in the United Kingdom.]]

Note: Paragraph 295A inserted from 2 October 2000 (Cm 4581). Subparagraph (i) substituted and sub-para (iv) deleted from 1 April 2003 (HC 538). Words in square brackets at the end of sub-para (viii) inserted from 18 September 2002 (Cm 5597). Subparagraph (iii) inserted from 25 August 2003 (Cm 5949). References to same-sex partners inserted from 5 December 2005 (HC 582).

[Leave to enter the United Kingdom with a view to settlement as the unmarried [or same-sex] partner of a person present and settled in the United Kingdom or being admitted on the same occasion for settlement

295B. Leave to enter the United Kingdom with a view to settlement as the unmarried [ro same-sex] partner of a person present and settled in the United Kingdom or being admitted on the same occasion for settlement, may [or, in the case of a person within paragraph 295A(i)(a),] be granted for an initial period not exceeding 2 years [or, in the case of a person admitted within paragraph 295A(i)(b), indefinite leave to enter may be granted] provided that a valid United Kingdom entry clearance for entry [in the appropriate] capacity is produced to the Immigration Officer on arrival.]

Note: Paragraph 295B inserted from 2 October 2000 (Cm 4581). Words in square brackets after 'for settlement, may' and words in square brackets after '2 years' inserted from 1 April 2003 (HC 538). Words in square brackets after 'entry clearance for entry' substituted from 1 April 2003 (HC 538). References to same-sex partners inserted from 5 December 2005 (HC 582).

[Refusal of leave to enter the United Kingdom with a view to settlement as the unmarried [or same-sex] partner of a person present and settled in the United Kingdom or being admitted on the same occasion for settlement

295C. Leave to enter the United Kingdom with a view to settlement as the unmarried [or same-sex] partner of a person present and settled in the United Kingdom or being admitted on the same occasion for settlement, is to be refused if a valid United Kingdom entry clearance for entry in this capacity is not produced to the Immigration Officer on arrival.]

Note: Paragraph 295C inserted from 2 October 2000 (Cm 4581). References to same-sex partners inserted from 5 December 2005 (HC 582).

Leave to remain as the unmarried [or same-sex] partner of a person present and settled in the United Kingdom

[Requirements for leave to remain as the unmarried partner of a person present and settled in the United Kingdom

295D. The requirements to be met by a person seeking leave to remain as the unmarried [or same-sex] partner of a person present and settled in the United Kingdom are that:

(i) the applicant has limited leave to remain in the United Kingdom [which was given in accordance with any of the provisions of these Rules]; and

(ii) any previous marriage (or similar relationship) by either partner has permanently broken down; and

(iii) the applicant is the unmarried [or same-sex] partner of a person who is present and settled in the United Kingdom; and

(iv) the applicant has not remained in breach of the immigration laws; and

[(v) the parties are not involved in a consanguineous relationship with one another; and]

(vi) the parties have been living together in a relationship akin to marriage which has subsisted for two years or more; and

(vii) the parties' relationship pre-dates any decision to deport the applicant, recommend him for deportation, give him notice under Section 6(2) of the Immigration Act 1971, or give directions for his removal under section 10 of the Immigration and Asylum Act 1999; and

(viii) there will be adequate accommodation for the parties and any dependants without recourse to public funds in accommodation which they own or occupy exclusively; and

(ix) the parties will be able to maintain themselves and any dependants adequately without recourse to public funds; and

(x) the parties intend to live together permanently.]

Note: Paragraph 295D inserted from 2 October 2000 (Cm 4581). Subparagraph (v) inserted from 25 August 2003 (Cm 5949). Words in square brackets in sub-para (i) inserted from 1 October 2004 (Cm 6339). References to same-sex partners inserted from 5 December 2005 (HC 582).

[Leave to remain as the unmarried [or same-sex] partner of a person present and settled in the United Kingdom

295E. Leave to remain as the unmarried [or same-sex] partner of a person present and settled in the United Kingdom may be granted for a period of 2 years in the first instance provided that the Secretary of State is satisfied that each of the requirements of paragraph 295D are met.]

Note: Paragraph 295E inserted from 2 October 2000 (Cm 4581). References to same-sex partners inserted from 5 December 2005 (HC 582).

[Refusal of leave to remain as the unmarried [or same-sex] partner of a person present and settled in the United Kingdom

295F. Leave to remain as the unmarried [or same-sex] partner of a person present and settled in the United Kingdom is to be refused if the Secretary of State is not satisfied that each of the requirements of paragraph 295D is met.]

Note: Paragraph 295F inserted from 2 October 2000 (Cm 4581). References to same-sex partners inserted from 5 December 2005 (HC 582).

Indefinite leave to remain as the unmarried [or same-sex] partner of a person present and settled in the United Kingdom

[Requirements for indefinite leave to remain as the unmarried [or same-sex] partner of a person present and settled in the United Kingdom

295G. The requirements to be met by a person seeking indefinite leave to remain as the unmarried [or same-sex] partner of a person present and settled in the United Kingdom are that:

(i) the applicant was admitted to the United Kingdom or given an extension of stay for a period of 2 years [in accordance with paragraphs 295AA to 295F of these Rules] and has completed a period of 2 years as the unmarried [or same-sex] partner of a person present and settled here; and

(ii) the applicant is still the unmarried [or same-sex] partner of the person he was admitted or granted an extension of stay to join and the relationship is still subsisting; and
(iii) each of the parties intends to live permanently with the other as his partner; and
(iv) there will be adequate accommodation for the parties and any dependants without recourse to public funds in accommodation which they own or occupy exclusively; and
(v) the parties will be able to maintain themselves and any dependants adequately without recourse to public funds.]

Note: Paragraph 295G inserted from 2 October 2000 (Cm 4581). Words in square brackets in sub-para (i) inserted from 1 October 2004 (Cm 6339). References to same-sex partners inserted from 5 December 2005 (HC 582).

[Indefinite leave to remain as the unmarried [or same-sex] partner of a person present and settled in the United Kingdom

295H. Indefinite leave to remain as the unmarried [or same-sex] partner of a person present and settled in the United Kingdom may be granted provided that the Secretary of State is satisfied that each of the requirements of paragraph 295G is met.]

Note: Paragraph 295H inserted from 2 October 2000 (Cm 4581). References to same-sex partners inserted from 5 December 2005 (HC 582).

[Refusal of indefinite leave to remain as the unmarried [or same-sex] partner of a person present and settled in the United Kingdom

295I. Indefinite leave to remain as the unmarried [or same-sex] partner of a person present and settled in the United Kingdom is to be refused if the Secretary of State is not satisfied that each of the requirements of paragraph 295G is met.]

Note: Paragraph 295I inserted from 2 October 2000 (Cm 4581). References to same-sex partners inserted from 5 December 2005 (HC 582).

Leave to enter or remain as the unmarried [or same-sex] partner of a person with limited leave to enter or remain in the United Kingdom under paragraphs 128–193; 200–239; or 263–270

[Requirements for leave to enter or remain as the unmarried [or same-sex] partner of a person with limited leave to enter or remain in the United Kingdom under paragraphs 128–193; 200–239; or 263–270

295J. The requirements to be met by a person seeking leave to enter or remain as the unmarried [or same-sex] partner of a person with limited leave to enter or remain in the United Kingdom under paragraphs 128–193; 200–239; or 263–270; are that:

(i) the applicant is the unmarried [or same-sex] partner of a person who has limited leave to enter or remain in the United Kingdom under paragraphs 128–193; 200–239; or 263–270; and

(ii) any previous marriage (or similar relationship) by either partner has permanently broken down; and

[(iii) the parties are not involved in a consanguineous relationship with one another; and]

(iv) the parties have been living together in a relationship akin to marriage which has subsisted for 2 years or more; and

(v) each of the parties intends to live with the other as his partner during the applicant's stay; and

(vi) there will be adequate accommodation for the parties and any dependants without recourse to public funds in accommodation which they own or occupy exclusively; and

(vii) the parties will be able to maintain themselves and any dependants adequately without recourse to public funds; and

(viii) the applicant does not intend to stay in the United Kingdom beyond any period of leave granted to his partner; and

(ix) if seeking leave to enter, the applicant holds a valid United Kingdom entry clearance for entry in this capacity or, if seeking leave to remain, was admitted with a valid United Kingdom entry clearance for entry in this capacity.

Note: Paragraph 295J inserted from 2 October 2000 (Cm 4581). Subparagraph (iii) inserted from 25 August 2003 (Cm 5949). References to same-sex partners inserted from 5 December 2005 (HC 582).

[Leave to enter or remain as the unmarried [or same-sex] partner of a person with limited leave to enter or remain in the United Kingdom under paragraphs 128–193; 200–239; or 263–270

295K. Leave to enter as the unmarried [or same-sex] partner of a person with limited leave to enter or remain in the United Kingdom under paragraphs 128–193; 200–239; or 263–270; may be granted provided that a valid United Kingdom entry clearance for entry in this capacity is produced to the Immigration Officer on arrival. Leave to remain as the unmarried [or same-sex] partner of a person with limited leave to enter or remain in the United Kingdom under paragraphs 128–193; 200–239; or 263–270; may be granted provided that the Secretary of State is satisfied that each of the requirements of paragraph 295J is met.]

Note: Paragraph 295K inserted from 2 October 2000 (Cm 4581). References to same-sex partners inserted from 5 December 2005 (HC 582).

[Refusal of leave to enter or remain as the unmarried [or same-sex] partner of a person with limited leave to enter or remain in the United Kingdom under paragraphs 128–193; 200–239; or 263–270

295L. Leave to enter as the unmarried [or same-sex] partner of a person with limited leave to enter or remain in the United Kingdom under paragraphs 128–193; 200–239; or 263–270; is to be refused if a valid United Kingdom entry clearance for entry in this capacity is not produced to the Immigration Officer on arrival. Leave to remain as the unmarried [or same-sex] partner of a person with limited leave to enter or remain in the United Kingdom under paragraphs 128–193; 200–239; or 263–270; is to be refused if the Secretary of State is not satisfied that each of the requirements of paragraph 295J is met.]

Note: Paragraph 295L inserted from 2 October 2000 (Cm 4581). References to same-sex partners inserted from 5 December 2005 (HC 582).

Indefinite leave to remain for the bereaved unmarried partner of a person present and settled in the United Kingdom

[Requirements for indefinite leave to remain for the bereaved unmarried [or same-sex] partner of a person present and settled in the United Kingdom

295M. The requirements to be met by a person seeking indefinite leave to remain as the bereaved unmarried [or same-sex] partner of a person present and settled in the United Kingdom, are that:

- (i) the applicant was admitted to the United Kingdom or given an extension of stay for a period of 2 years [in accordance with paragraphs 295AA to 295F of these Rules] as the unmarried [or same-sex] partner of a person present and settled in the United Kingdom; and
- (ii) the person whom the applicant was admitted or granted an extension of stay to join died during that 2 year period; and
- (iii) the applicant was still the unmarried [or same-sex] partner of the person he was admitted or granted an extension of stay to join at the time of the death; and
- (iv) each of the parties intended to live permanently with the other as his partner and the relationship was subsisting at the time of the death.]

Note: Paragraph 295M inserted from 2 October 2000 (Cm 4581). Words in square brackets in sub-para (i) inserted from 1 October 2004 (Cm 6339). References to same-sex partners inserted from 5 December 2005 (HC 582).

[Indefinite leave to remain for the bereaved unmarried [or same-sex] partner of a person present and settled in the United Kingdom

295N. Indefinite leave to remain for the bereaved unmarried [or same-sex] partner of a person present and settled in the United Kingdom, may be granted provided that the Secretary of State is satisfied that each of the requirements of paragraph 295M is met.]

Note: Paragraph 295N inserted from 2 October 2000 (Cm 4581). References to same-sex partners inserted from 5 December 2005 (HC 582).

[Refusal of indefinite leave to remain for the bereaved unmarried [or same-sex] partner of a person present and settled in the United Kingdom

295O. Indefinite leave to remain for the bereaved unmarried [or same-sex] partner of a person present and settled in the United Kingdom, is to be refused if the Secretary of State is not satisfied that each of the requirements of paragraph 295M is met.]

Note: Paragraph 295O inserted from 2 October 2000 (Cm 4581). References to same-sex partners inserted from 5 December 2005 (HC 582).

Children

[**296.** Nothing in these Rules shall be construed as permitting a child to be granted entry clearance, leave to enter or remain, or variation of leave where his parent is party to a polygamous marriage and any application by that parent for admission or leave to remain for settlement or with a view to settlement would be refused pursuant to paragraphs 278 or 278A.]

Note: Substituted from 2 October 2000 (Cm 4851).

Leave to enter or remain in the United Kingdom as the child of a parent, parents or a relative present and settled or being admitted for settlement in the United Kingdom

Requirements for indefinite leave to enter the United Kingdom as the child of a parent, parents or a relative present and settled or being admitted for settlement in the United Kingdom

297. The requirements to be met by a person seeking indefinite leave to enter the United Kingdom as the child of a parent, parents or a relative present and settled or being admitted for settlement in the United Kingdom are that he:

- (i) is seeking leave to enter to accompany or join a parent, parents or a relative in one of the following circumstances:
  - (a) both parents are present and settled in the United Kingdom; or
  - (b) both parents are being admitted on the same occasion for settlement; or
  - (c) one parent is present and settled in the United Kingdom and the other is being admitted on the same occasion for settlement; or
  - (d) one parent is present and settled in the United Kingdom or being

admitted on the same occasion for settlement and the other parent is dead; or

(e) one parent is present and settled in the United Kingdom or being admitted on the same occasion for settlement and has had sole responsibility for the child's upbringing; or

(f) one parent or a relative is present and settled in the United Kingdom or being admitted on the same occasion for settlement and there are serious and compelling family or other considerations which make exclusion of the child undesirable and suitable arrangements have been made for the child's care; and

(ii) is under the age of 18; and

(iii) is not leading an independent life, is unmarried [and is not a civil partner], and has not formed an independent family unit; and

[(iv) can, and will, be accommodated adequately by the parent, parents or relative the child is seeking to join without recourse to public funds in accommodation which the parent, parents or relative the child is seeking to join, own or occupy exclusively; and

(v) can, and will, be maintained adequately by the parent, parents or relative the child is seeking to join, without recourse to public funds; and

(vi) holds a valid United Kingdom entry clearance for entry in this capacity.]

Note: Subparagraphs (iv)–(vi) substituted from 2 October 2000 (Cm 4851). Words in square brackets in sub-para (iii) inserted from 5 December 2005 (HC 582).

Requirements for indefinite leave to remain in the United Kingdom as the child of a parent, parents or a relative present and settled or being admitted for settlement in the United Kingdom

298. The requirements to be met by a person seeking indefinite leave to remain in the United Kingdom as the child of a parent, parents or a relative present and settled in the United Kingdom are that he:

(i) is seeking to remain with a parent, parents or a relative in one of the following circumstances:

(a) both parents are present and settled in the United Kingdom; or

(b) one parent is present and settled in the United Kingdom and the other parent is dead; or

(c) one parent is present and settled in the United Kingdom and has had sole responsibility for the child's upbringing; or

(d) one parent or a relative is present and settled in the United Kingdom and there are serious and compelling family or other considerations which make exclusion of the child undesirable and suitable arrangements have been made for the child's care; and

(ii) has limited leave to enter or remain in the United Kingdom, and

(a) is under the age of 18; or

(b) was given leave to enter or remain with a view to settlement under paragraph 302; and

(iii) is not leading an independent life, is unmarried [and is not a civil partner], and has not formed an independent family unit; and

[(iv) can, and will, be accommodated adequately by the parent, parents or relative the child was admitted to join, without recourse to public funds in accommodation which the parent, parents or relative the child was admitted to join, own or occupy exclusively; and

(v) can, and will, be maintained adequately by the parent, parents or relative the child was admitted to join, without recourse to public funds.]

Note: Subparagraphs (iv) and (v) substituted from 2 October 2000 (Cm 4851). Words in square brackets in sub-para (iii) inserted from 5 December 2005 (HC 582).

Indefinite leave to enter or remain in the United Kingdom as the child of a parent, parents or a relative present and settled or being admitted for settlement in the United Kingdom

299. Indefinite leave to enter the United Kingdom as the child of a parent, parents or a relative present and settled or being admitted for settlement in the United Kingdom may be granted provided a valid United Kingdom entry clearance for entry in this capacity is produced to the Immigration Officer on arrival. Indefinite leave to remain in the United Kingdom as the child of a parent, parents or a relative present and settled in the United Kingdom may be granted provided the Secretary of State is satisfied that each of the requirements of paragraph 298 is met.

Refusal of indefinite leave to enter or remain in the United Kingdom as the child of a parent, parents or a relative present and settled or being admitted for settlement in the United Kingdom

300. Indefinite leave to enter the United Kingdom as the child of a parent, parents or a relative present and settled or being admitted for settlement in the United Kingdom is to be refused if a valid United Kingdom entry clearance for entry in this capacity is not produced to the Immigration Officer on arrival. Indefinite leave to remain in the United Kingdom as the child of a parent, parents or a relative present and settled in the United Kingdom is to be refused if the Secretary of State is not satisfied that each of the requirements of paragraph 298 is met.

Requirements for limited leave to enter or remain in the United Kingdom with a view to settlement as the child of a parent or parents given limited leave to enter or remain in the United Kingdom with a view to settlement

301. The requirements to be met by a person seeking limited leave to enter or remain in the United Kingdom with a view to settlement as the child of a parent or parents given limited leave to enter or remain in the United Kingdom with a view to settlement are that he:

(i) is seeking leave to enter to accompany or join or remain with a parent or parents in one of the following circumstances:
   (a) one parent is present and settled in the United Kingdom or being admitted on the same occasion for settlement and the other parent is being or has been given limited leave to enter or remain in the United Kingdom with a view to settlement; or
   (b) one parent is being or has been given limited leave to enter or remain in the United Kingdom with a view to settlement and has had sole responsibility for the child's upbringing; or
   (c) one parent is being or has been given limited leave to enter or remain in the United Kingdom with a view to settlement and there are serious and compelling family or other considerations which make exclusion of the child undesirable and suitable arrangements have been made for the child's care; and

(ii) is under the age of 18; and

(iii) is not leading an independent life, is unmarried [and is not a civil partner], and has not formed an independent family unit; and

[(iv) can, and will, be accommodated adequately without recourse to public funds, in accommodation which the parent or parents own or occupy exclusively; and

(iva) can, and will, be maintained adequately by the parent or parents without recourse to public funds; and]

(v) (where an application is made for limited leave to remain with a view to settlement) has limited leave to enter or remain in the United Kingdom; and

(vi) if seeking leave to enter, holds a valid United Kingdom entry clearance for entry in this capacity or, if seeking leave to remain, was admitted with a valid United Kingdom entry clearance for entry in this capacity.

Note: Subparagraph (iv) substituted and sub-para (iva) inserted from 2 October 2000 (Cm 4851). Words in square brackets in sub-para (iii) inserted from 5 December 2005 (HC 582).

Limited leave to enter or remain in the United Kingdom with a view to settlement as the child of a parent or parents given limited leave to enter or remain in the United Kingdom with a view to settlement

302. A person seeking limited leave to enter the United Kingdom with a view to settlement as the child of a parent or parents given limited leave to enter or remain in the United Kingdom with a view to settlement may be admitted for a period not exceeding [24 months] provided he is able, on arrival, to produce to the Immigration Officer a valid United Kingdom entry clearance for entry in this capacity. A person seeking limited leave to remain in the United Kingdom with a view to settlement as the child of a parent or parents given limited leave to enter or remain in the United Kingdom with a view to settlement may be given limited leave to remain for a period not exceeding [24 months] provided the Secretary of State is satisfied that each of the requirements of paragraph 301(i)–(v) is met.

Note: Words in square brackets substituted from 13 November 2004 (HC 1224).

Refusal of limited leave to enter or remain in the United Kingdom with a view to settlement as the child of a parent or parents given limited leave to enter or remain in the United Kingdom with a view to settlement

303. Limited leave to enter the United Kingdom with a view to settlement as the child of a parent or parents given limited leave to enter or remain in the United Kingdom with a view to settlement is to be refused if a valid United Kingdom entry clearance for entry in this capacity is not produced to the Immigration Officer on arrival. Limited leave to remain in the United Kingdom with a view to settlement as the child of a parent or parents given limited leave to enter or remain in the United Kingdom with a view to settlement is to be refused if the Secretary of State is not satisfied that each of the requirements of paragraph 301(i)–(v) is met.

[Leave to enter and extension of stay in the United Kingdom as the child of a parent who is being, or has been admitted to the United Kingdom as a fiancé(e) [*or proposed civil partner*]

Requirements for limited leave to enter the United Kingdom as the child of a fiancé(e) [or proposed civil partner]

303A. The requirements to be met by a person seeking limited leave to enter the United Kingdom as the child of a fiancé(e) [or proposed civil partner], are that:

- (i) he is seeking to accompany or join a parent who is, on the same occasion that the child seeks admission, being admitted as a fiancé(e), or who has been admitted as a fiancé(e) [or proposed civil partner]; and
- (ii) he is under the age of 18; and
- (iii) he is not leading an independent life, is unmarried [and is not a civil partner], and has not formed an independent family unit; and
- (iv) he can, and will, be maintained and accommodated adequately without recourse to public funds with the parent admitted or being admitted as a fiancé(e); and
- (v) there are serious and compelling family or other considerations which make the child's exclusion undesirable, that suitable arrangements have been made for his care in the United Kingdom, and there is no other person outside the United Kingdom who could reasonably be expected to care for him; and
- (vi) he holds a valid United Kingdom entry clearance for entry in this capacity.]

Note: Paragraph 303A inserted from 2 October 2000 (Cm 4851). References to civil partnership inserted from 5 December 2005 (HC 582).

Limited leave to enter the United Kingdom as the child of a parent who is being, or has been admitted to the United Kingdom as a fiancé(e) [or proposed civil partner]

[**303B.** A person seeking limited leave to enter the United Kingdom as the child of a fiancé(e) [or proposed civil partner], may be granted limited leave to enter the United Kingdom for a period not in excess of that granted to the fiancé(e) [or proposed civil partner], provided that a valid United Kingdom entry clearance for entry in this capacity is produced to the Immigration Officer on arrival. Where the period of limited leave granted to a fiancé(e) [or proposed civil partner] will expire in more than 6 months, a person seeking limited leave to enter as the child of the fiancé(e) [or proposed civil partner] should be granted leave for a period not exceeding six months.]

Note: Paragraph 303B inserted from 2 October 2000 (Cm 4851). References to civil partnership inserted from 5 December 2005 (HC 582).

Refusal of limited leave to enter the United Kingdom as the child of a parent who is being, or has been admitted to the United Kingdom as a fiancé(e) [or proposed civil partner]

[**303C.** Limited leave to enter the United Kingdom as the child of a fiancé(e) [or proposed civil partner], is to be refused if a valid United Kingdom entry clearance for entry in this capacity is not produced to the Immigration Officer on arrival.]

Note: Paragraph 303C inserted from 2 October 2000 (Cm 4851). References to civil partnership inserted from 5 December 2005 (HC 582).

Requirements for an extension of stay in the United Kingdom as the child of a fiancé(e) [or proposed civil partner]

[**303D.** The requirements to be met by a person seeking an extension of stay in the United Kingdom as the child of a fiancé(e) [or proposed civil partner] are that:

(i) the applicant was admitted with a valid United Kingdom entry clearance as the child of a fiancé(e) [or proposed civil partner]; and
(ii) the applicant is the child of a parent who has been granted limited leave to enter, or an extension of stay, as a fiancé(e) [or proposed civil partner]; and
(iii) the requirements of paragraph 303A (ii)–(v) are met.]

Note: Paragraph 303D inserted from 2 October 2000 (Cm 4851). References to civil partnership inserted from 5 December 2005 (HC 582).

Extension of stay in the United Kingdom as the child of a fiancé(e) [or proposed civil partner]

[303E. An extension of stay as the child of a fiancé(e) [or proposed civil partner] may be granted provided that the Secretary of State is satisfied that each of the requirements of paragraph 303D is met.]

Note: Paragraph 303E inserted from 2 October 2000 (Cm 4851). References to civil partnership inserted from 5 December 2005 (HC 582).

Refusal of an extension of stay in the United Kingdom as the child of a fiancé(e) [or proposed civil partner]

[303F. An extension of stay as the child of a fiancé(e) [or proposed civil partner] is to be refused if the Secretary of State is not satisfied that each of the requirements of paragraph 303D is met.]

Note: Paragraph 303F inserted from 2 October 2000 (Cm 4851). References to civil partnership inserted from 5 December 2005 (HC 582).

Children born in the United Kingdom who are not British citizens

304. This paragraph and paragraphs 305–309 apply only to [. . .] dependent children under 18 years of age [who are unmarried and are not civil partners and] who were born in the United Kingdom on or after 1 January 1983 (when the British Nationality Act 1981 came into force) but who, because neither of their parents was a British citizen or settled in the United Kingdom at the time of their birth, are not British citizens and are therefore subject to immigration control. Such a child requires leave to enter where admission to the United Kingdom is sought, and leave to remain where permission is sought for the child to be allowed to stay in the United Kingdom. If he qualifies for entry clearance, leave to enter or leave to remain under any other part of these Rules, a child who was born in the United Kingdom but is not a British citizen may be granted entry clearance, leave to enter or leave to remain in accordance with the provisions of that other part.

Note: Words deleted and words in square brackets inserted from 5 December 2005 (HC 582).

Requirements for leave to enter or remain in the United Kingdom as the child of a parent or parents given leave to enter or remain in the United Kingdom

305. The requirements to be met by a child born in the United Kingdom who is not a British citizen who seeks leave to enter or remain in the United Kingdom as the child of a parent or parents given leave to enter or remain in the United Kingdom are that he:

(i) (a) is accompanying or seeking to join or remain with a parent or parents who have, or are given, leave to enter or remain in the United Kingdom; or

(b) is accompanying or seeking to join or remain with a parent or parents one of whom is a British citizen or has the right of abode in the United Kingdom; or

(c) is a child in respect of whom the parental rights and duties are vested solely in a local authority; and

(ii) is under the age of 18; and

(iii) was born in the United Kingdom; and

(iv) is not leading an independent life, is unmarried [and is not a civil partner], and has not formed an independent family unit; and

(v) (where an application is made for leave to enter) has not been away from the United Kingdom for more than 2 years.

Note: Words in square brackets in sub-para (iv) inserted from 5 December 2005 (HC 582).

Leave to enter or remain in the United Kingdom

306. A child born in the United Kingdom who is not a British citizen and who requires leave to enter or remain in the circumstances set out in paragraph 304 may be given leave to enter for the same period as his parent or parents where paragraph 305(i)(a) applies, provided the Immigration Officer is satisfied that each of the requirements of paragraph 305(ii)–(v) is met. Where leave to remain is sought, the child may be granted leave to remain for the same period as his parent or parents where paragraph 305(i)(a) applies, provided the Secretary of State is satisfied that each of the requirements of paragraph 305(ii)–(iv) is met. Where the parent or parents have or are given periods of leave of different duration, the child may be given leave to whichever period is longer except that if the parents are living apart the child should be given leave for the same period as the parent who has day to day responsibility for him.

307. If a child does not qualify for leave to enter or remain because neither of his parents has a current leave (and neither of them is a British citizen or has the right of abode), he will normally be refused leave to enter or remain, even if each of the requirements of paragraph 305 (ii)–(v) has been satisfied. However, he may be granted leave to enter or remain for a period not exceeding 3 months if both of his parents are in the United Kingdom and it appears unlikely that they will be removed in the immediate future, and there is no other person outside the United Kingdom who could reasonably be expected to care for him.

308. A child born in the United Kingdom who is not a British citizen and who requires leave to enter or remain in the United Kingdom in the circumstances set out in paragraph 304 may be given indefinite leave to enter where paragraph

305(i)(b) or (i)(c) applies provided the Immigration Officer is satisfied that each of the requirements of paragraph 305(ii)–(v) is met. Where an application is for leave to remain, such a child may be granted indefinite leave to remain where paragraph 305(i)(b) or (i)(c) applies, provided the Secretary of State is satisfied that each of the requirements of paragraph 305(ii)–(iv) is met.

Refusal of leave to enter or remain in the United Kingdom

309. Leave to enter the United Kingdom where the circumstances set out in paragraph 304 apply is to be refused if the Immigration Officer is not satisfied that each of the requirements of paragraph 305 is met. Leave to remain for such a child is to be refused if the Secretary of State is not satisfied that each of the requirements of paragraph 305(i)–(iv) is met.

Adopted children

[**309A.** For the purposes of adoption under paragraphs 310–316C a de facto adoption shall be regarded as having taken place if:

(a) at the time immediately preceding the making of the application for entry clearance under these Rules the adoptive parent or parents have been living abroad (in applications involving two parents both must have lived abroad together) for at least a period of time equal to the first period mentioned in sub-paragraph (b)(i) and must have cared for the child for at least a period of time equal to the second period material in that sub-paragraph; and

(b) during their time abroad, the adoptive parent or parents have:
   (i) lived together for a minimum period of 18 months, of which the 12 months immediately preceding the application for entry clearance must have been spent living together with the child; and
   (ii) have assumed the role of the child's parents, since the beginning of the 18 month period, so that there has been a genuine transfer of parental responsibility.]

Note: Paragraph 309A inserted from 1 April 2003 (HC 538).

Requirements for indefinite leave to enter the United Kingdom as the adopted child of a parent or parents present and settled or being admitted for settlement in the United Kingdom

310. The requirements to be met in the case of a child seeking indefinite leave to enter the United Kingdom as the adopted child of a parent or parents present and settled or being admitted for settlement in the United Kingdom are that he:

(i) is seeking leave to enter to accompany or join an adoptive parent or parents in one of the following circumstances;
   (a) both parents are present and settled in the United Kingdom; or
   (b) both parents are being admitted on the same occasion for settlement; or
   (c) one parent is present and settled in the United Kingdom and the other is being admitted on the same occasion for settlement; or
   (d) one parent is present and settled in the United Kingdom or being admitted on the same occasion for settlement and the other parent is dead; or
   (e) one parent is present and settled in the United Kingdom or being admitted on the same occasion for settlement and has had sole responsibility for the child's upbringing; or
   (f) one parent is present and settled in the United Kingdom or being admitted on the same occasion for settlement and there are serious and compelling family or other considerations which make exclusion of the child undesirable and suitable arrangements have been made for the child's care[or]
   [(g) in the case of a de facto adoption one parent has a right of abode in the United Kingdom or indefinite leave to enter or remain in the United Kingdom and is seeking admission to the United Kingdom on the same occasion for the purposes of settlement; and]
(ii) is under the age of 18; and
(iii) is not leading an independent life, is unmarried [and is not a civil partner], and has not formed an independent family unit; and
[(iv) can, and will, be accommodated {and maintained} adequately without recourse to public funds in accommodation which the adoptive parent or parents own or occupy exclusively; and]
(v) . . .
[(vi) (a) was adopted in accordance with a decision taken by the competent administrative authority or court in his country of origin or the country in which he is resident, being a country whose adoption orders are recognised by the United Kingdom; or
   (b) is the subject of a de facto adoption; and;]
(vii) was adopted at a time when:
   (a) both adoptive parents were resident together abroad; or
   (b) either or both adoptive parents were settled in the United Kingdom; and
(viii) has the same rights and obligations as any other child of the [adoptive parent's or parents' family]; and
(ix) was adopted due to the inability of the original parent(s) or current carer(s) to care for him and there has been a genuine transfer of parental responsibility to the adoptive parents; and

(x) has lost or broken his ties with his family of origin; and

(xi) was adopted, but the adoption is not one of convenience arranged to facilitate his admission to or remaining in the United Kingdom; and

(xii) holds a valid United Kingdom entry clearance for entry in this capacity.

Note: Subparagraph (iv) substituted from 2 October 2000 (Cm 4851). Subparagraph (i)(g) inserted and words in curly brackets in sub-para (iv) substituted from 1 April 2003 (HC 538). Subparagraph (v) deleted from 1 April 2003 (HC 538). Subparagraph (vi) and words in square brackets in sub-para (i)(f) and (viii) substituted from 1 April 2003 (HC 538). Words in square brackets in sub-para (iii) inserted from 5 December 2005 (HC 582).

Requirements for indefinite leave to remain in the United Kingdom as the adopted child of a parent or parents present and settled in the United Kingdom

311. The requirements to be met in the case of a child seeking indefinite leave to remain in the United Kingdom as the adopted child of a parent or parents present and settled in the United Kingdom are that he:

(i) is seeking to remain with an adoptive parent or parents in one of the following circumstances:

(a) both parents are present and settled in the United Kingdom; or

(b) one parent is present and settled in the United Kingdom and the other parent is dead; or

(c) one parent is present and settled in the United Kingdom and has had sole responsibility for the child's upbringing; or

(d) one parent is present and settled in the United Kingdom and there are serious and compelling family or other considerations which make exclusion of the child undesirable and suitable arrangements have been made for the child's care[or]

[(e) in the case of a de facto adoption one parent has a right of abode in the United Kingdom or indefinite leave to enter or remain in the United Kingdom and is seeking admission to the United Kingdom on the same occasion for the purpose of settlement; and]

(ii) has limited leave to enter or remain in the United Kingdom, and

(a) is under the age of 18; or

(b) was given leave to enter or remain with a view to settlement under paragraph 315 [or paragraph 316B]; and

(iii) is not leading an independent life, is unmarried [and is not a civil partner], and has not formed an independent family unit; and

[(iv) can, and will, be accommodated {and maintained} adequately without recourse to public funds in accommodation which the adoptive parent or parents own or occupy exclusively; and

(v) . . .

[(vi) (a) was adopted in accordance with a decision taken by the competent administrative authority or court in his country of origin or the country in which he is resident, being a country-whose adoption orders are recognised by the United Kingdom; or

(b) is the subject of a de facto adoption; and]

(vii) was adopted at a time when:

(a) both adoptive parents were resident together abroad; or

(b) either or both adoptive parents were settled in the United Kingdom; and

(viii) has the same rights and obligations as any other child of the [adoptive parent's or parents' family]; and

(ix) was adopted due to the inability of the original parent(s) or current carer(s) to care for him and there has been a genuine transfer of parental responsibility to the adoptive parents; and

(x) has lost or broken his ties with his family of origin; and

(xi) was adopted, but the adoption is not one of convenience arranged to facilitate his admission to or remaining in the United Kingdom.

Note: Subparagraph (iv) substituted from 2 October 2000 (Cm 4851). Subparagraph (i)(e) inserted, sub-para (v) deleted and sub-para (vi) substituted from 1 April 2003 (HC 538). Words in square brackets in sub-para (i)(d) substituted, words in curly brackets in sub-para (iv) inserted and words in square brackets in sub-para (viii) substituted from 1 April 2003 (HC 538). Words in square brackets in sub-para (iii) inserted from 5 December 2005 (HC 582).

Indefinite leave to enter or remain in the United Kingdom as the adopted child of a parent or parents present and settled or being admitted for settlement in the United Kingdom

312. Indefinite leave to enter the United Kingdom as the adopted child of a parent or parents present and settled or being admitted for settlement in the United Kingdom may be granted provided a valid United Kingdom entry clearance for entry in this capacity is produced to the Immigration Officer on arrival. Indefinite leave to remain in the United Kingdom as the adopted child of a parent or parents present and settled in the United Kingdom may be granted provided the Secretary of State is satisfied that each of the requirements of paragraph 311 is met.

Refusal of indefinite leave to enter or remain in the United Kingdom as the adopted child of a parent or parents present and settled or being admitted for settlement in the United Kingdom

313. Indefinite leave to enter the United Kingdom as the adopted child of a parent or parents present and settled or being admitted for settlement in the United Kingdom is to be refused if a valid United Kingdom entry clearance for entry in this capacity is not produced to the Immigration Officer on arrival. Indefinite leave to remain in the United Kingdom as the adopted child of a parent or parents present and settled in the United Kingdom is to be refused if the Secretary of State is not satisfied that each of the requirements of paragraph 311 is met.

Requirements for limited leave to enter or remain in the United Kingdom with a view to settlement as the adopted child of a parent or parents given limited leave to enter or remain in the United Kingdom with a view to settlement

314. The requirements to be met in the case of a child seeking limited leave to enter or remain in the United Kingdom with a view to settlement as the adopted child of a parent or parents given limited leave to enter or remain in the United Kingdom with a view to settlement are that he:

(i) is seeking leave to enter to accompany or join or remain with a parent or parents in one of the following circumstances:

(a) one parent is present and settled in the United Kingdom or being admitted on the same occasion for settlement and the other parent is being or has been given limited leave to enter or remain in the United Kingdom with a view to settlement; or

(b) one parent is being or has been given limited leave to enter or remain in the United Kingdom with a view to settlement and has had sole responsibility for the child's upbringing; or

(c) one parent is being or has been given limited leave to enter or remain in the United Kingdom with a view to settlement and there are serious and compelling family or other considerations which make exclusion of the child undesirable and suitable arrangements have been made for the child's care; and

[{(d)} in the case of a de facto adoption one parent has a right of abode in the United Kingdom or indefinite leave to enter or remain in the United Kingdom and is seeking admission to the United Kingdom on the same occasion for the purpose of settlement; and]

(ii) is under the age of 18; and

(iii) is not leading an independent life, is unmarried [and is not a civil partner], and has not formed an independent family unit; and

[(iv) can, and will, be accommodated {and maintained} adequately without recourse to public funds in accommodation which the adoptive parent or parents own or occupy exclusively; and

[(v) (a) was adopted in accordance with a decision taken by the competent administrative authority or court in his country of origin or the country in which he is resident, being a country whose adoption orders are recognised by the United Kingdom; or

(b) is the subject of a de facto adoption; and]

(vi) was adopted at a time when:

(a) both adoptive parents were resident together abroad; or

(b) either or both adoptive parents were settled in the United Kingdom; and

(vii) as the same rights and obligations as any other child of the [adoptive parent's or parents' family]; and

(viii) was adopted due to the inability of the original parent(s) or current carer(s) to care for him and there has been a genuine transfer of parental responsibility to the adoptive parents; and

(ix) has lost or broken ties with his family of origin; and

(x) was adopted, but the adoption is not one of convenience arranged to facilitate his admission to the United Kingdom; and

(xi) (where an application is made for limited leave to remain with a view to settlement) has limited leave to enter or remain in the United Kingdom; and

(xii) if seeking leave to enter, holds a valid United Kingdom entry clearance for entry in this capacity.

Note: Subparagraph (iv) substituted from 2 October 2000 (Cm 4851). Subparagraph (i)(d) inserted, sub-para (iva) deleted and sub-para (v) substituted from 1 April 2003 (HC 538). Words in curly brackets in sub-para (iv) inserted and words in square brackets in sub-para (vii) substituted from 1 April 2003 (HC 538). Words in curly brackets in sub-para (i)(d) substituted from 30 May 2003 (Cm 5829). Words in square brackets in sub-para (iii) inserted from 5 December 2005 (HC 582).

Limited leave to enter or remain in the United Kingdom with a view to settlement as the adopted child of a parent or parents given limited leave to enter or remain in the United Kingdom with a view to settlement

315. A person seeking limited leave to enter the United Kingdom with a view to settlement as the adopted child of a parent or parents given limited leave to enter or remain in the United Kingdom with a view to settlement may be admitted for a period not exceeding 12 months provided he is able, on arrival, to produce to the Immigration Officer a valid United Kingdom entry clearance for entry in this capacity. A person seeking limited leave to remain in the United Kingdom with a view to settlement as the adopted child of a parent or parents given limited leave to enter or remain in the United Kingdom with a view to settlement may be granted limited leave for a period not exceeding 12 months provided the Secretary of State is satisfied that each of the requirements of paragraph 314(i)–(xi) is met.

Refusal of limited leave to enter or remain in the United Kingdom with a view to settlement as the adopted child of a parent or parents given limited leave to enter or remain in the United Kingdom with a view to settlement

316. Limited leave to enter the United Kingdom with a view to settlement as the adopted child of a parent or parents given limited leave to enter or remain in the United Kingdom with a view to settlement is to be refused if a valid United Kingdom entry clearance for entry in this capacity is not produced to the Immigration Officer on arrival. Limited leave to remain in the United Kingdom with a view to settlement as the adopted child of a parent or parents given limited leave to enter or remain in the United Kingdom with a view to settlement is to be refused if the Secretary of State is not satisfied that each of the requirements of paragraph 314(i)–(xi) is met.

[Requirements for limited leave to enter the United Kingdom with a view to settlement as a child for adoption

316A. The requirements to be satisfied in the case of a child seeking limited leave to enter the United Kingdom for the purpose of being adopted {(which, for the avoidance of doubt, does not include a de facto adoption)} in the United Kingdom are that he:

(i) is seeking limited leave to enter to accompany or join a person or persons who wish to adopt him in the United Kingdom (the 'prospective parent(s)'), in one of the following circumstances:
  (a) both prospective parents are present and settled in the United Kingdom; or
  (b) both prospective parents are being admitted for settlement on the same occasion that the child is seeking admission; or
  (c) one prospective parent is present and settled in the United Kingdom and the other is being admitted for settlement on the same occasion that the child is seeking admission; or
  (d) one prospective parent is present and settled in the United Kingdom and the other is being given limited leave to enter or remain in the United Kingdom with a view to settlement on the same occasion that the child is seeking admission, or has previously been given such leave; or
  (e) one prospective parent is being admitted for settlement on the same occasion that the other is being granted limited leave to enter with a view to settlement, which is also on the same occasion that the child is seeking admission; or
  (f) one prospective parent is present and settled in the United Kingdom or is being admitted for settlement on the same occasion that the child is seeking admission, and has had sole responsibility for the child's upbringing; or
  (g) one prospective parent is present and settled in the United Kingdom or is being admitted for settlement on the same occasion that the child is seeking admission, and there are serious and compelling family or other considerations which would make the child's exclusion undesirable, and suitable arrangements have been made for the child's care; and

(ii) is under the age of 18; and

(iii) is not leading an independent life, is unmarried [and is not a civil partner], and has not formed an independent family unit; and

(iv) can, and will, be maintained and accommodated adequately without recourse to public funds in accommodation which the prospective parent or parents own or occupy exclusively; and

(v) will have the same rights and obligations as any other child of the marriage [or civil partnership]; and
(vi) is being adopted due to the inability of the original parent(s) or current carer(s) (or those looking after him immediately prior to him being physically transferred to his prospective parent or parents) to care for him, and there has been a genuine transfer of parental responsibility to the prospective parent or parents; and
(vii) has lost or broken or intends to lose or break his ties with his family of origin; and
(viii) will be adopted in the United Kingdom by his prospective parent or parents [in accordance with the law relating to adoption in the United Kingdom], but the proposed adoption is not one of convenience arranged to facilitate his admission to the United Kingdom.

Note: Paragraph 316A inserted from 2 October 2000 (Cm 4851). Words in curly brackets and words in square brackets inserted from 1 April 2003 (HC 538). Words in square brackets in sub-para (iii) inserted from 5 December 2005 (HC 582).

Limited leave to enter the United Kingdom with a view to settlement as a child for adoption

316B. A person seeking limited leave to enter the United Kingdom with a view to settlement as a child for adoption may be admitted for a period not exceeding [24 months] provided he is able, on arrival, to produce to the Immigration Officer a valid United Kingdom entry clearance for entry in this capacity.

Note: Paragraph 316B inserted from 2 October 2000 (Cm 4851). Words in square brackets substututed from 30 May 2003 (Cm 5829).

Refusal of limited leave to enter the United Kingdom with a view to settlement as a child for adoption

316C. Limited leave to enter the United Kingdom with a view to settlement as a child for adoption is to be refused if a valid United Kingdom entry clearance for entry in this capacity is not produced to the Immigration Officer on arrival.]

Note: Paragraph 316C inserted from 2 October 2000 (Cm 4851).

Requirements for limited leave to enter the United Kingdom with a view to settlement as a child for adoption under the Hague Convention

316D. The requirements to be satisfied in the case of a child seeking limited leave to enter the United Kingdom for the purpose of being adopted in the United Kingdom under the Hague Convention are that he:
(i) is seeking limited leave to enter to accompany one or two people each of

whom is habitually resident in the United Kingdom and wishes to adopt him under the Hague Convention ('the prospective parents');

(ii) is the subject of an agreement made under Article 17(c) of the Hague Convention; and

(iii) has been entrusted to the prospective parents by the competent administrative authority of the country from which he is coming to the United Kingdom for adoption under the Hague Convention; and

(iv) is under the age of 18; and

(v) can, and will, be maintained and accommodated adequately without recourse to public funds in accommodation which the prospective parent or parents own or occupy exclusively; and

(vi) holds a valid United Kingdom entry clearance for entry in this capacity.

Note: Inserted from 30 May 2003 (Cm 5829).

Limited leave to enter the united Kingdom with a view to settlement as a child for adoption under the Hague Convention

316E. A person seeking limited leave to enter the United Kingdom with a view to settlement as a child for adoption under the Hague Convention may be admitted for a period not exceeding 24 months provided he is able, on arrival, to produce to the Immigration Officer a valid United Kingdom entry clearance for entry in this capacity.

Note: Inserted from 30 May 2003 (Cm 5829).

Refusal of limited leave to enter the United Kingdom with a view to settlement as a child for adoption under the Hague Convention

316F. Limited leave to enter the United Kingdom with a view to settlement as a child for adoption under the Hague Convention is to be refused if a valid United Kingdom entry clearance for entry in this capacity is not produced to the Immigration Officer on arrival.

Note: Inserted from 30 May 2003 (Cm 5829).

Parents, grandparents and other dependent relatives of persons present and settled in the United Kingdom

Requirements for indefinite leave to enter or remain in the United Kingdom as the parent, grandparent or other dependent relative of a person present and settled in the United Kingdom

317. The requirements to be met by a person seeking indefinite leave to enter or remain in the United Kingdom as the parent, grandparent or other dependent relative of a person present and settled in the United Kingdom are that the person:

(i) is related to a person present and settled in the United Kingdom in one of the following ways:
  (a) mother or grandmother who is a widow aged 65 years or over; or
  (b) father or grandfather who is a widower aged 65 years or over; or
  (c) parent or grandparents travelling together of whom at least one is aged 65 or over; or
  [(d) a parent or grandparent aged 65 or over who has entered into a second relationship of marriage or civil partnership but cannot look to the spouse, civil partner or children of that second relationship for financial support; and where the person settled in the United Kingdom is able and willing to maintain the parent or grandparent and any spouse or civil partner or child of the second relationship who would be admissible as a dependant;]
  (e) a parent or grandparent under the age of 65 if living alone outside the United Kingdom in the most exceptional compassionate circumstances and mainly dependent financially on relatives settled in the United Kingdom; or
  (f) the son, daughter, sister, brother, uncle or aunt over the age of 18 if living alone outside the United Kingdom in the most exceptional compassionate circumstances and mainly dependent financially on relatives settled in the United Kingdom; and

(ii) is joining or accompanying a person who is present and settled in the United Kingdom or who is on the same occasion being admitted for settlement; and

(iii) is financially wholly or mainly dependent on the relative present and settled in the United Kingdom; and

[(iv) can, and will, be accommodated adequately, together with any dependants, without recourse to public funds, in accommodation which the sponsor owns or occupies exclusively; and

(iva) can, and will, be maintained adequately, together with any dependants, without recourse to public funds; and]

(v) has no other close relatives in his own country to whom he could turn for financial support; and

(vi) if seeking leave to enter, holds a valid United Kingdom entry clearance for entry in this capacity.

Note: Subparagraph (iv) substituted from 2 October 2000 (Cm 4851). Subparagraph (i)(d) substituted from 5 December 2005 (HC 582).

Indefinite leave to enter or remain as the parent, grandparent or other dependent relative of a person present and settled in the United Kingdom

318. Indefinite leave to enter the United Kingdom as the parent, grandparent or other dependent relative of a person present and settled in the United Kingdom may be granted provided a valid United Kingdom entry clearance for entry in this capacity is produced to the Immigration Officer on arrival. Indefinite leave to remain in the United Kingdom as the parent, grandparent or other dependent relative of a person present and settled in the United Kingdom may be granted provided the Secretary of State is satisfied that each of the requirements of paragraph 317(i)–(v) is met.

Refusal of indefinite leave to enter or remain in the United Kingdom as the parent, grandparent or other dependent relative of a person present and settled in the United Kingdom

319. Indefinite leave to enter the United Kingdom as the parent, grandparent or other dependent relative of a person settled in the United Kingdom is to be refused if a valid United Kingdom entry clearance for entry in this capacity is not produced to the Immigration Officer on arrival. Indefinite leave to remain in the United Kingdom as the parent, grandparent or other dependent relative of a person present and settled in the United Kingdom is to be refused if the Secretary of State is not satisfied that each of the requirements of paragraph 317(i)–(v) is met.

Part 9

General Grounds for the Refusal of Entry Clearance, Leave to Enter or Variation of Leave to Enter or Remain in the United Kingdom

Refusal of entry clearance or leave to enter the United Kingdom

320. In addition to the grounds for refusal of entry clearance or leave to enter out in Parts 2–8 of these Rules, and subject to paragraph 321 below, the following grounds for the refusal of entry clearance or leave to enter apply:

Grounds on which entry clearance or leave to enter the United Kingdom is to be refused

(1) the fact that entry is being sought for a purpose not covered by these Rules;

(2) the fact that the person seeking entry to the United Kingdom is currently the subject of a deportation order;

(3) failure by the person seeking entry to the United Kingdom to produce to the Immigration Officer a valid national passport or other document satisfactorily establishing his identity and nationality;

(4) failure to satisfy the Immigration Officer, in the case of a person arriving in the United Kingdom or seeking entry through the Channel Tunnel with the intention of entering any other part of the common travel area, that he is acceptable to the immigration authorities there;

(5) failure, in the case of a visa national, to produce to the Immigration Officer a passport or other identity document endorsed with a valid and current United Kingdom entry clearance issued for the purpose for which entry is sought;

(6) where the Secretary of State has personally directed that the exclusion of a person from the United Kingdom is conducive to the public good;

(7) save in relation to a person settled in the United Kingdom or where the Immigration Officer is satisfied that there are strong compassionate reasons justifying admission, confirmation from the Medical Inspector that, for medical reasons, it is undesirable to admit a person seeking leave to enter the United Kingdom.

Grounds on which entry clearance or leave to enter the United Kingdom should normally be refused

(8) failure by a person arriving in the United Kingdom to furnish the Immigration Officer with such information as may be required for the purpose of deciding whether he requires leave to enter and, if so, whether and on what terms leave should be given;

[(8A) where the person seeking leave is outside the United Kingdom, failure by him to supply any information, documents, copy documents or medical report requested by an Immigration Officer;]

(9) failure by a person seeking leave to enter as a returning resident to satisfy the Immigration Officer that he meets the requirements of paragraph 18 of these Rules [or that he seeks leave to enter for the same purpose as that for which his earlier leave was granted;]

(10) production by the person seeking leave to enter the United Kingdom of a national passport or travel document issued by a territorial entity or authority which is not recognised by Her Majesty's Government as a state or is not dealt with as a government by them, or which does not accept valid United Kingdom passports for the purpose of its own immigration control; or a passport or travel document which does not comply with international passport practice;

(11) failure to observe the time limit or conditions attached to any grant of leave to enter or remain in the United Kingdom;

(12) the obtaining of a previous leave to enter or remain by deception;

(13) failure, except by a person eligible for admission to the United Kingdom for settlement or a spouse [or civil partner] eligible for admission under paragraph 282, to satisfy the Immigration Officer that he will be admitted to another country after a stay in the United Kingdom;

(14) refusal by a sponsor of a person seeking leave to enter the United Kingdom to give, if requested to do so, an undertaking in writing to be responsible for that person's maintenance and accommodation for the period of any leave granted.

(15) whether or not to the holder's knowledge, the making of false representations or the failure to disclose any material fact for the purpose of obtaining [an immigration employment document;]

(16) failure, in the case of a child under the age of 18 years seeking leave to enter the United Kingdom otherwise than in conjunction with an application made by his parent(s) or legal guardian, to provide the Immigration Officer, if required to do so, with written consent to the application from his parent(s) or legal guardian; save that the requirement as to written consent does not apply in the case of a child seeking admission to the United Kingdom as an asylum seeker;

(17) save in relation to a person settled in the United Kingdom, refusal to undergo a medical examination when required to do so by the Immigration Officer;

(18) save where the Immigration Officer is satisfied that admission would be justified for strong compassionate reasons, conviction in any country including the United Kingdom of an offence which, if committed in the United Kingdom, is punishable with imprisonment for a term of 12 months or any greater punishment or, if committed outside the United Kingdom, would be so punishable if the conduct constituting the offence had occurred in the United Kingdom;

(19) where, from information available to the Immigration Officer, it seems right to refuse leave to enter on the ground that exclusion from the United Kingdom is conducive to the public good; if, for example, in the light of the character, conduct or associations of the person seeking leave to enter it is undesirable to give him leave to enter.

[(20) failure by the person seeking entry into the United Kingdom to comply with a requirement relating to the provision of physical data to which he is subject by regulations made under section 126 of the Nationality, Immigration and Asylum Act 2002.]

[(21) Whether or not to the holder's knowledge, the submission of a false document in support of an application.]

Note: Words in square brackets in sub-para (9) inserted from 1 November 1996 (HC 31). Subparagraph 8A inserted from 30 July 2000 (HC 704). Subparagraph (20) inserted from 27 February 2004 (HC 370). Words in square brackets in sub-para (15) substituted from 1 October 2004 (Cm 6339). Words in square brackets in (21) inserted from 25 October 2004 (Cm 1112). Words in square brackets in sub-para (13) inserted from 5 December 2005 (HC 582).

Refusal of leave to enter in relation to a person in possession of an entry clearance

321. A person seeking leave to enter the United Kingdom who holds an entry clearance which was duly issued to him and is still current may be refused leave to enter only where the Immigration Officer is satisfied that:

(i) whether or not to the holder's knowledge, false representations were employed or material facts were not disclosed, either in writing or orally, for the purpose of obtaining the entry clearance; or

(ii) a change of circumstances since it was issued has removed the basis of the holder's claim to admission, except where the change of circumstances amounts solely to the person becoming over age for entry in one of the categories contained in paragraphs 296–316 of these Rules since the issue of the entry clearance; or

(iii) refusal is justified on grounds of restricted returnability; on medical grounds; on grounds of criminal record; because the person seeking leave to enter is the subject of a deportation order or because exclusion would be conducive to the public good.

[Grounds on which leave to enter or remain which is in force is to be cancelled at port or while the holder is outside the United Kingdom

321A. The following grounds for the cancellation of a person's leave to enter or remain which is in force on his arrival in, or whilst he is outside, the United Kingdom apply:

(1) there has been such a change in the circumstances of that person's case, since the leave was given, that it should be cancelled; or

(2) the leave was obtained as a result of false information given by that person or by that person's failure to disclose material facts; or

(3) save in relation to a person settled in the United Kingdom or where the Immigration Officer or the Secretary of State is satisfied that there are strong compassionate reasons justifying admission, where it is apparent that, for medical reasons, it is undesirable to admit that person to the United Kingdom; or

(4) where the Secretary of State has personally directed that the exclusion of that person from the United Kingdom is conducive to the public good; or

(5) where from information available to the Immigration Officer or the Secretary of State, it seems right to cancel leave on the ground that exclusion from the United Kingdom is conducive to the public good; if, for example, in the light of the character, conduct or associations of that person it is undesirable for him to have leave to enter the United Kingdom; or

(6) where that person is outside the United Kingdom, failure by that person to supply any information, documents, copy documents or medical report requested by an Immigration Officer or the Secretary of State.]

Note: Paragraph 321A inserted from 30 July 2000 (HC 704).

Refusal of variation of leave to enter or remain or curtailment of leave

322. In addition to the grounds for refusal of extension of stay set out in Parts 2–8 of these Rules, the following provisions apply in relation to the refusal of an application for variation of leave to enter or remain or, where appropriate, the curtailment of leave:

Grounds on which an application to vary leave to enter or remain in the United Kingdom is to be refused

(1) the fact that variation of leave to enter or remain is being sought for a purpose not covered by these Rules.

Grounds on which an application to vary leave to enter or remain in the United Kingdom should normally be refused

(2) the making of false representations or the failure to disclose any material fact for the purpose of obtaining leave to enter or a previous variation of leave;

(3) failure to comply with any conditions attached to the grant of leave to enter or remain;

(4) failure by the person concerned to maintain or accommodate himself and any dependants without recourse to public funds;

(5) the undesirability of permitting the person concerned to remain in the United Kingdom in the light of his character, conduct or associations or the fact that he represents a threat to national security;

(6) refusal by a sponsor of the person concerned to give, if requested to do so, an undertaking in writing to be responsible for his maintenance and accommodation in the United Kingdom or failure to honour such an undertaking once given;

(7) failure by the person concerned to honour any declaration or undertaking given orally or in writing as to the intended duration and/or purpose of his stay;

(8) failure, except by a person who qualifies for settlement in the United Kingdom or by the spouse [or civil partner] of a person settled in the United Kingdom, to satisfy the Secretary of State that he will be returnable to another country if allowed to remain in the United Kingdom for a further period;

[(9) failure by an applicant to produce within a reasonable time information, documents or other evidence required by the Secretary of State to establish his claim to remain under these Rules;]

(10) failure, without providing a reasonable explanation, to comply with a request made on behalf of the Secretary of State to attend for interview;

(11) failure, in the case of a child under the age of 18 years seeking a variation of his

leave to enter or remain in the United Kingdom otherwise than in conjunction with an application by his parent(s) or legal guardian, to provide the Secretary of State, if required to do so, with written consent to the application from his parent(s) or legal guardian; save that the requirement as to written consent does not apply in the case of a child who has been admitted to the United Kingdom as an asylum seeker.

Note: Subparagraph (9) substituted from 6 July 2005 (HC 104).

Grounds on which leave to enter or remain may be curtailed

[**323.** A person's leave to enter or remain may be curtailed:

(i) on any of the grounds set out in paragraph 322(2)–(5) above; or

(ii) if he ceases to meet the requirements of the Rules under which his leave to enter or remain was granted; or

(iii) if he is the dependant, or is seeking leave to remain as the dependant, of an asylum applicant whose claim has been refused and whose leave has been curtailed under section 7 of the 1993 Act, and he does not qualify for leave to remain in his own right.]

[(iv) on any of the grounds set out in paragraph 339A(i)–(vi) and paragraph (i)–(vi).]

Note: Paragraph 323 substituted from 1 September 1996 (Cm 3365). Subparagraph (iv) inserted from 9 October 2006 (Cm 6918).

Crew members

324. A person who has been given leave to enter to join a ship, aircraft, hovercraft, hydrofoil or international train service as a member of its crew, or a crew member who has been given leave to enter for hospital treatment, repatriation or transfer to another ship, aircraft, hovercraft, hydrofoil or international train service in the United Kingdom, is to be refused leave to remain unless an extension of stay is necessary to fulfil the purpose for which he was given leave to enter or unless he meets the requirements for an extension of stay as a spouse [or proposed civil partner] in paragraph 284.

Note: Words in square brackets inserted from 5 December 2005 (HC 582).

Part 10

Registration with the Police

Note: Paragraph 324A deleted from 4 February 2005 (HC 194).

[**325.** For the purposes of paragraph 326, a 'relevant foreign national' is a person aged 16 or over who is:

(i) a national or citizen of a country or territory listed in Appendix 2 to these Rules;
(ii) a stateless person; or
(iii) a person holding a non-national travel document.]

Note: Paragraph 325 substituted from 4 February 2005 (HC 194).

[**326.**—(1) Subject to sub-paragraph (2) below, a condition requiring registration with the police should normally be imposed on any relevant foreign national who is:
(i) given limited leave to enter the United Kingdom for longer than six months; or
(ii) given limited leave to remain which has the effect of allowing him to remain in the United Kingdom for longer than six months, reckoned from the date of his arrival (whether or not such a condition was imposed when he arrived).

(2) Such a condition should not normally be imposed where the leave is given:
(i) as a seasonal agricultural worker;
(ii) as a private servant in a diplomatic household;
(iii) as a minister of religion, missionary or member of a religious order;
(iv) on the basis of marriage to [or civil partnership with] a person settled in the United Kingdom or as the unmarried [same-sex] partner of a person settled in the United Kingdom;
(v) as a person exercising access rights to a child resident in the United Kingdom;
(vi) as the parent of a child at school; or
(vii) following the grant of asylum.

(3) Such a condition should also be imposed on any foreign national given limited leave to enter the United Kingdom where, exceptionally, the Immigration Officer considers it necessary to ensure that he complies with the terms of the leave.]

Notes: Paragraph 326 substituted from 4 February 2005 (HC 194). Words in square brackets in sub-para (iv) inserted from 5 December 2005 (HC 582).

PART 11

ASYLUM

Definition of asylum applicant

[**327.** Under the Rules an asylum applicant is a person who makes a request to be recognised as a refugee under the Geneva Convention on the basis that it would be contrary to the United Kingdom's obligations under the Geneva Convention for him to be removed from or required to leave the United Kingdom.]

Note: Paragraph 327 substituted from 9 October 2006 (Cm 6918).

Applications for asylum

328. All asylum applications will be determined by the Secretary of State in accordance with the United Kingdom's obligations under the [Geneva Convention]. Every asylum application made by a person at a port or airport in the United Kingdom will be referred by the Immigration Officer for determination by the Secretary of State in accordance with these Rules.

Note: Words in square brackets substituted from 9 October 2006 (Cm 6918).

[**329.** Until an asylum application has been determined by the Secretary of State or the Secretary of State has issued a certificate under Part 2, 3, 4 or 5 of Schedule 3 to the Asylum and Immigration (Treatment of Claimants, etc.) Act 2004 no action will be taken to require the departure of the asylum applicant or his dependants from the United Kingdom.]

Note: Paragraph 329 substituted from 25 October 2004 (Cm 1112).

330. If the Secretary of State decides to grant asylum and the person has not yet been given leave to enter, the Immigration Officer will grant limited leave to enter.

[**331.** [If a person seeking leave to enter is refused asylum, the Immigration Officer will consider whether or not he is in a position to decide to give or refuse leave to enter without interviewing the person further. If the Immigration Officer decides that a further interview is not required he may serve the notice giving or refusing leave to enter by post. If the Immigration Officer decides that a further interview is required, he will then resume his examination to determine whether or not to grant the person] leave to enter under any other provision of these Rules. If the person fails at any time to comply with a requirement to report to an Immigration Officer for examination, the Immigration officer may direct that the person's examination shall be treated as concluded at that time. The Immigration Officer will then consider any outstanding applications for entry on the basis of any evidence before him.]

Note: Paragraph 331 substituted from 1 September 1996 (Cm 3365). Words in square brackets substituted from 28 July 2000 (HC 704).

332. If a person who has been refused leave to enter applies for asylum and that application is refused, leave to enter will again be refused unless the applicant qualifies for admission under any other provision of these Rules.

333. . . .

Note: Paragraph 333 deleted from 2 October 2000 (Cm 4851).

Grant of asylum

[334. An asylum applicant will be granted asylum in the United Kingdom if the Secretary of State is satisfied that:

(i) he is in the United Kingdom or has arrived at a port of entry in the United Kingdom;

(ii) he is a refugee, as defined in regulation 2 of The Refugee or Person in Need of International Protection (Qualification) Regulations 2006;

(iii) there are no reasonable grounds for regarding him as a danger to the security of the United Kingdom;

(iv) he does not, having been convicted by a final judgment of a particularly serious crime, he does not constitute danger to the community of the United Kingdom; and

(v) refusing his application would result in him being required to go (whether immediately or after the time limited by any existing leave to enter or remain) in breach of the Geneva Convention, to a country in which his life or freedom would threatened on account of his race, religion, nationality, political opinion or membership of a particular social group.]

Note: Paragraph 334 substituted from 9 October 2006 (Cm 6918).

335. If the Secretary of State decides to grant asylum to a person who has been given leave to enter (whether or not the leave has expired) or a person who has entered without leave, the Secretary of State will vary the existing leave or grant limited leave to remain.

Refusal of asylum

336. An application which does not meet the criteria set out in paragraph 334 will be refused.

337. . . .

Note: Paragraph 337 deleted from 1 September 1996 (Cm 3365).

338. When a person in the United Kingdom is {notified that his asylum application has been refused} he may, if he is liable to removal as an illegal entrant[, removal under section 10 of the Immigration and Asylum Act 1999] or to deportation, at the same time be notified of removal directions, served with a notice of intention to make a deportation order, or served with a deportation order, as appropriate.

Note: Words in square brackets inserted from 2 October 2000 (Cm 4851). Words in curly brackets substituted from 9 October 2006 (Cm 6918).

[339. . . .

Note: Paragraph 339 deleted from 2 October 2000 (Cm 4851).

Revocation or refusal to renew a grant of asylum

[**339A.** A person's grant of asylum under paragraph 334 will be revoked or not renewed if the Secretary of State is satisfied that:

(i) he has voluntarily re-availed himself of the protection of the country of nationality;
(ii) having lost his nationality, he has voluntarily re-acquired it; or
(iii) he has acquired a new nationality, and enjoys the protection of the country of his new nationality;
(iv) he has voluntarily re-established himself in the country which he left or outside which he remained owing to a fear of persecution;
(v) he can no longer, because the circumstances in connection with which he has been recognised as a refugee have ceased to exist, continue to refuse to avail himself of the protection of the country of nationality;
(vi) being a stateless person with no nationality, he is able, because the circumstances in connection with which he has been recognised as a refugee have ceased to exist, to return to the country of former habitual residence;
(vii) he should have been or is excluded from being a refugee in accordance with regulation 7 of The Refugee or Person in Need of International Protection (Qualification) Regulations 2006;
(viii) his misrepresentation or omission or facts, including the use of false documents, were decisive for the grant of asylum;
(ix) there are reasonable grounds for regarding him as a danger to the security of the United Kingdom; or
(x) having been convicted by a final judgment of a particularly serious crime he constitutes danger to the community of the United Kingdom.

In considering (v) and (vi), the Secretary of State shall have regard to whether the change of circumstances is of such a significant and non-temporary nature that the refugee's fear of persecution can no longer be regarded as well-founded.

Where an application for asylum was made on or after the 21st October 2004, the Secretary of State will revoke or refuse to renew a person's grant of asylum where he is satisfied that at least one of the provisions in sub-paragraph (i)–(vi) apply.]

Note: Paragraph 339A inserted from 9 October 2006 (Cm 6918).

[**339B.** When a person's grant of asylum is revoked or not renewed any limited leave which they have may be curtailed.]

Note: Paragraph 339B inserted from 9 October 2006 (Cm 6918).

Grant of humanitarian protection

[**339C.** A person will be granted humanitarian protection in the United Kingdom if the Secretary of State is satisfied that:

(i) he is in the United Kingdom or has arrived at a port of entry in the United Kingdom;
(ii) he does not qualify as a refugee as defined in regulation 2 of The Refugee or Person in Need of International Protection (Qualification) Regulations 2006;
(iii) substantial grounds have been shown for believing that the person concerned, if he returned to the country of return, would face a real risk of suffering serious harm and is unable, or, owing to such risk, unwilling to avail himself of the protection of that country; and
(iv) he is not excluded from a grant of humanitarian protection.

Serious harm consists of:
(i) the death penalty or execution;
(ii) unlawful killing;
(iii) torture or inhuman or degrading treatment or punishment of a person in the country of return; or
(iv) serious and individual threat to a civilian's life or person by reason of indiscriminate violence in situations of international or internal armed conflict.]

Note: Paragraph 339C inserted from 9 October 2006 (Cm 6918).

Exclusion from humanitarian protection

[**339D.** A person is excluded from a grant of humanitarian protection under paragraph 339C (iv) where the Secretary of State is satisfied that:
(i) there are serious reasons for considering that he has committed a crime against peace, a war crime, a crime against humanity, or any other serious crime or instigated [sic] or otherwise participated in such crimes;
(ii) there are serious reasons for considering that he is guilty of acts contrary to the purposes and principles of the United Nations or has committed, prepared or instigated such acts or encouraged or induced others to commit, prepare or instigate such acts;
(iii) there are serious reasons for considering that he constitutes a danger to the community or to the security of the United Kingdom; and
(iv) prior to his admission to the United Kingdom the person committed a crime outside the scope of (i) and (ii) that would be punishable by imprisonment were it committed in the United Kingdom and the person left his country of origin solely in order to avoid sanctions resulting from the crime.]

Note: Paragraph 339D inserted from 9 October 2006 (Cm 6918).

[**339E.** If the Secretary of State decides to grant humanitarian protection and the person has not yet been given leave to enter, the Secretary of State or an Immigration Officer will grant limited leave to enter. If the Secretary of State decides to grant humanitarian protection to a person who has been given limited leave to enter (whether or not that leave has expired) or a person who has entered without leave, the Secretary of State will vary the existing leave or grant limited leave to remain.]

Note: Paragraph 339E inserted from 9 October 2006 (Cm 6918).

Refusal of humanitarian protection

[**339F.** Where the criteria set out in paragraph 339C is not met humanitarian protection will be refused.]

Note: Paragraph 339F inserted from 9 October 2006 (Cm 6918).

Revocation of humanitarian protection

[**339G.** A person's humanitarian protection granted under paragraph 339C will be revoked or not renewed if the Secretary of State is satisfied that at least one of the following applies:

(i) the circumstances which led to the grant of humanitarian protection have ceased to exist or have changed to such a degree that such protection is no longer required;

(ii) the person granted humanitarian protection should have been or is excluded from humanitarian protection because there are serious reasons for considering that he has committed a crime against peace, a war crime, a crime against humanity, or any other serious crime or instigated or otherwise participated in such crimes;

(iii) the person granted humanitarian protection should have been or is excluded from humanitarian protection because there are serious reasons for considering that he is guilty of acts contrary to the purposes and principles of the United Nations or has committed, prepared or instigated such acts or encouraged or induced others to commit, prepare or instigate such acts;

(iv) the person granted humanitarian protection should have been or is excluded from humanitarian protection because there are serious reasons for considering that he constitutes a danger to the community or to the security of the United Kingdom;

(v) the person granted humanitarian protection misrepresented or omitted facts, including the use of false documents, which were decisive to the grant of humanitarian protection; or

(vi) the person granted humanitarian protection should have been or is excluded from humanitarian protection because prior to his admission to the United Kingdom the person committed a crime outside the scope of (ii) and (iii) that would be punishable by imprisonment had it been committed in the United Kingdom and the person left his country of origin solely in order to avoid sanctions resulting from the crime.

In applying (i) the Secretary of State shall have regard to whether the change of circumstances is of such a significant and non-temporary nature that the person no longer faces a real risk of serious harm.]

Note: Paragraph 339G inserted from 9 October 2006 (Cm 6918).

[**339H.** When a person's humanitarian protection is revoked or not renewed any limited leave which they have may be curtailed.]

Note: Paragraph 339H inserted from 9 October 2006 (Cm 6918).

Consideration of applications 

[**339I.** When the Secretary of State considers a person's asylum claim, eligibility for a grant of humanitarian protection or human rights claim it is the duty of the person to submit to the Secretary of State as soon as possible all material factors needed to substantiate the asylum claim or establish that he is a person eligible for humanitarian protection or substantiate the human rights claim, which the Secretary of State shall assess in cooperation with the person.

The material factors include:

(i) the person's statement on the reasons for making an asylum claim or on eligibility for a grant of humanitarian protection or for making a human rights claim;
(ii) all documentation at the person's disposal regarding the person's age, background (including background details of relevant relatives), identity, nationality(ies), country(ies) and place(s) of previous residence, previous asylum applications, travel routes; and
(iii) identity and travel documents.]

Note: Paragraph 339I inserted from 9 October 2006 (Cm 6918).

[**339J.** The assessment by the Secretary of State of an asylum claim, eligibility for a grant of humanitarian protection or a human rights claim will be carried out on an individual basis. This will include taking into account in particular:

(i) all relevant facts as they relate to the country of origin or country of return at the time of taking a decision on the grant; including laws and regulations of the country of origin or country of return and the manner in which they are applied;
(ii) relevant statements and documentation presented by the person including information on whether the person has been or may be subject to persecution or serious harm;
(iii) the individual position and personal circumstances of the person, including factors such as background, gender and age, so as to assess whether, on the basis of the person's personal circumstances, the acts to which the person

has been or could be exposed would amount to persecution or serious harm;

(iv) whether the person's activities since leaving the country of origin or country of return were engaged in for the sole or main purpose of creating the necessary conditions for making an asylum claim or establishing that he is a person eligible for humanitarian protection or a human rights claim, so as to assess whether these activities will expose the person to persecution or serious harm if he returned to that country; and

(v) whether the person could reasonably be expected to avail himself of the protection of another country where he could assert citizenship.]

Note: Paragraph 339J inserted from 9 October 2006 (Cm 6918).

[**339K.** The fact that a person has already been subject to persecution or serious harm, or to direct threats of such persecution or such harm, will be regarded as a serious indication of the person's well-founded fear of persecution or real risk of suffering serious harm, unless there are good reasons to consider that such persecution or serious harm will not be repeated.]

Note: Paragraph 339K inserted from 9 October 2006 (Cm 6918).

[**339L.** It is the duty of the person to substantiate the asylum claim or establish that he is a person eligible for humanitarian protection or substantiate his human rights claim. Where aspects of the person's statements are not supported by documentary or other evidence, those aspects will not need confirmation when all of the following conditions are met:

(i) the person has made a genuine effort to substantiate his asylum claim or establish that he is a person eligible for humanitarian protection or substantiate his human rights claim;

(ii) all material factors at the person's disposal have been submitted, and a satisfactory explanation regarding any lack of other relevant material has been given;

(iii) the person's statements are found to be coherent and plausible and do not run counter to available specific and general information relevant to the person's case;

(iv) the person has made an asylum claim or sought to establish that he is a person eligible for humanitarian protection or made a human rights claim at the earliest possible time, unless the person can demonstrate good reason for not having done so; and

(v) the general credibility of the person has been established.]

Note: Paragraph 339L inserted from 9 October 2006 (Cm 6918).

[**339M.** The Secretary of State may consider that a person has not substantiated his asylum claim or established that he is a person eligible for humanitarian protection or substantiated his human rights claim if he fails, without reasonable explanation, to make a prompt and full disclosure of material facts, either orally or in writing, or otherwise to assist the Secretary of State in establishing the facts of the case; this includes, for example, a failure to attend an interview, failure to report to a designated place to be fingerprinted, failure to complete an asylum questionnaire or failure to comply with a requirement to report to an immigration officer for examination.]

Note: Paragraph 339M inserted from 9 October 2006 (Cm 6918).

[**339N.** In determining whether the general credibility of the person has been established the Secretary of State will apply the provisions in s.8 of the Asylum and Immigration (Treatment of Claimants, etc.) Act 2004.]

Note: Paragraph 339N inserted from 9 October 2006 (Cm 6918).

Internal relocation

[**339O.**—(i) The Secretary of State will not make:

- (a) a grant of asylum if in part of the country of origin a person would not have a well founded fear of being persecuted, and the person can reasonably be expected to stay in that part of the country; or
- (b) a grant of humanitarian protection if in part of the country of return a person would not face a real risk of suffering serious harm, and the person can reasonably be expected to stay in that part of the country.

(ii) In examining whether a part of the country of origin or country of return meets the requirements in (i) the Secretary of State, when making his decision on whether to grant asylum or humanitarian protection, will have regard to the general circumstances prevailing in that part of the country and to the personal circumstances of the person.

(iii) (i) applies notwithstanding technical obstacles to return to the country of origin or country of return.]

Note: Paragraph 339O inserted from 9 October 2006 (Cm 6918).

Sur place claims

[**339P.** A person may have a well-founded fear of being persecuted or a real risk of suffering serious harm based on events which have taken place since the person left the country of origin or country of return and/or activities which have been engaged in by a person since he left the country of origin or country of return, in particular where it is established that the activities relied upon constitute the expression and continuation of convictions or orientations held in the country of origin or country of return.]

Note: Paragraph 339P inserted from 9 October 2006 (Cm 6918).

Residence Permits

[**339Q.**—(i) The Secretary of State will issue to a person granted asylum in the United Kingdom a United Kingdom Residence Permit (UKRP) as soon as possible after the grant of asylum. The UKRP will be valid for five years and renewable, unless compelling reasons of national security or public order otherwise require or where there are reasonable grounds for considering that the applicant is a danger to the security of the UK or having been convicted by a final judgment of a particularly serious crime, the applicant constitutes a danger to the community of the UK.]

(ii) The Secretary of State will issue to a person granted humanitarian protection in the United Kingdom a UKRP as soon as possible after the grant of humanitarian protection. The UKRP will be valid for five years and renewable, unless compelling reasons of national security or public order otherwise require or where there are reasonable grounds for considering that the person granted humanitarian protection is a danger to the security of the UK or having been convicted by a final judgment of a serious crime, this person constitutes a danger to the community of the UK.

(iii) The Secretary of State will issue a UKRP to a family member of a person granted asylum or humanitarian protection where the family member does not qualify for such status. A UKRP will be granted for a period of five years. The UKRP is renewable on the terms set out in (i) and (ii) respectively.

(iv) The Secretary of State may revoke or refuse to renew a person's UKRP where their grant of asylum or humanitarian protection is revoked under the provisions in the immigration rules.]

Note: Paragraph 339Q inserted from 9 October 2006 (Cm 6918).

340.–344.

Note: Paragraphs 340–344 deteted from 9 October 2006 (Cm 6918).

Travel documents

[**344A.**—(i) After having received a complete application for a travel document, the Secretary of State will issue to a person granted asylum in the United Kingdom and their family members travel documents, in the form set out in the Schedule to the Geneva Convention, for the purpose of travel outside the United Kingdom, unless compelling reasons of national security or public order otherwise require.

(ii) After having received a complete application for a travel document, the Secretary of State will issue travel documents to a person granted humanitarian protection in the United Kingdom where that person is unable to obtain a national passport or other identity documents which enable him to travel, unless compelling reasons of national security or public order otherwise require.

(iii) Where the person referred to in (ii) can obtain a national passport or identity documents but has not done so, the Secretary of State will issue that person with a travel document where he can show that he has made reasonable attempts to obtain a national passport or identity document and there are serious humanitarian reasons for travel.]

Note: Paragraph 344A inserted from 9 October 2006 (Cm 6918).

Access to Employment

[**344B.** The Secretary of State will not impose conditions restricting the employment or occupation in the United Kingdom of a person granted asylum or humanitarian protection.]

Note: Paragraph 344B inserted from 9 October 2006 (Cm 6918).

Information

[**344C.** A person who is granted asylum or humanitarian protection will be provided with access to information in a language that they may reasonably be supposed to understand which sets out the rights and obligations relating to that status. The Secretary of State will provide the information as soon as possible after the grant of asylum or humanitarian protection.]

Note: Paragraph 344C inserted from 9 October 2006 (Cm 6918).

Third country cases

[**345.—(1)** In a case where the Secretary of State is satisfied that the conditions set out in Paragraphs 4 and 5(1), 9 and 10(1), 14 and 15(1) or 17 of Schedule 3 to the Asylum and Immigration (Treatment of Claimants, etc.) Act 2004 are fulfilled, he will normally decline to examine the asylum application substantively and issue a certificate under Part 2, 3, 4 or 5 of Schedule 3 to the Asylum and Immigration (Treatment of Claimants, etc.) Act 2004 as appropriate.

(2) The Secretary of State shall not issue a certificate under Part 2, 3, 4 or 5 of Schedule 3 to the Asylum and Immigration (Treatment of Claimants, etc.) Act 2004 unless:

(i) the asylum applicant has not arrived in the United Kingdom directly from the country in which he claims to fear persecution and has had an opportunity at the border or within the third country or territory to make contact with the authorities of that third country or territory in order to seek their protection; or

(ii) there is other clear evidence of his admissibility to a third country or territory. Provided that he is satisfied that a case meets these criteria, the

Secretary of State is under no obligation to consult the authorities of the third country or territory before the removal of an asylum applicant to that country or territory.

(3) Where a certificate is issued under Part 2, 3, 4 or 5 of Schedule 3 to the Asylum and Immigration (Treatment of Claimants, etc.) Act 2004 in relation to the asylum claim and the person is seeking leave to enter the Immigration Officer will consider whether or not he is in a position to decide to give or refuse leave to enter without interviewing the person further. If the Immigration Officer decides that a further interview is not required he may serve the notice giving or refusing leave to enter by post. If the Immigration Officer decides that a further interview is required, he will then resume his examination to determine whether or not to grant the person leave to enter under any other provision of these Rules. If the person fails at any time to comply with a requirement to report to an Immigration Officer for examination, the Immigration Officer may direct that the person's examination shall be treated as concluded at that time. The Immigration Officer will then consider any outstanding applications for entry on the basis of any evidence before him.

(4) Where a certificate is issued under Part 2, 3, 4 or 5 of Schedule 3 to the Asylum and Immigration (Treatment of Claimants, etc.) Act 2004 the person may, if liable to removal as an illegal entrant, or removal under section 10 of the Immigration and Asylum Act 1999 or to deportation, at the same time be notified of removal directions, served with a notice of intention to make a deportation order, or served with a deportation order, as appropriate.]

Note: Paragraph 345 substituted from 25 October 2004 (Cm 1112).

346. . . .

Note: Paragraph 346 deleted from 25 October 2004 (Cm 1112).

347. . . .

Note: Paragraph 347 deleted from 1 September 1996 (Cm 3365).

Rights of appeal

348. . . .

Note: Deleted from 2 October 2000 (Cm 4851).

Dependants

[**349.** A spouse, civil partner, unmarried or same-sex partner, or minor child accompanying a principal applicant may be included in his application for asylum as his dependant. A spouse, civil partner, unmarried or same-sex partner, or minor child may also claim asylum in his own right. If the principal applicant is granted asylum and leave to enter or remain any spouse, civil partner, unmarried or same-sex partner, or minor child will be granted leave to enter or remain for the same duration. The case of any dependant who claims asylum in his own right will be considered individually in accordance with paragraph 334 above. An applicant under this paragraph, including an accompanied child, may be interviewed where he makes a claim as a dependant or in his own right.

If the spouse, civil partner, unmarried or same-sex partner, or minor child in question has a claim in his own right, that claim should be made at the earliest opportunity. Any failure to do so will be taken into account and may damage credibility if no reasonable explanation for it is given. Where an asylum application is unsuccessful, at the same time that asylum is refused the applicant may be notified of removal directions or served with a notice of the Secretary of State's intention to deport him, as appropriate. In this paragraph and paragraphs 350–352 a child means a person who is under 18 years of age or who, in the absence of documentary evidence establishing age, appears to be under that age. An unmarried or same-sex partner for the purposes of this paragraph, is a person who has been living together with the principal applicant in a subsisting relationship akin to marriage or a civil partnership for two years or more.]

Note: Paragraph 349 substituted from 9 October 2006 (Cm 6918).

Unaccompanied children

350. Unaccompanied children may also apply for asylum and, in view of their potential vulnerability, particular priority and care is to be given to the handling of their cases.

351. A person of any age may qualify for refugee status under the Convention and the criteria in paragraph 334 apply to all cases. However, account should be taken of the applicant's maturity and in assessing the claim of a child more weight should be given to objective indications of risk than to the child's state of mind and understanding of his situation. An asylum application made on behalf of a child should not be refused solely because the child is too young to understand his situation or to have formed a well-founded fear of persecution. Close attention should be given to the welfare of the child at all times.

352. [An accompanied or unaccompanied child who has claimed asylum in his own right may be interviewed about the substance of his claim or to determine his age and identity.] When an interview is necessary it should be conducted in the presence of a parent, guardian, representative or another adult who for the time being takes responsibility for the child and is not an Immigration Officer, an officer of the Secretary of State or a police officer. The interviewer should have particular regard to the possibility that a child will feel inhibited or alarmed. The child should be allowed to express himself in his own way and at his own speed. If he appears tired or distressed, the interview should be stopped.

Note: Words in square brackets substituted from 18 September 2002 (Cm 5597).

[**352A.** The requirements to be met by a person seeking leave to enter or remain in the United Kingdom as the spouse {or civil partner} of a refugee are that:

(i) the applicant is married to {or the civil partner of} a person granted asylum in the United Kingdom; and

(ii) the marriage {or civil partnership} did not take place after the person granted asylum left the country of his former habitual residence in order to seek asylum; and

(iii) the applicant would not be excluded from protection by virtue of article 1F of the United Nations Convention and Protocol relating to the Status of Refugees if he were to seek asylum in his own right; and

[(iv) each of the parties intends to live permanently with the other as his or her spouse {or civil partner} and the marriage {or civil partnership} is subsisting; and]

(v) if seeking leave to enter, the applicant holds a valid United Kingdom entry clearance for entry in this capacity.]

Note: Paragraph 352(iv) inserted from 18 September 2002 (Cm 5597). Words in curly brackets inserted from 5 December 2005 (HC 582).

[**352AA.** The requirements to be met by a person seeking leave to enter or remain in the United Kingdom as the unmarried or the same-sex partner of a refugee are that:

(i) the applicant is the unmarried or same-sex partner of a person granted asylum in the UK on or after 9th October 2006; and

(ii) the parties have been living together in a relationship akin to either a marriage or a civil partnership which has subsisted for two years or more; and

(iii) the relationship existed before the person granted asylum left the country of his former habitual residence in order to seek asylum; and

(iv) the applicant would not be excluded from protection by virtue of paragraph 334(iii) or (iv) of these Rules or article 1F of the Geneva Convention if he were to seek asylum in his own right; and

(v) each of the parties intends to live permanently with the other as his or her unmarried or same-sex partner and the relationship is subsisting; and

(vi) if seeking leave to enter, the applicant holds a valid United Kingdom entry clearance for entry in this capacity.]

Note: Paragraph 352AA inserted from 9 October 2006 (Cm 6918).

[**352B.** Limited leave to enter the United Kingdom as the spouse {or civil partner} of a refugee may be granted provided a valid United Kingdom entry clearance for entry in this capacity is produced to the Immigration Officer on arrival. Limited leave to remain in the United Kingdom as the spouse {or civil partner} of a refugee may be granted provided the Secretary of State is satisfied that each of the requirements of paragraph 352A (i)–(iii) are met.]

[**352BA.** Limited leave to enter the United Kingdom as the unmarried or same-sex partner of a refugee may be granted provided a valid United Kingdom entry clearance for entry in this capacity is produced to the Immigration Officer on arrival. Limited leave to remain in the United Kingdom as the unmarried or same-sex partner of a refugee may be granted provided the Secretary of State is satisfied that each of the requirements of paragraph 352AA (i)–(v) are met.]

Note: Paragraph 352BA inserted from 9 October 2006 (Cm 6918).

[**352C.** Limited leave to enter the United Kingdom as the spouse of a refugee is to be refused if a valid United Kingdom entry clearance for entry in this capacity is not produced to the Immigration Officer on arrival. Limited leave to remain as the spouse of a refugee is to be refused if the Secretary of State is not satisfied that each of the requirements of paragraph 352A (i)–(iii) are met.]

[**352CA.** Limited leave to enter the United Kingdom as the unmarried or same-sex partner of a refugee is to be refused if a valid United Kingdom entry clearance for entry in this capacity is not produced to the Immigration Officer on arrival. Limited leave to remain as the unmarried or same-sex partner of a refugee is to be refused if the Secretary of State is not satisfied that each of the requirements of paragraph 352AA (i)–(v) are met.]

Note: Paragraph 352CA inserted from 9 October 2006 (Cm 6918).

[**352D.** The requirements to be met by a person seeking leave to enter or remain in the United Kingdom [in order to join or remain with the parent who has been granted asylum in the United Kingdom] are that the applicant:

- (i) is the child of a parent who has been granted asylum in the United Kingdom; and
- (ii) is under the age of 18, and
- (iii) is not leading an independent life, is unmarried {and is not a civil partner}, and has not formed an independent family unit; and
- (iv) was part of the family unit of the person granted asylum at the time that the person granted asylum left the country of his habitual residence in order to seek asylum; and
- (v) would not be excluded from protection by virtue of article 1F of the United Nations Convention and Protocol relating to the Status of Refugees if he were to seek asylum in his own right; and
- (vi) if seeking leave to enter, holds a valid United Kingdom entry clearance for entry in this capacity.]

Note: Words in square brackets substituted from 18 September 2002 (Cm 5597).

[352E. Limited leave to enter the United Kingdom as the child of a refugee may be granted provided a valid United Kingdom entry clearance for entry in this capacity is produced to the Immigration Officer on arrival. Limited leave to remain in the United Kingdom as the child of a refugee may be granted provided the Secretary of State is satisfied that each of the requirements of paragraph 352D (i)–(v) are met.]

[352F. Limited leave to enter the United Kingdom as the child of a refugee is to be refused if a valid United Kingdom entry clearance for entry in this capacity is not produced to the Immigration Officer on arrival. Limited leave to remain as the child of a refugee is to be refused if the Secretary of State is not satisfied that each of the requirements of paragraph 352D (i)–(v) are met.]

Note: Paragraph 352F inserted from 2 October 2000 (Cm 4851).

Interpretation

[352G. For the purposes of this Part:

(a) 'Geneva Convention' means the United Nations Convention and Protocol relating to the Status of Refugees;

(b) 'Country of return' means a country or territory listed in paragraph 8(c) of Schedule 2 of the Immigration Act 1971;

(c) 'Country of origin' means the country or countries of nationality or, for a stateless person, or [*sic*] former habitual residence.]

Note: Paragraph 352G inserted from 9 October 2006 (Cm 6918).

Part 12

Procedure

Fresh claims

[353. When a human rights or asylum claim has been refused and any appeal relating to that claim is no longer pending, the decision maker will consider any further submissions and, if rejected, will then determine whether they amount to a fresh claim. The submissions will amount to a fresh claim if they are significantly different from the material that has previously been considered. The submissions will only be significantly different if the content:

(i) had not already been considered; and

(ii) taken together with the previously considered material, created a realistic prospect of success, notwithstanding its rejection.

This paragraph does not apply to claims made overseas.]

Note: Paragraph 353 inserted from 25 October 2004 (Cm 1112).

Part 11A
Temporary Protection

Definition of Temporary Protection Directive

[354. For the purposes of paragraphs 355 to 356B, 'Temporary Protection Directive' means Council Directive 2001/55/EC of 20 July 2001 regarding the giving of temporary protection by Member States in the event of a mass influx of displaced persons.]

Note: Paragraph 354 inserted from 1 January 2004 (HC 164).

Grant of temporary protection

[355. An applicant for temporary protection will be granted temporary protection if the Secretary of State is satisfied that:

(i) the applicant is in the United Kingdom or has arrived at a port of entry in the United Kingdom; and

(ii) the applicant is a person entitled to temporary protection as defined by, and in accordance with, the Temporary Protection Directive; and

(iii) the applicant does not hold an extant grant of temporary protection entitling him to reside in another Member State of the European Union. This requirement is subject to the provisions relating to dependants set out in paragraphs 356 to 356B and to any agreement to the contrary with the Member State in question; and

(iv) the applicant is not excluded from temporary protection under the provisions in paragraph 355A.]

Note: Paragraph 355 inserted from 1 January 2004 (HC 164).

[355A. An applicant or a dependant may be excluded from temporary protection if:

(i) there are serious reasons for considering that:

  (a) he has committed a crime against peace, a war crime, or a crime against humanity, as defined in the international instruments drawn up to make provision in respect of such crimes; or

  (b) he has committed a serious non-political crime outside the United Kingdom prior to his application for temporary protection; or

  (c) he has committed acts contrary to the purposes and principles of the United Nations, or

(ii) there are reasonable grounds for regarding the applicant as a danger to the security of the United Kingdom or, having been convicted by a final judgment of a particularly serious crime, to be a danger to the community of the United Kingdom.

Consideration under this paragraph shall be based solely on the personal conduct of the applicant concerned. Exclusion decisions or measures shall be based on the principle of proportionality.]

Note: Paragraph 355A inserted from 1 January 2004 (HC 164).

[**355B.** If temporary protection is granted to a person who has been given leave to enter or remain (whether or not the leave has expired) or to a person who has entered without leave, the Secretary of State will vary the existing leave or grant limited leave to remain.]

Note: Paragraph 355B inserted from 1 January 2004 (HC 164).

[**355C.** A person to whom temporary protection is granted will be granted limited leave to enter or remain, which is not to be subject to a condition prohibiting employment, for a period not exceeding 12 months. On the expiry of this period, he will be entitled to apply for an extension of this limited leave for successive periods of 6 months thereafter.]

Note: Paragraph 355C inserted from 1 January 2004 (HC 164).

[**355D.** A person to whom temporary protection is granted will be permitted to return to the United Kingdom from another Member State of the European Union during the period of a mass influx of displaced persons as established by the Council of the European Union pursuant to Article 5 of the Temporary Protection Directive.]

Note: Paragraph 355D inserted from 1 January 2004 (HC 164).

[**355E.** A person to whom temporary protection is granted will be provided with a document in a language likely to be understood by him in which the provisions relating to temporary protection and which are relevant to him are set out. A person with temporary protection will also be provided with a document setting out his temporary protection status.]

Note: Paragraph 355E inserted from 1 January 2004 (HC 164).

[**355F.** The Secretary of State will establish and maintain a register of those granted temporary protection. The register will record the name, nationality, date and place of birth and marital status of those granted temporary protection and their family relationship to any other person who has been granted temporary protection.]

Note: Paragraph 355F inserted from 1 January 2004 (HC 164).

[**355G.** If a person who makes an asylum application is also eligible for temporary protection, the Secretary of State may decide not to consider the asylum application until the applicant ceases to be entitled to temporary protection.]

Note: Paragraph 355G inserted from 1 January 2004 (HC 164).

Dependants

[**356.** In this part:

'dependant' means a family member or a close relative.

'family member' means:

(i) the spouse {or civil partner} of an applicant for, or a person who has been granted, temporary protection; or

(ii) the unmarried {or same-sex} partner of an applicant for, or a person who has been granted, temporary protection where the parties have been living together in a relationship akin to marriage {or civil partnership} which has subsisted for 2 years or more; or

(iii) the {minor child (who is unmarried and not a civil partner)} of an applicant for, or a person who has been granted, temporary protection or his spouse,

who lived with the principal applicant as part of the family unit in the country of origin immediately prior to the mass influx.

'close relative' means:

(i) the {adult child (who is unmarried and not a civil partner)} of an applicant for, or person who has been granted, temporary protection; or

(ii) the {sibling (who is unmarried and not a civil partner)} or the uncle or aunt of an applicant for, or person who has been granted, temporary protection, who lived with the principal applicant as part of the family unit in the country of origin immediately prior to the mass influx and was wholly or mainly dependent upon the principal applicant at that time, and would face extreme hardship if reunification with the principal applicant did not take place.]

Note: Paragraph 356 inserted from 1 January 2004 (HC 164). Words in curly brackets inserted from 5 December 2005 (HC 582).

[**356A.** A dependant may apply for temporary protection. Where the dependant falls within paragraph 356 and does not fall to be excluded under paragraph 355A, he will be granted temporary protection for the same duration and under the same conditions as the principal applicant.]

Note: Paragraph 356A inserted from 1 January 2004 (HC 164).

[**356B.** When considering any application by a dependant child, the Secretary of State shall take into consideration the best interests of that child.]

Note: Paragraph 356B inserted from 1 January 2004 (HC 164).

[PART 11B]

Reception Conditions for non-EU asylum applicants

[**357.** Part 11B only applies to asylum applicants (within the meaning of these Rules) who are not nationals of a member State.]

Note: Paragraph 357 inserted from 4 February 2005 (HC 194).

Information to be provided to asylum applicants

[**358.** The Secretary of State shall inform asylum applicants within a reasonable time not exceeding fifteen days after their claim for asylum has been recorded of the benefits and services that they may be eligible to receive and of the rules and procedures with which they must comply relating to them. The Secretary of State shall also provide information on non-governmental organisations and persons that provide legal assistance to asylum applicants and which may be able to help asylum applicants or provide information on available benefits and services.]

Note: Paragraph 358 inserted from 4 February 2005 (HC 194).

[**358A.** The Secretary of State shall ensure that the information referred to in paragraph 358 is available inwriting and, to the extent possible, will provide the information in a language that asylum applicants may reasonably be supposed to understand. Where appropriate, the Secretary of State may also arrange for this information to be supplied orally.]

Note: Paragraph 358A inserted from 4 February 2005 (HC 194).

Information to be provided by asylum applicants

[**358B.** An asylum applicant must notify the Secretary of State of his current address and of any change to his address or residential status. If not notified beforehand, any change must be notified to the Secretary of State without delay after it occurs.]

Note: Paragraph 358B inserted from 4 February 2005 (HC 194).

Documentation

[**359.** The Secretary of State shall ensure that, within three working days of recording an asylum application, a document is made available to that asylum applicant, issued in his own name, certifying his status as an asylum applicant or testifying that he is allowed to remain in the United Kingdom while his asylum application is pending. For the avoidance of doubt, in cases where the Secretary of State declines to examine an application it will no longer be pending for the purposes of this rule.]

Note: Paragraph 359 inserted from 4 February 2005 (HC 194).

[**359A.** The obligation in paragraph 359 above shall not apply where the asylum applicant is detained under the Immigration Acts, the Immigration and Asylum Act 1999 or the Nationality, Immigration and Asylum Act 2002.]

Note: Paragraph 359A inserted from 4 February 2005 (HC 194).

[**359B.** A document issued to an asylum applicant under paragraph 359 does not constitute evidence of the asylum applicant's identity.]

Note: Paragraph 359B inserted from 4 February 2005 (HC 194).

[**359C.** In specific cases the Secretary of State or an Immigration Officer may provide an asylum applicant with evidence equivalent to that provided under rule 359. This might be, for example, in circumstances in which it is only possible or desirable to issue a time-limited document.]

Note: Paragraph 359C inserted from 4 February 2005 (HC 194).

Right to request permission to take up employment

[**360.** An asylum applicant may apply to the Secretary of State for permission to take up employment which shall not include permission to become self-employed or to engage in a business or professional activity if a decision at first instance has not been taken on the applicant's asylum application within one year of the date on which it was recorded. The Secretary of State shall only consider such an applicant if, in his opinion, any delay in reaching a decision at first instance cannot be attributed to the applicant.]

Note: Paragraph 360 inserted from 4 February 2005 (HC 194).

[**360A.** If an asylum applicant is granted permission to take up employment under rule 360 this shall only be until such time as his asylum application has been finally determined.]

Note: Paragraph 360A inserted from 4 February 2005 (HC 194).

Interpretation

[**361.** For the purposes of this Part—

(a) 'working day' means any day other than a Saturday or Sunday, a bank holiday, Christmas day or Good Friday;

(b) 'member State' has the same meaning as in Schedule 1 to the European Communities Act 1972.]

Note: Paragraph 361 inserted from 4 February 2005 (HC 194).

Part 12

Note: Part 12 omitted from 2 October 2000 (Cm 4851).

Part 13

Deportation (and Administrative Removal Under Section 10 of the 1999 Act)

A deportation order

362. A deportation order requires the subject to leave the United Kingdom and authorises his detention until he is removed. It also prohibits him from re-entering the country for as long as it is in force and invalidates any leave to enter or remain in the United Kingdom given him before the order was made or while it is in force.

[**363.** The circumstances in which a person is liable to deportation include:

- (i) where the Secretary of State deems the person's deportation to be conducive to the public good;
- (ii) where the person is the spouse [or civil partner] or child under 18 of a person ordered to be deported; and
- (iii) where a court recommends deportation in the case of a person over the age of 17 who has been convicted of an offence punishable with imprisonment.]

Note: Paragraph 363 substituted from 2 October 2000 (Cm 4851). Words in square brackets in sub-para (ii) inserted from 5 December 2005 (HC 582).

[**363A.** Prior to 2 October 2000, a person would have been liable to deportation in certain circumstances in which he is now liable to administrative removal. These circumstances are listed in paragraph 394B below. However, such a person remains liable to deportation, rather than administrative removal where:

- (i) a decision to make a deportation order against him was taken before 2 October 2000; or
- (ii) the person has made a valid application under the Immigration (Regulation Period for Overstayers) Regulations 2000.]

Note: Paragraph 363A inserted from 2 October 2000 (Cm 4851).

[**364.** Subject to paragraph 380, while each case will be considered on its merits, where a person is liable to deportation the presumption shall be that the public interest requires deportation. The Secretary of State will consider all relevant factors in considering whether the presumption is outweighed in any particular case, although it will only be in exceptional circumstances that the public interest in deportation will be outweighed in a case where it would not be contrary to the Human Rights Convention and the Convention and protocol relating to the Status of Refugees to deport. The aim is an exercise of the power of deportation which is consistent and fair as between one person and another, although one case will rarely be identical with another in all material respects. In the cases detailed in paragraph 363A deportation will normally be the proper course where a person has failed to comply with or has contravened a condition or has remained without authority.]

Note: Paragraph 364 substituted from 20 July 2006 (HC 1337).

Deportation of family members

[**365.** Section 5 of the Immigration Act 1971 gives the Secretary of State power in certain circumstances to make a deportation order against the {spouse, civil partner or child} of a person against whom a deportation order has been made. The Secretary of State will not normally decide to deport the spouse {or civil partner} of a deportee where:

(i) he has qualified for settlement in his own right; or
(ii) he has been living apart from the deportee.]

Note: Paragraph 365 substituted from 1 October 1996 (Cm 3365). Words in curly brackets inserted from 5 December 2005 (HC 582).

[**366.** The Secretary of State will not normally decide to deport the child of a deportee where:

(i) he and his mother or father are living apart from the deportee; or
(ii) he has left home and has established himself on an independent basis; or
(iii) he married {or formed a civil partnership} before deportation came into prospect.]

Note: Paragraph 366 substituted from 1 October 1996 by (Cm 3365). Words in curly brackets inserted from 5 December 2005 (HC 582).

[**367.** In considering whether to require a spouse {or civil partner} or child to leave with the deportee the Secretary of State will take account of [all relevant factors, including]:

(i) the ability of the spouse {or civil partner} to maintain himself and any children in the United Kingdom, or to be maintained by relatives or friends without charge to public funds, not merely for a short period but for the foreseeable future; and
(ii) in the case of a child of school age, the effect of removal on his education; and

(iii) the practicality of any plans for a child's care and maintenance in this country if one or both of his parents were deported; and

(iv) any representations made on behalf of the spouse {or civil partner} or child.]

Note: Paragraph 367 substituted from 1 October 1996 (Cm 3365). Words in curly brackets inserted from 5 December 2005 (HC 582). Words in square brackets after 'take account of' substituted from 20 July 2006 (HC 1337).

368. Where the Secretary of State decides that it would be appropriate to deport a member of a family as such, the decision, and the right of appeal, will be notified and it will at the same time be explained that it is open to the member of the family to leave the country voluntarily if he does not wish to appeal or if he appeals and his appeal is dismissed.

Note: Paragraph 369–77 deleted from 2 October 2000 (Cm 4851).

[**378.** A deportation order may not be made while it is still open to the person to appeal against the Secretary of State's decision, or while an appeal is pending. There is no appeal within the immigration appeal system against the making of a deportation order on the recommendation of a court; but there is a right of appeal to a higher court against the recommendation itself. A deportation order may not be made while it is still open to the person to appeal against the relevant conviction, sentence or recommendation, or while such an appeal is pending.]

Note: Substituted from 2 October 2000 (Cm 4851). Paragraphs 379 and 379A deleted from 2 October 2000 (Cm 4851).

380. A deportation order will not be made against any person if his removal in pursuance of the order would be contrary to the United Kingdom's obligations under the Convention and Protocol relating to the Status of Refugees [or the Human Rights Convention].

Note: Words in square brackets inserted from 2 October 2000 (Cm 4851).

Procedure

381. When a decision to make a deportation order has been taken (otherwise than on the recommendation of a court) a notice will be given to the person concerned informing him of the decision and of his right of appeal. . . .

Note: Words omitted from 2 October 2000 (Cm 4851).

382. [Following the issue of such a notice the Secretary of State may authorise detention or make an order restricting a person as to residence, employment or occupation and requiring him to report to the police, pending the making of a deportation order.]

Note: Substituted from 2 October 2000 (Cm 4851).

383. . . .

Note: Deleted from 2 October 2000 (Cm 4851).

384. If a notice of appeal is given within the period allowed, a summary of the facts of the case on the basis of which the decision was taken will be sent to the [appropriate] appellate authorities, who will notify the appellant of the arrangements for the appeal to be heard.

Note: Word in square brackets inserted from 2 October 2000 (Cm 4851).

Arrangements for removal

385. A person against whom a deportation order has been made will normally be removed from the United Kingdom. The power is to be exercised so as to secure the person's return to the country of which he is a national, or which has most recently provided him with a travel document, unless he can show that another country will receive him. In considering any departure from the normal arrangements, regard will be had to the public interest generally, and to any additional expense that may fall on public funds.

386. The person will not be removed as the subject of a deportation order while an appeal may be brought against the removal directions or such an appeal is pending.

Supervised departure

387. . . .

Note: Deleted from 2 October 2000 (Cm 4851).

Returned deportees

388. Where a person returns to this country when a deportation order is in force against him, he may be deported under the original order. The Secretary of State will consider every such case in the light of all the relevant circumstances before deciding whether to enforce the order.

Returned family members

389. Persons deported in the circumstances set out in paragraph 365–368 above (deportation of family members) may be able to seek re-admission to the United Kingdom under the Immigration Rules where:

(i) a child reaches 18 (when he ceases to be subject to the deportation order); or

(ii) in the case of a spouse or civil partner, the marriage or civil partnership comes to an end.]

Note: Subparagraph (iii) substituted from 5 December 2005 (HC 582).

Revocation of deportation order

390. An application for revocation of a deportation order will be considered in the light of all the circumstances including the following:

(i) the grounds on which the order was made;
(ii) any representations made in support of revocation;
(iii) the interests of the community, including the maintenance of an effective immigration control;
(iv) the interests of the applicant, including any compassionate circumstances.

391. In the case of an applicant with a serious criminal record continued exclusion for a long term of years will normally be the proper course. In other cases revocation of the order will not normally be authorised unless the situation has been materially altered, either by a change of circumstances since the order was made, or by fresh information coming to light which was not before the court which made the recommendation or the appellate authorities, or the Secretary of State. The passage of time since the person was deported may also in itself amount to such a change of circumstances as to warrant revocation of the order. However, save in the most exceptional circumstances, the Secretary of State will not revoke the order unless the person has been absent from the United Kingdom for a period of at least 3 years since it was made.

392. Revocation of a deportation order does not entitle the person concerned to re-enter the United Kingdom; it renders him eligible to apply for admission under the Immigration Rules. Application for revocation of the order may be made to the Entry Clearance Officer or direct to the Home Office.

Rights of appeal in relation to a decision not to revoke a deportation order

393. . . .

394. . . .

Note: Paragraphs 393–394 deleted from 2 October 2000 (Cm 4851).

395. [There may be a right of appeal against refusal to revoke a deportation order.] Where an appeal does lie the right of appeal will be notified at the same time as the decision to refuse to revoke the order.

[Administrative Removal

395A. A person is now liable to administrative removal in certain circumstances in which he would, prior to 2 October 2000, have been liable to deportation.

395B. These circumstances are set out in section 10 of the 1999 Act. They are:

(i) failure to comply with a condition attached to his leave to enter or remain, or remaining beyond the time limited by the leave;

(ii) where the person has obtained leave to remain by deception; and
(iii) where the person is the spouse{, civil partner,} or child under 18 of someone in respect of whom directions for removal have been given under section 10.

Note: Words in curly brackets inserted from 5 December 2005 (HC 582).

[**395C.** Before a decision to remove under section 10 is given, regard will be had to all the relevant factors known to the Secretary of State, {including:

(i) age;
(ii) length of residence in the United Kingdom;
(iii) strength of connections with the United Kingdom;
(iv) personal history, including character, conduct and employment record;
(v) domestic circumstances;
(vi) previous criminal record and the nature of any offence of which the person has been convicted;
(vii) compassionate circumstances;
(viii) any representations received on the person's behalf.}

In the case of family members, the factors listed in paragraphs 365–368 must also be taken into account.]

Note: Paragraph 395C substituted from 1 October 2004 (Cm 6339). Words in curly brackets inserted from 20 July 2006 (HC 1337).

395D. No one shall be removed under section 10 if his removal would be contrary to the United Kingdom's obligations under the Convention and Protocol relating to the Status of Refugees or under the Human Rights Convention.

Procedure

[**395E.** When a decision that a person is to be removed under section 10 has been given, a notice will be given to the person concerned informing him of the decision and of any right of appeal.]

Note: Paragraph 395E substituted from 1 October 2004 (Cm 6339).

395F. Following the issue of such a notice an Immigration Officer may authorise detention or make an order restricting a person as to residence, employment or occupation and requiring him to report to the police, pending the removal.]

Note: Words in square brackets in para 395 inserted and paras 395A–F inserted from 2 October 2000 (Cm 4851).

Appendix 1

Visa Requirements for the United Kingdom

1. Subject to paragraph 2 below the following persons need a visa for the United Kingdom:

(a) Nationals or citizens of the following countries or territorial entities:

Afghanistan
Albania
Algeria
Angola
Armenia
Azebbaijan
Bahrain
Bangladesh
Belarus
Benin
Bhutan
Bosnia-Herzegovina
Bulgaria
Burkina Faso
Burma
Burundi
Cambodia
Cameroon
Cape Verde
Central African Republic
Chad
[People's Republic of China (except for those referred to in sub-paragraphs 2(d) and (e) of this Appendix)]
[Colombia]
Comoros
Congo
Cuba
[Democratic Republic of the Congo (Zaire)]
Djibouti
Dominican Republic
[Ecuador]
Egypt
Equatorial Guinea
Eritrea
Ethiopia
Fiji
Gabon
Gambia
Georgia
Ghana
Guinea
Guinea-Bissau
Guyana
Haiti
India
Indonesia
Iran
Iraq
Ivory Coast
[Jamaica]
Jordan
Kazakhstan
Kenya
Kirgizstan
Korea (North)
Kuwait
Laos
Lebanon
Liberia
Libya
Macedonia
Madagascar
[Malawi]
Mali
Mauritania
Moldova
Mongolia
Morocco
Mozambique
Nepal
Niger
Nigeria
Oman
Pakistan
Papua New Guinea
Peru
Philippines
Qatar
Romania
Russia
Rwanda
Sao Tome e Principe
Saudi Arabia
Senegal
Sierra Leone
Somalia
Sri Lanka
Sudan
Surinam
Syria
Taiwan
Tajikistan
Tanzania
Thailand
Togo
Tunisia
Turkey
Turkmenistan
Uganda
Ukraine
United Arab Emirates
Uzbekistan
Vietnam
Yemen
Zambia
[Zimbabwe]

The territories formerly comprising the Socialist Federal Republic of Yugoslavia excluding Croatia and Slovenia.

(b) Persons who hold passports or travel documents issued by the former Soviet Union or by the former Socialist Federal Republic of Yugoslavia.

(c) Stateless persons.

(d) Persons who hold non-national documents.

2. The following persons do not need a visa for the United Kingdom:

(a) those who qualify for admission to the United Kingdom as returning residents in accordance with paragraph 18;

[(b) those who seek leave to enter the United Kingdom within the period of their earlier leave and for the same purpose as that for which leave was granted, unless it—

(i) was for a period of six months or less, or

(ii) was extended by statutory instrument] [or by section 3C of the Immigration Act 1971 (inserted by section 3 of the Immigration and Asylum Act 1999)];

(c) . . .

[(d) those nationals or citizens of the People's Republic of China holding passports issued by Hong Kong Special Administrative Region; or

(e) those nationals or citizens of the People's Republic of China holding passports issued by Macao Special Administrative Region.]

[(f) those who arrive in the United Kingdom with leave to enter which is in force but which was given before arrival so long as those in question arrive within the period of their earlier leave and for the same purpose as that for which leave was granted, unless that leave—

(i) was for a period of six months or less, or

(ii) was extended by statutory instrument or by section 3C of the Immigration Act 1971 (inserted by section 3 of the Immigration and Asylum Act 1999).]

Note: Appendix substituted from 4 April 1996 (HC 329); para 2(b) substituted from 1 November 1996 (HC 31); words in square brackets at the end of 2(b)(ii) inserted from 18 December 2002 (HC 104); paras 2(d) and (e) inserted from 17 April 2002 (HC 735); para 2(c) deleted from 11 February 2003 (HC 389); para 2(f) inserted from 18 December 2002 (HC104). Transitional provisions apply to certain nationals of Malawi: see HC 949 (March 2006).

Paragraph 324A.

[Appendix 2

Countries or Territories Whose Nationals or Citizens are Relevant Foreign Nationals for the Purposes of Part 10 of These Rules (Registration With the Police)

Afghanistan
Algeria
Argentina
Armenia
Azerbaijan
Bahrain
Belarus
Bolivia
Brazil
China
Colombia
Cuba
Egypt
Georgia
Iran
Iraq
Israel
Jordan
Kazakhstan
Kirgizstan
Kuwait
Lebanon
Libya
Moldova
Morocco
North Korea
Oman
Palestine
Peru
Qatar
Russia
Saudi Arabia
Sudan
Syria
Tajikistan
Tunisia
Turkey
Turkmenistan
United Arab Emirates
Ukraine
Uzbekistan
Yemen]

Note: Appendix 2 inserted from 11 May 1998 (Cm 3953).

Appendix 3

Note: Appendix 3 deleted from 13 November 2005 (HC 645).

[List of countries participating in the Working Holidaymaker Scheme

Antigua and Barbuda
Australia
The Bahamas
Bangladesh
Barbados
Belize
Botswana
Brunei Darussalam
Canada
Cameroon
Dominica
Fiji Islands
The Gambia
Ghana
Grenada
Guyana
India
Jamaica
Kenya
Kiribati
Malawi
Malaysia
Maldives
Mauritius
Mozambique
Namibia
Nauru

New Zealand
Nigeria
Pakistan
Papua New Guinea
Saint Christopher and Nevis
Saint Lucia
Saint Vincent and the Grenadines
Seychelles
Sierra Leone
Singapore
Solomon Islands
South Africa
Sri Lanka
Swaziland
Tanzania, United Republic of Tonga
Trinidad and Tobago
Tuvalu
Uganda
Vanuatu
Western Samoa
Zambia
Zimbabwe]

Note: List of countries participating in the Working Holidaymaker Scheme inserted from 8 February 2005 (HC 302).
Note: Paragraph 177C

APPENDIX 4

Points criteria needed to succeed under paragraph 135D(ii) of these Rules

Qualifications

Points	Qualifications (can include equivalent level professional qualifications) Applicants may claim points for only one qualification.
50	PhD
35	Masters degree
30	Bachelors degree

Previous Earnings

Points	Applicants whose previous grant of leave to enter/remain under HSMP was for a period of more than 12 months: Previous Earnings from 12 out of the 15 months preceding the application.
5	16–17,999 Pounds Sterling (£)
10	18–19,999
15	20–22,999
20	23–25,999
25	26–28,999
30	29–31,999
35	32–34,999
40	35–39,999
45	40+

UK Experience

Points	Applicants whose previous grant of leave to enter/remain under HSMP was for a period of more than 12 months:
5	At least £16,000 of the past earnings for which points have been claimed under the previous points scoring section, have been earned in the United Kingdom.

Points	Applicants whose previous grant of leave to enter/remain under HSMP was for a period of more than 12 months or less:
5	At least £10,650 of the past earnings for which points have been claimed under the previous points scoring section, have been earned in the United Kingdom.

Age

Points	Age (as at date of posting of application)
20	29 or under
10	30 or 31
5	32 or 33

Note: Appendix 4 inserted from 5 December 2006 (HC 1702).

Appendix 5
Documents referred to in paragraph 135D(ii) and 135D(iii)b:

Part I
Qualifications – if achieved after initial HSMP grant

Required evidence for those with an academic qualification

Original academic certificate showing:
- Title of the award;
- Date of award;
- Institution;
- Name of applicant.

Required evidence for those with a professional/vocational qualification

Original award certificate showing:
- Title of award;
- Date of award;
- Institution;
- Name of applicant; and

Letter from UK professional body confirming qualification's equivalence to UK academic level showing:

- Name of award including country and awarding body;
- Equivalence of award to UK academic levels.

Required evidence for those who have just graduated

Letter from institution on headed paper showing:

- Name of applicant;
- Qualification awarded;
- Date of award;
- Date certificate will be issued; and

Academic transcript showing:

- Name of applicant;
- Institution;
- Course details;
- Confirmation of award.

Previous Earnings

Required evidence for those who have been in salaried employment

Both the following covering the full period claimed for:

- Income tax returns;
- Wage slips.

Required evidence for those who worked in a country with no tax system

Any two of the following three to cover the full period claimed for:

- Bank statements;
- Wage slips;
- Letter from employer stating salary.

Required evidence for independent contractors

All of the following to cover the full period claimed for:

- Income tax return;
- Copies of contracts from employers covering the total amount of earnings claimed;
- Invoices covering the full amount claimed; and
- Bank statements showing incoming payments covering the full amount claimed.

Required evidence for those who have been self employed

Both the following to cover the full period claimed for:

- Applicant's individual personal income tax return; and
- Applicant's personal bank statements;

Plus one of the following combinations of documents covering the full period claimed for:

- Company audited accounts PLUS Company Tax return (one of these documents must confirm the total payment claimed by the applicant); OR
- Unaudited business/management accounts confirming the total payment claimed by the applicant.

PLUS either

- Business bank statements AND a business tax return; OR
- Copies of contracts totalling the full amount payable to the individual AND corroborating invoices.

UK Experience

Required evidence for those claiming points for previous earnings

Evidence will be assessed for that sent in to qualify for Previous Earnings criteria. No additional documents required.

Age Assessment

Required evidence for those claiming points under the age assessment

The original passport or travel document.

Part II
English Language

Required evidence for those claiming a degree taught in English to fulfil criteria

Both of the following:
Original degree certificate; and
Original letter on headed paper from the institution confirming the degree was taught in English showing:

- Name;
- Qualification awarded;
- Date awarded.

Note: Appendix 5 inserted from 5 December 2006 (HC 1702).

STATUTORY INSTRUMENTS

Immigration (Control of Entry through Republic of Ireland) Order 1972
(SI 1972, No. 1610)

1. This Order may be cited as the Immigration (Control of Entry through Republic of Ireland) Order 1972 and shall come into operation on 1st January 1973.

2.—(1) In this Order—

'the Act' means the Immigration Act 1971; and

'visa national' means a person who, in accordance with the immigration rules, is required on entry into the United Kingdom to produce a passport or other document of identity endorsed with a United Kingdom visa and includes a stateless person.

(2) In this Order any reference to an Article shall be construed as a reference to an Article of this Order and any reference in an Article to a paragraph as a reference to a paragraph of that Article.

(3) The Interpretation Act 1889 shall apply to the interpretation of this Order as it applies to the interpretation of an Act of Parliament.

3.—(1) This Article applies to—

(a) any person (other than a citizen of the Republic of Ireland) who arrives in the United Kingdom on an aircraft which began its flight in that Republic if he entered that Republic in the course of a journey to the United Kingdom which began outside the common travel area and was not given leave to land in that Republic in accordance with the law in force there;

(b) any person (other than a person to whom sub-paragraph (a) of this paragraph applies) who arrives in the United Kingdom on a local journey from the Republic of Ireland if he satisfies any of the following conditions, that is to say—

(i) he is a visa national who has no valid visa for his entry into the United Kingdom;

(ii) he entered that Republic unlawfully from a place outside the common travel area;

(iii) he entered that Republic from a place in the United Kingdom and Islands after entering there unlawfully, [or if he had a limited leave to enter or remain there, after the expiry of the leave, provided that in either case] he has not subsequently been given leave to enter or remain in the United Kingdom or any of the Islands; or

(iv) he is a person in respect of whom directions have been given by the Secretary of State for him not to be given entry to the United Kingdom on the ground that his exclusion is conductive to the public good.

(2) In relation only to persons to whom this Article applies, the Republic of Ireland shall be excluded from section 1(3) of the Act (provisions relating to persons travelling on local journeys in the common travel area).

Note: Words in square brackets in Art 3(1)(b)(iii) inserted by SI 1979/730.

4.—(1) Subject to paragraph (2), this Article applies to [any person who does not have the right of abode in the United Kingdom under section 2 of the Act] and is not a citizen of the Republic of Ireland and who enters the United Kingdom on a local journey from the Republic of Ireland after having entered that Republic—

(a) on coming from a place outside the common travel area; or

(b) after leaving the United Kingdom whilst having a limited leave to enter or remain there which has since expired.

(2) This Article shall not apply to any person [who arrives in the United Kingdom with leave to enter or remain in the United Kingdom which is in force but which was given to him before arrival or] who requires leave to enter the United Kingdom by virtue of Article 3 or section 9(4) of the Act.

(3) A person to whom this Article applies by virtue only of paragraph (1)(a) shall, unless he is a visa national who has a visa containing the words 'short visit', be subject to the restriction and to the condition set out in paragraph (4).

(4) The restriction and the condition referred to in paragraph (3) are—

(a) the period for which he may remain in the United Kingdom shall not be more than three months from the date on which he entered the United Kingdom; and

[(b) unless he is a national of a state which is a member of the European Economic Community, he shall not engage in any occupation for reward; and

(c) unless he is a national of a state which is a member of the European Economic Community other than [Portugal or Spain] he shall not engage in any employment.]

(5) In relation to a person who is a visa national and has a visa containing the words 'short visit' the restriction and the conditions set out in paragraph (6) shall have effect instead of the provisions contained in paragraph (4).

(6) The restriction and the conditions referred to in paragraph (5) are—

(a) the period for which he may remain in the United Kingdom shall not be more than one month from the date on which he entered the United Kingdom;

(b) he shall not engage in any occupation for reward or any employment; and

(c) he shall, unless he is under the age of 16 years, be required to register with the police.

(7) The preceding provisions of this Article shall have effect in relation to a person to whom this Article applies by virtue of sub-paragraph (b) of paragraph (1)

(whether or not he is also a person to whom this Article applies by virtue of sub-paragraph (a) thereof) as they have effect in relation to a person to whom this Article applies by virtue only of the said sub-paragraph (a), but as if for the references in paragraphs (4) and (6) to three months and one month respectively there were substituted a reference to seven days.

Note: Words in square brackets in Art 4(1) substituted by SI 1982/1028. Words in square brackets in Art 4(2) inserted by SI 1776/2000 from 30 July 2000. Art 4(4)(b) and (c) substituted by SI 1980/1859. Words in square brackets in Art 4(4)(c) inserted by SI 1985/1854.

Immigration (Exemption from Control) Order 1972
(SI 1972, No. 1613)

1. This Order may be cited as the Immigration (Exemption from Control) Order 1972 and shall come into operation on 1st January 1973.

2.—(1) In this Order—

'the Act' means the Immigration Act 1971; and

'consular employee' and 'consular officer' have the meanings respectively assigned to them by Article 1 of the Vienna Convention on Consular Relations as set out in Schedule 1 to the Consular Relations Act 1968.

(2) In this Order any reference to an Article or to the Schedule shall be construed as a reference to an Article of this Order or, as the case may be, to the Schedule thereto and any reference in an Article to a paragraph as a reference to a paragraph of that Article.

(3) In this Order any reference to an enactment is a reference to it as amended, and includes a reference to it as applied, by or under any other enactment and any reference to an instrument made under or by virtue of any enactment is a reference to any such instrument for the time being in force.

(4) The Interpretation Act 1889 shall apply to the interpretation of this Order as it applies to the interpretation of an Act of Parliament.

3.—(1) The following persons shall be exempt from any provision of the Act relating to those who are not [British citizens], that is to say:—

(a) any consular officer in the service of any of the states specified in the Schedule (being states with which consular conventions have been concluded by Her Majesty);

(b) any consular employee in such service as is mentioned in subparagraph (a) of this paragraph; and

(c) any member of the family of a person exempted under sub-paragraph (a) or (b) of this paragraph forming part of his household.

(2) In paragraph (1) and in Article 4 any reference to a consular employee shall be construed as a reference to such an employee who is in the full-time service of the state concerned and is not engaged in the United Kingdom in any private occupation for gain.

Note: Words in square brackets in Art 3(1) substituted by SI 1982/1649.

4. The following persons shall be exempt from any provision of the Act relating to those who are not [British citizens] except any provision relating to deportation, that is to say:—

(a) unless the Secretary of State otherwise directs, any member of the government of a country or territory outside the United Kingdom and Islands who is visiting the United Kingdom on the business of that government;

(b) any person entitled to immunity from legal process with respect to acts performed by him in his official capacity under any Order in Council made under section 3(1) of the Bretton Woods Agreements Act 1945 (which empowers Her Majesty by Order in Council to make provision relating to the immunities and privileges of the governors, executive directors, alternates, officers and employees of the International Monetary Fund and the International Bank for Reconstruction and Development);

(c) any person entitled to immunity from legal process with respect to acts performed by him in his official capacity under any Order in Council made under section 3(1) of the International Finance Corporation Act 1955 (which empowers Her Majesty by Order in Council to make provision relating to the immunities and privileges of the governors, directors, alternates, officers and employees of the International Finance Corporation);

(d) any person entitled to immunity from legal process with respect to acts performed by him in his official capacity under any Order in Council made under section 3(1) of the International Development Association Act 1960 (which empowers Her Majesty by Order in Council to make provision relating to the immunities and privileges of the governors, directors, alternates, officers and employees of the International Development Association);

(e) any person (not being a person to whom section 8(3) of the Act applies) who is the representative or a member of the official staff of the representative of the government of a country to which section 1 of the Diplomatic Immunities (Conferences with Commonwealth Countries and Republic of Ireland) Act 1961 applies (which provides for representatives of certain Commonwealth countries and their staff attending conferences in the United Kingdom to be entitled to diplomatic immunity) so long as he is included in a list complied and published in accordance with that section;

(f) any person on whom any immunity from jurisdiction is conferred by any Order in Council made under section 12(1) of the Consular Relations Act 1968 (which empowers Her Majesty by Order in Council to confer on certain persons connected with the service of the government of Commonwealth countries or the Republic of Ireland all or any of the immunities and privileges which are conferred by or may be conferred under that Act on persons connected with consular posts);

(g) any person (not being a person to whom section 8(3) of the Act applies) on whom any immunity from suit and legal process is conferred by any Order in Council made under section 1(2), 5(1) or 6(2) of the International Organisations Act 1968 (which empower Her Majesty by Order in Council to confer certain immunities and privileges on persons connected with certain international organisations and international tribunals and on representatives of foreign countries and their staffs attending certain conferences in the United Kingdom) except any such person as is mentioned in section 5(2)(c) to (e) of the said Act of 1968 [or by any Order in Council continuing to have effect by virtue of section 12(5) of the said Act of 1968];

(h) any consular officer (not being an honorary consular officer) in the service of a state other than such a state as is mentioned in the Schedule;

(i) any consular employee in such service as is mentioned in paragraph (h);

[(j) any officer or servant of the Commonwealth Secretariat falling within paragraph 6 of the Schedule to the Commonwealth Secretariat Act 1966 (which confers certain immunities on those members of the staff of the Secretariat who are not entitled to full diplomatic immunity);]

[(k) any person on whom any immunity from suit and legal process is conferred by the European Communities (Immunities and Privileges of the North Atlantic Salmon Conservation Organisation) Order 1985 (which confers certain immunities and privileges on the representatives and officers of the North Atlantic Salmon Conservation Organisation);]

[(l) any member of the Hong Kong Economic and Trade Office as defined by paragraph 8 of the Schedule to the Hong Kong Economic and Trade Office Act 1996,]

[(m) (i) Any member or servant of the Independent International Commission on Decommissioning ('the Commission') established under an Agreement between the Government of the United Kingdom of Great Britain and Northern Ireland and the Government of the Republic of Ireland concluded on 26th August 1997,

(ii) in sub-paragraph (i) above, 'servant' includes any agent of or person carrying out work for or giving advice to the Commission,

(n) any member of the family of a person exempted under any of the preceding paragraphs forming part of his household.']

[(o) any person falling within Article 4A below.]

[**4A.**—(1) In relation to the court ('the ICC') established by the Rome Statute of the International Criminal Court done at Rome on 17th July 1998 ('the Rome Statute');

(a) except in so far as in any particular case the exemption given by this Article is waived by the State or intergovernmental organisation they represent,
   (i) any representative of a State party to the Rome Statute attending meetings of the Assembly or one of its subsidiary organs,
   (ii) any representative of another State attending meetings of the Assembly or one of its subsidiary organs as an observer, and
   (iii) any representative of a State or of an intergovernmental organisation invited to a meeting of the Assembly or one of its subsidiary organs,

while exercising their official functions and during their journey to and from the place of the meeting;

(b) except in so far as in any particular case the exemption given by this Article is waived by the State they represent, any representative of a State participating in the proceedings of the ICC while exercising their official functions and during their journeys to and from the place of the proceedings of the ICC;

(c) except in so far as in any particular case the exemption given by this Article is waived by an absolute majority of the judges, any judge and the Prosecutor, when engaged on or with respect to the business of the ICC;

(d) except in so far as in any particular case the exemption given by this Article is waived by the Prosecutor, any Deputy Prosecutor, when engaged on or with respect to the business of the ICC;

(e) except in so far as in any particular case the exemption given by this Article is waived by the Presidency, the Registrar, when engaged on or with respect to the business of the ICC;

(f) except in so far as in any particular case the exemption given by this Article is waived by the Registrar, the Deputy Registrar, so far as necessary for the performance of his functions;

(g) except in so far as in any particular case the exemption given by this Article is waived by the Prosecutor, any member of the staff of the office of the Prosecutor, so far as necessary for the performance of their functions;

(h) except in so far as in any particular case the exemption given by this Article is waived by the Registrar, any member of the staff of the Registry, so far as necessary for the performance of their functions;

(i) except in so far as in any particular case the exemption given by this Article is waived by the Presidency and subject to the production of the certificate under seal of the Registrar provided to counsel and persons assisting defence counsel upon appointment, counsel and any person assisting defence counsel, so far as necessary for the performance of their functions;

(j) except in so far as in any particular case the exemption given by this Article is waived by the Presidency and subject to the production of a document provided by the ICC certifying that the person's appearance before the ICC is required by the ICC and specifying a time period during which such appearance is necessary, any witness, to the extent necessary for their appearance before the ICC for the purposes of giving evidence;

(k) except in so far as in any particular case the exemption given by this Article is waived by the Presidency and subject to the production of a document provided by the ICC certifying the participation of the person in the proceedings of the ICC and specifying a time period for that participation, any victim, to the extent necessary for their appearance before the ICC;

(l) except in so far as in any particular case the exemption given by this Article is waived by the head of the organ of the ICC appointing the person and subject to the production of a document provided by the ICC certifying that the person is performing functions for the ICC and specifying a time period during which those functions will last, any expert performing functions for the ICC, to the extent necessary for the exercise of those functions;

(m) any member of the family of a person exempted under any of paragraphs (c) to (h) above forming part of their household.

(2) In paragraph (1) above:

'the Assembly' means the assembly of State parties to the Rome Statute;

'the Presidency' means the organ of the ICC composed of the president and the first and second vice-presidents of the ICC elected in accordance with Article 38, paragraph 1, of the Rome Statute;

'the Prosecutor' and 'Deputy Prosecutors' mean the prosecutor and deputy prosecutors respectively elected by the assembly of State parties to the Rome Statute in accordance with Article 42, paragraph 4, of the Rome Statute;

'the Registrar' and 'the Deputy Registrar' mean the registrar and deputy registrar respectively elected by the ICC in accordance with Article 43, paragraph 4, of the Rome Statute.]

Note: First words in square brackets Art 4 substituted by SI 1982/1649. Words in square brackets Art 4(g) added by SI 1977/693. Article 4(j) substituted by SI 1977/693. Article 4(k) substituted by SI 1985/1809. Art 4(l) substituted by SI 1402/1997. Art 4(m) substituted by SI 2207/1997. Article 4(o) and Art 4A inserted from a date to be appointed (SI 2004/3171).

5.—(1) Subject to the provisions of this Article the following persons who are not [British citizens] shall, on arrival in the United Kingdom, be exempt from the provisions of section 3(1)(a) of the Act (which requires persons who are not [British citizens] to obtain leave to enter the United Kingdom), that is to say—

(a) any citizen of the United Kingdom and Colonies who holds a passport issued to him in the United Kingdom and Islands and expressed to be a British Visitor's Passport;

(b) any Commonwealth citizen who is included in a passport issued in the United Kingdom by the Government of the United Kingdom or in one of the Islands by the Lieutenant-Governor thereof which is expressed to be a Collective Passport;

(c) any Commonwealth citizen or citizen of the Republic of Ireland returning to the United Kingdom from an excursion to France or Belgium [or the Netherlands] who holds a valid document of identity issued in accordance with arrangements approved by the United Kingdom Government and in a form authorised by the Secretary of State and enabling him to travel on such an excursion without a passport;

(d) any Commonwealth citizen who holds a British seaman's card or any citizen of the Republic of Ireland if (in either case) he was engaged as a member of the crew of a ship in a place within the common travel area and, on arrival in the United Kingdom, is, or is to be, discharged from his engagement;

(e) any person who, having left the United Kingdom after having been given a limited leave to enter, returns to the United Kingdom within the period for which he had leave as a member of the crew of an aircraft under an engagement requiring him to leave on that or another aircraft as a member of its crew within a period exceeding seven days.

(2) Paragraph (1) shall not apply so as to confer any exemption on any person against whom there is a deportation order in force or who has previously entered the United Kingdom unlawfully and has not subsequently been given leave to enter or remain in the United Kingdom and sub-paragraphs (d) and (e) of that paragraphs shall not apply to a person who is required by an immigration officer to submit to examination in accordance with Schedule 2 to the Act.

(3) In this Article any reference to a Commonwealth citizen shall be construed as including a reference to a British protected person and in paragraph (1)(d) 'British seaman's card' means a valid card issued under any regulations in force under section 70 of the Merchant Shipping Act 1970 or any card having effect by virtue of the said regulations as a card so issued and 'holder of a British seaman's card' has the same meaning as in the said regulations.

Note: Words in square brackets in Art 5(1) substituted by SI 1982/1649. Words in square brackets in Art 5(1)(c) added by SI 1975/617.

6.—(1) For the purposes of section 1(1) of the British Nationality Act 1981 (which relates to acquisition of British citizenship by birth in the United Kingdom), a person to whom a child is born in the United Kingdom on or after 1st January 1983 is to be regarded (notwithstanding the preceding provisions of this Order) as settled in the United Kingdom at the time of the birth if—

(a) he would fall to be so regarded but for his being at that time entitled to an exemption by virtue of this Order; and

(b) immediately before he became entitled to that exemption he was settled in the United Kingdom; and

(c) he was ordinarily resident in the United Kingdom from the time when he became entitled to that exemption to the time of the birth;

but this Article shall not apply if at the time of the birth the child's father or mother is a person on whom any immunity from jurisdiction is conferred by or under the Diplomatic Privileges Act 1964

(2) Expressions used in this Article shall be construed in accordance with section 50 of the British Nationality Act 1981.

Note: Article 6 added by SI 1982/1649.

Article 3 and 4 SCHEDULE

STATES WITH WHICH CONSULAR CONVENTIONS HAVE BEEN CONCLUDED BY HER MAJESTY

Austria
Belgium
Bulgaria
[Czechoslovakia]
Denmark
France
[German Democratic Republic]
Greece
Federal Republic of Germany
Hungary
Italy
Japan
Mexico
[Mongolia]
Norway
Poland
Romania
Sweden
Spain
Union of Soviet Socialist Republics
United States of America
Yugoslavia

Note: Words in square brackets in the Sch added by SI 1977/693.

Immigration (Ports of Entry) Order 1987
(SI 1987, No. 177)

1.—(1) This Order may be cited as the Immigration (Ports of Entry) Order 1987 and shall come into force on 1st March 1987.

(2) The Immigration (Ports of Entry) Order 1972, the Immigration (Ports of Entry) (Amendment) Order 1975 and the Immigration (Ports of Entry) (Amendment) Order 1979 are hereby revoked.

2. The ports specified in the Schedule to this Order shall be ports of entry for the purposes of the Immigration Act 1971.

SCHEDULE

PORTS OF ENTRY

Seaports and Hoverports

Dover
Felixstowe
Folkestone
Harwich
Hull
London
Newhaven
Plymouth
Portsmouth
Ramsgate
Sheerness
Southampton
Tyne

Airports

Aberdeen
Belfast
Birmingham
Bournemouth (Hurn)
Bristol
Cardiff (Wales)
East Midlands
Edinburgh
Gatwick-London
Glasgow
Heathrow-London
Leeds/Bradford
Liverpool
Luton
Manchester
Newcastle
Norwich
Prestwick
Southampton
Southend
Stansted-London
Tees-side

The Asylum Support Regulations 2000
(SI 2000, No. 704)

Arrangement of Regulations

General

1. Citation and commencement.
2. Interpretation.

Initial application for support

3. Initial application for support: individual and group applications.
4. Persons excluded from support.

Schedule

General

Citation and commencement

1. These Regulations may be cited as the Asylum Support Regulations 2000 and shall come into force on 3rd April 2000.

Interpretation

2.—(1) In these Regulations—

'the Act' means the Immigration and Asylum Act 1999;

'asylum support' means support provided under section 95 of the Act;

'dependant' has the meaning given by paragraphs (4) and (5);

'the interim Regulations' means the Asylum Support (Interim Provisions) Regulations 1999;

'married couple' means a man and woman who are married to each other and are members of the same household; and

'unmarried couple' means a man and woman who, though not married to each other, are living together as if married.

[(2) The period prescribed under section 94(3) of the Act (day on which a claim for asylum is determined) for the purposes of Part VI of the Act is 28 days where paragraph (2A) applies, and 21 days in any other case.

(2A) This paragraph applies where:

(a) the Secretary of State notifies the claimant that his decision is to accept the asylum claim;

(b) the Secretary of State notifies the claimant that his decision is to reject the asylum claim but at the same time notifies him that he is giving him limited leave to enter or remain in the United Kingdom; or

(c) an appeal by the claimant against the Secretary of State's decision has been disposed of by being allowed.]

(3) Paragraph (2) does not apply in relation to a case to which the interim Regulations apply (for which case, provision corresponding to paragraph (2) is made by regulation 2(6) of those Regulations).

(4) In these Regulations 'dependant', in relation to an asylum-seeker, a supported person or an applicant for asylum support, means, subject to paragraph (5), a person in the United Kingdom ('the relevant person') who—

(a) is his spouse;

(b) is a child of his or of his spouse, is dependant on him and is, or was at the relevant time, under 18;

(c) is a member of his or his spouse's close family and is, or was at the relevant time, under 18;

(d) had been living as part of his household—

(i) for at least six of the twelve months before the relevant time, or

(ii) since birth,

and is, or was at the relevant time, under 18;

(e) is in need of care and attention from him or a member of his household by reason of a disability and would fall within sub-paragraph (c) or (d) but for the fact that he is not, and was not at the relevant time, under 18;

(f) had been living with him as a member of an unmarried couple for at least two of the three years before the relevant time;

(g) is living as part of his household and was, immediately before 6th December 1999 (the date when the interim Regulations came into force), receiving assistance from a local authority under section 17 of the Children Act 1989;

(h) is living as part of his household and was, immediately before the coming into force of these Regulations, receiving assistance from a local authority under—

(i) section 22 of the Children (Scotland) Act 1995; or

(ii) Article 18 of the Children (Northern Ireland) Order 1995; or

(i) has made a claim for leave to enter or remain in the United Kingdom, or for variation of any such leave, which is being considered on the basis that he is dependant on the asylum-seeker;

and in relation to a supported person, or an applicant for asylum support, who is himself a dependant of an asylum-seeker, also includes the asylum-seeker if in the United Kingdom.

(5) Where a supported person or applicant for asylum support is himself a dependant of an asylum-seeker, a person who would otherwise be a dependant of the supported person, or of the applicant, for the purposes of these Regulations is not such a dependant unless he is also a dependant of the asylum-seeker or is the asylum-seeker.

(6) In paragraph (4), 'the relevant time', in relation to the relevant person, means—

(a) the time when an application for asylum support for him was made in accordance with regulation 3(3); or

(b) if he has joined a person who is already a supported person in the United Kingdom and sub-paragraph (a) does not apply, the time when he joined that person in the United Kingdom.

(7) Where a person, by falling within a particular category in relation to an asylum-seeker or supported person, is by virtue of this regulation a dependant of the asylum-seeker or supported person for the purposes of these Regulations, that category is also a prescribed category for the purposes of paragraph (c) of the definition of 'dependant' in section 94(1) of the Act and, accordingly, the

person is a dependant of the asylum-seeker or supported person for the purposes of Part VI of the Act.

(8) Paragraph (7) does not apply to a person who is already a dependant of the asylum-seeker or supported person for the purposes of Part VI of the Act because he falls within either of the categories mentioned in paragraphs (a) and (b) of the definition of 'dependant' in section 94(1) of the Act.

(9) Paragraph (7) does not apply for the purposes of any reference to a 'dependant' in Schedule 9 to the Act.

Note: Regulation 2(2) substituted from 8 April 2002 (SI 2002/472).

Initial application for support

Initial application for support: individual and group applications

3.—(1) Either of the following—

(a) an asylum-seeker, or

(b) a dependant of an asylum-seeker,

may apply to the Secretary of State for asylum support.

(2) An application under this regulation may be—

(a) for asylum support for the applicant alone; or

(b) for asylum support for the applicant and one or more dependants of his.

(3) The application must be made by completing in full and in English the form for the time being issued by the Secretary of State for the purpose; and any form so issued shall be the form shown in the Schedule to these Regulations or a form to the like effect.

[(4) The application may not be entertained by the Secretary of State—

(a) where it is made otherwise than in accordance with paragraph (3); or

(b) where the Secretary of State is not satisfied that the information provided is complete or accurate or that the applicant is co-operating with enquiries made under paragraph (5).]

(5) The Secretary of State may make further enquiries of the applicant about any matter connected with the application.

[(5A) Where the Secretary of State makes further enquiries under paragraph (5) the applicant shall reply to those enquiries within five working days of his receipt of them.

(5B) The Secretary of State shall be entitled to conclude that the applicant is not co-operating with his enquiries under paragraph (5) if he fails, without reasonable excuse, to reply within the period prescribed by paragraph (5A).

(5C) In cases where the Secretary of State may not entertain an application for asylum support he shall also discontinue providing support under section 98 of the Act.]

(6) Paragraphs (3) and (4) do not apply where a person is already a supported person and asylum support is sought for a dependant of his for whom such support is not already provided (for which case, provision is made by regulation 15).

[(7) For the purposes of this regulation, working day means any day other than a Saturday, a Sunday, Christmas Day, Good Friday or a day which is a bank holiday under section 1 of the Banking and Financial Dealings Act 1971 in the locality in which the applicant is living.]

Note: Subparagraphs (5A), (5B), (5C) and (7) inserted from 5 February 2005, SI 2005/11.

Persons excluded from support

4.—(1) The following circumstances are prescribed for the purposes of subsection (2) of section 95 of the Act as circumstances where a person who would otherwise fall within subsection (1) of that section is excluded from that subsection (and, accordingly, may not be provided with asylum support).

(2) A person is so excluded if he is applying for asylum support for himself alone and he falls within paragraph (4) by virtue of any sub-paragraph of that paragraph.

(3) A person is so excluded if—
- (a) he is applying for asylum support for himself and other persons, or he is included in an application for asylum support made by a person other than himself;
- (b) he falls within paragraph (4) (by virtue of any sub-paragraph of that paragraph); and
- (c) each of the other persons to whom the application relates also falls within paragraph (4) (by virtue of any sub-paragraph of that paragraph).

(4) A person falls within this paragraph if at the time when the application is determined—
- (a) he is a person to whom interim support applies; or
- (b) he is a person to whom social security benefits apply; or
- (c) he has not made a claim for leave to enter or remain in the United Kingdom, or for variation of any such leave, which is being considered on the basis that he is an asylum-seeker or dependent on an asylum-seeker.

(5) For the purposes of paragraph (4), interim support applies to a person if—
- (a) at the time when the application is determined, he is a person to whom, under the interim Regulations, support under regulation 3 of those Regulations must be provided by a local authority;
- (b) sub-paragraph (a) does not apply, but would do so if the person had been determined by the local authority concerned to be an eligible person; or
- (c) sub-paragraph (a) does not apply, but would do so but for the fact that the

person's support under those Regulations was (otherwise than by virtue of regulation 7(1)(d) of those Regulations) refused under regulation 7, or suspended or discontinued under regulation 8, of those Regulations;

and in this paragraph 'local authority', 'local authority concerned' and 'eligible person' have the same meanings as in the interim Regulations.

(6) For the purposes of paragraph (4), a person is a person to whom social security benefits apply if he is—

(a) a person who by virtue of regulation 2 of the Social Security (Immigration and Asylum) Consequential Amendments Regulations 2000 is not excluded by section 115(1) of the Act from entitlement to—

(i) income-based jobseeker's allowance under the Jobseekers Act 1995; or

(ii) income support, housing benefit or council tax benefit under the Social Security Contributions and Benefits Act 1992;

(b) a person who, by virtue of regulation 2 of the Social Security (Immigration and Asylum) Consequential Amendments Regulations (Northern Ireland) 2000 is not excluded by section 115(2) of the Act from entitlement to—

(i) income-based jobseeker's allowance under the Jobseekers (Northern Ireland) Order 1995; or

(ii) income support or housing benefit under the Social Security Contributions and Benefits (Northern Ireland) Act 1992;

(7) A person is not to be regarded as falling within paragraph (2) or (3) if, when asylum support is sought for him, he is a dependant of a person who is already a supported person.

(8) The circumstances prescribed by paragraphs (2) and (3) are also prescribed for the purposes of section 95(2), as applied by section 98(3), of the Act as circumstances where a person who would otherwise fall within subsection (1) of section 98 is excluded from that subsection (and, accordingly, may not be provided with temporary support under section 98).

(9) For the purposes of paragraph (8), paragraphs (2) and (3) shall apply as if any reference to an application for asylum support were a reference to an application for support under section 98 of the Act.

Determining whether persons are destitute

Determination where application relates to more than one person, etc.

5.—(1) Subject to paragraph (2), where an application in accordance with regulation 3(3) is for asylum support for the applicant and one or more dependants of his, in applying section 95(1) of the Act the Secretary of State must decide whether the applicant and all those dependants, taken together, are destitute or likely to become destitute within the period prescribed by regulation 7.

(2) Where a person is a supported person, and the question falls to be determined

whether asylum support should in future be provided for him and one or more other persons who are his dependants and are—

(a) persons for whom asylum support is also being provided when that question falls to be determined; or

(b) persons for whom the Secretary of State is then considering whether asylum support should be provided,

in applying section 95(1) of the Act the Secretary of State must decide whether the supported person and all those dependants, taken together, are destitute or likely to become destitute within the period prescribed by regulation 7.

Income and assets to be taken into account

6.—(1) This regulation applies where it falls to the Secretary of State to determine for the purposes of section 95(1) of the Act whether—

(a) a person applying for asylum support, or such an applicant and any dependants of his, or

(b) a supported person, or such a person and any dependants of his, is or are destitute or likely to become so within the period prescribed by regulation 7.

(2) In this regulation 'the principal' means the applicant for asylum support (where paragraph (1)(a) applies) or the supported person (where paragraph (1)(b) applies).

(3) The Secretary of State must ignore—

(a) any asylum support, and

(b) any support under section 98 of the Act, which the principal or any dependant of his is provided with or, where the question is whether destitution is likely within a particular period, might be provided with in that period.

(4) But he must take into account—

(a) any other income which the principal, or any dependant of his, has or might reasonably be expected to have in that period;

(b) any other support which is available to the principal or any dependant of his, or might reasonably be expected to be so available in that period; and

(c) any assets mentioned in paragraph (5) (whether held in the United Kingdom or elsewhere) which are available to the principal or any dependant of his otherwise than by way of asylum support or support under section 98, or might reasonably be expected to be so available in that period.

(5) Those assets are—

(a) cash;

(b) savings;

(c) investments;

(d) land;

(e) cars or other vehicles; and
(f) goods held for the purpose of a trade or other business.

(6) The Secretary of State must ignore any assets not mentioned in paragraph (5).

Period within which applicant must be likely to become destitute

7. The period prescribed for the purposes of section 95(1) of the Act is—

(a) where the question whether a person or persons is or are destitute or likely to become so falls to be determined in relation to an application for asylum support and sub-paragraph (b) does not apply, 14 days beginning with the day on which that question falls to be determined;

(b) where that question falls to be determined in relation to a supported person, or in relation to persons including a supported person, 56 days beginning with the day on which that question falls to be determined.

Adequacy of existing accommodation

8.—(1) Subject to paragraph (2), the matters mentioned in paragraph (3) are prescribed for the purposes of subsection (5)(a) of section 95 of the Act as matters to which the Secretary of State must have regard in determining for the purposes of that section whether the accommodation of—

(a) a person applying for asylum support, or

(b) a supported person for whom accommodation is not for the time being provided by way of asylum support, is adequate.

(2) The matters mentioned in paragraph (3)(a) and (d) to (g) are not so prescribed for the purposes of a case where the person indicates to the Secretary of State that he wishes to remain in the accommodation.

(3) The matters referred to in paragraph (1) are—

(a) whether it would be reasonable for the person to continue to occupy the accommodation;

(b) whether the accommodation is affordable for him;

(c) whether the accommodation is provided under section 98 of the Act, or otherwise on an emergency basis, only while the claim for asylum support is being determined;

(d) whether the person can secure entry to the accommodation;

(e) where the accommodation consists of a moveable structure, vehicle or vessel designed or adapted for human habitation, whether there is a place where the person is entitled or permitted both to place it and reside in it;

(f) whether the accommodation is available for occupation by the person's dependants together with him;

(g) whether it is probable that the person's continued occupation of the accommodation will lead to domestic violence against him or any of his dependants.

(4) In determining whether it would be reasonable for a person to continue to occupy accommodation, regard may be had to the general circumstances prevailing in relation to housing in the district of the local housing authority where the accommodation is.

(5) In determining whether a person's accommodation is affordable for him, the Secretary of State must have regard to—
   (a) any income, or any assets mentioned in regulation 6(5) (whether held in the United Kingdom or elsewhere), which is or are available to him or any dependant of his otherwise than by way of asylum support or support under section 98 of the Act, or might reasonably be expected to be so available;
   (b) the costs in respect of the accommodation; and
   (c) the person's other reasonable living expenses.

(6) In this regulation—
   (a) 'domestic violence' means violence from a person who is or has been a close family member, or threats of violence from such a person which are likely to be carried out; and
   (b) 'district of the local housing authority' has the meaning given by section 217(3) of the Housing Act 1996.

(7) The reference in paragraph (1) to subsection (5)(a) of section 95 of the Act does not include a reference to that provision as applied by section 98(3) of the Act.

Essential living needs

9.—(1) The matter mentioned in paragraph (2) is prescribed for the purposes of subsection (7)(b) of section 95 of the Act as a matter to which the Secretary of State may not have regard in determining for the purposes of that section whether a person's essential living needs (other than accommodation) are met.

(2) That matter is his personal preference as to clothing (but this shall not be taken to prevent the Secretary of State from taking into account his individual circumstances as regards clothing).

(3) None of the items and expenses mentioned in paragraph (4) is to be treated as being an essential living need of a person for the purposes of Part VI of the Act.

(4) Those items and expenses are—
   (a) the cost of faxes;
   (b) computers and the cost of computer facilities;
   (c) the cost of photocopying;
   (d) travel expenses, except the expense mentioned in paragraph (5);
   (e) toys and other recreational items;
   (f) entertainment expenses.

(5) The expense excepted from paragraph (4)(d) is the expense of an initial journey from a place in the United Kingdom to accommodation provided by way of asylum support or (where accommodation is not so provided) to an address in the United Kingdom which has been notified to the Secretary of State as the address where the person intends to live.

(6) Paragraph (3) shall not be taken to affect the question whether any item or expense not mentioned in paragraph (4) or (5) is, or is not, an essential living need.

(7) The reference in paragraph (1) to subsection (7)(b) of section 95 of the Act includes a reference to that provision as applied by section 98(3) of the Act and, accordingly, the reference in paragraph (1) to 'that section' includes a reference to section 98.

Provision of support

Kind and levels of support for essential living needs

10.—(1) This regulation applies where the Secretary of State has decided that asylum support should be provided in respect of the essential living needs of a person.

[(2) As a general rule, asylum support in respect of the essential living needs of that person may be expected to be provided weekly in the form of [cash, equal to] the amount shown in the second column of the following Table opposite the entry in the first column which for the time being describes that person, [. . .].

[TABLE

Qualifying couple	£63.07
Lone parent aged 18 or over	£40.22
Single person aged 25 or over	£40.22
Single person aged at least 18 but under 25	£31.85
Person aged at least 16 but under 18 (except a member of a qualifying couple)	£34.60
Person aged under 16	£45.58]

(3) In paragraph (1) and the provisions of paragraph (2) preceding the Table, 'person' includes 'couple'.

(4) In this regulation—

(a) 'qualifying couple' means a married or unmarried couple at least one of whom is aged 18 or over and neither of whom is aged under 16;
(b) 'lone parent' means a parent who is not a member of a married or unmarried couple;
(c) 'single person' means a person who is not a parent or a member of a qualifying couple; and
(d) 'parent' means a parent of a relevant child, that is to say a child who is aged under 18 and for whom asylum support is provided.

(5) Where the Secretary of State has decided that accommodation should be provided for a person (or couple) by way of asylum support, and the accommodation is provided in a form which also meets other essential living needs (such as bed and breakfast, or half or full board), the amounts shown in the Table in paragraph (2) shall be treated as reduced accordingly.

(6) . . .

Note: Regulation 10(6) omitted from 8 April 2002 (SI 2002/472). Regulation 10(2) substituted from 7 April 2005 (SI 2003/755). Table substituted from 10 April 2006 (SI 2006/733). Words in square brackets in reg 10(2) substituted from 4 June 2004 (SI 2004/1313).

[Additional support for pregnant women and children under 3

10A.—(1) In addition to the [cash support which the Secretary of State may be expected to provide weekly as] described in regulation 10(2), in the case of any pregnant woman or child aged under 3 for whom the Secretary of State has decided asylum support should be provided, there shall, as a general rule, be added to the [cash support] for any week the amount shown in the second column of the following table opposite the entry in the first column which for the time being describes that person.

Pregnant woman	£3.00
Child aged under 1	£5.00
Child aged at least 1 and under 3	£3.00

(2) In this regulation, 'pregnant woman' means a woman who has provided evidence to satisfy the Secretary of State that she is pregnant.]

Note: Regulation 10A inserted from 3 March 2003 (SI 2003/241). Words in square brackets substituted from 4 June 2004 (SI 2004/1313).

Additional single payments in respect of essential living needs

11.—(1) . . .

Note: Regulation 11 revoked from from 4 June 2004 (SI 2004/1313), save to enable the Secretary of State to make a payment to a person whose qualifying period ends on or before that date.

(6) Where a person is, in the opinion of the Secretary of State, responsible without reasonable excuse for a delay in the determination of his claim for asylum, the Secretary of State may treat any qualifying period as extended by the period of delay.

Note: Words in square brackets in reg 11(1) inserted from 8 April 2002 (SI 2002/472).

Income and assets to be taken into account in providing support

12.—(1) This regulation applies where it falls to the Secretary of State to decide the level or kind of asylum support to be provided for—

(a) a person applying for asylum support, or such an applicant and any dependants of his.

(b) a supported person, or such a person and any dependants of his.

(2) In this regulation 'the principal' means the applicant for asylum support (where paragraph (1)(a) applies) or the supported person (where paragraph (1)(b) applies).

(3) The Secretary of State must take into account—

(a) any income which the principal or any dependant of his has or might reasonably be expected to have,

(b) support which is or might reasonably be expected to be available to the principal or any dependant of his, and

(c) any assets mentioned in regulation 6(5) (whether held in the United Kingdom or elsewhere) which are or might reasonably be expected to be available to the principal or any dependant of his, otherwise than by way of asylum support.

Accommodation

13.—(1) The matters mentioned in paragraph (2) are prescribed for the purposes of subsection (2)(b) of section 97 of the Act as matters to which regard may not be had when exercising the power under section 95 of the Act to provide accommodation for a person.

(2) Those matters are—

(a) his personal preference as to the nature of the accommodation to be provided; and

(b) his personal preference as to the nature and standard of fixtures and fittings; but this shall not be taken to prevent the person's individual circumstances, as they relate to his accommodation needs, being taken into account.

Services

14.—(1) The services mentioned in paragraph (2) may be provided or made available by way of asylum support to persons who are otherwise receiving such support, but may be so provided only for the purpose of maintaining good order among such persons.

(2) Those services are—

(a) education, including English language lessons,

(b) sporting or other developmental activities.

Change of circumstances

Change of circumstances

15.—(1) If a relevant change of circumstances occurs, the supported person concerned or a dependant of his must, without delay, notify the Secretary of State of that change of circumstances.

(2) A relevant change of circumstances occurs where a supported person or a dependant of his—

(a) is joined in the United Kingdom by a dependant or, as the case may be, another dependant, of the supported person;

(b) receives or gains access to any money, or other asset mentioned in regulation 6(5), that has not previously been declared to the Secretary of State;

(c) becomes employed;

(d) becomes unemployed;

(e) changes his name;

(f) gets married;

(g) starts living with a person as if married to that person;

(h) gets divorced;

(i) separates from a spouse, or from a person with whom he has been living as if married to that person;

(j) becomes pregnant;

(k) has a child;

(l) leaves school;

(m) starts to share his accommodation with another person;

(n) moves to a different address, or otherwise leaves his accommodation;

(o) goes into hospital;

(p) goes to prison or is otherwise held in custody;

(q) leaves the United Kingdom; or
(r) dies.

(3) If, on being notified of a change of circumstances, the Secretary of State considers that the change may be one—
(a) as a result of which asylum support should be provided for a person for whom it was not provided before, or
(b) as a result of which asylum support should no longer be provided for a person, or
(c) which may otherwise affect the asylum support which should be provided for a person, he may make further enquiries of the supported person or dependant who gave the notification.

(4) The Secretary of State may, in particular, require that person to provide him with such information as he considers necessary to determine whether, and if so, what, asylum support should be provided for any person.

Contributions

Contributions

16.—(1) This regulation applies where, in deciding the level of asylum support to be provided for a person who is or will be a supported person, the Secretary of State is required to take into account income, support or assets as mentioned in regulation 12(3).

(2) The Secretary of State may—
(a) set the asylum support for that person at a level which does not reflect the income, support or assets; and
(b) require from that person payments by way of contributions towards the cost of the provision for him of asylum support.

(3) A supported person must make to the Secretary of State such payments by way of contributions as the Secretary of State may require under paragraph (2).

(4) Prompt payment of such contributions may be made a condition (under section 95(9) of the Act) subject to which asylum support for that person is provided.

Recovery of sums by Secretary of State

Recovery where assets become realisable

17.—(1) This regulation applies where it appears to the Secretary of State at any time (the relevant time)—
(a) that a supported person had, at the time when he applied for asylum support, assets of any kind in the United Kingdom or elsewhere which were not capable of being realised; but

(b) that those assets have subsequently become, and remain, capable of being realised.

(2) The Secretary of State may recover from that person a sum not exceeding the recoverable sum.

(3) Subject to paragraph (5), the recoverable sum is a sum equal to whichever is the less of—

(a) the monetary value of all the asylum support provided to the person up to the relevant time; and

(b) the monetary value of the assets concerned.

(4) As well as being recoverable as mentioned in paragraph 11(2)(a) of Schedule 8 to the Act, an amount recoverable under this regulation may be recovered by deduction from asylum support.

(5) The recoverable sum shall be treated as reduced by any amount which the Secretary of State has by virtue of this regulation already recovered from the person concerned (whether by deduction or otherwise) with regard to the assets concerned.

[Recovery of asylum support

17A.—(1) The Secretary of State may require a supported person to refund asylum support if it transpires that at any time during which asylum support was being provided for him he was not destitute.

(2) If a supported person has dependants, the Secretary of State may require him to refund asylum support if it transpires that at any time during which asylum support was being provided for the supported person and his dependants they were not destitute.

(3) The refund required shall not exceed the monetary value of all the asylum support provided to the supported person or to the supported person and his dependants for the relevant period.

(4) In this regulation the relevant period is the time during which asylum support was provided for the supported person or the supported person and his dependants and during which he or they were not destitute.

(5) If not paid within a reasonable period, the refund required may be recovered from the supported person as if it were a debt due to the Secretary of State.]

Note: Regulation 17A inserted from 5 April 2005, SI 2005/11.

Overpayments: method of recovery

18. As well as being recoverable as mentioned in subsection (3) of section 114 of the Act, an amount recoverable under subsection (2) of that section may be recovered by deduction from asylum support.

Breach of conditions and suspension and discontinuation of support

Breach of conditions: decision whether to provide support

19.—(1) When deciding—

(a) whether to provide, or to continue to provide, asylum support for any person or persons, or

(b) the level or kind of support to be provided for any person or persons, the Secretary of State may take into account [the extent to which a] relevant condition has been complied with.

[(2) A relevant condition is one which makes the provision of asylum support subject to actual residence by the supported person or a dependant of his for whom support is being provided in a specific place or location.]

Note: Words in square brackets in paras (1) and (2) substituted from 5 February 2005, SI 2005/11.

[Suspension or discontinuation of support

20.—(1) Asylum support for a supported person and any dependant of his or for one or more dependants of a supported person may be suspended or discontinued if—

(a) support is being provided for the supported person or a dependant of his in collective accommodation and the Secretary of State has reasonable grounds to believe that the supported person or his dependant has committed a serious breach of the rules of that accommodation;

(b) the Secretary of State has reasonable grounds to believe that the supported person or a dependant of his for whom support is being provided has committed an act of seriously violent behaviour whether or not that act occurs in accommodation provided by way of asylum support or at the authorised address or elsewhere;

(c) the supported person or a dependant of his has committed an offence under Part VI of the Act;

(d) the Secretary of State has reasonable grounds to believe that the supported person or any dependant of his for whom support is being provided has abandoned the authorised address without first informing the Secretary of State or, if requested, without permission;

(e) the supported person has not complied within a reasonable period, which shall be no less than five working days beginning with the day on which the request was received by him, with requests for information made by the Secretary of State and which relate to the supported person's or his dependant's eligibility for or receipt of asylum support including requests made under regulation 15;

(f) the supported person fails, without reasonable excuse, to attend an interview requested by the Secretary of State relating to the supported person's or his dependant's eligibility for or receipt of asylum support;

(g) the supported person or, if he is an asylum seeker, his dependant, has not complied within a reasonable period, which shall be no less than ten working days beginning with the day on which the request was received by him, with a request for information made by the Secretary of State relating to his claim for asylum;

(h) the Secretary of State has reasonable grounds to believe that the supported person or a dependant of his for whom support is being provided has concealed financial resources and that the supported person or a dependant of his or both have therefore unduly benefited from the receipt of asylum support;

(i) the supported person or a dependant of his for whom support is being provided has not complied with a reporting requirement;

(j) the Secretary of State has reasonable grounds to believe that the supported person or a dependant of his for whom support is being provided has made a claim for asylum ('the first claim') and before the first claim has been determined makes or seeks to make a further claim for asylum not being part of the first claim in the same or a different name; or

(k) the supported person or a dependant of his for whom support is being provided has failed without reasonable excuse to comply with a relevant condition.

(2) If a supported person is asked to attend an interview of the type referred to in paragraph (1)(f) he shall be given no less than five working days notice of it.

(3) Any decision to discontinue support in the circumstances referred to in paragraph (1) above shall be taken individually, objectively and impartially and reasons shall be given. Decisions will be based on the particular situation of the person concerned and particular regard shall be had to whether he is a vulnerable person as described by Article 17 of Council Directive 2003/9/EC of 27th January 2003 laying down minimum standards for the reception of asylum seekers.

(4) No person's asylum support shall be discontinued before a decision is made under paragraph (1).

(5) Where asylum support for a supported person or his dependant is suspended or discontinued under paragraph (1)(d) or (i) and the supported person or his dependant are traced or voluntarily report to the police, the Secretary of State or an immigration officer, a duly motivated decision based on the reasons for the disappearance shall be taken as to the reinstatement of some or all of the supported person's or his dependant's or both of their asylum support.

(6) For the purposes of this regulation—

(a) the authorised address is—
   (i) the accommodation provided for the supported person and his dependants (if any) by way of asylum support; or
   (ii) if no accommodation is so provided, the address notified by the supported person to the Secretary of State in his application for asylum support or, where a change of address has been notified to the Secretary of State under regulation 15 or under the Immigration Rules or both, the address for the time being so notified;

(b) 'collective accommodation' means accommodation which a supported person or any dependant of his for whom support is being provided shares with any other supported person and includes accommodation in which only facilities are shared;

(c) 'relevant condition' has the same meaning as in regulation 19(2);

(d) 'reporting requirement' is a condition or restriction which requires a person to report to the police, an immigration officer or the Secretary of State and is imposed under—
   (i) paragraph 21 of Schedule 2 to the Immigration Act 1971 (temporary admission or release from detention);
   (ii) paragraph 22 of that Schedule; or
   (iii) paragraph 2 or 5 of Schedule 3 to that Act (pending deportation).

(e) 'working day' has the same meaning as in regulation 3(7) save that the reference to the applicant shall be a reference to the supported person or his dependant.]

Note: Regulation 20 substituted from 5 February 2005, SI 2005/11.

[**Temporary Support**

20A. Regulations 19 and 20 shall apply to a person or his dependant who is provided with temporary support under section 98 of the Act in the same way as they apply to a person and his dependant who is in receipt of asylum support and any reference to asylum support in regulations 19 and 20 shall include a reference to temporary support under section 98.]

Note: Regulation 20A inserted from 5 April 2005, SI 2005/11.

Effect of previous suspension or discontinuation

21.—(1) [Subject to regulation 20(5) where—]

(a) an application for asylum support is made,

(b) the applicant or any other person to whom the application relates has previously had his asylum support suspended or discontinued under regulation 20, and

(c) there has been no material change of circumstances since the suspension or discontinuation, the application need not be entertained unless the Secretary of State considers that there are exceptional circumstances which justify its being entertained.

(2) A material change of circumstances is one which, if the applicant were a supported person, would have to be notified to the Secretary of State under regulation 15.

(3) This regulation is without prejudice to the power of the Secretary of State to refuse the application even if he has entertained it.

Note: Words in square brackets in para (1) substituted from 5 February 2005, SI 2005/11.

Notice to quit

Notice to quit

22.—(1) If—

(a) as a result of asylum support, a person has a tenancy or licence to occupy accommodation,

(b) one or more of the conditions mentioned in paragraph (2) is satisfied, and

(c) he is given notice to quit in accordance with paragraph (3) or (4),

his tenancy or licence is to be treated as ending with the period specified in that notice, regardless of when it could otherwise be brought to an end.

(2) The conditions are that—

(a) the asylum support is suspended or discontinued as a result of any provision of regulation 20;

(b) the relevant claim for asylum has been determined;

(c) the supported person has ceased to be destitute; or

(d) he is to be moved to other accommodation.

(3) A notice to quit is in accordance with this paragraph if it is in writing and—

(a) in a case where sub-paragraph (a), (c) or (d) of paragraph (2) applies, specifies as the notice period a period of not less than seven days; or

(b) in a case where the Secretary of State has notified his decision on the relevant claim for asylum to the claimant, specifies as the notice period a period at least as long as whichever is the greater of—

(i) seven days; or

(ii) the period beginning with the date of service of the notice to quit and ending with the date of determination of the relevant claim for asylum (found in accordance with section 94(3) of the Act).

(4) A notice to quit is in accordance with this paragraph if—

(a) it is in writing;

(b) it specifies as the notice period a period of less than seven days; and

(c) the circumstances of the case are such that that notice period is justified.

Meaning of 'destitute' for certain other purposes

Meaning of 'destitute' for certain other purposes

23.—(1) In this regulation 'the relevant enactments' means—
(a) section 21(1A) of the National Assistance Act 1948;
(b) section 45(4A) of the Health Services and Public Health Act 1968;
(c) paragraph 2(2A) of Schedule 8 to the National Health Service Act 1977;
(d) sections 12(2A), 13A(4) and 13B(3) of the Social Work (Scotland) Act 1968;
(e) sections 7(3) and 8(4) of the Mental Health (Scotland) Act 1984; and
(f) Articles 7(3) and 15(6) of the Health and Personal Social Services (Northern Ireland) Order 1972.

(2) The following provisions of this regulation apply where it falls to an authority, or the Department, to determine for the purposes of any of the relevant enactments whether a person is destitute.

(3) Paragraphs (3) to (6) of regulation 6 apply as they apply in the case mentioned in paragraph (1) of that regulation, but as if references to the principal were references to the person whose destitution or otherwise is being determined and references to the Secretary of State were references to the authority or (as the case may be) Department.

(4) The matters mentioned in paragraph (3) of regulation 8 (read with paragraphs (4) to (6) of that regulation) are prescribed for the purposes of subsection (5)(a) of section 95 of the Act, as applied for the purposes of any of the relevant enactments, as matters to which regard must be had in determining for the purposes of any of the relevant enactments whether a person's accommodation is adequate.

(5) The matter mentioned in paragraph (2) of regulation 9 is prescribed for the purposes of subsection (7)(b) of section 95 of the Act, as applied for the purposes of any of the relevant enactments, as a matter to which regard may not be had in determining for the purposes of any of the relevant enactments whether a person's essential living needs (other than accommodation) are met.

(6) Paragraphs (3) to (6) of regulation 9 shall apply as if the reference in paragraph (3) to Part VI of the Act included a reference to the relevant enactments.

(7) The references in regulations 8(5) and 9(2) to the Secretary of State shall be construed, for the purposes of this regulation, as references to the authority or (as the case may be) Department.

SCHEDULE

Regulation 3(3)

. . .

The Immigration (Leave to Enter and Remain) Order 2000
(SI 2000, No. 1161)

PART I
GENERAL

1. Citation, commencement and interpretation

(1) This Order may be cited as the Immigration (Leave to Enter and Remain) Order 2000.

(2) Articles 1 to 12, 14 and 15(1) of this Order shall come into force on 28th April 2000 or, if later, on the day after the day on which it is made and articles 13 and 15(2) shall come into force on 30th July 2000.

(3) In this Order—

'the Act' means the Immigration Act 1971;

['ADS Agreement with China' means the Memorandum of Understanding on visa and related issues concerning tourist groups from the People's Republic of China to the United Kingdom as an approved destination, signed on 21st January 2005;]

'control port' means a port in which a control area is designated under paragraph 26(3) of Schedule 2 to the Act;

['convention travel document' means a travel document issued pursuant to Article 28 of the Refugee Convention, except where that travel document was issued by the United Kingdom Government;]

'the Immigration Acts' means:

(a) the Act;
(b) the Immigration Act 1988;
(c) the Asylum and Immigration Appeals Act 1993;
(d) the Asylum and Immigration Act 1996; and
(e) the Immigration and Asylum Act 1999.

['Refugee Convention' means the Convention relating to the Status of Refugees done at Geneva on 28th July 1951 and its Protocol;]

'responsible third party' means a person appearing to an immigration officer to be:

(a) in charge of a group of people arriving in the United Kingdom together or intending to arrive in the United Kingdom together;
(b) a tour operator;
(c) the owner or agent of a ship, aircraft, train, hydrofoil or hovercraft;
(d) the person responsible for the management of a control port or his agent; or
(e) an official at a British Diplomatic Mission or at a British Consular Post or at the office of any person outside the United Kingdom and Islands who has been authorised by the Secretary of State to accept applications for entry clearance;

'tour operator' means a person who, otherwise than occasionally, organises and provides holidays to the public or a section of it; and

'visit visa' means an entry clearance granted for the purpose of entry to the United Kingdom as a visitor under the immigration rules.

Note: Words in first square brackets inserted from 1 April 2005 (SI 2005/1159). Other words in square brackets inserted from 27 February 2004 (SI 2004/475).

Part II

Entry Clearance as Leave to Enter

2. Entry clearance as Leave to Enter

Subject to article 6(3), an entry clearance which complies with the requirements of article 3 shall have effect as leave to enter the United Kingdom to the extent specified in article 4, but subject to the conditions referred to in article 5.

3. Requirements

[(1) Subject to paragraph (4), an entry clearance shall only have effect as leave to enter if it complies with the requirements of this article.]

(2) The entry clearance must specify the purpose for which the holder wishes to enter the United Kingdom.

(3) The entry clearance must be endorsed with:

(a) the conditions to which it is subject; or
(b) a statement that it is to have effect as indefinite leave to enter the United Kingdom.

[(4) Subject to paragraph (5), an entry clearance shall not have effect as leave to enter if it is endorsed on a convention travel document.

(5) An entry clearance endorsed on a convention travel document before 27th February 2004 shall have effect as leave to enter.]

Note: Article 3(1) substituted and Art 3(4) and (5) inserted from 27 February 2004 (SI 2004/475).

4. Extent to which entry clearance is to be leave to enter

(1) A visit visa, [(other than a visit visa granted pursuant to the ADS Agreement with China) unless endorsed with a statement that it is to have effect as a single-entry visa] during its period of validity, shall have effect as leave to enter the United Kingdom on an unlimited number of occasions, in accordance with paragraph (2).

(2) On each occasion the holder arrives in the United Kingdom, he shall be treated for the purposes of the Immigration Acts as having been granted, before arrival, leave to enter the United Kingdom for a limited period beginning on the date of arrival, being:

(a) six months if six months or more remain of the visa's period of validity; or

(b) the visa's remaining period of validity, if less than six months.

[(2A) A visit visa granted pursuant to the ADS Agreement with China endorsed with a statement that it is to have effect as a dual-entry visa, shall have effect as leave to enter the United Kingdom on two occasions during its period of validity, in accordance with paragraph (2B).

(2B) On arrival in the United Kingdom on each occasion, the holder shall be treated for the purposes of the Immigration Acts as having been granted, before arrival, leave to enter the United Kingdom for a limited period, being the period beginning on the date on which the holder arrives in the United Kingdom and ending on the date of expiry of the entry clearance.]

(3) In the case of [any form of entry clearance to which this paragraph applies], it shall have effect as leave to enter the United Kingdom on one occasion during its period of validity; and, on arrival in the United Kingdom, the holder shall be treated for the purposes of the Immigration Acts as having been granted, before arrival, leave to enter the United Kingdom:

(a) in the case of an entry clearance which is endorsed with a statement that it is to have effect as indefinite leave to enter the United Kingdom, for an indefinite period; or

(b) in the case of an entry clearance which is endorsed with conditions, for a limited period, being the period beginning on the date on which the holder arrives in the United Kingdom and ending on the date of expiry of the entry clearance.

[(3A) Paragraph (3) applies to—

(a) a visit visa (other than a visit visa granted pursuant to the ADS Agreement with China) endorsed with a statement that it is to have effect as a single entry visa;

(b) a visit visa granted pursuant to the ADS Agreement with China unless endorsed with a statement to the effect that it is to have effect as a dual entry visa; and
(c) any other form of entry clearance.]

(4) In this article 'period of validity' means the period beginning on the day on which the entry clearance becomes effective and ending on the day on which it expires.

Note: Words in square brackets inserted from 1 April 2005 (SI 2005/1159).

5. Conditions

An entry clearance shall have effect as leave to enter subject to any conditions, being conditions of a kind that may be imposed on leave to enter given under section 3 of the Act, to which the entry clearance is subject and which are endorsed on it.

6. Incidental, supplementary and consequential provisions

(1) Where an immigration officer exercises his power to cancel leave to enter under paragraph 2A(8) of Schedule 2 to the Act or article 13(7) below in respect of an entry clearance which has effect as leave to enter, the entry clearance shall cease to have effect.

(2) If the holder of an entry clearance—
(a) arrives in the United Kingdom before the day on which it becomes effective; or
(b) seeks to enter the United Kingdom for a purpose other than the purpose specified in the entry clearance, an immigration officer may cancel the entry clearance.

(3) If the holder of an entry clearance which does not, at the time, have effect as leave to enter the United Kingdom seeks leave to enter the United Kingdom at any time before his departure for, or in the course of his journey to, the United Kingdom and is refused leave to enter under article 7, the entry clearance shall not have effect as leave to enter.

Part III
Form and Manner of Giving and Refusing Leave To Enter

7. Grant and refusal of leave to enter before arrival in the United Kingdom

(1) An immigration officer, whether or not in the United Kingdom, may give or refuse a person leave to enter the United Kingdom at any time before his departure for, or in the course of his journey to, the United Kingdom.

(2) In order to determine whether or not to give leave to enter under this article (and, if so, for what period and subject to what conditions), an immigration officer may seek such information, and the production of such documents or copy documents, as an immigration officer would be entitled to obtain in an examination under paragraph 2 or 2A of Schedule 2 to the Act.

(3) An immigration officer may also require the person seeking leave to supply an up to date medical report.

(4) Failure by a person seeking leave to supply any information, documents, copy documents or medical report requested by an immigration officer under this article shall be a ground, in itself, for refusal of leave.

8. Grant or refusal of leave otherwise than by notice in writing

(1) A notice giving or refusing leave to enter may, instead of being given in writing as required by section 4(1) of the Act, be given as follows.

(2) The notice may be given by facsimile or electronic mail.

(3) In the case of a notice giving or refusing leave to enter the United Kingdom as a visitor, it may be given orally, including by means of a telecommunications system.

(4) In paragraph (3), 'leave to enter the United Kingdom as a visitor' means leave to enter as a visitor under the immigration rules for a period not exceeding six months, subject to conditions prohibiting employment and recourse to public funds (within the meaning of the immigration rules).

9. Grant or refusal of leave by notice to a responsible third party

(1) Leave to enter may be given or refused to a person by means of a notice given (in such form and manner as permitted by the Act or this Order for a notice giving or refusing leave to enter) to a responsible third party acting on his behalf.

(2) A notice under paragraph (1) may refer to a person to whom leave is being granted or refused either by name or by reference to a description or category of persons which includes him.

10. Notice of refusal of leave

(1) Where a notice refusing leave to enter to a person is given under article 8(3) or 9, an immigration officer shall as soon as practicable give to him a notice in writing stating that he has been refused leave to enter the United Kingdom and stating the reasons for the refusal.

(2) Where an immigration officer serves a notice under the Immigration (Appeals)

Notices Regulations 1984 or under regulations made under paragraph 1 of Schedule 4 to the Immigration and Asylum Act 1999 in respect of the refusal, he shall not be required to serve a notice under paragraph (1).

(3) Any notice required by paragraph (1) to be given to any person may be delivered, or sent by post to—

(a) that person's last known or usual place of abode; or

(b) any address provided by him for receipt of the notice.

11. Burden of proof

Where any question arises under the Immigration Acts as to whether a person has leave to enter the United Kingdom and he alleges that he has such leave by virtue of a notice given under article 8(3) or 9, the onus shall lie upon him to show the manner and date of his entry into the United Kingdom.

12.—(1) This article applies where—

(a) an immigration officer has commenced examination of a person ('the applicant') under paragraph 2(1)(c) of Schedule 2 to the Act (examination to determine whether or not leave to enter should be given);

(b) that examination has been adjourned, or the applicant has been required (under paragraph 2(3) of Schedule 2 to the Act) to submit to a further examination, whilst further inquiries are made (including, where the applicant has made an asylum claim, as to the Secretary of State's decision on that claim); and

(c) upon the completion of those inquiries, an immigration officer considers he is in a position to decide whether or not to give or refuse leave to enter without interviewing the applicant further.

(2) Where this article applies, any notice giving or refusing leave to enter which is on any date thereafter sent by post to the applicant (or is communicated to him in such form or manner as is permitted by this Order) shall be regarded, for the purposes of the Act, as having been given within the period of 24 hours specified in paragraph 6(1) of Schedule 2 to the Act (period within which notice giving or refusing leave to enter must be given after completion of examination).

Part IV

Leave Which Does Not Lapse on Travel Outside Common Travel Area

13.—(1) In this article 'leave' means—

(a) leave to enter the United Kingdom (including leave to enter conferred by means of an entry clearance under article 2); and

(b) leave to remain in the United Kingdom.

(2) Subject to paragraph (3), where a person has leave which is in force and which was:

(a) conferred by means of an entry clearance (other than a visit visa) under article 2; or

(b) given by an immigration officer or the Secretary of State for a period exceeding six months,

such leave shall not lapse on his going to a country or territory outside the common travel area.

(3) Paragraph (2) shall not apply:

(a) where a limited leave has been varied by the Secretary of State; and

(b) following the variation the period of leave remaining is six months or less.

(4) Leave which does not lapse under paragraph (2) shall remain in force either indefinitely (if it is unlimited) or until the date on which it would otherwise have expired (if limited), but—

(a) where the holder has stayed outside the United Kingdom for a continuous period of more than two years, the leave (where the leave is unlimited) or any leave then remaining (where the leave is limited) shall thereupon lapse; and

(b) any conditions to which the leave is subject shall be suspended for such time as the holder is outside the United Kingdom.

(5) For the purposes of paragraphs 2 and 2A of Schedule 2 to the Act (examination by immigration officers, and medical examination), leave to remain which remains in force under this article shall be treated, upon the holder's arrival in the United Kingdom, as leave to enter which has been granted to the holder before his arrival.

(6) Without prejudice to the provisions of section 4(1) of the Act, where the holder of leave which remains in force under this article is outside the United Kingdom, the Secretary of State may vary that leave (including any conditions to which it is subject) in such form and manner as permitted by the Act or this Order for the giving of leave to enter.

(7) Where a person is outside the United Kingdom and has leave which is in force by virtue of this article, that leave may be cancelled:

(a) in the case of leave to enter, by an immigration officer; or

(b) in the case of leave to remain, by the Secretary of State.

(8) In order to determine whether or not to vary (and, if so, in what manner) or cancel leave which remains in force under this article and which is held by a person who is outside the United Kingdom, an immigration officer or, as the case may be, the Secretary of State may seek such information, and the production of such documents or copy documents, as an immigration officer would be entitled to obtain in an examination under paragraph 2 or 2A of Schedule 2 to

the Act and may also require the holder of the leave to supply an up to date medical report.

(9) Failure to supply any information, documents, copy documents or medical report requested by an immigration officer or, as the case may be, the Secretary of State under this article shall be a ground, in itself, for cancellation of leave.

(10) Section 3(4) of the Act (lapsing of leave upon travelling outside the common travel area) shall have effect subject to this article.

Part V

Consequential and Transitional Provisions

14. Section 9(2) of the Act (further provisions as to common travel area: conditions applicable to certain arrivals on a local journey) shall have effect as if, after the words 'British Citizens', there were inserted 'and do not hold leave to enter or remain granted to them before their arrival'.

15.—(1) Article 12 shall apply where an applicant's examination has begin before the date that article comes into force, as well as where it begins on or after that date.

(2) Article 13 shall apply with respect to leave to enter or remain in the United Kingdom which is in force on the date that article comes into force, as well as to such leave given after that date.

The Immigration (Removal Directions) Regulations 2000 (SI 2000, No. 2243)

1. Citation and commencement

These Regulations may be cited as the Immigration (Removal Directions) Regulations 2000 and shall come into force on 2nd October 2000.

2. Interpretation

(1) In these Regulations—

'the Act' means the Immigration and Asylum Act 1999;

'aircraft' includes hovercraft;

'captain' means master (of a ship) or commander (of an aircraft);

'international service' has the meaning given by section 13(6) of the Channel Tunnel Act 1987;

'ship' includes every description of vessel used in navigation; and

'the tunnel system' has the meaning given by section 1(7) of the Channel Tunnel Act 1987.

(2) In these Regulations, a reference to a section number is a reference to a section of the Act.

3. Persons to whom directions may be given

For the purposes of section 10(6)(a) (classes of person to whom directions may be given), the following classes of person are prescribed—

(a) owners of ships;
(b) owners of aircraft;
(c) agents of ships;
(d) agents of aircraft;
(e) captains of ships about to leave the United Kingdom;
(f) captains of aircraft about to leave the United Kingdom; and
(g) persons operating an international service.

4. Requirements that may be imposed by directions

(1) For the purposes of section 10(6)(b) (requirements that may be imposed by directions), the following kinds of requirements are prescribed—

(a) in the case where directions are given to a captain of a ship or aircraft about to leave the United Kingdom, a requirement to remove the relevant person from the United Kingdom in that ship or aircraft;
(b) in the case where directions are given to a person operating an international service, a requirement to make arrangements for the removal of the relevant person through the tunnel system;
(c) in the case where directions are given to any other person who falls within a class prescribed in regulation 3, a requirements to make arrangements for the removal of the relevant person in a ship or aircraft specified or indicated in the directions; and
(d) in all cases, a requirement to remove the relevant person in accordance with arrangements to be made by an immigration officer.

(2) Paragraph (1) only applies if the directions specify that the relevant person is to be removed to a country or territory being—

(i) a country of which he is a national or citizen; or
(ii) a country or territory to which there is reason to believe that he will be admitted.

(3) Paragraph (1)(b) only applies if the relevant person arrived in the United Kingdom through the tunnel system.

(4) 'Relevant person' means a person who may be removed from the United Kingdom in accordance with section 10(1).

The Asylum (Designated Safe Third Countries) Order 2000

SI 2000, No. 2245

1. This Order may be cited as the Asylum (Designated Safe Third Countries) Order 2000 and shall come into force on 2nd October 2000.
2. The Asylum (Designated Countries of Destination and Designated Safe Third Countries) Order 1996 is hereby revoked.
3. The following countries are designated for the purposes of section 12(1)(b) of the Immigration and Asylum Act 1999 (designation of countries other than EU Member States for the purposes of appeal rights):

   Canada
   Norway
   Switzerland
   United States of America.

The Immigration (Leave to Enter) Order 2001

(SI 2001, No. 2590)

1.—(1) This Order may be cited as the Immigration (Leave to Enter) Order 2001 and shall come into force on the day after the day on which it is made.

(2) In this Order—

(a) 'the 1971 Act' means the Immigration Act 1971; and

(b) 'claim for asylum' and 'the Human Rights Convention' have the meanings assigned by section 167 of the Immigration and Asylum Act 1999.

Note: Commencement 18 July 2001.

2.—(1) Where this article applies to a person, the Secretary of State may give or refuse him leave to enter the United Kingdom.

(2) This article applies to a person who seeks leave to enter the United Kingdom and who—

(a) has made a claim for asylum; or

(b) has made a claim that it would be contrary to the United Kingdom's obligations under the Human Rights Convention for him to be removed from, or required to leave, the United Kingdom.

(3) This article also applies to a person who seeks leave to enter the United Kingdom for a purpose not covered by the immigration rules or otherwise on the grounds that those rules should be departed from in his case.

(4) In deciding whether to give or refuse leave under this article the Secretary of State may take into account any additional grounds which a person has for seeking leave to enter the United Kingdom.

(5) The power to give or refuse leave to enter the United Kingdom under this article shall be exercised by notice in writing to the person affected or in such manner as is permitted by the Immigration (Leave to Enter and Remain) Order 2000.

3. In relation to the giving or refusing of leave to enter by the Secretary of State under article 2, paragraphs 2 (examination by immigration officers, and medical examination), 4 (information and documents), 7(1), (3) and (4) (power to require medical examination after entry), 8 (removal of persons refused leave to enter), 9 (removal of illegal entrants) and 21 (temporary admission of persons liable to detention) of Schedule 2 to the 1971 Act shall be read as if references to an immigration officer included references to the Secretary of State.

4.—(1) This article applies where—

(a) an immigration officer has commenced examination of a person ('the applicant') under paragraph 2(1)(c) of Schedule 2 to the 1971 Act (examination to determine whether or not leave to enter should be given);

(b) that examination has been adjourned, or the applicant has been required (under paragraph 2(3) of Schedule 2 to the Immigration Act 1971) to submit to a further examination;

(c) the Secretary of State subsequently examines the applicant or conducts a further examination in relation to him; and

(d) the Secretary of State thereafter gives or refuses the applicant leave to enter.

(2) Where this article applies, the notice giving or refusing leave to enter shall be regarded for the purposes of the 1971 Act as having been given within the period of 24 hours specified in paragraph 6(1) of Schedule 2 to that Act (period within which notice giving or refusing leave to enter must be given after completion of examination by an immigration officer).

The Immigration (Entry Otherwise than by Sea or Air) Order 2002

(SI 2002, No. 1832)

1. This Order may be cited as the Immigration (Entry Otherwise than by Sea or Air) Order 2002 and shall come into force on the day after the day on which it is made.

Note: Commencement 17 July 2002.

2.—(1) This article applies where—

(a) a person who requires leave to enter the United Kingdom by virtue of section 9(4) of the Immigration Act 1971 or by virtue of article 3 of the Immigration (Control of Entry through Republic of Ireland) Order 1972; or

(b) a person in respect of whom a deportation order is in force, has entered or is seeking to enter the United Kingdom from the Republic of Ireland.

(2) Where this article applies, paragraphs 8, 9 and 11 of Schedule 2 to the Immigration Act 1971 shall have effect in relation to persons entering or seeking to enter the United Kingdom on arrival otherwise than by ship or aircraft as they have effect in the case of a person arriving by ship or aircraft, with the modifications set out in the Schedule to this Order.

3. Article 2 shall apply where an illegal entrant entered the United Kingdom before the date when this Order comes into force, as well as where he entered the United Kingdom on or after that date.

(3) Article 2 shall not apply where a person has arrived in, but not entered, the United Kingdom before the date on which this Order comes into force.

Article 2(2)

Schedule

Modifications to Schedule 2 of the Immigration Act 1971

1. In this Schedule 'Schedule 2' means Schedule 2 to the Immigration Act 1971.

2. For paragraph 8 of Schedule 2, substitute:

'8.—(1) Where a person arriving in the United Kingdom is refused leave to enter, an immigration officer or the Secretary of State may give the owners or agents of any train, vehicle, ship or aircraft directions requiring them to make arrangements for that person's removal from the United Kingdom in any train, vehicle, ship or aircraft specified or indicated in the direction to a country or territory so specified being—

(a) a country of which he is a national or citizen; or

(b) a country or territory in which he has obtained a passport or other document of identify; or
(c) a country or territory in which he embarked for the United Kingdom; or
(d) a country or territory to which there is reason to believe that he will be admitted.

(2) The costs of complying with any directions given under this paragraph shall be defrayed by the Secretary of State.'.

3. In paragraph 9(1) of Schedule 2:
(a) after 'immigration officer', insert 'or the Secretary of State'; and
(b) after 'authorised by paragraph 8(1)', insert 'and the costs of complying with any directions given under this paragraph shall be defrayed by the Secretary of State'.

4. In paragraph 11 of Schedule 2, after 'on board any', insert 'train, vehicle,'.

The Immigration Appeals (Family Visitor) Regulations 2003
(SI 2003, No. 518)

1. These Regulations may be cited as the Immigration Appeals (Family Visitor) Regulations 2003 and shall come into force on 1st April 2003.

2.—(1) For the purposes of section 90(1) of the Nationality, Immigration and Asylum Act 2002, a 'member of the applicant's family' is any of the following persons—
(a) the applicant's spouse, father, mother, son, daughter, grandfather, grandmother, grandson, granddaughter, brother, sister, uncle, aunt, nephew, niece or first cousin;
(b) the father, mother, brother or sister of the applicant's spouse;
(c) the spouse of the applicant's son or daughter;
(d) the applicant's stepfather, stepmother, stepson, stepdaughter, stepbrother or stepsister; or
(e) a person with whom the applicant has lived as a member of an unmarried couple for at least two of the three years before the day on which his application for entry clearance was made.

(2) In these Regulations, 'first cousin' means, in relation to a person, the son or daughter of his uncle or aunt.

The British Nationality (General) Regulations 2003
(SI 2003, No. 548)

Arrangement of Regulations

PART I

GENERAL

Citation and commencement

1. These Regulations may be cited as the British Nationality (General) Regulations 2003 and shall come into force on 1st April 2003.

Interpretation

2.—(1) In these Regulations, the following expressions have the meanings hereby assigned to them, that is to say—

'the Act' means the British Nationality Act 1981;

'applicant' in relation to an application made on behalf of a person not of full age or capacity means that person;

'High Commissioner' means, in relation to a country mentioned in Schedule 3 to the Act, the High Commissioner for Her Majesty's Government in the United Kingdom appointed to that country, and includes the acting High Commissioner.

(2) In the application of the provisions of regulation 6(2) [6(3), 6A(1), (3) and (5), paragraph 3 of Schedule 3] or Schedule 4 where a function of the Secretary of State under the Act is exercised by the Lieutenant-Governor of any of the Islands by virtue of arrangements made under section 43(1) of the Act, any reference in those provisions to the Secretary of State shall be construed as a reference to the Lieutenant-Governor.

Note: Words in square brackets inserted from 1 January 2004 (SI 2003/3158).

PART II

REGISTRATION AND NATURALISATION

Applications

3. Any application for registration as a British citizen, British Overseas citizen or British subject or for a certificate of naturalisation as a British citizen shall—

(a) be made to the appropriate authority specified in regulation 4; and

(b) satisfy the requirements of Part I and, if made on behalf of a person not of full age or capacity, Part II of Schedule 1 and such further requirements, if any, as are specified in relation thereto in Schedule 2.

Authority to whom application is to be made

4.—(1) Except as provided by paragraphs (2) and (3), the authority to whom an application is to be made is as follows:

(a) if the application is in Great Britain or Northern Ireland, to the Secretary of State at the Home Office;

(b) if the applicant is in any of the Islands, to the Lieutenant-Governor;

(c) if the applicant is in a British overseas territory, to the Governor;

(d) if the applicant is in a country mentioned in Schedule 3 to the Act, to the High Commissioner or, if there is no High Commissioner, to the Secretary of State at the Home Office;

(e) if the applicant is elsewhere, to any consular officer, any established officer in the Diplomatic Service of Her Majesty's Government in the United Kingdom or any person authorised by the Secretary of State in that behalf.

(2) The authority to whom an application under section 4(5) of the Act (acquisition by registration: British overseas territories citizens, etc), on grounds of Crown Service under the government of a British overseas territory or service as a member of a body established by law in a British overseas territory, is to be made is in all cases the Governor of that territory.

(3) The authority to whom an application under section 5 of the Act (acquisition by registration: nationals for purposes of the Community Treaties) is to be made is in all cases the Governor of Gibraltar.

Persons not of full age or capacity

5. An application may be made on behalf of someone not of full age or capacity by his father or mother or any person who has assumed responsibility for his welfare.

[Knowledge of language and life in the United Kingdom

5A.—(1) A person has sufficient knowledge of the English language and sufficient knowledge about life in the United Kingdom for the purpose of an application for naturalisation as a British citizen under section 6 of the Act if—

(a) he has attended a course which used teaching materials derived from the document entitled 'Citizenship Materials for ESOL Learners' (ISBN 1–84478–5424) and he has thereby attained a relevant accredited qualification; or

(b) he has passed the test known as the 'Life in the UK Test' administered by an educational institution or other person approved for this purpose by the Secretary of State; or

(c) in the case of a person who is ordinarily resident outside the United

Kingdom, a person designated by the Secretary of State certifies in writing that he has sufficient knowledge of the English language and sufficient knowledge about life in the United Kingdom for this purpose.

(2) In this regulation, a 'relevant accredited qualification' is—

(a) an ESOL 'Skills for Life' qualification in speaking and listening at Entry Level approved by the Qualifications and Curriculum Authority; or

(b) two ESOL Units at Access Level under the Scottish Credit and Qualifications Framework approved by the Scottish Qualifications Authority.]

Note: Paragraph 5A substituted from 1 November 2005 (SI 2005/2785).

[Citizenship oaths and pledges

6.—(1) Where a citizenship oath or pledge is required by section 42 of the Act to be made by an applicant for registration or for a certificate of naturalisation, it shall be administered in accordance with the requirements of Schedule 3.

(2) If, on an application for a registration or for a certificate of naturalisation by an applicant who is required to make a citizenship oath or pledge, the Secretary of State decides that the registration should be effected or the certificate should be granted, he shall cause notice in writing of the decision to be given to the applicant.

(3) The requirement to make a citizenship oath or pledge shall be satisfied within three months of the giving of the notice referred to in paragraph (2) or such longer time as the Secretary of State may allow.

(4) Any notice required by paragraph (2) to be given to an applicant may be given—

(a) in any case where the applicant's whereabouts are known, by causing the notice to be delivered to him personally or by sending it to him by post;

(b) in a case where the applicant's whereabouts are not known, by sending it by post in a letter addressed to him at his last known address.

(5) In this regulation, references to the requirement to make a citizenship oath or pledge include the requirement to make a citizenship oath and pledge at a citizenship ceremony.

Arrangements for, and conduct of, citizenship ceremonies

6A.—(1) The Secretary of State may designate or authorise a person to exercise a function (which may include a discretion) in connection with a citizenship ceremony or a citizenship oath or pledge, and the reference in paragraph (3)(b) to 'designated person' shall be construed accordingly.

(2) Each local authority (within the meaning of section 41(3B) of the Act) shall—

(a) make available, or make arrangements for, premises at which citizenship ceremonies may be conducted; and

(b) arrange for citizenship ceremonies to be conducted with sufficient frequency so as to enable applicants in their area who are required to make a citizenship oath and pledge at a citizenship ceremony to meet the time limit laid down by regulation 6(3).

(3) Where an applicant is required by section 42 of the Act to make a citizenship oath and pledge at a citizenship ceremony, the Secretary of State shall—

(a) issue to the applicant an invitation in writing to attend a citizenship ceremony (a 'ceremony invitation');

(b) notify the applicant of the local authority or designated person which the applicant should contact to arrange attendance at a citizenship ceremony (the 'relevant authority'); and

(c) notify the relevant authority of his decision in relation to the applicant.

(4) An applicant who has arranged attendance at a citizenship ceremony shall bring with him to the ceremony his ceremony invitation; and if the applicant fails to do so, the person conducting the ceremony may refuse admittance to, or participation in, the ceremony if he is not reasonably satisfied as to the identity of the applicant.

(5) Where an applicant makes the relevant citizenship oath and pledge at a citizenship ceremony as required by section 42 of the Act—

(a) the person conducting the ceremony shall grant to the applicant a certificate of registration or naturalisation, duly dated with the date of the ceremony; and

(b) the relevant authority shall notify the Secretary of State in writing within 14 days of the date of the ceremony that the applicant has made the relevant citizenship oath and pledge at a citizenship ceremony and the date on which the ceremony took place.

(6) In this regulation, 'the person conducting the ceremony' is the person who administers the citizenship oath and pledge at the citizenship ceremony in accordance with paragraph 3 of Schedule 3.]

Note: Regulation 6 substituted from 1 January 2004 (SI 2003/3158).

Certificates of naturalisation

7. A certificate of naturalisation shall be in the form set out in Schedule 4.

Part III

Renunciation and Deprivation

Declarations of renunciation

8. Any declaration of renunciation of British citizenship, British Overseas citizenship or the status of a British subject shall—

(a) be made to the appropriate authority specified in regulation 9; and
(b) satisfy the requirements of Schedule 5.

Authority to whom declaration of renunciation is to be made

9. The authority to whom a declaration of renunciation is to be made is as follows:
(a) if the declarant is in Great Britain or Northern Ireland, to the Secretary of State at the Home Office;
(b) if the declarant is in any of the Islands, to the Lieutenant-Governor;
(c) if the declarant is in a British overseas territory, to the Governor;
(d) if the declarant is in a country mentioned in Schedule 3 to the Act, to the High Commissioner or, if there is no High Commissioner, to the Secretary of State at the Home Office;
(e) if the declarant is elsewhere, to any consular officer, any established officer in the Diplomatic Service of Her Majesty's Government in the United Kingdom or any person authorised by the Secretary of State in that behalf.

Notice of proposed deprivation of citizenship

10.—(1) Where it is proposed to make an order under section 40 of the Act depriving a person of a citizenship status, the notice required by section 40(5) of the Act to be given to that person may be given—
(a) in a case where that person's whereabouts are known, by causing the notice to be delivered to him personally or by sending it to him by post;
(b) in a case where that person's whereabouts are not known, by sending it by post in a letter addressed to him at his last known address.

(2) If a notice required by section 40(5) of the Act is given to a person appearing to the Secretary of State or, as appropriate, the Governor or Lieutenant-Governor to represent the person to whom notice under section 40(5) is intended to be given, it shall be deemed to have been given to that person.

(3) A notice required to be given by section 40(5) of the Act shall, unless the contrary is proved, be deemed to have been given—
(a) where the notice is sent by post from and to a place within the United Kingdom, on the second day after it was sent;
(b) where the notice is sent by post from or to a place outside the United Kingdom, on the twenty-eighth day after it was sent, and
(c) in any other case on the day on which the notice was delivered.

Cancellation of registration of person deprived of citizenship

11. Where an order has been made depriving a person who has a citizenship status by virtue of registration (whether under the Act or under the former nationality

Acts) of that citizenship status, the name of that person shall be removed from the relevant register.

Cancellation of certificate of naturalisation in case of deprivation of citizenship

12. Where an order has been made depriving a person who has a citizenship status by virtue of the grant of a certificate of naturalisation (whether under the Act or under the former nationality Acts) of that citizenship status, the person so deprived or any other person in possession of the relevant certificate of naturalisation shall, if required by notice in writing given by the authority by whom the order was made, deliver up the said certificate to such person, and within such time, as may be specified in the notice; and the said certificate shall thereupon be cancelled or amended.

Part IV

Supplemental

Evidence

13. A document may be certified to be a true copy of a document for the purpose of section 45(2) of the Act by means of a statement in writing to that effect signed by a person authorised by the Secretary of State, the Lieutenant-Governor, the High Commissioner or the Governor in that behalf.

Manner of signifying parental consent to registration

14. Where a parent, in pursuance of section 3(5)(c) of the Act, consents to the registration of a person as a British citizen under that subsection, the consent shall be expressed in writing and signed by the parent.

Revocation

15. The British Nationality (General) Regulations 1982 are hereby revoked.

Regulation 3

Schedule I

General Requirements As Respects Applications

Part I

All applications

1. An application shall be made in writing and shall state the name, address and date and place of birth of the applicant.

2. An application shall contain a declaration that the particulars stated therein are true.

Part II

Applications by persons not of full age or capacity

3. An application in respect of someone not of full age or capacity made by another person on his behalf shall state that that is the case and the name and address of that person.
4. An application made by a person on behalf of someone not of full age or capacity shall indicate the nature of that person's connection with him and, if that person has any responsibility for him otherwise than as a parent, the nature of that responsibility and the manner in which it was assumed.

Regulation 3

Schedule 2

Particular Requirements As Respects Applications

Application under section 1(3) of the Act

1. An application under section 1(3) of the Act shall contain information showing that the applicant's father or mother became a British citizen, or became settled in the United Kingdom, after the applicant's birth.

Application under section 1(4) of the Act

2. An application under section 1(4) of the Act shall contain information showing that the applicant possesses the requisite qualifications in respect of residence.
3. If the applicant was absent from the United Kingdom on more than 90 days in all in any one of the first 10 years of his life and it is desired that the application should nevertheless be considered under section 1(7) of the Act, it shall specify the special circumstances to be taken into consideration.

Application under section 3(2) of the Act

4. An application under section 3(2) of the Act shall contain information showing—
   (a) that the applicant's father or mother ('the parent in question') was a British citizen by descent at the time of the applicant's birth;
   (b) that the father or mother of the parent in question—
      (i) was a British citizen otherwise than by descent at the time of the birth of the parent in question; or
      (ii) became a British citizen otherwise than by descent at commencement; or
      (iii) would have become a British citizen otherwise than by descent at commencement but for his or her death;
   (c) either—
      (i) that the parent in question possesses the requisite qualifications in respect of residence; or
      (ii) that the applicant was born stateless.

5. If the application is not made within 12 months after the applicant's birth and it is desired that the application should nevertheless be considered under section 3(4) of the Act, it shall specify the special circumstances to be taken into consideration.

Application under section 3(5) of the Act

6. An application under section 3(5) of the Act shall contain information showing—
   (a) that the applicant's father or mother was a British citizen by descent at the time of the applicant's birth;
   (b) that the applicant and his father and mother possess the requisite qualifications in respect of residence;
   (c) that the consent of the applicant's father and/or mother (as required by section 3(5)(c) and (6) of the Act) has been signified in accordance with regulation 14 and, if the consent of one parent only has been signified, the reason for that fact.

Application under section 4(2) of the Act

7.—(1) An application under section 4(2) of the Act shall contain information showing—
   (a) that the applicant is a British overseas territories citizen, a British Overseas citizen, a British subject under the Act or a British protected person;
   (b) that the applicant possesses the requisite qualifications in respect of residence, freedom from immigration restrictions and compliance with the immigration laws.

(2) If the applicant does not possess the requisite qualifications in respect of residence, freedom from immigration restrictions and compliance with the immigration laws and it is desired that the application should nevertheless be considered under section 4(4) of the Act, it shall specify the special circumstances to be taken into consideration.

Application under section 4(5) of the Act

8.—(1) An application under section 4(5) of the Act shall contain information showing—
   (a) that the applicant is a British overseas territories citizen, a British Overseas citizen, a British subject under the Act or a British protected person;
   (b) that the applicant possesses the requisite qualifications in respect of service.

(2) The application shall specify the special circumstances to be taken into consideration.

Application under section 4A of the Act

9. An application under section 4A of the Act shall contain information showing—
   (a) that the applicant is a British overseas territories citizen who is not such a citizen by virtue only of a connection with the Sovereign Base Areas of Akrotiri and Dhekelia;
   (b) that the applicant has not ceased to be a British citizen as a result of a declaration of renunciation.

Application under section 4B of the Act

10. An application under section 4B of the Act shall contain information showing—
   (a) that the applicant is a British Overseas citizen, a British subject under the Act or a British protected person and has no other citizenship or nationality;

(b) that the applicant has not after 4th July 2002 renounced, voluntarily relinquished or lost through action or inaction any citizenship or nationality.

Application under section 4C of the Act

11. An application under section 4C of the Act shall contain information showing—

(a) that the application was born after 7th February 1961 and before 1st January 1983;

(b) that the applicant would at some time before 1st January 1983 have become a citizen of the United Kingdom and Colonies by virtue of section 5 of the British Nationality Act 1948 if that section had provided for citizenship by descent from a mother in the same terms as it provided for citizenship by descent from a father;

(c) that immediately before 1st January 1983 the applicant would have had the right of abode in the United Kingdom by virtue of section 2 of the Immigration Act 1971 had he become a citizen of the United Kingdom and Colonies as described in sub-paragraph (b) above.

Application under section 5 of the Act

12. An application under section 5 of the Act shall contain information showing that the applicant is a British overseas territories citizen who falls to be treated as a national of the United Kingdom for the purposes of the Community Treaties.

Application under section 6(1)

13.—(1) An application under section 6(1) of the Act shall contain information showing—

(a) that the applicant possesses the requisite qualifications in respect of residence or Crown service, freedom from immigration restrictions, compliance with the immigration laws, good character, knowledge of language [, knowledge about life in the United Kingdom] and intention with respect to residence or occupation in the event of a certificate of naturalisation being granted to him;

(b) that the applicant is of full capacity.

(2) If the applicant does not possess the requisite qualifications in respect of residence, freedom from immigration restrictions, compliance with the immigration laws and knowledge of language and it is desired that the application should nevertheless be considered under paragraph 2 of Schedule 1 to the Act, it shall specify the special circumstances to be taken into consideration.

Note: Words in square brackets substituted from 1 May 2006 (SI 2005/2785).

Application under section 6(2) of the Act

14.—(1) An application under section 6(2) of the Act shall contain information showing—

(a) that the applicant is married to a British citizen;

(b) that the applicant possesses the requisite qualifications in respect of residence, freedom from immigration restrictions, compliance with the [immigration laws, good character, knowledge of language and knowledge about life in the United Kingdom].

(c) that the applicant is of full capacity.

(2) If the applicant does not possess the requisite qualifications in respect of residence and

compliance with the immigration laws and it is desired that the application should nevertheless be considered under paragraph 4 of Schedule 1 to the Act, it shall specify the special circumstances to be taken into consideration.

(3) If the applicant does not possess the requisite qualifications in respect of residence and it is desired that the application should nevertheless be considered under paragraph 4(d) of Schedule 1 to the Act on the grounds of marriage to a person who is serving in Crown Service under the government of the United Kingdom or other designated service, it shall specify the nature of the service and contain information showing that recruitment for that service took place in the United Kingdom.

Note: Words in square brackets substituted from 1 May 2006 (SI 2005/2785).

Application under section 10(1) of the Act

15. An application under section 10(1) of the Act shall contain information showing—

(a) that the applicant renounced citizenship of the United Kingdom and Colonies;

(b) that at the time when he renounced it the applicant was, or was about to become, a citizen of a country mentioned in section 1(3) of the British Nationality Act 1948;

(c) that the applicant could not have remained or become such a citizen but for renouncing it or had reasonable cause to believe that he would be deprived of his citizenship of that country unless he renounced it;

(d) that the applicant possessed the requisite qualifying connection with the United Kingdom immediately before commencement or was married before commencement to a person who possessed the requisite qualifying connection with the United Kingdom immediately before commencement or would if living have possessed such a connection;

(e) that the applicant has not previously been registered under section 10(1) of the Act.

Application under section 10(2) of the Act

16. An application under section 10(2) of the Act shall contain information showing—

(a) that the applicant has renounced citizenship of the United Kingdom and Colonies and his reason for so doing;

(b) that the applicant possesses the requisite qualifying connection with the United Kingdom or has been married to a person who has, or would if living have, such a connection;

(c) that the applicant is of full capacity.

Application under section 13(1) of the Act

17. An application under section 13(1) of the Act shall contain information showing—

(a) that the applicant has renounced British citizenship;

(b) that, at the time when he renounced it, the applicant had or was about to acquire some other citizenship or nationality;

(c) that the renunciation of British citizenship was necessary to enable him to retain or acquire that other citizenship or nationality;

(d) that the applicant has not previously been registered under section 13(1) of the Act;

(e) that the applicant is of full capacity.

Application under section 13(3) of the Act

18. An application under section 13(3) of the Act shall contain information showing—

(a) that the applicant has renounced British citizenship and his reason for so doing;

(b) that the applicant is of full capacity.

Application under paragraph 3 of Schedule 2 to the Act

19.—(1) An application under paragraph 3 of Schedule 2 to the Act shall contain information showing—

(a) that the applicant is and always has been stateless;

(b) that the applicant seeks British citizenship and possesses the requisite qualifications in respect of residence.

(2) If the applicant does not possess the requisite qualifications in respect of residence and it is desired that the application should nevertheless be considered under paragraph 6 of Schedule 2 to the Act, it shall specify the special circumstances to be taken into consideration.

Application under paragraph 4 of Schedule 2

20.—(1) An application under paragraph 4 of Schedule 2 to the Act shall contain information showing—

(a) that the applicant is and always has been stateless;

(b) in respect of both the father and mother of the applicant, which of the following statuses, namely, British citizenship, British overseas territories citizenship, British Overseas citizenship or the status of a British subject under the Act, was held at the time of the applicant's birth;

(c) that the applicant possesses the requisite qualifications in respect of residence;

(d) if more than one of the statuses mentioned in sub-paragraph (b) above are available to the applicant, which status or statuses is or are wanted.

(2) If the applicant does not possess the requisite qualifications in respect of residence and it is desired that the application should nevertheless be considered under paragraph 6 of Schedule 2 to the Act, it shall specify the special circumstances to be taken into consideration.

Application under paragraph 5 of Schedule 2

21. An application under paragraph 5 of Schedule 2 to the Act shall contain information showing—

(a) that the applicant is and always has been stateless;

(b) if he was not born at a place which is at the date of the application within the United Kingdom and British overseas territories—

(i) that the applicant's mother was a citizen of the United Kingdom and Colonies at the time of his birth; or

(ii) that he possesses the requisite qualifications in respect of parentage or residence and parentage;

(c) that the applicant seeks British citizenship or British Overseas citizenship and that

that citizenship is available to the applicant in accordance with paragraph 5(2) of Schedule 2 to the Act.

Regulation 6

SCHEDULE 3

ADMINISTRATION OF [CITIZENSHIP OATH OR PLEDGE]

1. Subject to [paragraphs 2 and 3] [a citizenship oath or pledge] shall be administered by one of the following persons:
   (a) in England and Wales or Northern Ireland—any justice of the peace, commissioner for oaths or notary public;
   (b) in Scotland—any sheriff principal, sheriff, justice of the peace or notary public;
   (c) in the Channel Islands, the Isle of Man or any British overseas territory—any judge of any court of civil or criminal jurisdiction, any justice of the peace or magistrate, or any person for the time being authorised by the law of the place where the applicant, declarant or deponent is, to administer an oath for any judicial or other legal purpose;
   (d) in any country mentioned in Schedule 3 to the Act of which Her Majesty is Queen, or in any territory administered by the government of any such country—any person for the time being authorised by the law of the place where the deponent is to administer an oath for any judicial or other legal purpose, any consular officer or any established officer of the Diplomatic Service of Her Majesty's Government in the United Kingdom;
   (e) elsewhere—any consular officer, any established officer of the Diplomatic Service of Her Majesty's Government in the United Kingdom or any person authorised by the Secretary of State in that behalf.

2. If the deponent is serving in Her Majesty's naval, military or air forces, the oath [or pledge] may be administered by any officer holding a commission in any of those forces, whether the oath [or pledge] is made [. . .] in the United Kingdom or elsewhere.

[3. Where a citizenship oath and pledge is required by section 42 of the Act to be made at a citizenship ceremony, it shall be administered at the ceremony:
   (a) in the case of a ceremony held in England, Wales or Scotland, by a registrar (within the meaning of section 41(3B) of the Act); and
   (b) in the case of a ceremony held elsewhere, by a person authorised to do so by the Secretary of State.]

Note: Words in square brackets substituted and inserted, and words omitted from 1 January 2004 (SI 2003/3158).

Regulation 7 SCHEDULE 4

FORM OF CERTIFICATE OF NATURALISATION AS A BRITISH CITIZEN

British Nationality Act 1981
Certificate of Naturalisation as a British Citizen

The Secretary of State, in exercise of the powers conferred by the British Nationality Act 1981, hereby grants this certificate of naturalisation to the person named below, who shall be a British citizen from the date of this certificate.
Full name
Name at birth if different
Date of birth
Place and country of birth

Regulation 8 SCHEDULE 5

REQUIREMENTS AS RESPECTS DECLARATIONS OF RENUNCIATION

1. A declaration shall be made in writing and shall state the name, address, date and place of birth of the declarant.
2. A declaration shall contain information showing that the declarant—
   (a) is a British citizen, British Overseas citizen or British subject, as the case may be;
   (b) is of full age or, if not, has been married;
   (c) is of full capacity;
   (d) will, after the registration of the declaration, have or acquire some citizenship or nationality other than British citizenship, British Overseas citizenship or British subject status, as the case may be.
3. A declaration shall contain a declaration that the particulars stated therein are true.

The Immigration (Notices) Regulations 2003
(SI 2003, No. 658)

Citation and commencement

1. These Regulations may be cited as the Immigration (Notices) Regulations 2003 and shall come into force on the 1st April 2003.

Interpretation

2. In these Regulations—

'the 1971 Act' means the Immigration Act 1971;

'the 1997 Act' means the Special Immigration Appeals Commission Act 1997;

'the 1999 Act' means the Immigration and Asylum Act 1999;

'the 2002 Act' means the Nationality, Immigration and Asylum Act 2002;

'decision-maker' means—

(a) the Secretary of State;

(b) an immigration officer;

(c) an entry clearance officer;

'EEA decision' means an immigration decision within the meaning of section 109(3) of the 2002 Act or a decision under Regulation 1251/70 which concerns a person's—

(a) removal from the United Kingdom;

(b) entitlement to be admitted to the United Kingdom;

(c) entitlement to be issued with or to have removed, or not to have removed, a residence permit or residence document; [or

(d) on or after 30th April 2006, entitlement to be issued with or have renewed, or not to have revoked, a registration certificate, residence card, document certifying permanent residence or permanent residence card;]

'entry clearance officer' means a person responsible for the grant or refusal of entry clearance;

'immigration decision' has the same meaning as in section 82(2) of the 2002 Act;

'minor' means a person who is under 18 years of age;

'notice of appeal' means a notice in the appropriate prescribed form in accordance with the rules for the time being in force under section 106(1) of the 2002 Act;

'Procedure Rules' means rules made under section 106(1) of the 2002 Act;

'representative' means a person who appears to the decision-maker—

(a) to be the representative of a person referred to in regulation 4(1) below; and

(b) not to be prohibited from acting as a representative by section 84 of the 1999 Act.

Note: Paragraph (d) inserted from 30 April 2006 (SI 2006/1003).

Transitional provision

3. These Regulations apply to a decision to make a deportation order which, by virtue of paragraph 12 of Schedule 15 of the 1999 Act,—

(a) is appealable under section 15 of the 1971 Act (appeals in respect of deportation orders); or

(b) would be appealable under section 15 of the 1971 Act, but for section 15(3) (deportation conducive to public good), and is appealable under section 2(1)(c) of the 1997 Act (appeal to Special Immigration Appeals Commission against a decision to make a deportation order).

Notice of decisions

4.—(1) Subject to regulation 6, the decision-maker must give written notice to a person of any immigration decision or EEA decision taken in respect of him which is appealable.

(2) The decision-maker must give written notice to a person of the relevant grant of leave to enter or remain if, as a result of that grant, a right of appeal arises under section 83(2) of the 2002 Act.

[(2A) The decision-maker must give written notice to a person of a decision that they are no longer a refugee if as a result of that decision a right of appeal arises under section 83A(2) of the 2002 Act.]

(3) If the notice is given to the representative of the person, it is to be taken to have been given to the person.

Note: Paragraph (2A) inserted from 31 August 2006 (SI 2006/2168).

Contents of notice

5.—[(1) A notice given under regulation 4(1)—

(a) is to include or be accompanied by a statement of the reasons for the decision to which it relates; and

(b) if it relates to an immigration decision specified in section 82(2)(a), (g), (h), (i), (ia) or (j) of the 2002 Act—

(i) shall state the country or territory to which it is proposed to remove the person; or

(ii) may, if it appears to the decision-maker that the person to whom the notice is to be given may be removable to more than one country or territory, state any such countries or territories.]

(2) A notice given under regulation 4(2) is to include or be accompanied by a statement of the reasons for the rejection of the claim for asylum.

(3) Subject to paragraph (6), the notice given under regulation 4 shall also include, or be accompanied by, a statement which advises the person of—

(a) his right of appeal and the statutory provision on which his right of appeal is based;

(b) whether or not such an appeal may be brought while in the United Kingdom;

(c) the grounds on which such an appeal may be brought; and

(d) the facilities available for advice and assistance in connection with such an appeal.

(4) Subject to paragraph (6), the notice given under regulation 4 shall be accompanied by a notice of appeal which indicates the time limit for bringing the appeal, the address to which it should be sent or may be taken by hand and a fax number for service by fax.

(5) Subject to paragraph (6), where the exercise of the right is restricted by an exception or limitation by virtue of a provision of Part 5 of the 2002 Act, the notice given under regulation 4 shall include or be accompanied by a statement which refers to the provision limiting or restricting the right of appeal.

(6) The notice given under regulation 4 need not comply with paragraphs (3); (4) and (5) where a right of appeal may only be exercised on the grounds referred to in section 84(1)(b), (c) or (g) of the 2002 Act by virtue of the operation of section 88(4), 89(3), 90(4), 91(2), 98(4) or (5) of that Act.

(7) Where notice is given under regulation 4 and paragraph (6) applies, if the person claims in relation to the immigration decision or the EEA decision that—

(a) the decision is unlawful by virtue of section 19B of the Race Relations Act 1976 (discrimination by public authorities);

(b) the decision is unlawful under section 6 of the Human Rights Act 1998 (public authority not to act contrary to the Human Rights Convention) as being incompatible with the person's Convention rights; or

(c) removal of the person from the United Kingdom in consequence of the immigration decision would breach the United Kingdom's obligations under the Refugee Convention or would be unlawful under section 6 of the Human Rights Act 1998 as being incompatible with the person's Convention rights, the decision-maker must as soon as practicable re-serve the notice of decision under regulation 4 and paragraph (6) of this regulation shall not apply.

(8) Where a notice is re-served under paragraph (7), the time limit for appeal under the Procedure Rules shall be calculated as if the notice of decision had been served on the date on which it was re-served.

Note: Paragraph (1) substituted from 31 August 2006, (SI 2006/2168).

Certain notices under the 1971 Act deemed to comply with the regulations

6.—(1) This regulation applies where the power to—

(a) refuse leave to enter; or

(b) vary leave to enter or remain in the United Kingdom;

is exercised by notice in writing under section 4 of (administration of control), or paragraph 6(2) (notice of decisions of leave to enter or remain) of Schedule 2 to, the 1971 Act.

(2) If—

(a) the statement required by regulation 5(3) is included in or accompanies that notice; and

(b) the notice is given in accordance with the provision of regulation 7;

the notice is to be taken to have been given under regulation 4(1) for the purposes of these Regulations.

Service of notice

7.—(1) A notice required to be given under regulation 4 may be—

(a) given by hand;

(b) sent by fax;

(c) sent by postal service in which delivery or receipt is recorded to—

(i) an address provided for correspondence by the person or his representative; or

(ii) where no address for correspondence has been provided by the person, the last-known or usual place of abode or place of business of the person or his representative.

(2) Where—

(a) a person's whereabouts are not known; and

(b) (i) no address has been provided for correspondence and the decision-maker does not know the last-known or usual place of abode or place of business of the person; or

(ii) the address provided to the decision-maker is defective, false or no longer in use by the person; and

(c) no representative appears to be acting for the person,

the notice shall be deemed to have been given when the decision-maker enters a record of the above circumstances and places the signed notice on the relevant file.

(3) Where a notice has been given in accordance with paragraph (2) and then subsequently the person is located, he shall be given a copy of the notice and details of when and how it was given as soon as is practicable.

(4) Where a notice is sent by post in accordance with paragraph (1)(c) it shall be deemed to have been served, unless the contrary is proved,—

(a) on the second day after it was posted if it is sent to a place within the United Kingdom;

(b) on the twenty-eighth day after it was posted if it is sent to a place outside the United Kingdom.

(5) For the purposes of paragraph (4) the period is to be calculated—

(a) excluding the day on which the notice is posted; and
(b) in the case of paragraph (4)(a), excluding any day which is not a business day.

(6) In this regulation, 'business day' means any day other than Saturday or Sunday, a day which is a bank holiday under the Banking and Financial Dealings Act 1971 in the part of the United Kingdom to which the notice is sent, Christmas Day or Good Friday.

(7) A notice given under regulation 4 may, in the case of a minor who does not have a representative, be given to the parent, guardian or another adult who for the time being takes responsibility for the child.

The Nationality, Immigration and Asylum Act 2002 (Commencement No. 4) Order 2003
(SI 2003, No. 754)

Citation and interpretation

1.—(1) This Order may be cited as the Nationality, Immigration and Asylum Act 2002 (Commencement No. 4) Order 2003.

(2) In this Order—
'the 1971 Act' means the Immigration Act 1971;
'the 1988 Act' means the Immigration Act 1988;
'the 1993 Act' means the Asylum and Immigration Appeals Act 1993;
'the 1997 Act' means the Special Immigration Appeals Commission Act 1997;
'the 1999 Act' means the Immigration and Asylum Act 1999; and
'the 2002 Act' means the Nationality, Immigration and Asylum Act 2002.

Commencement and appointed date provisions

2.—(1) The provisions of the 2002 Act specified in column 1 of Schedule 1 to this Order shall come into force on the date specified in column 2 of that Schedule, but where a particular purpose is specified in relation to any such provision in column 3 of that Schedule, the provision concerned shall come into force on that date only for that purpose.

(2) The date appointed under section 162(4) of the 2002 Act for the purposes of section 8 of that Act is 1st April 2003.

Transitional provisions

3.—(1) Subject to Schedule 2, the new appeals provisions are not to have effect in relation to events which took place before 1st April 2003 and, notwithstanding their repeal by the provisions of the 2002 Act commenced by this Order, the old appeals provisions are to continue to have effect in relation to such events.

(2) Schedule 2, which makes further transitional provisions, has effect.

Definitions for transitional provisions

4.—(1) In this Order—

(a) 'the new appeals provisions' means sections 82 to 99 and sections 101 to 103 of the 2002 Act; together with any provision (including subordinate legislation) of—

(i) the 2002 Act;

(ii) the 1971 Act, the 1997 Act and the 1999 Act (all as amended by the 2002 Act);

which refer to those provisions;

(b) 'the old appeals provisions' means—

(i) sections 13 to 17 of the 1971 Act;

(ii) subsections (1) to (4) of section 8 of the 1993 Act;

(iii) the 1997 Act (without the amendments made by the 2002 Act);

(iv) Part IV of, and Schedule 4 (except paragraphs 10 to 20 and 23) to, the 1999 Act;

(v) section 115 of the 2002 Act;

together with—

(vi) any subordinate legislation which applies to those provisions (unless specific provision is made to the contrary); and

(vii) any provision of the old Immigration Acts which refers to those provisions;

(c) 'the old Immigration Acts' means the 1971 Act, the 1988 Act, the 1993 Act, the 1996 Act, the 1997 Act and the 1999 Act, all without the amendments made by the 2002 Act.

(3) For the purposes of article 3 and Schedule 2, an event has taken place under the old Immigration Acts where—

(a) a notice was served;

(b) a decision was made or taken;

(c) directions were given; and

(d) a certificate was issued.

(4) For the purposes of this Order—

(a) a notice was served;

(b) a decision was made or taken;

(c) directions were given; and
(d) a certificate was issued;

on the day on which it was or they were sent to the person concerned, if sent by post or by fax, or delivered to that person, if delivered by hand.

(5) In this article—
(a) 'the person concerned' means the person who is the subject of the notice, decision, directions or certificate or the person who appears to be his representative; and
(b) a reference to the issue of a certificate is a reference to the issue of a certificate under section 11, 12 or 72(2) of the 1999 Act or section 115 of the 2002 Act.

SCHEDULE 1

. . .

Note: Schedule 1 specifies the provisions of the 2002 Act which are commenced by Art 2 above.

Article 3

SCHEDULE 2

Transitional provisions relating to the 2002 Act

1.—(1) In this paragraph, a reference to a section or to a Schedule is to be read as a reference to a section of, or to a Schedule to, the 2002 Act, unless otherwise specified.

(2) Section 77 (no removal while claim for asylum pending) shall have effect in relation to a claim for asylum pending on 31st March 2003 as it has effect in relation to a claim for asylum pending under the 2002 Act.

(3) Section 78 (no removal while appeal pending) shall have effect in relation to an appeal pending under the old appeals provisions as it has effect in relation to an appeal pending under section 82(1) of the 2002 Act.

(4) Section 79 (deportation order: appeal) shall have effect in relation to an appeal pending under the old appeals provisions as it has effect in relation to an appeal pending under section 82(1) of the 2002 Act.

(4A) Section 101(1) shall apply to a party to an appeal to an adjudicator under Part 4 of the 1999 Act which is determined on or after 9th June 2003, as it applies to a party to an appeal to an adjudicator under section 82 or 83.

(4B) Where section 101(1) applies by virtue of sub-paragraph (4A) above—
(a) sections 101(2) and (3), 102 and 103 shall apply in relation to any appeal or application for permission to appeal under section 101(1) subject to the modifications that—
(i) in section 102(1)(d), the reference to section 87 shall be treated as being a reference to paragraph 21 of Schedule 4 to the 1999 Act; and
(ii) in section 102(3), the reference to section 82 shall be treated as being a reference to Part 4 of the 1999 Act; and

(b) paragraphs 7, 22 and 23 of Schedule 4 to the 1999 Act shall not apply.

(5) Section 115 (appeal from within the United Kingdom: unfounded human rights claim or asylum claim: transitional provision) shall continue to have effect in relation to any person who made an asylum claim or human rights claim (as defined in subsection (10)) on or after 1st April 2003.

Note: Subparagraphs (4A) and (4B) inserted from 9 June 2003 (SI 2003/1339).

Transitional provisions relating to the appeals provisions of the 1971 Act

2.—(1) In this paragraph, a reference to a section or to a Schedule is to be read as a reference to a section of, or to a Schedule to, the 1971 Act, unless otherwise specified.

[(2) Section 3C of the 1971 Act (continuation of leave pending variation decision), as substituted by section 118 of the 2002 Act, shall apply in relation to an application made before 1st April 2003, in respect of which no decision has been made on or before 1st April 2003, as it applies to such an application made after 1st April 2003.]

(3) Section 5 (procedure for, and further provisions as to, deportation) is to continue to have effect in relation to—

(a) any person on whom the Secretary of State has, before 2nd October 2000, served a notice of his decision to make a deportation order; and

(b) any person—

(i) who applied during the regularisation period fixed by section 9 of the 1999 Act, in accordance with the Immigration (Regularisation Period for Overstayers) Regulations 2000, for leave to remain in the United Kingdom; and

(ii) on whom the Secretary of State has since served a notice of his decision to make a deportation order;

and, for the purposes of section 5, such a person is to be taken to be a person who is liable to deportation under section 3(5).

(4) Section 13 (appeals against exclusions from the United Kingdom) is to continue to have effect where the decision to refuse leave to enter the United Kingdom, or to refuse a certificate of entitlement or an entry clearance, was made before 2nd October 2000.

(5) Section 14 (appeals against conditions) is to continue to have effect where the decision to vary, or to refuse to vary, the limited leave to enter or remain was made before 2nd October 2000.

(6) Section 15 (appeals in respect of deportation orders) is to continue to have effect in relation to—

(a) any person on whom the Secretary of State has, before 2nd October 2000, served a notice of his decision to make a deportation order; and

(b) any person—

(i) who applied during the regularisation period fixed by section 9 of the 1999 Act, in accordance with the Immigration (Regularisation Period for Overstayers) Regulations 2000, for leave to remain in the United Kingdom; and

(ii) on whom the Secretary of State has since served a notice of his decision to make a deportation order.

(7) Section 16 (appeals against validity of directions for removal) is to continue to have

effect where the directions for a person's removal from the United Kingdom were given before 2nd October 2000.

(8) Section 17 (appeals against removal on objection to destination) is to continue to have effect—

(a) where the directions for a person's removal from the United Kingdom were given, or the notice specifying the destination of his removal was served, before 2nd October 2000; and

(b) in relation to any person—

(i) who applied during the regularisation period fixed by section 9 of the 1999 Act, in accordance with the Immigration (Regularisation Period for Overstayers) Regulations 2000, for leave to remain in the United Kingdom; and

(ii) on whom the Secretary of State has since served a notice of his decision to make a deportation order.

(9) Section 21 (references of cases by Secretary of State for further consideration) (including that section as applied by paragraph 4 of Schedule 2 to the 1993 Act) is to continue to have effect where the Secretary of State has referred a matter for consideration under that section before 2nd October 2000.

(10) Where an appeal is made under Part II (including that Part as it applies by virtue of Schedule 2 to the 1993 Act)—

(a) paragraph 28 of Schedule 2 (stay on directions for removal) (including that paragraph as applied by paragraph 9 of Schedule 2 to the 1993 Act) is to continue to have effect;

(b) the following provisions are not to have effect—

(i) paragraph 29(1) of Schedule 2 (grant of bail pending appeal) (including that paragraph as applied by paragraph 9 of Schedule 2 to the 1993 Act and by section 3(6) of the 1996 Act), as amended by paragraph 66 of Schedule 14 to the 1999 Act;

(ii) paragraph 3 of Schedule 3 (effect of appeals) including that paragraph as applied by paragraph 9 of Schedule 2 to the 1993 Act), as amended by paragraph 69 of Schedule 14 to the 1999 Act.

Note: Subparagraph (2) substituted from 8 April 2003 (SI 2003/1040).

Transitional provision relating to the appeals provisions of the 1988 Act

3. Section 5 (restricted right of appeal against deportation in cases of breach of limited leave) is to continue to have effect—

(a) where the directions for a person's removal from the United Kingdom were given, or the notice specifying the destination of his removal was served, before 2nd October 2000,

(b) in relation to any person—

(i) who applied during the regularisation period fixed by section 9 of the 1999 Act, in accordance with the Immigration (Regularisation Period for Overstayers) Regulations 2000, for leave to remain in the United Kingdom; and

(ii) on whom the Secretary of State has since served a notice of his decision to make a deportation order.

Transitional provisions relating to the appeals provisions of the 1993 Act

4.—(1) In this paragraph, a reference to a section or to a Schedule is to be read as a reference to a section of, or to a Schedule to, the 1993 Act, unless otherwise specified.

(2) In section 8 (asylum appeals)—

(a) subsection (1) is to continue to have effect where the decision to refuse leave to enter was made before 2nd October 2000;

(b) subsection (2) is to continue to have effect where the decision to vary, or to refuse to vary, the limited leave to enter or remain was made before 2nd October 2000;

(c) subsection (3) is to continue to have effect where the decision to make a deportation order, or the decision to refuse to revoke a deportation order, was made before 2nd October 2000;

(d) subsection (4) is to continue to have effect where the directions for a person's removal from the United Kingdom were given before 2nd October 2000.

(3) Where an appeal is made under Part II of the 1971 Act (including that Part as it applies by virtue of Schedule 2)—

(a) section 9A (bail pending appeal from Immigration Appeal Tribunal), as amended by paragraphs 105 and 106 of Schedule 14 to the 1999 Act, is not to have effect;

(b) the reference in section 9A (without the amendments made by the 1999 Act) to section 9 (appeals from Immigration Appeal Tribunal) is to include a reference to paragraph 23 of Schedule 4 to the 1999 Act (appeals from Immigration Appeal Tribunal).

(4) Where an appeal is made under section 8, the section 8 appeals provisions are to continue to have effect.

(5) In this paragraph 'the section 8 appeals provisions' means—

(a) paragraph 1 of Schedule 2 (asylum appeal rights to replace rights under the 1971 Act);

(b) paragraph 2 of Schedule 2 (scope of asylum rights of appeal);

(c) paragraph 3 of Schedule 2 (other grounds for appeal);

(d) paragraph 5 of Schedule 2 (special appeals procedures for claims without foundation);

(e) paragraph 6 of Schedule 2 (exception for national security);

(f) paragraph 7 of Schedule 2 (suspension of variation of limited leave pending appeal);

(g) paragraph 8 of Schedule 2 (deportation order not to be made while appeal pending);

(h) paragraph 9 of Schedule 2 (stay of removal directions pending appeal and bail).

(6) Where an appeal is made under section 8, the reference in paragraph 5 of Schedule 2 to section 20(1) of the 1971 Act (appeals to the Immigration Appeal Tribunal) is to include a reference to paragraph 22(1) of Schedule 4 to the 1999 Act (appeals to the Immigration Appeal Tribunal).

Transitional provision relating to the 1997 Act

5.—(1) The amendments to the 1997 Act made by the provisions of the 2002 Act commenced by this Order are not to have effect in relation to an appeal which is pending, by virtue of section 7A of the 1997 Act, on 1st April 2003 and, notwithstanding their amendment by the provisions commenced by this Order, the old appeal provisions are to continue to have effect in relation to such an appeal.

Transitional provisions relating to the 1999 Act

6.—(1) In this paragraph, a reference to a section or to a Schedule is to be read as a reference to a section of, or to a Schedule to, the 1999 Act, unless otherwise specified.

(2) Section 10 (removal of certain persons unlawfully in the United Kingdom) is not to have effect in relation to—

(a) any person on whom the Secretary of State has, before 2nd October 2000, served a notice of his intention to make a deportation order; and

(b) any person—

(i) who applied during the regularisation period fixed by section 9 of the 1999 Act, in accordance with the Immigration (Regularisation Period for Overstayers) Regulations 2000 for leave to remain in the United Kingdom; and

(ii) on whom the Secretary of State has since served a notice of his decision to make a deportation order;

and, for the purposes of section 5, such a person is to be taken to be a person who is liable to deportation under section 3(5).

(3) Where a certificate is issued under section 11 (removal of asylum-seeker to third country), as substituted by section 80 of the 2002 Act, before 1st April 2003 and an allegation is made after 1st April the allegation may be certified under section 72(2) of the 1999 Act, notwithstanding its repeal by the provisions of the 2002 Act commenced by this Order, and that certification shall have effect for the purposes of an appeal under the old appeal provisions.

(4) Subject to the provisions of the Order and any other enactment sections 59 to 78 and Schedules 2 to 4 shall continue to have effect in relation to events which took place before 1st April 2003.

(5) Where a decision has been taken under the Immigration Acts relating to a person's entitlement to enter or remain in the United Kingdom before 1st April 2003 there shall only be a right of appeal under section 65(1) where an allegation is made before 1st July 2003.

The Immigration (Passenger Transit Visa) Order 2003
(SI 2003, No. 1185)

Citation, commencement and interpretation

1. This order may be cited as the Immigration (Passenger Transit Visa) Order 2003 and shall come into force on 2nd May 2003.

2.—(1) Subject to paragraph (4), in this Order a 'transit passenger' means a person to whom paragraph (2) or (3) applies and who on arrival in the United Kingdom passes through another country or territory without entering the United Kingdom.

(2) This paragraph applies to a person who is a citizen or national of a country or territory listed in Schedule 1 to this order.

(3) This paragraph applies to a person holding a travel document issued by:
  (a) the purported 'Turkish Republic of Northern Cyprus';
  (b) the former Socialist Republic of Yugoslavia;
  (c) the former Federal Republic of Yugoslavia; or
  (d) the former Zaire.

(4) A person to whom paragraph (2) or (3) applies will not be a transit passenger if he:
  (a) has the right of abode in the United Kingdom under the Immigration Act 1971;
  (b) is a national of an EEA State; or
  (c) in the case of a national or citizen of the People's Republic of China, holds a passport issued by either the Hong Kong Special Administrative Region or the Macao Special Administrative Region.

(5) In [this Order] 'EEA State' means a country which is a contracting party to the Agreement on the European Economic Area signed at Oporto on 2nd May 1992 as adjusted by the Protocol signed at Brussels on 17th March 1993.

Requirement for a transit passenger to hold a transit visa

3. [Subject to article 3A, a] transit passenger is required to hold a transit visa.

[Exemption from the requirement for a transit passenger to hold a transit visa

3A.—(1) A transit passenger is not required to hold a transit visa if he holds or a person with whom he arrives in the United Kingdom holds on his behalf:
  (a) a valid visa for entry to Canada or the United States of America and a valid airline ticket for travel via the United Kingdom [as part of a journey] from another country or territory to the country in respect of which the visa is held;
  [(b) a valid airline ticket for travel via the United Kingdom as part of a journey from Canada or the United States of America to another country or territory, provided that the transit passenger does not seek to travel via the United Kingdom on a date more than six months from the date on which he last entered Canada or the United States of America with a valid visa for entry to that country or territory;]
  (c) a valid USA I-551 Permanent Resident Card issued on or after 21st April 1998;

(d) a valid Canadian Permanent Resident Card issued on or after 28th June 2002;
(e) a valid common format Category D visa for entry to an EEA State;
(f) a valid common format residence permit issued by an EEA State pursuant to Council Regulation (EC) No. 1030/2002;
(g) a diplomatic or service passport issued by the People's Republic of China; or
(h) a diplomatic or official passport issued by India.
[(i) a diplomatic or official passport issued by Vietnam.]

(2) . . .]

Method of application for a transit visa

4. An application for a transit visa may be made to any British High Commission, Embassy or Consulate which accepts such applications.

Revocations

5. The Orders specified in Schedule 2 to this Order are hereby revoked.

Article 2

[SCHEDULE 1

COUNTRIES OR TERRITORIES WHOSE NATIONALS OR CITIZENS NEED TRANSIT VISAS

Afghanistan
Albania
Algeria
Angola
Bangladesh
Belarus
Burma
Burundi
Cameroon
Colombia
Democratic Republic of the Congo
Ecuador
Eritrea
Ethiopia
Former Yugoslav Republic of Macedonia
Gambia
Ghana
India
Iran
Iraq
Ivory Coast
[Kenya]
Lebanon
Liberia
[Malawi]
Moldova
Nepal
Nigeria
Pakistan
Palestinian Territories
People's Republic of China
Rwanda
Senegal
Serbia and Montenegro
Sierra Leone
Somalia
Sri Lanka
Sudan
[Tanzania]
Turkey
Uganda
Vietnam
Zimbabwe].

Note: Words in square brackets in Arts 2 and 3, and Schedule substituted, and Art 3A inserted from 1 October 2003 (SI 2003/2628). Words in square brackets in Art 3A (1)(a) and (1)(i) and Schedule inserted and Art 3A revoked from 13 May 2004 (SI 2004/1304). Second word in square brackets in Schedule inserted from 2 March 2006 (SI 2006/493).

Article 5

SCHEDULE 2

REVOCATIONS

. . .

The Immigration and Asylum Act 1999 (Part V Exemption: Relevant Employers) Order 2003

(SI 2003, No. 3214)

Citation and commencement

1. This Order may be cited as the Immigration and Asylum Act 1999 (Part V Exemption: Relevant Employers) Order 2003 and shall come into force on 1st January 2004.

Interpretation

2. In this Order—

'the Act' means the Immigration and Asylum Act 1999;

'immigration advice' and 'immigration services' have the same meanings as in section 82 of the Act;

'work permit' has the same meaning as in section 33(1) of the Immigration Act 1971;

'immediate family' means a person's spouse, and children below eighteen years of age;

'EEA national' means a person to whom the [Immigration (European Economic Area) Regulations 2006] apply;

'family member of an EEA national' has the same meaning as in the Immigration (European Economic Area) Regulations 2000.

Note: Words in square brackets inserted from 30 April 2006 (SI 2006/1003).

Exemption of relevant employers

3.—(1) Subject to paragraph (2), the following category of person is hereby specified for the purposes of section 84(4)(d) of the Act (provision of immigration services), namely, a person who provides immigration advice or immigration services free of charge to an employee or prospective employee who—

(a) is the subject of an application for a work permit submitted by the prospective employer;

(b) has been granted a work permit entitling him to work with the employer; or

(c) is an EEA national or the family member of an EEA national,

where the immigration advice or immigration services are restricted to matters which concern that employee or prospective employee or his immediate family.

(2) For the purposes of paragraph (1), the person providing the immigration advice or immigration services must be the employer or prospective employer of the person receiving the advice or services, or an employee of that employer acting as such.

The Accession (Immigration and Worker Registration) Regulations 2004

(SI 2004, No. 1219)

Part 1

General

Citation, commencement and interpretation

1.—(1) These Regulations may be cited as the Accession (Immigration and Worker Registration) Regulations 2004 and shall come into force on 1st May 2004.

(2) In these Regulations—

(a) 'the 1971 Act' means the Immigration Act 1971;

(b) 'the 2000 Regulations' means the immigration (European Economic Area) Regulations 2000;

[(ba) 'the 2006 Regulations' means the Immigration (European Economic Area) Regulations 2006;]

(c) 'accession period' means the period beginning on 1st May 2004 and ending on 30th April 2009;

(d) 'accession State worker requiring registration' shall be interpreted in accordance with regulation 2;

(e) 'authorised employer' shall be interpreted in accordance with regulation 7;

(f) 'EEA State' means a Member State, other than the United Kingdom, or Norway, Iceland or Liechtenstein, and 'EEA national' means a national of an EEA State;

(g) 'employer' means, in relation to a worker, the person who directly pays the wage or salary of that worker;

(h) 'registration certificate' means a certificate issued under regulation 8 authorising an accession State worker requiring registration to work for an employer;

(i) 'relevant accession State' means the Czech Republic, the Republic of Estonia, the Republic of Latvia, the Republic of Lithuania, the Republic of Hungary, the Republic of Poland, the Republic of Slovenia and the Slovak Republic;

(j) 'self-sufficient person' has the same meaning as in [regulation 4 of the 2006 Regulations];

(k) 'worker' means a worker within the meaning of Article 39 of the Treaty establishing the European Community, and 'work' and 'working' shall be construed accordingly.

Note: Words in square brackets substituted from 30 April 2006 (SI 2006/1003).

'Accession State worker requiring registration'

2.—(1) Subject to the following paragraphs of this regulation, 'accession State worker requiring registration' means a national of a relevant accession State working in the United Kingdom during the accession period.

(2) A national of a relevant accession State is not an accession State worker requiring registration if on 30th April 2004 he had leave to enter or remain in the United Kingdom under the 1971 Act and that leave was not subject to any condition restricting his employment.

(3) A national of a relevant accession State is not an accession State worker requiring registration if he was legally working in the United Kingdom on 30th April 2004 and had been legally working in the United Kingdom without interruption throughout the period of 12 months ending on that date.

(4) A national of a relevant accession State who legally works in the United Kingdom without interruption for a period of 12 months falling partly or wholly after 30th April 2004 shall cease to be an accession State worker requiring registration at the end of that period of 12 months.

(5) A national of a relevant accession State is not an accession State worker requiring registration during any period in which he is also a national of—

(a) the United Kingdom;

(b) another EEA State, other than a relevant accession State; or

(c) Switzerland.

(6) A national of a relevant accession State is not an accession State worker requiring registration during any period in which he is—

(a) a posted worker; or

[(b) a family member of a Swiss or EEA national (other than an accession State worker requiring registration) who has a right to reside in the United Kingdom under regulation 14(1) or 15 of the 2006 Regulations.]

(7) For the purpose of this regulation—

(a) a person working in the United Kingdom during a period falling before

1st May 2004 was legally working in the United Kingdom during that period if—

(i) he had leave to enter or remain in the United Kingdom under the 1971 Act for that period, that leave allowed him to work in the United Kingdom, and he was working in accordance with any condition on that leave restricting his employment; or

(ii) he was entitled to reside in the United Kingdom for that period under the 2000 Regulations without the requirement for such leave;

(b) a person working in the United Kingdom on or after 1st May 2004 is legally working during any period in which he is working in the United Kingdom for an authorised employer;

(c) a person shall also be treated as legally working in the United Kingdom on or after 1st May 2004 during any period in which he falls within paragraph (5) or (6).

(8) For the purpose of paragraphs (3) and (4), a person shall be treated as having worked in the United Kingdom without interruption for a period of 12 months if he was legally working in the United Kingdom at the beginning and end of that period and any intervening periods in which he was not legally working in the United Kingdom do not, in total, exceed 30 days.

(9) In this regulation—

(a) . . .

(b) 'posted worker' means a person whose employer is not established in the United Kingdom and who works for that employer in the United Kingdom for the purpose of providing services on his employer's behalf;

[(c) 'family member' has the same meaning as in regulation 7 of the 2006 Regulations.]

Note: Regulation 2 does not have effect in relation to an application for a registration certificate under regulation 8 made before 1 October 2005. Words in square brackets substituted from 30 April 2006 (SI 2006/1003).

Part 2
Immigration

3. . . .

Note: Amends SI 2000/2326.

Right of residence of work seekers and workers from relevant acceding States during the accession period

4.—**(1)** This regulation derogates during the accession period from Article 39 of the Treaty establishing the European Community, Articles 1 to 6 of Regulation

(EEC) No. 1612/68 on freedom of movement for workers within the Community and [Council Directive 2004/38/EC of the European Parliament and of the Council on the right of citizens of the Union and their family members to move and reside freely within the territory of the Member States, insofar as it takes over provisions of] Council Directive (EEC) No. 68/360 on the abolition of restrictions on movement and residence within the Community for workers of Member States and their families.

(2) A national of a relevant accession State shall not be entitled to reside in the United Kingdom for the purpose of seeking work by virtue of his status as a work seeker if he would be an accession State worker requiring registration if he began working in the United Kingdom.

(3) Paragraph (2) is without prejudice to the right of a national of a relevant accession State to reside in the United Kingdom under the [2006 Regulations] as a self-sufficient person whilst seeking work in the United Kingdom.

(4) [A national of a relevant accession State who is seeking employment and an] accession State worker requiring registration shall only be entitled to reside in the United Kingdom in accordance with the [2006 Regulations] as modified by regulation 5.

Note: Words in square brackets substituted from 30 April 2006, (SI 2006/1003).

[Application of 2006 Regulations in relation to accession State worker requiring registration

5.—(1) The 2006 Regulations shall apply in relation to a national of a relevant accession State subject to the modifications set out in this regulation.

(2) A national of a relevant accession State who is seeking employment in the United Kingdom shall not be treated as a jobseeker for the purpose of the definition of 'qualified person' in regulation 6(1) of the 2006 Regulations and an accession State worker requiring registration shall be treated as a worker for the purpose of that definition only during a period in which he is working in the United Kingdom for an authorised employer.

(3) Subject to paragraph (4), regulation 6(2) of the 2006 Regulations shall not apply to an accession State worker requiring registration who ceases to work.

(4) Where an accession State worker requiring registration ceases working for an authorised employer in the circumstances mentioned in regulation 6(2) of the 2006 Regulations during the one month period beginning on the date on which the work begins, that regulation shall apply to that worker during the remainder of that one month period.

(5) An accession State worker requiring registration shall not be treated as a qualified person for the purpose of regulations 16 and 17 of the 2006 Regulations (issue of registration certificates and residence cards).]

Note: Regulation 5 substituted from 30 April 2006 (SI 2006/1003).

6. . . .

Note: Revoked from 30 April 2006 (SI 2006/1003).

PART 3

ACCESSION STATE WORKER REGISTRATION

Requirement for an accession State worker requiring registration to be authorised to work

7.—(1) By way of derogation from Article 39 of the Treaty establishing the European Community and Articles 1 to 6 of Regulation (EEC) No. 1612/68 on freedom of movement for workers within the Community, an accession State worker requiring registration shall only be authorised to work in the United Kingdom for an authorised employer.

(2) An employer is an authorised employer in relation to a worker if—

(a) the worker was legally working for that employer on 30th April 2004 and has not ceased working for that employer after that date;

(b) the worker—

(i) during the one month period beginning on the date on which he begins working for the employer, applies for a registration certificate authorising him to work for that employer in accordance with regulation 8; and

(ii) has not received a valid registration certificate or notice of refusal under regulation 8 in relation to that application or ceased working for that employer since the application was made;

(c) the worker has received a valid registration certificate authorising him to work for that employer and that certificate has not expired under paragraph (5); or

(d) the employer is an authorised employer in relation to that worker under paragraph (3) or (4).

(3) Where a worker begins working for an employer on or after 1st May 2004 that employer is an authorised employer in relation to that worker during the one month period beginning on the date on which the work begins.

(4) Where a worker was, before 1st May 2004, issued with leave to enter the United Kingdom under the 1971 Act as a seasonal worker at an agricultural camp and the worker begins working for an employer on or after 1st May 2004 as a seasonal worker at such a camp, that employer is an authorised employer in relation to that worker during the period beginning on the date on which the work begins and ending on the date on which the worker ceases working for that employer, or on 31st December 2004, whichever is the earlier.

(5) A registration certificate—
   (a) is invalid if the worker is no longer working for the employer specified in the certificate on the date on which it is issued;
   (b) expires on the date on which the worker ceases working for that employer.

(6) Regulation 2(7)(a) shall apply for the purpose of determining whether a person is legally working on 30th April 2004 for the purpose of this regulation.

Registration card and registration certificate

8.—(1) An application for a registration certificate authorising an accession State worker requiring registration to work for an employer may only be made by an applicant who is working for that employer at the date of the application.

(2) The application shall be in writing and shall be made to the Secretary of State.

(3) The application shall state—
   (a) the name, address, and date of birth of the applicant;
   (b) the name and address of the head or main office of the employer;
   (c) the date on which the applicant began working for that employer;
   (d) where the applicant has been issued with a registration card, the reference number of that card.

(4) Unless the applicant has been issued with a registration card under paragraph (5), the application shall be accompanied by—
   (a) a registration fee of [£70];
   (b) two passport size photographs of the applicant;
   (c) the applicant's national identity card or passport issued by the applicant's State;
   (d) a letter from the employer concerned confirming that the applicant began working for the employer on the date specified in the application.

(5) In the case of an application by an applicant who has not been issued with a registration card under this paragraph, the Secretary of State shall, where he is satisfied that the application is made in accordance with this regulation and that the applicant—
   (a) is an accession State worker requiring registration; and
   (b) began working for the employer on the date specified in the application,
   send the applicant a registration card and a registration certificate authorising the worker to work for the employer specified in the application, and shall return the applicant's national identity card or passport.

(6) In the case of any other application, the Secretary of State shall, if he is satisfied as mentioned in paragraph (5), send the applicant a registration certificate authorising the worker to work for the employer specified in the application.

(7) A registration card issued under paragraph (5) shall contain—
   (a) the name, nationality and date of birth of the applicant;

(b) a photograph of the applicant;

(c) a reference number.

(8) A registration certificate issued under paragraph (5) or (6) shall contain—

(a) the name of the applicant;

(b) the reference number of the applicant's registration card;

(c) the name and address of the head or main office of the employer, as specified in the application;

(d) the date on which the applicant began working for the employer, as specified in the application; and

(e) the date on which the certificate is issued.

(9) Where the Secretary of State receives an application made in accordance with this regulation and he is not satisfied as mentioned in paragraph (5), he shall—

(a) send the applicant a notice of refusal; and

(b) return any documents and fee that accompanied the application to the applicant.

(10) Where the Secretary of State sends a registration certificate or notice of refusal to an applicant under this regulation he shall, at the same time, send a copy of the certificate or notice to the employer concerned at the address specified in the application for that employer.

(11) Certificates and notices, and copies of these documents, sent under this regulation shall be sent by post.

Note: Amount in square brackets in para (4)(a) substituted from 1 October 2005 (SI 2005/2400).

Restriction on employers of relevant accession State workers requiring registration

9.—(1) Subject to paragraph (2), if an employer employs an accession State worker requiring registration during a period in which the employer is not an authorised employer in relation to that worker, the employer shall be guilty of an offence.

(2) Subject to paragraph (4), in proceedings under this regulation it shall be a defence to prove that—

(a) there was produced to the employer during the one month period beginning on the date on which the worker began working for the employer a document that appeared to him to establish that the worker was not an accession State worker requiring registration; and

(b) the employer took and retained a copy of that document.

(3) Subject to paragraph (4), in proceedings under this regulation it shall be a defence to prove that—

(a) there was produced to the employer during the one month period beginning on the date on which the worker began working for the employer a document that appeared to him to establish that the worker had applied for a registration certificate in accordance with regulation 8 authorising the worker to work for that employer;

(b) the employer took and retained a copy of that document; and

(c) the employer has not received a copy of a registration certificate or notice of refusal in relation to that application.

(4) The defence afforded by paragraph (2) or (3) shall not be available in any case where the employer knew that his employment of the worker would constitute an offence under this regulation.

(5) A person guilty of an offence under this regulation shall be liable on summary conviction to a fine not exceeding level 5 on the standard scale.

(6) Where an offence under this regulation committed by a body corporate is proved to have been committed with the consent or connivance of, or to be attributable to any neglect on the part of—

(a) any director, manager, secretary or other similar officer of the body corporate; or

(b) any person purporting to act in such a capacity,

he as well as the body corporate shall be guilty of the offence and shall be liable to be proceeded against and punished accordingly.

(7) Where the affairs of a body corporate are managed by its members, paragraph (6) shall apply in relation to the acts and defaults of a member in connection with his functions of management as if he were a director of the body corporate.

(8) Where an offence under this regulation is committed by a partnership (other than a limited partnership) each partner shall be guilty of the offence and shall be liable to be proceeded against and punished accordingly.

(9) Paragraph (6) shall have effect in relation to a limited partnership as if—

(a) a reference to a body corporate were a reference to a limited partnership; and

(b) a reference to an officer of the body corporate were a reference to a partner.

(10) Section 28(1) of the 1971 Act (extended time limit for prosecution) shall apply in relation to an offence under this regulation.

(11) An offence under this regulation shall be treated as—

(a) a relevant offence for the purpose of sections 28B and 28D of that Act (search, entry and arrest); and

(b) an offence under Part III of that Act (criminal proceedings) for the purposes of sections 28E, 28G and 28H (search after arrest).

Note: Paragraphs (6)(b) and (9)(c)(i) of reg 6 substituted from 1 May 2004 (SI 2004/1236).

The Immigration (Claimant's Credibility) Regulations 2004 (SI 2004, No. 3263)

Citation and commencement

1. These Regulations may be cited as the Immigration (Claimant's Credibility) Regulations 2004 and shall come into force on the 1st January 2005.

Interpretation

2. In these Regulations—
   'the 2004 Act' means the Asylum and Immigration (Treatment of Claimants, etc) Act 2004;
   'representative' means a person who appears to the decision maker—
   (a) to be the representative of a person; and
   (b) not to be prohibited from acting as a representative by section 84 of the Immigration and Asylum 1999 Act.

Manner of notifying immigration decision

3.—(1) For the purpose of section 8(5) of the 2004 Act a person may be notified of an immigration decision in any of the following ways—
   (a) orally, including by means of a telecommunications system;
   (b) in writing given by hand; or
   (c) in writing
      (i) sent by fax to a fax number;
      (ii) sent by electronic mail to an electronic mail address; or
      (iii) delivered or sent by postal service to an address,
   provided for correspondence by the person or his representative.

(2) Where no fax number, electronic mail or postal address for correspondence has been provided by the person, notice of an immigration decision under paragraph (1)(c) may be delivered or sent by postal service to the last known or usual place of abode or place of business of the person or his representative.

(3) Notice given in accordance with paragraph (1) or (2) to the representative of the person, is to be taken to have been given to the person.

(4) In the case of a minor who does not have a representative, notice given in accordance with paragraph (1) or (2) to the parent, guardian or another adult who for the time being takes responsibility for the minor is taken to have been given to the minor.

Presumptions about receipt of notice

4.—(1) For the purpose of section 8(5) of the 2004 Act notice of an immigration decision shall, unless the contrary is proved, be treated as received;

(a) where the notice is sent by postal service in which delivery or receipt is recorded to an address, on the recorded date of delivery or receipt, or on the second day after the day it was posted, whichever is the earlier;

(b) in any other case in which the notice is sent by postal service on the second day after the day it was posted; or

(c) in any other case, on the day and time that it was communicated orally, given by hand or sent by electronic mail or fax.

(2) For the purposes of determining the second day after a notice is posted under paragraph (1) (a) and (b) any day which is not a business day shall be excluded.

(3) In this regulation 'business day' means any day other than Saturday or Sunday, a day which is a bank holiday under the Banking and Financial Dealings Act 1971 in the part of the United Kingdom from or to which the notice is sent, Christmas Day or Good Friday.

The Asylum Seekers (Reception Conditions) Regulations 2005
(SI 2005, No. 7)

Citation and commencement

1.—(1) These Regulations may be cited as the Asylum Seekers (Reception Conditions) Regulations 2005 and shall come into force on 5th February 2005.

(2) These Regulations shall only apply to a person whose claim for asylum is recorded on or after 5th February 2005.

Interpretation

2.—(1) In these Regulations—

(a) 'the 1999 Act' means the Immigration and Asylum Act 1999;

(b) 'asylum seeker' means a person who is at least 18 years old who has made a claim for asylum which has been recorded by the Secretary of State but not yet determined;

(c) 'claim for asylum' means a claim made by a third country national or a stateless person that to remove him or require him to leave the United Kingdom would be contrary to the United Kingdom's obligations under the Convention relating to the Status of Refugees done at Geneva on 28th July 1951 and its Protocol;

(d) 'family members' means, in so far as the family already existed in the country of origin, the following members of the asylum seeker's family who are present in the United Kingdom and who are asylum seekers or dependants on the asylum seeker's claim for asylum:

(i) the spouse of the asylum seeker or his unmarried partner in a stable relationship;

(ii) the minor child of the couple referred to in paragraph (2)(d)(i) or of the asylum seeker as long as the child is unmarried and dependent on the asylum seeker;

(e) 'Immigration Acts' has the same meaning as in section 44 of the Asylum and Immigration (Treatment of Claimants, etc.) Act 2004; and

(f) 'third country national' means a person who is not a national of a member State.

(2) For the purposes of these Regulations—

(a) a claim is determined on the date on which the Secretary of State notifies the asylum seeker of his decision on his claim or, if the asylum seeker appeals against the Secretary of State's decision, the date on which that appeal is disposed of; and

(b) an appeal is disposed of when it is no longer pending for the purposes of the Immigration Acts.

Families

3.—(1) When the Secretary of State is providing or arranging for the provision of accommodation for an asylum seeker and his family members under section 95 or 98 of the 1999 Act, he shall have regard to family unity and ensure, in so far as it is reasonably practicable to do so, that family members are accommodated together.

(2) Paragraph (1) shall only apply to those family members who confirm to the Secretary of State that they agree to being accommodated together.

(3) This regulation shall not apply in respect of a child when the Secretary of State is providing or arranging for the provision of accommodation for that child under section 122 of the 1999 Act.

Provisions for persons with special needs

4.—(1) This regulation applies to an asylum seeker or the family member of an asylum seeker who is a vulnerable person.

(2) When the Secretary of State is providing support or considering whether to provide support under section 95 or 98 of the 1999 Act to an asylum seeker or

his family member who is a vulnerable person, he shall take into account the special needs of that asylum seeker or his family member.

(3) A vulnerable person is—
  (a) a minor;
  (b) a disabled person;
  (c) an elderly person;
  (d) a pregnant woman;
  (e) a lone parent with a minor child; or
  (f) a person who has been subjected to torture, rape or other serious forms of psychological, physical or sexual violence;

who has had an individual evaluation of his situation that confirms he has special needs.

(4) Nothing in this regulation obliges the Secretary of State to carry out or arrange for the carrying out of an individual evaluation of a vulnerable person's situation to determine whether he has special needs.

Asylum support under section 95 or 98 of the 1999 Act

5.—(1) If an asylum seeker or his family member applies for support under section 95 of the 1999 Act and the Secretary of State thinks that the asylum seeker or his family member is eligible for support under that section he must offer the provision of support to the asylum seeker or his family member.

(2) If the Secretary of State thinks that the asylum seeker or his family member is eligible for support under section 98 of the 1999 Act he must offer the provision of support to the asylum seeker or his family member.

Tracing family members of unaccompanied minors

6.—(1) So as to protect an unaccompanied minor's best interests, the Secretary of State shall endeavour to trace the members of the minor's family as soon as possible after the minor makes his claim for asylum.

(2) In cases where there may be a threat to the life or integrity of the minor or the minor's close family, the Secretary of State shall take care to ensure that the collection, processing and circulation of information concerning the minor or his close family is undertaken on a confidential basis so as not to jeopardise his or their safety.

(3) For the purposes of this regulation—
  (a) an unaccompanied minor means a person below the age of eighteen who arrives in the United Kingdom unaccompanied by an adult responsible for him whether by law or custom and makes a claim for asylum;
  (b) a person shall be an unaccompanied minor until he is taken into the

care of such an adult or until he reaches the age of 18 whichever is the earlier;

(c) an unaccompanied minor also includes a minor who is left unaccompanied after he arrives in or enters the United Kingdom but before he makes his claim for asylum.

The Immigration (Procedure for Marriage) Regulations 2005
(SI 2005, No. 15)

Citation, commencement and interpretation

1. These Regulations may be cited as the Immigration (Procedure for Marriage) Regulations 2005 and shall come into force on 1st February 2005.
2. In these Regulations, 'the 2004 Act' means the Asylum and Immigration (Treatment of Claimants, etc) Act 2004.

Specified registration districts in England and Wales

3. The registration districts in England and Wales listed in Schedule 1 are specified for the purposes of section 19(2)(a) of the 2004 Act.

Prescribed registration districts in Scotland

4. Every registration district in Scotland is prescribed for the purposes of section 21(2)(a) of the 2004 Act.

Prescribed registrars in Northern Ireland

5. The registrar of every register office in Northern Ireland is prescribed for the purposes of section 23(2)(a) of the 2004 Act.

Specified classes of person

6.—(1) A person who is settled in the United Kingdom is hereby specified for the purpose of sections 19(3)(c), 21(3)(c) and 23(3)(c) of the 2004 Act.

(2) In this regulation, 'settled in the United Kingdom' has the meaning given in paragraph 6 of the immigration rules (which are the rules laid before Parliament under section 3(2) of the Immigration Act 1971).

Application for permission

7.—(1) A person seeking the permission of the Secretary of State to marry in the United Kingdom under section 19(3)(b), 21(3)(b) or 23(3)(b) of the 2004 Act shall—

(a) make an application in writing; and

(b) pay a fee on the submission of the application in accordance with regulation 8.

(2) The information set out in Schedule 2 is to be contained in or provided with the application.

8.—(1) The fee to be paid in connection with the application is £135.

(2) The fee is to be paid to the Immigration and Nationality Directorate of the Home Office—

(a) by a cheque or postal order crossed and made payable to 'Home Office Certificate of Approval'; or

(b) by means of any debit card or credit card which that Directorate accepts.

SCHEDULE 1

Regulation 3

SPECIFIED REGISTRATION DISTRICTS IN ENGLAND AND WALES

Aberconwy
Barking and Dagenham
Barnet
Birmingham
Blackburn with Darwen
Brent
Brighton and Hove
Bristol
Bury St Edmunds
Cambridge
Camden
Cardiff
Cardiganshire North
Carlisle
Colchester
Coventry
Crawley
Croydon
Dacorum
Ealing
Enfield
Exeter
Gloucester
Greenwich
Hackney
Hammersmith and Fulham
Hampshire North
Haringey
Harrow
Havering
Hillingdon
Hounslow
Hull
Islington
Kendal
Kensington and Chelsea
Kent
Kingston upon Thames
Lambeth
Leeds
Leicester
Lewisham
Lincolnshire
Liverpool
Manchester
Merton
Middlesbrough
Mid Powys
Milton Keynes
Newcastle upon Tyne
Newham
Northampton
North Surrey
Norwich

Nottingham
Oxfordshire
Pembrokeshire
Peterborough
Plymouth
Reading
Redbridge
Sheffield
Shrewsbury
Slough
Southampton
Southwark
Stoke on Trent
Swansea
Swindon
Tower Hamlets
Truro
Waltham Forest
Wandsworth
Westminster
Wrexham

SCHEDULE 2

Regulation 7

INFORMATION TO BE CONTAINED IN OR PROVIDED WITH AN APPLICATION FOR PERMISSION TO MARRY IN THE UNITED KINGDOM

(a) Information to be provided in respect of the applicant

Name
Date of birth
Name at birth (if different)
Nationality
Full postal address
Daytime telephone number
Passport or travel document number
Home Office reference number
Current immigration status
Date on which current leave to enter or remain in the United Kingdom was granted
Date on which that leave expires
Whether he has previously been married [or formed a civil partnership,] and if so, information showing that he is now free to marry
Two passport-sized photographs
Passport or travel document

(b) Information to be provided in respect of the other party to the intended marriage

Name
Date of birth
Name at birth (if different)
Nationality
Full postal address
Daytime telephone number
Passport or travel document number
Whether he is subject to immigration control, and if so:
  Home Office reference number

Current immigration status
Date on which current leave to enter or remain in the United Kingdom was granted
Date on which that leave expires
Whether he has previously been married [or formed a civil partnership,] and if so, information showing that he is now free to marry
Two passport-sized photographs
Passport or travel document

Note: Words in square brackets in Sch 2 inserted from 5 December 2005 (SI 2005/2917).

The Asylum and Immigration (Fast Track Time Limits) Order 2005

(SI 2005, No. 561 [L. 13])

The Lord Chancellor, in exercise of the powers conferred upon him by sections 26(8) and (9) of the Asylum and Immigration (Treatment of Claimants, etc.) Act 2004, after consulting in accordance with section 26(10) of that Act, hereby makes the following Order:

Citation and commencement

1. This Order may be cited as the Asylum and Immigration (Fast Track Time Limits) Order 2005 and shall come into force on 4th April 2005.

Interpretation

2.—(1) In this Order—
   (a) 'the 2002 Act' means the Nationality, Immigration and Asylum Act 2002;
   (b) 'the 2004 Act' means the Asylum and Immigration (Treatment of Claimants, etc.) Act 2004;
   (c) 'the Fast Track Procedure Rules' means the Asylum and Immigration Tribunal (Fast Track Procedure) Rules 2005;
   (d) 'the Tribunal' means the Asylum and Immigration Tribunal.

(2) Rule 3(5) of the Fast Track Procedure Rules applies for the purpose of articles 3 and 4 of this Order as it applies for the purpose of rules 5 and 15 of those Rules.

Time limit for making review application

3.—(1) This article applies in relation to an application under section 103A(1) of the 2002 Act for a review of the Tribunal's decision on an appeal where—

(a) Part 2 of the Fast Track Procedure Rules applied at all times to the appeal to the Tribunal; and
(b) the appellant has been continuously in detention under the Immigration Acts at a place or places specified in Schedule 2 to the Fast Track Procedure Rules since being served with notice of the immigration decision against which he is appealing.

(2) The period of time within which the application must be made in the cases specified in section 103A(3)(a) and (c) of the 2002 Act shall be 2 days beginning with the date on which the applicant is treated in accordance with rules under section 106 of the 2002 Act as receiving notice of the Tribunal's decision.

Time limit for notifying appropriate court following review by Tribunal member

4.—(1) This article applies in relation to an application under section 103A of the 2002 Act for a review of the Tribunal's decision on an appeal where—
(a) Section 1 of Part 3 of the Fast Track Procedure Rules applied at all times to the consideration of the application by a member of the Tribunal under paragraph 30(2) of Schedule 2 to the 2004 Act; and
(b) the appellant has been continuously in detention under the Immigration Acts at a place or places specified in Schedule 2 to the Fast Track Procedure Rules since being served with notice of the immigration decision against which he is appealing.

(2) The period of time within which the applicant must give notification to the appropriate court under paragraph 30(5)(b) of Schedule 2 to the 2004 Act shall be 2 days beginning with the date on which the applicant is treated in accordance with rules under section 106 of the 2002 Act as receiving notice under paragraph 30(4)(b) of that Schedule.

The Asylum and Immigration (Treatment of Claimants, etc.) Act 2004 (Commencement No. 5 and Transitional Provisions) Order 2005

(2005, SI No. 565 [c.25])

Citation and interpretation

1.—(1) This Order may be cited as the Asylum and Immigration (Treatment of Claimants, etc.) Act 2004 (Commencement No. 5 and Transitional Provisions) Order 2005.

(2) In this Order—

'the 2002 Act' means the Nationality, Immigration and Asylum Act 2002;

'the 2004 Act' means the Asylum and Immigration (Treatment of Claimants, etc.) Act 2004;

'adjudicator' means an adjudicator appointed, or treated as if appointed, under section 81 of the 2002 Act;

'appropriate appellate court' has the meaning given in section 103B(5) of the 2002 Act;

'appropriate court' has the meaning given in section 103A(9) of the 2002 Act;

'commencement' means the commencement date in article 2 of this Order;

'the old appeals provisions' means the following provisions, insofar as they continued to have effect immediately before commencement in relation to a pending appeal—

(i) Part IV of, and Schedule 4 to, the Immigration and Asylum Act 1999;

(ii) section 8(1) to (4) of the Asylum and Immigration Act 1993;

(iii) sections 13 to 17 of the Immigration Act 1971.

(3) In this Order, references to a section by number alone are to the section so numbered in the 2002 Act.

Commencement provisions

2. The following provisions of the 2004 Act shall come into force on 4th April 2005—

(a) section 26(1) to (5) and (7) to (10),

(b) section 26(6), except that the insertion of section 103D into the 2002 Act shall not come into force in Northern Ireland;

(c) Schedule 1; and

(d) Schedule 2.

Transitional provisions: general

3.—(1) Where, immediately before commencement, an adjudicator or the Immigration Appeal Tribunal—

(a) has completed the hearing of an appeal, but has not produced his or its written determination; or

(b) has produced a written determination of an appeal but that determination has not been served on all the parties,

the appeal shall continue after commencement as an appeal to an adjudicator or the Immigration Appeal Tribunal, as the case may be, until the determination has been served on all the parties.

(2) A member of the Asylum and Immigration Tribunal who, immediately before commencement was—

(a) an adjudicator; or

(b) a member of the Immigration Appeal Tribunal,

shall, notwithstanding section 26(1), (4) and (5) of the 2004 Act, be deemed to remain an adjudicator or member of the Immigration Appeal Tribunal after commencement, to the extent necessary for the purpose of completing the determination of an appeal in the circumstances specified in paragraph (1) of this article.

4. Subject to article 3—

(a) any appeal or application to an adjudicator which is pending immediately before commencement shall continue after commencement as an appeal or application to the Asylum and Immigration Tribunal; and

(b) any appeal to the Immigration Appeal Tribunal which is pending immediately before commencement shall continue after commencement as an appeal to the Asylum and Immigration Tribunal.

5.—(1) This article applies, subject to article 3, in relation to any appeal which immediately before commencement is—

(a) pending before an adjudicator, having been remitted to an adjudicator by a court or the Immigration Appeal Tribunal; or

(b) pending before the Immigration Appeal Tribunal.

(2) The Asylum and Immigration Tribunal shall, after commencement, subject to rules under section 106 of the 2002 Act deal with the appeal in the same manner as if it had originally decided the appeal and it was reconsidering its decision.

(3) Following the determination of the appeal by the Asylum and Immigration Tribunal, a party—

(a) may not apply to the appropriate court under section 103A(1); but

(b) may, subject to section 103B(3), bring a further appeal on a point of law to the appropriate appellate court under section 103B(1).

6.—(1) Where an application for permission to appeal to the Immigration Appeal Tribunal against an adjudicator's decision is pending immediately before commencement, it shall be treated after commencement as an application under section 103A(1) (subject to paragraph (4) and to article 9(4) below) for an order requiring the Asylum and Immigration Tribunal to reconsider the adjudicator's decision on the appeal.

(2) Where—

(a) an adjudicator has determined an appeal; and

(b) no application for permission to appeal to the Immigration Appeal Tribunal is pending immediately before commencement,

a party to the appeal may after commencement apply under section 103A(1) (as modified by paragraph (4) below) for an order requiring the Asylum and Immigration Tribunal to reconsider the adjudicator's decision on the appeal.

(3) Where, in a case to which paragraph (2) applies, a time period specified in rules under section 106 for applying for permission to appeal to the Immigration Appeal Tribunal has started to run before 4th April 2005, an application under section 103A(1) may, notwithstanding section 103A(3), be made at any time before the expiry of that time period.

(4) In relation to an application which, by virtue of this article, is made or treated as made under section 103A, that section shall apply with the modifications that—

(a) references to the Tribunal, except for the second such reference in section 103A(1), shall be interpreted as referring to the adjudicator who determined the appeal;

(b) references to the Tribunal's decision shall be interpreted as referring to the adjudicator's decision.

(5) Section 103D shall not apply in relation to a pending application which is treated as an application under section 103A by virtue of paragraph (1) of this article.

7.—(1) An application to a court under section 101(2) (review of Immigration Appeal Tribunal's decision upon application for permission to appeal) which is pending immediately before commencement shall continue after commencement as if that section had not been repealed.

(2) A party who, immediately before commencement, was entitled to make an application to a court under section 101(2), may make such an application after commencement as if that section had not been repealed.

(3) Where, by virtue of this article, an application under section 101(2) is made or continues after commencement—

(a) paragraphs (a) and (c) of section 101(3) shall apply in relation to the application, as if they had not been repealed; and

(b) the judge determining the application may—

(i) affirm the Immigration Appeal Tribunal's decision to refuse permission to appeal;

(ii) reverse the Immigration Appeal Tribunal's decision to grant permission to appeal; or

(iii) order the Asylum and Immigration Tribunal to reconsider the adjudicator's decision on the appeal.

8.—(1) An appeal to the Court of Appeal or Court of Session under section 103 (appeal from Immigration Appeal Tribunal), or an application to the Court of Appeal or Court of Session for permission to appeal under section 103, which is pending immediately before commencement shall continue after commencement as if that section had not been repealed.

(2) Where, immediately before commencement, an application to the Immigration Appeal Tribunal for permission to appeal under section 103 is pending—
   (a) the application shall, following commencement, be determined by the Asylum and Immigration Tribunal; and
   (b) section 103 shall continue to apply in relation to the application as if it had not been repealed, but with the modification in paragraph (5) below.

(3) A party who—
   (a) is granted permission to appeal under section 103; or
   (b) immediately before commencement, was entitled to apply to the Court of Appeal or Court of Session for permission to appeal under section 103,

   may, after commencement, appeal or apply for permission to appeal under section 103 (as the case may be) as if that section had not been repealed.

(4) A party who, immediately before commencement, was entitled to apply to the Immigration Appeal Tribunal for permission to appeal under section 103, may apply to the Asylum and Immigration Tribunal for permission to appeal under that section; and section 103 shall continue to apply in relation to the application as if it had not been repealed, but with the modification in paragraph (5) below.

(5) In relation to an application for permission to appeal under section 103 which is made to or determined by the Asylum and Immigration Tribunal pursuant to paragraph (2) or (4), section 103 shall apply with the modification that the references to the Tribunal in section 103(2) shall be interpreted as referring to the Asylum and Immigration Tribunal.

(6) Where, after commencement, the Court of Appeal or Court of Session determines an appeal under section 103, section 103B(4) shall apply in relation to the appeal as it would in relation to an appeal under section 103B(1), but with the modification that the references to the Tribunal in paragraphs (a), (b) and (f) shall be interpreted as references to the Immigration Appeal Tribunal.

Further transitional provisions: appeals under the old appeals provisions

9.—(1) Where, immediately before commencement, an appeal to an adjudicator is pending to which any of the old appeals provisions apply, those provisions shall continue to apply to the appeal after commencement, subject (except where article 3 applies) to the modification that any reference in those provisions to an adjudicator shall be treated as a reference to the Asylum and Immigration Tribunal.

(2) Subject to paragraphs (3) to (5), any provision in the old appeals provisions about appeals or applications to the Immigration Appeal Tribunal or to a court shall not have effect after commencement, and instead sections 103A to 103E shall have effect in relation to appeals decided under the old appeals provisions.

(3) Where sections 103A to 103E have effect by virtue of paragraph (2), they shall do so with the modification that references to section 82 or 83 shall be treated as including a reference to the old appeals provisions.

(4) Where an appeal or application for permission to appeal to the Immigration Appeal Tribunal under the old appeals provisions is pending immediately before commencement—

  (a) articles 4(b) and 5, or article 6(1), of this Order (as appropriate) shall apply; but

  (b) if, under the old appeals provisions, the appeal or application was not restricted to the ground that the adjudicator made an error of law, then it shall not be so restricted following commencement.

(5) In relation to an appeal which has been determined by the Immigration Appeal Tribunal under the old appeals provisions before commencement, article 8 of this Order shall apply with the references to section 103 being treated as including references to corresponding provisions in the old appeals provisions.

The Community Legal Service (Asylum and Immigration Appeals) Regulations 2005

(SI 2005, No. 966)

Citation and commencement

1. These Regulations may be cited as the Community Legal Service (Asylum and Immigration Appeals) Regulations 2005 and shall come into force on 4th April 2005.

Scope of these Regulations

2. These Regulations have effect only in relation to appeals decided in England and Wales.

Interpretation

3.—(1) In these Regulations—

'the 1999 Act' means the Access to Justice Act 1999;

'the 2002 Act' means the Nationality, Immigration and Asylum Act 2002;

'the 2004 Act' means the Asylum and Immigration (Treatment of Claimants, etc.) Act 2004;

'business day' means any day other than a Saturday or Sunday, a bank holiday, Christmas Day, 27th to 31st December or Good Friday;

'Commission' means the Legal Services Commission established under section 1 of the 1999 Act;

'contract' means a contract between the Commission and a supplier under section 6(3)(a) of the 1999 Act;

'counsel' means a barrister in independent practice;

'fast track proceedings' means any immigration review proceedings in relation to which, pursuant to an order under section 26(8) of the 2004 Act, the time period for making an application under section 103A(1) of the 2002 Act is a period of less than 5 days;

'Funding Code' means the code approved under section 9 of the 1999 Act;

'Immigration review proceedings' means—

(i) applications to the High Court under section 103A of the 2002 Act (including applications which are considered by a member of the Tribunal pursuant to paragraph 30 of Schedule 2 to the 2004 Act); and

(ii) proceedings for the reconsideration of an appeal by the Tribunal pursuant to an order under section 103A of the 2002 Act;

'Legal Representation' has the meaning given in the Funding Code;

'section 103D order' means an order under section 103D(1) or 103D(3) of the 2002 Act;

'supplier' means a solicitor or other person who is an authorised litigator within the meaning of section 119(1) of the Courts and Legal Services Act 1990, having a contract for the provision of services including Legal Representation in immigration review proceedings;

'Tribunal' means the Asylum and Immigration Tribunal.

(2) References to a section by number alone refer to the section so numbered in the 2002 Act.

General restrictions on power to make section 103D orders

4.—(1) The High Court or the Tribunal shall only make a section 103D order in immigration review proceedings where an appellant is represented by a supplier acting pursuant to a grant of Legal Representation.

(2) The High Court or the Tribunal shall not make a section 103D order in fast track proceedings.

(3) Regulations 5 to 8 apply in relation to immigration review proceedings in which the High Court or the Tribunal has power, under section 103D(1)–(3) and this regulation, to make a section 103D order.

Criteria for making orders under section 103D(1)

5.—(1) The appropriate court must exercise the power to make an order under section 103D(1) in accordance with this regulation.

(2) If, upon a section 103A application, the appropriate court makes an order for reconsideration, subject to paragraph (5) it must not make an order under section 103D(1)

(3) If the High Court makes a reference under section 103C of the 2002 Act, it must make an order under section 103D(1).

(4) If the appropriate court dismisses or makes no order on the section 103A application, it may make an order under section 103D(1) only if—

(a) there has been a change in any relevant circumstances or a change in the law since the application was made; and

(b) at the time when the application was made, there was a significant prospect that the appeal would be allowed upon reconsideration.

(5) The appropriate court may, on an application in writing by a supplier or counsel instructed by the supplier, make an order under section 103D(1) where it has made an order for reconsideration, but no reconsideration of the appeal takes place.

(6) In this regulation, 'the appropriate court' means—

(a) the High Court; or

(b) a member of the Tribunal who considers a section 103A application by virtue of paragraph 30 of Schedule 2 to the 2004 Act.

Criteria for making orders under section 103D(3)

6.—(1) The Tribunal must exercise the power to make an order under section 103D(3) in accordance with this regulation.

(2) If the Tribunal allows an appeal on reconsideration, it must make an order under section 103D(3).

(3) If the Tribunal does not allow an appeal, it must not make an order under section 103D(3) unless it is satisfied that, at the time when the appellant made the section 103A application, there was a significant prospect that the appeal would be allowed upon reconsideration.

(4) If, where paragraph (3) applies, the Tribunal decides not to make an order under section 103D(3), it must give reasons for its decision.

Review by Tribunal of decision not to make order under section 103D(3)

7.—(1) A supplier, or counsel instructed by a supplier, may apply to the Tribunal in writing for a review of a decision by the Tribunal not to make an order under section 103D(3).

(2) An application under this regulation must be filed within 10 business days after the supplier is served with the Tribunal's decision not to make an order, or such longer period as the Tribunal may allow.

(3) A review shall be carried out by a senior immigration judge who was not the member of the Tribunal, or a member of the constitution of the Tribunal, which made the original decision.

(4) The senior immigration judge may—

(a) carry out the review without a hearing; or

(b) hold an oral hearing, if one is requested by the supplier or counsel.

(5) The senior immigration judge may—

(a) make an order under section 103D(3); or

(b) confirm the Tribunal's decision not to make an order.

(6) The senior immigration judge must give reasons for his decision on a review.

Terms and effect of section 103D orders

8.—(1) Subject to paragraph (2), a section 103D order shall have effect as an order for payment of all the costs incurred by a supplier representing the appellant in the proceedings to which the order relates, including the fees of counsel instructed by the supplier, for which payment is allowable under the terms of the contract between the Commission and the supplier.

(2) In relation to proceedings in which a supplier has instructed counsel, the High Court or the Tribunal may in special circumstances make a section 103D order—

(a) in respect of counsel's fees only; or

(b) in respect of the costs incurred by the supplier excluding counsel's fees.

(3) A section 103D order must not specify—

(a) the amount to be paid by the Commission; or

(b) the person or persons to whom payment is to be made,

and the Commission shall determine those matters in accordance with the terms of its contract with the supplier.

Modification to the Funding Code, etc.

9.—(1) Where an appellant applies for Legal Representation to bring immigration review proceedings, the Funding Code shall apply subject to the modifications that—

(a) in Section 5 of the Funding Code Criteria, the criteria in section 5.4 (standard criteria for Legal Representation and Support Funding) shall not apply; and
(b) in Section 13 of the Funding Code Criteria, sections 13.4 (prospects of success) and 13.5 (cost benefit) shall not apply.

(2) Where Legal Representation is granted for immigration review proceedings to be brought by an appellant, the effect of the grant shall be that—
(a) the Commission shall, subject to the provisions of its contract with the supplier, pay for—
(i) services consisting of advising on the merits of making an application under section 103A; and
(ii) any disbursements incurred by the supplier, other than counsel's fees,
whether or not a section 103D order is made; but
(b) otherwise, payment by the Commission for services provided by the supplier, or by counsel instructed by the supplier, shall be conditional upon the High Court or the Tribunal making a section 103D order.

(3) Where Legal Representation has been granted for immigration review proceedings to be brought by an appellant, section 10(1) of the 1999 Act shall apply, notwithstanding that payment by the Commission for services is conditional upon a section 103D order being made.

(4) This regulation does not apply in relation to fast track proceedings.

The Immigration and Asylum (Provision of Accommodation to Failed Asylum-Seekers) Regulations 2005
(SI 2005, No. 930)

Citation and commencement

1.—(1) These Regulations may be cited as the Immigration and Asylum (Provision of Accommodation to Failed Asylum-Seekers) Regulations 2005 and shall come into force on 31st March 2005.

(2) These Regulations apply to a person who is receiving accommodation when these Regulations come into force to the same extent as they apply to a person provided with accommodation after these Regulations come into force.

Interpretation

2. In these Regulations—

'the 1999 Act' means the Immigration and Asylum Act 1999;

'destitute' is to be construed in accordance with section 95(3) of the 1999 Act; and

'reporting requirement' means a condition or restriction which requires a person to report to the police, an immigration officer or the Secretary of State, and is imposed under—

(a) paragraph 21 of Schedule 2 to the Immigration Act 1971 (temporary admission or release from detention),

(b) paragraph 22 of that Schedule, or

(c) paragraph 2 or 5 of Schedule 3 to that Act (pending deportation).

Eligibility for and provision of accommodation to a failed asylum-seeker

3.—(1) Subject to regulations 4 and 6, the criteria to be used in determining the matters referred to in paragraphs (a) and (b) of section 4(5) of the 1999 Act in respect of a person falling within section 4(2) or (3) of that Act are—

(a) that he appears to the Secretary of State to be destitute, and

(b) that one or more of the conditions set out in paragraph (2) are satisfied in relation to him.

(2) Those conditions are that—

(a) he is taking all reasonable steps to leave the United Kingdom or place himself in a position in which he is able to leave the United Kingdom, which may include complying with attempts to obtain a travel document to facilitate his departure;

(b) he is unable to leave the United Kingdom by reason of a physical impediment to travel or for some other medical reason;

(c) he is unable to leave the United Kingdom because in the opinion of the Secretary of State there is currently no viable route of return available;

(d) he has made an application for judicial review of a decision in relation to his asylum claim—

(i) in England and Wales, and has been granted permission to proceed pursuant to Part 54 of the Civil Procedure Rules 1998,

(ii) in Scotland, pursuant to Chapter 58 of the Rules of the Court of Session 1994 or

(iii) in Northern Ireland, and has been granted leave pursuant to Order 53 of the Rules of Supreme Court (Northern Ireland) 1980; or

(e) the provision of accommodation is necessary for the purpose of avoiding a breach of a person's Convention rights, within the meaning of the Human Rights Act 1998.

Community activities: general

4.—(1) Where the Secretary of State so determines, the continued provision of accommodation to a person falling within section 4(2) or (3) of the 1999 Act is to be conditional upon that person's performance of or participation in such community activity as is described in this regulation and is from time to time notified to the person in accordance with regulation 5.

(2) In making the determination referred to in paragraph (1), regard will be had to the following matters—
  (a) the length of time that he believes the person will continue to be eligible for accommodation,
  (b) the arrangements that have been made for the performance of or participation in community activities in the area in which the person is being provided with accommodation,
  (c) any relevant health and safety standards which are agreed between the Secretary of State and a person with whom he has made arrangements for the provision of community activities in the person's area,
  (d) whether the person is in the Secretary of State's belief unable to perform or participate in community activities because of a physical or mental impairment or for some other medical reason,
  (e) whether the person is in the Secretary of State's belief unable to perform or participate in community activities because of a responsibility for the care of a dependant child or of a dependant who because of a physical or mental impairment is unable to look after himself, and
  (f) any relevant information provided to the Secretary of State, regarding the person's suitability to perform or participate in particular tasks, activities or a range of tasks or activities.

(3) Paragraph (1) does not apply in relation to a person who is under the age of 18.

(4) No condition on the continued provision of accommodation will require a person to perform or participate in community activities for more than 35 hours in any week, including the weekend.

Community activities: Relevant information

5. A notice under regulation 4(1) falls within this regulation if it contains the following information—
  (a) the task, activity or range of tasks or activities in the area in which the person lives which are to be performed or participated in as community activities,
  (b) the geographical location at which the community activities will be performed or participated in,
  (c) the maximum number of hours per week that the person will be expected to perform or participate in community activities, where it is possible for the Secretary of State to so specify, and
  (d) the date upon which the task, activity or range of tasks or activities to be performed or participated in as community activities will commence and,

where it is possible for the Secretary of State to so specify, the length of time such community activities will last.

Other conditions on continued provision of accommodation

6.—(1) The continued provision of accommodation to a person falling within section 4(2) or (3) of the 1999 Act is to be subject to such other conditions falling within paragraph (2) as—

(a) the Secretary of State may from time to time determine, and

(b) are set out in a notice to that person in writing.

(2) A condition falls within this paragraph to the extent that it relates to—

(a) complying with specified standards of behaviour,

(b) complying with a reporting requirement,

(c) complying with a requirement—

(i) to reside at an authorised address, or

(ii) if he is absent from an authorised address without the permission of the Secretary of State, to ensure that that absence is for no more than seven consecutive days and nights or for no more than a total of fourteen days and nights in any six month period, or

(d) complying with specified steps to facilitate his departure from the United Kingdom.

The Immigration (Procedure for Formation of Civil Partnerships) Regulations 2005
(SI 2005, No. 2917)

Citation, commencement and interpretation

1.—(1) These Regulations may be cited as the Immigration (Procedure for Formation of Civil Partnerships) Regulations 2005.

(2) Subject to paragraph (3), these Regulations shall come into force on 5th December 2005.

(3) This regulation, regulations 2 and 3 and Schedule 1 shall come into force on 14th November 2005.

2. In these Regulations—

(a) 'the 2004 Act' means the Civil Partnership Act 2004; and

(b) 'civil partnership' means a civil partnership which exists under or by virtue of the 2004 Act.

Application for permission

3.—(1) A person seeking the permission of the Secretary of State to form a civil partnership in the United Kingdom under paragraph 2(1)(b) of Schedule 23 to the 2004 Act shall—

(a) make an application in writing; and

(b) pay a fee of £135 on the submission of the application.

(2) The information set out in Schedule 1 to these Regulations is to be contained in or provided with the application.

(3) The fee is to be paid to the Immigration and Nationality Directorate of the Home Office—

(a) by a cheque or postal order crossed and made payable to 'Home Office Certificates of Approval'; or

(b) by means of any debit card or credit card which that Directorate accepts.

Specified classes of person

4.—(1) The following persons are specified for the purpose of paragraph 2(1)(c) of Schedule 23 to the 2004 Act—

(a) persons who are settled in the United Kingdom; and

(b) persons to whom Schedule 3 to the 2004 Act applies.

(2) In this regulation, 'settled in the United Kingdom' has the meaning given in paragraph 6 of the immigration rules (which are the rules laid before Parliament under section 3(2) of the Immigration Act 1971).

Specified registration authorities in England and Wales

5.—(1) The registration authorities in England and Wales listed in the left-hand column of Schedule 2 to these Regulations are specified for the purposes of paragraph 4(1)(a) of Schedule 23 to the 2004 Act.

(2) An employee or officer or other person provided by a specified registration authority is a 'relevant individual' for the purposes of paragraph 4(1)(b) and (2) of Schedule 23 to the 2004 Act if he—

(a) is authorised by that authority to attest notices of proposed civil partnership; and

(b) is located at the office specified in relation to that authority in the right-hand column of Schedule 2 to these Regulations.

Specified registration districts in Scotland

6. Every registration district in Scotland is specified for the purposes of paragraph 9(1)(a) of Schedule 23 to the 2004 Act.

Prescribed registrars in Northern Ireland

7. The registrar of every register office in Northern Ireland is prescribed for the purposes of paragraph 13(1)(a) of Schedule 23 to the 2004 Act.

8. . . . Amends SI 2005/15.

Regulation 3

Schedule 1

Information to be Contained in or Provided with an Application for Permission to Form a Civil Partnership in the United Kingdom

(a) Information to be provided in respect of the applicant

Name
Date of birth
Name at birth (if different)
Nationality
Full postal address
Daytime telephone number
Passport or travel document number
Home Office reference number
Current immigration status
Date on which current leave to enter or remain in the United Kingdom was granted
Date on which that leave expires
Whether he has previously been married or formed a civil partnership, and if so, information showing that he is now free to form a civil partnership
Two passport-sized photographs
Passport or travel document

(b) Information to be provided in respect of the other party to the proposed civil partnership

Name
Date of birth
Name at birth (if different)
Nationality
Full postal address
Daytime telephone number
Passport or travel document number
Whether he is subject to immigration control and, if so:
  Home Office reference number
  Current immigration status
  Date on which current leave to enter or remain in the United Kingdom was granted
  Date on which that leave expires

Whether he has previously been married or formed a civil partnership, and if so, information showing that he is now free to form a civil partnership
Two passport-sized photographs
Passport or travel document

Regulation 5

Schedule 2

Specified Registration Authorities in England & Wales

Specified registration authorities	*Offices specified in relation to specified registration authorities*
The London Borough of Barking and Dagenham	The register office for Barking and Dagenham
The London Borough of Barnet	The register office for Barnet
City of Birmingham	The register office for Birmingham
Borough of Blackburn with Darwen	The register office for Blackburn with Darwen
London Borough of Brent	The register office for Brent
City of Brighton and Hove	The register office for Brighton and Hove
City of Bristol	The register office for Bristol
County of Cambridgeshire	The register office for Cambridge
London Borough of Camden	The register office for Camden
City and County of Cardiff	The register office for Cardiff
County of Ceredigion	The register office for Cardiganshire North
County Borough of Conwy	The register office for Aberconwy
County of Cornwall	The register office for Truro
City of Coventry	The register office for Coventry
London Borough of Croydon	The register office for Croydon
County of Cumbria	The register office for Carlisle or the register office for Kendal
County of Devon	The register office for Exeter
London Borough of Ealing	The register office for Ealing
London Borough of Enfield	The register office for Enfield
County of Essex	The register office for Colchester
County of Gloucestershire	The register office for Gloucester
London Borough of Greenwich	The register office for Greenwich
London Borough of Hackney	The register office for Hackney
London Borough of Hammersmith and Fulham	The register office for Hammersmith and Fulham
County of Hampshire	The register office for Hampshire North
London Borough of Haringey	The register office for Haringey
London Borough of Harrow	The register office for Harrow
London Borough of Havering	The register office for Havering

County of Hertfordshire	The register office for Dacorum
London Borough of Hillingdon	The register office for Hillingdon
London Borough of Hounslow	The register office for Hounslow
Royal Borough of Kensington and Chelsea	The register office for Kensington and Chelsea
County of Kent	The register office for Kent
City of Kingston upon Hull	The register office for Hull
Royal Borough of Kingston upon Thames	The register office for Kingston upon Thames
London Borough of Islington	The register office for Islington
London Borough of Lambeth	The register office for Lambeth
City of Leeds	The register office for Leeds
City of Leicester	The register office for Leicester
London Borough of Lewisham	The register office for Lewisham
County of Lincolnshire	The register office for Lincolnshire
City of Liverpool	The register office for Liverpool
Borough of Luton	The register office for Luton
City of Manchester	The register office for Manchester
London Borough of Merton	The register office for Merton
Borough of Middlesbrough	The register office for Middlesbrough
Borough of Milton Keynes	The register office for Milton Keynes
City of Newcastle upon Tyne	The register office for Newcastle upon Tyne
London Borough of Newham	The register office for Newham
County of Norfolk	The register office for Norwich
County of Northamptonshire	The register office for Northampton
City of Nottingham	The register office for Nottingham
County of Oxfordshire	The register office for Oxfordshire
County of Pembrokeshire	The register office for Pembrokeshire
City of Peterborough	The register office for Peterborough
City of Plymouth	The register office for Plymouth
County of Powys	The register office for Mid Powys
Borough of Reading	The register office for Reading
London Borough of Redbridge	The register office for Redbridge
City of Sheffield	The register office for Sheffield
County of Shropshire	The register office for Shropshire
Borough of Slough	The register office for Slough
City of Southampton	The register office for Southampton
London Borough of Southwark	The register office for Southwark
City of Stoke on Trent	The register office for Stoke on Trent
County of Suffolk	The register office for Bury St Edmunds
County of Surrey	The register office for North Surrey
City and County of Swansea	The register office for Swansea
Borough of Swindon	The register office for Swindon
London Borough of Tower Hamlets	The register office for Tower Hamlets
London Borough of Waltham Forest	The register office for Waltham Forest

London Borough of Wandsworth	The register office for Wandsworth
City of Westminster	The register office for Westminster
County of West Sussex	The register office for Crawley
County Borough of Wrexham	The register office for Wrexham

The Immigration (European Economic Area) Regulations 2006
(SI 2006, No. 1003)

CONTENTS

Part 4

Refusal of Admission and Removal etc

Part 5

Procedure in Relation to EEA Decisions

Part 6

Appeals Under These Regulations

Part 7

General

Schedules

Part 1

Interpretation etc

Citation and commencement

1. These Regulations may be cited as the Immigration (European Economic Area) Regulations 2006 and shall come into force on 30th April 2006.

General interpretation

2.—(1) In these Regulations—

'the 1971 Act' means the Immigration Act 1971;

'the 1999 Act' means the Immigration and Asylum Act 1999;

'the 2002 Act' means the Nationality, Immigration and Asylum Act 2002;

'civil partner' does not include a party to a civil partnership of convenience;

'decision maker' means the Secretary of State, an immigration officer or an entry clearance officer (as the case may be);

'document certifying permanent residence' means a document issued to an EEA national, in accordance with regulation 18, as proof of the holder's permanent right of residence under regulation 15 as at the date of issue;

'EEA decision' means a decision under these Regulations that concerns a person's—

(a) entitlement to be admitted to the United Kingdom;
(b) entitlement to be issued with or have renewed, or not to have revoked, a registration certificate, residence card, document certifying permanent residence or permanent residence card; or
(c) removal from the United Kingdom;

'EEA family permit' means a document issued to a person, in accordance with regulation 12, in connection with his admission to the United Kingdom;

'EEA national' means a national of an EEA State;

'EEA State' means—

(a) a member State, other than the United Kingdom;
(b) Norway, Iceland or Liechtenstein; or
(c) Switzerland;

'entry clearance' has the meaning given in section 33(1) of the 1971 Act;

'entry clearance officer' means a person responsible for the grant or refusal of entry clearance;

'immigration rules' has the meaning given in section 33(1) of the 1971 Act;

'military service' means service in the armed forces of an EEA State;

'permanent residence card' means a card issued to a person who is not an EEA national, in accordance with regulation 18, as proof of the holder's permanent right of residence under regulation 15 as at the date of issue;

'registration certificate' means a certificate issued to an EEA national, in accordance with regulation 16, as proof of the holder's right of residence in the United Kingdom as at the date of issue;

'relevant EEA national' in relation to an extended family member has the meaning given in regulation 8(6);

'residence card' means a card issued to a person who is not an EEA national, in accordance with regulation 17, as proof of the holder's right of residence in the United Kingdom as at the date of issue;

'spouse' does not include a party to a marriage of convenience;

'United Kingdom national' means a person who falls to be treated as a national of the United Kingdom for the purposes of the Community Treaties.

(2) Paragraph (1) is subject to paragraph 1(a) of Schedule 4 (transitional provisions).

Continuity of residence

3.—(1) This regulation applies for the purpose of calculating periods of continuous residence in the United Kingdom under regulation 5(1) and regulation 15.

(2) Continuity of residence is not affected by—

(a) periods of absence from the United Kingdom which do not exceed six months in total in any year;

(b) periods of absence from the United Kingdom on military service; or

(c) any one absence from the United Kingdom not exceeding twelve months for an important reason such as pregnancy and childbirth, serious illness, study or vocational training or an overseas posting.

(3) But continuity of residence is broken if a person is removed from the United Kingdom under regulation 19(3).

'Worker', 'self-employed person', 'self-sufficient person' and 'student'

4.—(1) In these Regulations—

(a) 'worker' means a worker within the meaning of Article 39 of the Treaty establishing the European Community;

(b) 'self-employed person' means a person who establishes himself in order to pursue activity as a self-employed person in accordance with Article 43 of the Treaty establishing the European Community;

(c) 'self-sufficient person' means a person who has—

(i) sufficient resources not to become a burden on the social assistance system of the United Kingdom during his period of residence; and

(ii) comprehensive sickness insurance cover in the United Kingdom;

(d) 'student' means a person who—

(i) is enrolled at a private or public establishment, included on the Department for Education and Skills' Register of Education and Training Providers or financed from public funds, for the principal purpose of following a course of study, including vocational training;

(ii) has comprehensive sickness insurance cover in the United Kingdom; and

(iii) assures the Secretary of State, by means of a declaration, or by such equivalent means as the person may choose, that he has sufficient resources not to become a burden on the social assistance system of the United Kingdom during his period of residence.

(2) For the purposes of paragraph (1)(c), where family members of the person concerned reside in the United Kingdom and their right to reside is dependent upon their being family members of that person—

(a) the requirement for that person to have sufficient resources not to become a burden on the social assistance system of the United Kingdom during his period of residence shall only be satisfied if his resources and those of the family members are sufficient to avoid him and the family members becoming such a burden;

(b) the requirement for that person to have comprehensive sickness insurance cover in the United Kingdom shall only be satisfied if he and his family members have such cover.

(3) For the purposes of paragraph (1)(d), where family members of the person concerned reside in the United Kingdom and their right to reside is dependent upon their being family members of that person, the requirement for that person to assure the Secretary of State that he has sufficient resources not to become a burden on the social assistance system of the United Kingdom during his period of residence shall only be satisfied if he assures the Secretary of State that his resources and those of the family members are sufficient to avoid him and the family members becoming such a burden.

(4) For the purposes of paragraphs (1)(c) and (d) and paragraphs (2) and (3), the resources of the person concerned and, where applicable, any family members, are to be regarded as sufficient if they exceed the maximum level of resources which a United Kingdom national and his family members may possess if he is to become eligible for social assistance under the United Kingdom benefit system.

'Worker or self-employed person who has ceased activity'

5.—(1) In these Regulations, 'worker or self-employed person who has ceased activity' means an EEA national who satisfies the conditions in paragraph (2), (3), (4) or (5).

(2) A person satisfies the conditions in this paragraph if he—

(a) terminates his activity as a worker or self-employed person and—

(i) has reached the age at which he is entitled to a state pension on the date on which he terminates his activity; or

(ii) in the case of a worker, ceases working to take early retirement;

(b) pursued his activity as a worker or self-employed person in the United Kingdom for at least twelve months prior to the termination; and

(c) resided in the United Kingdom continuously for more than three years prior to the termination.

(3) A person satisfies the conditions in this paragraph if—

(a) he terminates his activity in the United Kingdom as a worker or self-employed person as a result of a permanent incapacity to work; and

(b) either—

(i) he resided in the United Kingdom continuously for more than two years prior to the termination; or

(ii) the incapacity is the result of an accident at work or an occupational disease that entitles him to a pension payable in full or in part by an institution in the United Kingdom.

(4) A person satisfies the conditions in this paragraph if—

(a) he is active as a worker or self-employed person in an EEA State but retains his place of residence in the United Kingdom, to which he returns as a rule at least once a week; and

(b) prior to becoming so active in that EEA State, he had been continuously resident and continuously active as a worker or self-employed person in the United Kingdom for at least three years.

(5) A person who satisfies the condition in paragraph (4)(a) but not the condition in paragraph (4)(b) shall, for the purposes of paragraphs (2) and (3), be treated as being active and resident in the United Kingdom during any period in which he is working or self-employed in the EEA State.

(6) The conditions in paragraphs (2) and (3) as to length of residence and activity as a worker or self-employed person shall not apply in relation to a person whose spouse or civil partner is a United Kingdom national.

(7) For the purposes of this regulation—

(a) periods of inactivity for reasons not of the person's own making;

(b) periods of inactivity due to illness or accident; and

(c) in the case of a worker, periods of involuntary unemployment duly recorded by the relevant employment office,

shall be treated as periods of activity as a worker or self-employed person, as the case may be.

'Qualified person'

6.—(1) In these Regulations, 'qualified person' means a person who is an EEA national and in the United Kingdom as—
(a) a jobseeker;
(b) a worker;
(c) a self-employed person;
(d) a self-sufficient person; or
(e) a student.

(2) A person who is no longer working shall not cease to be treated as a worker for the purpose of paragraph (1)(b) if—
(a) he is temporarily unable to work as the result of an illness or accident;
(b) he is in duly recorded involuntary unemployment after having been employed in the United Kingdom, provided that he has registered as a jobseeker with the relevant employment office and—
(i) he was employed for one year or more before becoming unemployed;
(ii) he has been unemployed for no more than six months; or
(iii) he can provide evidence that he is seeking employment in the United Kingdom and has a genuine chance of being engaged;
(c) he is involuntarily unemployed and has embarked on vocational training; or
(d) he has voluntarily ceased working and embarked on vocational training that is related to his previous employment.

(3) A person who is no longer in self-employment shall not cease to be treated as a self-employed person for the purpose of paragraph (1)(c) if he is temporarily unable to pursue his activity as a self-employed person as the result of an illness or accident.

(4) For the purpose of paragraph (1)(a), 'jobseeker' means a person who enters the United Kingdom in order to seek employment and can provide evidence that he is seeking employment and has a genuine chance of being engaged.

Family member

7.—(1) Subject to paragraph (2), for the purposes of these Regulations the following persons shall be treated as the family members of another person—
(a) his spouse or his civil partner;
(b) direct descendants of his, his spouse or his civil partner who are—
(i) under 21; or
(ii) dependants of his, his spouse or his civil partner;
(c) dependent direct relatives in his ascending line or that of his spouse or his civil partner;

(d) a person who is to be treated as the family member of that other person under paragraph (3).

(2) A person shall not be treated under paragraph (1)(b) or (c) as the family member of a student residing in the United Kingdom after the period of three months beginning on the date on which the student is admitted to the United Kingdom unless—

(a) in the case of paragraph (b), the person is the dependent child of the student or of his spouse or civil partner; or

(b) the student also falls within one of the other categories of qualified persons mentioned in regulation 6(1).

(3) Subject to paragraph (4), a person who is an extended family member and has been issued with an EEA family permit, a registration certificate or a residence card shall be treated as the family member of the relevant EEA national for as long as he continues to satisfy the conditions in regulation 8(2), (3), (4) or (5) in relation to that EEA national and the permit, certificate or card has not ceased to be valid or been revoked.

(4) Where the relevant EEA national is a student, the extended family member shall only be treated as the family member of that national under paragraph (3) if either the EEA family permit was issued under regulation 12(2), the registration certificate was issued under regulation 16(5) or the residence card was issued under regulation 17(4).

'Extended family member'

8.—(1) In these Regulations 'extended family member' means a person who is not a family member of an EEA national under regulation 7(1)(a), (b) or (c) and who satisfies the conditions in paragraph (2), (3), (4) or (5).

(2) A person satisfies the condition in this paragraph if the person is a relative of an EEA national, his spouse or his civil partner and—

(a) the person is residing in an EEA State in which the EEA national also resides and is dependent upon the EEA national or is a member of his household;

(b) the person satisfied the condition in paragraph (a) and is accompanying the EEA national to the United Kingdom or wishes to join him there; or

(c) the person satisfied the condition in paragraph (a), has joined the EEA national in the United Kingdom and continues to be dependent upon him or to be a member of his household.

(3) A person satisfies the condition in this paragraph if the person is a relative of an EEA national or his spouse or his civil partner and, on serious health grounds, strictly requires the personal care of the EEA national his spouse or his civil partner.

(4) A person satisfies the condition in this paragraph if the person is a relative of an EEA national and would meet the requirements in the immigration rules (other than those relating to entry clearance) for indefinite leave to enter or remain in the United Kingdom as a dependent relative of the EEA national were the EEA national a person present and settled in the United Kingdom.

(5) A person satisfies the condition in this paragraph if the person is the partner of an EEA national (other than a civil partner) and can prove to the decision maker that he is in a durable relationship with the EEA national.

(6) In these Regulations 'relevant EEA national' means, in relation to an extended family member, the EEA national who is or whose spouse or civil partner is the relative of the extended family member for the purpose of paragraph (2), (3) or (4) or the EEA national who is the partner of the extended family member for the purpose of paragraph (5).

Family members of United Kingdom nationals

9.—(1) If the conditions in paragraph (2) are satisfied, these Regulations apply to a person who is the family member of a United Kingdom national as if the United Kingdom national were an EEA national.

(2) The conditions are that—

(a) the United Kingdom national is residing in an EEA State as a worker or self-employed person or was so residing before returning to the United Kingdom; and

(b) if the family member of the United Kingdom national is his spouse or civil partner, the parties are living together in the EEA State or had entered into the marriage or civil partnership and were living together in that State before the United Kingdom national returned to the United Kingdom.

(3) Where these Regulations apply to the family member of a United Kingdom national the United Kingdom national shall be treated as holding a valid passport issued by an EEA State for the purpose of the application of regulation 13 to that family member.

'Family member who has retained the right of residence'

10.—(1) In these Regulations, "family member who has retained the right of residence" means, subject to paragraph (8), a person who satisfies the conditions in paragraph (2), (3), (4) or (5).

(2) A person satisfies the conditions in this paragraph if—

(a) he was a family member of a qualified person when the qualified person died;

(b) he resided in the United Kingdom in accordance with these Regulations for at least the year immediately before the death of the qualified person; and

(c) he satisfies the condition in paragraph (6).

(3) A person satisfies the conditions in this paragraph if—

(a) he is the direct descendant of—

(i) a qualified person who has died;

(ii) a person who ceased to be a qualified person on ceasing to reside in the United Kingdom; or

(iii) the person who was the spouse or civil partner of the qualified person mentioned in sub-paragraph (i) when he died or is the spouse or civil partner of the person mentioned in sub-paragraph (ii); and

(b) he was attending an educational course in the United Kingdom immediately before the qualified person died or ceased to be a qualified person and continues to attend such a course.

(4) A person satisfies the conditions in this paragraph if the person is the parent with actual custody of a child who satisfies the condition in paragraph (3).

(5) A person satisfies the conditions in this paragraph if—

(a) he ceased to be a family member of a qualified person on the termination of the marriage or civil partnership of the qualified person;

(b) he was residing in the United Kingdom in accordance with these Regulations at the date of the termination;

(c) he satisfies the condition in paragraph (6); and

(d) either—

(i) prior to the initiation of the proceedings for the termination of the marriage or the civil partnership the marriage or civil partnership had lasted for at least three years and the parties to the marriage or civil partnership had resided in the United Kingdom for at least one year during its duration;

(ii) the former spouse or civil partner of the qualified person has custody of a child of the qualified person;

(iii) the former spouse or civil partner of the qualified person has the right of access to a child of the qualified person under the age of 18 and a court has ordered that such access must take place in the United Kingdom; or

(iv) the continued right of residence in the United Kingdom of the person is warranted by particularly difficult circumstances, such as he or another family member having been a victim of domestic violence while the marriage or civil partnership was subsisting.

(6) The condition in this paragraph is that the person—

(a) is not an EEA national but would, if he were an EEA national, be a worker, a self-employed person or a self-sufficient person under regulation 6; or

(b) is the family member of a person who falls within paragraph (a).

(7) In this regulation, 'educational course' means a course within the scope of Article 12 of Council Regulation (EEC) No. 1612/68 on freedom of movement for workers.

(8) A person with a permanent right of residence under regulation 15 shall not become a family member who has retained the right of residence on the death or departure from the United Kingdom of the qualified person or the termination of the marriage or civil partnership, as the case may be, and a family member who has retained the right of residence shall cease to have that status on acquiring a permanent right of residence under regulation 15.

Part 2
EEA Rights

Right of admission to the United Kingdom

11.—(1) An EEA national must be admitted to the United Kingdom if he produces on arrival a valid national identity card or passport issued by an EEA State.

(2) A person who is not an EEA national must be admitted to the United Kingdom if he is a family member of an EEA national, a family member who has retained the right of residence or a person with a permanent right of residence under regulation 15 and produces on arrival—

(a) a valid passport; and

(b) an EEA family permit, a residence card or a permanent residence card.

(3) An immigration officer may not place a stamp in the passport of a person admitted to the United Kingdom under this regulation who is not an EEA national if the person produces a residence card or permanent residence card.

(4) Before an immigration officer refuses admission to the United Kingdom to a person under this regulation because the person does not produce on arrival a document mentioned in paragraph (1) or (2), the immigration officer must give the person every reasonable opportunity to obtain the document or have it brought to him within a reasonable period of time or to prove by other means that he is—

(a) an EEA national;

(b) a family member of an EEA national with a right to accompany that national or join him in the United Kingdom; or

(c) a family member who has retained the right of residence or a person with a permanent right of residence under regulation 15.

(5) But this regulation is subject to regulations 19(1) and (2).

Issue of EEA family permit

12.—(1) An entry clearance officer must issue an EEA family permit to a person who applies for one if the person is a family member of an EEA national and—

(a) the EEA national—

(i) is residing in the UK in accordance with these Regulations; or

(ii) will be travelling to the United Kingdom within six months of the date of the application and will be an EEA national residing in the United Kingdom in accordance with these Regulations on arrival in the United Kingdom; and

(b) the family member will be accompanying the EEA national to the United Kingdom or joining him there and—

(i) is lawfully resident in an EEA State; or

(ii) would meet the requirements in the immigration rules (other than those relating to entry clearance) for leave to enter the United Kingdom as the family member of the EEA national or, in the case of direct descendants or dependent direct relatives in the ascending line of his spouse or his civil partner, as the family member of his spouse or his civil partner, were the EEA national or the spouse or civil partner a person present and settled in the United Kingdom.

(2) An entry clearance officer may issue an EEA family permit to an extended family member of an EEA national who applies for one if—

(a) the relevant EEA national satisfies the condition in paragraph (1)(a);

(b) the extended family member wishes to accompany the relevant EEA national to the United Kingdom or to join him there; and

(c) in all the circumstances, it appears to the entry clearance officer appropriate to issue the EEA family permit.

(3) Where an entry clearance officer receives an application under paragraph (2) he shall undertake an extensive examination of the personal circumstances of the applicant and if he refuses the application shall give reasons justifying the refusal unless this is contrary to the interests of national security.

(4) An EEA family permit issued under this regulation shall be issued free of charge and as soon as possible.

(5) But an EEA family permit shall not be issued under this regulation if the applicant or the EEA national concerned falls to be excluded from the United Kingdom on grounds of public policy, public security or public health in accordance with regulation 21.

Initial right of residence

13.—(1) An EEA national is entitled to reside in the United Kingdom for a period not exceeding three months beginning on the date on which he is admitted to the United Kingdom provided that he holds a valid national identity card or passport issued by an EEA State.

(2) A family member of an EEA national residing in the United Kingdom under paragraph (1) who is not himself an EEA national is entitled to reside in the United Kingdom provided that he holds a valid passport.

(3) But—

(a) this regulation is subject to regulation 19(3)(b); and

(b) an EEA national or his family member who becomes an unreasonable burden on the social assistance system of the United Kingdom shall cease to have the right to reside under this regulation.

Extended right of residence

14.—(1) A qualified person is entitled to reside in the United Kingdom for so long as he remains a qualified person.

(2) A family member of a qualified person residing in the United Kingdom under paragraph (1) or of an EEA national with a permanent right of residence under regulation 15 is entitled to reside in the United Kingdom for so long as he remains the family member of the qualified person or EEA national.

(3) A family member who has retained the right of residence is entitled to reside in the United Kingdom for so long as he remains a family member who has retained the right of residence.

(4) A right to reside under this regulation is in addition to any right a person may have to reside in the United Kingdom under regulation 13 or 15.

(5) But this regulation is subject to regulation 19(3)(b).

Permanent right of residence

15.—(1) The following persons shall acquire the right to reside in the United Kingdom permanently—

(a) an EEA national who has resided in the United Kingdom in accordance with these Regulations for a continuous period of five years;

(b) a family member of an EEA national who is not himself an EEA national but who has resided in the United Kingdom with the EEA national in accordance with these Regulations for a continuous period of five years;

(c) a worker or self-employed person who has ceased activity;

(d) the family member of a worker or self-employed person who has ceased activity;

(e) a person who was the family member of a worker or self-employed person where—

(i) the worker or self-employed person has died;

(ii) the family member resided with him immediately before his death; and

(iii) the worker or self-employed person had resided continuously in the United Kingdom for at least the two years immediately before his death or the death was the result of an accident at work or an occupational disease;

(f) a person who—

(i) has resided in the United Kingdom in accordance with these Regulations for a continuous period of five years; and

(ii) was, at the end of that period, a family member who has retained the right of residence.

(2) Once acquired, the right of permanent residence under this regulation shall be lost only through absence from the United Kingdom for a period exceeding two consecutive years.

(3) But this regulation is subject to regulation 19(3)(b).

Part 3
Residence Documentation

Issue of registration certificate

16.—(1) The Secretary of State must issue a registration certificate to a qualified person immediately on application and production of—

(a) a valid identity card or passport issued by an EEA State;

(b) proof that he is a qualified person.

(2) In the case of a worker, confirmation of the worker's engagement from his employer or a certificate of employment is sufficient proof for the purposes of paragraph (1)(b).

(3) The Secretary of State must issue a registration certificate to an EEA national who is the family member of a qualified person or of an EEA national with a permanent right of residence under regulation 15 immediately on application and production of—

(a) a valid identity card or passport issued by an EEA State; and

(b) proof that the applicant is such a family member.

(4) The Secretary of State must issue a registration certificate to an EEA national who is a family member who has retained the right of residence on application and production of—

(a) a valid identity card or passport; and

(b) proof that the applicant is a family member who has retained the right of residence.

(5) The Secretary of State may issue a registration certificate to an extended

family member not falling within regulation 7(3) who is an EEA national on application if—

(a) the relevant EEA national in relation to the extended family member is a qualified person or an EEA national with a permanent right of residence under regulation 15; and

(b) in all the circumstances it appears to the Secretary of State appropriate to issue the registration certificate.

(6) Where the Secretary of State receives an application under paragraph (5) he shall undertake an extensive examination of the personal circumstances of the applicant and if he refuses the application shall give reasons justifying the refusal unless this is contrary to the interests of national security.

(7) A registration certificate issued under this regulation shall state the name and address of the person registering and the date of registration and shall be issued free of charge.

(8) But this regulation is subject to regulation 20(1).

Issue of residence card

17.—(1) The Secretary of State must issue a residence card to a person who is not an EEA national and is the family member of a qualified person or of an EEA national with a permanent right of residence under regulation 15 on application and production of—

(a) a valid passport; and

(b) proof that the applicant is such a family member.

(2) The Secretary of State must issue a residence card to a person who is not an EEA national but who is a family member who has retained the right of residence on application and production of—

(a) a valid passport; and

(b) proof that the applicant is a family member who has retained the right of residence.

(3) On receipt of an application under paragraph (1) or (2) and the documents that are required to accompany the application the Secretary of State shall immediately issue the applicant with a certificate of application for the residence card and the residence card shall be issued no later than six months after the date on which the application and documents are received.

(4) The Secretary of State may issue a residence card to an extended family member not falling within regulation 7(3) who is not an EEA national on application if—

(a) the relevant EEA national in relation to the extended family member is a qualified person or an EEA national with a permanent right of residence under regulation 15; and

(b) in all the circumstances it appears to the Secretary of State appropriate to issue the residence card.

(5) Where the Secretary of State receives an application under paragraph (4) he shall undertake an extensive examination of the personal circumstances of the applicant and if he refuses the application shall give reasons justifying the refusal unless this is contrary to the interests of national security.

(6) A residence card issued under this regulation may take the form of a stamp in the applicant's passport and shall be entitled 'Residence card of a family member of an EEA national' and be valid for—

(a) five years from the date of issue; or

(b) in the case of a residence card issued to the family member or extended family member of a qualified person, the envisaged period of residence in the United Kingdom of the qualified person,

whichever is the shorter.

(7) A residence card issued under this regulation shall be issued free of charge.

(8) But this regulation is subject to regulation 20(1).

Issue of a document certifying permanent residence and a permanent residence card

18.—(1) The Secretary of State must issue an EEA national with a permanent right of residence under regulation 15 with a document certifying permanent residence as soon as possible after an application for such a document and proof that the EEA national has such a right is submitted to the Secretary of State.

(2) The Secretary of State must issue a person who is not an EEA national who has a permanent right of residence under regulation 15 with a permanent residence card no later than six months after the date on which an application for a permanent residence card and proof that the person has such a right is submitted to the Secretary of State.

(3) Subject to paragraph (5) and regulation 20(3), a permanent residence card shall be valid for ten years from the date of issue and must be renewed on application.

(4) A document certifying permanent residence and a permanent residence card shall be issued free of charge.

(5) A document certifying permanent residence and a permanent residence card shall cease to be valid if the holder ceases to have a right of permanent residence under regulation 15.

Part 4

Refusal of Admission and Removal etc

Exclusion and removal from the United Kingdom

19.—(1) A person is not entitled to be admitted to the United Kingdom by virtue of regulation 11 if his exclusion is justified on grounds of public policy, public security or public health in accordance with regulation 21.

(2) A person is not entitled to be admitted to the United Kingdom as the family member of an EEA national under regulation 11(2) unless, at the time of his arrival—

(a) he is accompanying the EEA national or joining him in the United Kingdom; and

(b) the EEA national has a right to reside in the United Kingdom under these Regulations.

(3) Subject to paragraphs (4) and (5), a person who has been admitted to, or acquired a right to reside in, the United Kingdom under these Regulations may be removed from the United Kingdom if—

(a) he does not have or ceases to have a right to reside under these Regulations; or

(b) he would otherwise be entitled to reside in the United Kingdom under these Regulations but the Secretary of State has decided that his removal is justified on the grounds of public policy, public security or public health in accordance with regulation 21.

(4) A person must not be removed under paragraph (3) as the automatic consequence of having recourse to the social assistance system of the United Kingdom.

(5) A person must not be removed under paragraph (3) if he has a right to remain in the United Kingdom by virtue of leave granted under the 1971 Act unless his removal is justified on the grounds of public policy, public security or public health in accordance with regulation 21.

Refusal to issue or renew and revocation of residence documentation

20.—(1) The Secretary of State may refuse to issue, revoke or refuse to renew a registration certificate, a residence card, a document certifying permanent residence or a permanent residence card if the refusal or revocation is justified on grounds of public policy, public security or public health.

(2) The Secretary of State may revoke a registration certificate or a residence card or refuse to renew a residence card if the holder of the certificate or card has ceased to have a right to reside under these Regulations.

(3) The Secretary of State may revoke a document certifying permanent residence or a permanent residence card or refuse to renew a permanent residence card if the holder of the certificate or card has ceased to have a right of permanent residence under regulation 15.

(4) An immigration officer may, at the time of a person's arrival in the United Kingdom—

(a) revoke that person's residence card if he is not at that time the family member of a qualified person or of an EEA national who has a right of permanent residence under regulation 15, a family member who has retained the right of residence or a person with a right of permanent residence under regulation 15;

(b) revoke that person's permanent residence card if he is not at that time a person with a right of permanent residence under regulation 15.

(5) An immigration officer may, at the time of a person's arrival in the United Kingdom, revoke that person's EEA family permit if—

(a) the revocation is justified on grounds of public policy, public security or public health; or

(b) the person is not at that time the family member of an EEA national with the right to reside in the United Kingdom under these Regulations or is not accompanying that national or joining him in the United Kingdom.

(6) Any action taken under this regulation on grounds of public policy, public security or public health shall be in accordance with regulation 21.

Decisions taken on public policy, public security and public health grounds

21.—(1) In this regulation a 'relevant decision' means an EEA decision taken on the grounds of public policy, public security or public health.

(2) A relevant decision may not be taken to serve economic ends.

(3) A relevant decision may not be taken in respect of a person with a permanent right of residence under regulation 15 except on serious grounds of public policy or public security.

(4) A relevant decision may not be taken except on imperative grounds of public security in respect of an EEA national who—

(a) has resided in the United Kingdom for a continuous period of at least ten years prior to the relevant decision; or

(b) is under the age of 18, unless the relevant decision is necessary in his best interests, as provided for in the Convention on the Rights of the Child adopted by the General Assembly of the United Nations on 20th November 1989.

(5) Where a relevant decision is taken on grounds of public policy or public security it shall, in addition to complying with the preceding paragraphs of this regulation, be taken in accordance with the following principles—

(a) the decision must comply with the principle of proportionality;
(b) the decision must be based exclusively on the personal conduct of the person concerned;
(c) the personal conduct of the person concerned must represent a genuine, present and sufficiently serious threat affecting one of the fundamental interests of society;
(d) matters isolated from the particulars of the case or which relate to considerations of general prevention do not justify the decision;
(e) a person's previous criminal convictions do not in themselves justify the decision.

(6) Before taking a relevant decision on the grounds of public policy or public security in relation to a person who is resident in the United Kingdom the decision maker must take account of considerations such as the age, state of health, family and economic situation of the person, the person's length of residence in the United Kingdom, the person's social and cultural integration into the United Kingdom and the extent of the person's links with his country of origin.

(7) In the case of a relevant decision taken on grounds of public health—
(a) a disease that does not have epidemic potential as defined by the relevant instruments of the World Health Organisation or is not a disease to which section 38 of the Public Health (Control of Disease) Act 1984 applies (detention in hospital of a person with a notifiable disease) shall not constitute grounds for the decision; and
(b) if the person concerned is in the United Kingdom, diseases occurring after the three month period beginning on the date on which he arrived in the United Kingdom shall not constitute grounds for the decision.

Part 5

Procedure in Relation to EEA Decisions

Person claiming right of admission

22.—(1) This regulation applies to a person who claims a right of admission to the United Kingdom under regulation 11 as—
(a) a person, not being an EEA national, who is a family member of an EEA national, a family member who has retained the right of residence or a person with a permanent right of residence under regulation 15; or
(b) an EEA national, where there is reason to believe that he may fall to be excluded from the United Kingdom on grounds of public policy, public security or public health.

(2) A person to whom this regulation applies is to be treated as if he were a person seeking leave to enter the United Kingdom under the 1971 Act for

the purposes of paragraphs 2, 3, 4, 7, 16 to 18 and 21 to 24 of Schedule 2 to the 1971 Act (administrative provisions as to control on entry etc), except that—

(a) the reference in paragraph 2(1) to the purpose for which the immigration officer may examine any persons who have arrived in the United Kingdom is to be read as a reference to the purpose of determining whether he is a person who is to be granted admission under these Regulations;

(b) the references in paragraphs 4(2A), 7 and 16(1) to a person who is, or may be, given leave to enter are to be read as references to a person who is, or may be, granted admission under these Regulations; and

(c) a medical examination is not to be carried out under paragraph 2 or paragraph 7 as a matter of routine and may only be carried out within three months of a person's arrival in the United Kingdom.

(3) For so long as a person to whom this regulation applies is detained, or temporarily admitted or released while liable to detention, under the powers conferred by Schedule 2 to the 1971 Act, he is deemed not to have been admitted to the United Kingdom.

Person refused admission

23.—(1) This regulation applies to a person who is in the United Kingdom and has been refused admission to the United Kingdom—

(a) because he does not meet the requirement of regulation 11 (including where he does not meet those requirements because his EEA family permit, residence card or permanent residence card has been revoked by an immigration officer in accordance with regulation 20); or

(b) in accordance with regulation 19(1) or (2).

(2) A person to whom this regulation applies, is to be treated as if he were a person refused leave to enter under the 1971 Act for the purpose of paragraphs 8, 10, 10A, 11, 16 to 19 and 21 to 24 of Schedule 2 to the 1971 Act, except that the reference in paragraph 19 to a certificate of entitlement, entry clearance or work permit is to be read as a reference to an EEA family permit, residence card or a permanent residence card.

Person subject to removal

24.—(1) This regulation applies to a person whom it has been decided to remove from the United Kingdom in accordance with regulation 19(3).

(2) Where the decision is under regulation 19(3)(a), the person is to be treated as if he were a person to whom section 10(1)(a) of the 1999 Act applied, and section 10 of that Act (removal of certain persons unlawfully in the United Kingdom) is to apply accordingly.

(3) Where the decision is under regulation 19(3)(b), the person is to be treated as if he were a person to whom section 3(5)(a) of the 1971 Act (liability to deportation) applied, and section 5 of that Act (procedure for deportation) and Schedule 3 to that Act (supplementary provision as to deportation) are to apply accordingly.

(4) A person who enters or seeks to enter the United Kingdom in breach of a deportation order made against him pursuant to paragraph (3) shall be removable as an illegal entrant under Schedule 2 to the 1971 Act and the provisions of that Schedule shall apply accordingly.

(5) Where such a deportation order is made against a person but he is not removed under the order during the two year period beginning on the date on which the order is made, the Secretary of State shall only take action to remove the person under the order after the end of that period if, having assessed whether there has been any material change in circumstances since the deportation order was made, he considers that the removal continues to be justified on the grounds of public policy, public security or public health.

(6) A person to whom this regulation applies shall be allowed one month to leave the United Kingdom, beginning on the date on which he is notified of the decision to remove him, before being removed pursuant to that decision except—

(a) in duly substantiated cases of urgency;
(b) where the person is detained pursuant to the sentence or order of any court;
(c) where a person is a person to whom regulation 24(4) applies.

Part 6

Appeals Under These Regulations

Interpretation of Part 6

25.—(1) In this Part—

'Asylum and Immigration Tribunal' has the same meaning as in the 2002 Act;

'Commission' has the same meaning as in the Special Immigration Appeals Commission Act 1997;

'the Human Rights Convention' has the same meaning as 'the Convention' in the Human Rights Act 1998; and

'the Refugee Convention' means the Convention relating to the Status of Refugees done at Geneva on 28th July 1951 and the Protocol relating to the Status of Refugees done at New York on 31st January 1967.

(2) For the purposes of this Part, and subject to paragraphs (3) and (4), an appeal is to be treated as pending during the period when notice of appeal is given and ending when the appeal is finally determined, withdrawn or abandoned.

(3) An appeal is not to be treated as finally determined while a further appeal may

be brought; and, if such a further appeal is brought, the original appeal is not to be treated as finally determined until the further appeal is determined, withdrawn or abandoned.

(4) A pending appeal is not to be treated as abandoned solely because the appellant leaves the United Kingdom.

Appeal rights

26.—(1) Subject to the following paragraphs of this regulation, a person may appeal under these Regulations against an EEA decision.

(2) If a person claims to be an EEA national, he may not appeal under these Regulations unless he produces a valid national identity card or passport issued by an EEA State.

(3) If a person claims to be the family member or relative of an EEA national he may not appeal under these Regulations unless he produces—

(a) an EEA family permit; or

(b) other proof that he is related as claimed to an EEA national.

(4) A person may not bring an appeal under these Regulations on a ground certified under paragraph (5) or rely on such a ground in an appeal brought under these Regulations.

(5) The Secretary of State or an immigration officer may certify a ground for the purposes of paragraph (4) if it has been considered in a previous appeal brought under these Regulations or under section 82(1) of the 2002 Act.

(6) Except where an appeal lies to the Commission, an appeal under these Regulations lies to the Asylum and Immigration Tribunal.

(7) The provisions of or made under the 2002 Act referred to in Schedule 1 shall have effect for the purposes of an appeal under these Regulations to the Asylum and Immigration Tribunal in accordance with that Schedule.

Out of country appeals

27.—(1) Subject to paragraphs (2) and (3), a person may not appeal under regulation 26 whilst he is in the United Kingdom against an EEA decision—

(a) to refuse to admit him to the United Kingdom;

(b) to refuse to revoke a deportation order made against him;

(c) to refuse to issue him with an EEA family permit; or

(d) to remove him from the United Kingdom after he has entered or sought to enter the United Kingdom in breach of a deportation order.

(2) Paragraph (1)(a) does not apply where—

(a) the person held an EEA family permit, a registration certificate, a residence card, a document certifying permanent residence or a permanent residence card on his arrival in the United Kingdom or can otherwise prove that he is resident in the United Kingdom;

(b) the person is deemed not to have been admitted to the United Kingdom under regulation 22(3) but at the date on which notice of the decision to refuse to admit him is given he has been in the United Kingdom for at least 3 months;

(c) the person is in the United Kingdom and a ground of the appeal is that, in taking the decision, the decision maker acted in breach of his rights under the Human Rights Convention or the Refugee Convention, unless the Secretary of State certifies that that ground of appeal is clearly unfounded.

(3) Paragraph (1)(d) does not apply where a ground of the appeal is that, in taking the decision, the decision maker acted in breach of the appellant's rights under the Human Rights Convention or the Refugee Convention, unless the Secretary of State certifies that that ground of appeal is clearly unfounded.

Appeals to the Commission

28.—(1) An appeal against an EEA decision lies to the Commission where paragraph (2) or (4) applies.

(2) This paragraph applies if the Secretary of State certifies that the EEA decision was taken—

(a) by the Secretary of State wholly or partly on a ground listed in paragraph (3); or

(b) in accordance with a direction of the Secretary of State which identifies the person to whom the decision relates and which is given wholly or partly on a ground listed in paragraph (3).

(3) The grounds mentioned in paragraph (2) are that the person's exclusion or removal from the United Kingdom is—

(a) in the interests of national security; or

(b) in the interests of the relationship between the United Kingdom and another country.

(4) This paragraph applies if the Secretary of State certifies that the EEA decision was taken wholly or partly in reliance on information which in his opinion should not be made public—

(a) in the interests of national security;

(b) in the interests of the relationship between the United Kingdom and another country; or

(c) otherwise in the public interest.

(5) In paragraphs (2) and (4) a reference to the Secretary of State is to the Secretary of State acting in person.

(6) Where a certificate is issued under paragraph (2); or (4); in respect of a pending appeal to the Asylum and Immigration Tribunal the appeal shall lapse.

(7) An appeal against an EEA decision lies to the Commission where an appeal lapses by virtue of paragraph (6).

(8) The Special Immigration Appeals Commission Act 1997 shall apply to an appeal to the Commission under these Regulations as it applies to an appeal under section 2 of that Act to which subsection (2) of that section applies (appeals against an immigration decision) but paragraph (i) of that subsection shall not apply in relation to such an appeal.

Effect of appeals to the Asylum and Immigration Tribunal

29.—(1) This Regulation applies to appeals under these Regulations made to the Asylum and Immigration Tribunal.

(2) If a person in the United Kingdom appeals against an EEA decision to refuse to admit him to the United Kingdom, any directions for his removal from the United Kingdom previously given by virtue of the refusal cease to have effect, except in so far as they have already been carried out, and no directions may be so given while the appeal is pending.

(3) If a person in the United Kingdom appeals against an EEA decision to remove him from the United Kingdom, any directions given under section 10 of the 1999 Act or Schedule 3 to the 1971 Act for his removal from the United Kingdom are to have no effect, except in so far as they have already been carried out, while the appeal is pending.

(4) But the provisions of Part I of Schedule 2, or as the case may be, Schedule 3 to the 1971 Act with respect to detention and persons liable to detention apply to a person appealing against a refusal to admit him or a decision to remove him as if there were in force directions for his removal from the United Kingdom, except that he may not be detained on board a ship or aircraft so as to compel him to leave the United Kingdom while the appeal is pending.

(5) In calculating the period of two months limited by paragraph 8(2) of Schedule 2 to the 1971 Act for—

(a) the giving of directions under that paragraph for the removal of a person from the United Kingdom; and

(b) the giving of a notice of intention to give such directions,

any period during which there is pending an appeal by him is to be disregarded.

(6) If a person in the United Kingdom appeals against an EEA decision to remove him from the United Kingdom, a deportation order is not to be made against him under section 5 of the 1971 Act while the appeal is pending.

(7) Paragraph 29 of Schedule 2 to the 1971 Act (grant of bail pending appeal) applies to a person who has an appeal pending under these Regulations as it

applies to a person who has an appeal pending under section 82(1) of the 2002 Act.

Part 7
General

Effect on other legislation

30. Schedule 2 (effect on other legislation) shall have effect.

Revocations, transitional provisions and consequential amendments

31.—(1) The Regulations listed in column 1 of the table in Part 1 of Schedule 3 are revoked to the extent set out in column 3 of that table, subject to Part 2 of that Schedule and to Schedule 4.

(2) Schedule 4 (transitional provisions) and Schedule 5 (consequential amendments) shall have effect.

Regulation 26(7)

Schedule 1
Appeals to the Asylum and Immigration Tribunal

The following provisions of, or made under, the 2002 Act have effect in relation to an appeal under these Regulations to the Asylum and Immigration Tribunal as if it were an appeal against an immigration decision under section 82(1) of that Act:

section 84(1), except paragraphs (a) and (f);
sections 85 to 87;
sections 103A to 103E;
section 105 and any regulations made under that section; and
section 106 and any rules made under that section.

Regulation 30

Schedule 2
Effect on Other Legislation

Leave under the 1971 Act

1.—(1) In accordance with section 7 of the Immigration Act 1988, a person who is admitted to or acquires a right to reside in the United Kingdom under these Regulations shall not require leave to remain in the United Kingdom under the 1971 Act during any period in which he has a right to reside under these Regulations but such a person shall require leave to remain under the 1971 Act during any period in which he does not have such a right.

(2) Where a person has leave to enter or remain under the 1971 Act which is subject to

conditions and that person also has a right to reside under these Regulations, those conditions shall not have effect for as long as the person has that right to reside.

Persons not subject to restriction on the period for which they may remain

2.—(1) For the purposes of the 1971 Act and the British Nationality Act 1981, a person who has a permanent right of residence under regulation 15 shall be regarded as a person who is in the United Kingdom without being subject under the immigration laws to any restriction on the period for which he may remain.

(2) But a qualified person, the family member of a qualified person and a family member who has retained the right of residence shall not, by virtue of that status, be so regarded for those purposes.

Carriers' liability under the 1999 Act

3. For the purposes of satisfying a requirement to produce a visa under section 40(1)(b) of the 1999 Act (charges in respect of passenger without proper documents), 'a visa of the required kind' includes an EEA family permit, a residence card or a permanent residence card required for admission under regulation 11(2).

Appeals under the 2002 Act and previous immigration Acts

4.—(1) The following EEA decisions shall not be treated as immigration decisions for the purpose of section 82(2) of the 2002 Act (right of appeal against an immigration decision)—

(a) a decision that a person is to be removed under regulation 19(3)(a) by way of a direction under section 10(1)(a) of the 1999 Act (as provided for by regulation 24(2));

(b) a decision to remove a person under regulation 19(3)(b) by making a deportation order under section 5(1) of the 1971 Act (as provided for by regulation 24(3));

(c) a decision to remove a person mentioned in regulation 24(4) by way of directions under paragraphs 8 to 10 of Schedule 2 to the 1971 Act.

(2) A person who has been issued with a registration certificate, residence card, a document certifying permanent residence or a permanent residence card under these Regulations or a registration certificate under the Accession (Immigration and Worker Registration) Regulations 2004, or a person whose passport has been stamped with a family member residence stamp, shall have no right of appeal under section 2 of the Special Immigration Appeals Commission Act 1997 or section 82(1) of the 2002 Act. Any existing appeal under those sections of those Acts or under the Asylum and Immigration Appeals Act 1993, the Asylum and Immigration Act 1996 or the 1999 Act shall be treated as abandoned.

(3) Subject to paragraph (4), a person may appeal to the Asylum and Immigration Tribunal under section 83(2) of the 2002 Act against the rejection of his asylum claim where—

(a) that claim has been rejected, but

(b) he has a right to reside in the United Kingdom under these Regulations.

(4) Paragraph (3) shall not apply if the person is an EEA national and the Secretary of State certifies that the asylum claim is clearly unfounded.

(5) The Secretary of State shall certify the claim under paragraph (4) unless satisfied that it is not clearly unfounded.

(6) In addition to the national of a State which is a contracting party to the Agreement referred to in section 84(2) of the 2002 Act, a Swiss national shall also be treated as an EEA national for the purposes of section 84(1)(d) of that Act.

(7) An appeal under these Regulations against an EEA decision (including an appeal made on or after 1st April 2003 which is treated as an appeal under these Regulations under Schedule 4 but not an appeal made before that date) shall be treated as an appeal under section 82(1) of the 2002 Act against an immigration decision for the purposes of section 96(1)(a) of the 2002 Act.

(8) Section 120 of the 2002 Act shall apply to a person if an EEA decision has been taken or may be taken in respect of him and, accordingly, the Secretary of State or an immigration officer may by notice require a statement from that person under subsection (2) of that section and that notice shall have effect for the purpose of section 96(2) of the 2002 Act.

(9) In sub-paragraph (1), 'family member residence stamp' means a stamp in the passport of a family member of an EEA national confirming that he is the family member of an accession State worker requiring registration with a right of residence under these Regulations as the family member of that worker; and in this sub-paragraph 'accession State worker requiring registration' has the same meaning as in regulation 2 of the Accession (Immigration and Worker Registration) Regulations 2004.

Regulation 31(2)

Schedule 3

Revocations and Savings

Part 1

Table of Revocations

. . .

Part 2

Savings

1. The—
   (a) Immigration (Swiss Free Movement of Persons) (No. 3) Regulations 2002 are not revoked insofar as they apply the 2000 Regulations to posted workers; and
   (b) the 2000 Regulations and the Regulations amending the 2000 Regulations are not revoked insofar as they are so applied to posted workers;

   and, accordingly, the 2000 Regulations, as amended, shall continue to apply to posted workers in accordance with the Immigration (Swiss Free Movement of Persons) (No. 3) Regulations 2002.

2. In paragraph 1, 'the 2000 Regulations' means the Immigration (European Economic Area) Regulations 2000 and 'posted worker' has the meaning given in regulation 2(4)(b) of the Immigration (Swiss Free Movement of Persons) (No. 3) Regulations 2002.

Regulation 31(2)

Schedule 4
Transitional Provisions

Interpretation

1. In this Schedule—
   (a) the '2000 Regulations' means the Immigration (European Economic Area) Regulations 2000 and expressions used in relation to documents issued or applied for under those Regulations shall have the meaning given in regulation 2 of those Regulations;
   (b) the 'Accession Regulations' means the Accession (Immigration and Worker Registration) Regulations 2004.

Existing documents

2.—(1) An EEA family permit issued under the 2000 Regulations shall, after 29th April 2006, be treated as if it were an EEA family permit issued under these Regulations.

(2) Subject to paragraph (4), a residence permit issued under the 2000 Regulations shall, after 29th April 2006, be treated as if it were a registration certificate issued under these Regulations.

(3) Subject to paragraph (5), a residence document issued under the 2000 Regulations shall, after 29th April 2006, be treated as if it were a residence card issued under these Regulations.

(4) Where a residence permit issued under the 2000 Regulations has been endorsed under the immigration rules to show permission to remain in the United Kingdom indefinitely it shall, after 29th April 2006, be treated as if it were a document certifying permanent residence issued under these Regulations and the holder of the permit shall be treated as a person with a permanent right of residence under regulation 15.

(5) Where a residence document issued under the 2000 Regulations has been endorsed under the immigration rules to show permission to remain in the United Kingdom indefinitely it shall, after 29th April 2006, be treated as if it were a permanent residence card issued under these Regulations and the holder of the permit shall be treated as a person with a permanent right of residence under regulation 15.

(6) Paragraphs (4) and (5) shall also apply to a residence permit or residence document which is endorsed under the immigration rules on or after 30th April 2006 to show permission to remain in the United Kingdom indefinitely pursuant to an application for such an endorsement made before that date.

Outstanding applications

3.—(1) An application for an EEA family permit, a residence permit or a residence document made but not determined under the 2000 Regulations before 30 April 2006 shall be treated as an application under these Regulations for an EEA family permit, a registration certificate or a residence card, respectively.

(2) But the following provisions of these Regulations shall not apply to the determination of an application mentioned in sub-paragraph (1)—

(a) the requirement to issue a registration certificate immediately under regulation 16(1); and
(b) the requirement to issue a certificate of application for a residence card under regulation 17(3).

Decisions to remove under the 2000 Regulations

4.—(1) A decision to remove a person under regulation 21(3)(a) of the 2000 Regulations shall, after 29th April 2006, be treated as a decision to remove that person under regulation 19(3)(a) of these Regulations.

(2) A decision to remove a person under regulation 21(3)(b) of the 2000 Regulations, including a decision which is treated as a decision to remove a person under that regulation by virtue of regulation 6(3)(a) of the Accession Regulations, shall, after 29th April 2006, be treated as a decision to remove that person under regulation 19(3)(b) of these Regulations.

(3) A deportation order made under section 5 of the 1971 Act by virtue of regulation 26(3) of the 2000 Regulations shall, after 29th April 2006, be treated as a deportation made under section 5 of the 1971 Act by virtue of regulation 24(3) of these Regulations.

Appeals

5.—(1) Where an appeal against an EEA decision under the 2000 Regulations is pending immediately before 30th April 2006 that appeal shall be treated as a pending appeal against the corresponding EEA Decision under these Regulations.

(2) Where an appeal against an EEA decision under the 2000 Regulations has been determined, withdrawn or abandoned it shall, on and after 30th April 2006, be treated as an appeal against the corresponding EEA decision under these Regulations which has been determined, withdrawn or abandoned, respectively.

(3) For the purpose of this paragraph—
(a) a decision to refuse to admit a person under these Regulations corresponds to a decision to refuse to admit that person under the 2000 Regulations;
(b) a decision to remove a person under regulation 19(3)(a) of these Regulations corresponds to a decision to remove that person under regulation 21(3)(a) of the 2000 Regulations;
(c) a decision to remove a person under regulation 19(3)(b) of these Regulations corresponds to a decision to remove that person under regulation 21(3)(b) of the 2000 Regulations, including a decision which is treated as a decision to remove a person under regulation 21(3)(b) of the 2000 Regulations by virtue of regulation 6(3)(a) of the Accession Regulations;
(d) a decision to refuse to revoke a deportation order made against a person under these Regulations corresponds to a decision to refuse to revoke a deportation order made against that person under the 2000 Regulations, including a decision which is treated as a decision to refuse to revoke a deportation order under the 2000 Regulations by virtue of regulation 6(3)(b) of the Accession Regulations;
(e) a decision not to issue or renew or to revoke an EEA family permit, a registration

certificate or a residence card under these Regulations corresponds to a decision not to issue or renew or to revoke an EEA family permit, a residence permit or a residence document under the 2000 Regulations, respectively.

Periods of residence under the 2000 Regulations

6.—(1) Any period during which a person carried out an activity or was resident in the United Kingdom in accordance with the 2000 Regulations shall be treated as a period during which the person carried out that activity or was resident in the United Kingdom in accordance with these Regulations for the purpose of calculating periods of activity and residence under these Regulations.

Regulation 31(2)

Schedule 5

Consequential Amendments

. . .

The Immigration (Leave to Remain) (Prescribed Forms and Procedures) Regulations 2006

(SI 2006, No. 1421)

Citation, commencement and interpretation

1. These Regulations may be cited as the Immigration (Leave to Remain) (Prescribed Forms and Procedures) Regulations 2006 and shall come into force on 22nd June 2006.

2. In these Regulations:

'asylum claimant' means a person making a claim for asylum (within the meaning given in section 94(1) of the Immigration and Asylum Act 1999) which claim either has not been determined or has been granted;

'dependant', of a person, means—

(a) the spouse, civil partner, unmarried partner or same sex partner, or

(b) a child under the age of eighteen,

of that person; and

'public enquiry office' means a public enquiry office of the Immigration and Nationality Directorate of the Home Office.

Prescribed Forms

3.—(1) Subject to paragraph (2), the form set out in Schedule 1 is prescribed for an application for limited or indefinite leave to remain in the United Kingdom as:

(a) a business person,
(b) a sole representative,
(c) a retired person of independent means,
(d) an investor, or
(e) an innovator,

for the purposes of the immigration rules.

(2) Paragraph (1) does not apply to an application for limited or indefinite leave to remain in the United Kingdom as a business person where the application is made under the terms of a European Community Association Agreement.

[4. The form set out in Schedule 2 is prescribed for an application for limited leave to remain in the United Kingdom:

(a) for work permit employment,
(b) as a seasonal agricultural worker,
(c) for the purposes of employment under the Sectors-Based Scheme, or
(d) for Home Office approved training or work experience,

for the purposes of the immigration rules.]

Note: Regulation 4 substituted from 8 November 2006, SI 2006/2899.

[4A. The form set out in Schedule 2A is prescribed for an application for limited leave to remain in the United Kingdom as a highly skilled migrant for the purposes of the immigration rules.]

Note: Regulation 4A inserted from 8 November 2006, SI 2006/2899.

5. The form set out in Schedule 3 is prescribed for an application for limited leave to remain in the United Kingdom as:

(a) the spouse or civil partner of a person present and settled in the United Kingdom, or
(b) the unmarried partner or same sex partner of a person present and settled in the United Kingdom,

for the purposes of the immigration rules.

6. The form set out in Schedule 4 is prescribed for an application for limited leave to remain in the United Kingdom:

(a) as a student,
(b) as a student nurse,
(c) to re-sit an examination,
(d) to write up a thesis,
(e) as a student union sabbatical officer, or

(f) as a prospective student,

for the purposes of the immigration rules.

7. The form set out in Schedule 5 is prescribed for an application for limited leave to remain in the United Kingdom as a participant in the Science and Engineering Graduates Scheme for the purposes of the immigration rules.

8. The form set out in Schedule 6 is prescribed for an application for limited leave to remain in the United Kingdom as a participant in the Fresh Talent: Working in Scotland Scheme for the purposes of the immigration rules.

9.—(1) The form set out in Schedule 7 is prescribed for an application for limited leave to remain in the United Kingdom as:

(a) a visitor,
(b) a visitor seeking to undergo or continue private medical treatment,
(c) a postgraduate doctor or dentist or a trainee general practitioner,
(d) an au pair,
(e) a teacher or language assistant under an approved exchange scheme,
(f) a representative of an overseas newspaper, news agency or broadcasting organisation,
(g) a private servant in a diplomatic household,
(h) a domestic worker in a private household,
(i) an overseas government employee,
(j) a minister of religion, missionary or member of a religious order,
(k) a visiting religious worker or a religious worker in a non-pastoral role,
(l) a member of the operational ground staff of an overseas-owned airline,
(m) a person with United Kingdom ancestry,
(n) a writer, composer or artist,
(o) an overseas qualified nurse or midwife, or
(p) the spouse, civil partner or child of an armed forces member who is exempt from immigration control under section 8(4) of the Immigration Act 1971,

for the purposes of the immigration rules.

(2) Subject to paragraph (3), the form set out in Schedule 7 is prescribed for an application for limited leave to remain in the United Kingdom for any other reason or purpose for which provision is made in the immigration rules but which is not covered by the forms prescribed in regulations 3 to 8.

(3) Paragraph (2) does not apply to an application for limited leave to remain in the United Kingdom where:

(a) the application is made under the terms of a European Community Association Agreement, or
(b) the basis on which the application is made is that the applicant is an asylum claimant or a dependant of an asylum claimant.

10. The form set out in Schedule 8 is prescribed for an application for indefinite leave to remain in the United Kingdom as:

(a) the spouse or civil partner of a person present and settled in the United Kingdom, or
(b) the unmarried partner or same sex partner of a person present and settled in the United Kingdom,

for the purposes of the immigration rules.

11. The form set out in Schedule 9 is prescribed for an application for indefinite leave to remain in the United Kingdom as:
(a) the child under the age of eighteen of a parent, parents or relative present and settled in the United Kingdom,
(b) the adopted child under the age of eighteen of a parent or parents present and settled in the United Kingdom, or
(c) the parent, grandparent or other dependent relative of a person present and settled in the United Kingdom,

for the purposes of the immigration rules.

12.—(1) The form set out in Schedule 10 is prescribed for an application for indefmite leave to remain in the United Kingdom:
(a) as a work permit holder,
(b) as a highly skilled migrant,
(c) as a representative of an overseas newspaper, news agency or broadcasting organisation,
(d) as a private servant in a diplomatic household,
(e) as a domestic worker in a private household,
(f) as an overseas government employee,
(g) as a minister of religion, missionary or member of a religious order,
(h) as a member of the operational ground staff of an overseas-owned airline,
(i) as a person with United Kingdom ancestry,
(j) as a writer, composer or artist,
(k) on the basis of long residence in the United Kingdom,
(l) as a victim of domestic violence, or
(m) as a foreign or Commonwealth citizen discharged from HM Forces,

for the purposes of the immigration rules.

(2) Subject to paragraph (3), the form set out in Schedule 10 is hereby prescribed for an application for indefinite leave to remain in the United Kingdom for any other reason or purpose for which provision is made in the immigration rules but which is not covered by the forms prescribed in regulations 10 or 11.

(3) Paragraph (2) does not apply to an application for indefinite leave to remain in the United Kingdom where:
(a) the application is made under the terms of a European Community Association Agreement,
(b) the basis on which the application is made is that the applicant is an asylum claimant or a dependant of an asylum claimant.

13. An application for leave to remain in the United Kingdom which is made by a person ('the main applicant') on a form prescribed in any of the regulations 3 to 12 above may include an application in respect of any person applying for leave to remain in the United Kingdom as a dependant of the main applicant, insofar as this is permitted by the immigration rules.

Prescribed procedures

14.—(1) The following procedures are hereby prescribed in relation to an application for which a form is prescribed in regulations 3 to 12:

(a) the form shall be signed and dated by the applicant, save that where the applicant is under the age of eighteen, the form may be signed and dated by the parent or legal guardian of the applicant on behalf of the applicant;

(b) the application shall be accompanied by such documents and photographs as specified in the form; and

(c) each part of the form shall be completed as specified in the form.

(2) The following procedures are hereby prescribed in relation to delivery of an application for which a form is prescribed:

(a) in relation to an application for which a form is prescribed in regulation 3, the application shall be sent by prepaid post or by courier to the Immigration and Nationality Directorate of the Home Office; it may not be submitted in person at a public enquiry office;

(b) subject to (3) in relation to an application for which a form is prescribed in regulation 4, the application shall be:

(i) sent by prepaid post or by courier to Work Permits (UK) at the Immigration and Nationality Directorate of the Home Office, or

(ii) submitted in person at the Croydon public enquiry office (but no other public enquiry office),

(c) in relation to an application for which a form is prescribed in regulations 5 to 12 above, the application shall be:

(i) sent by prepaid post to the Immigration and Nationality Directorate of the Home Office, or

(ii) submitted in person at a public enquiry office.

(3) An application for which a form is prescribed in regulation 4(b) (application for limited leave to remain in the United Kingdom as a highly skilled migrant) shall be sent by prepaid post or by courier to Work Permits (UK) at the Immigration and Nationality Directorate of the Home Office, and may not be submitted in person at a public enquiry office.

15.—(1) A failure to comply with any of the requirements of regulation 14(1) to any extent will only invalidate an application if:

(a) the applicant does not provide, when making the application, an explanation for the failure which the Secretary of State considers to be satisfactory,

(b) the Secretary of State notifies the applicant, or the person who appears to the Secretary of State to represent the applicant, of the failure within 28 days of the date on which the application is made, and
(c) the applicant does not comply with the requirements within a reasonable time, and in any event within 28 days, of being notified by the Secretary of State of the failure.

(2) For the purposes of this regulation, the date on which the application is made is:
(a) in the case of an application sent by post, the date of posting,
(b) in the case of an application submitted in person, the date on which the application is delivered to, and accepted by, a public enquiry office, and
(c) in the case of an application sent by courier, the date on which the application is delivered to Work Permits (UK) at the Immigration and Nationality Directorate of the Home Office.

Revocation and transitional provision

16. . . .

The British Nationality (Proof of Paternity) Regulations 2006

(SI 2006, No. 1496)

1. These Regulations may be cited as the British Nationality (Proof of Paternity) Regulations 2006 and shall come into force on 1st July 2006.
2. The following requirements are prescribed as to proof of paternity for the purposes of section 50(9A)(c) of the British Nationality Act 1981—
   (a) the person must be named as the father of the child in a birth certificate issued within one year of the date of the child's birth; or
   (b) the person must satisfy the Secretary of State that he is the father of the child.
3. The Secretary of State may determine whether a person is the father of a child for the purpose of regulation 2(b), and for this purpose the Secretary of State may have regard to any evidence which he considers to be relevant, including, but not limited to—
   (a) DNA test reports; and
   (b) court orders.

The Immigration (Provision of Physical Data) Regulations 2006

(SI 2006, No. 1743)

Citation, commencement and interpretation

1. These Regulations may be cited as the Immigration (Provision of Physical Data) Regulations 2006 and shall come into force on the day after they are made.

2. In these Regulations:

'application' means:

(a) an application for entry clearance; or

(b) an application for leave to enter the United Kingdom where the person seeking leave to enter presents a Convention travel document endorsed with an entry clearance for that journey to the United Kingdom;

'Convention travel document' means a travel document issued pursuant to Article 28 of the Refugee Convention, except where that travel document was issued by the United Kingdom Government;

'Refugee Convention' means the Convention relating to the Status of Refugees done at Geneva on 28th July 1951 and its Protocol.

Power for an authorised person to require an individual to provide a record of his fingerprints and a photograph of his face

3. Subject to regulations 4 and 5, an authorised person may require an individual who makes an application to provide a record of his fingerprints and a photograph of his face.

Provision in relation to applicants under the age of sixteen

4.—(1) An applicant under the age of sixteen shall not be required to provide a record of his fingerprints or a photograph of his face except where the authorised person is satisfied that the fingerprints or the photograph will be taken in the presence of a person aged eighteen or over who is—

(a) the child's parent or guardian; or

(b) a person who for the time being takes responsibility for the child.

(2) The person mentioned in paragraph (1)(b) may not be—

(a) an officer of the Secretary of State who is not an authorised person;

(b) an authorised person; or

(c) any other person acting on behalf of an authorised person as part of a process specified under regulation 6(2).

(3) An authorised person shall not require a person under the age of sixteen to provide a record of his fingerprints or a photograph of his face unless his decision to do so has been confirmed by a person designated for the purpose by the Secretary of State.

(4) This regulation shall not apply if the authorised person reasonably believes that the applicant is aged sixteen or over.

Provision in relation to section 141 of the Immigration and Asylum Act 1999

5. An applicant shall not be required to provide a record of his fingerprints or a photograph of his face under regulation 3 if he is a person to whom section 141 of the Immigration and Asylum Act 1999 applies, during the relevant period within the meaning of that section.

Process by which the applicant's fingerprints and photograph may be obtained and recorded

6.—(1) An authorised person who requires an individual to provide a record of his fingerprints or a photograph of his face under regulation 3 may require that individual to submit to any process specified in paragraph (2).

(2) A process by which the individual who makes the application:

(a) attends a British Diplomatic mission or British Consular post where a record of his fingerprints or a photograph of his face is taken;

(b) attends a Diplomatic mission or Consular post of another State where a record of his fingerprints or a photograph of his face is taken by an official of that State on behalf of an authorised person; or

(c) attends other premises nominated by an authorised person where a record of his fingerprints or a photograph of his face is taken by a person on behalf of an authorised person.

Consequences of failure to comply with these Regulations

7.—(1) Subject to paragraphs (2) and (3), where an individual does not provide a record of his fingerprints or a photograph of his face in accordance with a requirement imposed under these Regulations, his application may be treated as invalid.

(2) An application shall not be treated as invalid under paragraph (1) if it is for leave to enter the United Kingdom where the person seeking leave to enter presents a Convention travel document endorsed with an entry clearance for that journey to the United Kingdom.

(3) Where an application is of a type described in paragraph (2) and the applicant does not provide a record of his fingerprints or a photograph of his face

in accordance with a requirement imposed under these Regulations, that application may be refused.

Destruction of information

8. Subject to regulation 9, any record of fingerprints, photograph, copy of fingerprints or copy of a photograph held by the Secretary of State pursuant to these Regulations must be destroyed by the Secretary of State at the end of ten years beginning with the date on which the original record or photograph was provided.

9. If an applicant proves that he is—
   (a) a British citizen; or
   (b) a Commonwealth citizen who has a right of abode in the United Kingdom as a result of section 2(1)(b) of the Immigration Act 1971,

   any record of fingerprints, photograph, copy of fingerprints or copy of a photograph held by the Secretary of State pursuant to these Regulations must be destroyed as soon as reasonably practicable.

10.—(1) The Secretary of State must take all reasonably practicable steps to secure:
   (a) that data held in electronic form which relate to any record of fingerprints or photograph which have to be destroyed in accordance with regulation 8 or 9 are destroyed or erased; or
   (b) that access to such data is blocked.

(2) The applicant to whom the data relates is entitled, on written request, to a certificate issued by the Secretary of State to the effect that he has taken the steps required by paragraph (1).

(3) A certificate issued under paragraph (2) must be issued within three months of the date on which the request was received by the Secretary of State.

Revocation and transitional provisions

11.—(1) . . .

(2) For the purposes of paragraph (3) only, 'application' means an application within the meaning of regulation 2 of the Immigration (Provision of Physical Data) Regulations 2003 (the '2003 Regulations').

(3) Where a person made an application before these Regulations came into force, the 2003 Regulations will continue to apply for the purposes of that application as if they had not been revoked by paragraph (1).

The Immigration (Continuation of Leave) (Notices) Regulations 2006
(SI 2006, No. 2170)

Citation and Commencement

1. These Regulations may be cited as the Immigration (Continuation of Leave) (Notices) Regulations 2006 and shall come into force on 31st August 2006.

Decision on an application for variation of leave

2. For the purpose of section 3C of the Immigration Act 1971 an application for variation of leave is decided—
   - (a) when notice of the decision has been given in accordance with regulations made under section 105 of the Nationality, Immigration and Asylum Act 2002; or where no such notice is required,
   - (b) when notice of the decision has been given in accordance with section 4(1) of the Immigration Act 1971.

The Refugee or Person in Need of International Protection (Qualification) Regulations 2006
(SI 2006, No. 2525)

Citation and commencement

1.—(1) These Regulations may be cited as The Refugee or Person in Need of International Protection (Qualification) Regulations 2006 and shall come into force on 9th October 2006.

(2) These Regulations apply to any application for asylum which has not been decided and any immigration appeal brought under the Immigration Acts (as defined in section 64(2) of the Immigration, Asylum and Nationality Act 2006) which has not been finally determined.

Interpretation

2. In these Regulations—

   'application for asylum' means the request of a person to be recognised as a refugee under the Geneva Convention;

'Geneva Convention' means the Convention Relating to the Status of Refugees done at Geneva on 28 July 1951 and the New York Protocol of 31 January 1967;
'immigration rules' means rules made under section 3(2) of the Immigration Act 1971;
'persecution' means an act of persecution within the meaning of Article 1(A) of the Geneva Convention;
'person eligible for humanitarian protection' means a person who is eligible for a grant of humanitarian protection under the immigration rules;
'refugee' means a person who falls within Article 1(A) of the Geneva Convention and to whom regulation 7 does not apply;
'residence permit' means a document confirming that a person has leave to enter or remain in the United Kingdom whether limited or indefinite;
'serious harm' means serious harm as defined in the immigration rules;
'person' means any person who is not a British citizen.

Actors of persecution or serious harm

3. In deciding whether a person is a refugee or a person eligible for humanitarian protection, persecution or serious harm can be committed by:
   (a) the State;
   (b) any party or organisation controlling the State or a substantial part of the territory of the State;
   (c) any non-State actor if it can be demonstrated that the actors mentioned in paragraphs (a) and (b), including any international organisation, are unable or unwilling to provide protection against persecution or serious harm.

Actors of protection 

4.—(1) In deciding whether a person is a refugee or a person eligible for humanitarian protection, protection from persecution or serious harm can be provided by:
   (a) the State; or
   (b) any party or organisation, including any international organisation, controlling the State or a substantial part of the territory of the State.

(2) Protection shall be regarded as generally provided when the actors mentioned in paragraph (1)(a) and (b) take reasonable steps to prevent the persecution or suffering of serious harm by operating an effective legal system for the detection, prosecution and punishment of acts constituting persecution or serious harm, and the person mentioned in paragraph (1) has access to such protection.

(3) In deciding whether a person is a refugee or a person eligible for humanitarian protection the Secretary of State may assess whether an international

organisation controls a State or a substantial part of its territory and provides protection as described in paragraph (2).

Act of persecution 

5.—(1) In deciding whether a person is a refugee an act of persecution must be:

(a) sufficiently serious by its nature or repetition as to constitute a severe violation of a basic human right, in particular a right from which derogation cannot be made under Article 15 of the Convention for the Protection of Human Rights and Fundamental Freedoms; or

(b) an accumulation of various measures, including a violation of a human right which is sufficiently severe as to affect an individual in a similar manner as specified in (a).

(2) An act of persecution may, for example, take the form of:

(a) an act of physical or mental violence, including an act of sexual violence;

(b) a legal, administrative, police, or judicial measure which in itself is discriminatory or which is implemented in a discriminatory manner;

(c) prosecution or punishment, which is disproportionate or discriminatory;

(d) denial of judicial redress resulting in a disproportionate or discriminatory punishment;

(e) prosecution or punishment for refusal to perform military service in a conflict, where performing military service would include crimes or acts falling under regulation 7.

(3) An act of persecution must be committed for at least one of the reasons in Article 1(A) of the Geneva Convention.

Reasons for persecution 

6.—(1) In deciding whether a person is a refugee:

(a) the concept of race shall include consideration of, for example, colour, descent, or membership of a particular ethnic group;

(b) the concept of religion shall include, for example, the holding of theistic, non-theistic and atheistic beliefs, the participation in, or abstention from, formal worship in private or in public, either alone or in community with others, other religious acts or expressions of view, or forms of personal or communal conduct based on or mandated by any religious belief;

(c) the concept of nationality shall not be confined to citizenship or lack thereof but shall include, for example, membership of a group determined by its cultural, ethnic, or linguistic identity, common geographical or political origins or its relationship with the population of another State;

(d) a group shall be considered to form a particular social group where, for example:

(i) members of that group share an innate characteristic, or a common background that cannot be changed, or share a characteristic or belief that is so fundamental to identity or conscience that a person should not be forced to renounce it, and

(ii) that group has a distinct identity in the relevant country, because it is perceived as being different by the surrounding society;

(e) a particular social group might include a group based on a common characteristic of sexual orientation but sexual orientation cannot be understood to include acts considered to be criminal in accordance with national law of the United Kingdom;

(f) the concept of political opinion shall include the holding of an opinion, thought or belief on a matter related to the potential actors of persecution mentioned in regulation 3 and to their policies or methods, whether or not that opinion, thought or belief has been acted upon by the person.

(2) In deciding whether a person has a well-founded fear of being persecuted, it is immaterial whether he actually possesses the racial, religious, national, social or political characteristic which attracts the persecution, provided that such a characteristic is attributed to him by the actor of persecution.

Exclusion

7.—(1) A person is not a refugee, if he falls within the scope of Article 1D, 1E or 1F of the Geneva Convention.

(2) In the construction and application of Article 1F(b) of the Geneva Convention:

(a) the reference to serious non-political crime includes a particularly cruel action, even if it is committed with an allegedly political objective;

(b) the reference to the crime being committed outside the country of refuge prior to his admission as a refugee shall be taken to mean the time up to and including the day on which a residence permit is issued.

(3) Article 1F(a) and (b) of the Geneva Convention shall apply to a person who instigates or otherwise participates in the commission of the crimes or acts specified in those provisions.

EUROPEAN MATERIALS

EN 24.12.2002 Official Journal of the European Communities C 325/33

Consolidated Version of the Treaty Establishing the European Community

Part Two

Citizenship of The Union

Article 17

1. Citizenship of the Union is hereby established. Every person holding the nationality of a Member State shall be a citizen of the Union. Citizenship of the Union shall complement and not replace national citizenship.
2. Citizens of the Union shall enjoy the rights conferred by this Treaty and shall be subject to the duties imposed thereby.

Article 18([1])

1. Every citizen of the Union shall have the right to move and reside freely within the territory of the Member States, subject to the limitations and conditions laid down in this Treaty and by the measures adopted to give it effect.
2. If action by the Community should prove necessary to attain this objective and this Treaty has not provided the necessary powers, the Council may adopt provisions with a view to facilitating the exercise of the rights referred to in paragraph 1. The Council shall act in accordance with the procedure referred to in Article 251.
3. Paragraph 2 shall not apply to provisions on passports, identity cards, residence permits or any other such document or to provisions on social security or social protection.

Article 19

1. Every citizen of the Union residing in a Member State of which he is not a national shall have the right to vote and to stand as a candidate at municipal elections in the Member State in which he resides, under the same conditions as nationals of that State. This right shall be exercised subject to detailed arrangements adopted by the Council, acting unanimously on a proposal from the Commission and after consulting the European Parliament; these arrangements

[1] Article amended by the Treaty of Nice.

may provide for derogations where warranted by problems specific to a Member State.

2. Without prejudice to Article 190(4) and to the provisions adopted for its implementation, every citizen of the Union residing in a Member State of which he is not a national shall have the right to vote and to stand as a candidate in elections to the European Parliament in the Member State in which he resides, under the same conditions as nationals of that State. This right shall be exercised subject to detailed arrangements adopted by the Council, acting unanimously on a proposal from the Commission and after consulting the European Parliament; these arrangements may provide for derogations where warranted by problems specific to a Member State.

Article 20

Every citizen of the Union shall, in the territory of a third country in which the Member State of which he is a national is not represented, be entitled to protection by the diplomatic or consular authorities of any Member State, on the same conditions as the nationals of that State. Member States shall establish the necessary rules among themselves and start the international negotiations required to secure this protection.

Article 21

Every citizen of the Union shall have the right to petition the European Parliament in accordance with Article 194. Every citizen of the Union may apply to the Ombudsman established in accordance with Article 195. Every citizen of the Union may write to any of the institutions or bodies referred to in this Article or in Article 7 in one of the languages mentioned in Article 314 and have an answer in the same language.

Article 22

The Commission shall report to the European Parliament, to the Council and to the Economic and Social Committee every three years on the application of the provisions of this part. This report shall take account of the development of the Union. On this basis, and without prejudice to the other provisions of this Treaty, the Council, acting unanimously on a proposal from the Commission and after consulting the European Parliament, may adopt provisions to strengthen or to add to the rights laid down in this part, which it shall recommend to the Member States for adoption in accordance with their respective constitutional requirements.

Part Three

Community Policies

. . .

Title III

Free Movement of Persons, Services and Capital

Chapter 1

Workers

Article 39

1. Freedom of movement for workers shall be secured within the Community.
2. Such freedom of movement shall entail the abolition of any discrimination based on nationality between workers of the Member States as regards employment, remuneration and other conditions of work and employment.
3. It shall entail the right, subject to limitations justified on grounds of public policy, public security or public health:
   (a) to accept offers of employment actually made;
   (b) to move freely within the territory of Member States for this purpose;
   (c) to stay in a Member State for the purpose of employment in accordance with the provisions governing the employment of nationals of that State laid down by law, regulation or administrative action;
   (d) to remain in the territory of a Member State after having been employed in that State, subject to conditions which shall be embodied in implementing regulations to be drawn up by the Commission.
4. The provisions of this article shall not apply to employment in the public service.

Article 40

The Council shall, acting in accordance with the procedure referred to in Article 251 and after consulting the Economic and Social Committee, issue directives or make regulations setting out the measures required to bring about freedom of movement for workers, as defined in Article 39, in particular:

(a) by ensuring close cooperation between national employment services;
(b) by abolishing those administrative procedures and practices and those qualifying periods in respect of eligibility for available employment, whether resulting from national legislation or from agreements previously

concluded between Member States, the maintenance of which would form an obstacle to liberalisation of the movement of workers;

(c) by abolishing all such qualifying periods and other restrictions provided for either under national legislation or under agreements previously concluded between Member States as imposed on workers of other Member States conditions regarding the free choice of employment other than those imposed on workers of the State concerned;

(d) by setting up appropriate machinery to bring offers of employment into touch with applications for employment and to facilitate the achievement of a balance between supply and demand in the employment market in such a way as to avoid serious threats to the standard of living and level of employment in the various regions and industries.

Article 41

Member States shall, within the framework of a joint programme, encourage the exchange of young workers.

Article 42

The Council shall, acting in accordance with the procedure referred to in Article 251, adopt such measures in the field of social security as are necessary to provide freedom of movement for workers; to this end, it shall make arrangements to secure for migrant workers and their dependants:

(a) aggregation, for the purpose of acquiring and retaining the right to benefit and of calculating the amount of benefit, of all periods taken into account under the laws of the several countries;

(b) payment of benefits to persons resident in the territories of Member States.

The Council shall act unanimously throughout the procedure referred to in Article 251.

Chapter 2

Right of Establishment

Article 43

Within the framework of the provisions set out below, restrictions on the freedom of establishment of nationals of a Member State in the territory of another Member State shall be prohibited. Such prohibition shall also apply to restrictions on the setting-up of agencies, branches or subsidiaries by nationals of any Member State established in the territory of any Member State. Freedom of establishment shall include the right to take up and pursue activities as self-employed persons and to set up and manage undertakings, in particular companies or firms within the meaning of the second paragraph of Article 48, under the conditions laid down for its own nationals by the law of the country where such establishment is effected, subject to the provisions of the chapter relating to capital.

Article 44

1. In order to attain freedom of establishment as regards a particular activity, the Council, acting in accordance with the procedure referred to in Article 251 and after consulting the Economic and Social Committee, shall act by means of directives.
2. The Council and the Commission shall carry out the duties devolving upon them under the preceding provisions, in particular:
   (a) by according, as a general rule, priority treatment to activities where freedom of establishment makes a particularly valuable contribution to the development of production and trade;
   (b) by ensuring close cooperation between the competent authorities in the Member States in order to ascertain the particular situation within the Community of the various activities concerned;
   (c) by abolishing those administrative procedures and practices, whether resulting from national legislation or from agreements previously concluded between Member States, the maintenance of which would form an obstacle to freedom of establishment;
   (d) by ensuring that workers of one Member State employed in the territory of another Member State may remain in that territory for the purpose of taking up activities therein as self-employed persons, where they satisfy the conditions which they would be required to satisfy if they were entering that State at the time when they intended to take up such activities;
   (e) by enabling a national of one Member State to acquire and use land and buildings situated in the territory of another Member State, in so far as this does not conflict with the principles laid down in Article 33(2);
   (f) by effecting the progressive abolition of restrictions on freedom of establishment in every branch of activity under consideration, both as regards the conditions for setting up agencies, branches or subsidiaries in the territory of a Member State and as regards the subsidiaries in the territory of a Member State and as regards the conditions governing the entry of personnel belonging to the main establishment into managerial or supervisory posts in such agencies, branches or subsidiaries;
   (g) by coordinating to the necessary extent the safeguards which, for the protection of the interests of members and other, are required by Member States of companies or firms within the meaning of the second paragraph of Article 48 with a view to making such safeguards equivalent throughout the Community;

(h) by satisfying themselves that the conditions of establishment are not distorted by aids granted by Member States.

Article 45

The provisions of this chapter shall not apply, so far as any given Member State is concerned, to activities which in that State are connected, even occasionally, with the exercise of official authority. The Council may, acting by a qualified majority on a proposal from the Commission, rule that the provisions of this chapter shall not apply to certain activities.

Article 46

1. The provisions of this chapter and measures taken in pursuance thereof shall not prejudice the applicability of provisions laid down by law, regulation or administrative action providing for special treatment for foreign nationals on grounds of public policy, public security or public health.
2. The Council shall, acting in accordance with the procedure referred to in Article 251, issue directives for the coordination of the abovementioned provisions.

Article 47

1. In order to make it easier for persons to take up and pursue activities as self-employed persons, the Council shall, acting in accordance with the procedure referred to in Article 251, issue directives for the mutual recognition of diplomas, certificates and other evidence of formal qualifications.
2. For the same purpose, the Council shall, acting in accordance with the procedure referred to in Article 251, issue directives for the coordination of the provisions laid down by law, regulation or administrative action in Member States concerning the taking-up and pursuit of activities as self employed persons. The Council, acting unanimously throughout the procedure referred to in Article 251, shall decide on directives the implementation of which involves in at least one Member State amendment of the existing principles laid down by law governing the professions with respect to training and conditions of access for natural persons. In other cases the Council shall act by qualified majority.
3. In the case of the medical and allied and pharmaceutical professions, the progressive abolition of restrictions shall be dependent upon coordination of the conditions for their exercise in the various Member States.

Article 48

Companies or firms formed in accordance with the law of a Member State and having their registered office, central administration or principal place of business within the Community shall, for the purposes of this Chapter, be treated in the same way as natural persons who are nationals of Member States. 'Companies or firms' means companies or firms constituted under civil or commercial law, including cooperative societies, and other legal persons governed by public or private law, save for those which are non-profit-making.

Chapter 3
Services

Article 49

Within the framework of the provisions set out below, restrictions on freedom to provide services within the Community shall be prohibited in respect of nationals of Member States who are established in a State of the Community other than that of the person for whom the services are intended. The Council may, acting by a qualified majority on a proposal from the Commission, extend the provisions of the Chapter to nationals of a third country who provide services and who are established within the Community.

Article 50

Services shall be considered to be 'services' within the meaning of this Treaty where they are normally provided for remuneration, in so far as they are not governed by the provisions relating to freedom of movement for goods, capital and persons. 'Services' shall in particular include:

- (a) activities of an industrial character;
- (b) activities of a commercial character;
- (c) activities of craftsmen;
- (d) activities of the professions.

Without prejudice to the provisions of the chapter relating to the right of establishment, the person providing a service may, in order to do so, temporarily pursue his activity in the State where the service is provided, under the same conditions as are imposed by that State on its own nationals.

Article 51

1. Freedom to provide services in the field of transport shall be governed by the provisions of the title relating to transport.

2. The liberalisation of banking and insurance services connected with movements of capital shall be effected in step with the liberalisation of movement of capital.

Article 52

1. In order to achieve the liberalisation of a specific service, the Council shall, on a proposal from the Commission and after consulting the Economic and Social Committee and the European Parliament, issue directives acting by a qualified majority.
2. As regards the directives referred to in paragraph 1, priority shall as a general rule be given to those services which directly affect production costs or the liberalisation of which helps to promote trade in goods.

Article 53

The Member States declare their readiness to undertake the liberalisation of services beyond the extent required by the directives issued pursuant to Article 52(1), if their general economic situation and the situation of the economic sector concerned so permit. To this end, the Commission shall make recommendations to the Member States concerned.

Article 54

As long as restrictions on freedom to provide services have not been abolished, each Member State shall apply such restrictions without distinction on grounds of nationality or residence to all persons providing services within the meaning of the first paragraph of Article 49.

Article 55

The provisions of Articles 45 to 48 shall apply to the matters covered by this chapter.

...

Regulation (EEC) No. 1612/68 of the Council of 15 October 1968

on freedom of movement for workers within the Community

THE COUNCIL OF THE EUROPEAN COMMUNITIES,

Having regard to the Treaty establishing the European Economic Community, and in particular Article 49 thereof;

Having regard to the proposal from the Commission;

Having regard to the Opinion of the European Parliament;

Having regard to the Opinion of the Economic and Social Committee;

Whereas freedom of movement for workers should be secured within the Community by the end of the transitional period at the latest; whereas the attainment of this objective entails the abolition of any discrimination based on nationality between workers of the Member States as regards employment, remuneration and other conditions of work and employment, as well as the right of such workers to move freely within the Community in order to pursue activities as employed persons subject to any limitations justified on grounds of public policy, public security or public health;

Whereas by reason in particular of the early establishment of the customs union and in order to ensure the simultaneous completion of the principal foundations of the Community, provisions should be adopted to enable the objectives laid down in Articles 48 and 49 of the Treaty in the field of freedom of movement to be achieved and to perfect measures adopted successively under Regulation No 15 on the first steps for attainment of freedom of movement and under Council Regulation No 38/64/EEC of 25 March 1964 on freedom of movement for workers within the Community;

Whereas freedom of movement constitutes a fundamental right of workers and their families; whereas mobility of labour within the Community must be one of the means by which the worker is guaranteed the possibility of improving his living and working conditions and promoting his social advancement, while helping to satisfy the requirements of the economies of the Member States; whereas the right of all workers in the Member States to pursue the activity of their choice within the Community should be affirmed;

Whereas such right must be enjoyed without discrimination by permanent, seasonal and frontier workers and by those who pursue their activities for the purpose of providing services;

Whereas the right of freedom of movement, in order that it may be exercised, by objective standards, in freedom and dignity, requires that equality of treatment shall be ensured in fact and in law in respect of all matters relating to the actual pursuit of activities as employed persons and to eligibility for housing, and also that obstacles to the mobility of workers shall be eliminated, in particular as regards the worker's right to be joined by his family and the conditions for the integration of that family into the host country;

Whereas the principle of non-discrimination between Community workers entails that all nationals of Member States have the same priority as regards employment as is enjoyed by national workers;

Whereas it is necessary to strengthen the machinery for vacancy clearance, in particular by developing direct co-operation between the central employment services and also between the regional services, as well as by increasing and co-ordinating the exchange of information in order to ensure in a general way a clearer picture of the labour market; whereas workers wishing to move should also be regularly informed of living and working conditions; whereas, furthermore, measures should be provided for the case where a Member State undergoes or foresees disturbances on its labour market which may seriously threaten the standard of living and level of employment in a region or an industry; whereas for this purpose the exchange of information, aimed at discouraging workers from moving to such a region or industry, constitutes the method to be applied in the first place but, where necessary, it should be possible to strengthen the results of such exchange of information by temporarily suspending the above-mentioned machinery, any such decision to be taken at Community level;

Whereas close links exist between freedom of movement for workers, employment and vocational training, particularly where the latter aims at putting workers in a position to take up offers of employment from other regions of the Community; whereas such links make it necessary that the problems arising in this connection should no longer be studied in isolation but viewed as inter-dependent, account also being taken of the problems of employment at the regional level; and whereas it is therefore necessary to direct the efforts of Member States toward co-ordinating their employment policies at Community level;

Whereas the Council, by its Decision of 15 October 1968 made Articles 48 and 49 of the Treaty and also the measures taken in implementation thereof applicable to the French overseas departments;

HAS ADOPTED THIS REGULATION:

Part I
Employment and Workers' Families

Title I

Eligibility for employment

Article 1

1. Any national of a Member State, shall, irrespective of his place of residence, have the right to take up an activity as an employed person, and to pursue such activity, within the territory of another Member State in accordance with the provisions laid down by law, regulation or administrative action governing the employment of nationals of that State.
2. He shall, in particular, have the right to take up available employment in the territory of another Member State with the same priority as nationals of that State.

Article 2

Any national of a Member State and any employer pursuing an activity in the territory of a Member State may exchange their applications for and offers of employment, and may conclude and perform contracts of employment in accordance with the provisions in force laid down by law, regulation or administrative action, without any discrimination resulting therefrom.

Article 3

1. Under this Regulation, provisions laid down by law, regulation or administrative action or administrative practices of a Member State shall not apply:
   — where they limit application for and offers of employment, or the right of foreign nationals to take up and pursue employment or subject these to conditions not applicable in respect of their own nationals; or
   — where, though applicable irrespective of nationality, their exclusive or principal aim or effect is to keep nationals of other Member States away from the employment offered.

   This provision shall not apply to conditions relating to linguistic knowledge required by reason of the nature of the post to be filled.
2. There shall be included in particular among the provisions or practices of a Member State referred to in the first subparagraph of paragraph 1 those which:
   (a) prescribe a special recruitment procedure for foreign nationals;

(b) limit or restrict the advertising of vacancies in the press or through any other medium or subject it to conditions other than those applicable in respect of employers pursuing their activities in the territory of that Member State;
(c) subject eligibility for employment to condition of registration with employment offices or impede recruitment of individual workers, where persons who do not reside in the territory of that State are concerned.

Article 4

1. Provisions laid down by law, regulation or administrative action of the Member States which restrict by number or percentage the employment of foreign nationals in any undertaking, branch of activity or region, or at a national level, shall not apply to nationals of the other Member States.
2. When in a Member State the granting of any benefit to undertakings is subject to a minimum percentage of national workers being employed, nationals of the other Member States shall be counted as national workers, subject to the provisions of the Council Directive of 15 October 1963.

Article 5

A national of a Member State who seeks employment in the territory of another Member State shall receive the same assistance there as that afforded by the employment offices in that State to their own nationals seeking employment.

Article 6

1. The engagement and recruitment of a national of one Member State for a post in another Member State shall not depend on medical, vocational or other criteria which are discriminatory on grounds of nationality by comparison with those applied to nationals of the other Member State who wish to pursue the same activity.
2. Nevertheless, a national who holds an offer in his name from an employer in a Member State other than that of which he is a national may have to undergo a vocational test, if the employer expressly requests this when making his offer of employment.

Title II

Employment and equality of treatment

Article 7

1. A worker who is a national of a Member State may not, in the territory of another Member State, be treated differently from national workers by

reason of his nationality in respect of any conditions of employment and work, in particular as regards remuneration, dismissal, and should he become unemployed, reinstatement or re-employment;

2. He shall enjoy the same social and tax advantages as national workers.
3. He shall also, by virtue of the same right and under the same conditions as national workers, have access to training in vocational schools and retraining centres.
4. Any clause of a collective or individual agreement or of any other collective regulation concerning eligibility for employment, employment remuneration and other conditions of work or dismissal shall be null and void in so far as it lays down or authorises discriminatory conditions in respect of workers who are nationals of the other Member States.

Article 8

1. A worker who is a national of a Member State and who is employed in the territory of another Member State shall enjoy equality of treatment as regards membership of trade unions and the exercise of rights attaching thereto, including the right to vote; [and to be eligible for the administration or management posts of a trade union,] he may be excluded from taking part in the management of bodies governed by public law and from holding an office governed by public law. Furthermore, he shall have the right of eligibility for workers' representative bodies in the undertaking. The provisions of this Article shall not affect laws or regulations in certain Member States which grant more extensive rights to workers coming from the other Member States.
2. . . .

Note: Article 8 amended by EEC 312/76.

Article 9

1. A worker who is a national of a Member State and who is employed in the territory of another Member State shall enjoy all the rights and benefits accorded to national workers in matters of housing, including ownership of the housing he needs.
2. Such worker may, with the same right as nationals, put his name down on the housing lists in the region in which he is employed, where such lists exist; he shall enjoy the resultant benefits and priorities.

   If his family has remained in the country whence he came, they shall be considered for this purpose as residing in the said region, where national workers benefit from a similar presumption.

Title III

Workers' families

Article 10

. . .

Note: Article 10 repealed from 30 April 2006 (Directive 2004/38, Article 38).

Article 11

. . .

Note: Article 11 repealed from 30 April 2006 (Directive 2004/38, Article 38).

Article 12

The children of a national of a Member State who is or has been employed in the territory of another Member State shall be admitted to that State's general educational, apprenticeship and vocational training courses under the same conditions as the nationals of that State, if such children are residing in its territory.

Member States shall encourage all efforts to enable such children to attend these courses under the best possible conditions.

Part II

Clearance of Vacancies and Applications for Employment

Title I

Co-operation between the Member States and with the Commission

Article 13

1. The Member States or the Commission shall instigate or together undertake any study of employment or unemployment which they consider necessary for securing freedom of movement for workers within the Community.

   The central employment services of the Member States shall co-operate closely with each other and with the Commission with a view to acting jointly as regards the clearing of vacancies and applications for employment within the Community and the resultant placing of workers in employment.

2. To this end the Member States shall designate specialist services which shall be entrusted with organising work in the fields referred to above and co-operating with each other and with the departments of the Commission.

   The Member States shall notify the Commission of any change in the designation of such services; the Commission shall publish details thereof for information in the *Official Journal of the European Communities.*

Article 14

1. The Member States shall send to the Commission information on problems arising in connection with the freedom of movement and employment of workers and particulars of the state and development of employment.

[2. The Commission, taking the utmost account of the opinion of the Technical Committee, shall determine the manner in which the information referred to in paragraph 1 is to be drawn up.]

3. In accordance with the procedure laid down by the Commission [taking the utmost account of the opinion of the Technical Committee,] the specialist service of each Member State shall send to the specialist services of the other Member States and to the European Co-ordination Office such information concerning living and working conditions and the state of the labour market as is likely to be of guidance to workers from the other Member States. Such information shall be brought up to date regularly.

   The specialist services of the other Member States shall ensure that wide publicity is given to such information, in particular by circulating it among the appropriate employment services and by all suitable means of communication for informing the workers concerned.

Note: Amended by EEC 2434/92.

Title II

Machinery for vacancy clearance

[Article 15

1. The specialist service of each Member State shall regularly send to the specialist services of the other Member States and to the European Co-ordination Office:
   (a) details of vacancies which could be filled by nationals of other Member States;
   (b) details of vacancies addressed to non-Member States;
   (c) details of applications for employment by those who have formally expressed a wish to work in another Member State;
   (d) information, by region and by branch of activity, on applicants who have declared themselves actually willing to accept employment in another country.

   The specialist service of each Member State shall forward this information to the appropriate employment services and agencies as soon as possible.

2. The details of vacancies and applications referred to in paragraph 1 shall be circulated according to a uniform system to be established by the European Coordination Office in collaboration with the Technical Committee.

   If necessary, the European Co-ordination Office may adapt this system in collaboration with the Technical Committee.]

Note: Substituted by EEC 2434/92.

[Article 16

1. Any vacancy within the meaning of Article 15 communicated to the employment services of a Member State shall be notified to and processed by the competent employment services of the other Member States concerned.

   Such services shall forward to the services of the first Member State the details of suitable applications.
2. The applications for employment referred to in Article 15(1)(c) shall be responded to by the relevant services of the Member States within a reasonable period, not exceeding one month.
3. The employment services shall grant workers who are nationals of the Member States the same priority as the relevant measures grant to nationals vis-a'-vis workers from non-Member States.]

Note: Substituted by EEC 2434/92.

Article 17

1. The provisions of Article 16 shall be implemented by the specialist services. However, in so far as they have been authorised by the central services and in so far as the organisation of the employment services of a Member State and the placing teachniques employment make it possible:
   (a) the regional employment services of the Member States shall:
      (i) on the basis of the [details] referred to in Article 15, on which appropriate action will be taken, directly bring together and clear vacancies and applications for employment;
      (ii) establish direct relations for clearance:
         — of vacancies offered to a named worker;
         — of individual applications for employment sent either to a specific employment service or to an employer pursuing his activity within the area covered by such a service;
         — where the clearing operations concern seasonal workers who must be recruited as quickly as possible;
   [(b) the services territorially responsible for the border regions of two or more Member States shall regularly exchange data relating to vacancies and applications for employment in their area and, acting in accordance with their arrangements with the other employment services of their countries,

shall directly bring together and clear vacancies and applications for employment.

If necessary, the services territorially responsible for border regions shall also set up cooperation and service structures to provide:

— users with as much practical information as possible on the various aspects of mobility, and

— management and labour, social services (in particular public, private or those of public interest) and all institutions concerned, with a framework of coordinated measures relating to mobility;]

(c) official employment services which specialise in certain occupations or specific categories of persons shall co-operate directly with each other.

2. The Member States concerned shall forward to the Commission the list, drawn up by common accord, of services referred to in paragraph 1; the Commission shall publish such list, and any amendment thereto, in the Official Journal of the European Communities.

Note: Amended by EEC 2434/92.

Article 18

Adoption of recruiting procedures as applied by the implementing bodies provided for under agreements concluded between two or more Member States shall not be obligatory.

Title III

Measures for controlling the balance of the labour market

Article 19

[1. On the basis of a report from the Commission drawn up from information supplied by the Member States, the latter and the Commission shall at least once a year analyse jointly the results of Community arrangements regarding vacancies and applications.]

2. The Member States shall examine with the Commission all the possibilities of giving priority to nationals of Member States when filling employment vacancies in order to achieve a balance between vacancies and applications for employment within the Community. They shall adopt all measures necessary for this purpose.

[3. Every two years the Commission shall submit a report to the European Parliament, the Council and the Economic and Social Committee on the implementation of Part II of this Regulation, summarizing the information required and the data obtained from the studies and research carried out and highlighting any useful points with regard to developments on the Community's labour market.]

Note: Amended by EEC 2434/92.

Article 20

. . .

Note: Deleted by EEC 2434/92.

TITLE IV

European Co-ordination Office

Article 21

The European Office for Co-ordinating the Clearance of Vacancies and Applications for Employment, established within the Commission (called in this Regulation the 'European Co-ordination Office'), shall have the general task of promoting vacancy clearance at Community level. It shall be responsible in particular for all the technical duties in this field which, under the provisions of this Regulation, are assigned to the Commission, and especially for assisting the national employment services.

It shall summarise the information referred to in Articles 14 and 15 and the data arising out of the studies and research carried out pursuant to Article 13, so as to bring to light any useful facts about foreseeable developments on the Community labour market; such facts shall be communicated to the specialist services of the Member States and to the Advisory and Technical Committees.

Article 22

1. The European Co-ordination Office shall be responsible, in particular, for:
   (a) co-ordinating the practical measures necessary for vacancy clearance at Community level and for analysing the resulting movements of workers;
   (b) contributing to such objectives by implementing, in co-operation with the Technical Committee, joint methods of action at administrative and technical levels;
   (c) carrying out, where a special need arises, and in agreement with the specialist services, the bringing together of vacancies and applications for employment for clearance by these specialist services.
2. It shall communicate to the specialist services vacancies and applications for employment sent directly to the Commission, and shall be informed of the action taken thereon.

Article 23

The Commission may, in agreement with the competent authority of each Member State, and in accordance with the conditions and procedures which it shall determine on the basis of the Opinion of the Technical Committee, organise visits and assignments for officials of other Member States, and also advanced programmes for specialist personnel.

Part III

Committees for Ensuring Close Co-operation Between the Member States in Matters Concerning the Freedom of Movement of Workers and Their Employment

Title I

The Advisory Committee

Article 24

The Advisory Committee shall be responsible for assisting the Commission in the examination of any questions arising from the application of the Treaty and measures taken in pursuance thereof, in matters concerning freedom of movement of workers and their employment.

Article 25

The Advisory Committee shall be responsible in particular for:

(a) examining problems concerning freedom of movement and employment within the framework of national manpower policies, with a view to co-ordinating the employment policies of the Member States at Community level, thus contributing to the development of the economies and to an improved balance of the labour market;

(b) making a general study of the effects of implementing this Regulation and any supplementary measures;

(c) submitting to the Commission any reasoned proposals for revising this Regulation;

(d) delivering, either at the request of the Commission or on its own initiative, reasoned opinions on general questions or on questions of principle, in particular on exchange of information concerning developments in the labour market, on the movement of workers between Member States, on programmes or measures to develop vocational guidance and vocational training which are likely to increase the possibilities of freedom of movement and employment, and on all forms of assistance to workers and their families, including social assistance and the housing of workers.

Article 26

1. The Advisory Committee shall be composed of six members for each Member State, two of whom shall represent the government, two the trade unions and two the employers' associations.
2. For each of the categories referred to in paragraph 1, one alternate member shall be appointed by each Member State.
3. The term of office of the members and their alternates shall be two years. Their appointments shall be renewable.

   On expiry of their term of office, the members and their alternates shall remain in office until replaced or until their appointments are renewed.

Article 27

The members of the Advisory Committee and their alternates shall be appointed by the Council which shall endeavour, when selecting representatives of trade unions and employers' associations, to achieve adequate representation on the Committee of the various economic sectors concerned.

The list of members and their alternates shall be published by the Council for information in the *Official Journal of the European Communities.*

Article 28

The Advisory Committee shall be chaired by a member of the Commission or his alternate. The Chairman shall not vote. The Committee shall meet at least twice a year. It shall be convened by its Chairman, either on his own initiative, or at the request of at least one third of the members. Secretarial services shall be provided for the Committee by the Commission.

Article 29

The chairman may invite individuals or representatives of bodies with wide experience in the field of employment or movement of workers to take part in meetings as observers or as experts. The Chairman may be assisted by expert advisers.

Article 30

1. An opinion delivered by the Committee shall not be valid unless two-thirds of the members are present.

2. Opinions shall state the reasons on which they are based; they shall be delivered by an absolute majority of the votes validly cast; they shall be accompanied by a written statement of the views expressed by the minority, when the latter so requests.

Article 31

The Advisory Committee shall establish its working methods by rules of procedure which shall enter into force after the Council, having received an opinion from the Commission, has given its approval. The entry into force of any amendment that the Committee decides to make thereto shall be subject to the same procedure.

TITLE II

The Technical Committee

Article 32

The Technical Committee shall be responsible for assisting the Commission to prepare, promote and follow up all technical work and measures for giving effect to this Regulation and any supplementary measures.

Article 33

The Technical Committee shall be responsible in particular for:

(a) promoting and advancing co-operation between the public authorities concerned in the Member States on all technical questions relating to freedom of movement of workers and their employment;

(b) formulating procedures for the organisation of the joint activities of the public authorities concerned;

(c) facilitating the gathering of information likely to be of use to the Commission and for the studies and research provided for in this Regulation, and encouraging exchange of information and experience between the administrative bodies concerned;

(d) investigating at a technical level the harmonisation of the criteria by which Member States assess the state of their labour markets.

Article 34

1. The Technical Committee shall be composed of representatives of the Governments of the Member States. Each Government shall appoint as member of the Technical Committee one of the members who represent it on the Advisory Committee.

2. Each government shall appoint an alternate from among its other representatives—members or alternates—on the Advisory Committee.

Article 35

The Technical Committee shall be chaired by a member of the Commission or his representative. The Chairman shall not vote. The Chairman and the members of the Committee may be assisted by expert advisers.

Secretarial services shall be provided for the Committee by the Commission.

Article 36

The proposals and opinions formulated by the Technical Committee shall be submitted to the Commission, and the Advisory Committee shall be informed thereof. Any such proposals and opinions shall be accompanied by a written statement of the views expressed by the various members of the Technical Committee, when the latter so request.

Article 37

The Technical Committee shall establish its working methods by rules of procedure which shall enter into force after the Council, having received an opinion from the Commission, has given its approval. The entry into force of any amendment which the Committee decides to make thereto shall be subject to the same procedure.

Part IV

Transitional and Final Provisions

Title I

Transitional provisions

Article 38

Until the adoption by the Commission of the uniform system referred to in Article 15(2), the European Co-ordination Office shall propose any measures likely to be of use in drawing up and circulating the returns referred to in Article 15(1).

Article 39

The rules of procedure of the Advisory Committee and the Technical Committee in force at the time of entry into force of this Regulation shall continue to apply.

Article 40

Until the entry into force of the measures to be taken by Member States in pursuance of the Council Directive of 15 October 1968 and where, under the measures taken by the Member States in pursuance of the Council Directive of 25 March 1964 the work permit provided for in Article 22 of Regulation No 38/64/EEC is necessary to determine the period of validity and extension of the residence permit, written confirmation of engagement from the employer or a certificate of employment stating the period of employment may be substituted for such work permit. Any written confirmation by the employer or certificate of employment showing that the worker has been engaged for an indefinite period shall have the same effect as that of a permanent work permit.

Article 41

If, by reason of the abolition of the work permit, a Member State can no longer compile certain statistics on the employment of foreign nationals, such Member State may, for statistical purposes, retain the work permit in respect of nationals of the other Member States until new statistical methods are introduced, but no later than 31 December 1969. The work permit must be issued automatically and must be valid until the actual abolition of work permits in such Member State.

Title II

Final provisions

Article 42

1. This Regulation shall not affect the provisions of the Treaty establishing the European Coal and Steel Community which relate to workers with recognised qualifications in coalmining or steelmaking, nor those of the Treaty establishing the European Atomic Energy Community which deal with eligibility for skilled employment in the field of nuclear energy, nor any measures taken in pursuance of those Treaties.

   Nevertheless, this Regulation shall apply to categories of workers referred to in the first subparagraph and to members of their families in so far as their legal position is not governed by the above-mentioned Treaties or measures.
2. This Regulation shall not affect measures taken in accordance with Article 51 of the Treaty.
3. This Regulation shall not affect the obligations of Member States arising out of:
   — special relations or future agreements with certain non-European countries or territories, based on institutional ties existing at the time of the entry into force of this Regulation; or

— agreements in existence at the time of the entry into force of this Regulation with certain non-European countries or territories, based on institutional ties between them.

Workers from such countries or territories who, in accordance with this provision, are pursuing activities as employed persons in the territory of one of those Member States may not invoke the benefit of the provisions of this Regulation in the territory of the other Member States.

Article 43

Member States shall, for information purposes, communicate to the Commission the texts of agreements, conventions or arrangements concluded between them in the manpower field between the date of their being signed and that of their entry into force.

Article 44

The Commission shall adopt measures pursuant to this Regulation for its implementation. To this end it shall act in close co-operation with the central public authorities of the Member States.

Article 45

The Commission shall submit to the Council proposals aimed at abolishing, in accordance with the conditions of the Treaty, restrictions on eligibility for employment of workers who are nationals of Member States, where the absence of mutual recognition of diplomas, certificates or other evidence of formal qualifications may prevent freedom of movement for workers.

Article 46

The administrative expenditure of the Committees referred to in Part III shall be included in the budget of the European Communities in the section relating to the Commission.

Article 47

This Regulation shall apply to the territories of the Member States and to their nationals, without prejudice to Articles 2, 3, 10 and 11.

Article 48

Regulation No 38/64/EEC shall cease to have effect when this Regulation enters into force.

This Regulation shall be binding in its entirety and directly applicable in all Member States.

Done at Luxembourg, 15 October 1968.

Note: Annex deleted by EEC 2434/92.

Regulation (EEC) No. 1251/70 of the Commission of 29 June 1970

on the right of workers to remain in the territory of a Member State after having been employed in that State

THE COMMISSION OF THE EUROPEAN COMMUNITIES,

Having regard to the Treaty establishing the European Economic Community, and in particular Article 48(3)(d) thereof, and Article 2 of the Protocol on the Grand Duchy of Luxembourg;

Having regard to the Opinion of the European Parliament;

Whereas Council Regulation (EEC) No 1612/68 of 15 October 1968 and Council Directive No 68/360/EEC of 15 October 1968 enabled freedom of movement for workers to be secured at the end of a series of measures to be achieved progressively; whereas the right of residence acquired by workers in active employment has as a corollary the right, granted by the Treaty to such workers, to remain in the territory of a Member State after having been employed in that State; whereas it is important to lay down the conditions for the exercise of such right;

Whereas the said Council Regulation and Council Directive contain the appropriate provisions concerning the right of workers to reside in the territory of a Member State for the purposes of employment; whereas the right to remain, referred to in Article 48(3)(d) of the Treaty; is interpreted therefore as the right of the worker to maintain his residence in the territory of a Member State when he ceases to be employed there;

Whereas the mobility of labour in the Community requires that workers may be employed successively in several Member States without thereby being placed at a disadvantage;

Whereas it is important, in the first place, to guarantee to the worker residing in the territory of a Member State the right to remain in that territory when he ceases to be employed in that State because he has reached retirement age or by reason of permanent incapacity to work; whereas, however, it is equally important to ensure that right for the worker who, after a period of employment and residence in the territory of a Member State, works as an employed person in the territory of another Member State, while still retaining his residence in the territory of the first State;

Whereas, to determine the conditions under which the right to remain arises, account should be taken of the reasons which have led to the termination of employment in the territory of the Member State concerned and, in particular, of the difference between retirement, the normal and foreseeable end of working life, and incapacity to work which leads to a premature and unforeseeable termination of activity; whereas special conditions must be laid down where termination of activity is the result of an accident at work or occupational disease, or where the worker's spouse is or was a national of the Member State concerned;

Whereas the worker who has reached the end of his working life should have sufficient time in which to decide where he wishes to establish his final residence;

Whereas the exercise by the worker of the right to remain entails that such right shall be extended to members of his family; whereas in the case of the death of the worker during his working life, maintenance of the right of residence of the members of his family must also be recognised and be the subject of special conditions;

Whereas persons to whom the right to remain applies must enjoy equality of treatment with national workers who have ceased their working lives;

HAS ADOPTED THIS REGULATION:

Article 1

The provisions of this Regulation shall apply to nationals of a Member State who have worked as employed persons in the territory of another Member State and to members of their families, as defined in Article 10 of Council Regulation (EEC) No 1612/68 on freedom of movement for workers within the Community.

Article 2

1. The following shall have the right to remain permanently in the territory of a Member State:
   (a) a worker who, at the time of termination of his activity, has reached the age laid down by the law of that Member State for entitlement to an old-age pension and who has been employed in that State for at least the last twelve months and has resided there continuously for more than three years;
   (b) a worker who, having resided continuously in the territory of that State for more than two years, ceases to work there as an employed person as a result of permanent incapacity to work. If such incapacity is the result of an accident at work or an occupational disease entitling him to a pension for which an institution of that State is entirely or partially responsible, no condition shall be imposed as to length of residence;

(c) a worker who, after three years' continuous employment and residence in the territory of that State, works as an employed person in the territory of another Member State, while retaining his residence in the territory of the first State, to which he returns, as a rule, each day or at least once a week.

Periods of employment completed in this way in the territory of the other Member State shall, for the purposes of entitlement to the rights referred to in subparagraphs (a) and (b), be considered as having been completed in the territory of the State of residence.

2. The conditions as to length of residence and employment laid down in paragraph 1(a) and the condition as to length of residence laid down in paragraph 1(b) shall not apply if the worker's spouse is a national of the Member State concerned or has lost the nationality of that State by marriage to that worker.

Article 3

1. The members of a worker's family referred to in Article 1 of this Regulation who are residing with him in the territory of a Member State shall be entitled to remain there permanently if the worker has acquired the right to remain in the territory of that State in accordance with Article 2, and to do so even after his death.

2. If, however, the worker dies during his working life and before having acquired the right to remain in the territory of the State concerned, members of his family shall be entitled to remain there permanently on condition that:
   - the worker, on the date of his decease, had resided continuously in the territory of that Member State for at least 2 years; or
   - his death resulted from an accident at work or an occupational disease; or
   - the surviving spouse is a national of the State of residence or lost the nationality of that State by marriage to that worker.

Article 4

1. Continuity of residence as provided for in Articles 2(1) and 3(2) may be attested by any means of proof in use in the country of residence. It shall not be affected by temporary absences not exceeding a total of three months per year, nor by longer absences due to compliance with the obligations of military service.

2. Periods of involuntary unemployment, duly recorded by the competent employment office, and absences due to illness or accident shall be considered as periods of employment within the meaning of Article 2(1).

Article 5

1. The person entitled to the right to remain shall be allowed to exercise it within

two years from the time of becoming entitled to such right pursuant to Article 2(1)(a) and (b) and Article 3. During such period he may leave the territory of the Member State without adversely affecting such right.

2. No formality shall be required on the part of the person concerned in respect of the exercise of the right to remain.

Article 6

1. Persons coming under the provisions of this Regulation shall be entitled to a residence permit which:
   (a) shall be issued and renewed free of charge or on payment of a sum not exceeding the dues and taxes payable by nationals for the issue or renewal identity documents;
   (b) must be valid throughout the territory of the Member State issuing it;
   (c) must be valid for at least five years and be renewable automatically.
2. Periods of non-residence not exceeding six consecutive months shall not affect the validity of the residence permit.

Article 7

The right of equality of treatment, established by Council Regulation (EEC) No 1612/68, shall apply also to persons coming under the provisions of this Regulation.

Article 8

1. This Regulation shall not affect any provisions laid down by law, regulation or administrative action of one Member State which would be more favourable to nationals of other Member States.
2. Member States shall facilitate re-admission to their territories of workers who have left those territories after having resided there permanently for a long period and having been employed there and who wish to return there when they have reached retirement age or are permanently incapacitated for work.

Article 9

1. The Commission may, taking account of developments in the demographic situation of the Grand Duchy of Luxembourg, lay down, at the request of that State, different conditions from those provided for in this Regulation, in respect of the exercise of the right to remain in Luxembourg territory.
2. Within two months after the request supplying all appropriate details has been

put before it, the Commission shall take a decision, stating the reasons on which it is based.

It shall notify the Grand Duchy of Luxembourg of such decision and inform the other Member States thereof;

This Regulation shall be binding in its entirety and directly applicable in all Member States.

Done at Brussels, 29 June 1970.

Council Directive of 25 July 1977

on the education of the children of migrant workers (77/486/EEC)

THE COUNCIL OF THE EUROPEAN COMMUNITIES,

Having regard to the Treaty establishing the European Economic Community, and in particular Article 49 thereof,

Having regard to the proposal from the Commission,

Having regard to the opinion of the European Parliament,

Having regard to the opinion of the Economic and Social Committee,

Whereas in its resolution of 21 January 1974 concerning a social action programme, the Council included in its priority actions those designed to improve the conditions of freedom of movement for workers relating in particular to reception and to the education of their children;

Whereas in order to permit the integration of such children into the educational environment and the school system of the host State, they should be able to receive suitable tuition including teaching of the language of the host State;

Whereas host Member States should also take, in conjunction with the Member States of origin, appropriate measures to promote the teaching of the mother tongue and of the culture of the country of origin of the abovementioned children, with a view principally to facilitating their possible reintegration into the Member State of origin,

HAS ADOPTED THIS DIRECTIVE:

Article 1

This Directive shall apply to children for whom school attendance is compulsory under the laws of the host State, who are dependants of any worker who is a national of another Member State, where such children are resident in the territory of the Member State in which that national carries on or has carried on an activity as an employed person.

Article 2

Member States shall, in accordance with their national circumstances and legal systems, take appropriate measures to ensure that free tuition to facilitate initial reception is offered in their territory to the children referred to in Article 1, including, in particular, the teaching—adapted to the specific needs of such children—of the official language or one of the official languages of the host State.

Member States shall take the measures necessary for the training and further training of the teachers who are to provide this tuition.

Article 3

Member States shall, in accordance with their national circumstances and legal systems, and in cooperation with States of origin, take appropriate measures to promote, in coordination with normal education, teaching of the mother tongue and culture of the country of origin for the children referred to in Article 1.

Article 4

The Member States shall take the necessary measures to comply with this Directive within four years of its notification and shall forthwith inform the Commission thereof.

The Member States shall also inform the Commission of all laws, regulations and administrative or other provisions which they adopt in the field governed by this Directive.

Article 5

The Member States shall forward to the Commission within five years of the notification of this Directive, and subsequently at regular intervals at the request of the Commission, all relevant information to enable the Commission to report to the Council on the application of this Directive.

Article 6

This Directive is addressed to the Member States.

Done at Brussels, 25 July 1977.

Council Directive 2001/55/EC

of 20 July 2001

on minimum standards for giving temporary protection in the event of a mass influx of displaced persons and on measures promoting a balance of efforts between Member States in receiving such persons and bearing the consequences thereof

Note: Entered into force on 7 August 2001 (Article 33).

THE COUNCIL OF THE EUROPEAN UNION,

Having regard to the Treaty establishing the European Community, and in particular point 2(a) and (b) of Article 63 thereof,

Having regard to the proposal from the Commission[2],

Having regard to the opinion of the European Parliament[3],

Having regard to the opinion of the Economic and Social Committee[4],

Having regard to the opinion of the Committee of the Regions[5],

Whereas:

(1) The preparation of a common policy on asylum, including common European arrangements for asylum, is a constituent part of the European Union's objective of establishing progressively an area of freedom, security and justice open to those who, forced by circumstances, legitimately seek protection in the European Union.

(2) Cases of mass influx of displaced persons who cannot return to their country of origin have become more substantial in Europe in recent years. In these cases it may be necessary to set up exceptional schemes to offer them immediate temporary protection.

(3) In the conclusions relating to persons displaced by the conflict in the former Yugoslavia adopted by the Ministers responsible for immigration at their meetings in London on 30 November and 1 December 1992 and Copenhagen on 1 and 2 June 1993, the Member States and the Community institutions expressed their concern at the situation of displaced persons.

(4) On 25 September 1995 the Council adopted a Resolution on burden-sharing with regard to the admission and residence of displaced persons on a temporary

[2] OJ C 311 E, 31.10.2000, p. 251.

[3] Opinion delivered on 13 March 2001 (not yet published in the Official Journal).

[4] OJ C 155, 29.5.2001, p. 21.

[5] Opinion delivered on 13 June 2001 (not yet published in the Official Journal).

basis[6], and, on 4 March 1996, adopted Decision 96/198/JHA on an alert and emergency procedure for burden-sharing with regard to the admission and residence of displaced persons on a temporary basis[7].

(5) The Action Plan of the Council and the Commission of 3 December 1998[8] provides for the rapid adoption, in accordance with the Treaty of Amsterdam, of minimum standards for giving temporary protection to displaced persons from third countries who cannot return to their country of origin and of measures promoting a balance of effort between Member States in receiving and bearing the consequences of receiving displaced persons.

(6) On 27 May 1999 the Council adopted conclusions on displaced persons from Kosovo. These conclusions call on the Commission and the Member States to learn the lessons of their response to the Kosovo crisis in order to establish the measures in accordance with the Treaty.

(7) The European Council, at its special meeting in Tampere on 15 and 16 October 1999, acknowledged the need to reach agreement on the issue of temporary protection for displaced persons on the basis of solidarity between Member States.

(8) It is therefore necessary to establish minimum standards for giving temporary protection in the event of a mass influx of displaced persons and to take measures to promote a balance of efforts between the Member States in receiving and bearing the consequences of receiving such persons.

(9) Those standards and measures are linked and interdependent for reasons of effectiveness, coherence and solidarity and in order, in particular, to avert the risk of secondary movements. They should therefore be enacted in a single legal instrument.

(10) This temporary protection should be compatible with the Member States' international obligations as regards refugees. In particular, it must not prejudge the recognition of refugee status pursuant to the Geneva Convention of 28 July 1951 on the status of refugees, as amended by the New York Protocol of 31 January 1967, ratified by all the Member States.

(11) The mandate of the United Nations High Commissioner for Refugees regarding refugees and other persons in need of international protection should be respected, and effect should be given to Declaration No 17, annexed to the Final Act to the Treaty of Amsterdam, on Article 63 of the Treaty establishing the European Community which provides that consultations are to be established with the United Nations High Commissioner for Refugees and other relevant international organisations on matters relating to asylum policy.

[6] OJ C 262, 7.10.1995, p. 1.
[7] OJ L 63, 13.3.1996, p. 10.
[8] OJ C 19, 20.1.1999, p. 1.

(12) It is in the very nature of minimum standards that Member States have the power to introduce or maintain more favourable provisions for persons enjoying temporary protection in the event of a mass influx of displaced persons.

(13) Given the exceptional character of the provisions established by this Directive in order to deal with a mass influx or imminent mass influx of displaced persons from third countries who are unable to return to their country of origin, the protection offered should be of limited duration.

(14) The existence of a mass influx of displaced persons should be established by a Council Decision, which should be binding in all Member States in relation to the displaced persons to whom the Decision applies. The conditions for the expiry of the Decision should also be established.

(15) The Member States' obligations as to the conditions of reception and residence of persons enjoying temporary protection in the event of a mass influx of displaced persons should be determined. These obligations should be fair and offer an adequate level of protection to those concerned.

(16) With respect to the treatment of persons enjoying temporary protection under this Directive, the Member States are bound by obligations under instruments of international law to which they are party and which prohibit discrimination.

(17) Member States should, in concert with the Commission, enforce adequate measures so that the processing of personal data respects the standard of protection of Directive 95/46/EC of the European Parliament and the Council of 24 October 1995 on the protection of individuals with regard to the processing of personal data and on the free movement of such data[9].

(18) Rules should be laid down to govern access to the asylum procedure in the context of temporary protection in the event of a mass influx of displaced persons, in conformity with the Member States' international obligations and with the Treaty.

(19) Provision should be made for principles and measures governing the return to the country of origin and the measures to be taken by Member States in respect of persons whose temporary protection has ended.

(20) Provision should be made for a solidarity mechanism intended to contribute to the attainment of a balance of effort between Member States in receiving and bearing the consequences of receiving displaced persons in the event of a mass influx. The mechanism should consist of two components. The first is financial and the second concerns the actual reception of persons in the Member States.

[9] OJ L 281, 23.11.1995, p. 31.

(21) The implementation of temporary protection should be accompanied by administrative cooperation between the Member States in liaison with the Commission.

(22) It is necessary to determine criteria for the exclusion of certain persons from temporary protection in the event of a mass influx of displaced persons.

(23) Since the objectives of the proposed action, namely to establish minimum standards for giving temporary protection in the event of a mass influx of displaced persons and measures promoting a balance of efforts between the Member States in receiving and bearing the consequences of receiving such persons, cannot be sufficiently attained by the Member States and can therefore, by reason of the scale or effects of the proposed action, be better achieved at Community level, the Community may adopt measures in accordance with the principle of subsidiarity as set out in Article 5 of the Treaty. In accordance with the principle of proportionality as set out in that Article, this Directive does not go beyond what is necessary in order to achieve those objectives.

(24) In accordance with Article 3 of the Protocol on the position of the United Kingdom and Ireland, annexed to the Treaty on European Union and to the Treaty establishing the European Community, the United Kingdom gave notice, by letter of 27 September 2000, of its wish to take part in the adoption and application of this Directive.

(25) Pursuant to Article 1 of the said Protocol, Ireland is not participating in the adoption of this Directive. Consequently and without prejudice to Article 4 of the aforementioned Protocol, the provisions of this Directive do not apply to Ireland.

(26) In accordance with Articles 1 and 2 of the Protocol on the position of Denmark, annexed to the Treaty on European Union and to the Treaty establishing the European Community, Denmark is not participating in the adoption of this Directive, and is therefore not bound by it nor subject to its application,

HAS ADOPTED THIS DIRECTIVE:

Chapter I

General Provisions

Article 1

The purpose of this Directive is to establish minimum standards for giving temporary protection in the event of a mass influx of displaced persons from third countries who are unable to return to their country of origin and to promote a balance of effort between Member States in receiving and bearing the consequences of receiving such persons.

Article 2

For the purpose of this Directive:

(a) 'temporary protection' means a procedure of exceptional character to provide, in the event of a mass influx or imminent mass influx of displaced persons from third countries who are unable to return to their country of origin, immediate and temporary protection to such persons, in particular if there is also a risk that the asylum system will be unable to process this influx without adverse effects for its efficient operation, in the interests of the persons concerned and other persons requesting protection;

(b) 'Geneva Convention' means the Convention of 28 July 1951 relating to the status of refugees, as amended by the New York Protocol of 31 January 1967;

(c) 'displaced persons' means third-country nationals or state-less persons who have had to leave their country or region of origin, or have been evacuated, in particular in response to an appeal by international organisations, and are unable to return in safe and durable conditions because of the situation prevailing in that country, who may fall within the scope of Article 1A of the Geneva Convention or other international or national instruments giving international protection, in particular:

   (i) persons who have fled areas of armed conflict or endemic violence;

   (ii) persons at serious risk of, or who have been the victims of, systematic or generalised violations of their human rights;

(d) 'mass influx' means arrival in the Community of a large number of displaced persons, who come from a specific country or geographical area, whether their arrival in the Community was spontaneous or aided, for example through an evacuation programme;

(e) 'refugees' means third-country nationals or stateless persons within the meaning of Article 1A of the Geneva Convention;

(f) 'unaccompanied minors' means third-country nationals or stateless persons below the age of eighteen, who arrive on the territory of the Member States unaccompanied by an adult responsible for them whether by law or custom, and for as long as they are not effectively taken into the care of such a person, or minors who are left unaccompanied after they have entered the territory of the Member States;

(g) 'residence permit' means any permit or authorisation issued by the authorities of a Member State and taking the form provided for in that State's legislation, allowing a third country national or a stateless person to reside on its territory;

(h) 'sponsor' means a third-country national enjoying temporary protection in a Member State in accordance with a decision taken under Article 5 and who wants to be joined by members of his or her family.

Article 3

1. Temporary protection shall not prejudge recognition of refugee status under the Geneva Convention.
2. Member States shall apply temporary protection with due respect for human rights and fundamental freedoms and their obligations regarding non-refoulement.
3. The establishment, implementation and termination of temporary protection shall be the subject of regular consultations with the Office of the United Nations High Commissioner for Refugees (UNHCR) and other relevant international organisations.
4. This Directive shall not apply to persons who have been accepted under temporary protection schemes prior to its entry into force.
5. This Directive shall not affect the prerogative of the Member States to adopt or retain more favourable conditions for persons covered by temporary protection.

CHAPTER II

DURATION AND IMPLEMENTATION OF TEMPORARY PROTECTION

Article 4

1. Without prejudice to Article 6, the duration of temporary protection shall be one year. Unless terminated under the terms of Article 6(1)(b), it may be extended automatically by six monthly periods for a maximum of one year.
2. Where reasons for temporary protection persist, the Council may decide by qualified majority, on a proposal from the Commission, which shall also examine any request by a Member State that it submit a proposal to the Council, to extend that temporary protection by up to one year.

Article 5

1. The existence of a mass influx of displaced persons shall be established by a Council Decision adopted by a qualified majority on a proposal from the Commission, which shall also examine any request by a Member State that it submit a proposal to the Council.
2. The Commission proposal shall include at least:
   (a) a description of the specific groups of persons to whom the temporary protection will apply;
   (b) the date on which the temporary protection will take effect;
   (c) an estimation of the scale of the movements of displaced persons.

3. The Council Decision shall have the effect of introducing temporary protection for the displaced persons to which it refers, in all the Member States, in accordance with the provisions of this Directive. The Decision shall include at least:
   (a) a description of the specific groups of persons to whom the temporary protection applies;
   (b) the date on which the temporary protection will take effect;
   (c) information received from Member States on their reception capacity;
   (d) information from the Commission, UNHCR and other relevant international organisations.
4. The Council Decision shall be based on:
   (a) an examination of the situation and the scale of the movements of displaced persons;
   (b) an assessment of the advisability of establishing temporary protection, taking into account the potential for emergency aid and action on the ground or the inadequacy of such measures;
   (c) information received from the Member States, the Commission, UNHCR and other relevant international organisations.
5. The European Parliament shall be informed of the Council Decision.

Article 6

1. Temporary protection shall come to an end:
   (a) when the maximum duration has been reached; or
   (b) at any time, by Council Decision adopted by a qualified majority on a proposal from the Commission, which shall also examine any request by a Member State that it submit a proposal to the Council.
2. The Council Decision shall be based on the establishment of the fact that the situation in the country of origin is such as to permit the safe and durable return of those granted temporary protection with due respect for human rights and fundamental freedoms and Member States' obligations regarding non-refoulement. The European Parliament shall be informed of the Council Decision.

Article 7

1. Member States may extend temporary protection as provided for in this Directive to additional categories of displaced persons over and above those to whom the Council Decision provided for in Article 5 applies, where they are displaced for the same reasons and from the same country or region of origin. They shall notify the Council and the Commission immediately.
2. The provisions of Articles 24, 25 and 26 shall not apply to the use of the possibility referred to in paragraph 1, with the exception of the structural

support included in the European Refugee Fund set up by Decision 2000/596/EC[10], under the conditions laid down in that Decision.

CHAPTER III

OBLIGATIONS OF THE MEMBER STATES TOWARDS PERSONS ENJOYING TEMPORARY PROTECTION

Article 8

1. The Member States shall adopt the necessary measures to provide persons enjoying temporary protection with residence permits for the entire duration of the protection. Documents or other equivalent evidence shall be issued for that purpose.
2. Whatever the period of validity of the residence permits referred to in paragraph 1, the treatment granted by the Member States to persons enjoying temporary protection may not be less favourable than that set out in Articles 9 to 16.
3. The Member States shall, if necessary, provide persons to be admitted to their territory for the purposes of temporary protection with every facility for obtaining the necessary visas, including transit visas. Formalities must be reduced to a minimum because of the urgency of the situation. Visas should be free of charge or their cost reduced to a minimum.

Article 9

The Member States shall provide persons enjoying temporary protection with a document, in a language likely to be understood by them, in which the provisions relating to temporary protection and which are relevant to them are clearly set out.

Article 10

To enable the effective application of the Council Decision referred to in Article 5, Member States shall register the personal data referred to in Annex II, point (a), with respect to the persons enjoying temporary protection on their territory.

Article 11

A Member State shall take back a person enjoying temporary protection on its territory, if the said person remains on, or, seeks to enter without authorisation onto, the territory of another Member State during the period covered by the

[10] OJ L 252, 6.10.2000, p. 12.

Council Decision referred to in Article 5. Member States may, on the basis of a bilateral agreement, decide that this Article should not apply.

Article 12

The Member States shall authorise, for a period not exceeding that of temporary protection, persons enjoying temporary protection to engage in employed or self-employed activities, subject to rules applicable to the profession, as well as in activities such as educational opportunities for adults, vocational training and practical workplace experience. For reasons of labour market policies, Member States may give priority to EU citizens and citizens of States bound by the Agreement on the European Economic Area and also to legally resident third-country nationals who receive unemployment benefit. The country nationals who receive unemployment benefit. The general law in force in the Member States applicable to remuneration, access to social security systems relating to employed or self-employed activities and other conditions of employment shall apply.

Article 13

1. The Member States shall ensure that persons enjoying temporary protection have access to suitable accommodation or, if necessary, receive the means to obtain housing.
2. The Member States shall make provision for persons enjoying temporary protection to receive necessary assistance in terms of social welfare and means of subsistence, if they do not have sufficient resources, as well as for medical care. Without prejudice to paragraph 4, the assistance necessary for medical care shall include at least emergency care and essential treatment of illness.
3. Where persons enjoying temporary protection are engaged in employed or self-employed activities, account shall be taken, when fixing the proposed level of aid, of their ability to meet their own needs.
4. The Member States shall provide necessary medical or other assistance to persons enjoying temporary protection who have special needs, such as unaccompanied minors or persons who have undergone torture, rape or other serious forms of psychological, physical or sexual violence.

Article 14

1. The Member States shall grant to persons under 18 years of age enjoying temporary protection access to the education system under the same conditions as nationals of the host Member State The Member States may stipulate that such access must be confined to the state education system.

2. The Member States may allow adults enjoying temporary protection access to the general education system.

Article 15

1. For the purpose of this Article, in cases where families already existed in the country of origin and were separated due to circumstances surrounding the mass influx, the following persons shall be considered to be part of a family:
   (a) the spouse of the sponsor or his/her unmarried partner in a stable relationship, where the legislation or practice of the Member State concerned treats unmarried couples in a way comparable to married couples under its law relating to aliens; the minor unmarried children of the sponsor or of his/her spouse, without distinction as to whether they were born in or out of wedlock or adopted;
   (b) other close relatives who lived together as part of the family unit at the time of the events leading to the mass influx, and who were wholly or mainly dependent on the sponsor at the time.
2. In cases where the separate family members enjoy temporary protection in different Member States, Member States shall reunite family members where they are satisfied that the family members fall under the description of paragraph 1(a), taking into account the wish of the said family members. Member States may reunite family members where they are satisfied that the family members fall under the description of paragraph 1(b), taking into account on a case by case basis the extreme hardship they would face if the reunification did not take place.
3. Where the sponsor enjoys temporary protection in one Member State and one or some family members are not yet in a Member State, the Member State where the sponsor enjoys temporary protection shall reunite family members, who are in need of protection, with the sponsor in the case of family members where it is satisfied that they fall under the description of paragraph 1(a). The Member State may reunite family members, who are in need of protection, with the sponsor in the case of family members where it is satisfied that they fall under the description of paragraph 1(b), taking into account on a case by case basis the extreme hardship which they would face if the reunification did not take place.
4. When applying this Article, the Member States shall taken into consideration the best interests of the child.
5. The Member States concerned shall decide, taking account of Articles 25 and 26, in which Member State the reunification shall take place.
6. Reunited family members shall be granted residence permits under temporary protection. Documents or other equivalent evidence shall be issued for that purpose. Transfers of family members onto the territory of another Member

State for the purposes of reunification under paragraph 2, shall result in the withdrawal of the residence permits issued, and the termination of the obligations towards the persons concerned relating to temporary protection, in the Member State of departure.

7. The practical implementation of this Article may involve cooperation with the international organisations concerned.
8. A Member State shall, at the request of another Member State, provide information, as set out in Annex II, on a person receiving temporary protection which is needed to process a matter under this Article.

Article 16

1. The Member States shall as soon as possible take measures to ensure the necessary representation of unaccompanied minors enjoying temporary protection by legal guardianship, or, where necessary, representation by an organisation which is responsible for the care and well-being of minors, or by any other appropriate representation.
2. During the period of temporary protection Member States shall provide for unaccompanied minors to be placed:
   (a) with adult relatives;
   (b) with a foster-family;
   (c) in reception centres with special provisions for minors, or in other accommodation suitable for minors;
   (d) with the person who looked after the child when fleeing.

   The Member States shall take the necessary steps to enable the placement. Agreement by the adult person or persons concerned shall be established by the Member States. The views of the child shall be taken into account in accordance with the age and maturity of the child.

Chapter IV

Access to the asylum procedure in the context of temporary protection

Article 17

1. Persons enjoying temporary protection must be able to lodge an application for asylum at any time.
2. The examination of any asylum application not processed before the end of the period of temporary protection shall be completed after the end of that period.

Article 18

The criteria and mechanisms for deciding which Member State is responsible for considering an asylum application shall apply. In particular, the Member State responsible for examining an asylum application submitted by a person enjoying temporary protection pursuant to this Directive, shall be the Member State which has accepted his transfer onto its territory.

Article 19

1. The Member States may provide that temporary protection may not be enjoyed concurrently with the status of asylum seeker while applications are under consideration.
2. Where, after an asylum application has been examined, refugee status or, where applicable, other kind of protection is not granted to a person eligible for or enjoying temporary protection, the Member States shall, without prejudice to Article 28, provide for that person to enjoy or to continue to enjoy temporary protection for the remainder of the period of protection.

Chapter V

Return and measures after temporary protection has ended

Article 20

When the temporary protection ends, the general laws on protection and on aliens in the Member States shall apply, without prejudice to Articles 21, 22 and 23.

Article 21

1. The Member States shall take the measures necessary to make possible the voluntary return of persons enjoying temporary protection or whose temporary protection has ended. The Member States shall ensure that the provisions governing voluntary return of persons enjoying temporary protection facilitate their return with respect for human dignity.

   The Member State shall ensure that the decision of those persons to return is taken in full knowledge of the facts. The Member States may provide for exploratory visits.
2. For such time as the temporary protection has not ended, the Member States shall, on the basis of the circumstances prevailing in the country of origin, give favourable consideration to requests for return to the host Member State from persons who have enjoyed temporary protection and exercised their right to a voluntary return.

3. At the end of the temporary protection, the Member States may provide for the obligations laid down in CHAPTER III to be extended individually to persons who have been covered by temporary protection and are benefiting from a voluntary return programme. The extension shall have effect until the date of return.

Article 22

1. The Member States shall take the measures necessary to ensure that the enforced return of persons whose temporary protection has ended and who are not eligible for admission is conducted with due respect for human dignity.
2. In cases of enforced return, Member States shall consider any compelling humanitarian reasons which may make return impossible or unreasonable in specific cases.

Article 23

1. The Member States shall take the necessary measures concerning the conditions of residence of persons who have enjoyed temporary protection and who cannot, in view of their state of health, reasonably be expected to travel; where for example they would suffer serious negative effects if their treatment was interrupted. They shall not be expelled so long as that situation continues.
2. The Member States may allow families whose children are minors and attend school in a Member State to benefit from residence conditions allowing the children concerned to complete the current school period.

Chapter VI
Solidarity

Article 24

The measures provided for in this Directive shall benefit from the European Refugee Fund set up by Decision 2000/596/EC, under the terms laid down in that Decision.

Article 25

1. The Member States shall receive persons who are eligible for temporary protection in a spirit of Community solidarity. They shall indicate—in figures or in general terms—their capacity to receive such persons. This information shall be set out in the Council Decision referred to in Article 5. After that Decision has been adopted, the Member States may indicate additional reception capacity by notifying the Council and the Commission. This information shall be passed on swiftly to UNHCR.

2. The Member States concerned, acting in cooperation with the competent international organisations, shall ensure that the eligible persons defined in the Council Decision referred to in Article 5, who have not yet arrived in the Community have expressed their will to be received onto their territory.
3. When the number of those who are eligible for temporary protection following a sudden and massive influx exceeds the reception capacity referred to in paragraph 1, the Council shall, as a matter of urgency, examine the situation and take appropriate action, including recommending additional support for Member States affected.

Article 26

1. For the duration of the temporary protection, the Member States shall cooperate with each other with regard to transferral of the residence of persons enjoying temporary protection from one Member State to another, subject to the consent of the persons concerned to such transferral.
2. A Member State shall communicate requests for transfers to the other Member States and notify the Commission and UNHCR. The Member States shall inform the requesting Member State of their capacity for receiving transferees.
3. A Member State shall, at the request of another Member State, provide information, as set out in Annex II, on a person enjoying temporary protection which is needed to process a matter under this Article.
4. Where a transfer is made from one Member State to another, the residence permit in the Member State of departure shall expire and the obligations towards the persons concerned relating to temporary protection in the Member State of departure shall come to an end. The new host Member State shall grant temporary protection to the persons concerned.
5. The Member States shall use the model pass set out in Annex I for transfers between Member States of persons enjoying temporary protection.

Chapter VII

Administrative cooperation

Article 27

1. For the purposes of the administrative cooperation required to implement temporary protection, the Member States shall each appoint a national contact point, whose address they shall communicate to each other and to the Commission. The Member States shall, in liaison with the Commission, take all the appropriate measures to establish direct cooperation and an exchange of information between the competent authorities.

2. The Member States shall, regularly and as quickly as possible, communicate data concerning the number of persons enjoying temporary protection and full information on the national laws, regulations and administrative provisions relating to the implementation of temporary protection.

Chapter VIII

Special provisions

Article 28

1. The Member States may exclude a person from temporary protection if:
   (a) there are serious reasons for considering that:
      (i) he or she has committed a crime against peace, a war crime, or a crime against humanity, as defined in the international instruments drawn up to make provision in respect of such crimes;
      (ii) he or she has committed a serious non-political crime outside the Member State of reception prior to his or her admission to that Member State as a person enjoying temporary protection. The severity of the expected persecution is to be weighed against the nature of the criminal offence of which the person concerned is suspected. Particularly cruel actions, even if committed with an allegedly political objective, may be classified as serious non-political crimes. This applies both to the participants in the crime and to its instigators;
      (iii) he or she has been guilty of acts contrary to the purposes and principles of the United Nations;
   (b) there are reasonable grounds for regarding him or her as a danger to the security of the host Member State or, having been convicted by a final judgment of a particularly serious crime, he or she is a danger to the community of the host Member State.
2. The grounds for exclusion referred to in paragraph 1 shall be based solely on the personal conduct of the person concerned. Exclusion decisions or measures shall be based on the principle of proportionality.

Chapter IX

Final provisions

Article 29

Persons who have been excluded from the benefit of temporary protection or family reunification by a Member State shall be entitled to mount a legal challenge in the Member State concerned.

Article 30

The Member States shall lay down the rules on penalties applicable to infringements of the national provisions adopted pursuant to this Directive and shall take all measures necessary to ensure that they are implemented. The penalties provided for must be effective, proportionate and dissuasive.

Article 31

1. Not later than two years after the date specified in Article 32, the Commission shall report to the European Parliament and the Council on the application of this Directive in the Member States and shall propose any amendments that are necessary. The Member States shall send the Commission all the information that is appropriate for drawing up this report.
2. After presenting the report referred to at paragraph 1, the Commission shall report to the European Parliament and the Council on the application of this Directive in the Member States at least every five years.

Article 32

1. The Member States shall bring into force the laws, regulations and administrative provisions necessary to comply with this Directive by 31 December 2002 at the latest. They shall forthwith inform the Commission thereof.
2. When the Member States adopt these measures, they shall contain a reference to this Directive or shall be accompanied by such reference on the occasion of their official publication. The methods of making such a reference shall be laid down by the Member States.

Article 33

This Directive shall enter into force on the day of its publication in the *Official Journal of the European Communities.*

Article 34

This Directive is addressed to the Member States in accordance with the Treaty establishing the European Community.

Done at Brussels, 20 July 2001.

For the Council
The President
J. VANDE LANOTTE

Council Directive 2003/9/EC

of 27 January 2003

laying down minimum standards for the reception of asylum seekers

Note: Entered into force on 6 February 2003 (Article 27).

THE COUNCIL OF THE EUROPEAN UNION,

Having regard to the Treaty establishing the European Community, and in particular point (1)(b) of the first subparagraph of Article 63 thereof,

Having regard to the proposal from the Commission[11],

Having regard to the opinion of the European Parliament[12],

Having regard to the opinion of the Economic and Social Committee[13],

Having regard to the opinion of the Committee of the Regions[14],

Whereas:

(1) A common policy on asylum, including a Common European Asylum System, is a constituent part of the European Union's objective of progressively establishing an area of freedom, security and justice open to those who, forced by circumstances, legitimately seek protection in the Community.

(2) At its special meeting in Tampere on 15 and 16 October 1999, the European Council agreed to work towards establishing a Common European Asylum System, based on the full and inclusive application of the Geneva Convention relating to the Status of Refugees of 28 July 1951, as supplemented by the New York Protocol of 31 January 1967, thus maintaining the principle of non-refoulement.

(3) The Tampere Conclusions provide that a Common European Asylum System should include, in the short term, common minimum conditions of reception of asylum seekers.

(4) The establishment of minimum standards for the reception of asylum seekers is a further step towards a European asylum policy.

(5) This Directive respects the fundamental rights and observes the principles recognised in particular by the Charter of Fundamental Rights of the European Union. In particular, this Directive seeks to ensure full respect for human dignity and to promote the application of Articles 1 and 18 of the said Charter.

[11] OJ C 213 E, 31.7.2001, p. 286.

[12] Opinion delivered on 25 April 2002 (not yet published in the Official Journal).

[13] OJ C 48, 21.2.2002, p. 63.

[14] OJ C 107, 3.5.2002, p. 85.

(6) With respect to the treatment of persons falling within the scope of this Directive, Member States are bound by obligations under instruments of international law to which they are party and which prohibit discrimination.

(7) Minimum standards for the reception of asylum seekers that will normally suffice to ensure them a dignified standard of living and comparable living conditions in all Member States should be laid down.

(8) The harmonisation of conditions for the reception of asylum seekers should help to limit the secondary movements of asylum seekers influenced by the variety of conditions for their reception.

(9) Reception of groups with special needs should be specifically designed to meet those needs.

(10) Reception of applicants who are in detention should be specifically designed to meet their needs in that situation.

(11) In order to ensure compliance with the minimum procedural guarantees consisting in the opportunity to contact organisations or groups of persons that provide legal assistance, information should be provided on such organisations and groups of persons.

(12) The possibility of abuse of the reception system should be restricted by laying down cases for the reduction or withdrawal of reception conditions for asylum seekers.

(13) The efficiency of national reception systems and cooperation among Member States in the field of reception of asylum seekers should be secured.

(14) Appropriate coordination should be encouraged between the competent authorities as regards the reception of asylum seekers, and harmonious relationships between local communities and accommodation centres should therefore be promoted.

(15) It is in the very nature of minimum standards that Member States have the power to introduce or maintain more favourable provisions for third-country nationals and stateless persons who ask for international protection from a Member State.

(16) In this spirit, Member States are also invited to apply the provisions of this Directive in connection with procedures for deciding on applications for forms of protection other than that emanating from the Geneva Convention for third country nationals and stateless persons.

(17) The implementation of this Directive should be evaluated at regular intervals.

(18) Since the objectives of the proposed action, namely to establish minimum standards on the reception of asylum seekers in Member States, cannot be sufficiently achieved by the Member States and can therefore, by reason of the scale and effects of the proposed action, be better achieved by the Community, the Community may adopt measures in accordance with the

principles of subsidiarity as set out in Article 5 of the Treaty. In accordance with the principle of proportionality, as set out in that Article, this Directive does not go beyond what is necessary in order to achieve those objectives.

(19) In accordance with Article 3 of the Protocol on the position of the United Kingdom and Ireland, annexed to the Treaty on European Union and to the Treaty establishing the European Community, the United Kingdom gave notice, by letter of 18 August 2001, of its wish to take part in the adoption and application of this Directive.

(20) In accordance with Article 1 of the said Protocol, Ireland is not participating in the adoption of this Directive. Consequently, and without prejudice to Article 4 of the aforementioned Protocol, the provisions of this Directive do not apply to Ireland.

(21) In accordance with Articles 1 and 2 of the Protocol on the position of Denmark, annexed to the Treaty on European Union and to the Treaty establishing the European Community, Denmark is not participating in the adoption of this Directive and is therefore neither bound by it nor subject to its application,

HAS ADOPTED THIS DIRECTIVE:

Chapter I

Purpose, Definitions and Scope-

Article 1

Purpose

The purpose of this Directive is to lay down minimum standards for the reception of asylum seekers in Member States.

Article 2

Definitions

For the purposes of this Directive:

(a) 'Geneva Convention' shall mean the Convention of 28 July 1951 relating to the status of refugees, as amended by the New York Protocol of 31 January 1967;

(b) 'application for asylum' shall mean the application made by a third-country national or a stateless person which can be understood as a request for international protection from a Member State, under the Geneva Convention. Any application for international protection is presumed to be an application for asylum unless a third-country national or a stateless person explicitly requests another kind of protection that can be applied for separately;

(c) 'applicant' or 'asylum seeker' shall mean a third country national or a stateless person who has made an application for asylum in respect of which a final decision has not yet been taken;

(d) 'family members' shall mean, in so far as the family already existed in the country of origin, the following members of the applicant's family who are present in the same Member State in relation to the application for asylum:

   (i) the spouse of the asylum seeker or his or her unmarried partner in a stable relationship, where the legislation or practice of the Member State concerned treats unmarried couples in a way comparable to married couples under its law relating to aliens;

   (ii) the minor children of the couple referred to in point (i) or of the applicant, on condition that they are unmarried and dependent and regardless of whether they were born in or out of wedlock or adopted as defined under the national law;

(e) 'refugee' shall mean a person who fulfils the requirements of Article 1(A) of the Geneva Convention;

(f) 'refugee status' shall mean the status granted by a Member State to a person who is a refugee and is admitted as such to the territory of that Member State;

(g) 'procedures' and 'appeals', shall mean the procedures and appeals established by Member States in their national law;

(h) 'unaccompanied minors' shall mean persons below the age of eighteen who arrive in the territory of the Member States unaccompanied by an adult responsible for them whether by law or by custom, and for as long as they are not effectively taken into the care of such a person; it shall include minors who are left unaccompanied after they have entered the territory of Member States;

(i) 'reception conditions' shall mean the full set of measures that Member States grant to asylum seekers in accordance with this Directive;

(j) 'material reception conditions' shall mean the reception conditions that include housing, food and clothing, provided in kind, or as financial allowances or in vouchers, and a daily expenses allowance;

(k) 'detention' shall mean confinement of an asylum seeker by a Member State within a particular place, where the applicant is deprived of his or her freedom of movement;

(l) 'accommodation centre' shall mean any place used for collective housing of asylum seekers.

Article 3

Scope

1. This Directive shall apply to all third country nationals and stateless persons who make an application for asylum at the border or in the territory of a

Member State as long as they are allowed to remain on the territory as asylum seekers, as well as to family members, if they are covered by such application for asylum according to the national law.

2. This Directive shall not apply in cases of requests for diplomatic or territorial asylum submitted to representations of Member States.
3. This Directive shall not apply when the provisions of Council Directive 2001/55/EC of 20 July 2001 on minimum standards for giving temporary protection in the event of a mass influx of displaced persons and on measures promoting a balance of efforts between Member States in receiving such persons and bearing the consequences thereof[15] are applied.
4. Member States may decide to apply this Directive in connection with procedures for deciding on applications for kinds of protection other than that emanating from the Geneva Convention for third-country nationals or stateless persons who are found not to be refugees.

Article 4

More favourable provisions

Member States may introduce or retain more favourable provisions in the field of reception conditions for asylum seekers and other close relatives of the applicant who are present in the same Member State when they are dependent on him or for humanitarian reasons insofar as these provisions are compatible with this Directive.

Chapter II

General Provisions on Reception Conditions

Article 5

Information

1. Member States shall inform asylum seekers, within a reasonable time not exceeding fifteen days after they have lodged their application for asylum with the competent authority, of at least any established benefits and of the obligations with which they must comply relating to reception conditions.

   Member States shall ensure that applicants are provided with information on organisations or groups of persons that provide specific legal assistance and organisations that might be able to help or inform them concerning the available reception conditions, including health care.

[15] OJ L 212, 7.8.2001, p. 12.

2. Member States shall ensure that the information referred to in paragraph 1 is in writing and, as far as possible, in a language that the applicants may reasonably be supposed to understand. Where appropriate, this information may also be supplied orally.

Article 6

Documentation

1. Member States shall ensure that, within three days after an application is lodged with the competent authority, the applicant is provided with a document issued in his or her own name certifying his or her status as an asylum seeker or testifying that he or she is allowed to stay in the territory of the Member State while his or her application is pending or being examined.

   If the holder is not free to move within all or a part of the territory of the Member State, the document shall also certify this fact.
2. Member States may exclude application of this Article when the asylum seeker is in detention and during the examination of an application for asylum made at the border or within the context of a procedure to decide on the right of the applicant legally to enter the territory of a Member State. In specific cases, during the examination of an application for asylum, Member States may provide applicants with other evidence equivalent to the document referred to in paragraph 1.
3. The document referred to in paragraph 1 need not certify the identity of the asylum seeker.
4. Member States shall adopt the necessary measures to provide asylum seekers with the document referred to in paragraph 1, which must be valid for as long as they are authorised to remain in the territory of the Member State concerned or at the border thereof.
5. Member States may provide asylum seekers with a travel document when serious humanitarian reasons arise that require their presence in another State.

Article 7

Residence and freedom of movement

1. Asylum seekers may move freely within the territory of the host Member State or within an area assigned to them by that Member State. The assigned area shall not affect the unalienable sphere of private life and shall allow sufficient scope for guaranteeing access to all benefits under this Directive.
2. Member States may decide on the residence of the asylum seeker for reasons of public interest, public order or, when necessary, for the swift processing and effective monitoring of his or her application.

3. When it proves necessary, for example for legal reasons or reasons of public order, Member States may confine an applicant to a particular place in accordance with their national law.
4. Member States may make provision of the material reception conditions subject to actual residence by the applicants in a specific place, to be determined by the Member States. Such a decision, which may be of a general nature, shall be taken individually and established by national legislation.
5. Member States shall provide for the possibility of granting applicants temporary permission to leave the place of residence mentioned in paragraphs 2 and 4 and/or the assigned area mentioned in paragraph 1. Decisions shall be taken individually, objectively and impartially and reasons shall be given if they are negative.

   The applicant shall not require permission to keep appointments with authorities and courts if his or her appearance is necessary.
6. Member States shall require applicants to inform the competent authorities of their current address and notify any change of address to such authorities as soon as possible.

Article 8

Families

Member States shall take appropriate measures to maintain as far as possible family unity as present within their territory, if applicants are provided with housing by the Member State concerned. Such measures shall be implemented with the asylum seeker's agreement.

Article 9

Medical screening

Member States may require medical screening for applicants on public health grounds.

Article 10

Schooling and education of minors

1. Member States shall grant to minor children of asylum seekers and to asylum seekers who are minors access to the education system under similar conditions as nationals of the host Member State for so long as an expulsion measure against them or their parents is not actually enforced. Such education may be provided in accommodation centres.

The Member State concerned may stipulate that such access must be confined to the State education system.

Minors shall be younger than the age of legal majority in the Member State in which the application for asylum was lodged or is being examined. Member States shall not withdraw secondary education for the sole reason that the minor has reached the age of majority.

2. Access to the education system shall not be postponed for more than three months from the date the application for asylum was lodged by the minor or the minor's parents. This period may be extended to one year where specific education is provided in order to facilitate access to the education system.
3. Where access to the education system as set out in paragraph 1 is not possible due to the specific situation of the minor, the Member State may offer other education arrangements.

Article 11

Employment

1. Member States shall determine a period of time, starting from the date on which an application for asylum was lodged, during which an applicant shall not have access to the labour market.
2. If a decision at first instance has not been taken within one year of the presentation of an application for asylum and this delay cannot be attributed to the applicant, Member States shall decide the conditions for granting access to the labour market for the applicant.
3. Access to the labour market shall not be withdrawn during appeals procedures, where an appeal against a negative decision in a regular procedure has suspensive effect, until such time as a negative decision on the appeal is notified.
4. For reasons of labour market policies, Member States may give priority to EU citizens and nationals of States parties to the Agreement on the European Economic Area and also to legally resident third-country nationals.

Article 12

Vocational training

Member States may allow asylum seekers access to vocational training irrespective of whether they have access to the labour market.

Access to vocational training relating to an employment contract shall depend on the extent to which the applicant has access to the labour market in accordance with Article 11.

Article 13

General rules on material reception conditions and health care

1. Member States shall ensure that material reception conditions are available to applicants when they make their application for asylum.
2. Member States shall make provisions on material reception conditions to ensure a standard of living adequate for the health of applicants and capable of ensuring their subsistence. Member States shall ensure that that standard of living is met in the specific situation of persons who have special needs, in accordance with Article 17, as well as in relation to the situation of persons who are in detention.
3. Member States may make the provision of all or some of the material reception conditions and health care subject to the condition that applicants do not have sufficient means to have a standard of living adequate for their health and to enable their subsistence.
4. Member States may require applicants to cover or contribute to the cost of the material reception conditions and of the health care provided for in this Directive, pursuant to the provision of paragraph 3, if the applicants have sufficient resources, for example if they have been working for a reasonable period of time.

   If it transpires that an applicant had sufficient means to cover material reception conditions and health care at the time when these basic needs were being covered, Member States may ask the asylum seeker for a refund.

5. Material reception conditions may be provided in kind, or in the form of financial allowances or vouchers or in a combination of these provisions.

   Where Member States provide material reception conditions in the form of financial allowances or vouchers, the amount thereof shall be determined in accordance with the principles set out in this Article.

Article 14

Modalities for material reception conditions

1. Where housing is provided in kind, it should take one or a combination of the following forms:
   (a) premises used for the purpose of housing applicants during the examination of an application for asylum lodged at the border;
   (b) accommodation centres which guarantee an adequate standard of living;
   (c) private houses, flats, hotels or other premises adapted for housing applicants.
2. Member States shall ensure that applicants provided with the housing referred to in paragraph 1(a), (b) and (c) are assured:

(a) protection of their family life;

(b) the possibility of communicating with relatives, legal advisers and representatives of the United Nations High Commissioner for Refugees (UNHCR) and non-governmental organisations (NGOs) recognised by Member States. Member States shall pay particular attention to the prevention of assault within the premises and accommodation centres referred to in paragraph 1(a) and (b).

3. Member States shall ensure, if appropriate, that minor children of applicants or applicants who are minors are lodged with their parents or with the adult family member responsible for them whether by law or by custom.

4. Member States shall ensure that transfers of applicants from one housing facility to another take place only when necessary. Member States shall provide for the possibility for applicants to inform their legal advisers of the transfer and of their new address.

5. Persons working in accommodation centres shall be adequately trained and shall be bound by the confidentiality principle as defined in the national law in relation to any information they obtain in the course of their work.

6. Member States may involve applicants in managing the material resources and non-material aspects of life in the centre through an advisory board or council representing residents.

7. Legal advisors or counsellors of asylum seekers and representatives of the United Nations High Commissioner for Refugees or non-governmental organisations designated by the latter and recognised by the Member State concerned shall be granted access to accommodation centres and other housing facilities in order to assist the said asylum seekers. Limits on such access may be imposed only on grounds relating to the security of the centres and facilities and of the asylum seekers.

8. Member States may exceptionally set modalities for material reception conditions different from those provided for in this Article, for a reasonable period which shall be as short as possible, when:
   - an initial assessment of the specific needs of the applicant is required,
   - material reception conditions, as provided for in this Article, are not available in a certain geographical area,
   - housing capacities normally available are temporarily exhausted,
   - the asylum seeker is in detention or confined to border posts.

   These different conditions shall cover in any case basic needs.

Article 15

Health care

1. Member States shall ensure that applicants receive the necessary health care which shall include, at least, emergency care and essential treatment of illness.

2. Member States shall provide necessary medical or other assistance to applicants who have special needs.

Chapter III

Reduction or Withdrawal of Reception Conditions

Article 16

Reduction or withdrawal of reception conditions

1. Member States may reduce or withdraw reception conditions in the following cases:
   (a) where an asylum seeker:
   — abandons the place of residence determined by the competent authority without informing it or, if requested, without permission, or
   — does not comply with reporting duties or with requests to provide information or to appear for personal interviews concerning the asylum procedure during a reasonable period laid down in national law, or
   — has already lodged an application in the same Member State.

   When the applicant is traced or voluntarily reports to the competent authority, a duly motivated decision, based on the reasons for the disappearance, shall be taken on the reinstallation of the grant of some or all of the reception conditions;
   (b) where an applicant has concealed financial resources and has therefore unduly benefited from material reception conditions.

   If it transpires that an applicant had sufficient means to cover material reception conditions and health care at the time when these basic needs were being covered, Member States may ask the asylum seeker for a refund.

2. Member States may refuse conditions in cases where an asylum seeker has failed to demonstrate that the asylum claim was made as soon as reasonably practicable after arrival in that Member State.
3. Member States may determine sanctions applicable to serious breaching of the rules of the accommodation centres as well as to seriously violent behaviour.
4. Decisions for reduction, withdrawal or refusal of reception conditions or sanctions referred to in paragraphs 1, 2 and 3 shall be taken individually, objectively and impartially and reasons shall be given. Decisions shall be based on the particular situation of the person concerned, especially with regard to persons covered by Article 17, taking into account the principle of proportionality. Member States shall under all circumstances ensure access to emergency health care.
5. Member States shall ensure that material reception conditions are not withdrawn or reduced before a negative decision is taken.

Chapter IV

Provisions for Persons with Special Needs

Article 17

General principle

1. Member States shall take into account the specific situation of vulnerable persons such as minors, unaccompanied minors, disabled people, elderly people, pregnant women, single parents with minor children and persons who have been subjected to torture, rape or other serious forms of psychological, physical or sexual violence, in the national legislation implementing the provisions of Chapter II relating to material reception conditions and health care.
2. Paragraph 1 shall apply only to persons found to have special needs after an individual evaluation of their situation.

Article 18

Minors

1. The best interests of the child shall be a primary consideration for Member States when implementing the provisions of this Directive that involve minors.
2. Member States shall ensure access to rehabilitation services for minors who have been victims of any form of abuse, neglect, exploitation, torture or cruel, inhuman and degrading treatment, or who have suffered from armed conflicts, and ensure that appropriate mental health care is developed and qualified counselling is provided when needed.

Article 19

Unaccompanied minors

1. Member States shall as soon as possible take measures to ensure the necessary representation of unaccompanied minors by legal guardianship or, where necessary, representation by an organisation which is responsible for the care and well-being of minors, or by any other appropriate representation. Regular assessments shall be made by the appropriate authorities.
2. Unaccompanied minors who make an application for asylum shall, from the moment they are admitted to the territory to the moment they are obliged to leave the host Member State in which the application for asylum was made or is being examined, be placed:
   (a) with adult relatives;
   (b) with a foster-family;

(c) in accommodation centres with special provisions for minors;
(d) in other accommodation suitable for minors.

Member States may place unaccompanied minors aged 16 or over in accommodation centres for adult asylum seekers.

As far as possible, siblings shall be kept together, taking into account the best interests of the minor concerned and, in particular, his or her age and degree of maturity. Changes of residence of unaccompanied minors shall be limited to a minimum.

3. Member States, protecting the unaccompanied minor's best interests, shall endeavour to trace the members of his or her family as soon as possible. In cases where there may be a threat to the life or integrity of the minor or his or her close relatives, particularly if they have remained in the country of origin, care must be taken to ensure that the collection, processing and circulation of information concerning those persons is undertaken on a confidential basis, so as to avoid jeopardising their safety.
4. Those working with unaccompanied minors shall have had or receive appropriate training concerning their needs, and shall be bound by the confidentiality principle as defined in the national law, in relation to any information they obtain in the course of their work.

Article 20

Victims of torture and violence

Member States shall ensure that, if necessary, persons who have been subjected to torture, rape or other serious acts of violence receive the necessary treatment of damages caused by the aforementioned acts.

Chapter V

Appeals

Article 21

Appeals

1. Member States shall ensure that negative decisions relating to the granting of benefits under this Directive or decisions taken under Article 7 which individually affect asylum seekers may be the subject of an appeal within the procedures laid down in the national law. At least in the last instance the possibility of an appeal or a review before a judicial body shall be granted.
2. Procedures for access to legal assistance in such cases shall be laid down in national law.

Chapter VI

Actions to Improve the Efficiency of the Reception System

Article 22

Cooperation

Member States shall regularly inform the Commission on the data concerning the number of persons, broken down by sex and age, covered by reception conditions and provide full information on the type, name and format of the documents provided for by Article 6.

Article 23

Guidance, monitoring and control system

Member States shall, with due respect to their constitutional structure, ensure that appropriate guidance, monitoring and control of the level of reception conditions are established.

Article 24

Staff and resources

1. Member States shall take appropriate measures to ensure that authorities and other organisations implementing this Directive have received the necessary basic training with respect to the needs of both male and female applicants.
2. Member States shall allocate the necessary resources in connection with the national provisions enacted to implement this Directive.

Chapter VII

Final Provisions

Article 25

Reports

By 6 August 2006, the Commission shall report to the European Parliament and the Council on the application of this Directive and shall propose any amendments that are necessary.

Member States shall send the Commission all the information that is appropriate for drawing up the report, including the statistical data provided for by Article 22 by 6 February 2006.

After presenting the report, the Commission shall report to the European Parliament and the Council on the application of this Directive at least every five years.

Article 26

Transposition

1. Member States shall bring into force the laws, regulations and administrative provisions necessary to comply with this Directive by 6 February 2005. They shall forthwith inform the Commission thereof.

   When the Member States adopt these measures, they shall contain a reference to this Directive or shall be accompanied by such a reference on the occasion of their official publication. Member States shall determine how such a reference is to be made.
2. Member States shall communicate to the Commission the text of the provisions of national law which they adopt in the field relating to the enforcement of this Directive.

Article 27

Entry into force

This Directive shall enter into force on the day of its publication in the *Official Journal of the European Union.*

Article 28

Addresses

This Directive is addressed to the Member States in accordance with the Treaty establishing the European Union.

Done at Brussels, 27 January 2003.

For the Council
The President
G. PAPANDREOU

25.2.2003 L 50/1 Official Journal of the European Union EN

I

(Acts whose publication is obligatory)

Council Regulation

(EC) No 343/2003 of 18 February 2003

establishing the criteria and mechanisms for determining the Member State responsible for examining an asylum application lodged in one of the Member States by a third-country national

---

THE COUNCIL OF THE EUROPEAN UNION,

Having regard to the Treaty establishing the European Community; and in particular Article 63, first paragraph, point (1)(a),

Having regard to the proposal from the Commission,[16]

Having regard to the opinion of the European Parliament,[17]

Having regard to the opinion of the European Economic and Social Committee,[18]

Whereas:

(1) Common policy on asylum, including a Common European Asylum System, is a constituent part of the European Union's objective of progressively establishing an area of freedom, security and justice open to those who, forced by circumstances, legitimately seek protection in the Community.

(2) The European Council, at its special meeting in Tampere on 15 and 16 October 1999, agreed to work towards establishing a Common European Asylum System, based on the full and inclusive application of the Geneva Convention relating to the Status of Refugees of 28 July 1951, as supplemented by the New York Protocol of 31 January 1967, thus ensuring that nobody is sent back to persecution, i.e. maintaining the principle of non-refoulement. In this respect, and without affecting the responsibility criteria laid down in this Regulation, Member States, all respecting the principle of non-refoulement, are considered as safe countries for third-country nationals.

(3) The Tampere conclusions also stated that this system should include, in the short term, a clear and workable method for determining the Member State responsible for the examination of an asylum application.

(4) Such a method should be based on objective, fair criteria both for the Member

[16] Article amended by the Treaty of Nice.

[17] Article amended by the Treaty of Nice.

[18] OJ C 125, 27.5.2002, p.28.

States and for the persons concerned. It should, in particular, make it possible to determine rapidly the Member State responsible, so as to guarantee effective access to the procedures for determining refugee status and not to compromise the objective of the rapid processing of asylum applications.

(5) As regards the introduction in successive phases of a common European asylum system that should lead, in the longer term, to a common procedure and a uniform status, valid throughout the Union, for those granted asylum, it is appropriate at this stage, while making the necessary improvements in the light of experience, to confirm the principles underlying the Convention determining the State responsible for examining applications for asylum lodged in one of the Member States of the European Communities,[19] signed in Dublin on 15 June 1990 (hereinafter referred to as the Dublin Convention), whose implementation has stimulated the process of harmonising asylum policies.

(6) Family unity should be preserved in so far as this is compatible with the other objectives pursued by establishing criteria and mechanisms for determining the Member State responsible for examining an asylum application.

(7) The processing together of the asylum applications of the members of one family by a single Member State makes it possible to ensure that the applications are examined thoroughly and the decisions taken in respect of them are consistent. Member States should be able to derogate from the responsibility criteria, so as to make it possible to bring family members together where this is necessary on humanitarian grounds.

(8) The progressive creation of an area without internal frontiers in which free movement of persons is guaranteed in accordance with the Treaty establishing the European Community and the establishment of Community policies regarding the conditions of entry and stay of third country nationals, including common efforts towards the management of external borders, makes it necessary to strike a balance between responsibility criteria in a spirit of solidarity.

(9) The application of this Regulation can be facilitated, and its effectiveness increased, by bilateral arrangements between Member States for improving communications between competent departments, reducing time limits for procedures or simplifying the processing of requests to take charge or take back, or establishing procedures for the performance of transfers.

(10) Continuity between the system for determining the Member State responsible established by the Dublin Convention and the system established by this Regulation should be ensured. Similarly, consistency should be ensured between this Regulation and Council Regulation (EC) No 2725/2000 of 11 December 2000 concerning the establishment of 'Eurodac' for the comparison of fingerprints for the effective application of the Dublin Convention.[20]

[19] OJ C 254, 19.8.1997, p.1.

[20] OJ L 316, 15.12.2000, p.1.

(11) The operation of the Eurodac system, as established by Regulation (EC) No 2725/2000 and in particular the implementation of Articles 4 and 8 contained therein should facilitate the implementation of this Regulation.

(12) With respect to the treatment of persons falling within the scope of this Regulation, Member States are bound by obligations under instruments of international law to which they are party.

(13) The measures necessary for the implementation of this Regulation should be adopted in accordance with Council Decision 1999/468/EC of 28 June 1999 laying down the procedures for the exercise of implementing powers conferred on the Commission.[21]

(14) The application of the Regulation should be evaluated at regular intervals.

(15) The Regulation observes the fundamental rights and principles which are acknowledged in particular in the Charter of Fundamental Rights of the European Union.[22] In particular, it seeks to ensure full observance of the right to asylum guaranteed by Article 18.

(16) Since the objective of the proposed measure, namely the establishment of criteria and mechanisms for determining the Member State responsible for examining an asylum application lodged in one of the Member States by a third-country national, cannot be sufficiently achieved by the Member States and, given the scale and effects, can therefore be better achieved at Community level, the Community may adopt measures in accordance with the principle of subsidiarity as set out in Article 5 of the Treaty. In accordance with the principle of proportionality, as set out in that Article, this Regulation does not go beyond what is necessary in order to achieve that objective.

(17) In accordance with Article 3 of the Protocol on the position of the United Kingdom and Ireland, annexed to the Treaty on European Union and to the Treaty establishing the European Community, the United Kingdom and Ireland gave notice, by letters of 30 October 2001, of their wish to take part in the adoption and application of this Regulation.

(18) In accordance with Articles 1 and 2 of the Protocol on the position of Denmark, annexed to the Treaty on European Union and to the Treaty establishing the European Community, Denmark does not take part in the adoption of this Regulation and is not bound by it nor subject to its application.

(19) The Dublin Convention remains in force and continues to apply between Denmark and the Member States that are bound by this Regulation until such time an agreement allowing Denmark's participation in the Regulation has been concluded,

[21] OJ L 184, 17.7.1999, p.23.

[22] OJ C 364, 18.12.2000, p.1.

HAS ADOPTED THIS REGULATION:

Chapter I

Subject-Matter and Definitions

Article 1

This Regulation lays down the criteria and mechanisms for determining the Member State responsible for examining an application for asylum lodged in one of the member States by a third-country national.

Article 2

For the purposes of this Regulation:

(a) 'third-country national' means anyone who is not a citizen of the Union within the meaning of Article 17(1)of the Treaty establishing the European Community;

(b) 'Geneva Convention' means the Convention of 28 July 1951 relating to the status of refugees, as amended by the New York Protocol of 31 January 1967;

(c) 'application for asylum 'means the application made by a third-country national which can be understood as a request for international protection from a Member State, under the Geneva Convention. Any application for international protection is presumed to be an application for asylum, unless a third-country national explicitly requests another kind of protection that can be applied for separately;

(d) 'applicant' or 'asylum seeker' means a third country national who has made an application for asylum in respect of which a final decision has not yet been taken;

(e) 'examination of an asylum application' means any examination of, or decision or ruling concerning, an application for asylum by the competent authorities in accordance with national law except for procedures for determining the Member State responsible in accordance with this Regulation;

(f) 'withdrawal of the asylum application' means the actions by which the applicant for asylum terminates the procedures initiated by the submission of his application for asylum, in accordance with national law, either explicitly or tacitly;

(g) 'refugee' means any third-country national qualifying for the status defined by the Geneva Convention and authorised to reside as such on the territory of a Member State;

(h) 'unaccompanied minor' means unmarried persons below the age of eighteen who arrive in the territory of the Member States unaccompanied by an adult responsible for them whether by law or by custom, and for as long as they are not effectively taken into the care of such a person; it includes minors who are left unaccompanied after they have entered the territory of the Member States;

(i) 'family members' means insofar as the family already existed in the country of origin, the following members of the applicant's family who are present in the territory of the Member States:

(i) the spouse of the asylumseeker or his or her unmarried partner in a stable relationship, where the legislation or practice of the Member State concerned treats unmarried couples in a way comparable to married couples under its law relating to aliens;

(ii) the minor children of couples referred to in point (i) or of the applicant, on condition that they are unmarried and dependent and regardless of whether they were born in or out of wedlock or adopted as defined under the national law;

(iii) the father, mother or guardian when the applicant or refugee is a minor and unmarried;

(j) 'residence document 'means any authorisation issued by the authorities of a Member State authorising a third-country national to stay in its territory, including the documents substantiating the authorisation to remain in the territory under temporary protection arrangements or until the circumstances preventing a removal order from being carried out no longer apply, with the exception of visas and residence authorisations issued during the period required to determine the responsible Member State as established in this Regulation or during examination of an application for asylum or an application for a residence permit;

(k) 'visa 'means the authorisation or decision of a Member State required for transit or entry for an intended stay in that Member State or in several Member States. The nature of the visa shall be determined in accordance with the following definitions:

(i) 'long-stay visa 'means the authorisation or decision of a Member State required for entry for an intended stay in that Member State of more than three months;

(ii) 'short-stay visa 'means the authorisation or decision of a Member State required for entry for an intended stay in that State or in several Member States for a period whose total duration does not exceed three months;

(iii) 'transit visa 'means the authorisation or decision of a Member State for entry for transit through the territory of that Member State or several Member States, except for transit at an airport;

(iv) 'airport transit visa 'means the authorisation or decision allowing a third-country national specifically subject to this requirement to pass through the transit zone of an airport, without gaining access to the national territory of the Member State concerned, during a stopover or a transfer between two sections of an international flight.

Chapter II

General Principles

Article 3

1. Member States shall examine the application of any third-country national who applies at the border or in their territory to any one of them for asylum. The application shall be examined by a single Member State, which shall be the one which the criteria set out in Chapter III indicate is responsible.
2. By way of derogation from paragraph 1, each Member State may examine an application for asylum lodged with it by a third-country national, even if such examination is not its responsibility under the criteria laid down in this Regulation. In such an event, that Member State shall become the Member State responsible within the meaning of this Regulation and shall assume the obligations associated with that responsibility. Where appropriate, it shall inform the Member State previously responsible, the Member State conducting a procedure for determining the Member State responsible or the Member State which has been requested to take charge of or take back the applicant.
3. Any Member State shall retain the right, pursuant to its national laws, to send an asylum seeker to a third country, in compliance with the provisions of the Geneva Convention.
4. The asylum seeker shall be informed in writing in a language that he or she may reasonably be expected to understand regarding the application of this Regulation, its time limits and its effects.

Article 4

1. The process of determining the Member State responsible under this Regulation shall start as soon as an application for asylum is first lodged with a Member State.
2. An application for asylum shall be deemed to have been lodged once a form submitted by the applicant for asylum or a report prepared by the authorities has reached the competent authorities of the Member State concerned. Where an application is not made in writing, the time elapsing between the statement of intention and the preparation of a report should be as short as possible.
3. For the purposes of this Regulation, the situation of a minor who is accompanying the asylum seeker and meets the definition of a family member set out in Article 2, point (i), shall be indissociable from that of his parent or guardian

and shall be a matter for the Member State responsible for examining the application for asylum of that parent or guardian, even if the minor is not individually an asylum seeker. The same treatment shall be applied to children born after the asylum seeker arrives in the territory of the Member States, without the need to initiate a new procedure for taking charge of them.

4. Where an application for asylum is lodged with the competent authorities of a Member State by an applicant who is in the territory of another Member State, the determination of the Member State responsible shall be made by the Member State in whose territory the applicant is present. The latter Member State shall be informed without delay by the Member State which received the application and shall then, for the purposes of this Regulation, be regarded as the Member State with which the application for asylum was lodged. The applicant shall be informed in writing of this transfer and of the date on which it took place.
5. An asylum seeker who is present in another Member State and there lodges an application for asylum after withdrawing his application during the process of determining the Member State responsible shall be taken back, under the conditions laid down in Article 20, by the Member State with which that application for asylum was lodged, with a view to completing the process of determining the Member State responsible for examining the application for asylum. This obligation shall cease, if the asylum seeker has in the meantime left the territories of the Member States for a period of at least three months or has obtained a residence document from a Member State.

Chapter III
Hierarchy of Criteria

Article 5

1. The criteria for determining the Member State responsible shall be applied in the order in which they are set out in this Chapter.
2. The Member State responsible in accordance with the criteria shall be determined on the basis of the situation obtaining when the asylum seeker first lodged his application with a Member State.

Article 6

Where the applicant for asylum is an unaccompanied minor, the Member State responsible for examining the application shall be that where a member of his or her family is legally present, provided that this is in the best interest of the minor. In the absence of a family member, the Member State responsible for examining the application shall be that where the minor has lodged his or her application for asylum.

Article 7

Where the asylum seeker has a family member, regardless of whether the family was previously formed in the country of origin, who has been allowed to reside as a refugee in a Member State, that Member State shall be responsible for examining the application for asylum, provided that the persons concerned so desire.

Article 8

If the asylum seeker has a family member in a Member State whose application has not yet been the subject of a first decision regarding the substance, that Member State shall be responsible for examining the application for asylum, provided that the persons concerned so desire.

Article 9

1. Where the asylum seeker is in possession of a valid residence document, the Member State which issued the document shall be responsible for examining the application for asylum.
2. Where the asylum seeker is in possession of a valid visa, the Member State which issued the visa shall be responsible for examining the application for asylum, unless the visa was issued when acting for or on the written authorisation of another Member State. In such a case, the latter Member State shall be responsible for examining the application for asylum. Where a Member State first consults the central authority of another Member State, in particular for security reasons, the latter's reply to the consultation shall not constitute written authorisation within the meaning of this provision.
3. Where the asylum seeker is in possession of more than one valid residence document or visa issued by different Member States, the responsibility for examining the application for asylum shall be assumed by the Member States in the following order:
    (a) the Member State which issued the residence document conferring the right to the longest period of residency or, where the periods of validity are identical, the Member State which issued the residence document having the latest expiry date;
    (b) the Member State which issued the visa having the latest expiry date where the various visas are of the same type;
    (c) where visas are of different kinds, the Member State which issued the visa having the longest period of validity, or, where the periods of validity are identical, the Member State which issued the visa having the latest expiry date.
4. Where the asylum seeker is in possession only of one or more residence

documents which have expired less than two years previously or one or more visas which have expired less than six months previously and which enabled him actually to enter the territory of a Member State, paragraphs 1, 2 and 3 shall apply for such time as the applicant has not left the territories of the Member States. Where the asylum seeker is in possession of one or more residence documents which have expired more than two years previously or one or more visas which have expired more than six months previously and enabled him actually to enter the territory of a Member State and where he has not left the territories of the Member States, the Member State in which the application is lodged shall be responsible.

5. The fact that the residence document or visa was issued on the basis of a false or assumed identity or on submission of forged, counterfeit or invalid documents shall not prevent responsibility being allocated to the Member State which issued it. However, the Member State issuing the residence document or visa shall not be responsible if it can establish that a fraud was committed after the document or visa had been issued.

Article 10

1. Where it is established, on the basis of proof or circumstantial evidence as described in the two lists mentioned in Article 18(3), including the data referred to in Chapter III of Regulation (EC)No 2725/2000, that an asylum seeker has irregularly crossed the border into a Member State by land, sea or air having come from a third country, the Member State thus entered shall be responsible for examining the application for asylum. This responsibility shall cease 12 months after the date on which the irregular border crossing took place.
2. When a Member State cannot or can no longer be held responsible in accordance with paragraph 1, and where it is established, on the basis of proof or circumstantial evidence as described in the two lists mentioned in Article 18(3), that the asylum seeker—who has entered the territories of the Member States irregularly or whose circumstances of entry cannot be established—at the time of lodging the application has been previously living for a continuous period of at least five months in a Member State, that Member State shall be responsible for examining the application for asylum. If the applicant has been living for periods of time of at least five months in several Member States, the Member State where this has been most recently the case shall be responsible for examining the application.

Article 11

1. If a third-country national enters into the territory of a Member State in which the need for him or her to have a visa is waived, that Member State shall be responsible for examining his or her application for asylum.

2. The principle set out in paragraph 1 does not apply, if the third-country national lodges his or her application for asylum in another Member State, in which the need for him or her to have a visa for entry into the territory is also waived. In this case, the latter Member State shall be responsible for examining the application for asylum.

Article 12

Where the application for asylum is made in an international transit area of an airport of a Member State by a third-country national, that Member State shall be responsible for examining the application.

Article 13

Where no Member State responsible for examining the application for asylum can be designated on the basis of the criteria listed in this Regulation, the first Member State with which the application for asylum was lodged shall be responsible for examining it.

Article 14

Where several members of a family submit applications for asylum in the same Member State simultaneously, or on dates close enough for the procedures for determining the Member State responsible to be conducted together, and where the application of the criteria set out in this Regulation would lead to them being separated, the Member State responsible shall be determined on the basis of the following provisions:

(a) responsibility for examining the applications for asylum of all the members of the family shall lie with the Member State which the criteria indicate is responsible for taking charge of the largest number of family members;

(b) failing this, responsibility shall lie with the Member State which the criteria indicate is responsible for examining the application of the oldest of them.

Chapter IV

Humanitarian Clause

Article 15

1. Any Member State, even where it is not responsible under the criteria set out in this Regulation, may bring together family members, as well as other dependent relatives, on humanitarian grounds based in particular on family or cultural considerations. In this case that Member State shall, at the request of another

Member State, examine the application for asylum of the person concerned. The persons concerned must consent.

2. In cases in which the person concerned is dependent on the assistance of the other on account of pregnancy or a new-born child, serious illness, severe handicap or old age, Member States shall normally keep or bring together the asylum seeker with another relative present in the territory of one of the Member States, provided that family ties existed in the country of origin.
3. If the asylum seeker is an unaccompanied minor who has a relative or relatives in another Member State who can take care of him or her, Member States shall if possible unite the minor with his or her relative or relatives, unless this is not in the best interests of the minor.
4. Where the Member State thus approached accedes to the request, responsibility for examining the application shall be transferred to it.
5. The conditions and procedures for implementing this Article including, where appropriate, conciliation mechanisms for settling differences between Member States concerning the need to unite the persons in question, or the place where this should be done, shall be adopted in accordance with the procedure referred to in Article 27(2).

Chapter V

Taking Charge and Taking Back

Article 16

1. The Member State responsible for examining an application for asylum under this Regulation shall be obliged to:
   (a) take charge, under the conditions laid down in Articles 17 to 19, of an asylum seeker who has lodged an application in a different Member State;
   (b) complete the examination of the application for asylum;
   (c) take back, under the conditions laid down in Article 20, an applicant whose application is under examination and who is in the territory of another Member State without permission;
   (d) take back, under the conditions laid down in Article 20, an applicant who has withdrawn the application under examination and made an application in another Member State;
   (e) take back, under the conditions laid down in Article 20, a third-country national whose application it has rejected and who is in the territory of another Member State without permission.
2. Where a Member State issues a residence document to the applicant, the obligations specified in paragraph 1 shall be transferred to that Member State.

3. The obligations specified in paragraph 1 shall cease where the third-country national has left the territory of the Member States for at least three months, unless the third-country national is in possession of a valid residence document issued by the Member State responsible.
4. The obligations specified in paragraph 1(d) and (e) shall likewise cease once the Member State responsible for examining the application has adopted and actually implemented, following the withdrawal or rejection of the application, the provisions that are necessary before the third-country national can go to his country of origin or to another country to which he may lawfully travel.

Article 17

1. Where a Member State with which an application for asylum has been lodged considers that another Member State is responsible for examining the application, it may, as quickly as possible and in any case within three months of the date on which the application was lodged within the meaning of Article 4(2), call upon the other Member State to take charge of the applicant. Where the request to take charge of an applicant is not made within the period of three months, responsibility for examining the application for asylum shall lie with the Member State in which the application was lodged.
2. The requesting Member State may ask for an urgent reply in cases where the application for asylum was lodged after leave to enter or remain was refused, after an arrest for an unlawful stay or after the service or execution of a removal order and/or where the asylum seeker is held in detention. The request shall state the reasons warranting an urgent reply and the period within which a reply is expected. This period shall be at least one week.
3. In both cases, the request that charge be taken by another Member State shall be made using a standard form and including proof or circumstantial evidence as described in the two lists mentioned in Article 18(3) and/or relevant elements from the asylum seeker's statement, enabling the authorities of the requested Member State to check whether it is responsible on the basis of the criteria laid down in this Regulation. The rules on the preparation of and the procedures for transmitting requests shall be adopted in accordance with the procedure referred to in Article 27(2).

Article 18

1. The requested Member State shall make the necessary checks, and shall give a decision on the request to take charge of an applicant within two months of the date on which the request was received.
2. In the procedure for determining the Member State responsible for examining the application for asylum established in this Regulation, elements of proof and circumstantial evidence shall be used.
3. In accordance with the procedure referred to in Article 27(2) two lists shall be

established and periodically reviewed, indicating the elements of proof and circumstantial evidence in accordance with the following criteria:

(a) Proof:

(i) This refers to formal proof which determines responsibility pursuant to this Regulation, as long as it is not refuted by proof to the contrary.

(ii) The Member States shall provide the Committee provided for in Article 27 with models of the different types of administrative documents, in accordance with the typology established in the list of formal proofs.

(b) Circumstantial evidence:

(i) This refers to indicative elements which while being refutable may be sufficient, in certain cases, according to the evidentiary value attributed to them.

(ii) Their evidentiary value, in relation to the responsibility for examining the application for asylum shall be assessed on a case-by-case basis.

4. The requirement of proof should not exceed what is necessary for the proper application of this Regulation.

5. If there is no formal proof, the requested Member State shall acknowledge its responsibility if the circumstantial evidence is coherent, verifiable and sufficiently detailed to establish responsibility.

6. Where the requesting Member State has pleaded urgency, in accordance with the provisions of Article 17(2), the requested Member State shall make every effort to conform to the time limit requested. In exceptional cases, where it can be demonstrated that the examination of a request for taking charge of an applicant is particularly complex, the requested Member State may give the reply after the time limit requested, but in any case within one month. In such situations the requested Member State must communicate its decision to postpone a reply to the requesting Member State within the time limit originally requested.

7. Failure to act within the two-month period mentioned in paragraph 1 and the one-month period mentioned in paragraph 6 shall be tantamount to accepting the request, and entail the obligation to take charge of the person, including the provisions for proper arrangements for arrival.

Article 19

1. Where the requested Member State accepts that it should take charge of an applicant, the Member State in which the application for asylum was lodged shall notify the applicant of the decision not to examine the application, and of the obligation to transfer the applicant to the responsible Member State.

2. The decision referred to in paragraph 1 shall set out the grounds on which it is

based. It shall contain details of the time limit for carrying out the transfer and shall, if necessary, contain information on the place and date at which the applicant should appear, if he is travelling to the Member State responsible by his own means. This decision may be subject to an appeal or a review. Appeal or review concerning this decision shall not suspend the implementation of the transfer unless the courts or competent bodies so decide on a case by case basis if national legislation allows for this.

3. The transfer of the applicant from the Member State in which the application for asylum was lodged to the Member State responsible shall be carried out in accordance with the national law of the first Member State, after consultation between the Member States concerned, as soon as practically possible, and at the latest within six months of acceptance of the request that charge be taken or of the decision on an appeal or review where there is a suspensive effect. If necessary, the asylum seeker shall be supplied by the requesting Member State with a laissez passer of the design adopted in accordance with the procedure referred to in Article 27(2). The Member State responsible shall inform the requesting Member State, as appropriate, of the safe arrival of the asylum seeker or of the fact that he did not appear within the set time limit.
4. Where the transfer does not take place within the six months' time limit, responsibility shall lie with the Member State in which the application for asylum was lodged. This time limit may be extended up to a maximum of one year if the transfer could not be carried out due to imprisonment of the asylum seeker or up to a maximum of eighteen months if the asylum seeker absconds.
5. Supplementary rules on carrying out transfers may be adopted in accordance with the procedure referred to in Article 27(2).

Article 20

1. An asylum seeker shall be taken back in accordance with Article 4(5) and Article 16(1)(c), (d) and (e) as follows:
   (a) the request for the applicant to be taken back must contain information enabling the requested Member State to check that it is responsible;
   (b) the Member State called upon to take back the applicant shall be obliged to make the necessary checks and reply to the request addressed to it as quickly as possible and under no circumstances exceeding a period of one month from the referral. When the request is based on data obtained from the Eurodac system, this time limit is reduced to two weeks;
   (c) where the requested Member State does not communicate its decision within the one month period or the two weeks period mentioned in sub-paragraph (b), it shall be considered to have agreed to take back the asylum seeker;
   (d) a Member State which agrees to take back an asylum seeker shall be obliged

to readmit that person to its territory. The transfer shall be carried out in accordance with the national law of the requesting Member State, after consultation between the Member States concerned, as soon as practically possible, and at the latest within six months of acceptance of the request that charge be taken by another Member State or of the decision on an appeal or review where there is a suspensive effect;

(e) the requesting Member State shall notify the asylum seeker of the decision concerning his being taken back by the Member State responsible. The decision shall set out the grounds on which it is based. It shall contain details of the time limit on carrying out the transfer and shall, if necessary, contain information on the place and date at which the applicant should appear, if he is travelling to the Member State responsible by his own means. This decision may be subject to an appeal or a review. Appeal or review concerning this decision shall not suspend the implementation of the transfer except when the courts or competent bodies so decide in a case-by-case basis if the national legislation allows for this. If necessary, the asylum seeker shall be supplied by the requesting Member State with a laissez passer of the design adopted in accordance with the procedure referred to in Article 27(2). The Member State responsible shall inform the requesting Member State, as appropriate, of the safe arrival of the asylum seeker or of the fact that he did not appear within the set time limit.

2. Where the transfer does not take place within the six months' time limit, responsibility shall lie with the Member State in which the application for asylum was lodged. This time limit may be extended up to a maximum of one year if the transfer or the examination of the application could not be carried out due to imprisonment of the asylum seeker or up to a maximum of eighteen months if the asylum seeker absconds.

3. The rules of proof and evidence and their interpretation, and on the preparation of and the procedures for transmitting requests, shall be adopted in accordance with the procedure referred to in Article 27(2).

4. Supplementary rules on carrying out transfers may be adopted in accordance with the procedure referred to in Article 27(2).

Chapter VI

Administrative Cooperation

Article 21

1. Each Member State shall communicate to any Member State that so requests such personal data concerning the asylum seeker as is appropriate, relevant and non-excessive for:

(a) the determination of the Member State responsible for examining the application for asylum;
(b) examining the application for asylum;
(c) implementing any obligation arising under this Regulation.

2. The information referred to in paragraph 1 may only cover:
(a) personal details of the applicant, and, where appropriate, the members of his family (full name and where appropriate, former name; nicknames or pseudonyms; nationality, present and former; date and place of birth);
(b) identity and travel papers (references, validity, date of issue, issuing authority, place of issue, etc.);
(c) other information necessary for establishing the identity of the applicant, including fingerprints processed in accordance with Regulation (EC) No 2725/2000;
(d) places of residence and routes travelled;
(e) residence documents or visas issued by a Member State;
(f) the place where the application was lodged;
(g) the date any previous application for asylum was lodged, the date the present application was lodged, the stage reached in the proceedings and the decision taken, if any.

3. Furthermore, provided it is necessary for the examination of the application for asylum, the Member State responsible may request another Member State to let it know on what grounds the asylum seeker bases his application and, where applicable, the grounds for any decisions taken concerning the applicant. The Member State may refuse to respond to the request submitted to it, if the communication of such information is likely to harm the essential interests of the Member State or the protection of the liberties and fundamental rights of the person concerned or of others. In any event, communication of the information requested shall be subject to the written approval of the applicant for asylum.

4. Any request for information shall set out the grounds on which it is based and, where its purpose is to check whether there is a criterion that is likely to entail the responsibility of the requested Member State, shall state on what evidence, including relevant information from reliable sources on the ways and means asylum seekers enter the territories of the Member States, or on what specific and verifiable part of the applicant's statements it is based. It is understood that such relevant information from reliable sources is not in itself sufficient to determine the responsibility and the competence of a Member State under this Regulation, but it may contribute to the evaluation of other indications relating to the individual asylum seeker.

5. The requested Member State shall be obliged to reply within six weeks.

6. The exchange of information shall be effected at the request of a Member State and may only take place between authorities whose designation by each

Member State has been communicated to the Commission, which shall inform the other Member States thereof.

7. The information exchanged may only be used for the purposes set out in paragraph 1. In each Member State such information may, depending on its type and the powers of the recipient authority, only be communicated to the authorities and courts and tribunals entrusted with:
   (a) the determination of the Member State responsible for examining the application for asylum;
   (b) examining the application for asylum;
   (c) implementing any obligation arising under this Regulation.
8. The Member State which forwards the information shall ensure that it is accurate and up-to-date. If it transpires that that Member State has forwarded information which is inaccurate or which should not have been forwarded, the recipient

   Member States shall be informed thereof immediately. They shall be obliged to correct such information or to have it erased.

9. The asylum seeker shall have the right to be informed, on request, of any data that is processed concerning him. If he finds that this information has been processed in breach of this Regulation or of Directive 95/46/EC of the European Parliament and the Council of 24 October 1995 on the protection of individuals with regard to the processing of personal data and on the free movement of such data,[23] in particular because it is incomplete or inaccurate, he is entitled to have it corrected, erased or blocked. The authority correcting, erasing or blocking the data shall inform, as appropriate, the Member State transmitting or receiving the information.
10. In each Member State concerned, a record shall be kept, in the individual file for the person concerned and/or in a register, of the transmission and receipt of information exchanged.
11. The data exchanged shall be kept for a period not exceeding that which is necessary for the purposes for which it is exchanged.
12. Where the data is not processed automatically or is not contained, or intended to be entered, in a file, each Member State should take appropriate measures to ensure compliance with this Article through effective checks.

Article 22

1. Member States shall notify the Commission of the authorities responsible for fulfilling the obligations arising under this Regulation and shall ensure that those authorities have the necessary resources for carrying out their tasks and in

[23] OJ L281, 23.11.1995, p.31.

particular for replying within the prescribed time limits to requests for information, requests to take charge of and requests to take back asylum seekers.

2. Rules relating to the establishment of secure electronic transmission channels between the authorities mentioned in paragraph 1 for transmitting requests and ensuring that senders automatically receive an electronic proof of delivery shall be established in accordance with the procedure referred to in Article 27(2).

Article 23

1. Member States may, on a bilateral basis, establish administrative arrangements between themselves concerning the practical details of the implementation of this Regulation, in order to facilitate its application and increase its effectiveness. Such arrangements may relate to:
   (a) exchanges of liaison officers;
   (b) simplification of the procedures and shortening of the time limits relating to transmission and the examination of requests to take charge of or take back asylum seekers;
2. The arrangements referred to in paragraph 1 shall be communicated to the Commission. The Commission shall verify that the arrangements referred to in paragraph 1(b) do not infringe this Regulation.

Chapter VII

Transitional Provisions and Final Provisions

Article 24

1. This Regulation shall replace the Convention determining the State responsible for examining applications for asylum lodged in one of the Member States of the European Communities, signed in Dublin on 15 June 1990 (Dublin Convention).
2. However, to ensure continuity of the arrangements for determining the Member State responsible for an application for asylum, where an application has been lodged after the date mentioned in the second paragraph of Article 29, the events that are likely to entail the responsibility of a Member State under this Regulation shall be taken into consideration, even if they precede that date, with the exception of the events mentioned in Article 10(2).
3. Where, in Regulation (EC) No 2725/2000 reference is made to the Dublin Convention, such references shall be taken to be a reference made to this Regulation.

Article 25

1. Any period of time prescribed in this Regulation shall be calculated as follows:
   (a) where a period expressed in days, weeks or months is to be calculated from the moment at which an event occurs or an action takes place, the day during which that event occurs or that action takes place shall not be counted as falling within the period in question;
   (b) a period expressed in weeks or months shall end with the expiry of whichever day in the last week or month is the same day of the week or falls on the same date as the day during which the event or action from which the period is to be calculated occurred or took place. If, in a period expressed in months, the day on which it should expire does not occur in the last month, the period shall end with the expiry of the last day of that month;
   (c) time limits shall include Saturdays, Sundays and official holidays in any of the Member States concerned.
2. Requests and replies shall be sent using any method that provides proof of receipt.

Article 26

As far as the French Republic is concerned, this Regulation shall apply only to its European territory.

Article 27

1. The Commission shall be assisted by a committee.
2. Where reference is made to this paragraph, Articles 5 and 7 of Decision 1999/468/EC shall apply. The period laid down in Article 5(6) of Decision 1999/468/EC shall be set at three months.
3. The Committee shall draw up its rules of procedure.

Article 28

At the latest three years after the date mentioned in the first paragraph of Article 29, the Commission shall report to the European Parliament and the Council on the application of this Regulation and, where appropriate, shall propose the necessary amendments. Member States shall forward to the Commission all information appropriate for the preparation of that report, at the latest six months before that time limit expires. Having submitted that report, the Commission shall report to the European Parliament and the Council on the application of this Regulation at the same time as it submits reports on the implementation of the Eurodac system provided for by Article 24(5) of Regulation (EC)No 2725/2000.

Article 29

This Regulation shall enter into force on the 20th day following that of its publication in the Official Journal of the European Union. It shall apply to asylum applications lodged as from the first day of the sixth month following its entry into force and, from that date, it will apply to any request to take charge of or take back asylum seekers, irrespective of the date on which the application was made. The Member State responsible for the examination of an asylum application submitted before that date shall be determined in accordance with the criteria set out in the Dublin Convention. This Regulation shall be binding in its entirety and directly applicable in the Member States in conformity with the Treaty establishing the European Community.

Done at Brussels, 18 February 2003.

For the Council
The President
N. CHRISTODOULAKIS

Commission Regulation (EC) No 1560/2003

of 2 September 2003

laying down detailed rules for the application of Council Regulation (EC) No 343/2003 establishing the criteria and mechanisms for determining the Member State responsible for examining an asylum application lodged in one of the Member States by a third-country national

Note: Entered into force on 6 September 2003 (Article 23).

THE COMMISSION OF THE EUROPEAN COMMUNITIES,

Having regard to the Treaty establishing the European Community,

Having regard to Council Regulation (EC) No 343/2003 of 18 February 2003 establishing the criteria and mechanisms for determining the Member State responsible for examining an asylum application lodged in one of the Member States by a third-country national[24], and in particular Article 15(5), Article 17(3), Article 18(3), Article 19(3) and (5), Article 20(1), (3) and (4) and Article 22(2) thereof,

Whereas:

[24] OJ L 50, 25.2.2003, p. 1.

(1) A number of specific arrangements must be established for the effective application of Regulation (EC) No 343/2003. Those arrangements must be clearly defined so as to facilitate cooperation between the authorities in the Member States competent for implementing that Regulation as regards the transmission and processing of requests for the purposes of taking charge and taking back, requests for information and the carrying out of transfers.

(2) To ensure the greatest possible continuity between the Convention determining the State responsible for examining applications for asylum lodged in one of the Member States of the European Communities[25], signed in Dublin on 15 June 1990, and Regulation (EC) No 343/2003, which replaces that Convention, this Regulation should be based on the common principles, lists and forms adopted by the committee set up by Article 18 of that Convention, with the inclusion of amendments necessitated by the introduction of new criteria, the wording of certain provisions and of the lessons drawn from experience.

(3) The interaction between the procedures laid down in Regulation (EC) No 343/2003 and the application of Council Regulation (EC) No 2725/2000 of 11 December 2000 concerning the establishment of 'Eurodac' for the comparison of fingerprints for the effective application of the Dublin Convention[26] must be taken into account.

(4) It is desirable, both for the Member States and the asylum seekers concerned, that there should be a mechanism for finding a solution in cases where Member States differ over the application of the humanitarian clause in Article 15 of Regulation (EC) No 343/2003.

(5) The establishment of an electronic transmission network to facilitate the implementation of Regulation (EC) No 343/2003 means that rules must be laid down relating to the technical standards applicable and the practical arrangements for using the network.

(6) Directive 95/46/EC of the European Parliament and of the Council of 24 October 1995 on the protection of individuals with regard to the processing of personal data and on the free movement of such data[27] applies to processing carried out pursuant to the present Regulation in accordance with Article 21 of Regulation (EC) No 343/2003.

(7) In accordance with Articles 1 and 2 of the Protocol on the position of Denmark annexed to the Treaty on European Union and to the Treaty establishing the European Community, Denmark, which is not bound by Regulation (EC) No 343/2003, is not bound by the present Regulation or subject to its application, until such time as an agreement allowing it to participate in Regulation (EC) No 343/2003 is reached.

[25] OJ C 254, 19.8.1997, p. 1.
[26] OJ L 316, 15.12.2000, p. 1.
[27] OJ L 281, 23.11.1995, p. 31.

(8) In accordance with Article 4 of the Agreement of 19 January 2001 between the European Community and the Republic of Iceland and the Kingdom of Norway concerning the criteria and mechanisms for establishing the State responsible for examining an application for asylum lodged in a Member State or in Iceland or Norway[28], this Regulation is to be applied by Iceland and Norway as it is applied by the Member States of the European Community.

Consequently, for the purposes of this Regulation, Member States also include Iceland and Norway.

(9) It is necessary for the present Regulation to enter into force as quickly as possible to enable Regulation (EC) No 343/2003 to be applied.

(10) The measures set out in this Regulation are in accordance with the opinion of the Committee set up by Article 27 of Regulation (EC) No 343/2003,

HAS ADOPTED THIS REGULATION:

TITLE I

Procedures

CHAPTER I

PREPARATION OF REQUESTS

Article 1

Preparation of requests for taking charge

1. Requests for taking charge shall be made on a standard form in accordance with the model in Annex I. The form shall include mandatory fields which must be duly filled in and other fields to be filled in if the information is available. Additional information may be entered in the field set aside for the purpose.

   The request shall also include:

   (a) a copy of all the proof and circumstantial evidence showing that the requested Member State is responsible for examining the application for asylum, accompanied, where appropriate, by comments on the circumstances in which it was obtained and the probative value attached to it by the requesting Member State, with reference to the lists of proof and circumstantial evidence referred to in Article 18(3) of Regulation (EC) No 343/2003, which are set out in Annex II to the present Regulation;

   (b) where necessary, a copy of any written declarations made by or statements taken from the applicant.

[28] OJ L 93, 3.4.2001, p. 40.

2. Where the request is based on a positive result (hit) transmitted by the Eurodac Central Unit in accordance with Article 4(5) of Regulation (EC) No 2725/2000 after comparison of the asylum seeker's fingerprints with fingerprint data previously taken and sent to the Central Unit in accordance with Article 8 of that Regulation and checked in accordance with Article 4(6) of that Regulation, it shall also include the data supplied by the Central Unit.
3. Where the requesting Member State asks for an urgent reply in accordance with Article 17(2) of Regulation (EC) No 343/2003, the request shall describe the circumstances of the application for asylum and shall state the reasons in law and in fact which warrant an urgent reply.

Article 2

Preparation of requests for taking back

Requests for taking back shall be made on a standard form in accordance with the model in Annex III, setting out the nature of the request, the reasons for it and the provisions of Regulation (EC) No 343/2003 on which it is based.

The request shall also include the positive result (hit) transmitted by the Eurodac Central Unit, in accordance with Article 4(5) of Regulation EC) No 2725/2000, after comparison of the applicant's fingerprints with fingerprint data previously taken and sent to the Central Unit in accordance with Article 4(1) and (2) of that Regulation and checked in accordance with Article 4(6) of that Regulation.

For requests relating to applications dating from before Eurodac became operational, a copy of the fingerprints shall be attached to the form.

Chapter II
Reaction to Requests

Article 3

Processing requests for taking charge

1. The arguments in law and in fact set out in the request shall be examined in the light of the provisions of Regulation (EC) No 343/2003 and the lists of proof and circumstantial evidence which are set out in Annex II to the present Regulation.
2. Whatever the criteria and provisions of Regulation (EC) No 343/2003 that are relied on, the requested Member State shall, within the time allowed by Article 18(1) and (6) of that Regulation, check exhaustively and objectively, on the basis of all information directly or indirectly available to it, whether its responsibility for examining the application for asylum is established.

If the checks by the requested Member State reveal that it is responsible under at least one of the criteria of that Regulation, it shall acknowledge its responsibility.

Article 4

Processing of requests for taking back

Where a request for taking back is based on data supplied by the Eurodac Central Unit and checked by the requesting Member State, in accordance with Article 4(6) of Regulation (EC) No 2725/2000, the requested Member State shall acknowledge its responsibility unless the checks carried out reveal that its obligations have ceased under the second subparagraph of Article 4(5) or under Article 16(2), (3) or (4) of Regulation (EC) No 343/2003. The fact that obligations have ceased on the basis of those provisions may be relied on only on the basis of material evidence or substantiated and verifiable statements by the asylum seeker.

Article 5

Negative reply

1. Where, after checks are carried out, the requested Member State considers that the evidence submitted does not establish its responsibility, the negative reply it sends to the requesting Member State shall state full and detailed reasons for its refusal.
2. Where the requesting Member State feels that such a refusal is based on a misappraisal, or where it has additional evidence to put forward, it may ask for its request to be re-examined. This option must be exercised within three weeks following receipt of the negative reply. The requested Member State shall endeavour to reply within two weeks. In any event, this additional procedure shall not extend the time limits laid down in Article 18(1) and (6) and Article 20(1)(b) of Regulation (EC) No 343/2003.

Article 6

Positive reply

Where the Member State accepts responsibility, the reply shall say so, specifying the provision of Regulation (EC) No 343/2003 that is taken as a basis, and shall include practical details regarding the subsequent transfer, such as contact particulars of the department or person to be contacted.

Chapter III
Transfers

Article 7

Practical arrangements for transfers

1. Transfers to the Member State responsible may be carried out in one of the following ways:
   (a) at the request of the asylum seeker, by a certain specified date;
   (b) by supervised departure, with the asylum seeker being accompanied to the point of embarkation by an official of the requesting Member State, the responsible Member State being notified of the place, date and time of the asylum seeker's arrival within an agreed time limit;
   (c) under escort, the asylum seeker being accompanied by an official of the requesting Member State or by a representative of an agency empowered by the requesting Member State to act in that capacity and handed over to the authorities in the responsible Member State.
2. In the cases referred to in paragraph 1(a) and (b), the applicant shall be supplied with the laissez-passer referred to in Article 19(3) and Article 20(1)(e) of Regulation (EC) No 343/2003, a model of which is set out in Annex IV to the present Regulation, to allow him to enter the Member State responsible and to identify himself on his arrival at the place and time indicated to him at the time of notification of the decision on taking charge or taking back by the Member State responsible.

   In the case referred to in paragraph 1(c), a laissez-passer shall be issued if the asylum seeker is not in possession of identity documents. The time and place of transfer shall be agreed in advance by the Member States concerned in accordance with the procedure set out in Article 8.
3. The Member State making the transfer shall ensure that all the asylum seeker's documents are returned to him before his departure, given into the safe keeping of members of the escort to be handed to the competent authorities of the Member State responsible, or sent by other appropriate means.

Article 8

Cooperation on transfers

1. It is the obligation of the Member State responsible to allow the asylum seeker's transfer to take place as quickly as possible and to ensure that no obstacles are put in his way. That Member State shall determine, where appropriate, the location on its territory to which the asylum seeker will be transferred or

handed over to the competent authorities, taking account of geographical constraints and modes of transport available to the Member State making the transfer. In no case may a requirement be imposed that the escort accompany the asylum seeker beyond the point of arrival of the international means of transport used or that the Member State making the transfer meet the costs of transport beyond that point.

2. The Member State organising the transfer shall arrange the transport for the asylum seeker and his escort and decide, in consultation with the Member State responsible, on the time of arrival and, where necessary, on the details of the handover to the competent authorities. The Member State responsible may require that three working days' notice be given.

Article 9

Postponed and delayed transfers

1. The Member State responsible shall be informed without delay of any postponement due either to an appeal or review procedure with suspensive effect, or physical reasons such as ill health of the asylum seeker, non-availability of transport or the fact that the asylum seeker has withdrawn from the transfer procedure.
2. A Member State which, for one of the reasons set out in Article 19(4) and Article 20(2) of Regulation (EC) No 343/2003, cannot carry out the transfer within the normal time limit of six months provided for in Article 19(3) and Article 20(1)(d) of that Regulation, shall inform the Member State responsible before the end of that time limit. Otherwise, the responsibility for processing the application for asylum and the other obligations under Regulation (EC) No 343/2003 falls to the former Member State, in accordance with Article 19(4) and Article 20(2) of that Regulation.
3. When, for one of the reasons set out in Article 19(4) and Article 20(2) of Regulation (EC) No 343/2003, a Member State undertakes to carry out the transfer after the normal time limit of six months, it shall make the necessary arrangements in advance with the Member State responsible.

Article 10

Transfer following an acceptance by default

1. Where, pursuant to Article 18(7) or Article 20(1)(c) of Regulation (EC) No 343/2003 as appropriate, the requested Member State is deemed to have accepted a request to take charge or to take back, the requesting Member State shall initiate the consultations needed to organise the transfer.
2. If asked to do so by the requesting Member State, the Member State responsible

must confirm in writing, without delay, that it acknowledges its responsibility as a result of its failure to reply within the time limit. The Member State responsible shall take the necessary steps to determine the asylum seeker's place of arrival as quickly as possible and, where applicable, agree with the requesting Member State the time of arrival and the practical details of the handover to the competent authorities.

Chapter IV
Humanitarian Clause

Article 11

Situations of dependency

1. Article 15(2) of Regulation (EC) No 343/2003 shall apply whether the asylum seeker is dependent on the assistance of a relative present in another Member State or a relative present in another Member State is dependent on the assistance of the asylum seeker.
2. The situations of dependency referred to in Article 15(2) of Regulation (EC) No 343/2003 shall be assessed, as far as possible, on the basis of objective criteria such as medical certificates. Where such evidence is not available or cannot be supplied, humanitarian grounds shall be taken as proven only on the basis of convincing information supplied by the persons concerned.
3. The following points shall be taken into account in assessing the necessity and appropriateness of bringing together the persons concerned:
   (a) the family situation which existed in the country of origin;
   (b) the circumstances in which the persons concerned were separated;
   (c) the status of the various asylum procedures or procedures under the legislation on aliens under way in the Member States.
4. The application of Article 15(2) of Regulation (EC) No 343/2003 shall, in any event, be subject to the assurance that the asylum seeker or relative will actually provide the assistance needed.
5. The Member State in which the relatives will be reunited and the date of the transfer shall be agreed by the Member States concerned, taking account of:
   (a) the ability of the dependent person to travel;
   (b) the situation of the persons concerned as regards residence, preference being given to the bringing the asylum seeker together with his relative where the latter already has a valid residence permit and resources in the Member State in which he resides.

Article 12

Unaccompanied minors

1. Where the decision to entrust the care of an unaccompanied minor to a relative other than the mother, father or legal guardian is likely to cause particular difficulties, particularly where the adult concerned resides outside the jurisdiction of the Member State in which the minor has applied for asylum, cooperation between the competent authorities in the Member States, in particular the authorities or courts responsible for the protection of minors, shall be facilitated and the necessary steps taken to ensure that those authorities can decide, with full knowledge of the facts, on the ability of the adult or adults concerned to take charge of the minor in a way which serves his best interests.

   Options now available in the field of cooperation on judicial and civil matters shall be taken account of in this connection.

2. The fact that the duration of procedures for placing a minor may lead to a failure to observe the time limits set in Article 18(1) and (6) and Article 19(4) of Regulation (EC) No 343/2003 shall not necessarily be an obstacle to continuing the procedure for determining the Member State responsible or carrying out a transfer.

Article 13

Procedures

1. The initiative of requesting another Member State to take charge of an asylum seeker on the basis of Article 15 of Regulation (EC) No 343/2003 shall be taken either by the Member State where the application for asylum was made and which is carrying out a procedure to determine the Member State responsible, or by the Member State responsible.
2. The request to take charge shall contain all the material in the possession of the requesting Member State to allow the requested Member State to assess the situation.
3. The requested Member State shall carry out the necessary checks to establish, where applicable, humanitarian reasons, particularly of a family or cultural nature, the level of dependency of the person concerned or the ability and commitment of the other person concerned to provide the assistance desired.
4. In all events, the persons concerned must have given their consent.

Article 14

Conciliation

1. Where the Member States cannot resolve a dispute, either on the need to carry out a transfer or to bring relatives together on the basis of Article 15 of Regulation (EC) No 343/2003, or on the Member State in which the persons concerned should be reunited, they may have recourse to the conciliation procedure provided for in paragraph 2 of this Article.
2. The conciliation procedure shall be initiated by a request from one of the Member States in dispute to the Chairman of the Committee set up by Article 27 of Regulation (EC) No 343/2003. By agreeing to use the conciliation procedure, the Member States concerned undertake to take the utmost account of the solution proposed.

   The Chairman of the Committee shall appoint three members of the Committee representing three Member States not connected with the matter. They shall receive the arguments of the parties either in writing or orally and, after deliberation, shall propose a solution within one month, where necessary after a vote.

   The Chairman of the Committee, or his deputy, shall chair the discussion. He may put forward his point of view but he may not vote.

   Whether it is adopted or rejected by the parties, the solution proposed shall be final and irrevocable.

Chapter V

Common Provisions

Article 15

Transmission of requests

1. Requests, replies and all written correspondence between Member States concerning the application of Regulation (EC) No 343/2003 shall where possible be sent through the 'DubliNet' electronic communications network, set up under Title II of the present Regulation.

   By way of derogation from the first subparagraph, correspondence between the departments responsible for carrying out transfers and competent departments in the requested Member State regarding the practical arrangements for transfers, time and place of arrival, particularly where the asylum seeker is under escort, may be transmitted by other means.

2. Any request, reply or correspondence emanating from a National Access Point, as referred to in Article 19, shall be deemed to be authentic.

3. The acknowledgement issued by the system shall be taken as proof of transmission and of the date and time of receipt of the request or reply.

Article 16

Language of communication

The language or languages of communication shall be chosen by agreement between the Member States concerned.

Article 17

Consent of the persons concerned

1. For the application of Articles 7 and 8, Article 15(1) and Article 21(3) of Regulation (EC) No 343/2003, which require the persons concerned to express a desire or give consent, their approval must be given in writing.
2. In the case of Article 21(3) of Regulation (EC) No 343/2003, the applicant must know for what information he is giving his approval.

Title II

Establishment of the 'Dublinet' Network

Chapter I

Technical Standards

Article 18

Establishment of 'DubliNet'

1. The secure electronic means of transmission referred to in Article 22(2) of Regulation (EC) No 343/2003 shall be known as 'DubliNet'.
2. DubliNet is based on the use of the generic IDA services referred to in Article 4 of Decision No 1720/1999/EC[29].

Article 19

National Access Points

1. Each Member State shall have a single designated National Access Point.

[29] OJ L 203, 3.8.1999, p. 9.

2. The National Access Points shall be responsible for processing incoming data and transmitting outgoing data.

3. The National Access Points shall be responsible for issuing an acknowledgement of receipt for every incoming transmission.

4. The forms of which the models are set out in Annexes I and III and the form for the request of information set out in Annex V shall be sent between National Access Points in the format supplied by the Commission. The Commission shall inform the Member States of the technical standards required.

Chapter II
Rules For Use

Article 20

Reference number

1. Each transmission shall have a reference number making it possible unambiguously to identify the case to which it relates and the Member State making the request. That number must also make it possible to determine whether the transmission relates to a request for taking charge (type 1), a request for taking back (type 2) or a request for information (type 3).

2. The reference number shall begin with the letters used to identify the Member State in Eurodac. This code shall be followed by the number indicating the type of request, according to the classification set out in paragraph 1.

   If the request is based on data supplied by Eurodac, the Eurodac reference number shall be included.

Article 21

Continuous operation

1. The Member States shall take the necessary steps to ensure that their National Access Points operate without interruption.

2. If the operation of a National Access Point is interrupted for more than seven working hours the Member State shall notify the competent authorities designated pursuant to Article 22(1) of Regulation (EC) No 343/2003 and the Commission and shall take all the necessary steps to ensure that normal operation is resumed as soon as possible.

3. If a National Access Point has sent data to a National Access Point that has experienced an interruption in its operation, the acknowledgement of transmission generated by the IDA generic services shall be used as proof of the date and time of transmission. The deadlines set by Regulation (EC) No 343/2003

for sending a request or a reply shall not be suspended for the duration of the interruption of the operation of the National Access Point in question.

Title III

Transitional and Final Provisions

Article 22

Laissez-passer produced for the purposes of the Dublin Convention

Laissez-passer printed for the purposes of the Dublin Convention shall be accepted for the transfer of applicants for asylum under Regulation (EC) No 343/2003 for a period of no more than 18 months following the entry into force of the present Regulation.

Article 23

Entry into force

This Regulation shall enter into force on the day following that of its publication in the *Official Journal of the European Union.*
This Regulation shall be binding in its entirety and directly applicable in all Member States.

Done at Brussels, 2 September 2003.

For the Commission
António VITORINO
Member of the Commission

Council Directive 2004/83/EC
of 29 April 2004
on minimum standards for the qualification and status of third country nationals or stateless persons as refugees or as persons who otherwise need international protection and the content of the protection granted

Note: Entered into force on 20 October 2004 (Article 39). Implemented 10 October 2006, Article 38.

THE COUNCIL OF THE EUROPEAN UNION,

Having regard to the Treaty establishing the European Community, and in particular points 1(c), 2(a) and 3(a) of Article 63 thereof,

Having regard to the proposal from the Commission [30],

Having regard to the opinion of the European Parliament [31],

Having regard to the opinion of the European Economic and Social Committee [32],

Having regard to the opinion of the Committee of the Regions [33],

Whereas:

(1) A common policy on asylum, including a Common European Asylum System, is a constituent part of the European Union's objective of progressively establishing an area of freedom, security and justice open to those who, forced by circumstances, legitimately seek protection in the Community.

(2) The European Council at its special meeting in Tampere on 15 and 16 October 1999 agreed to work towards establishing a Common European Asylum System, based on the full and inclusive application of the Geneva Convention relating to the Status of Refugees of 28 July 1951 (Geneva Convention), as supplemented by the New York Protocol of 31 January 1967 (Protocol), thus affirming the principle of non-refoulement and ensuring that nobody is sent back to persecution.

(3) The Geneva Convention and Protocol provide the cornerstone of the international legal regime for the protection of refugees.

(4) The Tampere conclusions provide that a Common European Asylum System should include, in the short term, the approximation of rules on the recognition of refugees and the content of refugee status.

(5) The Tampere conclusions also provide that rules regarding refugee status should be complemented by measures on subsidiary forms of protection, offering an appropriate status to any person in need of such protection.

(6) The main objective of this Directive is, on the one hand, to ensure that Member States apply common criteria for the identification of persons genuinely in need of international protection, and, on the other hand, to ensure that a minimum level of benefits is available for these persons in all Member States.

(7) The approximation of rules on the recognition and content of refugee and subsidiary protection status should help to limit the secondary movements of applicants for asylum between Member States, where such movement is purely caused by differences in legal frameworks.

(8) It is in the very nature of minimum standards that Member States should have the power to introduce or maintain more favourable provisions for third

[30] OJ C 51 E, 26.2.2002, p. 325.

[31] OJ C 300 E, 11.12.2003, p. 25.

[32] OJ C 221, 17.9.2002, p. 43.

[33] OJ C 278, 14.11.2002, p. 44.

country nationals or stateless persons who request international protection from a Member State, where such a request is understood to be on the grounds that the person concerned is either a refugee within the meaning of Article 1(A) of the Geneva Convention, or a person who otherwise needs international protection.

(9) Those third country nationals or stateless persons, who are allowed to remain in the territories of the Member States for reasons not due to a need for international protection but on a discretionary basis on compassionate or humanitarian grounds, fall outside the scope of this Directive.

(10) This Directive respects the fundamental rights and observes the principles recognised in particular by the Charter of Fundamental Rights of the European Union. In particular this Directive seeks to ensure full respect for human dignity and the right to asylum of applicants for asylum and their accompanying family members.

(11) With respect to the treatment of persons falling within the scope of this Directive, Member States are bound by obligations under instruments of international law to which they are party and which prohibit discrimination.

(12) The 'best interests of the child' should be a primary consideration of Member States when implementing this Directive.

(13) This Directive is without prejudice to the Protocol on asylum for nationals of Member States of the European Union as annexed to the Treaty Establishing the European Community.

(14) The recognition of refugee status is a declaratory act.

(15) Consulations with the United Nations High Commissioner for Refugees may provide valuable guidance for Member States when determining refugee status according to Article 1 of the Geneva Convention.

(16) Minimum standards for the definition and content of refugee status should be laid down to guide the competent national bodies of Member States in the application of the Geneva Convention.

(17) It is necessary to introduce common criteria for recognising applicants for asylum as refugees within the meaning of Article 1 of the Geneva Convention.

(18) In particular, it is necessary to introduce common concepts of protection needs arising *sur place*; sources of harm and protection; internal protection; and persecution, including the reasons for persecution.

(19) Protection can be provided not only by the State but also by parties or organisations, including international organisations, meeting the conditions of this Directive, which control a region or a larger area within the territory of the State.

(20) It is necessary, when assessing applications from minors for international protection, that Member States should have regard to child-specific forms of persecution.

(21) It is equally necessary to introduce a common concept of the persecution ground 'membership of a particular social group'.

(22) Acts contrary to the purposes and principles of the United Nations are set out in the Preamble and Articles 1 and 2 of the Charter of the United Nations and are, amongst others, embodied in the United Nations Resolutions relating to measures combating terrorism, which declare that 'acts, methods and practices of terrorism are contrary to the purposes and principles of the United Nations' and that 'knowingly financing, planning and inciting terrorist acts are also contrary to the purposes and principles of the United Nations'.

(23) As referred to in Article 14, 'status' can also include refugee status.

(24) Minimum standards for the definition and content of subsidiary protection status should also be laid down. Subsidiary protection should be complementary and additional to the refugee protection enshrined in the Geneva Convention.

(25) It is necessary to introduce criteria on the basis of which applicants for international protection are to be recognised as eligible for subsidiary protection. Those criteria should be drawn from international obligations under human rights instruments and practices existing in Member States.

(26) Risks to which a population of a country or a section of the population is generally exposed do normally not create in themselves an individual threat which would qualify as serious harm.

(27) Family members, merely due to their relation to the refugee, will normally be vulnerable to acts of persecution in such a manner that could be the basis for refugee status.

(28) The notion of national security and public order also covers cases in which a third country national belongs to an association which supports international terrorism or supports such an association.

(29) While the benefits provided to family members of beneficiaries of subsidiary protection status do not necessarily have to be the same as those provided to the qualifying beneficiary, they need to be fair in comparison to those enjoyed by beneficiaries of subsidiary protection status.

(30) Within the limits set out by international obligations, Member States may lay down that the granting of benefits with regard to access to employment, social welfare, health care and access to integration facilities requires the prior issue of a residence permit.

(31) This Directive does not apply to financial benefits from the Member States which are granted to promote education and training.

(32) The practical difficulties encountered by beneficiaries of refugee or subsidiary protection status concerning the authentication of their foreign diplomas, certificates or other evidence of formal qualification should be taken into account.

(33) Especially to avoid social hardship, it is appropriate, for beneficiaries of refugee or subsidiary protection status, to provide without discrimination in the context of social assistance the adequate social welfare and means of subsistence.

(34) With regard to social assistance and health care, the modalities and detail of the provision of core benefits to beneficiaries of subsidiary protection status should be determined by national law. The possibility of limiting the benefits for beneficiaries of subsidiary protection status to core benefits is to be understood in the sense that this notion covers at least minimum income support, assistance in case of illness, pregnancy and parental assistance, in so far as they are granted to nationals according to the legislation of the Member State concerned.

(35) Access to health care, including both physical and mental health care, should be ensured to beneficiaries of refugee or subsidiary protection status.

(36) The implementation of this Directive should be evaluated at regular intervals, taking into consideration in particular the evolution of the international obligations of Member States regarding non-refoulement, the evolution of the labour markets in the Member States as well as the development of common basic principles for integration.

(37) Since the objectives of the proposed Directive, namely to establish minimum standards for the granting of international protection to third country nationals and stateless persons by Member States and the content of the protection granted, cannot be sufficiently achieved by the Member States and can therefore, by reason of the scale and effects of the Directive, be better achieved at Community level, the Community may adopt measures, in accordance with the principle of subsidiarity as set out in Article 5 of the Treaty. In accordance with the principle of proportionality, as set out in that Article, this Directive does not go beyond what is necessary in order to achieve those objectives.

(38) In accordance with Article 3 of the Protocol on the position of the United Kingdom and Ireland, annexed to the Treaty on European Union and to the Treaty establishing the European Community, the United Kingdom has notified, by letter of 28 January 2002, its wish to take part in the adoption and application of this Directive.

(39) In accordance with Article 3 of the Protocol on the position of the United Kingdom and Ireland, annexed to the Treaty on European Union and to the Treaty establishing the European Community, Ireland has notified, by letter of

13 February 2002, its wish to take part in the adoption and application of this Directive.

(40) In accordance with Articles 1 and 2 of the Protocol on the position of Denmark, annexed to the Treaty on European Union and to the Treaty establishing the European Community, Denmark is not taking part in the adoption of this Directive and is not bound by it or subject to its application,

HAS ADOPTED THIS DIRECTIVE,

Chapter I
General Provisions

Article 1
Subject matter and scope

The purpose of this Directive is to lay down minimum standards for the qualification of third country nationals or stateless persons as refugees or as persons who otherwise need international protection and the content of the protection granted.

Article 2
Definitions

For the purposes of this Directive:

(a) 'international protection' means the refugee and subsidiary protection status as defined in (d) and (f);

(b) 'Geneva Convention' means the Convention relating to the status of refugees done at Geneva on 28 July 1951, as amended by the New York Protocol of 31 January 1967;

(c) 'refugee' means a third country national who, owing to a well-founded fear of being persecuted for reasons of race, religion, nationality, political opinion or membership of a particular social group, is outside the country of nationality and is unable or, owing to such fear, is unwilling to avail himself or herself of the protection of that country, or a stateless person, who, being outside of the country of former habitual residence for the same reasons as mentioned above, is unable or, owing to such fear, unwilling to return to it, and to whom Article 12 does not apply;

(d) 'refugee status' means the recognition by a Member State of a third country national or a stateless person as a refugee;

(e) 'person eligible for subsidiary protection' means a third country national or a stateless person who does not qualify as a refugee but in respect of whom substantial grounds have been shown for believing that the person concerned, if returned to his or her country of origin, or in the case of a stateless person, to his or her country of former habitual residence, would face a real risk of suffering serious harm as defined in Article 15, and to whom Article 17(1) and (2) do not apply, and is unable, or, owing to such risk, unwilling to avail himself or herself of the protection of that country;

(f) 'subsidiary protection status' means the recognition by a Member State of a third country national or a stateless person as a person eligible for subsidiary protection;

(g) 'application for international protection' means a request made by a third country national or a stateless person for protection from a Member State, who can be understood to seek refugee status or subsidiary protection status, and who does not explicitly request another kind of protection, outside the scope of this Directive, that can be applied for separately;

(h) 'family members' means, insofar as the family already existed in the country of origin, the following members of the family of the beneficiary of refugee or subsidiary protection status who are present in the same Member State in relation to the application for international protection:
   — the spouse of the beneficiary of refugee or subsidiary protection status or his or her unmarried partner in a stable relationship, where the legislation or practice of the Member State concerned treats unmarried couples in a way comparable to married couples under its law relating to aliens,
   — the minor children of the couple referred to in the first indent or of the beneficiary of refugee or subsidiary protection status, on condition that they are unmarried and dependent and regardless of whether they were born in or out of wedlock or adopted as defined under the national law;

(i) 'unaccompanied minors' means third-country nationals or stateless persons below the age of 18, who arrive on the territory of the Member States unaccompanied by an adult responsible for them whether by law or custom, and for as long as they are not effectively taken into the care of such a person; it includes minors who are left unaccompanied after they have entered the territory of the Member States;

(j) 'residence permit' means any permit or authorisation issued by the authorities of a Member State, in the form provided for under that State's legislation, allowing a third country national or stateless person to reside on its territory;

(k) 'country of origin' means the country or countries of nationality or, for stateless persons, of former habitual residence.

Article 3

More favourable standards

Member States may introduce or retain more favourable standards for determining who qualifies as a refugee or as a person eligible for subsidiary protection, and for determining the content of international protection, in so far as those standards are compatible with this Directive.

Chapter II

Assessment of Applications for International Protection

Article 4

Assessment of facts and circumstances

1. Member States may consider it the duty of the applicant to submit as soon as possible all elements needed to substantiate the application for international protection. In cooperation with the applicant it is the duty of the Member State to assess the relevant elements of the application.
2. The elements referred to in of paragraph 1 consist of the applicant's statements and all documentation at the applicants disposal regarding the applicant's age, background, including that of relevant relatives, identity, nationality(ies), country(ies) and place(s) of previous residence, previous asylum applications, travel routes, identity and travel documents and the reasons for applying for international protection.
3. The assessment of an application for international protection is to be carried out on an individual basis and includes taking into account:
   (a) all relevant facts as they relate to the country of origin at the time of taking a decision on the application; including laws and regulations of the country of origin and the manner in which they are applied;
   (b) the relevant statements and documentation presented by the applicant including information on whether the applicant has been or may be subject to persecution or serious harm;
   (c) the individual position and personal circumstances of the applicant, including factors such as background, gender and age, so as to assess whether, on the basis of the applicant's personal circumstances, the acts to which the applicant has been or could be exposed would amount to persecution or serious harm;
   (d) whether the applicant's activities since leaving the country of origin were engaged in for the sole or main purpose of creating the necessary conditions for applying for international protection, so as to assess whether these activities will expose the applicant to persecution or serious harm if returned to that country;
   (e) whether the applicant could reasonably be expected to avail himself of the protection of another country where he could assert citizenship.
4. The fact that an applicant has already been subject to persecution or serious harm or to direct threats of such persecution or such harm, is a serious indication of

the applicant's well-founded fear of persecution or real risk of suffering serious harm, unless there are good reasons to consider that such persecution or serious harm will not be repeated.

5. Where Member States apply the principle according to which it is the duty of the applicant to substantiate the application for international protection and where aspects of the applicant's statements are not supported by documentary or other evidence, those aspects shall not need confirmation, when the following conditions are met:
   (a) the applicant has made a genuine effort to substantiate his application;
   (b) all relevant elements, at the applicant's disposal, have been submitted, and a satisfactory explanation regarding any lack of other relevant elements has been given;
   (c) the applicant's statements are found to be coherent and plausible and do not run counter to available specific and general information relevant to the applicant's case;
   (d) the applicant has applied for international protection at the earliest possible time, unless the applicant can demonstrate good reason for not having done so; and
   (e) the general credibility of the applicant has been established.

Article 5

International protection needs arising *sur place*

1. A well-founded fear of being persecuted or a real risk of suffering serious harm may be based on events which have taken place since the applicant left the country of origin.
2. A well-founded fear of being persecuted or a real risk of suffering serious harm may be based on activities which have been engaged in by the applicant since he left the country of origin, in particular where it is established that the activities relied upon constitute the expression and continuation of convictions or orientations held in the country of origin.
3. Without prejudice to the Geneva Convention, Member States may determine that an applicant who files a subsequent application shall normally not be granted refugee status, if the risk of persecution is based on circumstances which the applicant has created by his own decision since leaving the country of origin.

Article 6

Actors of persecution or serious harm

Actors of persecution or serious harm include:

(a) the State;
(b) parties or organisations controlling the State or a substantial part of the territory of the State;
(c) non-State actors, if it can be demonstrated that the actors mentioned in (a) and (b), including international organisations, are unable or unwilling to provide protection against persecution or serious harm as defined in Article 7.

Article 7

Actors of protection

1. Protection can be provided by:
   (a) the State; or
   (b) parties or organisations, including international organisations, controlling the State or a substantial part of the territory of the State.
2. Protection is generally provided when the actors mentioned in paragraph 1 take reasonable steps to prevent the persecution or suffering of serious harm, *inter alia*, by operating an effective legal system for the detection, prosecution and punishment of acts constituting persecution or serious harm, and the applicant has access to such protection.
3. When assessing whether an international organisation controls a State or a substantial part of its territory and provides protection as described in paragraph 2, Member States shall take into account any guidance which may be provided in relevant Council acts.

Article 8

Internal protection

1. As part of the assessment of the application for international protection, Member States may determine that an applicant is not in need of international protection if in a part of the country of origin there is no well-founded fear of being persecuted or no real risk of suffering serious harm and the applicant can reasonably be expected to stay in that part of the country.
2. In examining whether a part of the country of origin is in accordance with paragraph 1, Member States shall at the time of taking the decision on the application have regard to the general circumstances prevailing in that part of the country and to the personal circumstances of the applicant.
3. Paragraph 1 may apply notwithstanding technical obstacles to return to the country of origin.

Chapter III

Qualification for Being a Refugee

Article 9

Acts of persecution

1. Acts of persecution within the meaning of article 1 A of the Geneva Convention must:
   (a) be sufficiently serious by their nature or repetition as to constitute a severe violation of basic human rights, in particular the rights from which derogation cannot be made under Article 15(2) of the European Convention for the Protection of Human Rights and Fundamental Freedoms; or
   (b) be an accumulation of various measures, including violations of human rights which is sufficiently severe as to affect an individual in a similar manner as mentioned in (a).
2. Acts of persecution as qualified in paragraph 1, can, *inter alia*, take the form of:
   (a) acts of physical or mental violence, including acts of sexual violence;
   (b) legal, administrative, police, and/or judicial measures which are in themselves discriminatory or which are implemented in a discriminatory manner;
   (c) prosecution or punishment, which is disproportionate or discriminatory;
   (d) denial of judicial redress resulting in a disproportionate or discriminatory punishment;
   (e) prosecution or punishment for refusal to perform military service in a conflict, where performing military service would include crimes or acts falling under the exclusion clauses as set out in Article 12(2);
   (f) acts of a gender-specific or child-specific nature.
3. In accordance with Article 2(c), there must be a connection between the reasons mentioned in Article 10 and the acts of persecution as qualified in paragraph 1.

Article 10

Reasons for persecution

1. Member States shall take the following elements into account when assessing the reasons for persecution:
   (a) the concept of race shall in particular include considerations of colour, descent, or membership of a particular ethnic group;
   (b) the concept of religion shall in particular include the holding of theistic, non-theistic and atheistic beliefs, the participation in, or abstention from, formal worship in private or in public, either alone or in community with

others, other religious acts or expressions of view, or forms of personal or communal conduct based on or mandated by any religious belief;

(c) the concept of nationality shall not be confined to citizenship or lack thereof but shall in particular include membership of a group determined by its cultural, ethnic, or linguistic identity, common geographical or political origins or its relationship with the population of another State;

(d) a group shall be considered to form a particular social group where in particular:

— members of that group share an innate characteristic, or a common background that cannot be changed, or share a characteristic or belief that is so fundamental to identity or conscience that a person should not be forced to renounce it, and

— that group has a distinct identity in the relevant country, because it is perceived as being different by the surrounding society;

depending on the circumstances in the country of origin, a particular social group might include a group based on a common characteristic of sexual orientation. Sexual orientation cannot be understood to include acts considered to be criminal in accordance with national law of the Member States: Gender related aspects might be considered, without by themselves alone creating a presumption for the applicability of this Article;

(e) the concept of political opinion shall in particular include the holding of an opinion, thought or belief on a matter related to the potential actors of persecution mentioned in Article 6 and to their policies or methods, whether or not that opinion, thought or belief has been acted upon by the applicant.

2. When assessing if an applicant has a well-founded fear of being persecuted it is immaterial whether the applicant actually possesses the racial, religious, national, social or political characteristic which attracts the persecution, provided that such a characteristic is attributed to the applicant by the actor of persecution.

Article 11

Cessation

1. A third country national or a stateless person shall cease to be a refugee, if he or she:

(a) has voluntarily re-availed himself or herself of the protection of the country of nationality; or

(b) having lost his or her nationality, has voluntarily reacquired it; or

(c) has acquired a new nationality, and enjoys the protection of the country of his or her new nationality; or

(d) has voluntarily re-established himself or herself in the country which he or she left or outside which he or she remained owing to fear of persecution; or

(e) can no longer, because the circumstances in connection with which he or she has been recognised as a refugee have ceased to exist, continue to refuse to avail himself or herself of the protection of the country of nationality;
(f) being a stateless person with no nationality, he or she is able, because the circumstances in connection with which he or she has been recognised as a refugee have ceased to exist, to return to the country of former habitual residence.

2. In considering points (e) and (f) of paragraph 1, Member States shall have regard to whether the change of circumstances is of such a significant and non-temporary nature that the refugee's fear of persecution can no longer be regarded as well-founded.

Article 12

Exclusion

1. A third country national or a stateless person is excluded from being a refugee, if:
   (a) he or she falls within the scope of Article 1 D of the Geneva Convention, relating to protection or assistance from organs or agencies of the United Nations other than the United Nations High Commissioner for Refugees. When such protection or assistance has ceased for any reason, without the position of such persons being definitely settled in accordance with the relevant resolutions adopted by the General Assembly of the United Nations, these persons shall ipso facto be entitled to the benefits of this Directive;
   (b) he or she is recognised by the competent authorities of the country in which he or she has taken residence as having the rights and obligations which are attached to the possession of the nationality of that country; or rights and obligations equivalent to those.
2. A third country national or a stateless person is excluded from being a refugee where there are serious reasons for considering that:
   (a) he or she has committed a crime against peace, a war crime, or a crime against humanity, as defined in the international instruments drawn up to make provision in respect of such crimes;
   (b) he or she has committed a serious non-political crime outside the country of refuge prior to his or her admission as a refugee; which means the time of issuing a residence permit based on the granting of refugee status; particularly cruel actions, even if committed with an allegedly political objective, may be classified as serious non-political crimes;
   (c) he or she has been guilty of acts contrary to the purposes and principles of the United Nations as set out in the Preamble and Articles 1 and 2 of the Charter of the United Nations.

3. Paragraph 2 applies to persons who instigate or otherwise participate in the commission of the crimes or acts mentioned therein.

Chapter IV
Refugee Status

Article 13

Granting of refugee status

Member States shall grant refugee status to a third country national or a stateless person, who qualifies as a refugee in accordance with Chapters II and III.

Article 14

Revocation of, ending of or refusal to renew refugee status

1. Concerning applications for international protection filed after the entry into force of this Directive, Member States shall revoke, end or refuse to renew the refugee status of a third country national or a stateless person granted by a governmental, administrative, judicial or quasi-judicial body, if he or she has ceased to be a refugee in accordance with Article 11.
2. Without prejudice to the duty of the refugee in accordance with Article 4(1) to disclose all relevant facts and provide all relevant documentation at his/her disposal, the Member State, which has granted refugee status, shall on an individual basis demonstrate that the person concerned has ceased to be or has never been a refugee in accordance with paragraph 1 of this Article.
3. Member States shall revoke, end or refuse to renew the refugee status of a third country national or a stateless person, if, after he or she has been granted refugee status, it is established by the Member State concerned that:
   (a) he or she should have been or is excluded from being a refugee in accordance with Article 12;
   (b) his or her misrepresentation or omission of facts, including the use of false documents, were decisive for the granting of refugee status.
4. Member States may revoke, end or refuse to renew the status granted to a refugee by a governmental, administrative, judicial or quasi-judicial body, when:
   (a) there are reasonable grounds for regarding him or her as a danger to the security of the Member State in which he or she is present;
   (b) he or she, having been convicted by a final judgement of a particularly serious crime, constitutes a danger to the community of that Member State.
5. In situations described in paragraph 4, Member States may decide not to grant status to a refugee, where such a decision has not yet been taken.

6. Persons to whom paragraphs 4 or 5 apply are entitled to rights set out in or similar to those set out in Articles 3, 4, 16, 22, 31 and 32 and 33 of the Geneva Convention in so far as they are present in the Member State.

Chapter V

Qualification for Subsidiary Protection

Article 15

Serious harm

Serious harm consists of:
(a) death penalty or execution; or
(b) torture or inhuman or degrading treatment or punishment of an applicant in the country of origin; or
(c) serious and individual threat to a civilian's life or person by reason of indiscriminate violence in situations of international or internal armed conflict.

Article 16

Cessation

1. A third country national or a stateless person shall cease to be eligible for subsidiary protection when the circumstances which led to the granting of subsidiary protection status have ceased to exist or have changed to such a degree that protection is no longer required.
2. In applying paragraph 1, Member States shall have regard to whether the change of circumstances is of such a significant and non-temporary nature that the person eligible for subsidiary protection no longer faces a real risk of serious harm.

Article 17

Exclusion

1. A third country national or a stateless person is excluded from being eligible for subsidiary protection where there are serious reasons for considering that:
   (a) he or she has committed a crime against peace, a war crime, or a crime against humanity, as defined in the international instruments drawn up to make provision in respect of such crimes;
   (b) he or she has committed a serious crime;
   (c) he or she has been guilty of acts contrary to the purposes and principles of

the United Nations as set out in the Preamble and Articles 1 and 2 of the Charter of the United Nations;

(d) he or she constitutes a danger to the community or to the security of the Member State in which he or she is present.

2. Paragraph 1 applies to persons who instigate or otherwise participate in the commission of the crimes or acts mentioned therein.

3. Member States may exclude a third country national or a stateless person from being eligible for subsidiary protection, if he or she prior to his or her admission to the Member State has committed one or more crimes, outside the scope of paragraph 1, which would be punishable by imprisonment, had they been committed in the Member State concerned, and if he or she left his or her country of origin solely in order to avoid sanctions resulting from these crimes.

Chapter VI
Subsidiary Protection Status

Article 18

Granting of subsidiary protection status

Member States shall grant subsidiary protection status to a third country national or a stateless person eligible for subsidiary protection in accordance with Chapters II and V.

Article 19

Revocation of, ending of or refusal to renew subsidiary protection status

1. Concerning applications for international protection filed after the entry into force of this Directive, Member States shall revoke, end or refuse to renew the subsidiary protection status of a third country national or a stateless person granted by a governmental, administrative, judicial or quasi-judicial body, if he or she has ceased to be eligible for subsidiary protection in accordance with Article 16.

2. Member States may revoke, end or refuse to renew the subsidiary protection status of a third country national or a stateless person granted by a governmental, administrative, judicial or quasi-judicial body, if after having been granted subsidiary protection status, he or she should have been excluded from being eligible for subsidiary protection in accordance with Article 17(3).

3. Member States shall revoke, end or refuse to renew the subsidiary protection status of a third country national or a stateless person, if:

(a) he or she, after having been granted subsidiary protection status, should have been or is excluded from being eligible for subsidiary protection in accordance with Article 17(1) and (2);

(b) his or her misrepresentation or omission of facts, including the use of false documents, were decisive for the granting of subsidiary protection status.

4. Without prejudice to the duty of the third country national or stateless person in accordance with Article 4(1) to disclose all relevant facts and provide all relevant documentation at his/her disposal, the Member State, which has granted the subsidiary protection status, shall on an individual basis demonstrate that the person concerned has ceased to be or is not eligible for subsidiary protection in accordance with paragraphs 1, 2 and 3 of this Article.

Chapter VII

Content of International Protection

Article 20

General rules

1. This Chapter shall be without prejudice to the rights laid down in the Geneva Convention.
2. This Chapter shall apply both to refugees and persons eligible for subsidiary protection unless otherwise indicated.
3. When implementing this Chapter, Member States shall take into account the specific situation of vulnerable persons such as minors, unaccompanied minors, disabled people, elderly people, pregnant women, single parents with minor children and persons who have been subjected to torture, rape or other serious forms of psychological, physical or sexual violence.
4. Paragraph 3 shall apply only to persons found to have special needs after an individual evaluation of their situation.
5. The best interest of the child shall be a primary consideration for Member States when implementing the provisions of this Chapter that involve minors.
6. Within the limits set out by the Geneva Convention, Member States may reduce the benefits of this Chapter, granted to a refugee whose refugee status has been obtained on the basis of activities engaged in for the sole or main purpose of creating the necessary conditions for being recognised as a refugee.
7. Within the limits set out by international obligations of Member States, Member States may reduce the benefits of this Chapter, granted to a person

eligible for subsidiary protection, whose subsidiary protection status has been obtained on the basis of activities engaged in for the sole or main purpose of creating the necessary conditions for being recognised as a person eligible for subsidiary protection.

Article 21

Protection from refoulement

1. Member States shall respect the principle of non-refoulement in accordance with their international obligations.
2. Where not prohibited by the international obligations mentioned in paragraph 1, Member States may refoule a refugee, whether formally recognised or not, when:
   (a) there are reasonable grounds for considering him or her as a danger to the security of the Member State in which he or she is present; or
   (b) he or she, having been convicted by a final judgement of a particularly serious crime, constitutes a danger to the community of that Member State.
3. Member States may revoke, end or refuse to renew or to grant the residence permit of (or to) a refugee to whom paragraph 2 applies.

Article 22

Information

Member States shall provide persons recognised as being in need of international protection, as soon as possible after the respective protection status has been granted, with access to information, in a language likely to be understood by them, on the rights and obligations relating to that status.

Article 23

Maintaining family unity

1. Member States shall ensure that family unity can be maintained.
2. Member States shall ensure that family members of the beneficiary of refugee or subsidiary protection status, who do not individually qualify for such status, are entitled to claim the benefits referred to in Articles 24 to 34, in accordance with national procedures and as far as it is compatible with the personal legal status of the family member.

   In so far as the family members of beneficiaries of subsidiary protection status are concerned, Member States may define the conditions applicable to such benefits.

In these cases, Member States shall ensure that any benefits provided guarantee an adequate standard of living.

3. Paragraphs 1 and 2 are not applicable where the family member is or would be excluded from refugee or subsidiary protection status pursuant to Chapters III and V.
4. Notwithstanding paragraphs 1 and 2, Member States may refuse, reduce or withdraw the benefits referred therein for reasons of national security or public order.
5. Member States may decide that this Article also applies to other close relatives who lived together as part of the family at the time of leaving the country of origin, and who were wholly or mainly dependent on the beneficiary of refugee or subsidiary protection status at that time.

Article 24

Residence permits

1. As soon as possible after their status has been granted, Member States shall issue to beneficiaries of refugee status a residence permit which must be valid for at least three years and renewable unless compelling reasons of national security or public order otherwise require, and without prejudice to Article 21(3).

   Without prejudice to Article 23(1), the residence permit to be issued to the family members of the beneficiaries of refugee status may be valid for less than three years and renewable.
2. As soon as possible after the status has been granted, Member States shall issue to beneficiaries of subsidiary protection status a residence permit which must be valid for at least one year and renewable, unless compelling reasons of national security or public order otherwise require.

Article 25

Travel document

1. Member States shall issue to beneficiaries of refugee status travel documents in the form set out in the Schedule to the Geneva Convention, for the purpose of travel outside their territory unless compelling reasons of national security or public order otherwise require.
2. Member States shall issue to beneficiaries of subsidiary protection status who are unable to obtain a national passport, documents which enable them to travel, at least when serious humanitarian reasons arise that require their presence in another State, unless compelling reasons of national security or public order otherwise require.

Article 26

Access to employment

1. Member States shall authorise beneficiaries of refugee status to engage in employed or self-employed activities subject to rules generally applicable to the profession and to the public service, immediately after the refugee status has been granted.
2. Member States shall ensure that activities such as employment-related education opportunities for adults, vocational training and practical workplace experience are offered to beneficiaries of refugee status, under equivalent conditions as nationals.
3. Member States shall authorise beneficiaries of subsidiary protection status to engage in employed or self-employed activities subject to rules generally applicable to the profession and to the public service immediately after the subsidiary protection status has been granted. The situation of the labour market in the Member States may be taken into account, including for possible prioritisation of access to employment for a limited period of time to be determined in accordance with national law. Member States shall ensure that the beneficiary of subsidiary protection status has access to a post for which the beneficiary has received an offer in accordance with national rules on prioritisation in the labour market.
4. Member States shall ensure that beneficiaries of subsidiary protection status have access to activities such as employment-related education opportunities for adults, vocational training and practical workplace experience, under conditions to be decided by the Member States.
5. The law in force in the Member States applicable to remuneration, access to social security systems relating to employed or self-employed activities and other conditions of employment shall apply.

Article 27

Access to education

1. Member States shall grant full access to the education system to all minors granted refugee or subsidiary protection status, under the same conditions as nationals.
2. Member States shall allow adults granted refugee or subsidiary protection status access to the general education system, further training or retraining, under the same conditions as third country nationals legally resident.
3. Member States shall ensure equal treatment between beneficiaries of refugee or subsidiary protection status and nationals in the context of the existing

recognition procedures for foreign diplomas, certificates and other evidence of formal qualifications.

Article 28

Social welfare

1. Member States shall ensure that beneficiaries of refugee or subsidiary protection status receive, in the Member State that has granted such statuses, the necessary social assistance, as provided to nationals of that Member State.
2. By exception to the general rule laid down in paragraph 1, Member States may limit social assistance granted to beneficiaries of subsidiary protection status to core benefits which will then be provided at the same levels and under the same eligibility conditions as nationals.

Article 29

Health care

1. Member States shall ensure that beneficiaries of refugee or subsidiary protection status have access to health care under the same eligibility conditions as nationals of the Member State that has granted such statuses.
2. By exception to the general rule laid down in paragraph 1, Member States may limit health care granted to beneficiaries of subsidiary protection to core benefits which will then be provided at the same levels and under the same eligibility conditions as nationals.
3. Member States shall provide, under the same eligibility conditions as nationals of the Member State that has granted the status, adequate health care to beneficiaries of refugee or subsidiary protection status who have special needs, such as pregnant women, disabled people, persons who have undergone torture, rape or other serious forms of psychological, physical or sexual violence or minors who have been victims of any form of abuse, neglect, exploitation, torture, cruel, inhuman and degrading treatment or who have suffered from armed conflict.

Article 30

Unaccompanied minors

1. As soon as possible after the granting of refugee or subsidiary protection status Member States shall take the necessary measures, to ensure the representation of unaccompanied minors by legal guardianship or, where necessary, by an organisation responsible for the care and well-being of minors, or by any other appropriate representation including that based on legislation or Court order.

2. Member States shall ensure that the minor's needs are duly met in the implementation of this Directive by the appointed guardian or representative. The appropriate authorities shall make regular assessments.
3. Member States shall ensure that unaccompanied minors are placed either:
   (a) with adult relatives; or
   (b) with a foster family; or
   (c) in centres specialised in accommodation for minors; or
   (d) in other accommodation suitable for minors.

   In this context, the views of the child shall be taken into account in accordance with his or her age and degree of maturity.
4. As far as possible, siblings shall be kept together, taking into account the best interests of the minor concerned and, in particular, his or her age and degree of maturity. Changes of residence of unaccompanied minors shall be limited to a minimum.
5. Member States, protecting the unaccompanied minor's best interests, shall endeavour to trace the members of the minor's family as soon as possible. In cases where there may be a threat to the life or integrity of the minor or his or her close relatives, particularly if they have remained in the country of origin, care must be taken to ensure that the collection, processing and circulation of information concerning those persons is undertaken on a confidential basis.
6. Those working with unaccompanied minors shall have had or receive appropriate training concerning their needs.

Article 31

Access to accommodation

The Member States shall ensure that beneficiaries of refugee or subsidiary protection status have access to accommodation under equivalent conditions as other third country nationals legally resident in their territories.

Article 32

Freedom of movement within the Member State

Member States shall allow freedom of movement within their territory to beneficiaries of refugee or subsidiary protection status, under the same conditions and restrictions as those provided for other third country nationals legally resident in their territories.

Article 33

Access to integration facilities

1. In order to facilitate the integration of refugees into society, Member States shall make provision for integration programmes which they consider to be appropriate or create pre-conditions which guarantee access to such programmes.
2. Where it is considered appropriate by Member States, beneficiaries of subsidiary protection status shall be granted access to integration programmes.

Article 34

Repatriation

Member States may provide assistance to beneficiaries of refugee or subsidiary protection status who wish to repatriate.

Chapter VIII

Administrative Cooperation

Article 35

Cooperation

Member States shall each appoint a national contact point, whose address they shall communicate to the Commission, which shall communicate it to the other Member States.

Member States shall, in liaison with the Commission, take all appropriate measures to establish direct cooperation and an exchange of information between the competent authorities.

Article 36

Staff

Member States shall ensure that authorities and other organisations implementing this Directive have received the necessary training and shall be bound by the confidentiality principle, as defined in the national law, in relation to any information they obtain in the course of their work.

Chapter IX

Final Provisions

Article 37

Reports

1. By 10 April 2008, the Commission shall report to the European Parliament and the Council on the application of this Directive and shall propose any amendments that are necessary. These proposals for amendments shall be made by way of priority in relation to Articles 15, 26 and 33. Member States shall send the Commission all the information that is appropriate for drawing up that report by 10 October 2007.
2. After presenting the report, the Commission shall report to the European Parliament and the Council on the application of this Directive at least every five years.

Article 38

Transposition

1. The Member States shall bring into force the laws, regulations and administrative provisions necessary to comply with this Directive before 10 October 2006. They shall forthwith inform the Commission thereof.
   When the Member States adopt those measures, they shall contain a reference to this Directive or shall be accompanied by such a reference on the occasion of their official publication. The methods of making such reference shall be laid down by Member States.
2. Member States shall communicate to the Commission the text of the provisions of national law which they adopt in the field covered by this Directive.

Article 39

Entry into force

This Directive shall enter into force on the twentieth day following that of its publication in the *Official Journal of the European Union.*

Article 40

Addressees

This Directive is addressed to the Member States in accordance with the Treaty establishing the European Community.

Done at Luxembourg, 29 April 2004.

For the Council
The President
M. McDOWELL

Directive 2004/38/EC of the European Parliament and of the Council of 29 April 2004

on the right of citizens of the Union and their family members to move and reside freely within the territory of the Member States amending Regulation (EEC) No 1612/68 and repealing Directives 64/221/EEC, 68/360/EEC, 72/194/EEC, 73/148/EEC, 75/34/EEC, 75/35/EEC, 90/364/EEC, 90/365/EEC and 93/96/EEC

(Text with EEA relevance)

Note: Entered into force on 30 April 2004 (Article 41). To be implemented by 30 April 2006 (Article 40).

THE EUROPEAN PARLIAMENT AND THE COUNCIL OF THE EUROPEAN UNION,

Having regard to the Treaty establishing the European Community, and in particular Articles 12, 18, 40, 44 and 52 thereof,

Having regard to the proposal from the Commission[34],

Having regard to the Opinion of the European Economic and Social Committee[35],

Having regard to the Opinion of the Committee of the Regions[36],

Acting in accordance with the procedure laid down in Article 251 of the Treaty[37],

[34] OJ C 270 E, 25.9.2001, p. 150.

[35] OJ C 149, 21.6.2002, p. 46.

[36] OJ C 192, 12.8.2002, p. 17.

[37] Opinion of the European Parliament of 11 February 2003 (OJ C 43 E, 19.2.2004, p. 42), Council Common Position of 5 December 2003 (OJ C 54 E, 2.3.2004, p. 12) and Position of the European Parliament of 10 March 2004 (not yet published in the Official Journal).

Whereas:

(1) Citizenship of the Union confers on every citizen of the Union a primary and individual right to move and reside freely within the territory of the Member States, subject to the limitations and conditions laid down in the Treaty and to the measures adopted to give it effect.

(2) The free movement of persons constitutes one of the fundamental freedoms of the internal market, which comprises an area without internal frontiers, in which freedom is ensured in accordance with the provisions of the Treaty.

(3) Union citizenship should be the fundamental status of nationals of the Member States when they exercise their right of free movement and residence. It is therefore necessary to codify and review the existing Community instruments dealing separately with workers, self-employed persons, as well as students and other inactive persons in order to simplify and strengthen the right of free movement and residence of all Union citizens.

(4) With a view to remedying this sector-by-sector, piecemeal approach to the right of free movement and residence and facilitating the exercise of this right, there needs to be a single legislative act to amend Council Regulation (EEC) No 1612/68 of 15 October 1968 on freedom of movement for workers within the Community[38], and to repeal the following acts: Council Directive 68/360/ EEC of 15 October 1968 on the abolition of restrictions on movement and residence within the Community for workers of Member States and their families[39], Council Directive 73/148/EEC of 21 May 1973 on the abolition of restrictions on movement and residence within the Community for nationals of Member States with regard to establishment and the provision of services[40], Council Directive 90/364/EEC of 28 June 1990 on the right of residence[41], Council Directive 90/365/EEC of 28 June 1990 on the right of residence for employees and self-employed persons who have ceased their occupational activity[42] and Council Directive 93/96/EEC of 29 October 1993 on the right of residence for students[43].

(5) The right of all Union citizens to move and reside freely within the territory of the Member States should, if it is to be exercised under objective conditions of freedom and dignity, be also granted to their family members, irrespective of nationality. For the purposes of this Directive, the definition of 'family member' should also include the registered partner if the legislation of the host Member State treats registered partnership as equivalent to marriage.

[38] OJ L 257, 19.10.1968, p. 2. Regulation as last amended by Regulation (EEC) No 2434/92 (OJ L 245, 26.8.1992, p. 1).

[39] OJ L 257, 19.10.1968, p. 13. Directive as last amended by the 2003 Act of Accession.

[40] OJ L 172, 28.6.1973, p. 14.

[41] OJ L 180, 13.7.1990, p. 26.

[42] OJ L 180, 13.7.1990, p. 28.

[43] OJ L 317, 18.12.1993, p. 59.

(6) In order to maintain the unity of the family in a broader sense and without prejudice to the prohibition of discrimination on grounds of nationality, the situation of those persons who are not included in the definition of family members under this Directive, and who therefore do not enjoy an automatic right of entry and residence in the host Member State, should be examined by the host Member State on the basis of its own national legislation, in order to decide whether entry and residence could be granted to such persons, taking into consideration their relationship with the Union citizen or any other circumstances, such as their financial or physical dependence on the Union citizen.

(7) The formalities connected with the free movement of Union citizens within the territory of Member States should be clearly defined, without prejudice to the provisions applicable to national border controls.

(8) With a view to facilitating the free movement of family members who are not nationals of a Member State, those who have already obtained a residence card should be exempted from the requirement to obtain an entry visa within the meaning of Council Regulation (EC) No 539/2001 of 15 March 2001 listing the third countries whose nationals must be in possession of visas when crossing the external borders and those whose nationals are exempt from that requirement[44] or, where appropriate, of the applicable national legislation.

(9) Union citizens should have the right of residence in the host Member State for a period not exceeding three months without being subject to any conditions or any formalities other than the requirement to hold a valid identity card or passport, without prejudice to a more favourable treatment applicable to job-seekers as recognised by the case-law of the Court of Justice.

(10) Persons exercising their right of residence should not, however, become an unreasonable burden on the social assistance system of the host Member State during an initial period of residence. Therefore, the right of residence for Union citizens and their family members for periods in excess of three months should be subject to conditions.

(11) The fundamental and personal right of residence in another Member State is conferred directly on Union citizens by the Treaty and is not dependent upon their having fulfilled administrative procedures.

(12) For periods of residence of longer than three months, Member States should have the possibility to require Union citizens to register with the competent authorities in the place of residence, attested by a registration certificate issued to that effect.

[44] OJ L 81, 21.3.2001, p. 1. Regulation as last amended by Regulation (EC) No 453/2003 (OJ L 69, 13.3.2003, p. 10).

(13) The residence card requirement should be restricted to family members of Union citizens who are not nationals of a Member State for periods of residence of longer than three months.

(14) The supporting documents required by the competent authorities for the issuing of a registration certificate or of a residence card should be comprehensively specified in order to avoid divergent administrative practices or interpretations constituting an undue obstacle to the exercise of the right ofresidence by Union citizens and their family members.

(15) Family members should be legally safeguarded in the event of the death of the Union citizen, divorce, annulment of marriage or termination of a registered partnership. With due regard for family life and human dignity, and in certain conditions to guard against abuse, measures should therefore be taken to ensure that in such circumstances family members already residing within the territory of the host Member State retain their right of residence exclusively on a personal basis.

(16) As long as the beneficiaries of the right of residence do not become an unreasonable burden on the social assistance system of the host Member State they should not be expelled. Therefore, an expulsion measure should not be the automatic consequence of recourse to the social assistance system. The host Member State should examine whether it is a case of temporary difficulties and take into account the duration of residence, the personal circumstances and the amount of aid granted in order to consider whether the beneficiary has become an unreasonable burden on its social assistance system and to proceed to his expulsion. In no case should an expulsion measure be adopted against workers, self-employed persons or job-seekers as defined by the Court of Justice save on grounds of public policy or public security.

(17) Enjoyment of permanent residence by Union citizens who have chosen to settle long term in the host Member State would strengthen the feeling of Union citizenship and is a key element in promoting social cohesion, which is one of the fundamental objectives of the Union. A right of permanent residence should therefore be laid down for all Union citizens and their family members who have resided in the host Member State in compliance with the conditions laid down in this Directive during a continuous period of five years without becoming subject to an expulsion measure.

(18) In order to be a genuine vehicle for integration into the society of the host Member State in which the Union citizen resides, the right of permanent residence, once obtained, should not be subject to any conditions.

(19) Certain advantages specific to Union citizens who are workers or self-employed persons and to their family members, which may allow these persons to acquire a right of permanent residence before they have resided five years in the host Member State, should be maintained, as these constitute

acquired rights, conferred by Commission Regulation (EEC) No 1251/70 of 29 June 1970 on the right of workers to remain in the territory of a Member State after having been employed in that State[45] and Council Directive 75/34/EEC of 17 December 1974 concerning the right of nationals of a Member State to remain in the territory of another Member State after having pursued therein an activity in a self-employed capacity[46].

(20) In accordance with the prohibition of discrimination on grounds of nationality, all Union citizens and their family members residing in a Member State on the basis of this Directive should enjoy, in that Member State, equal treatment with nationals in areas covered by the Treaty, subject to such specific provisions as are expressly provided for in the Treaty and secondary law.

(21) However, it should be left to the host Member State to decide whether it will grant social assistance during the first three months of residence, or for a longer period in the case of job-seekers, to Union citizens other than those who are workers or self-employed persons or who retain that status or their family members, or maintenance assistance for studies, including vocational training, prior to acquisition of the right of permanent residence, to these same persons.

(22) The Treaty allows restrictions to be placed on the right of free movement and residence on grounds of public policy, public security or public health. In order to ensure a tighter definition of the circumstances and procedural safeguards subject to which Union citizens and their family members may be denied leave to enter or may be expelled, this Directive should replace Council Directive 64/221/EEC of 25 February 1964 on the coordination of special measures concerning the movement and residence of foreign nationals, which are justified on grounds of public policy, public security or public health[47].

(23) Expulsion of Union citizens and their family members on grounds of public policy or public security is a measure that can seriously harm persons who, having availed themselves of the rights and freedoms conferred on them by the Treaty, have become genuinely integrated into the host Member State. The scope for such measures should therefore be limited in accordance with the principle of proportionality to take account of the degree of integration of the persons concerned, the length of their residence in the host Member State, their age, state of health, family and economic situation and the links with their country of origin.

(24) Accordingly, the greater the degree of integration of Union citizens and their family members in the host Member State, the greater the degree of protection

[45] OJ L 142, 30.6.1970, p. 24.

[46] OJ L 14, 20.1.1975, p. 10.

[47] OJ 56, 4.4.1964, p. 850. Directive as last amended by Directive 75/35/EEC (OJ 14, 20.1.1975, p. 14).

against expulsion should be. Only in exceptional circumstances, where there are imperative grounds of public security, should an expulsion measure be taken against Union citizens who have resided for many years in the territory of the host Member State, in particular when they were born and have resided there throughout their life. In addition, such exceptional circumstances should also apply to an expulsion measure taken against minors, in order to protect their links with their family, in accordance with the United Nations Convention on the Rights of the Child, of 20 November 1989.

(25) Procedural safeguards should also be specified in detail in order to ensure a high level of protection of the rights of Union citizens and their family members in the event of their being denied leave to enter or reside in another Member State, as well as to uphold the principle that any action taken by the authorities must be properly justified.

(26) In all events, judicial redress procedures should be available to Union citizens and their family members who have been refused leave to enter or reside in another Member State.

(27) In line with the case-law of the Court of Justice prohibiting Member States from issuing orders excluding for life persons covered by this Directive from their territory, the right of Union citizens and their family members who have been excluded from the territory of a Member State to submit a fresh application after a reasonable period, and in any event after a three year period from enforcement of the final exclusion order, should be confirmed.

(28) To guard against abuse of rights or fraud, notably marriages of convenience or any other form of relationships contracted for the sole purpose of enjoying the right of free movement and residence, Member States should have the possibility to adopt the necessary measures.

(29) This Directive should not affect more favourable national provisions.

(30) With a view to examining how further to facilitate the exercise of the right of free movement and residence, a report should be prepared by the Commissionin order to evaluate the opportunity to present any necessary proposals to this effect, notably on the extension of the period of residence with no conditions.

(31) This Directive respects the fundamental rights and freedoms and observes the principles recognised in particular by the Charter of Fundamental Rights of the European Union. In accordance with the prohibition of discrimination contained in the Charter, Member States should implement this Directive without discrimination between the beneficiaries of thisective on grounds such as sex, race, colour, ethnic or social origin, genetic characteristics, language, religion or beliefs, political or other opinion, membership of an ethnic minority, property, birth, disability, age or sexual orientation,

HAVE ADOPTED THIS DIRECTIVE:

Chapter I
General Provisions

Article 1
Subject

This Directive lays down:

(a) the conditions governing the exercise of the right of free movement and residence within the territory of the Member States by Union citizens and their family members;

(b) the right of permanent residence in the territory of the Member States for Union citizens and their family members;

(c) the limits placed on the rights set out in (a) and (b) on grounds of public policy, public security or public health.

Article 2
Definitions

For the purposes of this Directive:

1) 'Union citizen' means any person having the nationality of a Member State;

2) 'Family member' means:
   (a) the spouse;
   (b) the partner with whom the Union citizen has contracted a registered partnership, on the basis of the legislation of a Member State, if the legislation of the host Member State treats registered partnerships as equivalent to marriage and in accordance with the conditions laid down in the relevant legislation of the host Member State;
   (c) the direct descendants who are under the age of 21 or are dependants and those of the spouse or partner as defined in point (b);
   (d) the dependent direct relatives in the ascending line and those of the spouse or partner as defined in point (b);

3) 'Host Member State' means the Member State to which a Union citizen moves in order to exercise his/her right of free movement and residence.

Article 3
Beneficiaries

1. This Directive shall apply to all Union citizens who move to or reside in a Member State other than that of which they are a national, and to their family members as defined in point 2 of Article 2 who accompany or join them.

2. Without prejudice to any right to free movement and residence the persons concerned may have in their own right, the host Member State shall, in accordance with its national legislation, facilitate entry and residence for the following persons:
   (a) any other family members, irrespective of their nationality, not falling under the definition in point 2 of Article 2 who, in the country from which they have come, are dependants or members of the household of the Union citizen having the primary right of residence, or where serious health grounds strictly require the personal care of the family member by the Union citizen;
   (b) the partner with whom the Union citizen has a durable relationship, duly attested.

   The host Member State shall undertake an extensive examination of the personal circumstances and shall justify any denial of entry or residence to these people.

Chapter II

Right of Exit and Entry

Article 4

Right of exit

1. Without prejudice to the provisions on travel documents applicable to national border controls, all Union citizens with a valid identity card or passport and their family members who are not nationals of a Member State and who hold a valid passport shall have the right to leave the territory of a Member State to travel to another Member State.
2. No exit visa or equivalent formality may be imposed on the persons to whom paragraph 1 applies.
3. Member States shall, acting in accordance with their laws, issue to their own nationals, and renew, an identity card or passport stating their nationality.
4. The passport shall be valid at least for all Member States and for countries through which the holder must pass when travelling between Member States. Where the law of a Member State does not provide for identity cards to be issued, the period of validity of any passport on being issued or renewed shall be not less than five years.

Article 5

Right of entry

1. Without prejudice to the provisions on travel documents applicable to national border controls, Member States shall grant Union citizens leave to enter their

territory with a valid identity card or passport and shall grant family members who are not nationals of a Member State leave to enter their territory with a valid passport.

No entry visa or equivalent formality may be imposed on Union citizens.

2. Family members who are not nationals of a Member State shall only be required to have an entry visa in accordance with Regulation (EC) No 539/2001 or, where appropriate, with national law. For the purposes of this Directive, possession of the valid residence card referred to in Article 10 shall exempt such family members from the visa requirement.

   Member States shall grant such persons every facility to obtain the necessary visas. Such visas shall be issued free of charge as soon as possible and on the basis of an accelerated procedure.

3. The host Member State shall not place an entry or exit stamp in the passport of family members who are not nationals of a Member State provided that they present the residence card provided for in Article 10.

4. Where a Union citizen, or a family member who is not a national of a Member State, does not have the necessary travel documents or, if required, the necessary visas, the Member State concerned shall, before turning them back, give such persons every reasonable opportunity to obtain the necessary documents or have them brought to them within a reasonable period of time or to corroborate or prove by other means that they are covered by the right of free movement and residence.

5. The Member State may require the person concerned to report his/her presence within its territory within a reasonable and non-discriminatory period of time. Failure to comply with this requirement may make the person concerned liable to proportionate and non-discriminatory sanctions.

Chapter III

Right of Residence

Article 6

Right of residence for up to three months

1. Union citizens shall have the right of residence on the territory of another Member State for a period of up to three months without any conditions or any formalities other than the requirement to hold a valid identity card or passport.

2. The provisions of paragraph 1 shall also apply to family members in possession of a valid passport who are not nationals of a Member State, accompanying or joining the Union citizen.

Article 7

Right of residence for more than three months

1. All Union citizens shall have the right of residence on the territory of another Member State for a period of longer than three months if they:
   (a) are workers or self-employed persons in the host Member State; or
   (b) have sufficient resources for themselves and their family members not to become a burden on the social assistance system of the host Member State during their period of residence and have comprehensive sickness insurance cover in the host Member State; or
   (c) — are enrolled at a private or public establishment, accredited or financed by the host Member State on the basis of its legislation or administrative practice, for the principal purpose of following a course of study, including vocational training; and
   — have comprehensive sickness insurance cover in the host Member State and assure the relevant national authority, by means of a declaration or by such equivalent means as they may choose, that they have sufficient resources for themselves and their family members not to become a burden on the social assistance system of the host Member State during their period of residence; or
   (d) are family members accompanying or joining a Union citizen who satisfies the conditions referred to in points (a), (b) or (c).

2. The right of residence provided for in paragraph 1 shall extend to family members who are not nationals of a Member State, accompanying or joining the Union citizen in the host Member State, provided that such Union citizen satisfies the conditions referred to in paragraph 1(a), (b) or (c).

3. For the purposes of paragraph 1(a), a Union citizen who is no longer a worker or self-employed person shall retain the status of worker or self-employed person in the following circumstances:
   (a) he/she is temporarily unable to work as the result of an illness or accident;
   (b) he/she is in duly recorded involuntary unemployment after having been employed for more than one year and has registered as a job-seeker with the relevant employment office;
   (c) he/she is in duly recorded involuntary unemployment after completing a fixed-term employment contract of less than a year or after having become involuntarily unemployed during the first twelve months and has registered as a job-seeker with the relevant employment office. In this case, the status of worker shall be retained for no less than six months;
   (d) he/she embarks on vocational training. Unless he/she is involuntarily unemployed, the retention of the status of worker shall require the training to be related to the previous employment.

4. By way of derogation from paragraphs 1(d) and 2 above, only the spouse, the registered partner provided for in Article 2(2)(b) and dependent children shall have the right of residence as family members of a Union citizen meeting the conditions under 1(c) above. Article 3(2) shall apply to his/her dependent direct relatives in the ascending lines and those of his/her spouse or registered partner.

Article 8

Administrative formalities for Union citizens

1. Without prejudice to Article 5(5), for periods of residence longer than three months, the host Member State may require Union citizens to register with the relevant authorities.
2. The deadline for registration may not be less than three months from the date of arrival. A registration certificate shall be issued immediately, stating the name and address of the person registering and the date of the registration. Failure to comply with the registration requirement may render the person concerned liable to proportionate and non-discriminatory sanctions.
3. For the registration certificate to be issued, Member States may only require that
   - Union citizens to whom point (a) of Article 7(1) applies present a valid identity card or passport, a confirmation of engagement from the employer or a certificate of employment, or proof that they are self-employed persons;
   - Union citizens to whom point (b) of Article 7(1) applies present a valid identity card or passport and provide proof that they satisfy the conditions laid down therein;
   - Union citizens to whom point (c) of Article 7(1) applies present a valid identity card or passport, provide proof of enrolment at an accredited establishment and of comprehensive sickness insurance cover and the declaration or equivalent means referred to in point (c) of Article 7(1). Member States may not require this declaration to refer to any specific amount of resources.
4. Member States may not lay down a fixed amount which they regard as 'sufficient resources' ' but they must take into account the personal situation of the person concerned. In all cases this amount shall not be higher than the threshold below which nationals of the host Member State become eligible for social assistance, or, where this criterion is not applicable, higher than the minimum social security pension paid by the host Member State.
5. For the registration certificate to be issued to family members of Union citizens, who are themselves Union citizens, Member States may require the following documents to be presented:

(a) a valid identity card or passport;
(b) a document attesting to the existence of a family relationship or of a registered partnership;
(c) where appropriate, the registration certificate of the Union citizen whom they are accompanying or joining;
(d) in cases falling under points (c) and (d) of Article 2(2), documentary evidence that the conditions laid down therein are met;
(e) in cases falling under Article 3(2)(a), a document issued by the relevant authority in the country of origin or country from which they are arriving certifying that they are dependants or members of the household of the Union citizen, or proof of the existence of serious health grounds which strictly require the personal care of the family member by the Union citizen;
(f) in cases falling under Article 3(2)(b), proof of the existence of a durable relationship with the Union citizen.

Article 9

Administrative formalities for family members who are not nationals of a Member State

1. Member States shall issue a residence card to family members of a Union citizen who are not nationals of a Member State, where the planned period of residence is for more than three months.
2. The deadline for submitting the residence card application may not be less than three months from the date of arrival.
3. Failure to comply with the requirement to apply for a residence card may make the person concerned liable to proportionate and non-discriminatory sanctions.

Article 10

Issue of residence cards

1. The right of residence of family members of a Union citizen who are not nationals of a Member State shall be evidenced by the issuing of a document called 'Residence card of a family member of a Union citizen' no later than six months from the date on which they submit the application. A certificate of application for the residence card shall be issued immediately.
2. For the residence card to be issued, Member States shall require presentation of the following documents:
   (a) a valid passport;
   (b) a document attesting to the existence of a family relationship or of a registered partnership;

(c) the registration certificate or, in the absence of a registration system, any other proof of residence in the host Member State of the Union citizen whom they are accompanying or joining;
(d) in cases falling under points (c) and (d) of Article 2(2), documentary evidence that the conditions laid down therein are met;
(e) in cases falling under Article 3(2)(a), a document issued by the relevant authority in the country of origin or country from which they are arriving certifying that they are dependants or members of the household of the Union citizen, or proof of the existence of serious health grounds which strictly require the personal care of the family member by the Union citizen;
(f) in cases falling under Article 3(2)(b), proof of the existence of a durable relationship with the Union citizen.

Article 11

Validity of the residence card

1. The residence card provided for by Article 10(1) shall be valid for five years from the date of issue or for the envisaged period of residence of the Union citizen, if this period is less than five years.
2. The validity of the residence card shall not be affected by temporary absences not exceeding six months a year, or by absences of a longer duration for compulsory military service or by one absence of a maximum of twelve consecutive months for important reasons such as pregnancy and childbirth, serious illness, study or vocational training, or a posting in another Member State or a third country.

Article 12

Retention of the right of residence by family members in the event of death or departure of the Union citizen

1. Without prejudice to the second subparagraph, the Union citizen's death or departure from the host Member State shall not affect the right of residence of his/her family members who are nationals of a Member State.

   Before acquiring the right of permanent residence, the persons concerned must meet the conditions laid down in points (a), (b), (c) or (d) of Article 7(1).
2. Without prejudice to the second subparagraph, the Union citizen's death shall not entail loss of the right of residence of his/her family members who are not nationals of a Member State and who have been residing in the host Member State as family members for at least one year before the Union citizen's death.

   Before acquiring the right of permanent residence, the right of residence of the persons concerned shall remain subject to the requirement that they are able to show that they are workers or self-employed persons or that they have sufficient resources for themselves and their family members not to become a burden on the social assistance system of the host Member State during their period of residence and have comprehensive sickness insurance cover in the host Member State, or that they are members of the family, already constituted in the host Member State, of a person satisfying these requirements. 'Sufficient resources' shall be as defined in Article 8(4). Such family members shall retain their right of residence exclusively on a personal basis.

3. The Union citizen's departure from the host Member State or his/her death shall not entail loss of the right of residence of his/her children or of the parent who has actual custody of the children, irrespective of nationality, if the children reside in the host Member State and are enrolled at an educational establishment, for the purpose of studying there, until the completion of their studies.

Article 13

Retention of the right of residence by family members in the event of divorce, annulment of marriage or termination of registered partnership

1. Without prejudice to the second subparagraph, divorce, annulment of the Union citizen's marriage or termination of his/her registered partnership, as referred to in point 2(b) of Article 2 shall not affect the right of residence of his/her family members who are nationals of a Member State.

   Before acquiring the right of permanent residence, the persons concerned must meet the conditions laid down in points (a), (b), (c) or (d) of Article 7(1).

2. Without prejudice to the second subparagraph, divorce, annulment of marriage or termination of the registered partnership referred to in point 2(b) of Article 2 shall not entail loss of the right of residence of a Union citizen's family members who are not nationals of a Member State where:
   (a) prior to initiation of the divorce or annulment proceedings or termination of the registered partnership referred to in point 2(b) of Article 2, the marriage or registered partnership has lasted at least three years, including one year in the host Member State; or
   (b) by agreement between the spouses or the partners referred to in point 2(b) of Article 2 or by court order, the spouse or partner who is not a national of a Member State has custody of the Union citizen's children; or
   (c) this is warranted by particularly difficult circumstances, such as having been a victim of domestic violence while the marriage or registered partnership was subsisting; or
   (d) by agreement between the spouses or partners referred to in point 2(b) of Article 2 or by court order, the spouse or partner who is not a national

of a Member State has the right of access to a minor child, provided that the court has ruled that such access must be in the host Member State, and for as long as is required.

Before acquiring the right of permanent residence, the right of residence of the persons concerned shall remain subject to the requirement that they are able to show that they are workers or self-employed persons or that they have sufficient resources for themselves and their family members not to become a burden on the social assistance system of the host Member State during their period of residence and have comprehensive sickness insurance cover in the host Member State, or that they are members of the family, already constituted in the host Member State, of a person satisfying these requirements. 'Sufficient resources' shall be as defined in Article 8(4).

Such family members shall retain their right of residence exclusively on personal basis.

Article 14

Retention of the right of residence

1. Union citizens and their family members shall have the right of residence provided for in Article 6, as long as they do not become an unreasonable burden on the social assistance system of the host Member State.
2. Union citizens and their family members shall have the right of residence provided for in Articles 7, 12 and 13 as long as they meet the conditions set out therein.

   In specific cases where there is a reasonable doubt as to whether a Union citizen or his/her family members satisfies the conditions set out in Articles 7, 12 and 13, Member States may verify if these conditions are fulfilled. This verification shall not be carried out systematically.
3. An expulsion measure shall not be the automatic consequence of a Union citizen's or his or her family member's recourse to the social assistance system of the host Member State.
4. By way of derogation from paragraphs 1 and 2 and without prejudice to the provisions of Chapter VI, an expulsion measure may in no case be adopted against Union citizens or their family members if:
   (a) the Union citizens are workers or self-employed persons, or
   (b) the Union citizens entered the territory of the host Member State in order to seek employment.

   In this case, the Union citizens and their family members may not be expelled for as long as the Union citizens can provide evidence that they are continuing to seek employment and that they have a genuine chance of being engaged.

Article 15

Procedural safeguards

1. The procedures provided for by Articles 30 and 31 shall apply by analogy to all decisions restricting free movement of Union citizens and their family members on grounds other than public policy, public security or public health.
2. Expiry of the identity card or passport on the basis of which the person concerned entered the host Member State and was issued with a registration certificate or residence card shall not constitute a ground for expulsion from the host Member State.
3. The host Member State may not impose a ban on entry in the context of an expulsion decision to which paragraph 1 applies.

Chapter IV

Right of Permanent Residence

Section I

Eligibility

Article 16

General rule for Union citizens and their family members

1. Union citizens who have resided legally for a continuous period of five years in the host Member State shall have the right of permanent residence there. This right shall not be subject to the conditions provided for in Chapter III.
2. Paragraph 1 shall apply also to family members who are not nationals of a Member State and have legally resided with the Union citizen in the host Member State for a continuous period of five years.
3. Continuity of residence shall not be affected by temporary absences not exceeding a total of six months a year, or by absences of a longer duration for compulsory military service, or by one absence of a maximum of twelve consecutive months for important reasons such as pregnancy and childbirth, serious illness, study or vocational training, or a posting in another Member State or a third country.
4. Once acquired, the right of permanent residence shall be lost only through absence from the host Member State for a period exceeding two consecutive years.

Article 17

Exemptions for persons no longer working in the host Member State and their family members

1. By way of derogation from Article 16, the right of permanent residence in the host Member State shall be enjoyed before completion of a continuous period of five years of residence by:
   (a) workers or self-employed persons who, at the time they stop working, have reached the age laid down by the law of that Member State for entitlement to an old age pension or workers who cease paid employment to take early retirement, provided that they have been working in that Member State for at least the preceding twelve months and have resided there continuously for more than three years.

   If the law of the host Member State does not grant the right to an old age pension to certain categories of self-employed persons, the age condition shall be deemed to have been met once the person concerned has reached the age of 60;

   (b) workers or self-employed persons who have resided continuously in the host Member State for more than two years and stop working there as a result of permanent incapacity to work.

   If such incapacity is the result of an accident at work or an occupational disease entitling the person concerned to a benefit payable in full or in part by an institution in the host Member State, no condition shall be imposed as to length of residence;

   (c) workers or self-employed persons who, after three years of continuous employment and residence in the host Member State, work in an employed or self-employed capacity in another Member State, while retaining their place of residence in the host Member State, to which they return, as a rule, each day or at least once a week.

   For the purposes of entitlement to the rights referred to in points (a) and (b), periods of employment spent in the Member State in which the person concerned is working shall be regarded as having been spent in the host Member State.

   Periods of involuntary unemployment duly recorded by the relevant employment office, periods not worked for reasons not of the person's own making and absences from work or cessation of work due to illness or accident shall be regarded as periods of employment.

2. The conditions as to length of residence and employment laid down in point (a) of paragraph 1 and the condition as to length of residence laid down in point (b) of paragraph 1 shall not apply if the worker's or the self-employed person's spouse or partner as referred to in point 2(b) of Article 2 is a national

of the host Member State or has lost the nationality of that Member State by marriage to that worker or self-employed person.

3. Irrespective of nationality, the family members of a worker or a self-employed person who are residing with him in the territory of the host Member State shall have the right of permanent residence in that Member State, if the worker or self-employed person has acquired himself the right of permanent residence in that Member State on the basis of paragraph 1.

4. If, however, the worker or self-employed person dies while still working but before acquiring permanent residence status in the host Member State on the basis of paragraph 1, his family members who are residing with him in the host Member State shall acquire the right of permanent residence there, on condition that:
   (a) the worker or self-employed person had, at the time of death, resided continuously on the territory of that Member State for two years; or
   (b) the death resulted from an accident at work or an occupational disease; or
   (c) the surviving spouse lost the nationality of that Member State following marriage to the worker or self-employed person.

Article 18

Acquisition of the right of permanent residence by certain family members who are not nationals of a Member State

Without prejudice to Article 17, the family members of a Union citizen to whom Articles 12(2) and 13(2) apply, who satisfy the conditions laid down therein, shall acquire the right of permanent residence after residing legally for a period of five consecutive years in the host Member State.

Section II

Administrative Formalities

Article 19

Document certifying permanent residence for Union citizens

1. Upon application Member States shall issue Union citizens entitled to permanent residence, after having verified duration of residence, with a document certifying permanent residence.

2. The document certifying permanent residence shall be issued as soon as possible.

Article 20

Permanent residence card for family members who are not nationals of a Member State

1. Member States shall issue family members who are not nationals of a Member State entitled to permanent residence with a permanent residence card within six months of the submission of the application. The permanent residence card shall be renewable automatically every ten years.
2. The application for a permanent residence card shall be submitted before the residence card expires. Failure to comply with the requirement to apply for a permanent residence card may render the person concerned liable to proportionate and non-discriminatory sanctions.
3. Interruption in residence not exceeding two consecutive years shall not affect the validity of the permanent residence card.

Article 21

Continuity of residence

For the purposes of this Directive, continuity of residence may be attested by any means of proof in use in the host Member State. Continuity of residence is broken by any expulsion decision duly enforced against the person concerned.

Chapter V

Provisions Common to the Right of Residence and the Right of Permanent Residence

Article 22

Territorial scope

The right of residence and the right of permanent residence shall cover the whole territory of the host Member State. Member States may impose territorial restrictions on the right of residence and the right of permanent residence only where the same restrictions apply to their own nationals.

Article 23

Related rights

Irrespective of nationality, the family members of a Union citizen who have the right of residence or the right of permanent residence in a Member State shall be entitled to take up employment or self-employment there.

Article 24

Equal treatment

1. Subject to such specific provisions as are expressly provided for in the Treaty and secondary law, all Union citizens residing on the basis of this Directive in the territory of the host Member State shall enjoy equal treatment with the nationals of that Member State within the scope of the Treaty. The benefit of this right shall be extended to family members who are not nationals of a Member State and who have the right of residence or permanent residence.
2. By way of derogation from paragraph 1, the host Member State shall not be obliged to confer entitlement to social assistance during the first three months of residence or, where appropriate, the longer period provided for in Article 14(4)(b), nor shall it be obliged, prior to acquisition of the right of permanent residence, to grant maintenance aid for studies, including vocational training, consisting in student grants or student loans to persons other than workers, self-employed persons, persons who retain such status and members of their families.

Article 25

General provisions concerning residence documents

1. Possession of a registration certificate as referred to in Article 8, of a document certifying permanent residence, of a certificate attesting submission of an application for a family member residence card, of a residence card or of a permanent residence card, may under no circumstances be made a precondition for the exercise of a right or the completion of an administrative formality, as entitlement to rights may be attested by any other means of proof.
2. All documents mentioned in paragraph 1 shall be issued free of charge or for a charge not exceeding that imposed on nationals for the issuing of similar documents.

Article 26

Checks

Member States may carry out checks on compliance with any requirement deriving from their national legislation for non-nationals always to carry their registration certificate or residence card, provided that the same requirement applies to their own nationals as regards their identity card. In the event of failure to comply with this requirement, Member States may impose the same sanctions as those imposed on their own nationals for failure to carry their identity card.

Chapter VI

Restrictions on the Right of Entry and the Right of Residence on Grounds of Public Policy, Public Security or Public Health

Article 27

General principles

1. Subject to the provisions of this Chapter, Member States may restrict the freedom of movement and residence of Union citizens and their family members, irrespective of nationality, on grounds of public policy, public security or public health. These grounds shall not be invoked to serve economic ends.
2. Measures taken on grounds of public policy or public security shall comply with the principle of proportionality and shall be based exclusively on the personal conduct of the individual concerned. Previous criminal convictions shall not in themselves constitute grounds for taking such measures.

   The personal conduct of the individual concerned must represent a genuine, present and sufficiently serious threat affecting one of the fundamental interests of society. Justifications that are isolated from the particulars of the case or that rely on considerations of general prevention shall not be accepted.
3. In order to ascertain whether the person concerned represents a danger for public policy or public security, when issuing the registration certificate or, in the absence of a registration system, not later than three months from the date of arrival of the person concerned on its territory or from the date of reporting his/her presence within the territory, as provided for in Article 5(5), or when issuing the residence card, the host Member State may, should it consider this essential, request the Member State of origin and, if need be, other Member States to provide information concerning any previous police record the person concerned may have. Such enquiries shall not be made as a matter of routine. The Member State consulted shall give its reply within two months.
4. The Member State which issued the passport or identity card shall allow the holder of the document who has been expelled on grounds of public policy, public security, or public health from another Member State to re-enter its territory without any formality even if the document is no longer valid or the nationality of the holder is in dispute.

Article 28

Protection against expulsion

1. Before taking an expulsion decision on grounds of public policy or public security, the host Member State shall take account of considerations such as how

long the individual concerned has resided on its territory, his/her age, state of health, family and economic situation, social and cultural integration into the host Member State and the extent of his/her links with the country of origin.

2. The host Member State may not take an expulsion decision against Union citizens or their family members, irrespective of nationality, who have the right of permanent residence on its territory, except on serious grounds of public policy or public security.

3. An expulsion decision may not be taken against Union citizens, except if the decision is based on imperative grounds of public security, as defined by Member States, if they:
   (a) have resided in the host Member State for the previous ten years; or
   (b) are a minor, except if the expulsion is necessary for the best interests of the child, as provided for in the United Nations Convention on the Rights of the Child of 20 November 1989.

Article 29

Public health

1. The only diseases justifying measures restricting freedom of movement shall be the diseases with epidemic potential as defined by the relevant instruments of the World Health Organisation and other infectious diseases or contagious parasitic diseases if they are the subject of protection provisions applying to nationals of the host Member State.
2. Diseases occurring after a three-month period from the date of arrival shall not constitute grounds for expulsion from the territory.
3. Where there are serious indications that it is necessary, Member States may, within three months of the date of arrival, require persons entitled to the right of residence to undergo, free of charge, a medical examination to certify that they are not suffering from any of the conditions referred to in paragraph 1. Such medical examinations may not be required as a matter of routine.

Article 30

Notification of decisions

1. The persons concerned shall be notified in writing of any decision taken under Article 27(1), in such a way that they are able to comprehend its content and the implications for them.
2. The persons concerned shall be informed, precisely and in full, of the public policy, public security or public health grounds on which the decision taken in their case is based, unless this is contrary to the interests of State security.

3. The notification shall specify the court or administrative authority with which the person concerned may lodge an appeal, the time limit for the appeal and, where applicable, the time allowed for the person to leave the territory of the Member State. Save in duly substantiated cases of urgency, the time allowed to leave the territory shall be not less than one month from the date of notification.

Article 31

Procedural safeguards

1. The persons concerned shall have access to judicial and, where appropriate, administrative redress procedures in the host Member State to appeal against or seek review of any decision taken against them on the grounds of public policy, public security or public health.
2. Where the application for appeal against or judicial review of the expulsion decision is accompanied by an application for an interim order to suspend enforcement of that decision, actual removal from the territory may not take place until such time as the decision on the interim order has been taken, except:
   - where the expulsion decision is based on a previous judicial decision; or
   - where the persons concerned have had previous access to judicial review; or
   - where the expulsion decision is based on imperative grounds of public security under Article 28(3).
3. The redress procedures shall allow for an examination of the legality of the decision, as well as of the facts and circumstances on which the proposed measure is based. They shall ensure that the decision is not disproportionate, particularly in view of the requirements laid down in Article 28.
4. Member States may exclude the individual concerned from their territory pending the redress procedure, but they may not prevent the individual from submitting his/her defence in person, except when his/her appearance may cause serious troubles to public policy or public security or when the appeal or judicial review concerns a denial of entry to the territory.

Article 32

Duration of exclusion orders

1. Persons excluded on grounds of public policy or public security may submit an application for lifting of the exclusion order after a reasonable period, depending on the circumstances, and in any event after three years from

enforcement of the final exclusion order which has been validly adopted in accordance with Community law, by putting forward arguments to establish that there has been a material change in the circumstances which justified the decision ordering their exclusion.

The Member State concerned shall reach a decision on this application within six months of its submission.

2. The persons referred to in paragraph 1 shall have no right of entry to the territory of the Member State concerned while their application is being considered.

Article 33

Expulsion as a penalty or legal consequence

1. Expulsion orders may not be issued by the host Member State as a penalty or legal consequence of a custodial penalty, unless they conform to the requirements of Articles 27, 28 and 29.
2. If an expulsion order, as provided for in paragraph 1, is enforced more than two years after it was issued, the Member State shall check that the individual concerned is currently and genuinely a threat to public policy or public security and shall assess whether there has been any material change in the circumstances since the expulsion order was issued.

Chapter VII

Final Provisions

Article 34

Publicity

Member States shall disseminate information concerning the rights and obligations of Union citizens and their family members on the subjects covered by this Directive, particularly by means of awareness-raising campaigns conducted through national and local media and other means of communication.

Article 35

Abuse of rights

Member States may adopt the necessary measures to refuse, terminate or withdraw any right conferred by this Directive in the case of abuse of rights or fraud, such as marriages of convenience. Any such measure shall be proportionate and subject to the procedural safeguards provided for in Articles 30 and 31.

Article 36

Sanctions

Member States shall lay down provisions on the sanctions applicable to breaches of national rules adopted for the implementation of this Directive and shall take the measures required for their application. The sanctions laid down shall be effective and proportionate. Member States shall notify the Commission of these provisions not later than . . .* and as promptly as possible in the case of any subsequent changes.

Article 37

More favourable national provisions

The provisions of this Directive shall not affect any laws, regulations or administrative provisions laid down by a Member State which would be more favourable to the persons covered by this Directive.

Article 38

Repeals

1. Articles 10 and 11 of Regulation (EEC) No 1612/68 shall be repealed with effect from . . .*.
2. Directives 64/221/EEC, 68/360/EEC, 72/194/EEC, 73/148/EEC, 75/34/EEC, 75/35/EEC, 90/364/EEC, 90/365/EEC and 93/96/EEC shall be repealed with effect from . . .*.
3. References made to the repealed provisions and Directives shall be construed as being made to this Directive.

Article 39

Report

No later than . . .† the Commission shall submit a report on the application of this Directive to the European Parliament and the Council, together with any necessary proposals, notably on the opportunity to extend the period of time during which Union citizens and their family members may reside in the territory of the host Member State without any conditions. The Member States shall provide the Commission with the information needed to produce the report.

* Two years from the date of entry into force of this Directive.

† Four years from the date of entry into force of this Directine.

Article 40

Transposition

1. Member States shall bring into force the laws, regulations and administrative provisions necessary to comply with this Directive by . . .*.

   When Member States adopt those measures, they shall contain a reference to this Directive or shall be accompanied by such a reference on the occasion of their official publication. The methods of making such reference shall be laid down by the Member States.

2. Member States shall communicate to the Commission the text of the provisions of national law which they adopt in the field covered by this Directive together with a table showing how the provisions of this Directive correspond to the national provisions adopted.

Article 41

Entry into force

This Directive shall enter into force on the day of its publication in the Official Journal of the European Union.

Article 42

Addresses

This Directive is addressed to the Member States.

Done at Strasbourg, 29 April 2004.

For the European Parliament
The President
P. COX

For the Council
The President
M. McDOWELL

* Two years from the date of entry into froce of this Directine.

Council Directive 2005/85/EC
of 1 December 2005
on minimum standards on procedures in Member States for granting and withdrawing refugee status

THE COUNCIL OF THE EUROPEAN UNION,

Having regard to the Treaty establishing the European Community, and in particular point (1)(d) of the first paragraph of Article 63 thereof,

Having regard to the proposal from the Commission[48],

Having regard to the opinion of the European Parliament[49],

Having regard to the opinion of the European Economic and Social Committee[50],

Whereas:

(1) A common policy on asylum, including a Common European Asylum System, is a constituent part of the European Union's objective of establishing progressively an area of freedom, security and justice open to those who, forced by circumstances, legitimately seek protection in the Community.

(2) The European Council, at its special meeting in Tampere on 15 and 16 October 1999, agreed to work towards establishing a Common European Asylum System, based on the full and inclusive application of the Geneva Convention of 28 July 1951 relating to the status of refugees, as amended by the New York Protocol of 31 January 1967 (Geneva Convention), thus affirming the principle of non-refoulement and ensuring that nobody is sent back to persecution.

(3) The Tampere Conclusions provide that a Common European Asylum System should include, in the short term, common standards for fair and efficient asylum procedures in the Member States and, in the longer term, Community rules leading to a common asylum procedure in the European Community.

(4) The minimum standards laid down in this Directive on procedures in Member States for granting or withdrawing refugee status are therefore a first measure on asylum procedures.

(5) The main objective of this Directive is to introduce a minimum framework in the Community on procedures for granting and withdrawing refugee status.

(6) The approximation of rules on the procedures for granting and withdrawing refugee status should help to limit the secondary movements of applicants for

[48] OJ C 62, 27.2.2001, p. 231 and OJ C 291, 26.11.2002, p. 143.

[49] OJ C 77, 28.3.2002, p. 94.

[50] OJ C 193, 10.7.2001, p. 77. Opinion delivered following non-compulsory consultation.

asylum between Member States, where such movement would be caused by differences in legal frameworks.

(7) It is in the very nature of minimum standards that Member States should have the power to introduce or maintain more favourable provisions for third country nationals or stateless persons who ask for international protection from a Member State, where such a request is understood to be on the grounds that the person concerned is a refugee within the meaning of Article 1(A) of the Geneva Convention.

(8) This Directive respects the fundamental rights and observes the principles recognised in particular by the Charter of Fundamental Rights of the EuropeanUnion.

(9) With respect to the treatment of persons falling within the scope of this Directive, Member States are bound by obligations under instruments of international law to which they are party and which prohibit discrimination.

(10) It is essential that decisions on all applications for asylum be taken on the basis of the facts and, in the first instance, by authorities whose personnel has the appropriate knowledge or receives the necessary training in the field of asylum and refugee matters.

(11) It is in the interest of both Member States and applicants for asylum to decide as soon as possible on applications for asylum. The organisation of the processing of applications for asylum should be left to the discretion of Member States, so that they may, in accordance with their national needs, prioritise or accelerate the processing of any application, taking into account the standards in this Directive.

(12) The notion of public order may cover a conviction for committing a serious crime.

(13) In the interests of a correct recognition of those persons in need of protection as refugees within the meaning of Article 1 of the Geneva Convention, every applicant should, subject to certain exceptions, have an effective access to procedures, the opportunity to cooperate and properly communicate with the competent authorities so as to present the relevant facts of his/her case and sufficient procedural guarantees to pursue his/her case throughout all stages of the procedure. Moreover, the procedure in which an application for asylum is examined should normally provide an applicant at least with the right to stay pending a decision by the determining authority, access to the services of an interpreter for submitting his/her case if interviewed by the authorities, the opportunity to communicate with a representative of the United Nations High Commissioner for Refugees (UNHCR) or with any organisation working on its behalf, the right to appropriate notification of a decision, a motivation of that decision in fact and in law, the opportunity to consult a legal adviser or other counsellor, and the right to be informed of his/her legal

position at decisive moments in the course of the procedure, in a language he/she can reasonably be supposed to understand.

(14) In addition, specific procedural guarantees for unaccompanied minors should be laid down on account of their vulnerability. In this context, the best interests of the child should be a primary consideration of Member States.

(15) Where an applicant makes a subsequent application without presenting new evidence or arguments, it would be disproportionate to oblige Member States to carry out a new full examination procedure. In these cases, Member States should have a choice of procedure involving exceptions to the guarantees normally enjoyed by the applicant.

(16) Many asylum applications are made at the border or in a transit zone of a Member State prior to a decision on the entry of the applicant. Member States should be able to keep existing procedures adapted to the specific situation of these applicants at the border. Common rules should be defined on possible exceptions made in these circumstances to the guarantees normally enjoyed by applicants. Border procedures should mainly apply to those applicants who do not meet the conditions for entry into the territory of the Member States.

(17) A key consideration for the well-foundedness of an asylum application is the safety of the applicant in his/her country of origin. Where a third country can be regarded as a safe country of origin, Member States should be able to designate it as safe and presume its safety for a particular applicant, unless he/she presents serious counter-indications.

(18) Given the level of harmonisation achieved on the qualification of third country nationals and stateless persons as refugees, common criteria for designating third countries as safe countries of origin should be established.

(19) Where the Council has satisfied itself that those criteria are met in relation to a particular country of origin, and has consequently included it in the minimum common list of safe countries of origin to be adopted pursuant to this Directive, Member States should be obliged to consider applications of persons with the nationality of that country, or of stateless persons formerly habitually resident in that country, on the basis of the rebuttable presumption of the safety of that country. In the light of the political importance of the designation of safe countries of origin, in particular in view of the implications of an assessment of the human rights situation in a country of origin and its implications for the policies of the European Union in the field of external relations, the Council should take any decisions on the establishment or amendment of the list, after consultation of the European Parliament.

(20) It results from the status of Bulgaria and Romania as candidate countries for accession to the European Union and the progress made by these countries

towards membership that they should be regarded as constituting safe countries of origin for the purposes of this Directive until the date of their accession to the European Union.

(21) The designation of a third country as a safe country of origin for the purposes of this Directive cannot establish an absolute guarantee of safety for nationals of that country. By its very nature, the assessment underlying the designation can only take into account the general civil, legal and political circumstances in that country and whether actors of persecution, torture or inhuman or degrading treatment or punishment are subject to sanction in practice when found liable in the country concerned. For this reason, it is important that, where an applicant shows that there are serious reasons to consider the country not to be safe in his/her particular circumstances, the designation of the country as safe can no longer be considered relevant for him/her.

(22) Member States should examine all applications on the substance, i.e. assess whether the applicant in question qualifies as a refugee in accordance with Council Directive 2004/83/EC of 29 April 2004 on minimum standards for the qualification and status of third country nationals or stateless persons as refugees or as persons who otherwise need international protection and the content of the protection granted[51], except where the present Directive provides otherwise, in particular where it can be reasonably assumed that another country would do the examination or provide sufficient protection. In particular, Member States should not be obliged to assess the substance of an asylum application where a first country of asylum has granted the applicant refugee status or otherwise sufficient protection and the applicant will be readmitted to this country.

(23) Member States should also not be obliged to assess the substance of an asylum application where the applicant, due to a connection to a third country as defined by national law, can reasonably be expected to seek protection in that third country. Member States should only proceed on this basis where this particular applicant would be safe in the third country concerned. In order to avoid secondary movements of applicants, common principles for the consideration or designation by Member States of third countries as safe should be established.

(24) Furthermore, with respect to certain European third countries, which observe particularly high human rights and refugee protection standards, Member States should be allowed to not carry out, or not to carry out full examination of asylum applications regarding applicants who enter their territory from such European third countries. Given the potential consequences for the applicant of a restricted or omitted examination, this application of the safe third country concept should be restricted to cases involving third countries

[51] OJ L 304, 30.9.2004, p. 12.

with respect to which the Council has satisfied itself that the high standards for the safety of the third country concerned, as set out in this Directive, are fulfilled. The Council should take decisions in this matter after consultation of the European Parliament.

(25) It follows from the nature of the common standards concerning both safe third country concepts as set out in this Directive, that the practical effect of the concepts depends on whether the third country in question permits the applicant in question to enter its territory.

(26) With respect to the withdrawal of refugee status, Member States should ensure that persons benefiting from refugee status are duly informed of a possible reconsideration of their status and have the opportunity to submit their point of view before the authorities can take a motivated decision to withdraw their status. However, dispensing with these guarantees should be allowed where the reasons for the cessation of the refugee status is not related to a change of the conditions on which the recognition was based.

(27) It reflects a basic principle of Community law that the decisions taken on an application for asylum and on the withdrawal of refugee status are subject to an effective remedy before a court or tribunal within the meaning of Article 234 of the Treaty. The effectiveness of the remedy, also with regard to the examination of the relevant facts, depends on the administrative and judicial system of each Member State seen as a whole.

(28) In accordance with Article 64 of the Treaty, this Directive does not affect the exercise of the responsibilities incumbent upon Member States with regard to the maintenance of law and order and the safeguarding of internal security.

(29) This Directive does not deal with procedures governed by Council Regulation (EC) No 343/2003 of 18 February 2003 establishing the criteria and mechanisms for determining the Member State responsible for examining an asylum application lodged in one of the Member States by a third-country national[52].

(30) The implementation of this Directive should be evaluated at regular intervals not exceeding two years.

(31) Since the objective of this Directive, namely to establish minimum standards on procedures in Member States for granting and withdrawing refugee status cannot be sufficiently attained by the Member States and can therefore, by reason of the scale and effects of the action, be better achieved at Community level, the Community may adopt measures, in accordance with the principle of subsidiarity as set out in Article 5 of the Treaty. In accordance with the principle of proportionality, as set out in that Article, this Directive does not go beyond what is necessary in order to achieve this objective.

[52] OJ L 50, 25.2.2003, p. 1.

(32) In accordance with Article 3 of the Protocol on the position of the United Kingdom and Ireland, annexed to the Treaty on European Union and to the Treaty establishing the European Community, the United Kingdom has notified, by letter of 24 January 2001, its wish to take part in the adoption and application of this Directive.

(33) In accordance with Article 3 of the Protocol on the position of the United Kingdom and Ireland, annexed to the Treaty on European Union and to the Treaty establishing the European Community, Ireland has notified, by letter of 14 February 2001, its wish to take part in the adoption and application of this Directive.

(34) In accordance with Articles 1 and 2 of the Protocol on the position of Denmark, annexed to the Treaty on European Union and to the Treaty establishing the European Community, Denmark does not take part in the adoption of this Directive and is not bound by it or subject to its application,

HAS ADOPTED THIS DIRECTIVE:

Chapter I

General Provisions

Article 1

Purpose

The purpose of this Directive is to establish minimum standards on procedures in Member States for granting and withdrawing refugee status.

Article 2

Definitions

For the purposes of this Directive:

(a) 'Geneva Convention' means the Convention of 28 July 1951 relating to the status of refugees, as amended by the New York Protocol of 31 January 1967;

(b) 'application' or 'application for asylum' means an application made by a third country national or stateless person which can be understood as a request for international protection from a Member State under the Geneva Convention. Any application for international protection is presumed to be an application for asylum, unless the person concerned explicitly requests another kind of protection that can be applied for separately;

(c) 'applicant' or 'applicant for asylum' means a third country national or stateless person who has made an application for asylum in respect of which a final decision has not yet been taken;

(d) 'final decision' means a decision on whether the third country national or stateless person be granted refugee status by virtue of Directive 2004/83/EC and which is no longer subject to a remedy within the framework of Chapter V of this Directive irrespective of whether such remedy has the effect of allowing applicants to remain in the Member States concerned pending its outcome, subject to Annex III to this Directive;
(e) 'determining authority' means any quasi-judicial or administrative body in a Member State responsible for examining applications for asylum and competent to take decisions at first instance in such cases, subject to Annex I;
(f) 'refugee' means a third country national or a stateless person who fulfils the requirements of Article 1 of the Geneva Convention as set out in Directive 2004/83/EC;
(g) 'refugee status' means the recognition by a Member State of a third country national or stateless person as a refugee;
(h) 'unaccompanied minor' means a person below the age of 18 who arrives in the territory of the Member States unaccompanied by an adult responsible for him/her whether by law or by custom, and for as long as he/she is not effectively taken into the care of such a person; it includes a minor who is left unaccompanied after he/she has entered the territory of the Member States;
(i) 'representative' means a person acting on behalf of an organisation representing an unaccompanied minor as legal guardian, a person acting on behalf of a national organisation which is responsible for the care and well-being of minors, or any other appropriate representation appointed to ensure his/her best interests;
(j) 'withdrawal of refugee status' means the decision by a competent authority to revoke, end or refuse to renew the refugee status of a person in accordance with Directive 2004/83/EC;
(k) 'remain in the Member State' means to remain in the territory, including at the border or in transit zones, of the Member State in which the application for asylum has been made or is being examined.

Article 3

Scope

1. This Directive shall apply to all applications for asylum made in the territory, including at the border or in the transit zones of the Member States, and to the withdrawal of refugee status.
2. This Directive shall not apply in cases of requests for diplomatic or territorial asylum submitted to representations of Member States.
3. Where Member States employ or introduce a procedure in which asylum applications are examined both as applications on the basis of the Geneva Convention and as applications for other kinds of international protection

given under the circumstances defined by Article 15 of Directive 2004/83/EC, they shall apply this Directive throughout their procedure.

4. Moreover, Member States may decide to apply this Directive in procedures for deciding on applications for any kind of international protection.

Article 4

Responsible authorities

1. Member States shall designate for all procedures a determining authority which will be responsible for an appropriate examination of the applications in accordance with this Directive, in particular Articles 8(2) and 9.

   In accordance with Article 4(4) of Regulation (EC) No 343/2003, applications for asylum made in a Member State to the authorities of another Member State carrying out immigration controls there shall be dealt with by the Member State in whose territory the application is made.

2. However, Member States may provide that another authority is responsible for the purposes of:
   (a) processing cases in which it is considered to transfer the applicant to another State according to the rules establishing criteria and mechanisms for determining which State is responsible for considering an application for asylum, until the transfer takes place or the requested State has refused to take charge of or take back the applicant;
   (b) taking a decision on the application in the light of national security provisions, provided the determining authority is consulted prior to this decision as to whether the applicant qualifies as a refugee by virtue of Directive 2004/83/EC;
   (c) conducting a preliminary examination pursuant to Article 32, provided this authority has access to the applicant's file regarding the previous application;
   (d) processing cases in the framework of the procedures provided for in Article 35(1);
   (e) refusing permission to enter in the framework of the procedure provided for in Article 35(2) to (5), subject to the conditions and as set out therein;
   (f) establishing that an applicant is seeking to enter or has entered into the Member State from a safe third country pursuant to Article 36, subject to the conditions and as set out in that Article.

3. Where authorities are designated in accordance with paragraph 2, Member States shall ensure that the personnel of such authorities have the appropriate knowledge or receive the necessary training to fulfil their obligations when implementing this Directive.

Article 5

More favourable provisions

Member States may introduce or maintain more favourable standards on procedures for granting and withdrawing refugee status, insofar as those standards are compatible with this Directive.

Chapter II

Basic Principles and Guarantees

Article 6

Access to the procedure

1. Member States may require that applications for asylum be made in person and/or at a designated place.
2. Member States shall ensure that each adult having legal capacity has the right to make an application for asylum on his/her own behalf.
3. Member States may provide that an application may be made by an applicant on behalf of his/her dependants. In such cases Member States shall ensure that dependant adults consent to the lodging of the application on their behalf, failing which they shall have an opportunity to make an application on their own behalf.

   Consent shall be requested at the time the application is lodged or, at the latest, when the personal interview with the dependant adult is conducted.
4. Member States may determine in national legislation:
   (a) the cases in which a minor can make an application on his/her own behalf;
   (b) the cases in which the application of an unaccompanied minor has to be lodged by a representative as provided for in Article 17(1)(a);
   (c) the cases in which the lodging of an application for asylum is deemed to constitute also the lodging of an application for asylum for any unmarried minor.
5. Member States shall ensure that authorities likely to be addressed by someone who wishes to make an application for asylum are able to advise that person how and where he/she may make such an application and/or may require these authorities to forward the application to the competent authority.

Article 7

Right to remain in the Member State pending the examination of the application

1. Applicants shall be allowed to remain in the Member State, for the sole purpose of the procedure, until the determining authority has made a decision in

accordance with the procedures at first instance set out in Chapter III. This right to remain shall not constitute an entitlement to a residence permit.

2. Member States can make an exception only where, in accordance with Articles 32 and 34, a subsequent application will not be further examined or where they will surrender or extradite, as appropriate, a person either to another Member State pursuant to obligations in accordance with a European arrest warrant[53] or otherwise, or to a third country, or to international criminal courts or tribunals.

Article 8

Requirements for the examination of applications

1. Without prejudice to Article 23(4)(i), Member States shall ensure that applications for asylum are neither rejected nor excluded from examination on the sole ground that they have not been made as soon as possible.
2. Member States shall ensure that decisions by the determining authority on applications for asylum are taken after an appropriate examination. To that end, Member States shall ensure that:
   (a) applications are examined and decisions are taken individually, objectively and impartially;
   (b) precise and up-to-date information is obtained from various sources, such as the United Nations High Commissioner for Refugees (UNHCR), as to the general situation prevailing in the countries of origin of applicants for asylum and, where necessary, in countries through which they have transited, and that such information is made available to the personnel responsible for examining applications and taking decisions;
   (c) the personnel examining applications and taking decisions have the knowledge with respect to relevant standards applicable in the field of asylum and refugee law.
3. The authorities referred to in Chapter V shall, through the determining authority or the applicant or otherwise, have access to the general information referred to in paragraph 2(b), necessary for the fulfilment of their task.
4. Member States may provide for rules concerning the translation of documents relevant for the examination of applications.

[53] Council Framework Decision 2002/584/JHA of 13 June 2002 on the European arrest warrant and the surrender procedures between Member States (OJ L 190, 18.7.2002, p. 1).

Article 9

Requirements for a decision by the determining authority

1. Member States shall ensure that decisions on applications for asylum are given in writing.
2. Member States shall also ensure that, where an application is rejected, the reasons in fact and in law are stated in the decision and information on how to challenge a negative decision is given in writing.

   Member States need not state the reasons for not granting refugee status in a decision where the applicant is granted a status which offers the same rights and benefits under national and Community law as the refugee status by virtue of Directive 2004/83/EC. In these cases, Member States shall ensure that the reasons for not granting refugee status are stated in the applicant's file and that the applicant has, upon request, access to his/her file.

   Moreover, Member States need not provide information on how to challenge a negative decision in writing in conjunction with a decision where the applicant has been provided with this information at an earlier stage either in writing or by electronic means accessible to the applicant.
3. For the purposes of Article 6(3), and whenever the application is based on the same grounds, Member States may take one single decision, covering all dependants.

Article 10

Guarantees for applicants for asylum

1. With respect to the procedures provided for in Chapter III, Member States shall ensure that all applicants for asylum enjoy the following guarantees:
   (a) they shall be informed in a language which they may reasonably be supposed to understand of the procedure to be followed and of their rights and obligations during the procedure and the possible consequences of not complying with their obligations and not cooperating with the authorities. They shall be informed of the time-frame, as well as the means at their disposal for fulfilling the obligation to submit the elements as referred to in Article 4 of Directive 2004/83/EC. This information shall be given in time to enable them to exercise the rights guaranteed in this Directive and to comply with the obligations described in Article 11;
   (b) they shall receive the services of an interpreter for submitting their case to the competent authorities whenever necessary. Member States shall consider it necessary to give these services at least when the determining authority calls upon the applicant to be interviewed as referred to in Articles 12 and 13 and appropriate communication cannot be ensured

without such services. In this case and in other cases where the competent authorities call upon the applicant, these services shall be paid for out of public funds;

(c) they shall not be denied the opportunity to communicate with the UNHCR or with any other organisation working on behalf of the UNHCR in the territory of the Member State pursuant to an agreement with that Member State;

(d) they shall be given notice in reasonable time of the decision by the determining authority on their application for asylum. If a legal adviser or other counsellor is legally representing the applicant, Member States may choose to give notice of the decision to him/her instead of to the applicant for asylum;

(e) they shall be informed of the result of the decision by the determining authority in a language that they may reasonably be supposed to understand when they are not assisted or represented by a legal adviser or other counsellor and when free legal assistance is not available. The information provided shall include information on how to challenge a negative decision in accordance with the provisions of Article 9(2).

2. With respect to the procedures provided for in Chapter V, Member States shall ensure that all applicants for asylum enjoy equivalent guarantees to the ones referred to in paragraph 1(b), (c) and (d) of this Article.

Article 11

Obligations of the applicants for asylum

1. Member States may impose upon applicants for asylum obligations to cooperate with the competent authorities insofar as these obligations are necessary for the processing of the application.

2. In particular, Member States may provide that:

(a) applicants for asylum are required to report to the competent authorities or to appear before them in person, either without delay or at a specified time;

(b) applicants for asylum have to hand over documents in their possession relevant to the examination of the application, such as their passports;

(c) applicants for asylum are required to inform the competent authorities of their current place of residence or address and of any changes thereof as soon as possible. Member States may provide that the applicant shall have to accept any communication at the most recent place of residence or address which he/she indicated accordingly;

(d) the competent authorities may search the applicant and the items he/she carries with him/her;

(e) the competent authorities may take a photograph of the applicant; and

(f) the competent authorities may record the applicant's oral statements, provided he/she has previously been informed thereof.

Article 12

Personal interview

1. Before a decision is taken by the determining authority, the applicant for asylum shall be given the opportunity of a personal interview on his/her application for asylum with a person competent under national law to conduct such an interview.

   Member States may also give the opportunity of a personal interview to each dependant adult referred to in Article 6(3).

   Member States may determine in national legislation the cases in which a minor shall be given the opportunity of a personal interview.

2. The personal interview may be omitted where:
   (a) the determining authority is able to take a positive decision on the basis of evidence available; or
   (b) the competent authority has already had a meeting with the applicant for the purpose of assisting him/her with completing his/her application and submitting the essential information regarding the application, in terms of Article 4(2) of Directive 2004/83/EC; or
   (c) the determining authority, on the basis of a complete examination of information provided by the applicant, considers the application to be unfounded in cases where the circumstances mentioned in Article 23(4)(a), (c), (g), (h) and (j) apply.

3. The personal interview may also be omitted where it is not reasonably practicable, in particular where the competent authority is of the opinion that the applicant is unfit or unable to be interviewed owing to enduring circumstances beyond his/her control. When in doubt, Member States may require a medical or psychological certificate.

   Where the Member State does not provide the applicant with the opportunity for a personal interview pursuant to this paragraph, or where applicable, to the dependant, reasonable efforts shall be made to allow the applicant or the dependant to submit further information.

4. The absence of a personal interview in accordance with this Article shall not prevent the determining authority from taking a decision on an application for asylum.

5. The absence of a personal interview pursuant to paragraph 2(b) and (c) and paragraph 3 shall not adversely affect the decision of the determining authority.

6. Irrespective of Article 20(1), Member States, when deciding on the application for asylum, may take into account the fact that the applicant failed to appear

for the personal interview, unless he/she had good reasons for the failure to appear.

Article 13

Requirements for a personal interview

1. A personal interview shall normally take place without the presence of family members unless the determining authority considers it necessary for an appropriate examination to have other family members present.
2. A personal interview shall take place under conditions which ensure appropriate confidentiality.
3. Member States shall take appropriate steps to ensure that personal interviews are conducted under conditions which allow applicants to present the grounds for their applications in a comprehensive manner. To that end, Member States shall:
   (a) ensure that the person who conducts the interview is sufficiently competent to take account of the personal or general circumstances surrounding the application, including the applicant's cultural origin or vulnerability, insofar as it is possible to do so; and
   (b) select an interpreter who is able to ensure appropriate communication between the applicant and the person who conducts the interview. The communication need not necessarily take place in the language preferred by the applicant for asylum if there is another language which he/she may reasonably be supposed to understand and in which he/she is able to communicate.
4. Member States may provide for rules concerning the presence of third parties at a personal interview.
5. This Article is also applicable to the meeting referred to in Article 12(2)(b).

Article 14

Status of the report of a personal interview in the procedure

1. Member States shall ensure that a written report is made of every personal interview, containing at least the essential information regarding the application, as presented by the applicant, in terms of Article 4(2) of Directive 2004/83/EC.
2. Member States shall ensure that applicants have timely access to the report of the personal interview. Where access is only granted after the decision of the determining authority, Member States shall ensure that access is possible as soon as necessary for allowing an appeal to be prepared and lodged in due time.

3. Member States may request the applicant's approval of the contents of the report of the personal interview.

   Where an applicant refuses to approve the contents of the report, the reasons for this refusal shall be entered into the applicant's file.

   The refusal of an applicant to approve the contents of the report shall not prevent the determining authority from taking a decision on his/her application.

4. This Article is also applicable to the meeting referred to in Article 12(2)(b).

Article 15

Right to legal assistance and representation

1. Member States shall allow applicants for asylum the opportunity, at their own cost, to consult in an effective manner a legal adviser or other counsellor, admitted or permitted as such under national law, on matters relating to their asylum applications.
2. In the event of a negative decision by a determining authority, Member States shall ensure that free legal assistance and/or representation be granted on request, subject to the provisions of paragraph 3.
3. Member States may provide in their national legislation that free legal assistance and/or representation is granted:
   (a) only for procedures before a court or tribunal in accordance with Chapter V and not for any onward appeals or reviews provided for under national law, including a rehearing of an appeal following an onward appeal or review; and/or
   (b) only to those who lack sufficient resources; and/or
   (c) only to legal advisers or other counsellors specifically designated by national law to assist and/or represent applicants for asylum; and/or
   (d) only if the appeal or review is likely to succeed.

   Member States shall ensure that legal assistance and/or representation granted under point (d) is not arbitrarily restricted.
4. Rules concerning the modalities for filing and processing requests for legal assistance and/or representation may be provided by Member States.
5. Member States may also:
   (a) impose monetary and/or time-limits on the provision of free legal assistance and/or representation, provided that such limits do not arbitrarily restrict access to legal assistance and/or representation;
   (b) provide that, as regards fees and other costs, the treatment of applicants shall not be more favourable than the treatment generally accorded to their nationals in matters pertaining to legal assistance.
6. Member States may demand to be reimbursed wholly or partially for any expenses granted if and when the applicant's financial situation has improved

considerably or if the decision to grant such benefits was taken on the basis of false information supplied by the applicant.

Article 16

Scope of legal assistance and representation

1. Member States shall ensure that a legal adviser or other counsellor admitted or permitted as such under national law, and who assists or represents an applicant for asylum under the terms of national law, shall enjoy access to such information in the applicant's file as is liable to be examined by the authorities referred to in Chapter V, insofar as the information is relevant to the examination of the application.

   Member States may make an exception where disclosure of information or sources would jeopardise national security, the security of the organisations or person(s) providing the information or the security of the person(s) to whom the information relates or where the investigative interests relating to the examination of applications of asylum by the competent authorities of the Member States or the international relations of the Member States would be compromised. In these cases, access to the information or sources in question shall be available to the authorities referred to in Chapter V, except where such access is precluded in cases of national security.
2. Member States shall ensure that the legal adviser or other counsellor who assists or represents an applicant for asylum has access to closed areas, such as detention facilities and transit zones, for the purpose of consulting that applicant. Member States may only limit the possibility of visiting applicants in closed areas where such limitation is, by virtue of national legislation, objectively necessary for the security, public order or administrative management of the area, or in order to ensure an efficient examination of the application, provided that access by the legal adviser or other counsellor is not thereby severely limited or rendered impossible.
3. Member States may provide rules covering the presence of legal advisers or other counsellors at all interviews in the procedure, without prejudice to this Article or to Article 17(1)(b).
4. Member States may provide that the applicant is allowed to bring with him/her to the personal interview a legal adviser or other counsellor admitted or permitted as such under national law.

   Member States may require the presence of the applicant at the personal interview, even if he/she is represented under the terms of national law by such a legal adviser or counsellor, and may require the applicant to respond in person to the questions asked.

   The absence of a legal adviser or other counsellor shall not prevent the competent authority from conducting the personal interview with the applicant.

Article 17

Guarantees for unaccompanied minors

1. With respect to all procedures provided for in this Directive and without prejudice to the provisions of Articles 12 and 14, Member States shall:
   (a) as soon as possible take measures to ensure that a representative represents and/or assists the unaccompanied minor with respect to the examination of the application. This representative can also be the representative referred to in Article 19 of Directive 2003/9/EC of 27 January 2003 laying down minimum standards for the reception of asylum seekers[54];
   (b) ensure that the representative is given the opportunity to inform the unaccompanied minor about the meaning and possible consequences of the personal interview and, where appropriate, how to prepare himself/herself for the personal interview. Member States shall allow the representative to be present at that interview and to ask questions or make comments, within the framework set by the person who conducts the interview.

   Member States may require the presence of the unaccompanied minor at the personal interview, even if the representative is present.
2. Member States may refrain from appointing a representative where the unaccompanied minor:
   (a) will in all likelihood reach the age of maturity before a decision at first instance is taken; or
   (b) can avail himself, free of charge, of a legal adviser or other counsellor, admitted as such under national law to fulfil the tasks assigned above to the representative; or
   (c) is married or has been married.
3. Member States may, in accordance with the laws and regulations in force on 1 December 2005, also refrain from appointing a representative where the unaccompanied minor is 16 years old or older, unless he/she is unable to pursue his/her application without a representative.
4. Member States shall ensure that:
   (a) if an unaccompanied minor has a personal interview on his/her application for asylum as referred to in Articles 12, 13 and 14, that interview is conducted by a person who has the necessary knowledge of the special needs of minors;
   (b) an official with the necessary knowledge of the special needs of minors prepares the decision by the determining authority on the application of an unaccompanied minor.

[54] OJ L 31, 6.2.2003, p. 18.

5. Member States may use medical examinations to determine the age of unaccompanied minors within the framework of the examination of an application for asylum.

   In cases where medical examinations are used, Member States shall ensure that:

   (a) unaccompanied minors are informed prior to the examination of their application for asylum, and in a language which they may reasonably be supposed to understand, of the possibility that their age may be determined by medical examination. This shall include information on the method of examination and the possible consequences of the result of the medical examination for the examination of the application for asylum, as well as the consequences of refusal on the part of the unaccompanied minor to undergo the medical examination;

   (b) unaccompanied minors and/or their representatives consent to carry out an examination to determine the age of the minors concerned; and

   (c) the decision to reject an application for asylum from an unaccompanied minor who refused to undergo this medical examination shall not be based solely on that refusal.

   The fact that an unaccompanied minor has refused to undergo such a medical examination shall not prevent the determining authority from taking a decision on the application for asylum.

6. The best interests of the child shall be a primary consideration for Member States when implementing this Article.

Article 18

Detention

1. Member States shall not hold a person in detention for the sole reason that he/she is an applicant for asylum.
2. Where an applicant for asylum is held in detention, Member States shall ensure that there is a possibility of speedy judicial review.

Article 19

Procedure in case of withdrawal of the application

1. Insofar as Member States provide for the possibility of explicit withdrawal of the application under national law, when an applicant for asylum explicitly withdraws his/her application for asylum, Member States shall ensure that the determining authority takes a decision to either discontinue the examination or reject the application.
2. Member States may also decide that the determining authority can decide to

discontinue the examination without taking a decision. In this case, Member States shall ensure that the determining authority enters a notice in the applicant's file.

Article 20

Procedure in the case of implicit withdrawal or abandonment of the application

1. When there is reasonable cause to consider that an applicant for asylum has implicitly withdrawn or abandoned his/her application for asylum, Member States shall ensure that the determining authority takes a decision to either discontinue the examination or reject the application on the basis that the applicant has not established an entitlement to refugee status in accordance with Directive 2004/83/EC.

   Member States may assume that the applicant has implicitly withdrawn or abandoned his/her application for asylum in particular when it is ascertained that:

   (a) he/she has failed to respond to requests to provide information essential to his/her application in terms of Article 4 of Directive 2004/83/EC or has not appeared for a personal interview as provided for in Articles 12, 13 and 14, unless the applicant demonstrates within a reasonable time that his/her failure was due to circumstances beyond his control;

   (b) he/she has absconded or left without authorisation the place where he/she lived or was held, without contacting the competent authority within a reasonable time, or he/she has not within a reasonable time complied with reporting duties or other obligations to communicate.

   For the purposes of implementing these provisions, Member States may lay down time-limits or guidelines.

2. Member States shall ensure that the applicant who reports again to the competent authority after a decision to discontinue as referred to in paragraph 1 of this Article is taken, is entitled to request that his/her case be reopened, unless the request is examined in accordance with Articles 32 and 34.

   Member States may provide for a time-limit after which the applicant's case can no longer be re-opened.

   Member States shall ensure that such a person is not removed contrary to the principle of non-refoulement.

   Member States may allow the determining authority to take up the examination at the stage where it was discontinued.

Article 21

The role of UNHCR

1. Member States shall allow the UNHCR:

(a) to have access to applicants for asylum, including those in detention and in airport or port transit zones;
(b) to have access to information on individual applications for asylum, on the course of the procedure and on the decisions taken, provided that the applicant for asylum agrees thereto;
(c) to present its views, in the exercise of its supervisory responsibilities under Article 35 of the Geneva Convention, to any competent authorities regarding individual applications for asylum at any stage of the procedure.

2. Paragraph 1 shall also apply to an organisation which is working in the territory of the Member State concerned on behalf of the UNHCR pursuant to an agreement with that Member State.

Article 22

Collection of information on individual cases

For the purposes of examining individual cases, Member States shall not:
(a) directly disclose information regarding individual applications for asylum, or the fact that an application has been made, to the alleged actor(s) of persecution of the applicant for asylum;
(b) obtain any information from the alleged actor(s) of persecution in a manner that would result in such actor(s) being directly informed of the fact that an application has been made by the applicant in question, and would jeopardise the physical integrity of the applicant and his/her dependants, or the liberty and security of his/her family members still living in the country of origin.

Chapter III

Procedures at First Instance

Section I

Article 23

Examination procedure

1. Member States shall process applications for asylum in an examination procedure in accordance with the basic principles and guarantees of Chapter II.
2. Member States shall ensure that such a procedure is concluded as soon as possible, without prejudice to an adequate and complete examination.

Member States shall ensure that, where a decision cannot be taken within six months, the applicant concerned shall either:
(a) be informed of the delay; or
(b) receive, upon his/her request, information on the time-frame within which

the decision on his/her application is to be expected. Such information shall not constitute an obligation for the Member State towards the applicant concerned to take a decision within that time-frame.

3. Member States may prioritise or accelerate any examination in accordance with the basic principles and guarantees of Chapter II, including where the application is likely to be well-founded or where the applicant has special needs.

4. Member States may also provide that an examination procedure in accordance with the basic principles and guarantees of Chapter II be prioritised or accelerated if:
   (a) the applicant, in submitting his/her application and presenting the facts, has only raised issues that are not relevant or of minimal relevance to the examination of whether he/she qualifies as a refugee by virtue of Directive 2004/83/EC; or
   (b) the applicant clearly does not qualify as a refugee or for refugee status in a Member State under Directive 2004/83/EC; or
   (c) the application for asylum is considered to be unfounded:
      (i) because the applicant is from a safe country of origin within the meaning of Articles 29, 30 and 31, or
      (ii) because the country which is not a Member State, is considered to be a safe third country for the applicant, without prejudice to Article 28(1); or
   (d) the applicant has misled the authorities by presenting false information or documents or by withholding relevant information or documents with respect to his/her identity and/or nationality that could have had a negative impact on the decision; or
   (e) the applicant has filed another application for asylum stating other personal data; or
   (f) the applicant has not produced information establishing with a reasonable degree of certainty his/her identity or nationality, or it is likely that, in bad faith, he/she has destroyed or disposed of an identity or travel document that would have helped establish his/her identity or nationality; or
   (g) the applicant has made inconsistent, contradictory, improbable or insufficient representations which make his/her claim clearly unconvincing in relation to his/her having been the object of persecution referred to in Directive 2004/83/EC; or
   (h) the applicant has submitted a subsequent application which does not raise any relevant new elements with respect to his/her particular circumstances or to the situation in his/her country of origin; or
   (i) the applicant has failed without reasonable cause to make his/her application earlier, having had opportunity to do so; or
   (j) the applicant is making an application merely in order to delay or frustrate

the enforcement of an earlier or imminent decision which would result in his/her removal; or

(k) the applicant has failed without good reason to comply with obligations referred to in Article 4(1) and (2) of Directive 2004/83/EC or in Articles 11(2)(a) and (b) and 20(1) of this Directive; or

(l) the applicant entered the territory of the Member State unlawfully or prolonged his/her stay unlawfully and, without good reason, has either not presented himself/herself to the authorities and/or filed an application for asylum as soon as possible, given the circumstances of his/her entry; or

(m) the applicant is a danger to the national security or public order of the Member State, or the applicant has been forcibly expelled for serious reasons of public security and public order under national law; or

(n) the applicant refuses to comply with an obligation to have his/her fingerprints taken in accordance with relevant Community and/or national legislation; or

(o) the application was made by an unmarried minor to whom Article 6(4)(c) applies, after the application of the parents or parent responsible for the minor has been rejected and no relevant new elements were raised with respect to his/her particular circumstances or to the situation in his/her country of origin.

Article 24

Specific procedures

1. Member States may provide for the following specific procedures derogating from the basic principles and guarantees of Chapter II:
   (a) a preliminary examination for the purposes of processing cases considered within the framework set out in Section IV;
   (b) procedures for the purposes of processing cases considered within the framework set out in Section V.
2. Member States may also provide a derogation in respect of Section VI.

Section II

Article 25

Inadmissible applications

1. In addition to cases in which an application is not examined in accordance with Regulation (EC) No 343/2003, Member States are not required to examine whether the applicant qualifies as a refugee in accordance with Directive 2004/83/EC where an application is considered inadmissible pursuant to this Article.

2. Member States may consider an application for asylum as inadmissible pursuant to this Article if:
   (a) another Member State has granted refugee status;
   (b) a country which is not a Member State is considered as a first country of asylum for the applicant, pursuant to Article 26;
   (c) a country which is not a Member State is considered as a safe third country for the applicant, pursuant to Article 27;
   (d) the applicant is allowed to remain in the Member State concerned on some other grounds and as result of this he/she has been granted a status equivalent to the rights and benefits of the refugee status by virtue of Directive 2004/83/EC;
   (e) the applicant is allowed to remain in the territory of the Member State concerned on some other grounds which protect him/her against refoulement pending the outcome of a procedure for the determination of status pursuant to point (d);
   (f) the applicant has lodged an identical application after a final decision;
   (g) a dependant of the applicant lodges an application, after he/she has in accordance with Article 6(3) consented to have his/her case be part of an application made on his/her behalf, and there are no facts relating to the dependant's situation, which justify a separate application.

Article 26

The concept of first country of asylum

A country can be considered to be a first country of asylum for a particular applicant for asylum if:
(a) he/she has been recognised in that country as a refugee and he/she can still avail himself/herself of that protection; or
(b) he/she otherwise enjoys sufficient protection in that country, including benefiting from the principle of non-refoulement;

provided that he/she will be re-admitted to that country.

In applying the concept of first country of asylum to the particular circumstances of an applicant for asylum Member States may take into account Article 27(1).

Article 27

The safe third country concept

1. Member States may apply the safe third country concept only where the competent authorities are satisfied that a person seeking asylum will be treated in accordance with the following principles in the third country concerned:
   (a) life and liberty are not threatened on account of race, religion, nationality, membership of a particular social group or political opinion;

(b) the principle of non-refoulement in accordance with the Geneva Convention is respected;
(c) the prohibition of removal, in violation of the right to freedom from torture and cruel, inhuman or degrading treatment as laid down in international law, is respected; and
(d) the possibility exists to request refugee status and, if found to be a refugee, to receive protection in accordance with the Geneva Convention.

2. The application of the safe third country concept shall be subject to rules laid down in national legislation, including:
   (a) rules requiring a connection between the person seeking asylum and the third country concerned on the basis of which it would be reasonable for that person to go to that country;
   (b) rules on the methodology by which the competent authorities satisfy themselves that the safe third country concept may be applied to a particular country or to a particular applicant. Such methodology shall include case-by-case consideration of the safety of the country for a particular applicant and/or national designation of countries considered to be generally safe;
   (c) rules in accordance with international law, allowing an individual examination of whether the third country concerned is safe for a particular applicant which, as a minimum, shall permit the applicant to challenge the application of the safe third country concept on the grounds that he/she would be subjected to torture, cruel, inhuman or degrading treatment or punishment.
3. When implementing a decision solely based on this Article, Member States shall:
   (a) inform the applicant accordingly; and
   (b) provide him/her with a document informing the authorities of the third country, in the language of that country, that the application has not been examined in substance.
4. Where the third country does not permit the applicant for asylum to enter its territory, Member States shall ensure that access to a procedure is given in accordance with the basic principles and guarantees described in Chapter II.
5. Member States shall inform the Commission periodically of the countries to which this concept is applied in accordance with the provisions of this Article.

Section III

Article 28

Unfounded applications

1. Without prejudice to Articles 19 and 20, Member States may only consider an application for asylum as unfounded if the determining authority has

established that the applicant does not qualify for refugee status pursuant to Directive 2004/83/EC.

2. In the cases mentioned in Article 23(4)(b) and in cases of unfounded applications for asylum in which any of the circumstances listed in Article 23(4)(a) and (c) to (o) apply, Member States may also consider an application as manifestly unfounded, where it is defined as such in the national legislation.

Article 29

Minimum common list of third countries regarded as safe countries of origin

1. The Council shall, acting by a qualified majority on a proposal from the Commission and after consultation of the European Parliament, adopt a minimum common list of third countries which shall be regarded by Member States as safe countries of origin in accordance with Annex II.
2. The Council may, acting by a qualified majority on a proposal from the Commission and after consultation of the European Parliament, amend the minimum common list by adding or removing third countries, in accordance with Annex II. The Commission shall examine any request made by the Council or by a Member State to submit a proposal to amend the minimum common list.
3. When making its proposal under paragraphs 1 or 2, the Commission shall make use of information from the Member States, its own information and, where necessary, information from UNHCR, the Council of Europe and other relevant international organisations.
4. Where the Council requests the Commission to submit a proposal for removing a third country from the minimum common list, the obligation of Member States pursuant to Article 31(2) shall be suspended with regard to this third country as of the day following the Council decision requesting such a submission.
5. Where a Member State requests the Commission to submit a proposal to the Council for removing a third country from the minimum common list, that Member State shall notify the Council in writing of the request made to the Commission. The obligation of this Member State pursuant to Article 31(2) shall be suspended with regard to the third country as of the day following the notification to the Council.
6. The European Parliament shall be informed of the suspensions under paragraphs 4 and 5.
7. The suspensions under paragraphs 4 and 5 shall end after three months, unless the Commission makes a proposal before the end of this period, to withdraw the third country from the minimum common list. The suspensions shall in any case end where the Council rejects a proposal by the Commission to withdraw the third country from the list.

8. Upon request by the Council, the Commission shall report to the European Parliament and the Council on whether the situation of a country on the minimum common list is still in conformity with Annex II. When presenting its report, the Commission may make such recommendations or proposals as it deems appropriate.

Article 30

National designation of third countries as safe countries of origin

1. Without prejudice to Article 29, Member States may retain or introduce legislation that allows, in accordance with Annex II, for the national designation of third countries other than those appearing on the minimum common list, as safe countries of origin for the purposes of examining applications for asylum. This may include designation of part of a country as safe where the conditions in Annex II are fulfilled in relation to that part.
2. By derogation from paragraph 1, Member States may retain legislation in force on 1 December 2005 that allows for the national designation of third countries, other than those appearing on the minimum common list, as safe countries of origin for the purposes of examining applications for asylum where they are satisfied that persons in the third countries concerned are generally neither subject to:
   (a) persecution as defined in Article 9 of Directive 2004/83/EC; nor
   (b) torture or inhuman or degrading treatment or punishment.
3. Member States may also retain legislation in force on 1 December 2005 that allows for the national designation of part of a country as safe, or a country or part of a country as safe for a specified group of persons in that country, where the conditions in paragraph 2 are fulfilled in relation to that part or group.
4. In assessing whether a country is a safe country of origin in accordance with paragraphs 2 and 3, Member States shall have regard to the legal situation, the application of the law and the general political circumstances in the third country concerned.
5. The assessment of whether a country is a safe country of origin in accordance with this Article shall be based on a range of sources of information, including in particular information from other Member States, the UNHCR, the Council of Europe and other relevant international organisations.
6. Member States shall notify to the Commission the countries that are designated as safe countries of origin in accordance with this Article.

Article 31

The safe country of origin concept

1. A third country designated as a safe country of origin in accordance with either Article 29 or 30 may, after an individual examination of the application, be considered as a safe country of origin for a particular applicant for asylum only if:
   (a) he/she has the nationality of that country; or
   (b) he/she is a stateless person and was formerly habitually resident in that country;

   and he/she has not submitted any serious grounds for considering the country not to be a safe country of origin in his/her particular circumstances and in terms of his/her qualification as a refugee in accordance with Directive 2004/83/EC.
2. Member States shall, in accordance with paragraph 1, consider the application for asylum as unfounded where the third country is designated as safe pursuant to Article 29.
3. Member States shall lay down in national legislation further rules and modalities for the application of the safe country of origin concept.

Section IV

Article 32

Subsequent application

1. Where a person who has applied for asylum in a Member State makes further representations or a subsequent application in the same Member State, that Member State may examine these further representations or the elements of the subsequent application in the framework of the examination of the previous application or in the framework of the examination of the decision under review or appeal, insofar as the competent authorities can take into account and consider all the elements underlying the further representations or subsequent application within this framework.
2. Moreover, Member States may apply a specific procedure as referred to in paragraph 3, where a person makes a subsequent application for asylum:
   (a) after his/her previous application has been withdrawn or abandoned by virtue of Articles 19 or 20;
   (b) after a decision has been taken on the previous application. Member States may also decide to apply this procedure only after a final decision has been taken.
3. A subsequent application for asylum shall be subject first to a preliminary

examination as to whether, after the withdrawal of the previous application or after the decision referred to in paragraph 2(b) of this Article on this application has been reached, new elements or findings relating to the examination of whether he/she qualifies as a refugee by virtue of Directive 2004/83/EC have arisen or have been presented by the applicant.

4. If, following the preliminary examination referred to in paragraph 3 of this Article, new elements or findings arise or are presented by the applicant which significantly add to the likelihood of the applicant qualifying as a refugee by virtue of Directive 2004/83/EC, the application shall be further examined in conformity with Chapter II.
5. Member States may, in accordance with national legislation, further examine a subsequent application where there are other reasons why a procedure has to be re-opened.
6. Member States may decide to further examine the application only if the applicant concerned was, through no fault of his/her own, incapable of asserting the situations set forth in paragraphs 3, 4 and 5 of this Article in the previous procedure, in particular by exercising his/her right to an effective remedy pursuant to Article 39.
7. The procedure referred to in this Article may also be applicable in the case of a dependant who lodges an application after he/she has, in accordance with Article 6(3), consented to have his/her case be part of an application made on his/her behalf. In this case the preliminary examination referred to in paragraph 3 of this Article will consist of examining whether there are facts relating to the dependant's situation which justify a separate application.

Article 33

Failure to appear

Member States may retain or adopt the procedure provided for in Article 32 in the case of an application for asylum filed at a later date by an applicant who, either intentionally or owing to gross negligence, fails to go to a reception centre or appear before the competent authorities at a specified time.

Article 34

Procedural rules

1. Member States shall ensure that applicants for asylum whose application is subject to a preliminary examination pursuant to Article 32 enjoy the guarantees provided for in Article 10(1).
2. Member States may lay down in national law rules on the preliminary examination pursuant to Article 32. Those rules may, *inter alia*:

(a) oblige the applicant concerned to indicate facts and substantiate evidence which justify a new procedure;
(b) require submission of the new information by the applicant concerned within a time-limit after he/she obtained such information;
(c) permit the preliminary examination to be conducted on the sole basis of written submissions without a personal interview.

The conditions shall not render impossible the access of applicants for asylum to a new procedure or result in the effective annulment or severe curtailment of such access.

3. Member States shall ensure that:
   (a) the applicant is informed in an appropriate manner of the outcome of the preliminary examination and, in case the application will not be further examined, of the reasons for this and the possibilities for seeking an appeal or review of the decision;
   (b) if one of the situations referred to in Article 32(2) applies, the determining authority shall further examine the subsequent application in conformity with the provisions of Chapter II as soon as possible.

Section V

Article 35

Border procedures

1. Member States may provide for procedures, in accordance with the basic principles and guarantees of Chapter II, in order to decide at the border or transit zones of the Member State on applications made at such locations.
2. However, when procedures as set out in paragraph 1 do not exist, Member States may maintain, subject to the provisions of this Article and in accordance with the laws or regulations in force on 1 December 2005, procedures derogating from the basic principles and guarantees described in Chapter II, in order to decide at the border or in transit zones as to whether applicants for asylum who have arrived and made an application for asylum at such locations, may enter their territory.
3. The procedures referred to in paragraph 2 shall ensure in particular that the persons concerned:
   (a) are allowed to remain at the border or transit zones of the Member State, without prejudice to Article 7;
   (b) are be [sic] immediately informed of their rights and obligations, as described in Article 10(1)(a);
   (c) have access, if necessary, to the services of an interpreter, as described in Article 10(1)(b);

(d) are interviewed, before the competent authority takes a decision in such procedures, in relation to their application for asylum by persons with appropriate knowledge of the relevant standards applicable in the field of asylum and refugee law, as described in Articles 12, 13 and 14;

(e) can consult a legal adviser or counsellor admitted or permitted as such under national law, as described in Article 15(1); and

(f) have a representative appointed in the case of unaccompanied minors, as described in Article 17(1), unless Article 17(2) or (3) applies.

Moreover, in case permission to enter is refused by a competent authority, this competent authority shall state the reasons in fact and in law why the application for asylum is considered as unfounded or as inadmissible.

4. Member States shall ensure that a decision in the framework of the procedures provided for in paragraph 2 is taken within a reasonable time. When a decision has not been taken within four weeks, the applicant for asylum shall be granted entry to the territory of the Member State in order for his/her application to be processed in accordance with the other provisions of this Directive.

5. In the event of particular types of arrivals, or arrivals involving a large number of third country nationals or stateless persons lodging applications for asylum at the border or in a transit zone, which makes it practically impossible to apply there the provisions of paragraph 1 or the specific procedure set out in paragraphs 2 and 3, those procedures may also be applied where and for as long as these third country nationals or stateless persons are accommodated normally at locations in proximity to the border or transit zone.

Section VI

Article 36

The European safe third countries concept

1. Member States may provide that no, or no full, examination of the asylum application and of the safety of the applicant in his/her particular circumstances as described in Chapter II, shall take place in cases where a competent authority has established, on the basis of the facts, that the applicant for asylum is seeking to enter or has entered illegally into its territory from a safe third country according to paragraph 2.

2. A third country can only be considered as a safe third country for the purposes of paragraph 1 where:

(a) it has ratified and observes the provisions of the Geneva Convention without any geographical limitations;

(b) it has in place an asylum procedure prescribed by law;

(c) it has ratified the European Convention for the Protection of Human

Rights and Fundamental Freedoms and observes its provisions, including the standards relating to effective remedies; and

(d) it has been so designated by the Council in accordance with paragraph 3.

3. The Council shall, acting by qualified majority on a proposal from the Commission and after consultation of the European Parliament, adopt or amend a common list of third countries that shall be regarded as safe third countries for the purposes of paragraph 1.

4. The Member States concerned shall lay down in national law the modalities for implementing the provisions of paragraph 1 and the consequences of decisions pursuant to those provisions in accordance with the principle of non-refoulement under the Geneva Convention, including providing for exceptions from the application of this Article for humanitarian or political reasons or for reasons of public international law.

5. When implementing a decision solely based on this Article, the Member States concerned shall:

(a) inform the applicant accordingly; and

(b) provide him/her with a document informing the authorities of the third country, in the language of that country, that the application has not been examined in substance.

6. Where the safe third country does not re-admit the applicant for asylum, Member States shall ensure that access to a procedure is given in accordance with the basic principles and guarantees described in Chapter II.

7. Member States which have designated third countries as safe countries in accordance with national legislation in force on 1 December 2005 and on the basis of the criteria in paragraph 2(a), (b) and (c), may apply paragraph 1 to these third countries until the Council has adopted the common list pursuant to paragraph 3.

Chapter IV

Procedures for the Withdrawal of Refugee Status

Article 37

Withdrawal of refugee status

Member States shall ensure that an examination to withdraw the refugee status of a particular person may commence when new elements or findings arise indicating that there are reasons to reconsider the validity of his/her refugee status.

Article 38

Procedural rules

1. Member States shall ensure that, where the competent authority is considering withdrawing the refugee status of a third country national or stateless person in accordance with Article 14 of Directive 2004/83/EC, the person concerned shall enjoy the following guarantees:
   (a) to be informed in writing that the competent authority is reconsidering his or her qualification for refugee status and the reasons for such a reconsideration; and
   (b) to be given the opportunity to submit, in a personal interview in accordance with Article 10(1)(b) and Articles 12, 13 and 14 or in a written statement, reasons as to why his/her refugee status should not be withdrawn.

   In addition, Member States shall ensure that within the framework of such a procedure:
   (c) the competent authority is able to obtain precise and up-to-date information from various sources, such as, where appropriate, from the UNHCR, as to the general situation prevailing in the countries of origin of the persons concerned; and
   (d) where information on an individual case is collected for the purposes of reconsidering the refugee status, it is not obtained from the actor(s) of persecution in a manner that would result in such actor(s) being directly informed of the fact that the person concerned is a refugee whose status is under reconsideration, nor jeopardise the physical integrity of the person and his/her dependants, or the liberty and security of his/her family members still living in the country of origin.
2. Member States shall ensure that the decision of the competent authority to withdraw the refugee status is given in writing. The reasons in fact and in law shall be stated in the decision and information on how to challenge the decision shall be given in writing.
3. Once the competent authority has taken the decision to withdraw the refugee status, Article 15, paragraph 2, Article 16, paragraph 1 and Article 21 are equally applicable.
4. By derogation to paragraphs 1, 2 and 3 of this Article, Member States may decide that the refugee status shall lapse by law in case of cessation in accordance with Article 11(1)(a) to (d) of Directive 2004/83/EC or if the refugee has unequivocally renounced his/her recognition as a refugee.

Chapter V
Appeals Procedures

Article 39

The right to an effective remedy

1. Member States shall ensure that applicants for asylum have the right to an effective remedy before a court or tribunal, against the following:
   (a) a decision taken on their application for asylum, including a decision:
      (i) to consider an application inadmissible pursuant to Article 25(2),
      (ii) taken at the border or in the transit zones of a Member State as described in Article 35(1),
      (iii) not to conduct an examination pursuant to Article 36;
   (b) a refusal to re-open the examination of an application after its discontinuation pursuant to Articles 19 and 20;
   (c) a decision not to further examine the subsequent application pursuant to Articles 32 and 34;
   (d) a decision refusing entry within the framework of the procedures provided for under Article 35(2);
   (e) a decision to withdraw of refugee status pursuant to Article 38.
2. Member States shall provide for time-limits and other necessary rules for the applicant to exercise his/her right to an effective remedy pursuant to paragraph 1.
3. Member States shall, where appropriate, provide for rules in accordance with their international obligations dealing with:
   (a) the question of whether the remedy pursuant to paragraph 1 shall have the effect of allowing applicants to remain in the Member State concerned pending its outcome;
   (b) the possibility of legal remedy or protective measures where the remedy pursuant to paragraph 1 does not have the effect of allowing applicants to remain in the Member State concerned pending its outcome. Member States may also provide for an ex officio remedy; and
   (c) the grounds for challenging a decision under Article 25(2)(c) in accordance with the methodology applied under Article 27(2)(b) and (c).
4. Member States may lay down time-limits for the court or tribunal pursuant to paragraph 1 to examine the decision of the determining authority.
5. Where an applicant has been granted a status which offers the same rights and benefits under national and Community law as the refugee status by virtue of Directive 2004/83/EC, the applicant may be considered as having an effective remedy where a court or tribunal decides that the remedy pursuant to

paragraph 1 is inadmissible or unlikely to succeed on the basis of insufficient interest on the part of the applicant in maintaining the proceedings.

6. Member States may also lay down in national legislation the conditions under which it can be assumed that an applicant has implicitly withdrawn or abandoned his/her remedy pursuant to paragraph 1, together with the rules on the procedure to be followed.

Chapter VI
General and Final Provisions

Article 40

Challenge by public authorities

This Directive does not affect the possibility for public authorities of challenging the administrative and/or judicial decisions as provided for in national legislation.

Article 41

Confidentiality

Member States shall ensure that authorities implementing this Directive are bound by the confidentiality principle as defined in national law, in relation to any information they obtain in the course of their work.

Article 42

Report

No later than 1 December 2009, the Commission shall report to the European Parliament and the Council on the application of this Directive in the Member States and shall propose any amendments that are necessary. Member States shall send the Commission all the information that is appropriate for drawing up this report. After presenting the report, the Commission shall report to the European Parliament and the Council on the application of this Directive in the Member States at least every two years.

Article 43

Transposition

Member States shall bring into force the laws, regulations and administrative provisions necessary to comply with this Directive by 1 December 2007. Concerning Article 15, Member States shall bring into force the laws, regulations and administrative provisions necessary to comply with this Directive by 1 December 2008. They shall forthwith inform the Commission thereof.

When Member States adopt those provisions, they shall contain a reference to this Directive or shall be accompanied by such a reference on the occasion of their official publication. The methods of making such reference shall be laid down by Member States.

Member States shall communicate to the Commission the text of the provisions of national law which they adopt in the field covered by this Directive.

Article 44

Transition

Member States shall apply the laws, regulations and administrative provisions set out in Article 43 to applications for asylum lodged after 1 December 2007 and to procedures for the withdrawal of refugee status started after 1 December 2007.

Article 45

Entry into force

This Directive shall enter into force on the 20th day following its publication in the *Official Journal of the European Union.*

Article 46

Addressees

This Directive is addressed to the Member States in conformity with the Treaty establishing the European Community.

Done at Brussels, 1 December 2005.

For the Council
The President
Ashton of UPHOLLAND

Annex I

Definition of 'determining authority'

When implementing the provision of this Directive, Ireland may, insofar as the provisions of section 17(1) of the *Refugee Act 1996* (as amended) continue to apply, consider that:

— 'determining authority' provided for in Article 2(e) of this Directive shall, insofar as the examination of whether an applicant should or, as the case may be, should not be declared to be a refugee is concerned, mean the *Office of the Refugee Applications Commissioner*; and

— 'decisions at first instance' provided for in Article 2(e) of this Directive shall include recommendations of the *Refugee Applications Commissioner* as to whether an applicant should or, as the case may be, should not be declared to be a refugee.

Ireland will notify the Commission of any amendments to the provisions of section 17(1) of the *Refugee Act* 1996 (as amended).

Annex II

Designation of safe countries of origin for the purposes of Articles 29 and 30(1)

A country is considered as a safe country of origin where, on the basis of the legal situation, the application of the law within a democratic system and the general political circumstances, it can be shown that there is generally and consistently no persecution as defined in Article 9 of Directive 2004/83/EC, no torture or inhuman or degrading treatment or punishment and no threat by reason of indiscriminate violence in situations of international or internal armed conflict.

In making this assessment, account shall be taken, *inter alia*, of the extent to which protection is provided against persecution or mistreatment by:

(a) the relevant laws and regulations of the country and the manner in which they are applied;
(b) observance of the rights and freedoms laid down in the European Convention for the Protection of Human Rights and Fundamental Freedoms and/or the International Covenant for Civil and Political Rights and/or the Convention against Torture, in particular the rights from which derogation cannot be made under Article 15(2) of the said European Convention;
(c) respect of the non-refoulement principle according to the Geneva Convention;
(d) provision for a system of effective remedies against violations of these rights and freedoms.

Annex III

Definition of 'applicant' or 'applicant for asylum'

When implementing the provisions of this Directive Spain may, insofar as the provisions of '*Ley 30/1992 de Régimen jurídico de las Administraciones Públicas y del Procedimiento Administrativo Común*' of 26 November 1992 and '*Ley 29/1998 reguladora de la Jurisdicción Contencioso-Administrativa*' of 13 July 1998 continue to apply, consider that, for the purposes of Chapter V, the definition of 'applicant' or 'applicant for asylum' in Article 2(c) of this Directive shall include '*recurrente*' as established in the abovementioned Acts.

A '*recurrente*' shall be entitled to the same guarantees as an 'applicant' or an 'applicant for asylum' as set out in this Directive for the purposes of exercising his/her right to an effective remedy in Chapter V.

Spain will notify the Commission of any relevant amendments to the abovementioned Act.

INTERNATIONAL MATERIALS

UNHCR Handbook on Procedures and Criteria for Determining Refugee Status

under the 1951 Convention and the 1967 Protocol relating to the Status of Refugees

Office of the United Nations High Commissioner for Refugees
Reedited Geneva, January 1992.

TABLE OF CONTENTS

PART TWO

ANNEXES

Foreword

I) Refugee status, on the universal level, is governed by the 1951 Convention and the 1967 Protocol relating to the Status of Refugees. These two international legal instruments have been adopted within the framework of the United Nations. At the time of republishing this Handbook 110 states have become parties to the Convention or to the Protocol or to both instruments.

II) These two international legal instruments are applicable to persons who are refugees as therein defined. The assessment as to who is a refugee, i.e. the determination of refugee status under the 1951 Convention and the 1967 Protocol, is incumbent upon the Contracting State in whose territory the refugee applies for recognition of refugee status.

III) Both the 1951 Convention and the 1967 Protocol provide for co-operation between the Contracting States and the Office of the United Nations High Commissioner for Refugees. This co-operation extends to the determination of refugee status, according to arrangements made in various Contracting States.

IV) The Executive Committee of the High Commissioner's Programme at its twenty-eighth session requested the Office of the High Commissioner 'to consider the possibility of issuing—for the guidance of Governments—a handbook relating to procedures and criteria for determining refugee status'. The first edition of the Handbook was issued by my Division in September 1979 in response to this request by the Executive Committee. Since then the Handbook has been regularly reprinted to meet the increasing demands of government officials, academics, and lawyers concerned with refugee problems. The present edition updates information concerning accessions to the international refugee instruments including details of declarations on the geographical applicability of the 1951 Convention and 1967 Protocol.

V) The segment of this Handbook on the criteria for determining refugee status breaks down and explains the various components of the definition of refugee set out in the 1951 Convention and the 1967 Protocol. The explanations are based on the knowledge accumulated by the High Commissioner's Office over some 25 years, since the entry into force of the 1951 Convention on 21 April 1954. The practice of States is taken into account as are exchanges of views between the Office and the competent authorities of Contracting States, and the literature devoted to the subject over the last quarter of a century. As the Handbook has been conceived as a practical guide and not as a treatise on refugee law, references to literature etc. have purposely been omitted.

VI) With respect to procedures for the determination of refugee status, the writers of the Handbook have been guided chiefly by the principles defined in this respect by the Executive Committee itself. Use has naturally also been made of the knowledge available concerning the practice of States.

VII) The Handbook is meant for the guidance of government officials concerned with the determination of refugee status in the various Contracting States. It is hoped that it will also be of interest and useful to all those concerned with refugee problems.

Michel Moussalli

Director of International Protection
Office of the United Nations
High Commissioner for Refugees

Introduction

International Instruments Defining the term 'Refugee'

A. Early Instruments (1921–1946)

1. Early in the twentieth century, the refugee problem became the concern of the international community, which, for humanitarian reasons, began to assume responsibility for protecting and assisting refugees.

2. The pattern of international action on behalf of refugees was established by the League of Nations and led to the adoption of a number of international agreements for their benefit. These instruments are referred to in Article 1A(1) of the 1951 Convention relating to the Status of Refugees (see paragraph 32 below).

3. The definitions in these instruments relate each category of refugees to their national origin, to the territory that they left and to the lack of diplomatic protection by their former home country. With this type of definition 'by categories' interpretation was simple and caused no great difficulty in ascertaining who was a refugee.

4. Although few persons covered by the terms of the early instruments are likely to request a formal determination of refugee status at the present time, such cases could occasionally arise. They are dealt with below in Chapter II, A. Persons who meet the definitions of international instruments prior to the 1951 Convention are usually referred to as 'statutory refugees'.

B. 1951 Convention relating to the Status of Refugees

5. Soon after the Second World War, as the refugee problem had not been solved, the need was felt for a new international instrument to define the legal status of refugees. Instead of ad hoc agreements adopted in relation to specific refugee situations, there was a call for an instrument containing a general definition of who was to be considered a refugee. The Convention relating to the Status of Refugees was adopted by a Conference of Plenipotentiaries of the United Nations on 28 July 1951, and entered into force on 21 April 1954. In the following paragraphs it is

referred to as 'the 1951 Convention'. (The text of the 1951 Convention will be found in Annex II.)

C. 1967 Protocol relating to the Status of Refugees

6. According to the general definition contained in the 1951 Convention, a refugee is a person who:

> 'As a result of events occurring before 1 January 1951 and owing to well-founded fear of being persecuted . . . is outside his country of nationality . . .'

7. The 1951 dateline originated in the wish of Governments, at the time the Convention was adopted, to limit their obligations to refugee situations that were known to exist at that time, or to those which might subsequently arise from events that had already occurred. [The 1951 Convention also provides for the possibility of introducing a geographic limitation (see paragraphs 108 to 110 below).]

8. With the passage of time and the emergence of new refugee situations the need was increasingly felt to make the provisions of the 1951 Convention applicable to such new refugees. As a result, a Protocol relating to the Status of Refugees was prepared. After consideration by the General Assembly of the United Nations, it was opened for accession on 31 January 1967 and entered into force on 4 October 1967.

9. By accession to the 1967 Protocol, States undertake to apply the substantive provisions of the 1951 Convention to refugees as defined in the Convention, but without the 1951 dateline. Although related to the Convention in this way, the Protocol is an independent instrument, accession to which is not limited to States parties to the Convention.

10. In the following paragraphs, the 1967 Protocol relating to the Status of Refugees is referred to as 'the 1967 Protocol'. (The text of the Protocol will be found in Annex III.)

11. At the time of writing, 78 States are parties to the 1951 Convention or to the 1967 Protocol or to both instruments. (A list of the States parties will be found in Annex IV.)

D. Main provisions of the 1951 Convention and the 1967 Protocol

12. The 1951 Convention and the 1967 Protocol contain three types of provisions:

(i) Provisions giving the basic definition of who is (and who is not) a refugee and who, having been a refugee, has ceased to be one. The discussion and interpretation of these provisions constitute the main body of the present Handbook, intended for the guidance of those whose task it is to determine refugee status.

(ii) Provisions that define the legal status of refugees and their rights and duties in their country of refuge. Although these provisions have no influence on the process of determination of refugee status, the authority entrusted with this process should be aware of them, for its decision may indeed have far-reaching effects for the individual or family concerned.

(iii) Other provisions dealing with the implementation of the instruments from the administrative and diplomatic standpoint. Article 35 of the 1951 Convention and Article II of the 1967 Protocol contain an undertaking by Contracting States to co-operate with the Office of the United Nations High Commissioner for Refugees in the exercise of its functions and, in particular, to facilitate its duty of supervising the application of the provisions of these instruments.

E. Statute of the Office of the United Nations High Commissioner for Refugees

13. The instruments described above under A-C define the persons who are to be considered refugees and require the parties to accord a certain status to refugees in their respective territories.

14. Pursuant to a decision of the General Assembly, the Office of the United Nations High Commissioner for Refugees ('UNHCR') was established as of 1 January 1951. The Statute of the Office is annexed to Resolution 428(V), adopted by the General Assembly on 14 December 1950. According to the Statutes the High Commissioner is called upon—*inter alia*—to provide international protection, under the auspices of the United Nations, to refugees falling within the competence of his Office.

15. The Statute contains definitions of those persons to whom the High Commissioner's competence extends, which are very close to, though not identical with, the definition contained in the 1951 Convention. By virtue of these definitions the High Commissioner is competent for refugees irrespective of any dateline [see paragraphs 35 and 36 below] or geographic limitation. [See paragraphs 108 to 110 below.]

16. Thus, a person who meets the criteria of the UNHCR Statute qualifies for the protection of the United Nations provided by the High Commissioner, regardless of whether or not he is in a country that is a party to the 1951 Convention or the 1967 Protocol or whether or not he has been recognized by his host country as a refugee under either of these instruments. Such refugees, being within the High Commissioner's mandate, are usually referred to as 'mandate refugees'.

17. From the foregoing, it will be seen that a person can simultaneously be both a mandate refugee *and* a refugee under the 1951 Convention or the 1967 Protocol. He may, however, be in a country that is not bound by either of these instruments, or he may be excluded from recognition as a 'Convention refugee' by the application of the dateline or the geographic limitation. In such cases he would still qualify for protection by the High Commissioner under the terms of the Statute.

18. The above mentioned Resolution 428(V) and the Statute of the High Commissioner's Office call for co-operation between Governments and the High Commissioner's Office in dealing with refugee problems. The High Commissioner is designated as the authority charged with providing international protection to refugees, and is required inter alia to promote the conclusion and ratification of international conventions for the protection of refugees, and to supervise their application.

19. Such co-operation, combined with his supervisory function, forms the basis for the High Commissioner's fundamental interest in the process of determining refugee status under the 1951 Convention and the 1967 Protocol. The part played by the High Commissioner is reflected, to varying degrees, in the procedures for the determination of refugee status established by a number of Governments.

F. Regional instruments relating to refugees

20. In addition to the 1951 Convention and the 1967 Protocol, and the Statute of the Office of the United Nations High Commissioner for Refugees, there are a number of regional agreements, conventions and other instruments relating to refugees, particularly in Africa, the Americas and Europe. These regional instruments deal with such matters as the granting of asylum, travel documents and travel facilities, etc. Some also contain a definition of the term 'refugee', or of persons entitled to asylum.

21. In Latin America, the problem of diplomatic and territorial asylum is dealt with in a number of regional instruments including the Treaty on International Penal Law, (Montevideo, 1889); the Agreement on Extradition, (Caracas, 1911); the Convention on Asylum, (Havana, 1928); the Convention on Political Asylum, (Montevideo, 1933); the Convention on Diplomatic Asylum, (Caracas, 1954); and the Convention on Territorial Asylum, (Caracas, 1954).

22. A more recent regional instrument is the Convention Governing the Specific Aspects of Refugee Problems in Africa, adopted by the Assembly of Heads of State and Government of the Organization of African Unity on 10 September 1969. This Convention contains a definition of the term 'refugee', consisting of two parts: the first part is identical with the definition in the 1967 Protocol (i.e. the definition in the 1951 Convention without the dateline or geographic limitation). The second part applies the term 'refugee' to:

> 'every person who, owing to external aggression, occupation, foreign domination or events seriously disturbing public order in either part or the whole of his country of

origin or nationality, is compelled to leave his place of habitual residence in order to seek refuge in another place outside his country of origin or nationality'.

23. The present Handbook deals only with the determination of refugee status under the two international instruments of universal scope: the 1951 Convention and the 1967 Protocol.

G. Asylum and the treatment of refugees

24. The Handbook does not deal with questions closely related to the determination of refugee status e.g. the granting of asylum to refugees or the legal treatment of refugees after they have been recognized as such.

25. Although there are references to asylum in the Final Act of the Conference of Plenipotentiaries as well as in the Preamble to the Convention, the granting of asylum is not dealt with in the 1951 Convention or the 1967 Protocol. The High Commissioner has always pleaded for a generous asylum policy in the spirit of the Universal Declaration of Human Rights and the Declaration on Territorial Asylum, adopted by the General Assembly of the United Nations on 10 December 1948 and on 14 December 1967 respectively.

26. With respect to the treatment within the territory of States, this is regulated as regards refugees by the main provisions of the 1951 Convention and 1967 Protocol (see paragraph 12(ii) above). Furthermore, attention should be drawn to Recommendation E contained in the Final Act of the Conference of Plenipotentiaries which adopted the 1951 Convention:

> 'The Conference
> Expresses the hope that the Convention relating to the Status of Refugees will have value as an example exceeding its contractual scope and that all nations will be guided by it in granting so far as possible to persons in their territory as refugees and who would not be covered by the terms of the Convention, the treatment for which it provides.'

27. This recommendation enables States to solve such problems as may arise with regard to persons who are not regarded as fully satisfying the criteria of the definition of the term 'refugee'.

Part One

Criteria for the Determination of Refugee Status

Chapter I

General Principles

28. A person is a refugee within the meaning of the 1951 Convention as soon as he fulfils the criteria contained in the definition. This would necessarily occur prior to the time at which his refugee status is formally determined. Recognition of his refugee status does not therefore make him a refugee but declares him to be one. He does not become a refugee because of recognition, but is recognized because he is a refugee.

29. Determination of refugee status is a process which takes place in two stages. Firstly, it is necessary to ascertain the relevant facts of the case. Secondly, the definitions in the 1951 Convention and the 1967 Protocol have to be applied to the facts thus ascertaine(d)

30. The provisions of the 1951 Convention defining who is a refugee consist of three parts, which have been termed respectively 'inclusion', 'cessation' and 'exclusion' clauses.

31. The inclusion clauses define the criteria that a person must satisfy in order to be a refugee. They from the positive basis upon which the determination of refugee status is made. The so-called cessation and exclusion clauses have a negative significance; the former indicate the conditions under which a refugee ceases to be a refugee and the latter enumerate the circumstances in which a person is excluded from the application of the 1951 Convention although meeting the positive criteria of the inclusion clauses.

Chapter II
Inclusion Clauses

A. Definitions

(1) Statutory Refugees

32. Article 1A(1) of the 1951 Convention deals with statutory refugees, i.e. persons considered to be refugees under the provisions of international instruments preceding the Convention. This provision states that:

> 'For the purposes of the present Convention, the term 'refugee' shall apply to any person who:
>
> (1) Has been considered a refugee under the Arrangements of 12 May 1926 and 30 June 1928 or under the Conventions of 28 October 1933 and 10 February 1938, the Protocol of 14 September 1939 or the Constitution of the International Refugee Organization;
>
> Decisions of non-eligibility taken by the International Refugee Organization during the period of its activities shall not prevent the status of refugees being accorded to persons who fulfil the conditions of paragraph 2 of this section.'

33. The above enumeration is given in order to provide a link with the past and to ensure the continuity of international protection of refugees who became the concern of the international community at various earlier periods. As already indicated (para. 4 above), these instruments have by now lost much of their significance, and a discussion of them here would be of little practical value. However, a person who has been considered a refugee under the terms of any of these instruments is automatically a refugee under the 1951 Convention. Thus, a holder of a so-called 'Nansen Passport' ['Nansen Passport': a certificate of identity for use as a travel document, issued to refugees under the provisions of pre-war instruments] or a 'Certificate of Eligibility' issued by the International Refugee Organization must be considered a refugee under the 1951 Convention unless one of the cessation clauses has become applicable to his case or he is excluded from the application of the Convention by one of the exclusion clauses. This also applies to a surviving child of a statutory refugee.

(2) General definition in the 1951 Convention

34. According to article 1A(2) of the 1951 Convention the term 'refugee' shall apply to any person who:

> 'As a result of events occurring before 1 January 1951 and owing to well-founded fear of being persecuted for reasons of race, religion, nationality, membership of a particular social group or political opinion, is outside the country of his nationality and is unable or, owing to such fear, is unwilling to avail himself of the protection of that country; or who, not having a nationality and being outside the country of his former habitual residence as a result of such events, is unable or, owing to such fear, is unwilling to return to it.'

This general definition is discussed in detail below.

B. Interpretation of terms

(1) 'Events occurring before 1 January 1951'

35. The origin of this 1951 dateline is explained in paragraph 7 of the Introduction. As a result of the 1967 Protocol this dateline has lost much of its practical significance. An interpretation of the word 'events' is therefore of interest only in the small number of States parties to the 1951 Convention that are not also party to the 1967 Protocol. [See Annex IV.]

36. The word 'events' is not defined in the 1951 Convention, but was understood to mean 'happenings of major importance involving territorial or profound political changes as well as systematic programmes of persecution which are after-effects of earlier changes'. [UN Document E/1618 page 39.] The dateline refers to 'events' as a result of which, and not to the date on which, a person becomes a refugee, not does it apply to the date on which he left his country. A refugee may have left his country before or after the datelines, provided that his fear of persecution is due to 'events' that occurred before the dateline or to after-effects occurring at a later date as a result of such events. [*loc. cit.*]

(2) *'Well founded fear of being persecuted'*

(a) General analysis

37. The phrase 'well-founded fear of being persecuted' is the key phrase of the definition. It reflects the view of its authors as to the main elements of refugee character. It replaces the earlier method of defining refugees by categories (i.e. persons of a certain origin not enjoying the protection of their country) by the general concept of 'fear' for a relevant motive. Since fear is subjective, the definition involves a subjective element in the person applying for recognition as a refugee. Determination of refugee status will therefore primarily require an evaluation of the applicant's statements rather than a judgement on the situation prevailing in this country of origin.

38. To the element of fear—a state of mind and a subjective condition—is added the qualification 'well-founded'. This implies that it is not only the frame of mind of the person concerned that determines his refugee status, but that this frame of mind must be supported by an objective situation. The term 'well-founded fear' therefore contains a subjective and an objective element, and in determining whether well-founded fear exists, both elements must be taken into consideration.

39. It may be assumed that, unless he seeks adventure or just wishes to see the world, a person would not normally abandon his home and country without some compelling reason. There may be many reasons that are compelling and understandable, but only one motive has been singled out to denote a refugee. The expression 'owing to well-founded fear of being persecuted'—for the reasons stated—by indicating a specific motive automatically makes all other reasons of escape irrelevant to the definition. It rules out such persons as victims of famine or natural disaster, unless they also have well-founded fear of persecution for one of the reasons stated. Such other motives may not, however, be altogether irrelevant to the process of determining refugee status, since all the circumstances need to be taken into account for a proper understanding of the applicant's case.

40. An evaluation of the subjective element is inseparable from an assessment of the personality of the applicant, since psychological reactions of different individuals may not be the same in identical conditions. One person may have strong political or religious convictions, the disregard of which would make his life intolerable; another may have no such strong convictions. One person may make an impulsive decision to escape; another may carefully plan his departure.

41. Due to the importance that the definition attaches to the subjective element, an assessment of credibility is indispensable where the case is not sufficiently clear from the facts on record. It will be necessary to take into account the personal and family background of the applicant, his membership of a particular racial, religious, national, social or political group, his own interpretation of his situation, and his personal experiences—in other words, everything that may serve to indicate that the predominant motive for his application is fear. Fear must be reasonable. Exaggerated fear, however, may be well-founded if, in all the circumstances of the case, such a state of mind can be regarded as justified.

42. As regards the objective element, it is necessary to evaluate the statements made by the applicant. The competent authorities that are called upon to determine refugee status are not required to pass judgement on conditions in the applicant's country of origin. The applicant's statements cannot, however, be considered in the abstract, and must be viewed in the context of the relevant background situation. A knowledge of conditions in the applicant's country of origin—while not a primary objective—is an important element in assessing the applicant's credibility. In general, the applicant's fear should be considered well-founded if he can establish, to a reasonable degree, that his continued stay in his country of origin has become intolerable to him for the reasons stated in the definition, or would for the same reasons be intolerable if he returned there.

43. These considerations need not necessarily be based on the applicant's own personal experience. What, for example, happened to his friends and relatives and other members of the same racial or social group may well show that his fear that sooner or later he also will become a victim of persecution is well-founded. The laws of the country of origin, and particularly the manner in which they are applied, will be relevant. The situation of each person must, however, be assessed on its own merits. In the case of a well-known personality, the possibility of persecution may be greater than in the case of a person in obscurity. All these factors, e.g. a person's character, his background, his influence, his wealth or his outspokenness, may lead to the conclusion that his fear of persecution is 'well-founded'.

44. While refugee status must normally be determined on an individual basis, situations have also arisen in which entire groups have been displaced under circumstances indicating that members of the group could be considered individually as refugees. In such situations the need to provide assistance is often extremely urgent and it may not be possible for purely practical reasons to carry out an individual determination of refugee status for each member of the group. Recourse has therefore been had to so-called 'group determination' of refugee status, whereby each member of the group is regarded *prima facie* (i.e. in the absence of evidence to the contrary) as a refugee.

45. Apart from the situations of the type referred to in the preceding paragraph, an applicant for refugee status must normally show good reason why he individually fears persecution. It may be assumed that a person has well-founded fear of being persecuted if he has already been the victim of persecution for one of the reasons enumerated in the 1951 Convention. However, the word 'fear' refers not only to persons who have actually been persecuted, but also to those who wish to avoid a situation entailing the risk of persecution.

46. The expressions 'fear of persecution' or even 'persecution' are usually foreign to a refugee's normal vocabulary. A refugee will indeed only rarely invoke 'fear of

persecution' in these terms, though it will often be implicit in his story. Again, while a refugee may have very definite opinions for which he has had to suffer, he may not, for psychological reasons, be able to describe his experiences and situation in political terms.

47. A typical test of the well-foundedness of fear will arise when an applicant is in possession of a valid national passport. It has sometimes been claimed that possession of a passport signifies that the issuing authorities do not intend to persecute the holder, for otherwise they would not have issued a passport to him. Though this may be true in some cases, many persons have used a legal exit from their country as the only means of escape without ever having revealed their political opinions, a knowledge of which might place them in a dangerous situation vis-à-vis the authorities.

48. Possession of a passport cannot therefore always be considered as evidence of loyalty on the part of the holder, or as an indication of the absence of fear. A passport may even be issued to a person who is undesired in his country of origin, with the sole purpose of securing his departure, and there may also be cases where a passport has been obtained surreptitiously. In conclusion, therefore, the mere possession of a valid national passport is no bar to refugee status.

49. If, on the other hand, an applicant, without good reason, insists on retaining a valid passport of a country of whose protection he is allegedly unwilling to avail himself, this may cast doubt on the validity of his claim to have 'well-founded fear'. Once recognized, a refugee should not normally retain his national passport.

50. There may, however, be exceptional situations in which a person fulfilling the criteria of refugee status may retain his national passport—or be issued with a new one by the authorities of his country of origin under special arrangements. Particularly where such arrangements do not imply that the holder of the national passport is free to return to his country without prior permission, they may not be incompatible with refugee status.

(b) Persecution

51. There is no universally accepted definition of 'persecution', and various attempts to formulate such a definition have met with little success. From Article 33 of the 1951 Convention, it may be inferred that a threat to life or freedom on account of race, religion, nationality, political opinion or membership of a particular social group is always persecution. Other serious violations of human rights—for the same reasons—would also constitute persecution.

52. Whether other prejudicial actions or threats would amount to persecution will depend on the circumstances of each case, including the subjective element to which reference has been made in the preceding paragraphs. The subjective

character of fear of persecution requires an evaluation of the opinions and feelings of the person concerned. It is also in the light of such opinions and feelings that any actual or anticipated measures against him must necessarily be viewed. Due to variations in the psychological make-up of individuals and in the circumstances of each case, interpretations of what amounts to persecution are bound to vary.

53. In addition, an applicant may have been subjected to various measures not in themselves amounting to persecution (e.g. discrimination in different forms), in some cases combined with other adverse factors (e.g. general atmosphere of insecurity in the country of origin). In such situations, the various elements involved may, if taken together, produce an effect on the mind of the applicant that can reasonably justify a claim to well-founded fear of persecution on 'cumulative grounds'. Needless to say, it is not possible to lay down a general rule as to what cumulative reasons can give rise to a valid claim to refugee status. This will necessarily depend on all the circumstances, including the particular geographical, historical and ethnological context.

(c) Discrimination

54. Differences in the treatment of various groups do indeed exist to a greater or lesser extent in many societies. Persons who receive less favourable treatment as a result of such differences are not necessarily victims of persecution. It is only in certain circumstances that discrimination will amount to persecution. This would be so if measures of discrimination lead to consequences of a substantially prejudicial nature for the person concerned, e.g. serious restrictions on his right to earn his livelihood, his right to practise his religion, or his access to normally available educational facilities.

55. Where measures of discrimination are, in themselves, not of a serious character, they may nevertheless give rise to a reasonable fear of persecution if they produce, in the mind of the person concerned, a feeling of apprehension and insecurity as regards his future existence. Whether or not such measures of discrimination in themselves amount to persecution must be determined in the light of all the circumstances. A claim to fear of persecution will of course be stronger where a person has been the victim of a number of discriminatory measures of this type and where there is thus a cumulative element involved. [See also paragraph 53.]

(d) Punishment

56. Persecution must be distinguished from punishment for a common law offence. Persons fleeing from prosecution or punishment for such an offence are not normally refugees. It should be recalled that a refugee is a victim—or potential victim—of injustice, not a fugitive from justice.

57. The above distinction may, however, occasionally be obscured. In the first place, a person guilty of a common law offence may be liable to excessive punishment, which may amount to persecution within the meaning of the definition. Moreover, penal prosecution for a reason mentioned in the definition (for example, in respect of 'illegal' religious instruction given to a child) may in itself amount to persecution.

58. Secondly, there may be cases in which a person, besides fearing prosecution or punishment for a common law crime, may also have 'well-founded fear of persecution'. In such cases the person concerned is a refugee. It may, however, be necessary to consider whether the crime in question is not of such a serious character as to bring the applicant within the scope of one of the exclusion clauses. [See paragraphs 144 to 156.]

59. In order to determine whether prosecution amounts to persecution, it will also be necessary to refer to the laws of the country concerned, for it is possible for a law not to be in conformity with accepted human rights standards. More often, however, it may not be the law but its application that is discriminatory. Prosecution for an offence against 'public order', e.g. for distribution of pamphlets, could for example be a vehicle for the persecution of the individual on the grounds of the political content of the publication.

60. In such cases, due to the obvious difficulty involved in evaluating the laws of another country, national authorities may frequently have to take decisions by using their own national legislation as a yardstick. Moreover, recourse may usefully be had to the principles set out in the various international instruments relating to human rights, in particular the International Covenants on Human Rights, which contain binding commitments for the States parties and are instruments to which many States parties to the 1951 Convention have acceded.

(e) Consequences of unlawful departure or unauthorized stay outside country of origin

61. The legislation of certain States imposes severe penalties on nationals who depart from the country in an unlawful manner or remain abroad without authorization. Where there is reason to believe that a person, due to his illegal departure or unauthorized stay abroad is liable to such severe penalties his recognition as a refugee will be justified if it can be shown that his motives for leaving or remaining outside the country are related to the reasons enumerated in Article 1A(2) of the 1951 Convention (see paragraph 66 below).

(f) Economic migrants distinguished from refugees

62. A migrant is a person who, for reasons other than those contained in the definition, voluntarily leaves his country in order to take up residence elsewhere. He

may be moved by the desire for change or adventure, or by family or other reasons of a personal nature. If he is moved exclusively by economic considerations, he is an economic migrant and not a refugee.

63. The distinction between an economic migrant and a refugee is, however, sometimes blurred in the same way as the distinction between economic and political measures in an applicant's country of origin is not always clear. Behind economic measures affecting a person's livelihood there may be racial, religious or political aims or intentions directed against a particular group. Where economic measures destroy the economic existence of a particular section of the population (e.g. withdrawal of trading rights from, or discriminatory or excessive taxation of, a specific ethnic or religious group), the victims may according to the circumstances become refugees on leaving the country.

64. Whether the same would apply to victims of general economic measures (i.e. those that are applied to the whole population without discrimination) would depend on the circumstances of the case. Objections to general economic measures are not by themselves good reasons for claiming refugee status. On the other hand, what appears at first sight to be primarily an economic motive for departure may in reality also involve a political element, and it may be the political opinions of the individual that expose him to serious consequences, rather than his objections to the economic measures themselves.

(g) Agents of persecution

65. Persecution is normally related to action by the authorities of a country. It may also emanate from sections of the population that do not respect the standards established by the laws of the country concerned. A case in point may be religious intolerance, amounting to persecution, in a country otherwise secular, but where sizeable fractions of the population do not respect the religious beliefs of their neighbours. Where serious discriminatory or other offensive acts are committed by the local populace, they can be considered as persecution if they are knowingly tolerated by the authorities, or if the authorities refuse, or prove unable, to offer effective protection.

(3) 'for reasons of race, religion, nationality, membership of a particular social group or political opinion'

(a) General analysis

66. In order to be considered a refugee, a person must show well-founded fear of persecution for one of the reasons stated above. It is immaterial whether the persecution arises from any single one of these reasons or from a combination of two or more of them. Often the applicant himself may not be aware of the reasons for the

persecution feared. It is not, however, his duty to analyse his case to such an extent as to identify the reasons in detail.

67. It is for the examiner, when investigating the facts of the case, to ascertain the reason or reasons for the persecution feared and to decide whether the definition in the 1951 Convention is met with in this respect. It is evident that the reasons for persecution under these various headings will frequently overlap. Usually there will be more than one element combined in one person, e.g. a political opponent who belongs to a religious or national group, or both, and the combination of such reasons in his person may be relevant in evaluating his well-founded fear.

(b) Race

68. Race, in the present connexion, has to be understood in its widest sense to include all kinds of ethnic groups that are referred to as 'races' in common usage. Frequently it will also entail membership of a specific social group of common descent forming a minority within a larger population. Discrimination for reasons of race has found world-wide condemnation as one of the most striking violations of human rights. Racial discrimination, therefore, represents an important element in determining the existence of persecution.

69. Discrimination on racial grounds will frequently amount to persecution in the sense of the 1951 Convention. This will be the case if, as a result of racial discrimination, a person's human dignity is affected to such an extent as to be incompatible with the most elementary and inalienable human rights, or where the disregard of racial barriers is subject to serious consequences.

70. The mere fact of belonging to a certain racial group will normally not be enough to substantiate a claim to refugee status. There may, however, be situations where, due to particular circumstances affecting the group, such membership will in itself be sufficient ground to fear persecution.

(c) Religion

71. The Universal Declaration of Human Rights and the Human Rights Covenant proclaim the right to freedom of thought, conscience and religion, which right includes the freedom of a person to change his religion and his freedom to manifest it in public or private, in teaching, practice, worship and observance.

72. Persecution for 'reasons of religion' may assume various forms, e.g. prohibition of membership of a religious community, of worship in private or in public, of religious instruction, or serious measures of discrimination imposed on persons because they practise their religion or belong to a particular religious community.

73. Mere membership of a particular religious community will normally not be enough to substantiate a claim to refugee status. There may, however, be special circumstances where mere membership can be a sufficient ground.

(d) Nationality

74. The term 'nationality' in this context is not to be understood only as 'citizenship'. It refers also to membership of an ethnic or linguistic group and may occasionally overlap with the term 'race'. Persecution for reasons of nationality may consist of adverse attitudes and measures directed against a national (ethnic, linguistic) minority and in certain circumstances the fact of belonging to such a minority may in itself give rise to well-founded fear of persecution.

75. The co-existence within the boundaries of a State of two or more national (ethnic, linguistic) groups may create situations of conflict and also situations of persecution or danger of persecution. It may not always be easy to distinguish between persecution for reasons of nationality and persecution for reasons of political opinion when a conflict between national groups is combined with political movements, particularly where a political movement is identified with a specific 'nationality'.

76. Whereas in most cases persecution for reason of nationality is feared by persons belonging to a national minority, there have been many cases in various continents where a person belonging to a majority group may fear persecution by a dominant minority.

(e) Membership of a particular social group

77. A 'particular social group' normally comprises persons of similar background, habits or social status. A claim to fear of persecution under this heading may frequently overlap with a claim to fear of persecution on other grounds, i.e. race, religion or nationality.

78. Membership of such a particular social group may be at the root of persecution because there is no confidence in the group's loyalty to the Government or because the political outlook, antecedents or economic activity of its members, or the very existence of the social group as such, is held to be an obstacle to the Government's policies.

79. Mere membership of a particular social group will not normally be enough to substantiate a claim to refugee status. There may, however, be special circumstances where mere membership can be a sufficient ground to fear persecution.

(f) Political opinion

80. Holding political opinions different from those of the Government is not in itself a ground for claiming refugee status, and an applicant must show that he has a fear of persecution for holding such opinions. This pre-supposes that the applicant holds opinions not tolerated by the authorities, which are critical of their policies or

methods. It also presupposes that such opinions have come to the notice of the authorities or are attributed by them to the applicant. The political opinions of a teacher or writer may be more manifest than those of a person in a less exposed position. The relative importance or tenacity of the applicant's opinions—in so far as this can be established from all the circumstances of the case—will also be relevant.

81. While the definition speaks of persecution 'for reasons of political opinion' it may not always be possible to establish a causal link between the opinion expressed and the related measures suffered or feared by the applicant. Such measures have only rarely been based expressly on 'opinion'. More frequently, such measures take the form of sanctions for alleged criminal acts against the ruling power. It will, therefore, be necessary to establish the applicant's political opinion, which is at the root of his behaviour, and the fact that it has led or may lead to the persecution that he claims to fear.

82. As indicated above, persecution 'for reasons of political opinion' implies that an applicant holds an opinion that either has been expressed or has come to the attention of the authorities. There may, however, also be situations in which the applicant has not given any expression to his opinions. Due to the strength of his convictions, however, it may be reasonable to assume that his opinions will sooner or later find expression and that the applicant will, as a result, come into conflict with the authorities. Where this can reasonably be assumed, the applicant can be considered to have fear of persecution for reasons of political opinion.

83. An applicant claiming fear of persecution because of political opinion need not show that the authorities of his country of origin knew of his opinions before he left the country. He may have concealed his political opinion and never have suffered any discrimination or persecution. However, the mere fact of refusing to avail himself of the protection of his Government, or a refusal to return, may disclose the applicant's true state of mind and give rise to fear of persecution. In such circumstances the test of well-founded fear would be based on an assessment of the consequences that an applicant having certain political dispositions would have to face if he returned. This applies particularly to the so-called refugee '*sur place*'. [See paragraphs 94 to 96.]

84. Where a person is subject to prosecution or punishment for a political offence, a distinction may have to be drawn according to whether the prosecution is for political *opinion* or for politically-motivated acts. If the prosecution pertains to a punishable act committed out of political motives, and if the anticipated punishment is in conformity with the general law of the country concerned, fear of such prosecution will not in itself make the applicant a refugee.

85. Whether a political offender can also be considered a refugee will depend upon various other factors. Prosecution for an offence may, depending upon the circumstances, be a pretext for punishing the offender for his political opinions or the expression thereof. Again, there may be reason to believe that a political offender

would be exposed to excessive or arbitrary punishment for the alleged offence. Such excessive or arbitrary punishment will amount to persecution.

86. In determining whether a political offender can be considered a refugee, regard should also be had to the following elements: personality of the applicant, his political opinion, the motive behind the act, the nature of the act committed, the nature of the prosecution and its motives; finally, also, the nature of the law on which the prosecution is based. These elements may go to show that the person concerned has a fear of persecution and not merely a fear of prosecution and punishment—within the law—for an act committed by him.

(4) *'is outside the country of his nationality'*

(a) General analysis

87. In this context, 'nationality' refers to 'citizenship'. The phrase 'is outside the country of his nationality' relates to persons who have a nationality, as distinct from stateless persons. In the majority of cases, refugees retain the nationality of their country of origin.

88. It is a general requirement for refugee status that an applicant who has a nationality be outside the country of his nationality. There are no exceptions to this rule. International protection cannot come into play as long as a person is within the territorial jurisdiction of his home country. [In certain countries, particularly in Latin America, there is a custom of 'diplomatic asylum', i.e. granting refuge to political fugitives in foreign embassies. While a person thus sheltered may be considered to be outside his country's *jurisdiction,* he is not outside its territory and cannot therefore be considered under the terms of the 1951 Convention. The former notion of the 'extraterritoriality' of embassies has lately been replaced by the term 'inviolability' used in the 1961 Vienna Convention on Diplomatic Relations.]

89. Where, therefore, an applicant alleges fear of persecution in relation to the country of his nationality, it should be established that he does in fact possess the nationality of that country. There may, however, be uncertainty as to whether a person has a nationality. He may not know himself, or he may wrongly claim to have a particular nationality or to be stateless. Where his nationality cannot be clearly established, his refugee status should be determined in a similar manner to that of a stateless person, i.e. instead of the country of his nationality, the country of his former habitual residence will have to be taken into account. (See paragraphs 101 to 105 below.)

90. As mentioned above, an applicant's well-founded fear of persecution must be in relation to the country of his nationality. As long as he has no fear in relation to the country of his nationality, he can be expected to avail himself of that country's protection. He is not in need of international protection and is therefore not a refugee.

91. The fear of being persecuted need not always extend to the whole territory of the refugee's country of nationality. Thus in ethnic clashes or in cases of grave disturbances involving civil war conditions, persecution of a specific ethnic or national group may occur in only one part of the country.

In such situations, a person will not be excluded from refugee status merely because he could have sought refuge in another part of the same country, if under all the circumstances it would not have been reasonable to expect him to do so.

92. The situation of persons having more than one nationality is dealt with in paragraphs 106 and 107 below.

93. Nationality may be proved by the possession of a national passport. Possession of such a passport creates a *prima facie* presumption that the holder is a national of the country of issue, unless the passport itself states otherwise. A person holding a passport showing him to be a national of the issuing country, but who claims that he does not possess that country's nationality, must substantiate his claim, for example, by showing that the passport is a so-called 'passport of convenience' (an apparently regular national passport that is sometimes issued by a national authority to non-nationals). However, a mere assertion by the holder that the passport was issued to him as a matter of convenience for travel purposes only is not sufficient to rebut the presumption of nationality. In certain cases, it might be possible to obtain information from the authority that issued the passport. If such information cannot be obtained, or cannot be obtained within reasonable time, the examiner will have to decide on the credibility of the applicant's assertion in weighing all other elements of his story.

(b) Refugees '*sur place*'

94. The requirement that a person must be outside his country to be a refugee does not mean that he must necessarily have left that country illegally, or even that he must have left it on account of well-founded fear. He may have decided to ask for recognition of his refugee status after having already been abroad for some time. A person who was not a refugee when he left his country, but who becomes a refugee at a later date, is called a refugee '*sur place*'.

95. A person becomes a refugee '*sur place*' due to circumstances arising in his country of origin during his absence. Diplomats and other officials serving abroad, prisoners of war, students, migrant workers and others have applied for refugee status during their residence abroad and have been recognized as refugees.

96. A person may become a refugee '*sur place*' as a result of his own actions, such as associating with refugees already recognized, or expressing his political views in his country of residence. Whether such actions are sufficient to justify a well-founded fear of persecution must be determined by a careful examination of the circumstances. Regard should be had in particular to whether such actions may have

come to the notice of the authorities of the person's country of origin and how they are likely to be viewed by those authorities.

(5) 'and is unable or, owing to such fear, is unwilling to avail himself of the protection of that country'

97. Unlike the phrase dealt with under (6) below, the present phrase relates to persons who have a nationality. Whether unable or unwilling to avail himself of the protection of his Government, a refugee is always a person who does not enjoy such protection.

98. Being *unable* to avail himself of such protection implies circumstances that are beyond the will of the person concerned. There may, for example, be a state of war, civil war or other grave disturbance, which prevents the country of nationality from extending protection or makes such protection ineffective. Protection by the country of nationality may also have been denied to the applicant. Such denial of protection may confirm or strengthen the applicant's fear of persecution, and may indeed be an element of persecution.

99. What constitutes a refusal of protection must be determined according to the circumstances of the case. If it appears that the applicant has been denied services (e.g., refusal of a national passport or extension of its validity, or denial of admittance to the home territory) normally accorded to his co-nationals, this may constitute a refusal of protection within the definition.

100. The term *unwilling* refers to refugees who refuse to accept the protection of the Government of the country of their nationality. [UN Document E/1618, page 39.] It is qualified by the phrase 'owing to such fear'. Where a person is willing to avail himself of the protection of his home country, such willingness would normally be incompatible with a claim that he is outside that country 'owing to well-founded fear of persecution'. Whenever the protection of the country of nationality is available, and there is no ground based on well-founded fear for refusing it, the person concerned is not in need of international protection and is not a refugee.

(6) 'or who, not having a nationality and being outside the country of his former habitual residence as a result of such events, is unable or, owing to such fear, is unwilling to return to it'

101. This phrase, which relates to stateless refugees, is parallel to the preceding phrase, which concerns refugees who have a nationality. In the case of stateless refugees, the 'country of nationality' is replaced by 'the country of his former habitual residence', and the expression 'unwilling to avail himself of the protection . . .' is replaced by the words 'unwilling to return to it'. In the case of a stateless refugee, the question of 'availment of protection' of the country of his former habitual residence does not, of course, arise. Moreover, once a stateless person has abandoned the country of his former habitual residence for the reasons indicated in the definition, he is usually unable to return.

102. It will be noted that not all stateless persons are refugees. They must be outside the country of their former habitual residence for the reasons indicated in the definition. Where these reasons do not exist, the stateless person is not a refugee.

103. Such reasons must be examined in relation to the country of 'former habitual residence' in regard to which fear is alleged. This was defined by the drafters of the 1951 Convention as 'the country in which he had resided and where he had suffered or fears he would suffer persecution if he returned'. [*loc. cit.*]

104. A stateless person may have more than one country of former habitual residence, and he may have a fear of persecution in relation to more than one of them. The definition does not require that he satisfies the criteria in relation to all of them.

105. Once a stateless person has been determined a refugee in relation to 'the country of his former habitual residence', any further change of country of habitual residence will not affect his refugee status.

(7) Dual or multiple nationality

Article 1A(2), paragraph 2, of the 1951 Convention:

> 'In the case of a person who has more than one nationality, the term 'the country of his nationality' shall mean each of the countries of which he is a national, and a person shall not be deemed to be lacking the protection of the country of his nationality if, without any valid reason based on well-founded fear, he has not availed himself of the protection of one of the countries of which he is a national.'

106. This clause, which is largely self-explanatory, is intended to exclude from refugee status all persons with dual or multiple nationality who can avail themselves of the protection of at least one of the countries of which they are nationals. Wherever available, national protection takes precedence over international protection.

107. In examining the case of an applicant with dual or multiple nationality, it is necessary, however, to distinguish between the possession of a nationality in the legal sense and the availability of protection by the country concerned. There will be cases where the applicant has the nationality of a country in regard to which he alleges no fear, but such nationality may be deemed to be ineffective as it does not entail the protection normally granted to nationals. In such circumstances, the possession of the second nationality would not be inconsistent with refugee status. As a rule, there should have been a request for, and a refusal of, protection before it can be established that a given nationality is ineffective. If there is not explicit refusal of protection, absence of a reply within reasonable time may be considered a refusal.

(8) Geographical scope

108. At the time when the 1951 Convention was drafted, there was a desire by a number of States not to assume obligations the extent of which could not be foreseen. This desire led to the inclusion of the 1951 dateline, to which reference has already been made (paragraphs 35 and 36 above). In response to the wish of certain Governments, the 1951 Convention also gave to Contracting States the possibility of limiting their obligations under the Convention to persons who had become refugees as a result of events occurring in Europe.

109. Accordingly, Article 1B of the 1951 Convention states that:

> '(1) For the purposes of this Convention, the words "events occurring before 1 January 1951" in Article 1, Section A, shall be understood to mean either
>
> (a) "events occurring in Europe before 1 January 1951", or
>
> (b) "events occurring in Europe and elsewhere before 1 January 1951";
>
> and each Contracting State shall make a declaration at the time of signature, ratification or accession, specifying which of these meanings it applies for the purposes of its obligations under this Convention.
>
> (2) Any Contracting State which has adopted alternative (a) may at any time extend its obligations by adopting alternative (b) by means of a notification addressed to the Secretary-General of the United Nations.'

110. Of the States parties to the 1951 Convention, at the time of writing 9 still adhere to alternative (a), 'events occurring in Europe'. [See Annex IV.] While refugees from other parts of the world frequently obtain asylum in some of these countries, they are not normally accorded refugee status under the 1951 Convention.

Chapter III
Cessation Clauses

A. General

111. The so-called 'cessation clauses' (Article 1C(1) to (6) of the 1951 Convention) spell out the conditions under which a refugee ceases to be a refugee. They are based on the consideration that international protection should not be granted where it is no longer necessary or justified.

112. Once a person's status as a refugee has been determined it is maintained unless he comes within the terms of one of the cessation clauses. [In some cases refugee status may continue even though the reasons for such status have evidently ceased to exist. Cf sub-sections (5) and (6) (paragraphs 135 to 139 below).] This strict approach towards the determination of refugee status results from the need to provide refugees with the assurance that their status will not be subject to constant review in the light of temporary changes—not of a fundamental character—in the situation prevailing in their country of origin.

113. Article 1C of the 1951 Convention provides that:

'This Convention shall cease to apply to any person falling under the terms of section A if:

(1) He has voluntarily re-availed himself of the protection of the country of his nationality; or
(2) Having lost his nationality, he has voluntarily re-acquired it; or
(3) He has acquired a new nationality, and enjoys the protection of the country of his new nationality; or
(4) He has voluntarily re-established himself in the country which he left or outside which he remained owing to fear of persecution; or
(5) He can no longer, because the circumstances in connexion with which he has been recognised as a refugee have ceased to exist, continue to refuse to avail himself of the protection of the country of his nationality;

Provided that this paragraph shall not apply to a refugee falling under section A(1) of this Article who is able to invoke compelling reasons arising out of previous persecution for refusing to avail himself of the protection of the country of nationality;

(6) Being a person who has no nationality he is, because the circumstances in connexion with which he has been recognized as a refugee have ceased to exist, able to return to the country of his former habitual residence;

Provided that this paragraph shall not apply to a refugee falling under section A(1) of this Article who is able to invoke compelling reasons arising out of previous persecution for refusing to return to the country of his former habitual residence.'

114. Of the six cessation clauses, the first four reflect a change in the situation of the refugee that has been brought about by himself, namely:

(1) voluntary re-availment of national protection;
(2) voluntary re-acquisition of nationality;
(3) acquisition of a new nationality;
(4) voluntary re-establishment in the country where persecution was feared.

115. The last two cessation clauses, (5) and (6), are based on the consideration that international protection is no longer justified on account of changes in the country where persecution was feared, because the reasons for a person becoming a refugee have ceased to exist.

116. The cessation clauses are negative in character and are exhaustively enumerated. They should therefore be interpreted restrictively, and no other reasons may be adduced by way of analogy to justify the withdrawal of refugee status. Needless to say, if a refugee, for whatever reasons, no longer wishes to be considered a refugee, there will be no call for continuing to grant him refugee status and international protection.

117. Article 1C does not deal with the cancellation of refugee status. Circumstances may, however, come to light that indicate that a person should never have been recognized as a refugee in the first place; e.g. if it subsequently appears that refugee status was obtained by a misrepresentation of material facts, or that the person concerned possesses another nationality, or that one of the exclusion clauses would have applied to him had all the relevant facts been known. In such cases, the decision by which he was determined to be a refugee will normally be cancelled.

B. Interpretation of terms

(1) Voluntary re-availment of national protection

Article 1C(1) of the 1951 Convention:

> 'He has voluntarily re-availed himself of the protection of the country of his nationality;'

118. This cessation clause refers to a refugee possessing a nationality who remains outside the country of his nationality. (The situation of a refugee who has actually returned to the country of his nationality is governed by the fourth cessation clause, which speaks of a person having 're-established' himself in that country.) A refugee who has voluntarily re-availed himself of national protection is no longer in need of international protection. He had demonstrated that he is no longer 'unable or unwilling to avail himself of the protection of the country of his nationality'.

119. This cessation clause implies three requirements:

(a) voluntariness: the refugee must act voluntarily;
(b) intention: the refugee must intend by his action to re-avail himself of the protection of the country of his nationality;
(c) re-availment: the refugee must actually obtain such protection.

120. If the refugee does not act voluntarily, he will not cease to be a refugee. If he is instructed by an authority, e.g. of his country of residence, to perform against his will an act that could be interpreted as a re-availment of the protection of the country of his nationality, such as applying to his Consulate for a national passport, he will not cease to be a refugee merely because he obeys such an instruction. He may also be constrained, by circumstances beyond his control, to have recourse to a measure of protection from his country of nationality. He may, for instance, need to apply for a divorce in his home country because no other divorce may have the necessary international recognition. Such an act cannot be considered to be a 'voluntary re-availment of protection' and will not deprive a person of refugee status.

121. In determining whether refugee status is lost in these circumstances, a distinction should be drawn between actual re-availment of protection and occasional and incidental contacts with the national authorities. If a refugee applies for and obtains a national passport or its renewal, it will, in the absence of proof to the contrary, be presumed that he intends to avail himself of the protection of the country of his nationality. On the other hand, the acquisition of documents from the national authorities, for which non-nationals would likewise have to apply—such as a birth or marriage certificate—or similar services, cannot be regarded as a re-availment of protection.

122. A refugee requesting protection from the authorities of the country of his nationality has only 're-availed' himself of that protection when his request has actually been granted. The most frequent case of 're-availment of protection' will be where the refugee wishes to return to his country of nationality. He will not cease to be a refugee merely by applying for repatriation. On the other hand, obtaining an entry permit or a national passport for the purposes of returning will, in the absence of proof to the contrary, be considered as terminating refugee status. [The above applies to a refugee who is still outside his country. It will be noted that the fourth cessation clause provides that any refugee will cease to be a refugee when he has voluntarily 're-established' himself in his country or nationality or former habitual residence.] This does not, however, preclude assistance being given to the repatriant—also by UNHCR—in order to facilitate his return.

123. A refugee may have voluntarily obtained a national passport, intending either to avail himself of the protection of his country of origin while staying outside that country, or to return to that country. As stated above, with the receipt of such a document he normally ceases to be a refugee. If he subsequently renounces either intention, his refugee status will need to be determined afresh. He will need to explain why he changed his mind, and to show that there has been no basic change in the conditions that originally made him a refugee.

124. Obtaining a national passport or an extension of its validity may, under certain exceptional conditions, not involve termination of refugee status (see paragraph 120 above). This could for example be the case where the holder of a national passport is not permitted to return to the country of his nationality without specific permission.

125. Where a refugee visits his former home country not with a national passport but, for example, with a travel document issued by his country of residence, he has been considered by certain States to have re-availed himself of the protection of his former home country and to have lost his refugee status under the present cessation clause. Cases of this kind should, however, be judged on their individual merits. Visiting an old or sick parent will have a different bearing on the refugee's relation to his former home country than regular visits to that country spent on holidays or for the purpose of establishing business relations.

(2) Voluntary re-acquisition of nationality

Article 1C(2) of the 1951 Convention:

> 'Having lost his nationality, he has voluntarily re-acquired it;'

126. This clause is similar to the preceding one. It applies to cases where a refugee, having lost the nationality of the country in respect of which he was

recognized as having well-founded fear of persecution, voluntarily re-acquires such nationality.

127. While under the preceding clause (Article 1C(1)) a person having a nationality ceases to be a refugee if he re-avails himself of the protection attaching to such nationality, under the present clause (Article 1C(2)) he loses his refugee status by reacquiring the nationality previously lost. [In the majority of cases a refuge maintains the nationality of his former home country. Such nationality may be lost by individual or collective measures of deprivation of nationality. Loss of nationality (statelessness) is therefore not necessarily implicit in refugee status.]

128. The re-acquisition of nationality must be voluntary. The granting of nationality by operation of law or by decree does not imply voluntary re-acquisition, unless the nationality has been expressly or impliedly accepted. A person does not cease to be a refugee merely because he could have re-acquired his former nationality by option, unless this option has actually been exercised. If such former nationality is granted by operation of law, subject to an option to reject, it will be regarded as a voluntary reacquisition if the refugee, with full knowledge, has not exercised this option; unless he is able to invoke special reasons showing that it was not in fact his intention to reacquire his former nationality.

(3) Acquisition of a new nationality and protection

Article 1C(3) of the 1951 Convention:

> 'He has acquired a new nationality and enjoys the protection of the country of his new nationality;'

129. As in the case of the re-acquisition of nationality, this third cessation clause derives from the principle that a person who enjoys national protection is not in need of international protection.

130. The nationality that the refugee acquires is usually that of the country of his residence. A refugee living in one country may, however, in certain cases, acquire the nationality of another country. If he does so, his refugee status will also cease, provided that the new nationality also carries the protection of the country concerned. This requirement results from the phrase 'and enjoys the protection of the country of his new nationality'.

131. If a person has ceased to be a refugee, having acquired a new nationality, and then claims well-founded fear in relation to the country of his new nationality, this creates a completely new situation and his status must be determined in relation to the country of his new nationality.

132. Where refugee status has terminated through the acquisition of a new nationality, and such new nationality has been lost, depending on the circumstances of such loss, refugee status may be revived.

(4) Voluntary re-establishment in the country where persecution was feared

Article 1C(4) of the 1951 Convention:

> 'He has voluntarily re-established himself in the country which he left or outside which he remained owing to fear of persecution;'

133. This fourth cessation clause applies both to refugees who have a nationality and to stateless refugees. It relates to refugees who, having returned to their country of origin or previous residence, have not previously ceased to be refugees under the first or second cessation clauses while still in their country of refuge.

134. The clause refers to 'voluntary re-establishment'. This is to be understood as return to the country of nationality or former habitual residence with a view to permanently residing there. A temporary visit by a refugee to his former home country, not with a national passport but, for example, with a travel document issued by his country of residence, does not constitute 're-establishment' and will not involve loss of refugee status under the present clause. [See paragraph 125 above.]

(5) Nationals whose reasons for becoming a refugee have ceased to exist

Article 1C(5) of the 1951 Convention:

> 'He can no longer, because the circumstances in connexion with which he has been recognized as a refugee have ceased to exist, continue to refuse to avail himself of the protection of the country of his nationality;
> Provided that this paragraph shall not apply to a refugee falling under section A(1) of this Article who is able to invoke compelling reasons arising out of previous persecution for refusing to avail himself of the protection of the country of nationality;'

135. 'Circumstances' refer to fundamental changes in the country, which can be assumed to remove the basis of the fear of persecution. A mere—possibly transitory—change in the facts surrounding the individual refugee's fear, which does not entail such major changes of circumstances, is not sufficient to make this clause applicable. A refugee's status should not in principle be subject to frequent review to the detriment of his sense of security, which international protection is intended to provide.

136. The second paragraph of this clause contains an exception to the cessation provision contained in the first paragraph. It deals with the special situation where a person may have been subjected to very serious persecution in the past and will not therefore cease to be a refugee, even if fundamental changes have occurred in his country of origin. The reference to Article 1A(1) indicates that the exception applies to 'statutory refugees'. At the time when the 1951 Convention was elaborated, these formed the majority of refugees. The exception, however, reflects a more general humanitarian principle, which could also be applied to refugees other than statutory refugees. It is frequently recognized that a person who—or whose family—has suffered under atrocious forms of persecution should not be expected to repatriate. Even though there may have been a change of régime in his country, this may not always produce a complete change in the attitude of the population, nor, in view of his past experiences, in the mind of the refugee.

(6) Stateless persons whose reasons for becoming a refugee have ceased to exist

Article 1C(6) of the 1951 Convention:

> 'Being a person who has no nationality he is, because the circumstances in connexion with which he has been recognized as a refugee have ceased to exist, able to return to the country of his former habitual residence;
> Provided that this paragraph shall not apply to a refugee falling under section A(1) of this Article who is able to invoke compelling reasons arising out of previous persecution for refusing to return to the country of his former habitual residence.'

137. This sixth and last cessation clause is parallel to the fifth cessation clause, which concerns persons who have a nationality. The present clause deals exclusively with stateless persons who are able to return to the country of their former habitual residence.

138. 'Circumstances' should be interpreted in the same way as under the fifth cessation clause.

139. It should be stressed that, apart from the changed circumstances in his country of former habitual residence, the person concerned must be *able* to return there. This, in the case of a stateless person, may not always be possible.

Chapter IV
Exclusion Clauses

A. General

140. The 1951 Convention, in Section D, E and F of Article 1, contains provisions whereby persons otherwise having the characteristics of refugees, as defined in Article 1, Section A, are excluded from refugee status. Such persons fall into three groups. The first group (Article 1D) consists of persons already receiving United Nations protection or assistance; the second group (Article 1E) deals with persons who are not considered to be in need of international protection; and the third group (Article 1F) enumerates the categories of persons who are not considered to be deserving of international protection.

141. Normally it will be during the process of determining a person's refugee status that the facts leading to exclusion under these clauses will emerge. It may, however, also happen that facts justifying exclusion will become known only after a person has been recognized as a refugee. In such cases, the exclusion clause will call for a cancellation of the decision previously taken.

B. Interpretation of terms

(1) Persons already receiving United Nations protection or assistance

Article 1D of the 1951 Convention:

> 'This Convention shall not apply to persons who are at present receiving from organs or agencies of the United Nations other than the United Nations High Commissioner for Refugees protection or assistance.
>
> When such protection or assistance has ceased for any reason, without the position of such persons being definitively settled in accordance with the relevant resolutions adopted by the General Assembly of the United Nations, these persons shall *ipso facto* be entitled to the benefits of this Convention.'

142. Exclusion under this clause applies to any person who is in receipt of protection or assistance from organs or agencies of the United Nations, other than the United Nations High Commissioner for Refugees. Such protection or assistance was previously given by the former United Nations Korean Reconstruction Agency (UNKRA) and is currently given by the United Nations Relief and Works Agency for Palestine Refugees in the Near East (UNRWA). There could be other similar situations in the future.

143. With regard to refugees from Palestine, it will be noted that UNRWA operates only in certain areas of the Middle East, and it is only there that its protection or assistance are given. Thus, a refugee from Palestine who finds himself outside that area does not enjoy the assistance mentioned and may be considered for determination of his refugee status under the criteria of the 1951 Convention. It should normally be sufficient to establish that the circumstances which originally made him qualify for protection or assistance from UNRWA still persist and that he has neither ceased to be a refugee under one of the cessation clauses nor is excluded from the application of the Convention under one of the exclusion clauses.

(2) Persons not considered to be in need of international protection

Article 1E of the 1951 Convention:

> 'This Convention shall not apply to a person who is recognized by the competent authorities of the country in which he has taken residence as having the rights and obligations which are attached to the possession of the nationality of that country.'

144. This provision relates to persons who might otherwise qualify for refugee status and who have been received in a country where they have been granted most of the rights normally enjoyed by nationals, but not formal citizenship. (They are

frequently referred to as 'national refugees'.) The country that has received them is frequently one where the population is of the same ethnic origin as themselves. [In elaborating this exclusion clause, the drafters of the Convention had principally in mind refugees of German extraction having arrived in the Federal Republic of Germany who were recognized as possessing the rights and obligations attaching to German nationality.]

145. There is no precise definition of 'rights and obligations' that would constitute a reason for exclusion under this clause. It may, however, be said that the exclusion operates if a person's status is largely assimilated to that of a national of the country. In particular he must, like a national, be fully protected against deportation or expulsion.

146. The clause refers to a person who has 'taken residence' in the country concerned. This implies continued residence and not a mere visit. A person who resides outside the country and does not enjoy the diplomatic protection of that country is not affected by the exclusion clause.

(3) Persons not considered to be deserving of international protection

Article 1F of the 1951 Convention:

> 'The provisions of this Convention shall not apply to any person with respect to whom there are serious reasons for considering that:
> (a) he has committed a crime against peace, a war crime, or a crime against humanity, as defined in the international instruments drawn up to make provision in respect of such crimes;
> (b) he has committed a serious non-political crime outside the country of refuge prior to his admission to that country as a refugee;
> (c) he has been guilty of acts contrary to the purposes and principles of the United Nations.'

147. The pre-war international instruments that defined various categories of refugees contained no provisions for the exclusion of criminals. It was immediately after the Second World War that for the first time special provisions were drawn up to exclude from the large group of then assisted refugees certain persons who were deemed unworthy of international protection.

148. At the time when the Convention was drafted, the memory of the trials of major war criminals was still very much alive, and there was agreement on the part of States that war criminals should not be protected. There was also a desire on the part of States to deny admission to their territories of criminals who would present a danger to security and public order.

149. The competence to decide whether any of these exclusion clauses are applicable is incumbent upon the Contracting State in whose territory the applicant seeks recognition of his refugee status. For these clauses to apply, it is sufficient to establish that there are 'serious reasons for considering' that one of the acts described has been committed. Formal proof of previous penal prosecution is not required. Considering the serious consequences of exclusion for the person concerned, however, the interpretation of these exclusion clauses must be restrictive.

(a) War crimes, etc.

> '(a) he has committed a crime against peace, a war crime or a crime against humanity, as defined in the international instruments drawn up to make provision in respect of such crimes.'

150. In mentioning crimes against peace, war crimes or crimes against humanity, the Convention refers generally to 'international instruments drawn up to make provision in respect of such crimes'. There are a considerable number of such instruments dating from the end of the Second World War up to the present time. All of them contain definitions of what constitute 'crimes against peace, war crimes and crimes against humanity'. The most comprehensive definition will be found in the 1945 London Agreement and Charter of the International Military Tribunal. The definitions contained in the above-mentioned London Agreement and a list of other pertinent instruments are given in Annexes V and VI.

(b) Common crimes

> '(b) he has committed a serious non-political crime outside the country of refuge prior to his admission to that country as a refugee.'

151. The aim of this exclusion clause is to protect the community of a receiving country from the danger of admitting a refugee who has committed a serious common crime. It also seeks to render due justice to a refugee who has committed a common crime (or crimes) of a less serious nature or has committed a political offence.

152. In determining whether an offence is 'non-political' or is, on the contrary, a 'political' crime, regard should be given in the first place to its nature and purpose i.e. whether it has been committed out of genuine political motives and not merely for personal reasons or gain. There should also be a close and direct casual link between the crime committed and its alleged political purpose and object. The political element of the offence should also outweigh its common-law character. This would not be the case if the acts committed are grossly out of proportion to the alleged objective. The political nature of the offence is also more difficult to accept if it involves acts of an atrocious nature.

153. Only a crime committed or presumed to have been committed by an applicant 'outside the country of refuge prior to his admission to that country as a refugee' is a ground for exclusion. The country outside would normally be the country of origin, but it could also be another country, except the country of refuge where the applicant seeks recognition of his refugee status.

154. A refugee committing a serious crime in the country of refuge is subject to due process of law in that country. In extreme cases, Article 33 paragraph 2 of the Convention permits a refugee's expulsion or return to his former home country if, having been convicted by a final judgement of a 'particularly serious' common crime, he constitutes a danger to the community of his country of refuge.

155. What constitutes a 'serious' non-political crime for the purposes of this exclusion clause is difficult to define, especially since the term 'crime' has different connotations in different legal systems. In some countries the word 'crime' denotes only offences of a serious character. In other countries it may comprise anything from petty larceny to murder. In the present context, however, a 'serious' crime must be a capital crime or a very grave punishable act. Minor offences punishable by moderate sentences are not grounds for exclusion under Article 1F(b) even if technically referred to as 'crimes' in the penal law of the country concerned.

156. In applying this exclusion clause, it is also necessary to strike a balance between the nature of the offence presumed to have been committed by the applicant and the degree of persecution feared. If a person has well-founded fear of very severe persecution, e.g. persecution endangering his life or freedom, a crime must be very grave in order to exclude him. If the persecution feared is less serious, it will be necessary to have regard to the nature of the crime or crimes presumed to have been committed in order to establish whether the applicant is not in reality a fugitive from justice or whether his criminal character does not outweigh his character as a *bona fide* refugee.

157. In evaluating the nature of the crime presumed to have been committed, all the relevant factors—including any mitigating circumstances—must be taken into account. It is also necessary to have regard to any aggravating circumstances as, for example, the fact that the applicant may already have a criminal record. The fact that an applicant convicted of a serious non-political crime has already served his sentence or has been granted a pardon or has benefited from an amnesty is also relevant. In the latter case, there is a presumption that the exclusion clause is no longer applicable, unless it can be shown that, despite the pardon or amnesty, the applicant's criminal character still predominates.

158. Considerations similar to those mentioned in the preceding paragraphs will apply when a crime—in the widest sense—has been committed as a means of, or concomitant with, escape from the country where persecution was feared. Such crimes may range from the theft of a means of locomotion to endangering or taking the lives of innocent people. While for the purposes of the present exclusion clause it may be possible to overlook the fact that a refugee, nor finding any other means of escape, may have crashed the border in a stolen car, decisions will be more difficult where he has hijacked an aircraft, i.e. forced its crew, under threat of arms or with actual violence, to change destination in order to bring him to a country of refuge.

159. As regards hijacking, the question has arisen as to whether, if committed in order to escape from persecution, it constitutes a serious non-political crime within the meaning of the present exclusion clause. Governments have considered the unlawful seizure of aircraft on several occasions within the framework of the United Nations, and a number of international conventions have been adopted dealing with the subject. None of these instruments mentions refugees. However, one of the reports leading to the adoption of a resolution on the subject states that 'the adoption of the draft Resolution cannot prejudice any international legal rights or duties of States under instruments relating to the status of refugees and stateless persons'. Another report states that 'the adoption of the draft Resolution cannot prejudice any international legal rights or duties of States with respect to asylum'. [Reports of the Sixth Committee on General Assembly resolutions 2645 (XXV) United Nations document A/8716, and 2551 (XXIV), United Nations document A/7845.]

160. The various conventions adopted in this connexion [Convention on Offences and Certain Other Acts Committed on Board Aircraft, Tokyo, 14 September 1963; Convention for the Suppression of Unlawful Seizure of Aircraft, the Hague, 16 December 1970; Convention for the Suppression of Unlawful Acts against the Safety of Civil Aviation, Montreal, 23 September 1971] deal mainly with the manner in which the perpetrators of such acts have to be treated. They invariably give Contracting States the alternative of extraditing such persons or instituting penal proceedings for the act on their own territory, which implies the right to grant asylum.

161. While there is thus a possibility of granting asylum, the gravity of the persecution of which the offender may have been in fear, and the extent to which such fear is well-founded, will have to be duly considered in determining his possible refugee status under the 1951 Convention. The question of the exclusion under Article 1F(b) of an applicant who has committed an unlawful seizure of an aircraft will also have to be carefully examined in each individual case.

(c) Acts contrary to the purposes and principles of the United Nations

> '(c) he has been guilty of acts contrary to the purposes and principles of the United Nations.'

162. It will be seen that this very generally-worded exclusion clause overlaps with the exclusion clause in Article 1F(a); for it is evident that a crime against peace, a war crime or a crime against humanity is also an act contrary to the purposes and principles of the United Nations. While Article 1F(c) does not introduce any specific new element, it is intended to cover in a general way such acts against the purposes and principles of the United Nations that might not be fully covered by the two preceding exclusion clauses. Taken in conjunction with the latter, it has to be assumed, although this is not specifically stated, that the acts covered by the present clause must also be of a criminal nature.

163. The purposes and principles of the United Nations are set out in the Preamble and Articles 1 and 2 of the Charter of the United Nations. They enumerate fundamental principles that should govern the conduct of their members in relation to each other and in relation to the international community as a whole. From this it could be inferred that an individual, in order to have committed an act contrary to these principles, must have been in a position of power in a member State and instrumental to his State's infringing these principles. However, there are hardly any precedents on record for the application of this clause, which, due to its very general character, should be applied with caution.

Chapter V

Special Cases

A. War refugees

164. Persons compelled to leave their country of origin as a result of international or national armed conflicts are not normally considered refugees under the 1951 Convention or 1967 Protocol. [In respect of Africa, however, see the definition in Article 1(2) of the OAU Convention concerning the Specific Aspects of Refugee Problems in Africa, quoted in paragraph 22 above.] They do, however, have the protection provided for in other international instruments, e.g. the Geneva Conventions of 1949 on the Protection of War Victims and the 1977 Protocol additional to the Geneva Conventions of 1949 relating to the protection of Victims of International Armed Conflicts. [See Annex VI, items (6) and (7).]

165. However, foreign invasion or occupation of all or part of a country can result—and occasionally has resulted—in persecution for one or more of the reasons enumerated in the 1951 Convention. In such cases, refugee status will depend upon whether the applicant is able to show that he has a 'well-founded fear of being persecuted' in the occupied territory and, in addition, upon whether or not he is able to avail himself of the protection of his government, or of a protecting power whose duty it is to safeguard the interests of his country during the armed conflict, and whether such protection can be considered to be effective.

166. Protection may not be available if there are no diplomatic relations between the applicant's host country and his country of origin. If the applicant's government is itself in exile, the effectiveness of the protection that it is able to extend may be open to question. Thus, every case has to be judged on its merits, both in respect of well-founded fear of persecution and of the availability of effective protection on the part of the government of the country of origin.

B. Deserters and persons avoiding military service

167. In countries where military service is compulsory, failure to perform this duty is frequently punishable by law. Moreover, whether military service is compulsory or not, desertion is invariably considered a criminal offence. The penalties may vary from country to country, and are not normally regarded as persecution. Fear of prosecution and punishment for desertion or draft-evasion does not in itself constitute well-founded fear of persecution under the definition. Desertion or draft-evasion does not, on the other hand, exclude a person from being a refugee, and a person may be a refugee in addition to being a deserter or draft-evader.

168. A person is clearly not a refugee if his only reason for desertion or draftevasion is his dislike of military service or fear of combat. He may, however, be a refugee if his desertion or evasion of military service is concomitant with other relevant motives for leaving or remaining outside his country, or if he otherwise has reasons, within the meaning of the definition, to fear persecution.

169. A deserter or draft-evader may also be considered a refugee if it can be shown that he would suffer disproportionately severe punishment for the military offence on account of his race, religion, nationality, membership of a particular social group or political opinion. The same would apply if it can be shown that he has well-founded fear of persecution on these grounds above and beyond the punishment for desertion.

170. There are, however, also cases where the necessity to perform military service may be the sole ground for a claim to refugee status, i.e. when a person can show that the performance of military service would have required his participation in military action contrary to his genuine political, religious or moral convictions, or to valid reasons of conscience.

171. Not every conviction, genuine though it may be, will constitute a sufficient reason for claiming refugee status after desertion or draft-evasion. It is not enough for a person to be in disagreement with his government regarding the political justification for a particular military action. Where, however, the type of military action, with which an individual does not wish to be associated, is condemned by the international community as contrary to basic rules of human conduct, punishment for desertion or draft-evasion could, in the light of all other requirements of the definition, in itself be regarded as persecution.

172. Refusal to perform military service may also be based on religious convictions. If an applicant is able to show that his religious convictions are genuine, and that such convictions are not taken into account by the authorities of his country in requiring him to perform military service, he may be able to establish a claim to refugee status. Such a claim would, of course, be supported by any additional indications that the applicant or his family may have encountered difficulties due to their religious convictions.

173. The question as to whether objection to performing military service for reasons of conscience can give rise to a valid claim to refugee status should also be considered in the light of more recent developments in this field. An increasing number of States have introduced legislation or administrative regulations whereby persons who can invoke genuine reasons of conscience are exempted from military service, either entirely or subject to their performing alternative (i.e. civilian) service. The introduction of such legislation or administrative regulations has also been the subject of recommendations by international agencies. [Cf Recommendation 816 (1977) on the Right of Conscientious Objection to Military Service, adopted at the Parliamentary Assembly of the Council of Europe at its Twenty-ninth Ordinary Session (5–13 October 1977).] In the light of these developments, it would be open to Contracting States, to grant refugee status to persons who object to performing military service for genuine reasons of conscience.

174. The genuineness of a person's political, religious or moral convictions, or of his reasons of conscience for objecting to performing military service, will of course need to be established by a thorough investigation of his personality and background. The fact that he may have manifested his views prior to being called to arms, or that he may already have encountered difficulties with the authorities because of his convictions, are relevant considerations. Whether he has been drafted into compulsory service or joined the army as a volunteer may also be indicative of the genuineness of his convictions.

C. Persons having resorted to force or committed acts of violence

175. Applications for refugee status are frequently made by persons who have used force or committed acts of violence. Such conduct is frequently associated with, or claimed to be associated with, political activities or political opinions. They may be the result of individual initiatives, or may have been committed within the framework of organized groups. The latter may either be clandestine groupings or political cum military organizations that are officially recognized or whose activities are widely acknowledged. [A number of liberation movements, which often include an armed wing, have been officially recognized by the General Assembly of the United Nations. Other liberation movements have only been recognized by a limited number of governments. Others again have no official recognition.] Account should also be taken of the fact that the use of force is an aspect of the maintenance of law and order and may—by definition—be lawfully resorted to by the police and armed forces in the exercise of their functions.

176. An application for refugee status by a person having (or presumed to have) used force, or to have committed acts of violence of whatever nature and within whatever context, must in the first place—like any other application—be examined from the standpoint of the inclusion clauses in the 1951 Convention (paragraphs 32–110 above).

177. Where it has been determined that an applicant fulfils the inclusion criteria, the question may arise as to whether, in view of the acts involving the use of force

or violence committed by him, he may not be covered by the terms of one or more of the exclusion clauses. These exclusion clauses which figure in Article 1F(a) to (c) of the 1951 Convention, have already been examined (paragraphs 147 to 163 above).

178. The exclusion clause in Article 1F(a) was originally intended to exclude from refugee status any person in respect of whom there were serious reasons for considering that he has 'committed a crime against peace, a war crime, or a crime against humanity' in an official capacity. This exclusion clause is, however, also applicable to persons who have committed such crimes within the framework of various non-governmental groupings, whether officially recognized, clandestine or self-styled.

179. The exclusion clause in Article 1F(b), which refers to 'a serious non-political crime', is normally not relevant to the use of force or to acts of violence committed in an official capacity. The interpretation of this exclusion clause has already been discussed. The exclusion clause in Article 1F(c) has also been considered. As previously indicated, because of its vague character, it should be applied with caution.

180. It will also be recalled that, due to their nature and the serious consequences of their application to a person in fear of persecution, the exclusion clauses should be applied in a restrictive manner.

Chapter VI

The Principle of Family Unity

181. Beginning with the Universal Declaration of Human Rights, which states that 'the family is the natural and fundamental group unit of society and is entitled to protection by society and the State', most international instruments dealing with human rights contain similar provisions for the protection of the unit of a family.

182. The Final Act of the Conference that adopted the 1951 Convention:

> 'Recommends Governments to take the necessary measures for the protection of the refugee's family, especially with a view to:
>
> (1) Ensuring that the unity of the refugee's family is maintained particularly in cases where the head of the family has fulfilled the necessary conditions for admission to a particular country.
>
> (2) The protection of refugees who are minors, in particular unaccompanied children and girls, with special reference to guardianship and adoption.' [See Annex I.]

183. The 1951 Convention does not incorporate the principle of family unity in the definition of the term refugee. The above-mentioned Recommendation in the

Final Act of the Conference is, however, observed by the majority of States, whether or not parties to the 1951 Convention or to the 1967 Protocol.

184. If the head of a family meets the criteria of the definition, his dependants are normally granted refugee status according to the principle of family unity. It is obvious, however, that formal refugee status should not be granted to a dependant if this is incompatible with his personal legal status. Thus, a dependant member of a refugee family may be a national of the country of asylum or of another country, and may enjoy that country's protection. To grant him refugee status in such circumstances would not be called for.

185. As to which family members may benefit from the principle of family unity, the minimum requirement is the inclusion of the spouse and minor children. In practice, other dependants, such as aged parents of refugees, are normally considered if they are living in the same household. On the other hand, if the head of the family is not a refugee, there is nothing to prevent any one of his dependants, if they can invoke reasons on their own account, from applying for recognition as refugees under the 1951 Convention or the 1967 Protocol. In other words, the principle of family unity operates in favour of dependants, and not against them.

186. The principle of the unity of the family does not only operate where all family members become refugees at the same time. It applies equally to cases where a family unit has been temporarily disrupted through the flight of one or more of its members.

187. Where the unity of a refugee's family is destroyed by divorce, separation or death, dependants who have been granted refugee status on the basis of family unity will retain such refugee status unless they fall within the terms of a cessation clause; or if they do not have reasons other than those of personal convenience for wishing to retain refugee status; or if they themselves no longer wish to be considered as refugees.

188. If the dependant of a refugee falls within the terms of one of the exclusion clauses, refugee status should be denied to him.

Part Two

Procedures for the Determination of Refugee Status

A. General

189. It has been seen that the 1951 Convention and the 1967 Protocol define who is a refugee for the purposes of these instruments. It is obvious that, to enable States parties to the Convention and to the Protocol to implement their provisions, refugees have to be identified. Such identification, i.e. the determination of refugee status, although mentioned in the 1951 Convention (cf. Article 9), is not specifically regulated. In particular, the Convention does not indicate what type of procedures are to be adopted for the determination of refugee status. It is therefore left to each Contracting State to establish the procedure that it considers most appropriate, having regard to its particular constitutional and administrative structure.

190. It should be recalled that an applicant for refugee status is normally in a particularly vulnerable situation. He finds himself in an alien environment and may experience serious difficulties, technical and psychological, in submitting his case to the authorities of a foreign country, often in a language not his own. His application should therefore be examined within the framework of specially established procedures by qualified personnel having the necessary knowledge and experience, and an understanding of an applicant's particular difficulties and needs.

191. Due to the fact that the matter is not specifically regulated by the 1951 Convention, procedures adopted by States parties to the 1951 Convention and to the 1967 Protocol vary considerably. In a number of countries, refugee status is determined under formal procedures specifically established for this purpose. In other countries, the question of refugee status is considered within the framework of general procedures for the admission of aliens. In yet other countries, refugee status is determined under informal arrangements, or *ad hoc* for specific purposes, such as the issuance of travel documents.

192. In view of this situation and of the unlikelihood that all States bound by the 1951 Convention and the 1967 Protocol could establish identical procedures, the Executive Committee of the High Commissioner's Programme, at its twenty-eighth session in October 1977, recommended that procedures should satisfy certain basic requirements. These *basic requirements*, which reflect the special situation of the applicant for refugee status, to which reference has been made above, and which would ensure that the applicant is provided with certain essential guarantees, are the following:

(i) The competent official (e.g., immigration officer or border police officer) to whom the applicant addresses himself at the border or in the territory of a Contracting State should have clear instructions for dealing with cases which might come within the purview of the relevant international instruments. He should be required to act in accordance with the principle of *non-refoulement* and to refer such cases to a higher authority.

(ii) The applicant should receive the necessary guidance as to the procedure to be followed.

(iii) There should be a clearly identified authority—wherever possible a single central authority—with responsibility for examining requests for refugee status and taking a decision in the first instance.

(iv) The applicant should be given the necessary facilities, including the services of a competent interpreter, for submitting his case to the authorities concerned. Applicants should also be given the opportunity, of which they should be duly informed, to contact a representative of UNHCR.

(v) If the applicant is recognized as a refugee, he should be informed accordingly and issued with documentation certifying his refugee status.

(vi) If the applicant is not recognized, he should be given a reasonable time to appeal for a formal reconsideration of the decision, either to the same or to a different authority, whether administrative or judicial, according to the prevailing system.

(vii) The applicant should be permitted to remain in the country pending a decision on his initial request by the competent authority referred to in paragraph (iii) above, unless it has been established by that authority that his request is clearly abusive. He should also be permitted to remain in the country while an appeal to a higher administrative authority or to the courts is pending. [Official Records of the General Assembly, Thirty-second Session, Supplement No. 12 (A/32/12/Add.1), paragraph 53(6)(e).]

193. The Executive Committee also expressed the hope that all States parties to the 1951 Convention and the 1967 Protocol that had not yet done so would take appropriate steps to establish such procedures in the near future and give favourable consideration to UNHCR participation in such procedures in appropriate form.

194. Determination of refugee status, which is closely related to questions of asylum and admission, is of concern to the High Commissioner in the exercise of his function to provide international protection for refugees. In a number of countries, the Office of the High Commissioner participates in various forms, in procedures for the determination of refugee status. Such participation is based on Article 35 of the 1951 Convention and the corresponding Article II of the 1967 Protocol, which provide for co-operation by the Contracting States with the High Commissioner's Office.

B. Establishing the facts

(1) Principles and methods

195. The relevant facts of the individual case will have to be furnished in the first place by the applicant himself. It will then be up to the person charged with determining his status (the examiner) to assess the validity of any evidence and the credibility of the applicant's statements.

196. It is a general legal principle that the burden of proof lies on the person submitting a claim. Often, however, an applicant may not be able to support his statements by documentary or other proof, and cases in which an applicant can provide evidence of all his statements will be the exception rather than the rule. In most cases a person fleeing from persecution will have arrived with the barest necessities and very frequently even without personal documents. Thus, while the burden of proof in principle rests on the applicant, the duty to ascertain and evaluate all the relevant facts is shared between the applicant and the examiner. Indeed, in some cases, it may be for the examiner to use all the means at his disposal to produce the necessary evidence in support of the application. Even such independent research may not, however, always be successful and there may also be statements that are not susceptible of proof. In such cases, if the applicant's account appears credible, he should, unless there are good reasons to the contrary, be given the benefit of the doubt.

197. The requirement of evidence should thus not be too strictly applied in view of the difficulty of proof inherent in the special situation in which an applicant for refugee status finds himself. Allowance for such possible lack of evidence does not, however, mean that unsupported statements must necessarily be accepted as true if they are inconsistent with the general account put forward by the applicant.

198. A person who, because of his experiences, was in fear of the authorities in his own country may still feel apprehensive vis-à-vis any authority. He may therefore be afraid to speak freely and give a full and accurate account of his case.

199. While an initial interview should normally suffice to bring an applicant's story to light, it may be necessary for the examiner to clarify any apparent inconsistencies and to resolve any contradictions in a further interview, and to find an explanation for any misrepresentation or concealment of material facts. Untrue statements by themselves are not a reason for refusal of refugee status and it is the examiner's responsibility to evaluate such statements in the light of all the circumstances of the case.

200. An examination in depth of the different methods of fact-finding is outside the scope of the present Handbook. It may be mentioned, however, that basic information is frequently given, in the first instance, by completing a standard questionnaire. Such basic information will normally not be sufficient to enable the examiner to reach a decision, and one or more personal interviews will be required. It will be necessary for the examiner to gain the confidence of the applicant in order to assist the latter in putting forward his case and in fully explaining his options and feelings. In creating such a climate of confidence it is, of course, of the utmost importance that the applicant's statements will be treated as confidential and that he be so informed.

201. Very frequently the fact-finding process will not be complete until a wide range of circumstances has been ascertained. Taking isolated incidents out of context may be misleading. The cumulative effect of the applicant's experience must be taken into account. Where no single incident stands out above the others, sometimes a small incident may be 'the last straw'; and although no single incident may be sufficient, all the incidents related by the applicant taken together, could make his fear 'well-founded' (see paragraph 53 above).

202. Since the examiner's conclusion on the facts of the case and his personal impression of the applicant will lead to a decision that affects human lives, he must apply the criteria in a spirit of justice and understanding and his judgement should not, of course, be influenced by the personal consideration that the applicant may be an 'undeserving case'.

(2) Benefit of the doubt

203. After the applicant has made a genuine effort to substantiate his story there may still be a lack of evidence for some of his statements. As explained above (paragraph 196), it is hardly possible for a refugee to 'prove' every part of his case and, indeed, if this were a requirement the majority of refugees would not be recognized. It is therefore frequently necessary to give the applicant the benefit of the doubt.

204. The benefit of the doubt should, however, only be given when all available evidence has been obtained and checked and when the examiner is satisfied as to the applicant's general credibility. The applicant's statements must be coherent and plausible, and must not run counter to generally known facts.

(3) Summary

205. The process of ascertaining and evaluating the facts can therefore be summarized as follows:

(a) The *applicant* should:

(i) Tell the truth and assist the examiner to the full in establishing the facts of his case.

(ii) Make an effort to support his statements by any available evidence and give a satisfactory explanation for any lack of evidence. If necessary he must make an effort to procure additional evidence.

(iii) Supply all pertinent information concerning himself and his past experience in as much detail as is necessary to enable the examiner to establish the relevant facts. He should be asked to give a coherent explanation of all the reasons invoked in support of his application for refugee status and he should answer any questions put to him.

(b) The *examiner* should:

(i) Ensure that the applicant presents his case as fully as possible and with all available evidence.

(ii) Assess the applicant's credibility and evaluate the evidence (if necessary giving the applicant the benefit of the doubt), in order to establish the objective and the subjective elements of the case.

(iii) Relate these elements to the relevant criteria of the 1951 Convention, in order to arrive at a correct conclusion as to the applicant's refugee status.

C. Cases giving rise to special problems in establishing the facts

(1) Mentally disturbed persons

206. It has been seen that in determining refugee status the subjective element of fear and the objective element of its well-foundedness need to be established.

207. It frequently happens that an examiner is confronted with an applicant having mental or emotional disturbances that impede a normal examination of his case. A mentally disturbed person may, however, be a refugee, and while his claim cannot therefore be disregarded, it will call for different techniques of examination.

208. The examiner should, in such cases, whenever possible, obtain expert medical advice. The medical report should provide information on the nature and degree of mental illness and should assess the applicant's ability to fulfil the requirements normally expected of an applicant in presenting his case (see paragraph 205(a) above). The conclusions of the medical report will determine the examiner's further approach.

209. This approach has to vary according to the degree of the applicant's affliction and no rigid rules can be laid down. The nature and degree of the applicant's 'fear' must also be taken into consideration, since some degree of mental disturbance is frequently found in persons who have been exposed to severe persecution. Where there are indications that the fear expressed by the applicant may not be based on actual experience or may be an exaggerated fear, it may be necessary, in arriving at a decision, to lay greater emphasis on the objective circumstances, rather than on the statements made by the applicant.

210. It will, in any event, be necessary to lighten the burden of proof normally incumbent upon the applicant, and information that cannot easily be obtained from the applicant may have to be sought elsewhere, e.g. from friends, relatives and other persons closely acquainted with the applicant, or from his guardian, if one has been appointed. It may also be necessary to draw certain conclusions from the surrounding circumstances. If, for instance, the applicant belongs to and is in the company of a group of refugees, there is a presumption that he shares their fate and qualifies in the same manner as they do.

211. In examining his application, therefore, it may not be possible to attach the same importance as is normally attached to the subjective element of 'fear', which may be less reliable, and it may be necessary to place greater emphasis on the objective situation.

212. In view of the above considerations, investigation into the refugee status of a mentally disturbed person will, as a rule, have to be more searching than in a 'normal' case and will call for a close examination of the applicant's past history and background, using whatever outside sources of information may be available.

(2) Unaccompanied minors

213. There is no special provision in the 1951 Convention regarding the refugee status of persons under age. The same definition of a refugee applies to all individuals, regardless of their age. When it is necessary to determine the refugee status of a minor, problems may arise due to the difficulty of applying the criteria of 'well-founded fear' in his case. If a minor is accompanied by one (or both) of his parents, or another family member on whom he is dependent, who requests refugee status, the minor's own refugee status will be determined according to the principle of family unity (paragraphs 181 to 188 above).

214. The question of whether an unaccompanied minor may qualify for refugee status must be determined in the first instance according to the degree of his mental development and maturity. In the case of children, it will generally be necessary to enrol the services of experts conversant with child mentality. A child—and for that matter, an adolescent—not being legally independent should, if appropriate, have a guardian appointed whose task it would be to promote a decision that will be in the minor's best interests. In the absence of parents or of a legally appointed guardian, it is for the authorities to ensure that the interests of an applicant for refugee status who is a minor are fully safeguarded.

215. Where a minor is no longer a child but an adolescent, it will be easier to determine refugee status as in the case of an adult, although this again will depend upon the actual degree of the adolescent's maturity. It can be assumed that—in the absence of indications to the contrary—a person of 16 or over may be regarded as sufficiently mature to have a well-founded fear of persecution. Minors under 16 years of age may normally be assumed not to be sufficiently mature. They may have fear and a will of their own, but these may not have the same significance as in the case of an adult.

216. It should, however, be stressed that these are only general guidelines and that a minor's mental maturity must normally be determined in the light of his personal, family and cultural background.

217. Where the minor has not reached a sufficient degree of maturity to make it possible to establish well-founded fear in the same way as for an adult, it may be necessary to have greater regard to certain objective factors. Thus, if an unaccompanied minor finds himself in the company of a group of refugees, this may—depending on the circumstances—indicate that the minor is also a refugee.

218. The circumstances of the parents and other family members, including their situation in the minor's country of origin, will have to be taken into account. If there is reason to believe that the parents wish their child to be outside the country of origin on grounds of well-founded fear of persecution, the child himself may be presumed to have such fear.

219. If the will of the parents cannot be ascertained or if such will is in doubt or in conflict with the will of the child, then the examiner, in cooperation with the experts assisting him, will have to come to a decision as to the well-foundedness of the minor's fear on the basis of all the known circumstances, which may call for a liberal application of the benefit of the doubt.

Conclusions

220. In the present Handbook an attempt has been made to define certain guidelines that, in the experience of UNHCR, have proved useful in determining refugee status for the purposes of the 1951 Convention and the 1967 Protocol relating to the Status of Refugees. In so doing, particular attention has been paid to the definitions of the term 'refugee' in these two instruments, and to various problems of interpretation arising out of these definitions. It has also been sought to show how these definitions may be applied in concrete cases and to focus attention on various procedural problems arising in regard to the determination of refugee status.

221. The Office of the High Commissioner is fully aware of the shortcomings inherent in a Handbook of this nature, bearing in mind that it is not possible to encompass every situation in which a person may apply for refugee status. Such situations are manifold and depend upon the infinitely varied conditions prevailing in countries of origin and on the special personal factors relating to the individual applicant.

222. The explanations given have shown that the determination of refugee status is by no means a mechanical and routine process. On the contrary, it calls for specialized knowledge, training and experience and—what is more important—an understanding of the particular situation of the applicant and of the human factors involved.

223. Within the above limits it is hoped that the present Handbook may provide some guidance to those who in their daily work are called upon to determine refugee status.

Annex I

Excerpt from the final act of the United Nations Conference of Plenipotentiaries on the Status of Refugees and Stateless Persons (United Nations Treaty Series, vol. 189, p. 37)

IV

The Conference adopted unanimously the following recommendations:

A.

'The Conference,

Considering that the issue and recognition of travel documents is necessary to facilitate the movement of refugees, and in particular their resettlement,

Urges Governments which are parties to the Inter-Governmental Agreement on Refugee Travel Documents signed in London 15 October 1946, or which recognize travel documents issued in accordance with the Agreement, to continue to issue or to recognize such travel documents, and to extend the issue of such documents to refugees as defined in article 1 of the Convention relating to the Status of Refugees or to recognize the travel documents so issued to such persons, until they shall have undertaken obligations under article 28 of the said Convention.'

B.

'The Conference,

Considering that the unity of the family, the natural and fundamental group of society, is an essential right of the refugee, and that such unity is constantly threatened, and

Noting with satisfaction that, according to the official commentary of the ad hoc Committee on Statelessness and Related Problems the rights granted to a refugee are extended to members of his family,

Recommends Governments to take the necessary measures for the protection of the refugee's family, especially with a view to:

(1) Ensuring that the unity of the refugee's family is maintained particularly in cases where the head of the family has fulfilled the necessary conditions for admission to a particular country,

(2) The protection of refugees who are minors, in particular unaccompanied children and girls, with special reference to guardianship and adoption.'

C.

'The Conference,

Considering that, in the moral, legal and material spheres, refugees need the help of suitable welfare services, especially that of appropriate non-governmental organizations,

Recommends Governments and inter-governmental bodies to facilitate, encourage and sustain the efforts of properly qualified organizations.'

D.

'The Conference,

Considering that many persons still leave their country of origin for reasons of persecution and are entitled to special protection on account of their position,

Recommends that Governments continue to receive refugees in their territories and that they act in concert in a true spirit of international co-operation in order that these refugees may find asylum and the possibility of resettlement.'

E.

'The Conference,

Expresses the hope that the Convention relating to the Status of Refugees will have value as an example exceeding its contractual scope and that all nations will be guided by it in granting so far as possible to persons in their territory as refugees and who would not be covered by the terms of the Convention, the treatment for which it provides.'

Annex II

1951 Convention relating to the Status of Refugees (United Nations Treaty Series, vol. 189, p. 137)

Preamble

The High Contracting Parties

Considering that the Charter of the United Nations and the Universal Declaration of Human Rights approved on 10 December 1948 by the General Assembly have affirmed the principle that human beings shall enjoy fundamental rights and freedoms without discrimination,

Considering that the United Nations has, on various occasions, manifested its profound concern for refugees and endeavoured to assure refugees the widest possible exercise of these fundamental rights and freedoms,

Considering that it is desirable to revise and consolidate previous international agreements relating to the status of refugees and to extend the scope of and the protection accorded by such instruments by means of a new agreement,

Considering that the grant of asylum may place unduly heavy burdens on certain countries, and that a satisfactory solution of a problem of which the United Nations has recognized the international scope and nature cannot therefore be achieved without international co-operation,

Expressing the wish that all States, recognizing the social and humanitarian nature of the problem of refugees, will do everything within their power to prevent this problem from becoming a cause of tension between States,

Noting that the United Nations High Commissioner for Refugees is charged with the task of supervising international conventions providing for the protection of Refugees, and recognizing that the effective co-ordination of measures taken to deal with this problem will depend upon the co-operation of States with the High Commissioner,

Have agreed as follows.

Chapter I
General Provisions

Article 1. Definition of the term 'Refugee'

A. For the purposes of the present Convention, the term 'refugee' shall apply to any person who:

(1) Has been considered a refugee under the Arrangements of 12 May 1926 and 30 June 1928 or under the Conventions of 28 October 1933 and 10 February 1938, the Protocol of 14 September 1939 or the Constitution of the International Refugee Organization;

Decisions of non-eligibility taken by the International Refugee Organization during the period of its activities shall not prevent the status of refugee being accorded to persons who fulfil the conditions of paragraph 2 of this section;

(2) As a result of events occurring before 1 January 1951 and owing to well-founded fear of being persecuted for reasons of race, religion, nationality, membership of a particular social group or political opinion, is outside the country of his nationality and is unable or, owing to such fear, is unwilling to avail himself of the protection of that country; or who, not having a nationality and being outside the country of his former habitual residence as a result of such events, is unable or, owing to such fear, is unwilling to return to it.

In the case of a person who has more than one nationality, the term 'the country of his nationality' shall mean each of the countries of which he is a national, and a person shall not be deemed to be lacking the protection of the country of his nationality if, without any valid reason based on well-founded fear, he has not availed himself of the protection of one of the countries of which he is a national.

B. (1) For the purposes of this Convention, the words 'events occurring before 1 January 1951' in Article 1, Section A, shall be understood to mean either:

(a) 'events occurring in Europe before 1 January 1951' or

(b) 'events occurring in Europe or elsewhere before 1 January 1951' and each Contracting State shall make a declaration at the time of signature, ratification or accession, specifying which of these meanings it applies for the purpose of its obligations under this Convention.

(2) Any Contracting State which has adopted alternative (a) may at any time extend its obligations by adopting alternative (b) by means of a notification addressed to the Secretary-General of the United Nations.

C. This Convention shall cease to apply to any person falling under the terms of Section A if:

(1) He has voluntarily re-availed himself of the protection of the country of his nationality; or

(2) Having lost his nationality, he has voluntarily re-acquired it; or

(3) He has acquired a new nationality, and enjoys the protection of the country of his new nationality; or

(4) He has voluntarily re-established himself in the country which he left or outside which he remained owing to fear of persecution; or

(5) He can no longer, because the circumstances in connexion with which he has been recognized as a refugee have ceased to exist, continue to refuse to avail himself of the protection of the country of his nationality;

Provided that this paragraph shall not apply to a refugee falling under section A(1) of this Article who is able to invoke compelling reasons arising out of previous persecution for refusing to avail himself of the protection of the country of nationality;

(6) Being a person who has no nationality he is, because the circumstances in connexion with which he has been recognized as a refugee have ceased to exist, able to return to the country of his former habitual residence;

Provided that this paragraph shall not apply to a refugee falling under section A(1) of this Article who is able to invoke compelling reasons arising out of previous persecution for refusing to return to the country of his former habitual residence.

D. This Convention shall not apply to persons who are at present receiving from organs or agencies of the United Nations other than the United Nations High Commissioner for Refugees protection or assistance.

When such protection or assistance has ceased for any reason, without the position of such persons being definitively settled in accordance with the relevant resolutions adopted by the General Assembly of the United Nations, these persons shall *ipso facto* be entitled to the benefits of this Convention.

E. This Convention shall not apply to a person who is recognized by the competent authorities of the country in which he has taken residence as having the rights and obligations which are attached to the possession of the nationality of that country.

F. The provisions of this Convention shall not apply to any person with respect to whom there are serious reasons for considering that:
  (a) he has committed a crime against peace, a war crime, or a crime against humanity, as defined in the international instruments drawn up to make provision in respect of such crimes;
  (b) he has committed a serious non-political crime outside the country of refuge prior to his admission to that country as a refugee;
  (c) he has been guilty of acts contrary to the purposes and principles of the United Nations.

Article 2 General obligations

Every refugee has duties to the country in which he finds himself, which require in particular that he conform to its laws and regulations as well as to measures taken for the maintenance of public order.

Article 3 Non-discrimination

The Contracting States shall apply the provisions of this Convention to refugees without discrimination as to race, religion or country of origin.

Article 4 Religion

The Contracting States shall accord to refugees within their territories treatment at least as favourable as that accorded to their nationals with respect to freedom to practise their religion and freedom as regards the religious education of their children.

Article 5 Rights granted apart from this Convention

Nothing in this Convention shall be deemed to impair any rights and benefits granted by a Contracting State to refugees apart from this Convention.

Article 6 The term 'in the same circumstances'

For the purpose of this Convention, the term 'in the same circumstances' implies that any requirements (including requirements as to length and conditions of sojourn or residence) which the particular individual would have to fulfil for the enjoyment of the right in question, if he were not a refugee, must be fulfilled by him, with the exception of requirements which by their nature a refugee is incapable of fulfilling.

Article 7 Exemption from reciprocity

1. Except where this Convention contains more favourable provisions, a Contracting State shall accord to refugees the same treatment as is accorded to aliens generally.

2. After a period of three years' residence, all refugees shall enjoy exemption from legislative reciprocity in the territory of the Contracting States.

3. Each Contracting State shall continue to accord to refugees the rights and benefits to which they were already entitled, in the absence of reciprocity, at the date of entry into force of this Convention for that State.

4. The Contracting States shall consider favourably the possibility of according to refugees, in the absence of reciprocity, rights and benefits beyond those to which they are entitled according to paragraphs 2 and 3, and to extending exemption from reciprocity to refugees who do not fulfil the conditions provided for in paragraphs 2 and 3.

5. The provisions of paragraphs 2 and 3 apply both to the rights and benefits referred to in articles 13, 18, 19, 21 and 22 of this Convention and to rights and benefits for which this Convention does not provide.

Article 8 Exemption from exceptional measures

With regard to exceptional measures which may be taken against the person, property or interests of nationals of a foreign State, the Contracting States shall not apply such measures to a refugee who is formally a national of the said State solely on account of such nationality. Contracting States which, under their legislation, are prevented from applying the general principle expressed in this article, shall, in appropriate cases, grant exemptions in favour of such refugees.

Article 9 Provisional measures

Nothing in this Convention shall prevent a Contracting State, in time of war or other grave and exceptional circumstances, from taking provisionally measures which it considers to be essential to the national security in the case of a particular person, pending a determination by the Contracting State that that person is in fact a refugee and that the continuance of such measures is necessary in his case in the interests of national security.

Article 10 Continuity of residence

1. Where a refugee has been forcibly displaced during the Second World War and removed to the territory of a Contracting State, and is resident there, the period of such enforced sojourn shall be considered to have been lawful residence within that territory.

2. Where a refugee has been forcibly displaced during the Second World War from the territory of a Contracting State and has, prior to the date of entry into force of this Convention, returned there for the purpose of taking up residence, the period of residence before and after such enforced displacement shall be regarded as one uninterrupted period for any purposes for which uninterrupted residence is required.

Article 11 Refugee seamen

In the case of refugee regularly serving as crew members on board a ship flying the flag of a Contracting State, that State shall give sympathetic consideration to their establishment on its territory and the issue of travel documents to them on their temporary admission to its territory particularly with a view to facilitating their establishment in another country.

Chapter II
Juridical Status

Article 12 Personal status

1. The personal status of a refugee shall be governed by the law of the country of his domicile or, if he has no domicile, by the law of the country of his residence.
2. Rights previously acquired by a refugee and dependent on personal status, more particularly rights attaching to marriage, shall be respected by a Contracting State, subject to compliance, if this be necessary, with the formalities required by the law of that State, provided that the right in question is one which would have been recognized by the law of that State had he not become a refugee.

Article 13 Movable and immovable property

The Contracting States shall accord to a refugee treatment as favourable as possible and, in any event, not less favourable than that accorded to aliens generally in the same circumstances as regards the acquisition of movable and immovable property and other rights pertaining thereto, and to leases and other contracts relating to movable and immovable property.

Article 14 Artistic rights and industrial property

In respect of the protection of industrial property, such as inventions, designs or models, trade marks, trade names, and of rights in literary, artistic and scientific works, a refugee shall be accorded in the country in which he has his habitual residence the same protection as is accorded to nationals of that country. In the territory of any other Contracting State, he shall be accorded the same protection as is accorded in that territory to nationals of the country in which he has habitual residence.

Article 15 Right of association

As regards non-political and non-profit-making associations and trade unions the Contracting States shall accord to refugees lawfully staying in their territory the most favourable treatment accorded to nationals of a foreign country, in the same circumstances.

Article 16 Access to courts

1. A refugee shall have free access to the courts of law on the territory of all Contracting States.
2. A refugee shall enjoy in the Contracting State in which he has his habitual residence the same treatment as a national in matters pertaining to access to the Courts, including legal assistance and exemption from cautio judicatum solvi.
3. A refugee shall be accorded in the matters referred to in paragraph 2 in countries other than that in which he has his habitual residence the treatment granted to a national of the country of his habitual residence.

Chapter III

Gainful Employment

Article 17 Wage-earning employment

1. The Contracting State shall accord to refugees lawfully staying in their territory the most favourable treatment accorded to nationals of a foreign country in the same circumstances, as regards the right to engage in wage-earning employment.
2. In any case, restrictive measures imposed on aliens or the employment of aliens for the protection of the national labour market shall not be applied to a refugee who was already exempt from them at the date of entry into force of this Convention for the Contracting States concerned, or who fulfils one of the following conditions:
   (a) He has completed three years' residence in the country;
   (b) He has a spouse possessing the nationality of the country of residence. A refugee may not invoke the benefits of this provision if he has abandoned his spouse;
   (c) He has one or more children possessing the nationality of the country of residence.
3. The Contracting States shall give sympathetic consideration to assimilating the rights of all refugees with regard to wage-earning employment to those of nationals,

and in particular of those refugees who have entered their territory pursuant to programmes of labour recruitment or under immigration schemes.

Article 18 Self-employment

The Contracting States shall accord to a refugee lawfully in their territory treatment as favourable as possible and, in any event, not less favourable than that accorded to aliens generally in the same circumstances, as regards the right to engage on his own account in agriculture, industry, handicrafts and commerce and to establish commercial and industrial companies.

Article 19 Liberal professions

1. Each Contracting State shall accord to refugees lawfully staying in their territory who hold diplomas recognized by the competent authorities of that State, and who are desirous of practising a liberal profession, treatment as favourable as possible and, in any event, not less favourable than that accorded to aliens generally in the same circumstances.

2. The Contracting States shall use their best endeavours consistently with their laws and constitutions to secure the settlement of such refugees in the territories, other than the metropolitan territory, for whose international relations they are responsible.

Chapter IV
Welfare

Article 20 Rationing

Where a rationing system exists, which applies to the population at large and regulates the general distribution of products in short supply, refugees shall be accorded the same treatment as nationals.

Article 21 Housing

As regards housing, the Contracting States, in so far as the matter is regulated by laws or regulations or is subject to the control of public authorities, shall accord to refugees lawfully staying in their territory treatment as favourable as possible and, in any event, not less favourable than that accorded to aliens generally in the same circumstances.

Article 22 Public education

1. The Contracting States shall accord to refuges the same treatment as is accorded to nationals with respect to elementary education.

2. The Contracting States shall accord to refugees treatment as favourable as possible, and, in any event, not less favourable than that accorded to aliens generally in the same circumstances, with respect to education other than elementary education and, in particular, as regards access to studies, the recognition of foreign school certificates, diplomas and degrees, the remission of fees and charges and the award of scholarships.

Article 23 Public relief

The Contracting States shall accord to refugees lawfully staying in their territory the same treatment with respect to public relief and assistance as is accorded to their nationals.

Article 24 Labour legislation and social security

1. The Contracting States shall accord to refugees lawfully staying in their territory the same treatment as is accorded to nationals in respect of the following matters:

(a) In so far as such matters are governed by laws or regulations or are subject to the control of administrative authorities: remuneration, including family allowances where these form part of remuneration, hours of work, overtime arrangements, holidays with pay, restrictions on home work, minimum age of employment, apprenticeship and training, women's work and the work of young persons, and the enjoyment of the benefits of collective bargaining;

(b) Social security (legal provisions in respect of employment injury, occupational diseases, maternity, sickness, disability, old age, death, unemployment, family responsibilities and any other contingency which, according to national laws or regulations, is covered by a social security scheme), subject to the following limitations:

(i) There may be appropriate arrangements for the maintenance of acquired rights and rights in course of acquisition;

(ii) National laws or regulations of the country of residence may prescribe special arrangements concerning benefits or portions of benefits which are payable wholly out of public funds, and concerning allowances paid to persons who do not fulfil the contribution conditions prescribed for the award of a normal pension.

2. The right to compensation for the death of a refugee resulting from employment injury or from occupational disease shall not be affected by the fact that the residence of the beneficiary is outside the territory of the Contracting State.

3. The Contracting States shall extend to refugees the benefits of agreements concluded between them, or which may be concluded between them in the future, concerning the maintenance of acquired rights and rights in the process of acquisi-

tion in regard to social security, subject only to the conditions which apply to nationals of the States signatory to the agreements in question.

4. The Contracting States will give sympathetic consideration to extending to refugees so far as possible the benefits of similar agreements which may at any time be in force between such Contracting States and non-contracting States.

Chapter V

Administrative Measures

Article 25 Administrative assistance

1. When the exercise of a right by a refugee would normally require the assistance of authorities of a foreign country to whom he cannot have recourse, the Contracting States in whose territory he is residing shall arrange that such assistance be afforded to him by their own authorities or by an international authority.

2. The authority or authorities mentioned in paragraph 1 shall deliver or cause to be delivered under their supervision to refugees such documents or certifications as would normally be delivered to aliens by or through their national authorities.

3. Documents or certifications so delivered shall stand in the stead of the official instruments delivered to aliens by or through their national authorities, and shall be given credence in the absence of proof to the contrary.

4. Subject to such exceptional treatment as may be granted to indigent persons, fees may be charged for the services mentioned herein, but such fees shall be moderate and commensurate with those charges to nationals for similar services.

5. The provisions of this article shall be without prejudice to articles 27 and 28.

Article 26 Freedom of movement

Each Contracting State shall accord to refugees lawfully in its territory the right to choose their place of residence and to move freely within its territory, subject to any regulations applicable to aliens generally in the same circumstances.

Article 27 Identity papers

The Contracting States shall issue identity papers to any refugee in their territory who does not possess a valid travel document.

Article 28 Travel documents

1. The Contracting States shall issue to refugees lawfully staying in their territory travel documents for the purpose of travel outside their territory unless compelling reasons of national security or public order otherwise require, and the provisions of

the Schedule to this Convention shall apply with respect to such documents. The Contracting States may issue such a travel document to any other refugee in their territory; they shall in particular give sympathetic consideration to the issue of such a travel document to refugees in their territory who are unable to obtain a travel document from the country of their lawful residence.
2. Travel documents issued to refugees under previous international agreements by parties thereto shall be recognized and treated by the Contracting States in the same way as if they had been issued pursuant to this article.

Article 29 Fiscal charges

1. The Contracting States shall not impose upon refugees duties, charges or taxes, of any description whatsoever, other or higher than those which are or may be levied on their nationals in similar situations.

2. Nothing in the above paragraph shall prevent the application to refugees of the laws and regulations concerning charges in respect of the issue to aliens of administrative documents including identity papers.

Article 30 Transfer of assets

1. A Contracting State shall, in conformity with its laws and regulations permit refugees to transfer assets which they have brought into its territory, to another country where they have been admitted for the purposes of resettlement.

2. A Contracting State shall give sympathetic consideration to the application of refugees for permission to transfer assets wherever they may be and which are necessary for their resettlement in another country to which they have been admitted.

Article 31 Refugees unlawfully in the country of refuge

1. The Contracting States shall not impose penalties, on account of their illegal entry or presence, on refugees who, coming directly from a territory where their life or freedom was threatened in the sense of Article 1, enter or are present in their territory without authorization, provided they present themselves without delay to the authorities and show good cause for their illegal entry or presence.

2. The Contracting States shall not apply to the movements of such refugees restrictions other than those which are necessary and such restrictions shall only be applied until their status in the country is regularized or they obtain admission into another country. The Contracting States shall allow such refugees a reasonable period and all the necessary facilities to obtain admission into another country.

Article 32 Expulsion

1. The Contracting States shall not expel a refugee lawfully in their territory save on grounds of national security or public order.

2. The expulsion of such a refugee shall be only in pursuance of a decision reached in accordance with due process of law. Except where compelling reasons of national security otherwise require, the refugee shall be allowed to submit evidence to clear himself, and to appeal to and be represented for the purpose before competent authority or a person or persons specially designated by the competent authority.

3. The Contracting States shall allow such a refugee a reasonable period within which to seek legal admission into another country. The Contracting States reserve the right to apply during that period such internal measures as they may deem necessary.

Article 33 Prohibition of expulsion or return ('refoulement')

1. No Contracting State shall expel or return ('refouler') a refugee in any manner whatsoever to the frontiers of territories where his life or freedom would be threatened on account of his race, religion, nationality, membership of a particular social group or political opinion.

2. The benefit of the present provision may not, however, be claimed by a refugee whom there are reasonable grounds for regarding as a danger to the security of the country in which he is, or who, having been convicted by a final judgement of a particularly serious crime, constitutes a danger to the community of that country.

Article 34 Naturalization

The Contracting States shall as far as possible facilitate the assimilation and naturalization of refugees. They shall in particular make every effort to expedite naturalization proceedings and to reduce as far as possible the charges and costs of such proceedings.

Chapter VI

Executory and Transitory Provisions

Article 35 Co-operation of the national authorities with the United Nations

1. The Contracting States undertake to co-operate with the Office of the United Nations High Commissioner for Refugees, or any other agency of the United Nations which may succeed it, in the exercise of its functions, and shall in particular facilitate its duty of supervising the application of the provisions of this Convention.

2. In order to enable the Office of the High Commissioner or any other agency of the United Nations which may succeed it, to make reports to the competent organs of the United Nations, the Contracting States undertake to provide

them in the appropriate form with information and statistical data requested concerning:

(a) the condition of refugees,
(b) the implementation of this Convention, and
(c) laws, regulations and decrees which are, or may hereafter be, in force relating to refugees.

Article 36 Information on national legislation

The Contracting States shall communicate to the Secretary-General of the United Nations the laws and regulations which they may adopt to ensure the application of this Convention.

Article 37 Relation to previous conventions

Without prejudice to article 28, paragraph 2, of this Convention, this Convention replaces, as between parties to it, the Arrangements of 5 July 1922, 31 May 1924, 12 May 1926, 30 June 1928 and 30 July 1935, the Conventions of 28 October 1933 and 10 February 1938, the Protocol of 14 September 1939 and the Agreement of 15 October 1946.

Chapter VII

Final Clauses

Article 38 Settlement of disputes

Any dispute between parties to this Convention relating to its interpretation or application, which cannot be settled by other means, shall be referred to the International Court of Justice at the request of any one of the parties to the dispute.

Article 39 Signature, ratification and accession

1. This Convention shall be opened for signature at Geneva on 28 July 1951 and shall thereafter be deposited with the Secretary-General of the United Nations. It shall be open for signature at the European Office of the United Nations from 28 July to 31 August 1951 and shall be reopened for signature at the Headquarters of the United Nations from 17 September 1951 to 31 December 1952.

2. This Convention shall be open for signature on behalf of all States Members of the United Nations, and also on behalf of any other State invited to attend the Conference of Plenipotentiaries on the Status of Refugees and Stateless Persons or to

which an invitation to sign will have been addressed by the General Assembly. It shall be ratified and the instruments of ratification shall be deposited with the Secretary-General of the United Nations.

3. This Convention shall be open from 28 July 1951 for accession by the States referred to in paragraph 2 of this Article. Accession shall be effected by the deposit of an instrument of accession with the Secretary-General of the United Nations.

Article 40 Territorial application clause

1. Any State may, at the time of signature, ratification or accession, declare that this Convention shall extend to all or any of the territories for the international relations of which it is responsible. Such a declaration shall take effect when the Convention enters into force for the States concerned.

2. At any time thereafter any such extension shall be made by notification addressed to the Secretary-General of the United Nations and shall take effect as from the ninetieth day after the day of receipt by the Secretary-General of the United Nations of this notification, or as from the date of entry into force of the Convention for the State concerned, whichever is the later.

3. With respect to those territories to which this Convention is not extended at the time of signature, ratification or accession, each State concerned shall consider the possibility of taking the necessary steps in order to extend the application of this Convention to such territories, subject where necessary for constitutional reasons, to the consent of the governments of such territories.

Article 41 Federal clause

In the case of a Federal or non-unitary State, the following provisions shall apply:

(a) With respect to those articles of this Convention that come within the legislative jurisdiction of the federal legislative authority, the obligations of the Federal Government shall to this extent be the same as those of Parties which are not Federal States,

(b) With respect to those articles of this Convention that come within the legislative jurisdiction of constituent States, provinces or cantons which are not, under the constitutional system of the federation, bound to take legislative action, the Federal Government shall bring such articles with a favourable recommendation, to the notice of the appropriate authorities of States, provinces or cantons at the earliest possible moment.

(c) A Federal State Party to this Convention shall, at the request of any other Contracting State transmitted through the Secretary-General of the United Nations, supply a statement of the law and practice of the Federation and its constituent units in regard to any particular provision of the Convention showing the extent to which effect has been given to that provision by legislative or other action.

Article 42 Reservations

1. At the time of signature, ratification or accession, any State may make reservations to articles of the Convention other than to articles 1, 3, 4, 16(1), 33, 36 to 46 inclusive.

2. Any State making a reservation in accordance with paragraph 1 of this article may at any time withdraw the reservation by a communication to that effect addressed to the Secretary-General of the United Nations.

Article 43 Entry into force

1. This Convention shall come into force on the ninetieth day following the day of deposit of the sixth instrument of ratification or accession.

2. For each State ratifying or acceding to the Convention after the deposit of the sixth instrument of ratification or accession, the Convention shall enter into force on the ninetieth day following the day of deposit by such State of its instrument of ratification or accession.

Article 44 Denunciation

1. Any Contracting State may denounce this Convention at any time by a notification addressed to the Secretary-General of the United Nations.

2. Such denunciation shall take effect for the Contracting State concerned one year from the date upon which it is received by the Secretary-General of the United Nations.

3. Any State which has made a declaration or notification under article 40 may, at any time thereafter, by a notification to the Secretary-General of the United Nations, declare that the Convention shall cease to extend to such territory one year after the date of receipt of the notification by the Secretary-General.

Article 45 Revision

1. Any Contracting State may request revision of this Convention at any time by a notification addressed to the Secretary-General of the United Nations.

2. The General Assembly of the United Nations shall recommend the steps, if any, to be taken in respect of such request.

Article 46 Notifications by the Secretary-General of the United Nations

The Secretary-General of the United Nations shall inform all Members of the United Nations and non-member States referred to in article 39:

(a) of declarations and notifications in accordance with Section B of Article 1;

(b) of signatures, ratifications and accessions in accordance with article 39;
(c) of declarations and notifications in accordance with article 40;
(d) of reservations and withdrawals in accordance with article 42;
(e) of the date on which this Convention will come into force in accordance with article 43;
(f) of denunciations and notifications in accordance with article 44;
(g) of requests for revision in accordance with article 45.

In faith whereof the undersigned, duly authorized, have signed this Convention on behalf of their respective Governments,

Done at Geneva, this twenty-eighth day of July, one thousand nine hundred and fifty-one, in a single copy, of which the English and French texts are equally authentic and which shall remain deposited in the archives of the United Nations, and certified true copies of which shall be delivered to all Members of the United Nations and to the non-member States referred to in article 39.

Schedule

Paragraph 1

1. The travel document referred to in article 28 of this Convention shall be similar to the specimen annexed hereto.

2. The document shall be made out in at least two languages, one of which shall be in English or French.

Paragraph 2

Subject to the regulations obtaining in the country of issue, children may be included in the travel document of a parent or, in exceptional circumstances, of another adult refugee.

Paragraph 3

The fees charged for issue of the document shall not exceed the lowest scale of charges for national passports.

Paragraph 4

Save in special or exceptional cases, the document shall be made valid for the largest possible number of countries.

Paragraph 5

The document shall have a validity of either one or two years, at the discretion of the issuing authority.

Paragraph 6

1. The renewal or extension of the validity of the document is a matter for the authority which issued it, so long as the holder has not established lawful residence in another territory and resides lawfully in the territory of the said authority. The issue of a new document is, under the same conditions, a matter for the authority which issued the former document.

2. Diplomatic or consular authorities, specially authorized for the purpose, shall be empowered to extend, for a period not exceeding six months, the validity of travel documents issued by their Governments.

3. The Contracting States shall give sympathetic consideration to renewing or extending the validity of travel documents or issuing new documents to refugees no longer lawfully resident in their territory who are unable to obtain a travel document from the country of their lawful residence.

Paragraph 7

The Contracting States shall recognize the validity of the documents issued in accordance with the provisions of article 28 of this Convention.

Paragraph 8

The competent authorities of the country to which the refugee desires to proceed shall, if they are prepared to admit him and if a visa is required, affix a visa on the document of which he is the holder.

Paragraph 9

1. The Contracting States undertake to issue transit visas to refugees who have obtained visas for a territory of final destination.

2. The issue of such visas may be refused on grounds which would justify refusal of a visa to any alien.

Paragraph 10

The fees for the issue of exit, entry or transit visas shall not exceed the lowest scale of charges for visas on foreign passports.

Paragraph 11

When a refugee has lawfully taken up residence in the territory of another Contracting State, the responsibility for the issue of a new document, under the terms and conditions of article 28, shall be that of the competent authority of that territory, to which the refugee shall be entitled to apply.

Paragraph 12

The authority issuing a new document shall withdraw the old document and shall return it to the country of issue, if it is stated in the document that it should be so returned; otherwise it shall withdraw and cancel the document.

Paragraph 13

1. Each Contracting State undertakes that the holder of a travel document issued by it in accordance with article 28 of this Convention shall be readmitted to its territory at any time during the period of its validity.
2. Subject to the provisions of the preceding sub-paragraph, a Contracting State may require the holder of the document to comply with such formalities as may be prescribed in regard to exit from or return to its territory.
3. The Contracting States reserve the right, in exceptional cases, or in cases where the refugee's stay is authorized for a specific period, when issuing the document, to limit the period during which the refugee may return to a period of not less than three months.

Paragraph 14

Subject only to the terms of paragraph 13, the provisions of this Schedule in no way affect the laws and regulations governing the conditions of admission to, transit through, residence and establishment in, and departure from, the territories of the Contracting States.

Paragraph 15

Neither the issue of the document nor the entries made thereon determine or affect the status of the holder, particularly as regards nationality.

Paragraph 16

The issue of the document does not in any way entitle the holder to the protection of the diplomatic or consular authorities of the country of issue, and does not confer on these authorities a right of protection.

Annex

Specimen travel document

The document will be in booklet form (approximately 15 × 10 centimetres).

It is recommended that it be so printed that any erasure or alteration by chemical or other means can be readily detected, and that the words 'Convention of 28 July 1951' be printed in continuous repetition on each page, in the language of the issuing country.

(*Cover of booklet*)
TRAVEL DOCUMENT
(Convention of 28 July 1951)

No.

(1)
TRAVEL DOCUMENT
(Convention of 28 July 1951)

This document expires on ______________________
unless its validity is extended or renewed.

Name ______________________

Forename(s) ______________________

Accompanied by ______________________ child (children)

1. This document is issued solely with a view to providing the holder with a travel document which can serve in lieu of a national passport. It is without prejudice to and in no way affects the holder's nationality.

2. The holder is authorized to return to ______________________ ______________________ [state here the country whose authorities are issuing the document] on or before ______________________ unless some later date is hereafter specified.

[The period during which the holder is allowed to return must not be less than three months]

3. Should the holder take up residence in a country other than that which issued the present document, he must, if he wishes to travel again, apply to the competent authorities of his country of residence for a new document. [The old travel document shall be withdrawn by the authority issuing the new document and returned to the authority which issued it.] [1]

(This document contains pages, exclusive of cover.)

[1] The sentence in brackets to be inserted by Governments which so desire.

---

(2)

Place and date of birth
Occupation
Present residence
* Maiden name and forename(s) of wife
* Name and forename(s) of husband

Description

Height ________________
Hair ________________
Colour of eyes ________________
Nose ________________
Shape of face ________________
Complexion ________________
Special peculiarities ________________

Children accompanying holder

Name	Forename(s)	Place and date of birth	Sex

* Strike out whichever does not apply.

(This document contains pages, exclusive of cover).

---

(3)

Photograph of holder and stamp of issuing authority
Finger-prints of holder (if required)

Signature of holder ________________

(This document contains pages, exclusive of cover).

---

(4)

1. This document is valid for the following countries:

____
____
____
____

2. Document or documents on the basis of which the present document is issued:

____
____
____

Issued at ________________
Date ________________

Signature and stamp of authority issuing the document:

Fee paid

(This document contains pages, exclusive of cover).

(5)

Extension or renewal of validity

Fee paid: From ______________________
To ______________________
Done at ______________ Date ______________________

Signature and stamp of authority extending or renewing the validity of the document:

____

Extension or renewal of validity

Fee paid: From ______________________
To ______________________
Done at ______________ Date ______________________

Signature and stamp of authority extending or renewing the validity of the document:

(This document contains pages, exclusive of cover.)

---

(6)

Extension or renewal of validity

Fee paid: From ______________________
To ______________________
Done at ______________ Date ______________________

Signature and stamp of authority extending or renewing the validity of the document:

____

Extension or renewal of validity

Fee paid: From ______________________
To ______________________
Done at ______________ Date ______________________

Signature and stamp of authority extending or renewing the validity of the document:

(This document contains pages, exclusive of cover.)

(7–32)

Visas

The name of the holder of the document must be repeated in each visa.

(This document contains pages, exclusive of cover.)

Annex III
1967 Protocol relating to the Status of Refugees (United Nations, Treaty Series, vol. 606, p. 267)

The States Parties to the present protocol,

Considering that the Convention relating to the Status of Refugees done at Geneva on 28 July 1951 (hereinafter referred to as the Convention) covers only those persons who have become refugees as a result of events occurring before 1 January 1951,

Considering that new refugee situations have arisen since the Convention was adopted and that the refugees concerned may therefore not fall within the scope of the Convention,

Considering that it is desirable that equal status should be enjoyed by all refugees covered by the definition in the Convention irrespective of the dateline 1 January 1951,

Have agreed as follows:

Article I General provision

1. The States Parties to the present Protocol undertake to apply articles 2 to 34 inclusive of the Convention to refugees as hereinafter defined.

2. For the purpose of the present Protocol, the term 'refugee' shall, except as regards the application of paragraph 3 of this article, mean any person within the definition of article 1 of the Convention as if the words 'As a result of events occurring before 1 January 1951 and . . .' and the words '. . . as a result of such events', in article 1A(2) were omitted.

3. The present Protocol shall be applied by the States Parties hereto without any geographic limitation, save that existing declarations made by States already Parties to the Convention in accordance with article 1B(1)(a) of the Convention, shall, unless extended under article 1B(2) thereof, apply also under the present Protocol.

Article II Co-operation of the national authorities with the United Nations

1. The States Parties to the present Protocol undertake to co-operate with the Office of the United Nations High Commissioner for Refugees, or any other agency of the United Nations which may succeed it, in the exercise of its functions, and shall in particular facilitate its duty of supervising the application of the provisions of the present Protocol.

2. In order to enable the Office of the High Commissioner, or any other agency of the United Nations which may succeed it, to make reports to the competent

organs of the United Nations, the States Parties to the present Protocol undertake to provide them with the information and statistical data requested, in the appropriate form, concerning:

(a) The condition of refugees;
(b) The implementation of the present Protocol;
(c) Laws, regulations and decrees which are, or may hereafter be, in force relating to refugees.

Article III Information on national legislation

The States Parties to the present Protocol shall communicate to the Secretary-General of the United Nations the laws and regulations which they may adopt to ensure the application of the present Protocol.

Article IV Settlement of disputes

Any dispute between States Parties to the present Protocol which relates to its interpretation or application and which cannot be settled by other means shall be referred to the International Court of Justice at the request of any one of the parties to the dispute.

Article V Accession

The present Protocol shall be open for accession on behalf of all States Parties to the Convention and of any other State Member of the United Nations or member of any of the specialized agencies or to which an invitation to accede may have been addressed by the General Assembly of the United Nations. Accession shall be effected by the deposit of an instrument of accession with the Secretary-General of the United Nations.

Article VI Federal clause

In the case of a Federal or non-unitary State, the following provisions shall apply:

(a) With respect to those articles of the Convention to be applied in accordance with article 1, paragraph 1, of the present Protocol that come within the legislative jurisdiction of the federal legislative authority, the obligations of the Federal Government shall to this extent be the same as those of States Parties which are not Federal States;
(b) With respect to those articles of the Convention to be applied in accordance with article I, paragraph 1, of the present Protocol that come within the legislative jurisdiction of constituent States, provinces or cantons which are not, under the constitutional system of the federation, bound to take legislative action, the Federal Government shall bring such articles with a favourable

recommendation to the notice of the appropriate authorities of States, provinces or cantons at the earliest possible moment;

(c) A Federal State Party to the present Protocol shall, at the request of any other State Party hereto transmitted through the Secretary-General of the United Nations, supply a statement of the law and practice of the Federation and its constituent units in regard to any particular provision of the Convention to be applied in accordance with article I, paragraph 1, of the present Protocol, showing the extent to which effect has been given to that provision by legislative or other action.

Article VII Reservations and Declarations

1. At the time of accession, any State may make reservations in respect of article IV of the present Protocol and in respect of the application in accordance with article I of the present Protocol of any provisions of the Convention other than those contained in articles 1, 3, 4, 16(1) and 33 thereof, provided that in the case of a State Party to the Convention reservations made under this article shall not extend to refugees in respect of whom the Convention applies.

2. Reservations made by States Parties to the Convention in accordance with article 42 thereof shall, unless withdrawn, be applicable in relation to their obligations under the present Protocol.

3. Any State making a reservation in accordance with paragraph 1 of this article may at any time withdraw such reservation by a communication to that effect addressed to the Secretary-General of the United Nations.

4. Declarations made under article 40, paragraphs 1 and 2, of the Convention by a State Party thereto which accedes to the present Protocol shall be deemed to apply in respect of the present Protocol, unless upon accession a notification to the contrary is addressed by the State Party concerned to the Secretary-General of the United Nations. The provisions of article 40, paragraphs 2 and 3, and of article 44, paragraph 3, of the Convention shall be deemed to apply *mutatis mutandis* to the present Protocol.

Article VIII Entry into force

1. The present Protocol shall come into force on the day of deposit of the sixth instrument of accession.

2. For each State acceding to the Protocol after the deposit of the sixth instrument of accession, the Protocol shall come into force on the date of deposit by such State of its instrument of accession.

Article IX Denunciation

1. Any State Party hereto may denounce this Protocol at any time by a notification addressed to the Secretary-General of the United Nations.
2. Such denunciation shall take effect for the State Party concerned one year from the date on which it is received by the Secretary-General of the United Nations.

Article X Notifications by the Secretary-General of the United Nations

The Secretary-General of the United Nations shall inform the States referred to in article V above of the date of entry into force, accessions, reservations and withdrawals of reservations to and denunciations of the present Protocol, and of declarations and notifications relating hereto.

Article XI Deposit in the Archives of the Secretariat of the United Nations

A copy of the present Protocol, of which the Chinese, English, French, Russian and Spanish texts are equally authentic, signed by the President of the General Assembly and by the Secretary-General of the United Nations, shall be deposited in the archives of the Secretariat of the United Nations. The Secretary-General will transmit certified copies thereof to all States Members of the United Nations and to the other States referred to in article V above.

Annex IV

Convention relating to the Status of Refugees of 28 July 1951

(Entry into force—22 April 1954)

Protocol relating to the Status of Refugees of 31 January 1967

(Entry into force—4 October 1967)

List of States Parties

States parties to the 1951 UN Convention: 106
States parties to the 1967 Protocol: 107
States parties to both the 1951 Convention and the 1967 Protocol: 103
States parties to either one both of these instruments: 110

I. Africa

Algeria
Angola
Benin
Botswana
Burkina Faso
Burundi
Cameroon
Cape Verde[(P)]
Central African Republic
Chad
Congo
Djibouti
Egypt
Equatorial Guinea
Ethiopia
Gabon
Gambia
Ghana
Guinea
Guinea Bissau
Ivory Coast
Kenya
Lesotho
Liberia
Madagascar[(C)]*
Malawi
Mali
Mauritania
Morocco
Mozambique
Niger
Nigeria
Rwanda
Sao Tome and Principe
Senegal
Seychelles
Sierra Leone
Somalia
Sudan
Swaziland[(P)]
Togo
Tunisia
Uganda
United Republic of Tanzania
Zaire
Zambia
Zimbabwe

II. Americas

Argentina
Belize
Bolivia
Brazil
Canada
Chile
Colombia
Costa Rica
Dominican Republic
Ecuador
El Salvador
Guatemala
Haiti
Jamaica
Nicaragua
Panama
Paraguay
Peru
Suriname
United States of America[(P)]
Uruguay
Venezuela[(P)]

III. Asia

China
Iran (Islamic Republic of)
Israel
Japan
Philippines
Yemen

IV. Europe

Austria
Belgium
Cyprus
Czechoslovakia
Denmark[2]
Finland
France[3]
Germany, Federal Republic of[4]

Greece
Holy See
Hungary*
Iceland
Ireland
Italy
Liechtenstein
Luxembourg
Malta*
Monaco(C)*
Netherlands[5]
Norway
Poland
Portugal
Romania
Spain
Sweden
Switzerland
Turkey*
United Kingdom[6]
Yugoslavia

V. Oceania

Australia[1]
Fiji
New Zealand
Papua New Guinea
Samoa(C)
Tuvalu

* The five States marked with an asterisk: Hungary, Madagascar, Malta, Monaco and Turkey have made a declaration in accordance with Article 1(B) 1 of the 1951 Convention to the effect that the words 'events occurring before 1 January 1951' in Article 1, Section A, should be understood to mean 'events occurring *in Europe* before 1 January 1951'. All other States Parties apply the Convention without geographical limitation. The following two States have expressly maintained their declarations of geographical limitation with regard to the 1951 Convention upon acceding to the 1967 Protocol: Malta and Turkey. Madagascar and Monaco have not yet adhered to the 1967 Protocol.

'(C)': the three States marked with a 'C' are Parties to the 1951 Convention only;
'(P)': the four States marked with a 'P' are Parties to the 1967 Protocol only.

1 Australia extended application of the Convention to Norfolk Island.

2 Denmark declared that the Convention was also applicable to Greenland.

3 France declared that the Convention applied to all territories for the international relations of which France was responsible.

4 The Federal Republic of Germany made a separate declaration stating that the Convention and the Protocol also applied to Land Berlin.

5 The Netherlands extended application of the Protocol to Aruba.

6 The United Kingdom extended application of the Convention to the following territories for the conduct of whose international relations the Government of the United Kingdom is responsible:

Channel Islands, Falkland Islands (Malvinas), Isle of Man, St. Helena.

The United Kingdom declared that its accession to the Protocol did not apply to Jersey, but extended its application to Montserrat.

Annex V

Excerpt from the Charter of the International Military Tribunal*

Article 6

'The Tribunal established by the Agreement referred to in Article 1 hereof for the trial and punishment of the major war criminals of the European Axis countries shall have the power to try and punish persons who, acting in the interests of the European Axis countries, whether as individuals or as members of organisations, committed any of the following crimes.

The following acts, or any of them, are crimes coming within the jurisdiction of the Tribunal for which there shall be individual responsibility:

(a) *Crimes against peace:* namely, planning, preparation, initiation or waging of a war of aggression, or a war in violation of international treaties, agreements or assurances, or participation in a common plan or conspiracy for the accomplishment of any of the foregoing;

(b) *War crimes:* namely, violations of the laws or customs of war. Such violations shall include, but not be limited to, murder, ill-treatment or deportation to slave labour or for any other purpose, of civilian population of or in occupied territory, murder or ill-treatment of prisoners of war or persons on the seas, killing of hostages, plunder of public or private property, wanton destruction of cities, towns or villages, or devastation not justified by military necessity;

(c) *Crimes against humanity:* namely, murder, extermination, enslavement, deportation and other inhumane acts committed against any civilian population, before or during the war; or persecutions on political, racial or religious grounds in execution of or in connection with any crime within the jurisdiction of the Tribunal, whether or not in violation of the domestic law of the country where perpetrated.

Leaders, organisers, instigators and accomplices participating in the formulation or execution of a common plan or conspiracy to commit any of the foregoing crimes are responsible for all acts performed by any persons in execution of such plan.'

Note: *See '*The Charter and Judgement of the Nürnberg Tribunal: History and Analysis*' Appendix II—United Nations General Assembly—International Law Commission 1949 (A/CN.4/5 of 3 March 1949).

Annex VI

International Instruments relating to Article 1F(a) of the 1951 Convention

The main international instruments which pertain to Article 1F(a) of the 1951 Convention are as follows:

(1) the London Agreement of 8 August 1945 and Charter of the International Military Tribunal;

(2) Law No. 10 of the Control Council for Germany of 20 December 1945 for the Punishment of Persons Guilty of War Crimes, Crimes against Peace and Crimes against Humanity;

(3) United Nations General Assembly Resolution 3(1) of 13 February 1946 and 95(1) of 11 December 1946 which confirm war crimes and crimes against humanity as they are defined in the Charter of the International Military Tribunal of 8 August 1945;

(4) Convention on the Prevention and Punishment of the Crime of Genocide of 1948 (Article III); (entered into force 12 January 1951);

(5) Convention of the Non-Applicability of Statutory Limitations of War Crimes and Crimes Against Humanity of 1968 (entered into force 11 November 1970);

(6) Geneva Conventions for the protection of victims of war of August 12, 1949 (Convention for the protection of the wounded, and sick, Article 50; Convention for the protection of wounded, sick and shipwrecked, Article 51; Convention relative to the treatment of prisoners of war, Article 130; Convention relative to the protection of civilian persons, Article 147);

(7) Additional Protocol to the Geneva Conventions of 12 August 1949 Relating to the Protection of Victims of International Armed Conflicts (Article 85 on the repression of breaches of this Protocol).

Convention for the Protection of Human Rights and Fundamental Freedoms

as amended by Protocol No. 11

Rome, 4.XI.1950

The text of the Convention had been amended according to the provisions of Protocol No. 3 (ETS No. 45), which entered into force on 21 September 1970, of Protocol No. 5 (ETS No. 55), which entered into force on 20 December 1971 and of Protocol No. 8 (ETS No. 118), which entered into force on 1 January 1990, and comprised also the text of Protocol No. 2 (ETS No. 44) which, in accordance with Article 5, paragraph 3 thereof, had been an integral part of the Convention since its entry into force on 21 September 1970. All provisions which had been amended or added by these Protocols are replaced by Protocol No. 11 (ETS No. 155), as from the date of its entry into force on 1 November 1998. As from that date, Protocol No. 9 (ETS No. 140), which entered into force on 1 October 1994, is repealed and Protocol No. 10 (ETS No. 146) has lost its purpose.

Protocol
Protocols: No. 4 | No. 6 | No. 7
No. 12 | No. 13 | No. 14

The governments signatory hereto, being members of the Council of Europe,

Considering the Universal Declaration of Human Rights proclaimed by the General Assembly of the United Nations on 10th December 1948;

Considering that this Declaration aims at securing the universal and effective recognition and observance of the Rights therein declared;

Considering that the aim of the Council of Europe is the achievement of greater unity between its members and that one of the methods by which that aim is to be pursued is the maintenance and further realisation of human rights and fundamental freedoms;

Reaffirming their profound belief in those fundamental freedoms which are the foundation of justice and peace in the world and are best maintained on the one hand by an effective political democracy and on the other by a common understanding and observance of the human rights upon which they depend;

Being resolved, as the governments of European countries which are like-minded and have a common heritage of political traditions, ideals, freedom and the rule of law, to take the first steps for the collective enforcement of certain of the rights stated in the Universal Declaration,

Have agreed as follows:

Article 1—Obligation to respect human rights[1]

The High Contracting Parties shall secure to everyone within their jurisdiction the rights and freedoms defined in Section I of this Convention.

Section I—Rights and freedoms[1]

Article 2—Right to life[1]

1. Everyone's right to life shall be protected by law. No one shall be deprived of his life intentionally save in the execution of a sentence of a court following his conviction of a crime for which this penalty is provided by law.

2. Deprivation of life shall not be regarded as inflicted in contravention of this article when it results from the use of force which is no more than absolutely necessary:

(a) in defence of any person from unlawful violence;

(b) in order to effect a lawful arrest or to prevent the escape of a person lawfully detained;

(c) in action lawfully taken for the purpose of quelling a riot or insurrection.

Article 3—Prohibition of torture[1]

No one shall be subjected to torture or to inhuman or degrading treatment or punishment.

Article 4—Prohibition of slavery and forced labour[1]

1. No one shall be held in slavery or servitude.

2. No one shall be required to perform forced or compulsory labour.

3. For the purpose of this article the term 'forced or compulsory labour' shall not include:
   (a) any work required to be done in the ordinary course of detention imposed according to the provisions of Article 5 of this Convention or during conditional release from such detention;
   (b) any service of a military character or, in case of conscientious objectors in countries where they are recognised, service exacted instead of compulsory military service;
   (c) any service exacted in case of an emergency or calamity threatening the life or well-being of the community;
   (d) any work or service which forms part of normal civic obligations.

Article 5—Right to liberty and security[1]

1. Everyone has the right to liberty and security of person. No one shall be deprived of his liberty save in the following cases and in accordance with a procedure prescribed by law:
   (a) the lawful detention of a person after conviction by a competent court;
   (b) the lawful arrest or detention of a person for non-compliance with the lawful order of a court or in order to secure the fulfilment of any obligation prescribed by law;
   (c) the lawful arrest or detention of a person effected for the purpose of bringing him before the competent legal authority on reasonable suspicion of having committed an offence or when it is reasonably considered necessary to prevent his committing an offence or fleeing after having done so;
   (d) the detention of a minor by lawful order for the purpose of educational supervision or his lawful detention for the purpose of bringing him before the competent legal authority;
   (e) the lawful detention of persons for the prevention of the spreading of infectious diseases, of persons of unsound mind, alcoholics or drug addicts or vagrants;

(f) the lawful arrest or detention of a person to prevent his effecting an unauthorised entry into the country or of a person against whom action is being taken with a view to deportation or extradition.

2. Everyone who is arrested shall be informed promptly, in a language which he understands, of the reasons for his arrest and of any charge against him.

3. Everyone arrested or detained in accordance with the provisions of paragraph 1.c of this article shall be brought promptly before a judge or other officer authorised by law to exercise judicial power and shall be entitled to trial within a reasonable time or to release pending trial. Release may be conditioned by guarantees to appear for trial.

4. Everyone who is deprived of his liberty by arrest or detention shall be entitled to take proceedings by which the lawfulness of his detention shall be decided speedily by a court and his release ordered if the detention is not lawful.

5. Everyone who has been the victim of arrest or detention in contravention of the provisions of this article shall have an enforceable right to compensation.

Article 6—Right to a fair trial[1]

1. In the determination of his civil rights and obligations or of any criminal charge against him, everyone is entitled to a fair and public hearing within a reasonable time by an independent and impartial tribunal established by law. Judgement shall be pronounced publicly but the press and public may be excluded from all or part of the trial in the interests of morals, public order or national security in a democratic society, where the interests of juveniles or the protection of the private life of the parties so require, or to the extent strictly necessary in the opinion of the court in special circumstances where publicity would prejudice the interests of justice.

2. Everyone charged with a criminal offence shall be presumed innocent until proved guilty according to law.

3. Everyone charged with a criminal offence has the following minimum rights:

(a) to be informed promptly, in a language which he understands and in detail, of the nature and cause of the accusation against him;
(b) to have adequate time and facilities for the preparation of his defence;
(c) to defend himself in person or through legal assistance of his own choosing or, if he has not sufficient means to pay for legal assistance, to be given it free when the interests of justice so require;
(d) to examine or have examined witnesses against him and to obtain the attendance and examination of witnesses on his behalf under the same conditions as witnesses against him;
(d) to have the free assistance of an interpreter if he cannot understand or speak the language used in court.

Article 7—No punishment without law[1]

1. No one shall be held guilty of any criminal offence on account of any act or omission which did not constitute a criminal offence under national or international law at the time when it was committed. Nor shall a heavier penalty be imposed than the one that was applicable at the time the criminal offence was committed.

2. This article shall not prejudice the trial and punishment of any person for any act or omission which, at the time when it was committed, was criminal according to the general principles of law recognised by civilised nations.

Article 8—Right to respect for private and family life[1]

1. Everyone has the right to respect for his private and family life, his home and his correspondence.

2. There shall be no interference by a public authority with the exercise of this right except such as is in accordance with the law and is necessary in a democratic society in the interests of national security, public safety or the economic well-being of the country, for the prevention of disorder or crime, for the protection of health or morals, or for the protection of the rights and freedoms of others.

Article 9—Freedom of thought, conscience and religion[1]

1. Everyone has the right to freedom of thought, conscience and religion; this right includes freedom to change his religion or belief and freedom, either alone or in community with others and in public or private, to manifest his religion or belief, in worship, teaching, practice and observance.

2. Freedom to manifest one's religion or beliefs shall be subject only to such limitations as are prescribed by law and are necessary in a democratic society in the interests of public safety, for the protection of public order, health or morals, or for the protection of the rights and freedoms of others.

Article 10—Freedom of expression[1]

1. Everyone has the right to freedom of expression. This right shall include freedom to hold opinions and to receive and impart information and ideas without interference by public authority and regardless of frontiers. This article shall not prevent States from requiring the licensing of broadcasting, television or cinema enterprises.

2. The exercise of these freedoms, since it carries with it duties and responsibilities, may be subject to such formalities, conditions, restrictions or penalties as are

prescribed by law and are necessary in a democratic society, in the interests of national security, territorial integrity or public safety, for the prevention of disorder or crime, for the protection of health or morals, for the protection of the reputation or rights of others, for preventing the disclosure of information received in confidence, or for maintaining the authority and impartiality of the judiciary.

Article 11—Freedom of assembly and association[1]

1. Everyone has the right to freedom of peaceful assembly and to freedom of association with others, including the right to form and to join trade unions for the protection of his interests.

2. No restrictions shall be placed on the exercise of these rights other than such as are prescribed by law and are necessary in a democratic society in the interests of national security or public safety, for the prevention of disorder or crime, for the protection of health or morals or for the protection of the rights and freedoms of others. This article shall not prevent the imposition of lawful restrictions on the exercise of these rights by members of the armed forces, of the police or of the administration of the State.

Article 12—Right to marry[1]

Men and women of marriageable age have the right to marry and to found a family, according to the national laws governing the exercise of this right.

Article 13—Right to an effective remedy[1]

Everyone whose rights and freedoms as set forth in this Convention are violated shall have an effective remedy before a national authority notwithstanding that the violation has been committed by persons acting in an official capacity.

Article 14—Prohibition of discrimination[1]

The enjoyment of the rights and freedoms set forth in this Convention shall be secured without discrimination on any ground such as sex, race, colour, language, religion, political or other opinion, national or social origin, association with a national minority, property, birth or other status.

Article 15—Derogation in time of emergency[1]

1. In time of war or other public emergency threatening the life of the nation any High Contracting Party may take measures derogating from its obligations under this Convention to the extent strictly required by the exigencies of the situation,

provided that such measures are not inconsistent with its other obligations under international law.

2. No derogation from Article 2, except in respect of deaths resulting from lawful acts of war, or from Articles 3, 4 (paragraph 1) and 7 shall be made under this provision.

3. Any High Contracting Party availing itself of this right of derogation shall keep the Secretary General of the Council of Europe fully informed of the measures which it has taken and the reasons therefor. It shall also inform the Secretary General of the Council of Europe when such measures have ceased to operate and the provisions of the Convention are again being fully executed.

Article 16—Restrictions on political activity of aliens[1]

Nothing in Articles 10, 11 and 14 shall be regarded as preventing the High Contracting Parties from imposing restrictions on the political activity of aliens.

Article 17—Prohibition of abuse of rights[1]

Nothing in this Convention may be interpreted as implying for any State, group or person any right to engage in any activity or perform any act aimed at the destruction of any of the rights and freedoms set forth herein or at their limitation to a greater extent than is provided for in the Convention.

Article 18—Limitation on use of restrictions on rights[1]

The restrictions permitted under this Convention to the said rights and freedoms shall not be applied for any purpose other than those for which they have been prescribed.

Section II—European Court of Human Rights[2]

Article 19—Establishment of the Court

To ensure the observance of the engagements undertaken by the High Contracting Parties in the Convention and the Protocols thereto, there shall be set up a European Court of Human Rights, hereinafter referred to as 'the Court'. It shall function on a permanent basis.

Article 20—Number of judges

The Court shall consist of a number of judges equal to that of the High Contracting Parties.

Article 21—Criteria for office

1. The judges shall be of high moral character and must either possess the qualifications required for appointment to high judicial office or be jurisconsults of recognised competence.

2. The judges shall sit on the Court in their individual capacity.

3. During their term of office the judges shall not engage in any activity which is incompatible with their independence, impartiality or with the demands of a full-time office; all questions arising from the application of this paragraph shall be decided by the Court.

Article 22—Election of judges

1. The judges shall be elected by the Parliamentary Assembly with respect to each High Contracting Party by a majority of votes cast from a list of three candidates nominated by the High Contracting Party.

2. The same procedure shall be followed to complete the Court in the event of the accession of new High Contracting Parties and in filling casual vacancies.

Article 23—Terms of office

1. The judges shall be elected for a period of six years. They may be re-elected. However, the terms of office of one-half of the judges elected at the first election shall expire at the end of three years.

2. The judges whose terms of office are to expire at the end of the initial period of three years shall be chosen by lot by the Secretary General of the Council of Europe immediately after their election.

3. In order to ensure that, as far as possible, the terms of office of one-half of the judges are renewed every three years, the Parliamentary Assembly may decide, before proceeding to any subsequent election, that the term or terms of office of one or more judges to be elected shall be for a period other than six years but not more than nine and not less than three years.

4. In cases where more than one term of office is involved and where the Parliamentary Assembly applies the preceding paragraph, the allocation of the terms of office shall be effected by a drawing of lots by the Secretary General of the Council of Europe immediately after the election.

5. A judge elected to replace a judge whose term of office has not expired shall hold office for the remainder of his predecessor's term.

6. The terms of office of judges shall expire when they reach the age of 70.

7. The judges shall hold office until replaced. They shall, however, continue to deal with such cases as they already have under consideration.

Article 24—Dismissal

No judge may be dismissed from his office unless the other judges decide by a majority of two-thirds that he has ceased to fulfil the required conditions.

Article 25—Registry and legal secretaries

The Court shall have a registry, the functions and organisation of which shall be laid down in the rules of the Court. The Court shall be assisted by legal secretaries.

Article 26—Plenary Court

The plenary Court shall:
(a) elect its President and one or two Vice-Presidents for a period of three years; they may be re-elected;
(b) set up Chambers, constituted for a fixed period of time;
(c) elect the Presidents of the Chambers of the Court; they may be re-elected;
(d) adopt the rules of the Court, and
(e) elect the Registrar and one or more Deputy Registrars.

Article 27—Committees, Chambers and Grand Chamber

1. To consider cases brought before it, the Court shall sit in committees of three judges, in Chambers of seven judges and in a Grand Chamber of seventeen judges. The Court's Chambers shall set up committees for a fixed period of time.

2. There shall sit as an ex officio member of the Chamber and the Grand Chamber the judge elected in respect of the State Party concerned or, if there is none or if he is unable to sit, a person of its choice who shall sit in the capacity of judge.

3. The Grand Chamber shall also include the President of the Court, the Vice-Presidents, the Presidents of the Chambers and other judges chosen in accordance with the rules of the Court. When a case is referred to the Grand Chamber under Article 43, no judge from the Chamber which rendered the judgment shall sit in the Grand Chamber, with the exception of the President of the Chamber and the judge who sat in respect of the State Party concerned.

Article 28—Declarations of inadmissibility by committees

A committee may, by a unanimous vote, declare inadmissible or strike out of its list of cases an application submitted under Article 34 where such a decision can be taken without further examination. The decision shall be final.

Article 29—Decisions by Chambers on admissibility and merits

1. If no decision is taken under Article 28, a Chamber shall decide on the admissibility and merits of individual applications submitted under Article 34.

2. A Chamber shall decide on the admissibility and merits of inter-State applications submitted under Article 33.

3. The decision on admissibility shall be taken separately unless the Court, in exceptional cases, decides otherwise.

Article 30—Relinquishment of jurisdiction to the Grand Chamber

Where a case pending before a Chamber raises a serious question affecting the interpretation of the Convention or the protocols thereto, or where the resolution of a question before the Chamber might have a result inconsistent with a judgment previously delivered by the Court, the Chamber may, at any time before it has rendered its judgment, relinquish jurisdiction in favour of the Grand Chamber, unless one of the parties to the case objects.

Article 31—Powers of the Grand Chamber

The Grand Chamber shall:

(a) determine applications submitted either under Article 33 or Article 34 when a Chamber has relinquished jurisdiction under Article 30 or when the case has been referred to it under Article 43; and

(b) consider requests for advisory opinions submitted under Article 47.

Article 32—Jurisdiction of the Court

1. The jurisdiction of the Court shall extend to all matters concerning the interpretation and application of the Convention and the protocols thereto which are referred to it as provided in Articles 33, 34 and 47.

2. In the event of dispute as to whether the Court has jurisdiction, the Court shall decide.

Article 33—Inter-State cases

Any High Contracting Party may refer to the Court any alleged breach of the provisions of the Convention and the protocols thereto by another High Contracting Party.

Article 34—Individual applications

Chart of Declarations under former Articles 25 and 46 of the ECHR

The Court may receive applications from any person, non-governmental organisation or group of individuals claiming to be the victim of a violation by one of the High Contracting Parties of the rights set forth in the Convention or the protocols thereto. The High Contracting Parties undertake not to hinder in any way the effective exercise of this right.

Article 35—Admissibility criteria

1. The Court may only deal with the matter after all domestic remedies have been exhausted, according to the generally recognised rules of international law, and within a period of six months from the date on which the final decision was taken.

2. The Court shall not deal with any application submitted under Article 34 that:
   (a) is anonymous; or
   (b) is substantially the same as a matter that has already been examined by the Court or has already been submitted to another procedure of international investigation or settlement and contains no relevant new information.

3. The Court shall declare inadmissible any individual application submitted under Article 34 which it considers incompatible with the provisions of the Convention or the protocols thereto, manifestly ill-founded, or an abuse of the right of application.

4. The Court shall reject any application which it considers inadmissible under this Article. It may do so at any stage of the proceedings.

Article 36—Third party intervention

1. In all cases before a Chamber or the Grand Chamber, a High Contracting Party one of whose nationals is an applicant shall have the right to submit written comments and to take part in hearings.

2. The President of the Court may, in the interest of the proper administration of justice, invite any High Contracting Party which is not a party to the proceedings or any person concerned who is not the applicant to submit written comments or take part in hearings.

Article 37—Striking out applications

1. The Court may at any stage of the proceedings decide to strike an application out of its list of cases where the circumstances lead to the conclusion that:
   (a) the applicant does not intend to pursue his application; or
   (b) the matter has been resolved; or
   (c) for any other reason established by the Court, it is no longer justified to continue the examination of the application.

However, the Court shall continue the examination of the application if respect for human rights as defined in the Convention and the protocols thereto so requires.

2. The Court may decide to restore an application to its list of cases if it considers that the circumstances justify such a course.

Article 38—Examination of the case and friendly settlement proceedings

1. If the Court declares the application admissible, it shall:
   (a) pursue the examination of the case, together with the representatives of the parties, and if need be, undertake an investigation, for the effective conduct of which the States concerned shall furnish all necessary facilities;
   (b) place itself at the disposal of the parties concerned with a view to securing a friendly settlement of the matter on the basis of respect for human rights as defined in the Convention and the protocols thereto.
2. Proceedings conducted under paragraph 1(b) shall be confidential.

Article 39—Finding of a friendly settlement

If a friendly settlement is effected, the Court shall strike the case out of its list by means of a decision which shall be confined to a brief statement of the facts and of the solution reached.

Article 40—Public hearings and access to documents

1. Hearings shall be in public unless the Court in exceptional circumstances decides otherwise.

2. Documents deposited with the Registrar shall be accessible to the public unless the President of the Court decides otherwise.

Article 41—Just satisfaction

If the Court finds that there has been a violation of the Convention or the protocols thereto, and if the internal law of the High Contracting Party concerned allows only partial reparation to be made, the Court shall, if necessary, afford just satisfaction to the injured party.

Article 42—Judgments of Chambers

Judgments of Chambers shall become final in accordance with the provisions of Article 44, paragraph 2.

Article 43—Referral to the Grand Chamber

1. Within a period of three months from the date of the judgment of the Chamber, any party to the case may, in exceptional cases, request that the case be referred to the Grand Chamber.

2. A panel of five judges of the Grand Chamber shall accept the request if the case raises a serious question affecting the interpretation or application of the Convention or the protocols thereto, or a serious issue of general importance.

3. If the panel accepts the request, the Grand Chamber shall decide the case by means of a judgment.

Article 44—Final judgments

1. The judgment of the Grand Chamber shall be final.
2. The judgment of a Chamber shall become final:
   (a) when the parties declare that they will not request that the case be referred to the Grand Chamber; or
   (b) three months after the date of the judgment, if reference of the case to the Grand Chamber has not been requested; or
   (c) when the panel of the Grand Chamber rejects the request to refer under Article 43.
3. The final judgment shall be published.

Article 45—Reasons for judgments and decisions

1. Reasons shall be given for judgments as well as for decisions declaring applications admissible or inadmissible.

2. If a judgment does not represent, in whole or in part, the unanimous opinion of the judges, any judge shall be entitled to deliver a separate opinion.

Article 46—Binding force and execution of judgments

1. The High Contracting Parties undertake to abide by the final judgment of the Court in any case to which they are parties.

2. The final judgment of the Court shall be transmitted to the Committee of Ministers, which shall supervise its execution.

Article 47—Advisory opinions

1. The Court may, at the request of the Committee of Ministers, give advisory opinions on legal questions concerning the interpretation of the Convention and the protocols thereto.

2. Such opinions shall not deal with any question relating to the content or scope of the rights or freedoms defined in Section I of the Convention and the protocols thereto, or with any other question which the Court or the Committee of Ministers might have to consider in consequence of any such proceedings as could be instituted in accordance with the Convention.

3. Decisions of the Committee of Ministers to request an advisory opinion of the Court shall require a majority vote of the representatives entitled to sit on the Committee.

Article 48—Advisory jurisdiction of the Court

The Court shall decide whether a request for an advisory opinion submitted by the Committee of Ministers is within its competence as defined in Article 47.

Article 49—Reasons for advisory opinions

1. Reasons shall be given for advisory opinions of the Court.

2. If the advisory opinion does not represent, in whole or in part, the unanimous opinion of the judges, any judge shall be entitled to deliver a separate opinion.

3. Advisory opinions of the Court shall be communicated to the Committee of Ministers.

Article 50—Expenditure on the Court

The expenditure on the Court shall be borne by the Council of Europe.

Article 51—Privileges and immunities of judges

The judges shall be entitled, during the exercise of their functions, to the privileges and immunities provided for in Article 40 of the Statute of the Council of Europe and in the agreements made thereunder.

Section III—Miscellaneous provisions[1,3]

Article 52—Inquiries by the Secretary General[1]

On receipt of a request from the Secretary General of the Council of Europe any High Contracting Party shall furnish an explanation of the manner in which its internal law ensures the effective implementation of any of the provisions of the Convention.

Article 53—Safeguard for existing human rights[1]

Nothing in this Convention shall be construed as limiting or derogating from any of the human rights and fundamental freedoms which may be ensured under the laws of any High Contracting Party or under any other agreement to which it is a Party.

Article 54—Powers of the Committee of Ministers[1]

Nothing in this Convention shall prejudice the powers conferred on the Committee of Ministers by the Statute of the Council of Europe.

Article 55—Exclusion of other means of dispute settlement[1]

The High Contracting Parties agree that, except by special agreement, they will not avail themselves of treaties, conventions or declarations in force between them for the purpose of submitting, by way of petition, a dispute arising out of the interpretation or application of this Convention to a means of settlement other than those provided for in this Convention.

Article 56—Territorial application[1]

1. [4]Any State may at the time of its ratification or at any time thereafter declare by notification addressed to the Secretary General of the Council of Europe that the present Convention shall, subject to paragraph 4 of this Article, extend to all or any of the territories for whose international relations it is responsible.

2. The Convention shall extend to the territory or territories named in the notification as from the thirtieth day after the receipt of this notification by the Secretary General of the Council of Europe.

3. The provisions of this Convention shall be applied in such territories with due regard, however, to local requirements.

4. [4]Any State which has made a declaration in accordance with paragraph 1 of this article may at any time thereafter declare on behalf of one or more of the territories

to which the declaration relates that it accepts the competence of the Court to receive applications from individuals, non-governmental organisations or groups of individuals as provided by Article 34 of the Convention.

Article 57—Reservations[1]

1. Any State may, when signing this Convention or when depositing its instrument of ratification, make a reservation in respect of any particular provision of the Convention to the extent that any law then in force in its territory is not in conformity with the provision. Reservations of a general character shall not be permitted under this article.

2. Any reservation made under this article shall contain a brief statement of the law concerned.

Article 58—Denunciation[1]

1. A High Contracting Party may denounce the present Convention only after the expiry of five years from the date on which it became a party to it and after six months' notice contained in a notification addressed to the Secretary General of the Council of Europe, who shall inform the other High Contracting Parties.

2. Such a denunciation shall not have the effect of releasing the High Contracting Party concerned from its obligations under this Convention in respect of any act which, being capable of constituting a violation of such obligations, may have been performed by it before the date at which the denunciation became effective.

3. Any High Contracting Party which shall cease to be a member of the Council of Europe shall cease to be a Party to this Convention under the same conditions.

4. [4]The Convention may be denounced in accordance with the provisions of the preceding paragraphs in respect of any territory to which it has been declared to extend under the terms of Article 56.

Article 59—Signature and ratification[1]

1. This Convention shall be open to the signature of the members of the Council of Europe. It shall be ratified. Ratifications shall be deposited with the Secretary General of the Council of Europe.

2. The present Convention shall come into force after the deposit of ten instruments of ratification.

3. As regards any signatory ratifying subsequently, the Convention shall come into force at the date of the deposit of its instrument of ratification.

4. The Secretary General of the Council of Europe shall notify all the members of

the Council of Europe of the entry into force of the Convention, the names of the High Contracting Parties who have ratified it, and the deposit of all instruments of ratification which may be effected subsequently.

Done at Rome this 4th day of November 1950, in English and French, both texts being equally authentic, in a single copy which shall remain deposited in the archives of the Council of Europe. The Secretary General shall transmit certified copies to each of the signatories.

[1] Heading added according to the provisions of Protocol No. 11 (ETS No. 155).

[2] New Section II according to the provisions of Protocol No. 11 (ETS No. 155).

[3] The articles of this Section are renumbered according to the provisions of Protocol No. 11 (ETS No. 155).

[4] Text amended according to the provisions of Protocol No. 11 (ETS No. 155).

Convention Relating to the Status of Stateless Persons

(New York, September 28, 1954)

Preamble

The High Contracting Parties,

Considering that the Charter of the United Nations and the Universal Declaration of Human Rights approved on 10 December 1948 by the General Assembly of the United Nations have affirmed the principle that human beings shall enjoy fundamental rights and freedoms without discrimination,

Considering that the United Nations has, on various occasions, manifested its profound concern for stateless persons and endeavoured to assure stateless persons the widest possible exercise of these fundamental rights and freedoms,

Considering that only those stateless persons who are also refugees are covered by the Convention relating to the Status of Refugees of 28 July 1951, and that there are many stateless persons who are not covered by that Convention,

Considering that it is desirable to regulate and improve the status of stateless persons by an international agreement.

Have agreed as follows:

Chapter I
General Provisions

Article 1 Definition of the term 'Stateless Person'

1. For the purpose of this Convention, the term 'stateless person' means a person who is not considered as a national by any State under the operation of its law.

2. This Convention shall not apply:
   (i) To persons who are at present receiving from organs or agencies of the United Nations other than the United Nations High Commissioner for Refugees protection or assistance so long as they are receiving such protection or assistance;
   (ii) To persons who are recognized by the competent authorities of the country in which they have taken residence as having the rights and obligations which are attached to the possession of the nationality of that country;
   (iii) To persons with respect to whom there are serious reasons for considering that:
      (a) They have committed a crime against peace, a war crime, or a crime against humanity, as defined in the international instruments drawn up to make provisions in respect of such crimes;
      (b) They have committed a serious non-political crime outside the country of their residence prior to their admission to that country;
      (c) They have been guilty of acts contrary to the purposes and principles of the United Nations.

Article 2 General obligations

Every stateless person has duties to the country in which he finds himself, which require in particular that he conform to its laws and regulations as well as to measures taken for the maintenance of public order.

Article 3 Non-discrimination

The Contracting States shall apply the provisions of this Convention to stateless persons without discrimination as to race, religion or country of origin.

Article 4 Religion

The Contracting States shall accord to stateless persons within their territories treatment at least as favourable as that accorded to their nationals with respect to freedom to practise their religion and freedom as regards the religious education of their children.

Article 5 Rights granted apart from this Convention

Nothing in this Convention shall be deemed to impair any rights and benefits granted by a Contracting State to stateless persons apart from this Convention.

Article 6 The term 'in the same circumstances'

For the purpose of this Convention, the term 'in the same circumstances' implies that any requirements (including requirements as to length and conditions of sojourn or residence) which the particular individual would have to fulfil for the enjoyment of the right in question, if he were not a stateless person, must be fulfilled by him, with the exception of requirements which by their nature a stateless person is incapable of fulfilling.

Article 7 Exemption from reciprocity

1. Except where this Convention contains more favourable provisions, a Contracting State shall accord to stateless persons the same treatment as is accorded to aliens generally.

2. After a period of three years' residence, all stateless persons shall enjoy exemption from legislative reciprocity in the territory of the Contracting States.

3. Each Contracting State shall continue to accord to stateless persons the rights and benefits to which they were already entitled, in the absence of reciprocity, at the date of entry into force of this Convention for that State.

4. The Contracting States shall consider favourably the possibility of according to stateless persons, in the absence of reciprocity, rights and benefits beyond those to which they are entitled according to paragraphs 2 and 3, and to extending exemption from reciprocity to stateless persons who do not fulfil the conditions provided for in paragraphs 2 and 3.

The provisions of paragraphs 2 and 3 apply both to the rights and benefits referred to in Articles 13, 18, 19, 21 and 22 of this Convention and to rights and benefits for which this Convention does not provide.

Article 8 Exemption from exceptional measures

With regard to exceptional measures which may be taken against the person, property or interests of nationals or former nationals of a foreign State, the Contracting States shall not apply such measures to a stateless person solely on account of his having previously possessed the nationality of the foreign State in question. Contracting States which, under their legislation, are prevented from applying the general principle expressed in this Article shall, in appropriate cases, grant exemptions in favour of such stateless persons.

Article 9 Provisional measures

Nothing in this Convention shall prevent a Contracting State, in time of war or other grave and exceptional circumstances, from taking provisionally measures which it considers to be essential to the national security in the case of a particular person, pending a determination by the Contracting State that that person is in fact a stateless person and that the continuance of such measures is necessary in his case in the interests of national security.

Article 10 Continuity of residence

1. Where a stateless person has been forcibly displaced during the Second World War and removed to the territory of a Contracting State, and is resident there, the period of such enforced sojourn shall be considered to have been lawful residence within that territory.

2. Where a stateless person has been forcibly displaced during the Second World War from the territory of a Contracting State and has, prior to the date of entry into force of this Convention, returned there for the purpose of taking up residence, the period of residence before and after such enforced displacement shall be regarded as one uninterrupted period for any purpose for which uninterrupted residence is required.

Article 11 Stateless seamen

In the case of stateless persons regularly serving as crew members on board a ship flying the flag of a Contracting State, that State shall give sympathetic consideration to their establishment on its territory and the issue of travel documents to them or their temporary admission to its territory particularly with a view to facilitating their establishment in another country.

Chapter II
Juridical Status

Article 12 Personal status

1. The personal status of a stateless person shall be governed by the law of the country of his domicile or, if he has no domicile, by the law of the country of his residence.

2. Rights previously acquired by a stateless person and dependent on personal status, more particularly rights attaching to marriage, shall be respected by a Contracting State, subject to compliance, if this be necessary, with the formalities required by the law of that State, provided that the right in question is one which would have been recognized by the law of that State had he not become stateless.

Article 13 Movable and immovable property

The Contracting States shall accord to a stateless person treatment as favourable as possible and, in any event, not less favourable than that accorded to aliens generally in the same circumstances, as regards the acquisition of movable and immovable property and other rights pertaining thereto, and to leases and other contracts relating to movable and immovable property.

Article 14 Artistic rights and industrial property

In respect of the protection of industrial property, such as inventions, designs or models, trade marks, trade names, and of rights in literary, artistic and scientific works, a stateless person shall be accorded in the country in which he has his habitual residence the same protection as is accorded to nationals of that country. In the territory of any other Contracting State, he shall be accorded the same protection as is accorded in that territory to nationals of the country in which he has his habitual residence.

Article 15 Right of association

As regards non-political and non-profit-making associations and trade unions the Contracting States shall accord to stateless persons lawfully staying in their territory treatment as favourable as possible, and in any event, not less favourable than that accorded to aliens generally in the same circumstances.

Article 16 Access to Courts

1. A stateless person shall have free access to the Courts of Law on the territory of all Contracting States.

2. A stateless person shall enjoy in the Contracting State in which he has his habitual residence the same treatment as a national in matters pertaining to access to the Courts, including legal assistance and exemption from *cautio judicatum solvi.*

3. A stateless person shall be accorded in the matters referred to in paragraph 2 in countries other than that in which he has his habitual residence the treatment granted to a national of the country of his habitual residence.

Chapter III
Gainful Employment

Article 17 Wage-earning employment

1. The Contracting States shall accord to stateless persons lawfully staying in their territory treatment as favourable as possible and, in any event, not less favourable than that accorded to aliens generally in the same circumstances, as regards the right to engage in wage-earning employment.

2. The Contracting States shall give sympathetic consideration to assimilating the rights of all stateless persons with regard to wage-earning employment to those of nationals, and in particular of those stateless persons who have entered their territory pursuant to programmes of labour recruitment or under immigration schemes.

Article 18 Self-employment

The Contracting States shall accord to a stateless person lawfully in their territory treatment as favourable as possible and, in any event, not less favourable than that accorded to aliens generally in the same circumstances, as regards the right to engage on his own account in agriculture, industry, handicrafts and commerce and to establish commercial and industrial companies.

Article 19 Liberal professions

Each Contracting State shall accord to stateless persons lawfully staying in their territory who hold diplomas recognized by the competent authorities of that State, and who are desirous of practising a liberal profession, treatment as favourable as possible and, in any event, not less favourable than that accorded to aliens generally in the same circumstances.

Chapter IV
Welfare

Article 20 Rationing

Where a rationing system exists, which applies to the population at large and regulates the general distribution of products in short supply, stateless persons shall be accorded the same treatment as nationals.

Article 21 Housing

As regards housing, the Contracting States, in so far as the matter is regulated by laws or regulations or is subject to the control of public authorities, shall accord to stateless persons lawfully staying in their territory treatment as favourable as possible and, in any event, not less favourable than that accorded to aliens generally in the same circumstances.

Article 22 Public education

1. The Contracting States shall accord to stateless persons the same treatment as is accorded to nationals with respect to elementary education.

2. The Contracting States shall accord to stateless persons treatment as favourable as possible and, in any event, not less favourable than that accorded to aliens generally in the same circumstances, with respect to education other than elementary education and, in particular, as regards access to studies, the recognition of foreign school certificates, diplomas and degrees, the remission of fees and charges and the award of scholarships.

Article 23 Public relief

The Contracting States shall accord to stateless persons lawfully staying in their territory the same treatment with respect to public relief and assistance as is accorded to their nationals.

Article 24 Labour legislation and social security

1. The Contracting States shall accord to stateless persons lawfully staying in their territory the same treatment as is accorded to nationals in respect of the following matters:

   (a) In so far as such matters are governed by laws or regulations or are subject to the control of administrative authorities: remuneration, including family allowances where these form part of remuneration, hours of work, overtime arrangements, holidays with pay, restrictions on home work, minimum age of employment, apprenticeship and training, women's work and the work of young persons, and the enjoyment of the benefits of collective bargaining;

   (b) Social security (legal provisions in respect of employment injury, occupational diseases, maternity, sickness, disability, old age, death, unemployment, family responsibilities and any other contingency which, according to national laws or regulations, is covered by a social security scheme), subject to the following limitations:

(i) There may be appropriate arrangements for the maintenance of acquired rights and rights in course of acquisition;

(ii) National laws or regulations of the country of residence may prescribe special arrangements concerning benefits or portions of benefits which are payable wholly out of public funds, and concerning allowances paid to persons who do not fulfil the contribution conditions prescribed for the award of a normal pension.

2. The right to compensation for the death of a stateless person resulting from employment injury or from occupational disease shall not be affected by the fact that the residence of the beneficiary is outside the territory of the Contracting State.

3. The Contracting States shall extend to stateless persons the benefits of agreements concluded between them, or which may be concluded between them in the future, concerning the maintenance of acquired rights and rights in the process of acquisition in regard to social security, subject only to the conditions which apply to nationals of the States signatory to the agreements in question.

4. The Contracting States will give sympathetic consideration to extending to stateless persons so far as possible the benefits of similar agreements which may at any time be in force between such Contracting States and non-contracting States.

Chapter V

Administrative Measures

Article 25 Administrative assistance

1. When the exercise of a right by a stateless person would normally require the assistance of authorities of a foreign country to whom he cannot have recourse, the Contracting State in whose territory he is residing shall arrange that such assistance be afforded to him by their own authorities.

2. The authority or authorities mentioned in paragraph 1 shall deliver or cause to be delivered under their supervision to stateless persons such documents or certifications as would normally be delivered to aliens by or through their national authorities.

3. Documents or certifications so delivered shall stand in the stead of the official instruments delivered to aliens by or through their national authorities, and shall be given credence in the absence of proof to the contrary.

4. Subject to such exceptional treatment as may be granted to indigent persons, fees may be charged for the services mentioned herein, but such fees shall be moderate and commensurate with those charged to nationals for similar services.

5. The provisions of this article shall be without prejudice to Articles 27 and 28.

Article 26 Freedom of movement

Each Contracting State shall accord to stateless persons lawfully in its territory the right to choose their place of residence and to move freely within its territory, subject to any regulations applicable to aliens generally in the same circumstances.

Article 27 Identity papers

The Contracting States shall issue identity papers to any stateless person in their territory who does not possess a valid travel document.

Article 28 Travel documents

The Contracting States shall issue to stateless persons lawfully staying in their territory travel documents for the purpose of travel outside their territory, unless compelling reasons of national security or public order otherwise require, and the provisions of the Schedule to this Convention shall apply with respect to such documents. The Contracting States may issue such a travel document to any other stateless person in their territory; they shall in particular give sympathetic consideration to the issue of such a travel document to stateless persons in their territory who are unable to obtain a travel document from the country of their lawful residence.

Article 29 Fiscal charges

1. The Contracting States shall not impose upon stateless persons duties, charges or taxes, of any description whatsoever, other or higher than those which are or may be levied on their nationals in similar situations.

2. Nothing in the above paragraph shall prevent the application to stateless persons of the laws and regulations concerning charges in respect of the issue to aliens of administrative documents including identity papers.

Article 30 Transfer of assets

1. A Contracting State shall, in conformity with its laws and regulations, permit stateless persons to transfer assets which they have brought into its territory, to another country where they have been admitted for the purpose of resettlement.

2. A Contracting State shall give sympathetic consideration to the application of stateless persons for permission to transfer assets wherever they may be and which are necessary for their resettlement in another country to which they have been admitted.

Article 31 Expulsion

1. The Contracting States shall not expel a stateless person lawfully in their territory save on grounds of national security or public order.
2. The expulsion of such a stateless person shall be only in pursuance of a decision reached in accordance with due process of law. Except where compelling reasons of national security otherwise require, the stateless person shall be allowed to submit evidence to clear himself, and to appeal to and be represented for the purpose before the competent authority or a person or persons specially designated by the competent authority.
3. The Contracting States shall allow such a stateless person a reasonable period within which to seek legal admission into another country. The Contracting States reserve the right to apply during that period such internal measures as they may deem necessary.

Article 32 Naturalization

The Contracting States shall as far as possible facilitate the assimilation and naturalization of stateless persons. They shall in particular make every effort to expedite naturalization proceedings and to reduce as far as possible the charges and costs of such proceedings.

Chapter VI
Final Clauses

...

United Kingdom of Great Britain and Northern Ireland

'I have the honour further to state that the Government of the United Kingdom deposit the present instrument of ratification on the understanding that the combined effects of Articles 36 and 38 permit them to include in any declaration or notification made under paragraph 1 of Article 36 or paragraph 2 of Article 36 respectively any reservation consistent with Article 38 which the Government of the territory concerned might desire to make.'

'When ratifying the Convention relating to the Status of Stateless Persons which was opened for signature at New York on September 28, 1954, the Government of the United Kingdom have deemed it necessary to make certain reservations in accordance with paragraph 1 of Article 38 thereof the text of which is reproduced below:—

(1) The Government of the United Kingdom of Great Britain and Northern Ireland understand Articles 8 and 9 as not preventing them from taking in time of war or other grave and exceptional circumstances measures in the interests of national security in the case of a stateless person on the ground of his former nationality. The provisions of Article 8 shall not prevent the Government of the United Kingdom of Great Britain and Northern Ireland from exercising any rights over property or interests which they may acquire or have acquired as an Allied or Associated Power under a Treaty of Peace or other agreement or arrangement for the restoration of peace which has been or may be completed as a result of the Second World War. Furthermore, the provisions of Article 8 shall not affect the treatment to be accorded to any property or interests which at the date of entry into force of this Convention for the United Kingdom of Great Britain and Northern Ireland are under the control of the Government of the United Kingdom of Great Britain and Northern Ireland by reason of a state of war which exists or existed between them and any other state.

(2) The Government of the United Kingdom of Great Britain and Northern Ireland in respect of such of the matters referred to in sub-paragraph (b) of paragraph 1 of Article 24 as fall within the scope of the National Health Service, can only undertake to apply the provisions of that paragraph so far as the law allows.

(3) The Government of the United Kingdom of Great Britain and Northern Ireland cannot undertake to give effect to the obligations contained in paragraphs 1 and 2 of Article 25 and can only undertake to apply the provisions of paragraph 3 so far as the law allows.'

Convention Against Torture and Other Cruel, Inhuman or Degrading Treatment or Punishment

(United Nations Headquarters, New York, 4 February 1985)

Note: Articles 1–4 only.

The States Parties to this Convention,

Considering that, in accordance with the principles proclaimed in the Charter of the United Nations, recognition of the equal and inalienable rights of all members of the human family is the foundation of freedom, justice and peace in the world,

Recognizing that those rights derive from the inherent dignity of the human person,

Considering the obligation of States under the Charter, in particular Article 55, to promote universal respect for, and observance of, human rights and fundamental freedoms,

Having regard to article 5 of the Universal Declaration of Human Rights and article 7 of the International Covenant on Civil and Political Right, both of which provide that no one shall be subjected to torture or to cruel, inhuman or degrading treatment or punishment,

Having regard also to the Declaration on the Protection of All Persons from Being Subjected to Torture and Other Cruel, Inhuman or Degrading Treatment or Punishment, adopted by the General Assembly on 9 December 1975,

Desiring to make more effective the struggle against torture and other cruel, inhuman or degrading treatment or punishment throughout the world,

Have agreed as follows:

Part I

Article 1

1. For the purposes of this Convention, the term 'torture' means any act by which severe pain or suffering, whether physical or mental, is intentionally inflicted on a person for such purposes as obtaining from him or a third person information or a confession, punishing him for an act he or a third person has committed or is suspected of having committed, or intimidating or coercing him or a third person, or for any reason based on discrimination of any kind, when such pain or suffering is inflicted by or at the instigation of or with the consent or acquiescence of a public official or other person acting in an official capacity. It does not include pain or suffering arising only from, inherent in or incidental to lawful sanctions.

2. This article is without prejudice to any international instrument or national legislation which does or may contain provisions of wider application.

Article 2

1. Each State Party shall take effective legislative, administrative, judicial or other measures to prevent acts of torture in any territory under its jurisdiction.

2. No exceptional circumstances whatsoever, whether a state of war or a threat of war, internal political instability or any other public emergency, may be invoked as a justification of torture.

3. An order from a superior officer or a public authority may not be invoked as a justification of torture.

Article 3

1. No State Party shall expel, return ('*refouler*') or extradite a person to another State where there are substantial grounds for believing that he would be in danger of being subjected to torture.

2. For the purpose of determining whether there are such grounds, the competent authorities shall take into account all relevant considerations including, where applicable, the existence in the State concerned of a consistent pattern of gross, flagrant or mass violations of human rights.

Article 4

1. Each State Party shall ensure that all acts of torture are offences under its criminal law. The same shall apply to an attempt to commit torture and to an act by any person which constitutes complicity or participation in torture.

2. Each State Party shall make these offences punishable by appropriate penalties which take into account their grave nature.

INDEX